MARKETING

WILLIAM ZIKMUND

Oklahoma State University

MICHAEL D'AMICO

Akron University

John Wiley and Sons

New York Chichester Brisbane Toronto Singapore

To TOBIN AND NOAH ZIKMUND
KATHY AND ALYSE D'AMICO

Library of Congress Cataloging in Publication Data:

Zikmund, William G.
  Marketing.

  Includes index.
  1. Marketing. I. D'Amico, Michael. II. Title.
HF5415.Z54 1984   658.8   83-23521
ISBN 0-471-86493-5

Printed in the United States of America

10 9 8 7 6 5 4 3 2 1

PREFACE

Marketing presents a lively picture of marketing as a dynamic, creative, and competitive field and as an activity that is part of our everyday lives. It is readable and practical in that it uses contemporary examples from the "real world" to enhance the marketing concepts and strategies being discussed. As a further aid to students, the various exhibits and boxes illustrate practical marketing activities as they occur, not only in advertisements, but in every facet of marketing. We hope that you will find *Marketing* interesting and that you will come to share our own enthusiasm for this fascinating field.

We emphasize *effective* marketing throughout, so that students are able to distinguish between intuitive decision-making and sound marketing management. We point out the right way to plan marketing strategy as well as what can go wrong.

Marketing is organized so that students can understand the role of both environmental factors and the marketing manager's adjustments of the marketing mix, which influence a product's success. Theoretical concepts, such as consumer behavior theory, are presented so students may understand their practical value for marketing managers. *Marketing* was also written to be teachable. A considerable effort was made to insure that the pedagogy meets the instructor's needs. Chapter scans, learning objectives, and chapter summaries are included to help students organize their thoughts. Color graphics experts and graphic designers assisted the authors by designing a book to highlight key concepts and ideas within the textbook.

The major features of the book include:

1 Numerous real-world examples. The inclusion of international, industrial, not-for-profit, and service examples throughout the book *and* in special industrial and international marketing chapters.

2 A straightforward prose style with a balanced coverage of marketing concepts and examples to make marketing easy to understand.

3 Interesting and relevant end-of-chapter materials. Cases and questions at the end of each chapter reflect practical marketing problems.

4 "What Went Wrong?" and "What Went Right?" boxes that reflect specific successes and failures in marketing organizations.

5 Color graphics and exhibits designed for student involvement and learning.

6 A complete package of instructor's aids available to adopters.

7 Auxiliary books to supplement student learning, including *Study Guide to Accompanying Marketing* by Jim Grimm and *Applied Marketing* by Don Sciglimpaglia.

This book was completed because of the hard work of many people. Our editor, Richard Esposito, coordinated an army of co-workers at John Wiley & Sons with Patton-like skill and Allen-like humor. The efforts of Elizabeth Doble, Joan Knizeski, Marsha Leest, and many other wordsmiths, made the book easy to read. Ed Burke and Karin Kincheloe, designers, and Stella Kupferberg and Kathy Bendo, photo researchers, were the artists responsible for the book's beauty. That we were able to get the book out on schedule still surprises us today. We express our deep appreciation to the people at the third oldest company in New York City.

A team of creative as well as critical reviewers from several universities and colleges added much to this book. We offer sincere thanks to John "Rusty" Brooks, Jr., West Texas State University; Jim Grimm, Illinois State University; Dillard Tinsley, Stephen F. Austin State University; and Don Sciglimpaglia, San Diego State University.

Our colleagues at Oklahoma State University and the University of Akron offered intellectual environments and constant encouragement to allow us to successfully complete the project. Colleagues Nancy Uhring, George Prough, and L. Lee Manzer made valuable contributions to parts of the book in their area of expertise. Robin Peterson of New Mexico State University helped by providing the first draft of the material for the physical distribution chapter.

Fred Beasley's assistance on the project was indispensable. Because of his efforts many errors are absent from the book. One could not ask for a more creative, energetic, and responsible graduate assistant.

Joan Kirkendall's contribution has been praised elsewhere. Anyone who can manage the scribblings of the manuscript stage on four books has more tolerance than Job. The manuscript was the true result of her labor. Patricia Johnson's patience was tested extensively, too.

There are many long-term debts owed as well. George Zikmund who spent his entire life in sales and sales management was responsible for leaving an indelible sense of the practical side of marketing to his son. Phil Campagna later served as a wise marketing mentor at Remington Arms Company. Learning to understand marketing takes many years and these long-term debts are hard to repay. We hope this book will pass on our parents', teachers', and mentors' insights to others.

WILLIAM ZIKMUND
MICHAEL D'AMICO

CONTENTS

PART 1

INTRODUCTION 3

PART 2

INFORMATION MANAGEMENT 123

PART 3

CONSUMER BEHAVIOR   173

PART 4

PRODUCT STRATEGY   229

PART 5

CHANNELS OF DISTRIBUTION 321

CHAPTER THIRTEEN   DISTRIBUTION INSTITUTIONS 361

PART 6

PRICING STRATEGY   419

PART 7

PROMOTION STRATEGY   485

PART 8

SPECIAL CONSIDERATIONS 593

MARKETING

PART 1

INTRODUCTION

Marketing is a major force in business and society. It impacts daily life in many ways. However, marketing operates within an environment which both limits what marketers can do and provides marketers with nearly limitless opportunities. The effective and successful organization is one whose managers understand marketing and its environment, and adjust to changes in that environment.

To do this, marketing managers develop strategies and tactics aimed at achieving goals. As must all managers, marketers develop plans that reflect the realities of the environment. The marketing planning process lays the groundwork for the marketing manager's most important task, preparation of an effective marketing mix.

Chapter 1 introduces marketing and its basic definition. Important concepts such as the marketing mix and the marketing concept are explored.

Chapter 2 considers the environment in which marketers must operate and stresses the important role marketing managers play in guiding the organization's operations within the environment.

Chapter 3 discusses not only the development of marketing strategies and the role the marketing environment plays in providing opportunities and information, but also constraints, with which the marketer must work.

Chapter 4 treats specifically the very important and very powerful marketing planning tool known as market segmentation. ∎

CHAPTER 1

The Nature of Marketing

CHAPTER SCAN

This chapter introduces marketing as a force in society and business.

The chapter defines marketing and the marketing mix and shows that marketing is an exchange process that is carried out in nonprofit as well as business dealings.

This chapter also describes the marketing concept, the business philosophy that, when properly applied, is the basis of all effective marketing.

WHEN YOU HAVE STUDIED THIS CHAPTER, YOU WILL:

Be able to discuss the importance of marketing in your daily life.

Be able to define effective marketing in the business sense and in the newer "broadened" sense.

Be able to show how marketing creates economic utility.

Be able to describe the marketing mix.

Be able to explain the marketing concept.

You are exposed to marketing activities almost every day of your life. Hearing a radio commercial, such as the one transcribed below, is a familiar experience.[1]

Waiter:	I got an order for you, chef.
Chef:	What is it?
Waiter:	Table six wants the blimp cocktail.
Chef:	You mean shrimp cocktail.
Waiter:	And the beer soup.
Chef:	Bean soup.
Waiter:	And a bowl of the beef glue.
Chef:	What? Let me see that menu.
Waiter:	Okay.
Chef:	Who made this copy. It's all smeared and wrinkled. I can hardly read it.
Waiter:	Booth four wants chicken frisbee.
Chef:	Fricassee.
Waiter:	What the heck is corn on the cat?
Chef:	Oh, these copies are terrible.
Waiter:	What do you want from me, our copier jams up all the time.
Chef:	Get me a Minolta.
Waiter:	I don't see Minolta on the menu. Oh, you mean the minestrone.
Chef:	I mean the Minolta EP 310 copier.
Waiter:	Ahhh.
Chef:	The Minolta EP 310 has this incredibly short paper path that virtually eliminates paper jam.
Waiter:	No kidding.
Chef:	And the Minolta EP 310 even has a self-diagnostic system.
Waiter:	How about the bowling banquet in the back room.
Chef:	Yeah?
Waiter:	They want the nude cake.
Chef:	You mean nut cake.
Waiter:	No, nude cake, where the girl jumps out at the . . .
Chef:	Oh, that.
Waiter:	Yeah.
Chef:	That.
Announcer:	The Minolta EP 310 copier. A business partner you can depend on.

The radio advertisement we've just read is an example of creative marketing that we can all recognize and appreciate. There are probably many other advertisements that we have enjoyed or disliked. However, advertising such as this is

---

[1] William D. Tyler, "The Sounds of Winners: Year's Best Radio Spots," *Advertising Age*, August 24, 1981, p. 54.

not the only marketing activity prominent in our lives. We all probably recognize brand names and corporate logos. They are extremely important in the marketing of products. We have seen and heard advertisements, visited shopping centers, examined retail displays, compared prices, dealt with salespeople, and evaluated and purchased products that were shipped from other states or from foreign countries. By doing these things we have, for most of our lives, played a role in the marketing system. Thus, everyone already knows something about marketing.

However, though most people are familiar with the marketing phenomena, they do not fully understand marketing's place in society or how marketing activities should be managed.

The brand names shown on the left are probably quite familiar, but the logos above are probably not. They identify corporations most consumers seldom encounter directly. These companies buy products and services in order to produce other products and services, thus performing important marketing activities "behind the scenes." Therefore, while most of us deal regularly with retailers and sales clerks, we less frequently encounter wholesalers, industrial sales representatives, and advertising agents. Thus, there are many aspects of marketing that we may have never considered in a systematic fashion.

Our purposes in writing this book are to introduce the concept of marketing as an academic discipline and to portray the many fascinating marketing practices which form the bases of our national and international economies.

MARKETING: WHAT IS IT?

As we will see, there are several ways to consider the subject of marketing, so there are also a number of ways to define the term itself. Since, for most people, marketing has a business connotation, it is best to begin by discussing marketing from a business perspective.

"Marketing," as the term implies, is focused on the marketplace. In fact, for many shoppers of past generations, the word "marketing" meant going to a store or market to buy groceries. If a business person was asked the question, "What is marketing?" the answer might be that marketing is selling, or advertising, or retailing. Notice that these are marketing activities, not definitions of marketing as a whole.

At the broadest level, the function of marketing activities is to bring buyers and sellers together. At the beach, the thirsty sunbather seeks the Pepsi stand owner who is, in turn, interested in selling soft drinks to satisfy the customer's thirst. Marketing activities such as locating the stand at the beach or advertising the price on a sign help bring buyers and sellers together. The owner's goal is to consummate a sale to satisfy a customer. This, of course, is a simple example. A more sophisticated situation requires more complex marketing activities.

Suppose you are the marketing vice-president of Sony Corporation of America. Sony markets products that have already been produced in Japan. Thus, production is not your major marketing concern. Instead, your marketing activities might be identified as product planning, determining prices, advertising, selling, distribution of products to consumers, and servicing the products after sales are made. Still, there is more to marketing than the activities named here.

A full understanding of marketing requires recognition of the fact that product development activities and product modifications are planned in response to the public's changing needs and wants. A major marketing activity is paying continuous attention to customers' needs and interpreting those needs *before* other steps, including production, are undertaken. Although most marketing activities are intended to direct the flow of goods and services from producer to consumer, the marketing process begins with customer analysis before the product is even manufactured. For instance, before Sony manufactured the Walkman cassette stereo player, the new product idea was discussed with high school and college students to refine the product to suit American students' needs. Thus, Sony of America does not merely import Japanese products; it interprets the American market's needs for electronic equipment and passes these interpretations on to manufacturing and other company personnel who attempt to incorporate consumer benefits into the company's product offering. Creation of the Sony Walkman was based on a recognition of a need for high quality sound when people were engaging in activities outside of the home.

NOT-FOR-PROFIT ORGANIZATIONS ARE MARKETERS TOO

"Perform a death-defying act—eat less saturated fat." The American Heart Association offered this admonition in an advertisement (see Exhibit 1-1), yet the Heart Association does not seek to make a profit nor does it charge a price for most services. Is the American Heart Association engaged in marketing? Are your university, church, or local police department marketers? If we take a broadened perspective of marketing, the answer is unquestionably "Yes."[2]

---

[2] Philip Kotler and Sidney J. Levy, "Broadening the Concept of Marketing," *Journal of Marketing*, January 1979, pp. 10–15.

JOIN, or DIE.

This example of not-for-profit marketing was published by Benjamin Franklin in his *Pennsylvania Gazette,* May 9, 1754. The broken parts of the snake are the divided American colonies.

When analyzing a politician's campaign, a zoo's fund-raising drive, or an anti-smoking group's program, we can see marketing in action. Whether a donation is made to the American Heart Association or to a zoo, to a political campaign, or to an anti-smoking effort, something is given and something is received. Even though the "something received" may be an intangible, such as a feeling of goodwill or a sense of satisfaction rather than a packaged good, there has been a transaction between either an individual and a group or between two individuals. In all these instances, marketing can be found. The characteristic common to each of these situations is the set of activities necessary to bringing about exchange relationships.[3]

If the concept of marketing is broadened to include not-for-profit organizations, then the primary emphasis of marketing involves an **exchange process** requiring that two or more parties exchange, or trade, things of value. An economic transfer of goods or services in exchange for a price expressed in monetary terms is the most frequently analyzed marketing exchange.

However, the offering of a vote or a volunteer effort in exchange for a candidate's pledge to work hard for his or her constituents, or the donation of blood to help the sick and injured, or

time spent working for a United Way campaign where the reward is a sense of satisfaction, are all exchange activities. As such, these activities may be viewed from a marketing perspective when they are planned to bring about an exchange.

EXHIBIT 1-1

The American Heart Association Engages in Marketing

Don't be a heartbreaker

Eat less saturated fat.

American Heart Association
WE'RE FIGHTING FOR YOUR LIFE

---

[3] Robert J. Holloway and Robert S. Hancock, *Marketing in a Changing Environment* (New York: John Wiley & Sons, 1973), p. 10.

A DEFINITION OF EFFECTIVE MARKETING

The Sony example illustrates what marketing is like in a well-managed business. The American Heart Association example illustrates that not-for-profit organizations engage in marketing. You now have enough marketing knowledge to understand our definition of effective marketing:

> **Effective marketing** consists of a consumer oriented mix of business activities planned and implemented by a marketer to facilitate the exchange or transfer of products, services, or ideas so that both parties profit in some way.

Thus, effective marketing requires the development of products, services, or ideas so they may be brought to market and purchased by buyers. Promotion, pricing, and distribution of these goods, services, or ideas facilitates the basic function of bringing marketers (suppliers) together with consumers (buyers). Each party must gain something; revenues for the marketers, products for the consumers.

MARKETING'S PURPOSE IN SOCIETY

Marketing should be considered from one additional viewpoint: the important role it plays in society. Before this is explained, a note on terminology is in order. When marketing is referred to as an *aggregate* of marketing activities within an economy or as the marketing system within a society, some prefer to use the term **macro-marketing.** Thus, marketing may be split the same way economics may be split into micro-economics and macro-economics. Our preference is to use the term **marketing** throughout, making its meaning clear by the context in which it is discussed. Marketing's role in society can be illustrated by the description of marketing (macro-marketing) as "the delivery of a standard of living to society."[4] It may seem a bit grandiose to describe marketing in such a way but some reflection will bear out the truth of that statement.

When we think of the *aggregate* of organizations' marketing activity, especially the aggregation of transportation and distribution activity, we see that the efficiency of the system for moving goods from producers to the people who will utilize the goods (consumers) may substantially affect a society's well-being.[5] In primitive societies and undeveloped countries, middlemen, such as retailers and wholesalers, may be nonexistent or inefficient. Thus, transportation, storage, and other distribution aspects of marketing are fundamental in the delivery of a standard of living to society. To reach a desired level of economic well-being, a country must trade with other countries or develop its domestic resources. International trade is performed and facilitated by marketing. In at least some cases, less-developed countries are "poor" because their international marketing systems are too primitive or inefficient to "deliver" an improved quality of life.

---

[4] Paul Mazur, "Does Distribution Cost Enough?" *Fortune*, November 1974, p. 138.

[5] The word "marketing" derives from the Latin term "mercatus," or "marketplace," which in turn comes from the term "mercari," "to trade."

Marketing provides time, place, and possession utility.

Marketing and Utility

A business or a nonprofit organization performs its role in society and survives only as long as it can provide utilities to its customers. **Economic utility** is the ability of a product or service to satisfy some aspect of a consumer's wants or needs. A product that can satisfy buyers has more economic utility than a product that is of little or no use to anyone. In Exhibit 1-2, we have constructed a hypothetical range of economic utility for several products to illustrate how most consumers evaluate the utility of various products.

Notice that of the five types of utility identified, only one, form utility, is not developed and enhanced mostly by marketing activities. In fact, place, time, possession, and information (communication) utility are created almost entirely by marketing. Provision of these utilities is marketing's justification for existence in society.

EXHIBIT 1-2

Economic Utility

The Range of Economic Utility

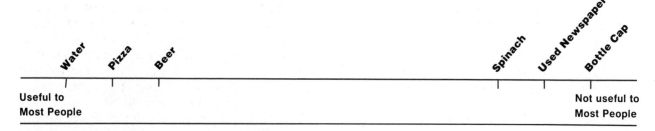

Useful to
Most People

Not useful to
Most People

Five specific types of utilities within economic utility

1. Form utility—created primarily by means of production

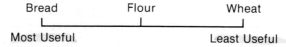

Bread Flour Wheat

Most Useful Least Useful

2. Place utility—created primarily by transportation and distribution

Beer in refrigerator Beer at retail store Beer at distributor Beer at brewery

Most Useful Least Useful

3. Time utility—created primarily by storage

Vegetables stored until demanded Vegetables available only at harvest time

Most Useful Least Useful

4. Possession utility—created primarily by the conclusion of a sale

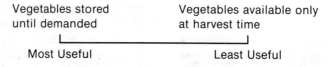

Car purchased through G.M.A.C. allows possession when car is desired Car desired but not purchased because credit is not available

Most Useful Least Useful

5. Information utility—created primarily by promotion

Motel located because of sign or yellow pages ad Motel not located, must drive 100 miles to next city

Most Useful Least Useful

THE MARKETING MIX

The term **marketing mix** describes the result of management's efforts to creatively combine interrelated and interdependent marketing activities. Faced with a wide choice of media, message, prices, distribution methods, and other marketing variables, the marketing manager must select and combine the "ingredients" of the organization's marketing mix.

To achieve organizational objectives, the marketing executive must be constantly engaged in fashioning a mix of marketing procedures and policies. This mix must be altered as new problems and environmental changes develop.[6] While the mix may have many facets, the basic categories of marketing mix elements are: **product, price, place (distribution),** and **promotion.** These are commonly referred to as the **"4 P's of Marketing"** and, since virtually every possible marketing activity can be placed in one of those categories, the 4 P's constitute a framework that may be utilized to develop a simple marketing plan.[7] Preparation of a marketing strategy would require consideration of each major mix area, and may involve the development of substrategies within each category. Since these marketing mix variables may be influenced by managers they are also called **controllable variables.**

Product

The term **product** refers to what the business or non-profit organization offers to its prospective customers or clients without regard to whether the offering is a tangible good such as a car, or a service such as an airline trip, or an intangible benefit such as being confident that you look your best.

Since customers often expect more from an organization than a simple, tangible product, the task of marketing management is to provide a complete offering—a "total product"—that includes not only the basic service or merchandise, but also all the "extras" that go with it. The product of a city bus line may be rides or transportation, but its total product offering should include courteous service, on-time performance, and assistance in finding appropriate bus routes. The Chairman of Binney and Smith, marketers of Crayola Crayons, says "We are no longer just a crayon company. We are in the business of providing assorted products that are fun to use and inspire creative self-expression."[8] This effective marketer realizes what a product is. The Burroughs Corporation's product is office equipment plus repair service, supplies, advice to customers, and other customer services. Their product extends beyond the initial sale. Burroughs' product definition allows the company to realize that the sale is not the end of the marketing process.

The product the customer receives in the exchange process is the result of a number of product strategy decisions. Product development and product planning involve making sure that the goods and services offered have the attributes which customers desire. Product strategy also includes such activities as selecting brand names, designing packages, and developing appropriate warranties and service plans.

As we will see, product strategies must take the other three elements of the marketing mix into consideration. The other elements enhance the attraction of the product offering.

Place

Determination of how goods get to the customer, how quickly, and in what condition, involves **place** or **distribution** strategy. Transporta-

---

[6]Neil H. Borden, "The Concept of the Marketing Mix," *Journal of Advertising Research*, June 1964, pp. 2–7.

[7]E. Jerome McCarthy, *Basic Marketing: A Managerial Approach* (Homewood, Ill.: Richard D. Irwin, 1971), p. 44.

[8]Quotation from Gay Jervey, "New Products Painting Rosy Future for Crayola," *Advertising Age*, January 11, 1982, p. 4.

tion, storage, materials handling, and the like are physical distribution, or "P.D.," activities. Selection of wholesalers, retailers, or other types of distributors is also a place problem since these intermediaries comprise channels of distribution.

The examples so far have shown that every organization engages in marketing. Every organization, however, does not have the resources or ability to manage all the activities required in the distribution process. Thus, organizations may concentrate on activities where they have a unique advantage. Wholesalers, retailers, and various other specialists, such as airlines, have developed to allow for specialization and to make the distribution process more efficient. For example, the Pepsi-Cola Corporation, which specializes in the production and promotion of soft drinks, finds it efficient to utilize independent bottlers and retailers to distribute their products to the ultimate consumer.

A **channel of distribution** is the complete sequence of marketing organizations involved in bringing a product from the producer to the ultimate consumer. Exhibit 1-3 illustrates a *basic* channel of distribution consisting of the manufacturer, the wholesaler, the retailer, and the ultimate consumer. Each of these four parties in the channel of distribution engages in making a transaction that involves movement of the physical product and/or a transfer of title (ownership) to that product.

Some formal definitions are in order:

Manufacturer. The organization that recognizes a consumer need and produces a service or product from raw materials, component parts, or labor to satisfy that need.

Wholesaler. The organization that serves as a mediator between manufacturer and retailer to facilitate the transaction of products themselves or the title to these products. Wholesalers neither produce nor consume the finished product.

Retailer. An organization that sells products

You can count on Sears serv

Few places in the U.S. are beyond the reach of Sears 16,000 service trucks—and even if you move to Ely, Nevada or Blairs Mills, Kentucky. Sears will arrange for your service and honor your warranties.

EVERY YEAR one American family in five moves to a new home. New address new phone number new schools, new friends—but if your appliances came from Sears, the same old reliable service is only a phone call away.

If you want help hooking up Sears appliances you've taken with you, call your new Sears store in advance and let them know when you expect to move in. Sears will do its best to be there that very day.

If you bought a Sears appliance from

any Sears store in the U.S. any store and service center in the country will service—and of course charge it on your Sears credit card.

If you bought a maintenance agreement from Sears, every Sears will honor it.

Sears operates 16,000 service trucks, each driven by a Sears-trained and stocked with parts for Sears. Chances are very good that a single call will have things humming a...

Sears provides place utility.

it obtained from the manufacturers or wholesalers to the ultimate consumer. Retailers neither produce nor consume the product.

Ultimate Consumer. The individual who buys or uses the product. The term industrial buyer refers to a consuming organization, such as an automobile manufacturer, purchasing a product like steel that will be utilized to produce or sell another good or service.

The actual path that a product or title takes may be much more complex than the one illustrated in Exhibit 1-3. These more complex distribution systems will be explained in Chapters 12, 13, and 14.

It is important to realize that distribution mixes vary widely, even among companies selling like products. For example, Avon and Amway use their own sales forces to sell directly to consumers while Gillette and Colgate-Palmolive, selling similar goods, utilize many wholesalers and retailers in their distribution systems. Other examples are Fuller Brush, which sells toothbrushes door-to-door, and Pepsodent, which uses intermediaries to place toothbrushes in drug stores.

Price

The amount of money, or sometimes goods or services, given in exchange for something is its **price.** In other words, price is what is exchanged for the product. Just as the customer buys a product with cash, so a manufacturer "buys" the customer's cash with the product.

According to economists, prices are always "on trial." Pricing strategies and decisions require establishing appropriate prices *and* careful monitoring of the competitive marketplace. Prices are always subject to change, in part because, unlike the other three elements of the marketing mix, price is relatively easy to change. Of course, changes that are poorly thought out can lead to disaster. In not-for-profit situations, price may be expressed in terms of volunteered time or effort, votes, or donations.

The numerous specialists performing specific facilitating activities for manufacturers, wholesalers, or retailers, such as the airline or the freight train company (*common carrier*) that transports the product from Boston to Philadelphia or the *advertising agency* on Madison Avenue creating the advertising message and selecting the appropriate media, are excluded from the channel of distribution. However, each of these specialists is hired because they can more efficiently or more effectively perform a certain marketing activity for an organization in a basic marketing channel. These **facilitating agents** are excluded from the term "organizations" in our definition of a channel of distribution.

Promotion

The essence of **promotion** is communication. Advertising, personal selling, publicity, and sales promotion are all forms of communication that are utilized to inform and to persuade. The firm's promotion mix is its particular combination of these communication tools. Some firms may emphasize advertising, while others hardly utilize advertising at all. Advertising "Coke is it!" reminds us of our experiences with a familiar cola. An IBM sales representative explains how a computer will help our organization. A supermarket display offers a free sample of Eckrich sausage. Promotion provides information that

Producers, wholesalers, retailers and consumers
are members of the channel of distribution.

EXHIBIT 1-3

Who Is Involved in a Basic Channel of Distribution

Flow of Product or Title	Definition	Example
Manufacturer	Producer of a finished product from raw materials or component parts.	Coors Beer Company Golden, Colorado
↓		
Wholesaler	A middleman who neither produces nor consumes the finished product, but sells to retailers or manufacturers or institutions that use the product for ultimate resale (perhaps in another product form).	Los Angeles Coors Distributor.
↓		
Retailer	A middleman who neither produces nor consumes the finished product, but sells to the ultimate consumer.	Safeway Stores
↓		
Consumer	A person who buys or uses the finished product.	You

encourages consumers to respond. Obviously, what is to be communicated is persuasive information about the *other* elements of the marketing mix, such as the uses for the product or the new low price being offered during a sale period.

The Art of Blending the Elements

A manager's selection of a marketing mix may be likened to the cook or chef who realizes that there is no "one best way" to make a dish. Instead, different combinations of ingredients may be utilized and the result will still be a satisfactory meal. In marketing, as in cooking, there is no standard formula for a successful combination of marketing elements. Marketing mixes will vary from company to company and from situation to situation.

Exhibit 1-4 provides examples of many marketing mix elements. While some experts claim marketing is, or could be, a science, the vast majority of marketers agree that the blending of the various elements of the marketing mix is a creative activity. For example, though both firms are successful, the marketing mix strategies of Honda motorcycles vary widely from those of Harley-Davidson motorcycles. Far greater differences in marketing mixes can be seen between different products, such as Seamco racquet balls and Steinway pianos. The field of marketing encompasses such differing approaches because the design, implementation, and revision of a marketing mix is a creative activity.

Certain aspects of marketing are scientific in nature, such as the gathering of information by marketing researchers. The fact remains, however, that there are no pat solutions in marketing. Even frequently encountered problems have unique aspects. This absence of certainty, or room for creativity, may annoy those who are accustomed to solving math or accounting problems and arriving at one "right" answer. But marketing is different. Its relationship to the ever-changing environment requires that it be dynamic, constantly altering its approaches to the marketplace.

EXHIBIT 1-4

Elements of the Marketing Mix—Creative Examples

Marketing Mix Element	Company or Organization	Example
Product		
Product development	Coors	Herman Joseph's 1868—Testing a new super premium beer.
Product modification	Hyatt Corp.	Park Hyatt—Remodeling a Chicago hotel into an elegant luxury hotel.
Branding	National Multiple Sclerosis Society	Help fight *MS*.
Warranty	Sears	"If any Craftsman hand tool ever fails to give complete satisfaction, Sears will replace it free."
Trademark	Playboy	Playboy Bunny.
Distribution		
Channel-of-distribution	IBM	Personal computers sold in retail stores.
Physical distribution	John Wiley & Sons, Publishers	Uses Federal Express to transport rush orders.
Promotion		
Advertising	Panasonic	Slightly ahead of our time.
	The Advertising Council	Remember only you can prevent forest fires.
Personal selling	Girl Scouts	Cookie sales door-to-door.
Sales promotion	Bloomingdale's	Irish heritage celebrated with exhibits of Irish homes and country cottages in 14 stores.
	Mattel	International "Astrosmash Shootoff" championship—computer game contest.
Publicity	Ford	Reporters test drive new cars in September.
Pricing	Southwest Airlines	Discounted tickets to travel agents buying in bulk.
	Chivas Regal	Tastes expensive and it is!
	Bell System	Long distance rates lower on weekends.

THE MARKETING CONCEPT— THE FOUNDATION OF EFFECTIVE MARKETING

The philosophy known as the **marketing concept** is central to all effective marketing thinking, planning, and action. It relates marketing to the organization's overall purpose—to survive and prosper by satisfying a clientele—and calls on management *and* employees to do three things.

1 To be consumer oriented in all matters, from product development to honoring warranties and service contracts.

2 To stress long-run profitability rather than short-term profits or sales volume.

3 To integrate and coordinate marketing functions and other corporate functions.

This is not as simple as it sounds at first. The historical developments of marketing point this out (see Exhibit 1-5). The marketing concept, common-sensical as it seems, was not practiced extensively by businesses until the middle of this century.

Production Era

Until the Great Depression (1929–1933) many American companies were able to do very well by following, not the marketing concept, but what might be called the production concept. Henry Ford's famous description of the Model T—"You can have any color you want as long as it's black"—sums up the prevailing attitude of the **production era.** Faced with a seller's market (manufacturers could turn out a decent product and expect to sell it rather easily), it was natural to be oriented toward production, not marketing.

Sales Era

The Depression spelled an end to the seller's market, leaving not a buyer's market so much as no market at all. With unemployment at 25 percent or more and the economy literally in shambles, Ford's approach to moving merchandise was replaced, as it was in many surviving businesses, with the slogan "Push! Push! Sell! Sell!" Many firms developed aggressive campaigns to "push" their products onto consumers. This was the **sales era.** Theaters gave away dishes and silverware, manufacturers stressed coupons, giveaways, slogan-writing contests, and free merchandise of all sorts. Sales-oriented organizations emphasized short-run increases in sales volume of their existing products rather than long-run profits.

Marketing Era

With the improvement of the economy after World War II came the realization that consumers would have to be approached in a new way. The "Push! Push!" method was no longer appropriate because of healthy market demand and rising educational levels. Increased production capacities and consumers' increasingly sophisticated tastes seemed to make Henry Ford's early slogan obsolete.

Thus, it was not until the mid-1950s, when businesspeople began reporting the successful use of a new idea called "marketing," that the *marketing era* began.[9] The old slogans and rules had, in a sense, changed, as illustrated by Exhibit 1-6.

Consumer Orientation

Consumer orientation is the first aspect of the marketing concept. The consumer or customer should be seen as "the fulcrum, the pivot point about which the business moves in operating for the balanced interests of all concerned."[10] Organizations that have accepted the marketing concept try to create products and services with

---

[9] Robert F. Keith, "The Marketing Revolution," *Journal of Marketing,* January 1960, pp. 35–38.

[10] Fred J. Burch, "The Marketing Philosophy as a Way of Business Life," in *The Marketing Concept: Its Meaning to Management,* Marketing Series, No. 99.

EXHIBIT 1-5

Three Eras of American Business

	Focus	Means	Goal
Production orientation	Manufacturing	Make quality products	Produce all that is possible.
Sales orientation	Existing products	Aggressive sales and persuasive advertising efforts	Profits through sales volume.
Marketing orientation	Actual and potential customer needs and wants	Integrated marketing	Profits through customer satisfaction.

Source: Adapted with permission from William Lazar, *Marketing Management: A Systems Perspective* (New York: John Wiley & Sons, 1971), p. 28 and Rom J. Markin, *Marketing* (New York: John Wiley & Sons, 1979), p. 33.

EXHIBIT 1-6

Philosophies of Three Eras

Production Era	Sales Era	Marketing Era
"You can have any color you want as long as it's black."	"You don't like black? I'll throw in a set of glassware!"	"Find out what consumers want before you make the product."
"Make the best product you can and people will buy it."	"Sell this inventory no matter what it takes."	"Maybe people don't want the 'best' product. Find out what they do want."
"Sell a lot of cars and each one at a profit."	"Sell some cars fast or we're out of business."	"Sell cars in a way that will make us profitable over the long haul."
"I know the people want my kind of product."	"Who cares what they want, sell what we've got."	"I'm going to find out what the people want."

the customer's needs in mind. It follows that the first determination must be what the customer wants. The marketing concept rightly suggests that it is better to find out what the customer wants and offer that product than it is to make a product and then try to sell it to somebody.

In a way, even Thomas Edison, usually thought of as an engineer or inventor, was a marketer. Though he did no formal marketing research, he did identify peoples' needs and sought to develop products that would fill those needs. Edison literally made a list of such poten-

COLLEGES MOVED THROUGH PRODUCTION AND SALES ERAS, TOO

Many, but unfortunately not all, American colleges and universities have experienced movement through the production and sales eras and on to their own marketing eras.

Until the 1970s, many institutions offered their degree programs with pretty much of a take-it-or-leave-it attitude. High school students worried about getting accepted to a "decent school," were kept guessing by admissions offices, and then expected to be grateful for a chance to earn a degree at Old Siwash. This was the *production era.*

A combination of overexpansion at many schools and a declining pool of high school students in the 1970s then drove many colleges into a *sales era.* Colleges sent recruiters to high schools far and wide, offered guaranteed admissions, and questionable academic programs in an effort to drag in students. Some went so far as to hire "headhunters" who toured foreign countries handing out student visas.

More recently colleges and universities have entered a *marketing era.* They have selected smaller groups to which to appeal (such as those interested in horse breeding or studies in Jewish history). They have permitted students to have a hand in designing their own programs, instituted long-term repayment plans, and offered course work at convenient locations near students' homes or jobs and, at times, convenient to the students' personal schedules. In other words, they have considered the market and developed marketing mixes that can satisfy that market.

tial products which included entries like these: a way to light houses without gas flames; a machine that could talk; and pictures that could move to tell a story.

According to most marketing thinkers, consumer orientation—the satisfaction of customer wants—is the justification for an organization's existence. Consider the following examples.

For years patrons of the United States Postal Service complained about slow package deliveries. Business customers and some private citizens wanted packages delivered overnight. The post office was not meeting these needs. Federal Express and some other firms stepped into the gap by offering private, overnight package courier services to customers who absolutely had to have next day package delivery.

The chairman of the board of McDonald's restaurants increased his company's consciousness of the importance of consumer orientation. While visiting one of McDonald's outlets, he encountered a sign ordering customers to "MOVE TO THE NEXT POSITION." He declared that such signs be removed from all McDonald's outlets, and stated, "It's up to us to move to the customer."[11] Progressive companies wisely spend a great deal of time and effort learning about consumers.

Burger King's long-lived "Have it your way" marketing strategy was developed after it was discovered that consumers were annoyed and frustrated when they had to wait for special orders at fast food places. Burger King learned that solving consumer problems is effective marketing and helps make sales.

Product success, industry leadership, even corporate survival, depend on satisfying the consumer. When a company defines the broad nature of its business it must take a consumer-oriented perspective. When setting a corporate mission, the company's style, its direction, and its goals, the company must avoid short-sighted, narrow-minded thinking that will lead it to define its purpose from a product orientation rather than a consumer orientation. A firm's failure to define its purpose from a broad consumer orientation is referred to as **marketing myopia.**[12] Thus

---

[11] Priscilla A. LaBarbara and Larry J. Rosenberg, "How Marketers Can Better Understand Consumers," *MSU Business Topics,* Winter 1980, p. 31.

[12] Theodore Levitt, "Marketing Myopia," *Harvard Business Review,* July–August 1960, pp. 45–56.

MERRILL LYNCH REALTY?
E. F. HUTTON LIFE INSURANCE?

Merrill Lynch is a stockbroker, right? A production-oriented management would have said yes. There would not have been any entry into a variety of new financial activities that compete with the banking business realtors and the like. Merrill Lynch realizes that someone's home is "the investment of your life." They did not take a myopic view of what services they should provide when they entered the realty business. In 1977 they diversified their services with Cash Management Account; a one stop financial service aimed at investors with at least $20,000 in cash or securities who wish to use the money from time to time. This service includes placing proceeds from securities sales and other forms of income into a money market fund. Loans with a debit card and withdrawals with one's checkbook are possible in the cash management account. Cash deposits may be made. Securities management and record keeping are part of the investment service. Merrill Lynch is involved in an investor's total money program. Merrill Lynch Realty is a marketing-concept oriented expansion by a company that understands the nature of consumers and their corporate mission. Merrill Lynch isn't the only company diversifying its financial services. American Express has acquired Shearson Loeb Rhoades. E.F. Hutton now sells life insurance. MasterCard offers travelers checks.

railroads should define their industry as transportation-oriented rather than railroad-oriented. People who make movies should see themselves as in the entertainment business rather than the movie business. The nature of the business must be defined with a broad consumer-oriented philosophy.

Profit Orientation

Even though the marketing concept stresses consumer orientation, this does not mean that every fleeting whim of every customer must be met. Implicit in the marketing concept is the assumption of the organization's continuity. Consumers would prefer that the price of a new Mercedes-Benz be under $500. But, since the manufacturing and marketing costs associated with such a car far exceed that figure, Mercedes' manufacturers and distributors would soon be out of business if they attempted to satisfy that particular consumer desire.

In other cases consumer wants must be considered in terms of cost and profit goals. Gillette, for example, found that the popular, adjustable flame feature on its Cricket lighter had to be dropped because high manufacturing expenses could not be justified. Freeze-dried ice cream—"Space Age Food Like the Astronauts Eat"—is a popular item sold at the National Air and Space Museum in Washington, D.C. But cleaning up ice cream and packages would raise maintenance costs and cause other difficulties. So, despite consumer desire for the ice cream, the package clearly states, "DO NOT OPEN IN THE MUSEUM." Consumer wants as well as costs *and* profits were *all* taken into consideration in determining this market offering.

The profit-oriented aspect of the marketing concept argues that sales volume for the sake of volume alone should not be sought. Sales volume can be profitless, and a firm can actually increase its sales volume while decreasing its profits, for example when big discounts attract more customers but result in less income.

It may be possible to "buy volume" with heavy advertising, price cutting, or other methods. Few industry analysts see this as a profitable strategy. Crown, a discount book store chain, offered best-sellers at up to 45 percent off list price and 25 percent off on other books. Competitors indicated "There's no way you can make money doing what Crown is doing."[13] As most aggressive price cutters find out, the profit

---

[13] "Booksellers Try Discounting," *Business Week*, October 26, 1981, p. 16; "How an Industry Is Getting Crowned," *Advertising Age*, May 30, 1983, p. m—4.

aspect of an operation regulates marketing activities over any but the shortest time periods.

Offering large discounts on books is nothing new. Books were offered at cut rate prices during the 1940s and 1950s by department stores such as Macy's and Gimbel's. Some best-sellers were sold at prices so low that other book retailers would buy large stocks for resale (at higher margins) in their own book stores. Ultimately, department stores found that profits from discount book sales failed to offset floor space costs or the cost of the voluminous paperwork that accompanied the shipping and ordering processes.

An approach to increasing profits that is more effective than price slashing is suggested by the fact that many firms have discovered that 20 percent of their customers are responsible for 80 percent of their profits and that too much marketing effort is expended on unprofitable accounts. The marketing concept suggests that marketing activities to smaller, possibly unprofitable, accounts be re-evaluated.

The same logic applies to product offerings. Republic Steel's industrial products division, a maker of lockers, shelving, and shop equipment, found that 95 percent of their sales came from some 3,000 items in a product line featuring 12,000 products. Republic trimmed three-fourths of its product line to increase its profits.[14]

Most retailers face problems similar to Republic Steel's. Ideally, a retailer would carry such a varied assortment of goods that customers would be offered a complete selection. Dial soap, for example, comes in three sizes and four colors, thus there are twelve "different" Dial soaps. Of the dozens of laundry detergents, the top five alone, with their four size choices, yield twenty "different" detergents. Consumers might want retailers to carry *all* of these choices and more, but this would increase shelf space requirements and raise other costs that can be

---

[14]Kevin Higgins, "Division of Republic Steel Earns Record Profits After Shift to Marketing Orientation," *Marketing News,* May 29, 1981, p. 4.

BETTER MOUSETRAPS— PRODUCT FAILURES

Producing a "better product" does not ensure success in the marketplace. Edsel automobiles by Ford and Corfam shoe material by DuPont are examples of gigantic failures. The list of products that did not meet company success standards could be substantially longer than the one listed below.

Apollo Video Games
New Cookery (diet food products)
Finger Frostings (candied frosting in cups to be eaten with fingers)
King Cola (soft drink)
Root 66 (soft drink)
Chelsea (soft drink)
Inside Sports Magazine
Output Magazine
Fruit-of-the-Loom (laundry detergent)
Free (cigarettes)
Fact (cigarettes)
Player (Miller's "Ultra Light" beer)
Chipper (Miller's dark, low calorie beer)
Altair 8800 (personal computer kit)
Ontrax Computer Disk Drives
House Dressings (salad dressings)
Happy Face (facial washing cream)
Small Miracle Shampoo
Vaseline Intensive Care Shampoo
Pink Panther Flakes (cereal)
Kream Krunch (cereal)
Great Loaf (bread mix for meat loaf)
Heaven's Gate (movie)
Golden Gate Commuter Airline
Mini Pearl's Chicken Restaurants
Jerry Lewis Cinemas
Susan B. Anthony dollar

reduced by stocking a limited selection of items . . . those that sell best. Despite the fact that some sales might be lost, the consumer's desire for a complete inventory must be balanced against the retailer's cost of carrying that inventory.

INTEGRATED MARKETING EFFORT

Marketing personnel do not work in a vacuum, isolated from other company activities. The actions of people in such areas as production, credit, and research and development, may have effects on the organization's marketing efforts. Similarly, the work of marketers will affect these other departments. Problems are almost certain to evolve if an integrated, company-wide effort is not maintained.

A prime example of things gone wrong is the W. T. Grant Company, one of the biggest retailing failures of all times. One of that chain

---

EXHIBIT 1-7

Marketing/Manufacturing Areas of Necessary Cooperation but Potential Conflict

Problem Area	Typical Marketing Comment	Typical Manufacturing Comment
1. Capacity planning and long-range sales forecasting	"Why don't we have enough capacity?"	"Why didn't we have accurate sales forecasts?"
2. Production scheduling and short-range sales forecasting	"We need faster response. Our lead times are ridiculous."	"We need realistic customer commitments and sales forecasts that don't change like wind direction."
3. Delivery and physical distribution	"Why don't we ever have the right merchandise in inventory?"	"We can't keep everything in inventory."
4. Quality assurance	"Why can't we have reasonable quality at reasonable cost?"	"Why must we always offer options that are too hard to manufacture and that offer little customer utility?"
5. Breadth of product line	"Our customers demand variety."	"The product line is too broad—all we get are short, uneconomical runs."
6. Cost control	"Our costs are so high that we are not competitive in the marketplace."	"We can't provide fast delivery, broad variety, rapid response to change, and high quality at low cost."
7. New product introduction	"New products are our life blood."	"Unnecessary design changes are prohibitively expensive."
8. Adjunct services such as spare parts inventory support, installation, and repair	"Field service costs are too high."	"Products are being used in ways for which they weren't designed."

Source: Reprinted by permission of the *Harvard Business Review*. An exhibit from "Can Marketing and Manufacturing Co-Exist?" by Benson Shapiro (September–October 1977). Copyright © 1977 by the President and Fellows of Harvard College; all rights reserved.

store's problems appears to have been a lack of integration between the credit department's policies and the needs of the company to maintain consumer-oriented charge plans which would encourage long-run profitability. Store managers were urged to push credit and given quotas to fill. One Grant executive stated that they "gave credit to every deadbeat who breathed."[15] Sales were increased, but the firm experienced losses because no integrated plan existed to accommodate this increase.[16]

Other difficulties arise when marketing is viewed as solely the problem of the enterprise's "Marketing Department." Other functional areas have goals which conflict with the overall goal of customer satisfaction. For example, the finance department may want fixed budgets, strict spending justifications, and prices that cover costs, whereas the marketing department may seek flexible budgets, spending rationales, and prices that may be less than cost so that markets can be quickly developed. The engineering and production department may want long lead time to design and produce products, but the marketing department may opt for short lead time so as to fulfill a perceived demand in the marketplace. The production department may prefer to make many units of a single model of a product, while the marketing department believes that customers will want multiple model options and custom components. Some additional aspects of marketing and manufacturing co-existence are illustrated in Exhibit 1-7.

Similar differences in outlook occur with the other functional areas of the organization, and these may be sources of serious conflicts.[17] The marketing concept seeks to resolve these conflicts by stressing customer satisfaction, long-

---

SUCCESSFUL MARKETING-ORIENTED ORGANIZATIONS CAN BE FOUND IN ALL FIELDS

Services	Holiday Inn is "Number 1 in people pleasing." Holiday Inn: "We want you to wake up feeling good."
Nonprofit	Chicago's Brookfield Zoo is portrayed as "In partnership with taxpayers in support of a unique leisure resource." Cleveland's Zoo invites citizens to "adopt" their very own zoo animal.
Industrial products	Compucorp Word Processor's "Correct 'n Spell" feature automatically inserts proper spellings.
Consumer products	Sony's Walkman provides entertainment for walkers and runners.

---

run profitability, and coordination of the firm's activities to achieve these overriding goals.

Many organizations have adopted the marketing concept, realizing that the organization must see itself not as producing goods and services but as "buying customers, as doing the things that will make people want to do business with it."[18] Unfortunately, not all firms have accepted the marketing concept as their philosophy or way of thinking. To some extent, the consumerism movement and people like Ralph Nader represent a backlash against firms that have *not* adopted the marketing concept but have remained sales- or production-oriented.

---

[15] "Investigating the Collapse of W.T. Grant," *Business Week*, July 19, 1976, p. 61.

[16] Joseph Barry Mason and Morris Lehman Mayer, *Modern Retailing: Theory and Practice* (Dallas, Tex.: Business Publications, Inc., 1978), p. 7.

[17] Philip Kotler, *Marketing Management: Analysis, Planning, and Control,* Third Edition (Englewood Cliffs, N.J.: Prentice-Hall, 1976), pp. 416, 417.

[18] Theodore Levitt, "Marketing Myopia," *Harvard Business Review,* July–August 1960, pp. 45–56.

SUMMARY

In this chapter we saw that marketing is an important influence on our lives and our society. Daily exposure to marketing activities of all sorts means that most consumers and students of business know a good deal about marketing before they ever consider the field in a formal way. Though some marketing organizations perform behind the scenes, marketing's major functions are apparent to all consumers.

Marketing deals with exchange. As such, it makes valuable contributions to all exchange processes be they profit-making, non-profit, political, or even charitable. All organizations, whether aware of it or not, create marketing mixes. The key, of course, is to develop a marketing mix which will satisfy customers.

Scholars and business people have developed the marketing concept, which provides a philosophy of business and a set of objectives for organizations to pursue. The concept offers guidelines for attaining success in exchange relationships of every sort.

THE MOST IMPORTANT CONCEPT IN THIS CHAPTER
Marketing deals with exchanges of all types. The marketing concept, if properly applied, will lead to successful, satisfying, and profitable exchanges.

KEY TERMS

Effective marketing	Possession utility	Promotion	Ultimate consumer
Macro-marketing (Marketing)	Information utility	Price	Marketing concept
Economic utility	Marketing mix	Channel of distribution	Facilitating agents
Form utility	4 P's of marketing	Manufacturer	Production era
Place utility	Controllable variables	Wholesaler	Sales era
Time utility	Product	Retailer	Marketing era
	Place (Distribution)		Marketing myopia

QUESTIONS FOR DISCUSSION

1 Define marketing in your own words.

2 If marketing activities involve exchange, what *isn't* marketing?

3 Think of a recent purchase you made and describe the economic utilities that you obtained?

4 Churches are not interested in increasing sales volume. What do churches market?

5 Do lawyers, accountants, and doctors need marketing?

6 Describe the marketing mix for:

(a) McDonald's
(b) Your local zoo
(c) A group interested in cleaning up air pollution
(d) The Xerox Corporation

7 British Airways hired a new chief executive officer. This new officer had no aviation experience, but he was formerly the president of Avis Incorporated. Did British Airways hire an inexperienced person?

8 Not all firms are in the marketing era. What organizations have been late to enter the marketing era or have not yet entered the marketing era?

9 Can you think of an example of a company that tried to reduce sales?

10 Should a newspaper company become involved in a cable TV business?

11 The American automobile industry did not emphasize small fuel-efficient cars for a long period of time. Is Detroit consumer-oriented?

12 What might be some potential areas of conflict between the marketers and manufacturing personnel in a production-oriented firm?

13 How might a firm such as Pillsbury have expressed their corporate mission in the different eras of marketing?

CASE 1-1 Success Rice

Success Rice is sold in grocery stores and supermarkets. Case Exhibit 1-1 shows a newspaper advertisement for Success Rice. Read this advertisement and think about the product and its marketing mix.

Questions

1 Is Success Rice a consumer-oriented product? Has the company adopted the marketing concept?

2 Identify and evaluate each of the elements of the marketing mix for Success Rice.

3 Is there an interrelationship between product, brand name, packaging, and advertising?

CASE 1-2 The Robert LaFortune North American Living Museum*

In 1972, the city of Tulsa had no natural history museum, botanical gardens, or aquarium. A master plan was designed to include a Living Museum of Natural History to provide the substance of the zoo and three other cultural institutions.

Today, five buildings constructed near the main entrance of the Tulsa Zoo house the Robert LaFortune North American Living Museum. Each building portrays a region of the North American continent (e.g., the Arctic). Displays and exhibits portray fauna, flora, soil, climate, native culture, and prehistory. After completion of the first of six planned regions, a newspaper reporter suggested that the living museum is not the taxpayers' idea of a zoo. The reporter thinks the zoo has gone too far.

The zoo director believes the zoo must be a partner with the taxpayer in providing a unique resource. He has often asked himself about the zoo's purpose. Is the purpose of the zoo to be merely a repository for animals or should it have a broader purpose?

Questions

1 What is the role of the zoo? What products and consumer benefits does the zoo provide?

2 Is the newspaper critic being myopic about the purpose of the zoo?

3 Should the zoo broaden its use of marketing techniques? So it may reach a wider audience?

4 What does the public exchange for a visit to the zoo?

CASE 1-3 Charlie O

Charlie O advertises that the six-cent soda has returned. Their brand name is written in a script reminiscent of the Coca-Cola trademark. Charlie O is a home carbonation system that allows customers to make soft drinks in their own homes. The carbonation system carbonates cold water and mixes soft drink syrups to produce inexpensive beverages. The amount of carbonation may be adjusted to any desired level. Cola, root beer, ginger ale, cream soda, grape, orange, and strawberry are some of the flavors. Charlie O advertises a flavor called "The Sting" because "we dare not mention the good doctor's name." Charlie O eliminates the need to lug heavy bottles home from the supermarket. "No more hefting those heavy six packs, or one- and two-liter bottles. No more bottle deposits, or bottle re-

turns. And no pouring drinks that have gone flat down the drain—because every Charlie O drink is made 'soda fountain fresh.' "

Local distributors (dealers) will provide free home demonstrations to prospective customers.

The price of syrups in 1982 was $3.85 for a half-gallon of syrup. Carousel package dispensers were priced at $27 for the eight-flavor carousel and $14.50 for the four-flavor carousel. Charlie O charges a $5 monthly rental fee and a $25 deposit for the carbonator.

Questions

1 Who are the prime customer prospects for Charlie O?

2 Is Charlie O consumer-oriented?

3 Evaluate Charlie O's marketing mix versus the Coca-Cola Company's marketing mix?

4 What market trends may have influenced the development of Charlie O?

---

*Source: Information based on David G. Zucconi and Joseph A. Nicholson, "Robert J. LaFortune North American Living Museum" International Zoological Yearbook, Vol. 21, 1982.

CHAPTER 2

Environmental Opportunities and Constraints

CHAPTER SCAN

This chapter portrays marketing as operating within a multifaceted ever-changing environment, which both restricts the actions marketing managers can take and presents them with new opportunities.

The chapter describes the several aspects of the environment and their interrelationships.

The chapter also describes the reactions of marketers to environmental changes as they adapt to these changes.

Demographic matters such as population totals, migrations, and other characteristics of the population are discussed.

WHEN YOU HAVE STUDIED THIS CHAPTER, YOU WILL:

Be able to portray, the environment in which marketing managers work, and describe how that environment affects the organization.

Be able to discuss the impact of the environment on an organization's marketing mix.

Be able to describe the interactions between the several aspects of marketing's environment.

Know a number of important demographic facts and figures, population totals, household totals, racial proportions, and other characteristics that impact the marketing manager's performance.

Be familiar with a number of major demographic trends and their importance to modern marketers.

Be able to discuss such matters as migration, urbanization, and changing age structures of the population, and to describe their implications for marketing.

Be able to comment on the special activity known as "demarketing."

Be able to relate social values, and changes in those values, to marketing.

Be able to give examples of how the three levels of law in the United States affect marketing activities.

THE ENVIRONMENT OF MARKETING

All organizations operate within environments. That is, all profit-making and not-for-profit organizations are surrounded by, and must contend with, external forces. These uncontrollable influences affect the behavior of consumers and the organization's development of effective marketing strategy. For example, economic forces, shortages of materials, or high land prices might lead to a decline in home building. Such a decline would then reduce the demand for bulldozers, concrete mixers, nails, and even work clothes. Organizations' reactions to high inflation rates are easy to spot in their pricing policies. The U.S. Postal Service provides a case in point. Its response to the environmental factor of inflation was to raise the price of a first-class stamp from 10 to 12 to 15 to 18 to 20 cents over the last few years. Increased postal charges, especially when these occur late in a calendar year, often contribute to declines in greeting card companies' sales.

Other environmental influences are more subtle than the direct impact of inflation or economic problems. Changes in our social environment also affect marketing. Not until the 1970s were birth control devices displayed openly in drug stores. Until that point, society would not "accept" such a thing. Hotel executives have responded to rising crime levels by replacing room locks with computerized electronic locks. These new locks are opened by simple strips of foil with patterns of holes representing lock combinations. Each lock's combination can be quickly changed when guests check out or report their key cards missing. Thus, a new product reduces the possibility of a burglary in high crime areas.

Environmental factors affect all organizations, even the largest and wealthiest companies. Anheuser-Busch, for example, attempted to diversify into soft drinks partly because of an environment shift. Changing consumer tastes, indicating an increased preference for wines and soft drinks, led to a lessening of growth opportunities in the beer business. Unfortunately, Chelsea, the soft drink developed by the company, failed because it ran up against other environmental forces. The product, a "not-so-soft" drink, having a 0.5 percent alcohol content and foaming like beer, was aimed at an adult market that was dissatisfied with sweet soft drinks. The result was a barrage of criticism from the Virginia Nurses Association and various religious groups which accused the brewery of encouraging children to grow up to be beer drinkers.[1] The company's response was to remove the alcohol from Chelsea. But the influence of the environment could not be so easily overcome and the product was withdrawn from the marketplace.

THE ENVIRONMENT AND THE MARKETING MIX

Reacting and adapting to competition, inflation, social influences and trends, government regulations, and the many other environmental influences surrounding an organization is a major part of the marketing manager's job. Two important terms are used to describe these changes. **Environmental dynamics** refers to the various dynamic forces influencing an organization which are external to that organization. The term **marketing dynamics** refers to the various activities and changes in an organization's marketing mix. Environmental dynamics are beyond the control of any individual organization, although the organization may have some influence on aspects of its environment. Marketing dynamics, on the other hand, are controllable by the organization because they are adjustments of the marketing mix made to reflect the effects of

---

[1]Christy Marshall, "A-B Withdraws Chelsea Ads but Says Products Stay in Test," *Advertising Age*, October 30, 1978, p. 2.

EXHIBIT 2-1

Managers Must Recognize the Influence of Environmental Forces on Marketing by Anticipating, Reacting, and Adapting to External Forces

changes in the environment. The proper timing of a marketing decision often is the essential factor that determines success. Determining the correct time to enter and to exit the market often rests on an analysis of the environment dynamics. While there are many forces influencing marketing timing decisions, these decisions remain in the hands of the marketing manager.

Exhibit 2-1 illustrates that marketing managers must anticipate, react, and adapt to environmental opportunities and constraints. As noted in Chapter 1, the marketer is like a chef, combining ingredients to develop a good "mix" of variables. The marketing mix is a puzzle as well; it must be fitted together with care before it

EXHIBIT 2-2

The Facets of the Marketing Mix Fit together like the Pieces of a Puzzle

CHANGING WITH THE TIMES

The Campbell Soup Kids in an era of fitness have slimmed down. Still cherubic, but no longer chubby, the kids still think Campbell's is "M'm M'm Good!"

can work. And the mix must be adjusted, even reassembled, periodically, as the external environment in which the organization operates changes. See Exhibit 2-2 for an illustration of how the marketing mix should fit together.

IDENTIFYING MAJOR ENVIRONMENTAL INFLUENCES

Marketing activities are performed within a large arena or environment. This environment is made up of two major parts, the physical environment and the cultural environment, and their subdivisions. A schema for investigating the forces that generate marketing change is given in Exhibit 2-3.

Exhibit 2-3 shows the relationship of the physical environment to the cultural environment. The exhibit also shows how both environments contribute to the development of a marketing mix, and provides a checklist of environmental forces that any marketing planner should consider.

EXHIBIT 2-3

Environmental Influences on the Marketing Mix

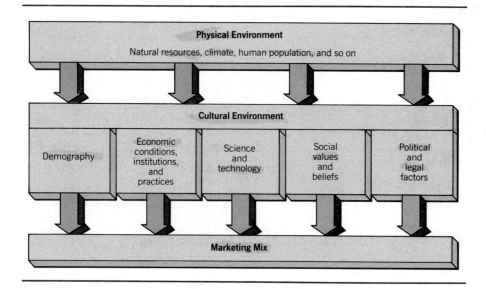

THE PHYSICAL ENVIRONMENT

The **physical environment** consists of natural resources such as minerals, climate, the human population, and other aspects of nature.[2]

Marketing is influenced by many aspects of the natural environment. Climate is one aspect of the physical environment that influences marketing. It is not difficult to imagine that umbrella sales are greater in rainy Seattle than in desert-like Tucson, or that more winter clothing is sold in Minneapolis than in Miami. The climate may have a direct or indirect effect on marketing activities. For example, a Brazilian shoe marketer, Interbras, the makers of Hippopotamus shoes,

---

[2]Robert J. Holloway and Robert S. Hancock, *The Environment of Marketing Management* (New York: John Wiley & Sons, 1974), p. 3.

The natural environment may have a devastating influence on marketing activities.

learned not to forget the physical environment in exporting ventures when the Soviets returned more than 100,000 pairs of shoes because the flimsy tropical footwear was not adapted for harsher Russian climes.[3]

Areas rich in petroleum may concentrate on the production and marketing of fuel oil, kerosene, benzene, naphtha, paraffin, and other products resulting from this natural resource.

The physical environment of marketing consists not only of what we think of as "natural resources," but also includes the earth's human population. The size and distribution of this population is a physical influence that is highly interrelated with the cultural environment.

THE CULTURAL ENVIRONMENT

Marketing in one form or another operates within every society, and every society has a culture that guides its everyday life. Thus, when discussing the environment of marketing, the word "culture" does not refer to classical music, art, and literature. Instead, **culture** refers to social institutions, values, beliefs, and behaviors. Culture includes, then, everything other than the basic drives with which we were born. For example, we are all born with a need to eat, but what, when, and where we eat, and whether we season our food with ketchup or curdled goat's milk, are learned as part of our culture. That many American women are "liberated," while few Saudi women are, is also cultural. The material artifacts and the meaning or symbols associated with these items also vary by culture.

The **cultural environment** is that complex whole which includes demographic factors, scientific and technical knowledge, social values and beliefs, economic conditions, institutions and practices, and political and legal factors.[4]

---

[3]"A High Style Brazilian Shoe Hotfoots in the U.S.," *Business Week*, November 8, 1982, p. 54.

[4]An adaptation of the definition of culture given by Edward B. Taylor in the opening paragraph of his *Primitive Culture* (London: John Murray Publishers, 1871), p. 1.

Demography

The terms "demography" and "demographics" come from the Greek word "demos" or "people," as does the English word "democracy." Hence, **demography** may be defined as the study of the size, composition (e.g., age, racial groups) and distribution of the human population in relation to social factors such as geographic boundaries. The size, distribution, and nature of the population in any geographic market is clearly a major influence on marketing. Since demography is clearly of great concern to marketing managers, some basic demographic information and trends will be discussed in this section. The appendix to this chapter provides a wealth of demographic statistics for the United States.

World Population. The world population is nearing 5 billion people. Much of this population is concentrated in certain areas on the globe (see Exhibit 2-4). Since, in general, markets consist of people willing and able to exchange something of value for goods and services, this total is quite impressive. However, the rapid (exponential) growth of population, particularly in

There are more than 225 million people living in the U.S.A.

third-world countries, puts a heavy burden on marketing. The distribution of food, for instance, is a marketing problem which may prove crucial to the survival of this planet. The world population is expected to grow by at least 80 million per year (see Exhibit 2-5). That's about 9,000 new people per hour.

Although the remainder of this section deals with the demography of the American market, it is important to remember that the future of both developing and developed economies is well-served by a vigorous international trade. This trade cannot be effectively implemented and maintained unless marketers concern themselves deeply with what is going on in "the rest of the world."

U.S. Population. The population of the United States is constantly changing. Since marketing's goal is to satisfy the wants and needs of that population, it is important that effective marketers be aware of the changes that are occurring and the directions in which those changes are moving our population. Despite the fact that much of the available demographic data is somewhat inaccurate because of the difficulties involved in keeping track of well over 225 million people, the overall, or "big picture," of U.S. demography is believed to be accurate.

The 1980 Census of the Population revealed that there were, at that time, more than 220 million people living in the United States. Statistically, a new resident is born every seven minutes and someone dies every four minutes. The birth rate is 15.8 per thousand and the death rate is 8.7 per thousand. About 51.5 percent of the population is female and 48.5 percent is male. Racial proportions of minority groups were: 11.1 percent black; 9.1 percent Hispanic; and 0.8 percent American Indian.[5]

Migration. Migration has always been an overwhelmingly important demographic factor

---

[5]These figures from the 1982–83 edition of the *Statistical Abstract of the United States*, U.S. Department of Commerce, Bureau of the Census, p. 432.

THE CULTURAL ENVIRONMENT
INFLUENCES WOMEN'S VALUES AND BEHAVIOR

International marketing is strongly influenced by social values. Consider the different marketing approaches required by clothing manufacturers in the United States and in the Mideast. In a number of eastern countries, the role of women and particularly the display of the female body, is radically different from what occurs in the United States.

in the United States. Much is heard about the effect of the recent Cuban and Haitian migrations into South Florida and about the general migration into the Sunbelt states. However, these migrations into and around the country have been going on for hundreds of years. The 1790 U.S. census showed the "center of population"—i.e., the point at which half the population lived north, south, east, and west—to be 23 miles east of Baltimore, Maryland (actually under the waters of the Atlantic Ocean). This was because of the virtually absolute concentration of populations along the East Coast and the curve of the coastline. The 1980 census moved that point to Jefferson County, Missouri. Each census traditionally moves the point farther south and west.

Urbanization. The United States, and in fact the entire world, has become increasingly urbanized since the 1800s. In the United States, the

EXHIBIT 2-4

World Population Distribution

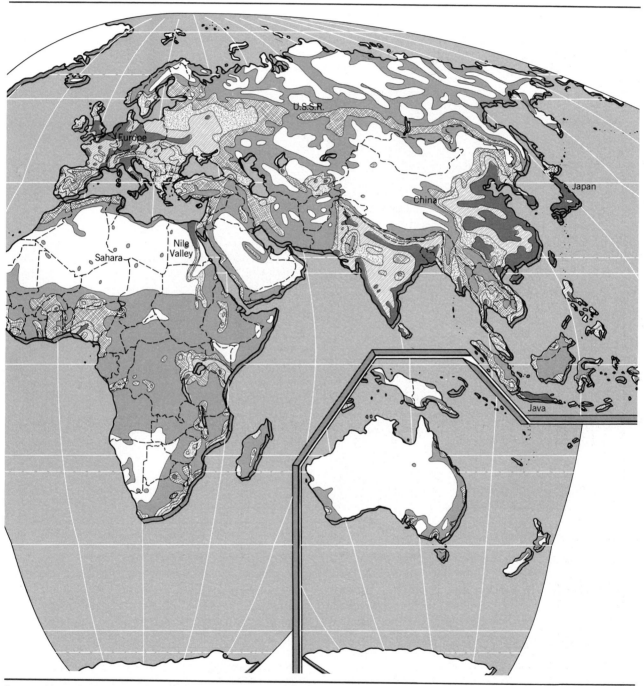

Source: Harm J. de Blij, *Human Geography* (New York: John Wiley & Sons, 1982), pp. 26–27.

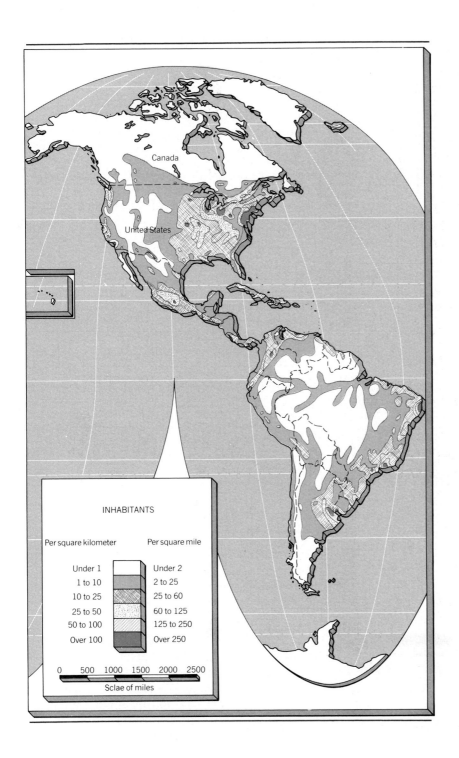

INHABITANTS

Per square kilometer   Per square mile

Under 1   Under 2
1 to 10   2 to 25
10 to 25   25 to 60
25 to 50   60 to 125
50 to 100   125 to 250
Over 100   Over 250

0   500   1000 1500 2000 2500
Sclae of miles

EXHIBIT 2-5

World Population Growth

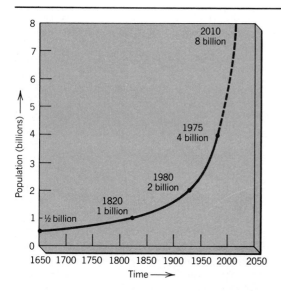

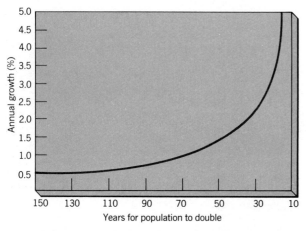

Source: Harm J. de Blij, *Human Geography* (New York: John Wiley & Sons, 1982), p. 36.

COUNTING UP BLACKS AND HISPANICS

One thing a decennial census does is puncture popular myths. Example: all the talk about Hispanics replacing blacks as the biggest minority market. Data from the 1980 census shows that although the Latino populace increased at a blistering pace in the 1970s (61% vs. 17% for blacks), there is a gap of almost 12 million between the two groups. A higher fertility rate contributed to Hispanic growth, and it is also likely that the bureau did a better job of counting undocumented aliens than it did in 1970. Still, if both minorities maintain their 1970–80 percentage growth rates, it won't be until the year 2000 that Hispanics overtake blacks, 37.8 million to 36.2 million. Of course, the bureau's Hispanic totals are hotly challenged by some ethnic spokespersons. Jorge Batista, head of the newly formed Hispanic Opinion and Preference Research, Inc., claims "there are approximately 20 million Hispanics in the U.S."

	1980	1970	Percent Increase 1970–80	Percent Distribution 1980	Percent Distribution 1970
Total population	226,504,825	203,211,926	11.5%	100.0%	100.0%
White	188,340,790	177,748,975	6.0	83.2	87.5
Black	26,488,218	22,580,289	17.3	11.7	11.1
Spanish origin	14,605,883	9,072,602	61.0	6.4	4.5

Note: Details will not add to totals because of omission of other minorities such as American Indian, Eskimo, and Asian.

Source: From "Changing Markets," *Sales and Marketing Management*, April 6, 1981, p. 24. Reprinted with permission.

expansion of metropolitan areas has brought neighboring cities and their suburbs so close together that they have, for all practical purposes, merged. Two examples of this phenomena are the "Northeast Corridor," which extends from Boston to Washington, D.C., and the string of communities from Los Angeles to Tijuana, Mexico.

Growth in the metropolitan areas has not meant growth in the central cities. Crowded conditions, crime rates, and other discomforts associated with city life, coupled with the great numbers of private cars owned by Americans have encouraged the much-discussed "flight to the suburbs" by people seeking to enjoy a blend of country and city living.

EXHIBIT 2-6

Populations of the 30 Largest Cities, 1970 and 1980 (figures rounded to 1000)

		1970	1980
1. New York	(−)	7,896,000	7,081,000
2. Chicago	(−)	3,367,000	2,970,000
3. Los Angeles	(+)	2,816,000	2,950,000
4. Philadelphia	(−)	1,950,000	1,680,000
5. Houston	(+)	1,233,000	1,555,000
6. Detroit	(−)	1,511,000	1,192,000
7. Dallas	(+)	844,000	901,000
8. San Diego	(+)	697,000	870,000
9. Baltimore	(−)	906,000	783,000
10. San Antonio	(+)	654,000	783,000
11. Phoenix	(+)	582,000	781,000
12. Indianapolis	(−)	734,000	695,000
13. San Francisco	(−)	716,000	674,000
14. Memphis	(+)	624,000	645,000
15. Washington, D.C.	(−)	757,000	635,000
16. Milwaukee	(−)	717,000	633,000
17. San Jose	(+)	446,000	626,000
18. Cleveland	(−)	751,000	573,000
19. Boston	(−)	641,000	562,000
20. Columbus	(+)	540,000	562,000
21. New Orleans	(−)	593,000	557,000
22. Jacksonville	(+)	504,000	541,000
23. Seattle	(−)	531,000	492,000
24. Denver	(−)	515,000	489,000
25. St. Louis	(−)	622,000	449,000
26. Kansas City	(−)	507,000	447,000
27. Nashville	(+)	426,000	440,000
28. El Paso	(+)	322,000	425,000
29. Pittsburgh	(−)	520,000	424,000
30. Atlanta	(−)	497,000	422,000

Source: United States Census Bureau, 1981.

Although there has been some migration back to the cities in recent years, Exhibit 2-6 shows that the populations of core cities has continued to decline. The number of suburbanites returning to the cities is less than half the number of people moving to the suburbs. The growth of suburban areas has meant that the populations of *areas* has been maintained, and even risen. Thus, while Chicago itself has lost population, the Chicago *area* has grown.

Sunbelt vs. Snowbelt. The states of the southern and western United States grew most rapidly during the period between 1970 and 1980. The populations of Nevada, Arizona, and Wyoming expanded at the highest rates, as the map in Exhibit 2-7 shows. However, the rate of population growth can be misleading since Wyoming and Nevada in particular have always been, and continue to be, small in terms of population. While there is a general perception that the Sun-

---

EXHIBIT 2-7

Population Growth Rates Vary by State

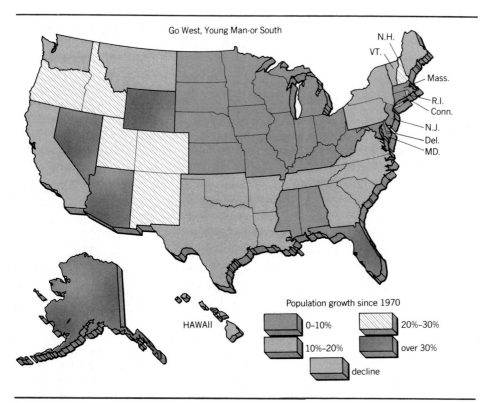

Go West, Young Man-or South

N.H.
VT.
Mass.
R.I.
Conn.
N.J.
Del.
MD.

HAWAII

Population growth since 1970

0–10%   20%–30%
10%–20%   over 30%
decline

Source: "Let The Great Head Count Begin," *Time*, March 31, 1980, p. 25.

---

belt is growing by leaps and bounds, the biggest growth in population (and in economic power) has taken place in California, Texas, and Florida. Analysts have pointed out that when these three states are removed from the figures cited by Sunbelt boosters, the glories of the Sunbelt lose much of their sheen.

Profile of the "Average American." What is the "average American consumer" like? Because of many variables involved, there is *no* true average American. But it is interesting to try to paint a picture of one. First, there are more women than men in the United States, so the average American is female. In 1981, the median age of Americans was 30.3 years. That means that half the population is older and half younger than that age. Although it is somewhat dangerous to deal with "averages," it is interesting to know that the typical American is a woman of about 30 years old.

How about the "average household?" Here, too, the picture may have some surprises. The average U.S. household, according to the most recent U.S. Census of Population, consists of 2.76 persons. Half the households have no children under 18 living at home. Households including one child represent 20.6 percent of all U.S. households, and only 13.8 percent of households include three or more children.

These figures paint quite a different picture of the "traditional family" than do the magazine

DEMOGRAPHIC QUIZ

Are you a demographic expert? Find out by taking the following quiz.

1 Baby Boom
In which year will the peak of the baby boom reach age 30?
(a) 1981 (b) 1984 (c) 1987 (d) 1990

2 Households
As of 1980, what was the average number of people per household?
(a) 1.91 (b) 2.48 (c) 2.76 (d) 3.14

3 Life Expectancy
What is the current average life expectancy for men and women combined?
(a) 69.3 (b) 71.2 (c) 73.2 (d) 77.1

4 Fertility
What was the total fertility rate in 1979?
(a) 1.5 (b) 1.9 (c) 2.1 (d) 2.4

5 Education
What is the median number of years of schooling for the population age 25 and older?
(a) 10.1 (b) 12.4 (c) 13.9 (d) 14.2

6 Farm Population
What percentage of Americans lived on farms in 1977?
(a) 3.6 (b) 6.3 (c) 9.6 (d) 12.3

7 Employment
What percentage of mothers with children under three years old were in the labor force in 1978?
(a) 24.7 (b) 27.3 (c) 34.6 (d) 39.1

8 Divorce
What was the divorce ratio in 1978?
(a) 23 (b) 51 (c) 74 (d) 91

Source: "Demographic Quiz," *American Demographics*, February 1980, pp. 8 and 47. Adapted with permission.

ANSWERS TO THE QUIZ

1 Baby Boom: *(c) 1987*
The peak of the baby boom was 1957, when there were 4,332,000 births. The boom began in 1946 and ended in 1964. From 1954 to 1964 there were more than 4 million births each year. In 1978, there were only about 3.3 million births.

2 Households: *(c) 2.76*
The average size of a household has steadily decreased. In 1940 the average household had four people in it; in 1970 the figure was 3.1.

3 Life Expectancy: *(c) 73.2*
Life expectancy has increased rapidly in recent years. It is 4.5 years higher today than it was only 25 years ago. Men have an average life expectancy of 69.3 years, women 77.1.

4 Fertility: *(b) 1.9*
Fertility is at near record low levels, close to the Census Bureau's "low" series of 1.7. The figure 2.1, which is the bureau's middle series, is replacement-level fertility.

5 Education: *(b) 12.4*
Educational attainment varies by age. Less than 40 percent of persons 65 and over attended high school, and only 8 percent graduated from college. But fully 85 percent of those between the ages of 25 and 29 completed high school, and 24 percent graduated from college.

6 Farm Population: *(a) 3.6*
The agricultural population has been shrinking for decades. In 1977 almost half of the agricultural work force did not live on farms, a substantial shift from 1960 when it was only one-quarter.

7 Employment: *(d) 39.1*
Total women's labor force participation increased from 42 percent in 1970 to 49.6 percent in 1978. But the most dramatic increases have been for mothers. In 1970, only 27.3 percent of women with children under three years old were in the labor force.

8 Divorce: *(d) 91*
The divorce ratio—the number of divorces per 1000 married people—has nearly quadrupled since 1960, when the figure was only 23. If divorces continue at the present pace, almost 40 percent of all marriages will end in divorce.

illustrators who portray a dining room full of people gathered about the Thanksgiving turkey. Where are the kids? Families are having fewer children and more couples than ever are having no children. Why is the average household so small? More career-minded single people, more divorced people, and more widowed people are living alone than ever before. Even as our population has stabilized somewhat in recent years, the number of households, abetted somewhat by changing patterns of culture which "permit" living alone and remaining childless, has risen quickly. More will be said about the family in Chapter 7.

And what about the "average income"? Inflation swelled the "average" income during the past decade. The median family income in the United States was $22,388 in 1981, up from $10,285 in 1971. The growth in per capita income between 1970 and 1980 was greatest in the Southwestern states (167 percent) and least in the middle-Atlantic states (129 percent) and New England states (134 percent).

Economics

Economic conditions, institutions, and practices determine how a society allocates its scarce resources. Under the Western World's modified capitalistic system, foreign and domestic competition influence the interaction of supply and demand forces. Rivalry in all areas of marketing is intensified by competition from substitutable goods and services. The term "substitutable" can be interpreted in two ways. First, it can mean that the consumer is choosing to spend discretionary family income on a new car, or a vacation, or putting an addition on the family home, or buying food. Second, it can mean that the consumer is choosing from among the various manufacturers and price ranges available.

The health of the economy, the amount of competition in several industries, the rate of inflation, consumer spending and savings patterns, and numerous other economic variables will affect how that spending decision is made.

Rivalry among competitors often leads to lower prices and the introduction of differentiated products. For example, hand-held electronic calculators sold for hundreds of dollars in the mid-1970s, but now sell for under ten dollars because of price cutting among competitors. Video tape recorders have gone the same route. The initial market entry, Betamax, sold for more than $1500. After a few short years, the price had been cut to less than one-third that figure. In addition, the first Betamax cassettes could record only two hours of programming, but today eight-hour video cassettes are available from Betamax and numerous new competitors.

In both cases, the high profits being earned when the products first hit the market attracted new competitors who offered lower prices and improved products.

Economic factors can, of course, serve to raise prices as well as lower them. The dramatic increase in petroleum costs in the mid-1970s resulted in gasoline prices becoming far higher than American consumers had ever experienced. Marketers adjusted their marketing mixes to reflect this change. Rising prices altered the price variable, but led many oil companies and independent dealers to change the form of their retail outlets from that of the traditional service station to that of self-service station, an approach to distribution formerly associated with small, "no name" companies. Many stations have further evolved into convenience food outlets with a few gas pumps.

Competitive Market Structures. The competitive market structure of an economy, that is the number of competing firms and size of market held by each competitor, strongly influences price strategies. *Monopoly, oligopoly, monopolistic competition*, and *pure competition* are the four basic types of competitive market structures.

Pure competition exists when there are no barriers to competition. This in turn means that there is a steady supply and demand for the product and, therefore, the price is not controlled by either the buyers or the sellers. Basic food commodities, such as rice or mushrooms, approximate this pure competition market structure.

BIG BUSINESS AND OLIGOPOLY

The Boeing Company, McDonnell Douglas, and Lockheed rank one, two, and three respectively in the manufacture and sale of commercial aircraft in the United States. Together they account for most of the large airplanes sold in this country (and a sizable fraction of those sold in the world; Boeing is America's top exporter). They make up what economists call an "oligopoly"—an industry dominated by a few big firms, with smaller competitors either nonexistent or vastly overshadowed by the giants.

Other examples of oligopoly are not hard to come by. General Motors, Ford, Chrysler, and American Motors manufacture virtually all of the American-made automobiles sold in this country. Goodyear, Firestone, Uniroyal, B.F. Goodrich, and General Tire make nearly all of the tires. Even an industry like breakfast cereals, where a wide variety of brands dot the supermarket shelves, is in reality an oligopoly: Kellogg's, General Foods, General Mills, and Quaker Oats account for virtually all the cereals we eat, from Special K (Kellogg's) to Count Chocula (General Mills). The steel industry, the oil industry, the meat-packing industry, and the cigarette industry are all, to a greater or lesser extent, oligopolies.

Oligopoly is not the same thing as large size, though the two often go hand in hand. Sears, Roebuck & Company, for example, is a huge corporation doing nearly $20 billion worth of business in a typical year. But it accounts for less than two percent of total retail sales in the country, and probably not much more than that in any given city. If Sears, K Mart, and one or two others could be found in every city and town—and if they were the only retailers around—they would constitute an oligopoly.

The distinguishing characteristic of an oligopoly is a measure of control over the marketplace— and in particular, some control over the prices at which it sells its good. Whenever there are a lot of enterprises trying to sell something—and whenever one seller's wares can't easily be advertised as different from another's— economists describe the situation as an "auction" market. Prices in such a market are set by supply and demand: how much is offered for sale and how much customers want to buy. The stock market is a good example of an auction market, as are the markets for most agricultural products. No one shareholder and no one farmer can hope to influence how much he or she gets in the marketplace. Instead, the goods are simply sold at the going price.

With an oligopoly, the situation is different. General Motors sets the prices for its cars; Coca-Cola sets the prices for its syrup. If business is slow the company may cut the price—or it may try a different strategy entirely, like launching a new ad campaign ("Have a Coke and a Smile"). Procter & Gamble doesn't try to undersell Colgate Palmolive, nor does Budweiser ordinarily compete with Miller by lowering its price. Rather, the competition takes place on different turf entirely—in those cases, mostly through advertising each product's special virtues. Each company in an oligopolistic industry has a measurable share of the market. Its goals revolve around both increasing its profit and increasing its market share.

An oligopoly arises not from any conspiracy but from the natural logic of the marketplace in some industries. If a given market can support only a few sellers— barbershops in a small town, say—then those sellers may act like an oligopoly and try to compete on grounds other than low price. More typically, the product being sold by an oligopolistic industry requires so much capital investment or so big a marketing network that, once a few firms get established, its hard for anybody else to break in. Setting up a company to compete with Kodak and Polaroid in the home-camera market is not quite the same as setting up a shoe-repair shop or even a necktie-manufacturing business. And even if you invented a cereal that tasted better or was more nutritious than those produced by the giants, you would have a hard time getting it on the supermarket shelves, let alone persuading anyone to give up their usual fare.

In recent years a lot of big firms—Boeing is an example, as are the auto companies—have faced stiff competition from abroad. Others, like Penn Central, have gone under because of changing tastes and technologies or bureaucratic sclerosis. So even big oligopolistic firms aren't immune to the dictates and requirements of the marketplace. But their large size and position in their industry gives them an asset that small, highly competitive firms can rarely match, namely the ability to absorb setbacks, plan new strategies, and in general to ride out rough economic weather. And in that, of course, lies the source of their strength.

Source: Reprinted with permission from *A Guide to Enterprise* (Boston: WGBH, 1980), p. 29.

On the other hand, the principal characteristic of **monopolistic competition** is product differentiation—a large number of sellers, for example, selling similar products differentiated only by minor changes in product design, style, or technology. Firms engaged in monopolistic competition have enough influence on the marketplace to exert some control over their own prices. The fast-food industry is a good example of monopolistic competition.

Oligopoly, the third type of market structure, is exemplified by an industry, such as the American automobile industry, that is controlled by a few large companies. Each of the companies in the oligopoly has a strong influence on product choice, price, and market structure within the industry.

Lastly, industries with only one producer firm, such as telephone companies or electric utilities, are called monopolies. A **monopoly** exists in a market situation where there are no suitable substitute products. Antitrust legislation strictly controls monopolies in this country.

Within each competitive market structure, there are many economic institutions. For example, the distribution structure within a country's economic system is a major factor influencing marketing managers' decisions. In many countries, such as Canada and the United States, there is a wide variety of wholesalers and retailers who can be used in the distribution of products. Consider the difficulties that would be encountered in distributing appliances in rural Angola or Peru. One of the strengths of the U.S. and Canadian system is that marketers are free *not* to use certain distribution methods if they believe others would be more efficient. Japan's high retail prices are blamed, in part, on a traditional distribution system which uses far more wholesalers to handle a given product than is really necessary.

Supply Problems and Demarketing. Only in recent years have American marketers concerned themselves with supply difficulties. It was once assumed that goods such as oil and metals were "givens" and that marketing's problems were simply promoting and distributing these things. It is now known that many goods cannot just be taken for granted.

Any organization can be greatly influenced by its suppliers. The power of the Oil and Petroleum Exporting Countries (OPEC) cartel illustrates the fact, sometimes painfully. In cases where supply is not restricted by an organization like OPEC, supply problems can still result from a supplier's inability to keep up with demand, from natural resource shortages, from a failure to accurately estimate demand, or from other reasons. In such situations, a marketing strategy aimed at *discouraging* buying may be appropriate.

Demarketing is the name which has been given to those activities which intentionally discourage all or some customers either on a temporary or permanent basis.[6] Demarketing adjusts marketing efforts to match the environment. Suppose, for example, that a manufacturing firm finds that it has a temporary shortage of finished goods available because of a scarcity of raw materials. The firm might use demarketing strategies such as reducing advertising, increasing prices, instituting a rationing system, or some other, more original activity. Is demarketing different from the first-come-first-served, take-it-or-leave-it attitude a marketer of goods in short supply might take? Yes. Demarketing stresses a key aspect of marketing, consumer satisfaction, even though shortages are unpleasant. It emphasizes trying to keep customers over the long run rather than antagonizing them with a take-it-or-leave-it attitude.

Environmental conditions that warrant demarketing strategies are encountered often. In periods of "money shortages," Visa, Master-Card, and other credit card companies demarketed their services by raising interest rates, charging annual membership fees, and cutting back on advertising and other efforts to recruit customers.[7] Gillette's introduction of Aapri fa-

---

[6]Philip Kotler and Sidney J. Levy, "Demarketing, Yes, Demarketing," *Harvard Business Review*, November–December 1971, pp. 74–80.

[7]Josh Levine, "Credit Cards Start to Unsell," *Advertising Age*, April 21, 1980, p. 1.

EXHIBIT 2-8

An Advertisement Demarketing Budweiser

Out of 'Bud'?

We're brewing more for you as slow as we can.

At Labatt's, we anticipated a warm welcome for Budweiser in Ontario. So we planned our brewing accordingly. But your response has been so overwhelming, supplies have run out in many areas.

If you've caught us in short supply, please be patient. We're brewing more 'Bud' as slow as we can. You see, the exclusive beechwood aging takes time.

So while we'll rush in fresh supplies as soon as we can, we won't rush the brewing. You still may find 'Bud' on draft and in pints at your favourite licensed establishments. If not, rest assured that in good time there'll be ample 'Bud' for you.

And thanks for making Budweiser such an overwhelming success in Ontario.

Budweiser. Brewed in Ontario by

cial scrub was flawed by a great *underestimation* of demand. Out-of-stock conditions quickly developed in retail outlets. Gillette developed newspaper ads headlined "Sold Out by Popular Demand," stressing that the shortages were temporary.[8] Budweiser's introduction into the Canadian provinces of Ontario and Quebec encountered similar difficulties caused by out-of-stock conditions. Because Bud stresses slow-brewed quality, its advertisements assured beer lovers that "We're brewing more for you as slow as we can"[9] (see Exhibit 2-8).

[8]Pat Sloan, "Gillette: Aapri Sold Out," *Advertising Age*, April 21, 1982, p. 1.

[9]Tony Thompson, "A Bud Blooms in Canadian Turf," *Advertising Age*, July 27, 1981, pp. 2–47.

In Washington, D.C., the Metro subway system engages in selective demarketing by raising rates during morning and evening rush hours. The fare increase discourages tourists, shoppers, and others who could use the subway in non-rush hours from travelling during peak periods. The Cleveland Zoo attempts to level out its patronage by charging an entrance fee, but allows those arriving before 11 A.M. to go in free.

Science and Technology

Though the two terms are sometimes used interchangeably, **science** is the accumulation of knowledge about human beings and the environment, while **technology** is the application of knowledge to practical purposes.[10] Thus, the discovery that certain diseases might be prevented by immunization is "scientific," but how and when such immunization is administered is "technical."

Like other changes in the environment of marketing, increases in scientific knowledge and technological advances can revolutionize or even destroy an industry. Think of the impact the development of the micro-computer chip has had on the electronics industry, or the effect on saccharin producers of the discovery that saccharin may be cancer-causing. A "real" example of this type of situation occurred when the "knowledge" that usage of Rely tampons was correlated with toxic shock syndrome became public. The giant Procter and Gamble Company withdrew that product from the market, even though subsequent studies suggested that the "knowledge" that Rely tampons were dangerous may have been incorrect.

Scientific and technological forces have a pervasive influence on the marketing of most goods and services. The development of improved cleaning devices, chemicals, and methods allow Service Master and other firms to claim that they can clean your home or office

[10]Richard L. Clewett, "Integrating Science, Technology and Marketing: An Overview," *Science and Technology and Marketing*, Raymond M. Hess, ed., Proceedings of the Fall Conference of the American Marketing Association, August–September 1966, pp. 3–20.

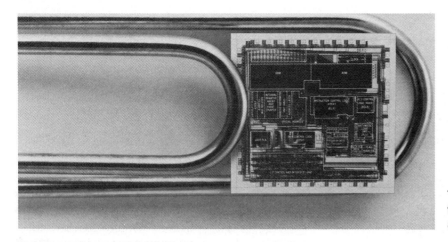

The micro-computer chip influenced much technological and marketing change.

"scientifically." Roachprufe, an insecticide which actually does get rid of roaches, is a highly successful, laboratory-developed product. Competition can be affected, too. For example, in 1962 Odyssey became the first video game marketer. Today, with the widespread distribution of this technology, there are more than forty producers of such equipment.[11]

Space exploration has also contributed to technological advances which have been seized by marketers. Besides Tang, freeze-dried ice cream, and some other food products, the space program yielded the micro-miniaturized computer chips which are found in word processors and hand-held computer games. In addition, space technology has found nonprofit applications: a fireman in a lightweight fire-fighting suit can now communicate with others through a built-in communication system. The nonfogging face protector the firefighter wears to improve visibility is also a product of space technology.

Because science and technology are particularly volatile parts of the environment of marketing, marketing organizations of all types must monitor these changes and adjust their marketing mix to meet them. For example, the development of the automobile and the building of improved roads are scientific changes that fostered the technological advances which led marketers to develop drive-in movies, drive-in dry cleaners, drive-in restaurants, and even drive-in churches and funeral homes.

There are numerous examples to be found of firms that did *not* adapt to changing technology, neighborhood restaurants that have fallen victim to more efficient, cheaper, and better-advertised organizations such as McDonald's, for instance. McDonald's production-line approach to food preparation and its heavy promotional efforts are made possible by scientific and technological advances. Timex's belated entry into the digital watch market is another example of a firm's not adapting to new technology. Timex waited too long; their watches did "keep on ticking" but many buyers were looking for watches that didn't tick at all. Timex's profitability was affected. The competition (Texas Instruments, and manufacturers from Hong Kong, Japan, and Taiwan) increased their own market shares by entering the market with newly developed quartz analog watches.[12]

Social Values and Beliefs

As a result of changing social values, organizations such as the American Red Cross and the

---

[11] "TV's New Super Hit: Jocktronics," *Time*, December 13, 1976, p. 80.

[12] "Falling Profits Prompt Timex to Shed Its Utilitarian Image," *Wall Street Journal*, September 17, 1981, p. 27.

Boy Scouts of America lost more than 25 percent of their volunteers during the 1970s.[13] The dwindling of volunteer helpers occurred because it was becoming increasingly acceptable for suburban women to work outside the home at the same time feminist groups were expressing negative attitudes toward the volunteer work activities that once dominated many women's lives.

A **social value** is a statement about a culture's shared ideas of what ought to be, an expression of a preferred way of acting. For example, we learn from those around us that it is wrong to lie or steal. A **belief** is a statement concerning the existence and characteristics of physical and social phenomena. We believe that cigarette smoking causes heart disease. Whether this belief is correct or not is not particularly important. Even a totally foolish belief may affect how people behave. It is the marketer's job to "read" the social environment and reflect the surrounding culture's values and beliefs in a marketing strategy.

Consider how Americans feel about time. There is a growing trend to place a premium on time because of an increased interest in leisure-time pursuits. One researcher suggests that (1) American consumers are less concerned with systems and order than they were in the past, and (2) there is a growing acceptance that it is perfectly all right to give in to moods and occasions.[14] Such changing social values could result in fewer shopping lists and more spur-of-the-moment or impulse purchases, as well as in less loyalty to weekly television programs or nightly newscast teams.

Social values influence not only marketing strategy but other environmental variables as well. The social values that lying and stealing are bad are reflected in laws dealing with deceptive advertising. The belief that smoking is injurious to health has led to regulations dealing with

---

Lifestyle Changes	+	Technological Advances	=	New Marketing Business

Today's fast-paced lifestyles and two-career families leave little time for shopping. Many consumers have come to view shopping by catalog as a time-saving necessity. A harried customer can look at hundreds of pieces of merchandise simply by flipping pages.

Retired entrepreneur and inventor Hazard Reeves took this concept into the electronic age by feeding the contents of hundreds of catalogs into a computer and opening "Catalogia," the country's first computer catalog store.

At this store, the customer can tell a clerk that she wants a pink negligee or a suit of armor and, in seconds, receive a print-out showing which catalogs carry the sought-after item. If the customer buys, the clerk places the order and Catalogia takes 20 percent of the sale as a commission. Reeves says the charge is quite reasonable since Catalogia creates "extra" sales for the catalog outfits.

Reeves plans to franchise additional stores and hopes to put a version of Catalogia on cable television.

Source: Adapted from "A Computerized Catalog of Catalogs," *Newsweek*, March 8, 1982, p. 82.

---

seating on airplanes, smoking in public places, and the barring of cigarette commercials from radio and television. The belief that children are more susceptible to persuasion than adults may ultimately lead to stringent laws governing advertising on children's television programs.

Social Values in Other Cultures. The significance of social values extends to the international marketplace. Understanding why people in foreign countries behave and react as they do means knowing something of their values and beliefs. A North American about to visit a Kentucky Fried Chicken restaurant in Canada or the United States is operating in an environment

---

[13]Seth Reichlin, "Economy Generates Change in Voluntarism," *Tulsa Tribune*, August 6, 1981, p. 1c.

[14]"New Rules: A Glimpse Into the New World," *Advertising Age*, July 20, 1981, p. 44.

A Kentucky Fried Chicken restaurant in Japan.

Political and Legal Environment

American athletes did not participate in the 1980 summer Olympics because the U.S. Government made a political decision in reaction to Russia's military involvement in Afghanistan. NBC-TV's loss of broadcasting the games was the most obvious impact of this uncontrollable political factor. However, all U.S. advertisers and marketers attempting to tie in with the Olympic theme or to utilize the Misha bear, symbol of the Moscow Olympics, were influenced.[15]

The political and legal environment can act in several ways. It can limit the actions marketers are allowed to take, for example, by restricting the percentage of foreign ownership of a company operating in another country. Some actions may be required, for example, the requirement that cookies called "chocolate chip cookies" contain chips made of real chocolate or the requirement that the surgeon general's warning be printed on all cigarette packages. Lastly, certain actions can be prohibited, including the legal sale of products such as opium, heroin, and nuclear weapons, except under the strictest of controls.

During the 1960s and 1970s, government increasingly intervened in and regulated marketing activities. In part, this was caused by the consumerism movement, but it was also due to the fact that some manufacturers, retailers, bankers, and other marketers *were* misleading and deceiving consumers. It is unfortunate that some regulations clearly went "overboard," as did some regulating agencies. It is also unfortunate that laws and rules served to annoy the honest business person even though they were aimed at the dishonest manager. In the 1980s, some easing of legal requirements has come about, though vast numbers of laws remain in effect, affecting each aspect of the organization's marketing mix.

Political processes in other countries may have dramatic impacts on international marketers. For example, political pressures within the United States led Japan to agree to limit for

quite different from that of a Japanese citizen contemplating a meal at a Kentucky Fried Chicken franchise in Tokyo. In Japan, the Kentucky Fried Chicken outlets are small because space is scarce. Poultry is also scarce, and therefore expensive. Thus, Kentucky Fried Chicken customers in Japan value a poultry dinner far differently from the Colonel's customers in North America.

Similarly, industrial buyers and government workers may behave differently in different cultures. In some countries business dealings are carried on so slowly that Americans are frustrated by what they perceive as delays. Yet, this customary slowness may be seen by their hosts as contributing to a friendly atmosphere. Government officials in some countries openly demand "gifts" or "tips" without which nothing gets done.

---

[15] *A Guide to Enterprise* (Boston: WGBH, Educational Foundation), 1980, p. 6.

WHEN GIRDLES WERE SLIPPING

The call for help went out to Daniel Yankelovich, Inc. research and consulting company.

"My wife is 40, she's not thin and she is not wearing a girdle all the time," explains the upset Playtex executive. "Can you please come over this afternoon."

The executive's distress was well founded, for the girdle industry was in a terrible bind in 1963. Despite figures suggesting that use of girdles should be expanding, sales were thinning at an alarming rate, and Playtex executives had been trying everything they could think of to reverse the trend.

Having risen to its dominant position on the strength of its marketing acumen, Playtex tried pouring more money into its advertising efforts. It established a program in which girdles would be displayed in multiple locations in grocery stores in hopes of attracting more consumer attention. The company even added more loops, belts and zippers to its already formidable products in case women felt the items were not providing much support.

None of the measures had helped.

"After we completed our research," recalls Florence Skelly, now president and chief executive of the company that changed its name to Yankelovich, Skelly & White in 1974, "it became clear that the main cause of the problem was the new set of social values that was emerging." It was not, she says, because of a direct product shortcoming or marketing failure.

The company's research showed that new attitudes toward naturalness and sexuality were beginning to emerge. Feminist books were stirring a reexamination of the role of women, especially among suburban women who were prime targets for girdle marketers. The new value system that would eventually reject the traditional American views of self-denial and discomfort were beginning to influence customers who were facing use of the uncomfortable and constraining girdles.

"Women simply weren't giving their 14-year-old daughters girdles as a rite of passage," says Ms. Skelly.

Considering the complexity of the social forces, the solution Yankelovich suggested to Playtex's problems was relatively simple: Shift away from zippers, heavy hardware, and the concept of constraining support. Move to the "control underwear" idea of women's undergarments. When the strategy was implemented, the sales slide was reversed.

The work done for Playtex was only one of the projects over the last 20 years that has earned Yankelovich, Skelly & White its prominent position in the market research community and have brought Mr. Yankelovich recognition as a pioneer in the field.

Source: From B. G. Yovovich, "Finding the Answers," *Advertising Age*, July 20, 1981, p. 41.

two years its automobile exports to the United States. Political forces were also clearly at play when China agreed to let the Coca-Cola Company market Coke in China after the Soviet Union agreed to permit the marketing of Pepsi in that country. And it may be merely coincidental, that Italy's FIAT Corporation produces autos in the U.S.S.R. and Italy has the largest communist party membership outside of Russia and its satellites.

Additional examples of political and legal constraints on marketing are easy to find. Here are a few examples.

■ Burger Chef won its case when it sued Wendy's for using the word "fun." Burger Chef had been promoting a kids' "fun meal" and charged that Wendy's "fun pack" and "fun feast" were trademark infringements and unfair competition.[16]

■ The Federal Trade Commission ordered that Anacin no longer could claim that it worked better than aspirin or that it had "the pain reliever

---

[16]"Burger Chef Takes Fun Out of Marketing," *Advertising Age*, October 5, 1981.

most recommended by doctors" unless ads also revealed that this pain reliever is, in fact, aspirin.[17]

■ The 1981 air traffic controllers' strike and the subsequent firing of the controllers dramatically reduced the number of flights and had major impacts on passenger air service and the cargo freight system.

■ The British-Argentine war over the Falkland Islands disrupted trade and shipping in the area of the islands and caused Europe's Common Market to halt all trade with Argentina for a short time. U.S. trade with Argentina was also affected.

■ The Federal Communication Commission's decisions, at various times, to permit FM broadcasts, encourage the development of UHF television stations, and raise the number of CB radio channels from 23 to 40 affected manufacturers and retailers of radios and television as well as marketers in the broadcasting business.

Three Levels of Law. Legislation intended to maintain a competitive business environment, protect consumers from dangerous products or unethical practices, and to preserve the natural environment can be found at the federal, state, and local levels. Since each of these levels have various departments, subdepartments, regulatory boards, and political subdivisions such as counties and townships, it is possible that a single marketing organization could confront some 78,000 sets of rules and regulations.[18]

Federal Level. At the Federal level of government, such agencies as the Department of Justice, the Food and Drug Administration, the Federal Trade Commission, and many others, have been established to enforce laws based on the Sherman Antitrust Act (1890), the Clayton Antitrust Act (1914), the Federal Trade Commission Act (1914), and the Wheeler-Lea Act (1938). **Federal antitrust legislation** prohibits acts such as restraint of trade and monopoly, price fixing, price discrimination, deceptive practices, misrepresentations in the labeling of products, and other behavior that tends to lessen competition. The degree of specialization of some laws and agencies is suggested by the examples in Exhibit 2-9.

EXHIBIT 2-9

A Sample of Specialized Federal Legislation Affecting Business-Government Relationships

Legislation	Major Provisions
Federal Hazardous Substances Act	Warning labels required on hazardous household chemicals.
Kefauver-Harris Drug Amendments	Manufacturers must prove drug effectiveness as well as safety.
Child Protection and Toy Safety Act	Allows FDA to ban products so dangerous that adequate safety warnings cannot be given.
Consumer Protection Credit Act	Banks, finance companies, and retailers must fully disclose true interest rates and all other charges to credit customers for loans, revolving charge accounts, and installment purchases.
Public Health Smoking Act	Prohibits cigarette advertising on TV and radio, and revised the health hazard warning on cigarette packages. (Advertising ban extended to include "little cigars" in 1973.)
Poison Prevention Labeling Act	Requires safety packaging for products that may be harmful to children.
Drug Listing Act	FDA is given access to wide information on drug manufacturers.

Source: Adapted with permission from Reed Moyer and Michael D. Hutt, *Macro Marketing: A Social Perspective*, second edition (New York: John Wiley & Sons, 1978), p. 175.

---

[17]"FTC Orders Fast Relief From Anacin Ad Claims," *The Tulsa Tribune*, September 24, 1981, p. 15a.

[18]Michael D. Hutt and Thomas W. Speh, *Industrial Marketing Management* (Chicago: Dryden Press, 1981), p. 35.

Jogging is just one manifestation of an exceedingly large environmental trend toward keeping fit. Diet Pepsi is a product that reflects this trend. Americans' preoccupation with looking good and feeling good is reflected in the sales of jogging shoes, diet drinks, stationary exercise bikes, health clubs, diet pills, barbells, and numerous other fitness extras. It is estimated that keeping fit is a $30 billion business in the United States.

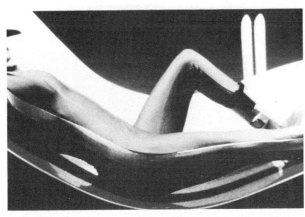

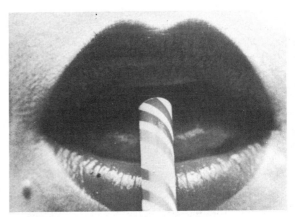

One major Federal agency, the **Federal Trade Commission** (FTC), which was established in 1914, affects virtually all marketers on a regular basis. The FTC was given broad powers of investigation and jurisdiction over "unfair methods of competition." Initially the FTC was supposed to draft a fixed list of "unfair practices." It soon became clear that no such list, covering all situations, could be developed. Thus, though the FTC does publish guidelines and uses past decisions as precedents for solving current problems, each situation investigated by the FTC is judged individually. Marketing managers, therefore, face considerable uncertainty in trying to develop programs that can withstand FTC scrutiny.

All U.S. legislation dealing with marketing would be impossible to discuss in this introductory treatment of the subject. Exhibit 2-10 summarizes selected Federal legislation which

EXHIBIT 2-10

Key Federal Legislation Affecting Marketers

Act	Purpose
The Sherman Act (1890)	Prohibits combinations, contracts or conspiracies to restrain trade or monopolize.
Clayton Act (1914)	The fundamental anti-trust statute prohibiting price discrimination, exclusive dealer arrangements and interlocking directorates which lessen competition.
Federal Trade Commission Act (1914)	Created the FTC and gave investigatory powers.
Robinson-Patman Act (1936) (See Chapter 17 for detailed discussion)	Expands Clayton Act to prohibit sellers from offering different deals to different customers.
The Wheeler-Lea Act (1938)	Expands powers of FTC to prevent injuries to competition *before* they occur.
The Celler-Kefauver Act (1950)	Expands anti-merger prohibitions of Clayton Act to include acquisition of physical assets as well as capital stock in another corporation when the effect is to injure competition.
The Magnuson-Moss Act (1975)	Confirms the FTC's right to regulate by industry-wide Trade Regulation Rules (TRR).
The Consumer Goods Pricing Act (1975)	Repealed "fair trade" laws and prohibited price maintenance agreements among producers and re-sellers.

affects most marketers. Additional milestone legislation affecting major portions of the marketing mix are discussed throughout the book.[19]

---

[19]For a survey of this topic, see Marshall Howard, *Legal Aspects of Marketing* (New York: McGraw-Hill, 1964).

State Level. Most states have created laws and agencies which parallel those at the federal level. State departments of agriculture, commerce, labor, and so on, are commonly found as are consumer protection laws dealing with foods, manufactured goods, lending, real estate, banking, and insurance.

All states have laws which can impact on organizations' marketing mixes. For example, in Oklahoma, distillers must sell their liquor brands to Oklahoma wholesalers at the lowest price in the country; New Jersey taxes take-out food, but not food consumed in restaurants, while Ohio does the opposite; and Texas prohibits banks from having branches. Some farm states do not apply sales taxes if the seller is the actual producer of the goods sold. Michigan prohibits bars from serving free peanuts or potato chips believing free food might encourage drinking, while New York requires that food be available where alcohol is served. California and Arizona prohibit the "importing" of certain fruits, plants, and vegetables. In addition, many states have laws mandating returnable beverage cans and bottles. Some states require beer sellers to hold to certain pricing practices to stabilize that product's price. Ohio and Pennsylvania control the sale of all hard liquors through a system of "state stores." A great number of businesses in Rhode Island close on September second. Why? It's Victory over Japan Day, a legal holiday only in Rhode Island!

Local Level. Cities, townships, villages, and counties are all empowered to pass laws and ordinances and create regulatory agencies. In most areas, health department inspectors check restaurants and motels, weights and measures inspectors check for honest scales, and city and county prosecutors investigate misleading and unfair business practices. Local government units may tax some products but not others, require that certain stores be closed on Sunday, or, as in New York City, legislate that all bars must be closed for at least one hour a day and all customers removed from the premises.

A common local control on marketing is the issuing of vendors' or other similar licenses. In

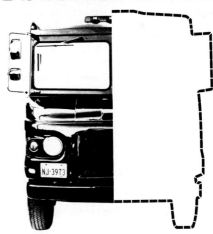
Federal, state, and local laws regulate marketing.

most cases, the licenses are not sold to make money for local governments, although this can be a factor, especially in the case of liquor licenses. The major reason for licensing is so that licenses can be *denied* to organizations which violate laws or local custom.

One common local law, which affects only door-to-door sellers, is the so-called *Green River Ordinance*, named for the town in Wyoming which pioneered its use. These ordinances vary widely from place to place since they are local town or city laws, but their purpose is always the same. They require peddlers to obtain a license while making such licenses very hard to get, or restrict door-to-door selling to certain neighborhoods or to specific hours of the day. Frequently, signs reading "Green River Ordinance in Effect" may be seen on the outskirts of towns.

ENVIRONMENTAL INTERACTIONS

Before ending this discussion of the different aspects of marketing's environment, we should note that parts of this environment interact with each other. Therefore, effective marketers must consider the whole of marketing's environment, not just its parts.

For example, natural phenomena such as the eruption of volcanoes can affect tourism, agriculture, weather patterns, radio and television transmission, heighten public interest in "disaster" movies and books, or inspire race track customers to bet on horses whose names suggest volcanic explosions.

Interactions between changes in the economic, technological, and social environments are relatively easy to spot. When the U.S. economy is in periods of decline, the divorce rate also declines because fewer couples can afford the expense of divorce. When medical science reduces the mortality rate in a country, that country's birth rate eventually declines because parents realize that their children can be expected to survive to adulthood.

These kinds of interactions make the job of environmental analysis a complex one. Nonetheless, marketing success cannot be achieved without a careful consideration of environmental constraints and opportunities.

SUMMARY

This chapter described the environment of marketing, the forces surrounding all organizations which affect everything those organizations do. Some aspects of the environment may limit the options marketers have, but many of them also provide marketers with opportunities.

The physical environment around us and the five major facets of our cultural environment (demography, economics, science and technology, social values and beliefs, and political and legal factors), were portrayed and discussed individually, but the focus was on the marketer's response to these forces and their interactions. For example, supply problems, an impact of the economic environment, resulted in the development of what are known as demarketing techniques.

This chapter reviewed some of the most significant aspects of America's demographic profile. Population totals as well as characteristics of the average American have also been examined. Most importantly, it was emphasized that marketers must keep track of changes in these demographic matters. All the facts and figures available find their greatest long-range value in the patterns by which these same figures change. The changes are caused by and reflect cultural forces, forces that are of major significance to marketers.

> THE MOST IMPORTANT CONCEPT IN THIS CHAPTER
>
> Marketing's environment changes constantly, creating new opportunities and eliminating old ones. Monitoring the environment and being willing and able to change with it is the only way to deal with its powerful forces.

KEY TERMS

Environmental dynamics

Marketing dynamics

Physical environment

Cultural environment

Culture

Demography

Economic conditions

Pure competition

Monopolistic competition

Oligopoly

Monopoly

Demarketing

Science

Technology

Social value

Belief

Federal antitrust legislation

Federal Trade Commission

QUESTIONS FOR DISCUSSION

1 What environmental factors might have the greatest influence on:
(a) General Motors
(b) McDonald's
(c) Your local zoo
(d) Boeing

2 What impact would the development of efficient solar energy have on:
(a) The housing industry
(b) The automobile industry
(c) Other industries of interest to you

3 What changing lifestyles do you envision in the next five years? How will they influence retailers?

4 How much influence do marketers have over political and legal influences on the marketing mix?

5 Identify and evaluate the major social trends that will influence the alcoholic beverages industry.

6 Evaluate the trend toward physical fitness from the point of view of:
(a) The manufacturer of packaged foods
(b) The marketer of athletic shoes
(c) The office building leasing agent

7 What geographic areas in North America seem to be bellweather states—that is, states predicting future environmental trends throughout the rest of the USA?

8 What are some examples of demarketing?

CASE 2-1 Aspen Skiing Corporation*

Aspen, Colorado has a population of 7,620. During the 1960s, when the ski boom hit, Aspen emerged as one of the skiing hot spots. The old Colorado Silver Mining town, at the base of 11,300 foot Aspen mountain, became the chic headquarters for the skiing crowds and a premier resort area. Throughout the 1960s and 1970s there were long lift lines at Ruthie's Run and every other lift in Aspen. Since 1979, however, empty chairs and runs appeared in Aspen as the number of skiers buying lift tickets declined 15 percent.

Profits and sales tax revenue have tumbled from the heady days of the mid-1970s, when business profits commonly grew at an annual rate of more than 15 percent. And in the 1982 season, even though Aspen had its best snowfall in many winters, business remained sluggish.

"That really got to people here," said the operator of a ski lodge. "People kept asking one another, 'If we've got such great snow, where are all the skiers?'"

---

*Source: Based on information in "Downhill Slope," *Time*, February 14, 1983, p. 19; and "Aspen: Acting Resort Faces Hard Choices," *Tulsa Tribune*, January 12, 1983, p. 4c.

In 1983, the landmark Red Onion Saloon was closed and five lodges, including the 170 unit Continental Inn, were in the midst of foreclosure. Retail sales growth was at a standstill and the retail sales of chic boutiques were significantly down from previous years. One retailer said "People are paying $200 a night and getting a dump."

A group of local residents argue that Aspen has not done a good job of marketing itself over the years. "We've been ho-humming it for years," says one resident. Another says, "Times have changed, Aspen is no longer unique." Another group of residents believes that Aspen is a mature resort with a solid product. If Aspen is marketed to everybody, Aspen will be spoiled.

Questions

1 What environment factors have influenced Aspen's problems?

2 Does Aspen have any marketing management problems?

3 What can Aspen do to be more in line with environmental trends?

CASE 2-2 Rockford Foods, Inc.

John B. Rockford was healthy and spry at 66 years of age. The old tennis buff regularly beat his son-in-law, Terry MacFarlane, six-three, six-two. Semi-retirement suited him.

Rockford had seen the grocery industry change dramatically since he purchased his first store when returning home after World War II. In his early years he was the first to suggest innovations. Innovation, hard work and a little luck allowed him to have a five-unit chain that continued to be successful. Over the last 10 or 12 years he tended to follow trends, rather than lead, but he kept informed about the latest occurrences in the grocery business. Three years ago, he went into semi-retirement. One of his biggest regrets in life was that his son, J.B. Rockford, Jr., didn't take over the stores. Of course, having a physician in the family was not a bad substitute. Old J.B. felt lucky that his daughter married Terry MacFarlane. A son-in-law with an interest in the grocery business was almost as good as a son running the business. Terry was pretty much in charge of the store these days. However, J.B. sat in on most of the important meetings.

At the last meeting J.B. attended, Terry proposed a new superstore located in the suburbs. Terry thought the next Rockford supermarket should feature a growing variety of non-food items. He believed that the general store concept "was returning." J.B. did not have any problems with the superstore concept. But when Terry suggested a restaurant, J.B. was flabbergasted. Because J.B. was letting Terry take over the reins, he did not want to create a great debate in the meeting. J.B. said only that the new store was important and that it was necessary to spend a considerable amount of time planning. The meeting ended on that note.

J.B. had been thinking about the restaurant concept for a number of days. Playing Terry two days after the meeting, J.B. served many double faults, something he rarely did. He would toss the ball saying "a restaurant in a grocery store?" In an effort to bring his tennis game back up to par, J.B. thought that he would suggest that Terry have a consultant provide suggestions for the new store.

Questions

1 What environmental factors and market trends have influenced MacFarlane's planning?

2 Are J.B.'s worries unfounded?

3 What consumer needs, if any, will the new superstore satisfy?

4 Should any additional information be gathered before the project gets underway?

APPENDIX USA Statistics in Brief, 1982–83

Population	Unit	1970	1975	1979	1980	1981
Total, incl. Armed Forces abroad	Mil.	204.4	216.0	225.1	227.0	229.8
Resident population	Mil.	203.3	215.5	224.6	226.5	229.3
Per square mile	No.	57.4	60.9	63.4	64.0	64.8
Under 5 years old	Mil.	17.2	16.1	16.1	16.3	16.9
5–17 years old	Mil.	52.5	51.0	48.0	47.4	46.2
18 years old and over	Mil.	133.5	148.3	160.5	162.8	166.1
25–34 years old	Mil.	24.9	31.3	36.0	37.1	38.8
35–44 years old	Mil.	23.1	22.8	25.1	25.6	26.5
45–64 years old	Mil.	41.8	43.8	44.4	44.5	44.5
65 years old and over	Mil.	20.0	22.7	25.1	25.5	26.3
Median age	Yr.	28.0	28.7	29.8	30.0	30.3
Male	Mil.	98.9	104.9	109.1	110.0	111.4
Female	Mil.	104.3	110.6	115.4	116.5	117.9
White	Mil.	178.1	187.2	193.7	194.8	196.6
Black	Mil.	22.6	24.7	26.3	26.6	27.2
Percent of resident population	Pct.	11.1	11.5	11.7	11.8	11.9
American Indian	Mil.	.8	(na)	(na)	1.4	(na)
Persons of Spanish origin	Mil.	9.1	(na)	(na)	14.6	(na)
Northeast	Mil.	49.1	49.4	49.2	49.1	49.3
North Central	Mil.	56.6	57.8	58.7	58.9	58.9
South	Mil.	62.8	69.6	74.3	75.3	76.9
West	Mil.	34.8	38.6	42.3	43.2	44.2
Urban	Mil.	149.3	(na)	(na)	167.1	(na)
Rural	Mil.	53.9	(na)	(na)	59.5	(na)
Metropolitan areas (318 SMSA's)[1]	Mil.	153.7	(na)	(na)	169.4	(na)
Percent of resident population	Pct.	75.6	(na)	(na)	74.8	(na)
Central cities	Mil.	67.9	(na)	(na)	68.0	(na)
Outside central cities	Mil.	85.8	(na)	(na)	101.5	(na)
Nonmetropolitan areas	Mil.	49.6	(na)	(na)	57.1	(na)
Males:[2] Single	Pct.	18.9	20.8	23.3	23.8	23.9
Married	Pct.	75.3	72.8	69.2	68.4	67.8
Divorced	Pct.	2.5	3.7	4.8	5.2	5.7
Females:[2] Single	Pct.	13.7	14.6	16.9	17.1	17.4
Married	Pct.	68.5	66.7	63.5	63.0	62.4
Divorced	Pct.	3.9	5.3	6.6	7.1	7.6
Households	Mil.	63.4	71.1	77.3	80.8	82.4
Average size (persons)	No.	3.14	2.94	2.78	2.76	2.73
One-person households	Pct.	17.0	19.6	22.2	22.7	23.0
Families	Mil.	51.6	55.7	57.8	59.6	60.3
Average size (persons)	No.	3.58	3.42	3.31	3.29	3.27
With own children under 18 yrs. old	Pct.	55.9	54.0	52.5	52.1	51.8
White	Mil.	46.3	49.5	50.9	52.2	52.7
Married couple	Pct.	88.7	86.9	85.7	85.7	85.1
Female householder[3]	Pct.	9.0	10.5	11.6	11.6	11.9
Black	Mil.	4.9	5.5	5.9	6.2	6.3
Married couple	Pct.	68.0	60.9	54.9	55.5	53.7
Female householder[3]	Pct.	28.3	35.3	40.5	40.3	41.7
Immigrants	Thous.	373	386	460	(na)	(na)
Rate per 1,000 population	Rate	1.8	1.8	2.1	(na)	(na)

(na) Not available.
[1] Standard metropolitan statistical areas as defined in June 1981.
Source: U.S. Department of Commerce: Bureau of the Census.

[2] Percent of total, 18 years old and over.
[3] With no spouse present.

Vital Statistics	Unit	1970	1975	1979	1980	1981
Births, live	Thous.	3,731	3,144	3,494	3,598	3,646
Percent to unmarried women	Pct.	10.7	14.2	17.1	(na)	(na)
Per 1,000 population	Rate	18.4	14.8	15.9	15.8	15.9
White	Rate	17.4	13.8	14.8	(na)	(na)
Black	Rate	25.3	20.9	22.3	(na)	(na)
Abortions	Thous.	(na)	1,034	1,498	1,554	(na)
Per 1,000 women, 15–44 yrs. old	Rate	(na)	22.2	28.8	29.3	(na)
Deaths	Thous.	1,921	1,893	1,914	1,986	1,987
Per 1,000 population	Rate	9.5	8.9	8.7	8.7	8.7
Infant deaths per 1,000 live births	Rate	20.0	16.1	13.1	12.5	11.7
White	Rate	17.8	14.2	11.4	(na)	(na)
Black	Rate	32.6	26.2	21.8	(na)	(na)
Deaths per 100,000 population	Rate	945	889	870	(na)	(na)
Diseases of heart	Rate	362	336	333	(na)	(na)
Malignancies	Rate	163	172	183	(na)	(na)
Cerebrovascular diseases	Rate	102	91	77	(na)	(na)
Accidents	Rate	56	48	48	(na)	(na)
Marriages	Thous.	2,159	2,153	2,331	2,413	2,438
Per 1,000 population	Rate	10.6	10.1	10.6	10.6	10.6
Per 1,000 unmarried women, 15 & over	Rate	77	67	64	(na)	(na)
Divorces	Thous.	708	1,036	1,181	1,182	1,219
Per 1,000 population	Rate	3.5	4.9	5.4	5.2	5.3
Per 1,000 married women, 15 & over	Rate	15	20	23	(na)	(na)

Health	Unit	1970	1975	1979	1980	1981
Life expectancy at birth, male	Yr.	67.1	68.7	69.9	69.8	(na)
Life expectancy at birth, female	Yr.	74.8	76.5	77.6	77.5	(na)
National health expenditures	$Bil.	74.7	132.7	215.0	249.0	286.6
Per capita	Dol.	358	604	938	1,075	1,225
Public, percent of total	Pct.	37.2	42.3	42.1	42.3	42.8
Hospital care	$Bil.	27.8	52.1	86.1	100.4	118.0
Physicians' services	$Bil.	14.3	24.9	40.2	46.8	54.8
Nursing home care	$Bil.	4.7	10.1	17.6	20.6	24.2
Private consumer expenditures for health	$Bil.	41.6	69.1	112.0	129.1	148.5
Met by private insurance	Pct.	37.5	43.6	44.8	44.2	45.0
Index of medical care prices	1967 = 100	120.6	168.6	239.7	265.9	294.5
Physicians' fees	1967 = 100	121.4	169.4	243.6	269.3	299.0
Hospital room rates	1967 = 100	145.4	236.1	370.3	418.9	481.1
Persons covered, private health insur.[1]	Mil.	154	162	171	(na)	(na)
Percent of civilian population	Pct.	75.9	76.4	77.8	(na)	(na)
Physicians, active M.D.'s[2]	Thous.	282	338	399	418	(na)
Rate per 100,000 population	Rate	138	156	176	182	(na)
Nurses, registered, active	Thous.	700	906	1,075	1,119	(na)
Dentists, active[2]	Thous.	96	107	118	121	(na)
Hospitals	No.	7,123	7,156	6,988	6,965	(na)
Beds per 1,000 population	Rate	7.9	6.8	6.1	6.0	(na)
Occupancy rate[3]	Rate	80.3	76.7	76.1	77.7	(na)
Days of hospital care per 1,000 persons[4]	Days	1,173	1,255	1,224	1,231	(na)
Bed disability, days per person: Male	Days	5.2	5.4	5.6	5.9	(na)
Female	Days	6.9	7.6	7.8	8.0	(na)

(na) Not available.
[1] For hospital benefits.
[2] Excludes Federal practitioners.
[3] Ratio of average daily census to every 100 beds.
[4] Non-Federal short-stay hospitals.

Education	Unit	1970	1975	1979	1980	1981
School enrollment	Mil.	60.4	61.0	57.9	57.3	56.9
Elementary (kindergarten & grades 1–8)	Mil.	37.1	33.8	30.9	30.6	30.1
Secondary (grades 9–12)	Mil.	14.7	15.7	15.1	14.6	14.3
Elementary & secondary in private school	Pct.	10.8	10.1	10.1	(na)	10.4
Higher education	Mil.	7.4	9.7	10.0	10.2	10.4
Female	Mil.	3.0	4.4	5.0	5.2	5.2
School expenditures, total	$Bil.	70.4	111.1	152.1	169.6	181.3
Elementary and secondary	$Bil.	45.7	72.2	98.0	108.6	116.3
Public	$Bil.	41.0	65.0	87.1	96.4	103.5
Average salary, public school teachers[1]	$Thous.	8.6	11.7	15.0	16.0	17.6
High school graduates, yearly	Mil.	2.9	3.1	3.1	3.1	(na)
College graduates, yearly	Mil.	.8	.9	.9	.9	(na)
Adult persons completed high school[2]	Pct.	55	63	68	69	70
Income and Prices						
Gross national product (GNP)	$Bil.	993	1,549	2,418	2,633	2,938
Per capita	Dol.	4,841	7,173	10,741	11,566	12,780
Personal consumption expenditures	$Bil.	622	976	1,507	1,667	1,843
Gross private domestic investment	$Bil.	144	206	423	402	472
Net exports of goods and services	$Bil.	7	27	13	25	26
Govt. purchases of goods and services	$Bil.	220	340	474	538	597
National income	$Bil.	811	1,239	1,967	2,117	2,353
Personal income	$Bil.	811	1,265	1,951	2,160	2,416
Disposable personal income	$Bil.	695	1,096	1,650	1,824	2,029
Per capita	Dol.	3,390	5,075	7,331	8,012	8,827
Personal savings	$Bil.	56	94	97	106	130
GNP, constant (1972) dollars	$Bil.	1,086	1,232	1,479	1,474	1,503
Per capita	Dol.	5,293	5,702	6,572	6,475	6,537
GNP implicit price deflator, index	1972 = 100	91.5	125.8	163.4	178.6	195.5
Median family money income	Dol.	9,867	13,719	19,587	21,023	22,388
White families	Dol.	10,236	14,268	20,439	21,904	23,517
Black families	Dol.	6,279	8,779	11,574	12,674	13,266
Median family income, 1981 dollars	Dol.	23,111	23,183	24,540	23,204	22,388
Families below poverty level	Mil.	5.3	5.5	5.5	6.2	6.9
Percent of all families	Pct.	10.1	9.7	9.2	10.3	11.2
Persons below poverty level	Mil.	25.4	25.9	26.1	29.3	31.8
Percent of all persons	Pct.	12.6	12.3	11.7	13.0	14.0
Producer price index (PPI):[3]						
Crude materials		112.3	196.9	274.3	304.6	329.0
Fuel		122.6	271.5	507.6	615.0	751.2
Immediate materials	1967 = 100	109.9	180.0	243.2	280.3	306.0
Finished goods		110.3	163.4	217.7	247.0	269.8
PPI, all commodities		110.4	174.9	235.6	268.8	293.4
Consumer price index, all items		116.3	161.2	217.4	246.8	272.4
Fuel oil, coal and bottled gas		110.1	235.3	403.1	556.0	675.9
Homeownership cost[4]		128.5	181.8	262.4	314.0	352.7
Gas and electricity	1967 = 100	107.3	169.6	257.8	301.8	345.9
Medical care		120.6	168.6	239.7	265.9	294.5
Transportation		112.7	150.6	212.0	249.7	280.0
Food		114.9	175.4	234.5	254.6	274.6
Rent		110.1	137.3	176.0	191.6	208.2
Urban intermediate budget:						
4-person family	$Thous.	10.7	15.3	20.5	23.1	25.4
Retired couple	$Thous.	4.5	6.5	8.6	9.4	10.2

(na) Not available.
[1] Elementary and secondary schools only.
[2] Persons 25 years old and over.
[3] By stage of processing.
[4] Includes home purchase, interest, taxes, insurance, maintenance, and repairs.

CHAPTER 3

Developing Marketing Strategy

CHAPTER SCAN

This chapter introduces the concepts of planning, strategies, and tactics as they apply to marketing management.

The chapter relates the many variables to be found within the environment of marketing to the marketing planning process.

The chapter shows how marketing managers can develop the effective plans of action that are necessary before attractive marketing mixes can be developed.

The chapter discusses marketing opportunity analysis, the process whereby marketers read the environment to locate threats and opportunities before they develop fully.

**WHEN YOU HAVE STUDIED
THIS CHAPTER, YOU WILL:**

Be familiar with the ideas and terminology associated with planning as these apply to marketing problems.

Be able to explain the planning and managing tasks performed by marketing executives.

Know how the three tasks of planning, execution, and control interrelate and form the basis of marketing management.

Be able to discuss the development of complete strategic plans, and to differentiate between strategy and tactics in the marketplace.

Be able to discuss the process of marketing opportunity analysis and its purpose in identifying trends and opportunities.

Know how marketing managers distinguish between opportunities in general and realistic opportunities that their organizations can profitably pursue.

Be able to explain how plans relate to "the strategic gap."

Near the end of the 1970s General Motors Corporation (GM) was happy with their long-range strategy.[1] GM had jumped two years ahead of its domestic competition in beginning the six-year shift to smaller automobiles and it was launching a new line of fuel-efficient cars, the X-cars, just as a fuel-conscious public was clammering for them. However, a few short years later, the world's largest automobile manufacturer was having problems. It suffered a loss of market share to both its domestic rivals and foreign competitors. One of GM's problems appeared to be the clutter of new, look-alike models that confused customers and blurred the traditional marketing distinctions among its five automotive divisions. Furthermore, the public was confused about GM's pricing, since the full-size Chevy Caprice cost the same as the tiny J-car. In 1983, Oldsmobile's mid-size, front-wheel drive Ciera was priced about $200 less than the big Oldsmobile 88. In 1982, when the Ciera was introduced, its price was $400 more than an Oldsmobile 88.

Another problem concerned consumers' view of the quality of domestic cars. Voluminous studies indicate domestic car makers lead in the durability of such components as engines, brakes, and transmissions. However, the Japanese plainly do a better job on "fit and finish"—the fit of doors, the finish of paint, and the lack of rattles—which consumers can sense at once. "Good quality is what the consumer thinks it is."

This situation required GM to consider their long-range marketing strategy. The cure GM came up with is a strategy straight from the 1920s. General Motor's view then was to market a car for every taste and pocketbook, spread across distinct Chevrolet, Pontiac, Oldsmobile, Buick, and Cadillac divisions. For years, each division's image corresponded to the size and price of its cars. Starting with Chevrolet and moving up through Pontiac, Oldsmobile, Buick, and Cadillac, the cars got bigger, fancier, and more expensive. Buyers moved up as their aspirations and incomes rose.

General Motors recognizes that those distinctions have now faded. They are preparing plans to eliminate the further dissolution of the "aspirational order" in GM's product line. Divisions are also trying to market more exclusive cars. For example, the Pontiac division introduced, in 1983, the Fiero, a two-seater automobile designed to be less sporty than the Chevrolet division's Corvette but appealing to young people.

As this example illustrates, developing a marketing strategy is crucial to an organization's success. Marketing management and marketing strategy are the subjects of this chapter.

MARKETING MANAGEMENT

Managers develop rules, principles, or ways of thinking that can be of use in attaining goals of all sorts. Charities, colleges, and universities must be managed in much the same way as the IBM Corporation. Executives must run the day-to-day marketing operations of the organizations in their care *and* plan future efforts *and*

improve on currently used methods and techniques.

Marketing executives, as managers of the marketing activities within an organization, must understand demand, consumer wants, and the environment which so strongly influences the development of an effective marketing mix. Since **marketing management** can be seen as a special application of general management techniques, marketers should utilize management concepts by adapting these concepts to marketing situations and problems.

---

[1]Based on "General Motors: The Next Move Is to Restore Each Division's Identity," *Business Week*, October 4, 1982, pp. 75–78.

Marketing Managers Plan, Execute, and Control Activities

As this chapter will show, successful marketing rarely, if ever, occurs without the careful planning, execution, and control of activities. Of course, the effort and risk connected with the introduction of a Dukes of Hazzard T-shirt differ from the effort and risk associated with the offering of a new automobile or an antibiotic. Yet some care in planning and execution is needed in all cases. Effective marketing is the result of good management.

What, exactly, is management? Because it is a human activity that covers a wide range of applications, **management** can be defined broadly as

a social function that gets things done. It takes us from some condition or state of affairs we do not want to one that we do want. Management does this by facilitating goal setting and integrating human and material resources to achieve goals.[2]

All organizations have goals to achieve. Within business organizations, executives may speak of corporate goals or "missions," while nonprofit organizations emphasize community service or other accomplishments. But, no matter what the context, good management remains the same. Planning, execution, and control activities are necessary to effective management in any area. They are functions performed by production executives, financial executives, and marketing executives alike (see Exhibit 3-1). Our purpose here is to investigate three general functions of the management process—**planning, execution, control**—as they are applied to marketing planning and management.

Marketing management is a decision making process concerned with planning, executing, and controlling a set of operating activities that help the firm achieve its goals.[3] What is our cor-

porate mission? Do new products need to be introduced? Do existing products need to be improved or modified? How much should be spent for advertising and personal selling? Is our price too high? Answering questions like these is the task of marketing management.

Marketing Planning

Marketing planning is the establishing of marketing goals and the design of marketing programs that are expected to be implemented in the future. Well-planned marketing goals and objectives provide a framework for future managerial decisions. Carefully stated goals and objectives serve as a standard to evaluate alternative courses of future action. The planning process consists of selecting those courses of action that will help achieve the marketing objectives in the most efficient manner. Planning is a forward-thinking activity, but marketing's environment is, as we have seen, constantly and rapidly changing. Thus, planning organizational goals and planning the means to attain those goals is not an easy task. It is not a hopeless one, however. Careful thought and consideration obviously have payoffs in *any* effort. Planning sufficient study time, locating a tutor, and hard work can get even the most "anxious" student through a statistics course. In business, designing a set of future actions that will be taken is a crucial ingredient of long-term success.

There are two general categories of marketing planning: **operational planning** and **strategic planning.** Operational planning concerns planning for day-to-day functional activities. It pertains to existing activities in existing markets with existing customers and facilities.[4] Operational planning is much shorter in range and in scope than strategic planning which concerns long-range considerations concerning an organization's mission, strategies, and objectives. Although strategic planning is considered

[2] Joseph A. Litterer, *An Introduction to Management* (New York: John Wiley & Sons, 1978), p. 4.

[3] Douglas J. Dalrymple and Leonard J. Parsons, *Marketing Management* (New York: John Wiley & Sons, 1980), p. 3.

[4] William Lazer and James D. Culley, *Marketing Management: Foundations and Practices* (Boston: Houghton Mifflin Co., 1983), p. 168.

EXHIBIT 3-1

Planning, Execution, and Control are the Three Functions of the Marketing Management Plan

Planning.

Execution.

Control.

in greater detail later on in this chapter, three examples are given below to help explain the general nature of marketing planning.

A classic story of how long-term planning influenced a corporation's success concerns the long-term plan for Montgomery Ward developed shortly after World War II. Since the president of Montgomery Ward expected a depression to follow World War II, the company did not expand its stores into growing suburban areas. Instead, the organization's assets were converted into short-term government obligations and other high-quality, highly liquid assets.

Sears Roebuck, conversely, developed a long-term marketing plan emphasizing rapid expansion which led to a dominance in retail markets during the prosperity of the 1950s and 1960s.[5] Sears' strategic planning for the 1980s is based on the long-term expectation that it will be unable to grow rapidly in retailing, and that there may be a decline in department store shopping in the future. In 1981, it radically redefined what business it was in and moved into the consumer financial services marketing area by buying a stock brokerage house, a real estate firm, and by marketing money market funds. Sears, while still a retailer, has planned for the long term by expanding its scope of retailing.

Both Montgomery Ward and Sears determined their long-term strategies based on the world economic situation. Consider another contemporary example, where the nub of the long-term plan is grounded in a comparison of brand differences. The 7-Up Company has made a decision to emphasize in all their promotion and packaging that 7-Up has no caffeine and an absence of artificial flavors and colorings. 7-Up is taking an enormous risk with this no additives campaign. They're putting their bottlers, who may also distribute colas with caffeine and other additives, in an almost adversarial position.[6] This long-term decision has tre-

---

[5] Henry O. Pruden, "The Kondratieff Wave," *The Journal of Marketing*, April 1978, p. 68.

[6] "7-Up Uncaps a Cola—and an Industry Feud," *Business Week*, March 22, 1982, p. 98; and "Another Wordball Campaign from 7-Up," *Business Week*, June 6, 1983, p. 300.

A CORPORATE MISSION STATEMENT THAT IS CONSUMER ORIENTED

Q. Can you tell me why American Express merged with the brokerage firm of Shearson Loeb Rhoades?

A. The goal of American Express has always been to deliver superior products and services to our customers. With high rates of inflation and a rapidly changing economic environment, our customers' needs are growing more and more complex.

Our merger with Shearson Loeb Rhoades greatly enhances American Express' abilities to meet these needs with sophisticated and flexible financial services.

Shearson's success in meeting its customers' needs has led it to become the second largest brokerage firm in America. The company, which was renamed Shearson/American Express in September, now has over 300 offices around the world serving some 700,000 individual, government and corporate clients. It has been a leader in the development of many contemporary financial service ideas and has a record of innovation in the investment community.

In addition to first-rate execution of customers' stock, bond and commodity trades, Shearson/American Express offers sophisticated money management, financial planning services and a wide range of tax-efficient investment opportunities in areas such as real estate and oil and gas drilling.

We believe the melding of the people, resources and ideas of American Express and Shearson will generate exciting financial opportunities which should benefit all of our customers.

Source: Used with the permission of *The American Express Newsletter*, November 1981, p. 2.

---

mendous implications for 7-Up's future, in terms of both its distributors' willingness to cooperate and its consumers' acceptance of the product.

7UP's long-term strategic planning is reflected in this advertisement.

The purpose of marketing planning is to go beyond diagnosis of the present and to predict the future by devising a means to adjust to some portion of the organization's environment before problems develop.[7] Planning helps an organization to shape its own destiny by anticipating changes in the marketplace rather than by merely reacting to those changes. Planning allows the marketing manager to follow the maxim, "Act! Don't react." In short, planning involves deciding *in advance.* The length of an organization's **planning horizon** is generally determined by the uncertainty of the environmental situation. In general, long-range strategic planning is more difficult than short-range operational planning because there is less certainty about the distant future. Whatever the length of the planning horizon, the essence of planning is establishing the relationship between an organization and its surroundings and anticipating how to meet new situations.

Planning, of course, must result in *plans,* specific courses of action to be taken when (or if) future events occur. Certain plans will ulti-mately be scrapped because of changes in the society or in other portions of marketing's environment. In the 1970s the developing energy crisis led makers of appliances, light bulbs, automobiles, trucks, and airplanes to market more energy efficient products. In the 1980s consumer worries about health problems related to high salt intake resulted in low-salt cheese, no-salt baby foods, and other low-salt products. No doubt some plans to introduce products which were high users of energy or high in salt had to be dropped as a result of the changing environment.

Execution of Marketing Plans

Once marketing plans have been developed and approved, they must be executed or carried out. In fact, the words "executive" and "execute" both mean to "follow out" or "carry out." Making a sales presentation, inspecting proofs of advertising copy, setting prices and discounts, and choosing distribution methods are all aspects of execution of a marketing plan.

Execution requires organizing and coordinating people, resources, and activities. Staffing, directing, developing, and leading subordinates are major activities used to implement

---

[7] Russell Ackoff, *A Concept of Corporate Planning* (New York: John Wiley & Sons, 1970), p. 1.

POOR PLANNING FOR THE ERECTOR SET

Without long-range planning many things can go wrong. While A. C. Gilbert and Company never became a very large firm—it did hold its own among the top ten toy manufacturers in the 1950s. It enjoyed one of the best reputations in science toys and was known to generations of boys and their fathers. During the 1960s, technology and science were becoming a national priority. What could be better for Gilbert?

As events later showed, lots could have been better for Gilbert. In the 1960s, the toy market was changing. And Gilbert was unaware of the changing marketplace and unfamiliar with the new nationwide promotional medium—TV. Television had taken a front-row place in toy marketing and was fast eclipsing Gilbert's old standbys—the toy catalog and the handsome window display.

The toy market was changing in yet another way. Customers were bypassing the "traditional" toy stores, hobby shops, and department stores in favor of self-service, high-volume supermarkets and discount stores. And what were these dealers pushing? Mainly low-priced, heavily advertised toys in attractive packages that functioned as selling tools.

When all of these changes finally dawned on Gilbert, there was frantic activity. The product line—a line that had gone relatively unchanged for decades—was expanded to include 50 new toys directed not only to the traditional target market of 6- to 14-year-old boys but also to girls and preschoolers.

But, having strayed from its time-honored base, Gilbert found itself in the business of toys it was not used to making. The new product line strained the company's engineering and production capabilities. The result could have been predicted: poorly designed toys of not very good quality, with disappointing customer appeal.

Nothing Gilbert later did served to restore the image of the reputable toy-maker. A company/brand image is a precious thing. Long in building, it can't for long take punishment and abuse. In 1967, a bankrupt A. C. Gilbert threw in the towel.

Source: Reprinted with permission from *Marketing Mistakes,* 2nd ed., by Robert F. Hartley, ed. (Columbus, Ohio: Grid Publishing, Inc., 1982), pp. 181–192.

Far left: **Boy playing with an erector set in the 1950s.** *Left:* **Boy playing with Legos in the 1980s.**

plans.[8] Clearly, the greatest of marketing plans, if not properly executed, is likely to result in failure. Speakers at sales meetings are fond of describing the salesperson who read every book on planning for success, who spent every waking hour developing approaches to customers and getting all aspects of his sales career in perfect order, but who never sold a thing and was fired. Why? He never got out of the house to sell anything! Planning, then, is extremely important, but it means little without execution.

Caution must always be taken, however, to assure that the environmental factors which suggested certain marketing plans, have not changed. Shifts in marketing's dynamic environment have caused the most carefully developed plans to fail miserably. The story of the Edsel automobile, which took years to bring to the market—years in which the marketing research it was based on had gone badly out of date—remains a famous example of the effects of the changing environment. "Booms" in certain product areas such as sports equipment, toys, shampoos, and vitamin supplements, often are short-lived, leaving products based on these booms to wither and die.

Execution is difficult to discuss because there are so many ways any one job may be accomplished. Mistakes may be made in the completion of any task. These mistakes are errors of execution. Great caution is needed to avoid such errors, some minor, some perhaps unavoidable, but all of them damaging to some degree.

■ A marketing textbook refers to a McDonald's "Quarter Pounder" as "two all beef patties, special sauce, etc., on a sesame seed bun." The readers know that that describes a "Big Mac" and wonder just how aware the text's author is.

■ T.V. advertisers generally use one model for "face shots" and another for "hand shots." Consumers frequently note that the "housewives" in advertisements have watches or rings on one hand at the start of the commercial which "move" to the other as the ad progresses.

■ An automotive trade magazine, *Tire Review,* ran an article on the glorious future ahead of Seiberling Tires, and published the magazine on the very day the company announced it was going out of business. Obviously, the reporter had not found out the whole story.

■ A J.C. Penney advertisement for a video game reads "reg. $34.95, new $27.96." "New" is erroneously substituted for "Now."

■ Joseph A. Banks Clothier Inc. wished to shorten the company name appearing in the yellow page ads. A corporate executive told the people at the phone company to make a change and to drop "incorporated" so the company name would be shorter. The name that actually appeared in the Atlanta phone book was "Drop Inc."[9]

An important aspect of the marketing manager's job is to supervise the implementation of marketing plans. These examples illustrate that execution errors do occur if the managers and employees are not careful in the performance of their tasks.

Control

The purpose of managerial **control** is to ensure that planned activities are completed and properly executed. Thus, the first aspect of control is to establish acceptable performance standards. Control also requires investigation and evaluation. Investigation involves "checking up" to determine whether the activities necessary to the execution of the marketing plan are in fact being performed. Actual performance must then be assessed. Performance may be evaluated, for example, in terms of the number of sales calls made or new accounts developed. Does the salesperson's performance equal or surpass a predetermined performance standard? Sales and financial figures may also be judged to appraise individual or organization successes.

---

[8]Joseph Litterer, *An Introduction to Management* (New York: John Wiley & Sons, 1978), p. 292.

[9]Based on a speech by Dan Robertson at the 1983 ABSEL Convention, Tulsa, Oklahoma, February 1983.

EXHIBIT 3-2

The Environment for Marketing Organization

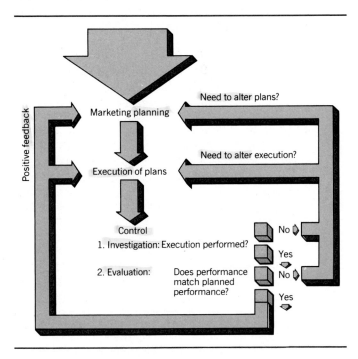

Marketing planning

Need to alter plans?

Execution of plans

Need to alter execution?

Control
1. Investigation: Execution performed?   No   Yes
2. Evaluation: Does performance match planned performance?   No   Yes

Positive feedback

Control activities provide feedback to alert managers since they indicate whether to continue with plans and activities or to change them and take corrective action. Marketing executives may discover, by means of the control activity, that the actions and results that were part of the marketing plan are not being matched "in the field." When this happens either the marketing plan must be corrected to reflect environmental realities or the persons responsible for carrying out the plan must be more strongly motivated to achieve organizational goals.

The **marketing audit** is a comprehensive review and appraisal of the total marketing operation. It requires a systematic and impartial review of an organization's recent and current operations and its marketing environment. The audit examines the company's strengths and weaknesses in light of problems and opportunities facing the organization. Since the effectiveness of marketing activities are being evaluated, it is often necessary to have an independent examination of marketing activity by outside consultants or otherwise unbiased personnel.

Planning, Execution, and Control Are Interrelated

It should be obvious from the above discussion of planning, execution, and control that these three functions are closely interrelated. A consideration of marketing's environment can lead to the formulation of marketing plans. These in turn must be executed. The execution of the plan must then be investigated and evaluated. It is the latter two steps that constitute the control function. The results or findings generated during the control phase serve as new inputs for both planning and execution, providing a basis for judging both the marketing plans and their execution. Thus a series of logical steps is maintained as is shown in Exhibit 3-2.

STRATEGIC MARKETING

Marketers, like admirals and generals, must develop strategies calculated to obtain the objectives they seek. The military planner's endeavors often lead to more disastrous results than do those of businesspeople, but the loss of the means to make a living, the closing of a factory, and the "defeat" of a product in the marketplace are serious matters indeed to the investors, executives, and workers involved. Therefore, a number of military terms—strategy, tactics, maneuvers, and so on—have been adopted by businesspeople, just as they have by football coaches.

What Is a Marketing Strategy?

Perhaps because of its widespread usage "strategy" has been broadly used and defined many different ways.[10] For our purposes, a specific definition is appropriate:

> A **marketing strategy** consists of the determination of basic long-range goals and objectives, the commitments of courses of action, and the allocation of resources necessary to achieve these goals.[11]

Hence, **strategic marketing planning** is a long-range, comprehensive framework formulated to accomplish brand, organizational, or divisional goals. A good example of a complete strategic plan was provided by the Smithfield Packing Company's introduction of its hot dog brand into the Washington-Baltimore market. Smithfield strategists carefully assessed the competitive environment and noted that many competitors were offering products that were

---

STRATEGIC VISIONS

A strategic vision is a clear image of what you want to achieve, which then organizes and instructs every step toward that goal. The extraordinarily successful strategic vision for NASA was "Put a man on the moon by the end of the decade." That strategic vision gave magnetic direction to the entire organization. Nobody had to be told or reminded of where the organization was going. Contrast the organizing focus of putting a man on the moon by the end of the decade with "We are going to be the world leader in space exploration," which doesn't organize anything.

In a constantly changing world, strategic planning is not enough; it becomes planning for its own sake. Strategic planning must be completely geared to a strategic vision and know exactly where it is going, with a clarity that remains in spite of the confusion natural to the first stages of change.

Source: John Naisbitt, *Megatrends* Copyright © 1982 by John Naisbitt, published by Warner Books. (New York: Warren Communications, 1982), p. 94. Used with permission.

---

not quite traditional versions of this traditional American food. Some competing products were made of chicken or turkey. Others were "franks that plump when you cook them."

Marketing strategists decided that Smithfield could develop and maintain a long-term position of strength in a competitive marketplace by stressing product quality and tradition. This assessment led to the introduction of "Luter's Original Old-Fashioned Hot Dogs," which were cured and smoked twice as long as "today's" hot dogs. The basic idea was to give a quality product a comfortable, somehow familiar image in a new market. As seen in Exhibit 3-3, this strategy was made complete by the use of a family name, a picture of a "traditional" hot dog maker, the notation that the product was "cured and

---

[10] H. Igor Ansoff, *Corporate Strategy* (New York: McGraw-Hill, 1965), p. 103; and Michael A. Hitt, R. Dennis Middlemist, and Robert L. Mathis, *Effective Management* (St. Paul: West Publishing, 1979), p. 143.

[11] Alfred D. Chandler, *Strategy and Structure* (Cambridge, Mass.: M.I.T. Press, 1962), p. 13.

EXHIBIT 3-3

A Marketing Strategy Stressing Product Quality and Old-Fashioned Traditional Values

smoked in Smithfield, Va." (an area famous for expensive, high-quality hams), and by the use of the terms "original" and "old-fashioned."[12]

Marketing Tactics and Strategy

The Armed Forces describe *strategy* as "what the generals do" and *tactics* as what lower officers such as captains and lieutenants do. This description rightly suggests that tactics are less comprehensive in scope than strategies. **Tactics** are specific actions intended to implement strategy. Therefore, tactics are most closely associated with the *execution* of plans rather than with planning itself. In the market introduction of Luter's Original Hot Dogs discussed earlier, the idea of projecting an old-time goodness image was a strategy; the actual selection of the term "old-fashioned" and the inclusion of a picture of an old-time butcher were

[12] "Luter's Takes Old-Fashioned Plan to Market," *Advertising Age,* April 27, 1981), p. 42.

tactics. The tactics were consistent with, and supported, the strategy.

McDonald's basic strategy is to have a family-type restaurant. The tactic not to have pay telephones that might encourage "hanging out" is one of the many tactics to implement the strategy.

A common pricing strategy is to be competitive with the market leader. Such a strategy could be carried out by utilizing one or several tactics. If the idea is to compete by dropping prices to win customers, a cents-off coupon or a rebate of some type might be appropriate. If the thought is to compete by suggesting a product quality equal to that of a high-priced market leader, raising the price could be the proper tactic.

Another strategy is to expand product usage. Renaming the product known as "Pretty Feet" to "Pretty Feet and Hands" was a tactic intended to expand product usage by including foot care *and* hand care in the name—thus reaching the larger hand care market.

DEVELOPING MARKETING STRATEGIES

Marketing strategies, and the tactics used to achieve the goals the strategies suggest, must always be developed with the consumer or buyer in mind. Every step of the marketing process, from strategy formulation to dealing with a single retail customer, must be aimed at satisfying the consumer. This is the key lesson of the marketing concept and foundation of effective marketing.

There are three major stages in the development of a marketing strategy (Exhibit 3-4). These are:

1 Identifying and evaluating opportunities.

2 Analyzing market segments and selecting target markets.

EXHIBIT 3-4

Three Stages of Marketing Strategy Development

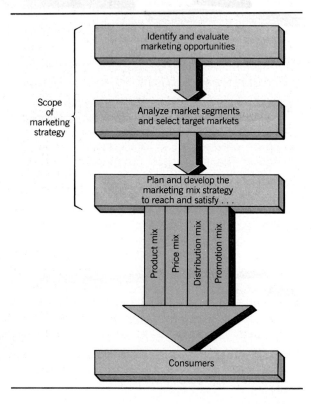

3 Planning a marketing mix strategy that will satisfy customers' needs *and* meet the objectives and goals of the organization.

The various activities involved in developing marketing strategy may, in fact, be carried out by a number of people over varying time periods, and the actual sequence of decisions may differ within different organizations. Nevertheless, each stage is crucial to effective strategy development.

Stage 1: Identifying and Evaluating Opportunities

The powerful and ever-changing impact of environmental factors on any organization is discussed in Chapter 2. Knowing that marketing activities are performed within a multifaceted environment and that this environment has a major impact on marketing is not enough to assure effective marketing. The marketer must be able to accurately "read" that environment, and any change in it, and to translate what is perceived into marketing opportunities. **Marketing opportunity analysis** is the diagnostic activity of interpreting environmental attributes and change. It serves as both a warning system to alert managers to the risk of potential problems and as an appraisal system to make managers aware of the benefits associated with certain opportunities.

Marketing opportunity analysis provides a well-built foundation for marketing planning and strategy development. Managers need to evaluate the environment in which they work and to estimate future environmental impacts on consumers. Consideration of trends, of what lies ahead, permits the marketing manager to act rather than to simply react. The environment must be carefully monitored and evaluated, and potential problems and opportunities identified, before any organization can begin strategic planning.

Effective managers facilitate the adapting of their strategies to shifts in its environment by analyzing situations and foreseeing problems that may result from unfavorable conditions. On the other hand, environmental changes may be

SOUP IS GOOD FOOD

Campbell's Soup Company is a dominant force in the condensed soup market. All competitors combined have less than 20 percent of the market. In recent years the demand for condensed soups has remained steady with a growth rate of only 1 percent a year. Campbell's marketing strategy is now to increase the demand for the soup category as a whole and reverse the lethargic trend. To do this, part of the advertising campaign stresses that "soup is good food."

Source: Based on Bill Abrams, "Campbell's New Ad Strategy: Make Folks Hungrier for Soup," *Wall Street Journal,* September 24, 1981, p. 25.

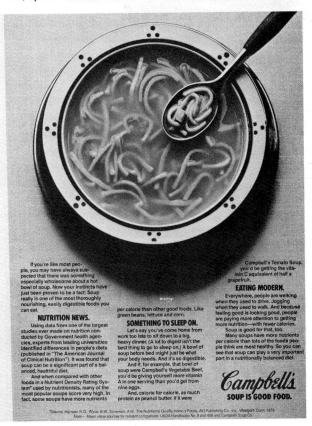

interpreted as opportunities rather than problems. Declining per capita coffee consumption may be seen as an unfavorable trend by coffee marketers, mug manufacturers, and coffee-cake bakers but as an opportunity to soft-drink marketers. The development of wash-and-wear clothing helped producers of certain fabrics and chemicals and contributed to the sale of laundry detergents, washing machines, and clothes dryers, but unfavorably impacted the dry cleaning industry.[13] A new technological development in the electronics industry may prove a boon to the marketers of hand-held electronic games and products such as Texas Instrument's "Speak and Spell" but impacts negatively on the tradi-

[13] Theodore Levitt, "Marketing Myopia," *Harvard Business Review,* July-August 1960, p. 45.

tional toy industry. Opportunity analysis helps spot trends like these.

Strengths and Weaknesses. Marketing opportunity analysis also entails identification of competitors and potential competitors as well as comparing their strengths and weaknesses relative to your own. Just as a football coach finds it useful to know that the opposing team has a strong pass defense but a weak rushing defense, so organizations need accurate analyses of their competitors' characteristics. For example, such a comparison may point out that a particular firm produces higher quality products than its competitors', but has a smaller sales force and a weaker advertising program. That firm might then follow a strategy of producing products for other retailers, such as Sears or Penney's, which are to be sold under the retailers' brands. Such a strategy makes the most of the company's manufacturing strengths and avoids the promotional areas where competitors appear to have an advantage.

Consider how company strengths and weakness were appraised in the situation facing the new president of Hazel Bishop Industries on the first day after he purchased the company. Hazel Bishop lipsticks and nail polishes were heavily advertised in the 1960s, but nearly disappeared from stores in the 1970s because of a lack of creative marketing, undercapitalization, and intense competition.[14] The main company strength was considered to be recognition of the brand and consumers' favorable memories associated with it. The product quality and manufacturing were perceived to be company weaknesses.

Since the company president believes that all lipsticks are the same, whether they retail for 89 cents or $10, he closed the company's own manufacturing facilities. Hazel Bishop became solely a purchaser and reseller of products made by other manufacturers under the Hazel Bishop brand name. The product line was expanded to include clear lipsticks, new colors with exotic names, and attractive packaging. The marketing strategy was then to market a low-priced lipstick

---

[14]Hazel Bishop, "Sudden Growth After a Decade of Obscurity," *Business Week*, March 15, 1982, pp. 54–56.

THE ANATOMY OF COMPETITION

The Boston Consulting Group, one of the country's most successful marketing consulting groups, has identified competition as a system of relationships. The more basic principals are:

■ All competitors who persist and survive have a unique advantage over all others. If they did not, then others would crowd them out. In biology this is known as Gause's principle of mutual exclusion.

■ The more similar competitors are to each other, the more severe their competition. This observation was made by Darwin in *The Origin of Species*.

■ If competitors are different and coexist, then each must have a distinct advantage over the other. Such an advantage can only exist if differences in the competitor's characteristics match differences in the environment that give those characteristics their relative value.

■ Competitors that coexist must be in equilibrium. Such equilibrium can exist only if any change produces forces that tend to restore the conditions prior to the disturbance.

■ If competitors must each have an advantage and each must match different environmental factors, then there must be a point or series of points where the advantage shifts from one competitor to the other. These points of no relative advantage define the "competitive segment" boundary.

Source: Used with the permission of The Boston Consulting Group. The excerpts appeared in Bruce D. Henderson, "The Anatomy of Competition," *Journal of Marketing*, Spring 1983, pp. 7–11.

(89 cents) that was an excellent value (about half the price of other brands) through drug stores and other variety stores selling to the low end of the market rather than department stores that once dominated the market with higher-priced merchandise. At the heart of this successful marketing strategy was the correct appraisal of

Hazel Bishop's strengths and weaknesses in light of the competition.

Matching Opportunities to the Organization. Of course, the world offers literally thousands of opportunities, but at least some of them may not be realistic given a particular organization's resources or interests. Procter and Gamble (P&G) may identify an opportunity to increase its sales among New York's Puerto Rican community and commit resources to development of an advertising campaign to reach that market. It is arguable that P&G is so large a company that it should take the "opportunity" to go into the nuclear power business, but Procter and Gamble is unlikely to make that move. Why not? Because its managers know that not all environmental opportunities are in fact *organizational* opportunities. Any organization can act profitably on *only* those opportunities which "fit" its capabilities. Procter and Gamble's strength lies in its experience in promoting and distributing superior consumer products, not in marketing energy to communities.

Anheuser-Busch's Eagle Snacks are a premium-price snack line consisting of smoked almonds, tortilla chips, and chip sticks that are packaged in stand-up foil bags.[15] The marketing strategy behind the Eagle Snack line capitalized on Anheuser-Busch's extensive distribution network. The snacks are marketed in places where Anheuser-Busch's beers are sold (e.g., hotels, restaurant bars, taverns, and airport lounges). The strategy to sell a high-priced product not distributed in food stores is intended to avoid direct competition with giant snack food marketers such as Frito-Lay. Management saw this opportunity as a perfect fit for Budweiser's resources and capabilities.

Many firms have developed guidelines to help distinguish between environmental opportunities and realistic, meaningful, organizational opportunities. Such guidelines are generally based on the firms' goals, strengths, or special competencies, and may be stated in the form of questions like these.

---

[15] Robert Reed, "Eagle Snacks Set to Roost in Twenty-five More Markets," *Advertising Age,* March 8, 1982, p. 37.

1 What competitive advantages will we have to aid our entry in this market? (For example: sales and advertising experience or a distribution system already in place.)

2 Do we have some special abilities to bring to this opportunity? (Technical know-how or particular skills.)

3 Do we have any weaknesses that will hurt us in this endeavor? (Lack of financial resources or management experience in the industry.)

4 Does the opportunity meet our organization's requirements? (Some companies require a certain return on investment or concentrate efforts only on leisure, growth, or energy markets.)

5 Does this opportunity fit our long-range plans? (For example: to become a vertically or horizontally integrated organization. Note: Oil producers that operate oil fields, refineries, distributors, and retail gas stations exemplify vertically integrated organizations. Department store operators who "buy out" and run other department stores are examples of horizontally integrated organizations.)

Thus, identification of opportunities involves not only assessment of the environment but also consideration of an organization's goals *and* its limitations. Once these things are done, it's time for strategic planning. But what information might be included in a strategic plan? Remember, strategy involves the "big picture."

Consider this summary statement offered by the president of an industrial instruments company.

We are going to put out the best, most reliable process monitoring equipment needed by the chemical and allied industries. We are not going to pioneer new products as that is risky and expensive. Instead, after someone else has introduced a new product we will either license it or design our own. In bringing out our product we shall stress reliability of performance and ease of maintenance. Our growth will be steady at between 10 and 15 percent a year. We could grow faster since the market is there but this way we will be able to finance our own growth and to select and train new employees, distributors, and

KENTUCKY FRIED CHICKEN: WE DO STRATEGIC PLANNING RIGHT

When Kentucky Fried Chicken (KFC) assumed it was a "dead bird," a redefined mission and strategic planning made the company "soar like an eagle," according to its chairman and chief executive officer. The top-to-bottom overhaul of KFC's system began with an intensive examination of the environment, the competition, and the resources available to both. Analyzing KFC's business and competition in excruciating detail pinpointed areas of strategic advantages and weaknesses.

KFC management had previously viewed the company as a food service conglomerate and diversified into various other businesses, including a seafood chain, a Mexican chain, and related equipment and supply companies. It attempted to offset declining sales by introducing new products and increasingly relied on discounting and price in-creases to meet short-term sales and profit goals. Despite seemingly overwhelming problems, KFC had several opportunities. The quick-service restaurant market was attractive, particularly in the fried chicken segment, and it had distribution and share advantages over competitors. Another advantage management saw was KFC's unique recipe which, when properly prepared, inspired "awesome" consumer loyalty.

Reviewing the environment served to identify critical issues that had to be resolved to reach the stated objectives. One of these issues became the principal marketing objective—to satisfy fried chicken customers better than KFC competitors other businesses were cut.

Turning around a 6,000-store, worldwide system was a mammoth job. In order to standardize its fried chicken recipe and procedures, KFC developed a systemwide training program and conducted inspections by mystery shoppers to rate product quality. The KFC management committee met monthly to review every element of the action plans and identify programs that weren't on schedule. Marketing became responsible for representing and interpreting consumer needs, and marketing management was charged with selling only the highest quality products, at a good value, and with an excellent financial return. Short-term profit tactics were rejected, and menu and pricing proposals were reviewed by top management and evaluated in accordance with KFC's long-term strategic goals rather than quarter-to-quarter earnings spikes. Strategic planning clarified KFC's direction and goals, facilitated the allocation of resources, and helped balance demands across all company functions.

Source: Based on and adapted with permission from "Chain's Fortunes Improve When It Rearticulated Its Mission and Strategic Plan," *Marketing News*, July 9, 1982, p. 14.

maintenance staff to continue to build customer faith in our reliability.[16]

Notice that this statement of strategy declares an organizational "mission," to offer the "best and most reliable" products, but also limits that mission to encompass only "process monitoring equipment." It further tells how this will be accomplished, *not* by pioneering, but by following others. This less exciting path is taken because the firm wants to avoid risk and expense. The strategy of stressing reliability and ease of maintenance is presented, but not the tactical points of *how* these qualities will be emphasized. Lastly, the statement lists growth goals and mentions that these are consistent with the "reliability" the company wants to offer its customers. Clearly, this firm has worked hard on strategic planning, devising a scheme by which an organization can meet certain goals.

Exhibit 3-5 illustrates that organizational goals are to be considered in light of the environment to determine the organization's *desired* position—where it wants to be. The company's strengths and weaknesses are also evaluated in terms of environmental factors during the process of *market opportunity analysis*. This

[16]Joseph A. Litterer, *An Introduction to Management* (New York: John Wiley & Sons, 1978), p. 349.

EXHIBIT 3-5

Strategic Planning Process

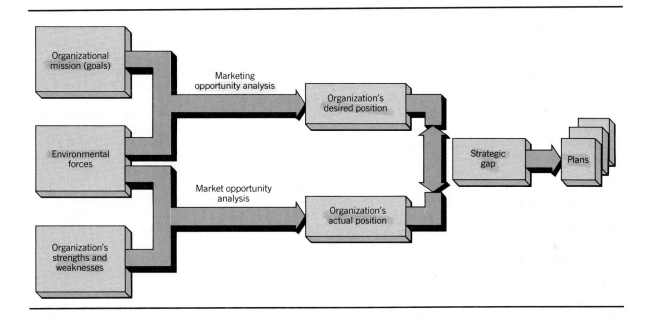

assesses the actual position—where the organization presently is.[17] Chances are good that the *desired* position differs somewhat from the *actual* position. The difference between the two can be called the **strategic gap.** Planning occurs so that the gap may be closed—that is, as was stated earlier, so the organization can move from a situation it doesn't want to one that it does want.

Stage 2: Analyzing Market Segments and Selecting Target Markets

A **market** is a group of individuals who are possible customers for the product being offered for sale. **Market segments** are portions of larger markets. Thus, black Americans constitute a segment of the total U.S. market. Black Americans between the ages of 30 and 40 years are a smaller, more narrowly defined segment. Female black Americans, ages 30 to 40, who use electric

[17]Lewis V. Gerstner, Jr., "Can Strategic Planning Pay Off?" *Business Horizons,* December 1972, pp. 5–16.

rather than gas stoves are a still smaller market segment. Market segments can be defined in terms of any number of variables from race or sex to cigarette smoking behavior. **Market segmentation** is defined as the dividing of a heterogeneous mass market into a number of smaller, more specific customer groups. Segments seen by analysts as having good potential for sales and services are likely to become the organization's **target markets** (that is, the specific group likely to buy the company's product). Although there are many tools and concepts used by marketers, market segmentation is one which virtually all marketers agree is extremely useful and valuable. Identifying and choosing "targets," rather than charging around trying to reach "everybody," allows the marketer to tailor marketing mixes to a group's specific needs. As the old adage states, "You can't be all things to all people." A firm selects a target market because it believes it will have a competitive advantage in that particular segment.

Market segmentation is such an important and powerful tool that it will be treated fully in

SEARS: A RETAILER'S CORPORATE MISSION AND SELECTED ASPECTS OF THEIR STRATEGIC PLAN

Excerpts from Sears' merchandising plan for 1979–1983 illustrate how strategy is related to Sears' corporate mission.

The corporate mission "Sears is a family store for middle-class, home-owning America."

"We are the premier distributor of durable goods for these families, their homes, and their automobiles. We are the premier distributor of nondurable goods that have their acceptance base in function rather than fashion, and, as a result of this, have increased our market share in nondurables over the past decade, reflective of an increased proportion of selling space devoted to them. We are valued by middle-class America for our integrity, our reputation for fair-dealing, and our guarantee."

What Sears *is not* is equally clear, the headquarters merchandising plan asserts. "We are not a fashion store. We are not a store for the whimsical, nor the affluent. We are not a discounter, nor an avant-garde department store. We are not, by the standards of the trade press or any other group of bored observers, an exciting store.

"We are not a store that *anticipates*. We *reflect* the world of Middle America, and all of its desires and concerns and problems and faults. And we must all look on what we are, and pronounce it good! And seek to extend it. And not to be swayed from it by the attraction of other markets, no matter how enticing they might be."

Aspects of the Strategy by Selected Product Groups

Home Improvements

■ *Home Modernization.* "The key strategy here is to market home improvements to the customer as a service rather than as individual products. We will differentiate product wherever possible to aid in our position vs. the local contractor, but our greatest superiority should come from a companywide commitment to professional installation."

Hardware

■ *Hardware Shop—Tools.* "Since this is a very mature business in which we are already strong, any

Sears, a family store for middle America.

real opportunity lies in more effective buying of our current products, and the expansion of the market through the introduction of new products.

"We also will position specialized products against significant consumer segments we have heretofore neglected . . . . While Craftsman is the most widely recognized name in the industry, the professional user does not equate it with top quality. We will therefore position Craftsman as a precision quality brand available only at Sears through the use of national franchise-building advertising."

Appliances

■ "Strengthen the everyday value image, while still using enough reduced price promotion to maintain our position of dominance. Accomplish sales goals at a lower promotional markdown cost."

Automotive

■ "Use national advertising to continue building strong brand awareness, as we have done in the Die Hard, Steady Rider, Muzzler, and Roadhandler. National advertising would also be used to position Sears as a center for professional automotive service and installation. This will help generate additional back shop income and help develop the sales of other lines such as brakes and front end."

the next chapter. Suffice it to say here that evaluation of marketing opportunities (step one in our three-stage development of marketing strategy) must be followed by a decision as to where marketing efforts will be directed (market segmenting and targeting), before the third and final step, planning and developing the marketing mix, can be undertaken.

The following example illustrates this point. Hyster, the Rolls Royce of forklift trucks, has a first-rate reputation in the industry.[18] For most of its history, Hyster has concentrated its efforts on manufacturing top-of-the line forklift trucks. Some of their custom-built luxury forklifts sell for as much as $250,000. Historically, Hyster's success stemmed from its skill at customizing trucks and from its ability to sell standard models with the most powerful engines, fastest lift speeds, tightest turning radii, and highest prices. In recent years, Hyster has faced indirect competition from new technology—automated storage and retrieval systems that are replacing some forklift-truck functions in factories and warehouses. Moreover, in the last decade Japanese companies (e.g., Toyota, Nissan, and Mitsubishi) have begun to market inexpensive (under $25,000) forklift models with heavy lifting capacity. The competition is also selling at a lower profit margin. These low-cost models do not compare in quality or durability to Hyster models, but they sell well to food warehouses, retail lumber stores, and other industrial customers that do not have sophisticated requirements for forklifts.

Hyster's managers must analyze the opportunities and problems facing the company. Then they must make a market segmentation decision. Should Hyster market a low-priced forklift truck to the food warehouse and retail lumber store segments? Should Hyster enter the automated business system business and to which market segment should these products be marketed? This situation requires that Hyster make some serious marketing strategy decisions for its future.

Stage 3: Planning and Developing a Marketing Mix

The construction of a marketing mix is the third step in the development of marketing strategy. Construction of the mix is discussed elsewhere in this book. To avoid repetition, it will not be repeated here except for the following reminders:

■ A marketing mix is the means by which a marketing manager achieves goals.

■ Some combination of the product, price, distribution, and promotion variables is always necessary in the solving of marketing problems.

■ In individual instances one or two of the four major mix components may have particular significance.

VARIOUS LEVELS OF PLANNING AND STRATEGY IN THE ORGANIZATION

There are many marketing functions within an organization. From an organizational standpoint these functions are performed by various departments at different levels of administrative responsibility. For simplicity's sake we will say that there are three levels of administration: top management, middle management, and supervisory

[18]Based on information in "Corporate Strategies: Hyster," *Business Week,* February 8, 1982, p. 101; and "Hyster Lifts the Stakes," *Sales and Marketing Management,* November 15, 1982, pp. 53–56.

management. Managers plan and develop strategy at each level of the organization. However, as we move downward from top management to supervisory management, the planning and strategic activities become a less important part of the job while tactical and executional activities become a more important job dimension. Thus, a vice-president of marketing will spend most of his or her time planning new products and strategy modifications for existing brands while a sales manager will concentrate on supervising and motivating the sales force.

SUMMARY

This chapter introduced the fact that marketing executives are managers. They are specialists in understanding demand, customer desires, and the environment that surrounds and strongly affects any organization's ultimate goal—the development of a successful marketing mix.

Marketing management is a decision-making process concerned with planning, execution and control. Planned marketing is central to an organization's success. This means that strategies and tactics must be developed with as much care as possible. But planning alone is not enough. Marketing managers must also make sure that plans are executed properly and must assess performance to determine whether what was planned is actually being carried out "in the field."

Development of marketing strategy hinges on the proper identification of realistic opportunities. Choosing appropriate opportunities sets the organization on the paths most likely to lead to success.

The three stages of marketing strategy are: 1) identifying and evaluating opportunities, 2(analyzing and selecting target markets, and 3) planning a marketing mix.

The term "marketing opportunity analysis" refers to the performance of one of any marketer's tasks—the analysis and reading of marketing's environment with the goal of discovering its impacts, trends, and the opportunities created. This analysis is clearly necessary to long-term organizational success and survival.

THE MOST IMPORTANT CONCEPT IN THIS CHAPTER
Effective marketing is not possible unless carefully developed guiding strategies are planned before an organization's marketing mix is created.

KEY TERMS

Management

Planning

Execution

Control

Marketing management

Marketing planning

Operational planning

Strategic planning

Planning horizon

Marketing audit

Marketing strategy

Tactics

Marketing opportunity analysis

Strategic gap

Market

Market segments

Market segmentation

Target markets

QUESTIONS FOR DISCUSSION

1 What are the three major tasks of marketing management?

2 Why are marketing planning activities important?

3 Identify several corporations, perhaps Digital Equipment Computers, Kodak, and Ford, and describe your interpretation of their corporate missions.

4 Several corporate slogans are listed below. Discuss how each reflects a corporate mission. (a) Federal Express—"When it absolutely positively has to be there overnight."

(b) Panasonic—"Just slightly ahead of our time."

(c) Radio Shack—"The biggest name in little computers."

(d) The Bell System—"The Knowledge Business."

(e) Paine Webber—"Working to Get the Right Information Fast."

5 Identify a retail store or a manufacturing company operation in your local area that has a sound marketing plan but poorly executes the plan.

6 Identify some typical execution errors.

7 What information is needed for a marketing audit? What questions might you ask in a marketing audit?

8 Distinguish between a strategy and a tactic.

9 McDonald's strategy is to be a family-type restaurant. What tactics do they utilize to implement this strategic goal?

10 Suppose you were the marketing manager for Walt Disney Productions in the late 1970s. What information might an opportunity analysis have identified? What marketing strategies would you have developed?

CASE 3-1 IBM

Study the IBM advertisement below.

This is the blueprint for an IBM Synergetix chair.

Every muscle you move. Every twist. Every turn.

All the motions you make went into designing the IBM Synergetix chair. It's just one component in IBM's revolutionary line of Synergetix office furniture, state-of-the-art modular furniture based on advanced research in ergonomics.

What's ergonomics? It's the science of creating work environments that adapt to individuals.

It's why we've designed our Synergetix furniture to flex, tilt, extend and retract in ways that provide greater comfort and less fatigue for your body, your eyes and your mind.

We think IBM Synergetix furniture makes the work station a more productive place. In fact, in a recent U. S. Government controlled laboratory study of ergonomic furniture which included the IBM Synergetix brand, productivity was found to improve by 24%.

The same effort that created such highly innovative furniture goes into making all IBM supplies and accessories. Quality products that you can conveniently order by contacting your IBM Systems Supplies representative. Or by calling IBM Direct, toll free, at 800-631-5582.*

From Synergetix printer stands to printer ribbons, you can depend on IBM.

Because confidence is the most important thing we supply.

For free product details and information on money saving special offers, call **IBM Direct toll free at 800-631-5582*** or mail this coupon today.

☐ Please send me an IBM Synergetix Furniture Brochure.

☐ Please add me to your mailing list for the IBM Computer & Office Supplies and Furnishings Catalog.

☐ Please have an IBM Marketing Representative contact me.

I have ☐ have not ☐ received an IBM catalog in the past year.

NAME_____TITLE_____

COMPANY_____TEL._____

STREET ADDRESS_____

CITY_____P.O. BOX_____

STATE_____ZIP_____

*(In Hawaii or Alaska 800-526-2484)

Mail to: IBM Corporation, Systems Supplies Division, Attn: IBM Direct, 1 Culver Road, Dayton, N.J. 08810

IN 3

IBM.

Questions

1 Why would a computer company like I.B.M. market office furniture?

2 Define IBM 's business.

CASE 3-2 Park Hyatt vs. La Quinta Inns*

Park Hyatt

The Park Hyatt Hotel emphasizes top-quality service. The hotel is located near Michigan Avenue's exclusive shopping on Chicago's "magnificent mile." The exact location is next to the Water Tower Plaza which landmarks the only building to survive the great Chicago fire.

The Park Hyatt is the result of a renovation of a downtown Chicago hotel (255 rooms). The hotel stresses personal service. They offer 24-hour maid service and continual room clean-up, bottled water (such as Perrier) in each room, special soaps and perfumes, and fresh flowers. The room rates exceed $100 per day. International travelers find staff members to speak a variety of foreign languages. The hotel contains two elegant restaurants.

La Quinta Motor Inns, Inc.

La Quinta was founded in Texas, but it is rapidly expanding. Today, it is one of the fastest growing lodging chains in the United States. La Quinta Inns are relatively small compared to other motel chains that erect large buildings. (The average size is 106 to 122 rooms.) They do not include a wide variety of amenities, such as restaurants, conference halls, or banquet rooms. Almost all units are located on major highways, close to airports, and within three miles of commercial centers.

Management believes restaurants are a burden that lower earnings. Freestanding restaurants are located nearby and leased to independent restaurant operators who are expected to run a 24-hour-a-day restaurant.

The rooms are comfortable and clean. 24-hour telephone service is provided. The Inns have swimming pools. Same-day laundry service

*Source: Based on information in "La Quinta Inns: How to Woo the Business Traveler," *Dunn's Review*, April 1980, pp. 146–147.

a small hotel
quite apart from the others.

Where guests have a drawing room
with a butler at their beck and call.

PARK HYATT.
ON WATER TOWER SQUARE, CHICAGO
312 280 2222

a small hotel
quite apart from the others.

Where Chicago puts its business heads together.

PARK HYATT.
ON WATER TOWER SQUARE, CHICAGO
312 280 2222

is available for an extra charge. To maintain a personal touch, each Inn tries to have a retired couple living on the grounds to provide day-to-day management.*

Questions

1 What market segment of the lodging market is the Park Hyatt trying to reach? La Quinta?

2 Does each marketing mix seem appropriate?

3 What other market segments might exist in the lodging industry?

---

*Theodore J. Gage, "Lull in Business Travel Makes Small Hotels Wince," *Advertising Age*, June 8, 1981, p. s-30.

CASE 3-3 Red Robin Restaurants*

The Red Robin Restaurants chain has recently begun selling franchises. This Seattle-based operation promotes both burgers and booze at its restaurants. There are 28 varieties of burger sandwiches and 33 exotic mixed drinks on the menu. The main menu item is a one-third pound chopped sirloin hamburger seasoned with 18 herbs. The definition of burger is somewhat liberal. A porkchop between two buns is called a porkchop burger. A chicken breast served with mozzarella and parmesan cheese is called a Sinatra burger. Exotic drinks, such as the screaming yellow banshee, are served in a decor of stained glass windows, Victorian ceiling fans, and carnival memorabilia. The owner believes that his customers want quality, service, and ambience. Adults "don't want to wait in the long lines and have their burgers handed to them in a bag."

Questions

1 Has the Red Robin adopted a viable marketing concept?

2 What is the Red Robin's target market?

3 Evaluate the Red Robin's marketing mix.

---

*Source: "Pattie Flipper Par Excellence," *Money Magazine,* December 1981, p. 27.

CHAPTER 4

Market Segmentation

CHAPTER SCAN

This chapter discusses market segmentation, one of the most powerful concepts in marketing. It also describes a related tool, target marketing. These techniques are applicable to virtually every marketing situation, and regularly provide the cornerstones of marketing success.

The chapter also outlines the many variables that can be used by a marketing manager to effectively identify, analyze, and target marketing opportunities.

WHEN YOU HAVE STUDIED THIS CHAPTER, YOU WILL:

Be able to define the term "market" and differentiate between the consumer and industrial/organizational markets.

Be able to explain the logic underlying the concept of market segmentation.

Be able to describe the processes of market segmentation and target marketing.

Be able to tell why successful segmentation must lead to the identification of meaningful target markets.

Be able to show the relationship between target marketing and the development of effective marketing mixes.

Be able to distinguish between undifferentiated, concentrated, differentiated, and custom marketing strategies.

Be familiar with the 80/20 rule and the majority fallacy, and their effects on marketing strategy.

Be able to describe the many market segmentation variables available to marketing managers, and tell which ones are the better ones.

WHAT *IS* A MARKET?

A market is a group of actual or potential customers for a particular product. More precisely, a **market** is a group of individuals or organizations who may want the good or service being offered for sale *and* who meet these three additional criteria:

1 Members of a market must have the purchasing power to be able to buy the product being offered.

2 Market members must be willing to spend their money or exchange other resources to obtain the product.

3 Market members must have the authority to make such expenditures.

There are many examples of shoppers or businesses who may seem to be "in the market" for certain types of products but who actually are *not* since they don't meet *all* of these conditions. For example, a child may want a particular toy but not have the money to buy it. Even if the child does have some money in a piggy bank, parental permission to break the bank and spend the money might be denied. A child in this situation is clearly not truly "in the market."

Real estate brokers selling residential housing constantly try to determine which customers are "buyers" and which are merely "lookers." The brokers say that "lookers" are not in the market because they lack the purchasing power to move or are really not willing to move. Realtors may try to convert lookers into buyers by locating the "ideal" house for them or by helping them to find financial assistance. However, the market categories of "lookers" and "buyers" still exist even though individual customers may move from one group to the other.

The term "market" can be somewhat confusing because it has been used to designate buildings (The Fulton Fish Market), places (The Greater Houston Metropolitan Market), institutions (the stock market), and stores (the supermarket), as well as many other things.[1] But each usage, even the name of a building in which trading is carried out, suggests people or groups with purchasing power who are willing to exchange it for something else.

THE MAJOR MARKETS: CONSUMER AND ORGANIZATIONAL

While there are many types of markets, the most fundamental distinction among them is drawn in terms of the buyer's use of the good or service being purchased. If the buyer is an individual who will use a product to satisfy personal or household needs, the product is being utilized by a consumer. Hence, the product is a *consumer* product sold in the **consumer market.** When a product is purchased by an organization or business, such as wood purchased by a furniture manufacturer, that organization or business is buying an *organizational* or *industrial* good in the **organizational** or **industrial market.**

The terms "organizational," and "industrial" are often used interchangeably. Both terms mean, in effect, the non-consumer market. Thus, all products other than consumer products are organizational or industrial products because they are used to help operate organizations or industries. The word "organizational" is broader and more inclusive than the term "industrial"

---

[1] Roland S. Vaile, "Some Concepts of Markets and Marketing Strategy," in *Changing Structure and Strategy in Marketing,* Robert V. Mitchell, ed. (Urbana: University of Illinois Bureau of Business and Economic Research, 1958), p. 17.

EXHIBIT 4-1

Is It a Consumer Good or an Organizational Good?

Question #1: Who bought it?	Question #2: Why did they buy it?	Answer
1. A consumer	⟶ for personal or household use	⟶ a consumer good
2. A business	⟶ to use in operating a business organization	⟶ organizational/industrial good
3. A non-profit organization	⟶ to use in operating a non- profit organization	⟶ organizational/industrial good
4. A wholesaler	⟶ for resale to retailers or use in business	⟶ organizational/industrial good[a]
5. A retailer	⟶ for sale to retail customers or use in running a store	⟶ organizational/industrial good[a]
6. A government	⟶ for use in operating a govern- ment (local, state, or national)	⟶ organizational/industrial good[b]

[a]When a good is bought to be sold to someone else, some marketers would call it a "reseller" good sold in the "reseller" market.

[b]A good used to help run a government organization is sometimes said to be sold in the "government" market.

but the latter remains in common use, even though the organizational buyer group includes governments, churches, and other nonindustrial entities, as well as manufacturers.

Faced with some indecision as to whether a product is a consumer or organization product, ask these two questions:

1 Who bought it?

2 Why did they buy it?

Exhibit 4-1 shows the possible answers to those questions.

Notice that it is not necessary to ask the question "What did they buy?" For example, airline travel may be a consumer or an organizational good, depending on who bought it and why it was purchased rather than what the actual service or product is.

For a good or service that has been classified as a consumer or organizational product, the marketer may want to identify smaller and more homogeneous submarkets. Though the consumer versus industrial/organizational classification is a general guideline, it is too broad to be of use to most organizations developing effective marketing strategies.

MARKET SEGMENTATION

Economics textbooks often give the impression that all consumers are alike. As long as there exists a willingness and ability to buy, economists frequently draw no distinctions among different types of buyers. Young buyers and old, men and women, people who drink twelve beers a day and those who drink one beer on New Year's Eve are all lumped together. A "demand

EXHIBIT 4-2

The "Typical" Economics Text Demand Curve

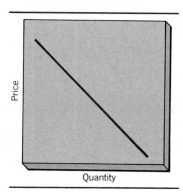

curve" is drawn, such as the one in Exhibit 4-2, to show how "the consumers" or "the market" behaves.

Experience tells us that in many cases, buyers differ from one another even though they may be buying the same products. Marketers try to identify groups and subgroups within total markets. Where the economist might show the demand for bottled water, such as Perrier, with a single curve, such as the one in Exhibit 4-2, the marketer sees many demand curves, such as those in Exhibit 4-3, each of which portrays the

behavior of a different submarket. Some consumers may buy more bottled water as price drops (*a*), others may buy less if the price drops below a certain level (*b*), while others may buy the same quantity no matter what the price is (*c*).

Increasing the complexity of the market is the fact that some buyers may buy only bottled water from France or bottled water from Texas, and some may use more bottled water in the winter than in the spring. The possibilities are, if not limitless, nearly so. It is possible that a given market may be so homogeneous that no meaningful submarkets can be identified. But, if everyone is not alike and if submarkets are identifiable, the strategy known as market segmentation may be appropriate.

Market segmentation consists of dividing a heterogeneous market into a number of smaller, more homogeneous submarkets.

Almost any variable—age, sex, product usage, lifestyle, expected benefit—may be used as a segmenting variable, but the logic of the strategy is always the same.

■ Not all buyers are the same.

■ Subgroups of people with similar behavior, values, and/or backgrounds may be identified.

EXHIBIT 4-3

Most Markets Constain Many Submarkets

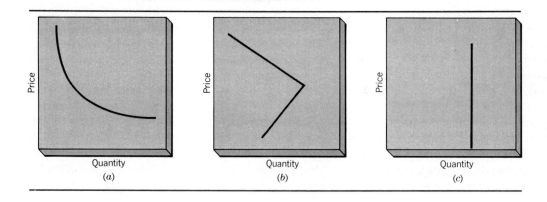

■ The subgroups will be smaller and more homogeneous than the group as a whole.

■ It should be "easier" to deal with smaller groups of similar customers than with large groups of dissimilar customers.

Thus, the game market may be divided into two segments: those buying children's games and those buying adult games. In fact, the buyers of children's games segment can be further divided into many other smaller, more homogeneous groups: children who buy games; adults who buy children's games as gifts; buyers purchasing boys' games; buyers purchasing girls' games; those purchasing games appropriate for both boys *and* girls; buyers who refuse to buy "violent" games; and so on. In the same way, sellers of condominiums may seek to segment the market and appeal to any or all of the following segments: singles; childless couples; families; the elderly; etc.

In some industrial markets, where products must be made to order for each buyer, the number of market segments is the same as the number of prospects. Such a situation is termed a **disaggregated market** because no groups or aggregates seem to be present. Usually, however, marketing executives are able to cluster similar customers into specific market segments with different, sometimes unique, market demands.

The number of market segments within the total market depends largely on the strategist's ingenuity and creativity in identifying those segments. Needless to say, a single marketing company is unlikely to pursue *all* possible market segments. In fact, the idea behind market segmentation is for the organization to choose one or a few meaningful segments and concentrate its efforts on satisfying those selected market parts. This enables an organization to effectively allocate its marketing resources by focusing attention on some portion of a market. It would be a rare circumstance if one product or one organization could succeed in being all things to all people. Concentrating efforts in a given market segment should mean a more precise program satisfying specific market needs.

WHAT SELLS WHERE?

According to research by A.C. Nielsen Co. and Sales Areas Marketing, Inc. (SAMI), certain products sell far better in some metropolitan areas than they do in the United States as a whole. For example, on a per capita basis, about five times as much dry cocktail mix, three times as many frozen lima beans, and twice as much canned milk is sold in the Baltimore/Washington market than in the nation as a whole.

Can you match the products on the left with the cities (on the right) in which they are especially popular?

Products	Cities
1. Insect repellents, insecticides, rodenticides, Mexican food, corn meal.	A. New York
2. Bluing, cleaning fluids, laundry detergents, kielbasa sausage.	B. Houston
3. Pickled herring, tomato sauce, tomato paste, bagels.	C. San Francisco
4. Fruit nectars, dried prunes, refrigerated herring, cream cheese, insecticide.	D. Cleveland
5. Figs, fireplace logs, ripe olives, frozen raspberries, apricots, deluxe frozen vegetables.	E. Miami

Answers

1B, 2D, 3A, 4E, 5C

Segmentation in an industrial market based on product use.

A market segment, or group of buyers, toward which the organization decides to direct its marketing plan is called the **target market.** The target market for Shower Shaver is that subgroup of women who shave their legs in the shower. Radio stations "target" their programming to market segments that prefer particular types of music. That is why rock, classical, and country music are not usually heard on the same station.

Target marketing opportunities abound because it is possible to segment markets in so many ways. For example, there are "left hander" shops specializing in products for left-handed people, tobacco shops catering to wealthy pipe smokers, and dress shops like the 5-7-9 Shops that target women who wear certain dress sizes. In addition, sports teams, such as the NFL's Rams or Eagles, license their names and symbols for numerous products marketed to team fans. Some companies even sell items to people who *hate* particular teams—A popular sports-related item in Cleveland is the "I Hate the Yan-

kees Hanky." Clearly, the very process of segmentation provides hints as to how to market to the targeted segments identified.

Selection of the target market (in some cases more than one could be selected) is a three-step process as shown in Exhibit 4-4. First, the total market, consisting of many different customers, is studied and then "broken down" into its component parts, i.e., individual customers. The customers are then regrouped by the marketing strategist into market segments on the basis of one or several characteristics that segment members have in common. Then the strategist must select segments to which to appeal. When that is done, the strategist has answered the question, "Who are our target markets?"

Determining Meaningful Market Segments

Target marketing, logical and popular as it is, rests on the assumption that the differences among buyers are related to meaningful differences in market behavior.[2] The identification of market segments which are not *meaningful* has little managerial value. The following four things make a segment meaningful:

1 The market segment has a characteristic or characteristics which distinguish the segment from the overall market.

2 A market potential of significant size.

3 The market segment is accessible through distribution efforts or reachable through promotional efforts.

4 The market segment's likelihood of favorably responding to a marketing mix tailored to a specialized need of the segment.

People born on October first form a possible subgroup or market segment. This is a large group. So let's assume it has unique market demands (even though it probably does not for most products). Since we cannot easily identify this group within the overall market, the marketer will find it difficult to reach this subgroup. It does not meet the *criterion of accessibility*.

Ease of measurement facilitates effective target marketing by helping to identify and quantify group size, and to indicate the differences between market segments. Although measurement is desirable, it is not absolutely mandatory that marketers be able to measure characteristics and attitudes of the different market segments.

It is possible to define a target market too narrowly and thus exclude potential customers. CBS cable television ceased operation in 1983. CBS cable television appealed to the narrow group of cable television viewers who preferred cultural programming. CBS cable's high-brow image excluded many potential customers, and, thus, the market for many of their programs was

---

[2]Christopher H. Lovelock, "A Market Segmentation Approach to Transit Planning, Modeling and Management," *Proceedings, Transportation Research Forum, Sixteenth Annual Meeting* (1975), p. 249.

EXHIBIT 4-4

The Major Steps in Market Segmentation and Selection of Target Markets

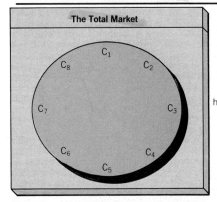

The Total Market

Consisting of heterogeneous customers

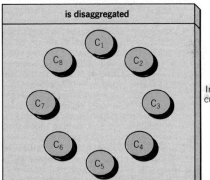

is disaggregated

Individual customers

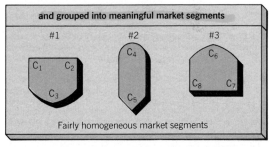

and grouped into meaningful market segments

Fairly homogeneous market segments

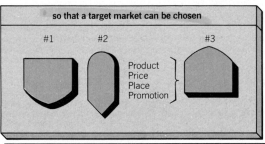

so that a target market can be chosen

Product Price Place Promotion

Source: Adapted with permission from J. G. Udell and G. R. Laczniak, *Marketing in an Age of Change* (New York: John Wiley & Sons, 1981), p. 56.

Donna Richards has a new slant for sizes 14 to 24 in a two tone dropped torso dress. The delicate tissue faille falls neatly into a trumpet skirt. Black/White $120.

The Forgotten Woman®

DESIGNER FASHIONS IN LARGE SIZES ONLY

The Crystal Tree
1201 U.S. Hwy. 1 • No. Palm Beach
411 Golf View Drive
Royal Palm Plaza Boca Raton
810 E. Las Olas Blvd. Ft. Lauderdale
NEW YORK • LONG ISLAND • FORT LEE • BEVERLY HILLS

Finding meaningful market segments is important.

too small. The market segment did not meet the criterion of *adequate size,* and, therefore, profitability.

A product which successfully appealed to a meaningful market segment was the First Alert Traveling Smoke and Fire Detector. The product was designed for frequent travelers, more particularly for the sizable number of frequent travelers who worry about hotel fires. Travelers frequently on vacations or business trips may be reached through promotion efforts (for example, in inflight magazines or on news programs). The marketing mix strategy offering a good portable

smoke alarm at a fair price by mail appealed to the specialized needs of this market segment.

Thus, First Alert met all the criteria. However, selecting a group that is not easily distinguishable or accessible in an efficient manner, or appealing to a segment that is too small to generate adequate sales volume, or that the company is unable to attract would seem to make little sense. Of course, the general criterion of profitability, which is influenced by each of these individual criteria, must be met. Exhibit 4-5 outlines the criteria for determining meaningful market segments.

The Market Segment Cross-Classification Matrix

Effective marketers segment the markets they address and then select attractive target markets. Some do this almost unintentionally, even unwittingly, as did the owner of a small grocery store located in the Seattle Metro-Market. The store serves only a small portion of that market, perhaps an area of a few blocks. In a sense, by choosing the store's location, the store's owner has "segmented" and "targeted" the market geographically. However, proper market segmentation and target marketing involves serious consideration of a total market, the variables that can be used to identify meaningful segments in that market, and the creation of marketing mixes aimed at satisfying chosen target segments.

It is a help to students, as well as to marketing managers, if a picture of a market and its segments can be assembled. Consider the marketing strategy utilized by a women's tennis shop in New York City. This marketer of tennis equipment has obviously decided to appeal to women, thus segmenting the market by gender. But other variables, such as geographic location and levels of tennis skill, may be used at the same time. All combine to create a **cross-classification matrix,** a market grid which helps isolate precise subdivisions in a market.[3]

---

[3] E. Jerome McCarthy, *Basic Marketing* (Homewood, Ill.: Richard D. Irwin, 1971), p. 39.

EXHIBIT 4-5

Determining If a Market Segment Is Meaningful

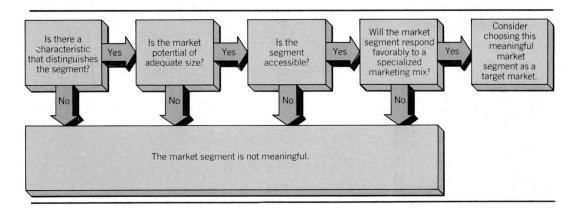

Exhibit 4-6 shows how the retail tennis equipment market might be segmented by the New York women's tennis shop's owners. First, the "total" group of people interested in tennis is cross-classified using a geographic variable and the variable of sex. Then, the chosen segment is "crossed with" level of tennis skill. It appears from Exhibit 4-6 that our tennis shop's selected target market is females interested in tennis who have access to shopping in Manhattan, are intermediate or advanced players, and have income levels in excess of $30,000 annually.

EXHIBIT 4-6

Cross-Classifications Used by a New York City Tennis Shop to Identify Market Segments

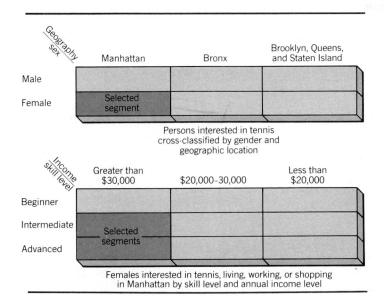

EXHIBIT 4-7

A Three-Dimensional Portrayal of the Cross-Classification Matrices Portrayed in Exhibit 4-6

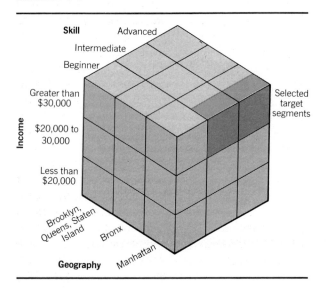

Of course, the variables used to segment the tennis market could have been portrayed on a single, three-dimensional figure as in Exhibit 4-7. However, the process of portrayal becomes increasingly difficult if more than three variables are employed. Thus, the cross-classification matrix concept is better understood when two dimensions are shown, as they are in Exhibit 4-6.

Matching the Mix to the Target Market

Having determined that its target segment will be intermediate and advanced tennis-playing women with incomes in excess of $30,000, the tennis shop owners must develop a marketing mix aimed at satisfying that group of consumers. This is a process that can be very difficult, even risky. Yet the segmentation effort itself simplifies some of the choices to be made.

1 What brands should be stocked? Those which appeal to female players who are not beginners. Names such as Prince Pro and Wilson's Chris Evert Autograph appeal to this segment.

GRID SYSTEMS INC.

The Compass is a portable personal computer with a large memory in a slim, nine-and-one-quarter pound carrying case. When Grid Systems Incorporated introduced the Compass (its first product), it looked as if Grid might become one of the big success stories of the 1980's. With tremendous reviews from the technical community, the product's prospects looked so bright that the company was easily able to generate twenty million dollars in venture capital. However, after three years the company had shipped only two hundred units of its high priced ($8,150) unit. Yet, a competitor, Compaq Computer Corporation, shipped between three hundred and four hundred units of its portable personal computers priced at $2,995 on the first day it was available for purchase, and they cannot keep up with demand. What went wrong at Grid Systems?

Grid's major problem was a market segmentation problem—their product strategy was targeted at too narrow of a market segment. The machine was aimed exclusively at top executives in corporations but there proved to be too few top executives ready to immerse themselves in personal computing.

Source: Based on "Ironing Out Grid's Marketing Mistakes," *Business Week*, February 28, 1983, p. 66.

2 Should credit cards be accepted? Probably so, since the shop is dealing with women who have good incomes and, therefore, good credit.

3 What newspapers should be used to advertise the store? The better choice is, likely, the *New York Times,* which appeals to "well off" readers, rather than the *Daily News* or *New York Post,* which appeal to "downscale" readers.

The above example shows how the tools known as market segmentation and target marketing can help tell not only to *whom* to appeal, but also give hints on *how* to make the appeal.

FOUR STRATEGIES FOR MARKET SEGMENTATION

The idea of narrowing in on a given market segment suggests analogies with rifles and shotguns. The shotgun approach spreads marketing efforts widely while the rifle allows for greater precision in focusing on one target market. The logic of this analogy may be more fully developed by identifying four segmentation strategies based on the uniqueness of consumer segments and organizational objectives.

Undifferentiated Marketing

Sometimes when a marketing manager asks "Who is our market?" the answer turns out to be "Almost *everyone* who has *any* use for our type of product." When marketers determine that there is little diversity among market segments, they may engage in mass marketing or undifferentiated marketing. A firm selling hacksaw blades, brass or silver polish, or garbage cans to consumers may find it more efficient not to distinguish between market segments. While a different appeal might be needed to sell these products to industrial buyers, it may simply be not worth the trouble to segment the consumer market according to any particular market segment's selective needs. Ths absence of segmentation, which is illustrated in Exhibit 4-8, is called **undifferentiated marketing.**

It can be argued that undifferentiated marketing may result in savings in production and marketing costs which can be passed on to consumers in the form of lower prices. After all, it should be cheaper to make and sell only one model car in one color, as Henry Ford did with the Model T, than to produce and sell tens of models in many colors and with various options, as General Motors does today. However, the attempt to appeal to everyone may make an organization extremely vulnerable to competition.

Even producers of a common, unexciting product like salt have found this out. Products like No-Salt, Lite Salt, sea salt, popcorn salt, flavored salts, and noniodized salt might chip away at a marketer of a single common salt. Facial tissues may be all pretty much alike, but a product marketed in a "Star Wars" package may appeal to buyers with small children. While "everyone" buys salt and tissues, the buyers' *secondary* desires (for example, to please a child with a Star Wars package) may provide the basis for segmentation. The undifferentiated brand cannot offer the same specialized benefits.

Undifferentiated marketing can succeed. A small grocery store in a small, isolated town seeks "all" the people in that town as its customers. The store operator must construct one well-prepared marketing mix to please "all," or at least "most," customers.

Concentrated Marketing

Suppose that a chain saw manufacturer identified three major market segments: the casual or occasional user (such as the suburban homeowner); the farm segment; and the professional lumberjack segment. Each of these users has special needs; each will utilize the chain saws in different ways; each reads different magazines and watches different television programs. If the chain saw marketer selects just one of these segments (say the farm user), develops an appropriate marketing mix, and directs its marketing efforts and resources toward that segment exclusively, it is engaged in **concentrated market-**

EXHIBIT 4-8

The Undifferentiated Marketing Approach

One well-prepared marketing mix

The marketing organization (the small store in an isolated town) → Product Price Place Promotion → Target market ("everybody")

EXHIBIT 4-9

The Concentrated Marketing Approach

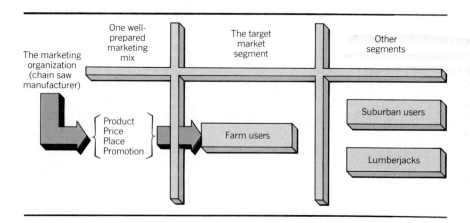

ing.[4] Exhibit 4-9 illustrates this concentration.

A firm might concentrate on a single market niche because management believes its company has a *competitive advantage* in dealings with the selected segment. Chain saws sold to the farm and professional segments are generally gasoline-powered. However, the casual user-suburban segment, with less demanding performance standards and far fewer acres to cover, may be content with less powerful electrical saws. A manufacturer of gasoline-powered lawnmowers may decide to produce gas-powered chain saws. A maker of electrical tools might find that its existing production facilities are compatible with the production of electrical chain saws. Each can select market segments which provide a match-up between company goals and abilities and customer needs. Thus, concentrated marketing strategies can be utilized by both firms.

Examples of firms that concentrate their marketing efforts are easy to find. There are jewelers and clothing manufacturers who produce products with what are, to most people,

---

[4]This terminology originally appeared in Philip Kotler, *Marketing Management* (Englewood Cliffs, N.J.: Prentice-Hall, 1976), pp. 151–154.

ridiculous price tags. Such products are sold to a small but wealthy market segment.

Big organizations can use the concentrated marketing strategy, too. Gillette, no small operation, decided to enter the shampoo market, introducing "For Oily Hair Only" in 1982. Realizing that as far as shampoo goes the company was really in no position to compete with Clairol and other firms known to shampoo buyers, Gillette's management selected a market segment and developed a marketing mix suited to that segment.

Can a service marketer practice concentrated marketing as do manufacturers? The answer is yes. An example: Leo Burnett is the sixth largest advertising agency yet it has only a very few clients (less than thirty). Burnett focuses its efforts on servicing a small number of well-heeled clients with huge advertising budgets. Specializing seems to work, for in this volatile business more than half of Burnett's clients have been with the agency for more than ten years.

Some Problems. Concentrated marketing is not without its risks. Sometimes these strategies do not work because the market segment is too narrow. The De Lorean Motor Company, with limited resources compared to those of General Motors, Nissan, or Volkswagen, concentrated its efforts on selling luxury cars to upper-income customers. More specifically, the target market was affluent people with several cars who never before owned a sports car. A sluggish economy and management's unwillingness to accept that the number of consumers like this was very small led to De Lorean's failure.

Another example of the risks involved in concentrated marketing may be found in the airline industry. People who regularly use the airlines have become increasingly concerned about price. Another way to say this is that there has been great growth in the economy-minded traveler segment. Some airlines, such as PanAm, which stressed expensive, full-service, and long-range flights, suffered as a result. They had to scramble to change their marketing mixes to meet this "unexpected" change in the marketplace.

Concentrating on the *wrong* target market segment can also lead to problems, or even failure. Texas Instruments (T.I.), a very successful company in most of its ventures, chose to target its "99/4" computer at the "typical" American family, while most competitors aimed at business professionals who utilize small computers for complicated work at home or at skilled hobbyists seeking a versatile home computer. The T.I. "family" computer packages emphasized games, teaching vocabulary and math to children, and keeping track of household finances. The product came to be seen as too high-priced

Lumberjacks and homeowners are two different segments in the chain saw market.

CHARMIN UTILIZES AN UNDIFFERENTIATED MARKETING STRATEGY

A vignette from a young ex-brand manager who had the Charmin brand of toilet paper illustrates the overwhelmingly positive side of P&G's reverence for quality. He was describing how customer complaints get sent back directly to the brand manager for action, and he recalled one intriguing incident. There are, it seems, three kinds of toilet paper dispensers: the kind you find in public washrooms, the kind that is typically mounted on the wall at home, and an old-fashioned type that is half built into the wall and fits into a semicylindrical wall cavity. It turns out that a roll of Charmin is about an eighth of an inch too thick to fit into the old-fashioned type. P&G's solution was most emphatically not to cut back on the number of sheets of paper, thereby compromising quality. Instead, the engineering department, R&D, and the brand manager got together and came up with an idea for tooling a machine so that it would wind the toilet paper faster, thereby reducing the diameter of the roll enough to fit into the dispenser.

Source: T.J. Peters and R.H. Waterman, Jr., *In Search of Excellence: Lessons from America's Best-Run Companies* (New York: Harper and Row, 1982), p. 175. © 1982 by Thomas J. Peters and Robert H. Waterman, Jr. Reprinted by permission of Harper and Row, Publishers, Inc.

for the family-use market *and* too unsophisticated for the professional or computer hobbyist. It was not a successful market entry for T.I.[5] A few years after the 99/4 was introduced the company changed its strategy by lowering its price, expanding its software, and using popular comedian Bill Cosby to endorse its use as a personal computer.

Eighty/Twenty Principle. Concentrating on one market segment is often made more attractive when it is known that a small percentage of all users of a product accounts for a great portion of sales of that product. The **80/20 principle** is the name given to this phenomenon because, typically, 20 percent of the customers buy 80 percent of the goods sold. This 20 percent may be called "heavy users" or "major customers," but the 80/20 situation (which may really be 75/25 or some other ratio) is found in both consumer and organizational markets.

For this reason, Miller Brewing changed from a strategy of aiming at the market segment seeking "The Champagne of Bottled Beer" to one focusing on blue-collar workers who are, stereotypes aside, the heavy beer drinkers. This group seems to do most of its beer drinking after work, hence the lines "It's Miller Time" and "When It's Time to Relax." Similar logic led Schaeffer, an East Coast regional beer, to the clever slogan "The One Beer to Have When You're Having More Than One." The 20 percent of that market segment drinking 80 percent of the beer will definitely have more than one! Similarly, Michelob changed its "Weekends Are Made for Michelob" strategy to "Put a Little More Weekend in Your Week" because the 20 percent who drink the most beer drink on days other than the weekend.

It happens that concentrating on the largest or heaviest-user segment may not be the best course of action. Some organizations mistakenly aim at such a segment *just* because it is so obviously attractive. These organizations have simply fallen hook, line, and sinker for the "majority fallacy." The **majority fallacy** is the name given to the blind pursuit of the largest, or most easily identified, or most accessible market segment. Why is it a fallacy? Simply because that segment is the one that *everybody* knows is the biggest or "best" segment. Therefore, it is the segment that probably attracts the most intense competition and may actually prove less profitable to firms competing for its attention.[6] For example, Procter and Gamble's Prell and Pert are aimed at broader markets than its dandruff-fighting Head

---

[5]Charles Alexander, "A Computer Whiz Short Circuits," *Time*, December 7, 1981, p. 59.

[6]A.A. Kuen and R.L. Day, "The Strategy of Product Quality," *Harvard Business Review*, November–December 1962, pp. 101–102.

Old and new advertisements reflect a change in Miller's target marketing.

and Shoulders, but Head and Shoulders sells more than the other two brands combined.

Clearly the point made by the majority fallacy idea is that it may be better for a marketer to go after a small, seemingly less attractive market segment than to pursue the same customers that everyone else is after. Thus, while most brewers seek the heavy user, some brewers will be able to succeed by offering smaller bottles of beer to people who *don't* drink much beer or very expensive beer to beer drinkers celebrating a special occasion. Lowenbrau successfully follows the "special occasion" strategy.

Differentiated Marketing

Of course, it is possible for an organization to target its efforts toward more than one market segment. Once the various segments likely to exist in a total market have been identified, specific

marketing mixes can be developed to appeal to all or some of the sub-markets. When an organization chooses *more* than one target market segment and prepares marketing mixes for each one, it is practicing **differentiated marketing** or **multiple market segmentation.** For example, Volkswagen markets many different vehicles in many different price ranges, each intended to appeal to a different sort of buyer. VW practices differentiated marketing.

Using a differentiated marketing strategy exploits the differences between market segments by tailoring a specific marketing mix for each segment.[7] For instance, the chain saw manufacturer who, earlier in this discussion, decided to concentrate on only one of three market seg-

---

[7]R.E. Frank, W.F. Massy, and Y. Wind, *Market Segmentation* (Englewood Cliffs, N.J.: Prentice-Hall, 1972), p. 7.

ments could have, given appropriate resources, attempted to appeal to each segment of the chain saw market. This would have meant a greater investment of money and effort since each segment would require its own specially tailored product, price, distribution, and promotion. Competitive conditions, corporate objectives, available resources, and alternative marketing opportunities for other product lines influence the decision to utilize a differentiated market segmentation strategy.

A good example of an industry facing a wide diversity of customers is the tobacco industry. Some customers smoke (pipes, cigarettes, cigars), some chew, and some place a pinch between cheek and gum. Within these large customer groups additional segments can be found. Exhibit 4-10 illustrates how Philip Morris segments the cigarette market. In this case, identifying the segments is not particularly difficult. The real work and expense comes in creating the marketing mixes which satisfy each segment.

The McDonald's fast-food chain, like Philip Morris, aims its efforts at multiple market seg-

ments. The marketing mix aimed at children includes promotions that feature fantasy characters like Ronald McDonald and the Gobblins, restaurants which include McDonaldland Parks, and meals targeted toward children (Happy Meals). Of course, portions of that mix appeal to adults, too. The playgrounds give adults a place to bring the kids or to chat with other adults while the kids play. Some of Ronald McDonald's T.V. commercials include hints on how to play safely and warnings not to leave toys on the floor. The marketing mix aimed primarily at adults emphasizes quality, service, convenience, cleanliness, and value. Several McDonald's products, such as Chicken McNuggets and McRib Sandwiches are intended mostly for adults, while the cheeseburgers are aimed at the youngsters. The restaurants themselves are adjusted to fit particular target markets. The contrast between a suburban Chicago McDonald's (with playground) and the outlet in a downtown area, such as Chicago's Watertower Plaza on the 6th floor of a highrise shopping center, is dramatic. The slogan "You deserve a break to-

EXHIBIT 4-10

The Differentiated Marketing Approach

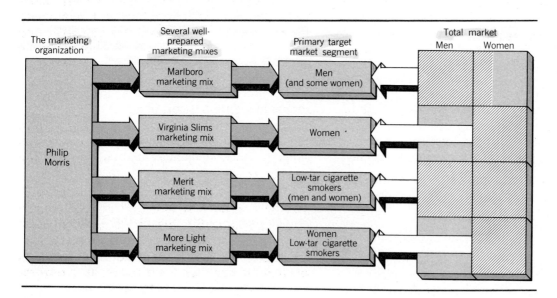

McDonald's uses differentiated marketing.

day'' is an attempt to appeal to harried adults, who, incidentally, eat the higher-priced Quarter Pounders and Big Macs rather than the smaller, less-expensive hamburgers.

The Coca-Cola Company has yet another approach to differentiated marketing. The company produces not only Coke but also Tab for the diet-conscious market and Diet-Coke for still another perceived segment. Further, each of these products is offered in caffeine-free versions for another segment. The company also offers Sprite to what's called the "green bottle" (i.e., Seven-Up) segment. Realizing that the beverage market is broader than the soft-drink market, Coca-Cola has diversified into orange juice (Minute Maid), bottled water (Great Bear and Arrowhead brands), coffee (Maryland Club), and wines (Taylor). By directing its marketing efforts at multiple market segments, the Coca-Cola Company expands its share of the beverage market, its total sales volume, and, management hopes, its profits.

Still another way for a manufacturer to attract a differentiated market—and one that requires relatively little effort—is by producing different sizes of the same product. For example, a ketchup manufacturer selling only 12-ounce bottles of its product through supermarkets might be able to appeal to various market segments by offering 26-ounce bottles for large families and 4-ounce bottles for use at picnics. Modified pricing, promotion, and so on, could be used to reinforce the various segment strategies.

This approach is applicable to many situations, but it is a tool that must be used with care. As differentiated marketing becomes more elaborate, costs increase. This fact, along with the competitive environment, must be taken into account as the marketing manager considers the value of focusing on different segment needs.

Custom Marketing

It could happen that the market facing a given marketing manager is so diverse, its members so different from one another, that *no* meaningful groups of customers can be identified. When this kind of diversity exists, when faced with **complete segmentation** in a disaggregated market, a special kind of marketing effort is necessary. This situation requires **custom marketing,** the attempt to satisfy each customer's unique set of needs. In this case, the marketer must develop a marketing mix suitable to *each* customer.

EXHIBIT 4-11

The Custom Marketing Approach

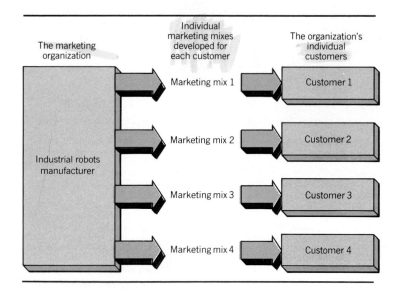

A manufacturer of industrial robots would face such a prospect. Industrial robots are usually custom-designed to fit the buyer's special manufacturing problems. Each buyer demands a unique product, with special size and strength characteristics, depending on the job to be done. Each will probably require delivery and installation at a given location, thus somewhat altering the marketer's distribution system. In addition, individual customers may have difficult technical questions, requiring sales people with broad technical knowledge who are the key element promotional efforts. The sales person may be required to alter the pricing variable to fit the custom-designed product's cost. In all, for our robot maker, each prospect may be considered as a market segment, as seen in Exhibit 4-11.

Exhibit 4-12 presents a summary of the typical characteristics of the four basic market segmentation strategies.

IDENTIFYING MARKET DIFFERENCES

Marketing is a creative activity, and many marketing success stories are the result of the creative identification of market segments with unsatisfied needs. No More Tangles creme rinse was developed to fill two needs: children's needs for "tangle-free hair without tears" and parents' needs to get through bathtime without a lot of crying and fussing. The product was developed and ready for market before competitors even identified the special needs addressed by the product. The result was a successful market entry.

The essence of market segmentation strategy is looking for differences within total markets on which to base the development of successful marketing mixes. Unfortunately, there

EXHIBIT 4-12

Summary of the "Typical" Characteristics of the Basic Market Segmentation Strategies

	Undifferentiated	Concentrated	Differentiated Marketing	Custom Marketing
Market segment	Everyone	One select segment	Multiple segments	Complete segmentation
Typical market characteristics	Little diversity	Special needs in end segment	Wide diversity of customers	Each customer unique
Company objectives	Production savings	Competitive advantage of specialization—match one well prepared marketing mix with special segment needs	Exploit differences between market segments—maximum market share	Satisfy each customer's unique needs
Major disadvantages	Competitors may identify segments	Majority fallacy—market segment too narrow	Large resources required	High marketing costs
Example of a company (brand) utilizing this strategy	Chicago Museum of Science and Industry	Curtis Mathis televisions	Eastman Kodak cameras	Hitachi industrial robots

are seldom any easy answers to this question, since the bases for differentiating market segments are virtually unlimited.

For example, Pepsi is aimed at the youth market. The Target chain of discount stores focuses on economy-minded customers. Virginia Slims and Eve Cigarettes appeal to women. Purina Puppy Chow is for puppy owners and Dog Chow is for owners of grown dogs. Mercedes automobiles are sold to the prestige auto segment. Merrill Lynch provides investment services for independent achievers who are "a breed apart."

The following discussion explores the variables that are used as bases for segmentation.

BASES FOR MARKET SEGMENTATION

Two things make the task of dealing with the almost limitless bases for market segmentation easier to handle. One is that the variables can be categorized into major groups, making them somewhat simpler to use and to remember. Exhibit 4-13 shows just such an arrangement. The other simplifying factor is that while the possible segmenting variables are numerous, there is a far smaller number of variables which are, in fact, the most commonly used.

Using Exhibit 4-13 and some imagination, the market for the Mazda RX-7 limited edition can be quickly identified. The variable of geography can be used to determine where sales of

EXHIBIT 4-13

Typical Bases for Market Segmentation

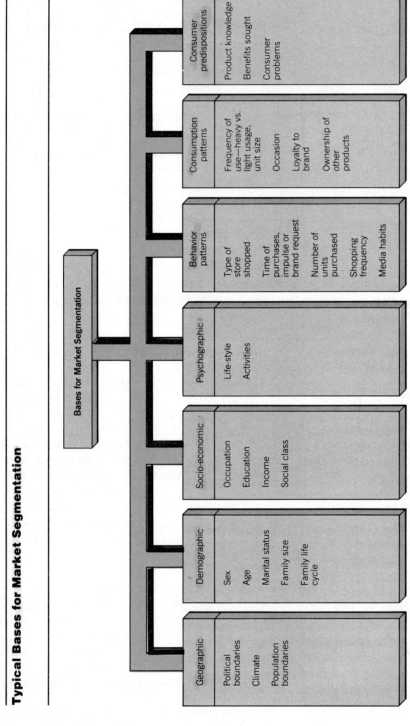

Source: Adapted from Jack Z. Sissors, "What is a Market?" *Journal of Marketing*, July 1966, p. 21; Philip Kotler, *Principles of Marketing* (Englewood Cliffs, N.J.: Prentice-Hall, 1980), p. 297; Rom Markin, *Marketing: Strategy in Management* (New York: John Wiley & Sons, 1982), p. 103.

imported automobiles are likely to be concentrated (e.g., West coast states where Japanese imports reach America). The socio-economic variable of income suggests that while many drivers might like to buy a Mazda RX-7, only those with enough money to do so are really in the market. Thus, although the automobile manufacturer *could* use any of thousands of market segmenting variables, perhaps only two or three variables might in fact prove the major focus of segmentation efforts.

Geographic Bases of Segmentation

Simple geography can be an important basis for market segmentation. The demand for suntan lotion is far greater in Florida, for example, than in Saskatchewan; the demand for farm plows is greater in Iowa than in New Mexico; Minnesota's demand for Snowmobiles exceeds that of Alabama. In some cases, a geographic variable might indicate to a marketer that there is absolutely no demand for a certain product, such as for snow shovels in Miami. Canada Dry concentrates the marketing of its ginger ale along the Eastern Seaboard because nearly 65 percent of all ginger ale is consumed in that area.[8]

Included in the general group of variables known as geographic segmentation bases are political boundaries (cities, counties, states, countries), climatic differences among areas, and population boundaries.

Population boundaries may require some explanation. Populations are not always adequately described by political boundaries. Marketers are most often concerned with the population map—where the people are—rather than such matters as the "line" that "separates" Billings Heights, Montana from Billings, Montana. Various expressions are used to reflect this fact—"Greater New York," "Dallas-Fort Worth Metro-Plex," "The Bay Area," "The Twin Cities."

These phrases, and others like them, indicate that there is no clear and distinct boundary line. Can an area like "Chicagoland," made up of hundreds of cities and towns stretching across three states, be found on a political map? No. But marketers know there is a unity to the Chicagoland market that is not obvious from the political boundary lines. Thus, terms like "mega-market," "metro-area," and even so broad a term as "Sunbelt," can have a significance to marketers that city and state boundaries do not express.

Demographic Bases of Segmentation

The word "demographic" comes from the Greek "demos" meaning "people" (as in "democracy"), plus "graphy" (as in "graphic" or "description"). Thus, demographic data describes "people things." **Demographics** is a commonly used marketing term because marketers are interested in the people and organizations that constitute markets.

Obviously, demographic variables, such as sex, age, marital status, and family size, provide segmentation variables that are easily understood and used. Families with six children generally buy more bicycles than families with one child. Further, information on demography is quickly found in almost any library. For these reasons, demographic variables are among the most commonly used by market segmenters. Demographic segmentation can be illustrated by utilizing an extended example of age as a demographic variable.

Segmentation Based on Age. The changing age distribution of the American population is one of the most dramatic demographic trends of this century.[9] The effects of age as a market segmentation variable may be far-reaching. For example, between 1977 and 1985 there will be four million persons in the 13 to 24 age group.

---

[8]"Drive to Begin Making Ginger Ale 'Soft Drink'," *Tulsa World*, April 12, 1981.

[9]J.O. Rentz, F.D. Reynolds, and R.G. Stout, "Analyzing Changing Consumption Patterns with Cohort Analysis," *Journal of Marketing Research*, February 1983, pp. 12–20.

BYE, BYE SMSA—HELLO MSA

Recognizing that marketers, and others, might be more interested in population boundaries than in political boundaries—that is, state or city lines—the Bureau of the Census has designations for an urban area (one or more cities) *plus* the surrounding areas economically and socially tied to the center city or "nucleus." Every state in the Union contains at least one MSA. SMSA (Standard Metropolitan Statistical Area), a term long used by marketers, had become too general. So Federal Bureaucrats have devised a new geographical classification scheme. These are the three basic metropolitan categories.

1. *Metropolitan Statistical Areas (MSAs)* are relatively free-standing and not closely associated with other metropolitan statistical areas. Typically, they are surrounded by nonmetropolitan counties. Areas qualifying for recognition must either have a city of 50,000 population *or* an urbanized area of 50,000 population *and* a total metropolitan area population of at least 100,000. For example, under this definition, the New Haven-Meriden, Connecticut area would be called an MSA, as would Syracuse, New York, Sheboygan, Wisconsin, Fargo, North Dakota, Moorhead, Minnesota, and Peoria, Illinois.

2. In areas with more than 1 million population, *Primary Metropolitan Statistical Areas (PSMAs)* are identified. These areas consist of a large urbanized county, or cluster of counties, with strong internal economic and social links, in addition to close ties to neighboring areas.

3. The large areas that include several PMSAs as component parts are now called *Consolidated Metropolitan Statistical Areas (CMSAs)*.

For example, under the new classification scheme Aurora-Elgin, Joliet, and Waukegan, Illinois, Gary-Hammond, Indiana, and Kenosha, Wisconsin are PMSAs. When they are lumped together with the Chicago PMSA the resulting region is a CMSA. Likewise, Anaheim-Santa Ana, Los Angeles-Long Beach, Oxnard-Ventura, and Riverside-San Bernardino are PMSAs that comprise the Los Angeles CMSA.

The purpose of the MSA concept is obvious. Marketers considering offering a product in the St. Louis area would most likely want to know how many people are in the St. Louis *market*, not how many are in the city of St. Louis itself. Instead of having to add up the populations, incomes, and other figures pertinent to every city and town in the St. Louis area, the marketer can think and do research in terms of the total market—that is, the MSA. Other data-gathering organizations have adopted the MSA and make their data available, as does the government, in terms of cities, towns, states and SMSAs.

Since the United States contains several "mega-markets," such as Los Angeles and New York, research data is also made available in terms of the CMSA.

As was the case with the SMSA, the MSA, PMSA, and CMSA terms may be of use in particular marketing problem situations. For example, the New York City-based television and radio stations cover the greater New York, New Jersey, and Connecticut markets—that is, the New York CMSA. CMSA data would be useful to advertisers about to employ these media.

Source: Based on *The Metropolitan Statistical Area Classification*, a report prepared by Federal Committee on Metropolitan Statistical areas, U.S. Department of Commerce, December 1979, and "Census Data to Reflect More Precise Geographical Definitions," *Marketing News*, January 21, 1983, p. 20.

Since this age group includes the heaviest users of soft drinks, this represents, among other things, an annual consumption loss of 3.3 billion cans of soft drinks.[10]

When the very first United States census of the population was taken in 1790, the median age was only 16 years. Today, the median age is more than 30. Exhibit 4-14 shows American age distributions for selected decades. Note the tremendous increase in pre-school and school-age children between 1945 and 1965. These are the children who constituted the "baby boom" of the twenty years following World War II.

---

[10]"The Graying of the Soft Drink Industry," *Business Week*, May 23, 1977, pp. 68–72.

Back in 1955 an unknown country singer named Bill Hayes released a record called "The Ballad of Davy Crockett." No one expected much: the song was a spinoff from a "Disneyland" TV series. But then, astonishingly, Crockett exploded: it became one of the biggest hits of all time, with versions in 16 languages. Meanwhile, kids across the country were pulling on buckskin and coonskin caps. The wholesale price of raccoon skins jumped from 25¢ a pound to $8 a pound, and more than 3,000 different Crockett items were moving off the shelves, including Crockett sweatshirts, sleds, blankets, snowsuits, toothbrushes, and lunch boxes.

What happened? The Crockett craze was the opening salvo of the Battle for the Baby Boom. Merchandisers discovered that those coonskin caps were warming the heads of the first wave of children born in the biggest population explosion in American history. All told, 75 million potential customers were born during the population surge that began in 1946 and lasted until 1964. Those kids have since grown up to become the biggest and most sought-after group of consumers in the world.[11]

Baby Boom women are growing older.

The impact of this market segment, or "age cohort" as demographers say, on American society has been far-reaching.

The baby boom led to booms in housing, education, and youth-related products. In the sixties sales of Levi's, lipstick, soft drinks, and acne preparations soared. So large was the number of youngsters during the 1960s that some analysts predicted that the average age in the United States would drop significantly before long. These projections proved false, however, and the average age rose in the last decade from 28.0 in 1970 to 30.0 in 1980 because of two underlying trends: first, all those baby boomers got older. Second, cultural changes in the United States led couples to have fewer children than was once considered "normal." (However, the U.S. birth rate has been rising slightly since 1976.)[12]

By the year 1990, America's citizens in the 25–44 age group will comprise the largest age segment of American society. While economic, social, or other forces may inhibit the start of a new baby boom à la the post-World War II boom, this age group will represent a sizable pool of people who will be of the proper ages to be forming households and having and raising children. They will constitute prime markets for homes, furniture, appliances, and other durable products.

Examples of market segmentation strategies emphasizing this shifting focus include the following: In response to baby-boom women growing into adulthood, the marketing strategies of the makers of Geritol changed significantly from a "tonic" for older people to a nutritional supplement for younger women who want to "take good care of themselves." Gillette's response to the larger adult woman segment was to target its Aapri Apricot facial scrub at grown-up baby

---

[11]Quote from Landon Y. Jones, "From Baby Boom to Buying Boom," *Enterprise* booklet, WGBH Boston.

[12]The U.S. birth rate had dropped to 25.0 per thousand in 1950 to 14.9 per thousand in 1975. It has been rising slowly since 1976 and in 1981 stood at 15.9 per thousand. The rate is expected to continue rising.

EXHIBIT 4-14

Age Distribution of the U.S. Population for Selected Years

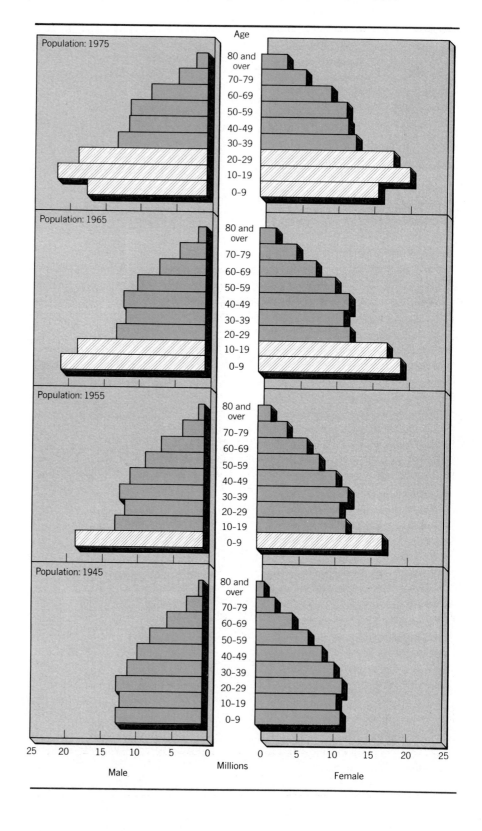

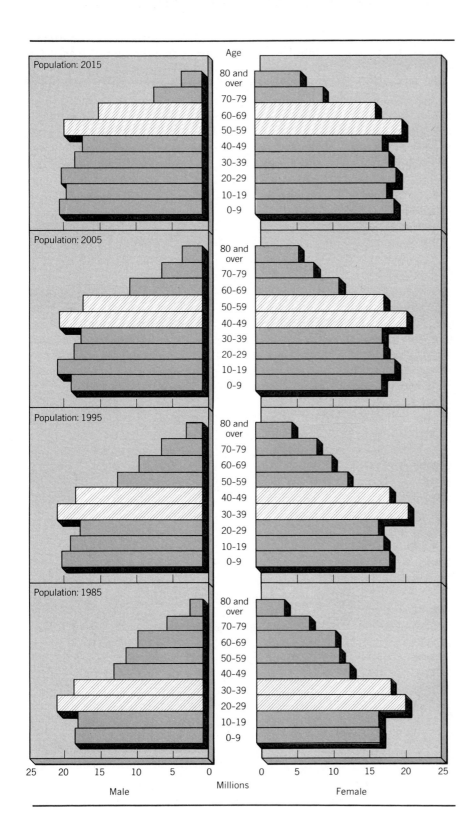

Age

Population: 2015

80 and over
70–79
60–69
50–59
40–49
30–39
20–29
10–19
0–9

Population: 2005

80 and over
70–79
60–69
50–59
40–49
30–39
20–29
10–19
0–9

Population: 1995

80 and over
70–79
60–69
50–59
40–49
30–39
20–29
10–19
0–9

Population: 1985

80 and over
70–79
60–69
50–59
40–49
30–39
20–29
10–19
0–9

25   20   15   10   5   0   0   5   10   15   20   25

Male   Millions   Female

boomers seeking skin care products. The marketing is aimed neither at very young women, as are medicated acne-fighters, nor at the older and richer women who use luxury-priced products such as Oil of Olay.[13]

In any case, the baby-boom cohort has grown into adulthood. This has had a significant effect on marketing segmentation strategies. Goods and services needed to meet the needs of the young have become less significant, while products desired by adults are becoming more important. The baby boom has become an "adult boom." Effective marketers, such as Gerber's, have met the challenges presented by this change by altering their product lines. Gerber's expanded into vaporizers, shampoos, and clothing. It began selling "baby food" to the elderly. Part of the reason is that there are fewer kids. Some organizations now market their "kids'" products to the adult segment as well. A classic example is Johnson & Johnson, who adopted a differentiated segmentation strategy and now markets their baby oil and shampoo as adult products as a result of their recognition of this demographic change. Other companies have met the challenge by seeking markets in foreign countries and offering, for example, baby-related goods in lands where birth rates have remained high.

Demographic trends also indicate that people over 65 years of age constitute a growing segment of the population (see Exhibit 14-15). This is so not only because of the normal aging process but also the fact that people are living longer today. The decline in the death rate has been faster than the corresponding decline in the birth rate. The average life span has increased to 74 years.

The "graying of America" has been as potent an influence on American marketing as was the baby boom of years past. There is an increasing awareness that many senior citizens do not fit the stereotype of an oldster sitting on a rocking chair waiting for a social security check. Many seniors are healthy and active, with

---

[13]"Challenge to Category Leader Noxema," *Marketing News*, May 29, 1981, p. 6.

sufficient finances to enjoy sports, entertainment, international travel, and other products they may have denied themselves while raising families. Some estimates indicate that nearly half of all savings account interest is earned by people over 65. This has particular interest to bank marketers, but should be considered by all other marketers as well.

Family Life Cycle. Demographic variables by themselves can be misleading. In a group of people aged 18 to 45, there may be some college students, some single people, some widows, and some married people with children of various ages. More specifically, there may be a 20-year-old who is single, one who is married, and one with two children aged 1 and 3. But there might also be a 40-year-old who is married with two children aged 1 and 3. These last two individuals, different though they are in age, are both buying diapers, baby food, and stuffed toys. In this regard, they are more alike than two 40-year-olds, one with small children and one with grown children. To allow for this fact, marketers have developed the **family life cycle,** a series of stages through which most people pass, though they may do so at different rates of speed. Exhibit 4-15 shows the stages of the family life cycle along with the age groups often found in those stages. Most important, certain products are more likely to be used during certain life cycle stages than in others. The life cycle helps identify markets. The concept of family is discussed further in Chapter 7.

Socio-economic Bases of Segmentation

Socio-economic variables reflect an individual's social position and/or economic standing within a society. A professor may have a low economic position, but a respectable social standing. A surgeon usually rates high in both areas. A dishwasher is probably low in both. Socio-economic factors such as occupation, income, or social class are often combined with demographic variables to describe consumers (e.g., white, male, professional, aged 35–40, making $45,000 or more).

EXHIBIT 4-15

Stages in the Family Life Cycle

Age	Developmental Level	Stage in the Family Life Cycle

18–34	Early adulthood	1. The **bachelor stage;** young, single people
		2. **Newly married** couples; young, no children
		3. The **full nest I;** young married couples with dependent children
		   a. Youngest child under 6
		   b. Youngest child over 6

35–54	Middle adulthood	4. The **full nest II;** older married couples with children living with them

55 and older	Later adulthood	5. The **empty nest;** older married couples with no children living with them
		   a. Head in labor force
		   b. Head retired
		6. The **solitary survivors;** older single people
		   a. In labor force
		   b. Retired

Source: F.D. Reynolds and W.D. Wells, *Consumer Behavior* (New York: McGraw-Hill Book Company, 1977), p. 41. Reproduced with permission.

Exhibit 4-16 portrays a socio-economic and demographic profile of the shotgun ammunition buyer versus the individuals who purchase little or no shotgun ammunition. Interpretation of this information leads to the conclusion that buyers of more than $11 worth of shells (defined by the researchers as heavy users) are younger, and more likely than non-users to be blue-collar craftsmen, to live in the rural South, and to have lower incomes than "light" or non-users of shells. The same type of socio-economic and demographic profile can be researched for other products.

Social Class and Marketing

Social class, discussed in greater depth in Chapter 7, is another socio-economic variable that can be used to distinguish groups of customers. Though Americans, perhaps disliking the term "class," tend to speak of rich and poor people rather than high- and low-class people, class distinctions do exist. There is a considerable difference between a married couple with high school educations making a combined annual income of $25,000 as toll collectors on the New Jersey Turnpike and a couple who are both graduates of the Harvard Medical School earning a combined income of $300,000 a year practicing in Beverly Hills, California. And the difference is not just in the money they make. The doctors may have considerable inherited wealth and come from families that have known the good life for generations. They may listen to classical music instead of the "easy listening" or "elevator" music probably favored by the toll collectors. The doctors may dine frequently at posh restaurants. The other couple probably does not. Consider this as a final comparison: If each couple were suddenly to earn an extra $10,000, how would each be likely to spend it? Would they spend it differently?

Psychographic Bases of Segmentation

Psychographics or "lifestyle" market segmentation was developed to provide a richer portrait of consumer groups than simple demographic information could yield. Psychographics, as the name suggests, represents an attempt to "get inside the customer's head" and find out what

---

EXHIBIT 4-16

Socio-economic and Demographic Profile of the Heavy User of Shotgun Ammunition

	Percent Who Spend $11+ per Year on Shotgun Ammunition	Percent Who Don't Buy
Age		
Under 25	9	5
25–34	33	15
35–44	27	22
45–54	18	22
55+	13	36
Occupation		
Professional	6	15
Managerial	23	23
Clerical sales	9	17
Craftsman	50	35
Income		
Under $6,000	26	19
$6,000–$10,000	39	36
$10,000–$15,000	24	27
$15,000+	11	18
Population Density		
Rural	34	12
2,500–50,000	11	11
50,000–500,000	16	15
500,000–2 million	21	27
2 million+	13	19
Geographic Division		
New England–Mid-Atlantic	21	33
Central (N.W.)	22	30
South Atlantic	23	12
E. South Central	10	3
W. South Central	10	5
Mountain	6	3
Pacific	9	15

Source: William D. Wells, "Psychographics: A Critical Review," *Journal of Marketing Research*, Vol. 12 (1975), pp. 196–213.

people actually think. Thus, **psychographics** enhances demographics by identifying patterns in the pursuit of life goals. For example, one father of young children may continue the activities which occupied him before the children arrived—golf, tennis, and partying. Another father, also in the full-nest stage of the family life cycle, may drop his sports and social activities to devote more time to the children. The two demographically similar men differ in terms of lifestyle or psychographic variables. **Lifestyle** is reflected in an individual's activities, interests, and opinions.[14]

Exhibit 4-16 presented a demographic and sociometric "picture" of the heavy user of shot-

gun shells. Exhibit 4-17 shows a psychographic profile of the same type of consumer. This portrait suggests a rugged, handyman-type who likes working with tools and doing things for himself, an outdoor lifestyle, and risks, adventure, and even violence. What does this tell the shotgun shell marketer? Well, interpret the profile and ask the questions confronting that marketer: Would newspapers be a good advertising medium? Would television? What kinds of programs would the heavy user watch? How about magazines? What magazines?

Psychographic variables are more difficult to deal with than demographic and socioeconomic variables. Library research can tell the marketer approximately how many male Hispanic-Americans there are in Delaware, but there are no statistics on the number of "carefree people" or "good family men." Therefore, marketers typically use psychographic variables in combination with other variables. For example, the buyer of a Porsche sportscar is probably a "swinger" rather than a "conservative traditionalist." "Swinger" might then be defined demographically as a male, 25 to 35, college educated, earning $25,000 or more a year. The psychographic lifestyle is thereby tied in with more concrete demographic and economic descriptions.

Behavioral Bases of Segmentation

Individual consumers exhibit different behavior patterns and habits. On a day-to-day basis behavior patterns worthy of a marketer's attention are easily found. Some individuals purchase apparel only at specialty men's or women's shops. Others buy their clothing at department stores, in discount shops, or from catalogs. Shopping habits and other behavioral differences may be used as bases for segmentation. Seven-Up increased efforts to have its products sold in fast food outlets and in vending machines. Why? Because marketing analysts found that these two types of outlets, which are aimed at people who behave in certain ways, accounted for 40 percent

---

[14]W.D. Wells and D.J. Tigert, "Activities, Interests and Opinions," *Journal of Advertising Research*, Vol. 11 (1971), pp. 27–35.

EXHIBIT 4-17

Psychographic Profile of the Heavy User of Shotgun Ammunition

Base	Percent Who Spend $11+ per Year on Shotgun Ammunition	Percent Who Don't Buy
I like hunting	33[a]	7
I like fishing	68	26
I like to go camping	57	21
I love the out-of-doors	90	65
A cabin by a quiet lake is a great place to spend the summer	49	34
I like to work outdoors	67	40
I am great at fixing mechanical things	47	27
I often do a lot of repair work on my own car	36	12
I like war stories	50	32
I would do better than average in a fist fight	38	16
I would like to be a professional football player	28	18
I would like to be a policeman	22	8
There is too much violence on television	35	45
There should be a gun in every home	56	10
I like danger	19	8
I would like to own my own airplane	35	13
I like to play poker	50	26
I smoke too much	39	24
I love to eat	49	34
I spend money on myself that I should spend on the family	44	26
If given a chance, most men would cheat on their wives	33	14
I read the newspaper every day	51	72

[a] Read as: of those who spent $11 or more per year on shotgun ammunition, 33 percent expressed agreement with the statement "I like hunting."
Source: William D. Wells, "Psychographics: A Critical Review," *Journal of Marketing Research*, Vol. 12 (1975), pp. 196–213.

of industry sales but only 20 percent of 7-Up's sales volume.[15]

Convenience food stores increased their summer soft drink sales by putting buckets filled with bottled drinks and ice near their entrances. This placement of the product increased sales because it appealed to certain behavior patterns. The displays attracted people who were thirsty as they passed by the store and liked being able

[15]"A Slow Rebound for 7-Up," *Business Week*, October 12, 1981, p. 107.

TRAILBLAZER MOTORCYCLE: PROFILING THE TARGET CUSTOMER

Several segmentation variables may be combined to portray a character sketch of the likely user of a product. Here is a customer profile for the Trailblazer Motorcycle. The target buyer is male, 26 to 34 years old, and married. He graduated from high school, speaks English, is white, and is employed full-time on the managerial level (professional). He lives in the East Central region of the country, in the suburban fringe of a city that has a population of 250,000 or more. The county has a large population. He heads a family unit that falls in the three- to four-member class. Household income is $10,000 to $24,000, and he is the only person in the family who works. He owns his own home. It is an unattached house. His social status is professional and managerial (and white collar).

The motorcycle rider's personality traits are: he wants to rival and surpass others, he likes to be the center of attention, he forms friendships and participates in groups, yet he seeks his freedom. He looks for new and different things to do, is attracted by the opposite sex, and has frequent daydreams.

In terms of life style, he is anxious to be busy, tries to stay out of the kitchen, and thinks a man should run the family. He believes he has the right to do nothing (or at least what he wants to do). He likes to wear comfortable clothes, is in good health, and uses few remedies. He takes what he considers calculated risks.

His buying style is based on need and convenience, but for an expensive item, he will study advertisements, shop around, and also heed the advice of friends. He reads newspapers, men's magazines, and enjoys news, sports, and travel shows on radio and television. From this description, a creative marketing team can visualize a prototype customer. The man is in his prime, with responsibilities but the means and ability to handle them. He is a leader and sociable, but he still wants to hang onto his freedom. The motorcycle gives him an outlet. His clothes are casual. He rides with a certain amount of care, and reacts to rational appeals, but the motorcycle also has emotional meaning for him.

Source: From *Advertising Today* by J. Douglas Johnson copyright © J. Douglas Johnson reprinted by permission of the publisher Science Research Associates, Inc. (Palo Alto: Science Research Associates, 1978), p. 31.

to make their purchase without having to walk through the store to the refrigerated display cases. Impulse buyers were also attracted to the display buckets.

Consumption Pattern Bases of Segmentation

The behavior of *consumption* is of most concern to marketers who would like all people who could use their products to do so. In this regard, the marketing mix can be seen, at base, to be a means to affect behavior. That is, to encourage people whose behavior is *not* to buy the product to change their behavior, while encouraging current customers *not* to change behaviors. Con-

sumers and other buyers can vary their consumption patterns from heavy-use to non-use. Therefore, in many cases, **consumption patterns** provide a good base for market segmentation.

Both the New York Mets and the New York Metropolitan Opera offer season tickets to heavy users of their products. Banks are aware that many of their customers are long-term clients who loyally deal with only one institution, thus the slogans like "A Full-Service Bank," and "The only bank you'll ever need." Light- or non-users of the same bank's services require a different marketing mix, perhaps one stressing convenient locations or free merchandise to new depositors.

Consumption patterns may also differ with particular circumstances. The **purchase occa-**

sion may prove to be the underlying force creating consumption patterns, and thus be useful in distinguishing among buyer groups. A holiday glass decorated with a Christmas tree or Santa Claus is obviously geared to buyers planning seasonal entertaining rather than to people looking for everyday glassware. The occasion of the United States Bi-Centennial earned the nickname "Buy-Centennial" because of the huge amounts of merchandise offered which tied in with that celebration. Lava soap and other hand cleaners are sold for use on the dirty, messy, or greasy occasion.

Of course, some buying patterns are strongly linked to other buying patterns. Ownership of one product may encourage the purchase of additional products. For example, marketers of custom sheepskin van seat covers can expect to sell very few products to people who don't own vans. Beer mugs are most commonly sold to people who drink beer. Storm windows are seldom bought by people who don't own houses. In many instances, consumption patterns can be the major clue in identifying meaningful marketing segments.

Consumer Predisposition Bases of Segmentation

Consumers generally vary widely with respect to product knowledge, beliefs about products and brands, and reasons for purchase. The sophis-

ticated, knowledgeable buyer of stereo equipment is, for marketing purposes, almost totally different from the novice buyer. The veteran buyer knows what to look for, what questions to ask, where to buy, where to get service, and even what the price should be. The novice knows almost nothing of these things and so looks to salespeople for guidance. The novice seeks a store with a good reputation and trustworthy salespeople. The veteran buyer trusts his own knowledge and judgment.

Further, the major benefits sought by consumers are likely to vary considerably. Seeking to identify groups of customers by the benefits they seek is called **benefit segmentation.** Even when two or more buyers are purchasing exactly the same product, the expected benefits may vary. Just as in the commercial, some people buy Miller Lite because it tastes good, others because it's less filling. A mouthwash might be bought because it kills germs or because it tastes "mediciney" and therefore must really work.

In the industrial sector, one study of benefits sought from electrical resistors uncovered two major benefit segments. Military engineers purchasing for the government and engineers purchasing for consumer electronic companies both sought performance stability and reliability. But military buyers were concerned with failure rate and promptness in review of specifications, while low price was the major benefit sought by the consumer products engineers.[16]

"BEST" SEGMENTATION VARIABLE

As shown by the discussion of market segmentation, the "best" segmentation variable is the one that leads the marketer to the identification of a meaningful target market segment. Some experts have argued that the benefits customers

seek from products are the basic reasons for the existence of market segments.[17] This may be so. After all, that idea suggests the consumer orientation that is the foundation of the marketing concept.

But contributing to the benefits sought are

---

[16]Jerome E. Scott, *An Empirical Investigation of the Formation of Product Preference in Industrial Markets*, doctoral dissertation, Pennsylvania State University (1971), p. 123.

---

[17]Russell I. Haley, "Benefit Segmentation: A Decision-Oriented Tool," *Journal of Marketing*, July 1968, pp. 30–35.

EXHIBIT 4-18

A "Bundle" of Segmenting Variables for Use by a Savings and Loan Association

Segmenting Variable \ Segment Identified	The Sophisticated Investor Segment	The Caution First Segment	The "Time" Consuming Segment	The "Rainy Day" Segment
Principal benefit sought	Best return per dollar invested	Assurance of the safety of their money	Convenience	Building a nest egg for the future
Demographic characteristics	Educated, professional, manager-occupation, higher income	Less educated, older age groups, lower income	Children at home, working wives	Less educated, clerical, foremen, craftsmen
Sociopsychological characteristics	Higher social classes, upwardly mobile	Lower social classes	Middle classes	Lower social classes
Special behavior characteristics	Intent on expressing financial acumen to others, beating inflation	Intent on conserving what he has, defers from trying new products, comfortable with the familiar	Always busy, club joiner, active in community affairs	Behaviorally conservative careful planner, budgeter
Preferred investment alternative	Stocks, real estate, mutual funds	Banks, savings and loans	Mutual funds, banks, savings and loans	Banks, savings and loans, mutual funds

Source: Leonard L. Berry, "Marketing—The Time is Now," *Savings and Loan News*, April 1969, pp. 58–62.

the buyers' demographic, psychographic, socio-economic, and other traits. That is, many segmentation variables may be found to be working together, complementing one another. For this reason, it is in the marketer's interest to seek the best bundle of segmenting variables—one or two or five or more—so that the most advantageous match-up of market and marketing mix can be achieved. Such a "bundle" approach is illustrated in Exhibit 4-18.

In other words, the best variables are the one's appropriate to the market situation.

SUMMARY

The purpose of this chapter is to provide some insight into the effective marketer's use of marketing segmentation and target marketing. These tools are extremely powerful, and most marketers agree that they are applicable to almost every situation and do, in fact, yield very positive results.

However, the identification of segments and targets is not enough. The marketer must also determine if the segments identified are *mean-*

ingful, and then develop marketing mixes appropriate to the satisfaction of each target market segment chosen.

Fortunately, as was seen in the discussion of the various segmentation variables available to marketing managers, the very process of identifying segments, of considering what it is that makes those segments different from other persons or organizations in the market place, often suggests to the marketer what steps must be taken to assemble an effective marketing mix.

> **THE MOST IMPORTANT CONCEPT IN THIS CHAPTER**
> Market segmentation is one of marketing's most powerful tools. It just makes good sense to try to use it, no matter what segmenting variables are employed, so that meaningful target segments can be identified and customer satisfying marketing mixes developed.

KEY TERMS

Market

Market segmentation

Disaggregated market

Consumer market

Organizational market

Industrial market

Target market

Meaningful market segments

Cross-classification matrix

Undifferentiated marketing

Concentrated marketing

80/20 principle

Majority fallacy

Differentiated market

Multiple market segmentation

Complete segmentation

Custom marketing

Demographics

Socioeconomic variables

Family life cycle

Psychographics

Lifestyle

Benefit segmentation

Consumption patterns

Purchase occasion

QUESTIONS FOR DISCUSSION

1 Identify and evaluate the target market for the following:
(a) Q*bert Video game
(b) The Chicago Cubs
(c) American Express Gold Card
(d) Perrier bottled water

2 Do the makers of industrial goods practice market segmentation? Think of some creative ways to segment the market for the following products?
(a) Rent-A-Car Company
(b) Zoo
(c) Personal Computer
(d) *Science* magazine

3 What are some unusual ways markets have been segmented?

4 Think of examples of companies utilizing undifferentiated marketing, concentrated marketing, differentiated marketing, and custom marketing. Why is the strategy appropriate in each instance?

5 What questions should be asked to determine if a market segment is meaningful?

6 What variable do you think is the best variable for segmenting the market?

7 How will the baby boom affect marketers in the year 2000?

8 What is benefit segmentation?

9 Should firms always aim at the largest market segment?

10 Kentucky Fried Chicken is testing a new menu tailored to location. For example, in Chicago a spicier chicken, scratch biscuits, "Dirty Rice," and collard greens are being served. Is this an appropriate market segmentation strategy?

11 How might Levi's segment the men's clothing market?

CASE 4-1 J.C. Penney: A Strategy for the Future*

J.C. Penney Co.'s future is on display now at the Perimeter Mall just outside of town.

Two Penney stores here have received the top-to-bottom overhaul that Penney plans for 450 of its larger stores over the next five years at a cost of more than $1 billion. Wood parquet floors and chocolate-colored carpeting have replaced tired linoleum. Aisle widths have nearly doubled, and departments have been partitioned off to suggest separate boutiques.

Gone are the paint, hardware, and lawn and garden-supply sections. In their place, glass display cases show off jewelry and pullover jerseys. Penney brand towels are stacked by color from floor to ceiling in a sleek display that looks from afar like a giant rainbow. Mirrors adorn every column on the selling floor, live plants encircle the escalators, and white walls and spotlights brighten everything.

The success of the overhaul isn't assured, but Penney probably couldn't avoid it. In recent years its profits have been squeezed by competition from fancy department stores on the high end of the retailing scale and mass discounters on the low end. Penney has chosen to try moving up. "We don't view what we're doing as a gamble because we've been doing this for a number of years," says Penney's chairman. "This is more of a case of accelerating our evolution rather than making an overnight transformation."

Penney started modernizing in the late 1970s, when its sales gains were shrinking. By closely monitoring operations and inventories, Penney was able to keep making money. But it realized it had to change direction. A venture into discounting, with the unprofitable Treasury division, wasn't panning out. And unlike Sears, Roebuck & Co., which is moving into financial services, Penney has only experimented with that.

Penney decided to concentrate on the business it knew best but to add a few trimmings. It may encounter problems, however, as it tries to sell its new image to American shoppers. "I think they're going to try to compete with department stores," says a department and specialty store retailer in New York. "But their biggest problem is their Penney name. It's going to be a tough one" to overcome. Others believe Penney will have trouble trying to take the lead in fashion because it has to buy for so many stores in so many geographical areas.

"They're making a wise move in strengthening their apparel," says the chief executive of a large retail chain. "But if they're thinking of going 'upscale,' that is infinitely more difficult. The worst sin a merchant can commit is to try to be all things to all people."

Questions

1 What market segment strategy has Penney adopted?

2 Do you foresee any problems that Penney will have to overcome?

3 To what alternative target markets could Penney appeal?

*Source: Excerpt from Claudia Ricci, "J.C. Penney Goes after Affluent Shoppers But Stores' New Image May Be Hard to Sell," *Wall Street Journal*, February 15, 1983, p. 27.

CASE 4-2 Analyzing Fashion Lifestyles*

A marketing analyst has suggested that there are eight fashion lifestyle types:

1 Clotheshorses (regular price, investment, novelty): Men and women of all ages and occupations can belong to this group, but they are especially likely to be in sales. Apparel spending is very high.

2 Executives (regular price, investment, conservative): More likely to be men than women, they have high incomes, tend to be in management, professional, or technical occupations, and spend a lot on apparel.

3 Savvy Shoppers (bargain price, investment, novelty): Primarily women age 25 and older with incomes of $20,000+, they are likely to be housewives or clerical workers. Apparel spending is moderately high, and they are the most frequent shoppers.

4 Sensibles (bargain price, investment, conservative): Primarily women over age 35 with incomes under $30,000, they are likely to be housewives or clericals, but their apparel spending is very low.

5 Daddy's Dollars (regular price, utility, novelty): People under age 25 of all income ranges, most likely students, belong to this group. Apparel spending is moderate.

6 Reluctants (regular price, utility, conservative): Primarily men, they are all ages and income ranges, although they tend to be blue-collar workers or retirees. They are infrequent shoppers and are low apparel spenders.

7 Trendy Savers (bargain price, utility, novelty): Primarily women age 18–45, they are in all income groups and are likely to be clericals, housewives, or students. Their apparel spending is low.

8 Make-Do Shoppers (bargain price, utility, conservative): Middle-aged and middle-income people, they are likely to have family responsibilities. All occupations are represented, but especially the skilled trades. Apparel spending is very low.

Questions

1 Do these segments seem appropriate for fashion marketing?

2 Are the demographic variables associated with each segment really the main basis for segmentation?

3 How might the developer of shopping centers utilize this information?

---

*Source: This case is based on excerpts from Rebecca C. Quarles, "Shopping Centers Use Fashion Lifestyle Research to Make Marketing Decisions," *Marketing News*, January 22, 1982, p. 18.

PART 2

INFORMATION MANAGEMENT

Marketing managers cannot rely exclusively on intuitive decision making if it is to consistently achieve its goals. Marketing research has a special place in effective marketing. Its purpose is to gather and organize the information managers need to make timely and proper decisions. In this way, marketing research adds dimensions to management's thinking, reduces risks, and lessens the impact of simple fortune on marketing plans. Other sources of information are also available to managers. Therefore, a means of organizing information—a marketing information system—is required in all organizations.

Chapter 5 explores the concepts, tools, and methods associated with a broad range of marketing research activities.

Chapter 6 shows how various sources of data can be brought together to produce a usable bank of pertinent marketing information. ∎

CHAPTER 5

Overview of the Marketing Research Process

CHAPTER SCAN

This chapter deals in general with the place of information in effective marketing but more specifically with the marketing research process.

Marketing research tools and techniques are many and varied. Describing how the researcher selects from among these, assuring that they are appropriate to the marketing problem being addressed by management, is the purpose of this chapter.

Although marketing research efforts must be adjusted to fit particular situations, in general these studies follow a progression of seven major steps. The seven steps, and some of the choices to be made as the research process unfolds, are the focus of much of this chapter.

WHEN YOU HAVE STUDIED THIS CHAPTER, YOU WILL:

Understand the importance of information in effective marketing.

Be able to explain the contribution marketing research makes to effective decision-making by management.

Understand the exploratory, descriptive, and causal types of marketing research and be able to show their relationships to particular marketing management problems.

Be able to describe each stage in the marketing research process and explain the logic of that process.

Be familiar with the possible uses of such tools as surveys, experiments, and observation.

THE PLACE OF INFORMATION IN EFFECTIVE MARKETING

Once a marketing problem or opportunity is identified, it is necessary to gather information that will help the marketing manager deal with the situation. To be effective, the marketer needs to gather enough information to understand past events, identify what is occurring *now,* and try to *predict* what might occur in the future.[1] Marketing information, whether or not gleaned through formal research programs, provides the basis for a wide variety of decisions. It is an extremely valuable management tool. Consider the following examples of how systematically gathered marketing information can lead the marketing manager to new products, to improvements on existing products, and to changes in price, promotion, or distribution strategies and methods.

Examples of Information's Value in Marketing

During the Christmas seasons of 1979 and 1980, hand-held electronic football, baseball, and other sports games were "hot," so hot that they sold out as quickly as they were placed on store shelves. Anxious Christmas shoppers hurried from store to store to find these types of games for their children and others on their gift lists. The games were a tremendous success. When the 1981 season approached, many retailers loaded up on new games and old favorites; but not Toys-Я-Us, a retail chain which continuously monitors its check-out counters with computerized cash registers. The company's marketing managers interpreted early sales trends as indicating a rapid decline in buyer preference for these hand-held games because of the corresponding rise in popularity of video game systems, such as Atari. Based on this information, Toys-Я-Us cleared its shelves of these items by cutting prices. The games were replaced with

Barbi dolls, Tonka trucks, and other toys in similar price ranges. Careful analysis of sales trends in a dynamic marketing situation helped Toys-Я-Us to its best sales in years while many other toy retailers had a terrible Christmas season.

Consider how Pepperidge Farm® utilized marketing information to introduce its Deli pastry sandwich line.[2] Analyzing information about consumer lifestyles suggested consumers' faster-paced patterns were changing eating habits. Trend information showed increasing numbers of working women; more people on the go meant less time to prepare meals. With this information in mind, Pepperidge Farm began reviewing available food products that combined bread or pastry with fillings, such as Cornish pasties and empanadas. Consumer research indicated that a broader, perhaps more sophisticated concept could be developed if Pepperidge Farm could use flaky pastry. Discussions with groups of consumers were used in order to define the still-nebulous product concept. Next, Pepperidge Farm investigated alternative promotional messages for stating the concept to zero in on the key product benefits and their importance to consumers. Then, selected households were given the product for use at home. This *home use test* of various flavors was conducted to determine whether consumers liked the product and, more importantly, whether they would buy it again.

For research purposes, the product was sold on a limited basis. These test marketing experiments proved to be a fertile learning ground. For one thing, Pepperidge Farm decided to make the products fairly simple, yet not easily duplicated by home cooking. Further, the product needed a new name and bold look. The initial name "Pastry 'n' . . ." did not exactly tumble easily off consumers' lips, and the packaging needed more vi-

---

[1] This chapter presents many of the concepts outlined in William G. Zikmund, *Exploring Marketing Research* (Hinsdale, Ill.: Dryden Press, 1982).

[2] Adapted with permission from "Case Histories: How Pepperidge Farm, . . . Met Existing Consumer Needs," *Advertising Age,* August 30, 1982, p. 54.

sual strength; it did not draw attention to itself on grocery shelves. Advertising showed the "light" (i.e., diet) concept did not have to be stressed, while the product's multiple-meal usage did. In turn, advertising, rather than pricing, stimulated purchases.

Pepperidge Farm began its commercial distribution in New England, two years after the initial conception of the product. Now nationally distributed, it is very successful. Pepperidge Farm's management contends that the Deli's effort would not have been so lucrative had Pepperidge Farm not listened to its research every step of the way (see Exhibit 5-1).

The Burger King "Have it your way" campaign is more than just a catchy (and successful) slogan. This marketing strategy was based on surveys of fast food restaurant patrons which asked for the patrons' biggest complaints about these outlets. Most customers said that their main *complaint* was too much ice in the soft drinks, but when they were asked to rank *problems,* "too much ice" was way down on the list. A problem much higher in the ranking was "having to wait for special orders." Seizing on this research finding, marketers decided to stress Burger King's willingness to "hold the pickle, hold the lettuce" so customers can have their food "their way." In the best marketing tradition, Burger King used research to identify a problem and to help in the development of an appropriate solution.[3]

The above examples show how a well-defined marketing research study should work. Unfortunately, failure to collect adequate information can lead to marketing failure. The American Animal Trap Company of Lititz, Pennsylvania found this out the hard way. The company developed what its production people were sure was a "better mousetrap." It was a plastic shell, not unlike an igloo. The bait, placed inside, attracted mice to put their heads inside the igloo, whereupon a spring-operated loop of wire cleanly strangled the creature. The trap was an improvement. It caught the mouse squarely

---

[3]"Have It Your Way," *Ad Week,* January 1981, p. 20.

EXHIBIT 5-1

A Product Developed with Extensive Marketing Research

across the neck rather than on the back or top of the head; it never missed the mouse; the "igloo" meant that squeamish trappers did not have to look their victims in the eye. The trap proved a marketing failure because customers bought it, used it, and never bought it again.

Company managers then surveyed customers to find out why. Simply stated, buyers of mousetraps usually throw the dead mouse *and* the trap into the trash, not bothering to remove the corpus to clean the trap. Buyers of the better mousetrap felt that the plastic trap looked too good to throw out, even if it was the same price as the old wooden trap. Buyers either didn't purchase the new trap to avoid the "guilt" of throwing it away or used the trap over and over. In either case, few new improved traps would be sold after the first purchase. The trap company went back to the old product design.

Each of the above examples, whether of success or disappointment, illustrates a marketing problem whose outcome was affected by systematically gathered information or the lack of marketing information. Each, in its way, illustrates a different technique for acquiring or analyzing information. The Burger King example illustrates how survey findings can be directly translated into product or advertising strategies. The Toys-Я-Us story draws attention to the value of the company's own well-kept records. Pepperidge Farms utilizes several tools, including a test market experiment, to help answer its marketing questions. The mousetrap tale points up the need to gather and analyze information about consumers and markets *before,* not after, the general introduction of a product.

Taken together, the examples show that marketing information is gathered in many ways—other tools, in addition to surveys, are required. Internal records, government and trade association figures, psychological tests, and test markets are among the valuable information sources available to marketers. The examples are intended to show that research information reduces uncertainty and improves the quality of the decision-making process. Too often, intuitive decisions based on personal experience, without research-based information, lead to costly mistakes.

SCOPE OF MARKETING RESEARCH

As shown above, marketing managers need information about a wide range of phenomena. Managers responsible for the marketing of personal care products like shampoo or shaving cream may ask whether a packaging change will improve sales. They may also want to know how to monitor wholesale and retail sales. Construction equipment manufacturers may be asking, "To whom am I losing sales? Whose sales am I taking away?" These marketing questions, as well as questions about *any* marketing situation, represent problems marketing research can help to solve by providing the information that managers need. Marketing research is one of the principal means used to answer the questions that face marketing managers. As will be seen later, however, it is not the only means.

Marketing Research Defined

As suggested above, the *task* of marketing research is to provide decision-makers with information about marketing phenomena. It is hoped that information will cause the managers to make their decisions based on objective, systematically gathered data rather than on intuition. This leads to the distinction between marketing research and other forms of marketing information. With or without a formal research program, a manager is going to have *some* information about what is going on in the world. He or she may discover that a competitor has announced a new product, that the inflation rate is stabilizing, or that a new highway will be built and a shopping mall erected north of town simply by reading the newspaper or watching TV news. All of these things may affect the marketer's business for good or for bad, and this information is certainly handy to have. But is this knowledge the result of marketing research?

The answer to this question is that it is not.

> **Marketing research** is usually defined as, "the systematic and objective process of gathering, recording, and analyzing of data for marketing decision making."[4]

---

[4] American Marketing Association, Committee on Definitions, *Marketing Definitions: A Glossary of Marketing Terms* (Chicago: American Marketing Association, 1960), p. 17.

This definition suggests that marketing research is a special effort, rather than haphazard attempt at gathering information. Thus, casual or accidental information gathering, such as glancing at a news magazine on an airplane or overhearing a rumor, is not marketing research.

But even a rumor or a fact casually overheard does provide the marketing manager with information. Such information might even prove to be the foundation of a marketing strategy. But it is *not* marketing research because it is not systematically and objectively gathered and recorded. The term "marketing research" suggests a specific, serious effort to do research. The term "research" suggests a patient, objective, and accurate search.

The researcher's role is to be detached from the question under study. Some researchers may lack this impersonal quality, and may be trying to prove something rather than trying to generate objective data. If bias of any type enters into the investigative process, the value of the findings must be questioned. Yet this sort of thing can happen with relative ease. For example, one developer, who owned a large parcel of land on which she wanted to build a high-priced, high-prestige shopping center, conducted a study to demonstrate to prospective mall occupants that there was an attractive market for such a center. By conducting the survey *only* in elite neighborhoods, she generated "proof" that area residents wanted a high-prestige shopping center. In another case, the Chamber of Commerce in a small city commissioned two professors to develop a survey to be administered to shoppers in that city's downtown area. The professors constructed an appropriate questionnaire, but the Chamber of Commerce spokesman rejected it.

The spokesman wanted a survey that would "prove" that the city was a good place to shop, not one which would uncover true shopper attitudes.

Misleading "research" of this kind must be avoided. Unfortunately, businesspeople with no knowledge of proper marketing research methods may inadvertently conduct poorly designed, biased studies, or may be sold such work by marketing research firms. All businesspeople should devote considerable effort to understanding marketing research to help avoid these mistakes.

Two other points should be mentioned. First, when the casual observer thinks of marketing research, "How do you like this product?" surveys come to mind. But marketing research is not restricted to product research. It can be used to facilitate decision-making in the pricing, promotion, distribution, *or* product areas. Secondly, marketing research should yield information that *helps* managers make decisions. It is not strictly survey research.

Both researcher and manager must understand that research is not intended to replace managerial judgment or to show a manager to be right or wrong. Further, research is essentially useless unless management actually puts it to work. It is the manager's responsibility to study the researcher's findings and to explain, if necessary, how they might better have been presented to marketing executives. It is the researcher's responsibility to present information in a usable format, such as a report that includes recommended actions. Marketing research cannot do its work unless researcher and marketing manager cooperate with one another.

THE PROCESS OF MARKETING RESEARCH

Marketing research is an important source of information as well as a major tool of marketing management. Its role in the marketing process is to provide information which serves to reduce uncertainty. It does *not* answer all questions or

eliminate the need for managerial judgment. It *does* broaden the manager's viewpoint and offers a way to see a marketing problem from more than one perspective. The marketer knows how he or she views a particular issue. Marketing research helps the marketer know how the *buyer* sees the same issue.

The definition of marketing research is the systematic and objective process of gathering, recording, and analyzing data for aid in marketing decision-making. This indicates that marketing research is generally seen as involving some special effort at gaining knowledge. It is something more than casual information gathering.

CONFUCIUS SAY . . .

To guess is cheap.
To guess wrongly is expensive.
Old Chinese Proverb

CLASSIFICATIONS OF MARKETING RESEARCH

Marketing research as a field of study includes many research techniques, each with its own special strengths and weaknesses. Researchers use observational and experimental studies as well as surveys in their efforts to understand buyers and potential buyers of products. These methods and tools may be classified in several ways, but here they are categorized in terms of their *purpose* to make the interrelationship between marketing problems and research techniques clearer. Certain methods are simply more suited to particular situations than are others.

In all, marketing research can have three major purposes: to explore a problem area, to describe a situation, and to find causes of particular behaviors. Thus the three-part classification system used in this chapter: (1) exploratory research; (2) descriptive research; and (3) causal research.

Exploratory Research

Before a research study can be designed to provide conclusive information, the marketer must know what information is needed. That is, the marketer must know what the problem being encountered actually is. Unfortunately, this is not always the case. If a retailer sees that fewer and fewer customers are visiting the store, a serious *symptom* of a problem has been noted. The real problem is *why* are people not coming to the store. Beyond the realization of the symptom, the retailer may know little or nothing about the

problem and may need to get a "handle" on the situation. In cases such as these, marketers need to perform what is called exploratory research.

The overriding purpose of **exploratory research** is to clarify and explain the nature of the marketing problems. This kind of research is often needed as a first step which leads to other, more specific, research efforts. Management may know, by noting a symptom such as declining sales or smaller order sizes, that some kind of problem is "out there." Exploratory research would be used to try to identify the problem. Or management may know *what* the problem is but not know how big or far-reaching it is. In either case, managers would need information to help analyze the situation.

Providing conclusions is *not* the purpose of exploratory research. Its purpose is simply to investigate and explore. Usually, exploratory research is undertaken with the expectation that other types of research will follow and that the subsequent research will be directed at finding possible problem solutions.

As is the case with other forms of marketing research, it is generally a mistake to begin an exploratory study by running off to conduct a detailed survey or experiment. Less expensive and handier sources of information can often be found. Some library work or a short series of interviews with a small number of customers may be in order. If a fast-food restaurant were considering adding a soup-and-salad bar or a line of tacos to its standard hamburger fare, marketing managers might begin their research by conducting some unstructured interviews with customers. It might happen that customers surprise management with negative comments on the proposed additions. Exploratory research thus could serve to identify problem areas or point to a need for additional information.

There are many techniques for exploratory research. Our discussion utilizes one popular method to illustrate the nature of exploratory techniques. The **focus group interview,** or technique, involves loosely structured interviews with groups of 10 to 12 people who "focus" on a product. During a group dynamics session individuals give their comments and reactions to new product ideas or explain why they buy (or do not buy) certain items. Researchers later analyze those comments for meaningful and useful ideas, such as "too high-priced" or "looks like it would break easily."

Focus group research is extremely flexible and may be utilized in many diverse exploratory studies. For example, focus groups were utilized to develop what became Arm and Hammer Baking Soda's most successful advertising campaign. Arm and Hammer was trying to promote increased usage of baking soda by advertising additional uses for the product. Historically, baking soda had been accepted as a mild cleanser for cleaning of refrigerator surfaces. Focus groups were utilized to explore alternative usages for cleaning. But, the theme of sweetening and freshening came up in the focus group.

At first, the researchers didn't pay much attention to the idea of using baking soda to clean the *air* within refrigerators; they were too preoccupied with looking for cleaning ideas. However, once they recognized the potential of the idea of putting a box of Arm and Hammer inside the refrigerator to remove odors, they again turned to focus groups to determine how to advertise the concept. "When we put the proposition to respondents directly 'your refrigerator smells, and baking soda will cure that' it didn't go over at all. . . . But when we came through the back door and worded the proposition in such a way that it didn't imply the woman was a lousy housekeeper, they showed a lot of interest in that

---

POETRY AND RESEARCH: AN ODD COUPLE?

The idea underlying this poem by Rudyard Kipling also is the basis of good marketing research. Researchers who ask these same questions will be started on the road to solving their marketing problems.

I keep six honest serving men,
(they taught me all I know),
their names are What, and Why, and When,
and How, and Where and Who.

---

idea." This led to the oblique "I've got a secret . . ." copy that is now famous.[5]

Descriptive Research

Descriptive research is undertaken in an effort to describe the nature of a market or of some marketing problem. Like the classic good newspaper story, descriptive studies tell "who, what, when, where, and how." Magazines, radio stations, and newspapers frequently conduct surveys to identify the characteristics of their audiences. They then use these descriptions to tell potential advertisers what they will be "buying" should they use these media.

Of course, a descriptive study in itself gives no explanation of *why* the situation described has occurred. Yet, in some instances, where the question "why" need not be answered, descriptive research may be all that's needed to solve marketing problems. Studies have shown that consumers in Pittsburgh, Cleveland, and Detroit use greater amounts of cleaning supplies than do "average Americans." Though it may be possible to *guess* why this is, the studies do not *tell* us why. If advertisers of cleansing products want to shift more advertising dollars to these parts of the country, they can support that decision with descriptive studies.

---

[5] The Ongoing Saga of Mother Baking Soda," by Jack Honomichl, *Advertising Age,* September 20, 1982, p. m–3.

In another case, descriptive research led the Gillette Company's safety razor division to market the Widget.[6] Descriptive research showed that 70 percent of American households utilize single-edge blades, but not for shaving. Almost all the blades purchased were for purposes of scraping and cutting. The survey indicated that users feared direct contact between their hands and the blades. Information and creative marketing led to the development of the Widget. This "real" widget is a disposable scraper and cutter consisting of a plastic holder and five single-edge stainless steel blades.

Unlike exploratory studies, descriptive studies require some basic comprehension of the problem under consideration. Otherwise, researchers wouldn't know what to describe. Thus, descriptive studies are often preceded by exploratory studies.

Performance Monitoring Research. One special type of descriptive research is performance monitoring research. It provides a continuous flow of information (market feedback) that permits management to evaluate and control marketing programs. Most organizations monitor sales and marketing activities to insure detection of sudden changes in sales or other abnormalities.

United Airlines' "Omnibus" survey provides a good example. United regularly administers written surveys to passengers on selected flights. Questions are asked about service, food and refreshments, the flight crew, and so forth. The questionnaire also deals with the passengers themselves—reasons for traveling, frequency of trips, and final destinations. This survey enables United to track, at a very low cost, characteristics of customers and their opinions of the airline.

Surveys like United's provide a test of new ideas and services by giving the company a series of measures taken at different times.

---

[6] "Gillette Sets Plans for Widget," *Advertising Age,* May 3, 1982, p. 24.

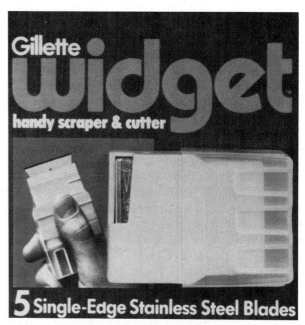

Descriptive research identified the use of single-edge blades to be scraping and cutting, not shaving.

United might decide to change the inflight menu by replacing hot lunches with sandwiches if subsequent Omnibus survey results show that consumer preferences for hot lunches have declined. Likewise, increasing dissatisfaction with ticketing services or boarding delays can be quickly spotted, thanks to performance monitoring research. Appropriate managerial actions can then be taken.

Causal Research

As the name suggests, **causal research** differs from exploratory or descriptive research in that it is designed to identify factors which *cause* certain market phenomena. More particularly, it seeks to identify cause and effect relationships among variables. In many cases, exploratory and descriptive research precede and lead to causal research. For example: exploratory studies may suggest that bagels and pickled herring seem to be bought in uneven patterns across the United

States; and descriptive research may uncover the fact that these items are purchased most heavily in large cities, particularly New York, Chicago, and Miami. The question of *why* this is so is left to causal research, i.e., research undertaken in the expectation that a cause and effect relationship will be ultimately explained. In the case of bagels and herring, the cause of heavy purchases appears to be the concentrations of Jewish consumers in the cities in question.

Other causal research studies, if successful, might show the relationship between price cuts and sales or between advertisements and orders for products. Ideally, marketing managers would prefer to establish that one event, such as a price reduction, clearly produces or causes another event, such as a sales increase. Causal research attempts to establish that those relationships exist.

Researchers engaged in causal studies must know a good deal about their subjects so that they can judge what sorts of variables might be related to other variables. It is one thing to "describe" the fact that refrigerated salad dressing is extremely popular in the Los Angeles area but quite another to tell *why* this is. Is it due to the area's ethnic make-up, its climate, or its economic base? These, or many other factors, could be "causes" of the refrigerated salad dressing consumption rate. Researchers must be knowledgeable enough to know which variables to focus on.

Researchers must also be cautious in claiming to have established causality. Retailers are fond of "experimenting" with prices, coupons, and so on. But if shirts don't sell this week at $25 a piece, and do sell next week at $30, has the retailer *proved* that sales increased because the price was raised? In fact, the weather may have changed, or Christmas may now be a week closer, or payday may have arrived. Care must be taken against going overboard with causal research in marketing. Strictly speaking, causal relationships are impossible to prove absolutely. Nevertheless, researchers can seek evidence that helps them to understand and predict market phenomena.

CAUSE AND EFFECT

Situation 1

A home-run hitting outfielder with the Seattle Mariners had 59 home runs going into the last two weeks of the season. Everywhere the Mariners played, the stadiums were full of fans. The ballplayer hit three homers in those last two weeks, breaking all records. He said, "That proved it. If the fans come to the ballpark, I hit home runs."

Do fans cause home runs? Or was it that the fellow was a good hitter and had 56 at bats in those last two weeks?

Situation 2

One morning at Atlantic City, a large number of ice cream cones were sold. That very afternoon there was a large number of drownings. Noting both figures, a hotel executive decided that eating ice cream causes drownings.

Was he correct? Or was it that the ice cream sales and the drownings were both caused by a *third* variable, the large number of people at the beach that day. And what caused the crowd? The nice, hot weather. And what caused *that*? The position of the sun in relation to the Earth. And that was caused by the Earth spinning and "tilting" on its axis, which is traceable to some law of the Universe. It gets complicated, doesn't it?

Which to Choose— Exploratory, Descriptive, or Causal?

There is one major factor which "tells" the researcher which of the three major types of research fits the problem at hand. That factor is uncertainty—uncertainty as to what the problem is, or how extensive it is, or what might be done about it. Exhibit 5-2 illustrates that as uncertainty decreases, as the researcher knows more about "what's going on," descriptive and causal research becomes more appropriate.

As a rule, then, exploratory research is con-

EXHIBIT 5-2

The Uncertainty Associated with the Research Problem Determines the Research Methodology

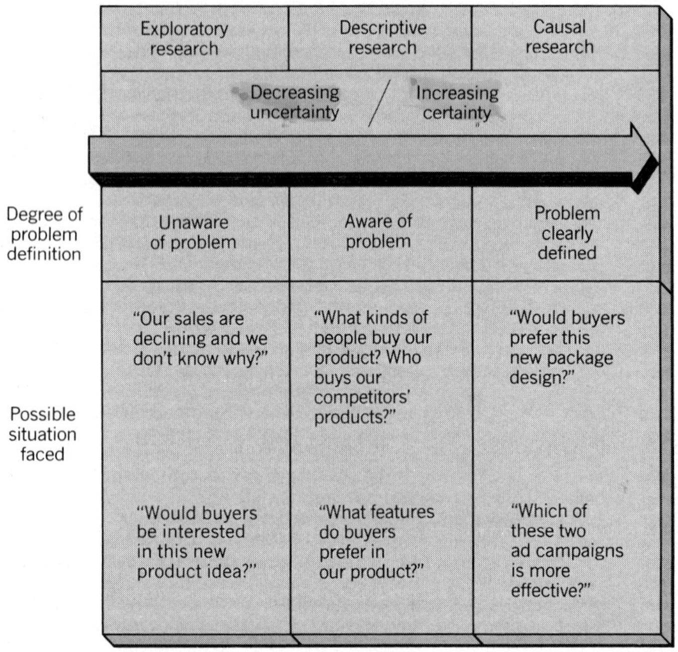

	Exploratory research	Descriptive research	Causal research
	Decreasing uncertainty / Increasing certainty		
Degree of problem definition	Unaware of problem	Aware of problem	Problem clearly defined
Possible situation faced	"Our sales are declining and we don't know why?"	"What kinds of people buy our product? Who buys our competitors' products?"	"Would buyers prefer this new package design?"
	"Would buyers be interested in this new product idea?"	"What features do buyers prefer in our product?"	"Which of these two ad campaigns is more effective?"

ducted during early stages of decision-making when the nature of the problem is unclear to managers. When management is aware of the problem, but not completely knowledgeable about the situation, descriptive research is usually conducted. Causal research studies require sharply defined problems so that cause and effect relationships can be explored.

THE STAGES IN THE RESEARCH PROCESS

Marketing is not a "true" or "exact" science such as mathematics or physics, but that does not mean that marketers and marketing researchers should not try to approach their jobs in a scientific manner. Marketing research is a form of systematic inquiry into the happenings of the marketplace just as astronomy is a systematic investigation of the stars and planets. Both make use of step-by-step approaches to gaining knowledge.

The steps in these processes are highly interrelated, and one step leads to the next. The stages in the research process often overlap. Disappointments encountered at one stage may mean returning to previous stages, or even starting over. Thus, it is something of an oversimplification to present a neatly ordered sequence of activities. Still, the stages of research, and of marketing research in particular, often follow a generalized pattern of seven stages. These stages are: (1) problem definition, (2) planning of the research design, (3) selection of a sample, (4) data collection, (5) data analysis, (6) drawing of conclusions and preparing of a report, and (7) follow-up.

Again, the stages overlap and affect one another. In some cases, the "later" stages may even be completed before the "early" ones. For example, the research objectives outlined as part of the problem definition stage will have an impact on the sample selection and data collection stages. A decision to sample people of low educational levels will affect the wording of the questions posed to these people. If the researcher has established that a computer will be used to analyze survey results, the questionnaire used will be designed to permit that analysis. The research process, in fact, often becomes a cyclical and on-going one, with the conclusions of one study generating new ideas and problems requiring further investigations.

Within each stage of the research process, the researcher faces a number of alternative methods or paths from which the best approach must be chosen. In this regard, the research process can be compared to a map.[7] On any map, some paths are more clearly charted than others. Some roads are direct and others are scenic. Some paths are free and clear, others costly or under construction. The point to remember is that there is no "right" or "best" path. The road taken depends on where the traveler wants to go and how much time, money, ability, and so forth are available for the trip.

The analogy of the map to marketing research is useful because the researcher must choose the appropriate path, i.e., one that best suits the particular problem at hand. In some situations, where time is short, the quickest path is best. In other circumstances, when money, time, and personnel are plentiful, the chosen path may be long and difficult.

Exploration of the various paths marketing researchers encounter is the main purpose of this chapter. The seven stages of the research process will be described. Exhibit 5-3 helps to illustrate the choices researchers face at each stage.

Stage One: Problem Definition

As shown earlier, there is a difference between a problem and the symptoms of that problem. Pain, for example, is the symptom of a problem. The cause of the pain is the problem. In marketing, the problem is not that sales are falling, but that the marketing mix is not properly matched to changing buyer preferences.

Research step 1, **problem definition,** is likely to begin with the discovery that *some* problem exists because symptoms have been detected. Exploratory research would follow in an effort to isolate the problem which underlies the symptoms. Finally, as Exhibit 5-3 shows, the problem would be defined, and a series of research objectives related to the problem would be developed.

The thought that problem definition is central to the marketing research process is so obvious that its importance is easily overlooked. Albert Einstein noted that "The formulation of a problem is often more essential than its solution."[8] This is valuable advice for marketing researchers who, in their haste to find the right answer, may fail to ask the right question. Too often, data is collected before the nature of the problem is carefully established. Except in cases of coincidence or good luck, such data will not help solve the marketer's difficulties.

The old adage, "a problem well-defined is a problem half-solved" puts all of this into perspective. Careful attention to problem definition allows the researcher to set proper research objectives. If the purpose of the research effort is made clear, the chances of collecting necessary and relevant information will be greater and the likelihood of gathering surplus data diminished.

---

[7] P.J. Runkel and J.E. McGrath, *Research on Human Behavior: A Systematic Guide to Method* (New York: Holt, Rinehart and Winston, 1972), p. 2.

[8] A. Einstein and L. Infeld, *The Evolution of Physics* (New York: Simon & Schuster, 1942), p. 95.

EXHIBIT 5-3

The Marketing Research Process

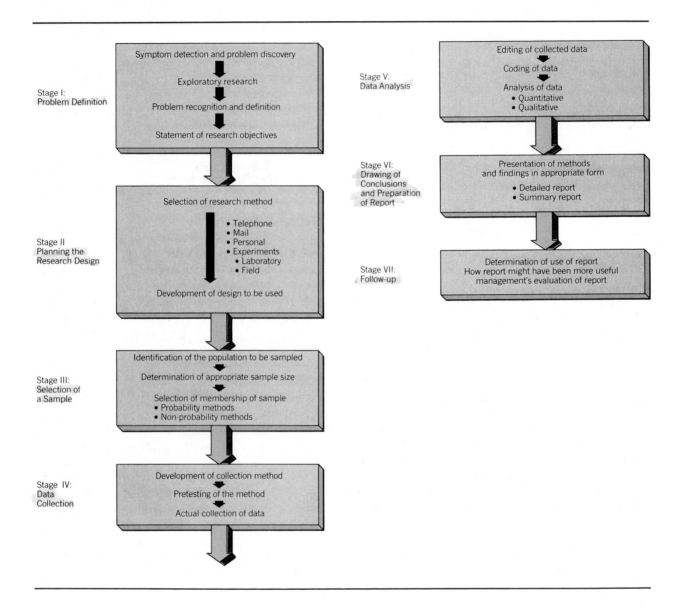

Stage I: Problem Definition
Symptom detection and problem discovery
Exploratory research
Problem recognition and definition
Statement of research objectives

Stage II Planning the Research Design
Selection of research method
• Telephone
• Mail
• Personal
• Experiments
  • Laboratory
  • Field
Development of design to be used

Stage III: Selection of a Sample
Identification of the population to be sampled
Determination of appropriate sample size
Selection of membership of sample
• Probability methods
• Non-probability methods

Stage IV: Data Collection
Development of collection method
Pretesting of the method
Actual collection of data

Stage V: Data Analysis
Editing of collected data
Coding of data
Analysis of data
• Quantitative
• Qualitative

Stage VI: Drawing of Conclusions and Preparation of Report
Presentation of methods and findings in appropriate form
• Detailed report
• Summary report

Stage VII: Follow-up
Determination of use of report
How report might have been more useful
management's evaluation of report

Stating Objectives. As has been suggested, and as is shown in Exhibit 5-3, the stage of the research process known as problem definition should culminate in a clear understanding of the objectives of the research about to be undertaken. Efficient marketing research work must have clear objectives and definite designs. Unfortunately, this is not always the case.

Consider the case of Ha-Psu-Shu-Tse (the name is the Pawnee Indian word for "red corn") brand fried Indian bread mix. The owner of the company thought that his product, one of the few American Indian food products sold in the United States, was selling poorly because it was not advertised heavily. His "feeling" about this led him to hire a management consulting group to research new advertising themes. The consultants suggested, instead, that the product's brand name (Ha-Psu-Shu-Tse) might be the main problem. They proposed that consumer attitudes toward the name and product should be the starting point of research. In effect, the consultants were reluctant to choose advertising, one component of the marketing mix, as *the* area of concern without checking for more basic causes of the firm's difficulties. The fact that the company's owner was Mr. Ha-Psu-Shu-Tse complicated matters somewhat, and no doubt colored his perceptions of the consultants' ideas. Despite the matter of the company owner's pride in his family name, the focus of the research was shifted away from the narrow objective of developing better advertising themes to the broader, but more basic, objective of determining how consumers perceived the product.

Similarly, when a professor at Wright State University in Dayton, Ohio was asked to have his marketing research class study nearby Trotwood to answer the question why nobody shopped in downtown Trotwood, he and his students discovered that there were no *stores* in downtown Trotwood. Thus, the problem to be faced by town officials was not why shoppers avoided Trotwood, but why retailers avoided Trotwood.

Problems Can Be Opportunities. It should be noted that there are many occasions when the research process is not focused on a problem but on an opportunity. In this happier circumstance, for example, a toy maker who developed a fabulous new item might face the "problem" of what age groups will most likely want the toy or of determining which of several advertising media is the best. In cases such as these, the problem definition stage of the research might well be called the "opportunity definition" stage. The point is that the problems addressed by marketing research are frequently "good" problems and not disasters.

Although the problem definition stage of the marketing research process is the first and probably most important stage, it is often neglected. In a sense, the best place to begin a process is at the end. Determining what is to be accomplished determines the process to be used. Errors or omissions at this early stage of the research process are likely to lead to costly mistakes later on, when it is harder to correct them.

What Is a "Good" Research Objective? Marketers contemplating a research project must decide *exactly* what they are looking for. A formal statement of the problem(s) and the research objective(s) must be the culmination of Step One of the research process. These provide the framework for the study as a whole.

The best way to express a research objective is as a well-constructed, testable hypothesis. A **hypothesis** is an unproven proposition or possible solution to a problem; a statement that can be supported or refuted by empirical data. It is a statement about the nature of the world and, in its simplest form, it is a guess. In times of inflation or economic recession, an auto manufacturer might hypothesize that lower income families are cutting back on car purchases more than are wealthy families. This is a hypothesis that can be tested by research. On the other hand, a maker of premium beer, in the same situation, may hypothesize that high-income families are reducing consumption of that product while low-income families, seeking some of life's "smaller pleasures," are not cutting down. This, too, is a hypothesis that can be tested.

Once researchers have developed testable hypotheses, they are ready to select a research design.

Stage Two: Planning the Research Design

After the researcher has clearly formulated the research problem and hypotheses, the next step is to develop a research design. The **research**

design is, as its name suggests, a master plan which specifically identifies the tools and procedures that will be used to collect and analyze information relevant to the research problem. The research design must be carefully compared against the objectives developed in Stage One of the process to assure that the sources of information, the data collected, the scheduling and costs involved, and so on, are consistent with the researcher's main goals. For example, if it has been determined that the research objective is to gather information about buyers of hospital beds in Little Rock, to have that information within two weeks, and to spend no more than $1,000 in the process, a nationwide survey that will take six months to complete would be totally incompatible with management's needs.

Researchers, at this stage of the process, are faced with choosing from among four basic techniques. They are:

1 Secondary data

2 Observation

3 Surveys

4 Experiments

Obviously, the matter of which one is "best" in any given case depends on the appropriateness of the technique, but also on time, cost, and other not-so-scientific considerations.

Secondary Data. Contrary to what the general public believes, marketing research studies do not always involve surveys or the generation of other new or original data. Previously gathered data, already in the researcher's files or in the library, may be enough to complete a meaningful and useful research effort. For example, a marketer of mobile homes might know that sales of this product rise as building permits issued for traditional homes decline. Using government figures showing permits issued and trends in home building, the mobile home seller can develop predictions of market behaviors, thus basing the research design entirely on secondary data sources.

Secondary data are those previously collected and assembled for some purpose other than the project at hand. Secondary data come from both internal sources and sources external to the organization. **Primary data** are those gathered and assembled specifically for the project at hand.

In any research situation, it is generally best to check available secondary data before beginning primary data collection. Such a check may result in a savings of time and money. The primary advantages of secondary data are that (1) they almost always are less expensive than primary data and (2) they can be obtained rapidly. Secondary sources must be used with care, however, as they have certain disadvantages.

■ Secondary data is previously collected data and is, therefore, "old" and possibly outdated.

■ Some data is collected only periodically. For example, the population census (Chapter 2) is taken only once a decade. Comparatively up-to-date estimates are often available in such cases.

■ Data may not have been collected in the form preferred. Sales figures for a county may be available, but not for a particular town within that county.

■ Users of secondary data may not be able to assess its accuracy. For example, previous researchers may have "bent" the data to "prove" some point or theory.

In general, the inherent disadvantage of secondary data is that they were not designed specifically to meet the researcher's needs. Thus, the manager's task is to determine if the secondary data are pertinent and accurate.[9]

Observation. If the purpose of a research effort is simply to note actions which are mechanically or visually recordable, observation techniques can form the basis of that effort. **Sci-**

---

[9]D.N. Bellenger and B.A. Greenberg, *Marketing Research: A Management Information Approach* (Homewood, Ill.: Richard D. Irwin, 1978), p. 128.

entific observation is systematic recording of behavior, objects, or events as they are witnessed.

Companies that sell space on outdoor billboards are particularly interested in traffic patterns, specifically the numbers of cars and people passing the billboard installations each day. Mass transit organizations may want to know the numbers of people riding each bus and at what stops most of them get on or off. In both cases, the information could be recorded by either human observers stationed on street corners or on buses or by mechanized counters.

Observation can be more complicated than these simple nose counting examples might suggest. "Mystery shoppers" can be used to check on the courtesy or product knowledge of retail salespeople. Researchers "disguised" as customers, store employees, or product demonstrators might subtly observe consumer reactions to prices, products, package designs, or display cases.

The greatest strength of observation is that it permits the recording of what actually occurred in a particular situation. Its biggest weakness is that the observer cannot be sure *why* the observed behavior occurred. Still, in some cases, it is enough to know that something happened. The Nielsen Company, for example, rates television shows in terms of how many people watch them. The networks are then paid more for advertisements on top-ten shows than on less popular shows. The questions of why a show is popular or why the ratings of old movies beat those of the President's State of the Union Address are often left to the critics.

Surveys. Primary data is most commonly generated by survey research. Survey results, on one topic or another, are reported almost daily by the news media. Most adult Americans have been stopped by interviewers at shopping centers or voting places or have received mailings or phone calls from survey-takers. In general, a **survey** is any research effort in which information is gathered from a sample of people by means of a questionnaire. As this broad definition suggests, survey techniques have many applications. For example, American automobile makers utilize style research clinics to appraise consumer reac-

Primary data is most commonly gathered by surveys.

tions to car designs. First, mock-ups of proposed designs are constructed, then consumers (or "respondents") are recruited by means of short telephone interviews. These respondents are brought in secret to a showroom and shown a car mock-up and competitive autos from around the world. As the "buyers" pore over the cars, professional interviewers ask for their reactions to virtually every detail. The survey results are then fed back to designers in Detroit.

Carrying the style clinic a step further, Ford spent two million dollars on style research for its Fiesta. One clinic was held in late 1967 in Lucerne, Switzerland, and attended by respondents from London, Paris, Madrid, Milan, and Düsseldorf. During the three-hour sessions, all participants were surveyed in their native languages as to how the Fiesta stacked up against six likely, non-Ford, competitors.[10]

Advantages of Survey Research. When surveys are properly planned and executed, they can prove to be quick, efficient, and accurate means of gathering information.[11] Furthermore, the Red Cross and Ford examples illustrate that surveys can be quite flexible. The marketing concept tells managers to provide buyers with what they want. How better to do that than to first *ask* them what they want?[12]

Problems with Survey Research. While survey techniques have been much improved in recent decades, careless researchers still use surveys improperly and produce incorrect or even worthless results. When surveys are properly conducted, their conclusions may come too late to solve the problem at hand, or may be in-

cluded in reports so bulky that no one will read them. It may well be that a majority of surveys conducted prove to be a waste of money.[13]

The most common survey errors are of two types: sampling and systematic. **Sampling errors** are a statistical phenomena. Impartial research attempts to portray a representative cross-section of a particular target population. Even with technically proper random probability samples, statistical errors will occur because of chance variation. Without increasing sample size, these statistical problems are unavoidable. However, random sampling errors can be estimated, and they may be taken into account by managers.

Systematic errors are those which occur in the design or execution of the research. Questions might be poorly worded, respondents might provide incorrect answers, or results might be misinterpreted. In some cases, the wrong people or organizations are included in the group surveyed. Sampling techniques have become increasingly scientific and accurate, but carelessness or ignorance can still lead to selection of samples which simply are not representative of individuals or companies in which the researcher is interested. Since the systematic error category includes all errors other than statistical sampling errors, systematic errors are referred to by some as non-sampling errors.

The specific advantages/disadvantages of surveys are best discussed in reference to each form of data collection (mail, personal interview, and telephone). These are outlined in Exhibit 5-4. This exhibit makes it obvious that there are trade-offs when one method is chosen rather than another. For instance, a low-cost mail survey takes more time and is less versatile than a higher-cost personal interview.

Each marketing problem for which surveys might provide useful information contains aspects which suggest the appropriate survey technique. An advertiser placing a message on a popular television program like the Super Bowl or the World Series might contact viewers in

---

[10] Ford Motor Company, *World Car: A Dramatic Automotive Concept for the 80's.*

[11] There is, however, some fear that the increasing surveys by marketers has lessened the public's willingness to participate in surveys. "The Public Clams Up on Survey Takers," *Business Week,* September 15, 1973, pp. 216–220.

[12] Paul B. Sheatsley, "Survey Design," in *Handbook of Marketing Research,* Robert Ferber, ed. (New York: McGraw-Hill, 1974), pp. 2–66.

---

[13] Paul B. Sheatsley, N. 11 *supra.*

EXHIBIT 5-4

Comparison of Typical Characteristics of the Three Survey Methods

	Personal	Mail	Telephone
Speed of data collection	Moderate to fast	Researcher has no control over the return of questionnaire	Quite fast
Respondent cooperation	Excellent cooperation	Moderate cooperation—poorly designed questionnaire will have low response rate	Good cooperation
Versatility of questioning	Very flexible	Highly standardized format	Moderate flexibility
Questionnaire length	Long	Varies depending on incentive	Moderate
Possibility for respondent misunderstanding	Lowest	Highest—no interviewer to clarify	Average
Influence of interviewer on answers	High	None	Moderate
Cost	Highest	Lowest	Low to moderate

their homes via telephone to gather reactions to its commercial. A manufacturer of industrial equipment might choose a mail survey because the executives it wishes to question are hard to reach on the phone. A political party might prefer to employ a door-to-door personal survey so that voters can, after some guidance by interviewers, formulate and voice their opinions on current issues. In these examples, the cost, time, and perhaps accuracy involved vary. It is the researcher's job to weigh the advantages and disadvantages involved and find the most appropriate way to collect the needed information.

Wording the Questions. Avoiding complexity and using simple, accurate, conversational language that does not confuse or bias the respondent is the goal of the questionnaire writer. The wording of questions should be simple and unambiguous so that the questions are readily understandable to all respondents.

For example, many respondents are susceptible to leading questions such as "You do agree that American automobiles are a better value than Japanese automobiles, don't you?"

Sometimes **rating scales** are utilized to measure consumers' attitudes. Two of the most common attitude scales are the *Likert Scale* and the *Semantic Differential*. A **Likert scale** asks respondents to indicate their degree of agreement with a statement such as:

Nike tennis shoes are expensive.

Strongly Agree
Agree
Undecided
Disagree
Strongly Disagree

A **semantic differential** identifies a company, store, brand, or other concept and asks the re-

KEEP THE RED CROSS READY

A survey conducted by the Red Cross revealed that only 3 of 10 respondents associated the Red Cross with blood collection work and very few connected the organization with lifesaving, water safety, and hospital volunteer work programs. Most were aware of Red Cross' disaster assistance efforts but also felt little personal identification with those efforts. Many people thought there was a close financial tie between the Red Cross and the federal government. (There isn't.) These survey results led to a harder sell "Keep the Red Cross Ready" ad campaign to replace the more passive "Good Neighbor" advertising efforts.

Once the advertising campaign had been initiated surveys were conducted by the Harris Poll organization to see if things had changed. The surveys showed that "collecting blood/maintaining blood banks" was now perceived by the public to be the most important service offered by service organizations. Most importantly, 86 percent of the total of 1,253 adults surveyed recognized that these services were supplied by the Red Cross. The Red Cross' association with teaching swimming and lifesaving was recognized by 46 percent of the respondents.

Source: Based on information in "Red Cross Drive Result of Research," *Advertising Age*, January 15, 1979, p. 36 and personal correspondence from Hildegard Herfurth, American Red Cross National Headquarters, January 26, 1983.

spondent to place a check mark on a bipolar rating scale such as:

Nike tennis shoes.

Expensive ——:——:——:——:——:——:—— : Inexpensive

Experiments. Experiments have long been used by scientists in attempts to discover cause and effect relationships. Almost every day we encounter news stories telling us about an experimental group of white mice that was exposed to some substance developing more cancers than a group not so exposed. The assumption, of course, is that the substance involved increased the chance of cancer. A properly run **experiment** allows the investigator to change one or two variables while observing the effects of those changes on another variable. Ideally, the experimenter holds all factors steady except the ones being manipulated, thus showing that changes can be caused by the factors being studied. Clearly, controlling the influence of environmental variables is more easily attained by a scientist working with mice than by a marketing researcher dealing with human beings and their reactions to changes. Yet marketing researchers can and do use experimental techniques. These may be used in marketplace or field experiments, or in a controlled or laboratory atmosphere.

For example, the leading American pickle marketer, Vlasic, learned through experimentation that the taste of their products should be varied by geographic region. Taste experiments showed that people on the West Coast tend to prefer sweeter pickles than do Americans in other areas. West Coasters also prefer less garlic in their kosher dill pickles than do East Coast residents.[14]

In another case, Schlitz experimented, by means of a *test market*, to determine if its Hawaiian beer Primo would sell in Southern states. The effect of the introduction of Primo on

---

[14] "Vlasic Foods: Sales Keep Barreling Along," *Sales and Marketing Management*, January 1978, p. 6.

WORDING THE QUESTION—THE RESEARCHER'S ART

1 The store should continue its excellent gift wrapping program.
(a) Yes
(b) No

Comment: The gift wrapping programs may not be excellent at all. By answering "yes," the respondent is implying that things are just fine as they are. By answering "no," he implies that the store should discontinue the gift wrapping. Don't place the respondent in that sort of a bind.

Better: How satisfied are you with the store's gift wrapping program?
(a) Very satisfied
(b) Somewhat satisfied
(c) Neither satisfied nor dissatisfied
(d) Somewhat dissatisfied
(e) Very dissatisfied

2 Do you understand and like the company's new pricing policy?
(a) Yes
(b) No

Comment: There are really two questions here:
(1) Do you understand the company's new pricing policy?
(2) Do you like it? The answers to the original question are ambiguous.

Better: Do you like the company's new pricing policy?
(a) I don't know what the company policy is.
(b) I don't like it.
(c) I neither like nor dislike it.
(d) I like it.

3 The government is handling the frequent and serious problems with the product safety of children's toys better now than six months ago.
(a) Strongly disagree
(b) Disagree
(c) Neither agree nor disagree
(d) Agree
(e) Strongly agree

Comment: The statement automatically puts respondents in a box, since it assumes that there were frequent serious problems with the product safety of children's toys six months ago.

Better: Compared with six months ago, how well does the government handle problems concerning the product safety of children's toys?
(a) Much better
(b) Somewhat better
(c) About the same
(d) Somewhat worse
(e) Much worse

4 What makes your sales job a good one?
(a) The good pay
(b) The opportunity for advancement
(c) A good supervisor
(d) Interesting work

Comment: This question assumes that the employee's sales job is a good one while the employee may not feel that it is particularly good. There is no provision for selecting one or more than one of the choices. If you really want to find out what the employee likes best about his job, you may want to ask an open-ended question. Or you may need to ask a series of questions about different aspects of the job.

Better: What do you like best about your sales job?
(a) The pay
(b) The opportunities for advancement
(c) The working conditions
(d) The people you work with
(e) Your supervisor
(f) The work
(g) The fringe benefits program

Source: Adapted with permission of Gloria E. Wheeler, "Yes; No; All of the Above," "Before You Conduct a Survey," *Exchange*, a publication of Brigham Young University School of Management Spring/Summer 1979, p. 21.

sales was noted and found to be quite small. Thus, the beer is not now sold in the South.

Advertisers use "laboratory" settings to test proposed new advertising copy. One group of subjects or participants is shown a television program that includes one version of the advertisement. In the same location or isolated setting, a second group views the same program

PITTSFIELD, MASS., A MARKETING LABORATORY

A Chicago-based company has turned Pittsfield, Mass., a city of some 50,000 people, into a marketing laboratory. Computers and the laser scanners that read the Universal Product Code in supermarkets have been linked together to tell reseachers who buys what.

If a consumer agrees to participate in the program, he or she is given a personal code number. Each supermarket purchase made is recorded against that code. No slip-ups, no need to rely on human memory. Each consumer provides the research firm, International Resources, Inc., with household statistics right down to the dog's age and sex. Participants are paid in "psychic income," the feeling that they are "telling marketers how they feel." Add to this a cable TV system that allows International Resources to send different commercials to its respondents than are seen by the rest of Pittsfield's citizenry, and you have a complete research package.

Weaknesses in the system are obvious. How to know, for example, if a given test commercial was actually seen by consumers in the panel? Improvements are being made in the Pittsfield "laboratory" and the other towns similarly "wired" by International. Other firms, such as A.C. Nielsen, are developing similar systems in other cities.

but with a different advertisement. Researchers compare the advertisements and the two groups. When research like this is *not* conducted in a natural setting to increase the control of environmental variables, the experiment is known as a **laboratory experiment.**

Scientists dealing with experiments in physics or chemistry might not be overly impressed with the experimental techniques used by marketers. Yet they are in fact true experiments within the limits imposed by dealing with people rather than animals or inanimate objects. As with surveys, careful planning and execution are required, but properly conducted experiments are valuable sources of marketing information.

Selecting the Research Design. After considering the many research alternatives included within the broad headings of secondary research, observation, surveys, and experimentation, the marketing researcher must ultimately pick the research design that will actually be used. Because there are so many alternatives, there is no one "best" research design. Certain techniques are simply more *appropriate* than others. The "feel" for what is appropriate develops from experience.

For example, which technique should be recommended to the Chicago Museum of Science and Industry to determine which of its exhibits were most popular? A survey? (Could you really expect visitors to remember and rate all the museum's exhibits?) Experimentation? (Would you close off the exhibits one at a time and count the complaints associated with each closing?) Study secondary data? (That *might* tell you what exhibits are most popular at *other* museums.) The Chicago Museum's researcher actually suggested the simple and inexpensive observation technique of keeping track of the frequency with which the floor tiles had to be replaced in front of each exhibit—indicating which exhibit drew the heaviest traffic. Of course, had the museum been in a hurry for information another method would have been proper, but the floor tile approach gave museum operators a good measurement over time at no real cost whatsoever. Incidentally, the chick hatching exhibit was the most popular.[15]

Once the researcher has determined what research design will best yield information useful in solving the marketing problem at hand, the next step is to select a sample (of people, organizations, or whatever is of interest) from which to gather information.

Stage Three: Selecting a Sample

Sampling was mentioned earlier in this chapter. However, further discussion of the methods for

---

[15] Stewart H. Britt, "Marketing Research: Why It Works and Why It Doesn't Work," Chicago Chapter, American Marketing Association, Conference on Marketing Research, 1972.

actually selecting the sample on which the accuracy and appropriateness of the study are based is important.[16]

Though sampling is a highly developed statistical science, its basic concepts are applied in daily life. For example, the first taste (or sample) of a bowl of soup may indicate that the soup needs salt, is too salty, or is "just right." Sampling, then, is any procedure in which a small part of the whole is used to draw conclusions regarding the whole.

A **sample** is simply a portion or "sub-set" of a larger **population.** It makes sense that a sample can provide a good representation of the whole. A well-chosen sample of lawyers in California should be representative of all California lawyers. Such a sample can be surveyed and conclusions drawn about California lawyers, making surveying *all* of them unnecessary. A survey of *all* the members of a group is called a **census.** If the group is small enough in number, as would be the presidents of colleges and universities in Nebraska, sampling is not needed. All the presidents can be easily identified and contacted.

Sampling essentially involves answering these three questions. Careful thought must precede each decision.

1 *Who is to be sampled?*

If a department store manager wants to analyze the store's image in the community at large, but uses credit card records to develop a survey mailing list, who will be surveyed? Only current, credit card-using clients, *not* non-credit customers, and certainly not non-customers, though those groups may be important parts of "the community at large." Specifically, identifying the **target population** is a crucial aspect of sampling.

2 *How big should the sample be?*

The traditional tongue-in-cheek response to this one is "big enough," but it suggests the

---

THE FIASCO OF 1936

A famous example of sampling error is the 1936 *Literary Digest* fiasco. The magazine conducted a survey and predicted that Republican candidate Alf Landon would win over Democrat Franklin Roosevelt by a landslide. History tells us there was a sampling error. The postmortems showed that the *Literary Digest* magazine had sampled telephone and magazine subscribers. In 1936, this was not a representative cross-section of voters, but one that was heavily loaded with Republican voters who, naturally, favored Landon.

---

true answer. The sample must be big enough to properly represent the target population. In general, bigger samples are "better" than smaller samples. Although larger samples are more precise than smaller samples, if proper probability sampling is utilized, a small proportion of the total population will give a reliable measure of the whole. For instance, the Nielsen TV survey, which appears to be highly accurate, involves sampling only a few hundred of America's 75 million households. The key here is that there is not much difference in most family's network viewing and those "Nielsen families" are selected with meticulous care to assure the representativeness of the sample.

3 *Who should be included in the sample?*

Many sampling methods are available, each aimed at selecting the individual people or organizations the researcher will contact.

Probability Sampling. There are two basic types of sampling: probability sampling and nonprobability sampling. A **probability sample** is defined as a sample in which every member of the population has a known, nonzero probability of selection.[17] If sample units are selected on the

---

[16]This is a short discussion of sampling techniques. It is not intended as a comprehensive discussion of these complex techniques. The interested student should investigate a marketing research textbook for additional details.

[17]Seymour Sudman, *Applied Sampling* (New York: Academic Press, 1976).

basis of convenience or personal judgment (e.g., Portland is selected as a test market because it appears to be typical), the sampling method is a **nonprobability sample.** In actuality, the sampling decision is not a simple choice between two methods. Simple random sampling, stratified sampling, and cluster sampling are the methods for drawing a probability sample.

In a **simple random sample,** drawing a particular individual's name from a complete list of all people in the same population is determined by chance selection procedures. Because there is only one stage in the sampling process this procedure is called *simple.* In a **stratified sample,** the researcher must first divide the complete list of all members of the population into subgroups or *strata.* Strata are chosen by determining some characteristics that are relevant to the study. A simple random sample is then taken for each stratum. A **cluster sample** may be utilized when there are no lists of the sample population available or when it is necessary to minimize the cost of sampling. If the purpose of a research study is to investigate behavior in the Western half of the United States, selecting Portland, Denver, and Salt Lake City as representative cities substantially reduces the amount of time spent traveling within this area. These *areas* or *geographical clusters* are first selected on a chance basis then individuals within those clusters are sampled with a probability sampling technique.

Nonprobability Sampling. There are three nonprobability sampling techniques. The first is a **convenience sample.** A professor or graduate student who administers a questionnaire to a class is using a convenience sample. It is convenient and economical to collect the sample data this way. Likewise, the interviewer intercepting consumers at a shopping mall or the reporter interviewing the man-on-the-street is using a convenience sample. The data is collected from people who are most conveniently available. A **judgment sample** utilizes judgment and experience to select the sample elements that will best contribute to the study. For example, test markets are often selected because they appear to

be typical of cities where the product is consumed. A **quota sample** is another nonprobability sample. When the sample elements are collected at the convenience of the interviewers but the characteristics of the sample are matched against certain quotas, the term quota sample is utilized. Thus, the researchers predetermine the pertinent sample characteristics (e.g., 10% with incomes above $80,000) and the data is collected so that the sample will exactly match these characteristics.

Stage Four: Data Collection

Up to this point in the research process, the problem has been defined, the research techniques have been chosen, and the sample to be analyzed selected. Now the researcher must actually collect the needed data. Whatever collection method is chosen, it is the researcher's task to minimize errors in the process—and errors are easy to make. Interviewers who are not carefully selected and trained, for example, may not phrase their questions properly, or may fail to record respondents' comments accurately.

Generally, the process of actually collecting the desired data is preceded by a pretesting of the collection method. A proposed questionnaire or "interview script" might be tried out on a small sample of respondents in an effort to assure that the instructions and questions are clear and comprehensible. It may develop that the survey instrument is too long, causing respondents to lose interest, or too short, yielding inadequate information. The pretest provides the researcher with a limited amount of data which can be used to develop an idea of what to expect from the upcoming full-scale study. In some cases, this data will show that the study is not answering the researcher's questions. The study may then have to be redesigned.

Pretesting is frequently used to develop the "answers" used for multiple-choice style questions. An open-ended question such as "What are your three favorite morning-hour radio programs?" might elicit, in the course of hundreds of interviews, perhaps fifty or more different responses. Pretesting that same question might

Identifying the target population is an important sampling decision.

well show that only eight or ten most popular programs are of significant importance and that all other programs should be relegated to the "Other" category.

The methods of data collection available to marketing research are many and varied. As the example of measuring interest in the Chicago Museum's various exhibits suggests, these methods are limited only by the researcher's inventiveness.

Stage Five: Data Analysis

Once the researcher has completed what is called the "fieldwork" by gathering the data germane to solving the research problem, that data must be manipulated or processed so that it is in a form that will answer the marketing manager's questions.

Editing. Data processing ordinarily begins with a job called **editing,** where surveys or other data collection forms are checked for omissions, incomplete or otherwise unusable responses, il-

legibility, and obvious inconsistencies. The editing process may result in certain collection forms being discarded. It is common in research reports to encounter phrases like, "One thousand people were interviewed yielding 856 usable responses." The process may also uncover correctable errors such as the recording of a usable response on the wrong line of a questionnaire.

Coding. Once the data collection forms have undergone editing, the data undergoes **coding.** That is, meaningful categories must be established so that responses can be grouped into usable classifications. In a survey where the focus is on minority group responses, the race code might be: 1 = white; 2 = black; 3 = Native American; 4 = Asiatic; 5 = Hispanic; 6 = other. In another situation, where only the responses of Hispanics are of concern, the code might be: 1 = Hispanic; 2 = Non-Hispanic. Such codes are especially useful when computer analysis of the data is to be employed, but they are also helpful when the results are hand-tabulated.

Analyzing. After the collected data is edited, coded, and stored, the researcher is ready to undertake the process of analysis. This analysis could involve statistical or qualitative (judgmental) analysis, or both. The type of analysis to be used should be based on the information requirements faced by management, the design of the research itself, the data collected, and the mathematical abilities of the people involved.

A review of the many statistical tools which can be used in marketing research is beyond the scope of this text, but it should be noted that they can range from simple comparisons of numbers and percentages ("100 people, or 25 percent of the sample agreed") to complex mathematical computations requiring a computer. Statistical tools such as the t-test of two means, the Chi square test, and correlation analysis are popular stand-bys used to analyze data. It may be surprising, in light of the availability of these and many other techniques, that a great number of studies use statistics no more sophisticated than averages and percentages.

Qualitative or judgmental analysis should not be ignored here. In fact, the whole study is called into question if the research project yields results that the marketing manager believes are unrealistic or just plain wrong. Ultimately, the researcher and the marketing manager will have to interpret the results of quantitative analysis.

Stage Six: Drawing Conclusions and Preparing the Report

Remember that the purpose of marketing research is to aid in the development of effective marketing decisions. The researcher's role is to answer the question, "What does this mean to marketing managers?" Therefore, the culmination of the research process must be a report that usefully communicates research findings to management. If the researcher is competent and the report makes good sense to management, decision-makers are not likely to want complicated recountings of technical aspects of the research effort. Typically, management is not interested in how the findings came about. Except in cases where the researcher's ability or trustworthiness is in question, management is likely to want only a summary of the findings. Presenting these clearly, using graphs, charts, and other forms of art work, is a creative challenge to the researcher and any others involved in the preparation of the final report.

If there are no employable interpretations of information, no conclusions for managerial decisions, the research process will have been of no use other than, perhaps, as a learning exercise. In addition, if the researcher's findings are unread by marketing managers, the often difficult research process has been, in effect, a total waste.

Stage Seven: Follow-up

After the researcher submits the report to management, he or she should follow-up to try to determine if and how management utilized the report. The researcher should ask how the report could have been improved and made more useful. This is not to say that the report's conclusions or suggested courses of action must be followed by management. Deciding such things is, after all, the role of management, not of researchers. Marketing management, for its part, should let researchers know how reports can be improved or how future reports might be of better use.

THE VALUE OF RESEARCH

This chapter began with a series of stories about how certain organizations used research to achieve success—Toys-Я-Us, Pepperidge Farm, and others—and how one company, the American Animal Trap Company, failed to do research and failed with their new product offering, the "better mousetrap." In tales of marketing success, the common element is the stress placed on consumer satisfaction. In the case of the mousetrap, the organization stressed a better *product,* not the satisfaction of consumers.

This thread runs throughout marketing. Clairol, an extremely successful consumer goods marketer, uses research to keep up with customer moods and problems. When Clairol found that women felt there was no simple, professional way to home-manicure fingernails with a single product, the company developed "Nail Works," an electric appliance that can shape fingernails, file toenails, buff and polish nails, and smooth calluses. A Clairol executive explained, with classic marketing insight, "Clairol doesn't sell appliance hardware. It sells solutions to beauty care problems."[18]

Research enables firms to fulfill the marketing concept. The concept stresses customer satisfaction as the key to any organization's success. No one can consistently know what will satisfy customers without research. In a sense, one of the most dangerous statements is "I *know* what my customers want!"—unless the marketer can satisfactorily answer the questions "How do you know?," "When did you check last?"

The marketing concept also accents profitability. Research, for example in test markets, can lead to the determination of an attractive *and* profitable price. Research can contribute to efficiency throughout the marketing mix by suggesting the most expedient distribution methods or the most effective promotional tools. An example which largely sums up this point is provided by the Exxon Chemical Company. Exxon salespeople carry briefcase-sized computer terminals that can provide telephone access from the prospect's office to the central computer at company headquarters. Thus, salespeople have access to the latest data, can run the complex calculations necessary to show the client the advantage of Exxon products over those of competitors, and can "deposit" information relating to customers' problems or needs. Use of research data in this way increases the firm's overall efficiency *and* improves the sales representative's batting average.[19]

Effective marketing management requires research. At Ford Motor Company, a marketing manager stated "Research is fundamental to everything we do, so much so that we hardly make any significant decisions without the benefit of some kind of market research. The risks are too big."[20] The prime managerial value of marketing research is that it reduces uncertainty. It may be used to define problems or to identify opportunities to enrich marketing ef-

---

[18] "Clairol Does Its Job by Solving Beauty Problems," *Marketing News,* June 2, 1978, p. 7.

NEW TECHNOLOGY IN INTERVIEWING

Problems in accurately recording and coding respondents' comments have long plagued researchers. New technologies are easing these problems and speeding up the research process in the bargain. Computer assisted, on-line telephone interviewing is one example. Telephone interviewers wearing headsets are seated at a CRT display (similar to a television screen) and a keyboard connected to a computer. Survey questions are printed out on the screen, thus increasing the likelihood that interviewers will present the survey items properly. The interviewer types the responses, as they are given, on the keyboard. This should increase accuracy of recording. The computer then codes the answers into the appropriate categories, stores them for later use, and, if desired, keeps "running totals."

This same technique can be adapted to nontelephone situations. In any situation where it is appropriate, however, the big advantages of this approach are the instantaneous collection, coding, and processing of data. More importantly, the technique eliminates steps in the process where errors can easily be made.

Source: "Phone Survey Benefits From New Technology," *ISR Newsletter*, Institute for Social Research, University of Michigan, Winter 1979, p. 2.

forts, and it can be used to identify alternative courses of action.

A second reason for using marketing research is to explain why something went wrong.[21] Detailed information about specific mistakes or failures is frequently sought. Exploring problems in depth may indicate which managerial judgments were erroneous.

A third way marketing research can aid managers is by predicting or forecasting future conditions in the constantly changing marketing environment. Information about changing environments helps marketing managers to adapt. While complete accuracy in assessing the future will never be possible, research can provide managers with more precise estimates than they otherwise would have.

Finally, mere description helps managers. In a number of situations, the purpose of marketing research is merely to describe what is occurring in the marketplace. Airwick Industries developed Shine Guard, a product designed to clean and protect non-waxed floors, based on descriptive research. Although no-wax floors ostensibly require no special treatment, descriptive research indicated that of the 40 million households with this type of floor, eight million were using some kind of wax or polishing liquid. Description of a possible market thus proved valuable, though no other information was available. Airwick, recognizing the potential market, developed Shine Guard to fill the need.

SUMMARY

There are many types of marketing research projects. The researcher decides which is appropriate to the marketing problem at hand by considering two major factors. The first factor is the degree of clarity with which the problem can be defined—should the research be exploratory, descriptive, or causal? The second factor is the nature of the problem and the information to be gathered—is secondary research, observation, survey, or experimentation most appropriate?

[19]Exxon Chemical Computer Tool Aids Salesmen," *Industrial Marketing*, August, 1978, p. 12.

[20]Harry V. Roberts, "The Role of Research in Marketing Management," *Journal of Marketing*, Vol. 22 (1957–1958), pp. 21–32.

[21]David K. Hardin, "Editorial: Marketing Research—Is It Used or Abused?" *Journal of Marketing Research*, Vol. 6 (1969), p. 239.

The research process itself follows a general pattern of seven stages, beginning with the attempt to define the marketing problem specifically and culminating with the preparation of a report and a follow-up effort to determine how the report was used by management. Throughout the process, the researcher has many opportunities to be inventive and creative in selecting and developing research tools. But the researcher must also approach the task as a scientist, seeking correct information as carefully as possible.

The overall goal of marketing research is to generate information which is correct *and* relevant to particular marketing problems. The researcher, though constrained somewhat by time and money factors, is free to use, and even invent, marketing research techniques, as long as they are appropriate to the problem at hand *and* generate useful information for marketing decision-making.

THE MOST IMPORTANT CONCEPT IN THIS CHAPTER

Marketing research can be conducted using a vast array of tools, but the common denominator is the use of a problem solving process to provide information to reduce uncertainty. The appropriate technique is one that results in information that contributes to effective marketing decision-making.

KEY TERMS

Marketing research

Exploratory research

Focus group interview

Descriptive research

Performance monitoring research

Causal research

Problem definition

Research design

Hypothesis

Secondary data

Primary data

Scientific observation

Survey

Experiment

Sample

Sampling errors

Systematic errors

Rating scales

Likert scale

Semantic differential

Laboratory experiment

Population

Census

Target population

Probability sample

Nonprobability sample

Simple random sample

Stratified sample

Cluster sample

Convenience sample

Judgment sample

Quota sample

Editing

Coding

Data analysis

QUESTIONS FOR DISCUSSION

1 How can marketing research help implement the marketing concept?

2 What types of marketing research might be utilized by the following organizations:
(a) Ford Motor Company
(b) Midway Airlines
(c) IBM

3 Think of a situation that might require:
(a) Exploratory research
(b) Descriptive research
(c) Conclusive research

4 How might an observation study be used to investigate consumer behavior?

5 What questions could a secondary data researcher ask himself/herself to determine if the secondary data is pertinent and accurate?

6 What types of surveys and experiments might be utilized to screen out poor advertisements from good advertisements?

7 What are the advantages and disadvantages of mail surveys versus telephone surveys?

8 How will computers be utilized to enhance marketing research?

9 If you had to answer these questions, would you use a mail survey, a phone survey, or a personal interview survey?
(a) What is the most popular TV show at 8 P.M. on Tuesdays in the Greater Boston area?
(b) What do shoppers like and dislike about the Rolling Hills Mall?
(c) How can we best reach a nationwide sample of 250,000 families to determine how much life insurance is carried on various family members?

10 Design a questionnaire to learn about the shopping behavior and attitudes toward a fast-food franchise in your town.

CASE 5-1 Sanz-O-Air*

Sanz-O-Air is an odor-neutralizing mineral packaged in a plastic mesh canister 3¾ inches tall and 2¾ inches in diameter. The Sun-Up Corp. claims Sanz-O-Air removes bacteria that cause odor, mildew, and food spoilage.

There are no moving parts and the container is placed where it's needed, such as inside a refrigerator or smoke-filled room. The product has been used successfully in garbage areas, bathrooms, basements and many other areas. When it begins to fail after six months, the mineral can be reactivated by placing it in a 180-degree oven for 15 minutes.

Sanz-O-Air is primarily composed of a mineral the firm won't identify. The firm calls it SOA. Sun-Up buys the plastic mesh which forms most of the Sanz-O-Air container but makes its own end caps. The product is manufactured by a firm composed of six men who do almost everything from mining the raw materials to making sales calls. The minerals come from near Wickenburg, Arizona, about 55 miles northwest of Phoenix, where Sun-Up leases 240 acres from the federal government for mining SOA. There are about 5¾

million tons of SOA available to the firm. When more SOA is needed, the six-man Sun-Up staff goes to Wickenburg, mines the SOA by hand, loads it on trucks and brings it to its headquarters in Tulsa—with equipment they designed—the mineral is put through a hammer mill, crushed, screened and packaged.

During the product's introduction in 1979 the firm asked its customers to participate in a do-it-yourself market study called "You Be The Judge." The $3.95 canisters were put on the Tulsa market and customers were asked to complete a five-point questionnaire within 48 hours of putting Sanz-O-Air into use. Buyers returning cards were to be paid $1 for their efforts.

The questionnaire, which is placed on a card located between the product label and the canister, is given in Case Exhibit 1. The product's exterior label is also shown. Note the statement: "see enclosed consumer reply card to receive $1 refund" on the label.

Questions

1 Evaluate the questionnaire for Sanz-O-Air.

2 What impact will the $1 refund for returning the questionnaire have on the survey's validity?

3 Is the sample design adequate?

---

*Source: Adapted by permission from Larry Levy, "Even Li'l Abner's Skunk Works Would Like Product," *Tulsa Tribune*, January 11, 1979, p. 1D.

CASE EXHIBIT 1

Example of a Product Label Questionnaire

You Be The Judge

Please put your Sanz-O-Air cannister in an interior area where you have a serious odor problem. After a maximum of 48 hours fill out the following questionnaire and mail.

You will receive $1 for your time and effort. This offer expires June 1980.

Thank you,

Ralph Lafferty Jr

Ralph Lafferty Jr.
President
Sun-Up Corporation

Where did you place your Sanz-O-Air? _____

How long did it take to remove existing odor? _____

Would you like to buy Sanz-O-Air in a
☐ larger or ☐ smaller size?

Would you like to buy SoA in loose form?
☐ Shaker ☐ Break Open Bag ☐ Resealable Cannister.

Are you planning to recharge your Sanz-O-Air?
☐ yes ☐ no.

Any further comments:

Mail To: Sun-Up Corporation
4308 East Pine Place
Tulsa, Oklahoma 74115

CASE 5-2 The Skool: Problem Definition*

The Skool was a singles bar in Chicago's "Rush Street" area. The Rush Street area, located on Chicago's Near North Side by the Gold Coast, is approximately seven blocks long and three blocks wide, and is a popular area for evening entertainment.

The Skool once was one of the most popular spots on "Rush Street." There had always been wall-to-wall people on Friday afternoons, but lately, the crowds had begun to go elsewhere.

A marketing research consultant who patronized The Skool because it was two blocks from his home knew the manager, Karen Stein, well. After some discussions with The Skool's manager, the consultant sent a letter that proposed The Skool conduct some marketing research. (See Case Exhibit 1.)

Case Exhibit 1 The Skool's Marketing Research Proposal

Dear Karen:

Here is a brief outline of what I believe The Skool must consider if it is to regain its popularity on Rush Street. As you know, The Skool's management has

---

*Copyright © 1981 by Dr. William G. Zikmund. Names are fictitious to protect confidentiality.

changed the decor and exterior of The S光ool, hired exceptional bands, and used various other promotions to improve business. In spite of this, a decline in The S光ool's popularity has been evidenced. As these efforts have not brought back the crowd The S光ool once had, I suggest The S光ool undertake a marketing research investigation of consumer behavior and consumer opinions among Rush Street patrons.

I recommend this project because The S光ool once had what it takes to be a popular bar on Rush Street and should still have the potential to regain this status. Most likely, the lack of patronage at The Skool is caused by one or both of the following factors:

1 A change in the people or type of people who patronize Rush Street bars.

2 The opinion of The S光ool held by people who patronize Rush Street has changed.

The problem for The S光ool's management is to determine the specifics of the change, either in different people, or in the opinions of the regular patrons of Rush Street and The S光ool.

Determining what type of information is desired by The S光ool's management depends upon some underlying facts about the popularity of the bars on Rush Street. An assumption must be made concerning the questions, "Does the crowd (weekend and Wednesday patrons) go where the regulars go or do the regulars go where the crowd goes?" If you believe that the regulars follow the crowd, a general investigation should be conducted to test why the mass goes to the popular bars. If the assumption is made that a popular bar is popular because there are always people (regulars) there, the best method to increase business is to get a regular following which will attract "the crowd."

Of course, the optimal position is to appeal to both the regulars and the crowd. Thus, there are numerous areas for investigation:

■ Who visits Rush Street bars? What are the group characteristics?

■ What motivates these people to go to the various bars and, thus, make them popular? For example, to what extent does the number of stag girls in the bars bring about more patrons? (Note: Remember that The S光ool, Rush-up, Filling Station, and Barnaby's had female waitresses at the start of their popularity. Could this have been a factor in their appeal?) How important is bartender rapport with the patrons?

■ What do drinkers like and dislike about The S光ool?

■ What is the awareness among beer drinkers of Watney's quality? Do they like it? How does having Bud on tap affect a bar's popularity?

■ What image does The S光ool project? Is it favorable or unfavorable? Has it lost the image it once had because it is trying to be the Store Annex, Barnaby's, Rush-up, and The S光ool combined? Is the decor consistent? How can a favorable image be put back into Rush Street drinkers' minds? You might think The S光ool can appeal to all Rush Street people, but you can't be all things to all people. A specialization of image and customers may bring back "the crowd" for The S光ool.

■ How important is it to be first with a new promotion? For example, did Barnaby's idea of starting a wine and chicken feast make it the place to go to—at least in the short run? If a food promotion would go over, what should The S光ool try?

There are many areas where The S光ool would benefit if it conducted a marketing research survey. Of course, the above suggestions for investigation are not all-inclusive, as I have not had a chance to talk with you to determine which areas are the most important. If you would like to have me submit a formal research proposal to determine how The S光ool can improve its business, I will be happy to talk with you any evening.

Sincerely yours,
Robert Millano

Questions

1 Has the problem been adequately defined?

2 Evelute the research proposal.

CHAPTER 6

The Marketing Information System and Sales Forecasting Methods

CHAPTER SCAN

This chapter deals with information and the organization of information into forms useful to marketing managers.

Effective marketing requires information of all sorts: facts and figures, survey results, forecasts, and even, occasionally, rumors. How these elements of information are found is one topic covered in this chapter.

An even more important concept is also dealt with—the Marketing Information System (M.I.S.). No organization can make use of the information it has gathered unless that information can be put into a meaningful form, retrieved when needed, and presented to decision-makers in a format they can use. This is the purpose of the M.I.S.

WHEN YOU HAVE STUDIED THIS CHAPTER, YOU WILL:

Understand the importance of information in effective marketing.

Be able to show how various formal and informal sources of data contribute to management's decision-making process.

Be able to describe the nature and functions of a Marketing Information System.

Be able to discuss the purposes of the sales forecast and be familiar with what forecasting involves.

MARKETING INFORMATION SYSTEMS

Until very recently, only clerical and factory workers equipped with word processors, electronic accounting systems, and computer-controlled tools really benefited from computer technology. Now, though, the personal computer explosion is changing the organizational structure of companies along with the function of marketing managers.[1]

Advances in technological sophistication have combined with the need for better, faster information to accelerate the use of computers. The technologies embodied in executive computer work stations are so new that only about 3 percent of all professional, technical, managerial, and administrative workers use them now. By 1990, however, that figure should climb to about 65 percent.

The advent of desk-top computers and other information tools, linked together by advanced telecommunications networks that provide access to widely diverse sources of data, heralds a huge surge in productivity for the approximately 10 million managers in the United States. Some of the new wizardry is already in place:

■ Individual managers now make decisions by combining information developed within their companies with outside data bases, including economic and industry statistics. Such data allow them to put together studies of their businesses, markets, competition, pricing, and forecasts in a few hours—studies that once took months of work.

■ New systems can turn reams of numbers into charts and colorful graphs that are easy for managers to understand. Information can thus be more quickly digested for faster action.

■ Electronic mail allows reports, memos, and drafts to be transmitted simultaneously to a number of people within the organization. Such systems greatly speed in-house communications. Managers can get signoffs on memos rapidly, making for faster decisions.

---

[1] The material under this topic is based on "How Computers Remake the Manager's Job," *Business Week*, April 25, 1983, p. 68.

The newest support systems let users tap information from both corporate and outside data bases. Because the computer calculates so fast, executives can play "what-if" games with figures to see how changes in various pricing or cost components could affect results.

At Pfizer Pharmaceuticals, a division of Pfizer Inc., Grant W. Denison, Jr., vice-president for planning and business development, uses microcomputers to analyze pricing, competitive product lines, and promotional allocations. A typical study might look at the potential impact of a 50 percent cut in promotion for a Pfizer product. To develop such a study, Denison would search his computer's memory to find out how a competitor that tried a similar strategy fared in the marketplace. "If you had to look through market research books, it would take four weeks," he notes. "Now you can do it right away. You ask more questions and get more analytic."

Although the information obtained via the systematic marketing research process is invaluable, there is much additional information known to marketers that is not the product of the marketing research department. As the first few paragraphs of this chapter indicate, computer systems may be a source of vast data bases. And, as computers grow increasingly sophisticated and their prices decrease, information support systems will become much more accessible to marketing managers. Still, information may be found in many places outside the computer or even the marketing research department. What is the place of casually encountered facts, information, rumor, news stories, and the like? The marketing decision-maker is not likely to reject these things, and is, in fact, likely to use them if they prove to be valuable. A sales representative's personal analysis of his or her sales territory is not likely to be disregarded. These are only a few of the many available sources of marketing information. How to manage all forms of information is the topic of this chapter.

Exhibit 6-1 shows the various sources of information that contribute to the marketing manager's knowledge of the environment in which

EXHIBIT 6-1

Sources of Marketing Information

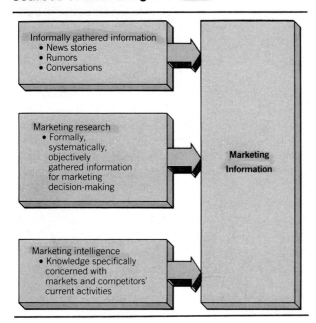

Informally gathered information
- News stories
- Rumors
- Conversations

Marketing research
- Formally, systematically, objectively gathered information for marketing decision-making

Marketing intelligence
- Knowledge specifically concerned with markets and competitors' current activities

Marketing Information

he or she operates. All of this information, taken together, might be termed **marketing information** since, regardless of the source, it represents all the data, facts, guesses, and so on, that the manager has to work with. Three sources contribute to that collection of marketing information: informally gathered information, data gathered by formal marketing research, and marketing intelligence information. **Marketing intelligence** refers to key information about the market with an emphasis on just what competitors are up to. Marketing intelligence often provided by sales personnel, derives its name from an analogy to military intelligence where spies provide information about the enemy. The term is included here because organizations do focus considerable attention on their competitors and because the term is frequently used in business.

The flow of information shown in Exhibit 6-1 does not end in the reservoir marked marketing information. Marketing information is of no use unless it is put to work. Thus, the information must flow on to the marketing decision-maker.

THE SCOPE OF MARKETING INFORMATION SYSTEMS

As we have seen, marketing managers have many sources of information on which to base their decisions, and the information is of many types. Certain data, such as daily sales figures and monthly or quarterly totals, are continuously and regularly supplied to managers. Other information, such as consumer survey results, is generated only upon special request. Still other information, generally informally gathered, comes to the manager on an unscheduled basis.

A problem that frequently faces managers is that while large amounts of information may be available, it may not be *exactly* what is needed. To people attempting to make a decision, the right kind of information is the information needed for the decision at hand. Managers can also find themselves overburdened with too much information, a good portion of which may be irrelevant to the problem they are addressing.

Exhibit 6-1 shows how various sources of data, facts, figures, and even rumors combine to create a reservoir of marketing information available to managers. It would be a rare case, indeed, when a manager would want to use *all* of the information. In any given decision situation much of it would be of little or no use.

Clearly, managers need some way to select what they need from the vast amount of information which confronts them. In other words, they need to manage information as they handle their other responsibilities.

Many managers are prone to leaping from one problem to another putting out fires rather than dealing with broader issues like controlling the flow of information that faces them daily. Marketing managers are as guilty of this as anyone, perhaps because marketing's changing environment contains so many variables which can generate "fires" to be put out.

Managers are often overburdened with too much information.

Some managers have come to recognize this problem and to realize that information can and should be managed systematically. Handling problems *un*systematically and charging off to get information relevant to each problem as it arises is less helpful in teaching executives to think more effectively than is the continuous gathering of information through inquiry.[2]

This way of viewing information for marketing decisions, combined with the increasing use of computers in business, led to the development of the Marketing Information System (M.I.S.). Recall for a moment the definition of marketing research and consider this definition of a M.I.S.[3]

A **marketing information system** is a continuing and interacting structure of people, equipment, and procedures designed to gather, sort, analyze, evaluate, and distribute pertinent, timely, and accurate information for use by marketing decision-makers to improve their marketing planning, execution, and control.

---

[2]R.H. Brien and J.E. Stafford, "Marketing Information Systems: A New Dimension for Marketing Research," *Journal of Marketing*, July 1968, pp. 19–23, and Joseph W. Newman, "Put Research in the Marketing Decision," *Harvard Business Review*, March–April 1962, p. 106.

[3]This definition appears in Philip Kotler, *Principles of Marketing*, (Englewood Cliffs, N.J.: Prentice-Hall, 1980), p. 136, and is adapted from Brien and Stafford's "Marketing Information Systems" cited at N. 2 *supra*.

BASEBALL'S PRODUCT RECORDS ARE NOW IN A SOPHISTICATED INFORMATION SYSTEM

Computers are becoming an integral part of major league baseball. Sports Team Analysis and Tracking Systems (STATS, of course), is now in use by the Oakland A's and the Chicago White Sox.

Under the information system, a statistician in the press box keeps a record of every pitch on a small Apple computer. When a ball is hit, he notes its precise direction and the number of feet it travels, which players field it, and the outcome of the play. This information is used to provide running statistical notes to broadcasters, who have their own screen, and to prepare an instant summary and box score for reporters covering the game. Within 15 minutes after the game (it used to take six hours), the information is provided to the press to generate publicity for the team.

Potentially more significant, the information is also sent by telephone to a master computer in Philadelphia that keeps pitch-by-pitch records for the entire season, and past seasons, too. Neither the A's nor the White Sox are yet making much use of this information for strategy, but the potential is there. White Sox manager Tony LaRussa, who thinks the data base is still too small, says, "In time the use of computers will be standard with all clubs. You're never going to have a computer making decisions for the manager, but the longer you use it the more uses you'll have for it."

The computer, for example, can draw a diagram of a baseball field and indicate where a particular batter has hit against a particular pitcher or a particular type of pitch. At present, managers must try to keep this sort of information on paper or in their heads. On the computer screen they can see it instantly and accurately, then select a pinch hitter or a relief pitcher, or reposition their fielders accordingly.

The system is also highly effective at analyzing defense. Outfielders Tony Armas, Rickey Henderson, and Dwayne Murphy are widely admired for their fielding, but it was the information system that documented their true value in the 1981 season. During the latter half of the season, these out-fielders caught so many of the line drives and fly balls hit into the outfield that they helped boost Oakland's pitching staff to the second best earned run average (ERA) in the league. With only average outfielders, Cramer calculates, the A's pitchers might have finished last in team ERA. "It may be the clearest statement anybody's been able to make about defense," Cramer says. It is also the kind of information that teams may eventually consider in negotiating salaries and making trades, the buying and selling of players. The system may also be utilized for the scouting function as it helps store and manage information on up to 6,000 minor league and free agent players.

Source: Adapted with permission from Kevin McKean, "Turning Baseball into a Science," *Discover,* June 1982, p. 31.

This definition of a M.I.S. emphasizes many of the same points and concepts—gathering accurate information, systematic evaluation, and analysis—as did the definition of marketing research. Perhaps the major difference between the two is the reference to "a continuing and interacting structure of people, equipment, and procedures." Many have interpreted this phrase to be a reference to computers and related computer programs.[4] Others, however, suggest that an information *system* could be put into effect using notebooks, pencils, and hand-held calculators. This last view has much to recommend it since the systematic treatment of information is clearly a good idea, one that can be recommended to both large and small organizations. Access to a computer would provide many advantages, but to say that there cannot be a M.I.S. without a computer is to remove a valuable tool and concept from the hands of many decision-makers.

Subsystems of the M.I.S.

A M.I.S. is an organizer of information, a means to allow decision-makers the chance to quickly find and use the facts and data relevant to a given problem. Since marketing research is "the systematic and objective process of gathering, recording, and analyzing of data for marketing decision-making," marketing research is *part* of the M.I.S. To use a more technical phrase, marketing research is a *subsystem* of the M.I.S.

Exhibit 6-2 shows that there are *three* subsystems within a M.I.S.: The marketing research system, the marketing intelligence system, and the system of data referred to earlier as "informally gathered information." While some might not wish to claim that informally gathered infor-

---

[4] Some scholars argue that a M.I.S. is simply a computer-based extension of marketing research, while others say it is a distinct activity. The argument may be mostly one of wording. However, since marketing research is generally seen as one source of information, and a M.I.S. is intended to order and manage information, the two terms would appear to refer to different concepts. For a discussion of this point, see William J. Stanton, *Fundamentals of Marketing* (New York: McGraw-Hill, 1978), pp. 44–46.

EXHIBIT 6-2

The Three Subsystems of a M.I.S.

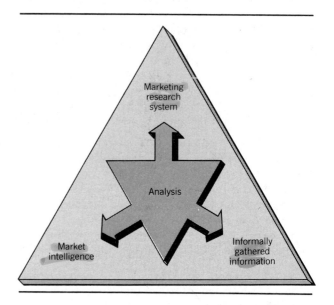

mation is a system, the fact remains that this information does play a part in decision-making. Exhibit 6-2 also indicates that managerial analysis is part of each subsystem, penetrating each and drawing out information useful in the particular problem being addressed.

Marketing Research System. Surveys of consumers, test market experiments, and other formal research projects undertaken to learn about a firm's external environment, and secondary data from the firm's accounting records, government sources, and the like, are the most commonly recognized aspect of an organization's **marketing research system.** These were discussed in the previous chapter.

Internal Records System. To understand the concept of a marketing information system it is useful to concentrate for a moment on internal records as part of the research subsystem. In fact, our definition of marketing research included what some authors treat separately as **internal records.**

Pacific Southwest Airlines (P.S.A), a California commuter line, introduced self-service passenger ticketing. Its "FASTICKET" machine permits a customer to use a credit card to quickly buy a P.S.A. ticket. With the push of a button and a wait of a few seconds, the rushed commuter is on the way. This innovation might have been based on a hunch that customers want to buy their airline tickets quickly and painlessly. But there was more to it than that. Pacific Southwest Airlines' internal company records indicated that about 60 percent of its customers purchased their tickets at the airport, not through mail order, travel agents, or airline offices. Furthermore, 40 percent used a credit card. Thus, marketing information from the company's own records helped P.S.A. develop "FASTICKET," a natural answer to its customers' needs.[5]

Sales reports, inventory statements, and back-orders are obvious examples of regularly kept internal records that managers can utilize in improving marketing performance. Typically, managers are provided with sales and profit reports broken down by sales territories, customer size, product line, and so forth. These types of numerical data lend themselves to computerization, thus allowing the generation of almost any breakdown imaginable.[6]

You may recall the significant role played by internal records from computerized cash registers in lowering the price of hand-held computer games in the Toys-Я-Us example (Chapter 5). Yet, internal records are often overlooked, even though they may yield the same information as survey work.

The Pillsbury Company's practices are typical of organizations that make good use of internal information. Each day reports are submitted by more than a hundred sales offices and warehouses on that day's sales. By eight o'clock the following morning, marketing management has a complete analysis of sales and inventories. In

Computer technology has advanced internal records systems.

another, but related information systems effort, a sample of salespeople periodically reports in-store data on 324 items. Included among the many factors reported are sales, shelf position, and shelf-facings.[7] In this, and many other instances, organizations use what some may view as simple record keeping to plan and control marketing operations.

Advances in computer technology have made internal reporting simpler than it once was and made the results easier to use. Computer graphics can be employed to convert endless columns of numbers to color charts, graphs, and maps.[8]

Market Intelligence System. Market intelligence has been defined in a variety of ways, but to differentiate it from other parts of the M.I.S.

---

[5]Jennifer Pendleton, "Pacific S.W. Airlines Kicks Off Push-Button Tickets," *Advertising Age,* September 11, 1978, p. 12.

[6]Marketing Management and the Computer," *Sales Management,* August 20, 1965, pp. 52–53.

[7]Shelf-facings refers to the exposure of the product on a retailer's shelf. Thus, Campbell's Soup, typically arrayed across a considerable width of shelf, ordinarily has far more facings than does Heinz vinegar.

[8]"The Spurt in Computer Graphics," *Business Week,* June 16, 1980, pp. 104–105.

Analysis transforms raw data into information.

this specialized and rather restrictive definition is useful.

> The **marketing intelligence system** is the set of sources and procedures by which marketing executives obtain their everyday information about developments in the external marketing environment.[9]

Marketing intelligence identified the need for the Corning Glass Corporation to recall its model E-1210 Corningware coffee percolators. Monitoring letters sent between customers and Corning's customer service department led to the discovery that the E-1210 was not proving durable in ordinary household use because the percolators separated from their handles due to faulty epoxy. Complaints had reached an unacceptable level. Keeping an eye on the marketplace, even after sales had been made, allowed Corning the chance to show customers that the company valued their patronage and would "do the right thing."[10]

Any organization can make good use of marketing intelligence. Salespeople or others dealing with members of target market segments are in good positions to keep abreast of changes in an organization's environment. In fact, salespeople are usually the major sources of marketing intelligence, especially when the information is gathered indirectly. For example, a sales representative's (rep's) call reports may alert home office managers to market changes in that rep's territory. Perhaps competitors in a particular area are altering prices, product offerings, or promotions and these are affecting the firm's own people in the field. Trade newspapers and magazines are another important source of information about "what's going on" in the marketplace.

---

[9] This treatment of marketing intelligence relies heavily on Philip Kotler's *Principles of Marketing* (Englewood Cliffs, N.J.: Prentice-Hall, 1980), pp. 134–135.

[10] Harland W. Warner, "Guidelines for Product Recall," *Public Relations Journal*, July 1977, pp. 11–13.

Analysis Is Required in Each Subsystem.
Analysis is the process of determining the nature, proportion, function, and relationships in the data. In a marketing information system, the managerial purpose of analysis is to transform raw data into information. **Raw data** are simply recorded measures of certain phenomena. **Information** refers to analyzed data in a form suitable for marketing decision-making. An analytical process is required in each information subsystem.

Some treatments of marketing information systems confuse computerized statistical banks or programs for computer models with the more general process of analysis. Although a complex computer simulation model is a quite different process from that of an executive evaluating the veracity of a rumor, the logical analysis that is utilized to transform the data into a marketing decision permeates both situations.

The Successful M.I.S.
In a successful M.I.S., information is systematically managed. This means that procedures are in place which expedite the flow of relevant information to the decision-makers. Facts and figures are kept current to provide regular assistance to the marketing manager. In addition, information that is not regularly "in the pipeline," such as the results of recent research projects, must be available to the manager when that manager needs it to make a decision. Lastly, the information, whether in verbal, numerical, or chart form, must be provided in a format that satisfies management's information requirements.

SALES FORECASTING

Sales forecasting is an application of marketing research which is utilized by most organizations. The **sales forecasting** process involves predicting an organization's sales totals over some specific future period of time. An accurate sales forecast is clearly one of the most useful pieces of information a marketing manager can have because so many plans and activities are influenced by estimates of market opportunity. A good forecast helps in the planning and control of production, distribution, and promotion activity. Forecasting may suggest that price structures need adjusting, or that there should be changes in budgeting procedures or inventory holdings. Since operational planning is highly dependent on the sales forecast, ensuring its accuracy is important. Mistakes in forecasting can lead to serious errors in other areas of the organization's management. For example, an overestimate of sales can cause the stockpiling of raw materials that will prove unusable, while an underestimate could mean lost sales due to material shortages.

The sales forecast performs a control function by establishing an evaluation standard. Management uses it for gauging the organization's marketing successes and failures. If no goal exists, there is no way to measure the success or failure of any achievement.

Forecast Types
Some forecasting attempts are aimed at anticipating general economic conditions, at estimating industry sales, or at determining the size of a market. Sales forecasts are focused on *company* sales, but may utilize these other kinds of forecasts as they work toward predicting an organization's sales over a period of time. A bank, for example, may use the Wharton forecast of the American economy to develop its own forecast for the banking industry. Based on that forecast, bank management would then try to estimate the demand for loans at its own various branch locations. This approach—that is, of starting with something big, like the U.S. Gross National Product (or G.N.P.—the value of all goods produced in a year), and working "down" to an *industry* forecast and then a *company* forecast, and even a *product* sales forecast—is very commonly employed. It is called the "break-down method."

Levels of Forecasting

Market potential, sales potential, and sales forecast are the three different levels at which forecasting takes place.

■ **Market potential** refers to the upper limit of industry demand or expected sales volume for all brands of a particular product type during a given time period. Market potential is usually defined for a given geographical area or market segment under certain assumed business conditions. It reflects the market's ability to absorb a type of product.

■ **Sales potential** is an estimate of an individual company's maximum share of the market or the company's maximum sales volume for a particular product during a given time period. Sales potential reflects company demand if maximum sales-generating activities were executed in a given time period under certain business conditions.

The **sales forecast** or expected actual sales volume is usually lower than sales potential because the organization is constrained by resources or because the managerial emphasis is on the highest profits rather than the largest sales volume.

Conditional Forecasting

A common forecasting approach is to assume that the upcoming time period will be much like the past and proceed on that assumption. Unfor-

---

EXHIBIT 6-3

Possible Relative Positions of Conditional Predictions under Various Economic Conditions

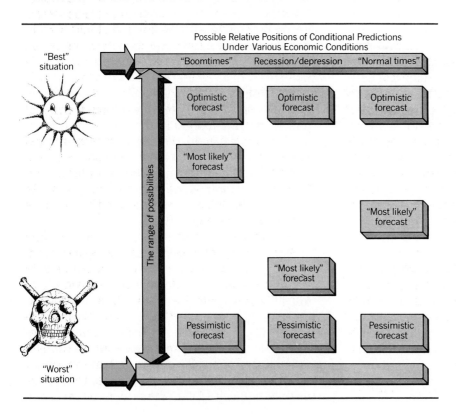

EXHIBIT 6-4

Forecasting Time Frames

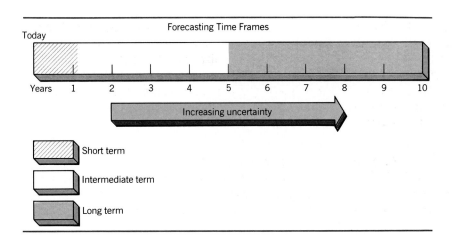

Forecasting Time Frames

Today

Years: 1 2 3 4 5 6 7 8 9 10

Increasing uncertainty

Short term

Intermediate term

Long term

---

tunately, this naive approach may be inadequate, especially since marketing is carried on in a dynamic environment.

A refinement of sorts is commonly used. The forecaster is likely to create three variants on each forecast needed, one based on optimistic assumptions, one based on pessimistic assumptions, and one based on conditions thought to be "most likely." As Exhibit 6-3 shows, the most likely forecast is *not* always halfway between the other two. In bad times, "most likely" might be awfully close to disaster. The advantage of this threefold forecasting approach is that the forecaster clearly distinguishes between what is actually *predicted* and what is *possible*.[11]

Forecasting by Time Periods

A good forecast includes some mention of a time frame during which the forecasted goal is to be met. Managers frequently use expressions like "short term," "long term," and "intermediate term" to describe these time periods. Such

expressions can mean almost anything depending on the marketing problem under discussion. For novelty items such as the Pet Rock, the difference between short and long term could be very short, indeed. Such products may have a life of only a month then disappear from the market. For established products like Wheaties or Lawn Boy lawn mowers, planners might expect to deal in years or even decades.

Though situations do vary, there is general agreement that a short term forecast covers a period of a year or less and that long term forecasts cover periods of five to ten years. As shown in Exhibit 6-4, the intermediate term is anywhere in between.

Generally, there aren't any forecasting time frames greater than ten years. For some products, such as automobile tires, it should be safe to assume that a market will exist ten, twenty, or even fifty years into the future. It is not safe to assume that any product—even automobile tires—will be around "forever." Some forecasters *do* make such long range forecasts. The problem, as Exhibit 6-4 shows, is that the longer the time period employed, the greater the uncertainty and risk involved. The level of uncertainty,

---

[11] Kenneth R. Davis, *Marketing Management* (New York: John Wiley & Sons, 1981), p. 73.

EXHIBIT 6-5

Uncertainty Increases as Forecasting Time Frames Are Increased

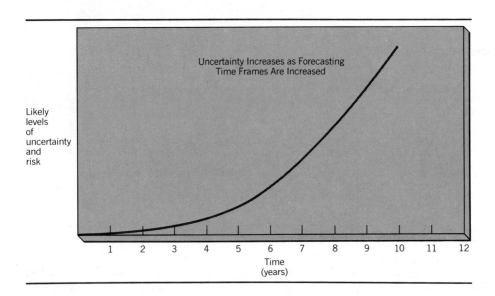

Uncertainty Increases as Forecasting
Time Frames Are Increased

Likely
levels
of
uncertainty
and
risk

1   2   3   4   5   6   7   8   9   10   11   12

Time
(years)

as shown in Exhibit 6-5, increases immensely for each year of the forecast.

As time frames are lengthened, at some point what was to be a forecast can become a guess, then a wild guess, and then a fantasy. The history of business is littered with stories of managers who encountered disasterous failure because they made such assumptions.[12] Marketing's dynamic environment does not offer the "safety" long term planners would like to have. Thus, many forecasters revise sales forecasts quarterly, monthly, or weekly, as the situation warrants.

Forecasting Tools and Methods

There is no best way to forecast sales. This does not mean that the researcher or sales manager faced with the need to forecast market demand or sales volume is also faced with chaos and confusion. It does mean that there are many different methods, ranging from simple to complex, for forecasting. Some methods that have been used to forecast sales are: executive opinion, sales force composite, customer expectations, projection of trends, and analysis of market factors.[13]

Executive Opinion. Top level executives with years of experience in an industry are well-informed. Surveying executives to obtain estimates of market potential, sales potential, or just to get a feel for the direction of demand may be a convenient and inexpensive way to forecast. However, it is not a scientific technique since executives may consciously or unconsciously be biased, and thus either be overly pessimistic or overly optimistic. Used in isolation, executive

---

[12]An entertaining, and widely reprinted, article which amply demonstrates this point is Theodore Levitt, "Marketing Myopia," *Harvard Business Review,* (July–August, 1960), pp. 45–46.

[13]W.J. Stanton and R.H. Buskirk, *Management of the Sales Force* (Homewood, Ill.: Richard D. Irwin, 1978), p. 428.

opinion has many pitfalls. However, when used in conjunction with one or more of the other methods, the seasoned opinion of industry executives may supplement more quantitative techniques.

Sales Force Composite. Asking each sales representative to project their own sales for the upcoming period is called the *sales force composite* method. A sales forecast is determined by combining each salesperson's estimate for his or her territory. The logic of this technique suggests the sales representative is the person most familiar with the local market area, especially competitive activity, and, therefore, is in the best position to predict local behavior. However, this method also allows for the possibility of subjective predictions and forecasting from a limited perspective.

Survey of Customers. Asking customers how many units they intend to buy is the basic logic underlying the survey of consumer expectations. This method is best when the product is established and consumers can relate their buying intentions to the particular product. For a new product concept, customer expectations may not adequately indicate actual behavior.

Projection of Trends. Identifying trends and extrapolating past performance into the future is a relatively uncomplicated quantitative forecasting technique. Time series data are identified, and even plotted on a graph, and the historical pattern is projected for the upcoming period. Thus, if sales have increased by 10 percent every year for the last five years, the trend suggests next year's sales should also increase by 10 percent. This common method of forecasting may work quite well in mature markets that do not experience dynamic changes. The underlying assumption is that the future will be somewhat like the past. If environmental change is quite radical, or if new competitors are entering the market, blindly projecting trends may be less useful and possibly detrimental. An advantage of projecting past sales trends is that data can

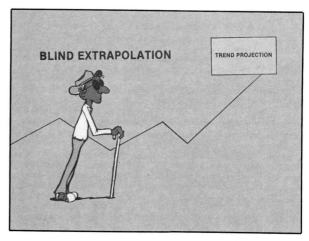
Trends should not be blindly extrapolated.

usually be found in the company's accounting records.

Analysis of Market Factors. The **market factor** method is utilized when there is an *association* between sales and another variable called a factor. For example, population is a general market factor that will help determine whether sales potential for Coca-Cola is higher in Albany, New York, or Las Vegas, Nevada. New housing starts may be a factor that predicts lumber sales. When a number of factors are combined into an index, they are referred to as a multiple **market factor index** or simply a **market index.** Correlation methods or regression methods are mathematical techniques that may be utilized to identify the degree of association between sales and the market factor.

The Sales Management Buying Power Index. The *Sales and Marketing Management* magazine's Survey of Buying Power is one of the most widely utilized market factor indexes. Exhibit 6-6 shows a page from the survey of buying power that portrays income, retail sales, and population data for a geographical area. The *Sales Management Buying Power Index* is a weighted index of three factors: *income,* weighted 5; *retail sales,* weighted 3; *popula-*

EXHIBIT 6-6

Sales Management's Survey of Buying Power

ARIZ.
S&MM ESTIMATES — POPULATION—12/31/80

METRO AREA County City	Total Population (Thousands)	% Of U.S.	Median Age of Pop.	% of Population by Age Group 18–24 Years	25–34 Years	35–49 Years	50 & Over	Households (Thousands)
TUCSON	549.5	.2405	30.2	14.4	16.1	15.5	26.9	204.7
Pima	549.5	.2405	30.2	14.4	16.1	15.5	26.9	204.7
·Tucson	335.5	.1468	29.9	15.0	16.4	14.8	26.9	128.3
SUBURBAN TOTAL	214.0	.0937	30.8	13.5	15.8	16.5	26.8	76.4
OTHER COUNTIES								
Apache	53.7	.0235	20.5	11.7	15.8	12.4	14.4	13.2
Cochise	88.6	.0388	27.8	14.2	15.3	16.1	23.0	30.1
Coconino	76.9	.0336	23.5	21.2	16.5	13.8	15.1	22.8
Gila	37.7	.0165	30.3	11.1	15.9	15.2	27.3	13.2
Graham	23.4	.0103	26.9	13.8	14.7	13.9	24.1	6.8
Greenlee	11.5	.0050	28.5	10.9	15.5	17.2	22.8	3.7
Mohave	58.0	.0254	34.5	8.4	16.2	16.0	33.1	22.2
Navajo	69.4	.0304	24.2	11.0	16.7	13.9	18.2	19.0
Pinal	92.6	.0405	28.0	12.0	16.6	15.8	22.6	29.3
Santa Cruz	21.0	.0092	28.8	10.3	15.1	16.3	24.4	6.2
Yavapai	70.6	.0309	40.4	8.5	12.1	14.6	40.6	27.8
Yuma	92.9	.0406	28.0	14.2	15.4	15.8	23.3	30.9
TOTAL METRO COUNTIES	2,109.3	.9231	30.2	13.6	16.9	16.1	25.7	774.4
TOTAL STATE	2,805.6	1.2278	29.6	13.4	16.6	15.8	25.3	999.6

ARIZ.
S&MM ESTIMATES — EFFECTIVE BUYING INCOME 1980

METRO AREA County City	Total EBI ($000)	Median Hsld. EBI	% of Hslds. by EBI Group (A) $8,000–$9,999 (B) $10,000–$14,999 (C) $15,000–$24,999 (D) $25,000 & Over — A	B	C	D	Buying Power Index
PHOENIX	12,235,244	18,890	5.4	14.4	29.8	32.2	.6762
Maricopa	12,235,244	18,890	5.4	14.4	29.8	32.2	.6762
Mesa	1,175,833	18,696	5.3	15.0	32.0	30.1	.0730
·Phoenix	6,227,290	18,822	5.1	14.2	30.5	31.5	.3375
Scottsdale	881,840	25,485	3.0	8.8	26.8	51.6	.0551
Tempe	922,855	22,622	4.1	12.2	28.1	43.4	.0526
SUBURBAN TOTAL	6,007,954	18,968	5.6	14.8	28.8	33.1	.3387
TUCSON	4,148,281	17,302	5.9	15.0	29.4	28.1	.2293
Pima	4,148,281	17,302	5.9	15.0	29.4	28.1	.2293
Tucson	2,420,177	16,371	6.2	16.2	30.0	24.7	.1486
SUBURBAN TOTAL	1,728,104	19,058	5.4	13.0	28.4	33.7	.0807
OTHER COUNTIES							
Apache	164,080	9,582	6.5	15.1	22.8	10.7	.0112

Source: Sales and Marketing Management's Survey of Buying Power, 1980.

RETAIL SALES BY STORE GROUP
1980

Total Retail Sales ($000)	Food ($000)	Eating & Drinking Places ($000)	General Mdse. ($000)	Furniture/ Furnish./ Appliance ($000)	Automotive ($000)	Drug ($000)
2,153,325	518,757	150,397	280,620	130,288	430,104	82,955
2,153,325	518,757	150,397	280,620	130,288	430,104	82,955
1,691,189	375,381	108,857	267,297	117,714	416,672	58,134
462,136	143,376	41,540	13,323	12,574	13,432	24,821
64,544	11,015	3,621	20,926	304	2,813	2,068
220,724	58,847	12,990	24,332	11,070	44,711	9,919
311,801	70,992	34,860	42,069	12,687	29,410	5,224
110,814	36,731	9,509	6,554	2,681	20,638	3,022
62,539	17,226	3,222	5,809	2,433	15,088	1,861
26,847	12,771	813	2,023	1,720	1,806	1,346
219,509	65,522	13,861	5,865	6,670	29,257	6,675
210,172	60,101	12,835	21,910	6,008	20,124	2,429
188,404	69,663	11,912	10,147	3,811	28,704	8,899
106,204	26,200	6,935	17,520	7,196	8,125	4,566
236,987	78,049	21,052	14,234	9,540	22,359	11,465
316,668	73,388	24,974	44,396	12,284	57,941	9,238
8,670,906	2,032,051	698,349	1,071,175	620,126	1,732,727	314,196
10,746,119	2,612,556	854,933	1,286,960	696,530	2,013,703	380,908

EFFECTIVE BUYING INCOME
1980

S&MM ESTIMATES

METRO AREA County City	Total EBI ($000)	Median Hsld. EBI	% of Hslds. by EBI Group: (A) $8,000–$9,999 (B) $10,000–$14,999 (C) $15,000–$24,999 (D) $25,000 & Over				Buying Power Index
			A	B	C	D	
Chochise	517,777	14,733	6.4	18.7	31.1	17.9	.0288
Coconino	390,072	14,738	5.9	18.5	30.6	18.4	.0272
Gila	226,693	16,088	6.1	15.4	35.4	19.3	.0130
Graham	124,641	15,455	5.7	15.8	27.4	24.0	.0074
Greenlee	75,735	20,318	3.0	7.9	51.0	23.6	.0039
Mohave	341,255	14,075	6.7	19.6	33.4	13.0	.0213
Navajo	274,350	12,481	5.9	15.2	27.0	14.9	.0202
Pinal	477,651	14,354	6.6	18.2	31.9	15.7	.0272
Santa Cruz	106,525	14,126	7.4	18.2	26.8	20.6	.0080
Yavapai	419,843	13,132	6.9	17.5	27.6	15.8	.0251
Yuma	591,365	16,110	6.3	17.4	29.2	24.5	.0343
TOTAL METRO COUNTIES	16,383,525	18,455	5.5	14.6	29.7	31.1	.9055
TOTAL STATE	20,093,512	17,433	5.7	15.2	29.7	28.1	1.1331

tion, weighted 2. A similar index for industrial purchasing power, which is of great use to industrial marketers, is also published by *Sales and Marketing Management.*

SUMMARY

This chapter stressed the importance of channeling all sorts of information to the marketing manager so that his or her decision-making process is more objective. It also stated that raw information, no matter how accurate or up-to-date, is of little use if it is not relevant to the particular problem at hand or if it cannot be easily accessed by the decision-maker.

This is where the Marketing Information System, or M.I.S., may help. The M.I.S. orders information so that needed facts and figures can be found quickly when they can do the most good. A good M.I.S. will usually contribute so much to marketing decisions that the effort taken to set it up will be paid back a thousandfold.

Sales forecasting is a valuable tool that facilitates marketing planning and control. Sales forecasting techniques range from rather simple and subjective methods, such as gathering the opinions of salespeople or executives, to relating past sales performance to multiple economic or other variables.

THE MOST IMPORTANT CONCEPT IN THIS CHAPTER
Information is necessary to effective marketing management. It's worth the trouble to get good information and arrange it so it can be used effectively.

KEY TERMS

Marketing information

Marketing intelligence

Marketing information system

Raw data

Marketing research system

Marketing intelligence system

Internal records

Information

Sales forecasting

Market potential

Sales potential

Sales forecast

Market factor

Market factor index

QUESTIONS FOR DISCUSSION

1 What is the difference between marketing research and a marketing information system?

2 What internal accounting records would you like to periodically see as a report of your marketing information system?

3 What are the advantages and disadvantages of each of the subsystems of a M.I.S.?

4 What is the difference between market potential, sales potential, and the sales forecast?

5 What market factors might help predict market potential for:
(a) Forklift trucks
(b) Chain saws
(c) Soft drinks
(d) Playground equipment

6 Why is it necessary to forecast market potential as well as individual company sales?

7 What forecasting method would be best for the following products:
(a) Cigar sales

(b) The Sony Watchman (miniature portable) television set
(c) Baseball attendance at your university

8 Why is trend extrapolation dangerous?

CASE 6.1 Space Wheyfers*

Space Wheyfers are new crispy snacks in the shapes of missiles, flying saucers, and rocket ships. They are made from whey. Whey is what is left over from cheese manufacturing. In the past, this waste from cheese-making was often dumped into streams by small cheese producers, where it polluted the water by inducing algae growth.

Space Wheyfers were developed as a snack food to compete with potato chips, pretzels, and other junk food that contains little more than empty calories. Space Wheyfers have fewer calories and less fat than the snack foods currently being marketed. Because of the protein-potent residue of whey, Space Wheyfers contain about 15 percent protein, substantially more than most potato chips. Space Wheyfers does not have the disadvantage of many snack foods—they do not contain too much starch.

The Blue Lake Cheese Corporation developed this product because it was a natural for their company. They felt that their dairy scientists' development—a yeast process to convert whey into protein for the Space Wheyfers—was a major breakthrough for the company.

Because teenagers often eat too much junk food, management believes that teenagers should be the prime market for Space Wheyfers. The space and galactic themes have been very popular since the movie *Star Wars* launched the space-cowboy era.

One of the best things about Space Wheyfers is that they can be given any appealing color or taste. The flavor of the food and the texture of the Wheyfers, however, need to be investigated in a taste test.

Questions

1 What is the marketing problem facing the management at Blue Lake Cheese Company?

2 Do you agree that the taste test should be the very first marketing research project?

3 What additional information would be useful to help the marketing of this product?

4 How can the company forecast sales?

---

*This is a fictitious name to assure confidentiality.

PART 3

CONSUMER BEHAVIOR

A study of consumer behavior is essential to the profession of marketing. After all, the consumer or buyer is the focal point about which all marketing activities revolve. To better understand the members of their markets, professional marketers draw heavily on the findings of such fields as psychology, sociology, social psychology, and even anthropology. In many ways the study of consumer behavior is the product of these varied disciplines with, however, a greater emphasis on the buying event.

In Chapter 7, the sociological or group aspects of consumer behavior are discussed.

Chapter 8 details the psychological factors that affect consumer behavior. ∎

CHAPTER 7

Sociological Factors in Consumer Behavior

CHAPTER SCAN

This chapter introduces the concept of consumer behavior.

The chapter illustrates how culture and major social institutions influence buying. Consumers are members of many groups. Within each of these, the buyer plays a role, holds a status, and shares values and norms that he or she cannot easily disregard.

The chapter includes many examples of advertisements, buyer actions, and interpretations of the symbolic natures of products, all of which are closely tied to the individual buyer's experience with the groups in which she or he holds membership.

WHEN YOU HAVE STUDIED THIS CHAPTER, YOU WILL:

Be able to describe buyer behavior in terms of human interaction with the surrounding environment.

Be able to describe how culture affects the behavior of individuals.

Be able to define the terms *role, status, self-concept, value,* and *norm* as they apply to buyer behavior.

Be able to discuss the different social classes in the United States.

Be able to analyze the impact groups have on the individual buyer.

Be able to identify the three roles played in the consumer decision-making process and to tell which of these is the most significant in terms of buyer choice.

The process of effective marketing must begin with the careful evaluation of the problems faced by potential customers. This is because the basic logic of the marketing concept is that marketing's efforts must be focused on the consumer. A good or service that does not provide an "answer" to a buyer's problem, no matter how frivolous that problem may seem to others, will not be sought or accepted by customers. This is true even if other aspects of the marketing mix, such as advertising, are perfectly designed and executed. Another aspect of the potential customers' problems is that it is simply smarter, easier, and more productive to find out what customers want in a product, and then to offer them that product, rather than to present a product and hope to convince customers that they need it. The study of consumer behavior gives the effective marketing manager information he or she can use to increase chances of success in the marketplace. In essence, this orientation lets the buyers tell the marketers what they want. Despite popular opinion, it rarely, if ever, works out that marketers tell buyers what the buyers want.

Buyers are the focus of marketing management; thus it is important that marketers understand buyer behavior. Buyer behavior or consumer behavior (the terms are essentially interchangeable) includes the behavior of ultimate consumers and the business behavior of organizational purchasers. **Consumer behavior** consists of the purchasing activities and decision processes that precede and determine the acts of buying and using products.[1] The study of consumer behavior is an emerging science. There are a number of good theories that can provide those in marketing with a means by which to organize their thinking and to predict future happenings. As French thinker Henri Poincaré wrote, "There is nothing more practical than a good theory." Marketing educators and practitioners, aided by research in other fields such as psychology, sociology, anthropology, and economics, are continually trying to advance the state of consumer behavior theories to improve their usefulness both as descriptors of that behavior and predictors of that behavior.

A SIMPLE START

This discussion of consumer behavior theories starts by presenting a basic building block which will be expanded. The building block is this: Consumer behavior is a subset of human behavior. Stated as a formula, behavior (B) is a function (f) of the interreaction between the person (P) and the environment (E) or $B = f(P,E)$.[2] Simple though it is, this formula says it all. Human behavior results when a person interacts with the environment. Though the behaviors may be simple or complex, they flow from the environmental variables: a person (P) touching a hot stove (E) will jump up and holler "Ouch!" (B).

The study of consumer behavior attempts to understand encounters more complex than that in the hot stove example. Though such physical encounters are important, psychological and social encounters are too. The decision process undertaken by individuals is more involved for social and psychological encounters than for physical encounters. The forces that influence behavioral reactions are difficult to directly observe and comprehend, but, at base, the behavior involved in an individual buying event results from persons interacting with their environments. An *individual buying* event, say the occurrence of purchasing a joystick controller for a video game, consists of the decision-making process of the individual consumer and the situational influence occurring at the time of the purchasing decision.

---

[1]J.F. Engle, R.D. Blackwell and D.T. Kollat, *Consumer Behavior* (Hinsdale, Ill.: Dryden Press. 1978), p. 1.

[2]Kurt Lewin, *A Dynamic Theory of Personality* (New York: McGraw-Hill, 1935).

SOCIAL FORCES

It is impossible to conceive of consumers in to-day's society acting alone, with no interaction with others in their social environment. Even a hermit in the woods, growing his own food and making his own shelter, functions as a part of society taken as a whole when he takes his once-a-year trip into town for tools and supplies. More ordinary people, the consumers or buyers with whom marketing is concerned, are clearly engaged in a social behavior—buying, selling, dealing with others in formal and informal situations and on levels ranging from intimate to aloof. In summary, the lives of consumers are subject to myriad social forces in their environment. **Sociology** is a discipline that investigates human behavior through the study of social institutions and their interrelationships. The individual is not discounted, but sociology's emphasis is on the family and various other social groups and institutions.

Exhibit 7-1 shows how an individual buying event (at the top of the pyramid) is influenced by culture, subcultures, social class, and groups. The nature and impact of these social institutions will be discussed individually.

EXHIBIT 7-1

**Sociological Influences
on the Individual Buying Event**

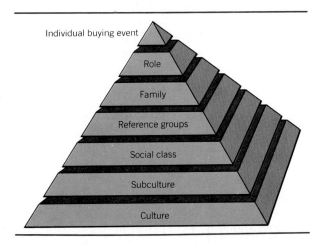

Culture

The term **culture,** though frequently used, is difficult to clearly define. Exhibit 7-2 provides a range of definitions. A common thread among these definitions is the notion that culture is manmade rather than innate. Thus, that children are born is "natural," but how the mating proc-

EXHIBIT 7-2

The Culture Concept Defined

Anthropologists have written various definitions of the culture concept. Several examples follow:

> That complex whole which includes knowledge, belief, art, morals, law, custom, and any other capabilities and habits acquired by man as a member of society.
>
> *E.B. Tylor (1871)*

> The sum total of the knowledge, attitudes and habitual behavior patterns shared and transmitted by the members of a particular society.
>
> *R. Linton (1940)*

> The mass of learned and transmitted motor reactions, habits, techniques, ideas, and values—and the behavior they induce.
>
> *A.L. Kroeber (1948)*

> The man-made part of the environment.
>
> *M.J. Herskovits (1955)*

> The learned pattern of thought and behavior characteristic of a population or society.
>
> *M. Harris (1971)*

> The acquired knowledge that people use to interpret experience and to generate social behavior.
>
> *J.P. Spradley and D.W. McCurdy (1975)*

> The sum of the morally forceful understandings acquired by learning and shared with the members of the group to which the learner belongs.
>
> *M.J. Swartz and D.K. Jordan (1976)*

Source: H.J. De Blij, *Human Geography* (New York: John Wiley & Sons, 1982), p. 179.

EMOTIONS AND SYMBOLS: THE SYMBOLIC ASSOCIATIONS OF SHAVING IN OUR CULTURE

Shaving is one of the most enduring male rituals of daily American life.

Those who are old enough remember how the ritual used to be conducted because many of us watched it every morning. Like a chemist with mortar and pestle, our father would whip up a rich lather by stirring his shaving brush around in his large ceramic mug. Like an orchestra conductor during a brisk allegro, he would strop his gleaming straightedge razor on a long strip of leather. Writer Richard Armour once recalled the scene: "I loved to watch him grimace and pull the skin taught with his fingers preparatory to a daring swipe from cheekbone to chin. I held my breath while he shaved his upper lip, coming perilously close to his nose, and when he started his hazardous course along his jawbone, risking an ear lobe. When he scraped around his Adam's apple, with a good chance of cutting his throat, I had to turn away until I thought the danger was past."

Armour lamented that safety razors and aerosol lathers had taken the "skill, fun, and danger" out of shaving. Though the audience, if there is an audience, may be less rapt, the morning ritual continues to occupy a very special place in most men's lives. Face shaving is one of the few remaining exclusively male prerogatives.

It is a daily affirmation of masculinity. One study indicated that beard growth is actually stimulated by the prospect of sexual relations. A survey by New York psychologists reported that while men complain about the bother of shaving, 95 percent of the sample would not want to use a cream, were one to be developed, that would permanently rid them of all facial hair. Gillette once introduced a new razor that came in versions for heavy, regular, and light beards. Almost nobody bought the light version, for nobody wanted to acknowledge in public his lackluster beard production. (Later, Gillette brought out an adjustable razor that enabled men with sparse whiskers to cope with their insufficiency in

private.) The first shave remains a rite of passage into manhood that is often celebrated by the gift of a handsome new razor (or the handing down of a venerable old razor) and a demonstration of its use from the father.

Though shaving may now require less skill and involve less danger than it once did, most men still want the razor they use to reflect their belief that shaving remains serious business. They regard their razor as an important personal tool, a kind of extension of self, like an expensive pen, cigarette lighter, attaché case, or golf club set. Gillette has labored hard, with success, to maintain the razor's masculine look, heft, and feel as well as its status as an item of personal identification worthy of, for instance, a Christmas gift. For seventy-six years, Gillette's perception of the shaving market and the psychology of shaving has been unerring. Though its products formally have only a 60 percent share, its technology and marketing philosophy have held sway over the entire market.

Source: Quoted from C. Welles, "The War of the Razors," *Esquire*, February 1980, p. 2.

ess is conducted and how the children are treated is "cultural."

It is important for marketers to understand cultural values—the things that people believe or "know"—and the symbols associated with that knowledge. Culture obviously varies from place-to-place around the globe and affects the success of marketing worldwide. When the

Tengelmann Group, West Germany's largest grocery chain, purchased the Great Atlantic and Pacific Tea Company (A&P), operations in America lost $75,000,000 in the next two years. Tengelmann converted many American stores into small, streamlined "box stores" which emphasized private labels, rather than well-known brands, and low prices with "no frills." Although this strategy worked well in West Germany, it did not work in the United States. Americans, for whatever reasons, prefer supermarkets with a full range of products.[3] Box stores work in the German culture but not in the American culture.

Individual products often fail because they challenge cultural beliefs or attitudes. What seems like a normal idea, or even a *great* idea to marketers in one country may be seen as unacceptable or even laughable to citizens of other lands. Campbell's Soup offered their familiar, to us, red-and-white labeled cans of soup in Brazil, but found cultural values there too difficult for this product to overcome. Brazilian housewives apparently felt guilty using the prepared soups that Americans take for granted. They believed that they would not be fulfilling their roles as homemakers if they served their families a soup they could not call their own.[4] Faced with this difficulty, Campbell's withdrew the product. However, Campbell's discovered that Brazilian women felt comfortable using a dehydrated "soup starter," to which they could add their own special ingredients and flare. If soup is marketed in Japan, the marketer must realize that soup is regarded as a breakfast drink rather than a dish served for lunch or dinner.

Cultural differences among countries are obvious to anyone who has seen TV commercials from other lands. What we would think of as too sexy, or private, or explicit, people from another culture might see as cute or of no interest at all. A famous Japanese commercial showing naked youngsters marching around and taking a communal bath concludes with a bubble of gas (?) rising from beneath one of the kids and bursting to the surface of the water. This advertisement, especially the punctuation mark employed, is shocking to many American viewers.

Certain advertising slogans are untranslatable for use in other cultures. The straightforward slogan, "Come alive with Pepsi!" translates to "Come out of the grave with Pepsi!" in Ger-

man. In other languages, the translation reads, "Pepsi brings your ancestors back from the grave."[5]

Subcultures

Cultural differences and language variations can, of course, be found within individual countries. In China, for example, five major and many minor languages are spoken. This makes for serious communication problems. Some countries have two (Canada and Belgium) or more (Switzerland has four) *official* languages. In the U.S.S.R., there are about 130 different spoken languages even though Russian is the official tongue.[6] A similar situation exists in the United States where many language groups can be identified, such as Spanish, which is now spoken by almost 20 percent of the population, and Black English. Differences in cultural values and complicating factors such as language provide marketers with challenges and segmentation possibilities that are rich in potential.

Within the American culture there are, then, many **subcultures.** Even within the majority group (white, English-speaking), there are subcultures: In the Northeastern states, people often eat lamb chops, but in West Texas beef is the staple and lamb chops are hard to find. Subcultures within racial or ethnic groups, such as the Black, Hispanic, or Jewish ethnics, are easiest to identify, but the marketer must recognize the many other subcultural differences to be found in the American culture.

The Cultural Symbols That Sell

The fact remains that mainstream *and* variant values must be considered by marketers. "Uncle Ben," the old porter, has disappeared from boxes of rice and has been replaced in TV commercials by a kindly riverboat captain. Marketers apparently determined, perhaps with some help

---

[3] "Golden Touches Turn to Lead," *Time,* November 30, 1981, p. 66.

[4] "Brazil Campbell's Soup Fails to Make it to the Table," *Business Week,* October 12, 1981, p. 66.

[5] "Oops, How's That Again?," *Time,* March 30, 1981, p. 85.

[6] Cullen Murphy, "Watching the Russians," *Atlantic Monthly,* February 1983, p. 38.

TASTE THE HIGH COUNTRY—SPANISH LANGUAGE PROMOTION TO THE HISPANIC SUBCULTURE

The emergence of the Hispanic American subculture as a substantial market was recognized by Coor's in the late 1970s. At this time Coor's was using an advertising campaign "Taste the High Country" throughout its market area. Management's initial Spanish language promotion translated Coor's "Taste the High Country" advertising theme. This advertising campaign did not appeal to the Hispanic American subculture. What went wrong? Research indicated that Hispanics did not relate to the Rocky Mountain life style. The advertising campaign was changed, and ultimately became "Otra Fria? Otra Coors!" (Another cold one? An-

other Coors!) This campaign, based on a mnemonic device common in the Hispanic community, was found to be on the right track. The gesture implies drinkability and lets Hispanics know that Coors is in tune with part of their life style. The Coors corporate campaign features black-and-white advertisements. A single Hispanic person in each reflects on his personal achievements while visiting the old neighborhood, farm place, etc. While the person in the ad may have achieved personal success, the message is that he has not forgotten his roots and the values that have made him what he is today.

Source: Based on "Yardang Capitalizes on Hispanic Growth, Buying Power," *Ad Week*, March 22, 1982, pp. 12 and 16.

from concerned consumers, that the symbolic value of "Uncle Ben" has been altered by cultural changes. Culture—our system of verbal and nonverbal symbols of the values shared by society—is of great importance in every effective marketing effort. Consumer behavior cannot be analyzed apart from its sociocultural environment.

SOCIAL INSTITUTIONS

In even the most primitive society, organized systems of practices are developed to deal with the recurrent problems and demands life makes on society. To further meet these demands, social institutions are developed. Though some of the institutions may "live" beyond their time of real usefulness, such as Britain's monarchy, for the most part they meet some social need and help solve the daily problems of group life. Each so-

cial institution develops a series of *values, norms, roles, statuses,* and other means to fulfill its central purpose. The family, for example, whose basic goal is to survive daily life, assigns roles or jobs to family members, agrees in some way on when meals will be served, and so on. The same sorts of steps are taken by other social institutions, as illustrated in Exhibit 7-3.

EXHIBIT 7-3

Major Social Institutions

All institutions have arisen over time as people develop social responses to the particular needs of their society. Each institution is a stable cluster of values, norms, statuses, roles, and participating groups, and it provides an established pattern of thought and action that offers a solution to the recurrent problems and demands of social living. This exhibit lists the major institutions of modern society, with examples of each of the elements involved.

Institution	Social Need	Some Values	Some Norms	Some Statuses/Roles	Some Groups
Family	Regulate sexual behavior; provide care for children	Marital fidelity	Have only one spouse	Husband; grandmother	Kinship group
Education	Transmit cultural knowledge to the young	Intellectual curiosity	Attend school	Teacher; student	High school clique; college seminar
Religion	Share and reaffirm community values and solidarity	Belief in God	Attend regular worship	Rabbi; cardinal	Synod; congregation
Science	Investigate social and natural world	Unbiased search for truth	Conduct research	Physicist; anthropologist	Research team; science society
Political system	Distribute power; maintain order	Freedom	Vote by secret ballot	Senator; lobbyist	Legislature; political party
Economic system	Produce and distribute goods and services	Free enterprise	Maximize profits	Accountant; vendor	Corporate board; labor union
Medical system	Take care of the sick	Good health	Save life if possible	Physician; patient	Hospital staff; ward of patients
Military	Aggress or defend against enemies of the state	Discipline	Follow orders	General; marine	Platoon; army division
Legal system	Maintain social control	Fair trial	Inform suspects of their rights	Judge; lawyer	Jury; cell mates
Sport	Recreation, exercise	Winning	Play by the rules	Umpire; coach	Baseball team; fan club

Source: I. Robertson, *Sociology* (New York: Worth Publishing, 1981), p. 84.

Values and Norms

Values are the goals that society views as important. As such, they reflect the moral order of a society or its institutions and give meaning to social life. The two major values of capitalistic economic institutions are to maintain a free economic system and to make a profit. Other institutions may have different values. A religious institution, for instance, might view salvation of the soul as its major goal.

Norms are rules of conduct to be followed in particular circumstances. Behavior appropriate to one situation may be inappropriate to another; norms are "situation specific." They reflect what one ought to do in a given situation. In the United States, the norm is for pedestrians to avoid touching each other. Jostling and crushing together is eschewed in most circumstances, and persons not following this norm are rewarded with angry stares or comments. At a parade, however, crowding and pushing are more acceptable. The norm changes with the situation.

Another example of a norm is the behavior we "expect" of others in elevators—low-speaking voices or silence, facing forward, gazing at the floor indicator. If we were to get on a

Norms vary by culture and reflect what we ought to do.

crowded elevator, face the back, look at people, and speak out loud, fellow passengers would probably stare in disbelief and move away.

Other cultures have different norms. The Japanese attending the new Tokyo Disneyland are far more restrained than Americans attending Disneyland in this country. For example, passengers on the rides in Japan do not raise their hands in the air and scream as do their American counterparts. It is not the accepted norm.

Values and norms strongly affect our day-to-day behavior patterns, life-styles, and consumer behavior. Many products and advertisements cater to the value of staying in good health. The increasingly commonplace norm of not smoking in certain public places influences the planning of service providers such as restaurants and airplanes.

Values and norms do change in our contemporary world and, abetted by better-than-ever communications, changes take place more rapidly than ever. Some examples of recent changes include: the commitment to "Buy American"; development of feelings of community; greater concern about the pollution of our air and water; anti-litter campaigns;[7] and a general agreement to "Save the Whale."

Roles and Status

Roles and status are closely allied concepts. They have been compared to opposite sides of the same coin. The traditional distinction is this: You occupy a status, but you play a role.

---

[7] O.S. Nordberg, "Lifestyle's Monitor," *American Demographics,* May 1981, p. 21.

Any group or social organization, from the smallest to the largest, creates and defines **roles** for its members. These, like norms, are essentially customary ways of doing things. A role, however, is associated with a *position* in a social setting. Roles include definitions of appropriate clusters of behavior patterns in reference to those found in other roles. Thus, the role of a son or daughter includes expected behavior patterns that differ from those expected of someone in a parental role. The role of a wage earner requires behaviors different from those required by the role of a student. The role of president of the company differs from that of a new management trainee.

Like norms, roles help tell us what to do and remind us that expected behavior differs for different roles. The group, by means of norms, values, roles, and so on, strives to organize and routinize its activities so that issues need not be decided over and over again each time they arise.

Roles obviously carry over into the marketing milieu. There are consumer and seller behavior patterns included in these roles. The shopper expects certain rights and obligations with regard to the store employee. The store employee in an expensive fur salon is expected to behave differently than a check-out clerk at K-Mart. In cases such as these, the individual fulfilling a role, be it K-Mart employee or fur salon manager, occupies a social position. The term **status,** though it may conjure up some unpleasant connotations, refers simply to the socially defined positions that an individual may hold. Age, sex, occupation, as well as social standing in the community or wealth, all are determinants of status. These matters of status affect the behavior of a consumer in many ways: We deal more informally with supermarket check-out clerks than with our psychiatrist's receptionist. Males are less likely to buy and wear two earrings than are females. Students may dress in jeans and sweatshirts to demonstrate their status as students. However, students of business administration may dress more formally or carry an attaché case to show their status as business students.

The term *status* itself is actually very neutral. It is the association with "higher" or "lower" status within a group or community that gives status its positive or negative connotation. That is a matter of prestige. **Prestige** is the assignment of value judgments about a status or a role. As such, it is one of the bases for social class.

In the service sector, the bank president and the bank teller play different roles and have different status. That one is higher than the other in our estimation is a matter of prestige. How much prestige is to be found in a role depends on who is doing the judging. Society grants more prestige to the president of a TV network than to the owner of a chain of gas stations. In the eyes of the high school student working at a station part-time, however, the gas station magnate has a great deal of prestige. In a marketing organization, prestige plays a major part in dealings between the regional manager and the local salesperson, and between the salesperson and the biggest customer in the territory. In short, the concepts of role, status, and prestige define the customary patterns for behaviors in marketing and other endeavors.

SOCIAL CLASS

A **social class** is a group of people with similar levels of prestige, power, and wealth who also share a set of related beliefs, attitudes, and values in their thinking and behavior.[8]

Exhibit 7-4, which summarizes one view of American social classes, shows five discrete groups. Class structure is actually more like an escalator since it runs from bottom to top without any major plateaus. The usefulness of social class to marketers has been demonstrated in

[8]G. Zaltman and M. Wallendorf, *Consumer Behavior: Basic Findings and Management Implications* (New York: John Wiley & Sons, 1979), p. 84.

Are there social classes in America?

thousands of situations. To get a feel for the influence of class on consumer behavior, answer the following questions:

■ Who shops at Neiman-Marcus, Brooks Brothers, and I. Magnin?

■ Who shops at K-Mart and Woolco?

■ Who buys Gucci loafers?

■ Who buys shoes at Discount Shoe City?

■ Who plays cribbage and goes to the opera?

■ Who goes bowling and watches wrestling on TV?

■ Who flies first-class from New York to San Diego?

■ Who rides the Greyhound bus from New York to San Diego?

Social class explains many differences in behavior patterns and life styles. Social class, as our questions illustrated, may have a major impact on shopping patterns or products purchased. An advertisement for Lucchese boots,

EXHIBIT 7-4

The American Class System in the Twentieth Century—An Estimate

Class (and percentage of population)	Income	Property	Occupation	Education	Personal and Family Life	Education of Children
Upper class (1–3%)	Very high income	Great wealth, old wealth	Corporate heads, high civil and military officials	Liberal arts education at elite schools	Stable family life, autonomous personality	College education by right for both sexes
Upper-middle class (10–15%)	High income	Accumulation of property through savings	Managers, professionals, high-level executives	Graduate training	Better physical and mental health	Educational system biased in their favor—reflects upper-middle class values
Lower-middle class (30–35%)	Modest income	Some savings	Small business people and farmers, semi-professionals, sales and clerical workers	Some college, high school	Longer life expectancy	Greater chance of college than working-class children
Working class (40–45%)	Low income	Some savings	Skilled labor, unskilled labor	Some high school, grade school	Unstable family life, conformist personality	Educational system biased against them, tendency toward vocational programs
Lower class (20–25%)	Poverty income	No savings	Highest unemployment	Illiteracy	Poorer physical and mental health, lower life expectancy	Little interest in education, high dropout rates

Source: Table used with permission from I. Robertson, *Sociology* (New York: Worth, 1981), p. 261.

which are exquisitely tooled from the finest leathers, states the boots are "available only at finer stores." This simple phrase may stop some readers from further consideration of these boots. Why? One of the classic studies in consumer behavior explains that the lower-status woman knows that if she goes into a high-status department store, the clerks will punish her in various subtle ways, making it clear that she does not "belong."[9] Members of different social classes know which stores and products are for people of their social class.

Social class often has an indirect impact on consumer behavior. For example the majority of people prefer to live in neighborhoods made up of people from their own class.[10] Thus, small membership groups which may directly influence purchases have been touched by the influence of social class.

In the upper-middle class, the *nouveaux*

[9] P. Martineau, "Social Class and Spending Behavior," *Journal of Marketing*, October 1958, pp. 121–130.

[10] "Social Class is a Major Source of Group Identity for Most Americans," *Institute for Social Research Newsletter*, Autumn 1982, pp. 4–5.

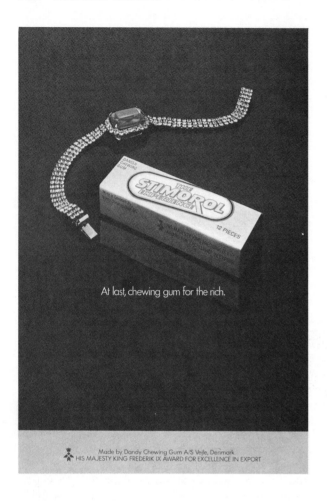

At last, chewing gum for the rich.

Made by Dandy Chewing Gum A/S Vejle, Denmark
HIS MAJESTY KING FREDERIK IX AWARD FOR EXCELLENCE IN EXPORT

riches are most likely to purchase furs or yachts because they are expressions of achievement. The expensive car, the bigger house, private college for the kids, and a summer home, boat, and frequent vacations are all symbolic expressions of success. This kind of behavior was well-described by American economist Thornstein Veblen, who coined the term "conspicuous consumption." Veblen meant to satirize and criticize persons who obtain products simply to *visibly* consume or openly display them, but he did hit on a fact of human nature. Consumption of certain items is a means to express one's social class status. Even if we snicker with Veblen at this behavior, the desire to express one's feelings (or show off) may be real and quite important to an individual who desires or has achieved social mobility. Marketers should not ignore this.

Packaged in a slim silver package Stimorol's price is 79 cents per pack. It is advertised as a chewing gum for the rich. This product, which met with approval of less than half the tasters in a taste test, has become the "in" gum of those who wish to show their affluence.[11] Stimorol provides an excellent example of the conspicuous consumption phenomenon.

Conspicuous consumption?

GROUPS

Each individual belongs to many groups, but all of them can be divided into one of two major categories. The first category is the intimate or small **primary group,** such as family or close friends where face-to-face contact endures over time. The second category consists of larger, more impersonal groups called **secondary groups.**

Behaviors, especially consumer behaviors, are influenced by the individual's interactions with both types of groups. Intimate primary

groups have influences that may persist for years after the group has been separated by geography or even death. For example, children tend to have the same political party and religious affiliations as their parents, as well as the same attitudes toward contributing to charities, and the same perceptions of stores (Bloomingdale's is "classy," Sears is for "regular people").

Larger secondary groups also have strong and lasting influences. Many students at a particular college, or many members of a social fraternity, may dress similarly to one another because of group behavior. Certain brands of products, such as cigarettes or toothpaste, are overwhelm-

---

[11]C. Endicott, "The Best Things in LIfe Are Not Free, Dear," *Advertising Age,* April 4, 1983, p. m–12.

ing favorites among certain ethnic groups even though the majority of the population does not favor them. Northerners may, on moving to the Sunbelt states of Dixie, develop a taste for regional food favorites and the expression "You all." The influence of groups large and small is obvious and undeniable.

Reference Groups

A reference group is used as a point of comparison to evaluate individual situations.[12] The expression **reference group** identifies groups that have an influence on an individual because that individual, whether willing to admit it or not, aspires to be a member of that group. Thus, a little brother may try to act like a big brother and his buddies, or a little sister may try to act like a big sister's teenage friends. An advertising campaign ("My big brother says . . .") for Sears' Winners basketball shoes was based on the knowledge that inner-city kids looked up to their big brothers more than to professional basketball stars. The influential people were in their own reference group.

Membership Groups. There are several sorts of reference groups or groups used as points of comparison by which individuals evaluate their situations.[13] One kind is the **membership group**—that is, a group of which the individual is actually a part. Examples might be fraternity brothers, fellow club members, members of the freshman class, or alumni of UCLA. Such groups strongly influence the consumer-group member's behavior by exerting pressure to conform, or *peer pressure.* In a **voluntary membership group,** such as college peers or a political party, the individual is free to join or withdraw from the group. Sometimes, the individual has little or no choice as to the selection of membership groups. People approaching middle-age may not like that fact, but they nevertheless make

[12]J.D. Thompson and D.R. Van Houten, *The Behavioral Sciences: An Interpretation* (Reading: Addison-Wesley Publishing, 1970), p. 53.

[13]H.H. Hyman, "The Psychology of Status," *Archives of Psychology,* Volume 38 (1942), p. 15.

changes in their lives as a result of the influence of their middle-aged peers. A Native American youth is unlikely to state that the invasion of whites into North America was a wonderful happening if only because peer pressure from other Native Americans would prohibit such comments. Yet the Native American had little choice in the matter of race and the middle-aged person did not choose the time he or she was born.

Aspirational Groups. The second major type of reference group is the **aspirational group.** Individuals may try to behave or look like the people whose group they *hope* to join. The young business manager may choose to "dress for success." This usually means dressing like the women and men the manager hopes to join one day in the organization's higher ranks. We may imitate groups to which we aspire. A negative aspirational group is one that we do not wish to be associated with.

Reference Groups Influence Some Products More Than Others. There are certain products whose use is subject to almost no group pressure. While clothing, cars, cigarettes, and beer consumed publicly are strongly subject to reference group pressure—"Are you man enough to smoke a Virginia Slim?"; "Are you brave enough to order a 'generic beer'?"—other products are so mundane or so lacking in consumption visibility that no one uses them to express their self-concept. The risks of using the "wrong" brand in private are small. One rarely hears comments about someone's eating Libby's canned peaches instead of Del Monte's. Similarly, some product categories can be subject to reference group influences without regard to brand name or design—"Why don't you break down and get an air conditioner, Harry?"; "You mean you use *instant* coffee? No, *thank* you." Reference groups may influence the types of products consumed, the brand purchased, or both.

Group or Opinion Leaders. It should be noted that groups frequently include individuals known as group leaders or **opinion leaders.**

Group leaders might be friends who are looked up to because of their intelligence, athletic abilities, appearance, or special abilities such as skill in cooking, mechanics, or languages. In any group, the role of opinion leader moves between and among several people, depending on the product involved. If someone is planning to buy a car, that person may seek the opinion or leadership of a friend or family member who is thought to know about cars. The same person might seek a different "expert" when he or she is buying stereo equipment, or good wines, or investment plans.

In certain situations, the most powerful determinant of buying behavior is the attitudes of those people the individual respects. Thus, word-of-mouth recommendations may be an important buying influence. One reason that marketers try to satisfy their customers is their hope for the customer's favorable recommendations about a product or organization to members of his or her social group. The "best" thing a homeowner can hear when hiring a house-painter is that the painter did a neighbor's or friend's house and that the former customer was satisfied with the job. Similarly, when choosing a bank, consumers like to hear that the bank they are considering has a "great reputation."

FAMILY

The family is an important social institution. Consequently, an individual's family is an important reference group. The family is characterized by frequent face-to-face interaction among family members who respond to each other on the basis of their total personalities rather than on the basis of a particular role. It is not surprising that values, self-concepts, and the products we buy are influenced by our family.

The family is responsible for the consumer **socialization process**—that is, passing down the cultural values and norms of the society or group to the children.

Children observe how their parents evaluate and select products in stores. They see how the exchange process takes place at the cash register, and quickly learn that money or a credit card changes hands there. That is how children learn the buying role. When children receive money as gifts or allowances, and are permitted to spend it, they act out the buying role, thus learning an activity they will perform throughout their lives. Members of the family in which we were raised may continue to be a strong influence throughout our lives. Parents may help with the down payment on the newlywed's first house or supply advice on how to raise their grandchildren.

The Changing American Family

A marketer of trash compactors, novel telephone apparatus, or home computers might concentrate efforts on households or families rather than on individual consumers. To these marketers, knowing the composition of households is important.

What is the typical American household like? Father, mother, and two children? Wrong! Only one-quarter of all "families" fit this traditional image. As Exhibit 7-5 shows, single-parent households and households composed of unmarried individuals under the age of 35 have proliferated in the last two decades. The number of such households increased by three times as much as the population. The average household declined in membership from 3.1 persons per household in 1970 to 2.7 in 1981.[14] There has been a tendency among baby boomers to postpone having a first child until age 30 or later, and to have fewer children. This is good news for makers of refrigerators and stoves, but not so good for sellers of toys and children's clothing.

---

[14] D.L. Kaplan and C. Russell, "What the 1980 Census Will Show," *American Demographics*, April 1980, p. 14.

EXHIBIT 7-5

**Composition of Households
by Type of Household: 1950 to 1990**

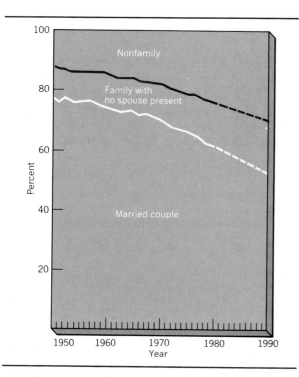

These trends promise to continue. The percentage of U.S. population living alone is growing. A larger number of people than ever before are never-have-been-marrieds, and young singles are remaining single longer than ever. There are growing numbers of divorces. The longer life expectancy of women over men means that widows constitute a sizable population segment.

Working Women

The advent of the modern career-oriented woman is, of itself, a major change in the American family. The increasing number of career-oriented working women affects the age at which women have children, whether they have children at all, and even whether they choose to live as single parents.

The number of people in the work force *has* grown rapidly. Exhibit 7-6 illustrates the anticipated growth in the work force, from 103 million people in 1979 to an anticipated 130 million in 1995. As shown in Exhibit 7-7, more than two-thirds of this growth will be due to the large influx of women entering the work force. Slightly more than 50 percent of American households currently include husbands and wives who both work. This is up from about 40 percent in 1960. Forecasters predict that by 1990, the "traditional" husband-wife household with only

Many working women choose to live as single parents.

EXHIBIT 7-6

The Growing Work Force

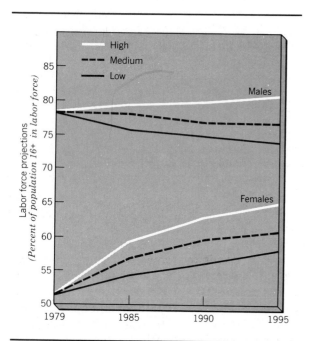

EXHIBIT 7-7

Labor Force Participation Rates for Persons by Sex: 1950 to 1990

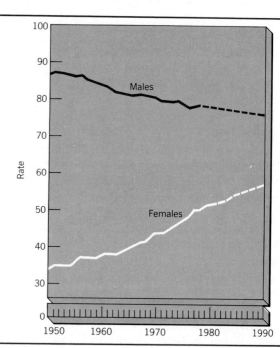

The labor force will grow from 103 million workers in 1979 to at least 122 million people in 1995 if growth is slow, or as many as 135 million if growth is rapid, according to the latest Bureau of Labor Statistics projections. Women, who will account for more than two-thirds of the growth, will represent 47 percent of the labor force by 1995, up from 42 percent today. In the high projection, the number of women in the labor force climbs to 64 million by 1995, up from 43 million in 1979.

Source: *American Demographics*, Vol. 3, No. 6, June 1981, p. 9.

one partner employed outside the home will account for only 14 percent of all such households.[15]

Obvious changes in the marketplace reflect these developments: Many stores are open weekends to permit shopping by working people, and it is the rare store that is not open late at least one or two nights per week. Easily prepared frozen dinners are increasingly commonplace. Take-out food, whether from a restaurant or from the prepared foods section of a supermarket, has gained great popularity. Soap operas, which were traditional afternoon TV fare, are now shown during nighttime TV viewing hours in the form of serials such as *Dallas, Falcon Crest,* and *Dynasty.*

For some marketers, such as convenience food manufacturers like Stouffer and Green Giant, these changes present great opportunities to meet and satisfy the needs of the two-career family. However, there are still traditional families whose needs must also be met. Reaching all kinds of customers offers a special challenge to marketers. Effective marketers can come up with the answers for all sorts of demographic groups, however, by adjusting the elements of their marketing mixes to meet the specific requirements of particular market segments. For example, makers of home care products, such as cleansers, effectively market their products to different demographic groups by advertising on both evening radio and TV programs *and* on afternoon soaps.

Joint Decison-Making

Some matters of consumer choice and behavior are not decided by individuals but by groups ranging in size from two on up. Families may, for example, choose a car or house together. This is referred to as **joint decision-making.** Or parents may sit down together to talk over insurance purchases, furniture purchases, or retirement plans. Despite this image of togetherness, most purchases are dominated by one group member. In the case of the family group, the parents domi-

---

PURCHASE BEHAVIOR MAY BE THE RESULT OF JOINT DECISION-MAKING

Third Grader
Come on, I want a T.V. for my own room. Come on. Please. Daddy, come on. Buy me a television. I want one for my room. Come on. Come on, Daddy. I want you to.

Seventh Grader
Oh Father—er, wait a minute—oh, Dad. I just was down shopping and I saw this most lovely, most beautiful TV I ever saw and it's a portable too. And I was wondering—it didn't cost very much, and you could put it on your charge account down there, and I was just wondering if you could kinda buy it for me, for my birthday or Christmas present to have in my own room. Ah—I'm sure that you'd like it, and well, if you want it, you buy one for your room too. They're kinda cheap. I mean, well, what you can get out of a TV, they're pretty nice, and oh, it'd just match all the furniture in my room. And I promise I wouldn't let any of my friends come in and watch it, or any of my sisters and brothers to wreck it.

Source: Used with permission, K.S. Berger, *The Developing Person* (New York: Worth, 1980), p. 434.

---

nate rather than the grade school kids. Older children may have greater influence—as when the teenage son, who "knows all about cars," advises his parents' selection of a new auto.

The **dominant role** in group decision-making is commonly taken by a particular group member when particular purchases are the topic of discussion. Stereotypes aside, in family groups, for example, the husband usually dominates decisions relating to purchases of insurance, while decisions regarding clothing for the children, food purchases, and furniture are most often wife-dominated.[16] This reflects our soci-

---

[15] "Study Indicates Dramatic Change Ahead for Families," *Tulsa Tribune,* May 29, 1980, p. 30.

[16] H.L. Davis and B.P. Rigaux, "Perception of Marital Roles in Decision Processes," *Journal of Consumer Research,* June 1974.

ety's norms and traditions. **Syncretic decisions,** those truly made by husband *and* wife together, are common when entertainment, housing, and vacation choices are being made. The comparative importance of individual family members have their parallels in non-family groups.

The locus of decision-making authority thus shifts with the issue of the purchase being addressed. This important fact is widely employed by marketers. For years insurance advertisements appeared mainly in publications such as *Business Week* and *Fortune* that (back then) were thought to appeal mainly to men. Marketers, then and now, seek out the *major* influences on purchases and direct most of their appeals to them.

Some investment and insurance advertisements now note that both husband *and* wife need to know about and to buy insurance, and seem to suggest that perhaps each spouse may want to choose his or her own plan. Changes taking place in our society are making the process of identifying the major "decision-influencer" more difficult.

THE THREE ROLES IN THE DECISION

To simplify the discussion in this chapter, the distinctions among the consumer's roles during the buying effort have not been mentioned. However, there are three roles to be played in any decision to buy, even if the product to be selected is commonly purchased, unexciting, and seemingly undebatable. These roles are: (1) the **buyer** who, narrowly defined, is the person who goes to the store and actually purchases the product; (2) the **consumer** who, narrowly viewed, is the person who actually uses the product; (3) the **decision maker** who decides which product or brand of product to buy. Think about it for a while. Each role could be played by different people, or by the same people, or by any combination of people.

The purchase of baby food is the classic example of different people playing each role. The baby *eats* the food, but is denied any comment on it. The *buyer* could be an older child sent to the store by Mom. Mom is the *decision-maker* who, by means of research, the influence of advertisements and news stories, or her own mother's suggestions, determined which brand of baby food to buy. The purchase of gum or cigarettes, however, may involve only one person performing all three roles.

When one person is involved, the job of marketing is more concentrated than when three people are involved. In the baby food example, who should the marketer attempt to reach? The decision-maker, who is the person with the real "say" in the matter, should be the target. Thus, baby food advertisements appear in publications read by mothers as well as on TV and radio programs that reach mothers. They stress information mothers care about, such as the foods' nutritional content. These are matters which

Parents may be the gatekeepers for the products children consume.

neither the baby nor the older sibling sent to the store really care about.

In the baby food example, the mother was the decision-maker, not the consumer. A similar role is widely found in organizational purchasing situations. A purchasing agent may buy, but not use, many items, and a committee may choose,

but not have to sell, the items stocked in a department store. This role is called the **gatekeeper function.** Decisions are made, and then the "gate" is opened or closed by someone having very little else to do with the process but to whom marketers must direct much of their efforts.

SUMMARY

The study of consumer behavior involves both the analysis of psychological factors affecting consumer decision-making and the analysis of environmental forces impinging on consumer behavior. This chapter discussed the sociological factors that influence consumer buying behavior.

Although the term *culture* has been defined in many ways, of central importance to marketers is the fact that culture is a mass of knowledge acquired by and shared with members of a group. It should be recognized that language and symbols are important aspects of culture. *Values* are a set of acts, customs, or goals that are deemed valuable and desirable by a society. *Norms* are rules or standards of conduct that reflect a society's perception of appropriate behavior. A *role* defines expected behavior within a social organization, while *status* refers to the socially defined positions that an individual may have. Judgments about role and status are the bases for social ranking and prestige. Marketers

should be cognizant of the changing nature of specific cultures and their roles, values, and norms.

Marketers should also know that consumer buying behavior is influenced by an individual's many reference groups. The groups that must be considered are membership groups, such as the family, and aspirational groups. Many purchases are the result of joint decision making. During the decision making process consumers may be classified into three roles: *buyer, consumer, decision maker.*

> THE MOST IMPORTANT CONCEPT IN THIS CHAPTER
> **Groups,** ranging in size from families to racial groups and age cohorts, are strong influences on the behavior of individuals. Thus, an effective marketer studies not only the individual buyer but the many groups to which the individual belongs or with which the individual identifies.

KEY TERMS

Consumer behavior
Sociology
Culture
Subculture
Values
Norms
Roles

Status
Prestige
Social class
Primary group
Secondary group
Reference group
Membership group

Voluntary membership group
Aspirational group
Opinion leaders
Socialization process
Joint decision-making
Dominant role

Buyer
Consumer
Decision maker
Syncretic decisions
Gatekeeper function

QUESTIONS FOR DISCUSSION

1 What is the subject matter of consumer behavior?

2 What is culture?

3 Have you ever been influenced by your culture in a buying situation? How did you recognize this influence?

4 How might the marketers of McDonald's be influenced by cultural forces in U.S. marketing? In international marketing?

5 Is a reference group likely to influence the purchase of the following brands or products:
(a) Laundry soap
(b) Hair shampoo
(c) Polo sports shirt
(d) Wrist watch
(e) Athletic club membership
(f) Milk

6 How likely is it that the following people will purchase a ticket to the ballet, a professional baseball game, and/or Disneyland:

(a) 34-year-old steel worker who graduated from high school
(b) 44-year-old college professor
(c) 21-year-old executive secretary
(d) 21-year-old counter helper at Burger King

7 Is social class useful in market segmentation?

8 How much joint decision-making would you expect for the following products?
(a) Life insurance
(b) Steam iron
(c) Trip to Europe
(d) Box of candy

9 What do *you* predict will be the nature of families in the year 2000?

10 Häagen-Daz is a rich ice cream shop located in upscale neighborhoods. The company advertises that their ice cream is "incredibly rich, outrageously delicious, and ridiculously expensive." They urge people to taste it so they'll know why. What social forces influence the trend toward ice creams such as Häagen-Daz?

CASE 7-1 IBM: International Business Machine

A TV advertisement for IBM personal computers is shown opposite. Study the storyboard and then answer the following questions.

Questions
1 Based on an evaluation of the script of this advertisement, what social forces influence the decision to purchase a computer?

2 What role does culture play in the decision? Reference groups?

CASE 7-2 Artesia*

Spurs janglin', boot heels clompin', the steely-eyed Texan bellies up to the bar, an' thumps the counter for—whiskey?
　　Nope.
　　Lone Star beer?
　　Nope.
　　Sparkling water.

Yep. At least, that's the way Rick Scoville has it figured—for Texas and the Southwest.
　　Scoville, of Bellaire, Texas, near Houston, is a former glue salesman who got his idea for

*Source: As quoted in Ron Wolfe, "Taking a Shot at Perrier," *Tulsa Tribune*, January 21, 1982, p. 10b.

(SFX: COWS, MUSIC UNDER)

SISTER 1: Look how dad's dressed. Snazzy.

SISTER 2: The cows won't recognize him.

DAD: I'm going to talk to IBM about a computer, for our farm.

SISTER 1: IBM?

SISTER 2: A computer?
DAD: It's a special demonstration. I'm invited. I'm going. OK?
SISTERS: OK.

ANNCR: (VO) As innovation brings down the cost of computers, more and more small businesses

have an opportunity to put this technology to work for them.

MAN: Where you headed, Jeff?

DAD: A meeting with IBM.

MAN: Well, excuse me!

ANNCR: (VO) And if you've never worked with computers before, we'll teach you the basics.

Soon you'll actually be able to demonstrate it to yourself.

DAD: I think I've got it...

This can help cut my costs.

SALESMAN: Easier than you thought, Jeff?

DAD: My cows are about to enter the computer age.
SALESMAN: You think they're ready?

DAD: They'll be tickled pink.

ANNCR: (VO) Computers for people who never thought they could afford them, but can.

Texas-style bubbling water while sitting around office lobbies here and there, waiting to sell glue.

He wasn't a big bubbling water drinker at the time. "As a matter of fact, I couldn't stand the stuff."

But the idea kept floating. "It occurred to me that everytime somebody bought a bottle of Perrier, that was more money going overseas. We have good water in America. I wondered why somebody didn't take a legitimate shot at Perrier," he said.

Scoville started out selling his Artesia bubbling water from a travel van "like a medicine man," he said. He got the hoo-rah time and again as he pumped for the idea that folks would rather have Texas Hill Country water than the elite French Perrier.

"Basically, nobody would listen to me, and I had to do the manufacturing, and the selling and delivering for myself," he said.

But he stayed in the saddle, bought what used to be a soda pop factory in San Antonio, and herded Artesia into the markets.

"Our first year in business (last year), we did a million dollars in sales," the red-bearded Scoville said.

"And, Pardner," he smiles when he says that "Perrier is still the top gun," but Scoville claims to have rustled away a third of the French water's sales in Texas.

"I was a gnat on the elephant's back. And before they knew it, I was an armadillo," he said.

Now, Artesia—the "Pure Texas Spirit" water from under the near-San Antonio area—is out to rope Oklahoma, Arkansas, New Mexico, and Louisiana.

"We're chic," Scoville said, branding Artesia the "perfect mixer" with everything from gin to orange juice. "But we're not so chic that a guy in Duke's is going to feel out of place to pick up one of our bottles."

Artesia comes bottled in brown glass, like a good cowboy beer, as opposed to Perrier's "foo-foo" green, as Scoville describes it.

And the carbonation level, like the price, is lower than the French bubbly, he said. "We allow you to taste the water and not the explosion."

Scoville discounts snobbish East Coast

ARTESIA—The Sparkling Mineral Water With Star-Spangled Spirit.

The alternative is downright UN-AMERICAN!

taste tests. The one he quotes—conducted in Big D Dallas—showed Artesia the favorite of 17 out of 47 gulpers, with even Dallas tap water ("Eau de Tap") preferred to imported French water.

"We're probably the most continental, chic nation in the world," he said. *"But people don't realize it."*

Water, barkeep. An' make it a straight.

Questions

1 What reasons might consumers give for buying Artesia? Are they likely to be the same for Perrier?

2 Use your knowledge of consumer behavior to explain the success of bottled water in the United States.

CHAPTER 8

Psychological Influences in Consumer Behavior

CHAPTER SCAN

This chapter discusses the psychological and situational factors that influence the consumer decision-making process.

Knowing how consumers react to stimuli is fundamental to an understanding of the individual buyer and the consumer decision-making process. The steps through which the consumer moves are, to a degree, hidden from view, as if within a "black box."

This chapter discusses the various explanations of what is inside this black box by exploring topics such as motivation, learning, perception, and attitude formation and change. It also investigates the five stages in a typical decision-making process—problem recognition, search, evaluation, purchase decision, and post-purchase evaluation.

WHEN YOU HAVE STUDIED THIS CHAPTER, YOU WILL:

Be able to show that buyer behavior is, in fact, a response to stimuli.

Be able to explain why much of the buyer decision-making process is described as being hidden in a "black box."

Be familiar with Maslow's needs hierarchy and with the importance of both rational and emotional motives.

Be able to discuss how self-concept and personality affect purchase behavior.

Have an understanding of learning models and the evoked set concept.

Know how and why perceptions differ among individuals, and be familiar with selective perception.

Be able to describe the three components of an attitude—affective, cognitive, and behavioral.

Be able to describe the five step "decision-making process," and tell why the outcome may be dissatisfaction as well as satisfaction.

Understand the importance of the phenomenon known as cognitive dissonance to marketing success.

Although many marketers may not have studied consumer psychology in a formal way, they must, and generally do, think about the buying process as they go about the task of managing effective marketing efforts. When marketers talk about "human nature" or their experience in "dealing with people" they are really discussing consumer behavior. Successful marketers, knowingly or not, have their own explanation of some buyer behavior, attitudes, learning, perception, and the other topics treated in this chapter.

In many cases, their intuitive feelings are consistent with consumer researchers' scientific findings, but many of their explanations of why people buy are dead wrong! While Chapter 7 focused on the social influences governing consumer behavior, this chapter investigates the personal factors that affect that behavior.

CONSUMER BEHAVIOR: THE STIMULUS–RESPONSE CONCEPT

This chapter investigates the personal factors that affect consumer behavior. Human behavior as a whole is a function of the interaction of a person with his or her environment. However, behavior is frequently triggered by some particular aspect or event within the environment rather than by the environment collectively.

Consumers act or respond psychologically to an event, object, or person that *acts* upon them in some way and causes a *re*action in a subsequent time period. Such an influence is called a *stimulus* or *cue.* If a shopper notices that a set of glassware decorated with Christmas trees is marked down 50 percent during the week before the holiday and subsequently considers buying the glasses, the shopper has been *stimulated* to take action. Should the act of considering the purchase actually lead to a purchase, so much the better for the retailer. In short, a **stimulus** is an aspect of the environment that triggers a behavioral response in a subsequent time period. In the glassware example, the sale information was received by the customer when he or she saw the sign announcing the price cut. The consideration given to the purchase, induced by the cue, is called the **response.** Another subsequent, more observable response is the actual purchase of the glasses.

Response follows cue. Human actions are almost always responses to cues. In the college classroom, for example, the closing of books, clicking of pens, and shuffling of feet are responses to the cue of the bell rung to signal the end of the hour. Rapid walking between classroom buildings may be brought on by a cue such as a clock showing two minutes until the start of the next class. A trip to the student union for a hamburger could be in response to the smell of food, the knowledge that it's lunchtime, or a growling stomach. All are cues (stimuli) which can bring about responses.

Internal tension from aroused needs increases attention to external stimuli.

Not all stimuli are as powerful or clear as the school bell or as basic as the growling tummy. In marketing, stimuli such as packaging, wording of a promotional message, or a friend's opinion about a product are rarely so obvious to those responding to them. However, subtle or obvious, the psychological explanation of human behavior is that the stimulus (S) operates on the consumer to produce a response (R). In more computer-oriented phrasing, the stimulus is the **input** and the response is the **output**.

The "Black Box" Concept

The simple stimulus–response concept does not totally describe the psychological and biological processes that contribute to a consumer's decision-making activities. Marketers cannot directly observe what is occurring "inside" the consumer. For this reason, the individual psychological process of the consumer is frequently represented as a **black box**. This name derives from a testing procedure used to examine electronics students. The students are given information

---

THE NOTION OF THE BLACK BOX AS SEEN BY THE GREAT THINKERS

If we asked some of the great thinkers "Why do people buy?" they might translate their grand theories into models of consumer behavior. In a creative and innovative article, Philip Kotler answered these questions about the black box for Alfred Marshall, Ivan Pavlov, Sigmund Freud, Thorstein Veblen, and Thomas Hobbes.

Marshallian Economic Model: Alfred Marshall, English Economist (1842–1924)

The economic man attempts to maximize his utility by rationally calculating the consequences of any purchase. While never addressing the question of how product preferences are formed, the economic explanation does indicate that buying behavior responds to logical norms, emphasizing that relative to prices and individual tastes, income is spent on goods that will produce the greatest "satisfaction."

Pavlovian Learning Model: Ivan Pavlov, Russian Physiologist (1849–1936)

The Pavlovian stimulus–response explanation is that human behavior is largely a learned, associative process. Containing four central concepts—drive, cue, response, and reinforcement—learning theory provides marketers knowledge to analyze and develop brand habit, and in using advertising cues that stimulate and arouse strong drives.

Freudian Psychoanalytic Model: Sigmund Freud, Austrian Physician (1856–1939)

The psychoanalytic model of human behavior stresses the importance of man's attempts to channel and express his basic instinctual drives and wages in socially acceptable modes. The human psyche (composed of the id, ego, and superego) must constantly balance the gratification of impulsive needs with demands for adherence to social norms. The

model's emphasis is on symbolic and unconscious motivations.

Veblenian Social-Psychological Model: Thorstein Veblen, American Economist (1857–1929)

Veblen saw man as being predominantly a social animal, his buying behavior strongly influenced by his membership in groups. In his work, *The Theory of the Leisure Class,* Veblen proposed that prestige-seeking, rather than need satisfaction, was the cause of much human buying behavior. Marketers must be acutely aware of social influences on individual tastes and preferences.

Hobbesian Organizational-Factors Model: Thomas Hobbes, English Philosopher (1588–1679)

The Hobbesian explanation focuses on the corporate man, and his attempts to satisfy both personal and organizational needs and goals.

Source: Adapted from P. Kotler, "Behavior Models for Analyzing Buyers," *Journal of Marketing,* October 1965, pp. 37–45.

EXHIBIT 8-1

The Black Box Problem in Marketing

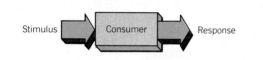

concerning the energies going *into* and *out of* the black box. They must then decide, using this information, what processes are at work *inside* the box.[1] Similarly, as Exhibit 8-1 shows, the individual consumer's psychological processes can be represented as a black box.

Even though the use of the black box idea to describe what goes on "inside" the consumer is not a particularly satisfying way of describing behavior, it remains a legitimate part of the study of consumer behavior. Consumer behavior theorists have presented elaborate models describing how various influences affect consumer behav-

iors and choices. All of these models include some form of black box even though it may be called by a different name.[2] Neither marketers nor anyone else can describe exactly what goes on inside the persons being studied. The element of surprise and mystery in human behavior remains whether it is called free will or human nature.

This does not mean that marketers are unable to predict likely consumer responses to stimuli. Marketers can draw inferences from the response side of the model in Exhibit 8-1. They can analyze consumer statements or behaviors and can study the environment in which these occurred for clues to possible future behaviors. Like detectives, they examine the evidence. Marketing activities would be more effective if marketing managers could peer into the black box, but, since they cannot, the input (stimulus) and the output (response) will have to serve as their sources of information. Many of the widely accepted inferences and theoretical concepts intended to explain consumer behavior are the subject for the remainder of this chapter.

PSYCHOLOGICAL THEORY AND CONSUMER NEEDS

Up to this point the word "need" has been used as a layperson would, rather than as someone closely associated with the field of consumer behavior might. Through everyday conversation, we all have a basic understanding of such terms as "needs," "wants," "desires," and "motives." Now, however, we are going to investigate these

concepts more deeply, from the *formal* perspective of psychological theory. It is important that no misconceptions are brought about by an inadequate or unscientific definition of terms. Critics of marketing who, for example, accuse advertisers of "creating needs" are not using a scientific vocabulary.

MOTIVATION

The term **motivation** refers to a consumer's psychological internal drive—it is the state which causes consumers to initiate behavior. Motivation directs behavior and keeps goal-directed behavior alive. Technically, a **need** is not a motive until it is aroused or stimulated. A need is an

innate desire, basic to human beings. Hunger or a desire to have friends are *needs*. But these needs are not always "activated." That is, they are always within the individual but do not al-

---

[1] R.P. Cuzzort, *Humanity and Modern Sociological Thought* (New York: Holt, Rinehart and Winston, 1969), p. 27.

[2] See for example: J.A. Howard and J.N. Sheth, *The Theory of Buyer Behavior* (New York: John Wiley & Sons, 1969), or J. Engel, D.T. Koflat, and R.D. Blackwell, *Consumer Behavior* (New York: Holt, Rinehart and Winston, 1968).

EXHIBIT 8-2

Simple Model of Motivated Behavior

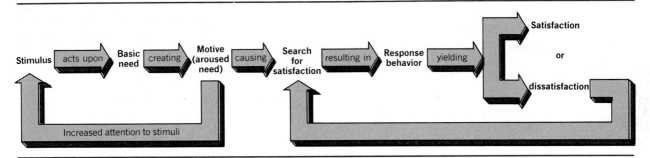

Source: Based on Henry L. Tosi and Stephen J. Carrol, *Management* (New York: John Wiley & Sons, 1982), p. 388.

ways cause the person to act. When, by whatever means, the need is "activated," it becomes a motive. Thus, we all need to eat, but hunger and the availability of food stimulates that basic need, which is always with us. Our **motive** to eat is a *stimulated need.*

What is it, then, that *arouses* motives? What gets us going? In general, it is either an external cue or internal force. For example, when we are hungry, our body's internal, biological mechanisms (grumbling stomach, empty feeling) arouse behaviors aimed at satisfying that hunger. Psychologists point out that individuals in such a situation are in a state of *tension.* Tension will be relieved when the appropriate steps are taken. The hungry person's motive is to alleviate the hunger. This motive is not fulfilled, however, without the person going through each step shown in Exhibit 8-2, which indicates the relationship between need arousal brought about by a stimulus and the ultimate response.

The unfulfilled motive, then, serves as an internal stimulus or **drive** that energizes behavior; the motivated person will take steps to satisfy the unfulfilled motive. This may be accomplished by reaching for a candy bar on the desk, a stroll to the refrigerator, or an automobile trip to a store or restaurant. However, the possibility exists that the stimulus which brought about all this action was *external* to the individual. A Long John Silver radio commercial, for example, may have aroused hunger motives or tensions that the

consumer acted on. The commercial may have had an effect unintended by the firm paying for it, such as leading people to the refrigerator or to a competitor like McDonald's or Pizza Hut. Before the consumer stopped at Pizza Hut, the stimulus may have made him or her more aware of a desire for food and thus more attentive to all fast-food commercials by Long John Silver and its competitors.

When considering Exhibit 8-2, remember that purchase behavior is only *one* possibility, as was going to Long John Silver's only one possible response for the consumer hearing the restaurant's commercial. A response will always come about to satisfy an aroused need—unfortunately it is often not the one hoped for by the marketer.

It is important to realize that although the series of steps shown in Exhibit 8-2 will be accomplished, they may be completed in varying lengths of time. Generally, the time frame gets longer as the product that might satisfy the need becomes more difficult to find, or more expensive, or requires consultation with others before the purchase is made. If that is the case, as it might be if the product is an automobile or a family vacation, the total decision-making process may require further thought or additional information. In effect, additional stimulus inputs may be complicating factors. Upcoming sections of this chapter will deal with such complicated situations.

Classifying Needs and Motives

Many psychologists have attempted to classify needs and motives. (See Exhibit 8-3 for an early classification scheme.) There is little agreement among these classifications. In fact, only one area of commonality can be found.

There is a general agreement that two basic groups of needs exist. The first group is called **physiological needs,** or needs stemming from our biological mechanisms. The second group consists of **social** and **psychological needs,** or needs resulting from an individual's interaction with the social environment. An example of marketers who deal with both sorts of needs are food marketers: Humans need food to live (*physiological need*), but the social environment of Americans leads them to be motivated to consume hamburgers and Coke rather than bugburgers and sour yak milk (*social need*).

EXHIBIT 8-3

An Early Scheme of Human Needs

Names of Instincts (synonyms in parentheses)	Names of Emotional Qualities Accompanying the Instinctive Activities
1. Instinct of escape (of self-preservation, of avoidance, danger instinct)	Fear (terror, fright, alarm, trepidation)
2. Instinct of combat (aggression, pugnacity)	Anger (rage, fury, annoyance, irritation, displeasure)
3. Repulsion (repugnance)	Disgust (nausea, loathing, repugnance)
4. Parental (protective)	Tender emotion (love, tenderness, tender feeling)
5. Appeal	Distress (feeling of helplessness)
6. Pairing (mating, reproduction, sexual)	Lust (sexual emotion or excitement, sometimes called love—an unfortunate and confusing usage)
7. Curiosity (inquiry, discovery, investigation)	Curiosity (feeling of mystery, of strangeness, of the unknown, wonder)
8. Submission (self-abasement)	Feeling of subjection (of inferiority, of devotion, of humility, of attachment, of submission, negative self-feeling)
9. Assertion (self-display)	Elation (feeling of superiority, of masterfulness, of pride, of domination, positive self-feeling)
10. Social or gregarious instinct	Feeling of loneliness, of isolation, nostalgia
11. Food-seeking (hunting)	Appetite or craving in narrower sense (gusto)
12. Acquisition (hoarding instinct)	Feeling of ownership, of possession (protective feeling)
13. Construction	Feeling of creativeness, of making, of productivity
14. Laughter	Amusement (jollity, carelessness, relaxation)

Source: W. McDougall, *An Introduction to Social Psychology* (Boston: J.W. Luce, 1920), p. 324, as quoted in H.R. Tosdal, *Principles of Personal Selling* (Chicago: A.W. Shaw Company, 1925).

Maslow's Hierarchy of Needs

Abraham Maslow, a psychologist, believed that even though each individual is unique, all humans have certain common needs. Maslow identified these needs and ordered them from the most basic need to the "highest" need. He thus created one of the most commonly cited and discussed categories of needs. His "needs hierarchy" provides the basis for many theories of motivation.

Maslow suggested that human needs range from such elemental biological needs as those for food and water to the most complex non-biological ones. These were categorized into the following five classes, which are also shown in Exhibit 8-4:[3]

1 *Physiological needs* (food, water, air, sex, control of body temperatures).

2 *Safety needs* (protection and security from threats).

3 *Love and social needs* (affection and feelings of belonging).

4 *Self-esteem needs* (feelings of self-worth, need for achievement, respect of others, prestige).

5 *Self-actualization needs* (seeking self-fulfillment, becoming increasing like one is capable of becoming).

Maslow also theorized that individuals will try to fill the most basic needs first. He also noted that a satisfied need is no longer a motivator of behavior. While 100 percent satisfaction of any one level of need is not necessary, people move on to higher levels of needs as lower levels are met. It follows from this that lower needs, such as hunger, if satisfied regularly, do not motivate people to the extent that they would if people were regularly concerned about the availability of food. Thus, in a society where people are comparatively unafraid of safety hazards, equipment which protects against those hazards has no

[3]A. Maslow, *Motivation and Personality* (New York: Harper & Row, 1954), p. 92.

EXHIBIT 8-4

Maslow's Hierarchy of Needs

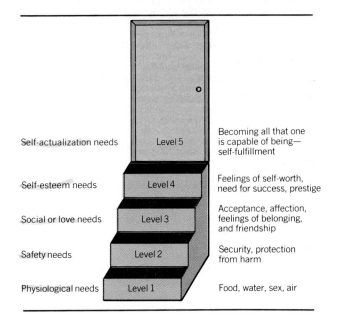

Self-actualization needs	Level 5	Becoming all that one is capable of being—self-fulfillment
Self-esteem needs	Level 4	Feelings of self-worth, need for success, prestige
Social or love needs	Level 3	Acceptance, affection, feelings of belonging, and friendship
Safety needs	Level 2	Security, protection from harm
Physiological needs	Level 1	Food, water, sex, air

great appeal. In the United States, where most citizens are *not* starving, food is marketed as "exciting" or "glamorous" or "a new taste treat." Food is not marketed as "filling" or "life-giving." But in countries where hunger and starvation are major problems, food is marketed almost entirely through simple distribution. No inducement other than availability is required.

Marketers know that the lower levels of needs, once satisfied, will not be as innately appealing. Thus Rice-a-Roni is "The San Francisco treat" and Minute Rice is "mistake proof." These products, which in fact satisfy the most basic need for food, have "moved" to other, higher levels of the hierarchy. After all, dining as San Franciscans do or making rice the quick and easy way, are not basic to human life, but they are appealing to consumers seeking affection or self-esteem.

Marketers must, however, be constantly alert for changes in the relative importance of needs. For example, until the 1960s, most people were unconcerned with automobile safety. In-

a

b

**Advertisements appealing to different needs in Maslow's hierarchy: (a) physiologi-
cal needs; (b) love and social needs; (c) safety needs; (d) self-actualization needs;
(e) self-esteem needs.**

c

d

e

creased awareness of safety risks led consumers to look for, or at least acknowledge, the importance of seat belts, air bags, collapsing steering columns, and other safety features in cars. Thus "safety," a need low on Maslow's scale, increased in importance for automobile manufacturers. Public awareness of crimes such as housebreaking and mugging have raised safety concerns in other areas. These concerns have resulted in increased sales of home alarm systems, pocket tear gas guns, and other safety-related products. The existence of an individual's "lower" concerns does not obviate the power of the other needs on the scale. The same person who is installing a home burglar or fire alarm system to satisfy a need for safety may also be seeking self-actualization by exercising, eating healthy foods, and dressing well so as to be all that she is "capable of becoming."

Needs, then, underlie all human behavior. When conditions of any sort *activate* or *stimulate* those needs, they become *motives* which move people to action.

Motivation and Emotion

Emotions, such as love, anger, fear, and hate, are complex reactions of subjectively experienced feelings of attraction or repulsion. There is a complex interrelationship between motivation and emotion. Early categorizations of motives by marketers presented classifications that sought to understand the role emotions play in motivation.[4] Therefore, motives were usually grouped as in categories such as "emotional" versus "rational." While distinctions are sometimes difficult to draw,[5] dichotomies of this sort continue in use. They persist because they serve to remind marketers that consumers, and even organizational buyers, are not strictly rational.

Many buyers appear not to want to be "rational." The average person looking for a new car does not want (or cannot understand) the kinds of facts and figures mechanical engineers might be able to provide. The typical car buyer wants very *simple* facts: the car "looks good"; the car dealer is a "good guy." The buyer does not want an analysis of the car's aerodynamics, an art expert's opinion of its looks, or a book on the history of car dealers in the old home town. In fact, Honda's "We make it simple" promotions are based on the findings that many consumers are confused about multiple optional accessories and mechanical details when purchasing. Offering only cars with "standard options," so that the buyer needs only to choose between red or black, simplifies the buying situation.

This is not to say that consumers actively try to allow their emotions to motivate them. It just happens that their behaviors are those which have been termed "emotional." Marketers need to be aware of those behaviors.

COGNITIVE PROCESSES

Once a motive has been aroused, a set of mental activities, or *cognitive* activities, begins to operate to reduce the tension state. Cognitive activities often begin so rapidly that we, as individuals, are not really conscious of the process.

The term **cognitive process** connotes a broad range of mental activities involving the interpretation of stimuli and the organization of thoughts and ideas. Among them are perception, learning, thinking, attitude formation, change of attitudes, processing of new knowledge and of information from the memory, reasoning, judging, and other mental functions that allow humans to know and be aware of their surroundings. It is difficult to separate these activities from one another because of their nearly

---

[4] M.T. Copeland, *Principles of Merchandising* (New York: Arch Shaw, 1924), pp. 155–167.

[5] Consider this: Is the purchase of a Cadillac, when a Chevrolet will do, rational or emotional? Many say it's emotional because one needn't have a Cadillac costing $15,000. The Chevrolet costs thousands less. Yet a stockbroker may want to drive a Cadillac to "prove" his success as a stockbroker to his clients. If you buy an American car, even though you think German cars are better, is your patriotism "irrational?"

simultaneous occurrence. However, we do have the opportunity to observe these activities in certain situations. For example, when we are at home the decision of what to eat at lunchtime can be made very quickly. At a new restaurant that offers a great array of dinner choices, however, our food decisions are reached more slowly and we are more aware of the "steps" in making a choice.

The discussion which follows focuses on the three aspects of the consumer's cognitive process—perception, learning, and attitude development and change—that are of particular importance to marketing.

PERCEPTION

Though the idea of "reality" at first seems simple, individuals perceive reality in different ways. A product, store, or advertisement will not be seen by everyone in exactly the same way. In fact, "reality" has been described as a dome built of pieces of glass, the pieces having many colors. Each individual in the world occupies just a small corner of the universe and sees a different combination of colors in the kaleidoscope.[6] Less poetically, but just as accurately stated, no two people see things exactly the same way.

Products offered by marketers provide many examples of this very phenomenon. A three-year-old car may appear to be just a used automobile, but a teenager may be thrilled to have it as a first car. The teenager's parents may see the car in a different light. The used-car dealer may view the car in still another. Their images of the automobile, their perceptions, are very different. **Perception,** then, is defined as the process of interpreting sensations and giving meaning to stimuli. In this case, it is meaning given to the used car. This process occurs because people constantly strive to make sense of the world and, when faced with new sensations or data, seek patterns or concepts that may relate new bits of information to each other and to past experience. Perception is the interpretation of reality, and each of us views reality from a different perspective.

Selective Perception

Individuals receive information about their world (stimuli) by hearing, seeing, touching, tasting, or smelling something, be it an object, an event, or an idea.[7] Organization and interpretation of these stimuli is influenced by factors such as the individual's abilities to experience the sensation, by personality, by the context in which the stimulus was encountered, by the person's intelligence and thought processes, and even by the person's moods.[8] These factors combine to create a mental phenomena known as **selective perception,** that is the individual tendency to screen out certain stimuli and to color or interpret other stimuli with meanings drawn from personal backgrounds. Selective perception is easily observable. When a politician gives a speech, for example, listeners who like the speaker based on their past experiences, agree with almost everything said and pronounce the speech a good one. They even remember more about the speech than the person who does not like the politician. To the listener who doesn't like the speaker, however, the speaker is a crook and a faker and not one word of the speech is factual. We cannot escape our past experiences, prejudices, or other limitations. That is why human perception of *everything* is influenced by selective perception.

---

[6]W. Durant, *The Pleasure of Philosophy* (New York: Simon & Schuster, 1953).

[7]P.T. Young, *Motivation and Emotion* (New York: John Wiley & Sons, 1961), pp. 298–299.

[8]G. Zaltman and M. Wallendorf, *Consumer Behavior* (John Wiley & Sons, 1979), p. 276.

ANALOZE

Analoze, a combination pain killer and antacid, was a new product introduced by Bristol-Myers some years ago. Analoze would relieve a headache and upset stomach without the need for water. The company believed it would be superior to pain killers, such as Bayer Aspirin, that the public took for relief of headaches by offering the benefits of successful antacids such as Rolaids. The company developed a cherry flavor for the combination tablet. Tests showed it to be an excellent product. The product was supported with advertising stating "Take it Without Water." What could go wrong with this antacid-pain killer in an easy to take form? Although the product was "technically sound," most consumers perceived this to be too different from most medicines. After all, doesn't a medicine, especially if it is a good pain killer, have to be taken with water? Consumers' beliefs about pain remedies, although not valid, killed a fine product.

Source: Based on information in J.U. McNeal, *An Introduction to Consumer Behavior* (New York: John Wiley & Sons, 1972), pp. 158–159.

The selectivity of human perception is important to marketers, as evidenced by these facts: People pay more attention to commercials for products they use than those they do not. (Often, after seeing a commercial for a particular brand of a product, the viewers report that the commercial was for *another* brand of the product, usually the brand they use.) An advertisement may contain a word or picture that offends the consumer, thereby making that advertisement "worthless" in its effects on the consumer. (An executive considering a major purchase may eliminate a particular supplier from the running because the salesman who presented that supplier's products is "a jerk.") There is nothing that escapes the effects of perception.

The *Time* magazine advertisement in Exhibit 8-5 shows how we all add symbolic meaning and interpretations to stimuli. The flower vase at-

EXHIBIT 8-5

**An Example of Closure
in the Selective Perception Process**

tracts attention because it is so different from the white letters. The picture actually contains these elements: T, flower in vase, M, and E. Yet we read "TIME" because of our tendency to "fill things in." This aspect of perception is called **closure.** We mentally "finish things off." In fact, many advertisements make use of this concept by *not* showing the product, showing only part of it, or showing only its shadow. The viewer supposedly becomes more involved with the advertisement through the process of closure. A per-

---

HOW DO WE PERCEIVE THE WORLD?

It is not a photographic representation of the physical world; it is, rather, a partial, personal construction in which certain objects, selected out by the individual for a major role, are perceived in an individual manner. Every perceiver is, as it were, to some degree a nonrepresentational artist, painting a picture of the world that expresses his individual view of reality.

Source: D. Krech, R.S. Crutchfield, and E.L. Ballachey, *Individual in Society* (New York: McGraw-Hill, 1962), p. 20.

---

son who can't perceive closure will be annoyed by the advertisement, so the closure idea is used only when the product in question is very well-known and the advertiser is sure that the viewer *can* complete the picture.

The Screening Process

The process of selective perception is much like a series of screens or sieves. The series is illustrated in Exhibit 8-6.

Selective exposure, the first of these screens, is perhaps the simplest. No individual is exposed to *all* stimuli. No one sees every advertisement. In Lubbock, Texas, for example, only some of the area's population pass by the billboards near the corner of 5th and Q; this is *selective exposure.*

One way consumers avoid information that is contrary to their existing attitudes is to avoid exposure to these messages. Some individuals do not want to receive certain messages or stimuli and either screen them out of their experience entirely or distort them by means of *perceptual defenses.*

Thus, even if a certain individual *does* pass the billboards at 5th and Q, he or she may not

notice the signs. The individual could be looking for an address, or at the traffic, and simply pay no attention—at least, no conscious attention—to the billboards; this is **selective attention.**

Selective interpretation occurs when perceptual defenses are operating because a newly encountered message is incompatible with the individual's established values or attitudes. For example, a person who has purchased a new Sony TV a week ago does not want to hear an advertisement announcing that Sony's prices have just been cut in half. In the same way, the owner of a Ford is likely to avoid information detailing why Chevys are better cars than Fords. Looking carefully at perception teaches the truth of the old adage, "It's not what you (marketer) say, it's what they (consumers) hear."

There is not much the marketer can do to overcome the difficulty of selective exposure other than to carefully plan the placement of advertisements and billboards so that the target customer *will* be reached. Selective attention may be overcome with attention-getting messages. The size of an advertisement, the colors used, the novelty of pictures included, and many other **stimulus factors,** have been shown to have considerable effects on the amount of attention a viewer will give an advertisement.

More subtly, an advertisement may gain increased attention by featuring aspects that "speak" to the viewer's needs, background, or hopes because perception is also influenced by **individual factors.** Thus, a full-page color advertisement probably will attract more attention than a quarter-page advertisement in black and white. However, a black and white advertisement offering hope of "a better appearance" to balding men is likely to attract a lot of attention among its target group, balding men.

Many rules of advertising (use color; don't be wordy) are profitably broken when the target consumers are willing to devote attention to a problem that means something to them. Advertisements promising aid for losing weight appeal to people who need this help be noticed by fat people, even if others may think the advertisements will lack attention getting color.

This illustrates a basic fact about the per-

EXHIBIT 8-6

The Screening Processes of Selective Perception

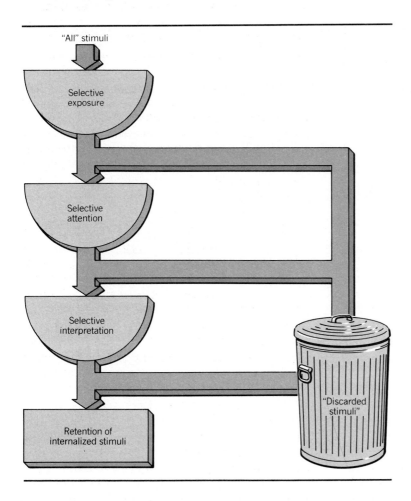

"All" stimuli

Selective exposure

Selective attention

Selective interpretation

Retention of internalized stimuli

"Discarded stimuli"

ception of advertising: Consumers pay attention to advertisements when the products featured interest them. When people readily forget messages for products for which they have no interest, they have **selectively retained** information. Different aspects of an individual's life are influenced by the way the brain deals with all stimuli, including advertising.

In summary, perception involves placing information within a framework as well as interpreting and giving meaning to stimuli. An individual's background, knowledge, personality, and other attributes influence perception. All stimuli that passes the "screens" of selective exposure and selective attention are selectively interpreted. This entire screening process is known as *selective perception*. As shown in Exhibit 8-6, the goal is to have the stimuli internalized. In marketing, this means that the aim is to ensure that consumers do not selectively screen out the marketer's messages. However, only a small number of the infinite number of stimuli each of us encounters daily can be internalized.

SUBLIMINAL PERCEPTION

Does the conscious mind perceive only part of what it is exposed to? In the 1950s, there was considerable controversy about the possibility of subliminal advertising or perception of advertising stimuli without conscious awareness. In a movie theater "experiment," the phrases "eat popcorn" and "drink Coca-Cola" were rapidly flashed on the screen so that people were unaware of the presence of a message. Sales in a Northern New Jersey movie theater were reported to have increased 58 percent for popcorn and 18 percent for Coca-Cola. Psychologists, alarmed at this result, seriously studied the adequacy of the initial study and concluded that it lacked scientific rigor. Subsequent investigations of "perception without

awareness" suggested the technical problems are so great in trying to achieve that effect that the public need not be apprehensive about subliminal perception. It appears that subliminal stimuli are too weak to be effective. For example, only very short messages can be communicated and the influence of selective perception tends to be stronger than the stimulus factors.

It is interesting to note that a resurfacing of this issue occurred in the 1970s when a popular book entitled *Subliminal Seduction* was published. The picture shown here allegedly hides an embedded "subliminal" sexual message. Can you see it? Even if you can, its effects on your subsequent purchase behaviors are, at least, debatable.

Perception: The Basis for Brand Image Marketing

One can conclude that product distinctions are often in the minds of the consumers and not in the products themselves. For these products, the symbolic meaning, developed through perception of "reality," is more important than the tangible ("real") product.[9] This is the concept of **brand image.** Though the "image" varies from consumer to consumer, a brand image remains a complex of symbols and meanings associated with the brand. People buy products not only for their functional purpose, but also for their symbolic meanings. Placing emphasis on certain symbols is part of the perception process.

That *perception* of reality is more important than "reality" itself is demonstrated in the various "taste test" ads we see on television. The "Pepsi Challenge" shows that many drinkers of Coke would, in blind taste tests, prefer Pepsi. Schlitz ran live "tests" that showed large numbers of beer-drinkers preferred Schlitz to their favorite brands. More recently, Blatz beer has done the same thing using individual consumers instead of the panels Schlitz utilized. In fact, it has been shown in casual and formal research that for a number of products, among them beer, cola, and brands of turkey, consumers cannot distinguish between the various brands once the labels have been removed.[10]

---

[9]S.J. Levy, "Symbols By Which We Buy," *Harvard Business Review*, July–August 1959.

[10]R.I. Allison and K.P. Uhl, "Impact of Beer Brand Identification on Taste Perception," *Journal of Marketing Research*, August 1964, pp. 36–39.

LEARNING

Learning occurs as a result of experience. Thus the expression "older and wiser" is not far from the mark since older people have had the opportunity to learn from their many experiences. Experiences related to product usage, shopping, and exposure to advertisements and other aspects of marketing, add to the consumers' banks of knowledge and influence their habits.

Learning is defined as any change in behavior or cognitions, such as attitudes, as a result of experience. That a child who was punished for writing on the walls no longer writes on the walls proves that he has learned not to do that foul deed. Similarly, in marketing, a package or display may attract the attention of a shopper who then gives a new product a try. If the product works to the customer's satisfaction, that buyer has learned, through experience, that the new product is acceptable. How humans behave in almost all instances is due to two major forces:

their basic biological makeup and what they have learned. Learning is having something you did not have before. Rather than being innate it can be demonstrated to have occurred.

Learning can also occur by observation of the consequences of others' behavior. For example, a younger child observes an older's punishments and learns to avoid that punishment by avoiding the situation that brought it about. Similarly, buyers often purchase products that were recommended by other people who have used those products. Much television advertising is based on this principle. We associate the satisfaction others receive from the product and, as we do, we are learning by observation.

There are many theories about how learning occurs. However, all of the widely accepted theories acknowledge the great importance of experience. Exhibit 8-7 illustrates the consumer learning process according to one theory called

EXHIBIT 8-7

**Effects of Reinforcement on Consumer Behavior:
First Trial and Repeat Purchase Situations**

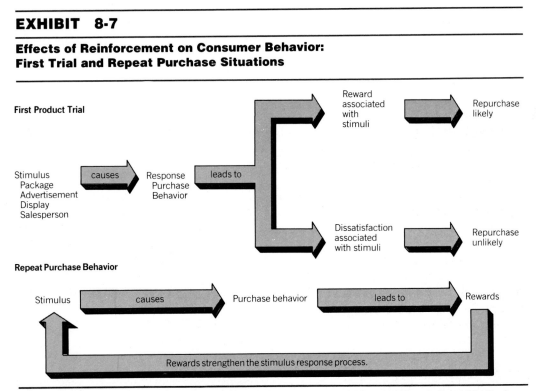

Source: Adapted from M.A. Hitt, R.D. Middlemist, and R.L. Mathis, *Effective Management* (St. Paul: West Publishing, 1979), p. 245.

operant conditioning. The new product is the *stimulus;* the purchase is the consumer's *response* to the stimulus. If the product proves to be satisfactory, the consumer receives a reward or payoff. Psychologists call this **reinforcement.** The fact is that the purchases were made in the hope that satisfaction would follow. When it did, the effect was to strengthen (reinforce) the stimulus-response process. Learning takes place as this phenomenon occurs over and over.

Needless to say, the rewards or reinforcements received by some buyers will not be clearcut. For example, Tide may in fact get one buyer's laundry cleaner and whiter than do other brands of detergents. This is a *functional reward.* However, the buyer may also find an intangible or *symbolic* satisfaction in using the laundry detergent that is "number one" or "the favorite for nearly forty years," or "the best for my family," or "the one my grandmother used." Thus, the rewards may be *functional* or *symbolic.* Rewards can be equally satisfying whether they are intangible or scientifically demonstrable.

Some theories of learning stress the importance of *repetition* in the development of habits. The more exposures you have to a television commercial, the more likely it is that you have learned the content of the sales message. For example, Mrs. Olsen's comments about Folger's coffee are probably familiar because of repetition of the advertising campaign. Repeatedly rewarding a behavior strengthens the stimulus-response relationship. More simply, repeated satisfaction creates buying habits and loyal customers. (See Exhibit 8-7.)

The **attribution theory** of learning stresses that consumers must attribute the obtained reward to their actions. Thus, purchasing of Tide must be perceived as instrumental in obtaining a reward if the stimulus-response relationship is to be strengthened. If the consumer thinks clean clothes are the result of a new washing machine rather than Tide, repurchase of Tide may not be as likely.

Learning Theories and Marketing

Most learning theories are compatible with marketing activities and marketing's key philosophy, the marketing concept.[11] The theories stress positive rewards or experiences which lead to repeated behaviors. The marketing concept stresses consumer satisfaction which leads to repeat purchases and long-term profitability for the organization.

The Evoked Set Concept. One model which seeks to explain consumer behavior largely in terms of learning is the **evoked set** concept developed by John Howard.[12] The model is simple, but it is so logical and makes such good sense that it is widely accepted in marketing literature. The underlying idea of the model is that throughout their lives people develop "lists" of things to do when a particular problem arises, that is, when a particular stimulus is encountered. Consider this example: a baby tries to eat everything from toys, furniture, and the cat's food to "adult" comestibles like horseradish and beer. However, the baby soon learns that certain things have appeal and others do not. Thus, the baby develops a "list" of things to eat. This list changes as the child's tastes change.

Exhibit 8-8 shows Howard's evoked set. Work through it considering the everyday problem of hunger. Faced with the stimulus hunger, we must eat. There are some things we could eat that do not come to mind because we are unaware of them as foods (for example chutney, tofu, and exotic plants). These are possibilities included in the *unawareness set.* However, among the foods we have learned are worthy of consideration, there are some that we like, some that we hate, and some that we tolerate. The idea of this model is that when we are hungry, we probably move directly to the *evoked set.* Thus, a marketer's goal would be to have his or her product first in the target customer's *awareness* set, then in the customer's *evoked set.*

What happens if a given product is not in our evoked set of foods? Is it permanently barred

---

[11] For an excellent consideration of applications of learning theory to marketing, see J.A. Howard, *Marketing Management: Analysis and Planning,* revised edition (Homewood, Ill.: Irwin, 1963).

[12] This discussion is adapted from J.A. Howard, *Marketing Management: Operating, Strategic and Administrative,* third edition (Homewood, Ill.: Irwin, 1973), pp. 62–71.

EXHIBIT 8-8

Evoked Set "Answer to the Hunger Stimulus

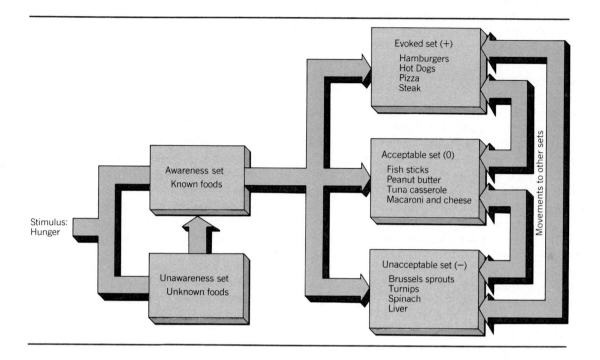

Evoked set (+)
Hamburgers
Hot Dogs
Pizza
Steak

Acceptable set (0)
Fish sticks
Peanut butter
Tuna casserole
Macaroni and cheese

Unacceptable set (−)
Brussels sprouts
Turnips
Spinach
Liver

Awareness set
Known foods

Unawareness set
Unknown foods

Stimulus:
Hunger

Movements to other sets

from consideration? No, because our tastes may change, or we may choose to try something new and like it, or we may react to a cultural change, such as the American emphasis on "healthy" foods such as tuna and liver.

A manufacturer can get its product into the *evoked set* by marketing. Advertising or other promotion can lead to potentially successful trials. Wider distribution can make the product easier to find. An appropriate price can make it more attractive. The product itself might be altered to achieve greater appeal: Tuna fish was once unsalable in the United States. It only became popular when its name was changed from "horse fish." Liver was once thrown away, but Americans ate kidneys. Now, kidneys are thrown away and Americans (some, at least) eat liver.

ATTITUDES

A marketing manager may state that a particular organizational customer has a very favorable attitude toward his firm's chemical products. Though that phrase seems clear enough, it is an everyday oversimplification of the concept of attitude. The customer's attitude is probably not 100 percent favorable. It probably contains both *positive* and *negative* elements. What the marketing manager actually meant was, "I think this customer has positive and negative beliefs about our products, but overall the customer has a favorable attitude because the positive beliefs outweigh the negative beliefs."

An **attitude** is a "learned predisposition to

respond in a consistently favorable or unfavorable manner with respect to a given object."[13] Notice that attitudes are *learned.* This is a bright spot for marketers because it suggests that it is possible to change attitudes. They are *not* innate. The definition also shows that attitudes are related to behavior in that they are a *predisposition to respond* in a certain way to a certain stimulus. It is easy to see that attitudes are the result of learning experiences. Socially unacceptable attitudes, such as racist attitudes, are also the result of learning. Learning is generally thought of in a positive way, but it has negative aspects as well.

Close examination of the definition points out that attitudes are *enduring* rather than momentary states. Stable, consistent attitudes help individuals organize mental processes and behavior. Finally, attitudes are *directed* toward some object. In marketing an attitudinal object may be a product, service, person, or idea.

Attitudes represent cognitive beliefs. If the industrial purchaser of chemicals believes that a supplier's product is of the highest quality, that customer service is good, and that delivery will be quick, this purchaser's attitude is likely to assure that the supplier of this product will have a very good chance to make a sale. Attitudes, in this situation, can lead to a particular desired behavior—that is, consideration of the chemical supplier.

Note that the behavior, in this example, is *not* that the product was purchased, but that it was included in the final consideration. The attitude of an individual serves as a general guide to behavior toward the attitudinal object. This does not necessarily mean a favorable attitude will result in a particular brand being purchased. Consumers have attitudes toward competing brands as well. Furthermore, attitudes are not the sole determinant of our behavior. Situational, financial, and motivational forces, as well as attitudes, influence our behavior.

Since attitudes are *situational,* the effects of attitudes are controlled by the circumstances which surround them. Most Americans have very favorable attitudes toward the Rolls Royce and Mercedes automobiles, yet not many own one of these cars. Many people admire, that is, have attitudes that favor, mansions surrounded by well-tended formal gardens. Few people live in such places, however. Attitudes may be affected by other attitudes. People who don't like winter weather will probably not like snow skiing, or buy a snowmobile, or plan to live out their days in Minnesota.

Thus, it is difficult to predict a *specific behavior* from an attitude toward a single object. One's specific behavior toward the purchase of a beverage for entertaining may be influenced by one's attitudes toward the time of the year, toward the guests, and toward saving money for that desperately needed vacation. Nevertheless, there are many situations where there is a consistency between attitudes and behavior. For example, we may think that the store personnel are friendly in our favorite department store. We may also think that the store is clean and the prices are reasonable. Purchasing behavior at this store may be consistent with our attitudes. Much managerial strategy is based on the assumption that "all other things being equal" a positive attitude toward a store or brand will predispose the consumer to shop at the store or utilize the brand.

Many products that we *don't* buy are avoided because of our *negative* attitudes toward these things. In short, our attitudes serve as a guide to our behavior toward the attitudinal object. Despite the complications entering into the consideration of attitudes, there are many situations where consistencies between attitudes and behavior occur. Effective marketing managers can put these consistencies to good use.

Thus far in this chapter we have been discussing the various elements which contribute to the decisions made by individuals, especially the decisions made by consumers evaluating products. The remainder of the chapter attempts to bring these elements together in a description of the decision-making process which *all* customers go through.

---

[13] M. Fishbein and I. Ajzen, *Beliefs, Attitudes, Intention and Behavior* (Reading, Mass.: Addison-Wesley, 1975), p.6.

A TRIPARTITE THEORY OF ATTITUDES

A tripartite approach to attitude has been very popular in recent years. There are three parts of an attitude. The **affective** component is the emotional component. It reflects a person's feelings toward the object. Is the brand good or bad? Is it desirable? Likeable? The **cognitive** component involves all beliefs, knowledge, and thoughts about the object—a consumer's perception of the product attributes or characteristics. Is it durable? Expensive? Suitable for a person like me? The third major component is the **behavioral** component (conative). It reflects the intended and actual behaviors toward the object. This component is a predisposition to action.

Let's investigate a perspective camera buyer's attitude toward the Canon AE-1 camera. The customer may hold several beliefs about the product. He may believe the camera takes clear shots and he may believe it is easy to use. He may know that the product is the "official camera" of the National Football League even though this may not be truly important to him. The light weight of the camera is evaluated as good. However, the belief that it is expensive is evaluated as bad. These cognitive aspects of the attitude influence whether there is a favorable emotional feeling toward the camera (affect) and the individual's predisposition toward purchase (behavioral aspect).

In any purchase situation, which component of attitude is most important? That varies from case to case. For jewelry and fashion apparel, "feelings" or "emotions" may be most important. For a couple building a new house, their study of materials, energy, and appliance alternatives may make the cognitive component most important. For an inveterate Chevrolet buyer whose car has just "died," the behavioral component ("Now it's time to go buy a new Chevy.") is clearly most important.

Thus, the "weights" of the components of attitude are product specific. They should also vary with the type of buyer. We would expect the organizational buyer to have attitudes but also expect the *cognitive* component of those attitudes to outweigh the *affective*.

Attitude		

(1)
Affective
Component
  Beliefs and feelings about products
	(2)
	Cognitive
	Component
	  Knowledge about products
		(3)
		Behavioral
		Component
		  Intended and actual behaviors toward products

THE DECISION-MAKING PROCESS

By this point, it is clear that behavior is an output influenced by myriad factors. That behavior is the resultant response to stimuli remains at the heart of consumer behavior theories. However, we have now seen some of the elements in the black box that separate the stimulus from the response, the input from the output. The workings of these elements are difficult to grasp, but they have been identified.

The process completed in the black box has been called by many names: thinking, reasoning, problem-solving, and decision-making. Whatever it is called, its outputs are readily observable. A stimulus can cause an individual to search for and select among various alternative solutions to a problem. The person must then make a choice: Pizza or a hamburger? Root beer or a glass of milk? How is that choice made?

CAN ATTITUDES BE CHANGED?

Changing another individual's firmly established attitudes can be very difficult, in part because the person is being asked to "toss aside" a belief that may have been a part of that person for a long time. Thus, many attitudes are unlikely to be much affected by outside influences. However, when attitude change is affected, it is believed to occur in three stages.

First comes what is called "thawing." The change influence breaks down or softens the existing attitude by raising questions which make the subject individual begin to wonder about the attitude he or she holds.

The second step, assuming the first has been successful, is to interject the desired new attitude. That is, the new idea or object is shown to answer the questions that were raised about the old attitudes.

The third step is to *refreeze* or solidify the "new" attitude by showing that some reward can be associated with accepting the new idea or object.

What sorts of people or groups frequently succeed in using this three-step process? The Armed Forces put their recruits in a rough situation (basic training) and break down some basic ideas the recruits may have. Taking them from familiar surroundings and off to a camp in the boondocks facilitates the process of removing the struts or supports which perpetuated the recruits' old beliefs and attitudes.

The agents of attitude change, drill sergeants and others, instill the "new" attitudes into the recruits. Finally, the refreezing or reinforcement step comes about in the form of a stripe on the sleeve, a parade in honor of the "new soldiers," the smiles of proud parents, and the assurance that "Now you are a true member of one of the greatest organizations the world has ever seen."

Decision-making is a cognitive process that brings together memory, thinking, information processing, and the making of evaluative judgments. The situation in which the decision is made determines the exact nature of the process. A cigarette smoker purchases a particular brand in a matter of seconds as a routine matter. The purchase of a new house by a consumer, or a fleet of trucks by an organization, however, usually requires extensive decision-making. The process may take months to finalize, with a series of identifiable decisions made at different points in the decision-making process.

The seeming "snap judgment" and the longer process are more closely related than it may seem at first. The "routine" decision in our example is likely to have been preceded by a series of trials and errors, with different brands of cigarettes being tested before the consumer is able to make routine choices. Both the routine choice and the extensive problem-solving procedure involve the same series of steps completed at different speeds. Again, the situation—routine or nonroutine purchase, major or minor outlay of funds, important or unimportant choice—determines the nature of the decision-making process.

While complex models of the consumer decision-making process are easily available in libraries such models are inappropriate in a first marketing textbook such as this one. Most colleges offer semester-long courses which "work through" such models. The five-step process shown in Exhibit 8-9 is enough for our purposes.

The following discussion focuses on the complete, five-step process shown in Exhibit 8-9. The stages or steps in that process are always present, though they be passed through at different rates of speed. A single step in the progression may be a "sticking point," slowing up the process. For example, if an individual's alarm clock pops a mainspring, he or she would know instantly that a new clock is needed and could visualize which store to buy it in. At the store, the person could quickly evaluate the available clocks and choose an electric model to replace

EXHIBIT 8-9

Steps in the Decision-Making Process

1. Problem
   recognition

2. Search for
   alternative
   solutions and information

3. Evaluation
   of alternatives

4. Purchase
   decision

Buy   Don't buy

Problem
still faced,
return to
Step 1

(or)

Stop

5. Postpurchase evaluation

Satisfaction   Dissatisfaction
Process   Frustration,
complete   possible return to Step 1

not reach the purchase stage if only because of a money shortage. Other reasons might include an *evaluation of alternatives* which ends with the feeling that no available alternatives will satisfy the decision-maker. Postponement or abandonment of the decision may result.

Step 1: Problem Recognition

A tire blows out on a car being driven on an interstate highway. This is a case of instantaneous problem recognition. Alternatively, problem recognition can be a more complex, long-term process. A person who has a car that occasionally "dies," and isn't very shiny or attractive any more, and whose friends express surprise that she's "still driving that old thing," might start to recognize a problem in the making.

Problem awareness is a result of inputs or stimuli. The individual becomes aware that a motive is not completely satisfied, that an aroused need requires some form of fulfillment. The person who has become aware that a new car is in order might take a bit of time in getting one. However, a smoker who realizes that he is lighting his last cigarette is likely to make a purchase

Problem awareness is the first stage in the consumer decision-making process.

the broken wind-up one. (Attitudes may have changed since the last clock purchase.) However, years might be spent regretting that the new clock doesn't have a snooze alarm and a night light. Although the final step is the sticking point here, a snafu might have occurred at any other step.

The five-step process need *not* be completed, even if it is begun. Frequently, buyers do decision very rapidly, passing through steps 2 and 3 of the decision-making process so speedily as to appear to have skipped them. For all practical purposes, these stages *have* been skipped. Marketers know that buyer behavior as routinized as this is difficult to alter. A buyer who devotes some time and consideration to decision-making opens up more opportunities for effective marketers to appeal to that buyer and to offer a product that may satisfy the buyer's need. Of course, marketers of the most popular brands of cigarettes, gum, and candy are happy that *their* regular customers have developed a routinized approach to solving problems.

Step 2: Search for Alternative Solutions and Information

Even the habitual buyer of Snickers candy bars is very likely to consider, however briefly, some other choices before selecting Snickers as usual. However, it is in cases where buyers are purchasing a product for the first time or making a purchase which could have major economic, social, or other consequences, that the search for alternatives and information about those alternatives is easily observed. That buyers in such positions behave as they do is explained by the theory of **perceived risk**—there is always a chance that the product will not do what it was expected to do. Consumers perceive risk in the sense that any action of a consumer will produce consequences that cannot be anticipated with anything approximating certainty, and some of which are likely to be unpleasant.[14] The amount of money to be spent or the social risks may be great, thus increasing the perceived risk. Both sorts of risk are encountered when expensive dress clothing is purchased: Is the clothing too expensive? Is it worth it? What will my friends say when they see this suit? Will I look good in this or look like an overdressed hick?

Buyers seek to reduce these feelings of uncertainty. They may bring family members or

---

[14] R.A. Bauer, "Consumer Behavior as Risk Taking," *Dynamic Marketing for a Changing World*, R. Hancock, ed. (Chicago: American Marketing Association, 1960), p. 389.

friends with them when shopping. They may want the salesman or a tailor or other expert to tell them that the product is a good one and that it looks good, too. This kind of information and help reduces consumer uncertainty, as does asking the opinions of relevant reference group members or opinion leaders.

Marketers can seek ways to satisfy this consumer need to reduce risk. Guarantees, a liberal return policy, store displays or advertisements that show that the products actually deliver what is promised, and a pledge that "We service what we sell," may reduce the risks. These are not "tricks." All of us prefer to deal with established companies, and to buy known rather than unknown brands of goods. Why? We are "reducing" our chances of injury, damage, or loss.

Step 3: Evaluation of Alternatives

The concept of perceived risk enters into the evaluation of the alternatives stage of the buyer decision-making process. Just as the individual seeks alternative solutions to a problem with an eye toward reducing risk, so he or she evaluates the located alternatives with the thought of reducing risk. In many ways, the "bottom line" in the process is a decision that the alternative chosen represents the least total risk (economic, social, even physical) given the decision-maker's beliefs, attitudes, and priorities.

In the evaluation of alternatives stage, the prospective buyer seeks to employ appropriate choice criteria in analyzing possible purchases. **Choice criteria** are those critical attributes utilized to evaluate a brand. Which choice criteria are used depends on the customer and the situation in which the customer is placed. For example, people needing automobile tires or a car battery might buy these things at the neighborhood service station even if prices there are higher than at other places. They may feel that the time saved in not seeking other sources of supply is worth the extra dollars spent. They may know the local station owner and want to "give him some business." They may be trying to keep on the station owner's good side just in case emergency help is ever needed. They may want to deal with a local seller so they can complain if something is wrong with the purchased goods. The choice criteria might even be, though for most consumers this is unlikely, the results and conclusions drawn from a serious study of the relative merits of different tires, batteries, warranties, and prices. The use of these "rational" criteria concerning functional features would be more likely to occur among organizational buyers than among consumers.

In some cases, the attributes of one brand may even be evaluated by comparison to other brands or product choices. Phillips Petroleum, for example, emphasizes that it is the "performance company" in most of its promotions. This implies that the company performs a useful social function. Phillips' advertising campaign is based on extensive consumer behavior research in which consumer choice criteria have been extensively investigated.

The convenience of stores, the prices posted, the personality of the gasoline dealer, and the premiums given away at the gas station are important choice criteria. But when those factors are considered equal among competitors, and research shows they generally are, the company's long-run performance image prevails in influencing the brand loyalty.[15]

Step 4: Purchase Decisions

Sooner or later the prospect must make a purchase decision. As Exhibit 8-9 shows, that decision may be *not* to buy any one of the alternatives available. In most cases, however, the "problem" that drove the person to begin the decision-making process still remains. Unless the problem has disappeared, as it conceivably could at any point in the process, the person who made the "don't buy" choice will either have to commence the process again or just "live with" the problem. How might the problem have "disappeared?" Well, Mom and Dad could have bought our decision-maker some new tires

or a neighbor may have given him some old but serviceable tires stored in a garage or basement.

Assuming that the problem persists and the decision-maker makes the "buy" choice, the mechanics of the purchase must be worked out. This may be a simple operation, especially if the buyer has either a credit card (and is within the credit limit) or a checkbook with a sizable balance. If the buyer is not in such happy circumstances, he or she may have to make another decision about the mechanics of a time payment. The decision to buy can also bring with it a few other related decisions: Should the buyer get new valve stems too? How about a lifetime wheel balancing agreement with the seller?

Step 5: Postpurchase Evaluation

Given that the decision-maker has made the choice to buy, the matter of **purchase satisfaction** (or dissatisfaction) remains. Satisfaction or dissatisfaction can occur only after the purchase is consummated. In some cases, the satisfaction is immediate, as when the buyer chews the just-bought gum or feels pleased that the decision-making decision process is over. Frequently, we think to ourselves, or tell others, after making a purchase, "Well, I bought a great house/set of tires/dog/pair of boots today." This patting ourselves on the back is an attempt to achieve satisfaction. We are telling ourselves that we are pleased with the purchase. In this case, marketing has achieved its goal of consumer satisfaction.

However, the opposite can occur and we may feel uneasy over the purchase. Is the roof on the house new? Are tires good on snow? Someone may mention their surprise that we bought this brand instead of that one. All of these things can create a feeling of unease, a sensation that the decision-making process may have yielded the wrong decision.

These feelings of uncertainty can be analyzed in terms of the theory of cognitive dissonance.[16] **Cognitive dissonance** is a postpur-

---

[15]"Phillips Tracy-Locke/BBDO Keep Up Their Performance," *Ad Week*, February 7, 1983, p. 6.

[16]L. Festinger, *A Theory of Cognitive Dissonance* (Stanford: Stanford University Press, 1957).

chase feeling that occurs after a commitment to purchase has been made. Individuals do not like to hold two or more beliefs or conflicting ideas at once in their minds. The car-owner bought the tires and has left the shop; there's no money back now. Should he have bought Michelin instead, even at a bit higher price? Dissonance theory describes these feelings as a sense of psychic tension, a tension that the individual will seek to relieve. Each alternative has some advantages and some disadvantages. Postpurchase evaluation of the alternatives to support one's choice is a psychological process buyers utilize to reduce dissonance. The buyer may seek reinforcement from friends or from the seller. The buyer may mentally downgrade the unselected alternatives and play-up the advantages of the selected brand to convince himself that the right choice was made.

Whether this phenomena is called psychic tension, dissonance, or just plain misgivings, effective marketers don't want dissatisfied customers. By understanding that any choice, even when it is undeniably the best choice, can make a customer wonder whether the right thing was done, marketers can seek to allay these concerns. The promise of good service, the statement that the buyer should come right back if there's any trouble and "we'll fix it up," or the giving of a toll-free "hot-line" number are good business. So is the practice of real estate agents who call or write customers a month or two after selling them a house to assure them one more time that the purchase was a wise one. Successful candidates for political office who recognize the good sense of this may post billboards with messages like "Thank you, neighbors," publish-

ing newsletters for voters, or even open "back home" offices with scheduled office hours for the home folks. Atari is one manufacturer that sought to reassure purchasers of its products. After Christmas of 1982, Atari paid for television advertisements showing families enjoying Atari games. The announcer said, "Atari would like to thank you for bringing us into your home." All of these ideas are good business that can increase satisfaction and lead to repeat purchasing behavior.

Summary of the Decision-Making Process

Exhibit 8-9 shows the things buyers do and it demonstrates the steps in the process, each of which provides an opportunity for effective marketing action. It also shows the points at which consumer satisfaction and dissatisfaction are created. Dissatisfaction might occur if the buyer seizes on the "wrong" problem, conducts an inappropriate search for alternatives and information, somehow misses an available alternative, makes a wrong purchase decision, or enters a state of cognitive dissonance. The effective marketer makes every effort to head-off these developments. Advertising, personal selling, and other promotional means serve to bring the consumer information and news about alternatives. A good product that is properly priced and sold will yield satisfaction.

Exhibit 8-10 summarizes and illustrates the flow of events and the effects of personal and nonpersonal variables in the consumer decision-making process.

PERSONALITY AND SELF-CONCEPT THEORIES

Personality

There are individual differences in human behavior. Personality reflects the individual's characteristics or consistent ways of responding to his or her environment.

As with many psychological terms, personality is used in nontechnical ways in our everyday vocabularies. When Bill says "Mike gets along well with others because he has a pleasing personality," the word is not used technically. In consumer behavior theory, **personality** is the general underlying dispositions of peo-

EXHIBIT 8-10

Psychological Aspects of Buying Behavior: Individual Response to Stimuli

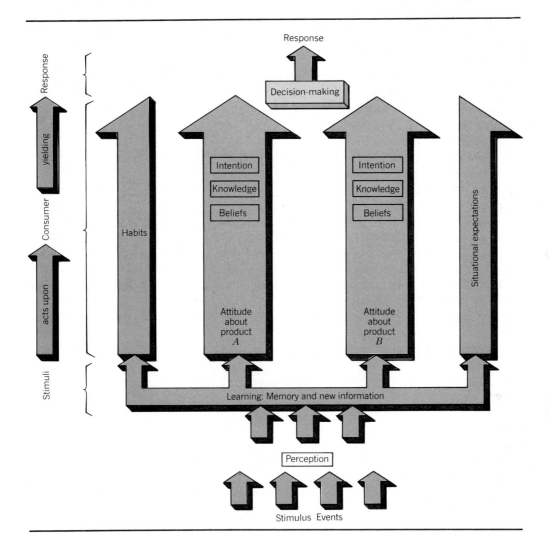

ple, especially the most dominant characteristics of individuals. It might be expected that introverts will purchase different types of automobiles than extroverts.

There are numerous theories of personality, and the list of personality traits seems endless. Traits such as dominance, gregariousness, self-confidence, masculinity, conservativeness, prestige-consciousness, independence, and numerous others have been suggested. Many con-

ceptions of personality are based on theories of motivation.

Freud's Personality Theory. One of the earliest personality theorists was Sigmund Freud. Freud held that there was an interplay or conflict between the three basic components of the personality: the id, the ego, and the superego. A sort of morality play developed according to Freud's thinking. The **id** represents basic instinctual cravings such as aggression drives for sex and food. Some of these urges may be observed in children's "uncontrolled behavior." The **ego** develops through learning about life as it is, not as the id wants it to be. The ego develops so that satisfaction may be obtained within the constraint of society. The ego is the *reality principal* because it must reconcile conflict between the id and superego. The **superego** represents socially accepted codes of behavior. When the individual violates a moral code, guilt or shame is represented in the superego. Conflict occurs because the id is developed biologically and the superego developed through experience, training, and parental influence. Because individuals feel guilty about basic drives, such as sex or aggression, they may repress these drives from the conscious down into the unconscious and treat them as if they were nonexistent. However they surface symbolically.

Freudian theory emphasizes the symbolic and the unconscious. Freudian thinkers argue that deep-seated forces lead to the purchase of certain products because of a symbolic association with repressed drives. A number of Freudian interpretations are quite interesting. For example:

■ A man buys a convertible as a substitute mistress.

■ People eat soup to call up positive images of childhood and their mother's love.[17]

■ A woman is very serious when she bakes a cake because unconsciously she is going through the symbolic act of giving birth.[18]

Perhaps the last item should be explained. To a Freudian, the cake-maker adds an egg (fertilization) to a mixture, then places it in the oven for gestation. Ultimately, the cake rises and "birth" occurs when the cake is removed.

---

[17] E. Dichter, *Handbook of Consumer Motivations* (New York: McGraw-Hill, 1964), p. 67.

[18] P. Kotler, "Behavior Models for Analyzing Buyers," *Journal of Marketing*, October 1956, p. 43.

AN INDEPENDENT BREED

Personality research led Merrill Lynch to drop its well-recognized "Bullish on America" theme. This campaign was created during the early seventies, when the country was in a glum mood. It appealed to people who like to think of themselves as belonging to a group. The heavy investor is a high need achiever; an individualist with a great deal of self-confidence. The new campaign theme, "Merrill Lynch—A Breed Apart," communicates the message that the investment firm is also individualistic and achievement oriented—a breed apart from the rest of the herd.

Source: Based on information in N. Giges, "Why Y and R Took Bull Out of the Herd," *Advertising Age*, November 9, 1981, p. 82.

Self-Concept

As a member of society, every individual has a certain status as well as roles to play. Everyone has been exposed to norms and values. Indeed, these things, plus the individual's mental and physical traits and experiences, combine to make up that individual. As Exhibit 8-11 shows, it is possible to "map" all the roles an individual plays so as to help in the identification of the "self." The term **self-concept** refers to the individual's perception and appraisal of himself or herself. Of course, the appraisal of others plays a part in this but, ultimately, our self-concept is created by each of us as individuals.

In simple terms, the self-concept is the person's own picture of who he or she is, and who

Self-concept is the individual's perception and appraisal of herself.

EXHIBIT 8-11

The Central Roles and Reciprocal Roles for a "Hypothetical Man"

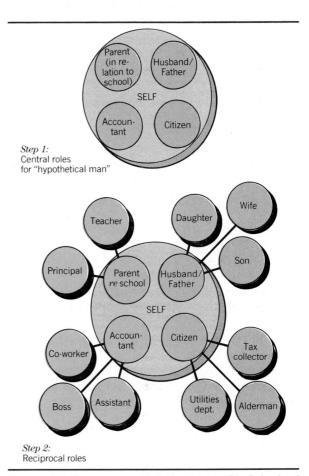

Step 1:
Central roles
for "hypothetical man"

Step 2:
Reciprocal roles

Source: J.D. Thompson and D.R. Van Houten, *The Behavioral Sciences: An Interpretation* (Menlo Park, Calif.: Addison-Wesley, 1970), pp. 86–87.

that person is in the process of becoming. The element of the future is nearly inescapable since most people automatically view themselves as becoming richer, poorer, older, stronger, or otherwise changing. This is reflected in the many advertisements which hold out the promise of a positive change in the individual brought about by a better car, exercise program, diet, appearance and so on.

Self-concept has two basic elements. The first is the internal, private picture of the self. It is the way one sees oneself. The individual may "know" that he or she is attractive no matter what others say, or "smart" no matter what the teacher says, or headed for "success" no matter what Dad says. The second part of self-concept is external. It is reflected in the way others behave toward the individual in question.[19] If the individual believes he or she is absolutely charming, but hasn't had a date in five years, other people are indicating that that individual's per-

ception may be off-base. A person whose style of dress is intended to show individualism may be perceived by others as a slob.

What does the alligator prominently shown on a preppy shirt say about the wearer? What do we surmise about someone whose shirt bears the J.C. Penney Fox? Self-concept is a potent influence in the matter of why someone buys, would like to buy, or does not buy a marketer's product. For many people, one's possessions

[19]J.D. Thompson and D.R. Van Houten, *The Behavioral Sciences: An Interpretation* (Reading: Addison-Wesley Publishing, 1970), p. 53.

are an expression of one's self-concept, as are the things they *hope* to have. Conversely, for some people, the absence of certain possessions serves to express their self-concepts. One example of this is the Volkswagen "Beetle," the ultimate practical, nonstylish car, which for many years was a "reverse status symbol." Some who drove one intended to show that their self-confidence was so great they did not need a fancy car to feed their ego.

SUMMARY

In this chapter, you have encountered the consumer decision-making process, looking at it, perhaps for the first time, from the "outside." It is a complex topic, though an underlying theory helps to put the process in perspective from both the buyer's point of view *and* the effective marketer's.

The concept of stimulus-response is the foundation of consumer behavior. Much of this behavior process is hidden from analysis, as is shown by the black box model. However, marketers can note the inputs flowing into the black box and the outputs which result. In this way, through careful analysis, they can approach an understanding of consumer and organizational buyer behavior.

Motivation refers to an individual's internal drive state, which causes the person to initiate behavior. Aroused yet unsatisfied motives may serve as an internal stimulus or drive. Motives may be classified as physiological (those motives stemming from biological needs) or psychological and social (those motives resulting from interaction with the social environment).

According to Maslow, there is a hierarchy of needs common to individuals. These needs are (1) physiological needs, (2) safety needs, (3) love or social needs, (4) self-esteem needs, and (5) self-actualization needs.

Aroused motives tend to heighten tension, and cognitive activities usually immediately begin to reduce the tension. Such activities include perception, learning, thinking, attitude formation and change, information processing, and reasoning. Perception is the process of interpreting sensations and giving meaning to stimuli, while selective perception refers to the discriminating aspects of an individual's perception. For marketers a basic fact regarding perception is that consumers pay attention to advertisements for products that interest them, either functionally or symbolically.

Learning has been defined as any change in behavior or cognitions as a result of experience. Three factors involved in the learning process are stimulus, response, and reinforcement. Compatible with learning theory, the marketing concept emphasizes consumer satisfaction (reward) and reinforcement with repeat purchases.

Attitudes are complex, learned predispositions that move us to make a favorable or unfavorable response to a given object. Although it is difficult to predict a specific behavior from an attitude, purchasing behavior is often quite consistent with attitudes. There are three distinguishing components of an attitude—affective, cognitive, and behavioral components.

Decision-making is a cognitive process involving thought, memory searching, information processing, and judgmental evaluation. There are several distinct stages in the decision-making process. These are problem recognition, search, evaluation, purchase decision, and post-purchase evaluation. The decision-making process may involve complex problem-solving, as in, say, the purchase of industrial equipment, or the decision-making process might be habitual, as in buying a soft drink.

The general dispositions of people, especially their dominant behavioral characteristics, are termed personality. One important theory of personality was developed by Sigmund Freud. Dividing the personality into three components, id, ego, and superego, Freud maintained that there was a constant interplay and conflict between the components. Freudian theory emphasizes the importance of symbolism and the unconscious in affecting behavior and personality.

THE MOST IMPORTANT CONCEPT IN THIS CHAPTER

Attempting to model consumer behavior is a difficult business, but the five-step buyer decision-making model, even when it is complicated by the addition of many personal and situational variables, provides a good guide to the process. Each step, and even each "confusing" variable, in the process provides effective marketers with knowledge of what's going on, and with opportunities to adjust the marketing mix to achieve customer satisfaction.

KEY TERMS

Stimulus (input)	Learning	Selective interpretation	Decision-making process
Response (output)	Operant conditioning	Stimulus factors	Perceived risk
Motivation	Reinforcement	Individual factors	Choice criteria
Need	Attribution theory	Selectively retained	Purchase satisfaction
Motive	Black box	Brand image	Cognitive dissonance
Drive	Perception	Evoked set	Personality
Physiological needs	Selective perception	Affective	Id
Social needs	Closure	Cognitive	Ego
Psychological needs	Selective exposure	Behavioral	Superego
Emotions	Selective attention	Attitude	Self-concept
Cognitive process			

QUESTIONS FOR DISCUSSION

1 List some rational and emotional buying motives for the selection of a product or the patronage of a store. Can you do this for industrial organizations?

2 What is selective perception?

3 Explain why products are repurchased by using a learning theory perspective.

4 Give some examples of where attitudes are consistent with behavior.

5 Will an unfavorable attitude lead to a behavior that is undesirable?

6 What type of attitudes might be most difficult to change?

7 Do radio stations and TV stations increase the volume to get a listener's attention during commercials?

8 Give an example of a situation in which secondary attributes become the key choice criterion.

9 How do you feel after you've just made a big purchase? What might a marketer do to reduce cognitive dissonance in the following situations:

(a) Automobile purchase
(b) A wholesaler takes on an industrial product line
(c) Purchase of an expensive video game
(d) Magazine subscription purchase where the subscriber is to be billed

10 Ernest Dichter's *Handbook of Consumer Motivation* is an interesting book. Go to your library and find out some reasons why people buy certain products.

CASE 8-1 Juicee Treat for Dogs*

Do dogs ever get tired of drinking water? The marketers of Juicee Treat, a "beefy flavored" dog drink, think so. The main ingredient of Juicee Treat is water. However, it is described as a "healthy alternative to water" because it also contains vitamin B, thiamin, niacin, protein, carbohydrates, and other ingredients. The product, which looks and smells like beef bouillon, is priced at 99 cents per quart. In addition to adding some variety to the dog bowl, the pet drink is said to prevent dry skin and kidney problems.

Questions

1 What would motivate someone to purchase this product? To what market segment does this product appeal?

2 Do you think the product benefits are worth the 99 cents per quart for Juicee Treat? Will this product be a success?

CASE 8-2 All-Star Baseball School of Chicago

The All-Star Baseball School of Chicago is a baseball camp for adult men up to the age of 63. For about $2,500 campers get to play hardball with professionals like the Chicago Cub pitcher Ferguson Jenkins for one week. The camp includes a Cub uniform, a single hotel room, meals, an awards banquet, and one week of hard work on the playing field. Most campers are far past the prime age of major-league ball players.

Questions

1 Why would a consumer spend $2,500 to go to spring training and work hard when there would

be no future chance to play professional baseball?

2 What social needs have influenced the success of these camps?

3 What part does culture play in the success of these camps?

4 Using your knowledge of consumer behavior, explain why these camps are successful.

---

*Source: Based on R. Keisman, "Is Exec Barking Up the Wrong Tree with Dog Juice? Buyers Say No," *Advertising Age*, January 11, 1982, p. 32.

PART 4

PRODUCT STRATEGY

Products are what marketers offer to consumers. They include goods, services, ideas, and any other things that can be exchanged by a supplier and a buyer or consumer. Marketers have come to realize that they must consider their "total products," viewing their market offerings as including perhaps elements unsuspected by the seller. The key to understanding "product" is to see what is bought, rented, accepted, or otherwise exchanged from the point of view of the customer.

Chapter 9 focuses on a definition and explanation of the marketing mix variable of product, with a discussion of such topics as the product as package and the product as brand name.

Chapter 10 reviews certain product-related planning tools. Among these are the product life cycle and the product portfolio.

Chapter 11 concentrates on the developing, managing, and commercialization of new products. ■

CHAPTER 9

The Elements of Products and Services

CHAPTER SCAN

This chapter is the first of three dealing with the marketing mix variable "product." In this first chapter the definition of "product" is discussed in terms of the concept known as "total product." This term reflects the fact that all products offer to buyers more than just a narrowly defined good or service. Many intangible aspects of products provide much of the satisfaction a buyer receives from a purchase.

The chapter also includes a discussion of such product-related matters as branding, trademarks, labeling, and packaging. These things are also part of the total product. Effective marketing requires that all these product-related factors be considered.

WHEN YOU HAVE STUDIED THIS CHAPTER, YOU WILL:

Be able to discuss the topic "product" as that term is broadly defined.

Be familiar with the concept of the total product and its importance to effective marketing.

Be able to categorize various products as being convenience, shopping, or specialty goods.

Be able to show how many marketing activities help to build brand image.

Be able to discuss the development of effective brand names and the occasional need to change brand names.

Understand such terminology as brand, brand name, brand mark, and trademark.

Be able to discuss the importance of packaging in the development of an effective product.

As the previous chapters of this book have established, every organization does some kind of marketing. Successful organizations, almost by definition, perform effective marketing. Some organizations, unfortunately, are not successful in developing effective marketing mixes. Whether or not the organization is effective, every marketing problem can be analyzed in terms of four variables: product, price, place, and promotion. In a sense, the preceding chapters of this textbook were an introduction to the remaining chapters, which deal specifically with the four variables of the marketing mix.

While all four marketing mix variables must fit and work together, it is logical to begin with a discussion of "product," since this is typically where most marketing planning begins. Understanding the nature of the product being offered to the market leads to questions of price, distribution, and promotion.

The simple phrase "exactly what the product is" is misleading in its straightforwardness. As we are about to see, the product an organization offers to its market is not simply a car or a soap or a charitable cause. Products have many facets, some of which are not always grasped by the people responsible for manufacturing or selling them. As with so many other things in marketing, there is more to "the product" than meets the eye.

UNDERSTANDING PRODUCT CONCEPTS

Consider this product, a cereal called Halfsies.[1] Quaker Oats Company has been marketing a cereal whose major physical characteristic is that it contains one-half the sugar of most other presweetened cereals. The basic idea behind Halfsies—its product concept—was developed because Quaker's management discovered that parents felt themselves caught in a bind over presweetened cereals. The parents wanted to please their children, but the children often prefer presweetened cereals. The parents also wanted to satisfy their own concerns over too much sugar in their children's diets, but no available presweetened cereal could address both concerns. Clearly, a new cereal that could, at least to some degree, respond to *both* concerns was in order. What better way than to split the difference and go halfway, with Halfsies?

The cereal itself is nutritious, containing corn flour, rice flour, and nine essential vitamins and minerals. Sweetness is supplemented with aspartane, a nutritive sweetener. The product, taken by itself, would seem to be an answer to

"I'M EATIN' LESS SUGAR AND LOVIN' EVERY BITE!"

He's eating new Quaker Halfsies.

Product concept is reflected in this Halfsies advertisement.

---

[1] Based on information in Larry Edwards, "Quaker Begins Wholehearted Tests of Halfsies," *Advertising Age,* August 6, 1979, p. 3.

the parents' dilemma over sweetened cereals.

Yet a cereal with one-half the sugar of other presweetened brands does not, by itself, solve *any* problems. It must reach the market. To reach the market, many marketing functions other than product development need to be performed.

Let's stick with the product itself for a moment. It needs a brand name. "Halfsies" is at least a good, descriptive, easy-to-say name. It must have a package that will attract buyers and also protect the product from damage and sogginess. At first, the new cereal was even packaged with a premium mini-microscope inside. This gift lent another aspect to the product being offered. The package also features "King of Half," who is featured on TV and in magazine ads.

In addition to tangible things, the buyer of Halfsies purchases intangibles such as the Quaker name and reputation. The fact that Halfsies are fortified with vitamins adds a product benefit that is both tangible and intangible: the vitamins (tangible benefits) are present and good for kids; the parents provide the kids with healthy food and get the feeling of being good parents (intangible benefit). Halfsies is more than just a cereal. It is a bundle of satisfactions.

What Is a Product?

Over the years, there have been many attempts to define what "a product" actually is. It *is* a thing, in the nuts and bolts sense. It *is* a reward offered to those willing to pay for it, in the sense that a mowed lawn is the payoff for someone who buys a lawn mower. A product is *both* the steak *and* the sizzle. As mentioned previously, the product is a bundle of satisfactions.

Defining a product as a bundle of satisfactions has a number of advantages. For one thing, this definition stresses the payoff provided by a product to its buyers. Thus, it is a customer-oriented definition—and very consistent with the marketing concept. Another good point about the bundle of satisfactions definition is that it stresses what the buyer gets, *not* what the seller

---

WHAT IS THE PRODUCT?

How would you answer these questions?

Are Calvin Klein jeans the same without the Calvin Klein name?

Is a gallon jug of Clorox the same product without the easy-to-hold handle on the side?

Is the lubricant WD-40 what do-it-yourselfers buy, or is it the convenience of the pressurized spray can?

Do children buy cereal for the toy spaceship inside?

Does anybody, apart from the Queen of England, really need to buy a Rolls Royce? What are "ordinary people" seeking when they buy one?

---

is selling. Why is this important? Because many buyers draw intangible or psychological benefits from these products of which the seller may be unaware.

The Total Product— A Broad View of the Product

What does a young married couple get when they buy their first house? They get much more than just a house. They get satisfactions, such as a sense of ownership, a place to start a family, nice neighbors, and a good school system. They get convenience if the house is near stores and work locations. In short, they get many things besides "a house."

It is because a product can have so many aspects and benefits that marketers have come to speak of and think in terms of what is called the **total product,** the broad spectrum of tangible and intangible benefits that a buyer might gain from a product once it has been purchased.

This broad interpretation of the product also allows marketers to segment markets. Because people are different in their needs, two different

THE BLUE JEANIUSES

Blue jeans were invented by two impoverished men—one a peddler, the other a tailor.

Levi Strauss, a Bavarian Jew, emigrated to America in 1848. At first, he made a meager living in New York City as a door-to-door dry goods peddler. Later, in San Francisco, Strauss cut and stitched a piece of heavy tent canvas and created the first pair of Levi jeans. The sturdy pants caught on, and he soon had a thriving business.

The brown cloth that Strauss dyed blue was imported from Nimes, France. It was called "serge de Nimes"—and thus was born the word "denims." A similar cloth was brought from Genoa, Italy. "Genes," the French name for Genoa, was Americanized to "jeans."

In 1872, Strauss received a letter from a struggling tailor named Jacob W. Davis. After years of hardship in Nevada, Davis had suddenly become successful selling his own brand of $3 denim and duck-cloth pants. He wrote to Strauss: "The secret of them Pents is the Rivits that I put in those Pockets."

The two men joined forces, and their riveted denims swept the country. There have been few changes in the pants design since 1873, though one notable alteration was made in 1933. Walter Haas, Sr., president of Levi Strauss, went camping wearing the original model 501 jeans, which had a copper rivet at the crotch. Relaxing by the campfire, Haas suffered "hot rivet syndrome" in a most sensitive area of his anatomy. The dangerous rivet was banished at the next Levi Strauss board of directors meeting.

Source: I. Wallace, D. Wallechinsky, and A. Wallace, "Significa," *Parade*, May 16, 1982, p. 20. Used with permission.

range of things from tangible items to services to ideas. Whether the organization's offering is largely tangible (a tape recorder), intangible (financial counseling), or even *more* intangible (ideas of zero population growth or world peace), their offering is a *product*. Products, therefore, include all manner of things that do not come immediately to mind when the seemingly simple word "product" is mentioned.

Services Are Products Too

Remember that services should be referred to as *products* just as we refer to the physical, tangible items we call goods. This is especially important since the service industry now accounts for about half of personal consumption expenditures.[2] If government is included as a service these figures swell.

If you think about an airlines' product, you will realize that it is difficult to separate goods from services entirely. This reality has led some marketing experts to array products along a continuum from "mostly good" to "mostly service." A steel girder is obviously a tangible good; a dentist clearly provides a service. But a restaurant provides both a good—the food it prepares—and a service—the cooking and serving of the food, as well as convenience, atmosphere, and other aspects of its total product offering. Thus you will find a restaurant in the middle of the goods-services scale in Exhibit 9-1.

While "service products" may be marketed somewhat differently from "goods products," the differences may not be as great as the marketing differences between a steel girder and a box of Tide. Nevertheless, there are some generalizations that may be made concerning how goods and services differ and some ramifications of those differences for marketers:

- **Services are intangible; goods are tangible.** Services, then, cannot be handled, examined, or

buyers may be receiving different sets of satisfaction from the same product.

In summary, any single product can be broadly defined in terms of its many possible benefits when the *total product* is considered. The word "product" itself suggests a broad

---

[2] Estimates of the importance of services vary because definitional problems exist. For example, the U.S. government statistics omit transportation from its definition of services and thus estimates services to account for approximately 30 percent of GNP.

tried out before they are purchased. This diminishes buyer confidence and necessitates the use, by marketers, of testimonials by respected persons or from previous buyers. Marketers may have to develop projections of what the service can deliver. Architects do this with models and drawings of proposed buildings.

■ Services "disappear" quickly. They cannot be stored. They are, in effect, highly perishable. If a car salesman loses a customer, the car remains to be sold to another. If a dentist's customer fails to make an appointment, a half-hour of the dentist's time, her product, is gone forever. The practice followed by many service marketers of lowering prices during non-peak hours, days, or seasons in an effort not to waste showtimes, hotel rooms, and resort facilities is one attempt to minimize this factor's impact.

■ Services vary widely in quality. This is because the skills of several providers of services may vary widely and because even a single provider can have a "bad day." Among a group of 10 tax consultants, considerable variation in skills and knowledge may be found. An individual tax advisor may not be as sharp at 6 P.M. as at 9:30 A.M. This problem is largely a matter of product quality control, a control that can come from the provider of the service or from the customer. The producer can screen service personnel and monitor them carefully. The producer can also monitor customer satisfaction and adjust procedures to maximize that satisfaction. Failure to do these things will result in a more direct input from consumers of services. They won't come back.

EXHIBIT 9-1

Goods-Services Continuum

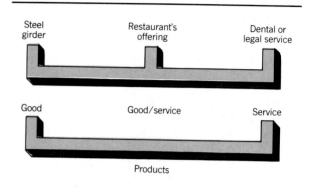

Source: Based on the concept presented in G. Lynn Shostack, "Breaking Free from Product Marketing," *Journal of Marketing*, April 1977, p. 76.

■ Services are not separable from their providers. The CPA cannot perform a service and store or ship it. The service is inseparable from the supplier of the service. If an opera buff expects to see Luciano Pavarotti in a performance and is told a substitute tenor is that night playing the lead role, certain feelings of disappointment may be encountered. Fortunately, most service marketers are not quite so unique as Pavarotti, nor are their roles so firmly constructed as an opera tenor's. The dentist can work faster, or hire a competent assistant or partner, or take any other step consistent with continuing customer satisfaction.

PRODUCT STRATEGY

Products have primary characteristics—that is, basic features and aspects, as well as auxiliary dimensions. **Auxiliary dimensions** include the product package, warranty, repair service contract, reputation, brand name, instructions for use, and so on. Each of these dimensions may provide supplementary benefits that, in combination with the functional product, fulfill buyer

needs. Any of these may be important to any particular buyer. However, the effective marketing strategist emphasizes certain benefits rather than others. The term **product concept** refers to the marketing strategist's selection and blending of a product's primary characteristics and auxiliary dimensions into a basic idea or concept emphasizing a particular set of consumer benefits.

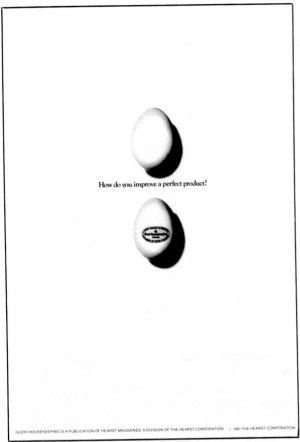

How do you improve a perfect product?

GOOD HOUSEKEEPING IS A PUBLICATION OF HEARST MAGAZINES, A DIVISION OF THE HEARST CORPORATION   c 1981 THE HEARST CORPORATION

Many subtle things—auxiliary dimensions—add supplementary benefits to products.

The product concept is the sum of a brand's benefits and attributes. Planning and developing this mix of product attributes is **product strategy.** As the discussion of Halfsies that began this chapter shows, successful product strategy requires that all aspects of the product be analyzed and properly treated. Deciding on which aspects to stress is the creative dimension of product strategy.

Who Is the Competition?

Effective marketers cannot plan their product strategies without giving close consideration to their competitors. When we realize how many dimensions a single product can have, it be-

comes clear that the question "Who are the competitors?" does not have an easy answer. Does Jell-O compete with frozen Sara Lee cheese cake? If a family buys three inexpensive cars rather than one Mercedes-Benz, are the cheaper cars in competition with the Mercedes? Marketers use three terms—product class, product category, and brand—to help put the matter of competition into perspective.

Product Class. The phrase **product class** is used to identify groups of items that may differ from each other while performing more or less the same function. Consider the product class of household cleaning products. This product class includes powdered cleaners such as Spic and Span and Soilax 3, spray cleaners such as Four Plus 1 concentrate and Fantastic, and bottled liquids such as Lysol and Murphy's Oil Soap. All of these products compete with each other, and, properly used, could perform each other's functions. That is, they provide similar benefits even though they are somewhat different.

Product Category. **Product categories** are the subsets of product types contained within a product class. In our household cleaner example, the cleaners, taken together, constitute the product class, but the subdivisions of liquids, powders, and sprays are product categories. As another example, consider the product class "beer." There are a number of product categories within that class, including light beer, regular beer, dark beer, imported beer, and so on.

Product Brand. To complete the view of competition, the marketing manager must consider the matter of *brand*. **Brands** identify and distinguish one marketer's product from its competitors. All of us are familiar with hundreds of brands of products. For example, the light beer *category* is made up of *brands* such as Miller Lite, Coors Light, Genessee Light, Stroh's Light, and many others.

We still must answer the question of just who the competition is. All three groupings or divisions—product class, category, and brand dis-

EXHIBIT 9-2

Automobiles: Product Class, Product Categories, and Product Brands

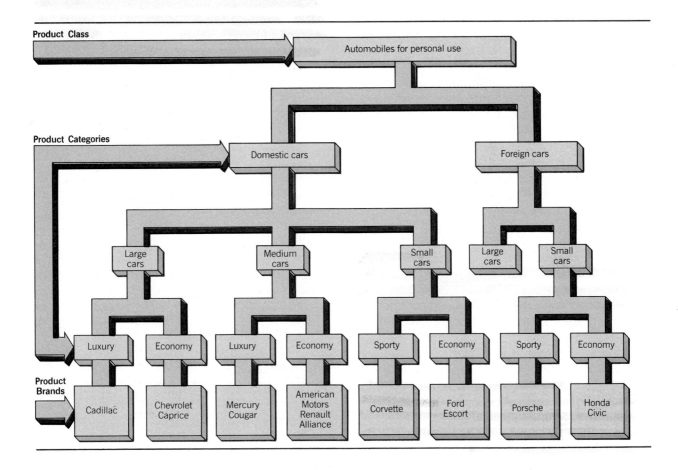

tinctions—must be considered in answering this question. A liquid cleaner like Top Job can be used to clean floors. So can a powdered cleaner like Spic and Span. Liquid Lysol can do anything that spray Lysol can do, except provide the convenience of the spray can itself.

In a sense, any cleaner, beer, or car can compete against any other member of its product class.[3] However, the realities of the market have led to the development of more finely shaped product categories consisting of products intended to meet specific consumer desires for convenience, ease of storage, light-weight

packaging, and so on. Brands of products compete primarily within categories of products, as illustrated in Exhibit 9-2. While the entire class of goods should be kept in mind, it is the product categories that contain the major competitors because the categories reflect specific consumer's wants, needs, and desires.

---

[3] In considering Exhibit 9-1, remember that the marketing analyst is free to alter the categories in any useful and meaningful way. If marketing research suggests, for example, that buyers view front-wheel and rear-wheel drive cars differently, those categories should be employed.

CLASSIFICATIONS OF CONSUMER GOODS

Many factors influence the buyer's decision-making process. One of the strongest factors is the type or nature of the product. Because, "nature of the product," involves so many physical, psychological, and purchase-behavior dimensions, the product itself is clearly one of the strongest influences on buyer behavior. For this reason, marketing managers have developed some widely accepted product classifications that are descriptive of both the products and, more importantly, how they are seen by buyers.

Many such classifications exist. However, the one believed to be developed first is the most widely recognized and the most useful. Therefore, without demeaning the efforts of others who developed improved classifications, we will concentrate on the classification scheme developed by Melvin T. Copeland in 1924. Copeland's plan suggested that there are three general classifications of consumer goods: convenience, shopping, and specialty.

Before we address Copeland's classification scheme, three important points should be made. First, the plan refers to *consumer* goods, not industrial goods. Second, and most significantly, though the classes are somewhat descriptive of the products involved, they are based on the *consumer's* reasons for buying, the *consumer's* need for information, and the *consumer's* shopping and purchase behaviors. The reason Copeland's plan, drawn up before the marketing concept was formalized, has remained popular for so long is that it is *consumer oriented.* Lastly, the classifications are somewhat generalized, based on a "typical" consumer's reasons for buying. They make good sense across the board though in the case of a specific shopper, especially if that shopper is very poor or very rich, the classification scheme is less useful.

Convenience Goods

The first of Copeland's categories is **convenience goods.** Bic disposable ballpoint pens are a convenience good. So are cigarettes. In most cases, so is gasoline. What do these items have in common? They are relatively inexpensive; they are purchased on a regular and recurring basis; they are bought almost reflexively without a great deal of thought. In fact, they are bought with a minimum of consumer shopping effort. But aren't buyers of a particular cigarette brand loyal? Yes, but the loyalty does not run very deep. Most smokers will settle for a brand that is similar to their regular brand rather than walk an extra block to get their preferred brand.

All of this boils down to the consumer behavior of buying convenience products such as these at the most *convenient* location. Hence the term convenience goods. Many disparate products, such as milk, cola, shoeshines, candy bars, and bread fit this class. How far out of your way would you go to buy a quart of a particular *brand* of milk? The answer to this question provides a guide to determining whether or not any given product is a convenience good.

Again, the key here is consumer attitudes and behaviors. Looking at these, marketers are provided with guidelines as to how to offer their convenience good products. Because extensive shopping effort rarely occurs, the marketing mix focuses in good measure on the matter of distribution. The object is to make the product available in almost every possible location. Thousands of retailers in every large city sell cigarettes and candy bars. These convenience goods are also common vending machine items. Convenience items that are purchased largely on impulse, such as razor blades, are sold in drug stores, discount houses, convenience outlets, and college bookstores. In fact, within individual stores, convenience items are usually placed at the most convenient spots, such as near the check-out counter. That many of these products can be sold through vending machines reflects the absence of a need for in-store persuasive selling. Distribution is a major element of the marketing mix for convenience goods.

Of course, the other three elements of the marketing mix must also support the convenience product. The price must be appropriate and the product itself must meet convenience criteria. Giant candy bars costing $5.50 do not meet the convenience criteria as well as the standard Snickers bar because the size of the package as well as its price places it into another product category. In the convenience goods classification, one brand is fairly easily substituted for another of a like type. Therefore, extensive advertising may be appropriate. The heavy advertising expenditures of Coca-Cola and Pepsi Cola attest to this.

Shopping Goods

Shopping goods, the second of Copeland's classifications, include those products for which consumers feel the need to make product comparisons, seek out additional information, examine merchandise, or otherwise reassure themselves before making a purchase. In other words, prospective buyers of these products want to shop around.

Decisions about shopping goods are not made on the spur of the moment. Buyers want to mull things over before committing themselves. This is due in part to the fact that shopping goods are generally priced higher than convenience goods. They also tend to be subject to the whims of fashion and are more likely to be noticed by the shopper's family and friends. Thus, the risks associated with shopping goods, both monetary and social, are fairly high. Clothing, shoes, furniture, and "everyday" silverware and china are examples of shopping goods.

Buyers of shopping goods are often brand loyal, or at least brand conscious. They are willing to search for the styles, brand names, or prices they want. Further, they may wish to purchase the products in a particular store. We hear friends say, "I got this suit at the Ivy League Shop." They seldom say, "I got this Doublemint gum at the 7-Eleven."

Thus, the distribution problem differs from that associated with convenience goods. Remembering that people are willing to shop around, the idea is not to place the product everywhere, but to place the product in the *proper* spots. The distribution strategy becomes one of selective distribution. Within a single store, it is likely that shopping goods will not be placed "up front." Furniture can be placed in distant areas of a department store because customers are willing to seek it out.

Marketing mix elements shift somewhat in relative importance when we move from the convenience to shopping goods classification. Product characteristics, including quality, become comparatively more important. Price must be appropriate, but it need not be as uniformly competitive with other brands as in the case of easily substitutable convenience goods. Retail marketers may, however, stress the price of these products since they are competing with other retailers of the same brands. The customer is shopping for a particular product category and will not buy one brand over another on the basis of price alone.

Specialty Goods

In some cases, consumers believe that they know exactly what they want. They will not accept substitutes. They don't *shop* for their purchases, they *plan* them. Goods that are the object of this sort of consumer concern fall into Copeland's third category. They are called **specialty goods.** Many of these products are seldom-purchased items such as engagement rings, pianos, or expensive cars. Potential buyers may seek a great amount of information, and spend considerable time looking at and comparing the various options. They may go so far as to buy and read books or magazines dealing with the product class.

Brand loyalty can be strong. A shopper may have decided, after considerable thought, that only Beleek china and Waterford crystal will do for the dining room. As a result, these may be the *only* acceptable brands. Sales personnel or advertising will not sway such a shopper. This is important to retailers since the customer will forego purchases if the desired brand is out of stock. For some specialty products, there is almost no brand loyalty, though loyalty to a particular *retail* marketer may be encountered. In the case of a diamond ring costing $20,000, the buyer is likely to choose the item not on the basis of brand, but on the basis of appearance bolstered by a trusted retailer's assurance that the ring is worth every penny of that price.

The marketer of a specialty good may develop a marketing mix which includes limited distribution of the brand. Dealers stocking Jaguar X-JS's are few and far between in part because a potential buyer will travel considerable distances to get one. Advertising and pricing policies must be appropriate to and support the brand's image.

INDUSTRIAL PRODUCTS

The subject of industrial marketing is covered in detail in Chapter 21. However, each of the seven classes of industrial products and some of the characteristics distinguishing them from consumer goods are outlined in Exhibit 9-3.

The Unifying Characteristics of Industrial Goods

All **industrial goods** have one thing in common: derived demand. **Derived demand** means that the demand for every industrial good depends on the demand for some *other* product. The auto mechanic's demand for metric tools is derived from the consumer's demand for imported cars. The demand for tempera paints, water colors, and chalk sold to the art departments of public schools is derived from the demand of students or their parents for a basic, well-rounded education. Many students are enrolled in a marketing course to earn credits towards a degree in business administration. The demand for the course is derived from the demand for the degree. When the economy slows down and consumer demand for products drops, the volume of business travel declines. Hilton Hotels, "America's business address," may suffer accordingly. Ultimately, the demand for all industrial goods depends on consumer demand for finished goods and services.

The Classifications of Industrial Goods

Industrial products can be categorized in much the same way as are consumer goods. Though the most commonly used classification system may at first glance appear to be more product oriented than the convenience-shopping-specialty goods plan, the categories do reflect buyer concerns. For example, major industrial purchases, such as a new factory building or a computerized assembly system, involve different problems and buyer concerns than do purchases of brooms and sweeping compound. In this sense, the categories of industrial products are buyer oriented.

The seven classes of industrial products are shown in Exhibit 9-3. Examples of each type of product are shown. While a discussion of the implications for marketing strategy appropriate to each class is postponed until Chapter 21, the following list outlines the basic characteristics of each class.

1 Raw materials. Raw materials are industrial products that are still very close to their natural states. That is, they have undergone almost no processing. Bars of aluminum, chunks of granite that will be made into statuary, and trees to be made into lumber or paper are good examples.

2 Component parts (fabricated materials). These goods are a step above raw materials in the processing chain. They include such things as screws, sheet metal, and parts of all sorts that end up in a finished product. To a maker of lawn mowers, spark plugs, wires, and bushings are all component parts. Notice that unlike raw materials, component parts and fabricated materials have undergone some considerable processing.

3 Process materials. One class of industrial products is used in making finished products but

EXHIBIT 9-3

Classification of Industrial Products

Product	Description	Example
Raw materials	Ingredients of the final product that must undergo processing	Zinc, pig iron, cotton
Component parts and fabricated materials	Manufactured items incorporated into the final assembled product	Electrical resistors, screws, electric motors
Process materials	Goods used in the production of a product but which do not become part of the finished product	Chemicals, oils, and other goods used to treat parts prior to their inclusion in the final product
Installations	Primary production equipment and major capital items	Buildings, computer hardware, assembly line
Accessory equipment	Accessory equipment that facilitates operations	Word processing machine, trucks
Operating supplies	Short-lived items that facilitate routine operations	Writing paper, lubricants, order forms, hand tools
Services	Work provided by others	Maintenance service, automobile rental, repair service, CPA accounting service

does not become part of these products. These goods are called process materials. They are used in the manufacturing process, but they are never encountered by later buyers in their original form. An example of such a product is an acid that is used to soak dirt and grime off machine parts.

4 Installations. Installations are capital items necessary to the manufacture of a final product. Buildings, assembly lines, heating plants, and other such major purchases are included in this category. Many of these products are made to order, such as an air conditioning system for a factory. "The product" is not on a shelf or in a warehouse where potential customers can view it.

5 Accessory equipment. Accessory equipment facilitates an organization's operations. Generally included in this category are such things as pick-up trucks, fork lifts, typewriters, word processors, and desk calculators. These items do not, as a rule, involve the large capital outlays associated with installations. They are not generally thought of as being specially built to do only one job, although a product such as a pick-up truck can be modified to handle certain specialized tasks.

6 Operating supplies. Operating supplies are the closest thing to a "convenience good" in the industrial goods classification scheme. This group includes paper, pencils, brooms, envelopes, and other short-lived items that are routinely bought and used up as the organization operates.

7 Services. Services may be broadly defined as work provided by others. Thus, the category is a general one including everything from janitorial service and machinery maintenance to the services of lawyers, CPAs, or medical providers.

THE PRODUCT LINE AND THE PRODUCT MIX

In discussing the classifications of consumer products and industrial products, we have treated each product type separately, as if a given organization offered just one good or service. The reality is that most organizations market more than one product. Even an industrial cleaning company, whose product would appear to be simply "cleaning," offers an array of services. Does the client want a daily clean-up or a weekly one? Did the client hire the company to do a once-a-year major cleaning or to clean-up after some remodeling work? Does the customer want the windows washed? What the cleaning firm has to offer is, in fact, a product line.

From a marketing company's perspective, then, the firm's **product line** is a group of products that are fairly closely related. McDonald's food product line has grown to include several hamburger variations, fish sandwiches, chicken nuggets, and several breakfast items. Each item in McDonald's product line is within the same product class.

The products which constitute a product line may be related to one another in several ways. They may be similar only in a broad sense because of product class. Procter & Gamble has, for example, a food products line, a paper products line, and a cleaning products line. Products in a line may perform some particular function such as grooming. Clairol's hair coloring product line is somewhat different from its shampoo and conditioner line and certainly different from its line of hair dryers, curlers, and other appliances. A product line may also be identified as a group of products that are sold to the same customer groups, as are Skill home shop tools, or a group of products marketed through the same outlets as are Ace Hardware and True Value Hardware products. A product line may be identified by price or quality. A&P divides its private label products into lines based on price. Its cheaper Iona brand products are distinct from its more expensive Ann Page brands. Sears has, from time to time, identified its products as Sears, Sears' better, and Sears' best.

What variable should be used to distinguish one product line from another? The answer depends on the organization's resources and the marketer's goals. A manufacturer of a full line of canned food products might find it useful to refer to its "generic" line, its "regular" line, and its "premium" line when the marketing goal is to show potential customers that a wide price and quality range of goods can be purchased from a single supplier. If the same manufacturer is dealing with a chain of supermarkets that stocks only high-quality products, it may be useful to speak only about the "premium" canned food line and the "diet" version of the same products. Big city

Consumers trust brand leaders

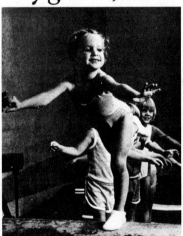

As Amy grows, so do we...

with leadership brands.

In packaged foods, casual footwear, children's apparel, cosmetics, fragrances, health and beauty products, Chesebrough-Pond's brands are the names Americans trust and turn to—day in, day out. This has helped us increase our sales and earnings for 24 years straight—and pay dividends without interruption since 1883.

For an independent investment analysis, call your stockbroker.

Chesebrough-Pond's Inc.

Consistent profitable growth... through leadership brands.

retailers may want to deal with food suppliers who carry a standard line and an ethnic line of products. In such circumstances, the marketer will present lines of goods that differ according to the different needs of the various groups.

Because any one marketing organization may be able to offer several classifications of products and define its various lines of products in many ways, there is a need for a term that encompasses all offerings of the organization no matter how unrelated these may be. That term is **product mix.** General Motors Corporation manufactures and sells large-, medium-, and small-sized cars, buses, Army tanks, locomotive engines, a wide range of parts and other products. It also provides repair services, training for mechanics and users of some of GM's more complicated products, and many other industrial products. The General Electric Company makes a wide range of consumer and industrial products. It also operates radio and TV stations. Many other organizations are similarly diversified. The term *product mix* is used to identify the entire group of products associated with one firm no matter how diverse they might be. Frequently, we are surprised to discover just how varied the product mix of a firm like Cheseborough-Ponds, Beatrice Foods, or Procter & Gamble really is.

BRANDING

There is a legend that the practice of branding products originated when an ancient ruler decided that goods should bear some sort of symbol so that, if something should go wrong, buyers and the authorities would know who was to blame. Forced to identify their products with themselves, the story goes, producers began to take greater pride in their products and to make them better than those of their competitors, thus reversing the negative intent of the king's order. Whether the story is true or not, it makes the point that branding serves many purposes within our society. It helps buyers to determine which manufacturer's products are to be avoided and which are to be sought.

Branding serves both the buyer and the seller. Without branding, a buyer would have difficulty recognizing products that had proved satisfactory in the past. Many consumers do not know enough about implications of the physical aspects of products they buy to be able to analyze competing items strictly on the basis of physical characteristics. They rely, therefore, on the brand's or firm's reputation as an assurance that the product being purchased meets certain standards. Branding also helps sellers to attract and build cadres of loyal customers and to show that the firm stands behind what it offers. A brand that has earned an association with a quality reputation may make introducing new products somewhat easier. Part of the attraction of Anacin-3 is its connection with the original Anacin, a branded product with a long record of public acceptance. In large measure, the free enterprise economy, with its accent on letting the market decide which firms will succeed and which will fail, would not be operable without branding. Even societies that have tried to do away with branding, such as the Soviet Union, have found that citizens will somehow determine which products are "good" and which are "bad" even if they have to use product serial numbers or other bits of information to differentiate between products.

Brands and Trademarks

Despite the common practice of speaking of brands, brand names, and trademarks as if all these terms mean the same things, there are some technical differences among them that should be noted.

Brands. A **brand** is any name, term, symbol, sign, design, or a unifying combination of these, that identifies and distinguishes one product

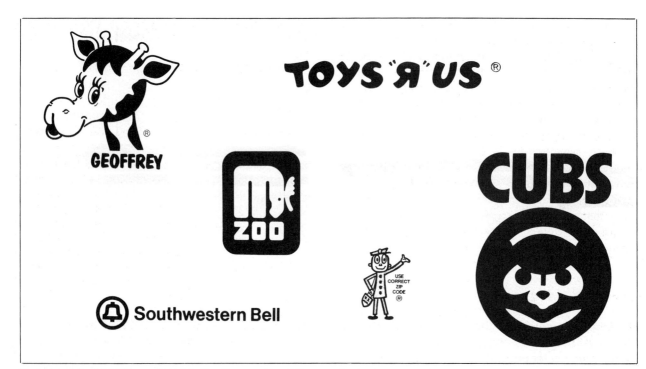

Brand marks identify and symbolically represent the product or company.

from another competitive product. Thus, we have Sanka *brand* coffee, with the emphasis on the word "brand" to distinguish this product from the many other decaffeinated coffees.

A **brand name** is the verbal part of the brand. Excedrin, Cover Girl, and IBM are brands. Whether verbalized or written, they are brand names.

Many branded products rely heavily upon some symbol for identification. Ford and Coca-Cola are brands that are closely associated with a certain style of script. White Horse scotch whiskey makes considerable use of a weathered tavern sign, and Apple Computers can be represented by a rainbow colored apple that has a bite out of it. The Olympic games' five-ring symbol is a similarly familiar rendering. Such unique symbols are referred to as **brand marks.** When a brand name or company name is written in a distinctive way, as are the TRW company's forward-leaning initials, this is called a **logo,** short for "logotype."

Trademarks. Thus far, the distinctions between these brand-related terms may not seem startlingly significant. While it is important to know these terms, the word that has a true legal significance is *trademark*. A brand or brand name can be almost anything a marketer wants it to be, but it may not have any legal status. A **trademark,** on the other hand, is a legally protected brand name or brand mark. The owners of trademarks have exclusive rights to their use. Thus, the word "trademark" is a legally defined term. A brand name is either a registered trademark or it is not.

The registered trademark gives a marketer proprietary rights to a symbol or name. The NBC peacock is a registered trademark. So is the name Coca-Cola *and* the script style in which it is written *and* its distinctive bottle. The holder of a trademark has exclusive right to utilize the trademarked name or symbol. A certain amount of protection is thus provided to the trademark holder. The name "Ball Park Frankfurters" is a registered trademark so no other franks with that name are likely to appear on the market.

If a legal authority can be induced to agree that the similarity is too great and constitutes an infringement of the original trademark, there is even some protection against similar names. A company selling "Ball *Game* Frankfurters" is thus very likely to hear from lawyers representing the "Ball *Park* Frankfurter" company. In the same way, Coca-Cola has fought off products with names like Cooka-Coola, Cola-Coola, and so on.

A trademark is an intellectual property. Just as an author owns the rights to a book or a composer the rights to a song, so the marketing company owns the rights to its products' legally protected trademarks.[4] Imitations, or even honestly accidental similarities, are usually evaluated in court. Judges have decided that "Old Kentucky Fried Chicken" is too similar to Colonel Sanders' "Kentucky Fried Chicken." Miller Lite tried to block the brewers who followed with their own "Light" beers. Miller was granted protection of the term "Lite," but the judge decided that "Light" may be used by anyone else since that is a common descriptive word. The company marketing Cadillac dog food was once hauled into court by the Cadillac Motor Division of General Motors. The judge decreed that the products involved were clearly not alike and protection of the Cadillac name could not be extended beyond the automotive trade. The law covering such matters, the **Lanham Act,** declares that brand names cannot be confusingly similar to or used for the same purpose as registered trademarks. This wording necessitates having someone—the judge—determine which names are confusingly similar and which are *un*confusingly similar.

Service Mark. One last term, *service mark*, should be mentioned. **Service marks** provide the same identifying function for services that trademarks provide for products. Like brands, they can be legally protected by registration. The

---

THE END OF A MONOPOLY

Monopoly is no longer a valid trademark held by Parker Brothers; Monopoly is now in the public domain. The U.S. Supreme Court refused to review the decision of the 9th Circuit of Appeals (San Francisco) judgment that said, in effect, that Parker Brothers had no monopoly on Monopoly. The Court implied that in order for a firm to have a valid trademark, the public must know the name of the company that produced the product. Thus, according to this ruling (which may be limited) people should have known that Monopoly is produced by Parker Brothers. Survey research evidence at the trial indicated that people did not know that Monopoly was produced by Parker Brothers. However, this appears to be contrary to other trademark law because most people do not know the name of the companies that produce Cheer laundry detergent and Lego toys.

Marketers have traditionally defended their trademarks by commissioning consumer surveys that identified the name as a bona fide trade name. DuPont Co. successfully defended its ownership of the Teflon mark with opinion research. DuPont listed eight names—STP, Thermos, Margarine, Teflon, Jell-O, Refrigerator, Aspirin, and Coke—and asked people to identify each as a brand or a common name. After 68 percent identified Teflon as a brand name, DuPont was able to enforce its trademark rights.

The Court also ruled that the term Monopoly was utilized to refer to a generic game and that few people referred to the game as Monopoly a "real estate trading game" as the company argued. Parker Brothers had failed to give consumers another word to use such as Scotch Brand cellophane tape utilizes to protect its trademark.

---

[4] Name Lab, Inc., *Everything You Need to Know About Trademarks*, 1982, p. 1.

NBC chimes and GM's Mr. Goodwrench are thus legally protected. Service marks may also include slogans like "Fly the Friendly Skies of United" or Holiday Inn's "Number One in People Pleasing."

Generic Names

Some words are so obviously part of our language that no one should be permitted to register rights to them. These terms, known as **generic names,** describe a product or item, that is part of our standard vocabulary, for example "flower" or "cat food." Other words and terms, such as nylon, kerosene, escalator, cellophane, and formica, were originally invented to name a particular product, but they have become legally generic and usable by anyone through common usage. Therefore, the 3M Company can call their tape "Scotch Brand cellophane tape," but 3M can no longer claim that it is the one and only cellophane tape. In many instances, a brand name becomes a generic term when a judge determines that a word, such as "formica," is in such common usage that the original formulator of the word can no longer hold the right to it.

It is because valuable brand names can and do become legally generic that Muzak advertisements stress that there is only one Muzak, with a capital M. Dictaphone advertisements call attention to the fact that there is only *one* Dictaphone. Coca-Cola bends every effort to make certain that you do not get a Pepsi when you ask a waiter for a Coke. Coke, Vaseline, Kleenex, Frisbee, and other commonly used names, names that are in fact employed to mean a generic product class, may one day be declared *legally* generic.

Do you call a copy machine a Xerox machine? The Xerox name is worth protecting.

The surf dashing upon the rocky shore sounded a cacophony in the disappearing night.

A lone gull swooped, a cackling reminder to the angry sea. Through the mist that crept along the edge of the cliff, two figures moved eerily toward a climactic confrontation.

A sliver of moonlight bathed their faces as he reached out and swept her up into his embrace.

And with the passion born of centuries he whispered, "Did you know that Xerox is a registered trademark of Xerox Corporation and, as a brand name, should be used only to identify its products and services?"

Please don't use our name in vain.

The name Xerox is one of the most famous in America. We're very flattered.

But we'd like to remind you that just as there are ways you can use our name, there are ways you shouldn't.

Despite what you may say, there is no such thing as a xerox.

In other words, you can't make a xerox. You can't go to the xerox. And you can't xerox anything. Ever.

On the other hand, you can make copies on the Xerox copier.

You can go to the Xerox copier or the Xerox computer.

And you can read a Xerox textbook. We're happy to have you use our name.

All we ask is that you use it the way the good law intended.

XEROX

XEROX is a trademark of XEROX CORPORATION

ALFRED E. PACKARD GRILL

At the University of Colorado—Boulder, the student union restaurant is named the Alfred E. Packard Grill. It is named after the only convicted cannibal in the history of the state of Colorado. Is this a good brand name? Why?

A "Good" Brand Name

What constitutes a "good" brand name? Instant Ocean, a synthetic sea salt for use in marine fish aquariums, has a good brand name. It is *easy to remember*. It is *easy to say*. It is *pronounceable*, at least in English, in only one way. It is a name with a *positive connotation*. It is a name that suggests what the product is supposed to do. Irish Spring deodorant soap, Orange Crush soda, and O.B. tampons from Johnson & Johnson, are also excellent names in that they *associate the product with an image* that is meaningful to consumers. Most names used for lipsticks, such as Love brands, suggest beauty or sensuousness. Cereal names, such as Fruit 'n Fibre, call to mind health and wholesomeness.

Brand names are often useful in reinforcing an overall product concept. Brands like Land O' Lakes Butter, L'Eggs, Duracell, Moist and Easy, or Nature Made may *communicate product attributes* far better than any other variable in the marketing mix. Consider, for example, the meanings and connotations associated with the Honda Motor Company's "Civic" automobile and Nissan Motors' "Sentra." The Civic is suggestive of a smaller car made for urban driving whose owner is civic-minded since the car doesn't use much gas. It may even suggest that the car is somehow a more civilized choice than a large, offensive gas-guzzler might be. Nissan Motors' "Sentra," on the other hand, may bring to mind the idea of a sentry, a safety preserver, counteracting some buyers' concerns about the car's small size and light weight. Notice, too, that many Japanese cars carry model names that

suggest other countries, such as Italy, Spain, or the United States. In fact, considerable marketing research was used when the name "Sentra" was chosen for the U.S. market in place of "Sunny," which was the name most people knew around the world. Research discovered that when people spelled "Centra" with a "C," they thought it was a domestic car; but when spelled with an "S," they thought it was an import car, though they weren't able to define whether it might be European or Japanese.

Notice that brand names and symbols say something about the product. Jiffy cake mix is quick. Ocean Freeze is fresh-frozen fish. Toast 'Em Pop-Ups tell what they are *and* how to cook them. Spic and Span and Beautyrest both tell what to expect from these products. But the brand name *also* says something about the buyers for which the product is intended. Narragansett is the beer for New Englanders. Lone Star is the beer for Texans. Rebel Yell is a brand name for a bourbon sold in the Deep South. If the market area of the bourbon is expanded, the brand name will appeal to displaced Southerners or to people who feel some affinity with Southern lifestyle. Eve and Virginia Slims are cigarette brand names that appeal to certain types of women.

A good brand name has a *mnemonic quality*, something that makes it *distinctive* and easily remembered. It has something that sticks in buyers' minds. To achieve this quality, most brand names are short, easy to pronounce, and unique. Exxon and Citgo, words coined by petroleum companies, are good brand names. Exxon's office systems division offered products called Qwip, Qyz, and Vydec, names that were unique but also something of a problem to pronounce. A name like Theragram-M is more difficult to remember than One-A-Day Vitamins, though the "medical" sound of Theragram may make the "extra" promotional efforts needed to make it "stick" worth the added effort. Toys-Я-Us, the children's supermarket, employs childlike backward R's to conjure an image of children *and* to make the name unique. When the sign on the first store, opened in 1954, led many customers to inform the manager that the R on the sign was backward, the founder of the firm knew he had hit on a name that people noticed and remembered. In fact, the R was used instead of the word "Are" to shorten the store's name, permitting bigger letters to be used on the first outlet's sign. Local ordinances prohibited enlarging the sign itself.

Brand names that are inappropriate to any market environment may "kill" an otherwise acceptable product. Recently, the restaurant chain Sambo's went under. This was partly due to the negative racial connotation associated with the name. Dr. Pepper, although a successful product, is believed by many consumers to be somehow medicinal—a fact that helps sell the product to certain buyers, but keeps others away.

Inventors of brand names must also be aware of linguistic traps. Cue toothpaste did not do well in French-speaking areas since "cue" is a slang expression for the human posterior. Conversely, a bubble gum maker attempting to crack the Italian market, succeeded when it changed its product name from "Big Bubble" to "Big Babol." Italian teens, the target market, would have read the first name as "Beeg Boob-leh" and not associate it with the product that they, in fact, know as bubble gum. "Babol" is read as "Bah-bowl," and the kids easily identified the product as bubble gum.

What steps should a company take when selecting a good brand name? The following steps have proven useful.[5]

1 Identify the objectives or criteria for the brand name, such as memorable (short, easy to say), descriptive of product attributes and benefits, positive connotation that fits with brand image, distinctive or unique name, or a criterion specific to the situation.

2 Generate brand name alternatives.

3 Screen the alternatives for appropriateness.

4 Research consumers' opinion, preference, image of brand name.

DRI-WEES, WINKS, TENDERS, TADS, SOLOS, OR ZEPHERS?

These were some of the brand names suggested for the disposable diapers now called Pampers. The name Pampers was selected because research showed the feeling of tender loving care parents give to their children was reflected in the name Pampers.

---

5 Conduct trademark search.

6 Select final brand name.

Many of the things that characterize a good brand name also apply to brand marks. A brand mark that is simple, contains few colors, and is unique and memorable is best. Thus, the Olympic rings, the Ballantine beer "Three Ring Sign," the camel on the Camel cigarette package, and the Chevrolet trapezoidal design are all good symbols. They can be made small or large and still be easily recognized. They do not involve complicated art work to render them in advertisements. Most importantly, they "stick" with the consumer.

Brand marks and other symbols may also be effective communicators. Elsie the Cow and Betty Crocker remain well-known and popular figures even though they have been around for more than 50 years. Elsie is "simple and honest, and reminds the public of gentler times when life was less confusing." Borden executives feel that "now, more than ever, people are buying products they know they can trust, and what better symbol can we use to gain trust?"[6] The Exxon Tiger suggests the smoothly powerful image Exxon officials want its gasoline to portray. The Tiger does this so well, in fact, that it was brought back from the "home for retired commercial characters" in a TV commercial when Exxon discovered that it was so well-remembered by customers.

---

[5]J.U. McNeil and L.M. Zeren, "Brand Names Selection for Consumer Products," *MSU Business Topics* (Spring 1981), pp. 35–39.

[6]Sam Harper, "Elsie Moo-ves Back into the Ad Limelight," *Advertising Age*, November 19, 1979, p. 91.

Black and Decker Versus Craftsman

Many of the brand names we are most familiar with are owned and advertised by the firms that actually manufacture these products. Black and Decker tools are made by the company of the same name. These brands are called **manufacturer brands** or **national brands,** though the latter name is less accurately descriptive.

We also frequently encounter products whose names are owned by retailers. Sears' respected line of Craftsman tools is a good example. Brands owned by Sears, A&P, Kroger, and other retailers are called **distributor brands** or **private brands.** (Here, again, the name distributor brand is more descriptive.) Brands owned by wholesalers, such as IGA, are also called distributor brands.

Why are there two types of brands, especially when Black and Decker, as a case in point, is likely to be the actual manufacturer of the Sears Craftsman line of electrical tools? The answer is that each brand serves a different purpose. The manufacturer's brand is intended to create customer loyalty toward the products of a particular manufacturer. Beyond this, it gives the manufacturer a means to control its own products. The products bear its name, are promoted in ways it deems appropriate, and the flow of profit is directed toward the firm. On the other hand, the distributor's brand is intended to build loyalty for a retailer or wholesaler. The retailer, having control over the brand, can advertise it or not, or change its price, label, and so forth, in any way necessary to please its own customers. Traditionally, private or distributor's brands provide the retailer with a higher margin than do manufacturer's branded goods. To retailers, and to other distributors supplying retailers, this is an undeniably attractive feature of private brand goods.

Why should Black and Decker or any other manufacturer supply a retailer with products to be sold under the distributor's brand rather than the manufacturer's? One reason is that the goods may be sold to the retailer on a fairly mechanical basis. The specifications are met, the dealer takes possession of the goods, and

Distributors often have their own private brands.

the manufacturer's job is finished. There is a certain appeal in letting the distributor handle the pricing, advertising, selling, and guaranteeing of these products. The manufacturer may also be able to smooth out production runs or make better use of assets by producing distributor's brand merchandise *and* its own manufacturer's brand goods. By the way, manufacturers who provide retailers and wholesalers with goods of this type refer to the products as "contract merchandise" since the products are made to order according to contract. Since a contract is involved, the manufacturer also gets the benefit of a guaranteed sale from such an arrangement.

Another reason exists for the manufacturer to provide a distributor-labeled product that will be sold, more cheaply, right next to its own nationally branded one: If Libby's doesn't want the business, Del Monte probably does.

Bare Bones and No Frills

As we have seen in recent years, it is possible for a product to carry neither a manufacturer's or a distributor's brand. These products, known as **generic products** or **generic brands,** feature a plain package, usually white, with stark, typically black lettering that simply lists the contents. These "no-name" brands offer no guarantees of high quality and are produced and distributed inexpensively. Some portion of the cost savings is passed on to consumers.

The concept of generic brands is not new. Many years ago, shoppers bought most food products from bins and barrels. These were truly generic goods. And, for years, a low-priced sun tan lotion named "No Ad," for "no advertising dollars were spent on this product," has been sold in the beach areas of Florida. However, during recent times, with increasing economic pressure on household budgets, many no frills products have been making significant gains in supermarket sales, particularly in such product categories as fabric softeners, tea bags, canned green beans, and facial tissues. Even among some products where brand identity is a major factor influencing purchases, such as cigarettes and beer, generics have had a modest success.[7] Many of the same factors that encourage manufacturers to supply distributor brand goods serve to make manufacturers interested in producing generic goods.[8] In fact, many manufacturers have found "contract work" so attractive that they have reduced their activities in the manufacturer's brand arena to concentrate on profitable work in the generic area. It is arguable that distributor's brands, and especially no-name brands, deny consumers the guarantee of consistent quality that a national brand provides. Consumers, however, are free to decide whether that guarantee is worth a higher retail price. Clearly, many have determined that it is not.

---

[7]Sam Harper, "L&M: Generics Rush to the Rescue," *Advertising Age*, June 1, 1981, p. 4.

[8]For an interesting discussion see K.B. Rotzoll, C.H. Patti, and R.P. Fisk, "Store Brand and National Advertiser: A Historical Perspective with Contemporary Options," *Journal of the Academy of Marketing Science* (Winter/Spring 1982), pp. 90–108.

Non-Consumer Generic Products. Before leaving the topic of generic products, we should note that the concept of generics has had long-standing acceptance in industrial and international marketing. Many industrial goods are interchangeable, regardless of who makes them, as long as they meet the buyer's specifications. Sheet metal with the necessary strength and alloy content is acceptable to a manufacturer of freezers no matter what its brand name. Similarly, many products traded internationally are virtually without brand name. When U.S. companies send wheat to the U.S.S.R. or oil to Japan, the nature and quality characteristics are important to the buyers, but not the supplier's name. However, as previously discussed, even in situations like this, effective marketing and a consideration of the total product being offered, can provide organizations opportunities to make themselves preferred suppliers.

Family Brands
Versus Individual Brands

When Mrs. Paul's Kitchens, a company known for its frozen fish products, decided to add a line of frozen fried chicken, management made the decision to utilize the Mrs. Paul's name on the new product. The company was thus able to capitalize on its well-known brand name while distinguishing the chicken products from the fish with the slogan "Even if you don't like fish, you can still love Mrs. Paul's."[9] This strategy is called **brand extension** in that it places an "old" name in use in "new" areas.

Family Brands. One form of brand extension is **family branding.** This practice involves using a single brand name like Hunt's, Del Monte, or Campbell's, over a whole line of fairly closely related items. The idea of family branding is to take advantage of a brand's reputation and the good will associated with the name. Introduction of a new product such as Jell-O Pudding Pops is made easier because of Jell-O's strong brand

---

[9]"New Wine in Old Bottles," *Time Magazine*, August 31, 1981, p. 41.

recognition. Similarly, family branding is used by Levi Strauss, General Electric, Volkswagen, and a host of other corporations.

Use of a family brand strategy does not guarantee success in the marketplace. In what was a relatively rare occurrence, a Campbell's product failed despite the Campbell's name. The product was ''Campbell's Very Own Special Special Sauce,'' a prepared spaghetti sauce. While many reasons can account for such a failure, the fact that Campbell's name is strongly associated with prepared ''American'' foods, such as franks and beans, probably had an impact here. Notice that most prepared spaghetti sauces on the market bear names like Mama Rosa's and Prégo.

Licensing. Licensing is a special case of family branding. As we have already indicated, a product's greatest strength may be an intangible quality or the symbols associated with it. Companies such as Binney and Smith have recently learned that their brand, 'Crayola' and logo type is their most valuable asset. A brand name may be a company's strongest asset. Thus, the company may **license** or make contractual arrangements with another firm so that the second firm may utilize the company's trademark. The proliferation of Star Wars, G.I. Joe, and other trademarks from movies and television shows are examples of licensing.

Individual Brands. Though the failure of its ''special'' sauce did no serious damage to the Campbell's reputation, a product that proves dangerous or of poor quality can hurt an organization's overall image. A company's other brands may suffer greatly because of quality problems with other brands of the same name. This is one reason why some firms utilize **individual brand** names rather than family brand names.

There are other reasons for adopting the individual brand strategy. One might be that the products produced by a single company differ substantially from one another. General Foods markets Maxwell House regular and instant coffees as well as Brim decaffeinated coffee. An organization may feel its products are different

THE SELLING OF THE SMURFS

In 1981, a tiny tribe of Belgium-born blue trolls made their appearance on NBC's Saturday morning television schedule. Soon, they were peddling all manner of kids' merchandise from bed sheets to bathing suits to toothbrushes. The Smurfs were in the business known as character licensing. Put another way, the Smurfs' managers appeared to be tie-in geniuses, with the Smurfs well on the way to catching up with Strawberry Shortcake, a girl who sold upwards of half a billion dollars' worth of merchandise a year.

During times of retrenchment, many companies find reasons to recruit little blue men and little pink girls to their marketing teams. In general, licensees (manufacturers of clothing, toothbrushes, etc.) rent the right to an image for a fee. Typically, the figure is 5 to 8 percent of sales.

Says Jack Chojnacki, co-president of the company which licenses Strawberry Shortcake, ''Licensing is advertising that makes money instead of costing money.'' The owners of the character get their percentage and the licensees receive a recognizable brand name and national marketing assistance. Sometimes these plans fizzle, as did the tie-in with the Robin Williams' movie, ''Popeye.'' Still, the payoffs, as with Strawberry Shortcake merchandise, have frequently been enormous. Wallace Berrie & Co., the Los Angeles novelty distributor who imported the Smurfs from Europe, did $600 million worth of Smurf business in 1982 while spending only $200 thousand on promotion.

Source: ''The Selling of the Smurfs,'' *Newsweek*, April 5, 1982, pp. 56–57.

enough that there is not much to be gained by identifying the products with one another. When products do differ significantly from others, such as Arm and Hammer baking soda deodorant, they may not flourish in the marketplace despite a familiar name.

Some organizations explain that they practice the individual branding approach because they wish to market several products that appeal to different market segments. There are many individual brands of detergents within the detergent lines of Procter & Gamble, Lever Brothers, and Colgate-Palmolive. Some contain bleaching crystals; some have fabric softeners; some have extra whitening power; some have extra strength; and some have low suds. Since these many products compete with each other, an individual brand name aids survival in the marketplace. This provides a strong reason to consider the individual branding strategy, especially when the competition is strong and the products are largely substitutable, as are detergents and candy.

Often, the reason a firm markets many brands in a product category is the belief that it is better to lose business to one of *our* other brands than to lose business to one of *their* brands. It follows, then, that an individual company may market several different brands. The Mars Company offers Snickers, Milky Way, Three Musketeers, M&M's, and many other candies. The matter of *shelf space* also enters into the decision to market multiple brands. A retailer may have room to display only 25 brands of candy bars. If 15 of them are Mars brands, the chances of a customer selecting a Mars product are obviously much improved by the use of the individual brands strategy.

Combining Family and Individual Brands.

One last alternative—using a combination of strategies—is available. The Kellogg's name is featured on Apple Jacks, Frosted Mini Wheats, Rice Krispies, and many other cereals whose brand names differ. The Willy Wonka name and brand mark appear on all packages of candies with more exotic names, including Everlasting Gobstopper, Oompas, Dinasour Eggs, Mixups, and Volcano Rocks. See Color Plate 3.

Brand Image

Jell-O's image reflects the nice lady who lives next door. She's not too old-fashioned, loves children and dogs, and has a streak of creativity

without being avant-garde. Similarly, studies showed that Dodge was perceived as a car for older people. The Chrysler Corporation is trying to offset that perception by developing sporty convertibles and other "exciting" cars.

When people say or think "this is my kind of product" or "this is my brand," they are really indicating that the *image* they have of the brand matches up with the image they would like to portray of themselves. This is because people tend to define themselves in terms of the symbolic value of their possessions. The symbolic value associated with a brand is referred to as **brand image.** Because this topic is highly interrelated with the topic of promotional strategy, an extensive discussion of this topic is postponed until Chapter 18. However, consider the corporate identity and image aspects associated with the new Sun Company's, formerly Sun Oil, corporate logo.

The lettering making up the word Sun gives an energy orientation and suggests positive movement.[10]

Changing a Brand Name

Though marketing planners spend considerable effort in developing brand names and symbols to be associated with their products, a change in the market environment or an initial "mistake" in brand name selection may mean that a name or symbol has to be changed. The original product name may have been a bad choice that was made worse over time. This was surely the case with Sambo's restaurants. The symbol served long and well, but it became inappropriate as times changed.

Some organizations have found that even well-known brand names should be changed because of pronunciation problems or because consumers do not have a good grasp of the or-

---

[10]"Why Companies Keep Changing Their Names," *U.S. News and World Report*, July 12, 1982, p. 73.

ganization's purpose. Datsun is turning to the name Nissan partly because U.S. customers seem unsure whether their cars are "Dotsuns" or "Datsuns" and partly because Datsun products are made by Nissan, a multi-national Japanese firm that wants a worldwide name. Some observers feel that the change will be a mistake. See Color Plate 2.

In the United States, the firm marketing gasoline as Cities Service Corporation changed its name to CITGO when it found that the public believed Cities Service Co. to be some sort of a water, sewage, and garbage collecting outfit that just happened to run a few gas stations as a sideline.

Around the world, organizations are chang-ing their names to include some indication of international interests. As international trade becomes ever more important, companies are adding words like "International" and "Worldwide" to their official names. Each name change, especially when the original name is well-established, involves many risks. Good will may be lost if clients fail to realize that the "new" company is the same as the "old" one.

Alternately, mergers or diversification may make an old name meaningless. When I.N.A. Corporation and Connecticut General merged, the company was renamed CIGNA Corporation. White Sewing Machine Company became White Consolidated Industries to reflect its diversified product lines.

PACKAGING

A package is basically an extension of the product offered for sale. In fact, it has frequently been pointed out that the packaging may be more important than the product it contains. The pump-top dispenser for Soft Soap and the hanging dispenser for Shower Mate are more than simple containers of a product. They, themselves, offer considerable consumer benefits. One brand of "drain opener" is packaged in a pressurized can that can be used to force a clogged drain open with compressed air. A legitimate question as to which is the product, the drain cleaner or the can, can be raised here.

Packages perform many functions. They contain a product and protect that product until it is ready for use. This function is frequently called protection in transit. Beyond this, packages facilitate the storage of products and, although perhaps not as importantly as the Soft Soap container, facilitate its use. Thus, packages should be designed with thought to ease of handling by consumers and by members of the channel of distribution. Products are often identified by their packages, and, because attractive packages on a shelf can attract the consumer's attention, they can play a major part in promotional strategy.

A package on the retailer's shelf may be surrounded by 10 or more packages competing for the consumers' attention. It has been said that the package is the product in these days of self-service. It is vital for every package design to convey an easily identifiable image. The product must have shelf impact. It must tell the consumer what the product is and why they should buy it— and that does not necessarily mean that the prettiest package design is the most effective.[11]

As all of this suggests, developing and designing a package is not unlike designing the product itself. The package designer must be as buyer oriented as the product designer. Research should be conducted to determine if customers have problems opening or closing the package. It should also determine how users handle the package, store it, and dispose of it. Channel members' concerns must also be researched. Does the package store well and stack well? Have there been problems with leakage or breakage? Effective marketers ask these questions *before* the product and its package are sent out to customers, and certainly before com-

---

[11]"Aseptic Packaging Elevates Milk Marketing to a New Level," *Marketing News*, January 7, 1983, p. 7.

ASEPTIC PACKAGING ELEVATES MILK MARKETING TO NEW LEVELS

Selling milk in a revolutionary container presents special problems for marketers, not the least of which is conveying through the packaging what exactly the product is.

Dairymen Inc., a farm cooperative based in Harrodsburg, Kentucky, recently introduced two nonrefrigerated liquid milk products. The products use an aseptic packaging system. Dairymen Inc. has not been able to keep up with demand.

Aseptic packaging has been around for many years in Europe, the Middle East, and Africa, but only recently has it appeared in the United States.

Aseptic packaging sometimes is referred to as UHT, which stands for ultra high temperature. In the case of milk, the product is heated to a temperature of 280 degrees Fahrenheit, effectively killing all the bacteria in the milk. The sterilized milk is placed in a carton made of a laminated material which seals the liquid in an airtight environment allowing the milk to stay fresh for 90 days without refrigeration and virtually forever with refrigeration. Regular milk stays fresh about seven days with refrigeration.

Dairymen Inc. offers Farm Best liquid milk, stocked in stores' milk sections, and Sip Ups, stocked in the soft drink and fruit drink sections. The milk comes in flavors such as chocolate, vanilla, banana, strawberry, and fruit punch.

Consumer resistance to and confusion about the products was anticipated, and Dairymen attempted to combat it with a package design that would gain acceptance. The package had to communicate to consumers that this was real milk. Farm Best opted for a design that is not revolutionary at all. It communicates that this is the same natural, wholesome product in a new package.

The production process required rectangular or triangular containers, so designing a package in milk's traditional tent-top container was impossible. This further compounded the difficulty of selling real liquid milk on unrefrigerated shelves. Dairymen could have opted for an elaborate, four-color gravure printing. It would have made the package look pretty, but it wouldn't have conveyed the effective sales message that "this is real liquid milk."

The solution was earthy graphics and extensive product information on the container, just like other liquid milk containers carry. The dairy industry's "Real" seal was affixed, and the industry's standard color-coding of red for whole milk and blue for lowfat was used. An additional problem was caused by the public's association of rectangular containers with powdered or condensed milk. To drive home the fact that this product is liquid and not powdered or condensed milk, a picture of a glass filled with milk appears on both Farm Best and Sip Ups packages.

The marketing problem was solved through an effective design. The successful package design succeeds at an aesthetic level, but its real measure of success is in communicating and selling the product.

Source: From "Aseptic Packaging Elevates Milk Marketing to a New Level," *Marketing News*, January 7, 1983, p. 7. Adapted with permission.

plaints start arriving. Package labeling, when appropriate, must tell buyers how to use the product contained within the package.

Labeling

The paper or plasticized sticker attached to a can of peas or mustard jar is technically called a **label.** But, as packaging technology improves and cans and bottles become less prominent, labels become incorporated into the protective aspects of the package. In the case of a box of frozen broccoli, for example, a good portion of the vegetable's protection comes from the label, more properly called, in this case, the *wrapper*.

Whether the label is a separate entity affixed to a package, or is, in effect, the package itself, it must perform certain tasks. It carries the brand

A warning label.

name and information concerning the contents of the package, including cooking instructions or information relating to safe and proper use of the product. Labels may also carry instructions on proper disposal of the product and its package, or at least the plea that littering be avoided. It must also contain any specific nutritional information, warnings, or legal restrictions required by law. Procter & Gamble labels also have an 800 telephone number for listening to customers' ideas and complaints. It is a major source of Procter & Gamble's product improvement ideas.

Most consumer goods are now labeled conspicuously with an appropriate **Universal Product Code** (UPC), the increasingly familiar array of black bars readable by optical scanners. The ad-

vantages of computerized checkouts and sales volume information that are a result of the UPC have become clear to distributors, retailers, and consumers in recent years.

Legal Guidelines for Packaging

Package designers are relatively free to develop any package design they believe will suit consumers and channel of distribution members. However, there are some legal guidelines and requirements that must be followed. Packages that are intentionally designed to mislead consumers, labels that bear false or misleading information, and packages that do not provide required warnings will soon draw the attention of the Federal Trade Commission, some other official body, or consumer groups. State and local laws, such as those requiring that soft drink bottles be clearly labeled as returnable, cannot be ignored. Some packaging requirements are not mandatory in the legal sense but flow from the less formalized influence of governmental offices and concerned interest groups. Packaging's biggest public relations problems are pollution and littering. Thus, the packaging industry has developed biodegradable packages that, unlike bottles and cans, decompose over time. Marketers like Burger King and McDonald's must spend considerable effort in keeping neighborhood litter under control even though their packages are biodegradable. Many other marketers operate recycling centers for aluminum cans and perform other litter or pollution reducing activities.

PRODUCT WARRANTIES

A **product warranty** provides a written guarantee of a product's integrity and the manufacturer's responsibility for repairing or replacing defective parts.[12] In offering the consumer a warranty the marketer may substantially reduce the risks the buyer perceives to be associated with

the purchase. In buying a new car, consumers look to the automobile's warranty for an assurance of quality. The maker would not, after all, provide a warranty on a product it thought would break down frequently. The warranty also provides the buyer with some assurance the necessary repairs will be paid for by someone else, thus reducing monetary risk. The stipulations contained in the warranty also diminish the

---

[12]R. Moyer and M.D. Hutt, *Macro-Marketing* (New York: John Wiley & Sons, 1978), p. 89.

You can count on Sears to replace it free if it fails to satisfy you—ever

"If any Craftsman® hand tool ever fails to give complete satisfaction, return it to the nearest Sears store in the U.S. and Sears will replace it free." This full unlimited warranty tells you a lot about Craftsman tools—and about Sears.

How can Sears offer such a sweeping warranty? Because Sears goes to such lengths to make sure you'll get complete satisfaction from any Craftsman hand tool you buy.

When you buy a Sears product, you should be able to count on Sears for good design, good workmanship, good materials, and good value.

So Sears digs into the details. If you were to visit the factory that makes the Craftsman pliers in our picture, you might run into a Sears engineer working to streamline production methods. Or a Sears tool buyer discussing possible improvements—perhaps a slight change to make the handle more comfortable.

At the Sears Laboratory, you would see some of the tests that over *ten thousand* of

Sears products go through every year. Tests of children's swing seats for strength, of bedding for flame resistance, of washing machines for performance.

After Sears approves a product and offers it for sale, Sears responsibility carries on. If what you've bought requires installation, Sears will make sure it's done right. And when it comes to service, Sears runs one of the world's largest service organizations, with Sears-trained repairmen buzzing around all fifty states in over 16,000 service trucks.

It all adds up to a sense of responsibility to you that starts with the development of the product—and stays alive and active after the product enters your home. From sewing machines to jeans to towels to tools, for products you can count on, you can count on Sears.

Sears
© Sears, Roebuck and Co. 1981

A warranty reflects the product's integrity.

buyer's responsibility of locating an appropriate repair shop since locations providing warranteed services are usually specified by the manufacturer. In general, the warranty communicates a message that suggests product quality and a lessening of purchase risk.

Unfortunately, consumers often find that warranties are difficult-to-understand documents written in legal jargon. Several manufacturers have made use of this fact by offering warranties advertised as simple, short, "plain English" documents.[13] Marketers who have not taken this approach may not be cognizant of the fact that terms like "fully guaranteed," "unconditionally guaranteed," and "lifetime guarantee" really don't mean much to buyers, especially to buyers who have been disappointed with the service received on other "guaranteed" goods.

Some of the difficulties associated with warranties have been mitigated by the **Magnuson-Moss Warranty Act** of 1975. This law requires that any guarantees provided by sellers be made

available to buyers prior to purchase of the product. It also grants power to the Federal Trade Commission to specifiy the manner and form in which guarantees may be used in promotional material. Further, the Act stipulates that the warranty must utilize simple language and disclose precisely *who* the warrantor is. The warranty must also indicate clearly what products or parts of products are covered by the terms of the guarantee, and which are excluded. The Act also specifies what the warrantor is obliged to do in the event of a product defect, how long the warranty applies, and what obligations the buyer has.[14] Unfortunately, the law has not cleared up all warranty-related problems. To require, for example, that something is to be stated "clearly" is one thing. To describe exactly what is a "clear" statement is another.

In short, the warranty is part and parcel of the total product. It should not be viewed as a nuisance to the seller. Effective marketers, such as Curtis Mathes televisions, may use the warranty as an opportunity to create satisfied customers and to offer an intangible product attribute desired by many buyers.

---

[13]For an interesting discussion of the readability of warranties, see John C. Lehman, L. Lee Manzer, James W. Gentry, and Hal W. Ellis, "The Readability of Warranties," in John C. Crawford and James Lumpkin (eds.), *Proceedings of the Southwest Marketing Association*, 1983, pp. 19–22.

[14]Moyer and Hutt, note 10 *supra*, at p. 91.

EXHIBIT 9-4

Illustrative Federal Legislation of Relevance for Product Planning

Informational

Pure Food and Drug Act (1906) prohibits misbranding of foods and drugs.

Wheeler-Lea Act (1937) Amended FTC Act of 1914 to give jurisdiction over advertising of foods, drugs, cosmetics, and therapeutic devices.

Federal Food, Drugs, and Cosmetics Act (1938) gives FTC more authority over packaging, misbranding, labeling.

Wool Products Act (1939) requires labels on wool products to indicate percent of wool, reprocessed and revised.

Fur Products Labeling Act (1951) prohibits false labeling and advertising of fur products.

Flammable Fabrics Act (1953) prohibits manufacture and sale of apparel which is dangerously flammable.

Textile Fiber Products Identification Act (1958) regulates labeling of textile products including synthetic fibers.

Hazardous Substances Labeling Act (1960) regulates proper labeling of toxic, corrosive, and irritating products.

Fair Packaging and Labeling Act (1966) requires mandatory and accurate labeling of kitchen and bathroom products concerning content, weight (truth in packaging).

Consumer Credit Protection Act (1968) requires disclosure of credit terms, annual rates and interest, finance charges on loans and installment purchases (truth in lending).

Consumer Protection Act (1970) provides for an individual to file class action suits for damages when deceptive practices involved; but Supreme Court (1974) ruled all members of class must be notified.

Magnuson-Moss Warranty-FTC Improvement Act (1974) provides minimum disclosure standards for written product warranties.

Perishable Agricultural Commodities Act (1974) protects from misbranding of fruits and vegetables.

Product Quality

Pure Food and Drug Act (1906) and the Federal Food, Drugs and Cosmetics Act (1938). The 1906 Act forbids adulteration of foods and drugs sold in interstate commerce, while the 1938 Act extends it to cosmetics.

Meat Inspection Act (1907) requires inspection of slaughtering, packing and canning.

Poultry Products Inspection Act (1957) upgrades poultry inspection practices.

Noise Control Act (1972) directs the EPA to set noise emission standards for a range of products.

Mobile Home Construction & Safety Standards Act (1974) directs HUD to establish appropriate federal mobile home construction and safety standards.

Product Safety

National Traffic and Motor Vehicle Safety Act (1966) permits secretary of transportation to issue safety standards.

Poison Prevention Packaging Act (1970) requires safety packaging for products.

Public Health Cigarette Smoking Act (1971) requires labeling of cigarettes as harmful to health.

Consumer Product Safety Act (1972) established the Consumer Product Safety Commission. A 1976 amendment adds that the commission has the power to conduct its own civil enforcement actions.

National Traffic & Motor Vehicle Safety Amendments (1972) encourages experimentation in new safety approaches and low auto emission systems and provides certain exceptions for smaller manufacturers.

Toxic Substance Control Act (1976) regulates commerce and protects human health and the environment by requiring testing and necessary use restriction on certain chemical substances.

Medical Devices Amendment (1976) provides for safety and effectiveness of medical devices intended for human use.

Source: Excerpts used with permission from Yoram J. Wind, *Product Policy: Concepts, Methods and Strategy* (Reading, Mass.: Addison-Wesley Publishing, 1982), pp. 183–184.

LEGAL CONCERNS

Exhibit 9-4 illustrates that there are several legal considerations in product strategy. There are laws requiring specific information on labeling and laws requiring certain quality and safety standards.

SUMMARY

In this chapter we have discussed the marketing mix variable "product," which refers to both goods and services. Products can be broadly defined to include many intangible aspects that may be as important to buyers as the physical products themselves. Because of the marketer's inability to know exactly what each buyer expects to receive from a product, the term "total product" has come to be used to name the totality of attributes connected with any good or service. It is by thinking of these many characteristics along with the payoffs sought by buyers that effective marketers can develop proper means of communicating and dealing with their customers.

A distinction must be made between consumer goods and industrial goods. Industrial goods, which are often described as raw materials, components, equipment, or supplies are always the result of derived demand.

One method of classifying consumer products categorizes them as convenience, shopping, or specialty goods. Convenience goods are typically inexpensive, frequently purchased items involving little decision-making. Shopping goods are typically items that are the subject of price and quality comparisons before a purchase is made. Specialty goods are items that usually have no substitutes and, therefore, develop considerable brand loyalty.

The following terms have also been discussed. A product brand is a name, term, sign, symbol, or design that distinguishes one product from another. A trademark is a legal protection of a brand name or brand mark. A good brand name should obviously be easy to remember, and should effectively communicate the attributes of the product. While national brands are the property of manufacturers, private brands are the property of wholesalers or retailers. A family brand connotes that multiple products utilize the same brand name in an effort to take advantage of that brand name.

Marketers should be aware that brand name, brand image, labeling, packaging, and warranty all are important determinants of a successful product strategy.

THE MOST IMPORTANT CONCEPT IN THIS CHAPTER
The definition of a product should be in terms of a total product concept that is far greater than the physical and tangible definition of the product.

KEY TERMS

Product concept	Product class	Shopping goods	Component parts
Total product	Product category	Specialty goods	Process materials
Auxiliary dimensions	Brand	Industrial goods	Installations
Product strategy	Convenience goods	Raw materials	Accessory equipment

↳ warranty

Operating supplies	Logo	National brands	Individual brand
Services	Trademark	Distributor brands	License
Product line	Lanham act	Generic products	Brand image
Product mix	Service mark	Generic brands	Label
Brand name	Generic name	Brand extension	Universal Product Code
Brand mark	Manufacturer brands	Family branding	Product warranty

QUESTIONS FOR DISCUSSION

1 Identify both the product class and product category for the following brands:
(a) Folger's coffee
(b) Space Shuttle video game by Activision
(c) Cheerios cereal
(d) Betamax video tape recorder

2 Evaluate the following brand names:
(a) Match Light Charcoal
(b) Arm and Hammer Pure Baking Soda
(c) Tums
(d) Scotch brand Video Cassette
(e) Kwik-Kopy Printing
(f) Sun-Maid Raisin Bread
(g) Yuban coffee
(h) Diehard batteries
(j) Handi-Wrap

3 Which of the following brand names for frozen Mexican food would you like to own? Why?

(a) Old El Paso
(b) Van deKamps Mexican Classics
(c) Happy Josés

4 Please identify which of the following are either common names or brand names.
(a) Aspirin (e) Thermos
(b) Betamax (f) Yo-Yo
(c) Zipper (g) Zomax
(d) Sanka (h) Kitty Litter

5 What characteristics distinguish convenience, shopping, and specialty goods?

6 Give some examples of trademarks that are not brand names.

7 When is it a good idea to use family branding?

8 What are the characteristics of an effective brand name?

9 What are the marketing management ramifications of the monopoly/antimonopoly case?

10 Converse brand holds approximately a 40 percent share of the basketball shoe market. Should they expand their product line in an attempt to become a major force in the running shoe market?

CASE 9-1 Standard Brands' Smooth and Easy

Standard Brands had not introduced a totally new product for two decades. The company had relied on its well-established products such as Blue Bonnet margarine to provide sales volume. Smooth and Easy resulted from management's efforts to increase consumers' use of margarine.

Smooth and Easy grew out of the desire to make the use of margarine more convenient for thickening things. The product was described as "the gravy stick with all the gravy basics in one refrigerated bar." To make homemade gravy, the cook must produce a thickening agent by melting margarine and adding flour. Smooth and Easy was a commercial product consisting of a flavored mixture in bar form. It required refrigeration. All a gravymaker had to do was slice off the proper amount of Smooth and Easy just like a margarine stick.

During early testing, enthusiastic executives, who had not had a new product for seven years, passed their optimism on to the sales force who tended to overstock retailers. During subsequent analysis, it was found that initial trial purchases were low and the repeat purchase rate was also low. After the product failed to meet sales expectations, it was concluded that consumers' natural bias against commercial gravies could not be overcome by advertising.

Questions

1 Did Standard Brands follow the prescriptions of the marketing concept?

2 What was Smooth and Easy's total product concept?

3 Identify the product class and product category for Smooth and Easy.

4 Was the brand name a good one?

CASE 9-2 American Telephone and Telegraph Company*

Would you like to have a telephone under your Christmas tree? Recently, AT&T offered gift certificates. AT&T thought a gift certificate, allowing the recipient to pay his or her monthly bill, purchase an extra phone, or utilize any service offered by the telephone company, would be an ideal gift product.

The major advantage of the gift certificates to the telephone company was that it was able to invest the money paid to them while waiting for the gift certificates to be used. In a regional test program, the company found that after 90 days approximately 30 to 40 percent of the certificates were still out. After nine months, there were still 5 percent of the certificates that had not been utilized. The company estimates that approximately 2 percent will never be turned in.

When the telephone company introduced the gift certificate program during the Christmas season they spent $5 million in advertising costs to sell $6 million in certificates.

Questions

1 Do you think this new service idea failed? Why?

2 How would your friends or family react to an AT&T gift certificate as a gift?

3 What is the total product concept?

---

*Source: Based on information in the *Tulsa World*, February 22, 1981.

CHAPTER 10

The Product Life Cycle and Related Strategies

CHAPTER SCAN

This chapter focuses on the marketing mix variable "product." A number of tools and concepts have been developed to help marketers channel their thinking on this key portion of the marketing mix. Two major planning tools, the product life cycle and the product portfolio, are discussed in this chapter with special attention toward their use as planning aids. Remember strategy development flows from the marketing manager's thinking. The tools used to help make strategy are not of themselves strategies.

The chapter concludes with a discussion of various strategy options that have been found to be of use to marketers.

WHEN YOU HAVE STUDIED THIS CHAPTER, YOU WILL:

Be familiar with a powerful marketing tool, the product life cycle.

Understand the role of managing and lengthening the product life cycle.

Be able to discuss the characteristics of the various stages of the product life cycle and what they suggest to marketing managers.

Understand the purpose of the product portfolio.

Be able to show how the interrelationships among products suggested by the product portfolio are useful to marketing management.

Be able to describe product- and market-related strategies used by effective marketers to support their market offerings.

Be able to discuss the overall marketing problem of matching products to markets and to show how effective marketers weigh and counterweigh the economic realities of this problem.

The fastest growing cigarette brand in the world is Camel, which increased its sales 13.3 percent worldwide in 1982.[1] Camel is the ninth most popular brand in the world.

Camel regular cigarettes were introduced by R.J. Reynolds Tobacco Co. in 1913. More than three trillion units have been sold since then. The brand was the leading seller in the United States for a long time but, in recent years, it has declined significantly, although introduction of the filtered version has helped the brand's sales in the American market. Its recent great resurgence is due, however, to overseas popularity.

In markets from South America to Southern Asia, but particularly in Europe, 1982 was a big year for Camel filters. Sales topped 20 billion for the second straight year thanks to the "Camel World" campaign and special events and promotions. For several years running, Camel has been the fastest growing brand in Switzerland and is one of the most important brands in Germany, Italy, Holland, France, Sweden, and Greece. In Germany, though tax and price changes have caused most brands to lose market volume, Camel has increased its market share.

In the Philippines, volume has been up by more than 200 percent in recent years. The company credits its "Camel World" campaign in TV advertisements with part of that success.

Faced with a tougher market at home, R.J. Reynolds has lengthened the Camel life cycle by altering the product by adding a filter *and* by strengthening its position overseas.

A number of product-related tools have been developed to assist management in the process of strategic marketing planning and execution. This chapter explores several of the most commonly utilized marketing management tools and the concepts related to them. More specifically, the product life cycle, the product portfolio, and some methods of developing product-based strategies will be discussed. These conceptual tools are somewhat related since, taken as a group, they consider products from their "birth" to their "death." Effective marketing requires that the marketing manager know both how to introduce new products and when to withdraw or to eliminate those goods or services that no longer enjoy meaningful market demand.

This chapter's major concern is strategic, focusing on what should be done in given marketing situations. But the product life cycle and product portfolio are not, of themselves, strategies. They are tools. They provide frameworks in which alternative strategies can be evaluated. They help marketing managers to think about and to visualize the situations in which they find themselves. Strategies are the plans based on creative thinking that marketers develop. This point must be stressed since human nature seems to make us think that once we have an understanding of a tool or concept, we also have "the answer" to our problem. In fact, at that point, problem-solving efforts have only begun.

THE PRODUCT LIFE CYCLE

The product life cycle (PLC) is an indispensable tool for product planners and for marketers in general. The product life cycle is based on the life process of all living things, beginning with "birth" and ending with "death," and, while it is obvious that there is quite a difference between biological life and the life of lemon-scented laundry detergents, the concept is useful nonetheless.

In general, the **product life cycle** is a graphic depiction of a product's sales history from its marketing inception to its withdrawal from the market. Product life cycles are, in effect, sales volume curves. Products begin their lives with the first sale of the product, rise to some peak, and then decline until their contributions to profits are insufficient to justify their presence in

---

[1] Used with permission, "Camel Cigarettes Enjoy Banner Year Worldwide," *Marketing News*, April 1, 1983, p. 9.

EXHIBIT 10-1

The General Pattern of the Product Life Cycle

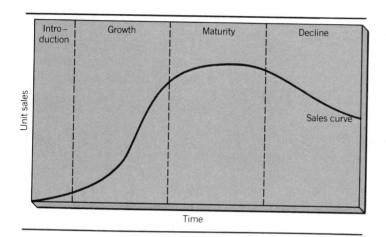

the market. While this pattern is common, it varies from product to product. Products such as salt and mustard have been used for thousands of years. Arm and Hammer baking soda has been used for over 125 years. Home computers and video games are mere youngsters by comparison. Some products, such as Instant Baby Food Flakes, a dehydrated food by Heinz, fail at the very start of their lives.

Traditionally, the product life cycle has been thought of as reflecting the life of a product class or product category as a whole. The life cycle of black and white television sets as a group, without regard to model or brand, would provide an excellent portrayal of the concept. However, marketing managers also use the product life cycle idea in evaluating specific brands of products. The ideas underlying the concept prove useful in such applications since most brands, as well as most products, have limited market lives.

Whether a product has a very short, short, long, or very long life, the pattern of that life may be portrayed by a charting of sales volume. For discussion purposes, the product life cycle is usually portrayed as in Exhibit 10-1. Each product's life, according to the life cycle concept, typ-

ically flows through several distinct product life cycle stages as sales volume is plotted over time. These stages are *introduction, growth, maturity,* and *decline.*[2] The length of time a product spends in each stage varies from case to case.

The General Sales Pattern of the Product Life Cycle

Before dealing with each product life cycle stage in detail, the reader should be familiar with the general course of the classic product life cycle (see Exhibit 10-1).

During the introduction stage, the new product is attempting to gain a foothold in the market. Sales are likely to be slow at the start of the period since the product is, by definition, new and untried. Some time spent in gaining accep-

---

[2]Some authors have identified five stages, placing "market saturation" between the maturity and decline stages, others have called attention to a "birth stage" and a "death stage." There have been efforts to show an "incubation stage" where the product life cycle curve is depicted as going *below* the X axis at the left side of the product life cycle. This presents a problem, however, in that it suggests negative sales. The four stages used in this text are the most common depiction of the product life cycle.

EXHIBIT 10-2

Industry Profits and the Product Life Cycle

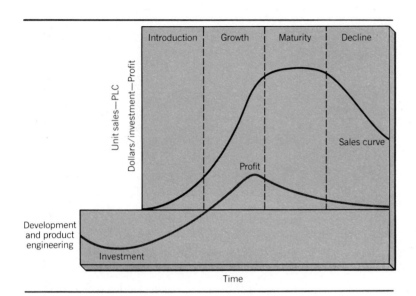

Profits and the Product Life Cycle

The product life cycle, displayed essentially as a graph, can be used to portray many other variables showing how these change over the life of a product. Among the most important of these is industry profit. Exhibit 10-2 shows how industry profit varies during the basic product life cycle.

During the period of product development and engineering, no sales are being made, yet assets are being spent. Thus, investments are being made in the belief that later profitable sales will justify them. When the product is introduced to the market and enters its growth stage, profit margins can be expected to be small. Sales volume and sales revenues are still low relative to the high expenses associated with developing the product and the marketing mix necessary to introduce a product to the market. Remember, *profit* is the consideration here, not prices.

As sales increase and the product moves to

tance is inevitable. If the product earns market acceptance, it should, at some point in time, launch into a period of comparatively rapid growth. Students may notice that the classic product life cycle portrays this growth stage as sales increasing at an increasing rate.

As the product approaches the end of its growth period, sales begin to level off. A change in the growth rate—indicated by sales increasing at a decreasing rate—heralds this change. When sales have peaked, the product passes into the maturity stage. For reasons such as diminished popularity, product obsolescence, or market saturation (i.e., most target customers now own the product), the product begins to lose market acceptance. The decline stage is underway, culminating, eventually, in the disappearance of the product from the market. In recent years the "health tonic" product class has passed through its final stages and approached "death." There are only a few surviving brands of these once popular tonics.

the growth stage, profits can be expected to increase, partly because sales are increasing but also because the "start-up" expenses encountered at the start of the product life cycle can be expected to diminish. As a rule, profits peak late in the growth period. As Exhibit 10-2 shows, they level off and then fall in the maturity stage. This is to be expected as competing firms try to operate within a static or slow growth market.

Ultimately, in the decline phase, survivor firms compete within an ever-smaller market, driving profit margins lower still. Ironically, the last surviving firm or firms may, as individual organizations, enjoy high profits at this point. This is because most competitors have withdrawn from the market leaving what is left to one or two suppliers. Since "what's left" is a group of extremely loyal buyers—the people who, for example, firmly believe that Father John's Tonic is the elixir of life—profits for the last firms can be high. However, profits for the *industry* will be low, since only one or two producers are left.

Do All Products Follow a Product Life Cycle?

The answer to the question of whether or not all products follow a product life cycle is "yes." All products are introduced and most eventually disappear. But the shape of the product life cycle, the rates of change in sales and profits, and the length and height of the cycles vary greatly. As Exhibit 10-3 shows, some products, like peanut butter, seem to be firmly ensconced in the maturity stage "forever," whereas others, such as novelty items like *The Secret of NIMH* lunch pails or Darth Vader Halloween masks, have very short cycles.

If a given novelty product's life cycle looks like that in Exhibit 10-3, did the product pass through all stages of the product life cycle? It can be argued that some products are so undesirable that sales of just a few items saturate the market, driving the product into a swift declining phase and on to rapid "death." It is also arguable that such products "died" in their introductory

EXHIBIT 10-3

The Long and Short of Product Life Cycles

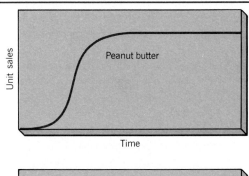

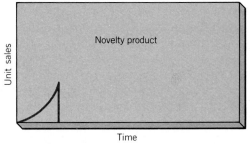

stages. However, the usefulness of the product life cycle as a planning tool can be understood without debating the fine points of product life cycle theory. Suffice it to say that the ultimate goal of a marketing planner is to bring the product into the maturity stage and to keep it there as long as it makes an acceptable financial return.

Failures may occur. But effective marketers research the market and plan to avoid such failures. It is worth noting that when a product does not become popular, analysts find that the reasons parallel the hallmarks of *in*effective marketing—not enough product research, failure to communicate with the target consumer, prices too high to gain market acceptance, faulty distribution, and so on.[3]

---

[3] The reasons for new product failure are explored in detail in the following chapter.

THE PRODUCT LIFE CYCLE AS A PLANNING TOOL

The product life cycle, while useful to visualize the stages of market acceptance a product is likely to encounter, has its greatest practical use as a planning tool. In fact, many successful marketing companies build their strategies around the concept, graphing financial and market data against product life cycles, and developing long- and short-range plans that complement each stage.

Furthermore, there have been a number of attempts to formulate marketing strategies that can be grouped as "appropriate" to one stage or another of the product life cycle. While such efforts prove useful in certain situations, blindly following the dictates of any tool or concept can make that concept a self-fulfilling prophecy. For example, it may be suggested that once a product is believed to have entered the decline stage, the appropriate steps to take are to cut back on promotion and other marketing activities. If this is done, *of course* the product will continue its declining course—but it may not have done so if marketing activities were not curtailed.

As mentioned earlier, problems arise when the PLC's influence on marketing strategies becomes confused with the strategies themselves. The true value of the product life cycle should flow from an understanding of the changes in competitive conditions that occur at each stage and a grasp of *why* they occur. The product life cycle also highlights the fact that conditions *will* change and that the product in question might well "die" unless careful planning is undertaken. Lastly, the PLC encourages the marketing planner to develop product improvements, or even totally new products, to protect the organization against the almost inevitable demise of their market offering. The history of business and of non-profit organizations is filled with stories of one-product companies that disappeared when their goods or services were no longer in demand. On the other hand, long-lived and successful companies have adjusted to inevitable change, saving themselves from a similar fate. The March of Dimes Organization, for example,

formed to raise funds to fight polio, redirected its efforts against birth defects once polio was brought under control.

The Introductory Stage

The introductory stage of the product life cycle is a period of attempting to gain market acceptance. The marketing mix appropriate to such an effort is focused not only on finding buyers, but also on creating channels of distribution—attracting retailers and other middlemen to handle the product. It is also a time when the bulk of research and development costs associated with the product need to be recouped. During this period, product alterations or changes in manufacturing may be needed to "get the bugs out" of the new market offering. The introduction stage is, then, typically a high cost/low profit period. Although it is an exciting time, it is also a time of uncertainty and anxiety, since the new product must survive this "now or never" situation.

Selecting strategies appropriate to the introductory stage of a product life cycle is an important matter, yet organizations differ widely in their strategy choices. Some companies believe that being a pioneer and risk-taker is the best approach—the greater the risk, the greater the reward. Thus, in many industries, such as tires and aircraft, the same companies are the leaders in new product development over and over again. Other companies quickly follow the pioneer's lead, and jump into the market during the introductory stage. Still others hold back, and wait to see whether the new product will actually take off into a growth period. Each approach has obvious advantages and risks which management must weigh.

The length of the PLC introductory stage varies dramatically. Personal computers and home video games have gained market acceptance rapidly. Television, on the other hand, took years to reach widespread popularity, although that delay was partly due to the diversion of technological assets necessitated by World War II.

The light beer product category presents yet another example of market acceptance. The idea of light or diet beer goes back many decades, but marketers believed that to even mention beer's fattening potential would be a mistake. The first serious effort to introduce such a product was made in the mid-1960s with the appearance of the Gablinger and Meister Brau Lite brands. But rapid sales growth for the category did not occur until 1975 when another brand, Miller Lite, was successfully introduced. Today, virtually every brewer has a light beer brand. The market for the product is mature.

Currently, many medical products are in their introductory stages. New classes of medicines are constantly being developed and the whole field of genetic engineering is new, at least to the marketplace.

The Growth Stage

When a product enters its growth stage, it has shown that it may have a future in the marketplace. As a result, the number of competitors and the level of marketing activity can be expected to increase. Pioneering firms are often required to alter their products since competitors, having the advantage of learning from the pioneer's mistakes and time to study the market, may have improved on the original. Competition also increases because of an industry's recognition of an untapped potential market. There is a feeling that there is enough profit to go around and that competing firms may be able to grab a sizable share of market without taking away from each other (as is the case during the maturity stage).

In recent years, the wine product class in the United States was clearly in a period of growth. Some producers, such as Blue Nun, Reunite, and Paul Masson were able to promote their brands to buyers who, for one reason or another, had little purchasing experience with wine. Consumers who lacked the confidence to select wines were attracted by growth-oriented promotions that described Blue Nun as the wine that goes with *everything* or by Orson Welles' assur-

ances that Paul Masson would never sell them a wine before its time. Many small wineries expanded production during this period to serve these new customers.

Products still in their growth stages include cable television service, alternative long-distance phone services such as Sprint and MCI, home video recorders, and home computers. During their growth stages, the profits associated with these products will rise (although not for every company) and peak at the end of the period. Distribution costs will be brought under control as channels become more organized and able to do their tasks routinely. Product quality will be stressed and improved. Promotion expenses will be adjusted as rising sales and profits indicate the product's potential.

The Maturity Stage

At any point in time, most products on the market are in their PLC's maturity phase. During this stage, competition among producers of a class of products is likely to be intense. After all, one of the goals of effective marketing is to achieve brand maturity status and to maintain it for as long as the market supports the product. Further, since a product in the maturity stage of the product life cycle is, by definition, one that has achieved wide market acceptance, the only way for any one company to increase its market share is to take market share away from competitors.[4] For example, in the mature automotive and television businesses, only a relatively few buyers of these products are buying their first car or TV. One strategy to increase market share is to produce private brands for distributors. Thus, private labels emerge in the mature stage because an organization selling a mature product may pick up new business in the price-conscious segment of the market as other less competitive companies withdraw from the market.

---

[4]Attainment of the maturity stage does not mean that "everyone" has the product, but does mean that everyone likely to buy the product has done so.

Organizations in mature markets have solved many of the problems encountered early in the product life cycle. Their products require little technological change. The "bugs" are gone, therefore changes in the product become largely a matter of style. Radios, for example, are now offered in tiny sizes and in big sizes, with tape decks and without, with belt clips for joggers and with handles for toting down the street. They run on house current, batteries, solar power, and by being plugged into car cigarette lighters. Designs and variations become important during the product's maturity, whereas early in the product life cycle the emphasis is on making sure that they work.

Although Exhibit 10-2 showed that industry profits generally peak near the end of the growth stage of the product life cycle, it should be recognized that many individual firms in mature market situations are very profitable. As we have noted, a major reason for this is the experience gained during the earlier stages. Development of economies of scale also play a part. Organizations in mature markets whose products are profitable typically use the funds these product items generate to support other items in the product mix. The laundry detergent industry is certainly in its mature stage, but industry leader Procter & Gamble uses the sizable profits generated by Tide and Cheer to pay for the development and introduction of new product items and lines.

Even though profitable products in the maturity stage are commonplace, successful marketing managers, recognizing the maturity pattern, conduct investigations into the *causes* of that maturity. Once sales have peaked, the possibility of decline starts to appear. The marketer may find that a product is in the mature stage because it has become and remains widely used, like roofing supplies or tires, and that sales volume remains stable. On the other hand, sales may have peaked because an alternative product or brand has become popular due to some environmental change. Candy and other sugared products may be used less because of health concerns. CB radio sales, after a few boom years, slowed and then fell as the fad wore off.

The demand for higher education has fallen somewhat as the pool of traditionally college-age citizens decreased in size. The effective marketer needs to know *why* a product is in its maturity stage, not just that it is there.

The Decline Stage

As the name denotes, the decline stage in the Product Life Cycle is one of falling sales and, on an industry-wide basis, falling profits. There is likely to be a shake-out in the number of firms in the industry as managers become aware that the product has entered the decline stage. A few firms, or even a single firm, many survive and even do well by catering to the remaining buyers. Makers of parts for Crosley, Kaiser, and Willys automobiles are neither large nor numerous, yet they can survive by catering to car collectors. Blacksmiths are not as common as they once were, but some still survive.

Marketing managers should take care to assure themselves that what they see as entry into the decline phase of their product's life cycle is in fact just that. A downward movement of sales may be due to some short term influence. For example, the PLC for television sets actually appeared to take a downward turn in the early 1960s. However, this was *not* the signal for RCA, Sony, and other television marketers to drop their marketing efforts. The product life cycle took an upward turn as soon as "perfected" color television sets came onto the market.

Again, it is clear that the key to using the PLC concept is understanding the *causes* of the cycles, shifts, and fluctuations, so that their implications for the organization's own industry and product can be considered.

Is There Life after Decline? Occasionally, a product life cycle changes slope, reversing the downward trend associated with the late maturity and decline stages. Some products and brands approach extinction only to suddenly achieve a new-found popularity. Such a turn of events may be due to nostalgia or to the sudden realization that an old, familiar brand or product was really pretty good after all. It may be a change in the marketing environment that brings

WHAT WENT WRONG?

SWANSON RELAXES IN MATURITY

In the highly competitive frozen food products industry, the Swanson line by Campbell's saw its volume slip 16 percent in the five-year period ending August 1, 1982. Sales of frozen dinners and entrees, once Swanson's mainstay, declined 23 percent, while industry sales of these particular products grew 58 percent to 2 billion dollars during the same period. What went wrong?

The market for convenience food is being exploited with new products by Stouffer's Lean Cuisine and Pillsbury's Green Giant division, who predicted significant changes among consumers. The growing numbers of working women and singles are now demanding better quality, more interesting entrees. Tired of Swanson's traditional TV dinners of Salisbury steak, mashed potatoes, and apple crisp, consumers in the 1980s want better tasting gourmet food on the order of chicken divan, beef burgundy, and steak teriyaki, and they want to cook their dinners in microwave ovens.

In an effort to breathe life into the Swanson line—still a substantial business—Campbell's initiated a program called project Fix. Initially, 10 million dollars was committed to overhaul the line with improved ingredients: less salt and more meat stock in gravies, new desserts, and more exciting

sauces. Advertising expenditures for the brand were doubled to 14 million dollars and new packaging and a redesigned logo were also planned.

Management had finally realized that "TV dinners were dangerously close to becoming an anachronism." In fact, "They had lost relevance to the consumer." With these changes underway the company projected at least a 10 percent increase in volume for Swanson.

Further fine-tuning was also initiated. Special advertising was created to target certain products such as sliced pork for adults and dinners featuring hot dogs or hamburgers for children. Aware of the increasing use of micro-

wave ovens, a gradual shift away from aluminum trays to paper or plastic by 1985 was planned.

Concluding that the long-term trend was away from traditional TV dinners, Swanson began testing a new line of high-priced dinners under the brand name of Le Menu. Test results were positive, and the introduction is now underway.

Swanson had failed to recognize the need to update and modify its product line, and more alert competitors seized the opportunity. Can Le Menu close the gap that Stouffer's and Pillsbury have opened up? Time will tell. One thing is certain—Swanson's has the most to lose.

this about. In the 1970s and 1980s, there was considerable medical attention given to proper nutrition as a means of maintaining good health. Fiber in the diet was the object of part of this concern. While some new products appeared in response to this, certain old products were suddenly more in demand. Granola, soups, and natural sweeteners such as honey were among these products, and they were marketed accordingly.

Products that appear to have stable or declining sales may increase in popularity because of their close tie-ins with other products or with difficulties facing society at large. The success and popularity of products such as the Betamax video recorder or the RCA video disc system should increase consumer interest in quality color television sets. Getting America "back in shape" helps the sales of jogging shoes, jump ropes, bicycles, and exercise machines. Purchases of wood-burning stoves increased immensely as oil and gas prices rose. The demand for services has also been affected by such changes: life insurance, and dry cleaning, both mature products, have been helped by the increased proportion of working women. The fitness "craze" has contributed to much of the success of health spas, gymnasiums, and sporting goods stores.

Marketing Strategy Changes Through the Product Life Cycle

As has been suggested throughout this discussion, marketers can use the product life cycle as a basis for developing market strategies. Exhibit 10-4 shows how various marketing mix aspects are likely to be adjusted as a product moves through the life cycle stages. Although it has been made clear that such patterns are intended for illustrative purposes only, it is also necessary to stress that marketing strategy formulation should *always* take the PLC into consideration. The PLC should not *tell* the strategist what to do, but it is too powerful a concept to be ignored.

Here are some examples of how close consideration of the product life cycle has influenced the decisions of marketing strategists:

Petrochemical companies pioneering in the marketing of styrene had to adjust their thinking as the two companies involved in the introduction of the product grew to five in the growth stage and nine in the maturity stage.[5]

---

[5]R.B. Stobaugh and P.L. Townsend, "Price Forecasting and Strategic Planning: The Case of Petrochemicals," *Journal of Marketing Research*, February 1975, p. 20.

Hewlett-Packard successfully introduced scientific pocket calculators. During the growth and mature stages of this product class, new models were introduced at the "top end" of the performance spectrum. This permitted price reductions on older models so as to meet new lower-priced competitors from Japanese producers.

Cigar sales are declining and have been since the mid-1960s. There are few young stogie smokers and, blessedly, advertising efforts aimed at attracting women to the product have been largely unsuccessful. The industry thus finds itself engaged in such decline state activities as price wars and numerous sales promotions. With few exceptions, cigar companies are diversifying into other product areas. One newer brand—Backwoods Smokes—does continue to woo younger smokers . . . Do you think that attempt will succeed?

During the maturity and decline stages firms often seek to introduce a new or improved version of the existing product. Canned fruits have been declining as a product category for several years. Libby's has sought to slow that trend with the introduction of light fruits after tests showed that consumers no longer wanted syrupy canned fruits but low-sugar products with a fresh taste. The new products apparently satisfy consumer needs since the sales of Libby's canned fruits have stopped their decline.

Shifts in the marketplace environment have led Hunt's, Del Monte, and Libby's to introduce no-salt-added ketchup, tomato sauce, canned fruits, and vegetables. These products are certainly in the mature or even decline stages but a response on the parts of these firms to a consumer awareness of the undesirability of excess salt in the diet may increase the sales of these products, at least in comparison to those manufactured by companies less aware of changes in the market.

The Intentionally Short Life Cycle. In general, marketing managers attempt to move their products successfully into the maturity phase of

EXHIBIT 10-4

How Product Life Cycle Advocates View the Implications of the Cycle for Marketing Activities

Effects and Responses	Stages of the PLC			
	Introduction	**Growth**	**Maturity**	**Decline**
Competition	None of importance	Some emulators	Many rivals competing for a small piece of the pie	Few in number with a rapid shakeout of weak members
Overall strategy	Market establishment; persuade early adopters to try the product	Market penetration; persuade mass market to prefer the brand	Defense of brand position; check the inroads of competition	Preparations for removal; milk the brand dry of all possible benefits
Profits	Negligible because of high production and marketing costs	Reach peak levels as a result of high prices and growing demand	Increasing competition cuts into profit margins and ultimately into total profits	Declining volume pushes costs up to levels that eliminate profits entirely
Retail prices	High, to recover some of the excessive costs of launching	High, to take advantage of heavy consumer demand	What the traffic will bear; need to avoid price wars	Low enough to permit quick liquidation of inventory
Distribution	Selective, as distribution is slowly built up	Intensive; employ small trade discounts since dealers are eager to store	Intensive; heavy trade allowances to retain shelf space	Selective; unprofitable outlets slowly phased out
Advertising strategy	Aim at the needs of early adopters	Make the mass market aware of brand benefits	Use advertising as a vehicle for differentiation among otherwise similar brands	Emphasize low price to reduce stock
Advertising emphasis	High, to generate awareness and interest among early adopters and persuade dealers to stock the brand	Moderate, to let sales rise on the sheer momentum of word-of-mouth recommendations	Moderate, since most buyers are aware of brand characteristics	Minimum expenditures required to phase out the product
Consumer sales and promotion expenditures	Heavy, to entice target groups, with samples, coupons, and other inducements to try the brand	Moderate, to create brand preference (advertising is better suited to do this job)	Heavy, to encourage brand switching, hoping to convert some buyers into loyal users	Minimal, to let the brand coast by itself

Source: Reprinted by permission of the Harvard Business Review. An exhibit from ''Forget the Product Life Cycle Concept'' by N.K. Khalla and Sonia S. Yuspen (January–February 1976). Copyright © 1977 by the President and Fellows of Harvard College; all rights reserved.

the product life cycle and then keep them there for considerable periods of time. However, certain products are *expected* to have short lives. Cereals, snack foods, and toys, for example, may gain considerable profits as fad items. Although it may surprise its makers with a long life, Strawberry Shortcake cereal, described as Kix with a strawberry coating, was expected to be a short term success.[6] Similarly, General Foods used carbonated confection technology to produce several fad bubble gum and candy items including Increda Bubble, Pop Rocks, and Space Dust. These fad candies, as well as some more familiar products, are marketed on a cyclical basis to reflect the belief that their faddish nature does not justify year-round marketing expenditures. Other products are "brought back" in essentially unchanged form once a new generation of buyers has replaced the old. Walt Disney comic books republish many stories from time to time once the given age cohort of readers has been replaced by a younger group. Some newspaper cartoonists also recycle their jokes, or slight variations on old jokes, apparently thinking that most readers will not remember a gag that last appeared a decade earlier. Just a few years ago, a popular advice columnist was discovered to be reprinting and reanswering letters that had, in fact, appeared in newspapers years before. These sorts of products have lives that are quite short. Marketers must be aware of this so they can develop strategies appropriate to intentionally short product life cycles.

BASIC PRODUCT/MARKET STRATEGIES

As has been stressed time and time again, no single facet of the marketing mix stands alone. Each facet must be viewed in light of what it contributes to the total mix and each must be consistent with and supportive of the other variables. Despite these strong interrelationships, a series of marketing strategies closely allied with the marketing mix variable of *product* has been developed. It is to these that we now turn our attention.

Market-Related Strategies for Existing Products

There are two major strategy paths available to any organization seeking to expand sales of existing products. Demand may be increased through a process called market penetration. **Market penetration** is the term used to describe growth of an established product via increased usage among existing customers in existing markets. Arm and Hammer has, with considerable success, appealed to existing customers to purchase more baking soda by showing these customers new and creative ways to use the product. One suggestion, offered in advertisements and on packages, was to put an opened box of baking soda in the home refrigerator to reduce food odors. Lest consumers feel that a box of baking soda would have to be thrown away without further use once it had remained in the refrigerator for a time, the company suggested that the product be poured down the kitchen drain to freshen the drain. This gave baking soda two new uses and gave buyers a way to dispose of the product in a manner that performed yet another odor-killing task. A similar technique is used by cereal companies. These frequently demonstrate how Cheerios or Rice Krispies can be used to make cookies, snack foods, and other non-breakfast items. Consumers are encouraged to try, for example, "Cooking with Kellogg."

A somewhat different strategy is the process known as **market development,** which designates an effort at drawing new customers to existing products or attracting potential buyers who need a little "nudge" to change them from lookers to buyers. The marketers of Mercury out-

---

[6]Janet Neiman, "General Foods Debuts 'Fad' Cereal," *Advertising Age,* July 13, 1981, p. 12.

Increased usage may be a PLC extension strategy.

board motors, as a case in point, found out that the population of outboard motor owners was aging rapidly as the industry failed to bring new customers, particularly younger people, into the market. Mercury targeted its market development effort toward "fence sitters"—people who wanted to own a boat but who had not actually committed themselves to buying one. Promotion for the company stressed that boat ownership was "the possible dream."[7]

The desire to expand the demand for an existing product need not come from the belief that a market is shrinking. It might derive from the fact that an organization has the capacity to produce more products or feels that its assets are not otherwise being utilized to the fullest. Restaurant managers typically search for ways to utilize their facilities for longer periods of time than just the lunch or dinner rush. Restaurants in downtown areas, where lunch traffic is high but dinner traffic low, often run special promotions, such as free cocktails or half-price dinners, during the dinner hour. Such plans are, in effect, attempts to sell more of the same basic product.

---

[7]"Mercury Explores New Waters," *Advertising Age,* April 27, 1981, p. 24.

Market-Related Strategies for New Products

If a restaurant's management seeks to increase its customer base by offering new products, the marketing strategy is somewhat different than those described so far. McDonald's has, over the past few years, expanded its menu to include non-hamburger items. The fish sandwich, Chicken McNuggets, and other such items are the results of **product development,** which refers to marketing innovative products to existing markets. At least part of McDonald's strategy in adding these products to its traditional menu was to provide loyal customers with greater food choices. Many McDonald's customers increased their purchases of McDonald's products as these options and varieties became available.

Of course, the expansion of the McDonald's menu also attracted some new customers. This was especially true of McDonald's decision to sell breakfast items and to open much earlier in the day than had been routine. Marketing new products to a new set of customers is called **product diversification.** The thrust of McDonald's breakfast plans was to attract new customers with new products. Before the move, no one was able to stop at McDonald's for breakfast. No consumers who regularly ate breakfast out could do so at McDonald's. Therefore, the new line was clearly intended to attract new customer groups. The strategy has paid off for McDonald's, and some of its competitors who adopted similar plans. McDonald's breakfast items now account for about 20 percent of the company's sales. Hardee's gets 25 percent of its sales from breakfast.

Product-Related Strategies

Products should be carefully designed to appeal to well-researched target markets. However, most products and brands enjoy limited lives because of the dynamic nature of those markets. Effective marketing does not fulfill its obligation to the product variable by contributing to the design of *the* product. Its role is on-going. Dynamic markets must be monitored and researched so that appropriate strategies, designed to keep old

EXHIBIT 10-5

Gillette Razor Blades' PLC

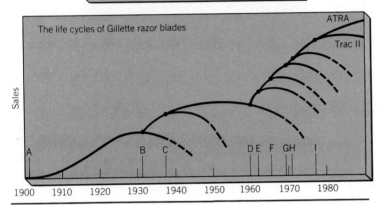

Blade	Year Introduced
A. Original Gillette blade	1903
B. Blue blade	1932
C. Thin blade	1938
D. Super Blue blade	1960
E. Stainless Steel blade	1963
F. Super Stainless Steel blade	1965
G. Platinum-Plus blade	1969
H. Trac II	1971
I. ATRA	1977

The life cycles of Gillette razor blades

Source: Redrawn from Douglas W. Mellott, Jr., *Marketing Applications and Cases* (Reston, Va.: Reston Publishing, 1978), p. 100.

customers and attract new ones and to extend the product life cycle, might be devised. This is an important aspect of product management. Pricing, promotion, and distribution also play their parts, as revealed in other chapters.

Several product strategies that typically do not stand alone are discussed in the following paragraphs.[8] These strategies are most often integrated with the four major market-related strategies discussed earlier.

Extension of the Product Life Cycle While many strategies can serve to extend a product's life cycle, it is important to focus on the extension strategy per se. Most organizations alter their products with an eye toward extending their lives. A master at this is the Gillette Com-

pany. A depiction of the product life cycle for Gillette razors is shown in Exhibit 10-5. Notice how the company has managed to keep its basic product alive by steadily developing new blades and new razors. DuPont, the developer of nylon, has accomplished much the same thing by showing that the basic product is usable in the production of everything from parachutes to automobile tires to underwear.

The basic dessert product, pudding, was helped to a longer life by the development of instant no-cook pudding. While this is, for some buyers, a product improvement, pudding manufacturers may view it as extending the life of the product because working mothers may now have time to make pudding. Similarly, pudding packaged in plastic tubs or in cans gives the consumer convenience of use—but for the marketer it extends the pudding product life cycle. "New and improved" products are intended to

---

[8]Our classification follows the thinking of Kenneth E. Runyon, *Advertising and the Practice of Marketing* (Columbus, Ohio: Charles E. Merrill, 1979), pp. 144–146.

The best pickle on your grocer's shelf isn't on your grocer's shelf.

Dr. Q. Cumbus Claussen
World renowned pickle expert.

Claussen® dill and sweet 'n sour pickles are in the refrigerated section, set apart from the others. To keep them fresh and crunchy, we keep them cold. And that can make the difference between a good pickle and a great pickle. You'll love 'em, once you find them. **In the refrigerated section. Where fresh things belong.** © 1979. Claussen Pickle Co.

A product with a differential advantage sets it apart from the ordinary.

breathe new life into the product or extend the product life cycle.

Product Differentiation. Calling the buyers' attention to aspects of a product that set it apart from its competitors is called **product differentiation.** This may be accomplished by making some adjustment in the product to vary it from the norm or by promoting one or more of its intangible attributes. A six-hour video cassette tape recorder with a seven-day programmable timer is likely to be more competitive than a basic two-hour recorder. Triple-protection Aquafresh toothpaste combines its ingredients in stripes that visually set that product apart from its competition. Gleem toothpaste does the same with little green "spots" in the dentifrice. Notice that the differences do not have to be scientifically demonstrable improvements. Color differences and shape differences, as well as technological differences, can all play a role in product differentiation. The bottom line is that if consumers see the variations as important then the variations, by definition, serve to differentiate the product from its competitors.

Claussen and Vlasic are two pickle-packers who stress product quality as their differential advantages. Claussen, however, emphasizes this quality by portraying its product as a cool, un-

cooked pickle, set apart from ordinary pickles on the grocer's shelf by its placement in the refrigerated cases. Some producers of salad dressings use exactly the same method to differentiate their products from dressings that do not require constant refrigeration. The need for special handling demonstrates the close relationship between product strategy, promotional strategy, distribution strategy, and ultimately, price.

Product Quality Strategies. Product design changes may improve product quality over product life cycle and may serve to both raise sales volume and extend the total product life cycle. Products on the market at any given time are generally improvements over the primitive early models first offered. Items offering basic features generally evolve into products of superior quality because of design changes. Today's marketing students may never have seen an "antique" television set with a four-inch screen and a 150-pound cabinet. These early sets broke down regularly. Today's TVs are obviously far superior to the early models. Adding features, shrinking or enlarging products, improving or varying flavors, and improving product quality are traditional product strategies.

Quality creep is a commonly encountered

A COMPUTER DIFFERENTIATES AND HELPS REVLON SELL THE PRODUCT LINE

American women may soon be able to choose their cosmetics by computer.

Revlon Inc. recently unveiled a countersize computer at Bloomingdale's. The machine, dubbed the Revlon Touch, suggests the proper makeup for customers, free of charge. Some four dozen computers are expected to be installed in department stores nationwide in at least 15 major cities.

The computer includes a sleekly packaged video screen and paper-tape printing device. Inside, a projector displays a dozen or so multiple-choice questions on the screen, questions dealing with the consumer's race, age, eyes, condition of hair and complexion, and clothing preferences. The customer responds by pressing her finger to the screen next to the answer she selects.

This five-minute dialogue is digested by the computer, which then prints out on paper one of 5,000 possible combinations for makeup, varied by clothing color preferences. The computer also flashes pictures of how the customer might look made up as suggested. Revlon has included several hundred faces, including those of its own employees as well as women chosen at random, in the computer display.

"Of course, if a 65-year-old woman punches in her age as 25, it isn't going to work," a Revlon official notes.

Revlon hopes to increase its clientele without expanding department store space. In test marketing, one-third to a half of the West Coast women who used the computer also made a Revlon purchase at that time.

The computer memory contains information on nearly 1,000 products including various colors. It can choose from 140 lipsticks, 110 nail polish colors, and up to 100 shades of eyeliner, as well as skin moisturizers, mascaras, and eyebrow sticks.

Source: Gail Bronson, "Computers Assume a Glamorous Role: Choosing Cosmetics," *Wall Street Journal,* August 1, 1980, p. 16.

---

phenomenon in the development of products. Assume that one manufacturer decides that a market exists for an inexpensive car, built along the most Spartan lines, and commits a design to paper. As the preparations are being made to manufacture that plainest of plain cars, people in the organization begin to make suggestions for "improving" the car. Why not add a radio? A strip of chrome here and there for eye appeal? Some fins? A bigger engine option? Chrome wheels? Etc.? Before you know it, the little super-economy car has been lost and something entirely different created. Making the product better destroyed the original good idea to appeal to the needs of a particular market segment. Quality creep has added useless quality to the product.

"Useless quality" sounds like a contradiction in terms until we realize that some products do not have to be of high quality, especially if customers are not really willing to pay for that quality. Does the homeowner need an electric saw that is as good as the one required by a professional carpenter? Probably not, so the line of saws offered should reflect the differing need. The manufacturer should make a high-quality, expensive saw for the carpenter, and a lower-quality, cheaper saw for the homeowner. To offer the homeowner the high-quality saw at a high price is to offer "useless quality."

The "Weakest Link" Concept. The part of a product that will be the first to wear out is the product's "weakest link." It makes sense to build the product around that part. A car's engine is difficult and expensive to replace. Within the bounds of safety then, the rest of the car should be built to be consistent with the life of the engine. Most buyers do not want to pay for a car

PLANNING JOE'S RETURN

The original, 11½ inch, gun-toting G.I. Joe doll was a casualty of anti-war sentiment during the Vietnam War. When sales fell from $22 million to under $6 million, Hasbro Company took Joe off the shelves and replaced him with Action Joe, an adventurer equipped with a space capsule and diving gear. In 1982, Hasbro returned G.I. Joe to the marketplace, but only after making several changes.

Rising plastic prices have forced Joe to shrink to less than four inches in height, and his clothes are painted on, not remov-

able. Joe no longer stands alone, but is part of the "G.I. Joe Mobile Strike Force," each member of which has a code name, military specialty, résumé, and a personality developed in comic books, which "tie in" to the "Strike Force." Each doll costs only $3, but the complete set of figures plus military hardware sells for about $200.

The "Strike Force" needed an enemy so Hasbro created the Cobra Command, members of which wear masks to conceal their ethnic origin. "When Joe

originally came out," Hasbro's marketing director said, "we had German and Japanese enemy soldiers. Today you never know what the enemy will look like."

Source: Adapted from "G.I. Joe Doll: Back in Action," *Newsweek*, February 1, 1982.

body that will outlive the engine. Matching the total product to the market requires consideration of the "weakest link."

In some situations, the concept is used by marketers other than the actual builders of the product that contains the weakest link. For example, several retailers sell high-quality auto batteries that are guaranteed for "as long as you

own your car" at premium prices. The car, not the battery, is the "weakest link" here because the batteries are being sold as replacement batteries and are installed in cars that are already three to five years old. Most Americans do not keep their cars much beyond that span of years. The car "link" is likely to give out long before the extra-strength battery does.

MATCHING PRODUCTS TO MARKETS: PRODUCT LINE STRATEGY

Ultimately, it is the goal of the marketing manager to develop a total product offering that satisfies the desires of target customers.[9] Ideally, since there are heterogeneous needs within

most markets, an organization would develop a series of products so that each target market's needs and desires would be mirrored in a product offering. However, as discussed in the chapter on market segmentation, the firm must select meaningful market segments that will be profitable. Offering an extreme proliferation of product items may involve an economic penalty to the organization.

---

[9] This discussion follows the logic of T.A. Staudt and D.A. Taylor, *A Managerial Introduction to Marketing* 2nd ed. (Prentice-Hall: Englewood Cliffs, N.J., 1970), Chapter 12, "Product-Market Integration."

A full product line matches product attributes with specific customer needs.

The depth of a product line—that is, the number of closely related product items—is influenced by the diversity of the market and the resources available to the marketing company. Consider the marketing organization that seeks to satisfy a wide range of customers with a broad array of product items only to discover that the sales force and other resources are not sufficient to reach all those different customers. Being spread too thin, the marketing effort results in cultivating *no* market properly. On the other hand, the marketing managers may have designed a product line that is too narrow to fulfill customer needs on a segment-by-segment basis. An automobile manufacturer, for example,

might offer five car models, only to find that the variations available for each of the five are too few to satisfy the market segments at which the five were initially targeted.

The answer to this problem usually involves a realignment of the product line and of the resources assigned to each product. Models and options offered to one market segment may be eliminated or pruned so as to better satisfy other segments or, if resources allow, the product line may be expanded.

In general, the broader the product line the higher the cost. Conversely, a narrow line may not ideally match the market's demands. A major product strategy decision to consider is: "What assortment of products should an organization offer?" That is, how many variations on a product can be presented to the market before the extra customer satisfaction achieved is no longer worth the expense to the company? The options the organization faces may be described in the following terms:

■ The **broad** or **full-line strategy** means offering a large number of variations of a product.

■ The **limited-line strategy** entails offering a smaller number of variations.

■ The **single product strategy** involves offering one product or one product with very few model options.

While these terms are not particularly technical in nature, they are commonly used to describe marketers of many types, including manufacturers, distributors, wholesalers, and others.

Although each of these strategy alternatives must be evaluated in terms of the market addressed, some general advantages and disadvantages are given in Exhibit 10-6. Two major product strategy decisions concerning product lines are mentioned here.

Product Line Extension

Ocean Spray Cranberries were once available in only two forms, either as a jelly or in traditional cranberry sauce form. Ocean Spray, however,

EXHIBIT 10-6

Full Line Versus Limited Line

Full Line	Limited Line

Full Line

Advantages

1 Customers may prefer to deal with one supplier, simplifying their buying.

2 More items carried should mean more opportunities to make a sale.

3 Shipping many items from one source may lower transportation costs.

4 A full line may permit coordination of product offerings—e.g., stove and refrigerator.

5 A supplier's image may be enhanced by being a source of a full line of merchandise.

Disadvantages

1 Manufacturing costs are greater as production must be adjusted to produce disparate items.

2 Handling and transportation costs should be greater than for standardized products.

3 Inventory costs may be higher as different items must be held for different customers.

4 Competitors practicing limited-line strategies may gain advantages related to specialization and economies of scale.

5 Sales force and other resources must be spread over a wider range of offerings.

Limited Line

Advantages

1 If line is limited to products sold in high volume, economies of scale in production and distribution should result.

2 Supplier's image may be enhanced if perceived as a "specialist."

3 Line can be limited to include only high-profit items.

4 A limited product offering may be more closely related to specific target markets or segments.

5 Buyers may prefer limited-line suppliers as a more certain source of supply or in the belief that savings due to specializing are passed on to buyers.

Disadvantages

1 Some sales lost due to lack of full line.

2 Channel members may prefer dealing with full-line supplier and resist dealing with limited-line dealers.

3 If customers buy in small lots, increased transportation costs could result because of small shipments.

4 There is no opportunity to offer a coordinated line of merchandise such as apparel items or appliances.

5 Consumer recognition problems could result. Due to advertising of many products, Kellogg's is a better known name than Maltex.

---

successfully developed and marketed Ocean Spray Cranberry Juice Cocktail. Then the organization extended or expanded that product into a whole line of juice drinks, such as Cranapple and Crangrape. These blends made use of several corporate assets including raw materials, manufacturing facilities, and the well-known Ocean Spray name. More recently, Ocean Spray has attempted to extend its juice line to include non-cranberry products, such as grapefruit juice, because the company recognized a potentially profitable market niche for a premium-priced, high-quality, natural juice packed in convenient containers. This portion of the market is broader than cranberry products alone can satisfy. Thus, it appeared logical to management to extend the product line. As an added benefit, these somewhat similar products, sometimes called **flanker brands,** are placed beside one another on grocery shelves, perhaps denying shelf space to competitors.

Sometimes a product line extension will

A product line based on line extensions in the juice drink product category.

cannibalize sales from other items in the product line. For example, *Playboy* magazine stopped publishing its semiannual *Playboy Fashion* and *Playboy Guide to Electronic Entertainment* guides when it discovered these items were taking sales away from the mainstay of its business—*Playboy* magazine. Introducing a new product to a line may take business away from one of your own products rather than from competitors. **Cannibalization** refers to a situation where one item eats into the sales revenues of another in the same line.

Eliminating Old Products

While an enormous amount of attention has been paid to new product development efforts, managers often neglect product elimination efforts.[10] Profits can be enhanced by eliminating certain costs associated with products in the later stages of the product life cycle as well as by increasing the productivity of the resources released from the older products. Hence, elimination of products should be a strategic move that

product managers should consider. Products that were once "winners" eventually become "old winners," and are either dropped entirely or replaced by other products that better satisfy changing market requirements. There is a need for marketing managers to devote systematic attention to the elimination of no-longer-profitable products, although this is sometimes a painful process necessitating the realignment of company personnel and other assets. Still, every organization works with a limited pool of talent and resources. Expending these on products which are in the final periods of the decline stage detracts from efforts that could be made pursuing new opportunities. Old winners can quickly become very costly in terms of resources and management time and effort.

Products may be dropped for reasons other than a lack of popularity in the market and low profits. Shortly after acquiring the Chore Boy and Chore Girl lines of scouring products, Airwick Industries reduced the number of items in the lines from 32 to 12.[11] The company went further and dropped most of the names so recently

[10]James T. Rothe, "The Product Elimination Decision," *MSU Business Topics*, Vol. 18 (Autumn 1970), p. 45.

[11]Nancy Giges, "Chore Boy Line Revamp," *Advertising Age*, April 13, 1981, pp. 3, 112.

purchased: Chore Girl, Chore Ready, Softy, Golden Fleece, and Scour Fresh. Increased profitability was certainly the object of these steps, but other goals were served as well: (1) Advertising could dwell on 12 brand names, rather than on 32; (2) thus the scouring products could be promoted to dealers as a single line of goods rather than as a collection of seemingly different items; and (3) management of the product mix, in general, was simplified.

THE PRODUCT PORTFOLIO

Marketing is a pragmatic discipline, ready to use any concept from any field of study if it will advance the cause of satisfying consumers. One such concept, clearly based in the field of finance, is the **product portfolio.**

Just as the investor or financial advisor seeks to assemble a group of stocks or other investments so that the total package of investments is considered sound, so can the marketing manager view the product mix as a collection of items to be balanced as a group. A balanced product mix might contain some good old standby products, some new products on the way up, some products that are in growth fields, and some products that may be a bit risky but which have a high payoff potential. The product portfolio concept stresses that the cash flows for a complete mix of products should be considered rather than concentration on isolated problems of the individual members of that mix. The primary contribution of the portfolio concept is that it focuses on the interrelationships between differing types of products within a product mix. Products grouped into subcategories within the portfolio will, of course, be subject to different marketing strategies and assignments of resources.

The product portfolio is such a useful concept that it has attracted much attention from marketing scholars and practitioners alike.[12] Among the variations on the portfolio model that have gained acceptance, the variant associated with the Boston Consulting Group (B.C.G.) is probably the best known and most easily understood version. It provides the basis of the discussion that follows.

The Portfolio Model

In its most common format, the product portfolio concept is illustrated in matrix form as shown in Exhibit 10-7. On the horizontal scale, the relative market shares of "high" and "low" are depicted. On the vertical scale, the same words refer to market growth. Thus, the following four combinations of these variables can be illustrated:

■ High market share product in a high growth market.

■ High market share product in a low growth market.

■ Low market share product in a high growth market.

■ Low market share product in a low growth market.

To put this in perspective, let's try to assign familiar products to each quadrant. The home computer market is a high growth one, and Apple computers has a high market share. The laundry detergent market is a low growth market and Tide has a high market share. The home video recorder market is growing rapidly and Sanyo has a low market share. The face soap market is a low growth one and Palmolive has a low market share.

As Exhibit 10-7 shows, some picturesque names have been assigned to products in each of the matrix cells. The names are descriptive. Tide detergent, for example, may not be involved

[12]Y. Wind and V. Mahajan, "Designing Product and Business Portfolios," *Harvard Business Review*, January–February 1981, p. 151.

EXHIBIT 10-7

The Cash Quadrant Approach to Describing the Product Portfolio

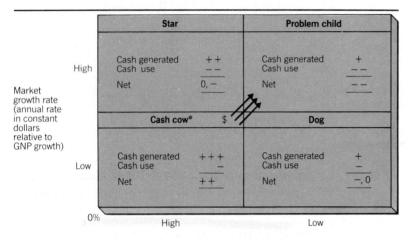

Market growth rate (annual rate in constant dollars relative to GNP growth)

High

Star

Cash generated ++
Cash use − −
Net 0, −

Problem child

Cash generated +
Cash use − −
Net − −

Cash cow* $

Low

Cash generated +++
Cash use −
Net ++

Dog

Cash generated +
Cash use −
Net −, 0

0%

High   Low

Market share dominance
(ratio of company share to share of largest competitor)

*Arrows indicate principal cash flows.

Source: Adapted with permission from George S. Day, "Diagnosing the Product Portfolio," *Journal of Marketing*, April 1977, pp. 28–38.

in an exciting and growing market, but it does make a lot of money for Procter & Gamble. Such a product is called a "cash cow." Products that are near the top of a growth market are called "stars." Products in high growth markets that seem to be having trouble picking up market share are, for their manufacturers, "problem children." But now we come to the low market share product in the low growth market. To name these products "dogs" is something of a disservice. (But that is what they are called.) After all, most industries are mature with comparatively low growth rates, and only one product can be number one in any given industry. Thus, many products on the market at any point in time fall into the "low-low" cell of the matrix.

While some marketing experts believe organizations should get rid of any dogs to free themselves to concentrate on more profitable projects, such an approach cannot work for every organization. Not every product can be a star. This does not mean that marketing managers should accept a role as a kennel keeper, but dogs do have some attractions. They might be profitable, even though there are few prospects for profit growth, in the sense that they contribute to overhead and administrative expenses. Consider how many home detergents are on the market. Most are dogs. Furthermore, such products may appeal to small market segments, and thus never attain the great sales totals other products do. Lastly, a dog product may occupy a safe and secure market niche that is easy to defend against any challenges from competitors.

Interrelationships

The four types of products shown in the portfolio can be found in a single organization. Ideally they fit together into an interrelated product mix. For example, stars are great to have, but, early in

KELLOGG MANAGES ITS PRODUCT PORTFOLIO OF CEREALS

Some of the snap, crackle and pop has gone out of the once booming market for so-called natural cereals. Most granola-type cereals, in fact, have disappeared from supermarket shelves. So how is Kellogg Co., the nation's No. 1 cereal-maker, reacting? It's coming out with a new natural cereal at a cost of $50 million.

Kellogg officials say they aren't worried about their timing. They insist that their "Nutri-Grain" cereal can fight the market trend. Not only have Kellogg researchers figured out a way to flake whole grains for the first time, they say, but the product is made without sugar—and the company says it doesn't need the sweetener added at breakfast time to make it taste good. "It's the biggest breakthrough in grain processing in 30 years, since Special K, since we learned how to mix protein and grains," says Gary E. Costley, Kellogg's senior vice president for sales.

The impetus for Nutri-Grain came when Kellogg chairman William E. LaMothe tried out some whole-grain cereals on a trip abroad. They didn't taste very good, but LaMothe thought that if this problem could be solved, the cereals had the right image for the '80s. Kellogg thinks it has licked the taste problem, but nonetheless its promotional efforts will be aimed primarily at nutrition-conscious adults.

The new cereal comes in four varieties—wheat, rye, barley and corn—a spread of choices that Kellogg hopes will end the "wear out" factor that hurt the granola-style cereals after their initial success. The cereal is packaged in plain boxes, and more than the usual amount of the advertising budget will go into print—and less into TV. LaMothe says the growing number of adults in the 18- to 45-year-old age bracket tends to buy foods that have a high nutrition content and are less processed. "And we're finding—right or wrong—people want to avoid sugar," he says.

Kellogg discovered that fact earlier when it test-marketed a flaked natural cereal, which customers found too much like one of the industry's usual sugary, highly processed concoctions. Researchers eliminated the sugar and found a new way to flake the grain so that it looked less processed. Not surprisingly, Kellogg will give no details on how it makes its whole-grain flakes tasty without the sugar. About all the company will reveal is that it added malt flavoring to the product to counteract the bitterness that results when the grain is toasted.

Kellogg has good reason to try to pep up its product line. The company still claims 40 percent of the American cereal business but has lost market share in recent years to its two leading competitors, General Mills and General Foods. General Mills has scored with two recent winners, Honey-Nut Cheerios and Crispy Wheat and Raisins. Analysts say Kellogg generally has not produced the steady stream of new products necessary to protect its traditional premier position in the industry. Some doubt that Nutri-Grain is a product that will send competitors scurrying to their labs. But the final judges will be the customers—who will soon find out for themselves if a cereal can taste good without sugar.

Source: *Newsweek*, July 27, 1981, p. 58. Used with permission.

their product life cycles, they use up more cash than they generate because of the financial effort needed to maintain a leading position in an attractive growth market. Although cash cows maintain a high market share since their markets are mature and less dynamic than high growth markets, cash cows are likely to have a long-standing record of popularity and to generate cash flow. Excess monies generated by the cows can be used to finance the growth of the products the organization hopes will become stars in the future.

Dogs may earn profits or be squeezed for any excess dollars they can generate. Products with low shares of low growth markets may continue to appeal to customers with special needs or who buy primarily on the basis of price. Many brewers maintain low-priced brands that appeal to bargain hunters. The investment made in marketing these products is small. Since there may be no advertising and no expenses incurred in improving the product, the brand that is simply placed on the shelf for sale may be profitable. A look around the supermarket will reveal many unadvertised foods, drinks, and other products marketed in just this way.

The ideal product mix would consist only of stars and possible future stars supported by a healthy barnful of cash cows. For this reason, many portfolio analysts suggest selling off the dogs—in other words, divestiture. In theory, this may be a good plan. But, as we have discussed, dogs are the most plentiful of products and they do hold attractions for organizations seeking a balanced product portfolio.

The Limits of the Product Portfolio Concept

As briefly described here, the product portfolio seems a reasonable and powerful description of product mix management. Within certain limits, it is. The first limitation of the concept is that it may give the inexperienced student of marketing an unjustified feeling of security. Simply placing the names of products in the appropriate boxes, however, is not the purpose of the portfolio. That merely helps to describe the problem. Once the matrix is formed, the marketing manager's difficult decisions are only beginning. If we have a star, is competition desperately trying to knock it down? Probably. So what steps come next? If we have a cash cow, how vulnerable is it to competition? Wouldn't the competitors like to have a cow of their own? They would. How about the dogs? Should we sell them off? Who would buy them? Should we keep them? How can that be done to maximize the cash flow? Should we hold on to them for a longer period since no competitor seems to be addressing their limited target markets? How much are we willing to spend trying to make the "problem child" into a star?

A second overriding problem that the portfolio concept only begins to address is the reality of the marketplace and of human nature. On the surface, the portfolio suggests that the marketing manager should work hard either to turn problem children into stars or to develop stars in some other way. However, keeping up a steady flow of stars is difficult, to say the least. Thus, many organizations and their marketing managers are tempted to build up the cows, increasing their market share to make sure they remain number one. Procter & Gamble seems very proud that Tide has been the premier detergent for decades. Anheuser-Busch becomes exceedingly concerned when some brand, such as Miller's, appears poised to take over the number one beer spot. This is not unreasonable since many such products are such big money makers, but it is not consistent with the notion of supporting the development of stars with cow money. Thus, while the idea of moving a mix of products in ways consistent with portfolio theory would seem to be useful, competition or other environmental forces may block total implementation of the concept, even for sizable, multiple-product organizations.

This is not meant to disparage the portfolio concept. Used as a theoretical tool, the portfolio concept provides valuable planning guidelines to marketing managers. No tool or theory, however, can replace managerial judgment based on close analysis of the marketing environment.

Portfolio Variations

The simple product portfolio shown in Exhibit 10-7 could be improved significantly. The "high" and "low" designations could be divided into three or more exact descriptors. A third dimension, such as profitability, could be added to the illustration. All these might be valuable additions to the model *if* they provide useful information. Any variation can be used by marketing managers. The key question is, however, will the variations or improvements make the tool more useful in the decision-making process?

SUMMARY

The purpose of this chapter was to narrow the focus of our study of marketing strategy to the single mix variable of *product*. While it is difficult to consider one marketing mix variable apart from the others, certain strategic tools are intended to be product oriented. These include the product life cycle, the product portfolio, and a range of product-based planning concepts.

The life cycle of a product is composed of a number of distinct stages—namely, introduction, growth, maturity, and decline. The introduction stage is characterized by large expenditures and an intensive marketing effort, yet profits are low. The primary concerns in the introduction stage are the generation of product awareness and the creation of channels of distribution.

The growth stage is typified by large expenditures and increasing competition as well as rapid sales growth. Emphasis in the growth stage is on creating brand preferences and promoting a product's differential features.

During the mature stage, there is a decrease in the growth of sales, reflecting intense competition to maintain profitability. The goal, during the mature stage, becomes one of maintenance or expansion of market share.

Decreasing profits and decreasing expenditures mark the decline stage. Although it may be possible to introduce a "new and improved" product to reverse the declining sales trend, termination is typically the final phase of the decline stage.

Sales of existing products may be increased by attraction of new customers or growth into new markets—that is, market development—or by increasing usage among existing customers (market penetration). Introducing a new product to an existing market is called product development, while introduction of a new product to a new set of customers is termed product diversification.

Ultimately, every marketing organization offers some product to the market place. Failure to gain market acceptance, while attributable to many causes, is often the result of a failure to match the product to the demands and needs of the buyer. In many respects, the product is the starting point and basis of marketing strategy. The tools and ideas discussed in this chapter become all the more useful when applied to the "total product" offered by the organization. That approach opens up the full range of applications of these concepts.

The product portfolio suggests that managers should manage cash flows for complete mixes of products rather than concentrating exclusively on strategies for isolated items.

THE MOST IMPORTANT CONCEPT IN THIS CHAPTER
The product life cycle is an important planning tool that presents general guidelines for the selection of a product strategy.

KEY TERMS

Product life cycle

Market penetration

Market development

Product development

Product diversification

Product differentiation

Full-line strategy

Limited-line strategy

Single product strategy

Flanker brands

Cannibalization

Product portfolio

QUESTIONS FOR DISCUSSION

1 At what stage of the product life cycle would you place the following products?
(a) Cigars
(b) Coffee
(c) Gasoline
(d) Amusement parks
(e) Tennis rackets

2 What are some typical pricing strategies during each stage of the product life cycle?

3 What are some typical distribution strategies during each stage of the product life cycle?

4 What are some typical promotion strategies during each stage of the product life cycle?

5 The Checker Taxi Cab is no longer in production. Why do you think this product was eliminated?

6 What guidelines would you suggest for rejuvenation of old brands in the mature stage of the product life cycle?

7 What are the pitfalls of a brand extension strategy that, for example, extends a name from a hair spray product to a facial cream?

8 Count Chocula and Boo Berry are marketed by the same company and have been featured together in a single television ad. What type of product strategy is this?

9 Pizza Hut added an individual serving pizza, that could be cooked within five minutes, to its product line. Why do you think they added this product to their product line?

10 Does marketing grow in importance as a product matures and moves from the introductory stage through the growth stage and into the maturity stage?

11 What is the relationship between market segmentation and choice of a single-line versus full-line product strategy?

12 Try to trace the product life cycle for a brand like Soft Soap (and its competitors).

13 Some homes are now being marketed with cable setups so that computer terminals may be installed. What product strategy does this reflect?

14 What is product differentiation and what relationship does it have to market segmentation?

CASE 10·1   Jefferson Bus Lines*

When buses joined the list of deregulated industries in the fall of 1982, many travelers feared that large bus companies like Greyhound and Trailways would abandon small-town stations where only a few passengers boarded. The giants plan to eliminate 1,300 stops, but dozens of small operators have entered the field, and in many places, bus service is improving.

One company that has profited handsomely from deregulation is Jefferson Lines of Minneapolis. The company was skidding into the red and facing a strike in 1978, when Louis Zelle, 59,

a Minneapolis real estate developer who owns 60 percent of the company, set out to find someone with "no background in the bus industry" to run the firm. He explains: "Most bus executives are only interested in meeting schedules. Passengers are incidental."

Daniel Prins, 40, was his choice. Born in Holland, Prins came to the U.S. in 1970 and worked in marketing for a variety of companies from TWA to Procter & Gamble. Prins knew nothing about buses, but figured that he "could market bus travel just like a box of Tide or Cheer."

Prins first persuaded his new employees to call off the strike, then talked them into accepting a profit-sharing plan instead of increases in

---

*Source: From "Front of the Bus," *Time*, May 2, 1983, p. 61. All rights reserved. Reprinted with permission.

salary and benefits. Next he traded in Jefferson's aging fleet of 120 buses for 100 new red-and-white ones that carry more passengers in greater comfort and at a lower cost.

Then Prins set out to fill the new buses. He installed sleeper seats for Kansas City ski buffs taking the overnight bus to Colorado resorts. He also put video games in some buses and movies on others. Prins' biggest revenue booster was special, cut-rate tours. Example: for $49.95, passengers can take a two-day trip from Des Moines to Minneapolis, complete with dinner and one night at a good hotel. Greyhound and Trailways charge more than $80 for the same round trip, without the hotel or the meal, and airfare is $100 one way. Jefferson now offers tours from coast to coast, and has even jumped the Atlantic to carry vacationers to Paris, Venice and the castles along the Rhine.

In addition to introducing imaginative marketing, Prins also found new sources of income inside the company. Jefferson began selling the service of its mechanics to competing firms. And while maintenance is usually a heavy drag on earnings in the industry, Jefferson's operation now produces $3 million in revenues. A training school for bus drivers that Prins started in 1980 also makes money and earns Jefferson a 30 percent reduction in insurance rates. The result of

the new services: in the past four years, the privately held company's revenues have increased by 33 percent, to $20 million, and profits have quadrupled.

Prins predicts his company will continue prospering despite the twin threats of increased competition and the prospect that falling gasoline prices and a strengthening economy will tempt passengers to drive their cars instead of taking the bus. One reason for Prins' optimism: "As the economy picks up, more people are planning to take tours." Indeed, Jefferson's 1983 tour bookings are already up 80 percent over last year's, and its European jaunts are almost sold out.

Prins now has a new plan to turn bus deregulation into still more profits. Last week Jefferson began offering new bus companies a package of services, ranging from the financing and maintenance of buses to advertising, promotion and accounting, to help them get started. Prins' fee: up to 15 percent of profits.

Questions

1 At what stage of the product life cycle is the Jefferson Bus Line?

2 What product strategies has Mr. Prins utilized?

CASE 10-2   RCA SelectaVision*

More than $150 million was spent developing the RCA SelectaVision video disc system. With SelectaVision consumers can purchase recorded movies or recorded programs on a recordlike platter and play them on the video disc machine. Unlike the video cassette recorders (VCRs), SelectaVision does not record programs from television broadcasts.

*Source: Based on information in Laura Landro, "Following a Slow Start: RCA Plans a New Push for Its Video Disc Player," The Wall Street Journal, October 13, 1981, p. 29 and "Three's a Crowd in Video Disc," Time, March 23, 1981, p. 71.

The SelectaVision discs, including the dust cover, are slipped into the player, then the cover is removed. A stylus detects signals from a grooved disc and transmits the signal to the TV screen. Magnavision, MCA, and Laser Disc are competitive models that read the pictures and the sound with a laser beam. These models cost approximately $200 more than the SelectaVision, which retails at about $500.

The available programs range from classic movies such as Gone With the Wind to video demonstrations of baby care by Dr. Benjamin Spock. However, recent movies account for the bulk of sales volume.

The product was test marketed for more than a year. The company estimated its first year's sales would be 200,000 player units. However only about 40,000 units were sold during the first year introduction.

Questions

1 At what stage of the product life cycle is the SelectaVision?

2 What reasons can you give for the slow sales of SelectaVision?

3 What product strategy would you recommend?

CASE 10-3 The Sony Mavica Electronic Camera*

Sony introduced its Mavica camera in Japan more than a year before it was marketed in the United States. The Sony Mavica is a major new product innovation. Mavica is an acronym for magnetic video camera. Although its appearance is similar to a conventional camera that can be fitted with various lenses, it has a different way of recording still pictures. It uses magnetic discs instead of rolled-film cartridges. The camera may replace slides and slide projectors. The magnetic discs are placed into a special player that reproduces the images on a standard television set. The magnetic disc produces better pictures and requires no processing. The disc may be either erased or reused almost indefinitely because the images will not fade. It is expected that a disc capable of 50 exposures will cost only $3. The initial retail price for the Mavica is expected to be between $900 and $1,000.

Questions

1 Why did Sony introduce Mavica in Japan before it was introduced in the larger U.S. market?

2 What marketing strategy would you expect Sony to utilize during the first five years of the product's life cycle?

3 What advantages does the Mavica brand name have? What disadvantages do you see? Suggest some alternate brand names for this product.

---

*Source: Based on information in "Pictures Without Film," by Bruce Schechter, *Discover*, November 1981, pp. 78–80 and "Kodak Fights Back," *Business Week*, February 1, 1982, pp. 50–53.

Both industrial robots, which are sold to automobile manufacturers, and tempra paints, which are sold to schools, are industrial products (see pages 238–239).

The "Datsun" name was changed to "Nissan" partly because consumers had a hard time pronouncing "Datsun" (see page 251).

Willy Wonka Brand—
a creative family bran[d]
based on a popular
movie character—
relies on its strong
appeal to the target
market and combines
individual brands for
items in the product
line (see page 250).

A package is an extension of the product. Coca-Cola spent considerable time and effort to design its Diet Coke package.

Attractive packaging may serve an important promotional function.

CHAPTER 11

Marketing New Products

CHAPTER SCAN

The main focus of this chapter is a discussion of the development and introduction of new consumer and industrial products to the marketplace. For most organizations, long-range success is based on new products or, at least, new forms of established products.

The chapter calls attention to the degrees of novelty a "new" product may possess, then turns to the characteristics of successful new products and some of the steps that may help to guard against new product failure.

Also covered in detail are the steps involved in the development and introduction of new products, ranging from the search for new product ideas to the commercialization of the selected and tested product itself. The related topic of the adoption process by which a market accepts and makes new products successful is also reviewed.

Finally, the major organizational designs that have been developed to permit firms to bring together the resources needed to develop, test, analyze, and ultimately market new products are presented.

WHEN YOU HAVE STUDIED THIS CHAPTER, YOU WILL:

Be able to discuss the idea that there are degrees of newness suggested by the term "new product" and to differentiate between those levels of newness.

Be able to comment on the chances of success and failure faced by new products in the marketplace, and to explain why these are likely to vary considerably from industry to industry.

Know and be able to define the general product characteristics associated with successful new products.

Be able to explain the stages of new product development and to describe the steps likely to be associated with each.

Be familiar with the new product diffusion process and the several groups of adopters to which marketing managers may ultimately have to appeal.

Be able to describe six organizational forms associated with the successful development and introduction of new products and the advantages associated with each.

New products are the shape of things to come.

At the Tokyo Motor Show, nine Japanese auto-makers demonstrated some new ideas amid fireworks and brass bands. Among the one million people in attendance the first day was a delegation of Detroit auto executives.

New cars were displayed on rotating platforms while mini-skirted models recited memorized sales spiels. Spectators gawked at, for example, a four-wheel-drive Toyota outfitted for bird watching that had a roof-mounted camera and sound equipment to record birdcalls.

In addition to the glitter and the glamour, the Tokyo show demonstrated some dazzling applications of modern electronics and semiconductor technology that make cars cheaper, safer, and easier to drive. Japanese manufacturers are using computers on a chip to improve fuel economy, monitor the engine, and even make a new electronically controlled transmission operate smoothly. Three separate companies exhibited an electronic map display, mounted on the dashboard, that points out the car's destination, gives instructions on the best route to follow, and notes the progress of the trip.

Toyota showed the shape of things to come in Japanese cars. Upon entering the automobile, the driver inserts a plastic card in the dashboard that adjusts the seats, air conditioning, and mirror to his or her specific desires. Shock absorbers automatically regulate the car's suspension to accommodate the number of passengers. Once the car is under way, a radar-activated cruise-control senses vehicles ahead and applies the brakes when necessary. In addition, an ultrasonic system warns the driver of any obstructions up to 10 feet behind the vehicle. If it starts to rain, electronic windshield wipers adjust their speed to the amount of precipitation.

Nissan presented a test vehicle that allows a handicapped person to drive literally without lifting a finger. The car is equipped with a "voiced word recognition system" that will carry out spoken commands from the driver. A disabled motorist can operate the lights and other instruments and adjust the driver's seat and rear-view mirrors simply by talking to the machine. The automobile is steered with a foot pedal. But the car will accept voice commands only from those whose voice it has been programmed to recognize.

WHAT IS A NEW PRODUCT?

This chapter concerns itself primarily with the marketing of new products. Therefore, we should come to some understanding of just what constitutes a new product. It would certainly appear that the voice-operated automobile just discussed is a new product but, before reading further, pause for a second to decide in your own mind what a **new product** is. Think of an example or two and try to identify what makes them new. To some marketers, a new product may be a major technological innovation new to the market. For example, the very first electronic computers introduced in the 1940s, though primitive by today's standards, were at one time new to the market, as were portable radios, frozen dinners, and filter cigarettes. To other marketers, new products might be simple additions to an otherwise unchanged product line, such as new shades of lipstick or hair colorings introduced by Revlon or Clairol. Even a "me, too" item, developed in imitation of a competitor's successful product, is a new product to the imitating company. Undoubtedly, management will treat it as new when introducing it to the market.

Lemon *juice* in dishwashing liquid makes a product different from the one that was merely lemon-*scented*. A product new on the market may be one that offers some benefit that other product offerings on the market do not offer. The marketing concept, after all, tells us to consider the product as a bundle of tangible and intangible benefits. If the bundle of benefits offered by a product differs from the bundle already available, then the product can be said to be new.

A consumer or industrial buyer may also consider a product to be new if it is something never before purchased, even if the item has been on the market for years. In international marketing, old products may become "new" again, especially when a manufacturer's established product is being offered to people in a less developed country. There are, for example, places in the world where television, and even moving pictures, are "new."

It is clear, then, that the term "new" and the related term "novel" are used in a relative sense.

They are influenced by our perceptions, whether we are marketing managers or consumers. Let's begin by taking the manager's perspective.

Management's Perspective of New Products

Recently, the management consulting firm of Booz, Allen, and Hamilton published the results of an extensive study of new product introductions in the United States using two dimensions, *newness to company* and *newness to market*.[2] The company identified how managers may classify the kinds of new products:

■ *New-to-the-world products:* New products that create an entirely new market.

■ *New product lines:* New products that, for the first time, allow a company to enter an established market.

■ *Additions to existing product lines*: New products or brand extensions that supplement a company's established product lines.

■ *Improvements in/revisions to existing products:* New products that provide improved performance of greater perceived value and that replace existing products.

■ *Repositionings:* Existing products that are targeted to new markets or market segments.

■ *Cost reductions:* New products that provide similar performance at lower cost.

Note that the graphic in Exhibit 11-1 includes the percentages of total new product introductions represented by each type of new product in the Booz, Allen, and Hamilton scheme. The study also indicates that the highest risk products, which accounted for 30 per-

---

[2] Booz, Allen, and Hamilton, Inc., *New Product Management for the 1980's: Phase I* (New York: Booz, Allen, and Hamilton, 1981).

EXHIBIT 11-1

The Booz, Allen, and Hamilton Six New Product Categories and Their Percent of Total New Product Introductions

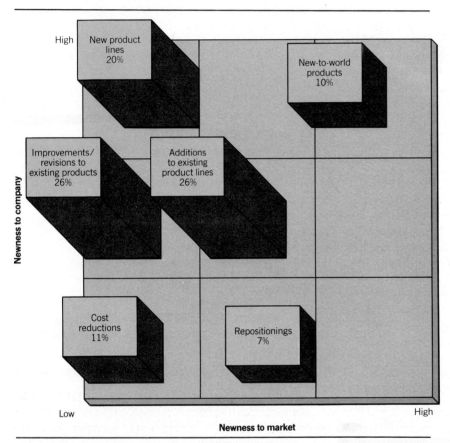

Source: Redrawn from Booz, Allen, and Hamilton, Inc., *New Product Management for the 1980s: Phase I* (New York, 1981), p. 3. Used with permission.

cent of all introductions, represent 60 percent of the "most successful" new products.

According to this consulting organization, there are two considerations associated with the new to the company dimension: *technology* and *investment.* The main consideration associated with the new to the market dimension is the nature of the market. Thus, from a company perspective, in making new product decisions managers must consider:

■ *Technology*—the fund of knowledge that makes the product possible.

■ *Investment*—the dollars and other resources necessary to develop the new product.

■ *Markets*—the people or the organizations to whom the product is marketed and how it is marketed.[3]

Using a slightly modified terminology, new products can be portrayed in terms of these three considerations.

[3]W. Lazer and J.D. Culley, *Marketing Management: Foundations and Practices* (Boston: Houghton-Mifflin, 1983), p. 510.

EXHIBIT   11-2

New Product Risk: A Function of Perceived Newness and Similarity to Existing Products

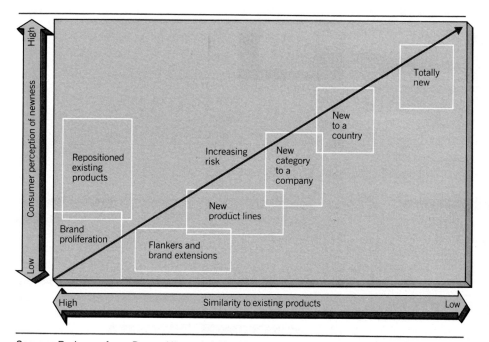

Source: Redrawn from Booz, Allen, and Hamilton, Inc., *New Product Management for the 1980s: Phase I* (New York, 1981), p. 3. Used with permission.

As the Exhibit 11-2 shows, a new product need not be totally fresh, unfamiliar, or exotic. It need not utilize the most advanced technology. Too, the risk associated with investments in new products can vary.

The more the buyer perceives the product as new and the less similar the product is to existing products, the greater the risk involved for both the buyer and, importantly for our purposes, the marketer.

The Consumer's Perspective of Newness

Was the filter cigarette really new or just a change developed in the nonfilter version? Is color TV, and eventually 3D TV, truly different from black and white TV? Does the ingenious, if controversial, nuclear power plant qualify as really new? New products vary with respect

to their *degrees* of newness. If we take a consumer or marketplace perspective, there are three types of innovations: discontinuous, dynamically continuous, and continuous. While it is probably impossible to find completely satisfactory examples of these types of innovations, the concept of degrees of newness is useful (see Exhibit 11-3).

Discontinuous Innovation. Discontinuous innovations are pioneering products so new that *no previous product performed an equivalent function.* As a result of this near-complete newness, *new consumption or usage patterns are required.* The lithium battery pacemaker implanted in heart patients is a discontinuous innovation. The original video tape recorder from Sony is another. Note that these products meet the test of doing things no products before them did *and* they necessitate extensive behavior

---

EXHIBIT 11-3

The Continuum of Newness

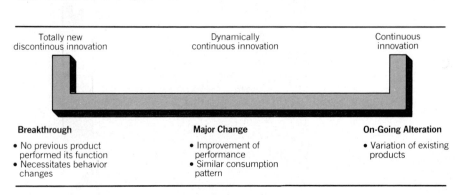

Totally new discontinuous innovation	Dynamically continuous innovation	Continuous innovation
Breakthrough	**Major Change**	**On-Going Alteration**
• No previous product performed its function • Necessitates behavior changes	• Improvement of performance • Similar consumption pattern	• Variation of existing products

---

changes in order to be used properly. Artificial hearts, kidneys, and other organs are still in their developmental stages, but once perfected and made available, they, too, will be discontinuous innovations.

Dynamically Continuous Innovation.

Thinking in terms of a newness continuum, somewhere between the breakthrough of the perfected artificial heart and the nearly commonplace newness of the "new and improved" consumer product is the **dynamically continuous innovation.** New products in this middle range are dynamically continuous because they represent changes and improvements that do not strikingly change buying and usage patterns.

The electric car is one example of a dynamically continuous innovation. The buying habits of those purchasing cars and fuel may be altered by successful and appealing electric automobiles, but virtually all driving behavior will remain much as it is. Consider, for example, the way the Model-T Ford affected society versus the lesser effects of the first compact cars. In the same way, the electric typewriter had a genuine newness about it, but its effect on the buyers and users of these machines was not anything like the effect of the first typewriter. Today the typerecorder is in this category.

Continuous Innovation.

As the name suggests, a **continuous innovation** is an on-going,

commonplace change such as a minor alteration of a product or the introduction of an imitative product. The creation of gel toothpaste or the introduction of a new, "orangier" version of Orange Crush are examples of continuous innovations. Marketers are constantly seeking to improve products because even minor improvements such as fewer calories or less salt provide a competitive advantage. Although this may be viewed as fine tuning the product, the new products are innovations of a sort, but they are certainly at the less innovative end of the newness continuum when compared to the artificial heart and the electric car.

The Slim Chances of Success

It is very difficult to determine the number of new product successes and failures since, like the idea of newness, the notion of success is hard to define. How *much* of a success must a new product be before it is truly "a success"? It is a widely accepted belief that relatively few new product ideas become commercial successes. Since most organizations would rather not talk about their failures, much of this belief must be based on *estimates* of product failures and successes. Moreover, some product ideas wither in their developmental stages; thus, a complete documentation of ideas that were suggested but never made it to market is not likely to be found. For our purposes, "failure" occurs when a product

A dynamically continuous innovation and a continuous innovation.

does not achieve the organization's expectations.[4]

A number of estimates of new product failure rates is available. Some of these suggest that 90 percent of all new product ideas do not become commercial successes. Booz, Allen, and Hamilton, after considerable study, suggest that only one successful product will be generated from 40 new product ideas. Once a new product actually appears on the market, the success rate, from that point, is much higher because of the research, planning, and effort that has gone into its introduction. For example, it is estimated that there is a one-in-three failure rate among new product *introductions*.[5]

---

[4]J.P. Guiltinan and G.W. Paul, *Marketing Management: Strategies and Programs* (New York: McGraw-Hill, 1982), pp. 160–161.

[5]"Survey Finds Sixty-Seven Percent of New Products Succeed," *Marketing News,* February 8, 1980, p. 1.

Clearly, failure and success rates vary from industry to industry. In the consumer package goods market, the failure rate is likely to be far higher than that in the electrical components field. This is because of the dynamic nature of the consumer marketplace and the unlikelihood of consumers being able to tell marketers exactly what new products will satisfy them. On the other hand, the buyers of electrical components are industrial buyers and able to give detailed information to component manufacturers. No wonder, then, that new product failure and success rates vary greatly.

Nevertheless, the chances of market success for any new product idea are relatively slim. Even a one-in-three chance of failure for a new product actually reaching the market is unattractive when the money, resources, jobs, and ambitions associated with each new venture are considered. Strangely, though, many organizations do not take the care to minimize their chances of market failure. Individual managers, for example, may be so convinced that a new product idea is "great" that they proceed to introduce it, blithely ignoring the warnings of market researchers, or even doing no marketing research at all. International marketing managers may similarly export a product doomed to failure overseas and then express surprise that such a product could fail "there" when it was so popular "here." Retail marketers encounter a similar problem when they stock new product offerings that *they* are sure will be popular, then find themselves stuck with shelves of unsalable goods. Great care must be taken to minimize the likelihood of new product failure.

THE CHARACTERISTICS OF SUCCESS

Product success is both difficult to define and difficult to achieve. Therefore, it is useful to consider new product successes and failures in terms of the situational characteristics that frequently surround them. No one can provide marketing managers with a checklist of do's and don'ts that will guarantee success in the marketplace. At best, such lists are catalogs of warnings; at worst, they are trite. Effective marketing skills are developed with practice and experience. However, by examining and discussing the characteristics of product successes, even the inexperienced student of marketing can gain some insight into situations of success and disappointment.

The five characteristics that influence a new product's chances for success in the marketplace are relative advantage, compatibility with existing consumption patterns, trialability, observability, and complexity.[6] When a product is lacking in one or more of the characteristics associated with success, the others might be used effectively to make up for these deficiencies. Furthermore, non-product portions of the marketing mix—price, promotion, and distribution—must be developed and adjusted with these same success characteristics in mind.

Consider the following characteristics of success.

Relative Advantage

Products that offer buyers clear-cut advantages over other existing, competing offerings are said to have **relative advantage.** In industrial markets relative advantage often arises from new products that perform exactly the same functions less expensively or faster than existing products. Experience and improved technology, for example, have made possible the replacement of many metal parts with cheaper and lighter plastic ones. Similarly, office materials such as calculators, word processors, and photocopiers have obvious advantages over earlier generations of the same tools.

These types of relative advantages are easily found among successful consumer products. Sony's Walkman provided customers with a lightweight tape cassette capable of remarkably good sound quality for use outside the home. The relative advantage of this product over bulkier tape players and in-home systems is readily apparent, especially to joggers and frequent travelers. New products appeal to their target markets in large part because they have relative advantages over other competing products.

Compatibility with Existing Consumption Patterns

Everything else being equal, a new product that is compatible with existing patterns of consumption behavior stands a better chance of market acceptance than does one which is *in*compatible. This is true even when the newer item has some relative advantage. Consider, for example, the new digital, laser-read recordings that pro-

---

[6]E.M. Rogers and F.F. Shoemaker, *Communication of Innovation* (New York: The Free Press, 1971).

NEW PRODUCTS PINCH THE SALT

It is found in everything from applesauce to antacid, from corn to cottage cheese. Statistically linked to high blood pressure and a host of other health problems, salt—sodium chloride—is used so heavily in American food processing that it is virtually impossible for concerned citizens to cut their consumption from the United States average of two-and-a-half teaspoons a day to the maximum one-and-a-half recommended by the National Academy of Sciences. But now corporate America is doing something about it. Del Monte, the nation's largest canner of fruits and vegetables, introduced a no-salt-added line of vegetables. Not to be left behind, Libby's also announced that it would convert virtually all its canned vegetables to low-sodium versions. "By taking the salt out of processing, we are letting the consumer choose how much," says the chairman of the company that owns Libby's. "It is well known that sodium is a bad thing to have too much of."

Salt-free vegetables are only the latest entry in the low-sodium sweepstakes. A Revlon, Inc., subsidiary introduced NoSalt—a potassium-chloride salt substitute, and the product has sold so well that grocers simply cannot keep it on the shelves. Campbell's began offering seven soups that contain a maximum of 35 milligrams of sodium per serving—far less than the 800 milligrams in a serving of regular chicken noodle soup. Ralston Purina is about to introduce a low-salt Chicken-of-the-Sea tuna, and General Mills, General Foods, and Quaker are considering low-sodium breakfast cereals. "It is the latest version of the new, improved product—only this time it's salt free."

Source: Adapted from "New Products Pinch the Salt," *Newsweek*, August 23, 1982, p. 52. Used with permission.

duce far better sound than do traditional records and, since they are not touched by a needle, last "forever." Unfortunately, the digital recordings cannot be played on the sorts of turntables most of us own. Instead, buyers of these recordings must also buy expensive equipment to play them. Digital recordings may, in fact, one day replace older-style records, but their incompatibility with existing usage patterns and in-use equipment will certainly slow their adoption.

Many products now taken for granted were slow to be adopted because of compatibility problems. Frozen vegetables and other foods were not sold in great quantities until home refrigerators with sizable freezer compartments were in wide use. In some areas of the world it is difficult to sell television sets because there are no television stations to watch. On the other hand, Kraft's Sun Seasons butterhead lettuce is specially packaged for freshness since the hydroponically grown lettuce continues its development within its "planter package." This new product is compatible with existing consumption patterns because no major changes in lifestyle are required for its use. No new kitchen equipment is necessary for its use. The problem of compatibility with existing consumption and life-style patterns once again shows the importance of close consideration of marketing's changing environment.

Trialability—The Opportunity for Buyer Testing

Somewhat related to the notion of compatibility is that of "trialability." A new product, such as Five Alive frozen juice, is trialable when it can be tested by possible future users with little risk or effort. Five Alive is not an expensive product, nor must the buyer invest in special equipment to use the product. Its trialability may also be enhanced by cents-off coupons in newspapers, magazines, and in the mail. New shampoos and laundry products are made available to shoppers in small, inexpensive packages to encourage trial at little monetary risk. Many companies, both consumer and industrial marketers, go so far as to give away free samples to possible

THE PAMPERS STORY

One of P&G's greatest paper breakthroughs began in 1956. Vic Mills, director of exploratory development, had just spent some time caring for his newborn grandchild. He had developed a profound (and understandable) dislike for cleaning diapers. Back at the laboratory, he assigned some of his most talented people to spend part of their time looking into the practicality of disposable diapers.

Months were devoted to studies of existing products (Chux, Drypers, Kleinerts, K.D.'s and so on) and how consumers felt about them. P&G learned that disposable diapers were used for less than 1 percent of the billions of diaper changes in the United States each year. The disposables were bought mainly by traveling parents when cloth diapers could not be laundered. Mothers simply didn't think they did as good a job. Besides, prices were high.

The initial idea was to develop a highly absorbent, pleated pad that could be inserted in a specially designed plastic panty, similar to a form used in Scandinavia. In six months R&D had a product ready for consumers to try. But the idea nearly died. In testing, Dallas was chosen for parent reaction. The average maximum temperature was 93°F and few mothers used plastic pants in such heat.

By March 1959, an exhausted research staff was ready to have its new version tested. Softer, more absorbent, with an improved "moisture barrier" between the infant and the wet wadding, the new diaper was tested in both a tape-on and pin-on design. The staff had laboriously assembled 37,000 diapers for a test in Rochester, New York. Parents in that city not only said they preferred the pin-on design but nearly two-thirds of them thought the product was as good as or better than cloth diapers. With such encouraging results, P&G engineers were asked to design machinery by which the new diaper could be made efficiently and speedily. "I think it was the most complex production operation the company had ever faced," said one engineer.

For some time the prospective product had no name, although thought was being given to Tads, Solos, and Larks. The name which became the favorite was Pampers. In December 1961, Pampers entered its first full marketing test in Peoria, Illinois. Within six months it was clear that this test, too, was a failure. Mothers liked Pampers well

Source: From "Pampers: How P&G Created a Market," *Advertising Age*, January 18, 1982, p. 50. Reprinted with permission.

buyers, bringing trialability to perhaps its highest level. When newly marketed products are given away in this manner, the process is termed **trial sampling.**

Effective marketing management demands careful consideration of steps that may contribute to buyer sampling of a new product. Items intended to be sold in cases or six-packs, like juices, sodas, and other drinks, might first be offered in single drink packages, or given away by the cupful in shopping malls. Customers may be reluctant to buy 12 of a given product but be willing to try just one. The concept of trialability is more appropriately referred to as a product's **divisibility** when there is an opportunity provided to try "a little bit." On the other hand, a $150 pair of running shoes has little divisibility. In-store trials, experienced salespeople, and guarantees of satisfaction may be used by the shoe marketer to overcome this deficit.

Observability—The Chance to See the Newness

Some new products enter the marketplace with attributes or characteristics that are visible to the customer. The Sony Walkman mentioned earlier has a relative advantage over other tape players, but, best of all for Sony, the advantage is easy to see. The collapsible, wind-up garden hose that enough, but the 10-cents-per-diaper price was too much to pay. Costs would have to be reduced, and the only practical way was to increase volume, more than doubling the original plans.

Further tests followed—a total of six markets in all—before consumer response indicated Pampers at six cents each might exceed P&G expectations.

In recounting Pampers' success in the late 1960s—after Paper Products had created its own sales force—Ed Harness told an annual meeting, "Pampers is a beautiful example of P&G's ability to look into the future and recognize tremendous opportunity. Disposable diapers had been sold in the United States for several generations, yet when the company launched the Pampers development program in the 1950s, less than 1 percent of the billions of diaper changes which take place in America every year were being made with disposables. Existing products were not good, their prices were too high and retail distribution was miniscule. Despite these negatives, company people had imagination and foresight enough to recognize that a really good disposable diaper at a reasonable price, backed with marketing know-how, could bring about an enormous change in one of motherhood's oldest chores. Today in some of Pampers' longer established markets about 25% of the diaper changes are made with disposables. This has been accomplished almost entirely by Pampers, since, with our head start, good competition is not yet very widespread."

What was the impact of a single new product in creating jobs? The figures were hard to project, but a financial analyst at P&G agreed to try. He based his estimate on one of P&G's most successful brands, Pampers.

"At the volume Pampers are doing, I estimate perhaps 2,400 jobs are required to manufacture Pampers," he said. "To that we must add the [research and development] people involved in maintaining quality and in making further improvements; the engineers who design and improve equipment; sales representatives, advertising, purchasing, traffic and financial people. It looks to me like between 2,850 and 2,900 P&G employees directly owe their jobs to Pampers. And that ignores sales in foreign countries. Outside P&G, I estimate an added 31,000 jobs are needed by various suppliers, equipment manufacturers, truckers and retail outlets to support Pampers. That is a total of 34,000 jobs on Pampers alone."

---

stores in a very small space is another product with observability. The Black & Decker Workmate, a collapsible work bench with adjustable legs, a built-in vise, and so on, is observable to customers, and the advantages that result from it are easily grasped.

Some products possess definite relative advantages that are *not* so easily grasped, necessitating development of a marketing mix that takes that fact into account. That a particular brand of boots will hold up under hard wear for 15 years is not observable by most buyers. Only a person who really knows something about boots could judge their quality by simply looking at them. Thus, advertisements for quality boots, and other long-lasting products, frequently feature expert users of the product who attest to its worth. A new candy bar, though inexpensive enough to be trialable, may be advertised via television on the basis of taste, an unobservable characteristic. Thus a sports hero, or even just a "regular kid," promises that the candy bar really tastes good and recommends a trial.

Complexity

Closely allied to most of our discussion thus far is the matter of new product complexity. A complex product, or one that requires complex procedures for storage or use, starts out with a disadvantage. Polaroid Land cameras, at their introduction, were viewed by consumers as minor miracles. Therefore, regardless of the complexity of the chemical processes that produced the pictures, the camera itself was designed for easy operation. The simplicity of *usage* thus offset the complexity of the product itself. The new digital recordings mentioned earlier are similarly surprising to consumers who find it difficult to grasp that these recordings are not played via the familiar needle and tone arm system. Makers of this new equipment must therefore carefully train salespeople to explain this wonder. Furthermore, they may arrange for newspaper and magazine columnists to try the new system so that they may explain it to their readers. The marketing mix for a complex new product differs greatly from that appropriate to a new flavor bubble gum.

NEW PRODUCT DEVELOPMENT

What is the source of innovations? How are new product ideas generated? There is no one answer to these questions. Some innovations are discovered by accident or luck, such as the vulcanization of the rubber process (discovered when a rubbery mixture was spilled on a hot stove), and Ivory's floating soap (first made when a mechanical mixer was left on overnight and whipped raw soap materials into a lightweight cleanser). Necessity, it seems, was the mother of invention for the ice cream seller in St. Louis who ran out of paper cups and rolled pancakes into serving cones—the first ice cream cones.

Sometimes, creative thinking and a crude prototype may influence new product development, as it did for the Bell & Howell zoom lens. The former president of Bell & Howell tells this story of how one new product idea was developed based on creative insight.[7]

Have you heard of zoom lenses? One of the great advantages of being new in a company is that you are thoroughly unaware of what cannot be done. I thought a zoom camera was something that you used for football games. That was my image—an extraordinarily expensive object. One day I was in the lab, and there was a zoom lens. I had never seen one in my life, and I put it up to my eyes, and—well, it is a very dramatic thing. They explained to me that this was not applicable to consumer products, because it

would cost a fair amount of money and so on. I asked, "What would it cost to make a camera for me—just one with a zoom lens on it?" They said, "Just one? Do you mean a crude modification? I think we would probably spend $500 on it." I said, "Well, suppose we do that; because my rates come pretty high, it will cost at least $500 for us to continue this discussion for another hour or two, so let's just do this." I took this camera home. At a dinner party that night, I put this zoom lens on the piano, and I asked everybody coming in if they wouldn't participate in a very sophisticated piece of market research; namely, to put the camera to their eye. To the man, the reaction was extraordinarily enthusiastic: "My, this is marvelous; I've never seen anything like this in my life." We did this for about $500. . . . If more industries would try out new ideas on a low-cost basis, perhaps their expectations of what the market will bear would go up.

On occasion, the "nut inventor" working in a basement comes up with an innovation that goes on to great success. However, there is general agreement that these days, when innovations require sizable financial investments and other resources for support and commercialization, most innovations come from serious research and development efforts undertaken with the support of formal organizations. The hobbiest-inventor may still enjoy considerable success, but this has become an increasingly rare occurrence.

The new product development process *can* be rather quick, the result of a sudden flash of insight. But in many cases, such as in the development of space satellites or other highly techni-

---

[7] P.G. Peterson, "Some Approaches to Innovation in Industry," in *The Creative Organization,* cited by Gary Steiner (Chicago: University of Chicago Press, 1965), pp. 191–192.

EXHIBIT 11-4

The General Stages in the Development of New Products

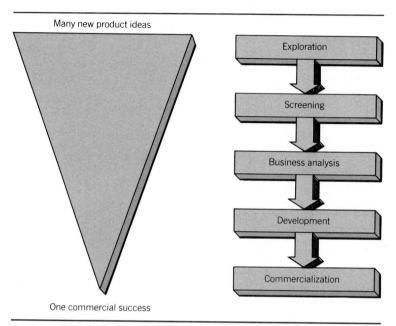

Many new product ideas

Exploration

Screening

Business analysis

Development

Commercialization

One commercial success

Source: Adapted from Roger A. Bengston, "Nine New Product Strategies: Each Requires Different Resources, Talent, Research Methods," *Marketing News*, March 19, 1982, p. 7.

cal products, the process can take years. In some cases—for example, instant coffee—the development process can be lengthy not so much because of technical problems but because of market resistance to the new product. Customer acceptance can be found lacking even when the new products have a technological advantage that will, eventually, succeed.

As illustrated in Exhibit 11-4, there are five general stages in the development process of new products. Individual new products may pass through these stages at varying rates of speed, perhaps stalling for a period of time in one and passing through another so quickly as to have appeared to skip it entirely.

Exploration

The exploration stage of new product development is, for dynamic organizations, less a period of time than an ongoing process.[8] Because mar-

kets are typically dynamic, even volatile, effective marketers are constantly searching for new products and are always open to new ideas. Attitudes of stability and close-mindedness are inconsistent with the marketing concept's stress on buyer satisfaction. Thus, the **exploration stage** involves a continuing search for product ideas that are consistent with target market needs and with the organization's objectives.

In many organizations, particularly those involved in industries where complex technology is the rule, generating ideas and searching for technological breakthroughs are likely to be the tasks of the research and development department. ITT research scientists, for example, have developed a sophisticated set of eight semiconductor chips that permit television sets to show two channels at once on a single screen. Individ-

---

[8] This discussion follows that in *Management of New Products*, Booz, Allen, and Hamilton, 1960, pp. 8–18.

AMDAHL'S APPROACH TO INNOVATION

Gene Amdahl is a former IBM executive. This computer designer is the founder of Amdahl Corporation and Acsys Limited, both in the scientific computing market. When asked by an interviewer for *INC* magazine about the founding of Amdahl Corporation and how he conceptualized the scientific computer product, Amdahl gave the following response.

Amdahl: I had a chance to do a lot of thinking about what I wanted to do next.

INC: Did you think in terms of a company, or product?

Amdahl: I thought in terms of problems—problems of product performance, function, and cost that were not being solved, and that needed to be solved to open up opportunities.

The nature of the problems wasn't obvious to the industry, but once I redefined them, it was clear they could be solved with known techniques.

I went through the same process when I left IBM to start Amdahl Corp. At IBM in the late 1960s, we were trying to build a high-performance computer with large-scale integration—more than 100 circuits on a chip. In those days, the world was working with small-scale integration, 20 to 30 circuits per chip. To achieve larger-scale integration, IBM and the rest of the industry thought you had to design new chips. IBM decided that wasn't economically feasible.

After I left IBM, I kept thinking about the problem. A very important breakthrough occurred to me. The problems caused by trying to put more circuits on a chip had been self-imposed by the semiconductor industry. People had made everything smaller and tried to pack things closer together. As a consequence, there was very little room for the interconnections between circuits on the chip.

What drove people to cram things together was the expense of silicon—the need to use as little silicon per chip as possible. What semiconductor people didn't see was that, if you could put more circuits on a chip, you would need fewer chips. You could afford to make the chips a little larger in order to cram more circuits on them.

What I had come up with was a nonsemiconductor solution. That may not sound like much, but a whole industry had beat its head on that problem for years. The logic that everybody had been trained in was preventing the problem from being solved. And the solution enabled Amdahl Corp. to produce a computer with large-scale integration—an advantage no other company had.

Source: Adapted from Susan Benner, "Starting Over," *INC,* January 1981, p. 34. Reprinted with permission. INC magazine, January 1981, Copyright © 1981 by INC Publishing Corporation, 38 Commercial Wharf, Boston.

ual viewers can pick the one they wish to watch without seeing the other or they can see both.

As we have seen, while most new products flow from research departments, other sources should not be ignored. New product suggestions may come from consumers or industrial buyers. Sales representatives may uncover or be told about new product opportunities. Marketing research can yield new product suggestions. Any employee or customer of an organization may come up with a good—or even brilliant—idea. Pampers, the disposable diaper, was suggested by an engineer working for Procter & Gamble because, in his role as a sometimes babysitter for his first grandchild, he realized that diaper changing could be made easier if disposable diapers were available. Others probably had this thought before him but he, and then his employer, acted upon it with great success. Many organizations, realizing that a good idea has to be brought to their attention before it can be acted upon, have instituted a rewards system to encourage employee suggestions.

New product ideas are sometimes the result of an organization's desire to make fuller use of its manufacturing facilities or its distribution facilities. A company selling common household products like brooms might want to expand its line to include expensive, medium-priced, and low-priced brooms as well as whisk brooms and brushes of various types. This would make better use of factory capacity and of the sales force which, after all, can probably offer a wider range of products without much additional effort. Along similar lines some organizations seek to develop new products that will permit them to make use of their existing product's by-products. Meat packers, for example, produce a wide range of people food but also make dog food containing "meat by-products." Manufacturers of canned pumpkin products seek ways to use pumpkin seeds. One such organization is currently trying to develop a honey-coated pumpkin seed candy.

Screening

The **screening stage** of the product development process involves analysis of new ideas to determine which are reasonable, pertinent to the organization's goals, and appropriate to the organization's target markets. This step is extremely important because the underlying assumption of the entire product development process is that risky alternatives—possibilities that do not offer as much promise for success as others—should be eliminated from consideration. Resources can then be concentrated on the best prospects, so that market failures can be avoided.

The screening stage is doubly important since it is the first stage in the product development process where effort at sorting alternative ideas is undertaken. At this stage, new ideas may be rejected. From time to time any management team is likely to reject some ideas that they later wish that they had accepted. Mistakes will be made. It is for this reason that caution must be exercised in the screening stage. Too quick a decision may be regretted later. In fact, because an idea rejected at this stage is eliminated from further consideration, some companies prefer to allow a marginal idea to progress to further stages of evaluation, rather than to risk rejecting it too early in the process. Balancing costs of additional investigation against loss of a viable product idea is one of management's most delicate tasks.

At Procter & Gamble, three basic questions are carefully answered before new product projects are approved.[9] These questions are general enough to be used by almost any organization in their own product screenings. Deceptively simple, these questions demand hard answers on which more than a few managers' careers may depend:

1 Is there a real consumer need for the product?

2 Does the organization have the scientific and technological ability to develop the product?

3 Is the potential for such a product large enough to offer some promise of making a profit?

While extensive marketing research is associated with later stages in the development process, some research tools, such as concept testing and discussions with salespeople, executives, and knowledgeable consumers, could be used to help answer questions such as these. The discussion on exploratory research in Chapter 5 suggested forms of research appropriate to this stage.

Business Analysis

A product idea that survives the screening process then enters the phase known as **business analysis**, where it is expanded into a concrete business recommendation. This recommendation includes such specifics as a listing of product features, information on resources needed to produce the product, and a basic marketing plan. Creativity and analysis come together at this stage.

Qualitative evaluations of the product and its likely success are still important, but business analysis requires quantitative facts and figures. Thus, during the business analysis stage, the new product idea begins to be evaluated with increasingly detailed quantitative data.

The business analysis stage is likely to include the development and implementation of formal buyer research studies, sales and market forecasts, break-even analyses, and other similar

---

[9]"Procter and Gamble Uses Pamper Story to Teach Consumers About Marketing," *Advertising Age*, April 4, 1977, p. 41.

research efforts. If these critical looks at the proposed product yield favorable results, the product may undergo transformation from a product concept, which is a verbal and/or pictorial description, to a product prototype. Such a prototype can then be shown to target customers, demonstrated to them, and perhaps used by the customers themselves. In short, the business analysis is a review of the new product from all significant perspectives, emphasizing practical applications and chances for success in the marketplace.

Development

A new product idea that has succeeded in passing through the first, largely evaluative stages in the product development process is ready for the fourth stage: development.

Products should be developed with the needs of the consumer or user in mind. For example, in General Electric's Video Products Division, design engineers are sent out to talk with dealers and customers to assure that market feedback goes directly to where it can do the most good—the engineers who design the products. GE describes this process in this way: "Engineers working at the drawing board are getting their directions from customers. The whole business is oriented toward bringing the technology and the consumer demand together."[10]

In the development stage, paper-and-pencil concepts become products in-hand that are producible and demonstrable. R&D or production engineers provide marketers with a product that can be tested, used in test markets, or investigated in other limited ways. This is not to say that the product is in final form. For example, soft drink marketers may taste test a new formulation on a limited number of consumers in a panel situation. If the product is less than well-accepted, it might be reformulated or its package changed. Then the product can be retested, until the proper set of characteristics has been discovered.

A good example of this phase of the new

product development process is provided by Dow Jones and Company. Seeking to develop a new business magazine and to link it to a very well-accepted existing product, Dow Jones developed *The Wall Street Journal Magazine.* Ultimately, sample copies were prepared. These were shown to test readers representative of the target market. But reaction from the test readers was not what the editors of the magazine expected. It revealed that potential readers simply desired a publication quite different from the one the editors wanted to provide. Ultimately, plans were scrapped for *The Wall Street Journal Magazine.*[11] Many consumer products, as we saw in Chapter 5, are test marketed in situations far more complex and elaborate than was *The Wall Street Journal Magazine.*

Because the organizational marketplace is likely to be more limited and its members more expert in their understanding of what they want, testing industrial products often can be carried out at an almost personal level. International marketers are well-advised to make no assumptions about the nature of unfamiliar markets without careful testing of the developed new product. Retail marketers constantly test market new products by buying "just a few units," then ordering more if those sell. When manufacturers provide retailers and other dealers with incentives to try a new product, such as by offering sales on consignment or cooperative advertising dollars, both manufacturer and dealer are helped in their efforts to gauge market acceptance.

Commercialization

After passing through the filtering stages in the new product development process, the new product is ready for the final stage, commercialization. **Commercialization** refers to the decision to produce and market a new product, to "go for it" and launch the new product's full-scale production and sales. Once this decision has been made, a great deal of money is at risk since this stage involves a serious commitment of re-

[10]"Listen to the Voice of the Marketplace," *Business Week*, February 21, 1983, p. 90.

[11]"WSJ Drops Magazine Idea," *Advertising Age*, October 26, 1981, p. 3.

sources and managerial effort. This is the last chance to stop the project if managers think the risks involved in commercialization do not justify the resources about to be committed. Many successful marketing firms, such as P&G, keep a finger on the "abort" button right to the last moment. Although a lot of money may have been spent in reaching the commercialization stage, that amount is quite small when compared to the sums full commercialization will demand.

Even when great caution is employed, product failures still result. It is not difficult to find products that should have been "killed" before being commercialized. Such products could have been tested just one more time to avoid a marketing debacle. For example, Dow Chemical Co. developed a compound of resins and methanol to be sprayed on car tires to increase their ability to maintain traction on ice. The product, Liquid Tire Chain, truly did work, as proved by in-use testing. Not surprisingly, however, buyers stored the pressurized cans of the product in their cars' trunks. When the aerosol containers froze in winter weather, the material within them solidified, making the product useless. The in-use tests Dow had undertaken somehow missed this factor. The product failed, unfortunately for Dow, *after* commercialization. Had testing been more complete, this could have been avoided.

Why Are There Failures?

The path to commercialization of a new product can be a long one, at least in terms of the care and effort that must be taken. Despite precautions, however, new product failures and near-failures occur with some regularity. For example, Texas Instruments failed after investing more than $50 million on the magnetic bubble memory; computer-makers preferred the microprocessor chips. The product had an early abandonment.

King Cola tried for three years to compete regionally against Pepsi and Coke but found the task impossible. Coke and Pepsi were beginning an intensive "cola war" with reduced prices and increased advertising. King Cola didn't have the resources.

McDonald's chopped beef steak sandwich was not successful in its initial testing. Yet the company continues to experiment with innovative new sandwiches.

A study of 148 companies published in 1980 by The Conference Board reported that new products, introduced during the previous five years, accounted for an average of 15 percent of current sales.[12] However, some firms indicated new products accounted for up to *50* percent of current sales. Yet these same companies had no trouble in naming the most common reasons for their product failures. Here, briefly stated, are those reasons.

■ *Inadequate top management involvement:* Often a problem in that management's expertise can contribute to product success and top management's influence may be necessary to commit adequate resources to the project.

■ *Departing from organization's expertise:* Some new products are judged to have failed because the organization's production or marketing strengths could not be brought to bear on those particular product classes.

■ *Assigning inadequate resources to market development:* Companies may devote considerable money and effort to development of a product but not enough on developing distribution and promotion, thinking that the product is so good it will "sell itself."

■ *Underestimating the competition:* Producers of a "good" new product, evaluating the marketplace as it is at the moment the new item will be introduced may forget to consider competitors' reactions or underestimate their abilities to respond quickly and strongly.

■ *Inadequate knowledge of costs:* Competitive reactions, lack of enthusiasm, inventory holding costs, and the need for sizable promotional budgets are among the many factors that may be underestimated by introducers of new products.

■ *Underestimating the diffusion rate:* The enthusiastic developer of a new product may be

[12]David S. Hopkins, *New Product Winners and Losers,* Research Report Number 773, The Conference Board, New York, N.Y., 1980, pp. 12–20.

surprised to find that the item does not sweep the market like wildfire. It often takes more time than expected to communicate a new concept and have it accepted.

Here are some additional reasons for new product failure.

- *Poor market research:* Misunderstanding consumers' needs, doing too little actual field testing, and developing overly optimistic forecasts of market need for and acceptance of the new product.

- *Poor timing:* The market may have changed before the new product was introduced or the company entered the market too early in the PLC or too late.

- *Technical problems:* Problems growing out of aspects of the product itself—failures in production or design.

While these and other reasons for new product failure are easily understood, pointing out common mistakes and resolving to avoid them may not be enough. After all, the very newness of the product complicates the planning process immensely. Planning the marketing of an *existing* product, identifying costs, and so on, gives the marketing manager the advantage of dealing with many known quantities. Planning the marketing of a new, untried product is clearly a far more difficult matter.

All new product introductions have one thing in common. They must attempt to predict the future. The product designed in 1984 and introduced to the market in 1986 may meet a somewhat different environment than that of two years earlier. Hence, marketing plans may not work as well as expected. New product marketing deals with forecasting the future and, as the old adage goes, "Forecasts are dangerous, particularly those about the future."

Cutting Down on Failures

The new product development process can be expensive, and failure can mean loss of a sizable investment. Even when a particular new product introduction has been comparatively inexpensive to complete, failure still means that the assets wasted on that product could have been put to better use somewhere else within the organization. At the very least, considerable managerial embarrassment results from such a failure. Since so many products do fail, these risks, of whatever magnitude, are always present.

Few organizations can rely, however, entirely on old, relatively risk-free products. For most firms, the inability to introduce successful new products from time to time means eventual decline and disappearance from the marketplace. It is one of marketing management's greatest challenges to determine which risks are acceptable and which are not. No organization "wins" all the time, but care and effort can improve the firm's batting average by increasing the number of winning products and holding down the number of losers. We have seen, and will continue to see all around us, products that fail and products that make it. The lessons to be learned from each should be utilized by effective marketing managers to raise their own batting averages. In summary, marketing managers can reduce failures by paying attention to their experiences and the experiences of others but, at the same time, they must not become "handcuffed" by fear of failure.

THE DIFFUSION PROCESS

Organizations introducing new products are very much concerned with the matter of who will actually buy, use, or in some other way *adopt* the product. When someone purchases a product never tried before, that person may ultimately become an *adopter*. The stages through which an adopter passes before actually making a purchase or placing an order were described in Chapter 8 when the buyer's decision-making process was discussed. Those stages were: awareness, interest, evaluation, trial, and, finally, adoption. When a new product is placed on the

EXHIBIT 11-5

The Product Adoption Process

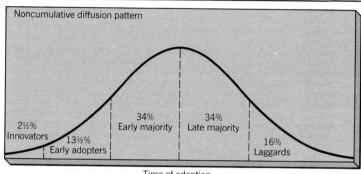

Noncumulative diffusion pattern

2½%
Innovators

13½%
Early adopters

34%
Early majority

34%
Late majority

16%
Laggards

Time of adoption
Average

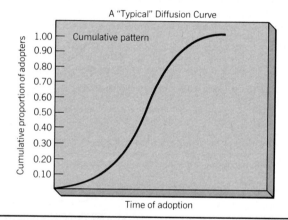

A "Typical" Diffusion Curve

Cumulative proportion of adopters

Cumulative pattern

1.00
0.90
0.80
0.70
0.60
0.50
0.40
0.30
0.20
0.10

Time of adoption

Source: Redrawn from E. M. Rogers, *Diffusion of Innovations* (Glencoe: The Free Press, 1962).

market, not all potential buyers go through the stages of the decision-making process at the same rate of speed. Some pass through them very quickly and are the first to adopt the new product. Others take a longer time to become aware of the product and to make up their minds to purchase it. Still others take a very long time to accept and to adopt the product.

This spread of the new product through the society is called the **diffusion process.** The stages in the diffusion process may be charted based on the differing time periods that individuals or groups of individuals take to adopt a new product. To clarify the difference between the terms *adoption process* and *diffusion process,* remember that individuals psychologically go through the various stages of *adoption* but the new product as it is purchased by the various groups of adopters is *diffused* through the social system or society at large.

Innovators

Whenever a new product appears on the market, some group of customers will be the first to buy it. These people are called the **innovators** because their purchase of the new product indicates their willingness to change their established ways of doing things.

Innovators are extremely important in get-

NO SMALL MIRACLE

In the late 1970s, Bristol-Myers researchers came up with what they thought was a break-through product, a hair conditioner that worked as others did except that its effects would last through several shampoos. The product could also be used on a daily basis.

The company hadn't had much to be happy about in recent years, with few new products being successfully introduced and the Clairol line of hair care products slipping. It was believed that the new conditioner could breathe new life into the Clairol line and combine with Clairol's "Condition II" to dominate the nearly seven hundred million dollar conditioner market. Bristol-Myers' plans and hopes were reflected in the name chosen for

the new product . . . "Small Miracle." But there was no miracle despite a product introduction that included one of the heaviest advertising and promotion budgets in the product class' history. By 1982, the product was on the way out with the company prepared to kill it once existing stocks had been worked off.

Why might such a "promising" product fail? Among the reasons suggested are these:

Maybe Small Miracle had characteristics people do not want.

Maybe Small Miracle had characteristics people did not understand.

Maybe Small Miracle failed just because its makers wanted so badly for it to succeed.

Here is the story as pieced together by Nancy Giges of *Advertising Age.*

At Bristol-Myers' Park Avenue offices in New York, volunteers are observed using hair care products at the company's test salon. This gives the company some sense of how consumers react to and use its products. The volunteers, who are watched through two-way mirrors, get free hair stylings for their help. While Small Miracle, code-named "Duco" at the time, was being salon tested, it was also being tested by Bristol-Myers' marketing research people. Throughout all this, it became clear to many Bristol-Myers employees that top management had a special interest in this project

Source: Used with permission, Nancy Giges, "No Miracle in Small Miracle: Story Behind Clairol Failure," *Advertising Age,* August 16, 1982, pp. 1, 76.

---

ting a new product accepted in the market. As Exhibit 11-5 shows, this venturesome group's membership is small in number, but they are willing to take a chance on an untried product. As might be expected, members of this group are likely to be younger and financially better-off buyers who can afford to take a chance on something new. They are generally better educated than the average consumer. This characteristic can be linked to their higher incomes and to their confidence in "thinking for themselves."

Early Adopters

A far larger group than the innovators, but a less adventurous one, is the early adopter group. However, for many products, to be an **early**

adopter requires the income, self-confidence, and education to use a product that has still not gained wide acceptance. Thus, the many characteristics of the innovative group are also to be found among the early adopters. Although members of this group follow the lead of the innovators, these people are more integrated into the social system and late adopters look to this group to determine what is "in." Early adopters are conceived of as opinion leaders who help to determine which new products are acceptable and which are not. They are a significant target for advertisements and other promotions aimed at creating a market where none existed before. Early adopters can be expected to influence their friends and co-workers and thus to contribute mightily to a new product's progress.

Developers of new products therefore spend

because it believed the product could be an exception to the dismal results the firm's consumer products group had shown of late.

The two sources of research information proved at odds. The marketing research people pronounced the product good for all types of hair. The salon-testers said it worked well only on thick and curly hair but gummed up thinner hair. Management ordered the salon people to try again and, when the same results were found, reprimanded them for disagreeing with the marketing research people. At first, the marketing research people were vindicated. Test markets in Green Bay, Wisconsin, and South Bend, Indiana, showed good results. But competitors like Gillette's Silkience and S.C. Johnson's Enhance were coming along and Bristol-Myers rushed Small Miracle into distribution, starting on the West Coast in June 1980, and working across the country.

As the marketing area expanded things went badly, perhaps because advertising was changed to suggest that the product could be used only twice a week *or* daily as the user preferred. Sales began to tail off after only a few weeks of success. Within six months, despite over $5 million spent in advertising and additional amounts in couponing and other promotion, sales were running less than 30 percent of projections. A new advertising agency was hired, but faced the problem of telling women that the product could be used only twice a week *or* daily *and* that daily users had better rinse very well to avoid greasy build-up.

It seems, in retrospect, that Bristol-Myers could never decide what Small Miracle's market position would be. Was it for daily use or weekly use? Was it for all hair types or only for thick and curly hair? Was it an "economy" product in that it did not necessitate daily use? As a matter of fact, some observers believed that women simply didn't *believe* the claim that Small Miracle could be used only twice a week. On one point most industry people do seem to agree: hair conditioners must be sold on their cosmetic virtues, consumers don't want economy, or twice a week usage, they want beautiful hair. Selling a conditioner that holds the promise of anything much more than beautiful hair seems to be a miracle no one can perform.

considerable time and resources in identifying and reaching this group. It is an effort to reach this group that fills the pages of such upscale magazines as, *The New Yorker* and *Esquire* with advertisements for imported wines, beers, bottled waters, perfumes, and other new-to-the-U.S. products.

This early adopter group, perhaps more than any other, is responsible for the long-range success of a product. No product, no matter how popular among innovators, will reach a mass market by appealing to that group alone. Moreover, some products adopted by innovators may be too "far out" to gain widespread acceptance. In a sense, the early adopter group filters the products accepted by the innovator group and popularizes them, leading the larger majority of buyers to accept the product.

Early and Late Majorities

The early and late majorities, taken together, constitute approximately 68 percent of the group that adopts a new product (see Exhibit 11-5). They make up the "mass market" on which many products depend. The two halves of this market are seen as having similar characteristics in differing degrees.

The membership of the **early majority** is usually the solid, middle-class consumer. Once a new product has been adopted by this group, it becomes an accepted part of the "American lifestyle." Hibachi grills, for example, were once owned primarily by apartment-dwelling urban young adults. Suburban dwellers cooked their steaks on brick barbecues. Acceptance of the hibachi by the early majority adopters made that cooking device part of the "American scene."

In general, people in this group who are members of the early rather than late majority are of average socio-economic status but may be slightly more educated and better-off financially than those in the **late majority** who are identified as older, more conservative, and more traditional.

Laggards

Laggards or final adopters are the last group to adopt a product. These people can make use of the product but for economic, social, or educational reasons have been slow to accept it. The laggard group is especially easily identified when the product in question is clothing. Frequently, a new clothing design is adopted by innovators, early adopters, and members of the majority groups, then dropped by them even as the laggard group begins to wear the style. Leisure suits are a good example of this phenomenon. Next time you visit a shopping mall, pay close attention to the various people and the clothing they are wearing. You will probably be able to make good guesses as to which shoppers are in this adopter group.

Non-adopters

No matter what the product under consideration, there are always some individuals who never buy that new product or adopt a new style. These people are termed **non-adopters.** This group contributes little to any product's success story, but is worth thinking about nonetheless.

A new alcoholic drink or tobacco product probably should not be advertised in a publication that reaches only members of abstemious religious groups. It probably makes little sense to advertise men's athletic products in women's magazines. However, for some products, it is conceivable that some non-adopters might be turned into adopters if some aspect of the product or its marketing mix could be changed to better appeal to them. For reasons such as these, then, non-adopters should at least be given some thought by marketing managers.

Use of the Adopter Categories

Planners about to introduce a new product should give close consideration to the diffusion process and the various adoption categories. The characteristics of the members of each stage are important in developing promotional and other marketing plans, including changes in prices and distribution processes, as the product moves through the diffusion process. It is no accident that the process shown in Exhibit 11-5 is reminiscent of the product life cycle, since gaining adopters is the cause of product movement from the low sales of the introductory period to the established market position of the maturity stage.

Characteristics of the various adopter groups may also provide the basis for market segmentation efforts. As we have seen, youth, economic resources, adventuresomeness, and other possible segmenting variables are usually not spread evenly among the adopter groups.

Lastly, the diffusion process is one which a successful product must navigate successfully. Thought and research intended to discover what sorts of adopters can help the new product on its way will surely pay off for marketing managers.

ORGANIZATION FOR NEW PRODUCT DEVELOPMENT

New product development is an important key to long term success in the marketplace. Therefore, the organization must be structured to permit and encourage new product development. However, many organizations are constructed around the day-to-day chores needed to keep operations moving smoothly and successfully in existing market areas. Managers in each functional area, such as manufacturing, marketing, and finance, understandably concentrate on meeting immediate objectives and solving current problems, such as filling orders, managing cash flows, or achieving sales and share-of-market goals. Despite the fact that "everyone" knows forecasting the future is important, current problems can easily blot the future from view. Individual managers may defend this situation with the observation that if today's problems are not solved, there will not *be* any future. Although there is the element of truth in this statement, long-range survival of the organization requires that long-range problems be solved.

The Booz, Allen, and Hamilton study of new product introductions cited earlier suggests that the organizations which encounter the most success in new product introductions are the ones that have given the greatest care to *organizing* for developing those products.[13]

Many organizational forms have been designed in an effort to encourage the smooth development and introduction of new products. We turn now to a description of several of these. Note that these organizational forms are generally intended to deal with new products developed within the organization itself. However, variations on these plans would be appropriate to handling products developed outside the firm—that is, products acquired from other firms or invented by outside individuals, laboratories, or other agencies. Organizations may also use more than one type of organization structure, choosing the one best fitted to a particular new product problem.[14]

The Product Manager

Many successful organizations employ a system built around the product manager concept. In this system, the **product manager,** sometimes called a **brand manager,** is responsible for planning and implementing the marketing of a single product or brand. The idea is to encourage coordination of the marketing effort through an individual who specializes in handling the assigned product. This format has the additional appeal of clearly identifying who is responsible for successes and failures.

A few companies have given responsibility for development of new products to their product managers, though the product manager concept was originally intended for the marketing of existing products. Many would argue that the two responsibilities do not fit together well. Others present the case that product managers are extremely knowledgeable individuals who are well-placed to detect market opportunities, to identify or conceptualize appropriate additions to product lines, and to evaluate the success–failure chances of new product offerings.

It is easy to see the other side of this. Product managers, as specialists, may be unlikely to develop product ideas outside their limited areas of specialization. They may be concerned that new products will undermine their established products. Product managers may be so busy assuring current success that they have no time for new product development. It can also be argued that the abilities needed to manage an existing product or brand are not necessarily those appropriate for developing new product ideas.

The New Product Manager

The new product manager form of organization for development of products is most likely to be found in a consumer goods company confronting a market in which marketing issues (rather than production or technical problems) predominate.

Individuals with the title "New Product Manager" are expected to be creative people who understand the unique problems of introducing new products to the market. Consider the new product manager at Bristol-Myers who conceived the notion that the existing deodorant product, Ban, could be improved with a larger application area (the ball that rolls on the product). Such a concept would have to be tested by building a prototype product which is presented to consumers for trial and approval. Then the target market, packaging strategy, and so on, would be chosen. But should the new product be introduced as "new, improved Ban" or as something else?

This is where the creativity and market sensitivity of the new product manager comes into

---

[13] *New Products Management for the 1980s*, Booz, Allen, and Hamilton, Inc., 1982, pp. 17–22.

[14] *New Products Management for the 1980s*, Booz, Allen, and Hamilton, Inc., 1982, p. 13.

play. It was determined that the existing product, Ban, had many loyal buyers. Instead of disrupting their buying patterns and Ban's market in general by introducing the new, larger applicator under the Ban name, a new brand of deodorant, using the new package, and sold in three new scents plus scentless, was introduced. The new brand was intended to win a new market position by appealing to buyers who were younger than established Ban users. The result was the new brand Tickle. Some Ban users probably switched to Tickle, *but* the share of market accounted for by Ban and Tickle *together* increased overall.

The role played by the new product manager—who knows both new product possibilities *and* the market to be approached—is a powerful one that allows a creative marketer a full creative challenge.

The Venture Team

As the term **venture team** may suggest, this approach involves constituting a group of specialists in the various functional areas of the organization intended to operate in an entrepreneurial environment. The team is supposed to develop a new business—a new venture—without operating as a closely controlled part of the whole organization. The team plays an independent role, therefore, in developing a new product, as well as in testing and commercialization. If the new product, or new business, is brought into full commercialization, the team members may be assigned to manage it. This assignment, as well as financial bonuses tied to the venture's success, may serve as significant rewards for team members.

The concept of an independent team developing a new product and plans for its future "on its own" has been successful for many organizations. It has been suggested that the independence of these teams, when it is genuine, results in more truly new products than do other systems. Monsanto Corporation, for example, used the method in the development and introduction of Astroturf. The Canon AE-1 program camera was also developed in this way. Studies seem to support the idea that a group set apart from daily organizational tasks can, in fact, very successfully complete the goals associated with the venture team concept.[15]

The New Products Department

A new products department is, unlike the venture team, a permanent department within an organization, headed by a director or even a vice-president. The attraction to this plan is that a high-ranking organizational official has clear-cut responsibility for new products and can, by virtue of the position, deal with other important officers as an equal. Furthermore, since the director is a high-level officer, dealing directly with the chief executive officer, it is possible to expedite matters related to product development.

In general, new product departments work in one of two ways. The department may be a fairly large one with its own research staff and other experts, or it may be quite small and call on people from other areas of the corporation as needed. Once a new product has reached the commercialization stage, in either type of organization, responsibility for the new product is turned over to the regular departments of the firm, perhaps with the new products department maintaining some coordinating role. Another difference from the venture team approach is evident here, since the venture team often maintains full responsibility for the new product or business.

The New Products Committee

A new products committee is a group similar to any other committee that is likely to be used to consider other matters. Usually, the heads of the organization's functional departments constitute the committee membership under the chairmanship of the chief executive officer. The committee would also include the new product director or other officer directly involved in such matters.

Despite popular jokes about the effectiveness of committees in general, the new product committee in various forms is a widely used product development tool. Such committees

---

[15]R.M. Hill and J.H. Hlavacek, "The Venture Team: A New Concept in Marketing Organization," *Journal of Marketing,* July 1977, pp. 44–50.

create and review new product policies, assign priorities to various new product options, evaluate progress and ultimately decide whether to commercialize new products. In fact, new product committees are frequently used in connection with some *other* new product management format, such as new product departments.[16] The existence of the committee can help the new product departments or new product managers by its input into the decision-making process. Most importantly, however, they help by putting the weight of its high-ranking, executive membership behind new product plans.

The Task Force

Task forces are used in new product development situations much as are task forces in government. A group whose membership spans numerous groups within the organization, typically the functional departments, is created. It is the job of a **task force** to see to it that the new project gets the support and resources that the various departments are able to offer. It is common for task force members to handle this responsibility *in addition* to their usual assignments. In this sense the members differ from the venture group. However, a few members are sometimes given leaves of absence from their regular jobs to devote their full attention to the task until it is completed. As was the case with the new products committee, the existence of a task force does not preclude the use of some other new product development system. The task force, might, for example, report to the new

product department's director or work under the aegis of a new products committee.

As is the case with most concepts, the task force approach offers advantages and certain disadvantages. On the advantage side, the task force approach does result in a group of knowledgeable people who are expected to stick with a new product idea, giving it continued attention until it is either commercialized or dropped. Furthermore, the task force cuts across organizational boundaries, bringing together individuals who otherwise might have little contact with one another. The situation in which its members thus find themselves forces them to work together to resolve differences that might hinder effective product development.

The major disadvantage of the task force is finding proper members to constitute the group. Making up one task force may not be too difficult, but if an organization wishes to consider many new product alternatives, a shortage of competent, cooperative, knowledgeable people may soon become apparent. The organization may find itself assigning less-than-perfect candidates to task forces, who may lack the influence to obtain full cooperation with different functional areas of the firm. One variation on the task force approach seeks to overcome this limitation. The makers of Johnson Wax use *two* sorts of task forces. The "sponsor group" guides the product through the developmental stages. If the product approaches commercialization, a "product committee," a more high-powered group, takes charge and brings the product through the final developmental stages.[17]

PUTTING IT ALL TOGETHER: THE DEVELOPMENT OF KODAK'S DISC CAMERA

The story of how Kodak marketing executives developed their new disc camera will illustrate the steps a new product idea undergoes before the actual product is marketed.[18]

The photographic industry is an "excellent example of widespread consumer satisfaction with existing products." According to an independent annual study of the industry, about 94

---

[16]Booz, Allen, and Hamilton, *New Products Management for the 1980's,* 1982, p. 13.

[17]S. Johnson and C. Jones, "How to Organize for New Products," *Harvard Business Review,* May–June, 1957, p. 56.

[18]Based on a speech by John J. Powers to Advertising Research Foundation, Chicago, 1982. Reprinted in *Marketing News,* January 21, 1983, pp. 1–8. Adapted with permission.

percent of U.S. families owned at least one camera in 1980. Simple-to-use, cartridge-loading cameras, introduced in the early 1960s, were the most popular type on the market, although sales peaked in 1978 and declined the next two years. The reason for the decline was that consumers were generally very happy with the cameras they had at home. Cartridge-loading pocket cameras were inexpensive and could be carried just about anywhere. Amateur photographers could conveniently take pictures in most situations. When photos taken under adverse conditions did not turn out, people accepted it. They were willing to live with some limitations in return for the convenience of easy picture-taking. Those who didn't want to accept the limitations joined the ranks of advanced amateurs and invested significantly more time and money in 35-mm photography. It was against this backdrop of high consumer satisfaction with current products that Kodak was challenged to "restimulate" the amateur photographic market, beginning the countdown toward the launch of disc cameras.

The initial objective was for Kodak's photographic engineers to design a camera that could take good pictures in a wide variety of situations. Over the years, Kodak had added numerous features to its basic roll-film camera to expand its range, but the results were nothing to write home about.

Adding more features also interfered with the automatic camera's simplicity and resulted in the picture-taker having to make more decisions about flash bulbs, batteries, focusing, film advance, etc. These comprised "more factors that could go wrong to disappoint the picture-taker."

Ten years ago, Kodak made the cartridge-loading camera "pocketable" by replacing mechanical devices with electronics: "We expanded the realm of photographic 'space' by allowing people to take more pictures in more situations with simple-to-use cameras. Sales were phenomenal, and what consumers told us in our surveys was that we had given them just what they wanted."

But Kodak did not agree. After the 1972 introduction of the Pocket Instamatic, the firm's research and development, manufacturing, and marketing personnel once again started to study photographic fundamentals and the ways in which people take pictures.

They began with a twofold objective: First, to determine under what conditions consumers were and were *not* taking pictures; and second, once they determined where they *weren't* taking pictures, they set out to develop a photographic system which could function in those areas of photographic space. Kodak was eventually led to the disc format and a number of breakthroughs in existing optics, electronics, and manufacturing technology. From a technical viewpoint, they were looking at a total systems approach to solving a photographic problem uncovered by behavioral research.

For example, a new manufacturing technology was developed to mass-produce the required glass lenses, and Kodak engineers custom-designed two integrated circuits that control and monitor the disc camera's automatic functions.

They had to virtually reinvent Kodacolor film with a new definition in sharpness and granularity to permit enlargements from a negative little more than one-sixth the size of a postage stamp. At the same time, they had to provide sufficient speed to expand the photographic space.

Kodak was aware of the engineering and manufacturing challenges involved in creating a new film format and camera, and felt it could meet them. But the firm still had to narrow down the alternatives and answer questions about product usage and features.

Another research effort, in the form of a feasibility study, was undertaken during which over 500 people put 64 different camera configurations through a battery of 14 tests. The basic design parameters of the disc camera began to emerge from this study. An upright camera with a built-in flash and a "calculator-feel" shutter button was decided on. A bezel was placed around the lens to keep stray fingers away. Other features were added to the camera's basic design for the two higher-priced models.

Kodak was pleased with the product design, but still did not know whether consumers would recognize the benefits and find them sufficiently attractive to be motivated to buy a new camera.

The new Kodak disc cameras were developed by going through every stage of the product development process.

This called for a major market research study to confirm and build on what the firm had already learned about consumer behavior and picture-taking needs.

Also, as with any new product launch, "it was vital that we know exactly who our target consumers are and how they perceived the new products." Kodak needed to determine (1) whether demographics dictated using different approaches among different consumer groups, and (2) which specific features people liked most and whether they would perceive these features as allowing them to take pictures where they previously did not.

The advantages turned up by the marketing research needed to be translated into benefits the consumer would quickly recognize. Complicating that was the knowledge that consumers needed to be educated about needs they probably never thought about or never associated with simple-to-use cameras.

As part of the market study, Kodak researchers took a representation of the prototype disc camera into more than 1,000 U.S. homes. Consumers were shown the camera's automatic advance, or "blink-and-whir" feature, as well as the plastic enclosure for the disc film. Kodak was not identified in the study, and the firm took additional security precautions.

Initially, respondents were asked for reactions based on visual observation alone. They were shown the camera representation and asked them to write down any features they recognized. Many respondents were quick to pick up on the camera's most sophisticated features.

Kodak researchers also explained the features in detail and asked consumers to rank 18 features in order of preference. In addition, researchers sought reactions to camera and film pricing variations and asked consumers to compare their perception of the disc camera with existing products.

One of the findings from the survey was that Kodak would not have to plan different communications programs based on demographics. Preferences for the camera's features were uniform, for the most part, among all demographic groups in the survey. All 18 features the people surveyed were asked to rank had at least some appeal, and 14 of the 18 features listed consistently ranked as *very* appealing.

While consumers found the camera's size and shape, five-year warranty, long-life power cell, automatic power-off, and automatic focusing features popular, the automatic flash, rapid flash recycling, and automatic film advance features were ranked at the top, along with overall ease of use.

The most significant result of the survey was that, after becoming familiar with all features of the disc camera, intent-to-purchase among respondents just about doubled. And the results helped narrow the scope of communications efforts by targeting those features that would have the broadest appeal. For example, marketing research suggested that Kodak could dispense with a description of "photographic space" in its advertising since the amateur photographic market wasn't equipment or gadget oriented. Amateurs want good pictures without fuss or bother. Discussion of sophisticated features is largely lost in advertising, unless it's translated into benefits, ideally consisting of more good pictures. Kodak addressed photographic space and tied the three most preferred benefits together by promising consumers that with the new disc camera "you'll be able to take pictures you may have been missing before."

But the real test was in the marketplace, and Kodak found a winner there. Actual sales of film, cameras, and photofinishing equipment far exceeded Kodak's most optimistic projections.

SUMMARY

In this chapter, we looked at several topics central to an understanding of new products. First, the issue of just what constitutes a new product was addressed, and it was shown that there are *degrees* of newness and novelty of which students of marketing should be aware. New products may be classified according to their degree of innovativeness. Discontinuous innovations connote products that have no functional equivalent. A product that is imitative in nature or that involves only minor alterations of an existing product is a continuous innovation. Attention was also drawn to the relatively high risks associated with developing and introducing new products. Explicit attention was given to the stages in new product development. Although new products may provide substantial profits for companies, the inherent risks of failure are also great. Some estimates indicate that 90 percent of all new products are not successful. The characteristics widely associated with successful new products were also reviewed, as were the general steps to be followed in the attempt to minimize chances of failure. Some characteristics of a successful new product are: (1) the relative advantage offered to a consumer, (2) compatibility of the product with existing consumption patterns, (3) complexity of the product, (4) trialability of the product, and (5) the degree of observable evidence of innovation.

The new product adoption or diffusion process was also presented. Different groups of buyers are encountered as marketers seek to expand market acceptance of their new products. Buyers can be classified as innovators, laggards, or non-adopters, or can be part of the early or late majority.

There are explicit stages in the process of new product development. These five stages are exploration, screening, business analysis, development, and commercialization.

Marketing managers have developed many forms of organizations intended to make the development and introduction of new products smoother. Six of the major forms were discussed: the brand manager system, new product manager, the venture team, new products department, new products committee, and the task force.

Lastly, a case study of a recent new product introduction, the disc camera by Kodak, was presented in an effort to bring the new product development process into sharper focus.

THE MOST IMPORTANT CONCEPT IN THIS
CHAPTER

Determining what is a new product depends on the perspective from which one views the product. Understanding what constitutes a new product and understanding the necessity of careful planning is essential to new product marketing. New products are the lifeblood of most organizations.

KEY TERMS

New product

Continuous innovation

Dynamically continuous innovation

Discontinuous innovations

Relative advantage

Trial sampling

Divisibility

Exploration stage

Screening stage

Business analysis

Commercialization

Diffusion process

Innovators

Early adopter

Early majority

Late majority

Laggards

Non-adopters

Product manager

Brand manager

Venture team

New products committee

Task force

QUESTIONS FOR DISCUSSION

1 What is your definition of a new product?

2 Classify the type of innovation used in the following products:
(a) A digital safe that uses a *LED* display and a six-digit computer code.
(b) A hand checker that consists of a magnetically coded card plus electronic sensors to check hand geometry to give absolute identity for banks and classified areas. Card coding and prerecorded hand data are checked in seconds.
(c) A new aerodynamically designed car that has a low wind resistance wedge-shaped body.
(d) Cow Patties brand of ice cream sandwich that contains a peanut butter cookie filled with chocolate ice cream and sprinkled with peanut chips.
(e) Penn brand two-tone tennis balls (orange *and* yellow rather than just orange or just yellow).
(f) Solar-powered electronic calculators.
(g) The disc camera by Kodak.

3 For the products in question 2, identify what salient product features might speed the acceptance of these innovations.

4 Identify the steps in the new product development process using the Pampers example given in the chapter.

5 What takes place in the business analysis stage of product development?

6 Procter & Gamble was testing a new feminine-hygiene product called Always just two and a half years after its $75 million write off from Rely tampons. What special care should Procter & Gamble take in the new product marketing of Always brand?

7 What type of product strategy did Coca-Cola utilize when it decided to introduce diet Coke? Caffeine-free Coke?

8 What are the limitations of brand extension as a new product strategy?

CASE 11·1 Glidden Paint Company*

How many of us have dreamed of painting a room without a spill, spot, or splash, with no drop cloth, no dustcovers—and no brush? Chemists at the Glidden Paint Company in To-

---

*Source: From "Paint Stick" by Doug Payne, *Technology Illustrated,* February–March 1982, p. 12. Used with permission.

ronto, Canada, are doing just that . . . with solid paint.

Their Spred Solid Paint comes in a cardboard box, goes on like lipstick, eliminates cleanups—and baffles consumers. Two test marketing campaigns have already been carried out in some Canadian cities, but the painting public apparently didn't catch on.

The idea of solid paint is not new; patents for such a product have already been taken out in 18 countries, including the United States and Japan, but no other company has advanced as far as Glidden. The multimillion-dollar project hinges on how paint is held together chemically. Many standard paints depend on a gel of bonded hydrogen atoms that keep the paint consistent enough to spread. The Glidden chemists at first followed this route and came up with a solid paint that solved all the problems but one: With denser hydrogen bonds, the paint would spread on a wall, then snap back onto the roller or brush as though it were attached by an elastic band.

Glidden abandoned hydrogen bonding and developed a new process that depends on electrostatic attraction—strong enough to keep the paint solid in storage but weak enough to let the paint flow when subjected to a shearing force, as in being drawn across a wall.

So far, Glidden has turned out an oil-base interior paint. It costs about 25 percent more than regular paint but saves the cost of brushes, rollers, and solvents. Solid paint dries quickly, stores for extended periods, and requires no mixing or shaking. The major drawback is that it doesn't work on textured surfaces or detailed trim.

A box about the size of a single-serving package of cereal holds the equivalent of a quart of liquid paint. Once applied, there is no difference between the solid paint and standard products. It even smells the same.

Questions

1 What type of innovation is the solid paint stick?

2 What features or characteristics does the product have that would speed the diffusion of the product? Inhibit the diffusion of the product?

3 What marketing activity is necessary to make this new product a success?

CASE 11-2 Ri-Le

Ri-Le is a Vietnamese restaurant. Although the furnishings are sparse, the restaurant serves gourmet food. Le was a helicopter pilot during the Vietnamese war. He and his wife escaped the country the day before the North Vietnamese took over Saigon. He enjoys life in America.

One dish served in the restaurant is the Lumpia dog, a hotdog with a touch of egg roll (won ton skin). A hotdog weiner is stuffed with egg roll filling, wrapped in egg roll paper to make a Lumpia dog, and deep fried. The Lumpia dog is served with a pineapple sauce for a dip.

Questions

1 Is the Lumpia dog a new product? Why or why not?

2 What research and analysis procedure would you take to develop this "new" product? As a restaurant item? As a frozen foods product?

PART 5

CHANNELS OF DISTRIBUTION

The general public, and even some students of marketing, often tend to ignore what is perhaps marketing's most significant task—distribution. The importance of this function, a function which accounts for about 25 percent of the cost of consumer goods, should not be underrated since it is distribution that delivers goods and services to those that need them. The distribution function of marketing encompasses the work of various intermediaries such as wholesalers, agents, brokers, and retailers, as well as the efforts of those who develop methods of physical distribution and channel management. The overall goal of all these marketers is always the same—efficiency of operation consistent with the desires of customers.

Chapter 12 provides an overview of channels of distribution and the general tasks these channels perform.

Chapter 13 discusses two major channel institutions—wholesalers and retailers, and many of the different kinds of marketing operations within those two categories.

In Chapter 14, instead of looking at technical detail, we present the physical distribution function with special attention to its overriding significance in marketing as a whole. ∎

CHAPTER 12

The Nature of Distribution

CHAPTER SCAN

This chapter introduces channels of distribution in general, with special emphasis on the important but often unnoticed functions performed by channel members.

We also examine the various functions performed by the marketing organizations known as channel intermediaries. The many structural possibilities of channels are also discussed. Issues dealing with channel management and the legal ramifications of certain aspects of distribution are reviewed.

WHEN YOU HAVE STUDIED THIS CHAPTER, YOU WILL:

Be able to discuss the general purpose of distribution in the marketing system.

Understand how distribution contributes to an effective marketing mix.

Know that all marketers engage in some distribution activities, even non-profit organizations and providers of services, including doctors and lawyers.

Be able to describe the major channels of distribution used by consumer goods and industrial goods marketers.

Be able to name and discuss the functions performed by channel intermediaries.

Know the major legal concerns associated with channel construction and management.

Be able to name the major vertical marketing systems and tell how they are organized.

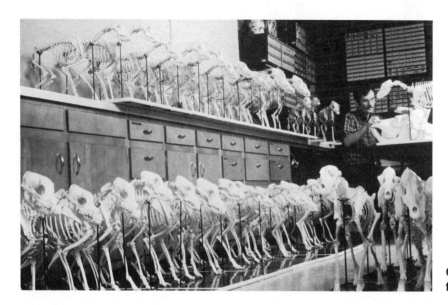

Carolina Biological Supply performs a distribution function.

When E.T. and his spaceship crew landed, seeking specimens of terrestrial life, they could have saved themselves a lot of trouble by taking their shopping list to the Carolina Biological Supply Company, in Burlington, North Carolina. There they could have bought more samples of the earth's animals, vegetables, and minerals than they could possibly have collected on their own.[1]

Carolina Biological sells more than 20,000 items, everything from human brains to the simplest and most primitive one-celled organisms. Live tarantulas, meat-eating plants, golden albino mystery snails, and tokay geckos are available, as well as 90 different types of fruit flies and fungi, 235 strains of algae, and 100 strains of bacteria. Any customer can buy the skull of a human being, a wallaby, or a baboon, or the complete skeleton of a mole, a marmoset, an armadillo, or a bush baby. Every manner of creeping, crawling, wriggling, strolling, biting, buzzing, sucking, stinging multi-legged creature and its neatly dissected innards have been vacuum-packed, freeze-dried, framed, pickled in alcohol or embalming fluid, or embedded in plastic for posterity. There is even a bat sealed in a plastic sphere, looking like misfortune seen in a crystal ball. What is not available in the flesh has been eerily reproduced in

plastic down to the last detail: life-sized models of flat feet, slipped discs, human ears (for teaching acupuncture), and a person choking on a bean are all for sale. The company also deals in fragments of the earth itself; quartz crystals, garnets, and glittering chunks of Muscovite mica are sold over the counter, by telephone, or by mail. Major credit cards are accepted.

Carolina Biological is one of the oldest and most respected scientific supply houses in the United States. Its 1,000-page catalogue is a bible for high school and college science teachers. It offers everything needed to equip a laboratory, from Bunsen burners to microscopes, along with kits that enable an entire class to carry out experiments in chemistry and physics, as well as biology. It has recently added computers and computer software packages to its inventory. The company sends a free four-page newsletter called *Carolina Tips* to 130,000 teachers every month; each issue carries a scientific article on subjects ranging from acid rain to cell biology, and a few advertisements for company products. During school vacations, groups of teachers often show up like pilgrims, seeking tours.

Because of the unusual products handled, you might wonder whether or not the Carolina Biological Supply Company is a typical marketing organization. Of course, its product sets the company apart from most others, but Carolina,

---

[1] Excerpts from Denise Grady, "The Sears, Roebuck of Science," *Discover*, September 1982, pp. 71–72. Used with permission.

like other marketing organizations, relies on a marketing mix to attract, satisfy, and keep customers. Much of the success Carolina has had can be traced to one particular feature of its marketing mix, the distribution function. Utilizing a number of channels of distribution and means of transportation, Carolina Biological Supply has built a sizable and successful wholesale trade.

DISTRIBUTION DELIVERS A STANDARD OF LIVING TO SOCIETY

In terms of society's needs, *the* major purpose of marketing is to satisfy human needs by delivering products of various types to buyers when and where they want them and at a reasonable cost. In fact, a key term in this statement of marketing's mission is *delivery*. In many ways, all marketing effort comes to nothing unless products are placed into the hands of those who need them. Thus, distribution is of overwhelming importance in any discussion of marketing's definitions and functions. Distribution is estimated to account for about one-quarter of the price of the consumer goods we buy. Most would agree that this is a cost well worth bearing. Distribution creates time utility and place utility.

With the development of the idea that efficiency could be gained, even in a primitive economy, if one person specialized in a certain activity, such as hunting, and another person specialized in a different activity, such as fishing or farming, distribution of products among the members of even primitive societies becomes necessary. Today, distribution is far more complex. For example, products shipped into Baltimore may ultimately be sold in Oregon, and Washington state apples may be consumed in Florida. The basic function of distribution, however, remains the same. One way or another, the distance between the grower or producer of a product and the final user of that product must be bridged. The distance to be covered can be quite long, as when Alaskan oil ends up in Australia. It can also be quite short, as when a farmer at a roadside stand sells the watermelon that grew just a few yards away. No matter what the distance required to move a good from a producer to a buyer or consumer, society relies on the marketing function of distribution to do the job—to provide products in the right place at the right time.

DISTRIBUTION IN THE MARKETING MIX: A KEY TO SUCCESS

Increasing levels of competition, cost-consciousness brought on by world and national economic developments, and consumer concerns with efficiency in marketing are among the main reasons why distribution has become increasingly important to organizations in recent years. For example, it used to be that the main business of the Hollywood movie studios was simply making films, that is, production. Today, the crucial factor determining a studio's profitability is the distribution of films. Major U.S. film studios produce only about one-half of the movies they distribute. Many films are purchased from independent studios. The large studios concentrate on distribution and other marketing functions and are compensated for these efforts via a fee system, usually 25 to 30 percent of a film's rentals. Film distribution itself has also changed in recent years. Supplying the films to theaters is no longer enough. Home Box Office, Show-Time, and other pay TV systems, as well as TV networks, independent stations, and video cassette makers, are now critical in the film marketing process. Distribution is the name of the game in Hollywood.[2] Distribution is also essential even when companies have expertise in managing the other areas of the marketing mix. When giant Coca-Cola decided to enter the fast-expanding wine business, its financial strength and marketing expertise made it capable of purchasing and operating just about any wine-producing firm. Coca-Cola chose the Taylor Wine Company. Taylor was eminently desirable for a number of reasons, although the big attraction for Coke was Taylor's superb distribution system covering every area of the country east of the Rocky Mountains. Taylor's fine reputation was also important, but, when carefully analyzed, the reputation and brand familiarity enjoyed by Taylor would not have been developed without its excellent distribution.[3] Although Coca-Cola recently sold its wine business because of short term return on asset considerations, its distribution system had allowed it to grow to number two in the industry (based on unit volume). The almost immediate success of Duncan Hines Cookies is strongly linked to the channels of distribution that were already in place between the manufacturer (Procter & Gamble) and the supermarkets expected to retail the products.

Some organizations compete successfully against much larger competitors basing their market appeal almost entirely on distribution. Amway, although it has grown to be a large firm in its own right, has done so while competing against such giants as Procter & Gamble, but by employing a distribution system much different from that of Procter & Gamble because the product goes right to the consumer's door. Mary Kay cosmetics has performed a similar feat.

---

[2]Based on "How TV Is Revolutionizing Hollywood," *Business Week,* February 21, 1983, pp. 78–89.

[3]John G. Given, "Coca-Cola Turning Taylor into Aggressive Wine Seller," *Tulsa Tribune,* August 15, 1982, p. G-5.

DENTISTS AND DISTRIBUTION

Dental vans? Ever hear of dentists making house calls? They do in the Denver and Detroit areas, where the National Foundation of Dentistry for the Handicapped—a public, non-profit corporation—sponsors two dentistry vans, each equipped with portable dental apparatus. The Henry J. Kaiser Family Foundation funds the van in Denver and the Michigan Department of Mental Health funds the one in the Detroit area. Dentists are hired on a time-available basis to visit and treat the handicapped and elderly who cannot visit them. Each van costs about $44,000. The dentists who have gone out on house calls find great satisfaction in their work.

Source: "Dental Vans," *Parade,* June 21, 1981, p. 8.

Non-profit and social service organizations such as the American Heart Association have used distribution effectively to better perform their functions. The American Heart Association makes blood pressure checks available in many locations including schools, libraries, and fire stations. The American Cancer Society distributes leaflets and other information at various locations and uses mass media and the mails to reach its target consumers.

Even activities not usually thought of as involving much in the way of distribution may rely heavily on this aspect of the marketing mix. Doctors, barbers, lawyers, and dentists are among the many providers of services who must decide where to locate their offices, whether or not to have several offices, whether to distribute their product in a traditional setting or in the middle of a shopping mall, indeed, whether or not to have any one place of business at all. It might be better for some organizations to operate out of a van or mobile office of some type. Some doctors and barbers, for example, have no home office and deliver their products only through house-calls.

DISTRIBUTION: A CAUSE OF FAILURE

The importance of distribution in effective marketing can be illustrated as strongly by marketing failures as by successes. Texas Instruments Incorporated (TI) nearly failed when it introduced its 99/4 home computer in 1980. The product carried a high price, nearly $1,200, but a bigger problem was TI's failure to line up a strong dealer network capable of properly distributing such an item. Research led to the discovery that (1) there is a limit to the number of brands a computer dealer is willing to carry, and (2) changes in the market for home computers necessitated changes in TI's distribution policies. Therefore, a new company president reassessed and revised the marketing strategy, stressing distribution. For a short time, TI's sales were revitalized through the use of mass market retailers, such as K-Mart, Gold Circle, Service Merchandise, and Toys-Я-Us. The company enhances this distribution effort by placing instore computers in these outlets so that customers could try them out.[4] Ultimately, however, its slow start in distribution, competitive pressures, and other problems forced TI to withdraw its home computer from the market.

CHANNEL OF DISTRIBUTION DEFINED

The channel of distribution can be referred to by other names, and terms vary from industry to industry. The simple term "channel," "trade channel," or any other variant may be used but the functions performed remain the same.

The term channel of distribution has its origins in the French word for canal. This suggests a path that goods take as they flow from producers to consumers. In this sense, the channel of distribution is defined by the organization(s) or individual(s) along the route from producer to consumer. Since the beginning and ending points of the route must be included, both producer and consumer are always members of the channel of distribution. However, there may be intermediate stops along the way. Several marketing institutions have developed to facilitate the flow of the physical product, or title to the product, from the producer to the consumer. Organizations that serve as marketing intermediaries (middlemen) specializing in distribution rather than production are *external* to the producing organization. When these intermediaries or middlemen join with a manufacturer in a loose coalition to engage in exploiting joint opportunities, a channel of distribution is formed.[5]

A channel of distribution consists of producer, consumer, and other intermediary organizations that are aligned to provide a vehicle that makes the passage of title or possession of the product from producer to consumer possible.[6]

The channel of distribution can also be seen as a system of interdependency within a set of organizations, a system that facilitates the exchange process.

All discussions of distribution channels concern a product that has taken on its final form. A channel of distribution for an automobile begins after the product becomes a finished automobile. It does not include the

---

[4]"Texas Instruments Come Roaring Back," *Business Week,* February 14, 1983, pp. 10–11.

[5]Wroe Alderson, *Marketing Behavior and Executive Action* (Homewood, Ill.: Richard D. Irwin, 1957).

[6]Definition adapted from David A. Revzan, "Marketing Organization Through the Channel," *Wholesaling and Marketing Organizations* (New York: John Wiley & Sons, 1961), pp. 107–142 and Ralph F. Breyer, "Some Organizations on Structural Formation and Growth in Marketing Channels," in R. Cox, W. Alderson, S. Shapiro, ed., *Theory in Marketing* (Homewood, Ill.: Irwin, 1964), pp. 163–175.

paths raw materials (such as steel) or component parts (such as tires) take to the automobile manufacturer who is an industrial user in these other channels. It should be emphasized that the channel's purpose of moving products to people is more than a simple matter of transportation. The channel of distribution must accomplish the task of transferring the title to the product as well as facilitating the physical movement of the goods to their ultimate destination. Although the task of title transfer and the exchange of physical possession (transportation) generally follow the same channel of distribution, they do not necessarily need to follow the same path.

What a Channel Involves

All but the shortest of channels (such as producer-direct-to-consumer channels) include one or more channel members who perform activities between the producer and the final user. These intermediaries are individuals or organizations specializing in distribution rather than production. These middlemen are distinct from the producers of goods. A distinction may be made between **merchant intermediaries** who take title to the product and **agent intermediaries** who do not take title to the product. Although agent intermediaries never own the goods, they perform a number of marketing functions, such as selling, that facilitates further transactions in the exchange process.

In most cases, intermediaries are independent organizations tied to the producers they deal with only by mutual agreements. They are not owned by the producers. Other intermediaries *are* owned by producers, such as the company-owned sales branches and sales offices that sell NCR office equipment. However, these company-owned sales offices and branches are easily identified as being separate from the production facilities operated by NCR.

In service marketing, there are cases where there appears to be *no* channel of distribution. When a beautician delivers a product such as a haircut or make-up advice, he or she deals directly with the customer. The shortest of distribution channels is found in these cases. However, though there may be no intermediaries involved, marketing functions are still being performed. Any required activities are simply performed by the provider of the service.

When identifiable intermediaries are present, the channel members form a coalition intended to discover joint opportunities in the marketplace. Each channel member, from producer to retailer, must see some opportunity for rewarding participation in the channel. Ultimately, for the channel to work properly the consumer, who is not a member of the commercial channel, must also perceive a likely reward. Thus, the large merchandise selection at low prices offered by a Venture or Target store must be seen as compensation for driving an extra mile or two to the store.

The coalition between the channel members may be a loose one resulting from negotiation or a formal set of contractual arrangements identifying each party's role in the distribution process of each individual product line. The **conventional channel** is characterized by loosely aligned, relatively autonomous marketing organizations that have developed a system to carry out a trade relationship. By way of contrast, *vertical marketing systems* are far more formally organized systems because channel members are either owned by a manufacturer or distributor, linked by strong contracts or agreements such as franchises, or managed and coordinated as an integrated system. Vertical marketing systems are discussed in greater detail later in this chapter.

It should also be pointed out that transportation companies, financial institutions, or other functional specialists who sell a service that helps the flow of goods and services are not included in the channel of distribution. They are merely **facilitators,** playing only a minor role by providing a limited service that is useful to the channel member.

MARKETING FUNCTIONS PERFORMED BY INTERMEDIARIES

Perhaps the most neglected, most misunderstood, and most maligned segment of the economy is the distribution segment. Retailers are seen by some as the principal cause of high consumer prices simply because retailers are the marketers with whom consumers come into most frequent contact. Retailers collect money from consumers so, even though much of that money is passed to other distributors, manufacturers, or the Internal Revenue Service, retailers often bear the brunt of citizens' complaints. Wholesalers are also seen as the cause of high prices, perhaps because much of what they do is done outside of the view of consumers. The well-known idea to "cut out the middleman" is posed by many as a means to lower the prices of consumer goods.

This kind of sentiment goes back thousands of years. The activities of those who perform the distribution function have been long misunderstood, and so it continues today. Students of marketing should try to develop an understanding that an efficient distribution system must somehow be financed. Most of the time, eliminating the middleman will *not* reduce prices since the dollars that go to intermediaries compensate them for the performance of tasks that *must* be accomplished regardless of the economic system in effect.

How Intermediaries Fit in Channels

In Chapter 1, we outlined a conventional channel of distribution consisting of a manufacturer, a wholesaler, a retailer, and the ultimate consumer. Not all channels include each of these marketing institutions. In some cases, a unit of product may pass directly from manufacturer to consumer. In other circumstances, it may be handled by not just one but two or more wholesalers. To see why these many variations are possible, the role of middlemen or intermediaries in marketing channels must be discussed.

Consider this conventional channel of distribution:

Manufacturer ⟶ Retailer ⟶ Ultimate consumer

It is possible to have a channel of distribution that does not include a separate wholesaler. A manufacturer *can* choose to sell directly to retailers, in effect eliminating the wholesaler. However, the marketing functions performed by the wholesalers must then be shifted to one of the other parties in the channel—that is, to the retailer or the manufacturer. If the manufacturer assumes some or all of these functions, they are said to have been shifted *backward* in the channel. If the retailer assumes them, they are said to have been shifted *forward* in the channel. For example, the manufacturer may decide to perform the function of breaking bulk, sending comparatively small orders on to individual retail customers. On the other hand, the retailer could be willing to accept carload lots of the product in question, to store large quantities of it, and to perform the activity of breaking down these larger quantities into smaller quantities. With the wholesaler out of the picture, the manufacturer that now sells in large quantities may have to create a sales force to call on the numerous retailers. In any case, the functions performed by the eliminated wholesaler do not disappear; they are simply shifted to another channel member.

The remaining channel members who assume these functions expect to be compensated in some way. The retailer may expect lower prices and higher margins. Sellers may expect larger purchase orders, more aggressive retail promotion, or more control over the distribution process.

The key to setting the structure of a channel of distribution is to determine how the necessary marketing functions can be carried out most efficiently and effectively. Certain variables, such as price, complexity of the product, or the number of customers to be served, can serve as guides to the appropriate channel structures. However, the functions to be performed should be the primary consideration in the marketing manager's distribution plans. Let us consider some of the major functions performed by intermediaries.

Physical Distribution Functions

Breaking-Bulk. With few exceptions, intermediaries perform a bulk-breaking function. The **bulk-breaking function** consists of buying in relatively large quantities and then selling in smaller quantities, passing the lesser amounts of merchandise on to retailers, industrial buyers, wholesalers, or other customers. By accumulating large quantities of goods and then breaking them into smaller amounts suitable to many buyers, one can reduce the cost of distribution for both manufacturers and consumers. Consumers need not buy and store great amounts of merchandise, increasing their own storage costs and running risks such as spoilage, fire, or theft. Manufacturers are spared the necessity of dividing their outputs into the small order sizes retailers or consumers might prefer.

This bulk-breaking or *sorting* function of intermediaries is sometimes termed a "resolution of economic discrepancies" in acknowledgment of the fact that manufacturers, as a rule, turn out amounts of merchandise that are vast in comparison to the quantity that an individual buyer might care to buy. Breaking-bulk thus resolves this discrepancy within the economy.

Accumulating Bulk. In the majority of cases, it is the task of the intermediary to *break* bulk. However, an intermediary may also *create* bulk, buying units of the same product from many small producers and offering the larger amount gathered to buyers preferring to purchase in large quantities; these intermediaries are then **accumulating bulk.** An intermediary performing

this function is called, not surprisingly, an **assembler.** The classic examples of assemblers are those encountered in the agriculture and fishing businesses. A maker of applesauce such as Mott's or a fish canner such as Bumble Bee would probably not want to have to deal with many comparatively small farming businesses or with independent owners of fishing boats. Assemblers gather large quantities of a product attractive to the large buyers. Exhibit 12-1 contrasts the operation of the assembler with that of other intermediaries.

Creation of Assortments. Another function that intermediaries perform is the creation of assortments of merchandise that would otherwise not be available. By performing the **assorting function,** the economic discrepancy resulting from the factory operator's natural inclination to produce a large quantity of a single product, or of a line of products, and the consumer's desire to select from a wide variety of choices is resolved. Wholesalers who purchase sizable amounts of goods from different manufacturers can offer retailers a greater assortment of items than the product line an individual manufacturer, is able to provide.

Consider how intermediaries are used by magazine publishers and retailers to solve a very big assorting problem. There are at least 30,000 different magazine titles available from American publishers. No newsstand operator or other retailer carries anything like that number, so a series of intermediaries is used to sort those many titles into appropriate groupings for individual stores. National wholesalers, such as Hearst, ICD, or Select Magazines, may be utilized to move the thousands of titles to the approximately 500 local wholesalers. Their reward for fulfilling this gargantuan task is about 6 percent of the magazines' retail prices, out of which they must pay all expenses involved.

The local distributors continue the task of breaking bulk, moving the magazines to countless supermarkets, newsstands, drugstores, and other retail spots. But there is more to the local wholesaler's task than simply breaking bulk and

EXHIBIT 12-1

The Breaking-Bulk and Creating-Bulk Functions

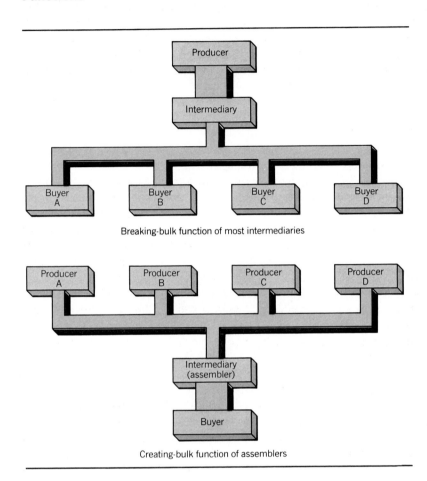

Breaking-bulk function of most intermediaries

Creating-bulk function of assemblers

making delivery. The local wholesaler must select, from among the 30,000 plus available titles, the ones that are appropriate for the individual retailer's operation. Then, this assortment of titles is assembled in the proper number of each magazine for each retailer. The local wholesaler is paid about 20 percent of the cover prices.

Complicated as this sounds, the system is so efficient that when *TV Guide* is printed, it is stocked by more than 150,000 retail establishments within 36 hours. Although the influence of wholesalers has declined in certain industries, it is obvious why wholesalers remain very important in the magazine distribution business.[7]

Reducing Transactions. There is one underlying reason why intermediaries can economically accumulate bulk, break bulk, and create assortments: the presence of intermediaries or middlemen within the distribution system actually *reduces the number of transactions* neces-

_____
[7]Bernice Kanner, "Wholesalers—Vital Cog in Magazine Machinery," *Advertising Age,* October 16, 1978, p. 30.

EXHIBIT 12-2

Reduction of Transactions by an Intermediary

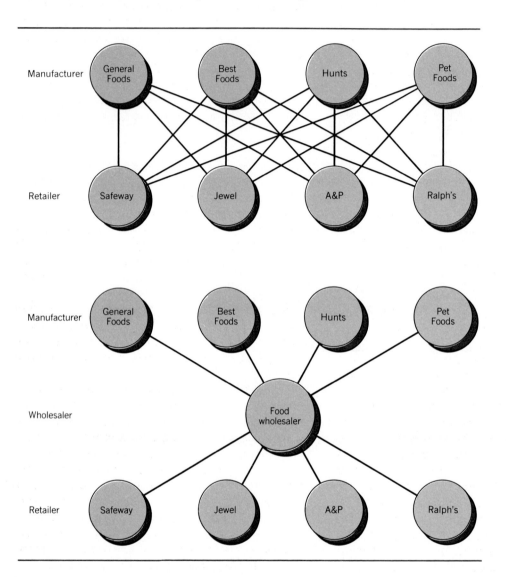

sary to accomplish the exchanges needed to keep the economy moving and consumers satisfied.

As Exhibit 12-2 indicates, even if only four suppliers of grocery items attempt to transact business with just four supermarket-buying headquarters, the number of interrelationships necessary is far greater than it is once an inter-mediary, such as a food wholesaler, is added to the system. Channel intermediaries, in their dual roles as buying agents for their customers and selling agents for the manufacturers with which they deal, simplify the necessary transaction pro-cess considerably.

Incidentally, intermediaries simplify the mar-keting process in more ways than reducing the number of transactions. They also reduce the geographic distances that buyers and sellers must travel to complete exchanges.

Intermediaries also simplify transactions by sparing manufacturers the trouble of locating and contacting individual potential customers. This job is done by the wholesalers who deal with retailers, and the retailers who deal with consumers. For this reason, and for the others mentioned above, the presence of intermediaries reduces the costs that would have to be borne if manufacturers and consumers had to perform all these activities themselves.

Transportation and Storage. Intermediaries, in most cases, perform two other marketing functions: **transportation** and **storage.** Merchandise must be physically moved from points of production to points of consumption. This process often involves storage or holding of the product at various spots along the way. As we have seen, intermediaries of all types, including retailers, are frequently engaged in storage of goods until they are demanded by customers further along in the channel of distribution. Stroh's beer, for example, is the most popular beer in the Cleveland, Ohio market. If each person wanting to buy Stroh's had to travel from Cleveland to the Stroh brewery in Detroit to make a purchase, the distances traveled by those hundreds of thousands of customers, or by Stroh's employees if they chose to make home deliveries, would add up to an incredible total. The presence of wholesalers and retailers provides storage in the Cleveland market. It also permits Stroh to send relatively few truckloads of beer to Cleveland, immensely reducing the total distance otherwise traveled, yet still satisfying the Cleveland area's demand for Stroh's beer. Although our example is far-fetched, it illustrates that one of the most important functions of intermediaries is to provide regional and local storage. The neighborhood Kroger's, Sears, or 7-Eleven all carry an inventory, thus each performs the storage function.

It should be mentioned that there are some types of intermediaries who do not take possession of the goods whose distribution they facili-tate. In such cases, the intermediary does not actually transport or store the merchandise. Instead, the intermediary may only coordinate transportation and storage or contribute in some other way to the creation of time and place utility. Thus, when we think of transportation and storage, we should do so in a broad way that permits consideration of the contribution of wholesalers who, for example, arrange for shipment of goods from a producer-owned place of storage to a buyer's home or place of business.

Communication Functions: Exchanging Information and Title

Wholesalers and other channel members perform important promotional functions for manufacturers so the title to the product may be exchanged. Most frequently, this communication is carried out by a sales force. However, intermediaries also use advertising and such sales promotion tools as retail displays. In other words, wholesalers perform a **selling function** for the manufacturer, often providing a sales force or other promotional efforts that can more efficiently perform the selling function than a supplier.

Consummating an exchange of title is the ultimate purpose of the *communication link* between the manufacturer and the retailer. The wholesaler provides a **buying function** for retailers, industrial users, or other customers. A wholesaler's contact with numerous manufacturers allows it to evaluate the product quality standards of wide assortments of goods from competing manufacturers. Thus, the retailer or other customer is free to specialize in the retailing or merchandising of its products. Intermediaries further serve as channels of communication in such ways as informing buyers on how products are to be sold, used, repaired, or guaranteed. They can even explain new product developments. In fact, retailers should pass along much of this same information to *their* customers, although it is unfortunately the case that many retail salespeople are unable to provide effective and meaningful communication of this sort. Intermediaries, who typically deal with a number of manufacturers or other suppliers of goods, are in unique positions to serve as conduits of information.

Intermediaries, being "in the middle," are uniquely placed not only to pass information from producers to other channel members, but to collect information from channel members and retail shoppers and return it to producers. For example, retailers may be faced with serious consumer complaints about a product or some product-related matter such as repair service. The retailers *should* then pass this information backwards in the channel to the other intermediaries, who bring the matter to the attention of the producer. "Should" is the key word here. Too often, whether because of apathy or the fear of somehow being blamed for a problem, intermediaries fail to perform this potentially valuable service. Marketers at all levels should encourage communication throughout channels of distribution because the satisfaction of all channel members and the consumer is at stake.

Facilitating Functions: The Intermediaries' "Hidden" Tasks

We have now discussed the marketing organization's performance of the major communication functions of buying and selling, or transferring of title, and the functions that comprise physical distribution, such as sorting, transportation, and storage. The transportation and storage functions of channel intermediaries are their most obvious contributions to the operation of the market system. However, intermediaries perform additional, so-called facilitating functions, which are not quite so apparent to observers of a channel in operation.

The tasks of a channel intermediary can be so varied that it is nearly an impossibility to list all the facilitating functions such a channel member might perform. However, there are three major categories of facilitating functions that should be mentioned specifically. There are the functions of providing "extra" services, offering credit, and risk-taking.

Extra Services Provided by Intermediaries. Channel members, particularly inter-

mediaries, can and do provide a whole range of "extra" services that increases the efficiency and effectiveness of the channel; intermediaries thus perform a **service function.** For many products, the availability of a post-sale *repair service* is an absolute necessity. Office photocopiers always seem to need either routine maintenance or minor and major overhauls. Wholesalers and retailers of such machines usually offer such repair services on a contract or "emergency" basis. They also carry necessary supplies like paper. Other products are not so prone to breakdowns, yet buyers of hand-held calculators or telephones like to know that repair service is available should it ever be needed. Honoring *manufacturers' guarantees* can be another responsibility of intermediaries.

A variety of *management services* can also be provided by channel intermediaries. In the food industry, for example, wholesalers offer a variety of such services including computerized accounting systems, inventory planning, store site selection, store layout planning, and management training programs. Of course, they also supply their customers with food products and help to stock the shelves.[8] The extra services offered are good business for the wholesalers, to be sure, in that (1) they attract customers to the wholesaler offering the services and (2) they help to keep those food retailer customers in business and successful. The services, if not offered by *every* competing wholesaler, can provide differential advantages to the food wholesaler willing to invest in them.

Wholesalers can draw patronage to themselves by other services, too. They may offer help in preparing advertisements. Wholesalers can offer a line of private brand goods or a wholesaler-owned label smaller retailers can use to create an image similar to that of larger chains. Some of the names of "behind the scenes" food wholesalers offering extensive management services are Scot-Lad Foods, Pacific Gamble Robinson, Scrivner, and Fleming Foods. Had you heard of them before?

---

[8]Carol Kurtis, "Bigger Slice of the Pie: Independent Grocers (and Their Suppliers) Carve One," *Barrons,* March 29, 1976, p. 11.

EXHIBIT 12-3

Summary of Marketing Functions a Channel Intermediary Performs for Its Suppliers and Its Customers

Marketing Functions	Suppliers	Customers
Physical distribution functions	Breaking bulk Accumulating bulk Creating assortments Transportation Storage	Sorting into desired quantities Assorting items into desired variety Delivery (transportation) Storage
Communication functions	Promotion, especially selling and communication of product information Gathering customer information	Buying based on interpretation of customer needs Dissemination of information
Facilitating functions	Financing customer purchases Service Risk-taking	Credit financing Repair service and management assistance Holding products and supplies until sale is made

Credit Services. Most channel intermediaries also perform a **credit function** by offering *credit service* of one kind or another. There are some wholesalers and retailers who operate exclusively on a cash-and-carry basis, promising to pass related savings on to their customers, but they are a relatively small number of the millions of channel intermediaries operating in the United States.

Some credit services provided by channel members may not be immediately obvious. Accepting MasterCard or Visa, in fact, costs the retailer a fee in the form of a percent of the sales made to be paid to the credit card company. Moreover, retailers run certain risks in accepting credit cards and may, in certain circumstances, be held responsible for non-payments. Sears, Montgomery Ward, and many other retailers offer their own credit plans, which are more clear-cut provisions of service than just accepting an "outside" card. Clothing and furniture stores typically offer credit plans that do not require the use of cards. This, too, is a more apparent credit service than MasterCard acceptance.

Wholesalers and other non-retailer channel members may provide credit in a number of obvious and not-so-obvious ways. A supplier may have a credit system so unique that buyers pay particular notice. However, supplier credit systems are generally so widespread throughout a trade that buyers scarcely see the credit system as a true service. Middlemen in many fields routinely offer 30, 60, or more days to pay for merchandise ordered. Often the days do not start "counting" until the goods are delivered to the buyer's place of business. Furthermore, it is common for sellers not to "enforce" the time period allowed for payment, thus extending more credit to the buyer. In effect, such a service permits the buyer to make some money on a product before having to pay for it. In short, most channel intermediaries favor their customers with sizable credit services even when those services are not particularly obvious.

Risk-Taking. In almost everything they do, channel intermediaries perform a **risk-taking function.** When purchasing a product from a manufacturer or supplier of any type, intermediaries run the risk of getting stuck with an item that falls out of favor with the buying public because of fashion shifts or quickly dying fads. It is also possible for the product to spoil while in storage or be lost through fire or some other disaster. Intermediaries bear these risks in addition to incurring market risk.

Intermediaries run obvious risks in offering credit to individuals and organizations to whom they sell. They take legal risks in that intermediaries, not just manufacturers, can be held responsible for problems caused by faulty products or misleading claims.

When intermediaries, for whatever reason, seek to avoid the channel service of risk-taking, the distribution system loses effectiveness. In hard economic times, for example, retailers and wholesalers are tempted to engage in hand-to-mouth buying, ordering small quantities of products and attempting to sell those before placing yet another small order. Such behavior defeats the whole purpose of the marketing channel by eliminating the "buy in large quantities—sell in smaller quantities" premise on which most channels are based.

Exhibit 12-3 summarizes the basic functions that channel intermediaries perform.

CHANNELS OF DISTRIBUTION: A SYSTEM OF INTERDEPENDENCY

We now turn to a discussion of typical channels of distribution used by marketers of consumer and industrial products. Before dealing with the construction of specific channels, attention should be drawn to the fact that any channel of distribution is a system of interdependency among all its members. If this is recognized by all channel participants, the channel operates properly and smoothly.

When a manufacturer seeks the help of an intermediary in distributing products, it relinquishes some measure of control over its own products. However, the manufacturer gains the benefit of not having to complete or finance the relinquished activities. It is thus freed to concentrate on the activities it can best perform. Some manufacturers, realizing that production is the activity they can best handle, surrender virtually all marketing activities to intermediaries. Thus, the use of channel intermediaries is a manifestation of specialization of labor or, in this case, specialization of management.

The efficiency of the distribution system is affected by **channel interdependency** because the actions of one channel member can greatly affect the performance of another or of the channel as a whole. Although the survival of intermediaries is in grave jeopardy if the manufacturer's operation fails, the manufacturer may also be driven out of business by the mistakes and failures of distributors. "The manufacturer is so dependent on the successful performance of the group of small suppliers and dealers that he cannot afford to let them sink or swim on their own merits."[9] Channel success is rooted in a community of interest and functional interdependency.

ALTERNATE CHANNELS OF DISTRIBUTION

Some organizations choose to sell their products directly to the consumer or industrial user; others make use of long channels that include numbers of wholesalers, agents, and retailers to reach buyers.[10] Channels may be distinguished by the number of intermediaries they include; the more intermediaries, the longer the channel is said to be.

The number of channel alternatives available to marketers is nearly limitless. Our discussion focuses on the most common channels of

---

[9]Valentine F. Ridgeway, "Administration of Manufacturer-Dealer Systems," *Administrative Science Quarterly*, March 1957, pp. 464–483.

[10]Because a retailer is a marketer who sells to an ultimate consumer, there can be, in fact, only one retailer of a single unit of a product though there could be any number of other kinds of intermediaries.

TAKING CARE OF OTHERS: THE WHOLESALER'S FUNCTION

The Morand Brothers Beverage Company, a wholesale liquor company, was founded in Chicago in 1884. It serves as a full-service wholesaler in the Chicago area for E. and J. Gallo Winery, Forman Distillers Company, Jack Daniels Distillery, and many other producers. Michael J. Romano, Jr., chairman of the company, explains how important the distributor is to the success or failure of a liquor brand.

"The distiller needs the distributor to execute the marketing ideas he has. Take Jack Daniels. We want to make sure the product is in distribution and exactly where it is. We ask the retailer to place it at eye level to encourage impulse buying." The company also makes sure its products are available in all sizes that can compete with similar products and that promotional material is prominently displayed.

Promotion is an effort necessary to the success of both sides. The distributor, by promoting the brands he carries, helps himself and the distiller. But the distributor needs a specific type of promotion. Morand Bros. does not promote Morand Bros. To the retailer, the company can only offer its price book and position prices competitively. Backed by good service and delivery, these are the nuts and bolts of attracting the retail business.

The wholesaler is important to both the manufacturer and retailer. Especially if it is an effective distributor such as Morand Bros.

Source: Anna Sobczynski, "Self-Made Plans Chicago Story," *Advertising Age*, August 16, 1982, p. m-37.

A neighborhood bakery is a direct channel of distribution.

distribution. Exhibit 12-4 shows the primary channels utilized by marketers of consumer and industrial goods. They range from the direct channel of manufacturer-to-consumer to far more complex models.

The Direct Channel

A good example of the direct channel is the neighborhood bakery that converts flour, water,

and other raw materials into a product and then retails the product, providing any other functions that might be necessary to complete the transaction. Although the direct channel is familiar to all of us because of the direct marketing activities of such firms as Avon Products, this channel of distribution is most commonly found in the marketing of industrial goods. A manufacturer-marketer of a technical product like fiber optic cables, or of any other industrial good, may find it necessary to have knowledgeable factory-trained sales representatives call directly on individual industrial users.

The Manufacturer-Retailer Channel

The manufacturer-retailer channel is a commonly employed one when the retailer involved is a sizable organization, such as a department

EXHIBIT 12-4

The Primary Channels of Distribution

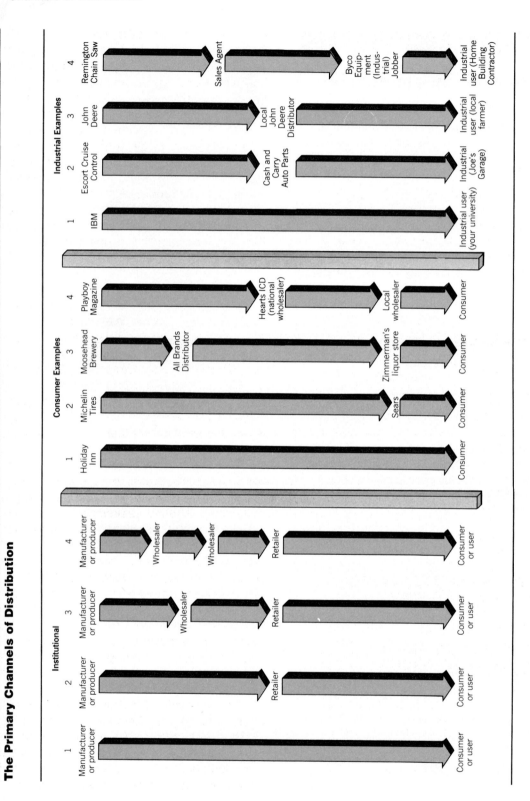

KING COLA'S KINGDOM SYSTEM

King Cola, founded by a former president of Pepsi Cola, had a short life during the late 1970s and early 1980s. The company was lost in the shuffle during a period of intensive comparative advertising and price warfare between Pepsi Cola and Coca-Cola. The company did innovate a unique distribution system for the soft drink industry. The management of King Cola believed that the big established cola companies, entrenched with hundreds of bottlers, were utilizing an old, restrictive distribution method. The store-door delivery method in which bottlers distributed the product they package in cans and bottles directly to the dealer was eliminated in the King Cola's distribution system. In King Cola's system, the United States was divided into 29 franchise areas, called Kingdoms. The Kingdom (wholesale distributor) operated under a franchise arrangement, buying the King Cola concentrate, produced at a central plant in New Jersey, from the parent company. Then custom packers, acting under contract to King Cola franchisers, added sugar and water to the concentrate and packaged the product in cans and bottles. The product was then shipped to the food chain's central warehouses which delivered the King Cola product to the individual stores in a manner similar to that utilized by most markets of nonperishables. Food brokers were utilized to maintain the product's positioning on the shelves.

Source: Based on "Here Comes King Cola," *Dunn's Review,* June 1979, pp. 72–76, "Now the King Cola Challenge," *Sales and Marketing Management,* November 1978, pp. 22–23, and "King Cola in Chapter 11," *Advertising Age,* November 9, 1981, p. 98.

store chain, or a mass merchandiser, such as a *Sears.* This type of retail marketing organization may prefer to deal directly with manufacturers to be able to order specially made or "spec" merchandise, or the retailer may prefer to deal direct because it may obtain a discount or other benefits that are important enough that the retailer is willing to perform many wholesaling functions. Alternatively, in an effort to please its large retailer customer, the manufacturer may agree to perform the wholesaler functions. Efficiencies that accrue to a manufacturer because of the large orders placed by a Sears or Penney's can more than offset the wholesaling costs the manufacturer may have to absorb.

The Manufacturer-Wholesaler-Industrial User Channel

Since, by definition, retailers deal with consumers, there is no industrial goods distribution channel that directly parallels the manufacturer-retailer channel. However, there is an industrial goods trade channel that utilizes just one wholesale intermediary who performs a function much like that of a retailer. This is the manufacturer-industrial distributor-industrial user channel. This type of wholesaler is also called by other names that vary from industry to industry; among the most common terms used is **jobber.**

Snap-On Tools, maker of socket wrenches and other hand tools, uses industrial distributors who, working out of well-stocked vans, call directly on Snap-On's customers, who are professional mechanics. Industrial distributors can also operate storelike facilities that industrial buyers such as electricians or plumbers may patronize. In either format, industrial distributors perform storage and communications functions. They may, as in the Snap-On example, provide delivery, and could also be engaged in credit or other functions.

The industrial distributor is classified a merchant intermediary because the industrial distributor takes title to the goods. The taking-of-title function is a major reason why this type of intermediary is found almost exclusively in channels handling relatively inexpensive or stan-

An industrial distributor is an important link in the manufacturer-wholesaler-industrial user channel of distribution.

dardized merchandise, such as hand tools or plumbing, electrical, or automotive parts. No middleman who had to buy the items to be offered for sale would want to stock up on very expensive or specialized goods. They might not sell, leaving the merchant "stuck" with hard-to-dispose-of inventory.

The Manufacturer-Wholesaler-Retailer Channel

The manufacturer-wholesaler-retailer channel of distribution is the most commonly used channel structure for consumer goods. This is because most consumer goods are widely used by many different individuals. It would be virtually impossible for the Wrigley Company, for example, to deal individually with every retailer stocking chewing gum, let alone every consumer of gum. Thus a long channel, using at least two intermediaries, is needed to distribute the product over the necessary areas.

The Manufacturer-Agent-Wholesaler-Retailer Channel

Some manufacturers, for reasons that might include a lack of experience or expertise in marketing a particular product line, choose to permit *manufacturers' agents* or *selling agents* to handle the marketing of their products. Such agents do not take title to the goods they sell, and usually earn commissions rather than a salary. These agents may, depending on circumstances and the product they offer, sell to retailers, wholesalers, or industrial users.

The wide range of customers to whom agents sell suggests their main attraction to manufacturers—flexibility. One type of agent intermediary, the broker, can be utilized on an off-and-on basis as needed. No continuing relationship, and, therefore, no continuing financial or other obligation, is necessary. Similarly, manufacturers' agents operate on a commission basis within fixed geographic territories. Therefore, they can be employed in "thin" market areas where potential sales do not seem to justify employment of a manufacturer's own sales force.

The Variety of Channels

As the foregoing discussion suggests, the variety of channel possibilities is extensive indeed. That is because marketers are constantly seeking new ways to perform the distribution function. Manufacturers and intermediaries have

7-UP BOTTLING COMPANIES

A 7-Up Bottling Company is typically a local, independently-owned business concern holding the right, by franchise agreement, to sell and distribute 7-Up. Of the 464 7-Up Bottling Companies in the United States the smallest may be family operations selling 100,000 to 200,000 cases annually in relatively small population areas. Larger 7-Up bottling operations in urban centers may sell more than a million cases of 7-Up in a month.

Bottlers purchase 7-Up Extract from The Seven-Up Company and convert the extract into bottled, canned or Fountain 7-Up. They are charged with selling, distributing and merchandising the product to retail stores, restaurants, and other outlets.

Typically, bottling plants are set up for a variety of rather different functions. The plants bottle and can 7-Up on sophisticated high-speed production lines, and maintain laboratory and line checks on purity and quality throughout the production process. Plant facilities include not only conveyors, fillers, sealers and packaging machinery, but also warehouse areas for container supplies and for the finished, packaged 7-Up products. A trucking fleet is maintained for delivery and distribution services.

Bottling company personnel coordinate local marketing, advertising, promotions, sales and merchandising activities with national 7-Up marketing programs developed by The Seven-Up Company. Bottling company employees in a community thus include sales and marketing executives, field sales staffs, clerical and accounting personnel, production and quality control technicians, production line and warehouse workers, route truck drivers and others. A 7-Up Bottler must be a well-rounded businessman or businesswoman to master the complexities of a modern, competitive soft drink industry.

Source: From "7-Up at a Glance," a pamphlet of the 7-Up Company, Corporate Affairs Department, 121 South Meramec, St. Louis, MO. 63105. Used with permission.

both contributed to this effort and have developed all sorts of variations on the basic theme of distribution. Some, therefore, operate from trucks, others from stores. Some grant credit, others do not. Some carry full lines of merchandise, others are specialists. Each variation was developed in an effort to better perform the distribution function and thereby to attract business.

ARE CHANNELS OF DISTRIBUTION WHAT TEXTBOOKS SAY THEY ARE?

As we have seen, there are many alternative channels of distribution available to marketing managers. Decisions concerning the selection of a channel or determining how many wholesalers or retailers or other channel intermediaries are needed to achieve the desired degree of market exposure are extremely important and difficult to make. Our discussion has focused on channel members as institutions. In actual practice, the determination of a channel may be complicated by less-than-perfect institutions.

A famous marketing management article raised the question: "Are Channels of Distribution What the Textbooks Say They Are?"[11] The

---

[11]Philip McVey, "Are Channels of Distribution What Textbooks Say They Are?" *Journal of Marketing,* January 1960, pp. 61–64.

EXHIBIT 12-5

Channel Arrangement: Wood Flush Door Suppliers

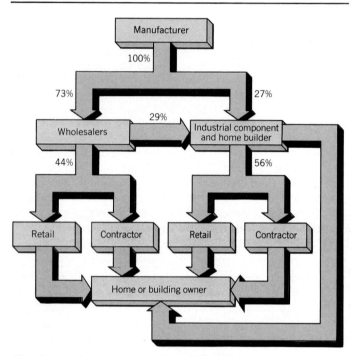

Note: Figures indicate percent of products distributed in this manner.

Source: W.G. Bowne and E.D Reiten, "Auditing Distribution Channels," *Journal of Marketing,* July 1978, p. 41.

point made was that orderly presentations of channel possibilities, such as the one in Exhibit 12-4, are somewhat misleading. The baker who sells his or her own products may also be a retailer of other producers' candy or specialty items.

Consider this complicated situation. General Cinema in Chestnut Hill, Massachusetts, is the nation's largest bottler of 7-Up and the developer of its own product, Sunkist orange soda. Is General Cinema a retailer because of its business as a theater operator, a middleman operation because of its 7-Up bottling franchise, or a manufacturer because of the Sunkist product?

Another reason that channels are not always what textbooks suggest they are is that many areas of the country are not served by the types of intermediaries a given manufacturer may wish to employ. Many manufacturers routinely use **multiple channels,** distributing different products or even a single product in several different ways, depending on the desires of particular customers. For example, the Simpson Timber Company's Columbia Door Division uses the channels shown in Exhibit 12-5 for its wood flush doors used in home and building construction. Sometimes a manufacturer has multiple channels of distribution because the product is sold in a variety of retail outlets such as both grocery stores and drugstores. **Scrambled merchandising** occurs when a product is sold in many different types of retail stores. A sports store selling tennis balls may utilize a different type of wholesaler or be involved in a different type of channel of distribution than a department store selling tennis balls. The manufacturer that wishes to satisfy the consumer's desire to have the product available in a variety of outlets will have to utilize a **multiple channel strategy.** Text-book descriptions, while accurate for many situations, generally cannot describe the complexity of channels unless a particular example warrants great detail.

VERTICAL MARKETING SYSTEMS

In many industries, such as the fast-food restaurant industry, the dominant distribution structure is the vertical marketing system. The concept of a vertical marketing system emerged along with the need to manage or administer the functions performed by intermediaries at two or more levels of the channel of distribution. **Vertical marketing systems** or vertically integrated marketing systems consist of networks of vertically aligned establishments that are managed as a centrally administered distribution system.[12] These vertical marketing systems are centrally administered to achieve technological, managerial, and promotional economies of scale through the integration, coordination, and synchronization of transactions and marketing activities necessary to perform the distribution function. There are three types of vertical marketing systems: *corporate, contractual* and *administered.*

Corporate Systems

The **corporate vertical marketing system** can be exemplified by a retailer, such as Sears, who integrates backward into manufacturing to assure quality control over production, and corporate control over the distribution system. A manufacturer may obtain complete control of the successive stages of distribution by vertically integrating through ownership. Sherwin-Williams administers a corporate vertical marketing system by owning more than 2,000 retail paint outlets.

Administered Systems

The second major model of a vertical market channel system is the administered system. Here a strong position of leadership is the source of influence over channel activities rather than outright ownership. The "administrator" could be any channel member who has the size or market clout to dominate the others.

Administered systems generally are constructed around a line of merchandise rather than the complete manufacturing, wholesaling, or retailing operation. For example, suppose that a manufacturer wishes to ensure that wholesalers and retailers follow its comprehensive program of marketing activities. In the **administered vertical marketing system,** the coordination of marketing activities is achieved through planning and management of a mutually beneficial program, made attractive (e.g., by offering attractive discounts or financial assistance) to all parties. Coordination is achieved through a dominant channel member or leader. Examples of strong channel leadership and administered marketing systems may be found in companies such as O.M. Scott and Sons Company (lawn products), Villager (women's apparel), and Magnavox (home entertainment). Recognize that this position of strength can be held by a wholesaler or a retailer as well as by a manufacturer.

Contractual Systems

The third vertical channel system is the contractual system. In a **contractual vertical marketing system,** channel leadership is assigned not by

---

[12]Bert C. McCammon, Jr., "Perspectives for Distribution Programming," in *Vertically Marketing Systems,* Louis P. Bucklin, ed. (Glenview, Ill.: Scott Foresman, 1970), p. 43, and William R. Davidson, "Changes in Distributive Institutions: A Reexamination, *The Canadian Marketer,* Winter 1975, pp. 7–13.

ownership or by less formal leadership, but by agreement in contract form. In such a channel, channel relationships are spelled out so that there is no question about distribution coordination. The relationship between McDonald's franchise holders and McDonald's headquarters is a contractual one wherein the rights and responsibilities of both parties are clearly identified. The idea behind such an approach to distribution is that if all parties live up to their sides of the agreement the system will work smoothly and well. In the main, this has certainly been the case for McDonald's, although the "secret" of McDonald's success is not merely the employment of a contractual vertical marketing system, but of working hard to make it succeed.

There are three subtypes of contractual systems: retailer cooperative organizations, wholesaler-sponsored voluntary chains, and franchises. A retail **cooperative organization** is a group of independent retailers that have combined their financial resources and their expertise in order to more effectively control their wholesaling needs. By capitalizing on economies of scale, they lower wholesaling costs by maintaining a centralized buying center. Yet these retailers are able to maintain their independence.

The **voluntary chain** is similar to the cooperative organization except that the wholesaler initiates the effort of combining services to a group of independent retailers. The retailers agree to utilize only the one wholesaler, while the wholesaler agrees to service all the organized retailers. Ace Hardware and Coast-to-Coast stores are examples.

A **franchise** is a contractual agreement between a *franchisor,* typically a manufacturer or a wholesaler, and a number of independent retailers (*franchisees*). The franchise agreement often gives the franchisor much discretion in controlling the operations of the small retailers. In exchange for fees, royalties, and a share of the profits, the franchisor offers assistance and often supplies. The franchisee is usually responsible for paying for insurance, property taxes, labor, and supplies. The franchise has been quite popular and often successful in the fast-food industry. Chuck E. Cheese Pizza Time Theaters, Pizza Hut, Godfather Pizza, and many others are franchises. McDonald's is the largest fast-food franchise operation. Of the 6,700 McDonald's outlets, 68 percent are franchised operations. In 1982, a 20-year franchise license for a McDonald's outlet cost about $325,000 plus 11.5 percent of annual sales.[13]

Franchising is prominent in the service industry as well. Consider such familiar names in the automotive field as Brakeman, Midas, and AAMCO. One of the main advantages of the contractual marketing system is the offering of a brand identity and a nationally recognizable storefront for a retail outlet. The Ethan Allen Carriage Houses, Holiday Inns, Burger Kings, and other franchise operations have strong identities. The person driving down the highway has a very clear conception of the products or services that will be found within the franchise.

MANAGING THE CHANNEL OF DISTRIBUTION

Distribution strategy requires the making of two major decisions. The first concerns *determining the structure of the channel of distribution.* The second concerns deciding on the *number of middlemen* or the *extent of distribution.*

Determining the Structure of the Channel

What determines whether a channel of distribution will be short or long? The selection criteria are influenced by the other elements of the marketing mix strategy, by organizational resources, and by a number of external environmental factors.

The Marketing Mix Strategy. The selection of the channel of distribution is just one of the vital strategic decisions concerning how to com-

---

[13]*Marketing and Media Decisions,* Spring 1982, p. 114.

EXHIBIT 12-6

The Business System: Xerox Versus Savin

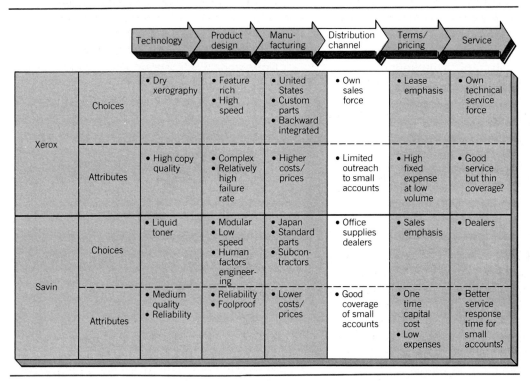

		Technology	Product design	Manu-facturing	Distribution channel	Terms/pricing	Service
Xerox	Choices	• Dry xerography	• Feature rich • High speed	• United States • Custom parts • Backward integrated	• Own sales force	• Lease emphasis	• Own technical service force
	Attributes	• High copy quality	• Complex • Relatively high failure rate	• Higher costs/prices	• Limited outreach to small accounts	• High fixed expense at low volume	• Good service but thin coverage?
Savin	Choices	• Liquid toner	• Modular • Low speed • Human factors engineer-ing	• Japan • Standard parts • Subcon-tractors	• Office supplies dealers	• Sales emphasis	• Dealers
	Attributes	• Medium quality • Reliability	• Reliability • Foolproof	• Lower costs/prices	• Good coverage of small accounts	• One time capital cost • Low expenses	• Better service response time for small accounts?

Source: Marketing News, January 21, 1983, p. 22.

pete with others offering the same product. For example, an organizational long-term strategic pricing plan may determine whether or not a company distributes the product through high margin outlets or through high volume outlets appealing to price-conscious consumers. Consider another example. Xerox utilizes its own sales force and sells direct, while Savin utilizes office supply dealers to help it market its product. Exhibit 12-6 shows that Savin Corporation is utilizing a distribution strategy that is part of its overall strategic plan to capture a major share of the low-end-office-copier business from its competitor Xerox.[14]

The *product's characteristics,* especially the tangible characteristics, play an important role in channel selection. For instance, if Maine lobsters are to be sold in Wichita, Kansas, the channel of distribution will be largely dictated by the perishability of the product. Many products require after-sale service; hence a middleman's technical repair service often is an important consideration when selecting a channel of distribution. The size, bulk, and weight of a product will determine whether short channels are necessary to reduce transportation and handling costs. Other product considerations such as the technical complexity, the replacement rate, the gross margin, and the image of the product will influence the type of channel selected.[15]

[14]"In Strategic Phase, Line Management Needs Business Research, Not Market Research," *Marketing News,* January 21, 1983, pp. 1, 22.

[15] See Leo Aspinwall, *Four Marketing Theories* (Boulder, Colo.: University of Colorado Bureau of Business Research, 1961), Chapter 3.

Organizational Resources. Arm and Hammer Heavy Duty Detergent is marketed by Church & Dwight, a small company when compared to Procter & Gamble and Colgate, its competitors. Church & Dwight utilizes 80 food brokers to market its product in supermarkets, whereas Procter & Gamble has the luxury of its own sales organization.[16]

Utilizing one or more marketing intermediaries disperses the responsibility for the performance of the distribution function. Thus, an organization that is unable or not interested in devoting large financial resources to have its own sales force, to store and hold a large inventory, or to provide other distribution functions, may utilize wholesalers or retailers to provide the resources or managerial expertise to handle these activities.

A company's existing channels of distribution for its other products are tremendous resources—they may be the main determinant in the selection of a channel of distribution. Fruit Roll-Ups, a new snack food item, will most likely be sold through the same channel of distribution as other General Mills products. The number of items in a manufacturer's product line helps determine the company's willingness to perform the distribution function. A large number of items will reduce the burden of overhead and other shared expenses that each brand must carry. Suppose a competitive manufacturer grants exclusive distribution rights to a wholesaler or retailer. The middleman carrying this line may not be willing to cooperate with another manufacturer. Moreover, it is possible that a competitive middleman will not be able to distribute the product of its choice because of these exclusive distribution rights.

In other situations a manufacturer may choose a strategy to differentiate its product from competitors by utilizing an alternate channel of distribution that is quite different. Thus, products sold by Land's End, a catalog reseller, compete differently from products sold in stores such as Macy's. The product gains a differential advantage because it has a unique channel of distribution. Or, when consumers frequently do comparison shopping, it may be important that the packaged goods product is displayed on the supermarket shelf next to its competitor.

External Environmental Criteria.

Consumer Preferences and Market Behavior. Customers' past behavior and preference for purchase location is a major selection criteria. Perhaps the ultimate consumer prefers to buy the product in a supermarket. If the supermarket prefers to purchase through wholesalers rather than directly from manufacturers, this has a dramatic impact on channel selection. At each market level, customer preferences must be considered. The trend toward scrambled merchandising has complicated the channel of distribution decision. Thus, if a manufacturer finds that some of its buyers prefer to purchase the product in drugstores and others prefer to buy the product in discount stores, multiple channels of distribution may be necessary.

The Nature and Availability of Middlemen. Most wholesalers and retailers specialize in regional or local geographical areas. In many cases, capable middlemen are either unavailable or unwilling to handle a product. When the Levi Strauss Company tried to market its Tailored Classic (high-quality, medium-price level) men's suits in 1980, the company found retailers resistant to handling the wool and wool-blended line because of the traditional Levi association with casual clothing. "Retailers envisioned the suit as a competitor to polyester clothing, not as a less expensive alternative to classier attire."[17] Retailers insisted on displaying the Levi's suit and sport coat line next to other low-priced clothing and demanded price reductions. Furthermore, many retailers would not carry the line because of the traditional Levi product line. When the preferred middleman is unavailable, a manufacturer may alter its channel of distribution, possibly by eliminating a wholesaler and going di-

---

[16] Jack J. Homichl, "The Ongoing Saga of Mother Baking Soda," *Advertising Age,* September 20, 1982, p. m–22.

[17] P. Solman and T. Friedman, *Life and Death on the Corporate Battlefield* (New York: Simon and Schuster, 1983), p. 126.

rectly to the ultimate consumer in a certain territory.

Other Environmental Factors. Any of the environmental forces discussed in Chapter 2 may have an impact on the channel of distribution. For example, the wholesaling and retailing structure in Japan is strongly influenced by political and legal factors. An organization must carefully consider all possible environmental forces before making the channel of distribution decision.

The Extent of Distribution: How Many Outlets?

Once the structure of the distribution channel has been determined, the manufacturer is faced with the problem of deciding on the intensity of distribution at each level within the channel. Determining the number of wholesalers and the number of retail outlets are important decisions that will determine the number of possible outlets where potential customers expect to find the product. The various degrees of distribution intensity are: (1) *intensive distribution,* (2) *selective distribution,* and (3) *exclusive distribution.*

Intensive Distribution. Products receiving intensive distribution may be presold with mass media advertising or presold by other means. Coca-Cola, for example, needs little personal selling and may be distributed in vending machines, supermarkets, drugstores, restaurants, and many other outlets.

Pennzoil intensively distributes its motor oil in service stations as well as in K-Mart's, Target stores, and other mass merchants where more than one-half of the U.S. car motor oil is sold. Furthermore, to increase the intensity of its distribution, Pennzoil purchased a large share of Jiffy-Lube International, the leading oil-change-while-you-wait franchise.[18]

The strategy of **intensive distribution** seeks to obtain maximum product exposure at the re-

tail level. When consumers will not go out of their way to purchase a product or will readily accept substitutes when the brand is not readily accessible, the appropriate strategy is to saturate every retail outlet with the product. Cigarettes, chewing gum, and other convenience goods normally receive intensive distribution. Intensive distribution at the wholesale level allows almost all appropriate wholesalers to carry the product.

Selective Distribution. At the retail level, a strategy of **selective distribution** restricts the sale of the product to a limited number of outlets. The manufacturers of Hathaway shirts focus their marketing efforts on certain selected outlets with the right store image. Each store selected must meet the company's performance standards while appealing to a select target market. As the intensity of distribution becomes more selective, the manufacturer may expect a greater effort on the part of the retailer (e.g., willingness to hold a larger inventory). Since retailers benefit from a limited number of competitors, they are expected to be more willing to accept the manufacturer's suggestions and control of the marketing strategy (e.g., supporting the list price).

Selective distribution is more commonly used for specialty and shopping goods as opposed to convenience goods. However, Noxell Corporation, the marketer of Noxzema and Cover Girl Brands of make-up and skin cream, selectively distributes its products in chain stores such as K-Mart and F.W. Woolco. It lets its competitors vie for distribution in the more prestigious department and specialty store business.[19] Its selective distribution strategy reaches its target market.

Exclusive Distribution. When a product requires aggressive personal selling, a complete inventory of the product line, repair service, or other special effort, a middleman may be granted an exclusive area. Generally, a manufac-

[18]"Pennzoil: Squeezing Out Lube-Oil Profits to Gamble on Natural Resources," *Business Week,* February 21, 1983, p. 119.

[19]"Noxell Glows in the Mass Market," *Business Week,* February 14, 1983, p. 148.

CATERPILLAR'S BACKBONE: A LONG DEALER NETWORK

Caterpillar Tractor Co.'s mammoth dealer network is probably the biggest obstacle to competitors who try to breach Caterpillar's markets. The dealerships are all independently owned, but a competitor's chances of wooing any dealer into his own camp seem almost nonexistent. "Our average dealer can count on a steady income from service, maintenance, and used-machine business generated by at least several thousand machines operating in his territory, and competitors who don't have that base can't afford the investment it takes to provide first-class services," maintains E.C. Chapman, executive vice-president for marketing.

Indeed, the 93 domestic and 137 overseas dealerships have blossomed into rich and diversified companies in their own right. With the strong encouragement of Caterpillar, many have established related businesses, such as refurbishing tractor parts and rebuilding diesel engines, that add to both their service capability and their own bottom lines. Average sales of $100 million and a typical net worth approaching $4 million give the dealerships the financial muscle to expand selling and service capabilities at the same pace that Caterpillar expands its product line. During the past year, dealers spent more than $200 million to add new buildings and equipment.

"We approach our dealers as partners in the enterprise, not as agents or middlemen," says Caterpillar Chairman Lee L. Morgan. "We worry as much about their performance as they do themselves." The dealers themselves are effusive in their praise of relations with Caterpillar. "They have consistently supplied us with superior products and a high-quality program of parts and product information," says Frank O. Moyle, executive vice-president of Patten Industries Inc., a dealer in Chicago's Elmhurst suburb.

But the strength of the dealer system lies less in the relations with Caterpillar than in the dealers' relations with customers. "It is our people—not Caterpillar's—who have to understand the customer's business well enough to match his needs with the right equipment," Moyle says.

Patten comes close to being an archetypal Caterpillar dealer. Besides making routine sales calls to promote business, Patten has added branches in Rockford, Ill., and Hammond, Ind., since its founding in 1933. Today it has more than 400 employees, a production line to rebuild Caterpillar engines, and a shop that refurbishes track shoes and other tractor parts. Its customers can buy rebuilt parts that last about 80% as long as new ones yet cost only half the price. Caterpillar loses some new-parts sales, but it encourages the practice because its equipment becomes more economical in the long run for the customer.

Caterpillar goes out of its way to make sure dealers' inventories are at the right level. There is a national computer network linking all dealers to the Morton (Ill.) distribution center, enabling them to order any part they need for delivery the next day. The company will buy back parts the dealers do not sell. And it tries to pace its introduction of new products according to dealers' capabilities. For example, because many dealers are still gearing up to handle the expansion of engine sales, Caterpillar will probably limit its new-product introductions over the next few years, although it has been developing a four-wheel drive farm tractor.

The company also conducts dozens of training programs for dealers and product demonstrations for their customers. Last year it assembled a large group of dealers and company personnel in Europe to demonstrate the competitive advantages of Caterpillar's excavating equipment. And it invited 300 mining executives from eight countries to New Mexico for a demonstration of Caterpillar machines in mining operations.

The company even conducts a course in Peoria to encourage dealers' children to remain in the business. "We had a dealer's son who was studying for the ministry and had a secondary interest in music," Chapman recalls. "By the time we sent him home, he changed his career plan. He has become one of our most successful dealers."

Source: From "Caterpillar's Backbone: A Long Dealer Network," *Business Week,* May 4, 1981, p. 77. Used with permission.

turer or wholesaler that grants a retailer **exclusive distribution** expects a maximum sales effort or expects to gain something from the prestige or efficiency of the retail outlet. Exclusive distribution agreements often involve contractual arrangements. Suppliers often will have written agreements with exclusive distributors stipulating certain responsibilities that are too important to be left to a mutual understanding. Contracts are signed, outlining tenure of appointment, trading area, sale conditions, warranty considerations, and extent of product line coverage. However, exclusive dealing may not be legal if it tends to lessen competition in the exclusive geographical area.

Caterpillar Tractor Company relies on a strong network of exclusive dealers. Its president and chairman made this statement:

We have a tremendous regard for our dealers. We do not bypass or undercut them. Some of our competitors do and their dealers quit. Caterpillar dealers don't quit, they die rich.[20]

It illustrates the nature of cooperation and degree of loyalty that can exist in an exclusive distribution system.

The extent of distribution must be determined at each level within the channel of distribution. For example, a manufacturer like Coca-Cola may execute an intensive distribution strategy at the retail level and a strategy of exclusive distribution at the wholesale level.

ISSUES CONCERNING THE INTERDEPENDENCY AMONG CHANNEL MEMBERS

Since the actions of one channel member may greatly influence the performance of another channel member, the relations among channel members are of considerable interest. The retailer relies on the manufacturer to create an adequate sales potential through advertising, product development, and other marketing strategies. An exclusive dealer's welfare is in jeopardy if a manufacturer's marketing strategy is not successful. A manufacturer may depend on the successful performance of a small group of wholesalers who cannot be left to sink or swim on their own merits.[21]

The objectives and marketing strategies of two channel members (e.g., manufacturer and retailer) may be in total harmony. Both parties recognize that their tasks are linked together, and by working together they can jointly exploit a marketing opportunity. The manufacturer promptly delivers a quality product with a good reputation; the retailer prices the product as expected and carries an inventory of the full product line. **Channel cooperation** is a situation in which the marketing objectives and strategies of two channel members are harmonious.

Channel Conflict

Channel conflict is a term utilized to discuss *vertical* conflicts among members of the same channel of distribution. This should not be confused with economic competition between two like intermediaries at the same level in the channel, such as Macy's and Gimbel's, which is sometimes referred to as *horizontal* conflict.[22] The term **channel conflict** refers to a situation in which the desires of channel members are not sufficiently integrated. The behavior of one channel member may be perceived to be inhibiting the attainment of another channel member's goals.[23]

---

[20] "Caterpillar—Sticking to the Basics to Stay Competitive," *Business Week,* May 4, 1981, p. 74.

[21] Valentine F. Ridgway, "Administration of Manufacturer-Dealer Systems," *Administrative Science Quarterly,* March 1957, pp. 464–483.

[22] See Joseph C. Palamountain, *The Politics of Distribution* (Cambridge, Mass.: Harvard University Press, 1955).

[23] L.W. Stern and R.H. Gorman, *Conflict in Distribution Channels,* in L.W. Stern, *Distribution Channels: Behavioral Dimensions* (Boston, Mass.: Houghton Mifflin Company, 1969), p. 156.

For example, consider the following instance of channel conflict. In 1982, Levi Strauss and Company, for the first time, sold its products to Sears, Roebuck and Company and the J.C. Penney Stores. This alignment with Sears and Penney's caused considerable channel conflict among many of Levi's department and specialty store accounts. The result of this conflict is that some major department store chains retaliated by paring their orders to include only the most popular Levi's items, such as the basic straight-leg jean and blue-jean jackets, thus eliminating clothes that were not being carried by the mass merchandisers.[24]

Vertical conflict can arise when a wholesaler is frustrated because the manufacturer bypasses it and sells directly to the larger accounts. Another typical instance may occur when a dealer believes its investment in inventory should be minimized, but its distributor's promise of speedy delivery cannot be relied on because the distributor does not maintain the proper inventory level. There may be vertical conflict when sales are down and, consequently, manufacturers accuse dealers or distributors of failing to promote aggressively. Other issues of conflict relate to manufacturers', wholesalers', or retailers' opinions that they are not making enough money on the product line.

In some cases, the causes of conflict are overt and readily identifiable because of differences in opinions, goals, or attitudes. For example, when Levi's started marketing its five-pocket jeans through Sears and the J.C. Penney Company, there was no question about the cause of the conflict. Furthermore, when department store chains such as R.H. Macy interpreted the new Levi channel strategy as damaging to the brand's fashion credibility and a threat to their mark-ups, they made the conflict more identifiable by ordering replacement brands such as Lee.[25] In other instances the cause of conflict is latent.

Channel conflict generally results from the

CHANNEL PROBLEMS AT BRANIFF

In 1982, while staring into the jaws of bankruptcy, the managers of Braniff Airways came up with what some observers termed an irresponsible, desperation plan to sell tickets. The airline offered its hometown market of Dallas a "Great Dollar Sale." For every round-trip Braniff ticket purchase, a customer received a second round-trip ticket for just a dollar. The promotion was a great short-term success, increasing advance bookings by 25 percent.

But Braniff sold more than half its tickets through travel agents and while agents' enthusiasm for the "Dollar Sale" in no way matched Braniff's. Agents, who had not been forewarned of the special promotion, were not ready for the ticket orders that poured into their offices. Their regular business customers were often neglected as agents sought to handle the hoards of pleasure travelers attracted by the dollar deal. Many agents ran out of ticket stock. The overriding problem, according to the president of a major agency, was that the airline did not understand the problems of the travel agents who sell their tickets. More tickets sold is not the measure of success. Commission earning on a $1 ticket are pretty slim. The promotion was a source of great channel conflict.

Source: Based on information in "Aviation: A New Braniff Gimmick the Agents Hate," *Business Week,* March 1, 1982, p. 29.

---

absence of a clearly identified locus of formal channel power and disagreements about the channel's common purpose. In the absence of a designated channel leader with a mutually agreed-on authority to reward, punish, plan, coordinate, or otherwise dictate the activities of its members, cooperation may break down.[26]

[24]"It's Back to Basics for Levi's," *Business Week,* March 8, 1982, p. 77.

[25]"How Levi's Is Helping Lee Sell More Jeans," *Business Week,* May 23, 1983, p. 46.

[26]R.D. Buzzell, R.E.M. Nourse, J.B. Mathews, Jr., and T. Levitt, *Marketing: A Contemporary Analysis* (New York: McGraw-Hill Book Company, 1972), p. 464.

If the causes of conflict are overt and readily identifiable, the management of conflict may be reasonably straightforward.[27] However, when the cause of conflict is latent, the issues of conflict are perceived as frustrations. In this type of situation, the managerial skills of channel members need improving. The need to manage channel conflict depends on the intensity of the conflict, and the intensity of conflict may vary considerably. At one extreme, conflict may approach "full-blown warfare." At the other extreme, conflict may be a latent frustration or slowly smoldering antagonism of one party for the other.[28]

Early theorists on channel conflict suggested that channel system goals should be to minimize conflict and maximize cooperation.[29] While excessive conflict is likely to be detrimental to efficient performance in the channel of distribution, there may be some instances where a certain level of conflict is desirable. Conflict may be regarded "as potentially beneficial to the system when it brings about a more equitable allocation of political power and economic resources by the formation of new countervailing forces, and greater balance and stability within the system. Conflict is destructive when a lack of recognition of mutual objectives results."[30]

While there is some question about the most efficient level of conflict, it is generally argued that conflict should not be unmanaged.[31] Unfortunately, Mark Twain's comment about the weather ("Everybody talks about the weather, but nobody does anything about it.") to some extent applies to discussions of conflict within channels of distribution.

---

[27]This paragraph is adapted from W.G. Zikmund and R. Catalanello, "Channel Development: An Operational System for Managing Channel Conflict," *Journal of the Academy of Marketing Science*, Vol. 141 (1976), pp. 801–814.

[28]Louis P. Bucklin, *A Theory of Distribution Structure* (Berkeley: University of California Press, 1966), p. 591.

[29]Bruce Mallen, "Theory of Retailer Supplier Control, Conflict and Cooperation," *Journal of Retailing,* Summer 1963, pp. 24–28.

[30]Henry Assael, "Constructive Role of Interorganizational Conflict," *Administrative Science Quarterly*, vol. 14 (1969), pp. 573–582.

[31]For a discussion of conflict in channel efficiency see Bert Rosenbloom, "Conflict in Channel Efficiency: Some Conceptual Models for the Decision Maker," *Journal of Marketing,* July 1973, pp. 26–30.

POSSIBLE CHANNEL CONFLICTS

Here are some possible channel conflicts.

■ A manufacturer may expect an intermediary, be it a wholesaler or retailer, to handle the manufacturer's products and to promote those products. The intermediary may prefer to put stress on another manufacturer's products if those are the ones its customers seem to prefer or if higher margins are provided on those items.

■ A retailer may purchase brand name soups from a wholesaler but also buy soup from a supplier which it then sells vigorously as a higher margin, private-label product.

■ Manufacturers often think in terms of national or international markets, while retailers and wholesalers almost always have a more local point of view. The role the manufacturer wants a local intermediary to play may fit well into that manufacturer's "big picture" but not suit the role the local marketer wishes to play.

■ A manufacturer or wholesaler may want to distribute a product as widely as possible; that is, have it for sale in many retail stores and, possibly, available through mail order, telephone sales, or other means. This often conflicts with the distribution approach local retailers would prefer—exclusive or nearly exclusive dealerships that protect the local retailer from competition.

■ Within a single market, many retailers may carry the same product. Many wholesalers may do the same. The high level of competition that can result from such a situation may lead to intermediaries resenting the manufacturer's distribution policies and each other as well.

Channel Power

When one organization in the channel of distribution is able to exert its **channel power** and influence over other channel members, this organization is referred to as the **channel leader** or **channel captain.** For instance, Home Box Office is the channel captain for the distribution of movies on pay TV. HBO virtually dictates how much it will pay for a film.[32] Furthermore, HBO may finance films while they are in production. In recent years HBO has become a major source of financing for independent movie producers. In a similar manner, a large retailer such as Sears may be able to exert such economic power, by the size of its purchase, that it may dictate the marketing strategy to less powerful channel members. By placing an order for a private label brand, Sears may insist on certain product specifications, prices, or delivery dates. A small manufacturer may be so dependent on the Sears order that it changes the specifications on its own brand so it can produce a product that meets Sears specifications.

An organization, such as a manufacturer of technical instruments, may also be able to wield channel power because of its expertise and ability to introduce technological innovations.[33]

Anheuser-Busch is a channel leader because of its marketing expertise. To support its wholesalers, Anheuser-Busch offers extensive training seminars on topics such as financial management and warehousing.[34] It has developed a computerized shelf-space management program for retailers that audits sales, margins, and turnover by brand and package.

REVERSE DISTRIBUTION

In recent decades, the recycling of waste has become a major ecological goal.[35] Whether recycling is viewed as a *backward channel of distribution,* or as somehow extending the channel from consumer *on to* a buyer or middleman participating in the recycling process, the ultimate consumer who seeks to recycle waste materials must undergo a role change.[36]

By recycling your old newspapers or metal cans, you become a "producer" of a usable product that has some economic utility. Thus, in this **backward channel,** the consumer has become the first link in a process rather than the last. The typical consumer probably does not create an elaborate strategy relating to the newspapers and cans given to the Boy Scouts or any other agency. Indeed, the backward channel is likely to be run by traditional manufacturers of paper or cans. Yet the flow of goods is the reverse of what most descriptions of marketing operations suggest.

Because our appreciation of environmental problems is relatively new, backward channels of distribution have historically been very primitive, although some recycling has always existed. For example, ecologically concerned civic groups have sponsored paper drives and community clean-up days. Such groups are, in essence, performing channel intermediary functions in primitive fashion. In some cases, traditional middlemen have long practiced as a side-line what have come to be recognized as recycling activities.[37] Soda bottlers have accepted returnable bottles for years, but this was not seen as either a major part of their business or a contribution to the economy. However, in

---

[32]"How TV Is Revolutionizing Hollywood," *Business Week*, February 21, 1983, p. 78.

[33]For a theoretical perspective on power in the channel of distribution, see R.A. Robicheaux and A.I. el-Ansary," "A General Model for Understanding Channel Member Behavior," *Journal of Retailing*, Winter 1975–1976, pp. 13–30.

[34]"Anheuser-Busch: The King of Beers Still Rules," *Business Week*, July 12, 1982, p. 52.

[35]This section is based on W.G. Zikmund and W.J. Stanton, "Recycling Solid Waste: A Channel of Distribution Problem," *Journal of Marketing*, July 1971, pp. 34–39.

[36]See, for example, J.L. Grimm and J.B. Spalding, "Is Channel(s) Theory Lagging?" in *Theoretical Developments in Marketing*, C.W. Lamb, Jr., and P.M. Dunne, eds. (Chicago: American Marketing Association, 1980), pp. 255–258. L.A. Crosby and J.R. Taylor, "Consumer Satisfaction with Michigan's Container Deposit Law—An Ecological Perspective," *Journal of Marketing*, Winter 1982, pp. 47–60, and Patrick E. Murphy, "A Cost/Benefit Analysis of the Oregon Bottle Bill," *Combined Proceedings* (Chicago: American Marketing Association, 1974), pp. 347–352.

[37]Ibid.

recent years, a growing sophistication has been brought to the operation of reverse channels of distribution. For example, brokers are often employed to negotiate the sale of used packaging cardboard to paper mills which can reprocess the product. Larger supermarkets ship the "waste" directly to the mills with the broker taking neither title nor possession but simply arranging the transfer. Such an operation shows considerable thought in its development and a sizable management effort to make it succeed. Some soda vending machines have been modified or designed from scratch to accept empty aluminum cans for recycling *and* to reimburse the recycling patron with a small reward. This is clearly a step or two beyond having Boy Scouts scour roadsides for old containers.

Recycling will surely grow in importance because of economic forces and because the citizenry has become increasingly concerned over maintenance of a clean and attractive environment. In most cases, our society prefers to achieve its goals through means based on private enterprise. For these reasons, and because

BUYING DISTRIBUTION

In January 1982, it was announced that Consolidated Foods had agreed to buy Sav-A-Shop, Inc., a Jacksonville, Florida wholesaler that supplies some 17,000 small merchants with housewares and beauty aids. The acquisition was made to give Consolidated's subsidiary Hanes Corporation an established distribution network to distribute L'eggs and L'erin products to small drug, convenience, and grocery stores. Hanes, to that point, had to rely on chains of large-volume supermarkets and discount stores to market those products.

Source: Based on "A Basket for L'eggs," *Business Week,* January 25, 1982, p. 36.

recycling just makes good sense, formalized backward channels of distribution can be expected to continue to grow in importance.

POLITICAL AND LEGAL FORCES IN DISTRIBUTION MANAGEMENT

In the United States, within many other countries, and in international trade, dealings in the area of distribution may be subject to numerous restrictions. For example, a manufacturer's ability to exercise power over channels is often regulated in an attempt to preserve the independence of intermediaries and to assure that unfair competition does not result.[38]

The Sherman Antitrust Act, the Clayton Act, the Federal Trade Commission Act, and other laws dealing with antitrust policy are the bases for much U.S. legislation influencing distribu-

tion. In the United States, the three main legal issues concerning distribution are exclusive dealing, exclusive territories, and tying agreements.

Exclusive Dealing

It is reasonable to assume that a manufacturer might want to pick and choose the dealers who will handle its product. It would also seem logical that a wholesaler or retailer might care to carry one manufacturer's products and not the competing brands of other manufacturers. The manufacturer, wholesaler, or retailer may wish to engage in **exclusive dealings** that restrict middlemen from selling products of two competing suppliers. No manufacturer should be required

---

[38]For an interesting discussion of restrained trade in channels of distribution, see Joseph Barry Mason, "Power and Channel Conflicts in Shopping Centered Development," *Journal of Marketing,* April 1975, pp. 28–35.

to deal with all possible channel intermediaries, nor should all intermediaries have to handle the goods of any manufacturer demanding such a service. However, it is easy to imagine situations in which a manufacturer or an intermediary might abuse these rights—for example, to force another business into an unattractive business option or to "punish" a business for some activity. A maker of a well-known and popular product might withdraw that product from a dealer, or threaten to do so, unless that dealer agrees to, say, an exclusive dealership. In situations where distributors have considerable market power, it is easy to imagine situations where middlemen could force manufacturers, who are dependent on the intermediaries' marketing strength, to "play ball."

The general purpose of legislation focused on exclusive dealing arrangements is to prevent channel of distribution members, including manufacturers, from abusing their rights as independent businesses. To their not unreasonable question—"It's my business, can't I do what I want?"—the answer is, in effect, "No." This negative response is forthcoming, however, only when the activity in question abuses the individual's right to act independently or the rights of other businesses to succeed, as in the following examples.

■ A manufacturer may restrict a middleman from selling products that compete with that manufacturer's products. But, such an activity is illegal if it tends to restrict competition. A new brand of automobile engine oil would never reach the marketplace if all makers of oil already in the market enforced exclusive dealing agreements with their wholesalers and retailers. Such an arrangement, in blocking entry of a new product, would appear to be restricting competition.

■ Powerful manufacturers have, on occasion, sought to use coercive power such as a "withdrawal" of a product from a distributor to make the intermediary limit its business' size or the territory covered by the intermediary. Since exercise of such power infringes on the right of the intermediary to operate the business as it wishes, such an action would likely be illegal.

Notice that in situations such as these phrases such as "appear to restrict competition" or "likely to be illegal" must be used. This is because, as will be seen in Chapter 23, most legal matters in marketing involve sizable gray areas to which there are no easy answers. How, then, are such matters decided? By legal actions, court decisions, and opinions of the appropriate regulating agencies.

Exclusive dealing arrangements are generally legal if it can be shown that the exclusivity is necessary for strategic reasons, such as the need to protect a product's image, or because of limited production capacity.[39] As you can imagine, certain channel members could, in fact, be seeking to restrict competition while claiming to be simply serving one of the acceptable strategic justifications. Thus, there is a need for laws and courts to deal with exclusive dealing arrangements.

Exclusive Territories

A manufacturer who grants a wholesaler or retailer an exclusive territory may be performing an illegal act. The key point, as it is in so many legal matters relating to business, is restriction of competition. If the granting of **exclusive territories** does not violate the statutes relating to this point, then limiting the number of outlets within an area or assignment of exclusive territories may be considered to be proper. Again, in many cases, this evaluation must be made by the legal system.

What about McDonald's, you may wonder, or Cadillac? Both of these organizations attract dealers in part by promising that other dealers will not be set up within particular areas. Such areas need not be defined geographically. Instead, they could be defined in terms of the number of people—that is, the number of potential customers—in an area rather than the physical size of the area. In the cases of supplying organizations such as McDonald's and Cadillac, a number of defenses, including the following, might be offered:

---

[39] James R. Burley, "Territorial Restrictions in Distribution Systems: Current Legal Development," *Journal of Marketing,* October 1975, pp. 52–56.

■ That the investment expected from new dealers is so great that dealers could not be recruited unless they are offered some sort of exclusive territory arrangement. In this case, the "defense" is that the nature of the business *demands* such exclusivity.

■ That the "image" associated with the product offered demands some exclusivity of territories. Cadillac, for example, is portrayed as a luxury automotive product. Excellent sales and service people are thus necessary. If Cadillac dealerships were allowed to open on every other street corner, this might destroy the luxury or elite image Cadillac Motor Division is trying to create.

■ That the quality image of the product is so important that, were exclusive territories not employed, potential customers would not believe it possible that quality has been maintained. McDonald's franchise owners and managers are sent to Hamburger University. Cadillac dealers and mechanics are carefully selected and trained. Thus, if some exclusivity of territories were not maintained, if "everybody" could be a Cadillac dealer or mechanic, then the very image of the dealers themselves is destroyed.

Again, while these defenses may sound reasonable, their ability to hold up in court is challenged periodically. Although McDonald's and Cadillac have not "lost" their cases, other companies seeking to maintain territory systems on the basis of interference with competition between its dealers have.

Tying Contracts

Tying contracts require a channel intermediary or a buyer to purchase lines of merchandise that the seller sees as supplementary to the merchandise the purchaser actually *wants* to buy. The seller tells the buyer, in effect, "If you want to have *these* products, you must also buy *those* products." In other words, two or more products are tied together. Not all tying agreements are illegal, although, in many cases, the practice has been struck down in the courts. The Clayton Act appears to make tying contracts illegal, but it is

open to debate whether or not a particular case, in fact, *is* a tying contract.

In the early part of this century, tying contracts were commonplace. A seller of printing presses might require buyers of the presses to *also* buy the seller's ink and paper for use with the press. Most would agree that there is something wrong with such a system *if* there are other inks and papers on the market that would perform equally as well. To require press buyers to purchase only one brand of supplies would appear to be a restriction on competitive trade. More recently, certain computer manufacturers have tried to suggest that only their cards, papers, ribbons, and so on, could be used with their brands of machines. If it is shown that independent suppliers of these items are offering products that equal the manufacturer's own quality, such tying contracts are nearly impossible to defend.

Despite the long history of legal defeats for tying contracts, they are frequently encountered. Some, no doubt, are defensible, but others are ludicrous (for example, "official" toilet paper tied to the sale of patented toilet paper dispensers). This suggests a key flaw in the logic of tying contracts. Just because a company has patented a computer or a toilet paper dispenser, should that company also be given the right to influence every buyer decision associated with such products? Where would such a progression end? Would the computer, for example, have to be housed in an "official" building, in a room decorated with "official" paint or carpets? The tying contract approach to marketing quickly exceeds the bounds of reason. Exhibit 12-7 summarizes how the legal aspects of tying contracts, exclusive dealing, and exclusive territory have been interpreted by the courts.

Legalities of International Distribution

The many restraints, limits, and problems associated with domestic distribution are compounded in the international marketplace. Domestic laws, the laws of the country *to* which goods are being shipped, the laws of the nations *through* which goods are being shipped, and the general con-

---

EXHIBIT 12-7

Former Versus Current Status with Respect to Key Legal Issues of Channel Control

Marketing Tactic	Issue	Former Status	Current Status
Tying agreements	Can suppliers use tied product arrangements?	Tied product arrangements are generally considered per se violations and should not be used. Conditions where it could be used or where the rule of reason would apply were unclear.	*Dunkin' Donuts* (1975) clarified that tying arrangements are not per se violations and that they may be justified when attempting to (1) maintain standards of quality, (2) enter a new market or industry, or (3) preserve market identity.
Exclusive dealing	Can middlemen sell the products of two competing suppliers?	Restrictive distribution arrangements prohibiting middlemen from selling the products of two competing suppliers have been determined to be illegal if they have resulted in a lessening of competition as judged by the rule of reason.	*American Motor Inns* (1973) and *Pitchford* (1975) further indicate that if a distributor carries competing lines the supplier does have the right to expect them to make an equal effort in displaying and promoting his product and to otherwise make a decent effort to sell it. The supplier may terminate his distributors if they do not produce adequate economic performance in this unrestricted situation.

Source: Adapted with permission from W.L. Trombetta and A.L. Page, "The Channel Control Issue under Scrutiny," *Journal of Retailing*, Summer 1978, pp. 54–56.

---

ventions associated with international trade must all be obeyed. This not only creates monumental problems, but raises questions which are very difficult to answer. Some coastal countries claim that ships passing within 500 miles of their shores are within their territorial waters and subject to their laws and, possibly, their taxes. Other countries recognize and observe far less extensive boundaries for territorial waters. Certain countries prohibit "dangerous materials" to pass through their territories, waters, or air space. In some foreign markets, payments that might be called "bribes" are necessary to the flow of trade, while the U.S. government, for one, prohibits the giving of such "bribes" even within the *foreign* countries, not simply within its own boundaries.

The many-faceted aspects of international constraints on distribution are beyond the scope of this chapter, but the immense problems that flow from them should be recognized by all students of marketing.

EXHIBIT 12-7 (Continued)

Former Versus Current Status with Respect to Key Legal Issues of Channel Control

Marketing Tactic	Issue	Former Status	Current Status
Exclusive dealing (cont.)	Can suppliers impose exclusive dealing arrangements on distributors?	Exclusive dealing arrangements have been viewed as antitrust violations if they (1) comprise a substantial share of the market, (2) if the dollar amount involved was substantial, or (3) if it is between large suppliers and a smaller distributor where the supplier's disparate economic power can be inherently coercive.	As indicated by *Whipple* v. *Shamrock Foods* (1976) exclusive dealing restrictions may not be violations if other equivalent merchandise is available in the market and if nothing more than the supplier's own sales are restricted to selected customers or franchised dealers.
Exclusive territories	Are exclusive territories and allocations valid for restricting where a product can be sold?	Territorial restrictions and allocations have not necessarily been antitrust violations but can be pro- or anticompetitive and have been subject to the rule of reason.	Recent decisions such as *Tomac* v. *Coca-Cola* (1976) have clarified when territorial restrictions and allocations are permissible. These include situations where they can be procompetitive, such as for a new or developing firm, or where it serves a legitimate business purpose or protects a distributor's interest. Furthermore, *Superior Bedding* (1972) established the legality of areas of responsibility and profit passovers as means for a supplier to retain some discretion over where and to whom his products are sold.

SUMMARY

In this chapter we looked at the marketing mix variable of distribution—a necessary but often misunderstood marketing function. The frequently heard notion of "eliminating the middleman" calls attention to the fact that the general public has little appreciation for the roles played by channels of distribution.

Channel intermediaries create time utility and place utility, as well as making other contributions to consumer satisfaction. A channel of distribution is the path that goods take as they flow from producer to consumer through the exchange process. Channel members perform a variety of functions including bulk-breaking, transportation, storage, promotion and communication, financing, and management services.

Although there are a wide variety of channels of distribution, every distribution system is marked by a high degree of functional interdependency. The advent of scrambled merchandising has necessitated the increased use of multiple channels of distribution for a particular product.

The marketing manager's determination of the structure of the channel is a crucial element of the marketing mix strategy. Marketers must choose either a strategy of intensive, selective, or exclusive distribution when determining the number of outlets at each level of distribution.

Vertical marketing systems consist of networks of vertically aligned establishments that are managed as centrally administered systems. There are three types: corporate, contractual, and administered.

Channel cooperation is a situation in which the marketing objectives and strategies of channel members are harmonious. However, channel conflict may characterize a channel of distribution. While there is some question about the influence of conflict on a channel of distribution, it is generally argued that conflict should not go unmanaged. When one organization in a channel of distribution is able to exert its power and influence over other channel members, this organization has channel power and is referred to as the channel leader.

The recycling of solid waste may be accomplished through a backward channel of distribution. This process of reverse distribution may accomplish a major ecological goal of society.

There are a number of legal restrictions that affect channels of distribution. The three main issues affecting the distribution process are: exclusive dealing arrangements, exclusive territorial arrangements, and tying contracts.

THE MOST IMPORTANT CONCEPT IN THIS CHAPTER

A channel of distribution provides a vehicle that makes possible the passage of title or possession of the product from producer to consumer. Channel members share the responsibility for performing the basic functions of marketing.

KEY TERMS

Channel of distribution

Merchant intermediaries

Agent intermediaries

Conventional channel

Facilitators

Physical distribution functions

Bulk-breaking function

Accumulating bulk

Assembler

Assorting function

Transportation

Storage

Selling function

Buying function

Service function

Credit function

Risk-taking function

Channel interdependency

Jobber

Multiple channels

Scrambled merchandising

Multiple channel strategy

Vertical marketing systems

Corporate vertical marketing systems

Administered vertical marketing system

Contractual vertical marketing systems

Cooperative organization

Voluntary chain

Franchise

Intensive distribution

Selective distribution

Exclusive distribution

Channel cooperation

Channel conflict

Channel power

Channel leader

Backward channel

Exclusive dealing

Exclusive territories

Tying contracts

QUESTIONS FOR DISCUSSION

1 What would happen if we eliminated the wholesalers (middlemen) for the following brands?
(a) Izod Lacoste shirts
(b) Cutty Sark Scotch Whiskey
(c) Weyerheuser Lumber

2 It has been suggested that banking and shopping be performed at home with personal computers. What are the implications for channels of distribution?

3 At a national bottlers meeting the vice-president of marketing for the Dr. Pepper Company said: "No matter how good a job we do, [consumers] can't get Dr. Pepper unless you [bottlers] have made the sale to retailers." Why would the vice-president say this?

4 A few years ago, Airwick professional products division, selling a variety of disinfectants, cleaning agents, insecticides, and environmental sanitation products, sold its products to a network of 65 distributors and 10 branch sales offices. The company decided to drop its sales branches. What circumstances might lead to such a change in channel strategy?

5 Only recently have medical professionals started to realize that they, like manufacturers, must give thought to their distribution systems. What distribution decisions might hospitals, dentists, and pediatricians have to make?

6 Goldman Sacs is the new distributor for the U.S. government's gold coins that will compete with Krugerrands. Originally, the gold coins were sold through the U.S. Postal Service, but the distribution situation was not satisfactory. What do you think went wrong?

7 What impact will a growing supermarket industry have on Procter & Gamble's distribution system?

8 If you were the manufacturer of the following products what channels of distribution would you select?
(a) Dictating machines
(b) Automobile mufflers
(c) Personal computers
(d) Telephones
(e) Toy dolls

9 Identify the channel of distribution for
(a) An airline
(b) A bakery
(c) A pizza restaurant

10 What advantages do vertical marketing systems have over conventional marketing systems?

11 Levi's jeans are now sold at Sears and Penney's as well as in department stores and specialty stores.
(a) Outline the channels of distribution for Levi Strauss.
(b) What potential channel conflict problems do you think may arise?

12 Would you use exclusive, selective, or intensive distribution for the following products? Why?
(a) Dr. Pepper
(b) Ford Tempo
(c) Panasonic video cassettes
(d) Ethan Allen furniture

CASE 12-1 The Apple Wear Company*

In the late 1960s and early 1970s, L'eggs products successfully carved out a market niche by selling nylons in supermarkets, drugstores, and mass merchandising outlets. The success of this product in a nontraditional distribution channel led to many imitative brands, such as No Nonsense. The Apple Wear Company intends to market bras and panties in attractively packaged Apple-type containers with a similar distribution strategy. The strategy is so similar that the prod-

---

* Source: George Lazarus, "Panty Hose's Supermarket Success Prompts Similar Push for Bra's," *Tulsa World*, June 12, 1983, p. 6–2 (Chicago Tribune Syndicate).

uct will be placed in rotary displays similar to those initially used by L'eggs. Although the intimate apparel products have never been marketed through this channel of distribution the President of Apple Wear is extremely optimistic. "We've patterned ourselves after L'eggs, and we think we've got a top sales opportunity."

Questions

1 How integral an element is the distribution system in Apple Wear's marketing strategy?

2 Outline the channel of distribution that Apple Wear will be utilizing.

3 Do you think that Apple Wear will be successful?

4 What impact will a success by Apple Wear have on the competitive structure of the intimate apparel industry?

CHAPTER 13

Distribution Institutions

CHAPTER SCAN

The major thrust of this chapter is to offer an understanding of the marketing management problems and opportunities presented by the marketing mix variable of *place.* It is necessary, for the sake of completeness, to discuss the major institutions performing the distribution function. These are of two general types. One group of intermediaries deals with final consumers of products. These are retailers. The second is the group of channel members who form a bridge between manufacturers and retailers and between manufacturers and the organizational users of their products. Actually, this group consists of two major types of wholesalers—merchant wholesalers and agents.

Retailers and wholesalers are examined with an eye toward gaining a grasp of their operations and of the way they fit into the big picture of channels management. Each of the intermediary types discussed represents marketing's response to developments within the marketplace it serves. Seeing them in this light will bring a fuller appreciation of how channels of distribution do their job.

WHEN YOU HAVE STUDIED THIS CHAPTER, YOU WILL:

Be able to describe the purposes of wholesaling and retailing in the distribution system and the activities performed by each.

Be aware of the various kinds of retailers and the several variables that can be used to classify them.

Be able to discuss the historical patterns found in American retailing and several theories that have been constructed to explain them.

Understand the difference between merchant wholesalers and agents and to describe how these organizations contribute to marketing goals.

Be able to show how full-service wholesalers and the many forms of limited-service wholesalers fit into the marketing system.

Be able to discuss the contributions to marketing of such agent intermediaries as brokers, auction companies, and selling agents.

Time Incorporated found the prospects for its *TV-Cable Week* magazine to be so poor that it decided to discontinue the troubled magazine after a six-month trial. The four-color magazine, which retailed at $2.95 a month, offered 32 pages weekly of news and features, wrapped around detailed "cable system-specific" program listings. Although there were some pricing problems, the failure seemed to be directly related to the channel of distribution. More specifically, cable TV operators never really gave the magazine much retailing support, and many declined to distribute the product to their subscribers. Industry observers thought that a primary reason for the resistance was that distributors felt the program guide might compete for subscription dollars with the more profitable pay TV services distributed by the cable operators. Furthermore, many cable systems publish their own directories or have contracts with rival guides, such as *TV Guide* or *Program Guide,* and *TV-Cable Week* was a direct competitor. A Time Incorporated executive stated "Our business plan depended upon high acceptance by cable systems and individuals. We thought the product would be so compelling that it would develop a new market." However, a cable operator saw it somewhat differently: "Our systems average 20,000 subscribers and they were going to make us pay a surcharge because these weren't large enough. Their approach didn't make economical sense."[1]

The previous chapter discussed how channels of distribution are constructed and how they are managed. However, the institutions that make up channels, the retailers and wholesalers, and other specialized intermediaries so vital to the marketing of many goods and services were not specifically analyzed. As the *TV-Cable Week* situation points out, these distribution institutions may make or break a product. These intermediaries are the major focus of this chapter.

The chapter has two major sections. The first section deals with retailers while the second concerns wholesalers who perform the function of operating "between" the manufacturer and the retailer or industrial user.

RETAILING

Retailing consists of all activities involved with the sale of products to ultimate consumers.

Some definitions use the term "consuming units" rather than "consumers" to include, for example, sales to a family member who does not actually consume the purchased product. Other definitions mention that most rental or leasing activities are included in retailing. By whatever definition, the basic concept is the same— *retailing* involves dealing with consumers who are acquiring products for their own use. If an intermediary does not deal with the ultimate consumer, that intermediary is not a retailer.[2] Viewed in a channel of distribution context, retailers are the important "final link" in the process that brings goods from manufacturers to consumers. Poor marketing on the part of retailers can negate all the planning and preparation that has gone into other marketing activities. We, as consumers, come into contact with a variety of retailers every day and are in a good position to see how retailers can make or break any consumer-oriented marketing plan.

As the definition of retailing shows us, Sears, K-Mart, Safeway, Marshall Field's, and

---

[1] Based on information in "The Demise of a Cable Directory," *Time,* September 26, 1983, p. 75; Stewart J. Elliott, "Time Gives up on Cable Book," *Advertising Age,* September 19, 1983, pp. 18 and 96; and "Right Decisions Give Given Problems Observers Say," *Advertising Age,* September 19, 1983, pp. 1 and 96.

[2] It is common to use sales figures to differentiate between retailers and other intermediaries. If an intermediary has more than 50 percent of sales to consumers, that intermediary is counted as a retailer in government business censuses.

other organizations selling products for resale to consumers are retailers. This includes some less-than-obvious institutions such as hotels, bars, restaurants, and ice cream truck operators. It also includes the enterprising students at the University of California-Berkeley who operate the Black Lightening Lecture Note Service that caters to the needs of students worried about the quality of their class notes. For a cost of about $10, a student receives an entire semester's worth of notes for particular courses. Typically, the notes are taken by graduate students employed to attend classes. They are typed within two days of the class lecture and distributed to subscribing students. Black Lightening's business is brisk, earning revenues approaching $200,000 annually. Black Lightening is a successful retailing institution, obtaining a product and selling it to ultimate users of that product.

Importance of Retailing

In the United States there are nearly 2 million retailing institutions accounting for almost $1 trillion in sales.[3] About 13 percent of American workers are employed in retailing, and retailers' sales account for approximately 97 percent of the sizable chunk of the Gross National Product known as personal income.

The 50 largest retailers had sales of $246 billion in 1982, representing an increase of 11 percent from the year before. Sears Roebuck and Company, with sales of $30 billion, remained number one.

Exhibit 13-1 lists the 20 largest retailing institutions in the United States and their sales volumes in 1982. The sales figures give the impression that giant companies dominate the field of retailing. However, small retail companies can and do fare very well. Such success requires careful selection of target market segments that can be better served by smaller companies, and then the development of an appropriate marketing mix.

---

[3] *Statistical Abstract of the United States 1982–83,* 103rd edition (Washington, D.C.: U.S. Department of Commerce, Bureau of the Census, 1983), p. 806.

EXHIBIT 13-1

The 20 Largest Retailing Companies (ranked by sales)

Rank 1982	Company	Sales ($000)
1	Sears Roebuck (Chicago)	30,019,800
2	Safeway Stores (Oakland)	17,632,821
3	K-Mart (Troy, Mich.)	16,772,166
4	Kroger (Cincinnati)	11,901,892
5	J. C. Penney (New York)	11,413,806
6	Lucky Stores (Dublin, Calif.)	7,972,973
7	Household International (Prospect Heights, Ill.)	7,767,500
8	Federated Department Stores (Cincinnati)	7,698,944
9	American Stores (Salt Lake City)	7,507,772
10	Winn-Dixie Stores (Jacksonville)	6,764,472
11	Southland (Dallas)	6,756,933
12	F. W. Woolworth (New York)	6,590,000
13	Great Atlantic and Pacific Tea (Montvale, N.J.)	6,226,755
14	Dayton Hudson (Minneapolis)	5,660,729
15	Montgomery Ward (Chicago)	5,583,861
16	Jewel Companies (Chicago)	5,571,721
17	Batus (Louisville)	5,165,439
18	Grand Union (Elmwood Park, N.J.)	4,137,447
19	Albertson's (Boise)	3,940,117
20	May Department Stores (St. Louis)	3,670,371

Source: Adapted from *Fortune,* June 13, 1983, p. 168. Used with permission.

Retailing Institutions

The great many retailing institutions in the United States can be divided into more easily analyzed groups by accenting certain differentiating characteristics. Retailing is dynamic, and retail institutions evolve constantly. For example, institutions such as "5 and 10's" are at the end of their life cycle. Individual companies like Sears, which began this century as a mail-order retailer of watches, are constantly evolving into new types of retailers. "No-frills" supermarkets and catalog showrooms are but two retailing innovations that have developed in recent

EXHIBIT 13-2

Retailers Differ in Variety and Selection

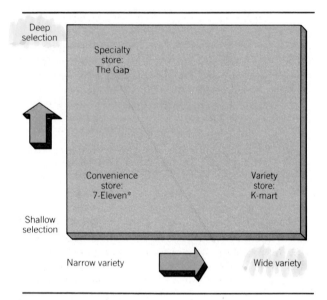

decades. In the next 20 years, we can expect retailers to adjust to their changing environments by making further transformations.

Types of Retailers and Product Variety

One method of differentiating among retailers is by the variety of products they sell. These types are familiar to all of us since we patronize them on a regular basis.

General merchandise retailers carry a wide variety of merchandise that cuts across generic lines of goods. Old-fashioned general stores are a good example. They carry "everything" from food items to electrical supplies to a limited line of clothing items, toys, and novelty items. Specifically, they carry a wide *variety* of products. Notice that many general merchandise retailers are not small-time operations. Even the largest department stores carry general merchandise. So do the major discount stores. The bigger general merchandise stores, such as

Sears or K-Mart, are commonly called *mass merchandisers,* although the variety of goods they carry links them to the much smaller general store. All types of general merchandise retailers share another thing in common: The wide variety of goods they carry means that they usually cannot afford to carry a large or deep selection of goods. As Exhibit 13-2 shows, retailers usually carry either wide variety or deep selection, but not both. The expense associated with having many kinds of goods and many choices of each kind makes the two possibilities largely mutually exclusive.

Single-line retailers and *limited-line retailers* are differentiated from general merchandise retailers by the degree of specialization reflected in their product lines. Grocery stores and clothing stores are **limited-line retailers** in that they carry a general line of goods *within* particular product classes. Computer stores and video recorder shops are limited-line retailers in that their lines of merchandise are even more narrowly restricted. These retailers, unlike department stores or other general merchandisers, do not try to be all things to all people.

Retail marketing managers contemplating opening shops with limited or single lines must be certain that there are enough potential customers who will seek the few items offered to support the operation. For this reason, general stores dominated American retailing until after the Civil War. Except in large cities, too few people could be found to justify limited-line retailers (such as jewelers or book sellers). Today, these single-line and limited-line stores represent the bulk of retailing operations. The major reason for their success is their development of considerable expertise in their particular product lines. Wallpapers to Go, for example, offers free wallpapering lessons to instruct consumers on wallpapering techniques *and* what to buy.

Specialty stores are narrower still in the merchandise lines they offer. These retailers specialize within a particular product line, selling only those items deemed appropriate to a narrow market segment or requiring a particular selling expertise. Retailers selling only children's shoes, automobile mufflers, or clocks exemplify

8 REASONS WHY NOBODY MAKES DECORATING EASIER THAN WALLPAPERS TO GO.

A single-line retailer.

this. Specialty stores have enjoyed remarkable success in recent years, illustrating the importance of effective market segmentation and target marketing.

Types of Retailer Ownership

Most retailers are **independent retailers** operating as single-unit entities. Independent operations may be proprietorships, partnerships, or corporations, but they are usually owned by one operator, a family, or a small number of individuals. They are not generally integrated into a larger corporation. Although these retailers are often thought of as small, some are quite sizable. Even though, as Exhibit 13-1 suggests, the large retailers account for vast chunks of U.S. retail sales, independent retailers, taken together, are

CONGLOMERCHANTS

These days when you ask "what does a company like such and such do?" you may find the answer is no longer simple and straightforward. The firm may be engaged in manufacturing for one product line and in retailing for another series of products. We all know Pillsbury is a flour and package goods manufacturer; yet it owns and operates Steak and Ale and Burger King restaurants.

The notion of *conglomerchants* reflects the increasing degree of disintegration of traditional classifications of retailers. Conglomerchants operate a variety of retailing concerns—each aiming at a different target market.

Classifying an organization like Dayton Hudson Corporation into one category is difficult. Consider a few of their operations: B. Dalton Bookstore and Team Electronics are both limited-line specialty stores. Mervyn's is a multiple-line specialty store emphasizing clothing and soft foods. Target is a discount store selling general merchandise. John A. Brown, Hudson's, Dayton's, and Diamond's are department stores, selling full-line general merchandise in limited regional areas.

This diversification of products and operations mirrors a prominent development in retailing in general. The consequence of such a strategy for the marketing student is that an accurate and precise delineation of classifications of retailers is all the more difficult.

an important part of the American retailing scene.

If a retail establishment is not an independent, it is classified into one of the two basic types of groups of retail institutions. The most familiar type is the **chain store**—one of a group of shops bearing the same name and having roughly the same store image. Chain store systems consist of two or more stores of a similar type that are centrally owned and operated. Chains have been successful for a number of reasons, but one of the most important is the opportunities they have to take advantage of economies of scale in buying and selling goods. They can then maintain their prices, thus increasing their margins, or they can cut prices and attract greater sales volume. Unlike small independents with lesser financial means, they can also take advantage of such tools as computers.

Chains fit the American culture. Sears, and other nationwide chains, can, for example, be found in nearly every population center. Thus, as our mobile citizenry moves from place to place, a familiar Sears store is "waiting" for them when they arrive.

Although chains possess many advantages over independents, some analysts say smaller retailers are more flexible. They may be better able to apply such marketing techniques as segmentation than bigger operations, whose appeal must be more general. We might expect that the greater financial resources of chains will assure their success, yet large organizations like W.T. Grant have vanished from the scene and others, such as A&P, have had to cut back their operations.

The other type of retailing organization is an ownership group. An **ownership group** is an organization made up of various stores or small chains each having a separate name, identity, and image, all the while operating under the ultimate control of a central owner. Typically, the members of the group are former independents bought out by the much larger ownership groups. Federated, May Co., and Carson, Pirie, Scott are among the ownership groups that operate stores with different names. For example, Federated operates Bloomingdale's, Foley's, Rich's, I. Magnum, Sanger-Harris, and many other department stores.

Classification of Retailers

Having considered retailer types by size and by ownership, let us turn to the various specific kinds of retailers operating in the United States today. Each has its particular advantages and disadvantages over the others, and each fits particular markets and situations. Try to envision the following store classes for what they represent—responses to particular marketing opportunities.

Supermarkets. The supermarket of today differs greatly from the "grocery store" from which it evolved. The grocery operator of the early 1900s knew most of his customers, personally filled customers' orders, and was likely to offer both delivery service and credit. With the advent of the telephone, the grocer accepted phone orders and dispatched a delivery boy to the customer's home. When the Great Atlantic and Pacific Tea Company[4] discontinued its delivery service in 1912, opting for self-service shopping, A&P began the transformation process from grocery to supermarket—an evolution that continues today.

Today's **supermarket** is a large departmentalized retail establishment selling a variety of products, mostly food items but also health and beauty aids, housewares, magazines, and much more. The inclusion of non-food items on supermarket shelves was once novel in that it represented the stocking of items that did not traditionally belong in the supermarket's group of offerings. The name given to this practice, **scrambled merchandising,** continues to be used even though the practice is no longer new. Scrambled merchandising permits the supermarket, and other types of retailing institutions, to sell items that carry a higher margin than do most food items and provides a means to increase profitability. Across the board, however, supermarket profits are slim—only 1 to 2 percent of total sales.

More recent additions to the supermarket include private and generic brands, bakeries, and delicatessens selling specialty items and precooked, take-home food items. While these additions are intended to increase profits, they are also aimed at attracting particular customer groups. For example, take-home prepared food has considerable appeal for the elderly, for working mothers, and for single people. All these de-

---

[4]It was called "The Tea Company" by its customers in the early days. It is still called that by its employees today.

velopments and additions have ballooned the number of products carried by the typical supermarket to more than 10,000. Accordingly, the recent emphasis in supermarket design is on larger stores ranging up to 50,000 square feet of floor space and beyond.[5]

Although there are many independently owned and operated supermarkets, supermarkets are often chain store operations. Safeway, a supermarket chain with more than $17 billion in sales in 1982, is the second largest retailer in the United States. However, the challenges presented by convenience stores and fast-food retailers have had their effects on the supermarket business, particularly on those supermarkets unable or unwilling to fight back. In good part because of this challenge, 5.5 percent more supermarkets closed in 1981 than in 1980.[6]

Convenience stores are, in essence, small supermarkets. They have rapidly developed as a major threat to their larger cousins. 7-Elevens, Quick-Trips, King Kwiks, and other imitative convenience stores have sprung up and multiplied across America. As their names generally imply, the major benefit to consumers is convenience—convenience of location and convenience of time. These stores specialize in adding "extra" time and place utility. As the prices found at most of these shops testify, consumers must pay for these conveniences and seem quite willing to do so. These stores carry a variety of consumer products priced to provide high profit margins. They are generally open 15-, 18-, or 24-hours a day, seven days a week.

Department Stores. A **department store** is typically a large store in comparison to most nearby retail outlets. Independent department stores do exist, but most department stores are members of chains or ownership groups. They carry a wide selection of products including furniture, clothing, home appliances, and housewares and, depending on the size of the operation, a good many other products as well. These stores are "departmentalized" both physically within the building and organizationally. Each department is operated largely as a separate entity headed by a *buyer* who has considerable independence and authority in buying and selling products and who is responsible for the particular department's profits.

Most department stores are characterized by a full range of services including credit plans, delivery, generous return policies, restaurants and coffee shops, and a host of other extras such as fashion clinics, closed-door sales for established customers only, and even etiquette classes for customers' little girls. Such services, as well as the need to carry a wide variety of merchandise and maintain a large building, increase store operating costs and necessitate higher prices than those at discount stores. Some consumers seek the service and atmosphere of the department store but then make actual purchases at a discount store. In short, discounters and other types of store operators are formidable competitors for traditional department stores.

Many of America's most famous retailers are old-line department stores. One of the largest and best-known of these is Macy's, whose popular "main" store is in the heart of Manhattan. However, in many cities, department store managers have withdrawn from downtown retailing and have located in suburban shopping malls. Typically, these stores are not as large or as well-stocked as the old downtown stores. Nonetheless, they are reflections of changes in the marketing environment and indications of the flexibility marketers must display to achieve survival.

Discount Stores. The **discount store** is a large self-service retail establishment selling a variety of high-turnover products at low prices. A good part of its ability to hold prices down stems from the practice of offering few services. Other than the costs of the goods they sell, most retailers find that personnel costs are their largest financial outlay. Thus, by eliminating most of the sales help, having no delivery staff, and hiring employees who are stock clerks and

[5]"Economy Puts Damper on Building Programs," *Chain Store Age Executive,* July 1, 1982, p. 37.
[6]Ibid.

cash register operators rather than true sales-people, discounters are able to take a big step toward reducing their sales prices.

The idea of using low prices to woo customers is not a new one. The modern discount store can be traced to the 1930s and 1940s when pioneering retailers began to open sizable outlets in low-rent locations, many of them suburban. These discounters offered appliances and other items on a cash-and-carry basis in a no-frills atmosphere. No credit plans, a minimum of shopping assistance, and extended store hours were the hallmarks of their operations. Today, such stores as Target and Venture continue the once revolutionary practices of the early discounters. Modern discounters may not go so far as having the plain cinder block walls of those pioneers, but today's discount stores stress neither interior design nor customer service in their efforts to reduce costs and maintain low prices. Some observers suggest that discounters should deliberately develop plain stores and hire even fewer people on the grounds that customer *inconvenience* heightens the belief that prices are being held to the minimum.

Toys Я Us stores utilize "supermarket retailing."

Varying Types of Discounters. Because the discount concept could be applied to almost any type of merchandise, many variations on the general theme of plain stores with low prices have been developed. Even such items as fur coats and rare jewels are sold at discount in many cities, although often these are good-condition used items.

The most important type of discount store is the general merchandise discount retailer. The largest of these is K-Mart, with sales of over $16 billion. Discount operators can also be found among specialty store retailers. Crown Books, a specialty retailer, is a bookstore chain that discounts every book on the *New York Times'* best-seller list by 35 percent. Crown has had problems, however, suggesting either that it pushed the discount concept too far or that book buyers prefer to browse and buy in a more traditional bookstore setting than a discounter is able to offer.

Although food retailers as a group operate

at low margins, discounters have also entered that field. The "no-frills" or "box store" supermarket is a discount store that, like its counterparts in discounting, offers few services. At many of these, customers must bring their own bags, mark their purchases with posted prices, and endure plain surroundings and minimal assistance from store employees. At some of these box stores even the shopping carts have been eliminated. It appears that certain customers are prepared to put up with these cutbacks to obtain lower prices; and yet many "box stores" have found that the discounting technique can be pushed too far and have reinstated a modicum of extras.

The term "supermarket retailing" has been used to describe many discount stores that have adopted the supermarket concept of large inventories displayed on self-service aisles. Toys-Я-

Us, Handy Dan, Forest City Lumber stores, and Oshman's illustrate the supermarket format applied to toys, lumber and building supplies, and sporting goods.[7]

Two other variations on the discounting concept are **warehouse retailers** and **catalog showrooms,** recent successful developments in mass merchandising. Retailers such as Levitz and Silo combine wholesaling and retailing functions as "warehouse retailers" although, since they deal with the retail consumer, they remain true retailers. For these marketers, the showroom facility doubles as a storage place or warehouse holding the retailer's stock in amounts far greater than regular retailers would retain.

For example, the basic Levitz strategy— cash-and-carry warehouse merchandising has each store stock everything it displays. By selling what Levitz terms "instant gratification"—the opportunity to walk out the door with furniture bought at a good price—Levitz has maintained its position as the nation's No. 1 independent furniture retailer.[8]

Catalog retailers, like Best Company, publish a large catalog identifying products for sale. Typically, these are high margin items. The catalog, or an accompanying price list, shows the "normal" retail price of the items and the catalog discounter's much lower price. Often, the discounter's price is printed without a dollar sign in a form of easily decipherable "code" to let the buyer know that a special deal—not available to just anyone—is being offered. Catalog discounters frequently operate out of spartan showrooms and offer no credit plans other than, perhaps, the acceptance of Visa or MasterCard. Like other discounters, they lack customer conveniences and salesperson assistance. Service is slowed by the need to wait for products selected to be delivered from some storage place. This permits lower prices, however, and the formula has been

successful. Service Merchandise, the second largest catalog showroom chain, operated 125 stores and had sales of $1.03 billion in fiscal 1982.[9]

Some discounters operate a special sort of catalog store called the *closed door house.* In this type of outlet, customers are asked to be "members" of the store and are issued cards that permit entry to the store. Some closed door houses require that customers already be members of some specific group such as a labor union or the civil service. While these operations may run the risk of being seen as discriminating against persons not in the target customer group, the membership idea has been found by some retailers to be effective in building store loyalty. Moreover, if membership involves developing an actual list of potential customers, direct-mail advertisements can be sent to these people eliminating, to a large extent, other forms of advertising with their large proportions of waste circulation.[10]

One last type of discounter has drawn attention in recent years. The *hypermarket* (or hypermarché as it was called in France, its country of origin) is a huge retail outlet, covering at least 50,000 square feet. The rough translation of the original term into "superstore" sums up the concept. The hypermarket sells food and health and beauty products, as well as appliances, clothing, furniture, and virtually everything a consumer might need—all at discount prices. As with any other discounter, this is achieved by holding customer services to a minimum and, in the superstore's case, performing certain wholesaling functions associated with the large quantities of merchandise bought from manufacturers and other suppliers.

Non-Store Retailing

In the public mind, retailing is almost totally associated with the operation of stores. However, as we have seen in this chapter, any marketer who sells to consumers is engaged in retailing

---

[7]B.C. McCammon, Jr. and W.L. Hammer, "A Frame of Reference for Improving Productivity and Distribution," *Atlanta Economic Review*, September–October 1974, pp. 9–13.

[8]"Levitz Furniture: Sitting Pretty as It Waits for the Recovery," *Business Week*, February 7, 1983, p. 76. Used with permission.

[9]*Chain Store Age Executive,* April 1982, p. 33.

[10]TV and radio advertisements, for example, are seen and heard by many people who will never shop at a given outlet.

FROM SIDELINE TO SERENDIPITY

Selling name brand merchandise at a low price is hardly a novel idea.

But it's precisely the formula that has propelled Service Merchandise Co. Inc. from a single catalog showroom in the 1960s into a $1 billion retail chain today.

According to Raymond Zimmerman, Service's chairman and president, it all began with a jobbing operation and a group of five and dime stores. "We originally got into the catalog business as a sideline. We wanted to trade up and sell better merchandise. But things were so good the first year that we got out of the jobbing business," Zimmerman says.

At the close of its 1982 fiscal year, Service had grown to be the second largest chain in one of the most rapidly expanding retail segments. It now has almost 125 units in 26 states, with clusters of showrooms in New England, the South and the Midwest.

Despite this prodigious growth, Service has remained remarkably faithful to its initial merchandising concept, says Zimmerman. "We have not changed our merchandising mix at all. The only thing that we may have beefed up is sporting goods and electronics. But other than that, we've still got the same assortment that we've always had."

In the early days, he continues, Service and the other fledgling catalogers had very little competition. "Everybody else was selling everything at full price then. The discounters had just started coming in, and there was little overlap of merchandise. It was a long time before we really began to feel the competition."

But how did Service and other catalogers introduce customers to that new brand of retailing? And what happened when many of those outlets became computerized in the 1970s?

As Zimmerman tells it, it is "not too extremely difficult" to orient shoppers in a new market where no cataloger has ever ventured before. Also, of course, if a chain opens a store in a previously tapped area, its customers will already be familiar with the showroom concept.

The rub comes when an existing store is computerized, says the Service executive, and the shoppers wait in line with a ticket instead of the merchandise. "Any time you change a customer's shopping habits, it's a traumatic experience," he observes.

Recent conversations have been smoother, he adds, and Service has probably won back the customers it lost—and then some. Zimmerman believes that some of the smaller or less fortunate catalogers may still go by the wayside, but that "the shakeout of the big guys has pretty much come and gone."

In other words, the catalog showroom industry will continue to grow, and Service Merchandise can be expected to get more than its share. But that's not surprising. The Nashville-based outfit outpaced its rivals in the 1960s and 1970s, and there's no reason for it to stop that strong performance now.

Source: From "From Sideline to Serendipity," *Chain Store Age*, April 1982, p. 33. Used with permission.

activities. Many of these marketers successfully offer the buying public a retail marketing mix that does not include a store at all. Among the many means of non-store retailing are mail-order, direct-response retailing, vending machines, and door-to-door selling.

Mail-Order and Direct-Response Retailing. Sears, Roebuck and Company began in the mail-order business and moved on to other types of selling. Today, the mail-order business is but a small portion of Sears' total business. Other companies, such as Spencer Gifts and Joseph Bank Clothiers, have combined both mail-order and in-store retailing. Still others, Spiegel of Chicago, for example, have remained fully committed to mail-order retailing.

The factor that most attracts consumers to mail-order retailing is convenience. Shopping at home, especially at such harried times of the year as the Christmas holidays, provides an undeniable attraction. So does the fact that many mail-order retailers will ship gift-wrapped orders directly to the person for whom the merchandise was bought, thus freeing the retail customer from wrapping and delivery chores. Some observers of the mail-order business have suggested that another attraction of mail-order shopping is the safety element. The shopper need not go to a possibly dangerous downtown or mall area. Certain target customers may be best reached by mail-order retailers. Purveyors of vitamins and other health aids for the senior citizens conduct a brisk business through advertisements placed in such magazines as *Modern Maturity,* the publication of the National Association of Senior Citizens. Many other carefully targeted magazines are similarly useful to mail-order retailers. Mail-order retailers also make extensive use of computer-generated mailing lists, available from companies specializing in developing them, that can be narrowly focused on selected interest groups, age groups, homeowners, renters, and so on.

Mail-order retailing offers many opportunities to reduce operating costs. No salespeople need be hired, trained, or paid. Businesses may be headquartered in low-rent areas that ordinary retailers would eschew. In fact, many corners can be cut by mail-order retailers simply because the way in which they conduct their business is never seen by their customers. On the other hand, mail-order retailers face considerable expenses in the preparation and mailing of catalogs. They must also attempt to expedite shipments in an effort to assure that customers receive their orders quickly and in good order lest customers buy the desired merchandise from some other source. Though mail-order retailing grows annually in the United States, the ever-present competition from other channels tends to limit its growth. Many buyers will not, for example, buy a suit or dress through the mail when they can go to a standard clothing store and personally examine the merchandise. In part to overcome the sense of unease some feel in buying through the mails, most mail-order retailers offer liberal return policies.

Mail-order retailers of the general merchandise sort are becoming over-shadowed in importance by mail-order specialty goods operations. These retailers succeed in part because at least some of the merchandise they offer is either "not available" or hard to find in stores. Television and telephone **direct-response retailers,** who fill orders via the mail, have proliferated by hawking everything from cutlery to Elvis Presley memorabilia. The familiar K-Tel television campaigns, called *saturation campaigns* for good reason, that urge viewers to write or call an 800 number, are good illustrations of this approach to retailing.

Vending Machines. The coin-operated vending machine is an old retailing tool that has become increasingly sophisticated in recent years. Computer-based technological innovations, as evidenced by the new talking Coke machines, have permitted these machines to reach new markets and to become more effective marketing tools.

It is believed that there is one vending machine for every 40 people in the United States. They can be found almost everywhere—and this is a big part of their appeal to the marketers who use them. Cigarettes, gum, and other items can be sold in subway stations, apartment houses, college dormitories, and church basements without an investment in a store or in personnel. Items sold through vending machines are generally small, easily preserved, high-turnover goods such as candy and soda pop. However, machines have also been used with success to dispense airline tickets, traveler's insurance, helium-filled balloons, and breathalyzer tests. Despite mechanical and electronic advances, however, items dispensed through vending machines remain relatively low priced, convenience goods.

Door-to-Door and In-Home Retailing. Bibles, vacuum cleaners, magazines, and cosmetics are among the many products sold successfully door-to-door. This kind of retailing is an expensive form of distribution. Labor costs, mostly in the form of commissions, are quite high. Yet many consumers appear to enjoy the personal in-home service provided by established companies like Electrolux, Fuller Brush, and Avon. In general, products sold door-to-door are of the type that particularly benefit from demonstration and a personal sales approach. Vacuums and

EXHIBIT 13-3

Summary of Selected Retailing Classifications

Retailer Classification	Brief Description
Product Variety	
General merchandise	Wide variety, shallow selection (department store)
Limited line (and single line)	Usually wide variety within a product class, large bulk of all retailing operations
Specialty	Narrow variety, deep selection (women's shoe store)
Ownership	
Independent	Can be proprietorship, partnership, or corporation
Chain	Two or more centrally owned stores with the same name, achieve economies of scale
Ownership group	Variety of stores with separate name and identity, centrally owned

Retailer Classification	Brief Description
Prominent Operational Activity	
Instore	
Supermarket	Wide variety of products, large departmentalized operation
Department store	Generally chain operations, wide variety, full range of services
Discount store	Wide variety of high-turnover products, low prices, few customer services
Nonstore	
Mail order	Low operating costs, emphasis on convenience, computerized lists utilized
Vending machine	High-turnover products, low priced
Door-to-door	High labor cost, image problems

carving knives are among the many products that lend themselves to such demonstration. Among the newer developments are the prospects of shopping at home by consumers who interact with retailers via personal computer or television systems such as the QUBE system, now in operation in Columbus, Ohio.

Unfortunately, for the many legitimate companies practicing this form of retailing, the image of the door-to-door approach has been tarnished by some unethical salespeople. However, in-home retailing is often performed by organizations with outstanding reputations, including Girl Scout cookies, Avon, and the several Tupperware-style "party" merchants.

A number of new developments make door-to-door selling even more difficult. For example, the *Green River Ordinances,* in effect in many local areas, put constraints on the activities of door-to-door salespeople by limiting the hours or neighborhoods in which they may call or by requiring stringently controlled licenses.

Exhibit 13-3 summarizes the various types of retailers based on selected classifications.

PATTERNS OF RETAIL DEVELOPMENT

Many types of retailing institutions have been developed by marketers. Many more will be developed as retail marketing continues to respond to changes in its environment. If some pattern of retail institutional development could be identified, retailers would be given a powerful management tool—a means of predicting what new forms of retailing institution will emerge.

Unfortunately, no hard and fast predictive method has yet been developed, but several "theories" have been formulated suggesting that cycles of past institutional development may be of some use to marketers attempting to foresee the future. Three such theories are discussed here.

EXHIBIT 13-4

**Current Positions on the "Wheel of Retailing"
in Order of Decreasing Markups**

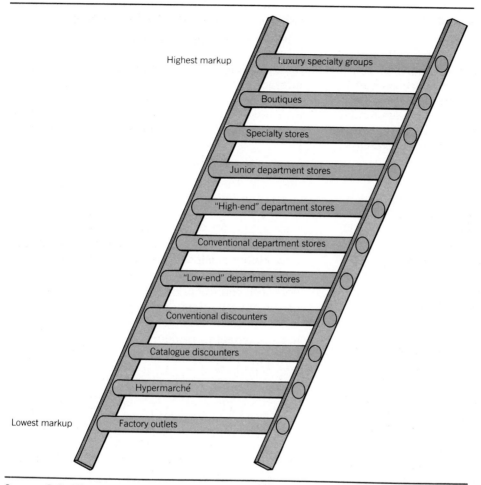

Highest markup — Luxury specialty groups

Boutiques

Specialty stores

Junior department stores

"High-end" department stores

Conventional department stores

"Low-end" department stores

Conventional discounters

Catalogue discounters

Hypermarché

Lowest markup — Factory outlets

Source: D.B. Tinsley, J.R. Brooks, Jr., and M.F. d'Amico, "Will the Wheel of Retailing Stop Turning?" *Akron Business and Economic Review*, Summer 1978, p. 26.

The Wheel of Retailing

The best known explanation or hypothesis relating to retail institutional development is the so-called **wheel of retailing**.[11] This theory states that new retailing institutions enter the marketplace as low-status, low-margin, low-price operations and then move toward higher status, margin, and price positions. Although the formulator of the theory viewed this process as the spinning of a wheel, a clearer notion of the idea is the ladder shown in Exhibit 13-4.

Analysts of retailing have observed that this pattern of "trading-up" exists with good reason. One cause of this phenomenon is the *American*

[11] The original wheel of retailing hypothesis was stated by Malcom P. McNair, "Significant Trends and Developments in the Post War Period," in A.B. Smith, ed., *Competitive Distribution in a Free High Level Economy and Its Impact for the University* (Pittsburgh, Pa.: University of Pittsburgh Press, 1958), pp. 1–25. See also Stanley C. Hollander, "The Wheel of Retailing," *Journal of Marketing*, July 1960, pp. 37–42.

dream which may drive retailers who start out small to attempt to end up operating businesses far larger and fancier than those with which they began. A small operator is thus likely to try to add services, buy a bigger building, or improve store appearances. This means that prices and margins will be raised to pay for such improvements. Another cause of trading-up is the American tradition of competing, at the retail level, more on the basis of non-price variables than on price variables. Americans do not have a tradition of haggling over prices; and retailers tend to compete with one another by such non-price means as offering trading stamps, free services, and more attractive stores. These things tend to drive up margins and prices.

Whatever the causes of trading-up, the wheel of retailing tells us that the end result is the same: A low spot on the wheel or ladder, once occupied by a low-margin retailer who has traded-up, is left open for an innovative retailer who realizes that it is possible to operate at a lower margin than that earned by existing retailers. The lower margin should attract customers. The innovator is thus tempted to snatch that lower spot, and the evolutionary process continues in this manner. Many of the discounters of the 1930s and 1940s followed this pattern and eventually ended up much like the department stores from which they sought to differentiate themselves. The discounters then became vulnerable to the newer, low-margin, low-price catalog stores and warehouse showrooms.

While the wheel hypothesis has much intuitive appeal and has been borne out in general by many studies of retail development, it should be noted that it only reflects a pattern. It is not a sure predictor of every change, nor was it ever intended to describe the development of every individual retailer. There are many non-conforming examples of retail managers who, for whatever reasons, have *not* traded-up their stores from the positions they originally occupied. Some observers also suggest that modern marketing methods, including research and positioning, will stop or slow the wheel of retailing when retail marketers resist abandoning market positions they have carefully selected.[12]

The Dialectic View of Retail Development

In the early 1800s, the German philosopher G.W. Hegel proposed a logical view of change, a pattern that fits nearly every situation: If a given institution exists, it will be challenged by another. The original **thesis** will be opposed by an **antithesis**. Except in rare cases, both sides will have something to recommend them. As they interact, a new idea—some combination of the two—will develop. Hegel called this hybrid concept the **synthesis**. The synthesis will be challenged by yet another antithesis, and so on. In fact, this is a good explanation of how ideas and institutions develop, and the pattern has been repeated throughout history.

Patterns like this can be discerned in retailing. As Exhibit 13-5 shows, one type of retailing institution can be challenged by another. What evolves from this confrontation is likely to be a new kind of institution combining elements of both. The challenge and response concept inherent in the dialectic process appeals to many observers of retailing because it suggests the competitive battles that retailers wage. Rethinking the wheel of retailing, we find the wheel hypothesis alone is insufficient to explain institutional change because it lacks the element of competition and response to that competition, which are inherent in retailing. Some combination of the wheel and the dialectic may therefore best explain retailing's changing patterns.

A General-Specific-General Explanation

We know that general stores once dominated the American retailing scene. Then, as populations grew and became concentrated in cities, more

---

[12] An interesting commentary suggested that one problem with "wheel" is that it considers only "producer costs" not "buyer costs." Buyer costs include travel parking, etc. These costs are disregarded by the "wheel" hypothesis. See J. Grimm, "Comments on the Dialectic Evolution of Retailing," in Barnett A. Greenberg, ed., *Proceedings: Southern Marketing Association*, 1974 Conference (Atlanta: Georgia State University, 1975), pp. 147–151.

EXHIBIT 13-5

The Challenge-Response Behavior of Retailing Institutions

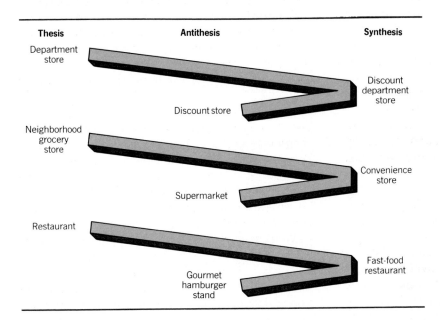

and more stores specializing in just a few products began to appear. Now we have seen the successful development of shopping malls that are combinations of smaller stores, many of them specialty shops, under one roof.

It is not too great a leap of the imagination to view these malls as giant general stores. Indeed, like the general stores of old, they are popular and successful in part because they offer one-stop shopping and something for everyone. While the general-specific-general explanation of retail institutional development may not be quite so appealing as the other two discussed, it is suggestive of a pattern worthy of some consideration.

Using These "Theories"

These explanations of retail institutional development do not and cannot explain how each and every change in our retailing system came about. Their predictive abilities are also imperfect if only because marketing is such a dynamic entity. The use of these theories lies not in the "answers" they give to planners, but in their abilities to raise questions. Their purpose is to generate thought. *Why* do these patterns appear to exist? What factors at play in the marketplace *contribute* to changes? Coming to grips with questions like these is far more important to planners than simply being familiar with theories and historical patterns.

RETAIL MANAGEMENT STRATEGIES

Like all marketers, retailers must develop a marketing mix. The concept of the marketing mix is essentially the same in all applications of marketing. Exhibit 13-6 shows some of the decision elements retail marketers face in developing a retail marketing mix.

Familiarity with the marketing mix concept should permit you to adjust the concept to fit the

EXHIBIT 13-6

Elements of the Retail Marketing Mix

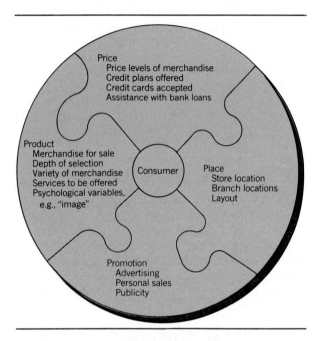

retail situation. For example, in which decision area would you place the variable store hours? Most would see it as a matter primarily concerned with ''place'' since the distribution of the store's total product offering clearly depends on the hours during which that product is available to customers.

This chapter cannot discuss all aspects of the retail marketing mix. Therefore, keeping the mix concept in mind, we will address three problem areas of special importance to retail marketers. These are *merchandise assortment, location,* and *store layout*. Image is another matter that transcends categories and is of concern to retailers. In a sense, image encompasses the three problem areas just mentioned as well as virtually every other aspect of a store's physical appearance and management. Personnel, merchandise, the store's immediate surroundings, its internal and external appearance, its prices, services, and so on, all contribute to image. Before reading on, consider familiar retailers and decide which features they possess contribute to your image of their operations.

SHOPPING CENTER VOCABULARY

You have observed that there are several kinds of shopping centers. Older models are often built as long strings of stores set in a parking area. This design is called a *strip*. A design that features stores built around a central area intended for strolling is called a *mall*. Technically, the heated and air-conditioned malls found in larger cities and towns are called *enclosed malls,* although most people simply call them malls.

You may also have noticed that shopping centers come in different sizes, essentially small, medium, and large. The official designations, however, are neighborhood, community, and regional. The *neighborhood shopping center* is likely to be a small strip containing such shops as a druggist, dry cleaner, and a small supermarket. The *community center* is larger with perhaps a variety store, clothing store, or small furniture dealer. The *regional center* is the largest, with 100 or even 200 stores, serving a large population and drawing customers from a wide geographic area. Although today we seldom think of it as such, the *downtown area* is, or at least used to be, a shopping center. For any number of reasons, including parking, crime, and a lack of public transportation, downtowns or *central business districts* (CBDs) have declined greatly in retailing importance since the post-World War II exodus of population to the suburbs. However, some city governments have successfully revitalized downtown areas. Minneapolis is a good example. The flight to the suburbs and the movement of retailers to suburban malls is difficult to overcome. Some observers feel that energy costs and changing tastes will ultimately lead to a rekindling of interest in downtown-based activities. In most cities, this has yet to occur, even though some ''downtown malls'' have been built.

Merchandise Assortment

One image that comes immediately to mind when the word ''store'' is mentioned is a physical place where merchandise for sale has been assembled. This is because one of a retailer's prime functions is to provide a product assortment for customers. Stated in different terms, retailers perform an **assorting function**—that is, they build desired assortments of varied goods so that manufacturers and customers need not. It is clearly in the interests of both consumers and producers to allow retailers to perform this service and to reward them for it. Since retailers also bear the risks associated with holding inventory, play important roles in channels of distribution, and provide flows of information, their markups or margins can seldom be seen as excessive.

From the individual customer's perspective, a major advantage of one retailer over a competitor is merchandise *assortment.* Other things are important, but no shopper will patronize a store without feeling that there is some chance that the merchandise sought will be found there. How does a retail marketer decide what merchandise assortment to carry? Information and suggestions are available from manufacturers and from intermediaries. Trade magazines and newspapers may offer useful insights. But, most importantly, the retailer must carefully consider the target market's needs and wants and match the merchandise selection with those desires. This truth is elemental to effective retail marketing. Yet retailers frequently make "buying mistakes," the costs of which must be absorbed through mark-downs or other means. Buying errors cannot be totally avoided, but careful planning can minimize their occurrence. The matter of aligning merchandise offerings with customer desires cannot be detailed here, but it is important to note that marketing—not guesswork—must be the basis of all decisions in this area.

Location, Location, and Location

There is an old line that the three most important factors in successful retailing are location, location, and location. Yet that is not absolutely the case. An out-of-the-way location can be compensated for by other means, especially huge selections and low prices. Nonetheless, the adage makes a point. Retailers are justifiably concerned about locating in the right part of the right town. They must monitor changes that may

---

THE DRIVE-IN DIALECTIC

Consider the evolution of the drive-in restaurant.

The early drive-in restaurant typically was "full-service" offering a broad menu, most meals prepared after ordered, and sit down as well as curb service. This thesis "begat" an antithesis, "The Fast Foods" restaurant in which many items were prepared in anticipation of orders and a limited menu in carryout service was the rule rather than the exception. Over time, both institutions have exhibited adaptive behavior as suggested by the dialectic hypothesis. Full service drive-in restaurants have reduced menu selections, added more prepared items, and set up carryout facilities. Limited menu drive-in restaurants meanwhile have increased the number of items on their menus and added sit-down eating accommodations. A synthesis type institution now prevails.

Source: This is quoted from T.J. Maronic and B.J. Walker, "The Dialectic Evolution of Retailing," in Barnett A. Greenberg, ed., *Proceedings: Southern Marketing Association,* 1974 Conference (Atlanta: Georgia State University, 1975), pp. 147–151.

---

affect the suitability of an existing location or make another site more attractive.

The right location depends on the type of business and the target customer, not on any formula or rule of thumb. As with merchandise assortment questions, the answer lies in careful marketing planning. Experience dictates certain guidelines, however. Toys-Я-Us requires that its outlets be placed in metropolitan areas with populations of at least one-quarter of a million people, of which an established percentage must be children. Ideally, the selected market should be large enough to support four stores, each of which can be located in an unattached or *free standing* building near a major mall.[13]

---

[13] Janet Neiman, "Retailers Should Know Their Place," *Advertising Age,* November 1, 1982, p. m-22.

THE SHOPPING MALL GOES URBAN

While most of the nation's retailers are waiting glumly for their too-silent cash registers to ring in the holiday season, merchants in downtown Milwaukee are dancing to the cheery beat of sales, sales, and more sales. A dazzling new inner-city shopping mall has given the city, its residents, and store owners a badly needed boost. Four blocks of the formerly seedy downtown area—known in its prosperous, turn-of-the-century days as the Grand Avenue—have been transformed into a mecca for shoppers. Only three months after it opened, the $70 million Grand Avenue complex, developed by Rouse Co., and its 135 shops are crowing that business is up some 35% over their projections.

More than 25,000 people a day stream in to enjoy the artful blend of the old and new. To develop a local theme, Rouse linked two "anchors" that underwent facelifts—Gimbels and Boston Store—with three historic buildings, including a Victorian retail arcade with a vaulted skylight and rotunda, and transformed them into a vibrant shopping area.

Brightly colored murals depicting the city's association with the beer industry and its ethnic heritage line the walls, while a beer-drinking bear on a unicycle traverses a wire in the upper reaches of the center. "Between the Brewers and Grand Avenue, the whole town is feeling a real uplift," says Gimbels Midwest Chairman Thomas G. Grime, who cheerily reports that sales at the downtown outlet are 25% ahead of last year's.

Grand Avenue is becoming a success story not only because its 245,000 square feet of retail space is 91 percent rented—in the middle of a recession—or because it surmounted the problems devastating the industrial Midwest. Rather, it has shown that canny marketing and an alliance of the public and private sectors can turn blighted and abandoned urban areas into pleasurable centers of commerce. More than 48 percent of its space is leased to local merchants who had given up on the area.

Milwaukee's is the latest in a new generation of downtown malls. Boston's Faneuil Hall Marketplace, once an abandoned landmark, is now a thriving, 365,000 sq. ft. bazaar that attracts 12 million people a year. Harborplace, on Baltimore's long-neglected waterfront, is such a tourist attraction that out-of-towners account for 35% of the 140,000 sq. ft. glassy center's business. Now, the International Council of Shopping Centers says that 25% of the projects proposed are pegged for in-city locations, compared with 10% five years ago.

Part of the reason for the emphasis on urban areas is simply that most of the choice suburban spots are pretty much "malled" over. But some developers believe that life in bedroom communities has lost its charm. "People are becoming bored with the suburbs and really want to return to the city," says Mathias J. DeVito, president of Rouse, which has similar complexes planned for downtowns in New York City, St. Louis, and Chicago. Edward J. DeBartolo Corp., a major builder of suburban malls, is also constructing downtown projects in San Antonio, New Orleans, and Pittsburgh. "We want attractions that only the city can offer—like interesting theme restaurants, art galleries, live theater, and even some jazz spots," says Howard S. Biel, vice-president for market research.

Urban centers, though, are tricky to master. They must appeal to a broad range of customers—office workers, tourists, and suburbanites—and offer extras that their off-the-main-highway rivals cannot. "Today, people have so many shopping alternatives that a trip to the city must be a special treat," says DeVito.

As a result, most downtown malls showcase a belt-loosening mélange of eating delights, a wide range of "events," diverse shops, easy transportation, and ample parking, as well as security. (Grand Avenue's 1,300-car, indoor garage offers free parking on weekends, after 5 p.m., or with proof of purchase; otherwise the

Source: From "The Shopping Mall Goes Urban," *Business Week*, December 13, 1982, p. 50. Used with permission.

fee is 25¢ an hour.) "Urban centers tend to fail when these fundamentals of marketing are not met," declares Robert C. Larson, president of Taubman Co., which recently opened the 900,000 sq. ft. Stamford Town Center in Connecticut and is planning to build five more downtown malls.

Achieving the right balance can be difficult. Renaissance Center in Detroit ran into problems soon after its opening in 1977 when its modernistic design reminded many of a fortress. That, plus an overabundance of ultrachic designer boutiques, had the $357 million center on the ropes. Center Companies Inc. took over

as manager early last year and has added more mass appeal retailers. But occupancy is still a puny 60%.

Knowing who the customers are and getting them to the mall is crucial, as the Gallery at Market East in Philadelphia found out. "When we opened in 1977, we envisioned that we could go to the suburbs [for customers], but we couldn't," says David C. Creighton, manager of the 200,000 square foot center. Instead, the Gallery was drawing city residents whose $23,000 average yearly income was not large enough to support the high-priced boutiques dotting the facility. A transit strike in 1981 hurt, too. "The key to our success is mass transit," asserts Creighton. "About 80 percent of our customers use it to get here." A new policy of renting to medium-priced merchants and running special events at least 40 weeks a year has the mall 98.5 percent leased.

Building downtown malls often involves political and economic wrangling. Grand Avenue finally got under way when 46 local Milwaukee companies kicked in $16 million for the project and the city coughed up $30 million. A $12.6 million Urban Development Action grant helped, but developers are not optimistic about future federal assistance. With development financing harder to find, Rouse and others are concentrating on mixed-use centers that will include office space,

hotels, and eateries. Grand Avenue already offers 200,000 square feet of office space, and its German-style dining area has 15 food shops and central seating that draws downtown workers at noon and after 5 P.M.

Strong anchor stores can also help inner-city malls. At Grand Avenue, Rouse's contract stipulated that both Gimbels and Boston Store modernize their aging plants. Gimbels turned its basement into a chic food emporium and upgraded throughout the store, while its co-anchor spiffed up its interior and selections to attract wealthy suburbanites who might otherwise drive 90 mi. to Chicago for such goods. Boston Store reports its sales are up 50 percent.

The outlook for the Milwaukee center is rosy. More than 100,000 people jammed it over the Thanksgiving weekend. So strong is Grand Avenue's pull that the surrounding suburban malls are feeling pressure: Three have just replaced their marketing managers, and another two have new general managers. Because local merchants are clamoring for more space in or near the Grand Avenue gold mine, the developer of a new federal building facing the complex is considering doubling its planned retail space. William Rush, senior vice-president of Gimbels, says happily, "In a tough retail year, this has been a real shot in the arm."

Retail site selection experts note that an important attribute of any intended site is the other types of outlets around it. Obviously, Toys-Я-Us expects major shopping malls to generate traffic near the toy store locations. Other retailers also seek what are called *complementary businesses.* Placing a diner near a gas station makes more sense than locating a dress shop near a gas station. The nature of the retailer's business operations may be important. Catalog discounters, for example, can rely on their customers to do some pre-shopping using the catalogs. This, plus the factors of lower prices and the immediate gratification of being able to take items home from the store, reduces the need for store locations in expensive, high-traffic areas. One catalog retailer says, "If we had our druthers, we'd be two blocks away from shopping centers. There's no use paying top dollar for the exposure because there is little impulse shopping."[14] On the other hand, the traffic generated by a shopping center would be far more important to a Haägen-Daz or Baskin-Robbins ice cream shop.

Layout

Retail management includes managing every aspect of the business. This includes the shop's layout, interior design, and overall atmosphere.

While as many factors contribute to store atmosphere as to store image, the ambiance of any store—the surroundings that the customer perceives as much as actually senses—is largely created by interior design and layout.

Modern supermarket design and layout, for example, seem to be aimed at avoiding an old-fashioned, stodgy atmosphere. The experimental Safeway in Arlington, Texas, creates an environment akin to a shopping mall, clustering convenience shops in the center of the store. The intense use of space, characteristic of most supermarkets' "grid" pattern, was sacrificed for the more attractive "free flow" design common to department stores and fashion goods shops to create a pleasant atmosphere for customers. This Safeway offers a variety of services including a deli, bakery, cafe, florist, and pharmacy. Atmospherics, such as lighting, music, colors, and the avoidance of a perception of crowding, are used to create favorable customer attitudes.[15] Supermarkets have changed to the point that some offer all the services and products of the Arlington Safeway and add lawyers' offices, emergency medical care centers, gift shops, and game rooms. It has been pointed out that today's mall serves many of the functions of old downtowns.[16] Supermarkets may be moving that way, too.

WHOLESALING

A wholesaler is a middleman that neither produces nor consumes the finished product but, instead, sells to retailers and other institutions that use the product for ultimate resale.

Its function is facilitating either the transportation or the transfer of title to the products. Our discussion in Chapter 12 indicated the functions

that all middlemen, including wholesalers, perform. Furthermore, because wholesaling activities fit the definition of industrial or organizational marketing, the discussion of industrial marketing in Chapter 21 includes a number of

[14] Stanley H. Slom, "The Catalogs Showroom Booms Reduce Cost, Make Shopping Easier," *Wall Street Journal,* July 5, 1972, pp. 1, 13.

[15] Kevin Higgins, "Safeway Enters Quest for Supermarket of the Future," *Marketing News,* January 7, 1983, p. 1 and "Safeway Goes for Modern Styling with Mall Layout," *Advertising Age,* November 29, 1982, p. 52s.

[16] J. Barry Mason, "First, Fifth and Fourteenth Amendments Rights: The Shopping Center Is a Public Forum," *Journal of Retailing,* Summer 1975, p. 21.

EXHIBIT 13-7

Wholesale Trade: Kinds of Business

Motor vehicles, automotive equipment	Paper, paper products
Furniture, home furnishings	Groceries and related products
Lumber, construction materials	Petroleum, petroleum products
Electrical goods	Farm product raw materials
Hardware, plumbing, heating equipment	Apparel, notions
Machinery, equipment, supplies	Metals and minerals

Source: *Statistical Abstract of the United States, 1982–83*, 103rd edition (Washington, D.C.: U.S. Department of Commerce, Bureau of the Census, 1983), p. 810.

special marketing strategies that trade wholesalers and other industrial marketers tend to utilize. The purpose of this section is to portray the different types of wholesaling establishments and institutions within the United States. Exhibit 13-7 lists the kinds of businesses involved in wholesaling.

The last *Census of Business* reported that there were 382,800 wholesale trade establishments in the United States.[17] Over 307,000 of these were merchant wholesalers. There were 40,500 manufacturers' sales branches and offices and 35,100 agents and brokers. Exhibit 13-8 shows the sales of merchant wholesalers by kinds of businesses.

Wholesalers have much in common with retailers; both of these types of marketers act as selling agents for their suppliers and as buying agents for their customers. Both are creators of time and place utility. Both must carefully evaluate the needs of their customers and deliver an appropriate total product of goods and services if they are to succeed in business. And both have developed ways of performing marketing functions that specially suit market environmental conditions.

[17] *Statistical Abstract of the United States, 1982–83*, 103rd edition (Washington, D.C.: United States Department of Commerce, Bureau of the Census), p. 810.

EXHIBIT 13-8

Merchant Wholesalers: Sales, by Kind of Business, 1982

	Sales (billions of dollars)
Durable Goods	
Motor vehicles and auto equipment	$ 87.7
Furniture and home furnishings	15.9
Electrical goods	54.6
Hardware, plumbing, and heating equipment	26.8
Machinery, equipment, and supplies	135.3
Nondurable goods	
Paper and paper products	22.8
Groceries and related products	179.8
Beer, wine, and distilled beverages	36.1
Miscellaneous	81.7
Total	$1,144.3

Source: Bureau of Census, *Current Business Reports, Monthly Wholesale Trade* (Washington, D.C.: U.S. Department of Commerce, 1983), p. 2.

Types of Wholesalers

Intermediaries performing wholesaling functions are traditionally divided into two groups—merchants and agents. The only distinction between these categories is whether their members take *title* to the goods they sell. Merchants middlemen take title; agent middlemen do not. This has nothing at all to do with the matter of possession of goods. Some merchants take possession of merchandise and others do not. Some agents take possession of the goods they sell, but most do not.

The distinction between a merchant and an agent is more than just a definitional matter. It is important to the behavior of these two types of intermediaries. After all, when title is taken to merchandise, the intermediary owns that merchandise and must be prepared to handle any risks associated with ownership—including that of getting stuck with merchandise which, for whatever reason, turns out to be unsalable.

Merchant Wholesalers

Merchant wholesalers account for slightly over 50 percent of all wholesale transactions.[18] **Merchant wholesalers** are independently owned concerns that take title to the goods they distribute. They represent about 80 percent of all wholesaling concerns in the nation. Since 80 percent of the institutions account for less than one-half the wholesale volume, many of these operations are fairly small. This is because the selling and transportation costs associated with wholesaling activities increase quickly as the area covered by a concern is enlarged. Therefore, many merchant wholesalers cover only single cities or areas stretching only 100 or 200 miles from the main office. This reduces or eliminates the need for overnight trips by trucks or sales personnel and holds down expenses.

Merchant wholesalers may be classified in terms of the numbers and types of services they provide to their customers. In this regard, they are perfect examples of how marketing firms adjust their total product offerings of goods and services to reflect the demands of particular situations and market segments.

Full-Service Merchant Wholesalers. As their name suggests, **full-service merchant wholesalers** provide their customers with a complete array of services in addition to the merchandise they offer. Such services include delivery of goods, extension of credit, providing marketing information and advice, and possibly even such managerial assistance as accounting aid or other non-marketing aids. Full-service wholesalers are also called *full-function wholesalers*.

Within this category, three subsets of wholesalers are identifiable by lines of goods offered. Like retailers, these intermediaries may be **general merchandise wholesalers** who sell a large number of different product types; **general line wholesalers,** who limit their offerings to a full array of products within one product line; and **specialty wholesalers,** who reduce their

Fleming Foods, a full-service merchant grocery wholesaler, utilizes modern technology.

lines still further. A coffee and tea wholesaler or a spice wholesaler would exemplify this last class.

Wholesalers determine how wide or narrow a line to carry by carefully considering the customers they serve and the industry in which they operate. When the target customers are operators of general stores, the decision to be a general merchandise wholesaler would be logical. In some industries, however, traditional marketing practices may require some degree of specialization. Occasionally, the specialization is required

---

[18]As a percentage of dollar sales volume, *Statistical Abstract of the United States 1982–83,* 103rd edition (Washington, D.C.: U.S. Department of Commerce, Bureau of the Census 1983), p. 810.

A cash-and-carry wholesaler.

by law, as in the case of beer wholesalers who, in many states, are not permitted to deal in any other alcoholic beverage.

Limited-Service Wholesalers. Regardless of the product line carried, full-service wholesalers provide an essentially complete line of extra services. However, some customers may not want, nor want to pay for, some or all of those services. Some buyers may prefer to sacrifice services to get lower prices. Since this is entirely likely, a group of **limited-service** or **limited function wholesalers** have developed.

Cash-and-Carry Wholesalers. Buyers not willing to pay for and not needing certain wholesale services, such as delivery and credit, may choose to patronize **cash-and-carry wholesalers.** Such an intermediary eliminates the delivery and credit functions associated with a full-service wholesaler and permits buyers to come to the warehouse or other point of distribution to pick up their merchandise and to pay cash. Resultant savings are then passed on to buyers who are, after all, performing several functions normally associated with wholesalers.

Truck Wholesalers. **Truck wholesalers,** also called **truck jobbers,** typically sell a limited line of items to comparatively small buyers. Most of these merchant wholesalers sell perishable

items. Their mode of operation, selling from a truckful of merchandise, can be justified by the increased freshness immediate delivery offers. Some truck wholesalers sell items which are not particularly perishable but which face keen competition. They might, for example, sell potato chips and other snack items to tavern owners. Although truck jobbing is an expensive means of distributing relatively small amounts of merchandise, it is an aggressive form of sales *and* provides instant delivery to buyers.

Mail-Order Wholesalers. **Mail-Order wholesalers** operate in much the same fashion as do mail-order retailers. They use catalogs or take phone orders, and then forward merchandise to buyers via the mails. Traditionally, these wholesalers have been most important in reaching remote rural locations where delivery services other than the U.S. mail may choose not to go. As delivery services have become better over the years, the importance of mail-order wholesaling has declined, even though it still is appropriate for servicing small-order customers.

Drop Shippers. **Drop shippers** are merchant wholesalers who take title to goods but do not take possession of the goods or handle them in any way. Drop shippers accept a buyer's order and pass it on to a producer or supplier of the desired commodity who then ships the product directly to the buyer, as shown in Exhibit 13-9.

EXHIBIT 13-9

Operation of a Drop Shipper

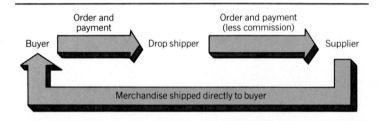

Order and payment → Buyer → Drop shipper → Order and payment (less commission) → Supplier — Merchandise shipped directly to buyer

The big advantage to this system is that the product escapes double handling. That is, it need not be loaded and unloaded several times. It goes directly to where it is needed, which also lowers transportation costs. These advantages are especially important when the product in question is bulky, unwieldy, and comparatively inexpensive. Thus, drop shipping is most commonly encountered for products such as coal, cement, building blocks, or logs.

Because the drop shipper does not physically handle any products, no investment in warehousing facilities or equipment is required. In fact, so little equipment of any sort is required that these wholesalers can often get by with little more than a small office, a desk, and a telephone. For this reason, they are also called **desk jobbers.**

Rack Jobbers. **Rack jobbers** are a form of merchant wholesaler that first came to prominence in the 1930s when many supermarket operators began to practice scrambled merchandising and started selling cosmetics and other items they had not previously carried. To do this easily, they contracted with wholesalers willing to come to the store, set up a display rack, stock and replenish it, and give the supermarket operator a percentage of the sales. Now rack jobbers sell many different product lines. Small items of clothing such as work gloves, paperback books, magazines, toys, cosmetics, and panty hose are among the items most commonly handled in this way.

The attraction of this system to the store operator is the chance to stock and sell certain items at little risk. The great attraction to the rack jobber is the chance to place merchandise in a high-traffic supermarket location. As with most relationships among channel of distribution members, theirs is a mutually beneficial, symbiotic one.

Agents

Agents, the second general category of wholesalers, take possession of goods they deal in but they do not take title to them. Agents, as a rule, do not carry an inventory or extend credit. They may help to *arrange* for delivery or extension of credit as part of their services, which can be generally described as bringing buyer and seller together. Agents typically receive commissions based on the selling prices of the products they help to sell. The commission percentage varies tremendously depending on the industry. They are expected to be familiar with those products and with who wants to sell and who wants to buy them. In short, they are expected to have an expert knowledge of the market in which they operate.

Brokers. **Brokers** are agent intermediaries who receive a commission for putting sellers in touch with buyers and assisting with contractual negotiations. While brokers generally portray themselves as "neutral" in their selling process, their commission is based on the selling price of the product involved, and, if the product is not sold, they get no commission whatsoever. For these reasons, brokers may be seen as working more for the seller than for the buyer in any transaction. Effective brokers are experts in the market for the products in which they deal. In effect, they sell their expertise. They have relatively low expenses. Their commissions are also small, likely to be 6 percent or less of the selling price.

Use of brokers holds particular appeal for sellers because brokers work strictly on commission and do not enter into long-term relationships with the companies that use them. A broker can be used only when needed and does not tie sellers to continuous expenses the way a fulltime sales force does.

Brokers are found in all fields. Such commodities as coffee, tea, crude petroleum, and scrap metal are frequently brokered, as are the financial instruments handled by the familiar stock broker. Many other things are sold in this way, however. Among them are time on commercial radio stations and used industrial equipment.

Because they are commonly used on a sporadic basis, brokers as a group do not constitute a major selling force in the day-to-day marketing activities of most organizations. A notable exception to this is the food broker who represents a number of manufacturers of food products on a constant basis and actively attempts to sell their products to wholesalers or supermarkets. However, such an operation really violates the standard description of a broker. In many ways, food brokers better fit other categories of agents. By tradition as much as anything else, they continue to be referred to as brokers.

Commission Merchants. The **commission merchant** is a type of agent intermediary similar to a broker. Unlike brokers, however, commission merchants are usually given certain powers by the sellers that use them. They might be empowered, for example, to attempt to bid up the selling price or to accept a selling price as long as it is above a previously agreed-on floor. Commission merchants thus perform a pricing function and more clearly work in league with the seller than do most brokers.

Commission merchants, despite the name, do not take title to the goods they sell. However, they often take possession of those goods. Since they are most commonly found representing producers of agricultural products, they frequently take possession of products for inspection by potential buyers. Once a sales agreement has been reached, the commission merchant deducts a commission from the selling price and returns the balance to the producer.

Auction Companies. Auction companies are agent intermediaries who perform valuable services in the buying and selling of livestock, tobacco, and other commodities, as well as artwork and used mechanical equipment. In a sense, these companies take possession of the goods they deal in since, frequently, some special place is provided in which the auction can take place. The products that are sold through auction might have been sold in some other manner, but auction companies offer a certain convenience in that they bring buyers together in one spot and facilitate a rather rapid bidding process that might otherwise have taken an extensive period of time to conduct. In addition, some industries, such as the tobacco industry, that have traditionally used auction companies continue to do so.

An auction company may be used to sell used equipment.

EXHIBIT 13-10

Wholesale Trade: Relative Positions of Merchant Wholesalers, Manufacturer Sales Branches and Offices, and Agents and Brokers

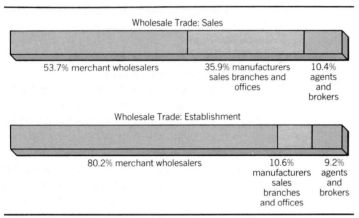

Wholesale Trade: Sales

53.7% merchant wholesalers | 35.9% manufacturers sales branches and offices | 10.4% agents and brokers

Wholesale Trade: Establishment

80.2% merchant wholesalers | 10.6% manufacturers sales branches and offices | 9.2% agents and brokers

Source: Department of Commerce, *Statistical Abstract of the United States, 1982–83,* 103rd edition (Washington, D.C.: U.S. Government Printing Office, 1982), p. 310.

The operation of the auction system provides some less-than-obvious advantages: (1) products can generally be examined by potential buyers; (2) sellers and buyers may, if they choose, remain anonymous; (3) buyers may enjoy the thrills involved with the auction approach to selling and savor their victory over other bidders for years to come. This last factor may not be important to a tobacco buyer, but it is to a patron of art auctions.

The auction company receives a commission based on the final, highest bid offered for an item or product provided that this bid is above a minimum agreed-on figure.

Manufacturers' Agents and Selling Agents. Two types of representatives are available to producers of products who, for whatever reasons, do not want to perform sales and marketing activities themselves. For example, a maker of photocopy equipment might want to handle only major markets itself, but not smaller cities or rural areas. It might decide to hire a series of manufacturers' agents to cover those areas with low market potential and to let the company's own sales force take the more important markets. **Manufacturers' agents,** also

called **manufacturers' representatives,** are agent intermediaries who represent one manufacturer or two or more non-competing producers within geographically limited areas, such as a few states or a portion of a state. Their familiarity with the local market and the fact that they are paid a commission rather than a salary make manufacturers' agents an attractive means to reach wholesalers, retailers, or industrial buyers.

The existence of markets with low market potential is not the only good reason to use manufacturers' agents. Another reason is that the producer may lack the interest or expertise to perform sales and marketing functions. Still another is finances: A company that has relatively few financial resources is more likely to use an agent since the agent need not be paid until a sale is made. This is not the case when the company must find, hire, train, and pay its own sales force.

Selling agents, like manufacturers' agents, may represent more than one producer and spread selling costs over the products produced by all of them. Selling agents are also paid a commission and are expected to be familiar with the products they handle and the markets they serve. However, they differ from manufacturers'

EXHIBIT 13-11

Summary Table: Wholesaling Classifications

Merchant Wholesalers

Full service
Deliver goods
Extend credit
Provide marketing information
Managerial assistance
Variety of lines of goods offered

Limited service
Cash and carry   No delivery or credit

Truck wholesaler   Limited product line, delivers goods (often perishable)

Mail-order wholesaler   Important in rural locations

Drop shipper   Doesn't handle products; generally bulky products

Rack jobber   Wide variety of small products; responsible for stocking products

Agent Wholesalers

Agents   May take possession but do not take title to products; receive commission based on selling price; usually do not extend credit

Brokers   Assist in contractual negotiations; bring buyers/sellers together

Commission merchants   May take possession but not title to goods; perform pricing function for sellers

Auction companies   Offer conveniences in bringing buyers/sellers together

Manufacturer's agents and selling agents   Assist manufacturer, often in "thin markets" to sell products, paid by commission; selling agents have greater responsibilities

Sales offices and branches   Manufacturers doing their own wholesaling, sales branch carries inventory but sales office does not; major benefit is greater control

---

agents in one major respect. They do not limit their activities to one geographic area, but sell *all* of the products manufactured by the producers they represent. Because they function as sales and marketing departments, they are often given more responsibility than are manufacturers' agents. They may be permitted to handle the advertising and pricing of the products sold and

determine any conditions of sale to be negotiated. When a selling agent is utilized, the manufacturer obtains what might be called an *external marketing department*.

Exhibits 13-10 and 13-11 give us an overview of the various wholesalers in the two basic classifications.

Manufacturers Who Do Their Own Wholesaling

Throughout this section we have been considering the performance of wholesaling as if done entirely by independent organizations other than manufacturers. Actually, although these various agents and merchant intermediaries are extremely important, especially within particular lines of trade, many manufacturers perform the wholesaling functions themselves. Some manufacturers have become disenchanted with wholesalers for a number of reasons. The feeling is widespread among them that wholesalers who handle the products of *many* manufacturers cannot push any *one* manufacturer's product as that producer feels it should be promoted. It has been estimated that more than one-third of all wholesale transactions carried out in the United States are performed by manufacturers themselves.

When manufacturers do their own wholesaling, be it to retailers or industrial users, they may use sales offices, sales branches, or both. (The U.S. Department of Commerce classifies sales branches and sales offices as wholesalers even though, according to our definition, they are not independent middlemen.) Sales offices and sales branches are wholesaling establishments maintained by producers of the products sold, and both could serve as headquarters for "outside" salespeople or as offices for "inside" salespeople. The *central difference* between the two is that the sales branch carries an inventory of products, while the sales office does not. The bulk of the product, the need for fast delivery, the technical aspects of the product, and the opportunity to sell a standardized product rather than a custom-made one would all contribute to the decision to use offices or branches.

The reasons manufacturers choose to do their own wholesaling can be expressed in one word: control. The maintenance of sales offices and branches permits manufacturers to control more effectively the flow of goods to their customers, the training of their salespeople and their selling activities, and the flow of information returned to "headquarters" by a staff that is actually out in the field.

Wholesaling in the Future

The successful independent wholesalers of the future will be those who most effectively adapt to the changing needs and requirements of the marketplace. Evolving trends in the distribution of goods and services demand innovations from tomorrow's wholesalers. Wholesalers perform functions that cannot easily be absorbed by other channel members, yet these services must continually be reexamined and redefined.

Wholesalers must maintain a particularly acute awareness of technological advances that affect the distribution of goods and services. They must be willing to adopt modernized materials-handling and information-processing systems if they are to remain efficient operators. The wholesaler of the future will be a more specialized wholesaler, targeting services to carefully identified target markets where success is most likely. The most apparent benefit a wholesaler can offer is extensive knowledge of the products of manufacturers and of the market where those products are bought and sold. The wholesaler must be willing to apply and sell this knowledge, and to provide greater assistance, in the form of accurate and pertinent information, to both the manufacturer and the retailer. If the wholesalers are able to adapt, the wholesaling industry will experience productive growth and success and evolve fully.

SUMMARY

Retailing involves all activities concerned with the sale of products to buyers who are also the ultimate users of those products. The nearly 2 million retailing establishments in the United States may be classified according to a number of criteria including the variety of products they sell, types of ownership, and style of operation, although accurate distinctions are difficult to draw given the continually evolving nature of these institutions. A number of hypotheses, such as the wheel of retailing, have been proposed to explain the evolutionary development of retailing institutions.

Retail marketers of all types must develop effective marketing mixes aimed at attracting and satisfying target markets. While the problems retailers face are somewhat distinct from those of manufacturers or of marketers operating in the industrial sector, the basic principles of effective marketing can be applied profitably in the retailing milieu. However, merchandise assortment, location, and store layout are of special importance to retailers.

Unlike retailers, wholesalers do not deal with final consumers but with industrial buyers, other wholesalers, and, of course, retailers themselves. Intermediaries performing the wholesaling function are either merchants or agents. Merchants take title to the goods they sell, while agents do not. In terms of numbers and sales totals, independent merchant wholesalers are the most important of these intermediaries, although wholesaling activities by manufacturers using sales branches and offices represent an important trend in this field. Agent intermediaries, such as brokers, manufacturers' representatives, and selling agents round out the portrait of wholesaling activities.

THE MOST IMPORTANT CONCEPT IN THIS CHAPTER

Retailing and wholesaling are the major distribution institutions that make our marketing system work. Classifying the various types of retailers and wholesalers into categories depends on the defined criteria, such as variety of products or type of ownership.

KEY TERMS

Retailing	Discount store	Full-service merchant wholesaler	Drop shipper
General merchandise retailer	Warehouse retailer	General merchandise wholesaler	Desk jobber
Limited-line retailer	Catalog showroom		Rack jobber
Specialty store	Direct-response retailer	Specialty wholesaler	Agent
Independent retailer	Wheel of retailing	Limited-service (limited function) wholesaler	Broker
Chain store	Dialectic theory		Commission merchant
Ownership group	General-specific-general	Cash-and-carry wholesaler	Auction company
Supermarket	Assorting function	Truck wholesaler (truck jobber)	Manufacturers' agent (manufacturers' representative)
Scrambled merchandising	Wholesaler		
Department store	Merchant wholesaler	Mail-order wholesaler	Selling agent

QUESTIONS FOR DISCUSSION

1 Give some examples of retailers in your local area that fit the following categories:
(a) General merchandise retailer
(b) Specialty store
(c) Chain store
(d) Catalog showroom or warehouse retailer

2 Which of the following retailers would tend to utilize free-standing locations? Why? Why not?
(a) K-Mart
(b) McDonald's
(c) Department store
(d) Popcorn shops

3 What are the advantages of franchising?

4 What are some of the disadvantages of using vending machines?

5 What trends do you predict in non-store retailing?

6 Take a look at furniture marketing in the United States and discuss the evolution and development of retailing innovations in this industry.

7 Do small independent retailing executives have the same growth orientation and business philosophies as large corporate executives?

8 Can you find local examples of the following:
(a) Cash-and-carry wholesaler
(b) Rack jobber
(c) Manufacturer's sales office
(d) Auction company

9 What is the major difference between agents and merchant wholesalers?

10 What would the advantages and disadvantages be of using manufacturers' agents in the following situations?
(a) New company marketing voice synthesizer for computers
(b) Large established company marketing truck axles
(c) West Virginia Coal Company selling coal in Pennsylvania

11 What trends do you predict in wholesaling?

CASE 13-1 Chief Auto Parts

Chief Auto Parts, Southland Corporation's auto parts convenience store chain, will test a service center concept. If successful, it will expand Chief's role as a retailer of do-it-yourself car-care products to include servicing those products. The test site will be in the Dallas area and will probably begin operation this year by offering light mechanical work. The combined service center and store will require twice the space of an existing Chief store, which is about 2,400 square feet. Marketing plans for the center have yet to be determined. It is expected the service center will be open 24 hours a day since Chief operates about 30 percent of its stores on a 24-hour basis. Chief will maintain a mix with some stores open all night and others open only during normal business hours.

Questions
1 What type of store is Chief Auto Parts?
2 Why do you think they are testing the service center concept?

CASE 13-2 The "VARs"*

In the beginning, entrepreneurs created systems houses to add software and customer support to computer manufacturers' unadorned hardware. The idea was a hit. Computer makers interested solely in moving their brute machines were so willing to unload such loathsome responsibilities that they offered big discounts to software and marketing specialists willing to handhold smallfry customers. Thousands of these value-added resellers (VAR) thrived. But as hardware prices have shrunk, so have manufacturers' discounts, and some observers are talking shakeout among the smaller systems houses.

Now, in an attempt to restore discounts to VARs, about 10 entrepreneurs have set themselves up as middlemen between manufacturers and VARs, buying in large quantities and reselling at still-major discounts to VARs, which then add software and marketing support. In return, these master VARs, as they are known, are getting some of the biggest discounts ever offered in the business. They make life easier for an IBM or a Honeywell, which can now sell in volume to a single buyer instead of to hundreds of dealers. And because master VARs get such big discounts from the manufacturers, they can pass along the savings to small dealers.

There are only about 10 master VARs that operate in a market said to account for perhaps $100 million to $200 million in sales this year, up from nothing just a few years ago. Master VARs are required to buy large volumes of computers and are prohibited from selling directly to end users.

Ultimate Corporation, Clark, New Jersey, the first master VAR, has grown to $38 million in sales for 1982, since its founding in 1979, by taking software that ran only on small-business computers made by Microdata and making it compatible with Honeywell computers.

In return for putting Honeywell into new markets, Honeywell gives Ultimate a hefty discount—between 35 percent and 50 percent, according to David Gould, senior vice-president for marketing at Ultimate. Gould's bread and butter is his network of 68 dealerships across the country and in Great Britain, Canada, Mexico, and Australia, which he is committed to expanding to 150 by 1985.

Perhaps no master VAR is more ambitious than Terry Marsh, 39, who started Western Business Computers Inc. in San Jose, California, in 1980. Marsh has already signed up 15 dealers who have written software for a single computer and make the program run on several brand-name machines. Marsh raised $8 million through an R&D limited partnership to develop translation programs that let software written for cer-

---

*Source: From Maisie McAdoo, "The Emerging 'Super' Systems Houses," *Venture*, May 1983, p. 100. Reprinted with permission.

tain lesser-known brands of small-business computers run on IBM and Honeywell machines. Marsh expects pretax profits of 15 to 20 percent on $20 million in sales this year.

The market for resellers is young because not all brand-name computer manufacturers are accustomed to dealing with master VARs. IBM, for example, traditionally sold directly to customers; so when it created a new unit to sell discounted hardware to master resellers, the change represented a major opportunity for reseller-entrepreneurs. Dennis Brown, 42, started Computer Distributors Inc. in Bellevue, Washing-

ton, as IBM's first master VAR in late 1981 with about $1 million. He could earn $1 million, pretax, this year on sales of $11 million, a big improvement over a first year loss on sales of $1 million.

Questions

1 Outline a channel of distribution that includes a VAR.

2 What marketing functions do the VARs perform? Estimate their value to manufacturers, retailers, and consumers.

CASE 13-3 J.C. Penney's*

A slimmed down, fashion-conscious J.C. Penney Stores, Inc. is flexing its muscles in preparation for entry into the even trendier arena of financial services.

In the last year, the nation's third-largest retailer has joined with a California savings and loan to open five financial service centers in Sacramento, acquired the videotext systems operations of a major Minneapolis bank, marketed the use of its huge electronic communications system to two oil companies, and purchased a Delaware bank.

Newly elected Chairman William R. Howell refused to rule out other financial service acquisitions, but he pointed out that Penney's efforts are designed "to see what role a retailer can play in the financial services arena.

"If it's appropriate, yes, we'll make an acquisition, but it's not probable in the near term," Howell said in an interview, explaining that Penney would digest and evaluate its ventures first.

Penney isn't quite a threat to Sears, Roebuck & Co., whose financial service centers include Allstate Insurance, the Dean Witter Reynolds Inc. brokerage firm, and Coldwell Banker

real estate operations, but clearly the company is working on it.

"If we rival Sears, it will be an accident of going after what the consumer wants," said Thomas J. Lyons, executive vice-president for J.C. Penney Financial Services. "We're trying to design to the consumer, to match our objectives with theirs."

But analysts see Penney's tentative thrusts into financial services as merely the latest move in a strategic plan to get its stores into the mainstream of affluent suburbia.

"It's in the development stage now," said Bruce Greer, an analyst with Drexel Burnham Lambert Inc. "But clearly Penney has to experiment in this area so they're current on what their customer wants and needs."

"In the last few years, Penney has undergone a major metamorphosis," said Bernard Sosnick, an analyst with L.F. Rothschild, Unterberg, Towbin. "The company is on the threshold of a major breakthrough."

Penney is embarking on its venture into financial services, which last year accounted for only $22 million of its $430 million in earnings, flush from the success of its campaign to upgrade itself into a shopping mall department store that offers fashionable merchandise at competitive prices.

"The nationwide debut of Halston's first

*Source: Based on "Penney Targets New Markets," *Tulsa World*, May 8, 1983, pp. 6–7 (Chicago Tribune Syndicate).

moderate price collection—also the couture designer's first effort for a mass merchandiser—on June 7 should fix Penney's new image in shoppers' minds," Sosnick said.

Encouraged by the success of the fashion program, which was begun in 1976 to dress up Penney's traditional private label image with such national names as Levi, Sassoon, Jordache, Russtogs, and Sergio Valente, the retailer began experimenting with a new upscale merchandise mix. By the end of last year, 42 prototype stores were sporting the new look—70 percent apparel and 30 percent hard goods.

"When judged against mid-range (in terms of price) department stores, Penney's remodeled stores put it in a position to gain considerable market share," Sosnick said.

That fact hasn't been lost on Penney's top management, which recently announced a record five-year, $1 billion capital spending program to modernize completely its 1,650 remaining stores.

The new merchandise mix will be installed in all stores by the end of 1984, with major appliance, paint and hardware, lawn and garden, and fabric and automotive centers discontinued. What's left will include family apparel, leisure lines, and softer home furnishings. That leaves Penney free to begin concentrating on financial services.

Questions

1 How would you classify J.C. Penney's as a type of retailer?

2 What factors have determined the change in Penney's merchandising assortment?

3 Is J.C. Penney's a direct competitor with Sears?

CHAPTER 14

Physical Distribution Management

CHAPTER SCAN

This chapter describes the marketing activity known as physical distribution. While this term is used by many to describe *all* distribution-related functions, distribution actually consists of three separate activities. Materials management is concerned with bringing raw materials and supplies to the point of production. Physical distribution, in its technical meaning, takes goods from the production point to the buyers. Logistics is the management activity that coordinates the entire process.

Physical distribution has been called the "last frontier" of marketing because computers, robots, and other modern management tools are applicable to it. Also, distribution goes on "behind the scenes," permitting marketing managers to seek and use all manner of means to reduce costs and meet environmental challenges as long as the basic goal —customer satisfaction—is met.

WHEN YOU HAVE STUDIED THIS CHAPTER, YOU WILL:

Be familiar with the important role played by physical distribution in the marketing mix.

Be able to discuss the major objective of physical distribution—satisfying buyers while reducing costs—and be able to explain what managers of distribution can do to bring about this partially self-contradictory goal.

Be able to explain the total cost approach to physical distribution.

Be familiar with the various modes of transportation of products available to shippers and their comparative advantages and disadvantages.

Understand the purposes of such distribution-related activities as warehousing, order processing, materials handling, and inventory control.

Be able to distinguish among the terms physical distribution, logistics, and materials handling as these terms are technically defined.

The physical distribution system for McDonald's Triple Ripple, a three-flavored ice cream product, was the major reason why the product was dropped. Experiments indicated that the product would freeze, defrost, and refreeze in the distribution system. Solving the problem would have required each McDonald's city to have an ice cream plant with special equipment to roll the three flavors into one.[1] As this example shows, physical distribution clearly has a dramatic influence on a product's success.

In every exchange situation, some aspect of the marketing function of physical distribution is to be found. Whether a West German steel company sells oil-storage tanks for use in Saudi Arabia or in New Jersey the steel company must distribute the tanks to the buyers' widely separated locations. In other instances, such as the distribution of services, physical distribution is equally important, but not as obvious. A rural university, considering distribution as a part of its marketing mix, may decide that its target markets can be better served if off-campus branches are installed in major cities around the state or even in other states. The school may also decide to offer an extension program conducted by

A city college recognized the importance of physical distribution.

mail, telephone, or closed-circuit television. Services, as well as physical products, must be physically distributed.

DEFINITIONS

As is suggested by the varied terms and activities that can be linked to physical distribution, there is no universally accepted definition. However, physical distribution has been defined by the National Council of Physical Distribution Management. **Physical distribution** is a term employed in manufacturing and commerce to describe the broad range of activities concerned with efficient movement of finished products from the end of the production line to the consumer.[2] In short, physical distribution refers to the flow of products from producers to consumers with the major focus on the *physical* aspects of that flow rather than the activities within channels of distribution dealing with changing title, facilitating exchanges, and negotiating with intermediaries. As part of the "place" portion of the overall marketing mix, physical distribution activities contribute time and place utility. A related term, **physical distribution management**, connotes the design and administration of systems to control the flow of products.

---

[1] Roger D. Blackwell and James F. Engle, "McDonald's Corporation," *Contemporary Cases in Consumer Behavior* (Hinsdale, Ill.: The Dryden Press, 1979).

[2] The National Council of Physical Distribution Management, in D.J. Bowersox, B.J. LaLonde, and E.W. Symkay, *Readings in Physical Distribution Management: The Logistics of Marketing* (New York: The Macmillan Company, 1969), p. x.

Materials management is concerned with bringing raw materials and supplies to the point of production. When discussing both physical distribution and materials management, it is appropriate to use the term **logistics,** which is broad in scope because it includes both planning and coordinating the physical distribution of finished goods and the management of the movement and storage of the raw materials and parts necessary during the procurement and production processes.[3] The armed forces, for example, use this term to describe the sizable efforts involved in moving personnel, weapons, and supplies during a war game or an actual conflict.

THE OBJECTIVES OF PHYSICAL DISTRIBUTION

Physical distribution has many objectives. They can all be condensed into one overall statement of purpose—*to minimize cost while maximizing customer service.* This goal is the statement of an ideal. Unfortunately, the lowest total cost and the highest levels of service almost always work at cross-purposes. For example, achieving high level customer service suggests that an appliance marketer should operate many warehouses, each carrying a large inventory so that local customers' orders can be filled rapidly. In lieu of that, the marketer should have a fleet of jet transports ready at all times to fly merchandise to customers within a few hours of receiving their orders. Both approaches to maximizing customer service are likely to prove inconsistent with the other half of the physical distribution objective that calls for minimizing cost. Minimizing cost generally suggests few warehouses, low inventories, and slow, inexpensive means of transportation.

The twin goals of maximum service and low cost cannot be fully met. Some compromising of one or both of them is necessary. Thus, physical distribution managers, while striving for the ideal, must work toward realistic objectives, performing a sort of balancing act in the process.

What Is a Realistic Objective?

How does marketing management develop reasonable objectives for physical distribution? A good place to start is with the marketing concept. The marketing concept dictates that marketing managers should strive for consumer satisfaction in all that they do, including physical distribution. Therefore, the distribution system is designed to fit the wants and needs of the customer.

Just as in any other element of the distribution system, cost should be evaluated in terms of customer wants. Suppose an analysis of the market shows that customers are most concerned with rapid and on-time deliveries. If the marketing company determines that such service can be provided and guaranteed only at an increase in the product's price, does that mean customers cannot be served? No. But it does mean that a further step—determining whether or not customers are willing to pay a premium price for that service—is in order. For example, Federal Express' customers seem to be willing to pay for quick service, as are the customers of the U.S. Postal System's Express Mail.

In many cases, however, customers may have some priority other than rapid delivery. Buyers of furniture and appliances, though perhaps anxious to possess their new purchases, often prefer to have the retailer from whom the purchase was made deliver, set up, or install the product even if this means waiting a week or two to actually take delivery. These buyers are willing to "pay" a premium of time, sacrificing quick delivery for the feeling that installation was done properly by skilled workers. Other kinds of buyers, such as purchasers of repair parts for machinery, fall somewhere in the middle, seek-

---

[3]Some texts, for simplicity's sake, do not differentiate between the terms "physical distribution" and "logistics". Yet, as you will see in this chapter, there is a significant difference between them.

ing parts both on a steady basis to maintain an in-shop inventory and on an emergency basis.

Therefore, marketing managers must research and calculate how the *customer* sees the problem of balancing maximum service and minimum cost. An important consideration in this is the competition's physical distribution policies. Emery Air Freight, Purolator, and other Federal Express competitors clearly have developed their distribution methods with Federal Express' market offering in mind. Each competitor is seeking a differential advantage over the other.

THE COMPONENTS OF A PHYSICAL DISTRIBUTION SYSTEM

Physical distribution consists of several identifiable concerns and activities that may be described as the components of physical distribution. Examples are:

1 *Inventory Management* A retailer determines how many men's suits is an adequate number and when to order.

2 *Order Processing* Customers' orders are received by sales office personnel who then arrange for the requested merchandise to be shipped and for the customer to be billed.

3 *Warehousing and Storage* Producers of seasonal goods, such as air conditioners, bathing suits, or mittens, hold products in storage for distribution from the best location as needed through the seasons.

4 *Materials Handling* Forklifts, conveyor belts, and other means are used to move merchandise into and within warehouses, retail stores, and wholesaler's facilities.

5 *Protective Packaging and Containerization* Sheets of paper for photocopiers are bound into packs of 200 sheets, placed in cardboard boxes containing ten packs, and placed on pallets.

6 *Transportation* Automobiles are shipped from Detroit and other assembly points to dealers around the United States and to certain overseas markets.

The *regular* physical distribution activities (e.g., excluding selection of a warehouse location) are shown in Figure 14-1.

Breaking physical distribution down into components permits us to concentrate on individual aspects of a complex subject. However, this approach is somewhat misleading because it suggests that each part operates separately, without interacting with the others. It is important to understand that the components operate as a system.

The **systems concept**—the idea that elements may be strongly interrelated and interact toward achieving one goal—is of special value in distribution. Even the casual observer can see that a warehouse is of no truly meaningful use unless it fills and empties as part of a system intended to achieve some distribution goal. No shipment of merchandise via railroad or plane is

Containerization and transportation are both important physical distribution activities.

EXHIBIT 14-1

Outlining the Physical Distribution Activities of a Wholesaler

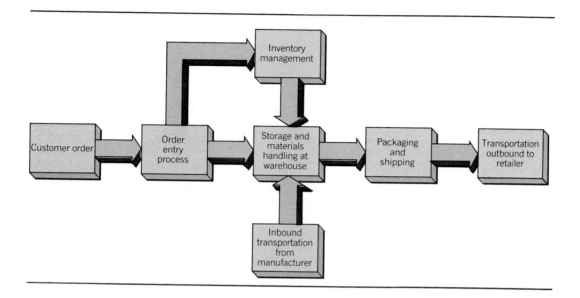

of any real value unless it is taken from the carrier and moved to where it is actually needed. In seeking to satisfy customer service demands at reasonable cost, marketing managers can use each part of a distribution system to help attain that goal, but only within the context of the system. Each part affects the others. That is the very meaning of *system*. The fastest mode of cross-country transportation does not contribute to customer satisfaction unless the other parts of the physical distribution system also contribute to getting the desired products into the customer's hands quickly.

THE TOTAL COST CONCEPT

The key ideas inherent in the systems approach to physical distribution have contributed to the development of the **total cost concept.** When this way of thinking is adopted by marketing managers, they see the answer to the distribution problem as a system—a system aimed at reducing *total* cost.

What factors need to be contemplated by the distribution manager seeking to follow the physical distribution objective to hold down total cost? The number of variables can become quite large, but consider this partial list:

- Handling costs at the point of production.

- Transportation to a wholesaler, if necessary.

- Handling costs at the wholesaler level.

- Transportation to a retailer or industrial user.

- Handling cost at the retailer level.

- Transportation to a buyer, if necessary.

Let's consider the case of an industrial good, a blade for a road scraper, produced in

California and intended for sale in New Hampshire. A partial list of associated physical distribution costs might include:

- Handling costs involved in moving the blade from the factory to a warehouse on the West Coast.

- Storage at the warehouse.

- Handling and shipping to a point of storage convenient to the New Hampshire buyer.

- Storage on the East Coast.

- Local transportation to move the blade from the East Coast warehouse, or another point of storage, to the road scraper owner.

- Paperwork, local inventory taxes, any additional handling or moving of the item, plus the further cost of customer concerns, worries, and dissatisfactions.

An observer of this list of costs would quickly see the basic lesson of the systems approach to distribution. A relatively slow means of transportation from West Coast to East Coast, such as ship or train, would only reduce the cost of the transcontinental shipment. If the purchaser of the road scraper blade cannot wait for a slow shipment, however, the distributor has a problem. Should a large inventory be warehoused on the East Coast, thus incurring the high cost of paperwork, inventory handling, handling costs, and local taxes? The cost in terms of lost sales could be even greater if the inventory was not available. Or can the problem be solved simply by using a more expensive means of transportation directly from the West Coast,

eliminating the need for an East Coast warehouse? Using air freight would likely reduce problems of storage and handling at both ends of the transaction and would probably lessen the *total* cost. Cheap transportation could prove more costly in the long run.

Clearly, minimizing the cost associated with only one or two steps of a multi-step process can result in increasing the total cost of the *whole* process. Systems-thinking managers make trade-offs, increasing the cost of some parts of the system to produce even greater cost reductions in other parts of the system—thus reducing the total cost.

Total cost is an important measure that was not always appreciated. At one time, shippers selected their transportation modes in a one-dimensional way. If management thought a product required quick delivery, the fastest mode of transportation was chosen. If quick delivery was thought not to be a major concern, the cheapest means of transportation, within reason, was selected. Looking back, we may wonder why transportation experts frequently did not bother to determine whether it were possible to lower the *total* cost of distribution even if that meant using a more expensive means of transportation, but this approach was uncommon until relatively recently in marketing history.

Sometimes, however, the customer's satisfaction may be more important than a dollars-and-cents cost reduction. One possible payoff of increasing some system costs may come in the form of greater buyer satisfaction. Unfortunately, it is easy for distribution managers to become so wrapped up in dealing with dollars that customer costs and payoffs are neglected.

THE "LAST FRONTIER" OF MARKETING

The area of physical distribution has been described as the "last frontier" of marketing. There are two very good reasons why this phrase has frequently appeared in the marketing literature.

The first of these reasons is that there is no area of marketing in which computerization,

automation, and modern quantitative techniques can be so extensively and profitably employed. Many of the marketing applications of computerization and automation are in the areas of handling inventory, doing paperwork, and other order-processing activities. Furthermore, quantitative techniques lend themselves far better to the simulation of transportation systems and the calculation of shipping costs than they do to producing a TV commercial or selecting a package design for a new lipstick.

The second reason why the "last frontier" phrase is appropriate is that the distribution function is performed behind the scenes. That is, most buyers, be they consumers or industrial users, do not ordinarily see the distribution process working, nor do they care to. They are concerned almost entirely with whether or not the products sought are delivered on time, in good shape, and at reasonable cost. Most other marketing functions are intentionally publicized. Promotion, price, and, of course, the product are seen and meant to be seen by buyers. But distribution's relative anonymity provides many opportunities for marketers to develop efficient tools and methods.

Establishing a Differential Advantage

In many cases, organizations can establish differential advantages over rivals through more effective physical distribution. This is especially true in industries where the products of one organization are essentially the same as those of competitors. This occurs in the coal and the steel industries. Marketers experience difficulty in establishing differential advantages through price differentials or through product superiority in such industries, but physical distribution offers an avenue to develop a differential advantage. Reliable delivery, faster delivery, avoiding errors in order processing, and delivering undamaged goods are all potential areas of differential advantage. Should competitors be weak in any of these areas, opportunities for differential advantage are especially attractive.

Many salespeople emphasize rapid delivery as a selling appeal. They make such statements as, "We can provide you with the goods within 24 hours of the order, whereas competitors cannot guarantee delivery in under three days." Rapid delivery is especially important in certain industries. Pharmacists, for instance, may insist on one- or two-hour service from suppliers. If this is not available, the pharmacist may lose a sale and possibly even a regular customer. Auto repair parts are likely to be available with 24-hour notice even in smaller towns. Produce marketers and bakery marketers realize that their products are perishable, and they may seek a differential advantage by establishing the image of products fresher than those of their rivals. Wonder Bread advertisements carry this appeal, emphasizing that it is baked locally and rushed to stores to ensure freshness.

Cutting Costs

As previously noted, many opportunities to cut costs in distribution present themselves to the effective marketing manager because so much of the distribution system operates beyond the observation of target buyers. Customers are concerned with the results of distribution, not how it is accomplished. Any cost-cutting measures that can be found can be utilized to lower prices to buyers, increase the seller's margin, or to achieve some combination of these goals.

Often, management finds that costs can be reduced through changes in existing physical distribution systems. Here are some examples.

■ Automating warehouses, thereby reducing payroll expenses.

■ Replacing numerous small warehouses located near markets with a few large national warehouses that serve multiple markets.

■ Correcting inefficient procedures in order processing, eliminating needless red-tape and paper handling.

■ Utilizing low-cost transportation carriers, such as barges.

■ Moving offices, plants, warehouses, and retail outlets to low-cost locations.

■ Requiring customers to perform some of the logistics functions, for example, when the marketer stipulates that retailers or wholesalers carry certain minimum inventories; this allows the marketer to shift part of the warehousing and storage costs to customers.

There are many ways of cutting costs through improvements in physical distribution. The extent of the possible savings is illustrated by the experience of one company that reported a potential savings of one-fifth of its total physical distribution costs of $40 million as the result of "a hardnosed physical distribution audit." Some of the problems that the audit uncovered were "small shipments moving separately to common destinations, fragmented inventories, different warehousing costs at different locations, and high costs per order."[4]

MANAGEMENT OF THE COMPONENTS OF PHYSICAL DISTRIBUTION

Managerial responsibilities associated with logistics may be categorized into three general areas: physical distribution management, materials management and logistical coordination.[5] Although these three, shown in Exhibit 14-2, must be organized and operated as an integrated system, our discussion will treat them separately. We concentrate our discussion on physical distribution management, the primary logistical concern of marketers.

Six major areas of concern may be isolated in the physical movement of products. Try to keep in mind their interrelationships as well as their individual contributions in the overall physical distribution system.

Transportation

Transportation decisions involve selecting the specific mode that will be used to physically move products from a manufacturer, grower, wholesaler, or other seller to the receiving facilities of the buyer. The major alternative modes of transportation include motor carrier, air freight, railroad, water transportation, and pipeline. One measure of their comparative importance, in terms of usage rate, is shown in Exhibit 14-3. Other means of transporting merchandise that may have come to mind, such as Parcel Post or "overnight" delivery services, are themselves users of one or more of these major transportation methods.

The physical distribution or transportation manager must consider the trade-offs mentioned earlier. The first of these is always the needs of the buyer. If these needs are extraordinarily difficult or expensive to meet, the willingness of the buyer to bear extra costs to satisfy those needs must be investigated. Other considerations include the nature of the product (bulk, perishability, weight, fragility), the necessary speed and dependability of delivery, and the cost and the availability of transportation methods and storage space. Alternatives may be evaluated in terms of these variables in selecting one of the following specific modes of transportation.

Motor Carrier. Prior to 1980, the trucking industry was tightly regulated by the federal government. Implementation of the Motor Carrier Act of 1980 dramatically transformed this by essentially deregulating the trucking industry. Motor carriers are now able to set rates for individual customers based on costs rather than having to comply with a uniform set of rates. Although not all trucking industry members favor deregulation, it seems to have resulted in heightened competition, greater efficiency, enhanced services, and innovative pricing.

Trucks, and even the far less important motor carrier operations like Greyhound's package service, which uses buses as carriers, are preferred over rail shipment, despite the fact that

---

[4]"A Hard-Nosed Physical Distribution Audit," *Marketing News,* Vol. 15, No. 10, November 15, 1973, p. 2.

[5]Donald Bowersox, *Logistical Management* (New York: Macmillan, 1974), pp. 14–15.

EXHIBIT 14-2

Areas of Managerial Responsibility in Logistics

1 Physical Distribution

- Transportation
- Warehousing
- Inventory control
- Materials handling
- Order processing
- Packaging

2 Materials Management

3 Logistical Coordination

Truck transportation is very accessible and flexible.

EXHIBIT 14-3

Percentage of Total Ton Miles by Various Modes of Transport in Domestic Intercity Traffic

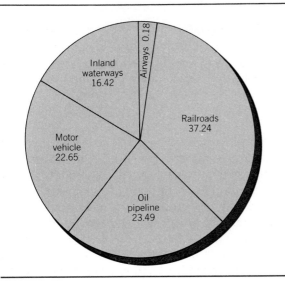

Airways 0.18

Inland waterways 16.42

Railroads 37.24

Motor vehicle 22.65

Oil pipeline 23.49

Source: Bureau of the Census, *Statistical Abstract of the United States* (Washington, D.C.: U.S. Government Printing Office, 1982), p. 607.

trains can move great quantities of products at lower prices. Damages in transit are less likely than when rail freight is used. Trucks are more accessible and have more flexibility than railroads, and they are generally more reliable in terms of delivery deadlines. Although they are most efficient moving comparatively small shipments over short distances, they are also effective for long distances.

While trucking companies may not fully believe it, times of economic recession make motor carriers more attractive to shippers. "Manufacturers, forced by high interest rates to reduce inventories, become increasingly vulnerable to delivery delays. With little or no cushion of spare parts or supplies, they are dependent on reliable trucking service."[6]

Air Freight. The primary advantages of air freight are speed and distance capabilities. For many shippers, these advantages compensate for the high costs associated with air transportation. However, as we saw when considering the *total cost* approach to physical distribution, fast transportation permits inventory reductions and

[6]"Shippers Are in the Driver's Seat," *Business Week,* October 18, 1982, p. 184.

The speed and distance capability of air freight may compensate for its high cost.

To establish a differential advantage of reliable delivery, bulky products such as coal are often routed after computer simulation of transportation systems.

savings in warehousing costs. Air freight has an excellent record for seldom damaging goods in transit. In remote areas that are inaccessible by truck or railroad, it may be the only transportation choice available. Traditionally, air transportation has been used primarily to move goods of high unit value, perishable goods, and emergency orders. The growth of international trade has contributed to a dramatic increase in the use of air transport during the past two decades.

As was the case with trucking, the recession and high interest rates of the early 1980s had a significant impact on the use of air freight. Manufacturers, especially producers of high technology products, chose to ship goods on demand via air freight rather than incur the costs of

carrying inventory. According to John C. Emery, Jr., chairman and president of Emery Air Freight, the nation's largest air freight forwarder, "Physical distribution is shifting away from the old ways of regional warehouses and trucks to an instant supply cycle."[7]

Railroads. Railroads demonstrate their comparative advantage over other transportation modes when the freight to be hauled consists of

---

[7] Helen L. Call, "Emery Is Very High on Air Freight," *San Diego Union,* November 14, 1980, p. D-1.

Road railer trains have vans with one set of rail wheels between them to facilitate piggyback service.

heavy and bulky items. These can be moved by rail over long distances at low cost. Shippers may find that unit costs of transporting *smaller* shipments are low if the goods are shipped by truck rather than rail. However, as shipment size increases, a point is reached where the economies of rail transport equal, and then exceed, those of truck shipment.

The major disadvantages of rail shipment are that delivery is relatively slow and that it can be used only where tracks are located. In addition, the industry has a reputation for damaging goods in transit and an unreliable delivery record. In some parts of the country, the tracks are so badly maintained that these disadvantages have been magnified. Still, in recent years some rail lines have attempted to modernize operations and have become more competitive with other means of transportation. Here are just two examples of such service improvements:

Piggyback service in which flatcars are used to carry loaded truck trailers, by rail, to distant destinations where they are then moved to local destinations by truckers. This combines the long-distance hauling attractions of the railroad with the local delivery flexibility of trucks.

Diversion-in-transit privileges that permit a shipper using rail transportation to direct the shipment to a destination that was not specified at the start of the trip. A fruit shipper may want to send California oranges or artichokes to the East Coast then, when the products are approaching that part of the country, divert them to the particular Eastern city where prices are highest or demand greatest.

These and other services and special rates have been introduced by railroads in an attempt to offset some of the advantages offered by their competitors, especially truckers.

Water Transportation. As a rule, water transportation offers a very low-cost means of moving products. It is most appropriate for bulky, low-value, nonperishable products such as gravel and coal. It is also appropriate for transporting fairly expensive items, such as cars from Germany or Japan being sent to the United States or Canadian markets, if they can be properly protected from damage during transit.

Delivery by water takes place on inland bodies of water, such as the Great Lakes or the Mississippi River, as well as on oceans. Considerable problems, however, such as the closing of some routes and ports by ice during winter, may arise. Water is also the slowest mode of transportation. However, where time constraints are not great, or where bulkiness and low unit value will not justify faster, more expensive transportation, it is extensively employed.

EXHIBIT 14-4

General Comparison of Attributes of Various Transportation Modes[a]

Low Cost	Speed	Reliable Delivery	Ability to Reach Inaccessible Areas	Specialized Facilities Available	Reputation for Undamaged Goods
(1) Water	(1) Air	(1) Pipeline	(1) Air	(1) Air	(1) Pipeline
(2) Pipeline	(2) Motor	(2) Air	(2) Motor	(2) Pipeline	(2) Air
(3) Rail	(3) Rail	(3) Motor	(3) Pipeline	(3) Motor	(3) Motor
(4) Motor	(4) Pipeline	(4) Rail	(4) Rail	(4) Rail	(4) Rail
(5) Air	(5) Water	(5) Water	(5) Water	(5) Water	(5) Water

Source: From Robin Peterson, *Marketing* (New York: John Wiley & Sons, 1977), p. 325.

[a]These comparisons are of a *very general nature* intended only to show the trade-offs involved when cost of use is compared to other attributes of modes of transportation.

Pipelines. Pipelines are the most specialized transportation means, since they are designed to carry only one or two products. They are used mainly to transport natural gas and crude petroleum, moving these from wells to storage or treatment facilities. Pipeline shipping is, generally, less expensive than rail but more expensive than waterway transportation.

A big part of the expense results from construction of the pipeline itself. Once in place, however, pipelines are a low-cost and reliable method of transportation. (See Exhibit 14-4 for a comparison of the different modes of transportation.)

As the specific applications of pipelines would lead you to expect, most of them are owned by the companies, such as gas and oil producers, who use them.

Attempts to ship non-liquid and non-gas products via pipeline have been made. Material such as coal may be broken up, mixed with water, then pumped through pipelines as a "slurry." Some success has been achieved with this method, but problems of pumping slurry mixes have kept the uses of slurry systems well below that of standard pipelines.

Warehousing

The second major aspect of physical distribution management is warehousing. **Warehousing** involves the holding and housing of goods between the time they are produced and the time they are shipped to the buyer. It includes all the activities that take place from the time the goods arrive at the warehouse until they are released for shipment to customers. Many large and small tasks are included in the warehousing function, but, taken together, they comprise two primary activities—storage and breaking bulk.

Storage. Storage consists of holding and housing goods in inventory. It is necessary because of the almost inevitable discrepancies that occur between production and consumption cycles. Consider this as an extreme example: The materials needed to operate mid-western steel mills come from the northern Great Lakes via ship or barge. But shipment is impossible in the winter since the Lakes freeze then. Therefore, the materials must be stored at locations that would not be blocked by ice in the winter. Such storage diminishes the effects that an uneven

CHANGING THE RULES FOR GAS PIPELINES

Transco Energy Company, of Houston, TX, was a gas pipeline company with the long term goal of operating as a carrier of natural gas owned by others. In November of 1982 however, still shaken from the extreme price swings in its chief competitor, oil, and tangled in a web of regulations, Transco found itself buying gas under long-term contracts with its suppliers at prices so high that it was losing customers.

In a bold shift in strategy Transco executives contacted all of the company's suppliers and the Federal Energy Regulatory Commission with a proposal to rewrite the rules of the industry. The company proposed the creation of a spot market in natural gas, allowing itself to buy gas from suppliers at prices set on a competitive basis. Such a new market arrangement would benefit all, argued Transco's top brass. If prices came down as a result, the continual loss of industrial customers to less expensive oil would be stopped, and new customers might be won. The increased demand would allow the suppliers to bring many of their shut-down wells back into production, improving their sagging cash flows. The natural gas pipeline industry has never been the same since.

The FERC, seeing a much needed solution to a serious problem, gave Transco the go-ahead. Other pipeline companies, also stuck with supplies of expensive gas they couldn't sell, quickly followed the Transco move.

Source: Based on information in *Business Week*, July 18, 1983, p. 126.

production cycle would have on the steel business. In some cases, marketers may store products when an opportunity to make a large quantity purchase has left them with more goods than they can sell at any one time. Again, this causes a discontinuity of supply and demand. Marketers may also store products in hopes that market prices for those products will be higher in the future.

There are any number of cases where the discontinuity to be overcome by storing products is brought about by cyclical demand rather than cyclical supply. Even though products of a seasonal nature, such as air conditioners, class rings, skis, and wedding gowns, are manufacturable throughout the year, regular schedules stabilize production and tend to minimize production costs. Storage permits the makers of these items to operate a steady production stream and hold the products until they are needed. Exhibit 14-5 illustrates this practice.

The Magic Chef Corporation became a leader in the marketing of soft-drink vending machines when they designed a machine that stores three cans in a row instead of two, boosting the capacity of the machines by one-third and cutting the frequency of restocking. The company realized the importance of storage considerations to its customers.

Breaking Bulk. The second key function of warehousing is the physical task of breaking bulk. Large shipments of any warehoused product are likely to arrive at the point of storage in large quantities and to leave in smaller quantities that are appropriate to the individual retailers or other buyers seeking them. A shipment of Toyotas arriving in California will be loaded on trucks and trains departing for various cities throughout the United States as the breaking bulk function is performed.

Warehousing Decisions. While the warehousing function can be a very complicated one, marketing managers can be viewed as facing two fundamental warehousing decisions. One is that of determining the optimum number, location, and types of warehouses needed. The other is calculating the proper levels of inventories to be stocked. As with so many of the problem areas in physical distribution, the question becomes largely one of minimizing costs while providing customer service that is satisfactory or at least adequate.

EXHIBIT 14-5

**Production, Storage, and Inventory Depletion
for Christmas Wrappings and Decorations**

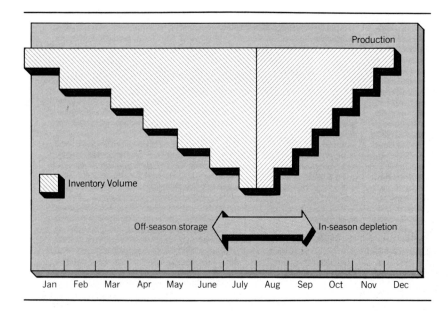

The choices open to marketing managers in this area may be demonstrated in terms of two strategy extremes between which many combinations of strategies lie. In one extreme case, the manufacturer makes large shipments over short distances to high-capacity *storage* warehouses located near manufacturing points. Shipments are then made, in smaller quantities, to retailers or other purchasers. At the other extreme lies the strategy alternative of making relatively large shipments over long distances to various *distribution* warehouses located near the buyers rather than near the manufacturer. The function of the warehouses then becomes to serve local buyers. These choices are illustrated in Exhibit 14-6.

If one or the other of these strikes you as "obviously" the better plan, remember that each alternative has certain cost and customer service advantages over the other. Locating warehouse facilities near buyers has a great deal of appeal, but it involves operating a larger number of storage points and dealing in smaller shipments be-cause local warehouses service only local markets. On the other hand, using a few large warehouses located near manufacturing points can yield economies of scale and other advantages, but may contribute to a reduction of service to buyers in far-off locales.

In warehouse-location decisions, consumer responsiveness to various degrees of speed and reliability in filling orders can be measured in terms of how quickly orders can be filled. An example of this occurs when management indicates that it can fill 20 percent of the orders within 24 hours and the remaining 80 percent within 72 hours, given a particular warehouse-location network.

The best warehouse location, then, is the one that maximizes customer service, gives the concern differential advantage over rivals, and minimizes cost. Finding the optimum location is difficult. Management, therefore, should turn to the marketing strategy for guidance as to the best site. If, for instance, the strategy calls for maximizing customer service, then cost consid-

EXHIBIT 14-6

Use of High-Capacity Storage Warehouses and Lesser-Capacity Distribution Warehouses to "Break Bulk"

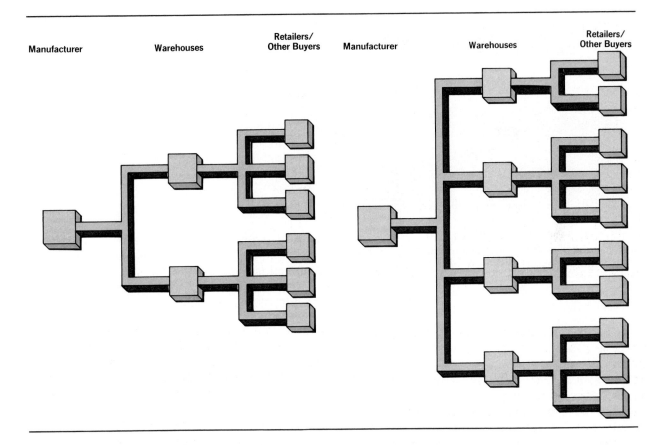

erations may be relatively unimportant. Where the strategy is to minimize cost and pass the resulting economies on to consumers in the form of low prices, however, cost may be the most important of the three variables.

Inventory Control

Another fundamental concern of physical distribution management is control of inventory levels. This problem is different than the question of whether inventory should be kept in large amounts in storage warehouses or smaller amounts in local distribution warehouses. **Inventory control** involves decisions concerning

how large or small inventories should be and how overstocking of inventory can be weighed against the dangers of costly stock-outs (which means that the product desired by the customer is not on hand). The ideal level of inventory is one that provides adequate service to customers while keeping suppliers' costs as low as possible. As is the case throughout the area of physical distribution, the presence of these twin goals, set at cross-purposes, complicates inventory decisions.

Valuable guidance on questions of inventory control can be found in sales forecasts, and consideration of a number of known facts, including how much inventory was needed in past plan-

WHAT IS A DISTRIBUTION CENTER?

For over two decades, writers in the area of physical distribution have been using the term *distribution center*. This term was intended to draw a distinction between the old image of a warehouse (a dusty place where goods lie stacked about collecting cobwebs) and the new perception of a storage place (a vibrant, bustling place where the emphasis is on "throughput").

Keeping products in a warehouse is not the goal of physical distribution managers. Their goal is to get products *out* of storage and into the hands of buyers. The phrase *distribution center* better suggests that outlook than does the term *warehouse*. While a warehouse *may* be a distribution center, not all warehouses are.

Both terms are used commonly today because the newer term has not fully replaced the old one. In any case, the name does not matter as much as what goes on in the warehouse/distribution center.

number of simple and sophisticated quantitative tools have been developed to help marketing managers deal with this problem area.

All risk cannot be removed from inventory control, but great strides have been made in the use of computerized inventory control systems. In fact, even seemingly impossible to gauge figures can be closely estimated. For example, the value of a lost sale could be viewed either as the selling price of the product or as the price plus expected service work income. Figures cannot accurately include the ill-will of a customer who could not be served, however.

Although no mathematical formulas are "perfect," the three major costs associated with holding inventory, which follow, can be dealt with more mechanically than can many areas of marketing management:

■ *Acquisition costs* are the expenses incurred in obtaining inventory. For a manufacturer, the acquisition costs are the costs of production; for an intermediary, they are the cost of the goods bought plus any transportation or handling assessments.

■ *Holding costs* are those incurred as a result of keeping inventory housed. Interest paid, taxes on inventory, and any costs associated with warehousing and spoilage are included.

■ *Out-of-stock* losses are those that occur when customers demand goods the marketer cannot provide. The loss of a sale may also mean the loss of customer goodwill or a long-term contribution to a bad reputation. Not all of these losses can be truly calculated.

Management can, with care, minimize total inventory costs by setting inventories at levels that take into account the behaviors of all three sets of costs. Computerized inventory control systems have facilitated this task greatly.

Materials Handling

We have referred in this chapter to "moving" goods from manufacturer to warehouse and to the "movement" of products from one spot to another. This movement does not simply occur

ning periods, how much was "left over" at the ends of past periods, the inventory turnover rates of the individual warehouses being used, the value of the inventories held, and the carrying costs, can also be used.

A great deal has been written on the matter of inventory control. The general approach involves reliance on data gathered in the past and on careful projections of future demand. Any

New technology in physical distribution aids materials handling.

on its own. Instead, it is carried out using personnel, machinery, and equipment to identify, check, load, and unload goods. These activities are fundamental to the operation of *materials handling,* which can be defined as the physical handling and moving about of inventory.

Throughout this century there has been an increasing mechanization of the materials handling process. Workers with hand trucks and carts have been largely replaced by operators of forklifts and other mechanical means such as conveyor belts, elevators, and cranes. Most recently, robots have been used to perform materials handling tasks. In many warehouses, orders can be assembled and packed with almost no human involvement. These systems have proved

faster, more accurate, and, in the main, cheaper than having human workers fill orders.

Order Processing

Like materials handling, this function is increasingly automated. Computerized order processing is common since speed and accuracy are vital to this activity. For many buyers, the quality of order-filling procedures is a primary purchasing criteria. Since order taking and processing is something of a first step in the process of getting merchandise to customers, mistakes made in this activity can carry through the whole process. Such mistakes result in lost time and money, as well as disgruntled customers. Expedient and reliable order processing can also enable an organization to realize economies in related physical distribution areas; for example, it may allow the organization to carry reduced inventories or to use lower-cost transportation modes, such as rail rather than air.

Packaging

Packaging must be considered in analyzing promotion, product, and price. But it also has an important place in the field of physical distribution, since products must be properly packaged to protect them during the distribution process. Damage is costly to marketers and can occur both during transportation or in storage. Protection, therefore, includes protection against breakage, spoilage, mildew, insects, dirt, and any other significant threat.

When designing packaging, marketing managers must evaluate container quality, appearance, and costs. Less obvious, but just as important, are the costs associated with *re*packaging products into larger or smaller quantities, such as cartons of grosses or dozens. Packages must also be designed to minimize difficulties in physical handling such as stacking in piles. For some products, like machine parts, packages are color coded or in some other way marked for ease of use to facilitate the process of order filling. The requirements of the Interstate Commerce Commission and other considerations specific to particular customers or products will present varying challenges for package design.

MATERIALS MANAGEMENT

The second area of managerial responsibility associated with physical distribution is materials management. In a simple model, three broad stages in the movement of products might be seen:

1 Getting materials to the factory.

2 Transporting semi-finished goods within the manufacturing facility.

3 Distributing finished goods to the customer.

The function of **materials management** within this overall system is to evaluate alternate sources of supplies and acquire needed raw materials necessary to ensure uninterrupted production at acceptable cost. The materials manager must procure materials of an acceptable quality that meet the organization's specifications, and obtain an assurance that the materials will arrive at the manufacturing facility at the right time. As this suggests, materials management is concerned with materials that are *inbound* to the point of production, whereas physical distribution management is focused on *outbound* products. Materials management is of major importance to marketing because shortages of any needed supply interrupt both production and distribution processes, making it impossible to supply customers with the products they want.[8]

LOGISTICAL COORDINATION

Logistics, dealing as it does with the "big picture" of an organization's distribution process, relies heavily on demand estimation (sales forecasting) to achieve its goal of smoothly controlling the physical flow of goods through the organization and its channel of distribution. Forecasting enables managers concerned with logistics to synchronize the activities that make up the distribution effort. With a properly constructed sales forecast at hand, indicating *what* sales totals are expected and *when* they are expected, the logistics manager can *plan* for the following, and many other, events and needs:

■ Handling and holding incoming inventories of raw materials, parts, etc.

■ Scheduling of production.

■ Monitoring of stocks, materials, and finished goods inventories.

■ Handling and shipping of finished goods to points of storage or to intermediaries.

■ Disposal of waste, by-products, and imperfectly manufactured output.

■ Monitoring and coordinating members of channels of distribution.

Note that logistical planning is market oriented. It does not start at the production-related plant operations and work toward the customers. It starts with the needs of the customers and works back to the plant.

Exhibit 14-7 shows the interrelationship of physical distribution, materials management, and logistics. It is common, as the exhibit indicates, to think of materials management as consisting of those activities performed up to the production point, and of physical distribution, narrowly defined, as activities that occur after production. Logistics management encompasses these two functions, assuring coordination of their activities.

---

[8]For a good overall treatment of materials management, see Harold E. Fearon, "Materials Management: A Synthesis and Current View," *Journal of Purchasing and Materials Management,* Summer 1975, pp. 37–43.

EXHIBIT 14-7

Materials Management, Physical Distribution Management, and Logistics Management Superimposed on an Organization's Flow of Materials

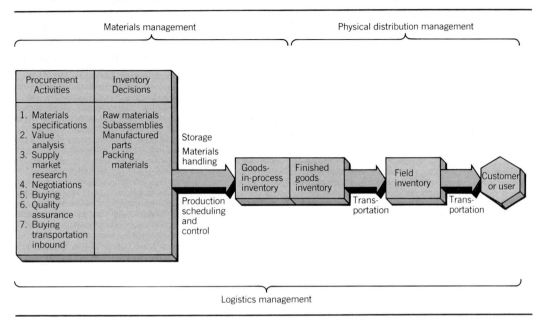

Source: L. Lee, Jr., and D.W. Dobler, *Purchasing and Materials Management: Text and Cases* (New York: McGraw-Hill, 1977), p. 25.

TRENDS IN PHYSICAL DISTRIBUTION

Like most of marketing, physical distribution operates within an ongoing state of change and development. Recent economic hard times have led many organizations to place a greater stress on cost control and increased efficiency. This has amplified the role of distribution management.

New Technology

Distribution managers have welcomed the use of computers because they make the job of distribution easier and more efficient, thus contributing significantly to the overall health of the organization. Computers provide distribution managers with detailed information that can be used to plan and control all types of decisions—from comparing sources of raw materials to determining the cheapest way to ship merchandise to retail dealers. Computer programs are available that simulate logistical problems, thus helping decision-makers to weigh the many alternatives that confront them. Programs can also analyze the complicated cost variables so common to distribution decisions and calculate lowest cost inventory levels and the most profitable warehouse location patterns.

As we have seen, automation of materials handling is common. In general, management of the entire field of physical distribution has become increasingly sophisticated.

Energy Costs

In recent years, the world has suffered through a number of energy shortages and rapidly rising costs of energy in general. These events, and fear of even higher prices, feed the drive for greater energy efficiency in all areas of distribution management, and especially in transportation. Many manufacturers of trucks and diesel railroad engines have dramatically increased the fuel efficiency of their products and, in some cases, radically redesigned them for greater aerodynamic sleekness. Other changes include the increasing use of tandem truck trailers, longer truck trailers, and lowered speed limits. These types of changes require legislative support at the state or local level, however, and the results are inconsistent.

Interorganizational Cooperation

Organizations heavily involved in distribution activities have deliberately sought ways to cooperate with one another and to share services. It makes little sense, for example, for every air freight company to support an entire complement of facilities and staff at every airport in the country. Realizing this, many companies sell ground support services to other cooperating organizations in an effort to eliminate duplicate investments. Other developments include increased use of freight consolidators, shipper's associations, and national chains of public warehouses.[9]

Other Trends

Not all trends in the physical distribution field are positive. Many organizations are faced with less-than-satisfactory profits, rising fuel costs, and revenues that are inadequate for the job of up-dating and replacing obsolete equipment. In the past few years, for example, many small and a few major trucking companies, such as Spector Freight, have either gone out of business entirely or sharply curtailed operations. In fact, within less than two years of the deregulatory Motor Carrier Act of 1980 the trucking industry witnessed a 25 percent decline in traffic, a series

---

[9]Public warehouses are, as the name implies, open to use by any organization willing to rent space in them. Private warehouses are operated by organizations for their own use. The existence of public warehouses permits any firm to perform distribution activities without having to build a series of storage spots.

PACKAGE DEAL: UNITED AIRLINES AND OVERNIGHT CARGO

United Airlines was the first major domestic airline to enter the overnight package delivery business. After a false start at the time of the 1981 air traffic controllers' strike, United committed $13 million dollars in 1982 to promote its service called United Air Express. With competitive overnight delivery services making billions of dollars in sales and growing at a 20 percent annual rate, the market was hard to resist. United's major competitors in the airline business, American, Delta, and Eastern, watched with interest but so far are staying out of the fray. One fear is that, in trying to compete with aggressive overnight freight forwarders, the airline will alienate cargo companies that use United aircraft to supplement their own fleets. Some cargo business has been lost in this way but not enough, apparently, to worry United's executives. Other airlines offer priority package service with no guarantee of overnight delivery. By fall of 1983, United was no longer offering the service. What went wrong? First, competition became intensive with Emery, Airborne and the U.S. Postal Service fighting tooth and nail against Federal Express. Further, United's approach was different from that of most other overnight services. It used its own fleet plus contracted ground services. United sought to expand its list of cities served by contracting with regional airlines. The major overnight services operate their own fleets of planes and trucks. Kent Freudenberger, Executive V.P.-Marketing, of Airborne Freight Corporation of Seattle, made two predictions as to how United would fare in this tough market. He declared that United's well-known name and extensive system would earn them a good number of user trials. "But," he added, "then it comes down to who can supply the service. Anytime you don't control it yourself, you create a greater propensity for screw-ups." His prediction about logistics came true.

Source: Adapted from Richard Kreisman, "Package Deal: United Lone Airline to Dent Overnight Cargo Area," *Advertising Age*, March 1, 1982, pp. 39–40. Used with permission.

A MARRIAGE OF CADILLACS IN MATERIALS HANDLING

Republic Steel's industrial products division (IPD) markets a stock-handling system which integrates Harnischfeger's Handi-Pak cranes with Republic shelving. Customers are assured of getting a compatible system that can be quickly installed at a competitive price. "The marriage of crane and shelving elements is a problem in materials handling, and we've made a marriage of Cadillacs." "The system can store and fetch items shelved from 18 to 40 feet high, and higher in aisles up to 500 feet long. The crane can operate in aisles as narrow as 45 inches, and it moves horizontally and vertically—simultaneously. We saw a certain amount of stodg- iness in the materials storage market, and our marketing orientation put us in a position to analyze the customers' needs." "The benefits of this system compound themselves and snowball. One manager said we're applying package goods techniques to the steel industry."

Source: From Kevin Higgins, "Division of Republic Steel Earns Record Profits After Shift to Marketing Orientation," *Marketing News,* May 29, 1981, p. 4. Used with permission.

of rate wars, and a record number of bankruptcies.[10]

Trends such as these, both good and bad, are simply further manifestations of marketing's changing environment. They offer many challenges to management to anticipate changes and to plan responses to them. The "last frontier" of marketing provides opportunities for effective marketing managers to successfully meet the challenges of their chosen profession.

SUMMARY

Physical distribution refers to the general flow of finished product from producers to customers. The function of physical distribution is to provide time and place utility; its objective is to define the wants and needs of target customers and provide services consistent with the demands of the market. The difficult-to-attain goal of physical distribution is to minimize distribution costs while maintaining the level of service specified by the customer.

Areas of managerial responsibility within a logistical system include physical distribution management, materials management, and logistical coordination. Each of the components requires extensive coordination, accurate fore- casting, and careful planning.

Transportation, warehousing, inventory control, materials handling, order processing, and packaging are the major areas of concern in physical distribution management.

Several trends in physical distribution are evident. These are the result of new technology, the energy crisis, and problems associated with attempts in physical distribution to compensate for rising costs in other areas of marketing.

---

[10]From "Shippers Are in the Driver's Seat," *Business Week,* October 18, 1982, p. 182.

THE MOST IMPORTANT CONCEPT IN THIS CHAPTER

Physical distribution deals with those activities concerned with efficient movement of finished products to the consumer. The physical distribution system should be managed to take *total* costs into account while attempting to satisfy consumers.

KEY TERMS

Physical distribution

Physical distribution management

Materials management

Logistics

Systems concept

Total cost concept

Transportation

Motor carrier

Air freight

Railroads

Piggyback service

Diversion-in-transit

Water transportation

Pipelines

Warehousing

Storage

Breaking bulk

Inventory control

Materials handling

Order processing

QUESTIONS FOR DISCUSSION

1 Define physical distribution. What are its components?

2 Indicate what is meant by the systems concept in physical distribution. In what ways does the use of this concept benefit marketers?

3 What are the major ways by which an organization can use physical distribution as a means of establishing differential advantage?

4 What is the difference between warehousing and storage? How do they differ from breaking bulk?

5 Discuss the total cost approach to distribution. What are its advantages and disadvantages?

6 An overnight package service and a petroleum pipeline are both common carriers. How do they differ? How are they similar?

7 What type of physical distribution system would you use for the following products:
(a) Bird of Paradise plants from Hawaii
(b) Kiwi fruit and avocados from California
(c) Barbie dolls

8 Why do organizations store goods? Provide an example of why a concern with which you are familiar engages in storage.

9 What factors should management consider in determining desired levels of inventory? What specific costs should management take into account?

10 Define order processing. Indicate how management can use this function to attain differential advantage over competitors.

11 Set forth the advantages and disadvantages of using each of the following:
(a) Railroads
(b) Motor trucks
(c) Airlines
(d) Water carriers
(e) Pipelines

12 What are the functions of freight forwarders? Why do shippers use them?

13 Describe the process for determining (a) the cities and metropolitan areas, and (b) specific sites for (1) retail and service units, and (2) warehouses.

14 Summarize the major trends in physical distribution.

15 For the class at large: What trends in physical distribution, other than those reported in the chapter, are evident? What are the major implications of these to marketers?

CASE 14-1 Adolph Coors Company*

Adolph Coors Company, a regional brewer, has been taking strides toward becoming a national beer marketer by expanding eastward into new territory. For years Coors had a "mystique" about it. The mystique began in the 1970s and helped give Coors Premium a reputation as a precious commodity. The brew was then available only in the West and had to be bootlegged into other parts of the country. The high point of this myth-making was the popular movie *Smokey and the Bandit,* in which the character played by actor Burt Reynolds fought the law and the clock in order to sneak a cargo of Coors into Atlanta.

"We really don't know what the mystique is all about," says Peter Coors, divisional president-sales, marketing and administration. "We believe it exists because Coors has a reputation for making quality products."

Coors has lined up an experienced wholesaler network to sell its beer in the new regions. Many of the distributors also carry the Schlitz brands and were around when the former Joseph Schlitz Brewing Company ruled the roost. Schlitz was taken over by Stroh Brewery of Detroit in 1981.

"They know what it takes to be No. 1," says Frank Spinoza, Coors vice-president of sales, referring to the distributors. "But they also learned a little humility and can recognize the mistakes the brewery made and the mistakes they made."

By working with veteran wholesalers, Coors also is seeking to avoid the dismal distribution problems encountered during its own previous expansion, when it moved into parts of Louisiana and Tennessee in that same year. During that trek, some key Coors distributorships were given to fledgling wholesalers who were forced to make hefty investments to build the refrigerated warehouses necessary to keep the ingredients within the Coors brews fresh. "Some of them had to invest nearly $500,000 in a refrigerated warehouse or trucks," notes Mr. Spinoza. "They had all their assets wrapped up in fixed costs and couldn't afford to back the brands." He adds that during this most recent expansion, Coors took on only veteran and es-

tablished distributors who thus have to make "a minimal investment" in refrigerated warehousing and trucks. They could "hit the ground running," the executive stresses.

But some observers question Coors staying power in the new territories.

Last year's wave of mergers and consolidations within the brewing industry has produced larger companies with bigger marketing budgets. The larger G. Heileman Brewing and Stroh Brewery are moving quickly to support their brands with multi-million-dollar advertising and promotional campaigns. And the "big guns," Anheuser-Busch and Miller Brewing, are fighting to retain their respective holds.

All these brewers have a decided advantage over Coors because each operates a brewery within the region. Coors has only the Colorado plant and, therefore, all beer must still be shipped by rail into the expansion areas. In addition, the distance could hinder communication between brewery and distributor, some observers contend.

"It doesn't take a genius to figure out that it is going to cost them a lot of money," says one Milwaukee-based analyst. "Also, it could hurt because the more they sell, the more it costs to ship."

Manny Goldman, analyst with Montgomery Securities, San Francisco, estimates the cost of shipping from Colorado into the Southeast is a "whopping $7 to $8 per barrel" (compared to normal $3-per-barrel costs). Those prohibitive costs are forcing Coors to consider either the construction or purchase of another brewery, he adds.

Coors officials dispute those figures, but do not release their own. They say that for the moment shipping beer by rail is satisfactory. A spot check of wholesalers found they have not had difficulty in getting the product from Golden, Colorado or in having local promotions approved quickly by headquarters.

---

*Source: Adapted with permission from Robert Reed, "Coors Charts Path over a Rocky Road to Growth," *Advertising Age,* July 11, 1983, pp. 4 and 59.

But Coors distributors and company executives concede a second brewery will eventually be needed. "It's no secret we cannot have a national presence with just one brewery," says Mr. Rechholtz.

Questions

1 What physical distribution problems will Coors encounter as they expand eastward?

2 What solutions can you suggest to avoid these problems?

PART 6

PRICING STRATEGY

The marketing function of pricing affects all of us whether we are consumers of goods and services or purchasers of products for use in operating an organization. The public attention devoted to prices makes this a particularly delicate area of marketing management. Prices are constantly under review by customers, customers whose main concern is what they must pay rather than how marketing managers determine the prices charged. For this reason, students of marketing must grasp the basics of pricing *and* see fully its importance as an integral part of the marketing mix. Thus this textbook devotes three chapters to price. We cannot stress too much the influence of price on buyers, government officials, international trading partners, organizations themselves, and the other marketing mix elements.

Chapter 15 provides an introduction to pricing and its contribution to the success of organizational objectives.

Chapter 16 shows the interplay of such variables as cost and demand in the determination of price.

Chapter 17 discusses pricing strategies used by marketers, including such matters as discounts and terms of sale. ∎

CHAPTER 15

Introduction to Pricing Concepts

CHAPTER SCAN

This chapter introduces the concept of price as a factor in our economy and as a marketing tool.

The chapter tells what price is, the names used to describe it, and how price is related to the other pieces of the marketing mix.

WHEN YOU HAVE STUDIED THIS CHAPTER, YOU WILL:

Be able to define price and discuss its place in our society.

Be able to show that price is both an economic and marketing tool.

Know how price interacts with the rest of the marketing mix.

Be able to discuss how inflation affects the consumer's view of price and the marketer's view of price.

Be able to explain how price is related to the organization's objectives.

For its first six years, Vector Graphic, Inc. did nothing but roll up sales and profits.[1] In its seventh year, however, the Thousand Oaks, California maker of personal computers ran into big trouble. It posted an operating loss of $1.3 million on a 15 percent drop in revenues for the first quarter of its fiscal year. Critical steps had to be taken to preserve cash flow: One-fourth of the staff—100 people—were quickly laid off, and the president and financial vice-president were ousted.

Vector Graphic is not the only manufacturer in the industry with such problems. Even though the personal computer has become the world's fastest-growing segment of the computer market, many of the hundred or more small producers are suddenly finding their sales and profits increasingly squeezed by the recent wave of price-cutting launched by the industry's major players, namely IBM and Apple Computer, Inc. Many industry experts, in fact, agree that these profit problems will precipitate the long-awaited industry shakeout. "IBM is putting pressure on just about everybody," says the chairman of American Computer Group, Inc., a Boston distributor. "The demise of the smaller companies is inevitable."

The president of the Westport, Connecticut, Computerworks store agrees: "The Vector Graphic and the North Stars of this world are really closed out. They are getting shoved off everyone's shelves." Doing most of the shoving is IBM. The giant "had 17 percent of the personal computer market in 1982, and approximately 26 percent in 1983," observes an industry analyst. Personal computer sales in 1983 grew about 43 percent, from $4.7 billion to $6.7 billion. And IBM's increase in market share will be "at the expense of the small companies."

Without a national brand name, small producers of personal computers must now offer better performance and a lower price to attract dealers and customers away from their big competitors. This point was driven home after IBM cut the price of its personal computer by 20 per-

cent, to $1,894. Since then nearly a dozen companies, including Vector Graphic, have dropped the prices of their personal computers to keep up. "IBM is getting very aggressive in pricing, and we—like smaller companies all over the country—have to keep ourselves just that much more price-competitive," declares the president of North Star Computers, Inc. which recently slashed its prices by 10 to 20 percent.

But many of the smaller manufacturers do not have margins wide enough to give them the latitude to cut prices so deeply. "Small manufacturers will face a lot of pressure because they do not have the [sales] volume to achieve economies of scale," says one Dataquest official. Intertec Data Systems, a 10-year-old company that shipped its first personal computer in 1978, saw its earnings plummet 69 percent to $1.9 million and its sales skid 31 percent to $15 million for the nine months ended December 31, 1982. Computer Devices, Inc. lost $4.9 million in 1982, primarily because of the heavy investment it made in developing and promoting a new portable personal computer.

The major producers of personal computers were able to make large price reductions because they could take advantage of much larger economies of scale. For instance, International Data Corp. estimates that IBM is now producing more than 30,000 Personal Computers a month. Because IBM and the other large companies can spread their investments over bigger production runs, they can afford to spend more money in designing their computers specifically to reduce manufacturing costs. Commodore International Ltd. is one example. It plans to cut the chip count in its Commodore 64 computer from 17 to 3 integrated circuits. Apple Computer is another example. It has just reduced the number of chips that it needs to assemble its Apple II computer from 110 in the original model to 31 in the Apple IIe—and reducing manufacturing costs by 35 percent. It is estimated Apple can now make the best-selling Apple IIe, which has a suggested list price of $1,395, for about $200 each.

Trimming manufacturing costs to keep up with the big guys is tougher all the time for the small companies, which typically have production runs of only 2,000 to 3,000 a month. "It is

---

[1]This material was adapted with permission from "The Squeeze Begins in Personal Computers," *Business Week*, May 30, 1983, pp. 91–92.

getting to be a hardball game. We're really look-ing for ways to drive costs down," acknowledges North Star's president.

So far, North Star has been able to success-fully compete with the large manufacturers. It was able to reduce manufacturing costs recently by investing in the computerized equipment needed to test computers on the production line. This cut the number of machines that needed repairs after they came off the assembly line by 20 percent. Thanks to improvements such as this, the privately-held company has been able to maintain profit margins of 10 percent and still give its dealers a 40 percent markup. Revenues nearly doubled, to $41 million, for the fiscal year ended January 31, 1983.

Unless the smaller producers can do what North Star has done and reduce their costs, they will find it impossible even to reach most retail outlets. Dealers are so eager to carry the most popular products—currently the IBM Personal Computer and the Apple IIe—that they are will-ing to wait for allocations when those models are in short supply. However, they can pick and choose their secondary product lines from among some 150 suppliers. "We now have a very valuable commodity—shelf space," declares a computer dealer in Columbus, Ohio. A Com-puterworks retailer adds: "There's zero loyalty [to manufacturers]. The guy who comes in with the next lower-priced computer gets the shelf space."

The battle to win shelf space is so important that some manufacturers are willing to cut profit margins to the bone to maintain dealer margins in the current 32-to-38 percent range. Intertec Data Systems, for example, recently dropped its profit margins to 15 percent from 28 percent to keep its dealers price-competitive. Even with that kind of help, dealers will look elsewhere if sales are slow. The president of Math Tech in Princeton, New Jersey, and one of Vector Graph-ic's largest and oldest dealers, praises the com-pany's dealer support. Nonetheless, he is look-ing for other, faster-moving products to sell. "There's nothing wrong in representing more than one company," he maintains.

The small manufacturers can avoid the profit-margin crunch altogether if they can find a niche in the market. Osborne Computer Corp. was selling 10,000 units a month in its second year by being the first to offer a portable com-puter. In 1982 it rang up sales of $70 million—up 600 percent over the previous year. (In 1983, Os-borne went bankrupt due to capitalization prob-lems.) And Compaq Computer Corp., a new company, has signed up 400 dealers to sell its portable computer. It has dealers excited be-cause it uses the same software as the IBM Per-sonal Computer. "You have to offer something else," warns Compaq's president. "Playing the price game is dangerous."

The description of aggressive price-cutting in the computer market illustrates the need for marketers to pay attention to the pricing aspects of the marketing mix; the organization's survival may be at stake.

WHAT IS PRICE?

As we have seen, marketing involves the ex-change of something of value. **Value** is the power one product or service has to attract an-other product or service in exchange. An auto mechanic could exchange four tune-ups for two months of coffee and doughnuts from a nearby diner. Such a trade is possible because the tune-ups, the coffee, and the doughnuts, all have value. When goods and services are exchanged for each other, the trade is called a **barter.**

Price is a statement of value, most com-monly expressed in dollars and cents. While it would be possible to value every product in the world in terms of every other product, such a system would be complicated and unwieldy. It is far easier to express these many values in terms of the single variable of money, or price. Even in a barter situation, the traders evaluate the items to be traded in terms of their monetary value.

Price has many names. These names vary according to tradition or the interests of the seller. For example, "rent," "fee," and "donation'' are terms used in specific exchange situations to express price. Some sellers avoid the use of the word "price" to make what is offered for sale appear to be of a quality that price cannot fully describe. Thus, the student pays tuition, not a price, for education. The commuter pays a toll. The professor who gives an off-campus speech "accepts an honorarium." The physician charges a fee for professional services. Universities, governments, professors, and doctors all sell their services for a price, no matter what that price is called.

In any case, marketing involves exchanges of things that have value. The name most commonly used to describe this value is "price."

PRICE IN THE ECONOMY

The major purpose of price within our relatively free market economy is to help allocate goods and services to various members of society. Most items of value are distributed to those who demand them *and* have the means to pay for them. As the price of gasoline has risen in recent years, some individuals have been willing *and* able to pay the higher prices while others have not. When products are scarce (e.g., if ordinary tap water is less than pure or "tastes funny"), wealthier citizens have been better able than poorer citizens to afford them (e.g., clean bottle water). Thus, price serves to allocate goods and services within our economy.

Inflation and the Price Variable

Recent periods of inflation have resulted in the decline of buying power among some groups of consumers as well as among many industrial and institutional buyers. This has made all buyers more price conscious and sensitive to price changes. Increased price awareness has not gone unnoticed by marketers. Products may be altered to permit the offering of lower-priced goods, as was done when the major coffee producers, such as Folgers, introduced "flaked" coffees. Distribution systems may be tightened in an effort to hold costs down. Advertising and personal selling messages stress lower prices and better values when buyers are known to be sensitive to price.

Surveys in 1964, 1975, and 1979 were conducted among executives to estimate the relative importance of the marketing mix variables in the meeting of marketing objectives. A comparison of these longitudinal surveys indicate that the ranking of pricing's importance in marketing strategy is relative to economic conditions, especially the inflation rate. Prices are the focus of increased executive attention when inflation rates are high.[2]

PRICING IN MARKETING STRATEGY

Price has a special significance in that it ultimately "pays" for all of the firm's activities. Since sales revenue equals price times unit sales volume, the price of a product is one of the prime determinations of sales revenues. If a price can be increased while unit volume and costs remain the same, revenues and profits will be increased. For this reason alone, pricing decisions are important. But price is important for another reason since it, like other marketing mix variables, influences unit sales volume. Thus, proper pricing of a product or service is expected to increase demand. Price is perhaps the most flex-

---

[2]Jon G. Udell, "How Important is Pricing in Competitive Strategy," *Journal of Marketing*, Vol. 28, January 1964, pp. 44–48; Robert A. Robicheaux, "How Important is Pricing in Competitive Strategy," H.W. Nash and D.P. Robin (eds.), *Proceedings of the Southern Marketing Association*, 1976, pp. 55, 57; and E. Boone and D. Kurtz, *Contemporary Marketing* (Hinsdale, Ill.: Dryden Press, 1980), p. 355.

ible element of the marketing mix because it can be changed rapidly in response to changes in the environment.

A price serves as a marketing tool by adding symbolic value to a good or service: A high price may suggest a status good, a low price may suggest a bargain, and a discount coupon or rebate may be used to encourage purchases by people who would otherwise not buy the product offered. Entire marketing themes may revolve around price. For example, Tiffany's, a chain of exclusive jewelry shops, maintains an image of the highest quality by stocking reliable products and providing special services, but also by charging comparatively high prices. K-Mart and Target stress bargains and must, therefore, keep prices at the lowest levels.

Price is closely related to the other marketing variables and cannot be discussed without simultaneous consideration of product, place, and promotion. Pricing strategies support the firm's other marketing strategies and must themselves be supported by these other strategies. In other words, all four pieces of the marketing mix must fit together to stimulate demand. For example, the Maytag product strategy—that customers have "ten years' trouble-free operation"—stresses the quality and reliability that is highlighted in their advertising strategy, which is reflected in Maytag's premium pricing strategy.

If Maytag planned to introduce a new, untried product, it would have to be offered to wholesalers and retailers at a price that would justify the risks involved in stocking a product that has no proven record of success. Likewise, a company like Maytag could not charge a high price for a poorly built appliance—at least not for long. Furthermore, Maytag could not reasonably advertise a special low price without having the brand in the stores when consumers come to buy it. Pricing must be coordinated with other aspects of marketing strategy.

Price bears a special relationship to promotion. One job of promotion is to show the potential buyer that an item is worth the price demanded. We can all think of products we bought or services we used because we believed that we were getting a good deal, a bargain, or high-quality workmanship. But, after a bit of thought, we might admit that the favorable price or statement of quality was identified with a familiar advertisement or a salesperson's presentation. Maybe the product's sturdy construction was demonstrated on television. Perhaps a salesperson convincingly explained that one diet center was better than another. In such instances, the asked-for price is paid more willingly primarily because promotion convinced us that the price charged was justified.

CONSIDERATIONS IN DETERMINING PRICING STRATEGIES

There are many mathematical tools that can be used to determine the specific price that should be assigned to a particular product. These will be discussed in the next two chapters. Most marketing managers, however, would be reluctant to trust such an important matter as price *exclusively* to any mechanical technique. Costs and demand need to be considered. Further, there remains an important role to be played by managerial judgment supported by marketing research, knowledge of competitors' actions, and anticipated buyer reactions to prices. When evaluating pricing alternatives it is important to[3]

1 Know your competition and the importance of price to your target market.
2 Determine your pricing objectives.
3 Know your costs.
4 Know your demand.
5 Know legal influences on pricing.

The remainder of the chapter discusses price competition and pricing objectives. Chap-

[3]This list is similar to the one found in Kent B. Monroe, *Pricing: Making Profitable Decisions* (New York: McGraw-Hill, 1979), pp. 272–273. •

AT EMERY AIR FREIGHT, PRICE ENSURES QUALITY SERVICE

Unwise managerial pricing judgments may be the result of simplistic thinking about the relationship between price and sales volume, overlooking the interaction between price and other elements of the product offering. Lower price is likely to require some reduction in costs, resulting in subtle changes in the product offering and a reduction in the resources available for promotion and market development.

This point was well made by the late John Emery, Sr., founder of Emery Air Freight Corporation. He explained that the company's objective was no more than 10 percent of the total airfreight market, and that its major commitment was to encouraging growth of the total air freight market. Mr. Emery, referring to the experience of the railroads where volume increases had been sought through drastic reductions in rates, believed that fighting for a larger market share would require price reductions inevitably leading to a reduction in the quality of the Emery service. Emery Air Freight Corporation consciously positioned itself as the premium-priced, quality service leader in the industry, aiming at the market segment that required superior service and was willing to pay for it. Refusing to lower rates and fight for larger market share, said Mr. Emery, "prevents our doing many foolish things." The wisdom of this philosophy is attested to by Emery's leadership position in the industry, sales growth, and profitability.

Source: Used with permission from Fredrick Webster, *Industrial Marketing* (New York: John Wiley & Sons, 1979), p. 125.

products are not distinctive, and price becomes the key marketing variable. In other product categories, price may be less important to the consumer than a distinctive product feature or a differentiated brand image. The firm that exclusively emphasizes low price in such a category may find competitors easily meet this low price.

Shortly after Tylenol was introduced, its maker, Johnson & Johnson, built a strong brand name recognition by emphasizing that acetaminophen was less irritating to the stomach. Datril was introduced as a "me too" brand. Datril utilized a price-cutting strategy with "low price" as its primary consumer benefit. Bristol-Meyers, the producers of Datril, sacrificed short-term profits so that reduced unit costs could be passed on to the consumer. Datril's price, approximately one-half the per unit price of Tylenol, was promoted heavily. The gist of the advertising campaign was that Datril was lower in price than the leading brand, Tylenol. Unfortunately for Datril, when Tylenol felt Datril was becoming serious competition, Tylenol met Datril's price and informed Bristol-Meyers that all of the Datril advertising had to be changed. The primary Datril strength, low price, was no longer an issue. If price is the sole basis of competition, competitors can easily take away the competitive advantage.[4] In July 1982, just before the Tylenol poisonings, Datril had less than a .2 percent share of the market.[5]

This example illustrates that price is extremely flexible. A price increase or decrease may be quickly made to adjust to changing competitive situations or changes in production costs.

Price: A Measure of Marketing Acumen

Ability to obtain and sustain a relatively high price for a product indicates that the marketing plan behind the item is sound and well-

ter 16 discusses pricing considerations associated with costs and related to demand. Chapter 17 discusses how to calculate a specific price and the related legal aspects of pricing.

Price Competition

There is considerable **price competition** in many industries. This is especially true with raw materials, such as crude petroleum, where competing

---

[4]"A Painful Headache for Bristol-Meyers?" *Business Week*, October 6, 1975, pp. 78–80.

[5]"A Bitter Pill for Aspirin Makers," *Business Week*, July 5, 1982, p. 78.

conceived.[6] Price is often indicative of overall marketing effectiveness. IBM gets a price substantially above that of many of its competitors, but, nevertheless, sells far more machines than any of them. This is fairly substantial proof that its overall marketing organization is far better than those of its competitors. The ability to maintain prices and volumes in the face of relatively stiff competition certainly indicates an excellent marketing organization. **Non-price competition** allows the marketer to emphasize other marketing mix elements rather than relying solely on a lower price to gain customers.

Federal Express has been so successful promoting a differential product that its competitors must lower their prices to compete. The United Parcel Service utilizes price to position itself as a competitor to Federal Express and other overnight delivery services. They offer a competitive price (slightly lower) for next day air service *and* a substantially lower price for second-day air service for those price-conscious customers who want quick service but do not necessarily need overnight delivery.

Properly priced goods facilitate all marketing activities. The marketing manager should realize that if products are too highly priced other marketing variables will be affected. Promotional efforts may not be as effective, for example, or it may be more difficult to obtain the desired channels of distribution. On the other hand, properly priced goods make the promotional program far more effective than it would otherwise be, and members of channels of distribution are usually more willing to handle items that represent good competitive values.

Target Market Considerations

The marketing manager's pricing decisions are affected by many factors. The most significant of these is demand from the organization's *target market*. Even when prices are changed in response to a *competitor's* change in price, target market considerations are important because

---

[6]This section is adapted with permission from R. H. Buskirk, D.J. Green, and W.C. Rodgers, *Concepts of Business: An Introduction to the Business System* (Richardson, Tex.: Oak Tree Press, 1976), p. 184.

A long-winded argument for MCI.

A short-winded argument.

LONG DISTANCE CALLS	MINS.	BELL	MCI	SAVINGS
St. Louis to Belleville	1	$ .32	$ .15	53.1%
New York City to Erie	1	.59	.36	39.0
Washington, D.C., to Atlanta	2	1.05	.75	28.6
San Francisco to Denver	3	1.52	1.15	24.3
Dallas to Milwaukee	5	2.34	1.87	20.1
Memphis to Fresno	9	4.16	3.46	16.8
Baltimore to Boston	4	1.85	1.45	21.6
Los Angeles to Chicago	7	3.28	2.69	18.0
Richmond to Baltimore	13	5.26	4.45	15.4
Cincinnati to Louisville	8	3.16	2.62	17.1
Cheyenne to Ft. Wayne	10	4.60	3.84	16.5
Houston to Phoenix	3	1.52	1.15	24.3
Atlanta to Cincinnati	6	2.69	2.18	19.0

A company can stress price competition because it offers a parity product without any "unique" features.

the competitor's move may affect the organization's *own* target market. In essence, the question the marketing manager faces is this, "Who are our customers and what do *they* want the price to be?"

The notion that the customer wants the lowest price is not always correct. Diamonds and Rolls Royce automobiles are expensive partly because people *expect* them to be expensive. A $100 bottle of perfume may contain only $4 to $16 of scent, while the rest of the price goes to advertising, packaging, distribution, and profit. When consumers buy such perfume, they are buying atmosphere, hope, the feeling of being someone special, and pride in having "the best."

The target market is a prime consideration in setting price.

Penney's Plain Pockets sell for $4 to $5 less than Levi Strauss brand.

More mundane products also fit this situation. The common household iron can be bought in many models, each with slightly different features. The top-of-the-line model typically sells for $55 or $60, perhaps $10 more than the next most expensive model. The top price model may, for example, have a light indicating when the iron is ready. The difference between the two in terms of manufacturing costs may be less than $3, but the *market segment* that wants "the best" seems to be willing to pay $10 for the light.

Even frequently-bought products can exemplify the customer's willingness to pay a higher price rather than a lower one. Parents do not usually brag about buying bargain-priced baby food for their infants, nor do most hosts offer their guests a drink while discussing what an inexpensive brand of whiskey they've been able to buy. In some demand situations marketers can

PRICING OF PRODUCTS IS STILL AN ART

Materials and labor costs plus overhead and other expenses plus profit equals price. But, in many cases, that equation includes psychological and other factors so subtle that pricing consultants are retained to help set appropriate market prices. The consultants, by the way, are themselves, high-priced.

One such firm is Management Decision Systems, Inc. (MDS), of Waltham, Massachusetts, which uses computers and consumer survey data to help marketers determine the most marketable prices for their products. The firm measures consumer reaction to two different prices on the same product and usually discovers that the lower price is preferred. But not always. An MDS vice president notes,

"The higher you price certain products like a Mercedes-Benz, the more desirable they become."

Fleischmann's gin was losing ground in the marketplace because recessionary conditions encouraged gin drinkers to drink at home and not in the bars and lounges where much of Fleischmann's gin was poured. Fleischmann raised its price from $4.50 per 750-millimeter bottle to $5.50. Fleischmann (a division of Nabisco Brands, Inc.) increased both its bottle sales and its revenues though the gin remained the same and the price increased. Another variable, the bottle itself, was altered to attract and appeal to the liquor store customers who were buying increasing amounts of gin for home consumption.

In a similar move with a dif-

ferent twist, Heublein increased the price of its Popov vodka by 8 percent in 1981, but kept it below that of its premium vodka Smirnoff. Outside analysts insist that the two products are one and the same. In Popov's case, sales fell, and the brand lost 1 percent of its market, but profits increased by 30 percent.

Although sellers of just about everything devote a great deal of time and study to determine what prices to put on their products, pricing remains largely an art. To decide prices, manufacturers usually weigh costs, prices on similar products, and other conditions and then "take a good guess." Everybody thinks people go about pricing scientifically, but often the process is incredibly arbitrary.

Source: Adapted with permission from "Pricing of Products Is Still an Art, Often Having Little Link to Costs," by Jeffrey H. Birnbaum, *Wall Street Journal*, November 25, 1981, p. 23.

expect to sell more at a higher price than at a lower one.

Most successful marketers do not employ high prices to appeal to buyers. Instead, they offer reasonably-priced products that prove popular to target markets. Among the more successful of these marketers is J.C. Penney. Penney's sells casual shirts with its "Fox" emblem in place of Lacoste's "Alligator." Its shirts sell for $5 less

than Lacoste's. Penny's insists that the shirts are *identical* except for the symbol. Penney's also offers "plain pocket" jeans at $4 or $5 less than the price suggested by Levi Strauss for its five pocket jeans. J.C. Penney's success with these efforts suggests that the company's pricing methods are appropriate for the *Penney* target market, while Lacoste and Levi Strauss also know *their* target markets.

PRICING OBJECTIVES

Each firm pricing a good or service must determine what is to be accomplished by its pricing plans. Managers should know *why* certain prices are being charged as well as why these

prices might differ from buyer to buyer and from time to time. Since many objectives are possible, various forms of pricing have been developed. A firm could face any number of problems and

EXHIBIT 15-1

Some Organizational Objectives and the Role Pricing Can Play in Attaining Them

Objectives Mainly Concerned With:	Pricing Steps Taken[a]	Why Take Such Steps?
Income		
■ **Achieve a target ROI**	Identify price levels that will yield the required return on investment.	Firm may have a required return on investment and may drop product lines that cannot reach that return.
■ **Increase cash flow**	Adjust prices and discounts to encourage purchases and rapid payment.	Company may face a serious cash flow problem and be unable to meet its obligations.
■ **Maximize profits**	Control costs and adjust prices to achieve point-of-profit maximization.	"All" companies would like to achieve profit maximization for obvious reasons. Some come close to this goal, particularly for certain items in their product mixes.
■ **Keep a going concern**	Adapt prices to permit the organization to "hold on" in periods of business downturns or until a buyer can be found.	The organization may be for sale, and it is easier to sell a going-concern than one which is out of business.
Sales		
■ **Maintain a share of market**	Assure that prices contribute to sales remaining in roughly the same proportion to those of competitors.	Many companies, G.M. in domestic autos and Procter and Gamble in detergents, are long-time number one companies and want to keep their positions of leaderhip.
■ **Encourage sales growth**	Adjust price and discounts to encourage more purchases by existing buyers and to attract new buyers.	The firm may need a larger group of customers to protect against disaster should some of their existing customers stop buying.
■ **"Survival"**	Set prices at a level that will allow the organization to "scrape by" in a current difficult situation.	The organization may be seeking to last out an economic storm or to simply hold on for a few years until the owners are ready to retire.

[a] *Important:* Notice that *no* consideration has been given here to possible actions by competitors or shifts in demand.

choose from among a great number of objectives. Some of these objectives are shown in Exhibit 15-1, along with possible pricing steps to be undertaken for each objective.

The important thing to note is that each price strategy, each type and level of price, has logic and reason behind it. Prices are set to help bring about a *result*. The hoped-for result is the **pricing objective.** Clearly the organization needs such objectives because "price" suggests a vast array of dollar values from one cent to millions of dollars. Objectives narrow the range of possibilities considerably and thus greatly facilitate the determining of price.

EXHIBIT 15-1 (Continued)

Objectives Mainly Concerned With:	Pricing Steps Taken[a]	Why Take Such Steps?
Competition		
■ Meet competition	Set prices about equal to those of competitors. Do the same with discounts offered.	A great number of American firms do this to avoid price competition and price cutting wars, and attempt to compete by means of non-price competitive moves.
■ Avoid competition	Set prices at a level that will discourage competition in the firm's markets.	A firm with a local monopoly might choose to keep prices on the low side so new competitors would not be attracted to its area.
■ Undercut competition	Set prices lower than the competition's.	The organization might undercut competition to project a bargain image or to draw customers away from competitors.
Social Concern		
■ Behave ethically	Due to special considerations, set prices at levels lower than they could have been.	A manufacturer of prescription medicines could charge almost any price for effective drugs but "does what's right," though this is partly to avoid government regulations.
■ Maintaining employment	Set prices at levels that will maintain production and employment of workers.	An organization with strong community ties may seek to keep townspeople employed at least until a buyer for the company can be found.

Objectives Must Be Consistent. Although we are concerned here with pricing, it should be remembered that pricing objectives must be coordinated with the firm's other marketing objectives. These must, in turn, flow from the company's overall objectives. Thus, if a firm seeks to become the major supplier of glass to U.S. automobile manufacturers, all of the marketing objectives, including the pricing objectives, must be consistent with that broad company goal. The relationship is shown in Exhibit 15-2.

Return on Investment Serves as Comparison Standard. Return-on-investment (ROI) is

AN ADMISSION AT THE BRITISH MUSEUM?

In the mid-1970s, the British Parliament passed an act requiring its top museums to charge admission for the first time in history. This created a storm of protest. The proponents of the admission price supplied the following arguments: (1) the government could no longer afford all of the annual cost of $44 million to maintain the museums; (2) visitors from abroad were getting something free by not being charged; (3) visitors would better appreciate the institutions if they were charged; (4) museum directors would have the incentive to put on better shows and be more responsive; (5) the money could be used to finance extensions and better collections; and (6) museums on the Continent and in the United States charged admission fees. Those who opposed the admission price countered with the following arguments: (1) the charge would discourage attendance by slum children, students, and the old; (2) the cost of collecting the money—more attendants, gates at the entrance, more paperwork—would reduce much of the benefit; and (3) museums should not be forced to go into the entertainment business to please the public but should concentrate on presenting serious exhibits. Despite these counterarguments, the act was passed, and the British museums began to consider the best form of charging admission. They examined three major pricing approaches:

1 Museums could charge daily admission except for one day of the week. A free day would allow the poor or young to visit the museum. The admission charge could be varied for different visitors, being lower (or waived) for children and students, people over 65, handicapped people, and veterans.

2 Museums could encourage donations from visitors rather than charge a fixed price. At the Metropolitan Museum in New York, people are encouraged to contribute $4.00, or anything they can. The voluntary nature of the donation allows the poor and young to enter without cost if they choose.

3 The museums could charge a small admission fee and also sponsor a membership plan which provides members with special benefits such as a monthly magazine, an annual report, invitation to exhibit openings, a discount at the gift shop, and a waiver of admission charges. The museum would establish different levels of membership and membership privilege, with dues going from $15 (regular membership) to $100 (special membership) to $500 (life membership).

The various museums considered these and other alternatives, and soon realized that the key issue was what objectives they were seeking to accomplish through the pricing mechanism.

Source: Philip Kotler, *Marketing for Nonprofit Organizations*, 2nd ed. (Englewood Cliffs, N.J.: Prentice-Hall), pp. 303–304, reprinted by permission of Prentice-Hall, Englewood Cliffs, N.J.

EXHIBIT 15-2

The Relationship of Pricing Decisions to Company Objectives

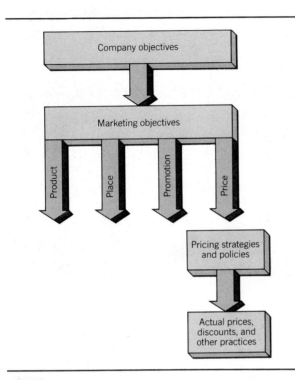

Revenue = X
Merchandise cost = $100,000
Selling expenses = $50,000
Required return = 25% (or .25)

Step 1. $100,000 + $50,000 + .25X = X
Step 2. $150,000 + .25X = X
Step 3. $150,000 = X − .25X
Step 4. $150,000 = .75X
Step 5. $150,000/.75 = X
Step 6. $200,000 = X
Step 7. $200,000 ÷ 10
= $20,000 price for each item

the ratio of profits to assets (or net worth) for an organizational segment (company, division, etc.), product line, or brand. The ROI is also called the *profit target.* If management has determined that a certain *ROI* is needed from each product or product line, the prices for those must be set with the return objective in mind. Such a price is referred to as an ROI price because it is chosen with a particular return on investment as its goal.

For example, if 10 computers cost a wholesaler $100,000, and $50,000 in selling expenses were also incurred, the wholesaler has "invested" $150,000 in those items. If the return required was 25 percent, the computers should have to generate $200,000 in revenue. Thus, each of the ten items should be priced at $20,000 ($200,000 ÷ 10). This price could be derived algebraically:

Turnover (sales divided by tangible assets) is an important factor in influencing the ROI of many organizations, especially retailers and wholesalers. Grocery store pricing strategies, for example, recognize that a higher return on investment may be generated if there is a rapid turnover of inventory. Thus, a grocery store might have a profit margin less than five percent but a high return on investment.

Exhibit 15-3 shows how cost and ROI determine the manufacturer's price for an automobile. Another factor, dealer markup, interacts to influence the final list price (sticker price) of the automobile.

What is the part played by the marketing manager's *judgment* and knowledge of the market in such mathematical calculation of price? For one thing, the ROI figure, 25 percent in our example, is itself something of a judgment call, since it is based on perceived risks, the expected condition of the economy, and other factors to be estimated.

Also, once the calculation has yielded the price, the marketing manager must make some decisions. Will the market pay that price? Is the ROI price too low? Should it be raised so that it can then be reduced if the market is accustomed to marked down prices? Should different prices be charged in different areas or to different sorts of customers? The answers to these questions and others like them must meet the organization's pricing objectives.

Return on investment considerations are important to many pricing decisions because they

EXHIBIT 15-3

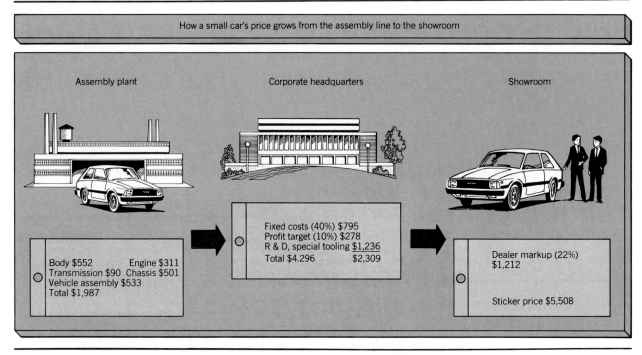

How a small car's price grows from the assembly line to the showroom

Assembly plant | Corporate headquarters | Showroom

Body $552   Engine $311
Transmission $90   Chassis $501
Vehicle assembly $533
Total $1,987

Fixed costs (40%) $795
Profit target (10%) $278
R & D, special tooling $1,236
Total $4.296 $2,309

Dealer markup (22%)
$1,212

Sticker price $5,508

Source: "Why Detroit Can't Cut Prices," *Business Week,* March 1, 1982, p. 111.

provide a means to evaluate *alternative* marketing opportunities. Assume two proposed products are expected to generate approximately the same sales volume. If one product is expected to yield an ROI of 10 percent and another is likely to offer an ROI of 30 percent, the choice between the two marketing opportunities is made easier. The ROI pricing method *suggests* a price that the marketing manager can use for reference as the decision-making process continues.

Sales Objectives. Prices may be set to encourage sales growth, to maintain or increase market share, or to allow the product to survive difficult economic times. (See Exhibit 15-1.) Sales objectives are often intertwined with competitive objectives and with the concepts of supply and demand (discussed in Chapter 16). We will limit our discussion of objectives to those concerning market share.

Protect or Improve Market Share. **Market share** refers to the percentage of total industry sales accounted for by a particular firm. Procter and Gamble accounts for a large portion of the total sales of the soap and detergent industry and thus has a large share of the market. In the soft drink industry, the same is true of Coca-Cola. These companies, for financial reasons or for reasons of pride, seek to protect their impressive shares of the market. They keep their prices at reasonable levels even when the popularity of certain items might appear to permit raising prices without loss of sales. The objective of this type of pricing is to *maintain market share.*

Price might also be used aggressively by firms seeking to *enlarge market shares.* Such firms could cut prices drastically in an attempt to attract customers away from competitors. However, such a move could backfire. Competitors might begin to lower their own prices, setting off a price war. Or customers could come to believe that the price reduction signaled a cutback in the product's quality. Thus, price cuts are generally used to attract more customers on a temporary basis. Cents-off coupons that expire on a certain date, auto rebates available for a short period of time, and January white sales are examples of temporary price cuts.

Competition Influences Most Pricing Objectives

The effective marketer invariably tempers pricing judgments with considerations of competition. Several situations in which competition frequently plays a very significant role are identified below.

Stabilize Prices. It could be a marketer's goal to stabilize prices by matching the competitors' prices—this is called **price stabilization.** This is fairly common, but is particularly evident in the retailing of gasoline and groceries. Though price wars in these fields are not unheard of, the normal course of events is for all gas stations in town to charge roughly equal prices for fuel and for all grocery stores to charge approximately the same prices for milk. A member of the business community seeking to avoid injurious price wars will set prices to help stabilize the general price level.

Avoid Competition. One pricing technique is to underprice goods and services to avoid attracting competitors. The logic goes like this: It is better to own the only store in the neighborhood and make a reasonable profit than to make a large profit that attracts other marketers to the service area.

Maximize Long-Term Profits. A form of pricing is suggested by the expression "all the traffic will bear." Perhaps this is a distasteful idea, but, in certain circumstances, it works. Faced with a shortage of apartments in Houston, newcomers are willing to pay *more* rent than they had planned to rather than have no place to stay. Victims of cancer or other serious diseases frequently demonstrate that they will pay *any* price for a "cure." In these, and many other situations, sellers might try to raise their prices to the highest levels. This is an understandable, if not always respected, course of action. The classic, but rare, monopolist who prices a product or service at the highest possible level comes to mind. But few, if any, businesses are free to behave in this manner.

Aside from the question of ethics, such practices may violate a major premise of the *marketing concept* . . . that consumer-orientation will lead to long-term profitability. An "all the traffic will bear" approach to pricing may be tempting in the short-run, but can be disastrous if it results in threats, boycotts, bad public relations, or government actions. Any firm that adopts this type of pricing attitude should be aware that the public may simply stop buying what is offered, may seek some different means for satisfying the need for what the firm offers, or may even demand government action against the firm.

Given the realities of our market economy, it is good marketing to maximize profits *over the long term* by charging prices that will keep customers and the government comparatively content. A business charging a very high price over a short period of time runs the risk of being driven out of business by competitors willing to provide the same service or a substitute good at a more reasonable price.

Match Competition. Businesses may find it necessary to price goods or services at approximately the levels charged by *competitors.* Unless the marketer is in the rare situation of holding an unbreakable patent on a product that is unique, difficult to copy, and in great demand, it is impossible to set prices without consideration of the competitors' prices. Many goods are so like one another that buyers can and do consider them to be virtually the same, forcing the individual firm to set its prices at the level established by competitors. New brands of coffee are generally priced at the going rate because one coffee is highly substitutable for another. Most con-

PRICE LEADERSHIP

Price leadership exists where one company is typically the first to announce price changes that others follow, although the leadership role sometimes rotates among several dominant producers.

The leader firm is able to effect a delicate price adjustment to changing cost and demand conditions without starting a price war and is able to make its announced price stick.

Successful price leaders tend to have most of the following 12 characteristics:

1 Large share of the industry's production capacity.
2 Large market share.
3 Commitment to a particular product class or grade.
4 New, cost-efficient plants.

5 Strong distribution system, perhaps including captive wholesale outlets.
6 Good customer relations such as technical assistance for industrial buyers, programs directed at end users, and special attention to important customers during shortage periods.
7 An effective market information system which provides analysis of the realities of supply and demand.
8 Sensitivity to the price and profit needs of the rest of the industry.
9 A sense of timing to know when price changes should be made.
10 Sound management organization for pricing.
11 Effective product-line financial controls, which are needed

to make sound price leadership decisions.
12 Attention to legal issues. The illegality of conspiring to fix prices is nothing new. Evidence of conspiracy is found in such company actions as disclosing and receiving from competitors the prices charged or quoted to buyers and threatening reprisals against wholesalers who don't conform to prices agreed upon by producers. To play it safe, some price leaders now avoid price announcements in trade journals and don't use speeches or interviews to express their ideas about when a price increase is needed and how large it should be. These firms also set up internal controls requiring division managers to document all sources of information on competitive prices.

Source: Used with permission of Stuart U. Rich, "Price Leaders: Large, Strong, but Cautious About Conspiracy," *Marketing News*, June 25, 1982, p. 11.

Matching the competition or offering competitive prices is a typical pricing strategy.

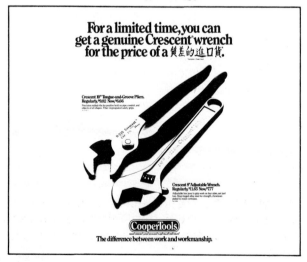

For a limited time, you can get a genuine Crescent wrench for the price of a 质差的进口货.

Crescent 10" Tongue-and-Groove Pliers. Regularly $9.82 Now $6.66

Crescent 8" Adjustable Wrench. Regularly $11.65 Now $7.77

CooperTools
The difference between work and workmanship.

sumers will not buy a brand of coffee costing $1 more per pound than the others. In cases where a brand is considerably more expensive than others, the higher pricing must be supported by other marketing strategies. These might include production of a genuinely better coffee blend, promotion of the brand by an extensive advertising campaign, or packaging the coffee in attractive reusable containers.

Many marketers of goods that are essentially substitutable with other brands depart from a policy of matching their competitors' prices by distributing cents-off coupons or temporarily reducing prices. Such tactics are more *promotional* than price-altering in nature since they are short-lived. Furthermore, competitors can quickly issue coupons or cut prices to match the special sale price.

SUMMARY

Marketing involves the exchange of something of value. Although what is exchanged could be goods or services, the values most commonly involved are expressed in dollars and cents, the usual expression of price.

Price is an economic force in our society, and a powerful influence in our lives, but it is, from a seller's viewpoint, also a marketing tool. Price can be altered by employing discounts, special sales, or rebates to make the purchase seem more attractive to the customer. Price can be raised to make some goods and services seem more desirable than others because customers often assume that something more expensive is better. Prices can be used to help firms attain financial and market-share objectives.

However, price is only one of the four major marketing variables. The others—product, place, and promotion—must be taken into account any time prices are set or changed. High prices that yield good profit provide the funds for developing better products, more efficient distribution, and more effective promotion. In certain situations, low prices may have equally beneficial results. While price "supports" these other areas of concern, it also must be supported by them. For example, a high price is supported by a satisfactory product, and a low price is supported by efficient means of production, distribution, and promotion. Thus, while a number of techniques can be used to determine price, the fact remains that price can never be considered without recognition of the importance of many variables. That these variables may be found both within and outside of the firm (for example, in the law) greatly complicates the marketing manager's job.

This chapter focused on the importance of knowing the competition and knowing the target market before pricing objectives are determined. Pricing objectives may be set to meet income, sales, or competitive goals. Social concerns also influence pricing objectives.

THE MOST IMPORTANT CONCEPT IN THIS CHAPTER

Although price is usually thought of in terms of dollars and cents, price is a statement of value and may include anything of value that is exchanged. As a marketing strategy variable, it must be determined with specific objectives in mind that reflect company objectives and other elements of the marketing mix.

KEY TERMS

Value	Non-price competition	Turnover
Barter	Pricing objective	Market share
Price	Return on	Price stabilization
Price competition	investment (ROI)	

QUESTIONS FOR DISCUSSION

1 What are some other names given to "price"? Why are these names used instead of "price"?

2 What is the major function of price within the economy as a whole? Differentiate between that function and the role price has as a marketing tool.

3 "A high price policy needs supporting policies." Explain.

4 Give some examples of situations where price might not be in sync with other aspects of a firm's marketing plan.

5 Why does the consumer often view price as the most important part of a transaction?

6 The prices a firm charges for its goods or services often depend primarily on how the customer is expected to react to the price charged. In what situations have you, as a customer or seller, encountered this approach to pricing?

7 How has inflation affected consumer awareness of price? How has it affected your family's shopping and buying habits?

8 Studies have shown that, in 1964, executives ranked promotion and pricing #2 and #3 in importance as marketing tools. In 1979, pricing was #1 and promotion #4. What changes have occurred to account for these shifts?

9 Differentiate between company objectives, marketing objectives, and pricing objectives.

10 Why must managerial judgment play a role in determining prices even though many mathematical techniques for that purpose have been developed?

11 How can target market considerations affect a firm's pricing policies?

12 What is meant by the expression "all the traffic will bear"? How does this practice relate to the marketing concept?

13 Is pricing an art or a science?

14 J.C. Penney sells its Fox shirts for several dollars less than Lacoste's alligator shirts. Why don't consumers simply buy the Fox and save themselves a good deal of money?

CASE 15-1   Magic Chef Incorporated

Magic Chef, a major producer of appliances, recently acquired Norge. It has been attempting to turn around Norge's sluggish sales. Norge was in desperate need of new production machinery and tooling when Magic Chef purchased it. Although Magic Chef has invested between $4 million and $7 million in each of the last few years, Norge lost $8 million in 1982. In addition to its manufacturing problems, Norge's product line was somewhat outdated. For example, its 30-inch dryers are larger than any competitive brand. Therefore, parts and material costs are higher.

Questions

1 What pricing objectives should Magic Chef have for its Norge line?

2 What short-term pricing strategy would you implement?

3 What long-term pricing strategy would you implement?

CASE 15-2 Datril vs. Tylenol: One More Time*

It's 1975 revisited: Bristol-Myers (B-M) is running a repeat performance of its classic Datril comparative advertising campaign. That campaign said Datril was superior to Extra-Strength Tylenol since the pain relievers were exactly the same and Datril costs less.

The revival is not due to an award-winning performance, since the original Datril campaign lost at least $10 million. But times have changed, say company officials, who now believe the 1975 campaign simply may have been ahead of its time. This time around, Datril, now known as Datril 500, will spend at an annual national rate

*Source: Based on "Datril Again Tries Price Versus Tylenol," *Advertising Age*, March 21, 1983, pp. 2 and 52.

of $26 million in its first six weeks on TV, with $1.5 million being spent during the first two weeks (which began March 15) and another $1.5 million going out during the next four weeks. "We will continue an aggressive program through 1983. It will be competitive and give us a presence," said John Loden, director of analgesics marketing. He also said that dollars would not be diverted from the company's other analgesic brands.

The Datril 500 TV commercial, by Kenyon & Eckhardt, features a woman who notes that Extra-Strength Datril works for her splitting headache just as well as Extra-Strength Tylenol "since I switched. And now I know why." She explains that the two products contain exactly the same pain-relieving ingredient and are the same strength. "Yet Extra-Strength Tylenol can cost so much more. So I'm staying with Datril. Why would I pay that much more for the same relief? Why would anybody?"

In one New York area store, a 50-tablet bottle of Datril was priced at $1.69 and a 60-tablet bottle of Tylenol at $3.79.

"Most people think of Tylenol as a generic drug," a B-M spokesman said, indicating B-M intends to change that impression. "When you go to the doctor, he says take two aspirin and go to bed or take two Tylenol and go to bed—never two acetaminophen," he said.

Newspaper advertisements are considered by B-M to be an educational effort that explains the differences, benefits, and disadvantages of both aspirin and acetaminophen. Another aspect will be a publicity tour by B-M spokesmen. The company hopes to have a medical staffer spreading the message during talk show appearances.

While the Datril advertising appears quite similar to the effort B-M made eight years ago, company executives said there are enough important differences to make them confident that Datril can become a successfully advertised brand. Frank Mayers, chairman, Bristol-Myers Products division, pointed out that many people forget that the Datril campaign was successful initially—at least until Johnson & Johnson spent $20 million within a matter of weeks to drop the price of Tylenol by 30 percent. The trade did buy millions of cases of Datril, but once the Tylenol price fell, B-M had to take a lot of returns. The returns plus heavy advertising outlays that had to be revised almost weekly as Tylenol's price gradually fell to Datril levels proved costly for B-M.

Mr. Loden pointed out that the analgesic market is much different today. The acetaminophen segment—largely Tylenol—has grown to 40 percent of the $1 billion category, big enough to accommodate more than one entry. He said research indicates that consumers are very loyal to whichever segment of analgesic they buy—either aspirin or acetaminophen—and he indicated that the business Datril gains will be from Tylenol or the other recent numerous smaller nonaspirin entries and not from its own aspirin brands.

As for share objectives, Mr. Loden said they don't have to be very high to consider the brand a success because the size of the category is so large. "If we achieve a 2%-to-3% market share, that would be terrific. Obviously, we hope to do even better," he said.

Questions

1 What pricing objective does Datril appear to have?

2 How has the change in the product life cycle affected Datril pricing strategy?

3 Should Johnson & Johnson try to stop the Datril advertisements with a strategy similar to their 1975 strategy?

CHAPTER 16

Costs and Demand: How They Influence Pricing Decisions

CHAPTER SCAN

This chapter investigates the economic theory of costs and demand and the contributions it has made to pricing.

This chapter also shows how marketers use costs and such accounting and financial tools as break-even and marginal analysis to determine the prices of their products.

WHEN YOU HAVE STUDIED THIS CHAPTER, YOU WILL:

Know how to use several tools employed in determining what a particular product's price will be.

Understand target return and full-line pricing.

Understand that as demand changes prices change.

Understand the price elasticity of demand.

Understand break-even analysis and marginal analysis.

Be able to show how managerial judgment is used to finally establish a product's market price.

"The majors are locked in almost mortal combat . . . nobody's taking any prisoners." So declared Southland Corporation's Vice-President for petroleum products in early 1983.[1] Even a large independent such as Southland which sells gasoline to 2,827 of its 7,165 7-Eleven convenience stores could not survive for long in the gasoline price war that kicked off the year. Shrinking demand and increased crude oil supply had dictated price competition and all but the very biggest organizations found it hard to stay alive. "There has never been such an extended period of tight or non-existent margins," said the Southland VP.

Diamond Shamrock Corporation, a Dallas-based independent refiner and retailer squeezed to the bone by the competition for market share had met prices as low as 94.9 cents a gallon for regular gasoline. On January 17, it attempted to call a truce in the war in Texas and raised prices to reestablish profitable margins. Experience had shown that, since such price wars were good for no one, the major oil companies would quickly follow. This time they did not, and within days Diamond Shamrock, despite its dominant position in the local market, was forced to lower prices again. The situation was much the same across the country.

As decades worth of efforts to conserve gasoline matured, the major oil producers were faced with steadily shrinking demand. Desperate to maintain volume by slashing prices, the industry's retail profits had all but disappeared. In

Southland, America's largest gasoline retailer, is strongly influenced by price competition.

some markets gasoline was selling at the price of crude oil, raising protests of predatory pricing from the rapidly failing independents. The majors "are all trying to buy market share," said a retired officer of Gulf Oil Corporation, "and it will be very costly."

DETERMINING PRICE LEVELS

While it is possible to set the price to be charged for a product or service simply by guesswork, marketing managers usually try to follow some logical pricing procedure. Such a procedure would take into account two major forces, *cost*

considerations and *market* or *demand* considerations. Even though some pricing methods focus on costs while others focus on demand, the marketing manager should use several methods to determine price rather than relying on one or two pricing tools. This chapter provides an explanation of various ways to determine price *level*. That is, what will the price be?

[1]Based on "It's War at the Gas Pumps," *Business Week*, February 7, 1983, p. 114.

COST-ORIENTED PRICING METHODS

Pricing methods involving only consideration of the seller's costs fail to include the all-important buyer in the pricing effort, but the seller's costs do provide a major area of concern. Although some products may be occasionally sold at a loss, costs must be recouped sooner or later. Cost provides the "floor" on which to build a pricing strategy.

Mark-Up on Selling Price and Mark-Up on Costs Are Different

Many marketers, especially retailers and wholesalers, rely on a comparatively uncomplicated method for determining their resale prices: The cost of the product is noted and a simple percentage **mark-up** is added to reach the selling price. For example, a cost, of $1 and a mark-up on selling price of 33.3 percent yields a selling price of $1.50. The 50-cent mark-up is expressed as 33.3 percent because 50 cents is one-third of the *selling* price of $1.50. The term **mark-up on selling price** is then used. Users of the mark-up method almost always use the *selling* price rather than the cost of the product or service in figuring the mark-up percentage. Certain industries have established traditional mark-ups for the various channel members.

If an item costs a retailer $50 and the retailer sold it for $100, what was the mark-up?

Solution 1. 100 percent ($50 added on divided by $50 cost = 100 percent)
or
Solution 2. 50 percent ($50 added on divided by $100 selling price = 50 percent)

The answer is 50 percent, since the mark-up is the amount *added* to the cost of the product divided by the *selling* price of the product.

Whenever the term mark-up is left unspecified, it refers to mark-up on the selling price. It is true that a mark-up can be calculated using cost rather than sales price, as was done in solution 1 above. That figure, however, is called a **mark-up on cost** as distinguished from the more common *mark-up on selling price.* Using a mark-up based on cost makes it appear that the marketer is charging more (100 percent versus 50 percent, for example), even though the dollar figures are exactly the same. The reason mark-up based on selling price is more commonly employed than mark-up based on cost is because many important figures such as gross sales, revenues, and so on, are *sales* figures, not cost figures.

The effective use of mark-up based on cost or selling price requires that the marketing manager calculate a *margin* which will ultimately provide adequate funds to cover selling expenses and profit. Once this is done, the technique has the major advantage of being easy to employ in determining price levels.

If a wholesaler bought a screwdriver for $5, and marked it up using a 20 percent mark-up based on cost, what would the selling price be? It would be a selling price of $6, because $5 × .20 = $1; $5 cost + $1 mark-up on cost = $6.

Cost-Plus

Manufacturers often choose to use a pricing method similar to mark-up in that they determine what *costs* were involved in producing an item then *add* an amount to the cost total to arrive at a price.

Like mark-up, *cost-plus* is easy to use once an appropriate addition to the cost has been determined.

Much government contracting is done on this basis, with the supplier of a product or service submitting the cost figures associated with a particular assignment and adding a reasonable profit margin to yield a total price for the project.

The Average-Cost Method

If a marketer identifies *all* the costs associated with the manufacturing and marketing of a product or provision of a service, it should be possible to determine what the average cost of a single unit of the product or service might be.

FORD CONSIDERS COSTS

According to Henry Ford mass production was the result, not the cause, of low prices.

Our policy is to reduce the price, extend the operations, and improve the article. You will notice that the reduction of price comes first. We have never considered any costs as fixed. Therefore we first reduce the price to the point where we believe more sales will result. Then we go ahead and try to make the prices. We do not bother about the costs. The new price forces the costs down. The more usual way is to take the costs and then determine the price, and although that method may be scientific in the narrow sense; it is not scientific in the broad sense, because what earthly use is it to know the cost if it tells you that you cannot manufacture at a price at which the article can be sold? But more to the point is the fact that, although one may calculate what a cost is, and of course all of our costs are carefully calculated, no one knows what a cost ought to be. One of the ways of discovering ... is to name a price so low as to force everybody in the place to the highest point of efficiency. The low price makes everybody dig for profits. We make more discoveries concerning manufacturing and selling under this forced method than by any method of leisurely investigation.

Source: Henry Ford, *My Life and Work* (New York: Doubleday, Page Company, 1923), pp. 146–147.

$$\frac{\text{All costs}\ (\$80,000)}{\text{Number of units produced (100)}} = \frac{\text{Average cost of}}{\text{a single unit}} = \$800$$

To do this, however, it is necessary to know how much of the product will be demanded and produced.

If a margin for profit was added to the total cost figures, a likely price for a unit of goods could be calculated. The example shown above can be changed as follows.

$$\text{All costs}\ (\$80,000) + \text{Margin for profit}\ (\$20,000) = \$100,000$$

$$\frac{\$100,000}{100\ \text{units}} = \frac{\text{Average cost of a single unit including the profit margin}}{} = \$1,000$$

Since the total cost figure of $100,000 now *includes* a margin for profit, the price of a single unit of the product might reasonably be $1,000.

While the average cost method can suggest a price that might be charged, there is a serious risk that the quantity demanded by the market (100 units in our example) might not match the predictions of the marketing manager. If it happened that only 50 units were demanded at the price of $1,000, the firm's income would be only $50,000 while the costs of production and marketing remained at $80,000. This demonstrates that it is extremely risky to base pricing decisions on costs alone. The market—the demand generated by customers—must be carefully considered in any calculation of price. Demand changes can turn profit into loss. The typical problem of cost overruns by companies with government contracts can occur because cost-plus-pricing offers little incentive to strive for improving cost efficiency.

Target Return Pricing

A marketing manager using **target return pricing** first calculates a total fixed cost figure. The total fixed cost figure includes such items as executive salaries, rents, and other expenses that must be paid even when no units of a product are being produced. A *target return,* usually represented as a percentage of investment, is added to total cost to get a figure representing total fixed costs and target return.

Now the marketer must estimate demand. If that estimate were 1,000 units, and if the total of fixed costs *and* target return were $500,000,

HOW TO SERVE UP
ROCK-BOTTOM PRICES: REDUCE COSTS

One feisty little carrier with rock-bottom prices has more business than its reservations clerks can handle. At People Express, callers sometimes find themselves talking to President Donald Burr. No wonder Burr is glad to pitch in wherever he can: In January of 1983, People flew 357,000 paying customers, a whopping 146% increase over traffic during the previous January.

In the 22 months since People Express started up, its home base—a former freight terminal—has become the busiest gateway at Newark International Airport, some 13 miles southwest of New York City. Flying passengers between cities from Boston to Palm Beach and as far west as Columbus, the pint-size airline earned a profit of $2.7 million in the first nine months of 1982, while the likes of Pan Am, Eastern and TWA were all showing losses. People's progress is mainly due to the lowest operating costs in the business, an average of 5.3¢ per seat per mile flown *vs.* up to 11¢

for other airlines. Says Burr: "We don't have any secret weapons. Our competitors can do it, and many of them are working day and night to get their costs down."

Burr, 41, formerly president of Texas International Airlines, gives much of the credit to his dedicated staff of 1,200 "race-horse types" who hire on for less and work hard. They have reason to: on the average, People Express workers own $20,000 worth of stock in the company. The one-time schoolteachers, anthropologists and art historians recruited by Burr seem to thrive in a company that has no secretaries or plush offices, and whose chief financial officer, Robert McAdoo, helps serve coffee on some flights. Says McAdoo: "We're all in this together."

Passengers seem to feel the same way. They do not mind paying 50¢ for a soft drink, or $3 for every bag checked. After all, there is plenty of room for carry-on luggage, and People's buy-while-you-fly on-board ticket sellers

eliminate those long waits at airport counters. But it is the fares that clinch customers' loyalty. Eastern Air Lines, once the king of the New York–Florida routes, is scrambling now to hold on to the business. Reason: People's $69 one-way fare ($49 at night). Eastern, whose standard coach fares are more than $200 for those flights, has retaliated with a $72 fare, but only for a few seats on night flights out of Newark. Moreover, Florida-bound Eastern customers boarding at nearby La Guardia Airport pay more, mainly because People flights are not available there.

Thanks to People's competitive punch, customers keep coming out of the woodwork. Says Burr: "We're getting people who wouldn't have traveled to New York to see a show, or buy clothes. If they did, they would have driven or taken a train." These days, at least on People Express, it is cheaper to fly.

Source: "How People Does It," *Time,* February 21, 1983, p. 53. Used with permission.

each unit produced costs $500 in fixed cost *and* target return.

$$\frac{\$500,000}{1,000} \quad \frac{\text{(Fixed costs + Target return)}}{\text{(Units to be sold)}} = \frac{\$500}{\text{per unit}}$$

However, production and sale of each unit involves additional costs, called *variable* costs, that are associated with production. These costs include raw materials, workers' wages, packag-

ing, and other costs that fluctuate with volume. If these costs were calculated to be $75 per unit, this figure could be added to the fixed cost and target return per unit of $500 to indicate that the price per unit should be $575.

Fixed costs and target return per unit ($500)	+	Variable costs per unit ($75)	=	Suggested price per unit ($575)

A hotel's building and lobby represent a major fixed cost.

As in the case of the average-cost method of pricing, a miscalculation of the demand for the product could be disastrous. If the firm's customers demanded only 500 units of the product, not the expected 1,000, the carefully calculated price of $575 would lead to a *loss* of $500 per unit since the fixed costs and target return per unit sold would now be $1,000, not $500.

$$\frac{\$500,000}{500} \frac{\text{(Fixed costs + Target return)}}{\text{(Units actually sold)}} = \$1,000 \text{ per unit}$$

Fixed costs and target return per unit ($1,000)	+	Variable costs per unit ($75)	=	Suggested price per unit ($1,075)

Therefore, the plan to sell at $575 would yield a *loss per sale* of $500.

Full-Line Pricing

Before moving on to demand-oriented pricing techniques, we must note that the above discussion centered on price setting for a *single* product or service. That is not always applicable to the "real world." This is not to say that these tools are invalid. In fact, marketing managers may adapt any of them to fit particular problems or simply use them to generate some guidelines. A serious difference arises, however, when the marketer has not one but many products to price. Imagine an electronics firm that produces a line of stereo equipment. Such questions as which portion of fixed costs (for example the office heating bill) should be assigned to one particular model in the product line are virtually impossible to answer accurately.

A compromise often used is to attempt to calculate the *variable* costs attributable to a product and use *that* figure as a pricing floor in the expectation that any money earned above that amount will make at least *some* contribution to fixed costs. It is this logic that allows airlines to accept stand-by passengers at much reduced fares. The pilots, stewardesses, ground crews, and landing fees must all be paid (fixed costs), whereas the stand-by passenger can be accommodated at the cost of one more sandwich and a Seven-Up (variable costs). *Any* price charged above the cost of the sandwich and Seven-Up is helping to pay the airline's fixed costs.

Even though using variable costs as a pricing floor does make good sense, a marketer seeking to price an entire line of goods, as was the stereo system manufacturer mentioned earlier, must give thought to how consumers will view the prices assigned to the *full line* of goods. This method is called **full-line pricing.** How much more expensive should the model EX Super be than the plain model EX? Does a cuing device on a turntable justify a price of $85 more than the price of the same turntable without the cuing device? These are the kinds of problems facing the marketer of a line of products rather than of a single product. These problems can only be resolved by the simultaneous use of cost-oriented pricing methods *and* demand or customer-oriented pricing techniques.

DEMAND-ORIENTED PRICING METHODS

Paramount Home Video offered its *Star Trek II: The Wrath of Khan,* on video cassette at a suggested retail price of $39.95—$40 less than its predecessor *Star Trek: The Movie,* which sold more than 50,000 video cassettes. Having taken costs into account, Paramount experimented to determine if a substantially lower price would greatly increase demand. Demand is a major factor determining prices.

No matter how much *quantitative* data is available to marketers attempting to price a product, *qualitative* elements generally enter into the pricing decision. Prices are frequently set primarily on the basis of the seller's "feel" for the market. Many business people have enough experience in their fields to be able to select prices that do prove attractive to customers. At the base of their thinking is the cost entailed in obtaining and marketing the product, but the price ultimately chosen may simply be the answer to the question, "What can I get for this?" Such a pricing technique is quick and easy to use and can be appropriate when the decision maker *truly* understands the market, however, in many cases an incorrect guess can be disastrous. For some marketers, such as small retailers, a wrong guess might not have particularly serious consequences because a price that proves unattractive can be changed quickly to one that might be more successful.

Having recognized that some demand-oriented pricing techniques may involve a minimum of formal analysis, let us move to other methods accenting customers rather than costs. These methods used by effective marketers include estimation of demand, break-even analysis, and marginal analysis.

Estimating Demand

An economist's explanation of demand is helpful in understanding pricing. While many marketers may not actually draw demand curves such as those found in economics texts, it remains that all marketers *do* face demand schedules. That is, customers *will* demand a certain amount of a product at a given price.

Usually, demand changes as price changes. The demand curve is merely a representation of this change. Thus, you might be willing to pay someone $10 to clean your messy bedroom each week. But you might have the room cleaned only every *two* weeks if the price rose to $25, and not at all at a price of $100. At $100, you would either clean the room yourself or leave it dirty! This demand schedule could be shown as a table or as a demand curve, as in Exhibit 16-1.

The demand schedule, in table or curve form, can be estimated using a number of different approaches, such as surveys of buyers' be-

EXHIBIT 16-1

Changes in Room Cleanings Demanded as Prices Increase

Demand schedule in:

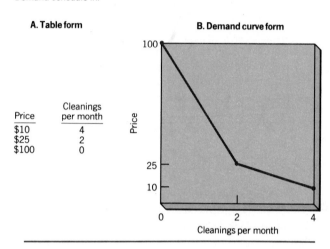

A. Table form

Price	Cleanings per month
$10	4
$25	2
$100	0

B. Demand curve form

(Graph with Price on the vertical axis showing values 100, 25, 10, and Cleanings per month on the horizontal axis showing 0, 2, 4)

liefs or intentions, analysis of past sales data to determine how buyers reacted to price changes, or asking experienced executives or salesmen to predict the effect of price change on sales.

The Demand Curve

The **demand curve,** or schedule of demand, is intended to graphically represent the relationship between the various prices a seller might charge for a product or service and the amount of that product or service that will be desired at those prices. Clearly, it would be a great help to a marketer to know what sort of a demand curve is to be confronted. While marketers seldom have an exact demand schedule showing how much they can sell at price 1, price 2, or price 3, these business people may have some demand information from marketing research. At the very least, when precise demand curves cannot be drawn, assumptions are made about them.

The most common portrayal of a demand curve is found in Exhibit 16-2. Note that as price (P) declines, more and more quantity (Q) of the product is demanded, and, one hopes, sold.

"FERNANDO THE GREAT"

The salary of a baseball player is a price—the price a team is willing to pay for his services.

After a successful rookie year in which he won fourteen games and became the first National League pitcher ever to win the Rookie of the Year Award *and* the Cy Young Award, Fernando Valenzuela offered to supply the Los Angeles Dodgers with his services for a second year for a mere million. The Dodgers, who wanted his services, were willing to pay a price of "only" $350,000. The Dodgers also had a strong bargaining position since Fernando was not a free agent and could play with no Major League club except the Dodgers.

It was at the price of $350,000 that supply was brought into equilibrium with demand. Still, since the agreed-upon price was $310,000 more than Fernando made during the rookie year, it wasn't a bad raise.

EXHIBIT 16-2

"Standard" Demand Curve Showing Quantity Demanded at Different Prices

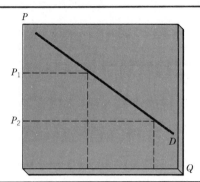

While logic tells us that things are not this simple in the real world, the graph in Exhibit 16-2 demonstrates that less of *most* goods will be demanded at a higher price than at a lower one.

Price Elasticity of Demand

Exhibits 16-3, 16-4, 16-5, and 16-6 illustrate the concept of price **elasticity of demand.** Logic leads us to conclude that (1) a decline in the price of a product might lead to a greater demand for it and (2) the rate of increase in sales would differ from case to case and from product to product. Bread sales, for example, might increase as price goes down, but the rise would be slight and would happen slowly because bread is a common, unexciting product that most people can afford and are already buying. There is also a limit to how much bread people can eat. This is demonstrated in Exhibit 16-3. A decrease in price from P_1 to P_2 increases demand from Q_1 to Q_2.

The gap between the two Qs is far less than the gap between the two Ps. This illustrates the situation of relative price *in*elasticity of demand. Demand is not very *flexible* when price is changed. Indeed, Exhibit 16-3 also illustrates that, when price is raised rather than lowered, from P_2 back to P_1, demand does not decrease rapidly because it is price *in*elastic.

The opposite situation is shown in Exhibit

EXHIBIT 16-3

Demand Curve Showing Relative Price Inelasticity

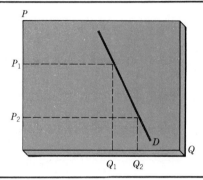

16-4, which shows that a downward change in price *does* increase demand significantly. More than that, the increase in demand appears to be greater than the decrease in price might warrant. This curve might apply in the case of filet mignon. This product is very much in demand even though most families buy it in limited amounts because of its high price. The shopper finding that the price of steak has been reduced is likely to stock up. Thus, the demand for the product is highly flexible or *elastic* in terms of price.

The demand curves in Exhibit 16-3 and 16-4 are of different slopes. If the slope of the line in Exhibit 16-3 were increased, so as to make it straight up and down as in Exhibit 16-5, the demand (*D*) line would show absolute and complete elasticity of demand. Regardless of the price charged, be it high or low, the *same* quantity is demanded. *No* change in price will affect demand. The classic example of this phenomenon is medicine. If a patient needs one dose per day of a certain drug, say insulin, to stay alive, that patient will pay virtually any price while demanding just the one shot of insulin per day. If the price fell, the patient would not buy more than the prescribed amount. If the price became extremely high, the same single treatment would be demanded, even if the patient had to seek charity or engage in dishonest endeavors to meet the bill.

Another special case is shown in Exhibit 16-

EXHIBIT 16-4

Demand Curve Showing Relative Price Elasticity

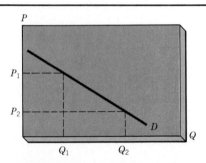

EXHIBIT 16-5

Demand Curve Showing Total Price Inelasticity

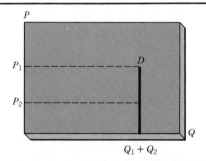

6, which shows the situation opposite to the one in Exhibit 16-5. The demand curve is perpendicular to the price axis, which illustrates that a single price is involved and that various quantities are demanded at that one price. *No* goods may be demanded or *many* units of goods may be demanded at a given point in time. Whereas the up-and-down curve showed absolute price *in*elasticity, the side-to-side line demonstrates total price *elasticity . . . no* change in price is needed to increase or decrease quantities demanded. The classic example of this situation is the wheat farmer who grows a product that is nearly identical to that of all competitors and who is unable to influence market price. Such a farmer can only earn the going price and sell as much wheat as he chooses at that price.

The demand schedules for most products lie somewhere between the extremes of total price inelasticity and total price elasticity. It is the often difficult task of each businessperson to determine the nature of the demand curve for each product or service offered to the market. Published trade association information should assist in this chore, as might research and experimentation with different price levels. Marketers do this every day, and when items don't sell at one price, they charge a different price or offer a discount. They move, either consciously or unconsciously, to a new point on their demand schedule.

Cross-Elasticity of Demand

One other aspect of elasticity of demand should be mentioned here. Many products depend partially on **cross-elasticity** for their sales. As an extreme example, consider that the demand for left shoes is closely related to the demand for right shoes—they are complementary, they go together. More realistic examples of cross-elasticity might be turkey and cranberry sauce or pork chops and apple sauce. As the demands for the meats go up and down, so do the demands for the trimmings. If the price of beef rises sharply, thereby reducing the demand for beef, the demand for lower-priced meat or for fish might increase. Therefore, effective marketers should study their own product's demand schedules as well as the demand schedule of substitute and complementary products.

In summary, the point to be remembered from economic theory is that demand *can* and *should* be estimated by marketers. After all, demand is the key concern of marketing management. Making no organized attempt to analyze demand is a prescription for disaster.

Break-Even Analysis

As we have seen, all marketers, whether of consumer goods, industrial goods, or services, face costs that must somehow be recovered. These include fixed costs and variable costs. *Variable*

EXHIBIT 16-6

Demand Curve Showing Total Price Elasticity

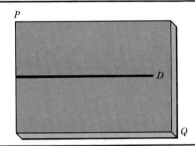

EXHIBIT 16-7

Costs, Revenues, and Break-Even Point

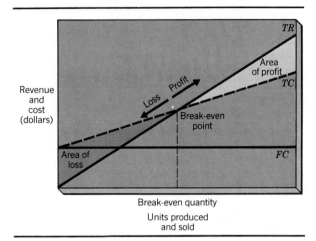

Break-even quantity
Units produced
and sold

costs would be zero if no products were produced and marketed, but *fixed* costs would remain at their established level even if production and sales were zero.

Exhibit 16-7 portrays fixed costs as the horizontal line *FC*. Variable costs added to fixed costs given the total cost figures showed by the line marked *TC*. This curve rises to the right because total costs should increase as production and sales increase.

With regard to revenue, the hope is that each additional unit of goods that is manufactured and sold or each additional service performed and paid for will raise the firm's total revenue. This is shown in Exhibit 16-7 by the total revenue curve labeled *TR*.

At the start of operations, zero units are being produced and total revenue is zero because no sales are being made. However, fixed costs such as rent are already being incurred. Therefore, the company is suffering a loss at this point. If all goes well, however, and sales rise, revenues will also rise. Revenues will continue to rise, if the firm is successful, until they meet and exceed the costs associated with production and marketing. Now, with revenue greater than costs, a profit is being made. The point at which costs and revenues meet is, logically, called the **break-even point.** The company has broken even: the money coming in is now equal to the money going out.

Price and Break-Even Analysis

Price clearly plays an important role in break-even analysis. For example, raising the price of the product may enlarge revenues allowing revenues to catch up to cost more quickly while lowering the price may have the opposite effect. It might also be demonstrated that a cost control program would enlarge profit by lowering the total cost curve. In any case, every organization has a break-even point. If that point is achieved and surpassed, the organization makes a profit. Price has an impact on when the break-even point is met. The concept, though simple, is important.

Demand and Break-Even Analysis

Break-even analysis deals with both demand and cost. The reason break-even analysis is discussed as a *demand*-oriented rather than a cost-oriented tool is that as price changes, the quantity demanded will probably change, too. It might be expected that a rise in price will lead to fewer sales and a drop in price will generate more sales. The marketing manager's problem in employing break-even analysis is to determine what effect a change in price will have on *demand*. Simple manipulation of cost and revenue figures

THE EXPERIENCE CURVE AND THE BOWMAR BRAIN

The Bowmar Brain was among the first of the electronic pocket calculators, produced by the Bowmar Instrument Company, which had been supplying precision mechanical counters and electromechanical systems to the U.S. Armed Forces and the aerospace industry.

With the development of the tiny semiconductor chip and the miniature light-emitting-diode display (LED), Edward White, president of Bowmar, spotted the potential for a mass-market consumer product and decided to enter the calculator market with a pocket-sized model featuring LED display numbers. When he couldn't sell the idea to any of the twenty or so companies in the consumer calculator business at the time, he decided to go it alone. Production began in 1971.

In the years 1963 to 1971, Bowmar's stockholders earned a return of approximately 3 percent after taxes. But as soon as the company began to produce the Bowmar Brain, sales—and profits—took off. In 1971, revenues were $13 million; by the end of 1972 they had more than doubled. After-tax earnings zoomed from $333,000 to more than $2 million. The rate of return became a stunning 30 percent after taxes.

But the pressure was on. There was pressure to expand in order to meet the seemingly insatiable demand and prevent competitors from filling the orders first

and beating Bowmar to the rush of new business.

There was pressure to produce in greater volume in order to get production costs down. According to the so-called "experience curve," for every doubling of production volume in manufacturing, the cost per unit drops about 20 percent—as workers become more adept, machines become more efficient, and the manufacturing system is continually improved. In the pocket-calculator market, that meant prices would be coming down fast. (It's why prices can come down fast on any new product that achieves sudden popularity—from color TVs to Rubik's cube.) The type of calculator Bowmar sold for $240 in September 1971, went for $110 by June 1973.

Bowmar had to increase its production capacity exponentially or lose out to competitors who were making more and cheaper calculators. There was also the pressure to invest in research and development to reduce costs further and increase the capability of the calculator, because the competition was doing the same. And finally, there was the pressure to find financing for all of the above.

What happened to Bowmar? It couldn't grow fast enough. Nor could it afford to price low enough quickly enough to keep pace with the competition, which included Japanese companies and Texas Instruments. The latter

was a primary manufacturer of semiconductor chips for Bowmar and hundreds of other companies. It specialized in chips, not consumer products. But when the pocket-calculator market took off, TI found itself in an enviable position. With resources to manufacture the LED calculators itself and price them *below cost,* it figured it could generate so much volume that the experience of mass production would bring its calculator cost back down below its price. Pursuing this strategy, TI soon had the lion's share of the business.

Bowmar simply did not have the resources to follow suit. It spent all the money it could on manufacturing, but with its competitors now producing in greater volume, it couldn't produce as cheaply as they could. Its sales dropped off. Meanwhile, it had financed its growth with borrowed money—money it had intended to pay back from future growth and profits. But the competition was squeezing profits. Bowmar was overextended and its creditors demanded payment, forcing the company into Chapter 11 bankruptcy.

Bowmar eventually worked out a debt-repayment plan with its creditors, and by 1982 it was back on its original track, a modest company making high-tech devices for the military and aerospace industries, and doing quite well at it. But its escape from "Brain death" was a narrow one.

THE LOGIC OF BREAK-EVEN ANALYSIS

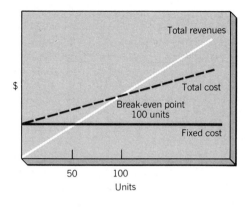

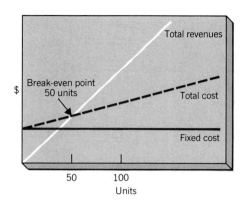

1 There are some bills that *must* be paid such as rent and electric bills. These are the *fixed costs.*

2 There are some costs that *vary* with the amount of goods or services produced. For example, the more cab rides produced, the more gasoline used. These are the *variable costs.* Total variable costs = variable cost per unit × total units produced.

3 The fixed costs *plus* the total variable costs equal the *total costs* involved in producing a given amount of products or services.

4 The income brought in by a firm, its *total revenues,* could be less than the amount the firm is spending. This is, of course, a *loss.* Total revenue = price per unit × total units sold.

5 The income brought in by the firm could be more than the firm is spending. This is a *profit.* Total profit = total revenues − total costs.

6 Once this income of the firm *equals* the money being spent by the firm, the firm has *broken even* and may go on to make a profit.

7 Manipulating the price upward may raise revenues and permit a lower break-even point, perhaps 50 units instead of 100.

8 *BUT,* the market (customers) may not pay the higher price or may begin looking for alternative products.

9 Thus, break-even calculations must be used with the customer in mind.

---

is not enough, nor are graphs, such as the one in Exhibit 16-7, which seem to portray ever-increasing profits as more and more units are sold. There is no built-in reason to assume that the product is going to sell at either a higher price or at a lower price. An effective marketer, aware of the changes and uncertainties operating in the marketplace, knows that raising prices will not necessarily increase revenues and lower the break-even point.

In short, determining a break-even point is only the beginning. The analysis may be of most use in conducting preliminary studies to eliminate certain extreme pricing situations. For example, a restaurant might be so poorly run that its costs necessitate menu prices that start at $5 for a hot dog—a price at which few are likely to be sold. Break-even points are also of use in evaluating alternative marketing strategies, but the underlying problem of estimating demand remains no matter how carefully costs and revenues are portrayed on a graph.

Using Break-Even and Demand Analysis

In this chapter we have seen that demand *can* be analyzed and estimated, and that break-even analysis is useful when it is applied with caution. Combining the two forms of analysis shows how these tools can be of real use to marketing decision-makers. Stated another way, if an analyst knew the company's costs of production and marketing, or could estimate them, the analyst could determine what those costs would be for various levels of production. In other words, a series of break-even points could be developed and portrayed on a table or graph showing that at 100 units the break-even point would be *X* dollars, while at 1,000 units it would be *Y* dollars. And, as we have seen, demand schedules can also be estimated showing expected sales at various price levels.

The marketing analyst can then "overlap" the estimated demand curve and the series of break-even points, as is done in Exhibit 16-8.[2] In short, the demand curve shows the analyst what

EXHIBIT 16-8

Using Estimated Demand and Break-Even Points To Determine Profitable Prices

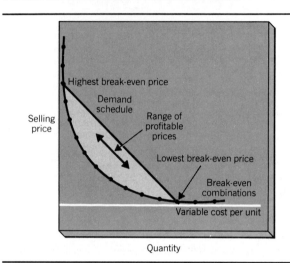

Source: This figure is based on Jon Hawes and Michael F. d'Amico, "Pricing: Using Breakeven and Demand Analysis," paper presented at the American Marketing Association Educators Conference, 1982.

range of prices would be acceptable to the organization if it wants to make a profit.

MARGINAL ANALYSIS

The technique of **marginal analysis** is aimed at attempting to determine the cost and revenue connected with the production and sale of each *additional* unit of a product. It does not eliminate the need for the manager to estimate the relationships between demand and price, but does focus attention on the fact that profit maximization, not breaking even or some other goal, is the aim of most business organizations.

The concept of marginal analysis can be demonstrated by example: If *one* unit of a prod-

uct or service is produced, all the costs of production and marketing must be assigned to that single unit. Thus, covering all cost associated with the very first brake repair job performed by a Brakeman franchise would amount to an immense amount of money because all of the fixed costs (that is, the expenses associated with entering the business) went into that first repair job. However, each *additional* brake repair carries some portion of the cost of the equipment, office facilities, and so forth. Thus, when there are many brake repair jobs, only a small portion of the fixed cost has to be allocated to each job.

The costs and revenues associated with the production of "one more unit" of a product or service are the **marginal costs** and **marginal revenues.** That these combine to create a point of

[2]Jon M. Hawes and Michael F. D'Amico, "Using Theory to Understand Product Pricing Applications of Break-Even Analysis," in Bruce J. Walker, et al. (eds.), *An Assessment of Marketing Thought and Practice* (Chicago: American Marketing Association, 1982), pp. 132–135.

EXHIBIT 16-9

Behaviors of Costs and Revenues as Demand and Quantities Produced Increase

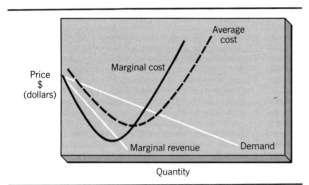

Quantity

maximum profitability for a firm is the basis of marginal analysis. As shown in Exhibit 16-9, that point is where marginal cost equals marginal revenues.

Move a pencil point along the horizontal or quantity axis of Exhibit 16-9 and note the behavior of the variables shown. The logic becomes clear. Moving from the left, where the quantity produced and sold is zero, average cost declines as quantity increases because the "cost" of the first repair job was far greater than the "cost" of

EXHIBIT 16-10

Intersection of Marginal Cost and Marginal Revenue Curves

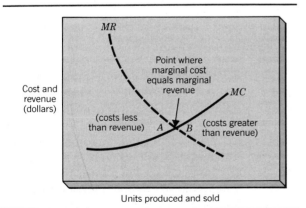

Units produced and sold

CONCEPT OF THE MARGIN

Throughout economic theory, the term "marginal" is used to modify various nouns such as revenue, costs, utility, firm, worker, efficiency of capital, operations, or any other thing one wishes to describe as being marginal. Margin originally referred to a border or edge, but its meaning has been broadened in economics to designate what happens at the "edge" of the activity being described—the last unit brought into play. Thus:

Marginal revenue is the net addition to the total revenue of the firm from selling one more unit of a product.

Marginal costs are the net addition to total costs caused by making one more unit of a product.

Marginal utility is the satisfaction received by the consumer from using one more unit of a product. Marginal utility of the dollar is the utility provided by earning one more dollar.

Marginal efficiency of capital is the profit made from the last dollar invested.

A *marginal firm* is one making the least profit in the industry.

Source: Reprinted from R.H. Buskirk, D.J. Green, and W.C. Rodgers, *Concepts of Business: An Introduction to the Business System* (Richardson, Tex.: Oak Tree Press, 1976), pp. 186–187. Used with permission.

the thousandth. Likewise, the marginal cost and the marginal revenue are seen to decline as we move along the quantity axis. In the case of the Brakeman franchise, this is because an increasing number of cars, using the same equipment and instruments as was the first, can be handled from the same garage. The revenue generated from the most recent sale is a comparatively small portion of the Brakeman's total income. The two cost curves eventually move upward because, after a time, a new and larger office may be needed, more help may be hired, and more equipment may be purchased.

THE LOGIC OF MARGINAL ANALYSIS

1 "Marginal" means "just one more."

2 Each time a firm produces and sells "just one more" unit, it receives *marginal income* but it also pays *marginal costs.*

3 If the cost of one more unit is *less* than the revenue to be gained, the firm made a *profit* on that unit, so it produces "one more."

4 If the cost of one more unit is *greater* than the revenue to be gained, that one more unit means a *loss.*

5 Therefore, the firm will try to produce more units up to the point where it does not lose money on "one more unit," that is, the point where there is no more opportunity for profit.

6 That point is where the cost of the unit and the revenue brought in by the unit are the same—where marginal cost equals marginal revenue.

If in looking at this table you decide the firm should not stop producing with the seventh unit, where marginal cost equals marginal revenue and profit is zero, but should stop with the *sixth* unit where the profit is still $1, you are *right.*

Others have noted that. But the firm would not know that the sixth unit was the last to make a profit until the seventh was produced and the firm "noticed" that profits had stopped. Thus, economists say that profits are maximized where *marginal cost equals marginal revenue.*

An Illustration of Marginal Costs and Revenues

Unit Produced	Marginal Cost	Marginal Revenue	Profit
1	1	2	+
2	1	2	+
3	1	2	+
4	1	2	+
5	1	2	+
6	1	2	+
7	2	2	0 ← Marginal cost equals
8	2	2	0 marginal·revenue here
9	3	2	—
10	3	2	—

But the point to be made is that profit is maximized where marginal cost equals marginal revenue ($MC = MR$). Consider Exhibit 16-10, which shows only these two variables. If a seller of any good or service discovered that the cost of producing one more unit was *less* than the revenue to be realized by producing that one unit (that the firm was at point *A*), management would logically decide to produce and sell that additional unit. That is, there is still some profit to be made since the cost is *less* than the revenue to be gained. However, if management discovered its operation to be at point *B,* where costs per unit are *greater* than revenue, there would be a realization that the "one more" unit costs *more* than it will bring in, and that a loss is being taken on that unit. The sensible thing to do would be to cut back, not to point *A* where the cost is still less than the revenue to be made, but to the point where cost and revenue levels come together. That is, where $MC = MR$.

In the economist's ideal world, where variables and customers cooperate fully, all that would need to be done to attain maximum profits would be to produce and sell the amount of goods or services that would make marginal revenue equal marginal cost. To do this, the marketer would have to know *exactly* what the market would demand and at what price. While this kind of information is almost never available, the logic of marginality focuses attention on the need to estimate demand as specifically as pos-

sible so that the important technique of marginal analysis might be employed. Some marketing managers, drawing upon research data, experience, and feel for the market *are* able to closely estimate the demand situation they face. In the future, improved information processing techniques may make marginal analysis a more exact tool. Currently, however, considerable amounts of intuition, guesswork, and luck are involved in its use.

SUMMARY

This chapter investigates cost and demand issues—two basic factors influencing the pricing function. Rather than setting the price to be charged for a good or service simply by guesswork, marketing managers should attempt to follow some logical pricing procedure. As some pricing methods focus on costs while others focus on demand, it is appropriate to use several methods and not rely on one pricing tool. The goal of the chapter was to portray some of the variables, considerations, and choices faced by real-world marketers as they attempt to establish and administer prices.

Pricing methods involving only consideration of costs fail to include the buyer in the pricing effort. Yet, at the least, cost provides a floor on which to build a pricing strategy. Prominent cost-oriented pricing methods discussed were mark-up on selling price, mark-up on costs, cost-plus, the average-cost method, target return pricing, and full-line pricing.

The demand curve represents the relation-

ship between the various prices a seller might charge for a product and the amount of product that will be desired at those prices. It is crucial that marketers attempt to estimate the demand and elasticity of demand for their products. Break-even analysis and marginal analysis both consider the effect of price and price changes on the quantity of product demanded.

THE MOST IMPORTANT CONCEPT IN THIS CHAPTER

Although the price set for a product or service is often the result of intuition, marketers should attempt to follow some logical pricing procedure involving methods that consider cost and demand. Such methods, which involve mechanical techniques and mathematical formulas, while not necessarily generating appropriate prices, do suggest courses of action attuned to the realities of the marketplace.

KEY TERMS

Mark-up on selling price	Demand curve	Marginal analysis
Mark-up on cost	Elasticity of demand	Marginal costs
Full-line pricing	Cross-elasticity	Marginal revenues
Target return pricing	Break-even point	

QUESTIONS FOR DISCUSSION

1 If the manufacturing cost of an item is $250, the selling expenses associated with the item $75, and the required return is 25 percent, what would the selling price of the item be?

2 How is return on investment of use in evaluating alternative marketing opportunities?

3 What is the logic behind the statement that profit is maximized where marginal cost = marginal revenue?

4 (a) Describe the concept behind break-even analysis.
(b) What is "wrong" with break-even analysis?

5 Why wouldn't a "reasonable monopolist" raise his prices to the highest level, gouging the consumer as much as possible? Or would he?

6 Using the average cost method, what price would you recommend for a product if the costs associated with its production and marketing were $150,000; the margin for profit $50,000; and anticipated sales were 5,000 units?

7 A marketer using the target return method miscalculated expected demand and the actual demand turned out to be *half* the expected demand. What would be the resulting loss per unit if the marketer used the following data to calculate price?

Expected demand	2,000 units
Fixed cost and target return	$200,000
Variable cost per unit	$100

CASE 16-1 Dude's Duds—Pricing a New Product Line*

Dude's Duds is a large, well-known clothing store chain with more than 400 retail outlets located throughout the United States and Canada. Appealing to the teenage and young adult consumer, the success enjoyed by Dude's Duds is based largely on the firm's ability to market fadish and fashionable merchandise at reasonable and competitive prices. While Dude's Duds stocks a limited selection of national manufacturer's brands (e.g., Levi's and Haggar) to enhance its store image and to generate consumer traffic, the vast majority of each outlet's merchandise consists of the firm's own private retailer brands. To ensure a reliable source of supply for their private labels, Dude's Duds purchased the Fashion-Plus Clothing Company (FPCC) in 1968. At the time of the takeover, FPCC was a well-established national manufacturer of high quality, fashionable apparel. FPCC's product mix consisted of a wide line of both men's and women's wearing apparel.

The recent increase in the popularity and ac-

ceptance of western wearing apparel by many diverse consumer groups throughout all market areas of the country prompted Ralph West, the General Merchandise Manager for Dude's Duds, to investigate the possibility of adding a new line of men's western style shirts. Preliminary results of that investigation led Ralph to conclude that such a line would appeal to the consumer group the firm identified as "the swingers"—a consumer market segment that wants fadish and stylish clothing of good quality but whose discretionary income requires certain economic considerations (i.e., affordable prices). As far as Ralph is concerned, the addition of a new line of men's western shirts makes good merchandising sense. However, it will be up to the production people at Fashion-Plus to determine whether the new line is feasible given the price, cost, and profit constraints under which they must produce the product.

---

*Source: This case was prepared by Jon M. Hawes, The University of Akron. Used by permission.

While Fashion-Plus is a wholly-owned subsidiary of Dude's Duds, Inc., FPCC's management is responsible for making all production decisions. Presently under consideration is Ralph's request for a new line of western shirts. To determine the feasibility of new product lines, Bill Morris (Manager for New Product Development) must collect the necessary information to make a cost and break-even analysis, to project expected profits, and to recommend a suggested retail price as well as a manufacturer's price (the price that Fashion-Plus should charge Dude's Duds). Having spent the last two weeks collecting data, Bill feels he now has the necessary information to make the required evaluations of the new western shirt project. Before proceeding with his analysis, Bill reviews the following information he has collected:

1 Several competitors have introduced similar lines of men's western shirts. Market research indicates that these lines are selling at a brisk pace at competitive retail stores for the following prices:

Retail Selling Prices	Number of Times Observed
$14.00	2
15.00	7
16.00	5
17.00	3

2 Dude's Duds will apply a 40 percent initial mark-up on the retail selling price of shirts.

3 Production costs for the new shirt are estimated to be

Cloth	$2.20 per shirt
Buttons	.05 per shirt
Thread	.05 per shirt
Direct labor	20 minutes per shirt
Shipping weight	2 pounds per packaged shirt

4 Basic marketing costs for introducing the new line of shirts are estimated to be $300,000 the first year if a low initial pricing policy is used or $340,000 if a high initial pricing policy is employed.

5 Being a large company, FPCC has fifteen production facilities strategically located throughout the USA. Last year, the average round trip distance from FPCC production facilities to Dude's Duds outlets was 225 miles. Current plans are to produce the new line of shirts at each of FPCC's production facilities.

6 An examination of FPCC's annual report reveals the following information:

Managerial salaries	$ 1,500,000
Rent and utilities expense	1,200,000
Transportation costs (1,250,000 miles)	750,000
Depreciation on plant and equipment	1,300,000
Other overhead	2,000,000
Direct labor costs (2,000,000 hours)	8,000,000
Total company sales	45,000,000
Average order size	1,000 pounds

7 The Kurt Behrens Market Research Corporation was hired to develop a sales forecast for the new line of western shirts. Their research findings estimate that if a high initial pricing policy were used, Dude's Duds could expect to sell approximately 110,000 to 130,000 shirts. Under a low initial pricing policy, the Behrens organization estimates a unit sales volume of approximately 130,000 to 150,000 shirts.

Question

Assume that Bill Morris was unexpectedly called out of town and he has asked you to prepare the analysis and written report on the feasibility of the project and then to make a recommendation for the pricing strategy he should use. At a minimum, your analysis should include a cost analysis (variable cost per shirt, fixed cost allocation for the line, and total cost per shirt), a break-even analysis in units and dollars, a determination of the manufacturer's price and suggested retail price, and a statement as to expected profit the company can derive from the new line.

CASE 16-2 The Micro Computer Price War*

In June 1983, at Olympic Sales in downtown Los Angeles, an Atari home computer that cost $630 three years ago carried a price tag of $77.95. At Lechmere Sales in Cambridge, Massachusetts, Texas Instrument micros that retailed for $525 in 1981 could be had for less than $100. Gemco stores in California were selling Commodore 64 computers for $199 each, two-thirds off their price of six months earlier. In Chicago, K-Mart was unloading tiny Timex Sinclair 1000s, listed last year at $99.95, for $29.97 each.

In 1983 the market for the smallest computers, always competitive, had finally blossomed into a full-scale price war. Manufacturers were trumpeting price cuts and rebates and spending heavily on TV advertising.

Questions

1 How important do you think costs, demand, and competitive considerations are in determining the price of a micro computer?

2 In what stage of the product life cycle are micro computers?

3 How has the product life cycle affected the pricing decisions of micro computers?

4 What pricing strategy would you recommend for a company such as Texas Instruments or Commodore?

---

*Source: Based on "Shake Out in the Hardware Wars," *Time Magazine,* June 27, 1983, p. 64.

CHAPTER 17

Pricing Strategies and Tactics

CHAPTER SCAN

The contributions that economics and pricing tools can make to the decision-making process were discussed in Chapter 16. This chapter focuses on those aspects of pricing in which the marketing manager's judgment plays a major role.

The chapter identifies the target market and competitive considerations that pricing decision-makers must evaluate.

This chapter also shows the range of pricing strategies and discount policies faced by the marketer.

The chapter concludes with a brief review of the major legal influences on pricing.

WHEN YOU HAVE STUDIED THIS CHAPTER, YOU WILL:

Be able to show how price must be related to the intended target market.

Understand how the marketing manager determines actual prices to be charged using judgment as well as cost and return-on-investment considerations.

Be able to describe the many price options available to marketing managers.

Be able to explain how time, geography, and other factors influence pricing decisions.

Be familiar with the major legal restrictions on pricing freedom.

In 1982, the University of Oklahoma Sooners were Number 1, and they voted themselves that honor. They were Number 1 in ticket prices, charging $15 for the cheapest football ticket, up from $12.50 in the previous year.

Other universities raised ticket prices, too. The University of Texas hiked its basic price to $12. "We have a great home schedule," said Texas business manager, Al Lundstedt. "We want to take advantage of it." In fact, when Texas met Oklahoma at the Cotton Bowl in a regular season game, the price was $18, though some officials thought $20 was more appropriate.

The Oklahoma price hike didn't affect sales. Season-ticket holders were happy to pay an extra $2.50 every other week for the status of being Sooner season ticketholders.

On the other side of the coin, a fan could attend a N.Y. Giant N.F.L. game for $14, attend three Slippery Rock State College contests for $15, buy a University of Wisconsin at Eau Clair season ticket for $15, or a University of Akron season ticket for $9.

Downtrodden Vanderbilt University offers an interesting variable price plan, a "menu" of games with prices to match the quality of the opponent. When Vanderbilt plays Tennessee, the price is $15, but $12 for Florida, Ole Miss, or Tennessee at Chattanooga. For Virginia Tech, it's $11, and only $10 for Tulane.[1]

PRICING STRATEGIES

In this chapter, many types of prices and forms of discounts are presented. Management's ultimate role in pricing is to choose from among these alternatives, though quantitative methods can be used to establish pricing *guidelines*. Even if the decision-maker selects a price generated by some quantitative method, the choice to go with that price rests with the decision-maker's *judgment*. The marketing manager must determine prices and discounts that reflect market realities as well as cost and other considerations.

The following descriptions of pricing strategies show the range of pricing goals and pricing strategies that are available to marketing managers. The marketer may use several of these price strategies in order to arrive at a combination of prices with strong appeal to buyers.

One-Price Policy
Versus Variable-Price Policies

A basic pricing decision is whether to maintain a fixed price regardless of who the customer is or to vary the price from buyer to buyer. Holding the price the same for all buyers is termed a **one-**price policy. In the United States, most retailers tend to follow a one-price policy. Whether a millionaire or a child with 50 cents enters the candy store, the price of the candy bar is the same. Some marketers defend this policy on the grounds that it is fair and democratic not to charge prices that might favor one customer over another.

However, many marketers do allow customers to haggle in an attempt to secure a favorable price. Major companies usually find themselves in a better position than weaker firms to drive a hard bargain when dealing with suppliers. Even at the retail level, consumers sometimes find themselves in a position where they can talk down a price. This is known as **variable pricing.** Automobile and real estate purchases often present such an opportunity.

Federal legislation prohibits the use of variable pricing policies when these might give large or powerful organizational buyers great competitive advantages over small organizational buyers (see the discussion of the Robinson-

---

[1] Adapted from "The Oklahoma Sooners are Number 1," *The Sunday Oklahoman*, January 10, 1982.

**Most American companies
utilize a one-price policy.**

Patman Act later in this chapter). However, there are many situations where seller and buyer engage in a bit of give and take. The variable pricing policy allows for this.

Consumers are all aware that theaters, airlines, and utilities vary their prices among buyers. The theater's matinee price is ordinarily less than the evening price; a plane ticket is less expensive if one flies during off hours; the industrial user generally pays less for electricity than the home owner. Such differences are not illegal under the Robinson-Patman Act because consumers are not considered to be competing buyers. Organizational buyers may obtain different prices because they are perceived as different *types* of customers. The price differences are usually treated as *discounts* rather than price variants.

A one-price policy provides the advantage of simplicity of administration that leads, in turn, to lower personnel expenses. This is the major reason most retailers use it. Salespeople and clerks need not debate the price of a loaf of bread or a yard of cloth with each customer. On the other hand, when variable prices are used, each salesperson must be able to handle customer questions, complaints, and attempts to have the price reduced. Thus, the supermarket's

one-price policy allows it to employ less experienced, lower-paid clerks. The automobile dealer, however, must hire active salespeople—and pay them comparatively high commissions—to administer its variable price policy.

Skimming Versus Penetration Price Strategies

A **skimming price** is a high price intended to "skim the cream off the market." It is best employed at the start of a product's life in the marketplace when the product is novel and consumers are uncertain about the product's value. For example, hand-held calculators and digital watches first sold at prices of hundreds of dollars. They can be purchased now for as little as $5. When they were first introduced, the least expensive ball point pen sold at a price equal to $100 today, but now they are priced as low as 29 cents. This pattern allows the companies involved to establish a flow of revenue that can be used to cover research and development expenses, as well as the initial high costs of bringing the product to market. A skimming policy assumes a relatively strong inelastic demand for the product, often because the product has status value or because it is a truly new, break-

OPERATING ON PRICES

People usually want "the best" when they are dealing with matters of health. But price adjustment can be used by hospitals to encourage the scheduling of operations during hospital "slack times" and by insurance companies seeking to hold down the costs of health care.

Doctors and patients tend to schedule surgery early in the week, especially on Mondays and Tuesdays, thus operating rooms are often unused late in the week and on weekends except for emergency procedures. Several hospitals have instituted "bonus plans" such as reduced operating room charges for "off day" usage, and some have gone so far as to award prizes to patients operated on during the slack times. Trips to Hawaii or other vacation spots have been offered by some West Coast hospitals.

With the cooperation of Melrose-Wakefield Hospital near Boston, Massachusetts Blue Cross and Blue Shield has been offering "rebates" to new mothers who leave the hospital within 24 hours after an uncomplicated delivery. The $100 rebate, in the form of a check, saves Blue Cross about seven times that amount by cutting the usual four-day stay down to one. The plan includes several follow-up care services at the patient's home.

Since obstetrical and gynecological care is the second most costly service provided by Massachusetts Blue Cross and Blue Shield (after psychiatric benefits), the company also offers financial incentives to women who leave the hospital earlier than usual after Caesarean sections or hysterectomies.

Source: Adapted with permission from "Leave the Hospital Early, Collect $100," *Newsweek*, May 25, 1981.

A **penetration price** is a low introductory price. It may even be a price which results in a loss. It is the result of the marketer's realization that a competitive situation is well-established (or soon will be) and that a low price in the introduction stage of the product life cycle will be necessary to break into the market. Its objective is to enable the product to become established and survive in the long run. Before American automotive companies entered the small car market, the Volkswagen "Beetle" dominated. Ford Pinto and other new cars were introduced at prices below that of the Volkswagen in an attempt to *penetrate* the small car market and establish the American products as alternatives to imported small cars. The low prices allowed the American firms to advertise list prices below those of the foreign competitors, and to establish a believable position in the small car market. More recently, the Subaru was offered at an astoundingly low price to help Subaru penetrate the small car market and quickly gain a position. The Toyota Tercel employed a similar strategy.

Penetration pricing is likely to be the most effective and desirable approach under one or more of the following conditions:[2] (1) when sales volume of the product is very sensitive to price (*elastic demand*); (2) when it is possible to achieve substantial economies in unit cost of manufacturing and/or distributing the product by operating at large volume (*economies of scale*); (3) when a product faces threats of strong competitive imitation soon after introduction because there is no patent protection, no high capital requirement for production or other factors to keep competition out of the market (*strong competitive threat*); (4) there is a mass market that will readily accept the product, thus market segmentation does not appear to be a major factor (*mass market acceptance*).

When Texas Instruments introduced semiconductor chips for computers, it utilized a penetrating pricing strategy. It priced the computer chips at an extremely low level assuming that its production cost per chip would be dramatically

[2]Joel Dean, "Techniques for Pricing New Products and Services," in *Handbook of Modern Marketing,* Victor Buell, ed. (New York: McGraw-Hill, 1970), pp. 5–51 to 5–61.

through item. Price is utilized as a means to segment the market on the basis of discretionary income or degree of need for the product. As anticipated price reductions due to competitive pressures result, new market segments become the key targets.

Status goods are often priced high.

A reduced price may be used so that a new or un-tried product may penetrate a market.

lowered if the company obtained a large volume and high market share in the long run. This turned out to be a successful pricing strategy that eliminated many would-be competitors. Thus, penetration pricing reduces the threat of competitive imitation because the small profit margin discourages low-cost imitators from entering the market. Furthermore, by increasing the size of the total market and/or market share, the marketer establishes a strong brand loyalty and increases the brand's dominance within consumers' minds.

Item Profit Pricing Versus Total Profit Pricing

A camera manufacturer may price its cameras at a low price in the hope of making significant profits on film for those cameras. Firms such as Schick and Gillette sell their razors at low prices

to encourage *long-term* purchase of blades that fit the razor. A newspaper costs more to produce and distribute than the price charged subscribers, but increased circulation encouraged by the low price leads to more advertising revenue and greater overall profit. In all these cases, the marketer charges a reduced price on particular *items* in order to increase *total profit*.

Leader Pricing and Bait Pricing

A commonly used pricing policy which sacrifices item profit for total profit is leader pricing. While most consumers are familiar with the concept of the **loss leader,** the product which the seller prices at a loss so as to attract customers who might buy other goods, the general public is less aware of the *cost leader* and the *low-profit* *leader.* In each instance, the product is priced to attract bargain-hunting customers who might make other purchases, but the leader item is sold at the seller's cost or at a very small profit. For example, when Target discount stores priced selected Atari video games at $6, they tripled store traffic. Goods so priced are usually frequently purchased, familiar items so that customers will be able to recognize that a bargain is available. Reduced prices on caviar and camel meat would not be appreciated by most American buyers.

Bait pricing is used to attract customers by advertising low-priced models of, for example, televisions. Although the bait item is available for sale in sufficient quantity, the expectation is to trade the customer up to a higher margin model that is also available for sale. This strategy may be an effective means to sell higher margin items.

The term **bait and switch,** however, is used when the merchant has no intention of selling the bait merchandise but attempts to convince the customer to buy more expensive goods. In fact, the item used in the bait and switch scheme is sometimes referred to as the ''nailed down model,'' so unlikely is it that it will be sold. Bait and switch has an unsavory reputation and is often the target of attention from the Federal Trade Commission.

Traditional Pricing

Certain prices are set largely by *tradition* rather than by individual marketers. These *customary* prices may remain unchanged for long periods of time. The 5-cent candy bar, although now a thing of the past, was priced at the same level for decades. As chocolate and sugar prices rose and fell, the bars got smaller or larger, but the price remained. It was only when the candy bar had diminished to near invisibility that manufacturers broke with tradition and raised the price to 10, then 15, then 30 cents, and more. Until that time, only a few bars were priced higher than the traditional price, and these were backed by appropriate *supporting* policies. The 10-cent bar in the 5-cent era was bigger than the others, of better quality, and was heavily promoted. Today,

EXHIBIT 17-1

Kinked Demand Curve Facing Marketers of Products Sold at a Traditional Price

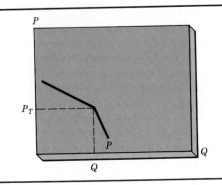

candies that break with the going rate price have similar attributes.

Exhibit 17-1 portrays the demand situation faced by firms in industries where prices have become established at particular levels. Should a company attempt to raise prices above the traditional level, the result will be considerably decreased sales. On the other hand, notice that a reduction of price will not produce sales increases that justify the price cut.

Demand is elastic above the traditional price but inelastic below it. When this condition occurs, it is because consumer beliefs and habits are so ingrained that price reductions are attributed to a negative reason, such as a perceived lowering of quality, rather than to competitive market pressures.

This kinked demand curve may also occur in oligopolistic markets where a small number of marketers must price at traditional market levels to maximize profits. Oligopolists, who are highly sensitive to competitive price shifts, generally respond in kind to price reductions. Thus, there is no advantage to price reductions that will only lead to a lower market price adhered to by all of the oligopolists.

Price Lining Policies

In some marketing situations, there appear to be prices that are more attractive to customers than

EXHIBIT 17-2

Assumed Demand Curve Facing Users of Price Lining Policies

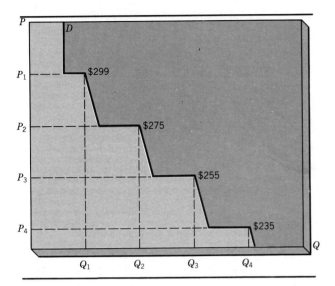

others. Many years ago, the five-and-ten-cent store actually sold *all* merchandise at those prices because management believed that the prices involved were particularly good in terms of ability to attract customers.

While the five-and-ten is no longer, clothing retailers, among many others, still practice **price lining.** A dress store ordinarily does not stock dresses from $300 to $55, pricing them at $299.99, $299.87, $299.76, etc., on down to $55. Instead, the prices offered are, for example, $299, $275, $255, $235. These prices are "points" believed by the store owner to be "strong price points" or prices which are greatly attractive to buyers.

Exhibit 17-2 shows the demand curve assumed by these store owners. Notice that the belief expressed is that a good number of dresses will be sold at $275, but, if the price is lowered, not many more will be sold *until* the price reaches the next strong price point, $255. Similarly, if the price is raised from $275, there will be a rapid drop in sales until the next strong price point is reached. Similar thinking leads bicycle, automobile, and television manufacturers to price their products at several distin-

guishable levels. Likewise, carpet-cleaning services establish price points by advertising "any living and dining room carpet cleaned for $42." Once the individual price points are established, the organization can simply "plug in" the price to be assigned to any particular item.

Price lining leads to serious risks. For one thing, a firm may become tied to the price points, making price competition difficult to ward off. As a case in point, a men's shop featuring suits priced at $200, $150, and $125 might find that a competitive store has opened across the street selling suits at $180, $140, and $115. In addition, no matter what price points are selected, rising costs and inflation will lead to a profit squeeze. The old five-and-ten provides an obvious example of this.

Odd Prices

Odd prices have become so common that the adjective may no longer be warranted. One seldom sees products priced at $2, $5, or $10. Instead, they are normally priced at odd prices such as $1.99, $4.98, and $9.99. Odd prices have, in fact, become traditional. The logic that led to the use of odd prices should be noted. The price of $1.95 is believed by some to suggest that the product's price is only a dollar plus some small change. However, there are those who suggest that a price of $1.98 is *seen* as $2 and that deeper cuts, say to $1.75, are necessary to achieve the intended *psychological* effect.

The odd price is said to make it appear that management shaved a few pennies off a price that could well have been $2. The practical purpose of forcing clerks to use the cash registers to make change, thus creating a record of the sale and discouraging employee dishonesty, is also served.

The practice of odd pricing assumes a demand curve such as the one shown in Exhibit 17-3. Note that the implication is that more sales will result at certain prices than would have resulted had the price been just one or two cents higher. This means the demand curve is very elastic just below the round number. The jags to the right side of the demand curve show the quantity demanded increasing even though the price has

EXHIBIT 17-3

Assumed Demand Curve Facing Users of Odd Prices

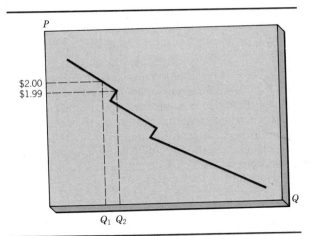

been changed hardly at all. Immediately below the odd price, however, demand may decrease slightly until potential customers perceive a significant price drop from the odd price.

Exceptions to the logic of odd pricing immediately come to mind. **Even prices** may result in *more* sales, especially if the marketer is dealing in relatively inexpensive items. More bottles of soda will be sold from a machine that accepts 50 or 75 cents than from a machine that accepts 49 or 73 cents. More raffle tickets will probably be sold for 50 cents than for 45 cents. In both cases, the bother of coming up with the proper change will lessen purchases even at the lower price.

Some Additional Pricing Strategies

Pricing strategies represent logical responses to individual marketing situations. Because of this, a great number of pricing strategies and tactics can be identified. Here are some of the wide choices of prices available to marketers.

As was shown earlier in this chapter, it is thought that certain products are demanded in part *because* of their high prices. Perfumes, furs,

Southwest Airlines
11th Anniversary

Friday Night Fun Fare

$11

Lowest fare in the air
on our last flight every
Friday night!

Midland/Odessa to Dallas Love Field

Flight	Depart	Arrive	Fare
975	11:10pm	12:05am	$11

Call Southwest Airlines 563-0750

or your travel agent for reservations.

A promotional price with a special discount for off hours.

and gems are among these. These products are *status* goods, and marketers often charge a high *prestige price* for them to portray a quality image for the brand.

The services of many professionals, such as doctors and lawyers, are often priced at a figure which suggests that the physician or attorney has been involved totally in the client's case and therefore will present a bill that is free of

AAIRPASS: PROTECTION AGAINST AIR FARE INCREASES

For a limited time, September 1981 to March 1982, American Airlines gambled that it could win hundreds of millions of dollars from frequent airline travelers by offering a hedge against rising airfares. Travelers were offered the opportunity to buy years of travel *at a fixed price* if they were willing to pay that price up front. By paying $19,900, $39,500, or $58,000, frequent flyers could guarantee a cost-per-mile rate for the next 5, 10, or 15 years. A lifetime, unlimited mileage pass could be had for $250,000, and several "leisure plans," aimed at senior citizens, were also available. Besides an expected saving, the purchasers of AAirpasses received membership in America's Admiral's Club, free cocktails and headsets in flight, plus several ticketing and boarding privileges.

American's assistant to the vice-president of marketing, Tom Kiernan, admitted that the move was a bold one. "We are moving into uncharted territory," he said, "but we have designed the AAirpass to be flexible enough to reach every corner of the market." Actually, American had some information on which to base sales estimates. For example, American offered an AAdvantage program to frequent travelers who logged over 25,000 miles per year. Some 75,000 people were enrolled in that program at the time the AAirpass system was announced.

Kiernan suggested that the AAirpass had a strong marketing appeal in that it was a breakthrough that created opportunities for new marketing programs. However, he predicted that AAirpass usage would not exceed 2 percent of the airline's total annual revenue passenger miles. At that rate American's exposure to fixed rates would be minimal. Kiernan also thought that the plan was an especially effective marketing tool because other airlines would find it "difficult to match in the near term. It's not as easy to match as a discount."

Source: Adapted from "AAirpass: a Ticket to Upfront Dollars?" Tom Bayer, *Advertising Age,* September 28, 1981.

itemized, penny-counting entries. Thus, the professional charges $1,000 for a gall bladder operation or $400 for a quick divorce. Such a price strategy results in a *professional price* or a *gentleman's price.*

Somewhat related to the professional price is the *ethical price.* This is a price purported to be lower than what could have been charged because of ethical or humanitarian reasons. Drug companies claim that the price of insulin is set at a reasonable level, even though more could be charged, because that is the right thing to do.

Special marketing situations demand *special prices,* prices such as "two for the price of one," "buy one get one free," and the long-running Rexall Drug "penny sales." In recent years discount stores have begun to run sales at special prices that last for only 15 minutes after being announced over the store's loudspeaker system.

Another special situation, that of a period of wildly fluctuating prices, can encourage the use of the *guarantee against price decline* price. When prices are going up and down rather than remaining comparatively steady, buyers might be tempted to make no purchases in the hope that tomorrow's price may be lower than today's. To overcome buyer resistance in such a situation some marketers have offered to sell to buyers at the current price, and to refund money or provide additional goods to those purchasers should the price be reduced during some period of time in the future.

In recent years, relatively few buyers have been concerned that prices will *drop,* and have instead sought assurance that prices will not *rise.* Sellers have been asked to guarantee some special rate in the future. Magazine subscription offers usually propose that the buyer purchase a three-, five-, even 10-year subscription "at today's low rates," or recommend a "charter subscriber" subscription to protect against prices that are certain to rise.

Lastly, some marketers believe that certain numbers are more likely to influence customers favorably than are other numbers. For example, it has been proposed that numbers that are rounded, such as zero, eight, and nine, are more attractive than fives and sevens which have jagged appearances.

DISTRIBUTION-BASED PRICE POLICIES

Many prices are based on the geographic distances separating the buyer from the point of sale or point of production. The prices are not *always* higher as the buyer gets farther from the seller. However, in most cases, geographic pricing policies reflect management's attempt to recover some or all of the costs involved in shipping products over distances.

F.O.B.

A common form of geographic pricing is **F.O.B.,** which may be read as "freight on board" or "free on board." The letters never stand alone but always are followed by a specific place such as "F.O.B. Baltimore" or "F.O.B. factory." This place name tells the buyer to *what point* the seller will be responsible for shipping. At that point, the buyer takes title to the goods and becomes responsible for shipping charges. A consumer in Kansas City might buy a Swedish auto "F.O.B. New York." This means that the price quoted includes shipment to New York. All other transportation costs will be extra.

Delivered Pricing

When a department store advertises that the price of a sofa is "$1,000 delivered in our area," that store is practicing **delivered pricing** or **freight allowed pricing.** The delivery charges are built into the price paid by the consumer. Occasionally, ill-will may develop when customers located just beyond the delivery zone lines must be charged a price higher than the advertised prices.

A variation on this is **zone pricing,** where geographic zones are delineated and prices increase as the number of zone lines crossed in completion of the transaction accumulate. The parcel post system employs zone pricing, charging a customer mailing a package a rate which depends on the weight of the parcel *and* the number of zones it will travel through before arriving at its destination. "Slightly higher west of the Rockies" is a phrase which reflects a zone pricing policy.

A company that views the entire country as its delivery zone, and charges the same prices in *every* location, is practicing a special form of delivered pricing called **uniform delivered pricing.** Candy bars, Timex watches, and postage stamps are priced at the same level throughout the nation. Such prices are, in fact, also called *postage stamp prices,* and are attractive to marketers in that they simplify pricing and nation-wide advertising.

Basing Point Pricing

This pricing system involves the selection of one or more locations to serve as *basing points.* Customers are charged prices and shipping fees as if their orders were shipped from these points *regardless* of where the merchandise actually originated. That is, if the basing point is Chicago and a buyer in Shreveport makes a purchase from a supplier in New Orleans, the buyer is charged as if the goods came from Chicago. The true shipping charge could have been $100, but the buyer must pay a charge of, say, $500. The seller is able to pocket the extra $400 because of

EXHIBIT 17-4

Basing Point Pricing

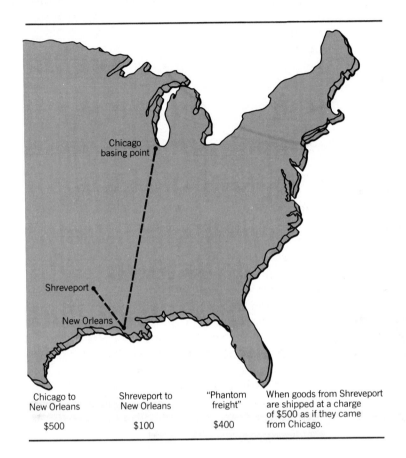

Chicago
basing point

Shreveport

New Orleans

Chicago to New Orleans	Shreveport to New Orleans	"Phantom freight"	When goods from Shreveport are shipped at a charge of $500 as if they came from Chicago.
$500	$100	$400	

basing point pricing (see Exhibit 17-4). This extra money is known as *phantom freight*.

Because this system is clearly not in the buyer's best interest, and because it smacks of collusion on the parts of suppliers, it has been the subject of court cases for more than 60 years. Although Supreme Court rulings made in the 1940s forbid industry-wide pricing systems that include phantom freight, cases involving basing point pricing are still encountered.

LIST PRICES

A manufacturer offering a product line of 10 items to wholesalers will prepare a list of prices to establish the basic price normally quoted to customers. Hence, **list prices** are basic price quotes without any price adjustments for change of season or other reason. In many industries, it is common for list prices to be adjusted with discounts or rebates depending on the competitive environment or season of the year. For example, retailers often mark down (i.e., reduce) the list

EXHIBIT 17-5

Rebates Are a Means of Ensuring That the Consumer Gets the Full Benefit of Price Reduction

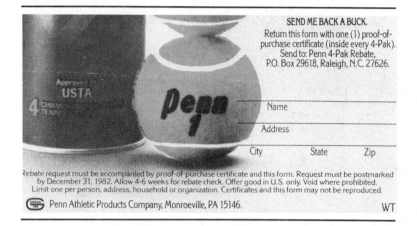

SEND ME BACK A BUCK.
Return this form with one (1) proof-of-purchase certificate (inside every 4-Pak).
Send to: Penn 4-Pak Rebate, P.O. Box 29618, Raleigh, N.C. 27626.

Name

Address

City   State   Zip

Rebate request must be accompanied by proof-of-purchase certificate and this form. Request must be postmarked by December 31, 1982. Allow 4-6 weeks for rebate check. Offer good in U.S. only. Void where prohibited. Limit one per person, address, household or organization. Certificates and this form may not be reproduced.

Penn Athletic Products Company, Monroeville, PA 15146.   WT

price when merchandise is out-of-season or slow-moving.

Rebates reduce the list price by giving back part of an amount paid. Rebates generally are reimbursements from the manufacturer rather than the retailer. A rebate policy assures that the consumer, and not the retailer, will benefit from the price adjustment by passing the savings on directly to the consumer.

The most common price adjustments are in the form of discounts.

Service marketers must pay special attention to price adjustments. Why? Because they can't store their products for sale at some other time. When prices fall, a dentist's services cannot be "warehoused" until prices rise again. The hotel in Florida cannot suspend operations without considerable cost while waiting for customers to return during the winter season. The service marketer must keep busy, and cannot keep busy building inventory. Price and discount adjusting provide an important tool leveling for the service marketer's demand.

DISCOUNT POLICIES

In addition to determining what prices are to be assigned to products and services, marketing managers must also decide what sorts of discounts are to be offered to potential buyers. A discount is a reduction from the list price or a reimbursement for performing a specific action, such as maintaining a sales force or carrying inventory. A number of discount schemes are commonly used. These are discussed briefly below. Notice that each discounting technique provides an incentive to potential buyers, but also yields some advantage, such as speedier payment of bills, to sellers.

Cash Discounts

Cash discounts may take the form of the common 2/10 net 30, which indicates that payment made within 10 days may be discounted 2 percent, and full payment, with no discount, must be made within 30 days. The amount of discount, the time allowed, and when the counting of days begins usually vary from industry to industry. The discount offered is usually large enough that it pays the buyer to borrow from a bank to pay what is owed to the supplier. An *anticipation* discount, an additional discount to encourage even faster payment, may also be offered. The pur-

KEYSTONING

Private label brands are becoming more popular with retailers who have become progressively disenchanted with name designer labels. The private brands are a means of enhancing the retailer's profitability because the change in merchandising/stocking has a pricing strategy implication. Keystoning is the term for the retailer's policy of doubling the wholesale price of an item and making this the regular price. During Christmas season, many stores will price their merchandise at keystone plus another fifteen percent. Thus, when the product goes on sale, the price is only marked down to the traditional keystone price. For example, an item bought for twenty dollars that is marked up to sell for fifty dollars is then put "on sale" for forty dollars. However, consumers have realized that the real price is forty dollars and they are now waiting for the products to go on sale below the forty dollar level before purchasing.

A Sakowitz executive says "There is no such thing any more as a 'retail price,' since everyone is scrambling to make whatever they can over wholesale cost. Stores are marking up and down quickly, and we have a problem with price credibility."

Source: Based on information in "Why Designer Labels are Fading," *Business Week*, February 21, 1983, pp. 70–71.

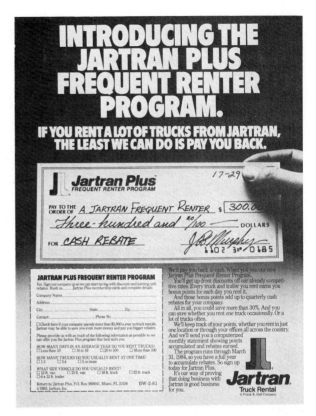

A quantity discount in the form of a rebate for the heavy user.

pose of each form of cash discount is to encourage prompt payment of bills. All forms of cash discounts are legal if offered equally to all similar buyers.

Trade Discounts

Trade discounts are discounts given to members of the trade. Electricians receive discounts on wire and tape because they are in the electrical trade. The electrical distributors (wholesalers) get even larger discounts because they must make a profit on the products they sell to electri-

cians. Since the recipient of the discount is performing a function, such as holding an inventory of electrical parts, these discounts are also called **functional discounts**.

The types and size of discounts for wholesale, retail, or other trade vary considerably by industry. Generally, the discount rate, which reflects the middleman's percentage margin on the goods sold, increases as the middleman's role in marketing to the customer increases. Thus, discounts are higher in the furniture industry than in the grocery industry.

Quantity Discounts

There are two types of quantity discounts, non-cumulative quantity discounts and cumulative quantity discounts. In the case of **non-cumulative quantity discounts,** each order is

FRONT ROW—THE OFF LIST PRICE SUPERSTORE

Front Row—the discount apparel store—has four stores in Houston, two in Chicago, and is rapidly expanding. Its penetration pricing strategy is aimed at the "thrifty shopper" market segment. Owned by U.S. Shoe Corporation, Front Row stresses that its prices are below list price. It claims to be "the most unusual, decidedly remarkable, eminently affordable way to shop." Advertisements explain that the retailer has men's, children's, women's, domestics, and shoe departments.

Front Row advertisements further claim to offer the "very same apparel, shoes, accessories, and domestics at 20 to 50 percent less than fine department and specialty stores, day in and day out." Some advertisements list prices to support the claim.

The store is a second-generation, off list price store that offers a continuity and depth of merchandise unlike other traditional off list price outlets. For example, there are no seconds or irregulars in stock. All merchandise is for the current season and includes the name brands and designer labels one would find at a competitor such as Foley's in Houston, a Federated Department Store.

Front Row can do this because of the experience and leverage U.S. Shoe has built with its other off list price units. It is really five stores under one roof—all united by a pricing strategy. The development of Front Row may be compared to the evolution of second-generation discount stores such as Dayton-Hudson's Target stores.

Front Row outlets are carpeted, have individual dressing rooms, and leave all labels on the products, although they can't be named in advertising.

The first TV spot featured an architect in his office, drawing plans for Front Row, buyers eagerly wait in the background to see the plans. When they see them, they stream into the architect's office telling him there isn't enough room for the menswear or the womenswear, or for any of the other merchandise.

Following that introductory campaign, the store's new spots will address the marketing concept. Advertising will ask consumers why they would shop at a department store when they could have the same merchandise at a reduced price.

Source: Adapted with permission from Tom Baker, "Front Row Targets Thrifty Shoppers," *Advertising Age*, September 5, 1983, p. 30S.

treated separately. The buyer's discount is calculated in terms of the size of that single purchase, without consideration of past purchases or future planned purchases. Obviously, the purpose of this discount is to encourage large orders.

Cumulative quantity discounts, on the other hand, allow the buyer an ever-increasing discount with each purchase made over some period of time, say a year. That is, the more the buyer orders, the larger the discount becomes. The major intent of the cumulative quantity discount is to keep the customer coming back. Stated another way, the supplier's aim is to tie the buyer to him.

Seasonal Discounts

As one would guess, the **seasonal discount** is intended to help level out the marketing workload by encouraging buyers to make purchases and take delivery of merchandise which is out-of-season. Products such as bathing suits, winter clothing, paint, and lawn furniture are obvious candidates for seasonal discounting at various times during the year.

Chain Discounts

In many purchasing situations the buyer will qualify for a series of discounts. When a wholesale buyer sees terms quoted as 40/10/5

EXHIBIT 17-6

Discounts and Objectives

Discount	Objective
Cash discount	To encourage customers to pay their bills within a given period of time, such as 10 days.
Anticipation	To encourage even faster payment of bills by offering additional discounts if the customer pays within, for example, 5, rather than 10 days.
Trade or functional discount	To "reward" a customer for functions performed, such as installation of a particular brand of storm windows in houses being built, or stocking a particular brand of clothing in a store.
Non-cumulative quantity discounts	To encourage buyers to place larger orders each time they buy merchandise.
Cumulative quantity discounts	To encourage buyers to return to a particular supplier to earn ever-larger discounts.
Seasonal discounts	To encourage buyers to make purchases during the "off season." Examples: house paint and bathing suits in the fall and winter and visits to winter resort areas during the summer.
Promotional allowance	To encourage middlemen to promote the product to their local customers.

net 30 the buyer realizes that she will face a series of discounts if all the appropriate options are utilized. For example, if the list price of a machine is $995, the chain discount would be calculated as follows:

List price	$995.00
Less trade discount (40 percent of $995)	− 398.00
Balance	$597.00
Less seasonal discount (10 percent of $597)	− 59.70
Balance	$537.30
Less cash discount (5 percent of $537.30)	− 26.86
Price wholesaler pays	$510.44

An adjustment from list price.

Promotional Allowances

A manufacturer may partially reimburse wholesalers or retailers for promotional assistance at the local level. These reimbursements may be cash or merchandise with the value commonly restricted to a percentage of sales or a discount off the list price.

A summary of the various discounts and allowances is given in Exhibit 17-6.

PRICING AND THE LAW

Because price is a tool of marketing that could be used in ways injurious to competition, and because price so clearly affects the consumer-voter as well as the business person, a number of national and local laws have been passed which influence pricing practices. The Sherman Antitrust Act (1890) and the Clayton Act (1914) were early attempts to curb price-fixing, restraint of trade, and other unfair and monopolistic practices. In many other cases legislation has amended these acts for purposes of clarification of what constitutes an antitrust action.

Fair Trade Acts

Until 1975, the states were empowered under federal law to pass *fair trade* or *resale price maintenance* acts. Most states enacted such laws. These allowed manufacturers to fix the prices of their goods and to *prohibit* wholesalers and retailers from charging reduced or discount prices. Though it was argued that these laws would protect small companies by forcing all businesses to charge the same prices for goods, their main purpose was to stabilize prices at comparatively high levels. Enforcement of these laws was difficult and growing consumer awareness that certain prices were being kept artificially high contributed to the repeal (1975) of the legislation that permitted the individual states to allow price maintenance.

Unfair Sales Practices Acts

Unfair sales practices acts are state laws that specify that certain items must be sold at prescribed mark-ups. The mark-ups may range from zero (thus eliminating loss leaders) to a relatively high percentage. Generally, some provision is made to allow the sale of old or out-of-style merchandise at a reduced price. Dealers covered by such laws may charge more, but *not less,* than the specified mark-ups allow. Thus, the laws are also termed *minimum mark-up laws.* These acts are intended to protect the small business using a relatively high mark-up by assuring that even a discount chain must mark-up its merchandise by the minimum amount. The small dealer then has a cushion which brings the price charged by the chain store closer to that charged by the independent.

Robinson-Patman Act

Price discrimination occurs when a manufacturer or supplier charges a lower price to one customer than another similar customer. The **Robinson-Patman Act** of 1936 is a federal law that makes it illegal to give, induce, or receive discriminatory prices. The act's sponsors believed it would wipe out chain stores. Under the law, a supplier of meat products may not give a large discount to a supermarket chain *just* because that chain is an important customer. But the supplier *may* give the discount if a "proportional" discount is offered to the corner grocer. In the event of litigation, a judge must decide what is proportional and what is not.

The law also prohibits the granting of a *wholesaler's discount* or a *broker's discount,* to a business which does not meet criteria identifying it as a true wholesaler. The effect of this *brokerage provision* is that a large retailing organization cannot demand to be given a wholesaler's discount even though it may buy merchandise in larger quantities than do typical wholesalers. The law does allow for the offering of cooperative advertising and other promotional assistance if the promotional help is offered to all customers on proportionally equal terms.

The Robinson-Patman Act itself includes two provisions which can be used to defend prices that could *appear* to be discriminatory. One of these allows for the use of several prices to customers if the *competitive situation* demands it. Thus, a lower price may be charged to one customer than another if this price is granted to meet the equally low price of a competitor. For example, a buyer in one city may be faced with a price war while a buyer in another city is not. The second provision is the so-called *cost justification provision*. If the seller can prove that the lower price to one buyer represents simply a passing on of cost savings, for example, as a result of producing and shipping in larger quantities, the seller has successfully employed the cost justification.

The Robinson-Patman Act, along with the Federal Trade Commission Act (discussed in Chapter 2) which established that watchdog agency, is one of the two most important laws affecting the daily dealings of marketers. Mere observance of its major provisions is not enough to avoid legal troubles. As with all legislation, its content is open to interpretation and reinterpretation by the courts and government agencies.[3]

State and Local Laws

Many states and cities have laws and ordinances that restrict the pricing freedom of firms within their boundaries. For example, several states set limits on the number of times per year that wholesale beer prices may be changed. Many cities require that a "fire sale" actually follow a

---

[3]For an excellent reference on the Robinson-Patman Act see "Those Who Can, Do . . . Those Who Can't . . . : Marketing Professors and the Robinson-Patman Act," by James C. Johnson and Kenneth C. Schneider, *Journal of the Academy of Marketing Science* (forthcoming).

In many areas, unit pricing is the result of pricing legislation.

fire, and that "going out of business" sales be followed by a cessation of business operations.

A service industry has grown up to supply companies with the latest information on legislation and court cases which may affect their pricing and other marketing plans.

Government Influences

Instances of government influence on pricing that are not in the form of legislation are easy to find. The *threat* of legislation is often enough to affect pricing policies. Government agencies frequently issue "advice" which, though backed by law, is not actual legislation, even though it has an effect not unlike that of a specific law.

BOTTLE BATTLE

Anheuser-Busch said "baby beer" would save the free-enterprise system in New Mexico, but beer drinkers there aren't buying that. They aren't buying much "baby beer" either.

It all started when Republican state Sen. Murray Ryan decided to come to the aid of his beer-drinking constituents, who pay as much as $2 a case more for beer than drinkers in some other states. That is because in other states, especially in the East and the northern Midwest, the big national-brand breweries must compete with local brewers that sell cheaper beer. There are no local brewers in New Mexico.

But there is the state legislature, which embraced Mr. Ryan's plan for confronting the problem in a straightforward manner: It passed an "affirmation law," forbidding a brewer to sell beer to its wholesalers at a price higher than the lowest price it charges anywhere in the country.

The law took effect in June 1979. Are prices lower? Are beer drinkers happy? They are not. The main effect so far is a legal battle between the state and the brewers in which the losers seem to be the wholesale distributors and the hapless drinkers.

A Simple Strategy

Anheuser-Busch Inc., maker of Budweiser and Michelob, attacked the law with marketing as well as legal parries. The marketing strategy was as simple and direct as the law, and just about as successful. The brewery switched to 10-ounce from 12-ounce containers, which it normally sold only in Louisiana. This vastly simplified Anheuser-Busch's problems in complying with the law.

Unfortunately, the price stayed the same, so tipplers were getting 10 ounces for what they previously paid for 12. This didn't escape their notice or their ire. Sales sank as much as 50% ("After all," said one Bud fancier, "there *are* other beers"). And, worse for the company's image in that land of macho sensibilities, people began scornfully referring to the Anheuser-Busch suds as "baby beer."

Joseph Schlitz Brewing Co. escaped opprobrium and increased its sales as well by taking the opposite approach, offering more beer for the same price. It squirted an extra quarter ounce into each 12-ounce container, making that size unique to the New Mexico market. Consumers were pleased.

But Anheuser-Busch paints the issue in broader strokes than a mere sales slump in a minor marketing territory. The company says it is taking a stand for free

Source: Kate Pound, "Anheuser-Busch's Baby Beer Flops as Brewers in New Mexico Fight a Law Meant to Cut Prices," *The Wall Street Journal*, September 9, 1980, p. 48. Used by permission.

Instances of government holding prices *down* are fairly common. For example, from time to time, presidents of the United States have privately, or on television, demanded that the United States Steel Company, and other large firms, roll back price increases. Another example is government price *support* programs, especially in the area of agriculture, that are aimed at keeping prices stable. Thus, farmers taking land out of production may receive wheat or other payment in kind.

It is even possible to identify instances where government influence has served to *raise* prices. Oil prices have been allowed to rise in recent years as a means of encouraging conservation. It was rumored for years that General Motors had the financial power to reduce the prices on its cars and drive the other U.S. manufacturers out of business. It was said that the firm's prices were kept higher than necessary to preserve competition and avoid government actions against it.

In any case, prices are subject to many government influences that are not spelled out in the law.

enterprise and for the common-wealth of beer drinkers across the land. It felt it had no choice but to fight the law with smaller bottles or pull out of New Mexico.

The Battle in Court

It is also fighting in the courtroom. Anheuser-Busch joined with Schlitz, Adolph Coors Co., Miller Brewing Co. and the U.S. Brewers Association to challenge the affirmation law. They argue that the law interferes with interstate commerce because promotional discounts or competitive pricing in other states would violate it. The brewers say they would have to respond by raising prices elsewhere rather than trimming them in New Mexico.

Anheuser-Busch is also trying less lofty and reasoned approaches to counter the angry drinkers' boycott. It has begun advertising the "Perfect 10" with pictures of pretty women, hoping the glamorous image will displace the noxious "baby beer" characterization. So far it hasn't.

At the Line Camp Tavern in Santa Fe, you can't even buy a Bud or Michelob any more, and the manager, Julian Harvey, says he quit selling the products to protect his customers' interests. "It's my opinion that big business is just trying to rape the public," he says.

Such sentiments are hurting Anheuser-Busch, but not nearly as much as they are hurting its distributors. One, Richard Matteucci, is fighting back, and he says survival of his $10-million-a-year business is at stake. Mr. Matteucci has filed suit charging Anheuser-Busch with disastrously damaging his business through its "corporate arrogance" in switching to 10-ounce containers. His lawyer, Mark Rodman, says the company is sacrificing its wholesaler to "teach other people they had better not try laws like this," a state-ment with which the brewer apparently agrees: In a deposition it says one reason for the switch was to "discourage other states from passing similar legislation."

Mr. Matteucci and others insist that Anheuser-Busch is sticking its (and their) neck out unnecessarily and could have avoided trouble by confining its fight to the courtroom.

On the legal front, the brewers were able to get an injunction barring enforcement of the pricing law pending the outcome of their suit against it. Under the injunction, they can ignore the law by posting bond and promising that if they lose they will pay the state any profits they have made in the interim.

If the law is upheld, the penalty for violating it would be a ban on sales for up to 30 days, but that may never happen. There's a chance the legislature may end the controversy by rescinding the law when it meets in January.

SUMMARY

The area of pricing is an important part of marketing that requires that both numbers and judgment be employed by the decision-maker. However, it is probably the most logical part of marketing in that most situations addressed by an organization actually "suggest" the pricing course to be taken. Whether it be matching competition or altering discounts, the decision-maker's response to the environment is usually one that is defensible and understandable.

A wide range of pricing goals and pricing strategies available to marketing managers were presented, including one-price policy versus variable price policy, skimming versus penetration, leader pricing versus bait pricing, odd pricing, price lining, and others. Pricing policies based on the geographical distances separating the buyer from the point of sale or point of production, such as F.O.B., delivered pricing, basing point pricing, and zone pricing were also discussed.

In addition to price determination, marketing managers must also make decisions concerning what price discounts are to be offered to potential buyers. Various discounting techniques discussed included cash discounts, quantity discounts, trade discounts, seasonal discounts, and promotional allowances.

Finally, because pricing strategies and tactics can have potentially injurious effects on consumers, a number of national and local laws have been enacted that influence pricing practices and that are important to the marketing manager involved in pricing decisions.

> **THE MOST IMPORTANT CONCEPT IN THIS CHAPTER**
> There are a wide variety of pricing goals and strategies available to the marketing manager. Determining the appropriate pricing strategy and price discounts is a delicate task influenced by target market selection, geographical factors, and legal considerations requiring the expert judgment of the marketing manager.

KEY TERMS

One-price policy

Variable pricing

Skimming price

Penetration price

Loss leader

Bait pricing

Bait and switch

Price lining

F.O.B.

Odd prices

Even prices

Delivered pricing

Freight allowed pricing

Zone pricing

Basing point pricing

Uniform delivered pricing

Cash discounts

List prices

Trade discounts

Functional discounts

Non-cumulative quantity discounts

Cumulative quantity discounts

Seasonal discounts

Unfair sales practices acts

Robinson-Patman Act

QUESTIONS FOR DISCUSSION

1 What are the relative advantages and disadvantages of variable prices versus a one-price policy?

2 In what competitive situation would you recommend using a penetration price? A skimming price?

3 Why are some prices based in part on the geographic distances the products must travel to reach the customer?

4 What is an unfair sales practices act? How can such an act help small retailers compete against larger retailers?

5 Give three examples of a sacrifice of item profit for the sake of total profit.

6 What are some possible influences that competitors might have on a firm's pricing activities?

7 What is a trade discount? Why is it sometimes called a functional discount?

8 Describe three instances of government-influenced prices found within the U.S. "free economy."

9 Match each pricing style with the logic behind it:

(a) Skimming
(b) Penetration
(c) Customary
(d) Odd

(e) Status
(f) Professional

(g) Ethical
(h) Leader
(i) Special
(j) Minimization of loss
(k) Price lining
(l) Guarantee against price decline

_____ "We'll get the customers worked up with a buy-one-get-one-at-half-price sale."

_____ "People will buy this because it's expensive and they can put it right in front of their houses and show off."

_____ "We've got to get rid of this stuff. Instead of just throwing it out, let's charge only two dollars apiece and get rid of it that way, even if we do lose a dollar on each one."

_____ "Look, people aren't going to pay two dollars for this can of dog food. Price it at $1.98 or so, and it may move."

_____ "Oil has been less than a dollar a can in discount houses _forever_. We can't be the only discounter in town charging over that."

_____ "I tell you, Jack, this is going to be a very big item. Very popular. So, we charge a lot for it now when it's still new to the market. Later we can lower the price."

_____ "Price, schmice. It's not the price that's so important. We gotta price this thing low enough to attract some attention. We just can't walk out into an established market without a price that's low enough for us to get our foot in the door."

_____ "So we cut the price on the mufflers, see? Then when people come in for the muffler, we hit 'em for new pipes, manifolds, shocks, and all like that."

_____ "For god's sake, if we start asking that kind of price for insulin, the government will start investigating our profit picture. We better charge a lower price so as to appear more 'fair'. "

_____ "Customers aren't buying just now, J.B. With the prices going up and down the way they are, they are holding back figuring that the price might go down tomorrow."

_____ "Shirts. Now shirts we're going to price this way. Some for right around twenty dollars. Some for around thirteen dollars. And the rest at about eight dollars."

_____ "O.K., so this is one of those new legal clinics. But we're just as good as the other lawyers. We don't want prices that sound like we're counting pennies. Let's charge fees for our services that are lower than the other lawyers' fees, but prices like $20 an office visit, $50 a divorce, $25 a will."

CASE 17-1 The Attack on Federal Express*

Probably only cave-dwellers without televisions have missed the fact that there is a new, particularly ferocious aspect to the marketing war for the business of those who must get small packages delivered from one city to another overnight.

Since the fall of 1982 prices have dipped to as low as $9 for door-to-door delivery of an envelope that weighs a few ounces. Rates can be even lower for lightweight multi-envelope shipments that leave from the same address. The U.S. Postal Service offers overnight delivery—but no pickup service—of packages weighing as much as two pounds for $9.35.

The overnight package-delivery industry is only 10 years old, and the number of companies

*Source: Used with permission from Tom Belden, "Package Delivery Marketing War Rages," _Knight-Ridder Newspapers, Tulsa World_, June 12, 1983, p. g–6.

getting into the competition for light shipments has grown sharply, especially in the last three years. But it is not clear whether the industry can remain a solid money-maker as it matures. Some fear that it could go the way of the passenger airline business, in which discount fares, brought on by excessive competition, have ravaged profits for three years.

According to analysts and officials of the air-freight business, the low rates for delivering a two-ounce or three-ounce envelope have not yet fallen to the level of a loss leader. The low rates for the smallest packages might even be considered overpriced, one analyst said, given the fact that the Postal Service can still deliver a one-ounce letter for only 20 cents.

Most industry executives and some independent analysts, however, do not expect to see rates for the small shipments fall much lower. Reliable service has been just as crucial, if not more so. "Price for someone who absolutely, positively has to have it overnight is always secondary" to dependable service, said industry analyst John V. Pincavage of the Paine Webber Mitchell Hutchins Inc. brokerage house in New York.

"You ship with us because you have a problem," said Armand Schneider, a spokesman for Federal Express. "Our business is carrying someone else's headache. We're selling peace of mind."

An aviation-industry analyst for a Philadelphia brokerage suggested that the end was near for the industry's "easy-growth stage," in which increases in business come largely from a rapidly expanding market for the service. Until recently, there was little price competition in the business. The market was growing and reliable service was indeed more important than price. "It is going to get more competitive," said the analyst. "They could cut each other's throats. If someone breaks rank and does it, all of them may follow. I just don't trust anyone in this business (aviation) to maintain a price structure."

Federal Express invented the overnight package service and is the leader of those that use only air delivery, with an estimated 40 percent of that business. Its growth rate has been phenomenal. Revenues went from $258 million in the fiscal year that ended May 31, 1979, to $804 million in fiscal 1982. Revenues in fiscal 1983 are expected to be almost $1 billion. At the same time, however, net income for the company, which was $78.4 million in fiscal 1982, will only be about the same level as this year.

Some industry executives, such as Chairman John C. Emery, Jr. of Emery Air Freight Corp., believe that because of the cost of getting into the business, competition in the air-express business will slow down and prices will stabilize.

To provide reliable overnight-delivery service, Emery said in a recent interview, requires a company to own all of its planes, have a large fleet of trucks in each city where it offers service, maintain a sophisticated computer system to coordinate the business and have a large "hub" where packages are sorted every night.

Emery was founded in 1946 as a "freight forwarder," using commercial airline flights to deliver any size shipment worldwide. But it did not decide until the late 1970s that it could not afford not to be in the overnight package business, too, since it owned its own aircraft fleet. Now, unlike Federal Express, which operates only in North America, Emery officials believe they are in a position to prosper because they are better established throughout the world than most companies.

Airlines have been using regional hub cities to feed passengers into their flight networks for years. Until the early 1980s, Federal Express was the only package service with a single, national hub—Memphis—in which virtually all packages from its system were ferried each night for sorting and put back on other planes to their destinations. One of the keys to making money at the low rates lies in the relatively low overhead costs of moving a lightweight, envelope-sized package—if an efficient hubbing system is in place. Putting such a system in place, however, has become an increasingly expensive proposition.

Building the Memphis hubbing center cost Federal Express $70 million in the late 1970s. Emery Air had to spend $130 million to set up a similar major hub in Dayton, Ohio, in 1981. If another company tried to do the same now, it would cost close to $250 million.

The biggest of the overnight services, Purolator Courier Corp., which delivers about 200,000 packages daily, has been able to hold its costs down by chartering rather than owning aircraft. It also makes deliveries of less than 400 miles by truck rather than air, spokesman Hollis McLaughlin said.

Questions

1 How important is price to the consumer in the overnight package delivery industry?

2 What pricing objectives should Federal Express implement?

3 What pricing strategy should Federal Express implement?

CASE 17-2 Century Cigarettes

Century cigarettes, produced by R.J. Reynolds, were marketed in approximately two-thirds of the nation in 1983. Statewide laws that tax cigarettes based on multiples of 10 force Century to limit its distribution to 33 states. This new brand of cigarettes features 25 cigarettes in a package; it retails for the same price as regular cigarette packages consisting of 20 cigarettes. A 9-pack (225 unit) carton of Century will be priced about the same as a 10-pack (200 unit) carton of other cigarettes. This 20 percent increase in cigarettes per package translates to a discount of 20 percent on a cost per cigarette basis. Generic brands of cigarettes are 30 percent less per cigarette than the regular cigarettes.

Questions

1 What is R.J. Reynolds' pricing strategy for Century?

2 What competitive implications will the introduction of the Century brand have on other cigarette marketers?

3 How is product strategy interrelated with pricing strategy?

PART 7

PROMOTION STRATEGY

Promotion is probably the most glamorous of the four ingredients of the marketing mix. Advertising surrounds us each day and much of it is clever, exciting, and colorful. Moreover, advertisers take understandable pride in the messages they create and pay for since these are obviously intended to be seen. Promotion in general is no behind-the-scenes activity. But people find it easy to forget, in the bright light of advertising, that other promotional activities such as personal selling, publicity, and sales promotion are also part of the communication process. These four major forms of promotion must be coordinated by marketing managers, not only with one another, but with the other elements of the marketing mix as well.

Chapter 18 offers an overview of the promotion process, its role as communication, its major components, and its basic place in marketing strategy.

Chapter 19 specifically examines the marketing activity of personal selling and the function of managing the selling effort.

Chapter 20 covers advertising, showing not only how advertising campaigns are developed but also how those campaigns, if they are to be effective, must tie in closely with an organization's total marketing plan. ∎

CHAPTER 18

An Overview of Promotion

CHAPTER SCAN

This chapter introduces the topic of promotion and draws attention to its purpose as a tool for external communication in marketing. It discusses the four major facets of promotion—personal selling, advertising, publicity, and sales promotion—and shows how each of these can be seen as an important part of the organization's promotional mix. Effective marketing depends on effective communication. Each promotional tool gives support to the others.

This chapter discusses several general promotional strategies from which marketing planners may select. Budgeting methods commonly employed by marketing managers are also examined.

WHEN YOU HAVE STUDIED THIS CHAPTER, YOU WILL:

Be able to discuss the key role played by promotion in any successful marketing effort.

Understand that, despite the comments of critics of advertising, promotion is necessary to the basic operation of our economy.

Be able to define each of the four major elements of promotion and comment on their interrelationships within a promotional plan.

Be familiar with the basic model that describes all communication processes, including promotion.

Know how promotional messages are varied to appeal to different target markets—customers ranging from those who are unaware of the product being offered to those who regularly purchase it.

Be able to discuss the appropriateness of using specific promotional tools for particular products and marketing situations.

Be familiar with the various promotional strategies, such as push versus pull and the hard sell versus the soft sell.

Be able to describe how the elements of promotion can be brought together to support one another in a promotional campaign.

Be able to name and describe the major approaches used by marketing managers to set promotional budgets.

At dusk, outside Feibel's Bowling Alley in Teaneck, New Jersey, a half-dozen limousines added a touch of glamour to a quiet strip of Palisades Avenue.[1] Inside, under hot lights, the shooting had moved into its ninth wearying hour.

The script called for Ben Davidson, former defensive tackle for the Oakland Raiders, to hand a bowling ball to a quivering Rodney Dangerfield and say, in his most menacing growl, "All we need is one pin, Rodney."

The cameras rolled for an umpteenth take, and Davidson handed over the ball. It promptly slid through Dangerfield's fingers and crashed onto the lane. Davidson did not miss a beat, "All we need is one broken foot, Rodney."

Welcome to one of the most successful long-running shows on television: the 30- and 60-second television commercials for Miller Lite beer. Pure American hucksterism at its best. This one was No. 74.

Philip Morris Inc. introduced Miller Lite beer in 1975, but no product succeeds without a pitch. It was McCann-Erickson, the advertising agency, that came up with the ingenious idea of promoting low-calorie beer—a virtual contradiction in terms—with big, beery-looking retired athletes bantering and bickering in neighborhood bars.

The message was simple. You do not have to be a sissy to drink Lite. And its success has been nothing short of phenomenal. From a standing start, Lite has become the third-largest selling beer, behind Budweiser and Miller's High Life. Miller, with more than 50 percent of the low-calorie market, sells approximately 12.5 million barrels of Lite each year.

The Lite advertising campaign may be an even bigger success. According to Video Storyboard Tests, Inc., a company that rates commercials by interviewing 5,000 viewers, the advertisements for Lite are the most popular on television.

The commercials for Lite also feature a sprinkling of non-sports celebrities such as Dangerfield and Mickey Spillane, the mystery writer. But retired athletes such as Bubba Smith and Deacon Jones and fiery managers like Billy Martin and Red Auerbach are the main Lite attractions.

Miller calls its group the Lite All Stars. Some of them find they are more celebrated and better paid as pitchmen than during their playing careers. Take "Marvelous" Marv Throneberry, an original member of the New York Mets most renowned for his reputation for ineptitude—and now for his line, "I still don't know why they chose me for a commercial."

When Throneberry was tracked down six years ago, he was working as general manager of an insulating company in Memphis. But doing the commercials proved to be more fun, glamourous and lucrative than insulation. A year and a half ago, he left his job to work full-time for Lite.

"We try to choose the sort of guys you'd love to have a beer with," said Bob Lenz, the advertising executive who conceived the Lite campaign, and now oversees it for the Backer and Spielvogel Agency. "We didn't want actors, or superstars, but macho guys who could make fun of themselves. We wouldn't use someone like Roger Staubach, for instance. He's just not beery enough."

The success story behind Miller Lite illustrates the fascinating world of promotion. Accomplishments credited to the advertising are even more impressive when one recalls that other low-calorie beers had fared miserably in the marketplace until the Miller advertising teamed light beer with "real men" such as Dick Butkus and Boog Powell, instead of dieters. The advertising is reinforced with other forms of promotion such as celebrity spokesmen's public appearances and personal selling by Miller's sales force. It was this stroke of promotional creativity that made Miller Lite one of America's most popular beers and opened the way for almost every brewer to market their own low-calorie products.

---

[1] Excerpts from Tony Schwartz, "Banter Between Brew Keeps Lite Sales Bubbling," *New York Times* News Service, *Tulsa Tribune*, December 28, 1981. Used with permission.

THE NATURE AND PURPOSES OF PROMOTION

Effective marketers know that the old adage—"Build a better mousetrap and the world will beat a path to your door"—contains a basic flaw. If "the world" doesn't find out that there *is* a better mousetrap, the manufacturer will be a very lonely person, indeed. Some form of *promotion* is necessary to make consumers, and other publics with which an organization interacts, aware of the existence of a product. Having a great product is not enough. People must be made familiar with the product's benefits.

Promotion is applied communication used by marketers to exchange persuasive messages and information between buyers and sellers.

Personal selling, advertising, publicity, and sales promotion are promotional methods that may be used to communicate a message.

Promotion Communicates Information

Although promotion, and advertising in particular, is often singled out as a part of the marketing mix that society could well do without, a moment's reflection shows that this criticism is unwarranted. The job of marketing is to identify consumer wants and to move to fill those wants by developing appropriate products—priced right, packaged for convenience, and properly distributed. The role of promotion in the marketing function is to convey news, to tell consumers about the benefits of the product. This communication is often termed "selling the product." Promotion is an inseparable part of the marketing function.[2]

Even critics of advertising might feel more comfortable with the job promotion performs in society once they realize that *the essence of pro-*

motion is communication. If the management of Macy's is planning a sale, communicating price savings to potential customers must be part of the plan. The lowering of prices will not be beneficial to anyone unless promotion communicates to consumers the fact that a sale is underway. On a more commonplace level, the store's promotions will provide other information, such as store hours, whether or not returns will be allowed on sale merchandise, and whether purchases can be made with credit cards. Thus, informing potential buyers is a broad goal of promotion.

Persuasive Communication

Marketers rarely face a situation where simple and plain communication of information is enough for effective promotion. In the era of the production concept, where many organizations faced a sellers' market, this may have been the case. But today's world is full of messages and distractions of all sorts. This is in part due to the free enterprise system which encourages organizations to develop and offer new and better products. Consumers are often faced with many competing options. People also seem to find themselves increasingly rushed and harried. With less time for comparative shopping, consumers turn to advertising for product information. It would be the generous commentator indeed who would suggest that "pure information" is all there is to be found in marketing communications. Marketing managers exist in a competitive environment and as competitors they want consumers to buy their brands. Thus, persuasion is a primary goal of promotion. It is management's hope that the information that Macy's is having a big sale will persuade consumers to visit Macy's and see for themselves. In fact, a traditional definition of promotion is *persuasive communication.*

Promotion Serves as a Reminder

Consider the customer who shops at Macy's regularly or the consumer who always buys Tide de-

---

[2] B.M. Kendal, Testimony Before the Federal Trade Commission in 1971 as quoted in F.M. Nicosia, *Advertising Management and Society: Business Point of View* (New York: McGraw-Hill, 1974), p. 25.

Leading brands may be promoted to remind consumers of their satisfaction with the brand.

tergent. Do marketers advertise to them? Yes. Is that a waste of money? The answer is no, for the very practical reason that even the most loyal customers must be reminded that a store or product has served them well over time and of the features that make that store or product attractive. This is especially so in a society wherein competitors are free to "tempt" loyal customers with their own informative and persuasive messages. Thus, reminding customers, in addition to informing and persuading them, may be a promotional objective. Morton salt, Bayer aspirin, and Coca-Cola are all number one in their fields. They have achieved their goals to inform and persuade. The major goal of their promotion is to sustain their customers' preference for their products. Attracting new customers is a secondary promotional goal. Even someone who believes totally that Coke is the best cola may be influenced by the message that "Coke is it"—the "real thing" and not an imitation.

In summary, the three basic purposes of promotion are to *inform, persuade,* and *remind.*

THE ELEMENTS OF PROMOTION

A city zoo or a refurnished downtown theater is usually seen as a community asset, worthy of being helped along. Such organizations may benefit from publicity via news media or public service announcements on radio and television. This publicity serves to inform the public about the services offered by the organization, perhaps by persuading some members of the community to patronize or contribute to the upkeep of this community asset, or by reminding others that they have not been to the zoo or the theater for years.

Some drug stores and discount houses have installed computerized machines to test blood pressure. These machines may serve to draw customer traffic into the store. They also offer the customer a service that was not available until the devices were installed. And they certainly indicate that the merchants who provide the service are concerned with their customers' well-being. Similarly, some city fire departments offer free blood pressure checks at selected stations.

There are many ways to promote products and services. Companies like Burger King or Lever Brothers spend millions of dollars on television, radio, magazine, and newspaper advertisements. IBM, and other firms selling complicated and expensive equipment, invests great sums in selecting, training, and paying personal salespeople.

Obviously, the zoo, the fire department, Burger King, and IBM are all engaged in promotion. Just as clearly, they differ in their approach to communication, and not just in terms of the money they invest. There are four major subsets of promotion. They are formally defined below.

A TELEVISION COMMERCIAL FOR BEEF?

A television commercial pictures a rugged cowboy returning from a hard day's work on the range and fantasizing: "Just look at this steak, cooked just the way I like it. It's pink'n juicy and it cuts like butter." The commercial ends with the slogan "Somehow, nothing satisfies like beef." Advertising beef to Americans? There was a time when the Beef Industry Council did not have to advertise like trade associations for other food groups. What went wrong? Why have consumers been spending a smaller portion of their disposable income on beef? The answer lies in changing environmental influences on beef consumption. There has been a steadily rising cost of beef combined with the consumer's perception that beef costs are rising higher than they actually have. Furthermore, there is an increase in public concern about the cholesterol in beef. Americans in the 1980s are concerned with health and fitness. They have changed their eating habits. The need for persuasive promotion was not anticipated or recognized by the Beef Industry Council until people began to eat less beef.

Four Subsets of Promotion

Personal selling, advertising, publicity, and sales promotion are the four subsets of promotion. These promotional efforts are of two general types. They involve either direct communication, on a face-to-face basis, or indirect communication via some medium, such as television. It is up to the marketer to determine which approach is best for each situation. The nature of the message and the context in which it is to be delivered provide powerful clues about which method to choose. Few industrial buyers would feel comfortable buying plant equipment solely on the basis of direct mail or telephone communication. Few consumers need to talk to a salesperson to choose a certain brand of canned peas, but rely on advertising for most product information.

Personal Selling.

Personal selling is a person-to-person dialogue between buyer and seller where the purpose of the face-to-face interaction is to persuade the buyer to accept a point of view or to convince the buyer to take a specific course of action.

In many instances, the one-to-one nature of this communication technique means that it is quite expensive to employ. The salesperson must be properly trained. He or she may have to spend considerable time in developing and delivering a message suited to the individual customer. Time may also be spent traveling or waiting for the opportunity to deliver the message.

These "disadvantages" are compensated for by the fact that personal selling is the most flexible means of delivering a promotional message. Questions can be answered, pauses taken at appropriate spots to allow an idea to sink in, and responses made to particular customer objections or reluctance to complete a purchase. Furthermore, the personal salesperson, unlike a TV or radio communication, can focus on the best prospects—those most likely to buy the product being offered. Direct, and usually immediate, feedback from customers is among the major advantages of personal selling. The other elements of promotion are essentially one-way communications delivered to potential buyers. They provide little or no interpersonal activity. Feedback information is not immediate. Reactions, in the form of refusals to buy, are slow in coming, although they are potentially devastating to the marketing organization.

Advertising.

Advertising includes any persuasive message carried by a mass medium and paid for by a sponsor who signs the message.[3]

---

[3]Douglass Johnson, *Advertising Today* (Chicago, Ill.: Science Research Associates, 1978), p. 1.

Statistical Abstract of the U.S

It consists of paid messages by identified sponsors through nonpersonal channels (media). Advertising bears a signature, in the form of a company or brand name. Any medium other than a live salesperson may be used. (A live salesperson would mean personal selling was used.) Almost anything else, however, could be an advertising medium. Later in this section of the text, you will see that, while most advertising is carried by common media like radio and television, effective marketers have developed some very clever and inventive media for delivering their messages.

Publicity.   Advertising is a *paid* form of message delivery.

> **Publicity** is similar to advertising except that it involves an *unpaid* and *unsigned* message, even though it may use the same mass media as advertising does.

When information about a product is considered newsworthy, mass media tend to communicate that information "for free." Thus, the organization being publicized neither signs nor pays for the message.[4] When Randall Park Mall near Cleveland, Ohio, opened, it received, as would any large, new business operation, a great deal of regional publicity. But, at the time it was built, the Mall was the largest in the United States, so stories about it were carried in newspapers and other media across the country. Randall Park was able to communicate its message free of charge.

Publicity can be positive or negative. In fact, since the message is in the hands of the media and not in the hands of the business or other organization having something newsworthy to report, publicity can be terrible. News stories concerning the Walt Disney movie production *Tron* provide an example of negative publicity. Several stock analysts, who were not profes-

---

[4]Although publicity is described as "free," it is true that some firms pay publicity agents or face other publicity-related expenses. However, the media carry the stories for "free," thus the term "unpaid" is associated with publicity.

NUMBER PLEASE

Friendly people, cleanliness of a store, the company letterhead, and every aspect of an organization communicates a message. Creative marketing managers manage these communications for promotional purposes. For example, consider the promotional value of these phone numbers:

National Car Rental	800-CAR-RENT
Chicago Motor Club	312-THE-CLUB
United Air Express	800-PACKAGE
Holiday Inns	800-HOLIDAY

---

sional movie reviewers, previewed *Tron,* a "breakthrough" movie employing extensive use of computer-generated graphics. The stock analysts were not impressed with the film's prospects and predicted that *Tron* would result in a drop in Disney's stock price. Because this was newsworthy business news, the story was widely broadcast on radio and TV and printed in newspapers. Disney, the marketer, had little influence on what was written or said by unidentified newswriters, editors, and producers. Another example of negative publicity is the publicity surrounding the Hooker Chemical Company when the Love Canal chemical dump story broke. The effects on the company were devastating.

Every recall of a popular product for repair or replacement makes the evening news and results in negative publicity. The makers of the Concorde plane, Firestone tires, and Ford automobiles spend millions of dollars to develop fine products. Bad publicity about defects, however minor, is an occupational hazard.

Marketers may take considerable time and effort in getting news releases and interviews with company spokespersons placed in newspapers and on broadcasts so that a favorable corporate organizational image may result. It often develops, however, that no publicity at all is better than negative publicity.

BRANDSTANDING

"Brandstanding" is a public relations technique that links a product to an event, an issue, or an idea of interest to consumers. According to Art Stevens, President of a public relations firm, marketers of products in the mature stage of the product life cycle frequently fail in efforts to attract new market segments to their products. Often there are no new segments for such goods as disposable diapers or denture adhesives. Further, management is often reluctant to invest sizable sums of money in an effort to increase product awareness since a majority of consumers are probably already very aware of the product.

These factors have contributed to the growth, in recent years, of "brandstanding," the seeking of ways to keep products before the public eye, and to have them viewed in a beneficial manner.

Brandstanding differs from simply seeking publicity for a product in that it does not focus on particular product features such as durability or low calorie content. In fact, it seldom features brand characteristics at all. It tries to link the product to an area of public concern, creating a rapport between the consumer and the product.

Clearly the best known brandstanding campaigns are sports-related. The Virginia Slims Tennis Tournament, the Volvo

Brandstanding

Classic, the Colgate Women's Games, and the Playtex Challenge provide examples. But other brandstanding efforts have also been successfully developed: the Kool Jazz Festival and the Ford College Cheerleading Championship are examples. Clearly the Ronald McDonald Houses for families of seriously ill children are not intended to sell hamburgers but to provide consumers with an image of McDonald's as a concerned and caring corpora-

tion willing to give its share for the public good. Hertz, trading on its "number one" image participates in a Number One program to honor top high school athletes in all 50 states. This program generates stories in almost every major newspaper in the country when Number One athletes are selected and honored at a banquet. One bonus to Hertz was a seven-minute segment on the popular "Good Morning, America" program.

Other brandstanding programs have linked Eagle Rare brand whiskey to campaigns to save the American bald eagle from extinction and Mazola Corn Oil to good health through its sponsorship of the New York Mini-marathon.

It is important to note that well-operated brandstanding efforts like these can support mature products on an ongoing, year-after-year basis. Brandstanding can be designed to meet specific marketing objectives. It can be scaled in size to local or national promotions. It can carry any message about a product including those which would not be conveyed by other promotional techniques. It blends well with other promotional efforts and has excellent media power. Its dollar effectiveness often exceeds other forms of promotion. "Consider brandstanding," says Stevens, "before sending your mature brand to a retirement home."

Source: Art Stevens, "Don't 'Retire' Mature Products, Promote Them with 'Brandstanding' PR Technique," *Marketing News,* March 18. 1983, pp. 2, 14.

EXHIBIT 18-1

Characteristics of the Four Elements of Promotion

	Personal Selling	**Advertising**	**Publicity**	**Sales Promotion**
Mode of communication	Direct and face-to-face	Indirect and nonpersonal	Indirect and nonpersonal	Indirect and nonpersonal
Regular and recurrent activity	Yes	Yes	No—only for newsworthy activity	No—short-term stimulation
Message flexibility	Personalized and tailored to prospect	Uniform and unvarying	Beyond marketer's control	Uniform and unvarying
Direct feedback	Yes	No	No	No
Control over message content	Yes	Yes	No	Yes
Sponsor identified	Yes	Yes	No	Yes
Cost per contact	High	Low to moderate	None	Varies

Sales Promotion. The phrase "sales promotion" is used to describe the last of the four major elements of promotion.

> **Sales promotion** can be defined as those promotional activities *other* than personal selling, advertising, and publicity that are intended to stimulate buyer purchases or dealer effectiveness in a specific time period.

Thus, special offers of free goods, coupon deals, display items for store use, training programs, in-store demonstrations, and trips to attractive vacation spots for top salespeople are examples of sales promotions. These offers are, in short, selling efforts not in the ordinary routine of things.[5] Although these promotions typically involve programs paid for by an identified sponsor, they are distinguished from advertising since they are *temporary* offers of a material reward to customers, salespeople, or sales prospects.

The intent of sales promotion programs is to amplify or bolster the advertising and personal selling messages offered by the organization. More often than not, the effects occur at the point of purchase.[6] Sales promotion is not a poor cousin of the other elements of promotion since American marketers spend millions of dollars on sales promotion, just as they do on advertising and personal selling.

A recent entertainment phenomenon provides an interesting and extremely effective example of a sales promotion. The bits of candy used to lure the extra-terrestrial space creature out of hiding in the movie *E.T.* were not the Mars

[5]Adapted from the Committee on Definitions, *Marketing Definitions: A Glossary of Marketing Terms,* American Marketing Association (Chicago, Ill., 1960), p. 20.

[6]Kenneth A. Longman, *Advertising* (New York, N.Y.: Harcourt Brace Jovanovich, 1971), p. 19.

Company's M & M's. Mars was unable to come to a proper agreement with the filmmakers. The candy used was the Hershey Company's Reese's Pieces. Lucky for Hershey. The success of what are called "tie-ins" was stupendous. Hershey gave away E.T. stickers with every bag of Reese's Pieces purchased in theaters. A child, or any other customer, who saved five of these could get a free set of stickers. E.T. T-shirts and posters could also be obtained. The result of this movie tie-in was that the candy's sales rose immensely—by 65 percent during the first month of the movie's release alone. All of this sales promotion contributed to publicity as well. For years to come, Reese's Pieces will be "E.T.'s candy" to many people.

Despite E.T.'s comparatively long-lasting appeal, the main purpose of such sales promotions is to achieve short-term objectives. Free samples or cents-off coupons may be utilized to encourage a first-time try of a product. The use of a premium offer or sweepstakes may stimulate interest in a product and be used to encourage off-season sales. Whether the sales promotion takes the form of a trade show, a consumer rebate, a point-of-purchase display for retailers, or pens and calendars for wholesalers to give away, the best sales promotions support and are coordinated with other promotional activities.

The characteristics of the four elements of promotion are summarized in Exhibit 18-1.

Packaging: The Illegitimate Element of Promotion

It is customary in marketing literature to discuss packaging as an element of the product portion of the marketing mix. This tradition has been followed in this textbook. However, it seems necessary to mention that packaging often has strong promotional aspects as well. This is particularly true in the case of consumer goods where the color or design of the packages is intended to attract attention. The package performs the function of protecting the product in storage and distribution, yet the promotional value of the package is undeniable.

Effective marketing requires that the promotional dimensions of a package, its graphics, shape, and so on, be remembered when a promotional strategy is being developed. The package should reflect the same unity of message communicated in other promotional methods.

THE COMMUNICATION PROCESS

Communication is the process of exchanging information and conveying meaning to others. But communication of even a single, apparently simple, idea is not easy. Effective promotional strategists need to understand this fact so they can carefully construct methods to get sales messages to customers and sales-related information to other organizations with which they must deal.

The goal of communication is a common understanding of the meaning of the information being transmitted. That is, the goal is to have the *receiver* of the information understand as closely as possible the meaning intended by the *sender* of the message. It is, for the most part, the send-er's responsibility to see that this goal is accomplished. In marketing, after all, the sender of an advertisement or other promotional message wants the intended receiver to be able to grasp the information offered and act upon it. In order for this goal to be accomplished, the sender, or message *source,* must understand the characteristics of the target audience, thus enabling the sender to tailor the message and choose the appropriate media to reach that audience. If necessary, the audience must have opportunities to supply the proper feedback.

One communication theorist described the matter of communication as "*who* says *what* to *whom* through *which channels* with *what ef-*

EXHIBIT 18-2

Basic Features of the Communication Process

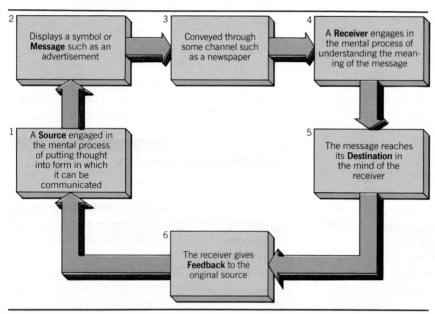

Source: G. Zaltman and M. Wallendorf, *Consumer Behavior* (New York: John Wiley & Sons, 1979), p. 216.

fect."[7] Each of these matters must be considered by the marketing communicator. Exhibit 18-2 summarizes in visual form these basic components of the communication process.[8] In considering the exhibit, remember that it describes all types of communication—words, gestures, pictures, and so on. Advertising is not the only medium that may be described by this communications model. The model may be used to describe a telephone sales call, a point-of-purchase display, or any promotional communication.

Encoding the Message

Evaluate the Marlboro advertisement shown in Exhibit 18.3 in terms of the model in Exhibit 18-2. *Who* says *what* to *whom*? The communica-

tion source (the advertiser) wishes to communicate the notion that Marlboro is a masculine cigarette. This idea is *what* is being symbolically displayed. It is the *message* of the advertisement. This is not an easy idea to get across, but the Marlboro advertisement effectively communicates this message. Excluding the small print included in the Surgeon General's warning, the advertisement has only a few words. The message is primarily visual and symbolic. In the situation portrayed, the rugged, masculine cowboy is shown to be a smoker of Marlboro cigarettes and to be out in "Marlboro Country." The sender's idea has been *encoded* by means of this picture even though Marlboro Country is an imaginary place. (At least, it does not appear on any maps.) **Encoding** is the process of translating the idea to be communicated into a symbolic message consisting of words, pictures, numbers, gestures, etc. This is a necessary step since with current technology there is no way to send an idea from one person to another in its raw or "pure" form.

---

[7]H.D. Lasswell, *Power and Personality* (New York, N.Y.: W.W. Norton, 1948).

[8]G. Zaltman and M. Wallendorf, *Consumer Behavior: Basic Findings and Management Implications* (New York, N.Y.: John Wiley & Sons, 1979), p. 216.

EXHIBIT   18-3

What Is Communicated in the Advertisement?

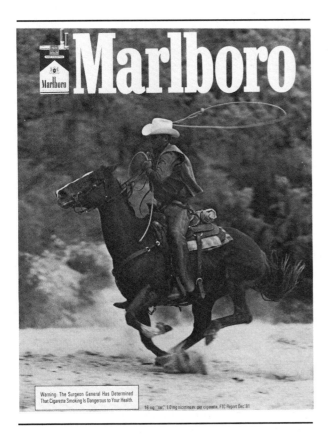

Warning: The Surgeon General Has Determined That Cigarette Smoking Is Dangerous to Your Health.

16 mg "tar," 1.0 mg nicotine av. per cigarette, FTC Report Dec '81

Transmitting the Message

Once the sender has created the message by encoding it into a transmittable form, it must be somehow conveyed to the receiver. It must be sent through a *channel* of communication, such as a magazine or other medium. Even our own casual conversations are sent in this way, though the medium is the less obvious one of vibrating vocal cords and movements of sound through air.

The message now arrives at the receiver via the channel of communication. Some receivers will be people who for one reason or another will never buy and smoke Marlboros. It is thus the sender's job to pick the medium that will reach a maximum number of target customers and a minimum number of non-target customers.

Decoding the Message

The message arrives and is viewed, heard, or otherwise sensed by the receiver. But the receiver must engage in the mental process of *decoding*. **Decoding** is the process by which the receiver *interprets* the meaning of the message. The difficulty encountered at this stage of the communication process is that receivers may interpret the message in different ways given their particular biases, backgrounds, and other characteristics. Nonsmokers may pass over the message entirely; anti-smokers may be angered by it; smokers satisfied with another brand may note the advertisement only casually. Some who see the advertisement may not "get it" at all. For whatever reason, the intended imagery may escape them completely.

Feedback

In many communications situations, the process will include **feedback,** the receiver's reaction to the message being communicated back to the source. In the case of the Marlboro advertisement, feedback may take the form of purchases of the product. If a new advertising program seems to result in an upswing in sales, the marketer has received positive feedback. A downturn in sales also tells the marketer something. So does a letter from an anti-smoking group condemning the advertisement.

In a personal selling situation, the feedback may be direct and immediate, as when the customer raises questions about the product or states why no purchase will be made. The great attraction of personal selling is that there can be a two-way conversation that will ensure greater understanding between the people involved. Such direct feedback cannot be developed when advertising is the medium in use.

Perfect Communication

Ideally, if perfect communication is to take place the message that is decoded and enters the mind of the receiver is exactly the same as the one the sender had in mind, encoded, and transmitted.[9] Communication is facilitated when the sender and the receiver have some *commonality in their psychological fields of experience.* In other words, if the sender and receiver share a common social background and have similar needs, it is more likely that they will similarly interpret the meaning of the words and symbols in the message. This perfect transmission is never possible, although in some familiar cases, such as that of the Marlboro advertisement, the sender may have developed messages that are decoded by the target audience in ways approximating what the sender had in mind.

It is likely—even inevitable—that any communication process will be interrupted or distorted by factors that communication experts term "noise." **Noise** is an interference or distraction that may disrupt any stage of the communication process. Noise may come in the form of conflicting messages, misunderstood terminology, inadequacies in the channel of communication, and so on. A radio advertisement might not be heard because of loud traffic noises outside of the car. In the Marlboro advertisement, the Surgeon General's warning is noise. The sources of noise may be external to the individual, such as traffic noises, or internal, such as daydreaming that interrupts concentration on a sales presentation. Many advertising messages cause people to think of a competing product. Brand loyalties and past learning may be internal distractions that interfere with the decoding process.

All of this points to the importance of the marketer's understanding of how communication takes place. *Message content* is not the only important factor in promotion. The model in Exhibit 18-2 shows us the steps in the communication process. Each step is another spot where something can go wrong. If the source is wrong, if the intended message was encoded poorly, if the wrong transmission medium is chosen, if the decoding process does not work properly be-

[9]William M. Kincaid, Jr., *Promotion: Products, Services, and Ideas* (Columbus, Ohio: Charles E. Merrill, 1981), p. 25.

SYMBOLS COMMUNICATE

Although language is perhaps the crowning accomplishment of the human race, it is nevertheless hopelessly inadequate to express our emotional human nature. Language barely touches the world of feeling at certain marginal points with names for some vague and crude states, and that is all. There are just no words to express the various nuances of sensation and feeling, to express such things as mood and aesthetic impression. Try to describe to a child how a strawberry tastes as compared to a raspberry, how a carnation smells, why it is pleasurable to dance, what a pretty girl looks like.

There are countless areas where the precise meanings and definitions have to be conveyed by nonverbal, nonrational symbols. A drawing, a photograph, a pantomime of gestures, such as the traffic policeman or the orchestra conductor uses—these are everyday obvious examples of nonverbal symbols. We determine the feelings and inner thinking of other people almost entirely from facial expressions; from movements of the body, such as the hands; from the general state of excitement such as weeping, blushing, or anger; from tone of voice; and from involuntary exclamations and sounds such as whistling or singing.

Source: From Pierre Martineau, *Motivation in Advertising* (New York: McGraw-Hill, 1957), p. 134. Used with permission.

cause of distractions, if the receiver lacks experience with the product, or if the receiver has a poor vocabulary, the message transmittal system cannot work well. The marketer's problem is to perform each step carefully along the way while trying to reduce the chance of ineffectiveness.

In short, the effective communication comes from the right *who* saying the right *what* to the right *whom* through the right *channel.*

THE HIERARCHY OF COMMUNICATION EFFECTS

Mrs. Olsen has extolled the virtues of Folgers' mountain grown coffee hundreds, maybe thousands, of times. Mr. Whipple has made nearly 500 different advertisements for Charmin toilet tissue. Why are there so many commercials for the same product? Creativity aside, the major reason is that a single communication, no matter how cleverly designed and implemented, may not be enough to persuade a customer to change an attitude or to make a purchase. Promotion, as a general rule, becomes more effective with repetition. Promotion usually seeks to change people, and people tend to change very slowly. The habits and beliefs developed over long periods of time will not be altered quickly by just a few messages. The presentation of a message may be varied, as in the Charmin example, because the effectiveness of a promotion may wear out as the repetitive presentation becomes boring. Marketers have come to expect various responses to their communications. To understand the various effects that promotion may bring about, the promotion process will be discussed as a "staircase," or a series of steps.

The Promotion "Staircase"

Conceive of promotion as a force that moves people up a series of steps.[10] This "staircase" is shown in Exhibit 18-4.

1 Near the bottom of the steps stand potential purchasers who are completely *unaware of the existence* of the product or service in question.

2 Closer to purchasing, but still a long way from the cash register, are those who are merely *aware of its existence*.

3 Up one step are prospects who *know what the product has to offer*.

4 Still closer to purchasing are those who have favorable attitudes toward the product—those who *like the product*.

5 Those whose favorable attitudes have developed to the point of *preference* over all other possibilities are up still another step.

6 Even closer to purchasing are consumers who couple preference with a desire to buy and the *conviction* that the purchase would be wise.

7 Finally, of course, is the step which translates this attitude into actual *purchase*.

Thus, consumers may move through a seven-step hierarchy, ranging from total ignorance of a product's existence to purchase of that product.[11] Eventually, as we saw earlier in this book, a satisfied or *reinforced* customer is the result when the purchase decision leads to a reward.

The hierarchy model shown in Exhibit 18-4 suggests two concepts to marketers. One concept is that promotion can be used to induce buyers to change—that is, to move up the staircase steps. The other is that particular buyers may already be at different stages along the staircase. Therefore, advertisers for a totally new product, such as the home video recorder was just a few years ago, face a different set of communication problems than do marketers of fluoride toothpaste. The toothpaste communication need not include an extensive discussion of the fact that fluoride helps to prevent cavities. Most consumers are already aware of fluoride's benefits. On the other hand, the seller of a near-revolutionary product may need to devote considerable effort to explaining what that product is, how it works, and even *that* it works.

The stair-step diagram in Exhibit 18-4 suggests that the organization seeking to create an effective promotional message will have to begin with one of marketing's most basic rules of

---

[10]R.J. Lavidge and G.A. Steiner, "A Model for Predictive Measure of Advertising Effectiveness," *Journal of Marketing* (October 1961), pp. 59–60.

[11]The hierarchy of communication effects model has been portrayed in several other forms. A common one is as follows: awareness, interest, evaluation, trial, adoption and attention, interest, desire, action (A.I.D.A).

EXHIBIT 18-4

Promotion Moves Customers to Ascend These Steps

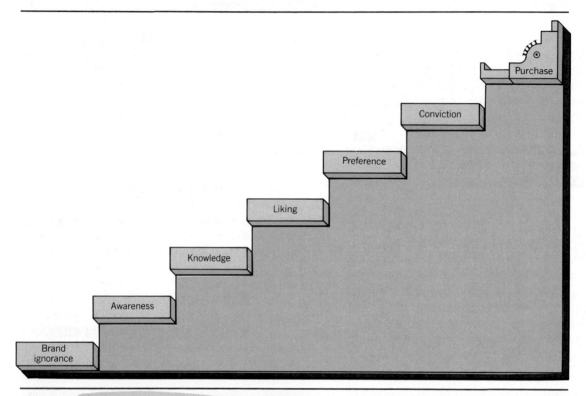

action—identification of the target market or, in this case, the target audience.

As discussed earlier, the whole communications process must be built around the intended receiver of the message. A key question, then, is what is the target audience's psychological state? If the marketing organization is attempting to influence those who are currently "on" the *awareness* and *knowledge* steps, a primary promotional objective will be to provide information of a factual sort. According to many petroleum companies, most citizens are totally unaware of how oil company revenues are utilized. Some of these companies spend a good portion of their advertising budgets in an effort to inform people of the true nature of the oil business. They demonstrate that a large portion of revenues are spent on additional explorations or on the development of products that enhance the lives of consumers.

Appealing to consumers on the *liking* or *preference* steps calls for promotional messages aimed at encouraging these favorable feelings toward the good or service offered. General Electric's "Go Dry" advertisement shown in Exhibit 18-5 exemplifies this. The target customer in this case already knows what a hair dryer is, and probably knows that GE is a respected manufacturer of appliances. Thus, the advertisement stresses emotional feelings toward the product. Similarly, advertisements for many soft drinks, beers, and wines accent the fun or sophistication associated with the drinks. Some wine advertisements, interestingly enough, stress *avoidance* of an emotion, that of embarrassment. Thus "Blue Nun" goes with "everything," permitting the customer to avoid buying the "wrong" wine.

Target customers who are on the *conviction* step of the model are very close to action, although they may need a little shove to get them to act. A bit of encouragement may be all that is

EXHIBIT 18-5

An Example of How Promotion Influences Our Emotional Mood Toward a Product.

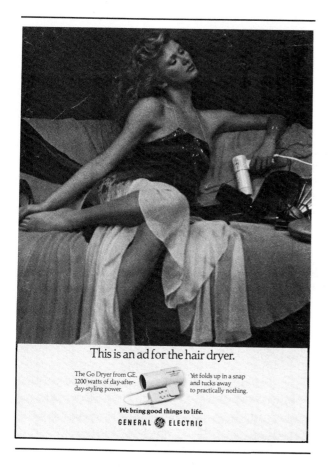

This is an ad for the hair dryer.

The Go Dryer from GE. 1200 watts of day-after-day-styling power.

Yet folds up in a snap and tucks away to practically nothing.

We bring good things to life.
GENERAL ⊗ ELECTRIC

required. Notification that now is the time to buy, or that prices may go up, or that a two-for-one coupon is available may motivate the consumer to move up the staircase to the final step, the

purchase. As we've seen in Chapter 8, this is not the end of the line. The marketer may continue to use promotional messages to reinforce the buyer in the belief that a good buy was made or, later on, to remind the customer of the product and its value or effectiveness.

Sophisticated consumer behavior research suggests that some consumer purchasing decisions, especially those when consumers have low involvement in the product, do not follow the steps in the hierarchy of communication effects.[12] Nevertheless, this approach is useful in understanding how many promotions work.

Promotional Messages at Several Levels

For convenience sake, promotional communications have been discussed as if they came from one source or one marketer. In fact, within any promotional campaign, messages may be found at several levels. Promotions may include *national* or *manufacturer* advertising in support of the manufacturer's own product or they may involve *local* advertising by retailers and wholesalers. As demonstrated in Exhibit 18-6,[13] this occurs even when the product involved is as common as soap.

Notice that Exhibit 18-6 illustrates personal selling at two levels. Additional personal communication takes place as customer feedback. The consumer not only expresses satisfaction to supermarket personnel (who, ideally, pass this information on to suppliers), but may also express opinions directly to the manufacturer. Information about purchase behavior, in the aggregate, may also be provided to marketing researchers.

THE PROMOTIONAL MIX

As has been suggested in the discussion to this point, the effective marketer must seek to develop an integration of all the elements of pro- motion—advertising, publicity, personal selling, and sales promotion. This integration is termed a **promotional mix** or a **promotion mix.** Such a pro-

---

[12]See for example Michael L. Ray, *Marketing Communications and the Hierarchy of Effects* (Cambridge, Mass.: Marketing Science Institute, 1973).

[13]Adapted from testimony to the Federal Trade Commission (1971) by A.A. Acheandbaum, Senior Vice President and Director of Advertising, J. Walter Thompson and Co.

EXHIBIT 18-6

A Packaged Goods Transaction—A Soap Sale

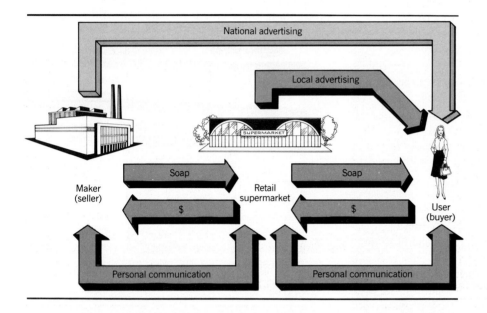

gram ideally would be planned to meet the information requirements of all target customers. That is, the mix is not ordinarily designed to satisfy only the new buyer *or* only the regular buyer. Some elements of the mix may be aimed at the target customer at a lower stage of the communication needs hierarchy, while others are aimed at potential customers near the top of the staircase. Even marketers of innovative, new products, such as the personal or home computer, must keep this in mind: Although some customers are first-time buyers of this product, there *are* some people who are owners of two or three computers. Potential buyers are to be found at all steps of the hierarchy staircase.

Suppose you are interested in the purchase of a personal computer. You have probably advanced beyond total brand ignorance and are increasingly aware of the different brands and their advertised benefits. Your interest in the product has led you to pay more attention to computer advertising and to magazine stories about computers. Newspaper columnists may be writing about their own home computers (pub-

licity). Sales promotions, such as the offer of a free software package or lessons on computer use, may ultimately bring you into the store where personal selling communicates to you the benefits associated with a particular brand of computer. A decision is then made to buy a particular brand, be it Apple, IBM, or Atari.

Which aspect of the promotional mix brought you to the decision to buy the brand of computer you chose? Perhaps one factor, such as the expertise of the salesperson, was a major influence, but the fact is that all elements of the mix did their parts in bringing about the sale. Each had a role to play and a function to perform. In this case, advertising proved effective in generating awareness and, perhaps, positive attitudes toward the product. The sales promotion offer of software led to the decision to visit the store. Personal selling proved, as it usually does, most effective in consummating the sale. This is because only the flexibility which personal selling can provide permitted the product to be "altered" to meet particular customer requirements. The potential buyer may need a program that balances checkbooks so the salesman "throws that in." The customer may wonder if he or she can learn to work the computer properly, so the salesperson either uses assurances that anyone can work it or informs the customer that classroom instruction on the machine's operation will be available in the evenings.

Computers are complex and expensive products, so personal selling is important in their promotional mix. Other product sales are well served by advertising's ability to reach a mass audience. Bic disposable pens and lighters have been sold around the world with personal selling contributing comparatively little to their success at the consumer level.

Certain target customers may be best attracted by sales promotions aimed at them specifically. Ford Motor Company has successfully used sales promotions to increase the numbers of women visiting Ford showrooms. Showroom parties at which invited female customers sip wine, receive such items as bracelets as gifts, and inspect new car models in a no-pressure setting were instituted after Ford planners noted that more than 25 percent of U.S. households are headed by women. The goal is to reduce feelings of intimidation that the technical aspects of cars may cause these particular women.[14]

The General Relationships Within the Mix

Exhibit 18-7 illustrates, in general terms, the relationship between advertising and personal selling at the pre-transaction, transaction, and post-transaction stages of the buying process.[15] The transaction may be roughly defined as that period in which the exchange agreement or the negotiation of the terms of sale are finalized.

[14]"Wine, Baubles, and Glamour Are Used to Help Lure Female Consumers to Ford's Showrooms," *Marketing News,* August 6, 1982, p. 1.

[15]Based on William Lazer, *Marketing Management: A Systems Perspective* (New York: John Wiley & Sons, 1971), p. 379, which was adapted from H.C. Cash and W.J.E. Crissy, *The Salesman's Role in Marketing, The Psychology of Selling* (Vol. 12, 1965), p. 68.

EXHIBIT 18-7

The Mix of Advertising and Personal Selling

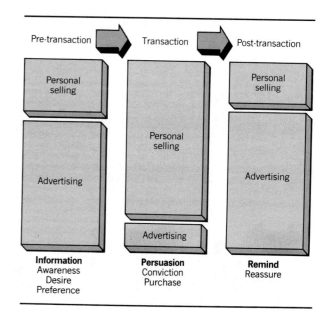

This relationship is strongly influenced by the many forces that contribute to the purchase decision. The characteristics of the marketplace, the state of the economy, the nature of the product, and the seller's overall marketing strategy vary from case to case, but some general statements may be made about the roles advertising and personal selling play at each stage. Exhibit 18-8 shows how the roles of personal selling and advertising decrease and increase in significance as products vary from complex industrial goods to consumer goods that are frequently repurchased.

Commonly, there is a strong interaction of the variables within the promotional mix. While consumers are strongly influenced by the advertising for cold remedies, in-store displays, packaging, sales promotions aimed at retailers, and the activities of a personal salesforce may all play some role in the ultimate purchase of a given medicine. The interaction of promotion mix variables is more obvious in the organizational market. Here advertising alone is unlikely

---

EXHIBIT 18-8

The Spectrum of Relationships That Exists Between Advertising and Personal Selling

---

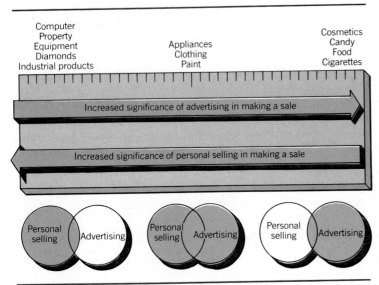

Source: William Lazer, *Marketing Management: A Systems Perspective* (New York: John Wiley & Sons, 1971), p. 378.

to sell many products, yet it performs an important function in supplementing and supporting the personal sales force. The McGraw-Hill Publishing Company's advertisements have been illustrating this fact for years. Their advertisement suggests that the salesperson will get nowhere at all with a tough industrial buyer unless the buyer is at least familiar with the salesperson's company or line of goods. The moral is that companies dealing with organizational buyers had better advertise in McGraw-Hill business publications.

PROMOTIONAL STRATEGIES

Since promotion is one of the four major elements of the marketing mix, effective marketing requires that promotion strategies be carefully formulated to fit within the organization's overall marketing strategy. If, for example, marketing research shows that middle-aged men believe that they should buy more life insurance, but feel that the price is prohibitively high, insurance companies clearly need to develop a marketing mix that can appeal to these target customers. A new type of insurance policy could be developed (*product*), sold by agents who are willing to visit clients in their home, office, or other convenient spot (*place*), and offered at a lower-than-expected price or on some sort of easy payment basis (*price*). Promotion would then be used to make the target market aware of the new insurance plan, its price, and its convenience. Advertising or promotion via mail or telephone could be used to generate lists of likely buyers or leads. Personal selling, another aspect of the promotional mix, could then be used to explain and sell the new insurance option.

The number of promotional strategies avail-

"I don't know who you are.

I don't know your company.

I don't know your company's product.

I don't know what your company stands for.

I don't know your company's customers.

I don't know your company's record.

I don't know your company's reputation.

Now–what was it you wanted to sell me?"

MORAL: Sales start **before** your salesman calls–with business publication advertising.

McGRAW-HILL MAGAZINES
BUSINESS • PROFESSIONAL • TECHNICAL

Advertising and personal selling go hand in hand.

able to an organization is limited mainly by the creativity of the individuals responsible for developing them. However, some common and quite basic strategies are widely practiced. Some of these will be discussed below.

Push and Pull Strategies

The prime target of a promotional strategy may be either the ultimate consumer or a member of the distribution channel. Using this as a basis for classification, the basic strategies of *push* (pushing) and *pull* (pulling) have developed. There is no single strategy of either type but, in general, they are described as follows. A **push strategy** is one that emphasizes personal selling, advertising, and other promotional efforts aimed at members of the channel of distribution. Thus,

the manufacturer of a product heavily promotes that product to wholesalers or other dealers. The wholesalers then promote the product heavily to retailers who, in turn, direct their selling efforts to consumers. Not infrequently, the wholesalers and retailers are offered strong price incentives or discounts as part of this process. The term "push" comes from the fact that the manufacturer, with the help of other channel members, pushes the product through the channel of distribution. The push strategy may be thought of as a step-by-step approach to promotion, with each channel member organizing the promotional efforts necessary to reach the channel member next in line (Exhibit 18-9).

An alternative strategy, the pull strategy, takes an opposite approach. Under the **pull strategy,** the manufacturer attempts to stimulate demand for the product by promotional efforts aimed at the consumer or buyer located at the other end of the channel of distribution. The goal is to generate demand at the retail level in the belief that such demand will encourage retailers and wholesalers to stock the product. Each channel member will "pass back" the demand. In other words, the demand at the buyer end of the channel pulls the product through the channels of distribution.

Consumers are most familiar with the pull strategy, since promotional messages that say, in effect, "go to the store and ask for this" are encountered so frequently. However, a moment's thought suggests products sold to us by the push approach. An imported watch or an expensive perfume might be purchased because the salesperson mentioned that these products are "the best" even though the brand names are totally unfamiliar. The push strategy suggests a step-by-step promotional effort. The pull strategy attempts to develop ultimate buyer demand and a smooth flow of products from the manufacturer to the buyer via cooperative middlemen.

Combination Strategies

Clearly, a marketing organization would not limit itself to using only a push or only a pull strategy. Buyers of many products, such as clothing and

EXHIBIT 18-9

Flow of Promotional Dollars and Effort: Push, Pull, and Combination Strategies

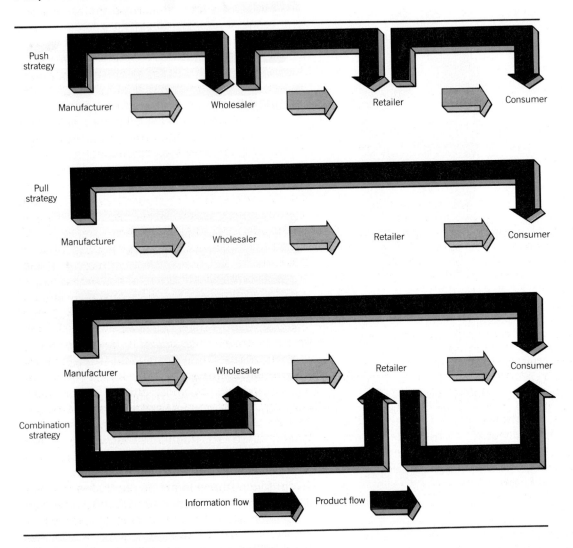

automobiles, receive promotional messages from manufacturers *and* from retailers. Marketers may orchestrate a combination of approaches, relying on elements of each strategy type. Indeed, each channel member, including the wholesaler, is a marketer who could use push or pull strategies, or some combination of these.

Push or Pull: Which Strategy to Emphasize?

As with most matters of choice, the "correct" promotional strategy to select as appropriate to a particular marketing problem depends on the situation in which the marketer must operate. If the marketing strategist has limited funds, paying for advertisements on the Super Bowl broad-

A COMBINATION STRATEGY

Effective marketing plans generally make use of both push and pull strategies. Consider these remarks by Dr. Pepper executives.

"We are a sales company."

"The Dr. Pepper bottler is the key to our success."

"No matter how good a job we do, (consumers) can't get Dr. Pepper unless you (bottlers) have made the sale to the retailer."

These comments indicate that a push strategy is being used to motivate local salesmen. Yet Dr. Pepper commercials are frequently seen on television, in magazines and newspapers, and heard on radio. These are obviously aimed at pulling the product through the channels of distribution by exciting consumer demand for the soft drink. Here the combination strategy employed acknowledges that the makers of Dr. Pepper have more than one type of customer. Thus, the promotional campaign has several parts. A portion of it is geared toward channel members and has the promotional objective of encouraging aggressive promotion of Dr. Pepper by local bottlers. Another portion is intended to generate purchases by ultimate consumers and the development of favorable consumer attitudes toward the product.

Source: Statements made by Dr. Pepper's Chairman of the Board at stockholders meeting (1980) and Vice President of Marketing at National Bottlers meeting (1979) as quoted in Thomas E. Barry, "The Dr. Pepper Company" in W.G. Zikmund, W. Lundstrom, and D. Sciglimpaglia, *Cases in Marketing Research* (Hinsdale, Ill.: Dryden Press, 1982), p. 131.

The choice of a strategy may also depend on where the product is in its life cycle. A product just beginning its product life cycle may be better served by a pushing strategy aimed at attracting wholesalers and retailers so that a distribution network can be established. Later, if the product catches on, the popularity of the product can be maintained by the pulling strategy of advertising directly to consumers. If the popularity can be thus maintained, dealers will carry the product because of its consumer appeal.

Many other situation-specific variables can be seen as affecting the appropriateness of the emphasis given to these promotional strategies. Goods sold primarily to housing contractors are promoted to those contractors and to building-supply dealers. This is because these dealers are seen by house buyers as the experts to depend on for advice. However, in a time of sharply rising home heating bills, some makers of windows, doors, and insulation advertise directly to home buyers and owners in attempts to encourage these ultimate consumers to specify and insist on particular brands of insulation, insulated doors, and triple-track windows. In this case, the manufacturer—marketers have decided to move somewhat to a pull strategy because the environment in which they operated changed when consumers became conscious of heating fuel costs. Yet they must still promote their products to contractors and other channel members so that these dealers will react positively to consumer inquiries about products advertised in non-trade publications or on television.

Similar situations are found in the international marketplace. Sony can afford to advertise directly to the American consumer, even when the product being advertised is a new one, because Sony's financial resources and well-respected name permit it to use a pulling strategy. Other Asian electronics firms are not so fortunate and must sell their products to American dealers via push strategies. Dealers, in turn, may sell these brands to consumers with the assurance that "this is as good as Sony, but a lot cheaper."

Recognize, however, that even a firm that seems eminently able to use a pull-type strategy

cast, or using any other high-cost medium, is essentially out of the question. The funds should probably be used in a pushing method to raise margins offered to dealers or to provide them with some other direct incentive to stock and sell the product in question.

still must have its products in the stores when consumers go looking for them. Some push-style methods may be necessary to assure this.

As consumers, we might tend to think that the pull strategy is better, or at least more ethical, than the push strategy. Shouldn't we, for example, be able to see advertisements and then choose for ourselves what we wish to buy? Do we want merchandise "pushed" at us? Unfortunately, even the term "push" has a bad connotation. Despite this, there are certain situations in which a push strategy makes a great deal of sense. For example, operators of a sports stadium may feel that they have no particular reason to sell Armour rather than Tobin hot dogs, or to offer Budweiser rather than Pabst beer. They may be correct in assuming that the products are similar enough that people attending sports events will buy hot dogs and beer regardless of the brands offered. What can a marketer of such products do? It is unreasonable to think sports fans will boycott their favorite teams until the stadium sells Pabst, and unlikely that the fans will refuse to buy non-Armour hot dogs at the stadium. Thus, the marketers of these products adopt a push rather than a pull strategy. In cases like this, aggressive personal selling, coupled with excellent price deals, is the general practice.

If the push strategy still seems a bit distasteful, consider this. As businesspeople or as marketers in the non-profit sector, you will have a certain promotional budget with which to work. From a strictly practical point of view, it does not matter if available dollars are spent on promotion in a pulling strategy or on a pushing strategy. The promotional dollars remain the same no matter how they are assigned. It is the marketer's job to assign the available advertising dollars to the most effective promotional means possible.

Again, there is no one correct promotional strategy, be it push, pull, or a combination of these, until the product, its stage in the product life cycle, the firm's financial situation, and the environment in which the marketer operates are fully and correctly assessed.

INSURANCE: DON'T CALL ME, I'LL CALL YOU

Life insurance salespeople are often stereotyped as hard sell individuals, but we should consider the selling situations in which they find themselves before we condemn them. First, the insurance business is very competitive and may necessitate a hard sell promotional scheme to even be recognized by potential customers. Second, most consumers really do not want insurance. This is not to suggest that insurance companies attempt to sell products that are not good for buyers or are in other ways undesirable. It is simply a fact that insurance customers do not want to think about their inevitable deaths or what will happen to their families once they are gone. Third, even otherwise rational people somehow believe that while other people have to die eventually, they do not.

In such a situation, the hard sell may be necessary to effect a sale, even though the customer is being sold a useful and valuable policy that can provide many considerable benefits.

Hard Sell and Soft Sell Strategies

Some marketers may think of the *hard sell* and the *soft sell* as sales techniques rather than strategies. However, they can also be termed promotional strategies in as much as some companies employ them on a long-term, continuing basis.

Proponents of the **hard sell** believe aggressive persuasion of individuals is the best way for consumers to learn the true benefits of the product. Sales personnel believe the repetitive promotional efforts emphasizing the same benefits over and over will ultimately be effective. They attempt to prove to prospective buyers that they need the product offered. Sales personnel do not accept "No" for an answer under a hard sell strategy.

Car dealerships and insurance salespeople are frequently seen as proponents of the hard sell. But they are not the only proponents of the hard sell promotional strategy. Many retail clerks, manufacturers, wholesalers, and creators of television commercials also use this approach. K-Tel, the television purveyor of records, vegetable choppers, and pocket-sized fishing rods, has become nationally recognized for hard sell commercials. While some consumers bemoan the repetitive nature of many radio and TV commercials, the advertisers of certain brands of kitchen knives and vegetable choppers believe that emphasis of the same benefits, over and over again, will ultimately be effective.

The hard sell promotional strategy, whether adopted by a TV advertiser or a salesperson, in essence makes "No" an unacceptable response. Comments like "buy now," "you can't afford to pass this up," "you will need this eventually," and "pay me now or pay me later" are typical of this never-say-die promotional strategy.

Actually, few marketers can totally avoid the hard sell strategy. Makers of extremely popular products holding large shares of markets may be able to advertise their products to consumers simply by showing happy people using the items. Campbell's soups and Coca-Cola are advertised on TV in this manner. Even these products, however, are also promoted more aggressively by salespeople calling on retailers, displays in

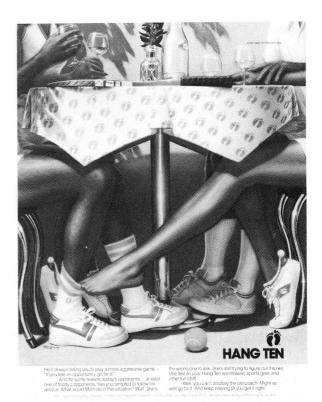

HANG TEN

Nonverbal symbols may be an important part of the promotional message in the soft sell. What is the nonverbal message in this advertisement?

supermarkets, cent-off deals, and coupons in newspapers. The levels of competition fostered by our economic system make a total reliance on soft sell approaches almost impossible.

The Marlboro advertisement previously discussed is an example of the soft sell strategy. Explaining the *soft sell* is more difficult than explaining the *hard sell*, not only because the communications and sales messages are more subtle but because the soft sell takes many forms. The soft sell is not as blatant or conspicuous in the direct asking for the order. While repetition may be utilized, there are subtle variations in the way things are communicated. The only way to define the **soft sell** is to say it is not the hard sell. Unfortunately, the difference between the hard and soft sell is not a black-and-white issue but one in that gray area where the difference is in the eye of the beholder.

Determining whether a promotional strategy is a hard or soft sell one is largely a matter of perception. Many consumers feel that advertising by dentists and lawyers, including the mentioning of prices for specific services, is simply informing the public of facts buyers have a clear right to know. Lawyers and dentists who do not advertise in this manner often state that the hard sell tactics of their more publicized colleagues give "their profession" a bad name.

PROMOTIONAL CAMPAIGNS

Throughout this chapter, the individual aspects of promotion have been considered, and the fact that the parts of the promotional effort must fit together and complement each other has been stressed. A trade magazine mailed to owners of automobile muffler shops promotes itself to its readers as the "voice" of the muffler industry. It also promotes itself to potential buyers of advertising space as *the* place to advertise to reach target customers. The magazine's management may sponsor race cars or make awards to outstanding people in the muffler business to build up the magazine's image as a major force in the trade. All of these activities fit together into a *unity of presentation* that could be called the magazine publisher's total promotional effort or promotional mix.

Military terminology is commonly used in football and business. This is seen once again in the term *promotional campaign*. A *promotional campaign* is a part or portion of a firm's promotion mix just as a military campaign is a portion of a total war effort. Thus, a **promotional campaign** is a series of promotional activities with a particular objective.

The phrase *particular objective* is important here since it is this objective that indicates the goal to be reached. The campaign must be constructed to achieve that goal. The task of introducing a new product requires a promotional campaign considerably different from that intended to increase the sales of an established or widely recognized product. Comparing advertisements for Prince tennis rackets during the product-launch stage of the product life cycle with those in the product's mature stage shows just how different these campaigns may be.

Because most products are in the mature stage of their product life cycles, this section of the text focuses primarily on promotional campaigns utilized for these products. However, aspects of these strategies could also be applied to product introductions or to products in the growth stage of the life cycle.

Three Promotional Approaches

There are three major approaches to developing a promotional campaign for a mature product. These are: image building, product differentiation, and positioning.

Image Building. Buyers frequently prefer one product or brand over another because of its symbolic meaning or brand image. As we have seen, products are often purchased or avoided not because of what they cost or how they work, but because of what they say about the buyer—user. The product image or brand image is an individual's net impression of "what the product or brand is all about." It is the symbolic value associated with the product. Products and brands of products often symbolize the user's personality or life-style. Marketers, who sell brands of products, are properly concerned with this symbolic value or "image." Thus, many promotional campaigns are aimed at **image building.**

Over the years, General Mills has established a strong image for its Betty Crocker brand. The image is one of dependability and honesty—valuable images for a food product. There never was a real Betty Crocker, but the General Mills products were good and reliable, just like Betty herself. Note that regardless of what some marketing critics might think, *no* promotional campaign could have imparted this good image to Betty Crocker products unless the products were in fact wholesome and trustworthy.

Despite Betty Crocker's long-lasting success, recent research showed that increasing numbers of consumers were viewing the product line as being somewhat out-of-date. The long-term popularity of the product itself contributed to a potentially undesirable image—the image that Betty Crocker products were old-fashioned, old-standby products, good but not very modern or exciting. General Mills management set out to build a new image that might appeal to the younger buyers who were replacing those who had grown old with Betty. The company altered the old-fashioned image by modifying product lines to include different products not offered by competitors. Although Betty Crocker's picture had been changed over the years to reflect new dress and hair styles, she was again given a fresh appearance. General Mills products were promoted as modern and innovative. Advertising reflected the emotional nature of dessert making with the ''Bake Someone Happy'' musical theme, and pictures which suggested that making a good dessert is a way to show others that you ''care.''

General Mills did not invent the idea that dessert preparation, especially cake-baking, is an important duty of a good homemaker, but it is useful to associate Betty Crocker products with that notion. After all, desserts, especially Betty Crocker desserts, have long been associated with happy family moments.[16] The image-building promotional campaign demonstrated to target consumers that Betty Crocker products are modern and that the company understood both homemakers and the importance of des-

---

[16]Stanley E. Cohen, ''New Betty Crocker Ads Star in Briefing for FTC,'' *Advertising Age,* May 14, 1979, p. 6.

sert. Betty Crocker products were shown to fit into a modern life-style.

In general, image-building promotional campaigns do not focus on product features, but emphasize creating impressions. The Marlboro campaign is a classic example. These may be impressions of status, sexuality, masculinity, femininity, reliability, or some other aspect of the brand's character thought to be alluring to target customers. Note, for example, that most advertisements for perfumes (e.g., Chanel No. 5 and Calandre) and jeans (Calvin Klein and Jordache) concentrate almost entirely on these characteristics. However, in noticing these promotional campaigns, do not forget the other less obvious marketing activities that contribute to the success of these efforts.

Product Differentiation. A promotional campaign aimed at developing a degree of **product differentiation** focuses on some dimension of the product that competing products do not enjoy or that accents in some way the solution of a customer problem through usage of the product. As gasoline prices rose during the 1970s, some automobile manufacturers began to stress strongly their products' miles per gallon (mpg) benefits. Promotional campaigns emphasized mpg. Other manufacturers noted that buyers feared running out of gas in a remote spot where no gas stations were open. They advertised cars with larger gas tanks. Their promotional campaigns emphasized the number of miles per tankful rather than miles per gallon. The focus on promotional campaigns for these products was on the *product,* not its image or price. Salespeople and dealer promotions stressed mileage. Booklets were produced showing customers the benefits of higher mpg and suggesting ways to achieve that goal through better driving habits and auto upkeep after the car was purchased. All portions of the promotional campaign focused on the product's differential advantage.

Product differentiation and its related promotional efforts often take the form of the **unique selling proposition** (USP). As the name of this concept suggests, the basic idea of the USP is to identify and promote an aspect of the prod-

WHEN SHOULD <u>YOU</u> TAKE THE VISINE TEST?

AFTER SUN AND SWIM

AFTER WAKE-UP

AFTER PARTYING

AFTER STUDYING

If you've seen the Visine® Test on television, then you've seen people just like you discover how Visine really gets the red out. Visine, with tetrahydrozoline, soothes itching, cools burning and gets the red out. So any time minor irritation makes your eyes sore and red...put Visine to the test and see for yourself. Visine gets the red out.

TAKE THE VISINE TEST AND SEE FOR YOURSELF.

c 1980, Pfizer Inc.

Visine: A unique selling proposition.

uct that the competition does not offer or, due to patents or other reasons, cannot easily offer. Visine eyedrops were the first to "get the red out" using tetrahydrozoline. Initially, Murine, the former market leader, had no such ingredient and no such benefit. Although Murine eventually did come out with its own similar product, Visine had successfully exploited the unique aspect of its product and made it a successfully promoted market offering.

Coors beer is portrayed as a unique product that offers advantages many brewers apparently do not see as matchable. Coors "Beats the heat that kills beer taste" and is aged "at the brewery, not at the store." The special handling required by Coors is a unique selling proposition around which to build a promotional campaign.

The USP often forms the foundation of promotional campaigns whose goal is product differentiation. There is only one soft drink that allows you to "Be a Pepper." There is only one orange soda that bears the familiar orange juice name of Sunkist. Chrysler Corporation, for good or for bad, has stressed "Chrysler engineering" for decades. These are all unique claims not made by the competition. The USP tells buyers that if they buy these products, they will receive a specific, exclusive benefit.[17]

Generally, products are not truly unique, especially from a performance point of view. Yet a parity product (one with ingredients nearly identical to competitors' brands) like Tylenol has been promoted as if it was special. Products have aspects other than the strictly functional ones that may be promoted as effectively as the functional features. Elmer Wheeler illustrated this fact in the classic statement "Don't sell the steak, sell the sizzle."[18] This is not to suggest that the point stressed in the unique selling proposition does not have to be meaningful to the potential buyer. It is possible to "sell the sizzle" only if the sizzle *means* something to the buyer. A USP buyers do not care about is of no use in effective marketing.

Positioning. *Business Week* positions itself as giving a complete, well-thought-out perspective to business news compared to the instant news of the *Wall Street Journal*. Jeep Wagoneer positions itself in a special automotive class—

---

[17]Rosser Reeves, *Reality in Advertising* (New York: Alfred A. Knopf, 1961), pp. 47–48.

[18]Elmer Wheeler, *Tested Sentences That Sell* (Englewood Cliffs, N.J.: Prentice-Hall, 1937).

★★★★★.

First Class excellence is the hallmark of TWA's Royal Ambassador Service to Europe and the Middle East.

From the very start of your trip, you'll be treated to the highest standards of personalized service.

In major airports, you'll find a special Royal Ambassador desk to speed you through check-in. And a special lounge to relax in before your flight. You'll even receive our Priority Baggage™ service to ensure that your luggage is first off the plane when you arrive.

★★★★★
Gourmet dining.

Once our transatlantic flights take off each evening, you'll be leisurely wined and dined.

You'll whet your appetite with champagne and caviar. Tempt it with an entrée like Chateaubriand. And sate it with a fine ripe cheese or deliciously rich dessert.

You'll satisfy your thirst with a vintage wine from France or California. Or with a selection from our cognac and fine liqueurs.

★★★★★
Room with a view.

After dining, you'll be ready to relax in comfort in your First Class Sleeper-Seat™.

Just settle back. The seat stretches out with you for a restful sleep under the stars all the way across the Atlantic. You'll awake refreshed—ready to face the new day.

So call your travel agent, corporate travel department, or TWA.

And experience for yourself the five-star quality that gives TWA's Royal Ambassador Service the mark of excellence.

You're going to like us TWA

The Total Campaign

As we have mentioned many times before, an organization's marketing effort must be carefully coordinated so that each promotional element supports and complements the others—so that each is concentrated on the same target market. This is especially true for the promotional campaign since this portion of the marketing effort is most obvious to the target consumer.

Aspects of a promotional campaign for Trans World Airlines (TWA) are illustrated in this color section. Notice that the corporate logo ("You're going to like us") stressing service and the Getaway themes are prominent throughout the advertising. The red and white that appears on the airplanes is also reflected in all trademarks and designs shown on promotional items, ranging from timetables to containers for cargo. Sales personnel consist of travel agents, ticket agents, and flight attendants who contribute to promoting the total travel experience.

Plate 5

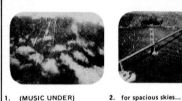

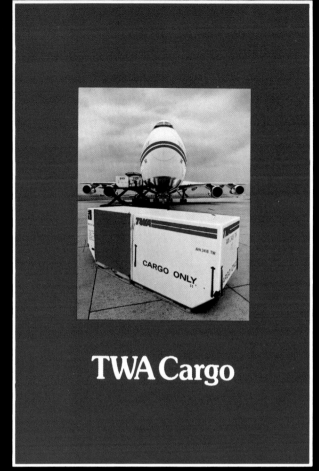

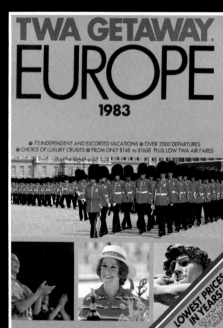

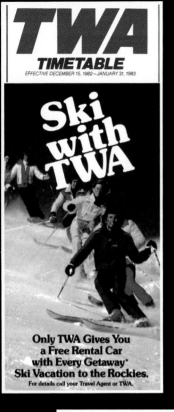

Perked vs. Instant

BusinessWeek

THE WALL STREET JOURNAL

Instant news.
It's what the daily press does so well.
But in their rush to beat the clock, the instant media have little time to spare for demanding business analysis. So they sometimes fail to report to you the relation between a late news item and a bigger, more important story.
Business Week editors and reporters concentrate on making this connection. They view business as a continuum. Not simply as a series of sudden events.

They take the full measure of a story. And give meaning and perspective to a business world that is complex and constantly evolving.
This is why over six million business leaders read Business Week's award-winning blend of worldwide business reporting and analysis. Useful information they can count on every week to satisfy them beyond the instant.
Business Week. It tells you what's really brewing.

BusinessWeek

For information on ordering a subscription to Business Week, please call toll-free 1-800-257-5112. In New Jersey, call 1-800-792-0570.

An example of a positioning campaign.

"Anyone who'd call Wagoneer a station wagon has obviously never driven one." By promoting the slogan "We do chicken right," Kentucky Fried Chicken positions itself as an exclusive specialist in the chicken business. Other fast-food franchises are portrayed in Kentucky Fried Chicken advertising as mass producers of a wide variety of inferior items. The **positioning** approach promotes a brand's "position" in relation to the competition in a buyer's mind.

It is assumed that consumers have so much information about other brands, advertising, and similar products that the company must create a distinct position for the brand in the prospect's mind. The Avis campaign advertising "We're

Only Number Two" is a classic example of this strategy. By positioning itself as the second largest automobile rental company, it dramatically increased market share. Business was taken away from the smaller rent-a-car companies, rather than Hertz, because consumers remembered the Avis and Hertz positions.

The positioning approach slots a brand, in

relation to its competition, within the target customer's mind. Avis made great marketing strides with its "We're Number Two" campaign because customers remembered that, while Hertz was Number One, Avis was in the Number Two slot, where a company had to "try harder" to succeed.

Campaign Overlaps. For simplicity sake, the three types of promotional campaigns have been discussed as if they were entirely unique and separate from one another. However, there is some overlap in these three approaches. For example, the positioning of Nyquil as the nighttime cold medicine is somewhat related to its chemical make-up and characteristics. In this case, product differentiation and positioning are closely allied.

DETERMINING THE PROMOTIONAL BUDGET

Marketers attempting to determine the size of their promotional budgets are often reminded of the adage, "If you can't make a splash, don't make a ripple." This old bromide seems to suggest that a very small amount of promotion may not effectively transmit the message the marketer wants to send to buyers. The giant organizations placing promotional messages in many media and utilizing other promotional tools are in an enviable position indeed, but even smaller organizations can mount successful promotional campaigns by carefully setting advertising budgets and selecting those messages, media, and timings that most effectively transmit the desired message. These matters will be dealt with more fully in later chapters since they specifically concern advertising and personal selling rather than promotion in general. Regardless of the promotional tool employed, the marketer must determine how much money will be available in the promotional fund before these other matters can be considered closely. Thus, before moving on to other topics, let us close this chapter by considering some methods used to determine the size of a promotional budget.

The Task Method or Objective Approach

The **task method,** also called the objective approach, of setting a promotional budget is probably the most logical of the budget-setting techniques. It calls for first identifying the task or objective to be accomplished and then determining the costs and efforts required to attain that objective. An appropriate objective for a retail marketer budgeting for 1986 might be to double the 1985 furniture sales. Assuming that this objective is a reasonable one, the retailer would then budget the promotional resources necessary to achieve it. The logical appeal of such an approach is greater than would be entrusting these important decisions to some mathematical formula based on strictly quantitative data. Here the *objective,* rather than sales figures or industry tradition, determines the size of the budget. This process is seldom easy, and it may require a great deal of time. Mainly because it is difficult for the planner to develop good objectives and then calculate what it takes to achieve these goals, and despite the lucidity of the task approach, it is not the most commonly used method of setting a promotional budget.

The Percent of Sales Method

The percent of sales method is probably the most commonly applied means of setting advertising budgets. The planner using the **percent of sales method** need only know a sales figure, take a percentage of that amount, and use that percentage as the promotional budget. For example, in the men's clothing business, 7 percent is considered a "reasonable" percentage of sales to spend on promotion. If sales for a period of time are $100,000, then the promotional budget "should" be $7,000. The percentage used varies from industry to industry, for example the food marketing industry typically uses

1 percent of sales for promotion, and movie theaters generally spend about 14 percent for promotion.

The attractiveness of this method is obvious. First, the marketer needs to know only sales totals to be able to easily calculate the resultant budget. Moreover, the appropriate percentage can be obtained from trade associations or other sources that indicate that the average organization in a given line of trade spends X percent of sales on promotion. The user of this budgeting method is thus spared having to determine what percent of sales figures to use. He or she may also feel comfortable knowing that the budget developed is reasonable, and is similar to that of other companies. These industry averages or standards are simple to use, but have many disadvantages. First, there is the logical problem presented by deriving a promotional budget from a sales figure. Supposedly, sales result from promotion. This method makes promotion a result of sales. In fact, the percent of sales method seems to suggest that the sales would have occurred with or without promotional expenditures. There is also the problem that such a method cannot cover all circumstances. For example, if sales are declining, it might be better to increase promotional expenditures, rather than reduce them as the formula would have us do.

Beyond the attraction of simplicity, there are two other advantages of this method. One, given that promotion is tied to sales, it is reasonable to assume that the sales have generated sufficient money to pay for the promotion. The logical flaws of the method, however, make this defense quite unsatisfying. Second, it is possible to defend the method for use in certain circumstances. Some industries—for example, the electric power companies—are mature and face predictable market changes. A mathematical formula is more appropriate here than in more dynamic marketing environments.

The Comparative Parity Method

The **comparative parity method** for determining a promotional budget boils down to doing what the competitors do. Brewers compare their dollars-per-barrel promotional expenditures with those of competitors in an effort to assure th they are not falling behind. Supermarkets operating in a given city commonly spend almost precisely what their competitors in that city spend. In a two-department-store town, it is common to see each store represented in the Sunday newspaper in nearly identical forms—similar in size, placement, and cost.

The comparative parity method for determining promotional budgets is based on the notion that the moves made by competitors or industry leaders somehow must be matched. Like the percent of sales method, this technique takes little note of changes in the marketplace or of opportunities that may suddenly arise. In fact, the method makes one firm's promotion a near mirror image of another's. The competitor is thus determining the promotional budget of the other firm. When the percent of sales method is based on industry standards, problems similar to the problems of comparative parity approach arise.

The Marginal Approach

Theoretically, the **marginal approach** to almost anything in business is "the best." When applied to the setting of promotional budgets, such a method would have the organization spend promotional dollars until the payoff from the last dollar spent indicates that it is no longer worth it to continue to raise the budget.

Unfortunately, though this method makes perfectly good sense, the dynamic nature of markets, the actions of competitors, and difficulty of the determination of exactly how much benefit was purchased with the "last promotional dollar spent" make this method of little practical value for most organizations.

The All-You-Can-Afford Method

The name of this technique is self-explanatory. Using this method, the marketer spends whatever is available to be spent on promotion. Organizations using this method typically do not have enough of a cash flow to justify utilization of other methods. A new business, just starting out and facing the frightening statistics on new

EXHIBIT 18-10

Horizontal and Vertical Cooperative Promotional Programs

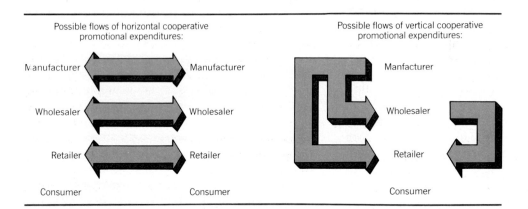

Possible flows of horizontal cooperative promotional expenditures:

Manufacturer ⟷ Manufacturer

Wholesaler ⟷ Wholesaler

Retailer ⟷ Retailer

Consumer   Consumer

Possible flows of vertical cooperative promotional expenditures:

Manfacturer

Wholesaler

Retailer

Consumer

business failures, for example, would be well-advised to spend, in effect, as much as is available for promotion. This method further implies that the promotional dollars are not borrowed but represent "cash on hand" that remains available.

The Combination Approach

Solutions to real-world problems, such as determining an advertising budget, are seldom left to one formula or one method of analysis. Even a planner who is able to utilize the task or objective approach effectively might still employ a percent of sales formulation to generate some ball park figures to be considered as the planning process progresses. A planner relying on the comparative parity method may be brought back to reality by the all-you-can-afford method when calculations yield a budget figure that is unreasonable given the organization's assets.

Cooperative Promotional Programs

Many marketers, at all levels in the distribution process, employ what is termed a cooperative approach to advertising and other promotional activities. These are of two general types, verti-

cal and horizontal (see Exhibit 18-10). **Vertical cooperative promotion** involves channel members at different levels, as when a manufacturer of tape recorders offers to pay for a portion of a retailer's advertising with the understanding that the advertisements will feature that particular brand of recorder. **Horizontal cooperative promotion** involves channel members at the same levels, as when retailers in a town get together to promote downtown shopping in general or a "sidewalk" promotion.

The attractiveness of these programs is clear. Every channel member gets some of the benefits of a promotional program, but no individual channel member must bear the full cost. Savings are realized by all concerned parties. In some situations, the rates charged by advertising media may also be reduced since some newspapers and broadcasting stations charge lower rates to local businesses than they charge to national advertisers. If a manufacturer paying part of the cost of the advertisement has the local retailer actually place the advertisement, this lower rate may be realized. Such an advertisement, placed by the local retailer, is termed a retailer-initiated cooperative ad. If, for whatever reasons, the manufacturer places the advertisement, it is termed a manufacturer-initiated cooperative advertisement.

Lest the idea of sharing the costs of advertising and other promotional tools, such as premiums and displays, seems to be a plan whereby everybody comes out ahead, some potential problem areas should be mentioned. For one thing, manufacturers often tie their cooperative advertising dollars to the amounts of merchandise purchased by retailers. This means that retailers must buy the goods before they get the desired help in selling the merchandise to consumers. Furthermore, manufacturers commonly place some total dollar limitation on the amount of aid to be granted. As a result, small retailers may be annoyed that they receive few cooperative dollars since their purchases and sales of the product in question are limited. Large retailers may be bothered by the fact that a ceiling on cooperative help has been placed on them even though they sell vast quantities of the manufacturer's product.

A more common complaint is the "strings" attached to most cooperative promotional campaigns. Retailers believe that they know the best ways to advertise to the familiar local markets. They therefore tend to feel that they should be given free rein to spend those dollars in the ways they know to be "best." Manufacturers or other suppliers for their parts hold that, since they are giving these cooperative dollars to channel members, they have the right to specify how those dollars are spent. Many manufacturers, therefore, attempt to specify the type of advertising to be used and exactly how the products are to be displayed. They commonly provide newspaper advertisements that are fully constructed and ready for insertion into local papers. Local merchants, though happy to receive cooperative advertising dollars or other benefits, are frequently annoyed at the restrictions placed on them by their cooperative partners.

SUMMARY

The essence of promotion is communication. Promotional strategy is designed to inform, persuade, and remind consumers about the existence and benefits of a product, service, or idea. Promotion is composed of four elements: personal selling, advertising, sales promotion, and publicity. The elements of promotion each have individual functions to perform and must be integrated into an effective promotional mix.

Understanding various components of the communication process—encoding, channel, message, decoding, feedback, and noise—is essential to the development of an effective promotional strategy. There is a psychological hierarchy in the communication process of awareness, knowledge, liking, preference, conviction, and purchase through which consumers climb. Marketers should take this into account when determining promotional strategies.

There are three major promotional approaches to developing a promotional campaign for a mature product: image building, product differentiation, and positioning.

Finally, there are various methods available by which to determine the promotional budget. Among these methods are percentage of sales, comparative parity, all-you-can-afford, and the task method.

THE MOST IMPORTANT CONCEPT IN THIS CHAPTER

Effective marketing requires effective communication. Promotion is the means by which marketers communicate with their customers; thus the strictest attention must be paid to developing and effecting a coordinated promotional effort.

KEY TERMS

Promotion	Promotional campaign	Noise	Horizontal cooperative promotion
Persuasion	Hard sell	Decoding	
Personal selling	Soft sell	Encoding	Task method
Advertising	Marginal approach	Communication	Comparative parity method
Pull strategy	Positioning	Sales promotion	
Push strategy	Image building	Vertical cooperative promotion	Percent of sales method
Promotion mix	Product differentiation		
Feedback	USP		

QUESTIONS FOR DISCUSSION

1 Using a communication model, give examples of the encoding and decoding that might take place during the personal selling process.

2 What is "noise" in the communication process?

3 How does selective perception enter into the communication process?

4 How does a push strategy differ from a pull strategy? Give some examples from your experience.

5 What is sales promotion? What are some creative examples of sales promotion?

6 What telephone number would you choose if your telephone number is used as a promotional device for the following companies:
(a) A florist
(b) A soccer team
(c) Merrill Lynch Stock Brokers
(d) Internal Revenue Service

7 Comment on the following: "Promotion mirrors the values and life-styles of the target consumers."

8 For the following brands indicate whether the primary promotional strategy is image building, positioning, or unique selling proposition.
(a) Sunkist soft drink
(b) Cooper Tools (e.g., Crescent Wrench, Lumpkin measuring tapes, Nichols saws, etc.)
(c) Sinclair/Timex personal computers.

CASE 18-1 Wolf Brand Chili Hot Dog Sauce*

Wolf Brand products markets canned chili and a chili hotdog sauce (used to make chili dogs). Traditionally, sales of chili are seasonal. In 1981, Wolf Brand found one competitor, Hormel Chili, had been experimenting with summer advertising. During the 1981 summer, sales for Wolf Brand were down and sales for Hormel were up. The company decided that a promotional campaign needed to be developed for "greater consumer and trade impact for Wolf Brand" during the summer months.

Questions
1 What type of promotional program would you suggest?
2 Outline the campaign.

*Source: Based on "Wolf Brand Gives Sauce New Spice," *Ad Week*, pp. 1–3, 1982.

CASE 18-2 Ken's Restaurant System*

True to an entrepreneur's spirit, Ken Selby thought he could make a better pizza than anyone else, and so to prove it he opened his first pizza parlor in 1961. That one store has grown into Ken's Restaurant System, which after a decade of relatively slow growth has become a thriving company-owned/franchise system that has taken a firm stance in the intensely competitive fast-food industry. In addition, KRS claims to be the only private pizza restaurant company in the country that has two pizza chains—with entirely different concepts and marketing strategies—operating successfully under the same corporate umbrella. KRS is continuing to stress an ambitious growth pattern through system-wide expansion, new advertising and marketing directions (advertising budgets for both chains have more than doubled in the past few years), and a new name, which until recently was Ken's Pizza. The new name takes into account Mazzio's, the second and newest chain under the KRS umbrella. Founded almost two years ago, the chain now has 39 stores with an additional 16 under development. Mazzio's has just embarked on its first full-scale ad campaign. The theme of the broadcast campaign is "Get into the thick of it," with "good" and "fun" substituted for "thick" as subthemes in various cases. Product quality is stressed—especially extra toppings—and television spots feature young families and singles enjoying the Mazzio's experience. Since five years of pizza industry research showed the continuing existence of a "pizza craving" among target audiences, copy includes many words intended to trigger that craving.

Mazzio's, developed in 1980, and Ken's both stress product quality. A major difference between the two chains is that Mazzio's touts limited self-service while Ken's emphasizes table service—the full restaurant experience. But the Mazzio's selling points—limited self-service and product quality—were not stressed heavily through advertising in the past because the chain has not had a full-scale, continuous ad program until recently. Both restaurants also feature drive-through windows, a rarity for the pizza industry. To further attract a younger de-

mographic target, Mazzio's also includes video games on the premises as a secondary attraction. Mazzio's restaurants are built either free-standing or in mall formats, while Ken's restaurants are all free-standing except for a mall version of Ken's called Pizza-by-the-Slice, of which there are currently three outlets.

While Mazzio's emphasizes limited self-service and skews to the younger end of the 18–34 market, Ken's advertising promotes the full restaurant experience with table service and targets the middle and higher ends of the age group, primarily younger families.

The theme for this year's Ken's campaign is "The pizza that brings you back." The ad program is intended to bring customers back and to remind them that Ken's has been in the community a long while.

By 1986, KRS plans to have 145 company-operated restaurants and 336 franchised operations in the system. This includes a 25 percent annual increase in franchise stores and a 12 percent annual increase for company-owned stores. There are now 62 company-owned Ken's restaurants and 14 company-owned Mazzio's outlets. Also in the plan is a projection of $60 million by 1986 for total company sales, which is currently the figure for total system sales.

Although pizza will continue to remain the mainstay of the business, KRS may one day also be branching out into other food-item restaurants. "The name change typifies this."

Questions

1 Evaluate the ad campaigns for Ken's and Mazzio's.

2 Why would a restaurant like Mazzio's have video games as part of its merchandising mix? Should this be stressed in promotional efforts?

3 Do Mazzio's and Ken's compete with each other? What promotional campaign changes or additions would you suggest for these two pizza restaurants?

---

*Source: Adapted from Debra Farst, "Ken's System Plans for a Bigger Bite of the Pizza Market," *Ad Week*, July 19, 1982, p. 9. Used with permission.

CHAPTER 19

Personal Selling and Sales Management

CHAPTER SCAN

This second chapter dealing with promotion, presents several aspects of personal selling as a tool for effective communication with customers. It discusses the purposes and goals of personal selling and identifies the several general types of sales positions. Also considered is the ''new'' role of the salesperson. The application of the marketing concept to the task of selling has made the salesperson's approach to the customer one of identifying customer problems and solving those problems with the products, terms of sale, and distribution options the organization has to offer.

This chapter also deals with sales management, the tasks and duties of the executives who select sales personnel, develop sales territories and compensation plans, and maintain standards of performance for the sales force. It concludes with a portrayal of a likely career path within an organization, beginning with hiring as a sales trainee and ending . . . as far along as hard work can take you.

WHEN YOU HAVE STUDIED THIS CHAPTER, YOU WILL:

Be able to discuss the role of personal selling in the marketing mix.

Be able to identify marketing situations in which personal selling rather than advertising or other means of communication would be most effective in reaching and influencing target buyers.

Be able to describe the role of the professional salesperson in a modern marketing firm.

Be able to discuss the several steps involved in a personal selling effort from prospecting for clients to closing the sale.

Be aware that the marketing process does not stop when the sale is made and be able to tell why this is the case.

Be familiar with the major aspect of the sales manager's job.

Understand why personal selling positions are frequently the first steps on a successful career path.

Bill Kelly, Manager, Information Systems for Amoco Production Company (USA), one of the world's largest energy corporations, began his career with IBM in marketing, initially as a systems engineer and eventually as a salesman. He feels that his start in sales was helpful in many ways.

The primary benefit of a start in sales is a firm and practical grounding in interpersonal skills. If you can't work with and communicate with a wide variety of people with diverse backgrounds, you don't sell anything and that gets very lonely. These skills are absolutely essential to the effective manager and businessman. The sales training supplied by an organization like IBM speeds development of those skills. Of course, many individuals have good skills to start with, but I have seen them passed by salesmen who have worked at their craft.

The second benefit of a sales career is the ability to understand and appreciate business decision processes from an executive viewpoint. The nature of the products I sold brought me into contact with customer management much earlier than I would have had I worked for those organizations. Marketing training on the products as well as personal development courses prepared me for that role more thoroughly than some organizations train their staffs. The marketing objective was to allow me to sell products to customer executives. In the process I became comfortable in the company of decision makers and find I work easily with them. Without the sales training, I am convinced this would have taken much longer, if it ever happened at all.

A third benefit which may be most important is the acceptance of individual responsibility for performance. The sales job by its nature is quantified and measured—you make your quota or you don't. This fact is impressed on the individual very early in his career in sales and leads to better personal organization. The salesman's role as the company representative to the customer requires him to coordinate the activities of many others, often without direct authority, to meet his commitments to his customer. The focus on measured results forces the salesman to concentrate his time and effort and the efforts of others on specific objectives. The salesman understands that he has to make things happen if the ob-

Personal selling is a person-to-person dialogue between buyer and seller.

jectives are to be met. He expects he will be rewarded for achievement and is prepared to accept that responsibility and challenge.

Salesmen are, to say it nicely, not universally loved and accepted. I had many prejudices about being a salesman when I started. (IBM refers to theirs as Marketing Representatives, possibly to alleviate the problem.) However, the salesman is the catalyst that makes our economy function. There are very few of us who have ever bought a car from a plant engineer or financial manager; we buy cars from salesmen. The critical role of selling for most organizations

should not be overlooked as a good place to start a career.

The selling experience and the lessons permeate my day-to-day life. As Manager, Information Systems, I am still dealing with computers but that is incidental to the task of planning and managing. I am responsible for leading a team of people, none of whom work for me, to develop APC (USA)'s Information System. This involves some 1600 people and a budget of some $175 million in 1982. Without the selling skills, I don't think I could handle the job. In fact, I don't think I would have the job.[1]

THE CHARACTERISTICS OF PERSONAL SELLING

Personal selling has been defined as a person-to-person dialogue between buyer and seller where the purpose of the face-to-face interaction is to persuade the buyer to accept a point of view or to convince the buyer to take a specific course of action.[2]

Selling is a promotional activity consisting of human contact and personal, oral communication rather than impersonal mass communication.

The salesperson's job may be to remind, to inform, or to persuade. In general, the salesperson's responsibility is to keep *existing customers* abreast of information about the company's products and services and to persuasively convey a sales message to *potential customers*. Salespeople are also expected to be aware of changes in the markets they serve and to report important information to their home offices. Professional sales personnel are vitally important as business' "front-line troops in the battle for customers' orders."[3] They communicate the company's offer and show prospective buyers how their problems can be solved by the product.

Closing

Ultimately, salespeople make the sale. In selling, the term **closing** indicates that the sale is being brought to a finish. The main advantage of personal selling versus other forms of promotion is that the salesperson is in a position to conclude negotiations by actually asking for an order. Closing or completing the sale, needless to say, is crucial in the marketing process.[4] The old adage "nothing happens until a sale is made" reflects the importance of selling to all aspects of a business. However, modern marketers view the closing of the sale not as the end of a process, but as the start of an organization's relationship with a customer.

---

[1] Personal correspondence to William G. Zikmund, February 11, 1983.

[2] Though some forms of personal-contact selling, such as telephone sales, are not literally face-to-face, these kinds of selling are still considered to be forms of personal selling.

[3] D.J. Dalrymple and L.J. Parsons, *Marketing Management* (New York: John Wiley & Sons, 1980), p. 538.

[4] Some businesspeople use the football terms "conversion" or "converting" to denote a sale being consummated. This reflects the fact that a sales prospect, a potential customer, has been "converted" into a buyer.

Personal Selling Is Flexible

Perhaps the key word used to describe a number of personal selling's advantages over other means of promotion is flexibility. For example, **flexibility** means that the salesperson can situationally *adapt a sales presentation*. When a sales prospect has a particular problem or series of problems he or she wishes to solve, the professional salesperson can adjust the presentation to show how the product or service offered can solve these problems and satisfy the individual needs of the potential customer. Similarly, the salesperson can answer questions and overcome customer objections that may arise. The salesperson can even "read" the customer. Sensing that the client agrees with a certain aspect of the presentation or is not interested in a given point, for example, the salesperson can shift gears and move to another consumer benefit or adjust the manner in which the sales talk is presented. The sales message can be adjusted because personal selling entails a two-way flow of communication. *Direct* and *immediate feedback* is elicited. An advertisement or a publicity announcement cannot obtain direct and immediate feedback.

Consider the following examples of how feedback allows the salesperson to gather information from the customer as well as to impart information to the buyer. The salesperson might discover in casual conversation that potential buyers have problems that no products on the market can solve. Customers may also suggest how existing products can be modified to better suit client needs. Customers might provide salespeople with new sales leads by mentioning other firms that could use the salesperson's merchandise. A personal approach may elicit a customer's view of the competition's sales presentation and use it to good advantage.

Concentrating on the Best Prospects

Personal selling is also flexible because it allows the carrier of an organization's message to concentrate on the best sales prospects. For example, a television advertisement might be seen

---

WHAT WENT RIGHT

PERSONAL SELLING IS FLEXIBLE AT BOEING

Nearly every operator of Boeing aircraft has a story about the company's coming through in a pinch. When tiny Alaska Airlines needed landing gear that could put a jet down on a dirt strip, Boeing was there. When Air Canada had a problem with ice clogging in some air vents, Boeing flew its engineers to Vancouver, where they worked around the clock to solve the problem and minimize disruption of the airline's schedule. Boeing's attention to customer relations has paid off. In December 1978, Alitalia lost a DC9 airliner into the Mediterranean Sea and the Italian national carrier vitally needed a replacement aircraft. Umberto Nordio, Alitalia's president, telephoned T.A. Wilson, Boeing's chairman, with a special request: Could Alitalia quickly get delivery on a Boeing 727? At the time there was a two-year wait for such aircraft, but Boeing juggled its delivery schedule and Alitalia got the plane in a month. Mr. Nordio returned the favor six months later, when Alitalia cancelled plans to buy McDonald Douglass DC10s and ordered nine 747 Jumbos [from Boeing], valued at about $575 million.

Source: Victor F. Sonana, "Boeing's Sale to Delta Gives It a Big Advantage over U.S. Competitors," *Wall Street Journal*, November 13, 1980, p. 1.

---

by just about anyone, including many people who will never be interested in the product offered for sale. This "waste circulation," as it is termed by marketers, can be reduced or even eliminated by effective personal sellers. With personal selling, large volume buyers can be visited or called on frequently. Personal selling allows efforts to be concentrated on the profitable accounts because it is a *selective medium*.

Some Limitations of Personal Selling. Our emphasis on the advantages of personal selling as an effective communication form should not overshadow its major limitations. Personal selling cannot economically reach a mass audience and, therefore, cannot be used efficiently in all marketing situations. Face soaps, such as Ivory or Dove, may be used by tens of millions of people while millions more are potential users. Reaching these target customers by personal selling is too expensive. Advertising via mass media is the appropriate tool in cases like these because it can reach a mass audience economically. Personal selling can play some role in marketing these products, for example, when sales representatives call on major retailers or other channel of distribution members who are relatively small in number.

Because personal selling utilizes personal communications, another limitation associated with personal selling is its cost. An expensive TV advertisement seen by a vast audience causes the *cost per thousand* viewers and *cost per sale* to be quite small. On the other hand, the recruiting, training, and paying of salespeople typically results in a very high *cost per call* or appointment associated with the sales efforts. In 1983, the average cost per call was approximately $200 for industrial products.[5] When one considers how many sales calls may be needed to generate a sale, the *cost per sale* can be tremendous. Part of this high cost is associated with the nature of the sales job. For example, considerable time can be spent driving to and from appointments or waiting in the reception room while the prospect finds time to see the salesperson. The many advantages of personal selling, however, often offset the high cost per sale. In some cases, such as selling machinery custom made for the buyer, personal selling is the only way a sale can be made.

Another major difficulty associated with personal selling is the problem of recruiting, selecting, training, and monitoring salespeople. These activities fall under the general topic of *sales management* and are treated later in this chapter.

IMPORTANCE OF PERSONAL SELLING

Personal selling is the most widely used means by which organizations communicate with their customers. It is possible to think of profit or nonprofit organizations that make no use whatsoever of advertising: For decades, the Hershey company did not advertise. Certainly, there are companies so obscure that they get no publicity at all. It is, however, almost impossible to imagine any organization making *no* personal contact with its clients. Even the one-man machine shop deals with clients via some kind of personal contact and sales effort. Thus, personal selling, in its various forms, is the most commonly used promotional tool. You may not think of it in this way, but accountants, stockbrokers, dentists, lawyers, and other professionals are personal salespeople in that they deal with clients and sell a service. For example, many hardworking accountants (who generally were not marketing majors in college) promoted to a partnership in an accounting firm find that they spend more time trying to generate new business than they spend working out accounting problems. Robert Louis Stevenson was not far from the mark when he said, "Everyone lives by selling something."

In terms of dollars spent, personal selling is also the foremost promotional tool. Money spent on personal selling far exceeds money spent on advertising, despite advertising's costs and visibility. This becomes clear when one considers the numbers of people engaged in selling and the expenses of training, compensation, and expense accounts associated with selling.

Personal selling is the most significant of promotional tools in terms of the numbers of people employed. It is estimated that at least 8

---

[5] Neesa Sweet, "Let the Salesmen do the Talking," *Advertising Age,* June 20, 1983, p. m-28.

million people, or 10 percent of the U.S. work-force, are engaged in sales. There are fewer than 200 thousand people working in advertising. As impressive as these statistics are, they underestimate the importance of personal selling in our economy and in other aspects of our social life. Professional selling is an activity of many individuals whose job titles may obscure this fact. Company presidents, advertising executives, and marketing researchers are frequently engaged in personal selling.

In general, personal selling is the most widely used element among the promotional mix possibilities. Yet, the importance of personal selling varies considerably across organizations. Some organizations may rely almost entirely on their sales forces to generate sales while others use them to support a pulling strategy based on advertising. Some organizations employ salespeople, such as the store clerks at Woolworth's or K-Mart, who do little professional selling, while others employ engineers and scientists as technical sales representatives. These two types of sales representatives are not comparable, thus it is necessary to discuss these sorts of individuals and the roles they play in organizations.

THE TYPES OF PERSONAL SELLING

It is useful to differentiate between the different types of selling jobs. After all, the marketing manager must decide which selling skills and job descriptions are appropriate to the sales objectives to be accomplished. Assignment of an over-qualified salesperson to a task that could be accomplished as efficiently by a less-qualified individual is a waste of an important resource. On the other hand, putting a salesperson into a selling spot where his or her skills are inappropriate is unfair to the individual and virtually guarantees that the organization's sales objectives will remain unfulfilled.

There are three basic categories of selling positions. These are commonly referred to as order-taking, order-getting, and sales support positions.

Order-Taking

Many millions of people are employed in sales jobs of a routine nature. These people, who do very little creative selling, are called order-takers. Their primary responsibilities involve writing up orders, checking invoices for accuracy, and assuring timely order processing. The term *order-taking* is appropriate to these situations since it is the customer who does most of the work. The customer decides on the appropriate products and prices and then tells the salesperson what the order is to be.

Without slighting the contributions made by people in order-taking capacities, it should be stressed that they do not require a great deal of persuasive skill or human relations talent. While order-takers must be pleasant and helpful to customers, they seldom generate sales beyond those which the customer was prepared to give. It is often said that the job of the order-taker is to *keep* sales rather than to *make* sales.

Types of Order-Taking Sales Jobs. In general, order-taking salespeople are divided into the "inside" sales group and the "outside" or "field" sales groups. Inside sales of this type are exemplified by auto parts salespeople who provide some advice on product quality or installation of the part. The fact is that the customer came to the shop seeking the part—the salesperson did not seek the customer. The inside salesperson could enlarge the total sale to any customer by suggesting that additional parts or tools would make the job easier or that the customer might as well change the oil filter while handling the other repairs. To the degree that the salesperson does expand on the basic order presented by the customer, that salesperson is departing from the standard order-taking mode of sales.

Outside or field salespeople may also be of the order-taking type. Manufacturer or wholesaler representatives selling such well-known products as Campbell's soups find themselves in this position. The question they ask their customers is essentially "How much do you want?" Since nearly every grocery store stocks Campbell's soups, there is little need for aggressive selling. Some sales representatives holding sales positions of this sort do a better job than others in enlarging order size, tying the product to special sales opportunities, and so on. Such efforts are likely to be rewarded with a promotion or a bigger bonus. Overall, however, since order-taking sales jobs require less sales talent and effort than selling expensive computer systems to corporate executives or new airplanes to the transportation industry, order-takers in general make less money than do the next group of salespersons—order-getters.

Order-Getting

In order-getting (also called creative selling) situations, the sales job is not routine. **Order-getters** must seek out customers, analyze their situations, discover how the products for sale might solve those problems, and then bring these solutions to the attention of the customer.

> **Creative selling** is the ability to interpret product and service features in terms of benefits and advantages to the buyer and to persuade and motivate the buyer to purchase the right quality and volume of products or service.[6]

Notice how this differs from the job of the order-taker. Whereas the order-taker's job is to *keep* the sale, the order-getter's job is to *make* the sale. Put another way, the primary function of the creative salesperson is to generate a sale that might not occur without the efforts of the salesperson. The salesperson, in this case, is virtually required to interpret the prospect's need and to convince the prospect of the benefits the product being offered can provide.

To this end, creative salespeople generally invest far more time and effort in making a sale

---

[6]K.B. Haas and J.W. Ernest, *Principles of Creative Selling* (Encino, Calif.: Glencove Publishing, 1974), p. 10.

than do the order-takers. And, while it is possible to engage in creative selling in either an inside or a field environment, the field environment is far more common, with creative salespeople going to the customer's place of business to evaluate the needs to be addressed. This process can take a very long time. A salesperson for IBM, attempting to demonstrate that a particular computer system is the best available to meet the needs of the bank holding company, can literally spend years preparing to make a sale. Needless to say, the compensation offered to effective creative salespeople generally exceeds that offered to order-taking salespeople.

Sales Support

Many salespeople hold jobs whose titles suggest that they are involved in special selling situations. One commonly encountered salesperson of this sort is the so-called "missionary." **Missionary sales personnel** in fact rarely take or actively seek orders; their primary responsibility is to build goodwill by distributing information to customers and prospective customers and "checking in" to be sure that buyers are being satisfactorily serviced by company representatives and other relevant channel members such as wholesalers. They are employed by the manufacturer to perform a kind of public relations function. For example, McDonald's has a missionary selling system they call the "STAR," or "Store Trading Area Representative" system. Under that system, a missionary salesperson is assigned to work the territory and go to each local community institution to help make them loyal McDonald's consumers. The salesperson may go to an old-age home with McDonald's Golden Arches' Club cards, offering significant discounts on McDonald's foods, and give them out to everyone there. They may go to the local public school and offer to bring Ronald McDonald and his friends to put on a show on safety. They may help with local Boy Scout activities or appear at McDonald's birthday parties. It is the responsibility of the STAR to really work the territory. The STARs are one of the real secrets of McDonald's sales strength.

Pharmaceutical manufacturers utilize mis-

"I WANTED TO MAKE A LOT OF MONEY."

That's how *Darla Longo* describes her motivation for choosing a career in commercial real estate. *"I like nice things. I have three sisters. My parents taught all of us a simple lesson: Nice things don't come easy. If you want things, you have to earn them."*

After only three years with Coldwell Banker, Darla is earning more than $100 thousand dollars a year—straight commission. That's not bad for a twenty-five year old woman. It's not bad for a man or woman of any age. Darla describes herself as a goal setter. *"Now my goal is to become a consistent top producer."* Asked to define a top producer, Darla set three levels.

■ Top top producers—consistently earn $200,000 plus

■ Top producers—consistently earn $100,000 to $200,000

■ Okay producers—consistently earn $50,000 to $100,000

It seems that anyone earning less than $50,000 doesn't last with the firm.

Coldwell Banker agents specialize in both a type of commercial real estate and in a geographic district. The major break is between users and investors. There are three divisions in the user category: office, commercial/retail, and industrial. The investor category is split between apartments and "everything else."

Darla specializes in industrial properties in the San Gabriel Valley just outside of Los Angeles. *"As a specialist I can overwhelm* them with my knowledge. I know every building and every owner. I know about every deal, I can drive down the streets and point out buildings as I give their histories. I feel like an encyclopedia.

"I don't sell anybody anything. I think of myself as an advisor, a consultant. I'm there to help them to find what they need. My job is a little different from traditional sales because I have to find more than buyers. I have to find the product to sell."

Any job in which you can earn in excess of $100,000 a year and earnings are virtually unlimited must have some costs attached. Darla is quick to point out that her work has it share of stress and aggravation. *"There are lots of ups and downs. It's a daily roller coaster ride. Things you've*

Source: From *Successful Saleswoman* (September 1982), p. 5, the monthly publication of the National Association For Professional Saleswomen, Sacramento, Cal.

sionaries, called "detailers," to call on doctors and provide them with information on the latest prescription and non-prescription products. Such detailers do not take orders; sales occur only when the doctor prescribes medication for patients. In fact, even missionary salespeople working for consumer goods companies and calling on retailers do not directly sell anything. If a retailer insisted on placing an order, the missionary would not refuse to accept it, but would simply pass it on to the salesperson who regularly handles the retailer's account.

Other specialized sales support people can be found in particular industries where appropriate scientists and engineers may be ready to serve as technical specialists to support the regular field sales force. The credentials and expertise of these sales engineers, applications programmers, and other technical support personnel are often helpful in concluding sales of complicated products such as nuclear reactors, computer installations, or advanced jet engines.

Some firms, especially those whose customers may require a little extra push at some point in the selling process, have master salesmen or sales experts on their selling staffs. These salespeople are held in reserve until less senior or less capable salespeople find themselves in need of help. Real estate sellers frequently find a sales expert helpful when, for example, a customer on the verge of buying a new house gets cold feet because of financing worries. At such a worked on for months can fall apart."

Coldwell Banker Sales Manager Ken Green concurs. "We have someone who's been doing real well. Then one day we find him or her totally wiped out—down in the dumps. Something that's been in the works for months has fallen through with a loud crash." But as Ken continues, "It's a numbers game. If you do the things you're supposed to time and time again, some of the deals will turn out."

Even when everything goes right, the pressure is on. "I'm always on call—center stage." But Darla knew what to expect. While a student at UCLA, Darla decided on a career in commercial real estate. She got her real estate license and her first job in commercial real estate even before graduation.

"But I knew I needed more training. I looked around and just knew that Coldwell Banker was for me. They have a great training program. It's the only place I interviewed." In fact, Coldwell Banker invests between $70 and $80 thousand in each trainee. But they don't have that many trainees. An average office may add only 3 to 5 people per year.

Coldwell Banker's training includes both on-the-job and classroom segments. Since Darla's business experience was limited, she went through "Presales." During this year, she spent 90 days at four different Coldwell Banker offices in the Los Angeles area. At the Beverly Hills office she got a taste of commercial/retail. In Newport Beach she spent her time in the industrial area.

At the end of the year, she actually reinterviewed with each of the area sales managers to find the office and the specialty where she fit best. She chose to specialize in industrial properties be-

cause she felt she could make more money there and she felt more comfortable with the clientele.

Darla's second year was spent as a runner. She served as a shadow-like assistant to a senior salesperson learning everything she could. Persons entering the Coldwell Banker organization with at least three years of top sales performance or three years of professional experience go into the runner program in their first year. A lot of Coldwell Banker salespeople have training and experience in accounting or law.

Being the number one rookie in the nation is a notable achievement. What made the difference? "I think it's my attitude. I never let anything get in my way. That includes my ego. I'll seek out advice before I'll blow a deal. I'm in a people business. That means I have to be the kind of person people want to deal with."

Selling may be supported by a sales team.

point, the salesperson may call on the owner of the agency to "clinch" the sale through the use of contacts at the bank or simply by lending an expert helping hand in moving the customer to the purchase point. Dealers in automobiles and major appliances also use this approach at the consumer level. Suppliers of industrial goods adapt the technique to their selling situations.

In all but the smallest organizations, the salesperson in contact with the customer is supported by a **sales team.** If a creative salesperson successfully closes a deal, he or she has perhaps called upon a technical specialist or master salesperson for aid. Perhaps the path to a successful selling experience was made easier by a missionary or detailer. After the sale, the missionary may play a further role in keeping the buyer content and certain that the best choice was made. Order-takers, whether in the field or at the home office, may see to it that orders are handled with dispatch and without error. The customer may be provided with the name and phone number of a **sales correspondent,** someone at company headquarters who can answer questions about delivery, post-sale service, installation, and repair parts, when the salesperson is away from the home office. A toll-free 800 number may be provided to buyers or inquiring customers.

However it is constructed and operated, the effective sales team is a good representation of the marketing concept in action. It reflects an effort to satisfy customers, not just to sell products.

THE CREATIVE SELLING PROCESS

As we have seen, there are some selling jobs wherein the salesperson does very little true selling. Perhaps the *least* creative selling situation is that of the "canned presentation."[7] Here, the salesperson memorizes a descriptive or persuasive speech and is directed to give that speech to any and all potential customers without variation. Such an approach is common in door-to-door or telephone selling. While such a strategy may have little appeal to most people, it should be mentioned that encyclopedia companies and other direct marketers frequently devote much time and effort to developing what is thought to be the "best" sales talk. These organizations obviously believe that the method's likelihood of success justifies the lack of individual selling creativity. Furthermore, since the canned approach seems to assume that anybody can succeed if they memorize the speech, inexperienced, low-paid individuals can be hired to fill these sales positions.

Except perhaps for the extreme situation of the canned sales talk deliverer, all salespeople can benefit from a consideration of the plan known as the *creative selling process.* This process is a series of steps intended to provide guidelines for the salesperson. It suggests that the true nature of professional selling is an adaptive process that begins with the identification of specific potential customers, and tailors the sales dialogue and product offering to the particular prospect's needs.

The **creative selling process** includes the following steps: (1) locating and qualifying the prospect; (2) approaching the prospect; (3) making the sales presentation; (4) handling complaints; (5) closing the sale; and (6) following-up. They are portrayed in Exhibit 19-1 in a manner intended to suggest a focus on the final goal of customer satisfaction. Again, these steps are a guideline that helps salespeople to think about the tasks that face them. Unlike the canned sales presentation, they are not to be slavishly followed.

---

[7] For two points of view on canned sales presentations, see Marvin A. Jolson, "The Underestimated Potential of Canned Sales Presentation," *Journal of Marketing* (January 1975), pp. 75–78, and Jim D. Reed, "Comments on the Underestimated Potential of the Canned Sales Presentation," *Journal of Marketing* (January 1976), pp. 67–68.

EXHIBIT 19-1

The Creative Selling Process

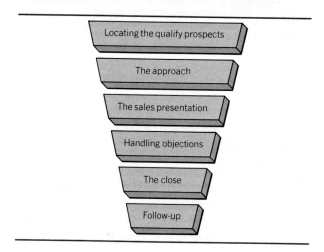

Locating the qualify prospects

The approach

The sales presentation

Handling objections

The close

Follow-up

Step One: Locating and Qualifying Prospects

An established sales representative may have many regular customers to rely on for a certain amount of business, but a successful salesperson is not one who is content to service only existing accounts. Sales calls to regular customers are only part of the sales job. New customers or new accounts must be sought. However, making a sales presentation to someone who has no need for the product, who has insufficient funds to pay for it, or who is not empowered to purchase the product, is not an efficient utilization of time unless the person being addressed may become a customer sometime in the future.

Locating Prospects. Locating likely prospects is called *prospecting.* Like the experienced prospector in Western movies, the professional salesperson knows how to find likely customers. **Prospecting,** then, refers to activities to identify likely buyers from lists of previous customers, referrals, trade lists, advertising inquiries (such as postcards or coupons returned to the sales office by interested parties), and other sources.

While each industry or line of business has its traditional means of generating "leads," such

as membership lists published by trade associations, good salespeople are prepared to dig harder for prospects. Government publications providing breakdowns of business patterns in particular counties and states can be used, and perhaps even cross-referenced with other sources, to develop lists of likely buyers. Some salespeople spend considerable time on the telephone screening possible clients. Others talk with organizations that supply or buy from the firms that the salesperson thinks may turn up possible customers. The number of prospecting tools is nearly unlimited.

Qualifying Prospects. Identification of possible prospects is only the beginning of effective creative selling. Prospects must be shown to be in need of the product and to be able to pay for it. Moreover, the prospect contacted by the salesperson must be in a position to make, or at least contribute to, the buying decision. Determining that conditions such as these are met is termed **qualifying the prospect.**

Another consideration in the qualifying process includes determining whether the prospective buyer's order will be of sufficient size. That is, does the account have an adequate sales potential? A potential customer may be assigned to a qualified group, a not-qualified group, or a group falling somewhere in between. For example, careful consideration of a prospect may lead to the conclusion that either there is insufficient potential for a specified sales volume and the prospect should be eliminated from further attention, or that the prospect is worthy of close attention and a series of sales calls and presentations, or that the prospect is worth a phone call or two but not a full presentation. Care must be taken to assure that a highly qualified prospect is not relegated to the wrong category due to inadequate or insufficient investigation methods.

Another important fact to be learned through qualifying is the specific person that a salesperson should contact. Who has the authority to make the purchase decision? Who else strongly influences the purchase decision? A plant superintendent may be a "boss," but call-

Can you spot the hot prospect? Bell can show you how.

When you qualify prospects and find out which ones are for real, you eliminate unnecessary sales visits. You save a lot of money and get to the prospects who are ready to buy.

You can do this with a Telemarketing center. The center can also support your salespeople on the road, taking messages for them, making appointments, relaying messages when they call in. It can handle paperwork and free up your salespeople for the job they do best: selling.

A Telemarketing center fuses telecommunications technology with systematic management. Your advertising or catalog stimulates a lead. The lead calls in on your 800 Service number, and you can qualify it at once.

If the lead comes in by mail, you use Long Distance or your Outward WATS line to contact and qualify your prospect. In either case, you have the Bell network, the world's largest and most advanced information management system, at your disposal.

No matter whether your company is small or large, Bell can show you how to set up a center. We can discuss Telemarketing programs and network services that will help you sell with precision and impact.

All you have to do is call now 1 800 821-2121
1 800 821-2121, toll free.

Put our knowledge to work for your business. Bell System.

The knowledge business

Locating and qualifying prospects are important tasks in selling.

ing on the superintendent exclusively is the wrong tactic if the vice-president makes all the buying decisions. The process of qualifying is difficult and may require considerable tact and effort.

The process of qualifying a prospect is sometimes called the *preapproach*. This is because the information gained in this step lays the foundation for planning the other steps in the selling process, including the actual approaching of potential clients.

Step Two: The Approach

The **approach** deals with making an initial contact and establishing rapport with the prospect. With established accounts or individuals already familiar with the salesperson and the company, the approach may be as simple as making a tele-

phone call to request an appointment or knocking on the prospect's door with a friendly greeting.

In dealing with new accounts, the salesperson may have to be more creative in attracting the attention of the prospect or in getting past the prospect's secretary. The image of the aggressive salesman either rushing past a secretary who is barring the boss's door, or claiming to be a government official in order to reach the boss, is not representative of the professional salesperson. The best way for a salesperson to build a creative sales approach is to do some homework on the prospect, learning some specific information about the prospect's needs for the products being offered. Once these needs are identified, they can provide the basis for effective personal communication by phone, letter, or direct personal contact.

The salesperson may approach the prospect by mentioning an offer that can benefit the prospective client. For example, the would-be seller may have discovered through investigation that the prospect is paying fairly high rates for advertising time on a rock music radio station appealing to young adults. The salesperson might then show that a middle-aged audience that *also* buys the advertised product can be reached far more cheaply through advertising on the classical music radio station that the salesperson represents. The approach, then, is intended to attract the buyer's *attention*. What better way to attract attention than to offer a benefit that will save money for the customer, make the customer's products more attractive to buyers, or add prestige to the customer's good name?

Effective sales personnel recognize that gaining favorable attention must be followed by making a good impression during the first few seconds of the sales presentation. Experience is a great helper in this matter, but research and caution can serve the seller well, too. For example, smoking a cigar or cigarette in a nonsmoker's office may lose a sale before the presentation has even begun. Not wearing a hard hat in a location where protective gear is required may make the salesperson appear too unfamiliar with the situation in which he or she is supposedly going to solve a client's problem. The importance of making a "good impression" should not be underestimated.

Step Three: The Sales Presentation

The **sales presentation** is the salesperson's attempt to persuasively communicate the product's benefits and to explain appropriate courses of action to the potential buyer. Typically, effective presentations begin with gaining the prospect's attention. Some salespeople do this by producing some physical object, such as the product itself (if it is both portable and eye-catching), a model of the product, or something that relates to the product in an interesting or even humorous way. It is more common, however, to have an opening statement designed to attract attention. Thus, opening lines such as, "I'm here to show you how we can save $5,000 a week in your factory," or, "I've got a furnace to show you that can burn newspapers and old socks instead of expensive oil" are frequently encountered.

After gaining the prospect's attention, the salesperson's job is to generate interest in the product being offered. An opening comment that the salesperson can save the client a great deal of money in income taxes may gain attention, but it must then be followed by the development of *interest* in the product being sold as the means to save the tax money. Describing the product in an interesting way, explaining how it works, or demonstrating the product's use can all be part of an effective presentation.

Notice that arousing interest in the product itself is not enough to make a sale. A *desire* to purchase the product must also be generated. A scale model of an executive jet plane may be interesting, but it is of little use if it does not help bring about a desire to own the plane itself.

In assembling effective sales presentations, the inclusion of visual aids such as flip charts, slide presentations, and sound and video recordings is not unusual. In recent years, some salespeople have come to rely on computers in their presentation. They either operate portable units

The approach.

at the place of presentation or offer computer-generated data that answers the customer's "what if" questions. For example, representatives of an industrial robotics firm may bring a computer terminal right into the prospect's office, ask for information such as production schedules, delivery requirements, and so on, and, via phone lines, communicate with the computer at headquarters. Within minutes, the terminal can yield an output that shows exactly how the salesperson's product will affect the prospect's business operations.

It should be noted that some of the communication in the sales presentation may not be verbal. Many successful salespeople use body language, seating arrangements, and clothing colors to communicate important non-verbal messages to their clients.

Step Four: Handling Objections

Most sales presentations do not occur in an atmosphere in which the salesperson makes a one-way presentation of information while the customer passively listens. The customer, no matter how friendly or interested in the product, may have reservations about making a commitment of money or other resources in a purchase agreement. Questions or strong objections are likely to arise. Since objections explain reasons

The presentation at a trade show.

for resisting or postponing purchase, the salesperson should listen and learn from them.

When an objection indicates that the prospect has failed to fully understand some point that was made, the objection allows the salesperson to comment on the area of uncertainty. A question about a product characteristic may mean that the prospect has not grasped how the product works or seen the benefits it can provide. Accepting and acting upon an objection of this type allows the salesperson to provide additional persuasive information, to clarify the sales presentation, or to offer the basic argument for the product in a different manner.

The sales call should be a dialogue or conversation in which objections may frequently arise. It is undesirable to have the prospect sit quietly until the end of the talk and then say "No" without any explanation. Effective salespeople encourage prospects to voice reasons why they are resisting the purchase. Even though the well-prepared sales presentation covers such topics as the quality of the product, the reputation of the seller, post-sale services, and the like, the objection or question tells the salesperson which point is most important to the

customer. Occasionally, such points are almost a surprise to the salesperson. For example, a representative of a pest control company may launch into a lengthy discourse on company reputation and demonstrate the product by poisoning a bug right before the prospect's eyes. It may take an objection to discover that the prospect is quite willing to buy the exterminator's service, but is concerned that neighbors will see the pest-killer's truck parked in front of the house or place of business. In such a case, the salesperson can respond by promising to have a nonuniformed exterminator drive to the client's location in an unmarked truck.

Objections can also be turned into counterarguments by experienced sales representatives. A stockbroker might say,

You are right, Dr. Williams. The price of this stock *has* dropped 50 percent in the last six months. That is exactly why I am recommending it to you. At this low price, it is now underpriced and is an excellent buy in the opinion of our analysts.[8]

---

[8] Albert W. Frey, *Marketing Handbook* (New York: Ronald Press, 1965), pp. 9, 24–25.

One tactic for handling objections is to agree with the prospect, as did the stockbroker mentioned above, accepting the objection *with reservation*. This is consistent with the marketing concept's prescription to sell the product from the customer's point of view. The salesperson's counter-argument is intended to refute the objection. "Yes, that is true, but *this* is also the case." The purpose of this method of dealing with objections is to avoid getting into an argument with the prospect. If the customer says the price is high and the salesperson says it is low, the discussion gets nowhere fast. But if the salesperson responds, "Yes, it is priced higher than many but our product quality is higher than the competitor's, so you get more for your money," the salesperson has both agreed and counter-argued at the same time. More importantly, the seller has given a comprehensible reason for the higher price.

The prospect's questions, objections, and other comments may reveal how close the prospect is to making a purchase decision. Good salespeople use such clues to determine whether they should attempt to enter the closing stages of the sales presentation.

Step Five: Closing the Sale

Unfortunately, many salespeople are knowledgeable and convincing when making sales presentations, but they never get around to asking for the order. Sometimes this is due to the presenter's genuine belief in the product being offered—a belief so strong that he or she can barely stop talking about it. In other cases, worry about receiving a negative answer or misreading the client's willingness to deal may be the cause.[9] In any case, there comes a point when the presentation must be drawn to its logical

---

[9] Experienced salespeople know that they will hear the word "No" *most* of the time, or at least more than they hear "Yes." Rejection is never a source of enjoyment, but there are many times when the sales representative is better off accepting a negative response gracefully and moving on to prospects who may be more likely to buy.

conclusion. In fact, many sales managers say that they wait for applicants to "close the sale," that is, to actually ask for the job, when they interview prospective sales representatives.

Because closing the sale is so vital, experienced sales personnel constantly try to read the prospect's reactions to the presentation for signs that a conclusion is in order. Occasionally, the prospect can be helpful, as, for example, when he or she asks "When can you make a delivery?" Should an opening like this occur, the sales representative should quickly answer the question and ask for the prospect's signature on the order.

When the prospect's willingness to close is not so clearly revealed, the salesperson may utilize what is called the "trial close." A **trial close** is a tactic intended to draw from the prospect information that will signal if a sale is imminent or not. For example, the salesperson may attempt to focus the conversation on closing the sale by asking whether the customer prefers the standard model or the deluxe. If the customer indicates a preference in a positive way, the sale may almost be made. Should the customer be unable to decide, or ask for another comparison of the two models, more information is necessary.

When a customer does not clearly indicate that the time has come to make the sale, the salesperson may use one of the following closing techniques:

1 Narrow the alternatives to a choice. This involves the salesperson asking, "Do you want alternative A or alternative B?"

2 The direct, straightforward approach. The salesperson requests the order.

3 The assumptive closing technique. The salesperson takes out the order forms or in some other way implies that an agreement has been reached saying something like, "Let's see here, you'll need 20 units by the first of the month."

4 The "standing room only" closing technique. Here the sales representative indicates that time

CONVERSATION: PART OF THE SALES ART

"The only proper intoxication is conversation," said Oscar Wilde. But many people feel that conversation is a dying art, partially being replaced by TV. Ironically, some of the most stimulating conversations being held today are *on* television. Dick Cavett, hosting *The Dick Cavett Show* on PBS (Public Broadcasting Service), has become a master of conversation. He has exchanged ideas with dozens of writers, actors, and newsmakers. *The American Express* newsletter asked Dick to converse with Cardmembers—about how to carry on good conversations in social, business, and travel situations. His comments are reprinted here.

What is a "good" conversation?

"It's several people talking about something that really interests them. It might include jokes, opinions, debates. But a good conversation has a shape, and it grows as you build on each other's ideas.

"You may not remember what was said a few weeks later. But you do remember that feeling of having experienced a good conversation."

How do you make conversation with new business associates?

"It's very helpful if you know something about them before you meet them. You can read their biographies or resumés. Or talk with someone who knows them.

"That gives you an opportunity to start a conversation by talking about what interests the other person.

"Business people also should read more about things outside their own field of interest. It provides them with a greater range of subjects to discuss.

"Business conversations and business letters should always start with the 'you.' It's the one word guaranteed to keep people listening. People are invariably interested in themselves."

What mistakes do people make?

"You shouldn't be afraid to start a conversation on a light, even superficial level.

"Some people launch into 'meaningful' conversations from the first breath. I hate it at parties when some intense person comes up to me and says, 'What are you *really* looking for?'

"People who can't get to the point can also be irritating. They seem to feel they score points with you if they use big words and take a tedious, complicated trip to their point.

"Anyone who uses words such as 'parameters' and 'interface' should never be invited to a dinner party.

"You have to learn to *listen* to what others are saying—instead of just waiting for the pause so you can jump in with your comment. You know what I mean. One person might say, 'I opened the trunk, and you'll never guess what I found.' And the other person says, 'Do you have any hobbies?'"

Any other ways to keep people's interest?

"Yes, mention their name frequently. It's magical. If you can develop the habit of remembering and using the other person's name, you almost don't have to worry about anything else in conversation."

Source: Dick Cavett, "The Art of Conversation," *The American Express,* August 1981, pp. 1, 4.

is an important factor and supply is limited. Typical phrases used are: "We've been selling a lot of these lately and I want to make sure that you get what you need," or "This offer will be withdrawn soon and it's back to the old higher prices," or "Inflation has been driving the prices up so your purchase should be made now."

5 The summative approach. Here the salesperson summarizes, usually with pencil and paper, the benefits of buying the product, perhaps mentioning some disadvantages which the advantages overcome. When the product's benefits are summarized, the salesperson asks for the order.

Step Six: The Follow-Up

Organizations that have truly adopted the marketing concept do not view the getting of an order as the end of the selling process. It can, in fact, be seen as a beginning. A satisfied customer will return to the sales organization that treated it best if it needs to repurchase the same product at some time in the future, or needs a related item. A happy customer may even recommend the sales representative to new sales prospects. The professional salesperson knows these things and **follows-up** after the sale, to make sure that everything was handled as promised and that the order was shipped promptly and received on schedule. Few things are worse than promising a delivery date and having the goods arrive weeks or months late. Sales personnel should also check with the customer as to whether there were any problems such as missing parts or damage to the merchandise during shipping. The customer, once in possession of the product, may still need added help in integrating it into his or her operations. Post-sale services such as parts, repairs, supplies, or returns may also be necessary.

In a sense, the follow-up and how well it is performed represents the difference between a simple selling job and marketing. After all, customer satisfaction is the goal of all properly run organizations. If it is not achieved, or if the organization appears not to even *try* to achieve it, anything more than a one-shot sale is unlikely.

A TOP SALESMAN'S SECRET OF SUCCESS

The sale begins after the sale. Don't take their money if you aren't going to service the account. People advertise for you. They tell other people. Sales are made one at a time. The reason I'm in the Guinness Book of World Records is because I don't just take people's money. I let them know that I think of them as human beings.

The secret of success is that the elevator to success is broken. You have to take the stairs—one step at a time.

Source: "Sales Tip from the Pros: Joe Girard on the Secrets of Success," From *Successful Saleswoman*, (Spring 1982), p. 2, the monthly publication of the National Association for Professional Saleswomen, Sacramento, Cal.

SALES MANAGEMENT

Thus far in this chapter we have concentrated on salespeople, the several types of sales positions they fill, and the creative sales process employed by many of them in the successful completion of their assignments. Now, we turn to the general field of sales management.

Sales Management Examined

Sales personnel, like most employees, require some degree of supervision and management. However, the typical salesman or saleswoman, especially the many salespeople operating outside of the retail store environment, are more or less on their own most of the time. They work away from the presence of their direct supervisors. This is the major reason why the task of the sales manager differs significantly from that of other managers. Indeed, a large part of the sales manager's job is to attempt to create a situation in which the salesperson can be placed and then monitored only periodically. Close supervision by managers is not only resented by many salespersons, it is also often impossible to achieve.

Sales management is the marketing management activity dealing with the planning, direction, and control of the sales force or personal selling effort.

CLOSING SIGNALS

Salespeople look for signs revealed by their prospects when they are ready to buy. These are called **closing signals.** Physical actions indicating readiness to purchase are:

1 The prospect reexamines the product carefully.

2 The prospect takes possession of the item—as, for example, strapping on a wristwatch.

3 The prospect begins to read the order form.

4 The prospect nods in agreement as the salesperson summarizes.

5 The prospect points at the samples on display.

Statements or comments indicating a readiness to buy are:

1 "I always wanted a video tape recorder."

2 "These new machines should reduce the number of breakdowns we've been having."

3 "The output from the dot-matrix printer is clear and attractive."

4 "I've always liked dealing with your company."

Questions signaling a closing are:

1 "When must you have the full downpayment?"

2 "When can you make delivery?"

3 "In what colors is it available?"

Source: Adapted with permission by Albert W. Frey, *Marketing Handbook* (New York: Ronald Press, 1965), pp. 9–26.

Sales managers are responsible for a number of tasks. These include planning and organizing the efforts of the sales force, recruiting and maintaining a well-trained sales force, and evaluating and controlling the sales force. Sales management emphasizes planning and developing a sales team rather than stressing a direct day-to-day supervision of activities.

The sales manager's responsibilities may also include selling activities. After all, virtually every sales manager earned the job by performing well "in the field." Sales managers may accompany less-experienced sales personnel during training periods or work with a veteran salesperson when a particularly significant account needs to be sold. Thus, while sales managers are primarily responsible for planning, organizing, directing, and controlling the sales force, they have ample opportunity to engage in the personal selling process.

Sales managers, like other managers, are assigned to specific corporate responsibilities. The nature of sales is such that the areas of responsibility are often expressed in geographic terms. District sales managers and regional sales managers, held accountable for the activity of sales personnel operating within specific areas, are referred to as **field sales managers** because of their direct concern for salespeople "out in the field." Their primary concern is management of the field sales personnel who report to them. Exhibit 19-2 provides a list of sales job titles and the varied job descriptions that go with them. These descriptions are common among sales organizations. However, titles are often altered by companies seeking to provide their people with positions appropriate to the selling situations in which they find themselves. Advertising agencies, for example, typically appoint many vice-presidents because clients entrusting these firms with considerable sums of money want to deal with highly placed agency people. Magazine publishers may overwork the titles of publisher, associate publisher, and so on because corporations placing advertisements in magazines prefer to deal with an executive rather than a "salesman."

EXHIBIT 19-2

Typical Job Titles

Top-Level Marketing Management
Marketing vice president Typically the top marketing executive in the company or division.

Sales vice president Sometimes another title for marketing vice president but sometimes the top sales executive who will report to either the president or the marketing vice president.

Top-Level Line Sales Management
National sales manager The top sales executive responsible for all sales force related activities.

General sales manager Another title for national sales manager.

Middle-Level Line Sales Management
National account sales manager Usually responsible for a separate, high-quality sales force which calls on national accounts. Often the only person in the national account sales force and responsible for actual selling, but the accounts are so large that the position needs a relatively high-level manager.

Regional, divisional, or zone sales manager These are titles for high-level field sales managers to whom other field sales managers report. Occasionally, the titles are used for first-level sales management jobs in which salespeople are managed.

Market sales manager A sales manager responsible for salespeople calling on a specific group of accounts. Often this position has marketing responsibility in addition to sales management and perhaps sales responsibility. A company which specializes its sales force by market will have one market sales manager to head each separate sales force.

Product sales manager The same as market sales manager except that the job is organized around a product line instead of a customer category. Both positions are more likely to occur in industrial companies than in consumer-goods companies. The product sales managers are usually more involved with product-oriented decisions than are market managers.

Lower-Level Line Sales Management
District or field sales manager The first line sales manager to whom the salespeople report.

Upper-Level Sales Positions
Account executive, key account salesperson, national account salesperson, major account salesperson These people are responsible for selling to major accounts. In the consumer-goods field, the title sometimes involves chain stores, meaning usually the three large national general merchandise chains (Sears, Penney, Montgomery Ward), food chains, or mass merchandisers such as discount department stores.

Typical Sales Positions
Salesperson, field salesperson, territory manager, account representative, sales representative All are typical titles for the salesperson responsible for selling and servicing a variety of accounts.

Staff Sales Management
These positions are usually functionally oriented and include titles such as manager of sales training, sales analyst, etc. The typical staff responsibilities include training, recruiting, and sales analysis. More general staff positions include the title *assistant to the national sales manager*. Assistant national sales managers may be either line or staff managers. Staff positions may occur at any level in the organization. Some companies with divisional sales forces, for example, have a job of corporate vice president of sales who has no line sales management responsibility. Other companies have regional or area sales vice presidents responsible for aiding salespeople from various divisions with major account sales. This is found, for example, in some weapons marketers where various product-oriented divisions call upon the same buying organization.

Source: Reprinted with permission from Benson P. Shapiro, *Sales Program Management: Formulation and Implementation* (New York: McGraw-Hill, 1977), p. 7.
Note: The titles and descriptions above are generalities. Different industries and different companies in many cases use different titles for the same job and organize job content differently.

The Retail Sales Force

Few direct references to *retail* sales forces were made in the preceding discussion. **Retail sales forces** must be organized and administered just as outside sales forces are. However, because most retail salespeople operate within a rather controlled setting, the job of managing them is more clearcut, if not easier, than managing outside people. The accounts serviced by retail salespeople are the people who visit their section of the store. Thus, delineating accounts, analyzing territories, and performing other sales management tasks become more manageable than they would be if a country-wide or even a world-wide sales force had to be developed and maintained.

Obviously, sales management is important in retail marketing. But the limitations of an introductory text require that we deal with sales management in general, and dwell on the field sales force in particular. The planning and thinking associated with managing a field sales force is appropriate and applicable to many aspects of retail sales force management.

Setting Sales Objectives

All good managers, before setting out to accomplish a task, first give considerable thought to what that task should or must be. In other words, they set objectives. The reason a statement of **sales objectives** is so important is that much of sales management is the assignment of resources. How can the manager know, for example, how many salespeople to hire unless the tasks to be accomplished are understood first? Sales objectives should meet the criteria by which objectives are generally evaluated in the marketing world. They should be precise, quantifiable, include a time frame, and be reasonable given the organization's resources and the competitive environment in which it operates. If they are *not* precise, managers really don't know what they are trying to accomplish. If they are *not* quantifiable, managers cannot know when the objective has been reached. If *no* time frame is included, the manager has "forever" to reach the goals. If they are *not* reasonable, the manager can waste time and effort in a pursuit that was doomed to failure at the start.

An example of a sales objective stated in terms of sales volume might be to expand annual sales in the Virginia/West Virginia sales territory by 10 percent over last year's dollar volume. A market share objective might be to increase market share by 1 percent every year for the next five years.

Sales objectives can be expressed in many ways. Among these are sales totals in dollars, sales totals in units of products, increases over previous sales totals, market share, sales calls completed, sales calls on new customers, and dollar or unit sales per sales call made.

Organizing the Sales Force

Since non-retail sales forces typically must contact their customers either face-to-face or by telephone, sales departments are generally organized so that sales personnel are responsible for certain accounts. Calling regularly on the same organizations and individuals leads to a better understanding of customers' problems and needs and provides the sales representative with an opportunity to develop a personal relationship with the client. Further, some form of organization is required to minimize or eliminate having several company representatives calling on the same customers where this is unnecessary. Duplication of calls is a waste of resources and can serve to annoy clients.

A **sales territory** is commonly thought of as a geographical area. Territories are not always so defined, however. For example, salespeople may be assigned to large or small accounts by product line with one group of salespeople handling buyers of large machinery while another group serves buyers of small machinery. Every method of creating territories has advantages and disadvantages. Whatever the method employed, the basis for structuring the characteristics and needs of the customers to be served should always take precedence over the convenience of the sales force.

EXHIBIT 19-3

Example of a Geographic Sales Organization

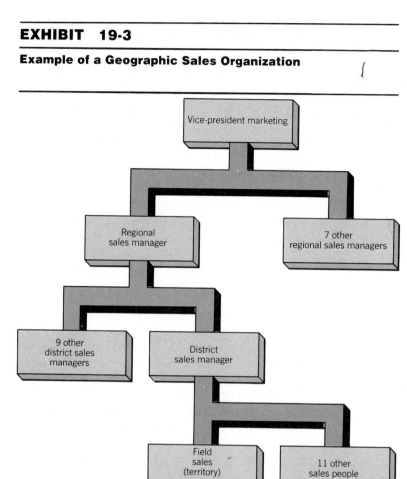

Geographically Based Sales Territories. Although other means of developing sales responsibilities are available, sales personnel are frequently assigned to particular geographical sales territories. Exhibit 19-3 shows an organization chart for a company utilizing this approach. Notice that as an individual manager moves higher in the organizational scheme, he or she becomes responsible for increasingly larger territories, with the vice-president for marketing ultimately responsible for the entire country, or even world, market.

Much attention has been given to the design of geographic sales territories. A number of variables should be considered as the market is being "cut up" into sections for assignment to individual sales representatives. Clearly, even though each company's situation is different, the same factors must be weighed. Some sales managers have adapted computers to perform the task of territory development. No matter how the task is handled, however, a major problem is creating territories that are roughly equal in terms of the following variables: physical size of the territory; transportation within the territory; the number of current and potential customers within the territory; the general economic state of the territory; and the size of the territory's sales and sales potential.

Personnel problems result when one salesperson gets a "bad" territory and another gets the "best" territory. Equality and fairness are important goals in this process.

A related goal is the development of geographic territories that allow the sales manager to maintain as close a working relationship with the sales representatives as is necessary. However, communication may involve telephone conversations or the filing of reports rather than actual face-to-face meetings. For example, a consumer goods company, such as Clairol, may typically have a very large territory, including Montana, Idaho, Wyoming, the Dakotas, Nebraska, and parts of other states, in the sparsely populated western United States. When a sales territory is that large, the opportunity for close personal contact between supervisor and salesperson is small. Personal encounters may be limited to occasional meetings at the home office. To encourage closer contact between sales manager and sales representative, some firms require that the manager travel with individual salespeople in their territories periodically.

Organization by Customer Type. When a sales organization specializes by customer type, for example, users of petrochemicals versus users of all other chemicals, two or more salespeople may cover the same geographical area. For example, a textbook publishing company may cover the Midwest with one sales representative who calls on business and engineering professors and another who deals with professors in colleges of arts and sciences. Notice the two facts present in both these cases: (1) more than one company representative calls on a single firm or university and (2) the representatives call on different individuals within these organizations. Obviously, the chemical company and the publisher both feel that the customer is better served by dealing with a salesperson who is a specialist rather than a generalist. The second point is that, even though the assignment of salespeople is by customer type, the matter of geog-

---

THE SALES PERSONALITY?

According to the president of the BATA Shoe Company, two shoe salesmen were sent to a poverty-stricken country. The first salesman cabled, "Returning home immediately. No one wears shoes here." The second, more optimistic salesman cabled, "Unlimited possibilities. Millions still without shoes."

Source: Eric Sevareid, *Enterprise: The Making of Business in America* (New York: McGraw-Hill, 1983), p. 13.

---

raphy still enters the picture. The bookseller specializes by buyer type *within* the Midwestern territory. The chemical company's representatives also call within a specific area, and not world-wide, in search of customers. Thus, a *combination* of geography and customer type is in use in these organizations. In fact, the inescapability of the geographic factor makes a *combination* approach to the assignment of sales territories the most commonly employed.

Organization by Product Line. Within large, multi-product companies, it is not uncommon for each corporate division or product line to have its own sales force. As with the customer-type organization plan, the stress is on specialization. Multi-line organizations often find that their salespeople must know a great many technical details about their products and customers. The selling points associated with each product may be finely detailed in a technical way. Too many products and too many details will almost certainly reduce the salesperson's ability to sell a product effectively. The sales forces may be organized according to product line so as to provide an opportunity for meaningful specialization.

Despite the attraction of specialization, the net result is a situation in which several sales representatives from a single company may call on the same client organization. As in the situation of organization by customer type, this may not be a source of annoyance to clients because the specialized nature of the products may be reflected in specialization of the *buyers.* A single purchaser may *not* have to deal with several of the same firm's representatives. Organizations whose sales forces specialize by product line have determined that the payoff associated with specialization offsets the waste of having several salespeople calling on a single client.

Organization by Selling Tasks. Sales forces can also be organized according to the selling tasks each is expected to perform. Some salespeople are judged to be best at *sales development*—that is, at bringing in new accounts. Others seem best at *sales maintenance*—that is, calling on existing accounts and making sure that these customers continue to purchase the products being offered. Again, we see the dichotomy between sales *getting* and sales *keeping.* Individual attitudes, aptitudes, and personalities would appear to play a great part in determining who are the getters and who are the keepers.

Recruiting and Selecting the Sales Force

One of the most important functions that sales managers perform is the personnel function, starting with finding and hiring individuals for sales slots in the organization.

Finding the person who is both interested in a sales job and qualified to fill it requires that the sales manager systematically evaluate the sales position to determine what it requires. Contrary to the old expression describing someone as a "born salesman," salespeople, no matter what their qualifications, are not universally acceptable in all selling situations. Thus, the sales manager must decide what characteristics a given sales position requires. IBM might need engineers attired in three-piece suits, while the person selling manure spreaders to Iowa farmers may require another form of dress. The job requirements for an order-taker may be quite different than those for an order-getter. These requirements must be carefully thought out and

YOUR DEGREE AND A SALES CAREER

Contrary to the beliefs of many students, a college degree may be required for many creative selling positions, though many successful salespeople do not have degrees. The degree may serve as a door opener, however, or a means to advancement to sales management, or to win a position over another applicant who has no degree. Meeting educational standards is very important. Not everyone is qualified for a selling career.

matched with job candidates, not only for the sake of the sales organization but also for the sake of the individuals hired. In some sales positions, employee turnover is fairly high, yet there are always some people who successfully hold these high turnover slots for long periods of time. Clearly, the lesson here is that the matter is one of getting the right person for the job.

Since selling situations vary tremendously from case to case, the analysis of a sales position is not complete without developing a related list of traits that an appropriate applicant should have. Some traits and accomplishments commonly considered when recruiting sales personnel are educational background, intelligence, self-confidence, problem-solving ability, speaking ability, appearance, achievement orientation, friendliness, empathy, and involvement in school or community organizations. These things do not guarantee that an applicant will be a successful sales representative, but they may be used as indicators of otherwise difficult to determine attributes. For example, if a friendly and helpful personality is thought to be a meaningful trait, membership in clubs and service organizations may suggest that trait is present. If the applicant's resumé shows that he or she is a loner, an area that may prove worthy of further investigation is flagged.

Related to this point is the matter of testing. Certainly no personality or other test *proves* that

Sales training has a big payoff.

an individual will or will not be a good salesperson. This fact annoys job applicants who feel that they have been denied a position they really wanted on the basis of a pencil-and-paper quiz. Sales managers understand this point and are willing to admit that no test is right in every case. However, many sales organizations continue to use these tests because the test results have indicated *some* validity over a long period of time. The tests are not right all the time. They simply serve to stack the odds in favor of making a correct choice.

Training the Sales Force

After sales personnel have been recruited and selected, they must be trained. Training programs vary from company to company. Some companies use an apprentice-type system by sending the newcomer into the field with an experienced salesperson to "learn the ropes." Others put the recruit through an intensive training program at headquarters or at a regional office before actually putting him or her out in the field. A few organizations believe in a "sink or swim" method whereby new people are sent out on their own to succeed or fail.

A typical sales training program for a recent college graduate hired by an office photo copier company is likely to cover the following areas: (1) company policies and practices; (2) industry and competitors' background; and (3) product knowledge and selling techniques. The graduate may receive several weeks of instruction at a center run by staff who specialize in training recruits. The instruction will probably feature guest lectures by both field salespeople and company executives. The next stage may require the graduate to work as a sales correspondent for several months, becoming familiar with customer needs and complaints and handling these by telephone or letter. The next phase may be on-the-job training while making sales presentations under the supervision and guidance of the sales manager or a senior salesperson. Programs like this are usually varied to suit the needs of the incoming employee. If the new person is experienced in sales, for example, less emphasis will be placed on selling skills than on company policies and product information.

In many successful sales organizations, training is an on-going process. Most sales representatives can benefit from a refresher course, a few days learning about new products, or just a break from their regular schedules. Thus, continuing training is often carried out at the home office, at sales conventions, or even at a local hotel or conference center.

Compensating the Sales Force

Saleswork, unlike certain other business professions such as accounting or personnel work, is generally highly visible. It involves the attempt to achieve clearly measurable results: Did sales go up or did they fall? How many new accounts were opened? How many calls were made? For this reason, most sales managers feel that salespeople who achieve the highest performances, in terms of some specific measure, should receive the largest compensation. Financial incentives are not the only motivators of a salesperson, but they are important and deserve the sales manager's close attention.

What would be the *ideal* compensation plan for salespeople? It would be *simple* so that disagreements over the size of paychecks and bonuses might be avoided. It would be as *fair* as possible to avoid petty jealousies among the sales team members. It would be *regular* so salespeople would be able to count on a reasonable reward coming to them steadily. It would provide *security* to the salesperson, and yet provide a degree of *incentive* to work harder. It would give management some *control* over the sales representative's activities. For example, it would be unfair to ask a salesperson to spend time conducting a marketing research effort if the representative gets paid only for sales actually made. Lastly, the ideal plan would encourage *optimal purchase orders by the customer.* For example, a heavily incentive-based plan might encourage salespeople to engage in extra hard-sell activities including selling customers items that they really do not need. Incentive should help in the development of a *long-term* profitable relationship with clients.

Having described the ideal plan of compensation, it is necessary to state that, unhappily, no compensation plan completely satisfies *all* these criteria. As a result, depending on the desires of the sales manager and his or her salespeople,

WHAT MAKES A SUCCESSFUL SALESPERSON?

As you would suspect, there is no easy or widely accepted answer to this question. Some "experts" claim that tall people fare better than short people, or that the key to successful selling is having a "winning personality." Other notions are harder to dismiss, such as the belief that a good salesperson needs to have a strong grasp of the product's benefits, or to be a hard worker, or to be hard to discourage. *All* these things probably have some truth to them.

One interesting result, and one that should be considered, has come out of many studies of the question of who succeeds as a salesperson: people who are successful as salespeople are *more like the people to whom they are trying to sell* than those who are not. In other words, if the buyer is a college-educated person, perhaps the sales representative should be, too. If the buyer is a technically trained executive, perhaps the seller should also be a technically trained individual.

The underlying reason for this belief is that people who are alike are more likely than those who are not to form a relationship, something like a trusting friendship. Buyers are thought to feel "I can believe this person; she is like *me.*" Thus, the buyer feels the salesperson is trustworthy, and the seller feels he or she should not mislead the buyer who is like a friend to the sales representative. The resulting mutual respect and understanding is thought by many to lead to a lasting, mutually beneficial, successful selling relationship.

and depending also on the nature of the selling job under consideration, management must select from among the available compensation plans described below.

The Compensation Continuum. The range of compensation plans used in selling situations represents a continuum (see Exhibit 19-4). At one end is the straight salary or straight wage

EXHIBIT 19-4

The Compensation Continuum and Conditions When Each Approach Is Most Useful

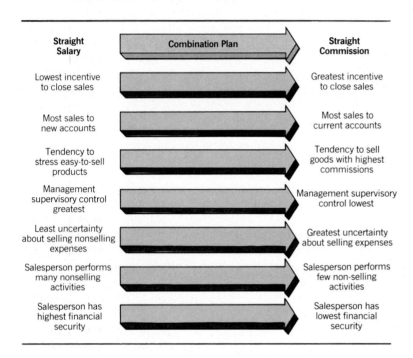

approach. At the other end of the scale is the straight commission plan. All other possible compensation plans are arrayed between these two extremes; they attempt to borrow the good points from both salary and commission.

Straight Salary or Wage. The **straight salary method** or hourly wage plan offers the salesperson compensation that is not immediately tied to sales performance. Many creative salespeople actually dislike this plan, preferring to accept the risks of commission in the hope of achieving high earnings. However, there are some selling situations that require use of the straight wage or salary plan. The common denominators among these situations are unequal selling opportunities and/or performance of non-selling activities. The sales clerks employed in a Target, K-Mart, or other similar store exemplify both of these situations. The selling oppor-tunities are grossly unequal. The employees at the back of the store are likely to make few sales, while those at the front of the store, where the most popular merchandise is displayed, would make most of the sales. Retail sales personnel may be expected to arrange stock, clean up spills, feed the fish in the display tank, or fill in wherever there is a need for an extra worker. To pay these people on anything other than a straight wage or salary plan would be unfair.

Many outside order getters also receive a salary, especially in situations where the salespeople are expected to engage in non-selling activities. Management has the greatest control over sales personnel under straight salary plans and the least uncertainty about selling expenses.

Straight Commission. Unlike the salary plan, the **straight commission plan** rewards only one thing—sales performance. A clearcut financial incentive is its prime advantage. On the surface, this plan would seem to have considerable appeal to most managements but, as we have seen, salespeople paid this way cannot be expected to do anything but sell. They may be reluctant to try to sell to new accounts that may develop slowly or to sell merchandise that is difficult to move, preferring instead to raise their short-term compensation by concentrating on goods they know they can sell quickly. While this approach may not be admirable, it is certainly understandable. Management may decide to discourage this behavior by lowering the commissions on "easy to sell" goods and raising it on "hard to sell goods." Notice, however, that this destroys one of the straight commission plan's other advantages, simplicity. In addition, salespeople may well resent changes that have the potential to reduce their incomes.

Straight commission has other shortcomings, too. The salesperson has little security. If the economy slows down, or if sales fall off for some other reason beyond the salesperson's control, the "incentive" in the plan may be lost because the sales representative may fail to achieve a satisfactory income over a period of a few weeks or more. Salespeople are less likely to allow managers to control their activities, especially if long-term non-selling activities are seen as a hindrance to earning higher commissions. Managers, who do not know exactly what sales expenses will be, cannot plan.

Commission with Draw. Management, seeking to keep the incentive of the commission plan, while softening the blow that a run of bad luck might deal a salesperson, can move toward the middle of the compensation continuum. One possibility is the plan known as **commission with draw.** Under this plan, the salesperson is still on straight commission but can dip into a "drawing account" to increase his or her pay during slack seasons. This pay plan is especially common when the product being sold has a seasonal demand, as certain construction materials might. The important thing to remember about commission with draw is that it is, at base, a true commission plan since the amount taken as a "draw"

must be paid back into the drawing account once the sales representative's commission returns to higher levels.

Quota-Bonus Plan. Under the **quota-bonus plan,** each salesperson is assigned a sales quota. However, an incentive is built in because a bonus is offered to any salespeople who exceed their quotas. A base salary is related to the quota total while the bonus provides a commission-like incentive. This plan, like others in the compensation continuum, attempts to provide aspects of straight salary and straight commission.

While the quota-bonus has a good deal of appeal, inherent in it are possibilities for friction between salespeople and management. For example, expert sales representatives may find they can "make their quota" very quickly. They then are tempted to take it easy for a time if there is no additional incentive beyond the minimum quota. Or if the bonus is progressive they may sell like mad to maximize the bonus. Either approach has little attraction for management, which might either suggest raising the quota or reducing the size of the sales representative's territory. Unfortunately, though it is the job of sales managers to handle such situations smoothly, the opportunities for controversy are clear.

Salary Plus Commission. As the name suggests, the **salary plus commission** compensation plan combines two pay methods by granting the salesperson a straight salary or wage *and* a commission on the sales generated by that person. Typically, since a salary is provided, the commission is smaller than would be expected in a straight commission pay package. The intent of this plan is to allow management to ask salespeople to engage in non-selling work (since they are on salary) but also reward them for successful sales efforts (with a commission). This method is commonly found in the retail selling environment where salespeople may be asked to perform non-selling chores. Because there are so many retail sales workers in the United States, this is the most commonly employed sales compensation plan.

Motivating the Sales Force

As mentioned above, many salespeople work alone in the field, often at great distances from their home offices and far from direct supervision. This unique situation, this feeling of working for oneself, draws many talented individuals into selling. But it also can create problems and thereby strongly influence the role of supervision.

Many salespeople are high achievement-oriented individuals, and may seldom require supervision from sales managers. For these people, selling itself is highly motivating. There is the challenge intrinsic in the selling process and the related challenge of trying to understand and solve the customer's problems using the salesperson's products. Despite these excitements and the feeling of being of service to clients, most salespeople need at least occasional support from management. Sales personnel are often subject to broad fluctuations in morale and motivation, from the lows that may accompany a string of customer rejections or a sense of being alone on the road, to the highs of obtaining major orders, big success, and substantial commissions and bonuses.[10] Sales personnel, especially young trainees, may become discouraged if they are not given proper help, supervision, and attention to morale.

While experienced sales managers may know how, by words and actions, to properly supervise and encourage salespeople to keep them fresh and interested in the job, many corporations use another element of their promotional mixes to help in this matter, the element of *sales promotion*. Sales contests, bonus plans, prizes and trips to be won, and sales conventions in exciting cities, can all be of great help to the sales manager who is seeking to keep sales force motivation high. Periodic sales meetings are also useful, both for creating a feeling of group support and mutual interest, as well as for providing a time for training and informational transmittal.

---

[10]Frederick E. Webster, Jr., *Industrial Marketing Strategy* (New York: John Wiley & Sons, 1979), p. 201.

"NOT MY JOB!"

An executive with a publisher of business textbooks remembers a young salesman who struck out early. He never recovered from a goof at a cocktail party held in the company's suite at the national convention of one of the academic associations. They had run out of glasses. So the executive rolled up his sleeves and started washing some in the little sink at the wet bar. He looked up to see that this first year salesperson was cheerfully chatting with a salesperson from a competing publishing company.

"If he had been talking with one of our authors, would-be authors or even a professor who might buy a book, I could have handled it. I would have understood why I was washing dishes while he was having a good time. But he wasn't. It was clear that I was there to work and he was there to have a good time. It wasn't too long before we decided to let him have his good time on someone else's payroll." A simple error in judgment brought on an unshakable impression of lack of devotion to task—lack of responsibility.

Source: From "Seek Out Responsibilities," From *Successful Saleswoman* (September 1982), p. 3, the monthly publication of *National Association for Professional Saleswomen,* Sacramento, Cal.

Sales organizations such as Tupperware rely on sales meetings as the primary means of motivation of the sales force. Every Monday night distributors hold a rally to announce sales successes with considerable hoopla and celebration. In another case, the field sales manager of a New Jersey territory rented the Meadowlands football stadium. Corporate executives, family, and friends were assembled to cheer as each salesman emerged from the players' tunnel. The electric scoreboard bearing the salesperson's name and the cheering crowd motivated the salesmen to keep excelling at their jobs.[11]

Evaluation and Control of the Sales Force

An organization's overall marketing plan must be translated into a series of territorial plans or sales plans that specify regional, district, or other territorial goals. In fact, it is safe to say that the national or even international sales goal must be viewed as a collection of smaller, relatively local objectives that must be met if the overall plan is to be fulfilled. Regional plans, in turn, ultimately rest on local performances. If the objective is to expand sales in the north-east region of the United States by 10 percent during the up-coming year, the resultant sales plan may involve adding an additional salesperson to the region and placing that person where he or she can best contribute to the attainment of the prescribed goal.

On an individual basis, the sales manager and the salesperson may work together to set certain objectives for the sales representative. These are not always expressed in terms of sales generated, but can involve increasing the number of sales calls made per week or raising the representative's number of orders per sales call (the sales "batting average").[12]

Specific and measurable objectives such as these serve as the basis for reviewing an individual salesperson's performance and progress. Because salespeople are often a bit leary of how sales or other goals are set for them, the system of evaluation must be fair and based on a mutual understanding of the performance standards and how they were determined. Note that the actual performance should be measured against predetermined standards, not standards set after the fact. It does not do much good to tell the sales representative that his or her performance this past year was "not too good" when no quota or indication of what was expected was given at the start of the year. To cover this point, many salespeople are assigned a **sales quota,** a specific goal or sales volume expectation for a given period of time. During progress reviews, actual sales for the period can then be compared with the quota.

At IBM, sales quotas are used as a motivational tool. IBM sets their sales quotas at a level to ensure that 70 to 80 percent of its salespeople reach their goals. The company wants their sales force to be confident and to consider themselves winners rather than losers. The logic goes something like this: If a person perceives himself as a winner he will start acting like one. The IBM quota system reinforces a positive attitude in individuals.[13] Nothing succeeds like success.

Sales managers, in order to do their jobs properly and meet their own goals or quotas, must develop instruments of control which provide feedback from salespeople in the field. This feedback tells managers if they should proceed with plans as scheduled, change course, look into particular problems, or check in with local sales personnel to take corrective action. For example, a simple but fundamental aspect of the sales manager's job is to assure that each salesperson is calling on an appropriate number of customers. In most companies, therefore, sales representatives keep a log, **call report,** or activity report that must be filed, weekly or monthly, to indicate the number of calls made and to relate special information about their accounts. Sales managers then evaluate this "paperwork" to determine whether or not the sales representative is working at an appropriate intensity.

An evaluation of the sales representative's paperwork may indicate to management that the salesperson enjoys calling on old stand-by accounts but seems to avoid trying to develop new accounts. This could indicate a need for additional motivation or training on approaching non-current customers. Perhaps a change in the

---

[11] T.J. Peters and R.H. Waterman, Jr., *In Search of Excellence: Lessons from America's Best-Run Companies* (New York: Harper & Row, 1983), p. xxiv.

[12] For an innovative approach to allocate selling efforts, see R. LaForge and D. Cravens, "Steps in Selling-Effort Deployment," *Industrial Marketing Management*, 1982, Vol. 11, pp. 183, 194.

---

[13] Based on data in T.J. Peters and R.H. Waterman, Jr., *In Search of Excellence, Lessons from America's Best-Run Companies* (New York: Harper & Row, 1982), pp. 56–57.

compensation plan, for example raising the commission on new business, could be in order.

Management of Sales Agents

As was discussed in the chapters dealing with channels of distribution, many marketing organizations have no sales force of their own because they use selling agents or manufacturers' agents. This presents a special problem to sales managers within these organizations in that they must devise means to "manage" salespeople who are not under their direct control. These agents, in fact, need sales training or other guidance as much as do company salespeople but, as independent agents, they may be understand-ably less than enthusiastic to take time off from selling. These kinds of conflicting goals and viewpoints can lead to stormy relationships.

There is hope in all this, however. Sales managers dealing with agents can and do adopt management tools for this special situation. Calling attention to the importance of a manufacturer's product to the agent's livelihood is not the only means to gain cooperation. Agents respond to monetary incentives such as commission rates and bonuses, sales promotion programs, and trips to Hawaii the same way company salespeople do. Dealing with agents may require special care and skill, but good sales managers can prove their worth by handling these relationships fairly and smoothly.

SALES: THE STARTING POINT FOR A MARKETING CAREER

The current president of IBM, John R. Opel, began his career at IBM as a salesman. He was so successful in sales that he was called to corporate headquarters to become assistant to Tom Watson, Jr., son of the company's founder and its then-president.[14] In fact, the chief executives of many organizations, large and small, "came up" through sales. What better way to learn about the markets on which the organization depends?

Jobs in personal selling are often utilized as starting places for individuals expected to be corporate marketing managers, vice-presidents, and presidents. The salesperson must learn the company's products *and* the company's customers to be successful. Thus, selling is an effective training ground for sales management and other management careers. Yet some individuals maintain a negative attitude towards sales positions.[15] This is partially due to a lack of under-standing of professional selling. It is particularly unfortunate since many organizations expect virtually "everybody" to start in sales. Partially because of this corporate attitude, the great majority of persons entering the business world do so in some sales-related capacity. Firestone Rubber Company, for example, hires many new college graduates, some 75 percent of them, as *retail* sales management trainees.

This chapter concludes with a description of a sales-based career path at the Kodak Corporation. While Kodak may not exemplify the attitudes of all organizations toward sales, the story is a typical enough one to merit attention. Anyone contemplating a career in the business world in general, or in marketing in particular, cannot afford to say, without proper investigation, "I don't want to be in sales."

Career Planning at Kodak

Many persons interested in a marketing career begin as salespeople.[16] Generally, there are many selling positions open to young, inex-

---

[14] "Other Maestros of the Micro," *Time*, January 3, 1983, p. 28.

"SELL" IS A FOUR LETTER WORD

Sell is a four letter word. To many it means forceful, aggressive, and high pressure persuasion. There are few figures in America that are more maligned than the salesperson. He is accused of sins ranging from running off with the farmer's daughter to convincing poor, helpless people that they should buy products for which they have no need. In reality, the salesperson has no more fascination for the farmer's daughter than does an accountant, a banker, or a wandering rock star. And, since the salesperson has not mastered the intricacies of the human mind, he is, therefore, seldom able to impose unwanted products onto the helpless public. Just because it is a four letter word doesn't mean that "sell" should have a negative connotation. Unfortunately, even the authors have used the term "sales orientation" in a negative context to make a point (Chapter 1). We did so to emphasize the true nature of effective marketing. However, at this point, you must realize ever, at this point, you must realize does a disservice to those who are involved in personal selling within organizations operating under the marketing concept. Sales is a profession of the utmost importance in marketing. This does not mean to imply that there are no aggressive, hard-hitting sales representatives, but the drummer of dubious social values such as Willy Loman (in *Death of a Salesman*) is no longer wanted or needed in today's economy. The contemporary professional salesperson requires different qualities than Willy's for a successful career in selling.

Source: Adapted with permission from W.J.E. Crissy, W.H. Cunningham, and I.C.M. Cunningham, *Selling the Personal Force in Marketing* (New York: John Wiley & Sons, 1977), pp. 3–4.

perienced persons. Furthermore, since selling provides such valuable firsthand experience with the marketing process, a sales position can become the springboard for promotions into various other marketing positions. The variety of opportunities available to a person starting in industrial sales can be seen in the Eastman Kodak organization where a number of career paths are open to a sales representative (Exhibit 19-5).

Note that there are four levels of technical sales representatives at Kodak, and a person preferring to remain in sales could be promoted three times. The more typical career path is to spend six years as a technical representative and then to move to the corporate headquarters as an instructor in the marketing education center. After two years in this assignment, a person would move to a staff job in sales development, customer service, product development, market research, or advertising. Three years later, the successful individual would become a district sales manager, a senior sales representative (grade 43 or 45), or a staff assistant to a regional sales manager. At Kodak, it usually takes five years before a district sales manager is promoted to regional sales manager. In another five years, a regional sales manager may be promoted to national sales manager or to manager of a staff marketing department. The position of administrative assistant to the regional sales manager is a two-year assignment, and these staff people usually become district sales managers or senior sales representatives (grade 45). After a period of time, people may move from staff marketing positions to manager of one of these departments in the Kodak organization.

---

[15] The reasons for student negativism toward personal selling are reviewed in Alan J. Dubinsky, "Perceptions of the Sales Job: How Students Compare with Industrial Salespeople," *Journal of the Academy of Marketing Science* (Fall, 1981), pp. 352–367.

[16] This section is used with permission from Douglas J. Dalrymple, *Sales Management: Concepts and Cases* (New York: John Wiley & Sons, 1982), pp. 15–16.

EXHIBIT 19-5

Alternative Career Paths at Eastman Kodak

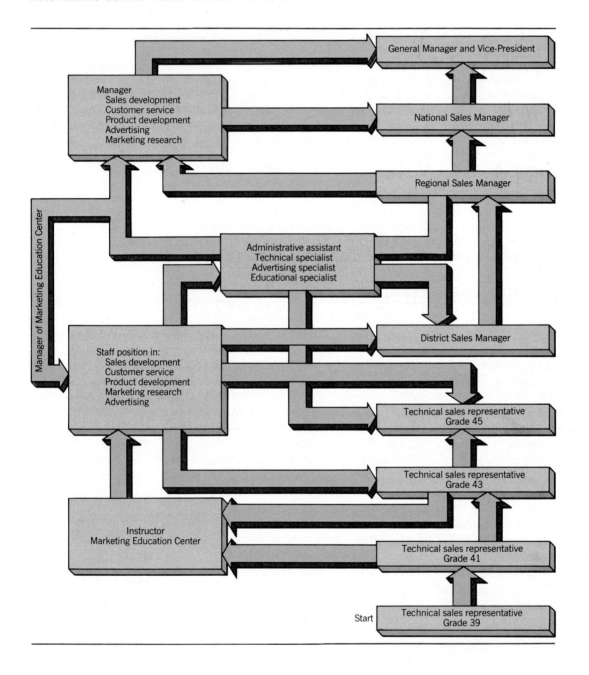

SUMMARY

Personal selling is a person-to-person dialogue between buyer and seller, where the purpose of the interaction is personal persuasion. Many marketing situations require the involvement of a personal salesperson, a professional who can effectively communicate the benefits of the products being offered. The salesperson's focus of concern should be to keep existing customers abreast of information about the company's products and services and also convey a sales message to potential customers. This sales message must be made flexible—that is, adaptable to the individual needs of each prospective customer.

There are three categories of selling positions: order-takers, order-getters, and sales support positions. The chapter also reviewed the steps through which a professional salesperson successfully finds, approaches, and makes a presentation to a customer, finally bringing about a sale. These steps are: (1) locating and qualifying prospects, (2) the approach, (3) the sales presentation, (4) handling objectives, (5) closing the sale, and (6) the follow-up. Salespersons are often supported in their jobs by technical specialists or sales correspondents.

This chapter also reviewed some of the major tasks of sales managers. The management of sales personnel is an important job that requires the ability to effectively organize, recruit, train, motivate, and evaluate a sales force.

Finally, compensation for sales personnel may be a straight salary, a commission based on sales, or a combination of these plans.

In concluding, the chapter presented a portrait of a sales position as the first step in a marketing management career.

THE MOST IMPORTANT CONCEPT IN THIS CHAPTER

Professional selling is the basis on which most organizational successes are built. Selling is most effective when it reflects the marketing concept—that is, when it is viewed as a flexible process whereby customer needs are identified and fulfilled on an individual basis.

KEY TERMS

Order-takers

Order-getters

Creative selling

Missionary sales

Prospecting

Creative selling process

Sales presentation

Closing

Sales team

Sales correspondent

Qualifying the prospect

Approach

Sales presentation

Handling objections

Trial close

Follow-up

Closing signals

Sales management

Field sales managers

Retail sales forces

Sales objectives

Sales territory

Straight salary method

Straight commission plan

Commission with draw

Quota-bonus plan

Salary plus commission

Sales quota

Call report

QUESTIONS FOR DISCUSSION

1 Would you expect the salesperson to be an order-taker or an order-getter in the following situations:
(a) Selling cable TV subscriptions to home-owners.
(b) Sales of industrial power tools to purchasing agents in the aircraft industry.
(c) Selling blocks of Oakland A's season tickets to businesses who entertain customers at the games.
(d) Sale of paper product supplies to office supply stores.

2 How would you prospect and qualify customer accounts if you were selling:
(a) Chain saws to hardware wholesalers.
(b) Installations of cables for computer networks to offices.

3 "Salesmen are born not made." Comment.

4 What are the steps in the personal selling process? Which is the most important step?

5 Handle the following objections:
(a) "The price is too high."
(b) "I don't have enough money I'll have to wait a month or two."
(c) "I'm just not certain if I need one or not."

6 The sales volume of a man with 25 years selling experience begins to slip. How would you motivate him to work hard?

7 Be creative. How can a sales manager determine the number of salespeople to hire?

8 Over a five-year period, a company keeps the same sales personnel in the same geographical territories. What problems might this create?

9 Why do most college students avoid careers in personal selling?

10 How much do you think the average cost per contact is when personal visits are utilized?

CASE 19-1 Food Dynamics*

Food Dynamics Inc. was born in 1976 when Bob Galvin, Bob Beaudry, and Florence Busch decided to strike out on their own, leaving a large New England food brokerage firm where they had been star salespeople. Within 30 days, they'd signed on seven product lines—which meant a total of $8,000 a month in commissions.

Their move, though, presented them with an important question: How could they keep top salespeople from eventually leaving their new company? If Food Dynamics was going to grow, the three partners knew they'd have to give their salespeople a reason to stay.

At first, there were no employees to worry

about losing. Galvin, Beaudry, and Busch, representing their manufacturers' food lines, traveled around New England with their sample cases; they called mainly on buyers from hospitals, restaurants, schools, and food distribution companies. Since they put any profits into building up Food Dynamics's image, they ran a lean operation.

"I remember when Beaudry and I first began going down to Connecticut for overnight stays," Galvin recalls. "One of us would check into a motel room and the other would sneak up later. It worked out fine until one night we got to the room only to find a single bed." Then, he remembers with a laugh, "we learned just how close a partnership we had."

After two years, the partners decided they were ready to expand. They wanted to hire individuals who were not just good salespeople, but

---

*Source: From Eileen B. Brill, "Making Sales People into Entrepreneurs," *INC*, July 1982, p. 87. Used with permission.

would also become almost as loyal to the company as they themselves were. All three believed that the best salespeople were entrepreneurs at heart who wanted a sense of participation in the business as well as a paycheck. One way to inspire loyalty, they felt, was to give the people they hired a stake in the company by tying commissions to the salesperson's contribution to overall profits.

According to Michael King, a vice-president of the National Food Brokers Association, most food brokers pay their salespeople on a salary basis, with a bonus arrangement. The problem then, says Galvin, "is that there is really no accountability. Salespeople may know how much they do in sales, but they have no idea what their contribution is to the profitability of the company."

So when Galvin, Beaudry, and Busch hired their first seasoned professional, John Vaillancourt, they decided to offer a compensation plan that would give him a stake in the company's growth and to use this plan as a prototype when it came to compensating future employees.

Under the system set up by Food Dynamics's owners, a salesperson would not only develop sales in a territory, but would also take charge of maximizing the territory's profitability for the firm, in return for a portion of the profits earned. Vaillancourt, for example, took total responsibility for the North Country market of Maine, New Hampshire, and Vermont. Food Dynamics, which specializes in providing food for restaurants, hospitals, and schools, among other institutions, had barely penetrated the three northern states and hoped Vaillancourt could increase its sales there to distributors and large-scale consumers.

Vaillancourt received a salary, plus a quarterly bonus based on a careful calculation of the profits he brought in from his area. The owners issued regular reports, advising Vaillancourt of the direct expenses that Food Dynamics had paid out for his salary and expenses. They also added in indirect expenses, figured as a percentage of the cost of maintaining the company's Wellesley, Mass., headquarters and its sales and service staff. After all expenses were subtracted from total sales for the territory, Vaillancourt then received an agreed-upon percentage of the profit.

Vaillancourt found the system gave him incentive to develop his territory—and an equally strong incentive to stay with Food Dynamics once he had developed it. "They treat my territory like another branch of the company," he says. "I've been given a great deal of autonomy, but when I need help the company is right there beside me."

"By making our salespeople responsible for their costs," says Galvin, "we make them more conscious of what's involved in the day-to-day running of our operation. People tend to think that items such as typewriter ribbons don't cost anything. Our financial reports also show the cyclical nature of the business—that we rely on the third and fourth quarters to carry us through the slower half." Moreover, tying bonuses directly to profits conserves Food Dynamics's cash flow in unprofitable periods.

Food Dynamics now has 3 key salespeople—out of a total staff of 19—managing portions of New England. The share of the firm's overhead and sales-support costs that each salesperson must cover varies, depending on the owners' assessment of his territory's potential. Once a year, each of these salespeople meets with the owners to discuss the projected revenues the company can expect from his territory. Expenses are also estimated for the coming year, and the difference represents the profit likely to be shared with the salesperson.

The company had to work closely with its salespeople in adjusting the profit-based compensation system to the firm's changing needs. Occasionally the company decides to invest in expanding its influence in a given territory; initially there may be no profits for the salesperson to share. That happened when Food Dynamics first hired Vaillancourt to develop the North Country. The solution: an agreement that for the first few pay periods, Food Dynamics's headquarters budget would absorb some of the expenses that would normally have been charged against Vaillancourt's territory.

Finding a compensation system that gave salespeople a stake in the company was a major step for the three partners, but they also recognized that they needed to go beyond dollars and cents if they were going to hang on to their top performers. "At some point," says Galvin, "salary becomes a moot question. More money is not always the way to secure a salesperson's loyalty."

Thus the partners structured the company so that salespeople in the field could count on a maximum of support and personal attention from the three owners. As additional salespeople were hired, each was assigned to the partner who knew the territory best and who could offer the most expert help whenever it was needed. Several times a year, for example, Beaudry visits Vaillancourt's territory to make special presentations to local distributors. And at trade shows at least one partner always works side by side with Food Dynamics's salespeople.

Constant telephone contact is the rule. "When we talk with our salespeople by phone, often three to four times a day, they don't feel that we're checking up on them," Galvin says. "Usually we discuss things like 'How can we increase distribution here?' or 'What's the quickest way to ship a product?' There are no mandates sent down from a central office."

The three partners have placed a great deal of emphasis on developing the skills and knowledge of their salespeople. They send them on trips to manufacturing plants to get a firsthand view of how products are made, and encourage direct contacts between salespeople and the manufacturers whose lines they represent—considered a risky tactic in the food brokerage business, since good salespeople often use their connections with manufacturers to launch their own firms. "We have faith in our ability to pick the right people," says Galvin. "In six years, we've lost only one line through a salesperson's leaving the company—and that salesperson came into our company with three lines."

The results of Food Dynamics's approach to managing salespeople have been financial success and team spirit. Only one salesperson has resigned in the company's history. Today annual sales are $30 million, and 22 top food manufacturers are represented.

"I guess the possibility that we could lose a key salesperson always exists, but I don't lose any sleep over it." Galvin says. "We feel pretty confident that our salespeople enjoy their work, are motivated, and have little reason to move someplace else."

Questions

1 Evaluate the compensation program at Food Dynamics.

2 Is sales management doing a good job of motivating the sales force?

CASE 19-2 Wally Boyce Retires

Wally Boyce, known as the Dean of college textbook sales among his peers, had been in his Southwestern territory longer than just about anyone could remember. He always made his quota of calls every day, giving book information to the professors he called upon. During his 26 years with McGraw-Hill Book Company, Wally had made many friends in the universities on which he called. He stressed service and the building of long-term relationships. An avid tennis player, Wally cultivated a group of tennis playing professors on almost every campus. Business with pleasure seemed to work for Wally who had been McGraw-Hill's top salesperson several times. So he always treated for a few beers after the match. Stories of deans' and professors' idiosyncrasies were a frequent topic, along with jokes and discussions about the textbooks in the field.

The "year" Wally was supposed to retire a fellow salesman sent the following letter. Wally knew nothing about it.

Questions

1 Why do professors adopt textbooks? What buying motives does the letter appeal to?
2 Why is Wally Boyce a successful salesman?
3 Will the letter work?

March 26th, 1982

W.G. Zikmund
Marketing
Oklahoma State University
Stillwater, OK 74078

Dear Professor Zikmund:

Wally Boyce is going to retire.........Let me introduce myself and explain why I'm writing. (Professor Zikmund, I'm not going to try and "kid" you, I'm using a little "home-brew" computer technology to compose and print this letter.) Anyway, my name is Don Sannes. I'm a friend and colleague of Wally's. (That means that I am the McGraw-Hill rep based in Austin.) I'm writing because I had this idea that seems like a no lose proposition.

I feel that all of us, as we consider retirement, would like to leave our job while making a final significant contribution. Well in the book business, at McGraw-Hill, no single sales rep has ever achieved a one million dollar sales year. To us, a $1,000,000.00 sales year is a really big deal. It is our 1,000 yards rushing, a hole in one, and four minute mile wrapped into one shot. Wally has a very real chance to attain that sales goal this year. However, I thought that if I would bring his goal to your attention (I'm sending this letter to people listed on Wally's calling records having a lot of checkmarks behind their names - I hope that adds up to people who know him.) you might, as you and your colleagues at Oklahoma State University decide on books for next falls classes, take a closer look at McGraw-Hill texts. (I know that you use many of our books, but there's always another course.) Part one of my proposition is that McGraw-Hill is the leading publisher of business, economics and engineering books, and in many cases using one of our books means that you are adopting a best selling book. Second, Wally's sales quota is high this year, in the range of seven hundred and fifty thousand dollars. He'll make his quota, he usually does, and by doing so will earn a bonus. But if he really hits (makes the one million dollar goal) his bonus will be in the twenty thousand dollar range. Not a bad retirement present. Third, as Wally's agent I stand to........No, seriously, I'm not sure if Wally would be upset if he knew I was writing this or if he would love it. (I suspect the latter.) In any case, if Wally decides to stick around and bask in the limelight and not retire next year I have your address and this letter on disk and I'll send it again next year. I'll just up the ante. Thank you for your support.

Sincerely,

Don Sannes

CHAPTER 20

Advertising

CHAPTER SCAN

We have said that marketing is both art and science. Advertising is the area of marketing where the art of marketing is most visible. This chapter traces the development of advertisements from the setting of communication goals to be achieved through the weighing of the advantages and disadvantages of the various advertising media.

Any description of advertising technique is flawed by the inherent problem of describing the "spark of creativity" so important to the construction of an attractive, attention-getting advertisement. However, the description of the tools and techniques used by advertisers, the models around which they can build their appeals, and the goals they seek to accomplish, do serve to give a good picture of what effective advertising involves.

WHEN YOU HAVE STUDIED THIS CHAPTER, YOU WILL:

Know how to define and use such terms as product advertising, institutional advertising, and direct-action advertising.

Know the difference between primary demand and selective demand advertising.

Be able to discuss the process followed in the development of an advertisement.

Be familiar with the role communication objectives play in the advertising process.

Be able to show how advertisements are likely to change over the course of a product life cycle.

Be able to explain the nature of an advertising appeal and to name and describe several commonly used formats to execute these appeals.

Be familiar with the various measures of advertising effectiveness, and advertising research techniques.

Be able to identify the advantages and disadvantages of different advertising media.

Insurance is a tough sale. Nobody likes to pay for something they cannot see or feel. Nobody likes to think about the loss that makes paying premiums necessary. Because it is difficult to depict such loss, it is often done in a humorous way to avoid upsetting potential customers—you know, the tree falling across the neighbor's house. To believably depict the probabilities of incurring such loss, insurance advertising stays conservative by showing corporate strength or building name awareness and identity.[1]

One Allstate commercial is notable. It has drama and emotion. It hits home. The scene is a burning house. The flames crackle. The camera, however, stays on the family that lived in that home. The sky is red, reflected in their eyes and in the windows of the fire department vehicles behind them. Finally, the family gets into the police car to be taken away. Their blank faces show their loss—as few advertisements have. The announcer makes the "home replacement guarantee . . . brick for brick" sales point in a voice that shows concern.

This television advertisement for Allstate illustrates the emotion, drama, and fascination of advertising. But television commercials for consumer goods are, despite their appeal and familiarity, only a small part of the advertising world. Advertising is utilized for a wide variety of purposes by many diverse organizations including businesses, non-profit and charitable groups, religious organizations, and all levels of govern-

---

CORVAIR FOR SALE

The authors have a friend (ahem) who was once the owner of a 14-year-old Chevrolet Corvair, an interesting but rusted-out rear-engine small car that was becoming increasingly difficult to keep operating. Deciding to sell it and wrongfully, it seems, figuring that a potential car buyer either really wants a 14-year-old Corvair or does not, he ran a simple newspaper advertisement reading, "1966 Corvair for sale. Call xxx-xxxx." Though he received a few calls, no prospective buyers came to see the car and it remained unsold.

A week later his wife ran an advertisement in the paper for the same car. This advertisement read, "Prove Ralph Nader wrong. Drive a classic Corvair and be the envy of the neighborhood." You get the idea, and you have probably guessed that the car sold within two days.

---

ment. Individual citizens use advertising in two ways. One is as a source of information about available products and services, the other as a means to publicize garage sales, club meetings, and lost pets.

All advertising has two basic components in common: creation of a message and selection of a media to carry the message.

PRODUCT AND INSTITUTIONAL ADVERTISING

As was shown in Chapter 18, promotion, including advertising, is a form of communication. Communication specialists have, therefore, developed many concepts and theories having application to advertising. These specialists have pointed out that messages can be viewed as being either consummatory or instrumental. **Con-**

summatory messages are delivered with the intent that something must be done right now, that is, some action must be consummated. "Come here!" and "Watch out!" are such messages. **Instrumental messages,** on the other hand, are intended to have some longer-term effect rather than to induce an immediate action. If a woman mentions that her favorite color is blue, her husband, remembering this months later, may present her with a blue dress.

---

[1] From "Critics Corner," *Advertising Age*, August 9, 1982, p. M-15. Adapted with permission.

These two types of messages are also found in the advertising world. Although the names used to describe them are different, the intents are the same.

Product Advertising

Advertisements for Wrigley's gum, Special-K cereal, and many other brands are clearly intended to suggest purchasing a particular product. When Sears advertises a special price on refrigerators, the message is that the refrigerators must be bought now if the low price is desired. The Sears advertisement is a **product advertisement** because it features a specific product. Since the Sears refrigerator advertisement suggests an immediate purchase, it is also what is termed a **direct-action advertisement.** Many advertisements seen on television and many direct-mail advertisements are of this type. Record companies frequently advertise that a special album can be purchased using Visa or MasterCard by calling a toll-free 800 number. The Book-of-the-Month Club mails announcements of its latest offering to club members' homes and includes a return envelope so that the latest selections can be ordered. Both cases are representative of direct-action advertising. Direct-action advertisements, in general, utilize coupons, toll-free telephone numbers, or invitations to call collect in order to facilitate action and encourage people to "buy now." Much retail advertising emphasizes direct action. Less aggressive advertisements, designed to sell products as well as to build brand image or position a brand rather than to sell merchandise right this minute, are also forms of product advertising. This type of advertising calls for *indirect action.* The **indirect-action advertisement** makes use of a soft sell approach calculated to stimulate sales over the longer run.

Institutional Advertising

"Baseball fever . . . catch it" is an institutional advertising slogan. So is DuPont's "Better living through chemistry" and Sears Roebuck's "Sears has everything." **Institutional advertising** does

CORPORATE ADVERTISING

Tell Me Quick and Tell Me True
I see that you've spent quite a big wad of dough
To tell me the things you think I should know.
How your plant is so big, so fine, and so strong;
And your founder had whiskers so handsomely
  long.
So he started the business in old '92!
How tremendously interesting that is—to you.
He built up the thing with the blood of his life?
(I'll run home like mad, tell that to my wife!)
Your machinery's modern and oh so complete;
Your "rep" is so flawless; your workers so neat.
Your motto is "Quality"—capital "Q"—
No wonder I'm tired of "Your" and of "You"!
So tell me quick and tell me true
Less—"how this company came to be"
More—"what it can do for me!"

Anonymous

Source: As quoted in John H. Hoefer, "Corporate Institutional Advertising: What's Wrong With It?" Vol. 42, No. 2, *The Stanford Business School Bulletin,* 1974.

not stress a particular ball team or game, or an individual product. Instead, it accents the sponsoring institution. The baseball advertisement, for example, attempts to build primary or generic demand for the sport. The advertisements paid for by DuPont and Sears stress how wonderful, responsible, or efficient those companies, taken as wholes, actually are. Contrasting the "baseball fever" slogan with such team slogans as "The Cubs are coming out of hibernation" or "Meet the Mets" makes the difference between institutional advertising and product advertising quite clear.

In general, institutional advertisements aim to promote a corporate image, to stimulate generic demand for a product, or to build goodwill for an industry. Phillips Petroleum has been running institutional advertising for some years, calling attention to itself as "The Performance Company" and stressing its lesser-known activities beyond those of oil exploration and refining.

MILK.
THE FRESHEST PART
OF THE BIG APPLE.

american dairy association

This institutional advertisement promotes many brands of milk.

The intention is to demonstrate that the firm is socially responsible and productive. It just might have some connection with the negative public image oil companies have been saddled with since the shortage periods of the 1970s. Letting it be known that "Tomorrow is taking place at TRW" should promote goodwill and increase investment in the company. These advertisements, and similar advertisements of other organizations, are aimed at the roles we all play as citizens, conversationalists, investors, and voters, rather than our roles as consumers or buyers.

PLANNING AND DEVELOPING ADVERTISING CAMPAIGNS

Development of an effective advertising campaign requires a stream of interconnected decisions on such matters as budgeting and media strategy as well as a strong creative strategy. The process followed in planning and developing an advertising program is shown in Exhibit 20-1. Each of the activities involved in the process is discussed in the following sections.

Overall Advertising Objectives

As we have seen throughout this book, goals must be decided before any work on plans or actions is begun. This edict is equally true where advertising is involved. Before developing a single advertisement, management must ask what the advertising is expected to do.

The ultimate answer, where advertising is concerned, is that "advertising is supposed to sell the product." That statement is too broad; the objective is too demanding to be truly useful to marketing planners. Advertising is, after all, only one element of the marketing mix. It affects and is affected by the product, the price, the packaging, the distribution, and the other promotional mix elements. All of these elements combine to sell the product; advertising does not do the job alone.

EXHIBIT   20-1

Advertising Planning and Development

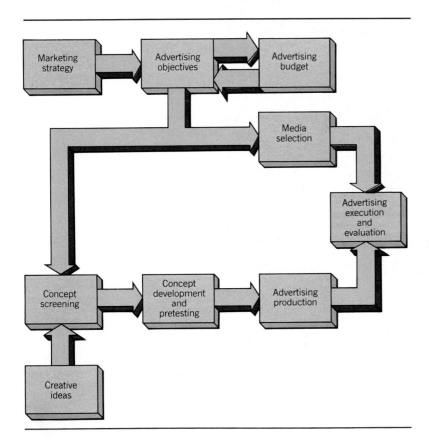

Regardless of the appeal and longevity of advertising campaigns such as Miller Lite's, Hathaway's, or Folger's, successful advertisements do not stand by themselves. Effective advertising campaigns are developed as part of an overall marketing strategy, and are tightly coordinated with the other facets of the promotional mix.

Four Communication Goals for Advertisements

Advertising can certainly be expected to contribute to sales totals or other measures of an organization's success. However, advertising is only a method of communication. Therefore, objectives directly related to advertising should be communication goals. In general, advertisers expect to accomplish four broad **communication goals:** Advertisements are expected to generate *attention*, to be *understood*, to be *believed*, and to be *remembered*. These goals relate to sales, but they are primarily matters of communication. If these broad objectives are not considered and met, the more specific objectives will not be met either. If attention is not paid to an advertisement, the more specific objective, such as to enhance a romantic brand image, cannot be achieved. Likewise, an advertisement must be understood and believed if it is to reinforce or change perceptions about a brand's characteristics. If it is not remembered, it will have little effect on buyer behavior. Although these broad objectives permeate most of advertising,

THE GIANT ARMADILLO AND LONE STAR BEER

It was a memorable advertising campaign that featured a fictitious (off screen) giant armadillo that rambled across the Lone Star State terrorizing Texans in its search to satisfy its unquenchable thirst for Lone Star Beer. Everyone loved the advertisements. They generated a great deal of interest. Texans loved to talk to friends about the armadillo's (the state's favorite animal) exploits.

What went wrong? The advertisements, while humorous and attention getting, did not sell the product. Research showed the giant armadillo advertising stirred some interest at the onset, but did not have a lasting impact. The campaign did not have staying power. Since the ultimate objective is to sell the product, the advertisement moved on into never-never land.

Source: From "The Giant Armadillo—R.I.P.," *Ad Week*, April 18, 1983, p. 4. Used with permission.

the development of advertising campaigns requires that objectives be more specific.

Specific Advertising Objectives

Encouraging increased consumption of a product by current users, generating more sales leads, increasing brand awareness, increasing repeat purchases, and supporting the personal selling effort are typical objectives for specific advertisements. As Exhibit 20-1 illustrates, the specific objectives that are developed from these goals provide the framework for the creative strategy. Many advertisements have disappeared from the media, even though "everybody liked them" because they did not contribute to accomplishment of these specific objectives. Advertising based strictly on creativity and not on a marketing objective frequently does not contribute to achievement of the goals that must be accomplished. When a "great advertisement" does not contribute to a better share of the market,

the introduction of a new product, or other like objectives, it is only great in the creative sense. In the business sense, however, it is far from great.

Opportunities in the marketplace, competitive advertising campaigns, and prior marketing strategy decisions, such as selection of a target market segment, all influence the development of specific advertising objectives. Clearly, Pepsi's advertising for the "original" Pepsi-Cola is aimed at regular, brand-loyal users of the product. It has a substantially different purpose than the advertising campaign used to introduce new Pepsi Free, the caffeine-free cola. Promotion to regular customers requires a campaign built around the objective of reminding customers of regular Pepsi's image and of their satisfaction with the product. Regular buyers do not need detailed information about the product and its contents. Further incentives, such as 50-cents off coupons, are nice—but the regular Pepsi-drinker will buy the product with or without them.

Other objectives must be served, however, when advertising the newer Pepsi Free. The product must be "explained." Potential customers need to know what the product does and does not contain. They must be told why they should try the product. And further incentives, such as a cents-off deal, may encourage people unfamiliar with Pepsi Free to try the new cola. The persuasion needed to woo loyal 7-Up drinkers to Pepsi Free is another matter that may require a separate objective. Each situation will dictate different advertising objectives.

Advertising Objectives and the Product Life Cycle

Advertising objectives change with varying environmental conditions, as do all other aspects of marketing. Marketing is dynamic; advertising, as one of its most visible components, must be especially reflective of change.

The concept of the product life cycle usefully illustrates the notion of change. As Exhibit 20-2 shows, advertising objectives change over the course of a product's life. During the in-

EXHIBIT 20-2

Changes in Advertising Objectives during the Product Life Cycle

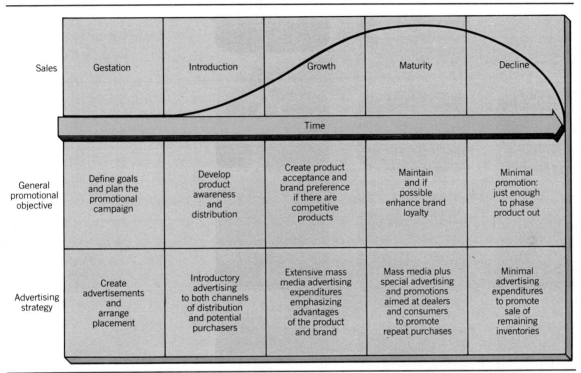

Sales	Gestation	Introduction	Growth	Maturity	Decline
General promotional objective	Define goals and plan the promotional campaign	Develop product awareness and distribution	Create product acceptance and brand preference if there are competitive products	Maintain and if possible enhance brand loyalty	Minimal promotion: just enough to phase product out
Advertising strategy	Create advertisements and arrange placement	Introductory advertising to both channels of distribution and potential purchasers	Extensive mass media advertising expenditures emphasizing advantages of the product and brand	Mass media plus special advertising and promotions aimed at dealers and consumers to promote repeat purchases	Minimal advertising expenditures to promote sale of remaining inventories

Source: J.G. Udell and G.R. Laczniak, *Marketing in an Age of Change* (New York: John Wiley & Sons, 1981), p. 371. Used with permission.

troductory stage of the product life cycle, developing consumer brand awareness and getting customers to try the product are normal advertising objectives. Trade advertising to attract and interest distributors in carrying the product is equally important, although less obvious, during this stage. Additional trade advertising may be developed later, with the objective of increasing the numbers of distributors and retail outlets. At the start of a product life cycle, it is necessary to develop **generic demand** for the product—that is, demand for the product class as a whole must be stimulated. This kind of advertising, which often must be so basic as to explain what a product is and how it works, is called **primary demand advertising.** It seeks to introduce the product without particular concern for different brands of the product. Advertising of this sort is also called *pioneering advertising.*

The Mature Product

As products move through their product life cycles, the expectations that marketing managers have for their advertising campaigns inevitably change. "Times like these are made for Taster's Choice" is a good example of an advertising campaign for a product in the maturity stage of the product life cycle. The advertisements no longer have to explain why freeze-dried coffee is different from ordinary instant coffee. They dwell, instead, on **selective demand advertising**—promoting a specific brand. These advertisements reflect the psychological or emotional dimensions of the brand and the situations in

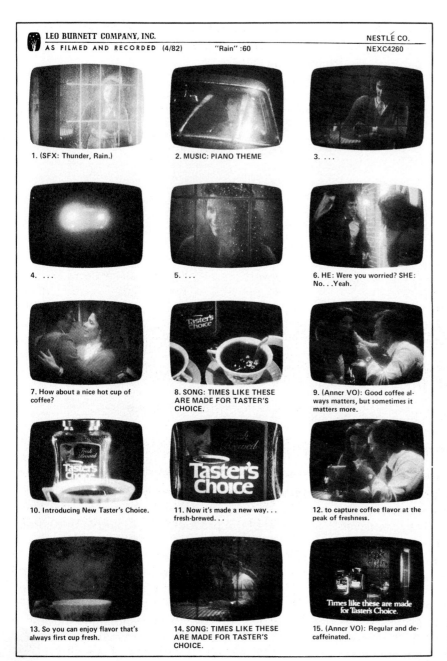

LEO BURNETT COMPANY, INC. NESTLÉ CO.
AS FILMED AND RECORDED (4/82) "Rain" :60 NEXC4260

1. (SFX: Thunder, Rain.)

2. MUSIC: PIANO THEME

3. . . .

4. . . .

5. . . .

6. HE: Were you worried? SHE: No. . .Yeah.

7. How about a nice hot cup of coffee?

8. SONG: TIMES LIKE THESE ARE MADE FOR TASTER'S CHOICE.

9. (Anncr VO): Good coffee always matters, but sometimes it matters more.

10. Introducing New Taster's Choice.

11. Now it's made a new way. . . fresh-brewed. . .

12. to capture coffee flavor at the peak of freshness.

13. So you can enjoy flavor that's always first cup fresh.

14. SONG: TIMES LIKE THESE ARE MADE FOR TASTER'S CHOICE.

15. (Anncr VO): Regular and decaffeinated.

Advertising for a mature product focusing on emotional dimensions of the brand.

which it is consumed. Since most products on the market *are* in their maturity stages, much advertising tends to emphasize psychological benefits. Advertisements stress the reasons brand X is better than its competitors instead of emphasizing the newness or uniqueness of the generic product, as is done at the start of the product life cycle.

In the case of mature products, there is relatively little emphasis on advertising product features. Messages that are increasingly symbolic accompany the product's "aging process." Partly, this reflects the fact that mature products have found their niche in the marketplace. They have been positioned, either by marketers or by the forces of the market itself, to appeal to smaller and more specialized market segments than when they were new and lacked intense competition.

The most commonly encountered advertising objectives for mature products may be summarized as follows.

1 Increase the number of buyers.

- Create brand awareness among previously unaware consumers.

- Convert buyers of competitive brands.
- Reduce brand switching among current customers.
- Appeal to new market segments.

2 Increase rate of usage among current users.

- Remind customers to use the brand.
- Inform consumers of new uses.[2]

CREATIVE STRATEGY

To develop the copy or message takes a creative spark—a feeling of about how a product when presented in print or over the airwaves will, in fact, persuade a consumer to act. It is probably in the execution where persuasion is built into the advertising.[3]

In advertising, the generation of ideas and the development of the advertising message or concept is called **the creative process.** Actually, creativity is necessary to all aspects of the marketing mix, but the term has come to be particularly associated with the people who actually develop and construct advertisements. Whether creative activity is based on information gathered by marketing research or on analysis by management, the basic thrust of an advertising message is largely developed by the creative departments of advertising agencies. As a result, this aspect of advertising receives a good deal of glory.

Discussing a process such as creativity is a difficult task. However, it is possible to describe schematically the steps involved in the creative process, as illustrated in Exhibit 20-3. The role played by that elusive something called creativity, however, can only be shown as the occurrence of a "creative spark."

As Exhibit 20-3 shows, information, insight, and the framework for marketing decisions combine with the creative spark in the production of an advertisement. When these tangible and intangible elements are present, the advertising copy writers, art directors, and other creative people are left with the task of answering two questions: *What* to say and *how* to say it.[4] These questions reflect the two basic parts of the creative strategy.

What to Say—The Appeal

The central idea of an advertising message is referred to as the **advertising appeal.** As the name suggests, the purpose of the appeal, and of the advertisement, is to tell potential buyers what the product offers and why the product is or should be appealing to them. Thinking about advertisements we have seen brings to mind the many kinds of appeals advertisers employ. It may be that the product offered has sex appeal, is compatible with the target customer's life-style (or desired life-style), or solves some particular problem such as "morning mouth," "medicine breath," or the need to protect teeth with a fluoride mouthwash.

Commercial messages making firm promises like, "Never again will you have to weed your lawn, thanks to Jiffy Kill" are frequently heard. Many advertisers believe an approach that

---

[2]Kenneth A. Longman, *Advertising* (New York: Harcourt Brace Jovanovich, 1971), p. 121.

[3]A.A. Achenbaum, Senior Vice President, J. Walter Thompson Advertising Agency, Testimony to the Federal Trade Commission, 1971.

[4]Michael L. Ray, *Advertising and Communications Management* (Englewood Cliffs, N.J.: Prentice-Hall, 1982), pp. 311–312.

WHO HANDLES ADVERTISING?

Advertising departments vary from one-man organizations to hundreds, depending on the size of the advertising budget, the importance of advertising to the company, and the industry within which it competes. A typical advertising department within a large company marketing consumer goods might resemble Diagram A. The Marketing Director has reporting to him the Sales Manager with his staff, as well as the Advertising Manager and his staff, in addition to Sales Promotion and Merchandising personnel.

The advertising staff might have as many as 100 people or more and might include specialists in research, copy, media, etc., in addition to people [the so-called product or brand managers] assigned directly against specific brands which the company markets.

Now let's look at a typical advertising agency structure (Diagram B). Reporting to the President are four main divisions: (a) Creative Services, which includes writers, artists, TV and print production people, as well as traffic personnel; (b) Client Service people, which include account supervisors and executives; (c) Marketing Services, within which media, research, and sales promotion functions are performed, and (d) Administrative and Finance, which includes personnel, accounting, finance, etc.

Two functions, unique to advertising, are discussed here:

Creative Services

It is the job of the creative person to put into words and pictures a unique, attention-getting and persuasive message for the advertiser's product or service. The creative process is a highly cooperative one. Other agency departments supply information and objectives; writers and art directors work as a team to conceive, write, design, and produce commercials or print ads.

Production: From the moment an ad is designed and written to the time it actually appears in magazines, newspapers, or on television, it is in the hands of the production people. They know what's practical for reproduction and work with the creative department in planning their work. They may purchase the graphic art services and materials and otherwise see assignments through to completion.

Traffic: It is the responsibility of this group to see that all production of the agency flows on a predetermined timetable. They also are responsible for the delivery of engravings, recordings, and films to publications, radio, and TV stations.

Client Services

The key to the working relationship between the advertiser and its agency is in the account staff of the agency. In charge of each account is an *account supervisor,* sometimes assisted by one or more account executives. These people are the basic coordinating point between the agency and the advertiser . . . [and are] responsible for interpreting the needs of an advertiser and communicating these needs to the staff people in the various departments of the agency. . . . [They] are usually responsible, in conjunction with the advertiser, for the development of marketing and advertising strategies also.

It is the account staff which interprets these strategies to the copywriters, artists, media planners and buyers, researchers, and others in the agency who do the work of executing the strategies into finished advertising. The account staff is also responsible for presenting the finished advertising to the client's advertising department for approvals (including medical, legal, and policy considerations). After such approvals, they see that the advertising is placed in media according to the approved plan.

Advertising agencies are compensated in a variety of ways for their services. This compensation includes fees from advertisers, but the great bulk of agency income is derived from commissions paid by media to the agency on advertising placed by the agency for a client. Historically, this commission has been 15% of the gross time or space cost of advertising placed.

Source: Excerpts from E.M. Thiele, Vice Chairman of the Board of Leo Bernett Company and Chairman of the Board Association of Advertising Agency's Testimony to the Federal Trade Commission in 1971.

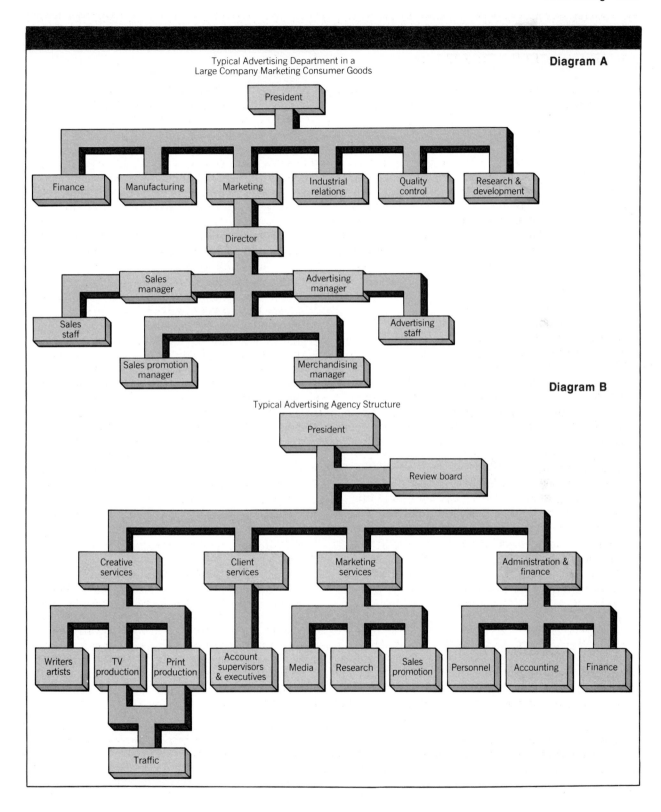

Typical Advertising Department in a
Large Company Marketing Consumer Goods

Diagram A

President

Finance · Manufacturing · Marketing · Industrial relations · Quality control · Research & development

Director

Sales manager · Advertising manager

Sales staff

Advertising staff

Sales promotion manager · Merchandising manager

Diagram B

Typical Advertising Agency Structure

President

Review board

Creative services · Client services · Marketing services · Administration & finance

Writers artists · TV production · Print production · Account supervisors & executives · Media · Research · Sales promotion · Personnel · Accounting · Finance

Traffic

EXHIBIT 20-3

Executing and Creating the Advertisement

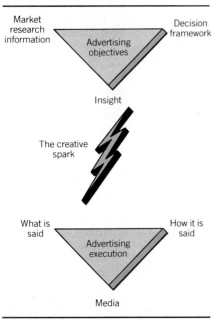

Source: Adapted from A.A. Achenbaum, Testimony to the Federal Trade Commission, 1971.

specifically describes the answer to a problem in this manner is the most effective. Other advertisements are built around an appeal that is less straightforward, such as the cigarette, beer, and hotel advertisements that stress brand image. When the same advertising appeal is used in several different advertisements to provide continuity to an advertising campaign, it is referred to as an **advertising theme.** The Army, for example, utilizes the theme, "Army—Be all you can be," in its advertising to both high school dropouts and college graduates.

Creativity is clearly the lifeblood of advertising. Its purpose is to effectively say things to people, both with and without words. The slogan, "At sixty miles an hour, the clock on the dash is the loudest thing you hear," tells the target customer something about the excellent construction of the Rolls Royce automobile. "I'm a Pepper," is a catchy phrase, as is "You've come a long way, Baby." The Hathaway man's eye patch is a symbol rich in meaning. So is the

INSIDE A MEAT PIE IS A LESSON IN THE POWER OF ADVERTISING

A few years ago, a prominent meat packer came to an advertising agency with a great new product—a delicious meat pie inside a steel container that simply had to be popped into an oven to prepare. The agency created advertising that was tested and found effective. But so enthusiastic was the meat packer, it didn't test the product in home use. The product got strong trade support from wholesalers and retailers in a three-state area, and advertising brought in the initial sales. Then the bottom fell out of the pie—the product was returned by the thousands because homemakers did not have the tools to open an all-metal container. This story points out what advertising *cannot* do—sell a product that can't meet a need.

To counter this sad episode, let's look at examples of what advertising can do. Advertising can induce trial. Crest toothpaste did this with its American Dental Association endorsement. Advertising can intensify usage. V-8 vegetable juice did this by repositioning as an enjoyable, rather than healthy, drink. Advertising can sustain preference. Parkay has been assaulted by margarine competitors for 30 years, but still holds top spot. Advertising confirms imagery. Chivas Regal backs its premier Scotch image with premier advertising. Advertising can build line acceptance. Kraft exudes a feeling of wholesomeness that benefits everything from cheese to mayonnaise. Advertising opens doors for salespersons. Avon ladies are welcome because of the lilting "Avon calling" theme. Advertising creates ambience. McDonald's is no longer millions of factory hamburgers, but a "friendly" place for the family.

Source: Adapted with permission from *Product Marketing,* February 1977, p. 10.

Marlboro man's cowboy hat and horse. One mark of the talent and success of creative types is that much of their work is so powerful that it can be used effectively in advertisements for decades. Many slogans, pictures, and other com-

Our favorite worm stand.

One thing will never change.

As we look out on a string of tomorrows, we can be sure of at least one thing.

The great idea, put purely and simply, is going to remain our reason for being around.

It may be brought to you by satellite, laser or moonbeam. Or some other equally awesome thingamajig.

But reaching for ideas that touch both mind and heart is, and will continue to be, what Leo Burnett is all about.

By the way, you know why there's no little kid up there in our picture?

He's gone fishing. Sold out, you know.

LEO BURNETT COMPANY, INC.
ADVERTISING

Advertising appeal will never be unimportant.

ponents of advertisements can be immediately identified with particular products by generations of consumers. These successes depend on the creative person's ability to capture a feeling or fact with just the right phrase and the right symbols. Compare, for example, these common advertising phrases with the way they might have been written.

"Does she or doesn't she?"
"Do you think that lady dyes her hair?"

"Are you a saltaholic?"
"Is it possible that you ingest undesirable levels of salt?"

"Come to Marlboro country."
"Please smoke Marlboros."

WHAT IS APPEAL?

"If our goal is to increase the quantity of purchase, what reasons can we give our target market for buying more of our product? If our goal is to take customers from competing brands, what reasons can we give customers for switching from their present brand to ours? If we want to stimulate people to change an old attitude and adopt a new one that will lead to future action, we must supply them with a reason for doing so. This reason is our appeal."

Source: Lewis Kaufman, *Essentials of Advertising* (New York: Harcourt Brace Jovanovich, 1980), pp. 311–312.

"Catch that Pepsi spirit."
"Pepsi is a drink for youthful individuals."

"Promise her anything, but give her Arpège."
"When you don't have time to shop or can't think of a present for your wife, buy some Arpège perfume."

An Example from the Brewing Industry

To get a feel for how creative advertising appeals vary across an industry, it is useful to consider several brands of the same type of product and the advertisements developed for each. Chapter 19 began with a discussion of the successful advertising developed for Miller's Lite beer. Let us now compare that advertising appeal with those intended to sell other brands of beer. (See color plates 9 through 12.)

Dixie beer's very name demonstrates its intended appeal to a particular region of the country. It is positioned and advertised as a part of the life-style known as "southern living." As we discussed earlier, Lone Star beer claimed a different, even narrower regional identity as "The National Beer of Texas" to generate high brand awareness with a humorous "Giant Armadillo."

Lowenbrau's and Natural Light's situational appeals are unlike Dixie's and Lone Star's re-

WHY IRON EYES?

An advertising campaign for Keep America Beautiful Inc., produced by the Advertising Council, illustrates the objectives, theme, and creative strategy of a public service advertising campaign. The "help fight pollution" campaign is designed to replace negative attitudes toward pollution with positive, personal values that make litter bugging, spoiling the landscape, or wasting energy unacceptable. The theme of the message is responsible citizen action. The desired effect is action. It seeks to stimulate citizens to initiate local efforts to solve issues of littering, waste handling, recycling, resource recovery, and energy conservation—relying on their own efforts rather than expecting action from government and other institutions.

The central character of the advertising is Iron Eyes Cody, the famous "crying" Indian. In one television commercial, the announcer delivers the message with a voiceover. The slogan is "the cure for pollution is people working together."

Source: Based on "Report to the American People 1980–1981," *The Advertising Council*, p. 5.

gional appeals. Lowenbrau is a "special occasion beer." Its advertisements stress sociability with the "Here's to good friends" theme and the suggestion that "Tonight"—but not every night—"let it be Lowenbrau." Natural Light emphasizes that it is light and less filling, thus the perfect accompaniment for food.

Coors, on the other hand, stresses product quality and focuses its appeal on the differential advantage of being packaged and shipped cold from the brewery. Even the occasional beer drinker appreciates that the cost involved in such an undertaking indicates, at the very least, that Coors is given special treatment that other beers are not.

The important thing to note here is that each of these products, as well as the others mentioned throughout this chapter, has a different appeal built into its advertisements. If every brewer said, "Our beer tastes great," there would be no uniqueness and no creativity associated with any individual brand. The advertising would not stand out as memorable. Many of these advertisements are part of positioning promotional campaigns. Claims—perfectly true claims—that a producer might want to make would not be believable because other brands are more established in the marketplace and hold certain positions in consumers' minds. Creativity, then, is more than an advertising tool. It is a competitive tool without which our competitive economic system would be stagnant.

How to Say It— The Execution of the Appeal

Even when a copywriter or artist has an important and meaningful message to relate, its effect can be lost if it is not presented in the right way and in the right context. Marketing research can help in this regard. For example, an advertising agency's research indicated that many women who buy TV dinners lead hectic lives and, because of time constraints, have trouble coping with everyday problems. So far so good. On this basis, advertising was developed for Swanson TV dinners showing a rundown woman flopping into a chair just before her family is to arrive home demanding dinner. Suddenly realizing that she has a problem, the woman gets the bright idea of cooking a TV dinner. The problem was real enough, but the appeal was wrong. The last thing harried women want is to be reminded of how tired they are.[5] Swanson changed its advertising appeal.

Television viewers are fond of pointing out that housewives on commercials are almost always peppy and well-groomed even when they are doing the laundry or washing the floor. This image brings the solution to a problem to the target customer's attention without making her feel like cursing the laundry or the dirty floor. What to say is one thing; how to say it is another.

[5]Peter W. Bernstein, "Psychographics Is Still an Issue on Madison Avenue," *Fortune*, January 16, 1978, p. 84.

Advertising decisions require determining what to say and how to say it.

How to say something is as important—and sometimes more important—as what to say. This is perhaps doubly true in advertising. The person delivering the message, the emotional tone of the advertisement, and the situation in which the action takes place, all influence the effectiveness of advertisements. Although some advertisements are simple, straightforward statements about the characteristics of a product, creating advertisements that grab the intended audience's attention often requires some embellishment. As seen in the previous chapter, the same was true of personal sales presentations. Advertisements are non-personal sales presentations, and some of the same things that make for good sales talks contribute to effective advertising.

The basic appeal of an advertisement, such as a product's good taste, may be implemented in a number of ways. The characters in Dr. Pepper commercials use a singing and dancing format to present the sales message. A Prudential Insurance Company commercial tells a short story about a fellow who actually dies and goes to heaven. The **execution format,** or style of presentation, of these sales messages is quite different. The execution formats selected by the people assembling the advertisements, and how they use those formats, are matters of creativity. Looking at some of the major formats or execution styles used in advertisements, especially TV commercials, helps put the creative strategies behind advertisements into perspective. The major formats are: storyline, product uses and problem solutions, slice-of-life, demonstrational, testimonial, use of a spokesperson, life-style, association, montage, and jingle.

Storyline. The **storyline** advertisement gives a history or tells a story about the product. For example, when the Coors organization introduced Killian's Irish Red, one advertisement gave the brand's history and explained a heritage dating back over a century. In television commercials, unseen announcers (this is called a *voiceover*) often narrate stories with recognizable beginnings, middles, and ends. As the stories unravel, the audience learns how to do something, such as solve a common problem, or is given some background about the product. Some copywriters attempt to make the product the ''hero'' of the story. Certain brands of whiskeys, for example, are shown in all their historical glory from the time of Camelot to the present.

Product Uses and Problem Solutions. A straightforward discussion of a product's uses, attributes, benefits, or availability is a frequently utilized advertising format. A unique selling proposition—some advantage of the product or special terms of its sale—is the central focus of such an advertisement. Comparatively simple advertisements for products ranging from Florsheim shoes to Merle Norman cosmetics explain uses of the product and how the product can be a solution to a problem.

The makers of exercise equipment may point out that being fat and out-of-shape is a problem ("your chest doesn't belong on your stomach") and may show that their product is a solution to the problem. Crest fights tooth decay problems. Texaco stops your car from "pinging."

Slice-of-Life. The **slice-of-life format** dramatizes a "typical" setting wherein people use the product being advertised. Most of these commercials center on some personal, household, or business problem. Two homemakers talking about a laundry problem and Mrs. Olson's happening upon situations where her comments on coffee are appropriate are examples of slice-of-life advertisements.

The slice-of-life commercial begins with a person *just before* the discovery of an answer to a problem. Whether the trouble is dandruff, bad breath, or ring-around-the-collar, emotions are running high. The protagonist may know of his problem or may be told about it by another character. The product is then introduced, recommended, and tried by the needy person. Just before the end of the commercial we are told and, indeed, can see for ourselves, that the new user of the product is now a better, sweeter-breathed, happier person.[6]

While this advertising format is most common in TV commercials, similar real-life situations can be developed in print media through the use of a series of pictures, and in radio advertisement through the use of character voices. The slice-of-life format is essentially a dramatized variation on the problem-solution format.

Demonstration. Certain products lend themselves to demonstration-type advertising efforts. The Master Lock advertisement, for example, where bullets are repeatedly fired into a lock that does not open is suspenseful and self-explanatory. The **demonstration format** makes its sales pitch by showing a clear-cut example of how the product can be used to benefit the consumer by either dramatically illustrating product features or by proving some advertised claim. The Master Lock advertisement certainly seems to prove that product's claim to toughness.

Unusual situations, although occasionally bordering on the fantastic, do draw attention to product benefits. When Bic throw-away ballpoint pens were new to the market, their high quality was "proven" with rifle champions shooting Bic pens through blocks of wood. The pens still wrote. Perhaps this advertisement had real meaning only for people who planned to shoot their pens through wood, but the situation drew the ordinary viewer's attention and demonstrated Bic's quality.

Comparative advertising, where one brand of a product is directly contrasted with another, is a form of demonstration advertising. In this type of advertisement, the sponsor's product is shown to be superior to other brands, or to Brand X, in a taste test, laundry whiteness test, toughness test, or other appropriate contest.

This format is somewhat controversial on two counts. First, some advertisers believe that calling attention to the other fellow's product helps that competitive product by giving it free exposure. Indeed, brands that do not have a high market share are intentionally compared with the best-known products to suggest that the two brands are equal. Pepsi, the number two cola, thus urges comparisons with Coke.

Second, some people do not believe that comparisons are fair and sporting. The recent Burger King versus McDonald's "war" raised a lot of hackles. In Burger King commercials, the "MacDonald family" urges hamburger lovers to switch from McDonald's to Burger King. On the other side, McDonald's supporters are encouraged to closely scrutinize Burger King's cooking methods. Much was then made of the fact that Burger King keeps its hot sandwiches

---

[6]A.C. Book and N.D. Cary, *The Television Commercial* (New York: Decker Communications, 1970), pp. 9–28.

MAKING COMPARISONS: TOP-SIDER VERSUS TIMBERLAND

Along with Lacoste alligators and chino trousers, Sperry Top-Sider shoes have come to epitomize the popular preppie look. Invented in the 1930s by a Connecticut yachtsman to help sailors keep their footing on slick decks, the white-soled, dark brown deck shoes have become a favorite with landlubbers from Newport, R.I., to Newport, Calif., who wear them more for status than for safety.

Sperry's dominance of the booming boat-shoe market is not unchallenged, however. The Timberland Co., a family-owned business that operates out of a former mill in Newmarket, N.H., is aggressively going after the no-skid business.

Timberland's assault started last year, with an advertising campaign under the headline THE BOAT SHOE THAT'S ABOUT TO BLOW SPERRY TOP-SIDER OUT OF THE WATER. The full-page ads claimed that the Sperry shoe had a "painted on" pigment that dries and cracks, was often machine made, used painted metal eyelets that chip, and had a less durable sole.

Top-Sider kicked back with a lawsuit filed in Massachusetts Superior Court, charging that the comparison in the ads was inaccurate. The suit was settled when Timberland agreed to change the text of the ads, but not the headline. Timberland has since filed a suit of its own in the U.S. district court in Concord, N.H., after discovering that the three sets of patent numbers on the Top-Sider sole had expired in 1955, 1957 and 1959. While Top-Sider has since removed the numbers from its soles, its attorneys contend that the use of the expired patent numbers was not illegal.

This year Timberland made another advance on the advertising front with a poll of "world-class sailors" that claimed to show overwhelming preference for its shoe. Crowed the headline: 151 WORLD-CLASS SAILORS PROVE SPERRY TOP-SIDER IS LOSING ITS GRIP. Meanwhile, Timberland is happily handing out reprints of a *Playboy Fashion Guide* interview in which Conservative Columnist William F. Buckley, Jr., a transatlantic sailor who always tries to put his right foot forward, calls Timberland's product "the world's most comfortable shoe."

Sperry has been trying to stay above the fray by ignoring Timberland's offensive. Sperry's ads stress the "classic" and "traditional" aspects of its shoe. After all, it really is just not preppie to pay much attention to the competition.

Source: "No-Skid Scuffle," *Time,* August 23, 1982, p. 44.

---

warm in steam tables, even though their commercials suggest that "flame broiling" is the only cooking medium used.

Overall, however, advertisements using the direct comparison format have been increasing in use in recent years. The Federal Trade Commission, believing that honest comparisons will help the consumer to make choices, has supported this trend.

Testimonials. Testimonials and endorsements have an individual, usually a prominent, show business or sports figure, make a statement establishing that he or she owns, uses, or supports the brand of product advertised. The idea is that people who identify with the celebrity will want to be like that person and use the same product. Alternatively, it is hoped that consumers will see the endorser as an honest person who would not lend his or her name to a product that is not good. Some celebrities, by virtue of their training or abilities, may be seen as "experts" on the products being advertised.

A variation on the testimonial appeal is the spokesperson. The **spokesperson** represents the company and directly addresses the audience about a product and urges us to buy it. James Garner and Mariette Hartley are the spokespersons for Polaroid. Their personable and warm manner are associated with a camera intended for family use. Leonard Nimoy, the actor who played the science officer, Mr. Spock, on

Star Trek, is the spokesman for a television set claiming space age technology. The personal recognition of Mr. Nimoy and his association with space age technology is strong. The spokesperson, often the commercial's central character, need not be a real person. Brother Dominic for Xerox, the Poppin' Fresh Dough Boy for Pillsbury, the Keebler elves, Captain Krunch, and Tony-the-Tiger are well-known spokespersons.

Life-Style. The **life-style advertisement** combines scenes or sequences of situations intended to reflect a particular target market's life-style. Soft drink and fast food advertisements, as well as those of many other consumer goods, frequently show product users in a sequence of daily activities. Young people might be shown enjoying some weekend activity and topping off a perfect day with a visit to a Burger King or Kentucky Fried Chicken shop. Thus, the enjoyable aspects of teenage life are shown in association with product usage. Important to such advertisements are the sorts of people displayed.

Association. The **association advertising format** concentrates on drawing an analogy or other relationship to convey its message. This creative strategy in effect "borrows interest" from another, more exciting product or situation. Thrilling activities, such as skydiving or windsurfing, and scenes of beautiful places, such as the coast of Maine or a mountain wilderness, are used in this way. An emotional mood is created. The psychological benefits of the product are communicated by the associations drawn by the viewer. The product thus becomes exciting, exotic, and symbolic in some other way.

Fantasy is a special associative format. The long-lived series of advertisements for Maidenform bras is a perfect example of the fantasy approach. The fantasy appeal seeks not to associate the product merely with a glamorous setting, but to associate it with the target buyer's wildest dreams and hopes.

Montage. The **montage format** blends a number of situations, demonstrations, and other vi-

---

THE MONTAGE MAY COMBINE SEVERAL FORMATS

The Coca-Cola Company introduction of Diet Coke is a line extension to intensify market segmentation efforts. Tab appeals to females of above-average education and income who are diet conscious. Marketing research indicated a large number of men who would also be receptive to a low-calorie soft drink by Coca-Cola. Appeals to this market utilized an advertising theme "Just for the taste of it." The promotional campaign ties the new product in with regular Coke using the bold, red graphics—a color that often appeals to males—and the Coke name.

The television commercials show a series of typical New York street scenes—a dog walker with at least five animals, joggers, Times Square's outdoor sign promoting Coca-Cola, lights, a stick ball game, a woman taking in the sun using a reflector. Interspersed throughout the montage of scenes, celebrities such as TV's Judd Hirsch and hockey star, Phil Esposito give their endorsement to Diet Coke, but they are not identified because the commercial wants to portray them as people who really like Diet Coke, not as paid employees.

This commercial is the result of extensive advertising research. Several copy themes were tested such as "This is it," "This is the real one," "One calorie Coca-Cola Style," "Ain't misbehaven."

Source: From "It's Coke Versus Pepsi—Again," *Business Week,* August 2, 1982, p. 64; Nancy Gides, "New York Tastes Diet Coke's Spot," *Advertising Age,* August 9, 1982.

---

sual effects into one commercial. The effect may be one of a swirl of colors or an exciting array of possibilities associated with product usage. Typical of such a format would be travel advertisements for places like Jamaica. In these TV spots, the varied sights and sounds of an island paradise are strung together, not only to show the many activities that are to be found there, but also to suggest the excitement of the place and

COLD FACTS ABOUT WARM BEER

You've been hearing a lot about Coors. Especially that it has to be kept cold to be good.

Well, the truth is, Coors is no more affected by heat than any other beer.

But it's also true that any beer kept cold longer will taste fresher. Not just Coors. But any beer.

That's why we go to such extremes to package and ship Coors cold. Not because we have to, but because we want to deliver the freshest possible beer to you.

So when you buy Coors warm, don't worry. It will always have a head start on freshness.

COORS. THE BEST OF THE ROCKIES IS YOURS.

There's nothing more southern than DIXIE

Four different advertising appeals for the same product category (see page 571).

Here's to good friends.

Löwenbräu

Ahh, the beer with the taste for food!

Guess who couldn't punch his way out of a St. Regis paper bag?

We put former heavyweight champion, Smokin' Joe Frazier in a bag made with our shipping sack paper and he couldn't get through it. No wonder.

This is the kind of performance you can expect from a new kind of Kraft paper soon to be available in volume from St. Regis. New Stress Kraft™ paper will absorb 18% more energy than other Kraft papers of equivalent weight. And since Stress Kraft paper will be so tough, we'll be able to give you shipping sacks with two plies that perform as well as shipping sacks made with three plies of regular Kraft.

What makes Stress Kraft paper so tough? It's easy to describe but not easy to achieve. Traditionally, Kraft paper is dried over a series of rollers that pull the paper taut.

Research showed that if the paper could be dried in a tension free way, it would have considerably more stretch, and, hence, more ability to absorb energy.

So we will dry new Stress Kraft paper on a special machine that does just that. St. Regis will be the only U.S. company to have Stress Kraft paper. And this is another example of why St. Regis is a leader in packaging technology. All this reflects the marketing stance of St. Regis toward all our packaging, paper and construction products. To use the full weight of

our technology and marketing in serving our customers and in renewing the forest resource our products come from.

St. Regis—serving Man and Nature to the benefit of both.

Demonstration

Couldn't you go for a mouth-watering, lip-smacking, flame-broiled Whopper right now?

Aren't You Hungry? BURGER KING

Still life

We teach you how to be beautiful...free.

At participating Studios.

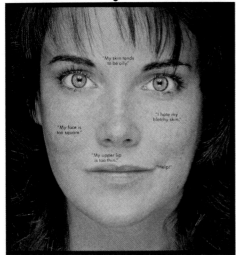

"My skin tends to be oily."

"I hate my blotchy skin."

"My face is too square."

"My upper lip is too thin."

"Help!"

Today's Face is created from:
Medium Neutral Total Finish.
Amberwood Sheer Powder Blusher. Persian Sage Creamy Powder Shadow. Copper Opal Creamy Powder Shadow. Loden Green Eye Pencil Plus. Black Creamy Flo-matic Mascara. Perfect Peach Lip Pencil Plus.

The beautiful faces you see all around you are not simply born that way. Beauty is something that is learned. Models learn how to be beautiful. Beauty Editors learn. And now Merle Norman will teach you how. Free. It starts with your own individual makeover. Our accomplished Beauty Advisors will teach you the shades and shapes that bring out the hidden beauty of your eyes. Your cheeks. Learn the fresh new shape of a prettier mouth. Eyes that are wider. Your jawline slimmer. Merle Norman has one of the most exclusive and individual makeup and skincare collections in the world. You may try every shade, every color on your own special face ... taking it home only if you feel it looks beautiful on you. Our no-nonsense makeover. Our no-nonsense way to buy. For the fun of it. For the beauty of it. At Merle Norman free. Do ask for our other lessons in: Complexion Care: *The care and cleansing of beautiful skin.* Eye Makeup: *Shape and* placement of color for your own specific eye type. New Fashion Shades: *Makeup to match your favorite wardrobe colors.*

MERLE NORMAN

The Place for the Custom Face®
For the Merle Norman Studio nearest you call (800) 421-2010.
In California call (800) 262-1734.

IVORY BAR

TITLE: "WRITE-IN #2"
EILEEN ROPER

LENGTH: 60 SECONDS

COMM'L NO.: PGIB 5746

EILEEN ROPER: My name is Eileen Roper. I'm a school teacher not an actress.

You know how I ended up in a television commercial?

My husband sent my picture in to the Ivory people... without telling me.

ROBERT: I think Eileen's complexion is just as healthy looking as any of those Ivory girls on T.V.

EILEEN: You know it really makes me feel good that Robert likes the way I look.

I do try t'take care of my skin. And I like it that he notices.

I mean I exercise and I try t'watch what I eat and I keep my skin really clean.

I've used Ivory soap for... for as long as I can remenber.

(VO) I just like Ivory purity...

(DV) Skin doesn't need things like heavy perfumes and deodorants to stay healthy looking.

Skin needs gentle cleaning like Ivory gives.

ANNCR: (VO) Helping skin stay healthy looking is what Ivory's all about. Shouldn't you get down to basics with Ivory?

EILEEN: I really believe in it. I really use Ivory,

and it's not hard for me to say all these things about it because they're all true.

ANNCR: (VO) If you know a healthy looking Ivory girl, like Eileen, write us. Maybe we'll make a commercial about her too.

---

estimonial

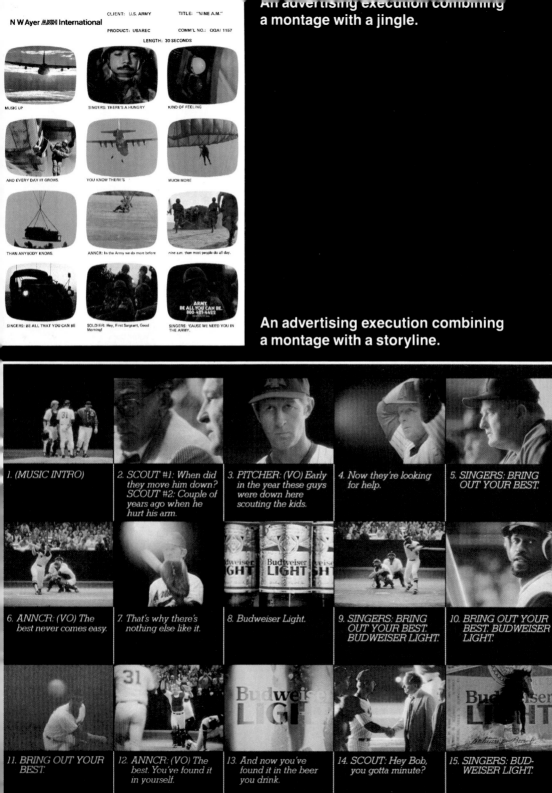

An advertising execution combining
a montage with a jingle.

An advertising execution combining
a montage with a storyline.

the sense that there is so much to do that the trip will surely be worth the investment.

Jingles. "My bologna has a first name . . . It's O.S.C.A.R." Can you remember the rest of this jingle? What restaurant do you think of if you hear "You deserve a break today?" What does one have to do if one wants to "Reach out, reach out and touch someone?" **Commercial jingles,** many of them written by well-known composers, have what could be termed "memory value." You literally cannot get them out of your head. We find ourselves thinking of them or, at least, able to remember them almost word for word

once our memories are jarred, even when they have been withdrawn from the market. Product names, phone numbers, and addresses, in jingle form, are remembered. The purpose best served by the jingle is as a memory aid; they can have an undeniable effect on product recall.

Other Formats. This short list of advertising formats is far from exhaustive. Animation and special effects, for example, have not been mentioned. However, this discussion should help you to think of other advertising formats and of the ways they work in developing an effective marketing program. (See color plates 9 to 12.)

PRODUCING THE ADVERTISEMENT

A full treatment of the process involving the actual creation of an advertisement is beyond the scope of this book. The purpose of this section is a quick overview. Readers interested in more detailed information should review the fine advertising textbooks available.

Advertisements consist of visual elements, verbal elements, and/or audio elements.[7] The exact combination of these elements depends on the people who design the advertisement. Their choices are strongly influenced by the advertising medium to be used. In fact, the interrelationship between media and advertisement is so strong that it is impossible to decide whether the selection of the medium or the development of the advertisement comes first. In this section, however, the creation of the advertisement will be treated first. This is a reasonable approach because the promotional mix should be a unified whole, employing all appropriate means of delivering a message. Thus, we see that many TV, radio, and print media advertisements for a product advance virtually the same message or appeal, but the advertisements, although they may

share a common theme, are constructed differently to fit each media.

Copy

The term **copy** refers to any words contained within an advertisement. The words may be printed or verbalized by a character in a commercial or by an announcer. In certain advertisements, such as radio advertisements, the copy makes the biggest contribution to the advertisement's effectiveness. Even in a visual medium, such as television, copy is likely to retain its supremacy since many of the claims an advertiser might make must be supported by the comments of the announcers or the characters. For example, advertisements for laundry detergents may show two piles of wash. It is the copy that assures viewers that the pile washed in Oxydol is the whitest. The fact that a man is relaxing in a hammock drinking lemonade does not, of itself, tell the viewer that he can relax because he has a Lawnboy mower. The man in the advertisement, or an unseen announcer, tells us that is the case.

Some advertisements are absolutely loaded with copy and have few illustrations. Success with that type of advertisement is possible because many people are so interested in the prod-

---

[7]In rare instances, such as utilization of scratch-and-sniff technology, the senses of touch and smell may be taken into consideration when developing advertisements.

Art represents part of the creative aspect of advertising.

uct's possible benefits that they are willing to read long paragraphs of information.

Art

The term **art** is broadly used to mean all aspects of an advertisement other than its verbal portions. Thus, pictures, graphs and charts, layout (the arrangement of the visual elements of an advertisement), and even whitespace (places where neither pictures nor words appear), all fall under the heading of art.

The function of pictures in an advertisement is to illustrate a fact or idea or to attract attention. Whitespace and layout are more subtle in their purposes. Layout can be effectively used to focus the viewer's attention on the picture of the product. Layout can also be used to draw attention to the brand name, the price, or the place of sale.

Whitespace can be used in similar ways, but is more commonly used to suggest quality. Notice that many newspaper and magazine advertisements employ considerable whitespace to accent the product. A great deal of whitespace says that the pictured item is special, probably expensive, and certainly of high quality. It implies that the product is deserving of the "spotlight" given it by a white field that accents its appeal. Thus, many advertisements for expensive jewelry picture the watch on a plain-colored velvet cloth; only a few words are included to distract from the beauty and perfection of the jewelry. On the other hand, a busy advertisement featuring a jumble of words and pictures and a small amount of whitespace may suggest low price and low quality. Look closely at the advertisements in your newspaper or favorite magazines and notice how layout is used in ways such as these.

Copy and Art Working Together: The AIDA Formula

Most advertisements, with the exception of radio advertisements, feature both copy and art. The two elements must work together and complement each other to accomplish the communication objectives set by management. To do this, most advertisers follow a "hierarchy of effects" model known as the AIDA formula. **AIDA** stands for **attention, interest, desire,** and **action.**

Attention. An effective advertisement must draw *attention* from the very first glance or hearing. Whatever follows will prove of little use if the target viewer has not been influenced to pay attention to the message first. Copy can be used to accomplish this, and the copy can be enhanced by illustration. Often a person, acting much like the target customer, is shown in situations that makes the viewer think, "What's going on here?" or "What happened to these people?"

For example, to attract the attention of luggage users, Samsonite luggage company has for years run advertisements showing such things as suitcases falling out of airplanes or supporting automobiles that have flipped over on top of the bags. Copy can also be used to gain attention. Notice, for example, how many radio advertisements start out sounding like soap operas or mystery stories to draw attention to them.

Interest. After attention has been attracted, the arousal of *interest* is next. If the attention-getter is powerful enough, interest should follow fairly automatically. However, it may be necessary to focus the viewers or listeners on how the product or service being advertised actually pertains to them.

Desire. Immediately following the arousal of interest is the attempt to create a *desire* for the product. Recent TV commercials for ChemLawn demonstrate this. The viewer sees one homeowner carrying tools and bags of lawn chemicals. One of the bags breaks and the exhausted do-it-yourselfer looks on helplessly. The viewer at home sees, however, that the unfortunate fellow's neighbor has a very nice-looking lawn but does not look harried and sweaty. Certainly he has no piles of spilled lawn care products around his property. The viewer is interested in this story: Why is one fellow miserable while his neighbor smilingly pities him? The contented homeowner is a subscriber to the ChemLawn service, of course. The viewer is treated to some scenes of the ChemLawn man applying liquid lawn chemicals in one easy step. The ChemLawn people know what and when to spray—another load off the homeowner's mind. Thus, the interest in and desire for the product are established in nearly simultaneous steps.

Action. *Action* is the last part of the AIDA formula. Continuing with the ChemLawn advertisement, we find that the last thing in the commercial is a call to action. "Phone the ChemLawn man in your phonebook for an estimate of what it takes to make you as happy as the man who has a nice lawn with no effort. Call this toll-free num-

THE CREATIVE PHILOSOPHIES OF DIFFERENT AD AGENCIES

The Ted Bates Advertising Agency believes in U.S.P.—the Unique Selling Proposition—as the keystone for successful advertising (the U.S.P. is a unique difference in a product or in the use of a product that distinguishes it from competition). Ogilvy, Benson, and Mather tout "image advertising," as exemplified by the "Man in the Hathaway Shirt." Norman B. Norman of Norman, Craig, and Kummel believes that conscious suggestion is a waste of the advertiser's money, and that effective advertising taps the *un*conscious, resulting in *empathy* (the personal identification of the reader with the product being advertised). Doyle Dane Bernbach depends on *execution,* insists that "execution becomes content," and argues that a good advertisement is a different advertisement. McCann-Erickson's orientation is toward *motivational* advertising "built on the 'real reason' why people use this kind of product." And, an executive of Batten, Barton, Dursten, and Osborn summed up his agency's position with the humorous observation: "You can always tell an Ogilvy ad or a Bates ad, but you can't spot a BBDO ad because we'll steal from everybody."

Source: From Kenneth E. Runyon, *Advertising and the Practice of Management* (Columbus, Ohio: Charles E. Merrill, 1979), p. 187.

ber. Etc." Thus, the means to *act* is provided. Usually, the action is made as effortless as possible, by giving a phone number or by closing with a note that credit cards are accepted.

How the AIDA Formula Works. The AIDA formula is based on a consumer behavior theory about the mental activities of consumers. The formula describes consumers' behavior and serves as a guideline for writing advertising copy. AIDA makes good sense as a copy-writing tool and is widely known and followed. It must be understood that it may not be possible for every advertisement to move the reader or viewer through the four stages to action with a single exposure.

Repetition is usually necessary so that the advertisement's message can "sink in" or so that distractions affecting the target customer on other occasions might be absent. Also, the target buyer's situation may have changed since the advertisement was first seen. In subsequent exposure situations, the customer may have just been paid or have received a tax return, and he or she may perceive the advertisement in a different light. Eventually, if the advertisement is an effective one aimed at the proper people, buyers are likely to move psychologically through the AIDA stages, and then act.

MEASURING THE EFFECTIVENESS OF ADVERTISING

An advertiser about to commit $500,000 or more for a 30-second commercial on the Super Bowl or for the development of a series of advertisements created especially for the Christmas season will be concerned about the effectiveness of those advertisements. Measuring the effectiveness of advertisements in terms of the sales dollars generated is difficult. Despite that fact, several approaches to measuring effectiveness have been developed. These tools, which are discussed in the next two sections, do not provide *exact* measures of effectiveness, but they do provide a means by which advertisers can develop and test advertisements to see whether they are accomplishing their intended objectives. Concerns about advertising effectiveness are simply too great to allow marketing managers to ignore these testing procedures. Advertising research may be divided into two phases: (1) the pretesting stage of development and refinement of advertising copy and (2) the post-testing stage that evaluates its effectiveness.

Developing Messages and Pretesting Advertisements

Effective marketers are reluctant to spend large sums of money running advertisements that have not been carefully pretested. Before advertisements are put on TV or in magazines, they may have gone through several stages of testing.

Pretesting may be conducted in the earliest stages of the development of an advertisement and continue virtually until the advertisement is printed or broadcast. First, the basic appeal of an advertisement, or a song around which the advertisement will be built, may be tested. Then a headline, picture, or slogan can be similarly tested. A "rough" version of the advertisement, featuring still photos in the case of a television commercial or a story acted out by nonprofessional actors in the case of a radio advertisement, can be assembled rather inexpensively and shown to a sample audience to measure its appeal and believability. It does no good to create a funny, clever, or dramatic advertisement unless the impact of the advertisement comes through to the people it is supposed to affect. Consider this story about the pretest of a television commercial for American Telephone and Telegraph.

"It was an earlier commercial we did for A.T.&T.," he says. **"We called it 'Fishing Camp.' The idea was this: These guys go off to a fishing camp in the north woods, somewhere far away, where they're going to have a terrific time together and do all this great fishing, only what happens is that it rains all the time and the fishing is a bust. Mind you, this was a humorous ad. The emphasis was on the humor. Anyway, the big moment occurs when the fishing guys are talking on the phone to their jealous friends back home—who naturally want to know how great the fishing is—and what you see are the fishing guys, huddled in this cabin, with the rain pouring down outside, and one of the guys is staring at a frying pan full of hamburgers sizzling on the stove while he says into the phone, 'Boy, you should see the great**

trout we've got cooking here.' O.K., so we made a photomatic of the commercial and we decided we'd test it. Our test audience generally gave the first part very positive responses, but when it came to the question 'What was cooking in the frying pan?' just about every person answering said 'Trout.' I mean, it was definitely and unmistakably hamburger in the frying pan, but the guy in the ad had said, 'Boy, you should see the great trout we've got cooking here,' so the test audience all said 'Trout.' I have to tell you, we were very discouraged. Some of our guys were even talking of junking the commercial, which was a good one, with a nice humorous flow to it. Well, we ended up making it, but what we had to do was, when we came to that segment, we put the camera almost inside the frying pan, and in the frying pan we put huge, crude chunks of hamburger that were so raw they were almost red. I mean, just about all you could see was raw meat. This time, when we took it to the audience, it tested O.K. That is, most of the test audience—though in fact, still not everybody—finally said 'Hamburger.' But the experience taught me an important lesson. It taught me not to worry about being too obvious visually, and that a lot of things can go wrong in thirty seconds."[8]

The value of pretesting—to limit, or even eliminate, mistakes—becomes obvious.

Videotaping possible spokespersons for products and showing these tapes to panels of consumers in an attempt to determine the appropriateness of the spokesperson to the product being offered is a worthwhile pretest. Consider, for example, the manufacturer of a hair-coloring kit who developed an advertisement featuring Raquel Welch endorsing the product. Tests of rough commercials showed that, while Ms. Welch was easily recognized and was perceived as an outstanding personality, she was not seen as an authority on the product or as a user of a home hair-coloring kit.[9] The pretesting indicated that, to enhance believability, advertisements for home-use products such as this should feature "real people" rather than movie stars. Similar

---

[8] From Michael J. Arlen, *30 Seconds* (New York: Farrar, Straus and Giroux, 1980), pp. 185–186. Used with permission. Copyright © 1980 by Farrar, Straus and Giroux.

[9] From "Pick Product Presenter Prudently," *Marketing News*, September 8, 1978, p. 12.

HELP STOP THE GREASIES ADVERTISING COPY DEVELOPMENT RESEARCH

Extensive marketing research preceded the introduction of S.C. Johnson's Agree Shampoo. Then pretesting research was utilized for advertising copy development.

Early advertising research focused on *advertising copy development*. Focus group interviews gave the company an insight into the ultimate theme—oiliness was indicated as a major problem. After this was determined, reasons why a shampoo would keep hair cleaner longer were explored. Users were found to be uncomfortable with heavy scientific reasoning. S.C. Johnson concluded that the communication task was really a simple one—to talk about cleaning.

Next came *concept tests* to quantify consumer reaction to the product and to the advertising ideas. The researchers found that an ad with "a laundry list of benefits, something for everyone" turned people off because of its emphasis on special ingredients. Instead, they focused on "the greasies" theme in the advertisement.

The first shampoo commercial was *rough produced* and *copy tested*. The initial draft of the ultimate advertising claim promised Agree would help keep hair cleaner longer. After copy testing, S.C. Johnson's staff went back to writing new copy. After the successful introduction of Agree Creme rinse and establishment of the term "the greasies," the advertising claim was modified to "help stop the greasies between shampoos." In all, 17 new commercials were copy-tested before the one offering the best blend of communication, motivation, and diagnostic help was found.

Source: Based on information in "Key Role of Research in Agree's Success Is Told," *Marketing News*, January 12, 1979, pp. 14–15.

tests are frequently run to test the music portions of advertisements intended for radio and TV.[10]

Many of the marketing research tools discussed in Chapter 5 are used or modified for pretest advertisements. Focus groups, discussions with consumers in malls, experiments, and other techniques can all be helpful. No matter which method is used, pretesting attempts to evaluate the effectiveness of an advertisement before that advertisement is placed in the mass media. Rough or finished versions of television commercials may be shown in consumers' homes (*in-home projector test*) or in specially equipped busses or trailers parked in shopping malls (*trailer tests*). After the commercial is shown, survey questionnaires or personal interviews are utilized to obtain the reaction to the advertisements.

Post-Testing Commercials and Advertisements

Once an advertisement is developed and run in the chosen media, **post-testing research** should be used to determine if it has met the objectives set by management. There are many different types of objectives for post-testing, and many kinds of post-tests, however. Determining whether objectives are met usually will take the form of measurement of brand awareness, changing attitudes toward the product, or generation of inquiries about the product. Our discussion here will be of a few standard post-testing techniques.

Brand Recognition and Recall. Since advertisers must gain the attention of buyers and have them remember the names of brands, or the stores in which they can be found, many post-tests are designed to evaluate recognition or recall. This is important even to advertisers of

well-known products since each advertisement for such products is intended to reinforce previously established good images. At the very least, a test which shows advertisers that particular advertisements were remembered gives a feeling that money devoted to the campaign had some impact in the marketplace.

Recall tests can take many forms. For example, a telephone survey may be conducted during the 24-hour period following the airing of a television commercial to measure day-after recall. In such studies, the telephone interviewer poses questions such as these:

"Did you watch 'Sixty Minutes' last night?"

If the answer is positive, the next question might be:

"Do you recall whether or not there was a commercial on that program for an automobile?"

If the answer is again positive, the interviewer would ask:

"What brand of automobile was that?"

To this point, what has been measured is *un*aided recall. The interviewer gives no clue as to the brand of car advertised. In an *aided recall* test, the questions might be phrased differently, as in these examples:

"Do you recall the brand of automobile advertised? Was it an American compact car?"

"I'm going to read you a list of automobile brand names. Can you pick out the name of the car that was advertised on the program?"

While aided recall is not as strong a test of attention and memory as unaided recall, it still provides valuable information. After all, remembering the brand when it is seen on the supermarket shelf may be all that is necessary.

Advertisers are also interested in what is termed *related recall*. Related recall refers to the ability of a person who has seen the advertisement to repeat or "play back" specific sales messages or images. Some advertisers set up booths in shopping malls and ask target customers to

---

[10]Well-known composers actively compete for these lucrative jobs, just as actors compete for spokesperson roles. These tests are usually not publicized so that the composer or actor is spared the embarrassment of being turned down because they are not "good enough" to write a song about toilet disinfectant or act alongside Ronald McDonald.

view one or more advertisements, and then comment on or describe the advertisements. Researchers then are able to determine which advertisements, or portions thereof, were most memorable to these subjects. This type of post-test allows researchers to determine if the advertisements accomplished their goals.

Many variations on this basic method are possible. Respondents could be shown a TV or magazine advertisement with the brand name of the product removed or blackened out. The respondent would then be asked to identify the product. If the respondent can, the advertisement may be considered memorable and effective in attracting attention and in "sticking with" the viewers.

Another form of measuring recognition involves showing an advertisement to a respondent and simply asking whether the respondent remembers seeing it before. If the answer is yes, the respondent is then asked questions about particular portions of the advertisement that were noted or read with care. The Starch Advertisement Readership Service is a syndicated supplier of this type of recognition information. They classify readers into three types:[11]

"Noted reader: A person who remembered having previously seen the advertisement in the magazine issue being studied.

"Association" reader: A person who not only "Noted" the advertisement but also saw or read some part of it, which clearly indicated the brand or advertiser.

"Read most" reader: A person who read at least one-half of the written material in the advertisement.

Certainly tests such as these are not perfect measures of recall and recognition. However, when they are conducted carefully, they provide marketing managers with helpful information.

Changing Attitudes about a Product. Effective advertisements can contribute to changing buyer attitudes about a product. However, in order to measure such changes, something must be known about buyers' attitudes before they are exposed to the relevant advertisement. Thus, a two-part study must be undertaken. This need not be as great a task as it might first appear.

In dealing with individual buyers, it may be possible to measure their changing attitudes toward a product in an experimental or interview situation. The subject may be asked to discuss the product in question verbally or through a written series of questions in, for example, a multiple-choice format. Nutrigena hand cream is said to have great powers to heal badly irritated skin. It is said to be a good foot treatment, too. Target buyers might be asked to check through a list of benefits of Nutrigena, could then be shown an advertisement making the two important points, and then finally asked to evaluate the product in light of the new information they have been given.

In a more general way, the effectiveness of Nutrigena's new advertisement could be measured by conducting before and after surveys among target buyers. The result of the first survey may show that few know that the product heals hands *and* feet. Next, advertisements should be shown. If the results of the second survey show recognition of the product's healing properties after the advertisements have run, some measure of success is credited to the advertisements.

Generating Inquiries about the Product

In certain situations, such as evaluation of one direct-mail piece versus another, the generation of inquiries is a good measure of an advertisement's effectiveness. Counting the number of inquiries generated by one magazine advertisement versus another is commonly used by industrial advertisers to measure advertising effectiveness. Many suppliers of industrial goods advertise in trade magazines that reach precisely those people and organizations most likely to be interested in their products. Many of these advertisements include a phone number to be called for additional information or a coupon to be returned for the same purpose. Certainly, the

---

[11]Based on information provided by the Starch Readership Service.

numbers of calls and coupons the advertiser receives can suggest the effectiveness of the advertisements. Some business magazines encourage readers to order as much additional information as they want on *any* of the magazine's advertisers by mailing in a single form that is provided at the back of the magazine. The reader need only circle the numbers or names of the advertisements in the particular issue. These cards, by the way, are called "bingo cards." They serve to show the advertisers that the magazine is useful in generating inquiries.

Inquiries usually come primarily from persons who are actually interested in the products being offered. Therefore, they are of particular use to marketing organizations whose promotional mix includes personal selling. Such organizations can use those inquiries to focus their sales force's efforts on the most-likely-to-buy customers. Thus, the number of inquiries gives a measure of an advertisement's pulling power and supports the activities of the personal sales force. This exemplifies how the elements of a marketing mix fit together and support one another.

Sales as a Measure of Advertisement Effectiveness.   After seeing some of the ways in which marketers try to measure the effectiveness of their advertising, the question arises: "Why not just use sales figures?" Unfortunately, not all organizations can use sales as directly as this in assessing advertising effectiveness. Many factors other than advertising influence sales. It is often nearly impossible to separate the effects on sales of the economy, the price, the wholesalers and other dealers, and so on, from the effects of the advertisements. Nevertheless, most marketers ultimately do use this measure. Many popular advertising campaigns have been removed from circulation when it was found that the advertisements were memorable and popular, but did not positively effect sales. In the case of advertisements designed to produce inquiries, a specific measure of effectiveness can be developed by tallying the numbers of inquiries that actually resulted in *sales*.

Sales remain the bottom line for all advertisements. However, only in special cases, such as sales as the result of a coupon or via an 800 phone number, will sales be a reasonably accurate measure of advertising effectiveness. Marketers must recall that tools intended to measure advertising's effects must be used carefully and with the understanding that they are usually very far from perfectly accurate.

MEDIA SELECTION

Suppose that you have decided to open a retail store. You have already decided that it is necessary to have a Yellow Pages advertisement but are undecided about whether to use radio, television, or newspaper advertising as well. This choice, which is made from among this wide variety of media, is a matter of selecting a communications channel for your message. A **media selection strategy** involves consideration of the message you wish to transmit, the audience you want to reach, the effect you want to have, and the budget you have to support this effort.

Developing a media strategy requires answers to these two questions: (1) Which media will efficiently get the message to the desired audience, (2) What scheduling of these media will neither bore people with too frequent repetition of the message nor let too many people forget the message?[12]

Which Media?

Certain media lend themselves to certain tasks. If we assume, for the moment, that budget considerations can be set aside, certain factors become

---

[12]Kenneth A. Longman, *Advertising* (New York: Harcourt Brace Jovanovich, 1971), p. 345.

KJRH NBC 2	KTVT Ft. Worth 3	KSHB Kansas City 4	Movie Five 5	KOTV CBS 6	CBN CABLE NETWORK 7	KTUL ABC 8	USA CABLE NETWORK 9	SPN 10	PBS 11	THE WEATHER CHANNEL 12	Program Guide 13
HBO 14	Cinemax 15	(Playboy) 16	THE DISNEY CHANNEL 17	CNN 18	CNN Headline News 19	WTBS Atlanta 20	WGN Chicago 21	Religion 22	KOKI 23	Education Channel: Colleges & Univs. 24	ESPN 24-Hour Sports 25
MTV MUSIC TELEVISION 26	Education: Public Schools 27	Education: Public Schools 28	Nickelodeon & arts 29	THE NASHVILLE NETWORK 30	UPI Sports News KWAB Radio 31	KGCT & Black Entertainment Television 32	DAYTIME COUNTRY MUSIC TV 33	Financial News Net & Tulsa Cablesports 34	Cable Health Network 35	Local & National Government 36	Tulsa Cable For Service Call 665-0200

Cable television is changing Americans' viewing habits.

dominant in choosing the medium to carry a sales message. If demonstration or visual comparison of one brand with another is the goal, television becomes the most logical contender. If a lengthy explanation of sales points is required, print advertisements (magazines and newspapers) come to mind. If consumers require a message to remind them of package identification or to be reminded of a short sales idea, outdoor advertising (billboards) makes sense. Thus, before a marketing planner starts thinking about what medium to use, he or she must know what is to be said. Once what is to be said is decided, the marketer's attention can turn to which media form can best say it.[13] Ultimately, several different media may be selected to communicate the multiple messages marketers may want to communicate.

Several media choices may appear to be able to do the job. When this is so, the marketing planner can narrow the choice by considering which media will hit the all-important target market. At this point, the media expert becomes a market expert. Knowing the target market—who buys the product, who are the heaviest buyers, what are their demographic characteristics—leads to a determination of which media will deliver these prospects. For example, the media planner in the insurance industry may be trying to target young males, 18 to 34; a European airline may be targeting well-educated, higher-income men and women ages 18 to 49; the primary customer for a laundry detergent may be women 18 to 49 years old.

Most products can be related to a demographic profile. The data gathered pertaining to media are geared to that same profile information. Thus, if the target is men and women, and it has been decided that television will do the best job and that the media budget permits such an expensive choice, the media planner may go for prime time television—from 8 P.M. to 11 P.M. The next question becomes which television vehicles (shows) have audiences whose profiles most clearly match those of the target customer.[14]

Careful analysis of any organization's marketing communication efforts might show that what appears to be the most appropriate advertising media is, in fact, quite inappropriate. Where should one advertise a product like children's crayons? Saturday morning television shows, with their ability to show happy children drawing and coloring, and with their excellent demographics, would seem to be the obvious choice. But when Crayola's marketing managers discovered that *mothers* were the prime factors in the purchase of crayons, they shifted $1 million of their advertising budget out of children's TV and into women's magazines. The copy theme developed, ''Give them a fresh box of crayons and see how they grow,'' reflected the shift in audience and the new media strategy. This is not to say that TV advertisements were not useful, but that TV advertisements *coupled with* women's magazine advertisements were better.

Media Strengths and Weaknesses
Each medium has its advantages and disadvantages. Direct-mail advertising can be very selective and can reach a clearly defined market such

[13]Based on H.D. Maneloveg, Testimony to the Federal Trade Commission, 1971.

[14]Based on H.D. Maneloveg, Testimony to the Federal Trade Commission, 1971.

TARKENTON TACKLES A NEW AD MEDIUM

Fran Tarkenton, 42, often flies as many as 20,000 miles a month setting up seminars for his Atlanta-based consulting firm, Tarkenton & Co. Realizing that paper airline ticketholders "are always with you," the former quarterback for the Minnesota Vikings has spawned a new advertising medium: Ticketholders with advertising pages.

It all started in April 1981, when he and longtime friend, Tony Jacobs, owner of Wessel Co., a Chicago printing company, got together and designed a ticketholder with 13 pages for advertising, only a few millimeters thicker than the regular jacket. Tarkenton then led a 10-day blitz on 11 major airlines, lining up nine major carriers with a promise of free airline jackets and a substantial percentage of the profits.

Tarkenton's next play called for lining up potential advertisers. His efforts chalked up $7.5 million in advertising from 11 major companies, including Hertz, Kodak, Chevrolet, and A.T.&T. The rates, based on 12-month distribution, range from $11 to $16 per thousand jackets. Each client was required to commit $100,000 per page per month, with a four-month obligation.

Ticket Holder Marketing officially kicked off in January with distribution of 9.5 million ticket jackets. With three more airlines due on board, Tarkenton expects distribution to increase to 16 million.

Tarkenton and Jacob, equal partners who hint they invested more than $1 million in the company, expect to see black ink the first year on revenues of $15 million to $20 million. Says Tarkenton: "I always wanted to be a pro football player and own my own business."

Source: From Mark Beffart, "Tarkenton Tackles a New Ad Medium," *Venture*, April 1982, p. 6. Used with permission.

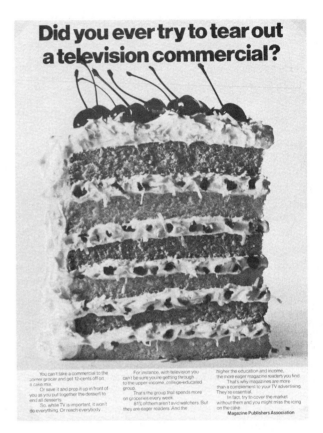

This advertisement reaches businesses that would use magazine advertising.

as families within a certain zip code or all holders of American Express cards. But it can also end up in the wastepaper basket. Television reaches a mass audience, although some specialization by type of show is possible. For example, *American Bandstand* appeals to teenagers and *Over Easy* appeals to older folks. Television allows the advertisers to show and tell because it can involve sight, sound, movement, cartoons, actors, and announcers who are not seen at all. Its strengths, however, may be outweighed by its relative expensiveness. Even when the advertising rates on a particular program or station are relatively low, the costs to develop and produce a commercial keep many potential users away from TV.

Newspapers have the advantages of mass appeal within selected geographical markets, a general respect in the community, and a short lead time. That is, newspaper advertisements can be inserted, withdrawn, or altered quickly. Magazines have relatively long lead times, but offer the advantages of selectivity of audience and far better reproduction of print and pictures

EXHIBIT 20-4

Selected Advantages and Disadvantages of Advertising Media

Newspapers

Advantages
Geographic market selectivity
Flexibility—ease of ad insertion and change
Editorial support

Disadvantages
Lack of permanence of advertising message
Poor quality of printing production
Limited demographic orientation

Magazines

Advantages
Demographic market selectivity
Long-life ad capability
Good quality print production
Editorial support

Disadvantages
Lack of flexibility— difficult to make last-minute changes
Limited availability
Expensive—especially for color

Radio

Advantages
Geographic and demographic market selectivity
Flexibility
Inexpensive on a relative basis

Disadvantages
Lack of permanence— perishability
Clutter
Lack of visual support
Limited impact—background medium

Television

Advantages
Show and tell—demonstration is possible
Geographic market selectivity
Market penetration due to large viewing audience

Disadvantages
Perishable ad message unless repeated
Expensive on a relative basis
Clutter—message may become lost in group of advertisements

Direct Mail

Advantages
Long life—permanence
Flexibility
Impact—few competing ads
Easy-to-measure results
Market selectivity

Disadvantages
Expensive—especially on a cost-per-person basis
Little or no editorial support
Limited reader interest in business market

Outdoor

Advantages
High reach and frequency potential
Market selectivity
Impact due to size
Inexpensive on a relative basis

Disadvantages
Brevity of message
Image is thought to be poor for certain markets
Clutter is often present
Location choices may be limited

Transit

Advantages
High reach and frequency potential
Impact—total bus may be ad
Geographic market selectivity
Inexpensive on a relative basis

Disadvantages
Limited demographic selectivity
Limited availability— does not exist in many markets
Image is thought to be poor for certain markets

Point-of-Purchase

Advantages
Promotes impulse buying
"Sells" in nonpersonal selling environment
Ties together product and ads

Disadvantages
Difficult to obtain desired placements
Clutter
Limited creative possibilities

Directory

Advantages
Permanence—long life
High reach and frequency potential

Disadvantages
Limited customer usage
Market coverage limited to phone customers

Source: From William H. Bolen, *Advertising* (New York: John Wiley & Sons, 1981), pp. 465–466. Used with permission.

than can be found in newspapers. Radio provides geographic and demographic selectivity because the programming of different stations attracts different sorts of listeners. Its lead time is short, and its use as a means to expose listeners to frequent messages is obvious. Exhibit 20-4 highlights the general characteristics of each medium.

MEDIA SCHEDULING

The **reach**—that is, the number of people exposed to an advertisement in a given medium—is an important factor in determining which media to use. So is the amount of repetition or *frequency* of the advertising message. The problem of scheduling requires that decisions be made about reach, frequency, and the timing of advertising messages. Should advertising be spaced steadily throughout the year, concentrated in a particular season, or pulsed at regular or irregular intervals so that the company spends heavily during a periodic pattern and then withdraws for a given time period? These are important questions that marketing managers must consider when choosing media.

In 1982, more than $17 billion was spent on media for national advertising. Exhibit 20-5 details these national expenditures by the various media.

In summary, the characteristics of each media vary greatly. These variations play a strong role in the marketing manager's choice from among the media. Most important of all, however, are the communication objectives the marketer determined at the start of the advertising planning process. These objectives dictate which medium will have the best impact. Then the choices of reach, frequency, and timing must be evaluated in terms of the realities of the budget. Cost is always a consideration in any organizational decision. We see, again, however, that careful and effective marketing planning can yield a communications effort that is creative and successful.

SUMMARY

This chapter explains the purpose of different types of advertising, how effective advertising is created and evaluated, and the role of the various advertising media.

Product advertising involves an emphasis on a particular product or service with the intent of stimulating direct or indirect action. Institutional advertising, on the other hand, is utilized to promote a corporate image, build goodwill, or stimulate generic demand for a product category.

Effective advertising is developed in coordination with the overall marketing strategy. Advertising objectives must be specific and must change with varying environmental conditions.

Much of advertising's success is due to that difficult-to-define concept of creativity. For that reason, this chapter explored the answers to the questions: "What to say?" and "How is it said?"

Some of the major execution formats for advertising are: storyline, product uses and problem solution, slice-of-life, life-style, demonstration, testimonial, spokesperson, association, montage, and the jingle.

Because advertisements are often quite costly, it is important that some measure of the effectiveness of an advertisement be obtained. Pretesting attempts to evaluate effectiveness before an advertisement is placed in the mass media, while post-testing is utilized to determine if the actual media-run advertisement achieved its objectives. Advertisers are also interested in related recall—that is, the ability of viewers of an advertisement to give feedback on specific sales messages from the advertising copy.

An important consideration in advertising development is the selection of the most appropriate medium by which to communicate the

EXHIBIT 20-5

**National Advertising Expenditures
for Eight Media**

Medium for National Advertisers	Thousands of Dollars in National Expenditures
Newspapers	$ 2,556,250
Magazines	3,222,883
Network TV	5,592,819
Spot TV	4,223,259
Farm publications	183,076
Network radio	224,661
Spot radio	896,000
Outdoor	355,939
Total for all eight media	$17,254,880

Source: From *Advertising Age,* September 9, 1982, p. 131.

message. There are inherent advantages and disadvantages with each medium. The advertiser's goal is to match the characteristics of the media audience with the desired target market for the advertisement. The appropriate mix of advertising media is ultimately dependent on the advertising budget and the advertising objectives.

THE MOST IMPORTANT CONCEPT IN THIS CHAPTER

Because advertising is the most "public" thing a marketing organization does, it cannot stand alone. It must reflect and mesh with the other parts of the marketing mix. As with everything else, planning and good execution will make advertising an effective means of communicating with target markets.

KEY TERMS

Consummatory messages

Instrumental messages

Product advertisement

Direct-action advertisement

Indirect-action advertisement

Institutional advertising

Communication goals

Generic demand

Primary demand advertising

Selective demand advertising

The creative process

Advertising appeal

Advertising theme

Execution format

Storyline

Slice-of-life format

Demonstration format

Comparative advertising

Testimonials

Spokesperson

Art

AIDA

Pretesting

Post-testing research

Recall tests

Media selection strategy

Life-style advertisement

Association advertising format

Fantasy

Montage format

Commercial jingles

Copy

Reach

QUESTIONS FOR DISCUSSION

1 Indicate whether the advertising in the following instances is indirect or direct action:
(a) Macy's holds its July 4th sale.
(b) Atari advertises that its home unit would be a nice Christmas gift.
(c) "Hertz is number one for everyone" car rental ad is launched.

2 When does advertising stimulate primary demand? When should it?

3 Inspect several TV commercials and determine what the advertising objective is for each one.

4 Identify three institutional advertisements and explain their purpose.

5 Identify some beer advertising other than those mentioned in the textbook and compare them to the ones shown in the textbook.

6 Does the AIDA formula have more appeal for the writing of advertising copy or the visual art aspect of advertising?

7 Describe the steps in developing a creative strategy.

8 What advertising media would you select for the following products? Why?
(a) Local zoo
(b) Local amusement park
(c) Local clothing store
(d) National soft drink advertiser

9 Of what value is an advertising agency?

10 What are some reasons for pretesting and post-testing specific advertisements? What are the best ways to do the testing?

11 An urban university is planning on advertising its educational programs in local newspapers. What type of creative strategy would you utilize? Be specific.

12 What type of spokesperson would you utilize in a testimonial advertisement for the following products:
(a) Campaign against alcohol abuse
(b) Campaign to encourage cigar smoking
(c) Campaign for Pizza Time Theater, a pizza restaurant with a video game arcade

CASE 20-1   KBTL or KYST*

Prior to May 1983, KYST, an AM stereo radio station drew less than 1 percent of the Houston/Galveston market. In May 1983, the station decided to switch to an all-Beatles format. They changed the name to KBTL.

Station owner, Roy Henderson, obtained the Beatles format, complete with play list, marketing plans, promotional ideas, call letters, and scripts from Phoenix-based Todd Wallace and Associates.

Todd Wallace, principal in the radio programming company, says he plans to market the all-Beatles format concept to failing AM radio stations nationally. Mr. Wallace contends the all-Beatles formula has the potential to raise a low-rated station's market share up to four points for a period of at least two years. The Beatles play list provided by Mr. Wallace's company consists of more than 500 songs played by the Beatles as a group and as individual artists.

Mr. Henderson says that, though some people may assume the Beatles songs become overly repetitious, "that's just not true."

"Most stations play from a call list of about 300 songs," he says. "We have more than 500 songs to choose from and that list keeps growing. Paul McCartney will come out with a new album this summer that we'll play from."

---

*Source: From "Beatles Format Sells as Short-Term and AM Fix," *Advertising Age*, July 4, 1983, p. 22s.

And, during any given hour, Mr. Henderson said the station also plays four separate vignettes of Beatles memorabilia.

"The format isn't designed for the long-term listener," Mr. Henderson says. "It's programmed to the 'button pusher.' If we can get people to just push their 'Beatle button' two to three times a day for a couple of songs, we'll get the couple of points' increase in market share we're after."

KYST has taken on the Wallace-provided station call letters of KBTL, for promotional purposes only, and is touting Mr. Wallace's suggested station slogan of, "All Beatles, all the time."

Questions

1 What appeal would this station have to listeners?

2 What advertisers would be likely to select this as an advertising medium?

3 How successful do you think the radio station will be?

CASE 20-2 Chanel #5—Share the Fantasy*

A pool, large and magical. The shadow of a plane skims across its surface. A woman in a bathing suit reclines at its edge, waiting. The thin figure of a man appears on the other side. He dives in, materializing near her. We do not see her reaction. They never touch. There is a suspension of time. Music tingles like wind chimes from another world. A man's voice softly asks us to "Share the fantasy."

Questions

1 What might the purpose of this advertisement be?

2 What type of commercial is it? What format does it have?

*Source: From Theodore Halki, "Reflections on a New Wave," *Advertising Age*, March 8, 1982, p. m-24.

PART 8

SPECIAL CONSIDERATIONS

This section of the book includes chapters dealing with special topics, each very important and deserving of close attention. The first of these is industrial or organizational marketing. This area of marketing activity is unfamiliar to most consumers even though it constitutes a market that is far larger than the consumer market. While the organizational market ultimately depends on consumers to buy the products produced by organizations, it also brings consumers the products that support their life-styles. International marketing is important to consumers and government as well but, like organizational marketing, is not ordinarily a matter of daily concern to most. How marketers contribute to international trade is the second special topic. Marketing's social responsibilities is the third. In spite of the occasional, justifiable complaints, it remains true that marketers do fulfill major roles in our society and must play those roles well if only to assure their own continued success.

Chapter 21 develops an understanding of the industrial or organizational marketplace.

In Chapter 22, the activity of international marketing is described and the special problems faced by international marketers are highlighted.

Chapter 23 discusses the place of marketing and marketers within our society and the ethical dimensions of the marketing function. ∎

CHAPTER 21

Industrial/Organizational Marketing

CHAPTER SCAN

Although considerable attention has already been given to industrial marketing throughout this textbook, and many examples have demonstrated how marketing concepts apply to non-consumer goods and service marketing, the sheer size and importance of the industrial market requires that special attention be devoted to it.

Industrial marketing, also called organizational marketing, encompasses the provision of products to all sorts of buyers *except* consumers. Thus a marketer may deal with manufacturers, farmers, churches, schools, and governmental units as organizational customers. Because the demand for industrial products is derived demand, and because of the special buying motives and ways in which industrial buyers think and behave, industrial marketing requires certain skills and information not generally associated with the more familiar marketing of consumer goods. It is the purpose of this chapter to investigate the industrial or organizational marketplace and the marketing management activities appropriate to succeeding in that marketplace.

WHEN YOU HAVE STUDIED THIS CHAPTER, YOU WILL:

Understand why demand for industrial products is derived demand.

Be able to discuss the buying criteria and motives at work in the industrial market.

Have noted some of the major characteristics of the industrial marketplace in general.

Have become familiar with the three basic buying situations that occur in industrial buying: the straight rebuy, the modified rebuy, and the new task purchase.

Understand what a buyer of organizational products seeks in the products to be purchased, and be able to explain how marketers can react to these needs.

Be familiar with the basics of the SIC system and its usefulness to marketers.

Know the basic categories of industrial goods and be able to relate them to the marketing approaches associated with each.

Grasp the importance of the buying center concept to industrial marketing.

The Caterpillar Corporation focuses its efforts on industrial marketing by determining customer needs and how to meet them quickly. In the industrial, construction machinery market, they know that building high quality, reliable products backed up by complete servicing is the key to success. To implement its marketing strategy Caterpillar has developed a series of complex, yet workable, arrangements with an extensive dealer network that allows Caterpillar to provide exemplary service to its customers while enhancing Caterpillar dealers' positions as entrepreneurs. Offering extensive training to dealers is part of Caterpillar's industrial marketing strategy to show dealers how they can establish profitable side businesses in rebuilt parts. Not only does this training help keep dealers profitable but it also makes repair of Caterpillar construction machinery more economical for Caterpillar customers.

Caterpillar carefully plans its introduction of new products. Introduction of a new machine will not occur until a two month's supply of spare parts is built up. This allows dealers to service the new product immediately. An extensive computerized inventory system keeps tight control of parts inventories so that any replacement part can be shipped to a customer anywhere in the world within 48 hours. Dealers are encouraged to keep a full stock of items because Caterpillar has the policy of repurchasing parts or equipment that dealers cannot sell.

Caterpillar emphasizes research and development efforts to improve existing products. Rarely does the company innovate with a completely new product offering to the market. It lets its competitors go through the trial and error, hit and miss process of introducing new products. Then Caterpillar imitates them with the most troublefree product on the market.

Caterpillar's marketing strategy is to establish and retain a customer loyalty through long term relationships with a quality dealer network. While its price tag is rarely the lowest, it relies on

---

[1]Based on information in "Caterpillar Sticking to Basics to Stay Competitive," *Business Week,* May 4, 1981, pp. 74–80.

EXHIBIT 21-1

Industrial/Organizational Markets

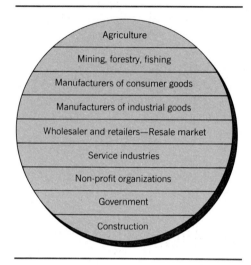

quality and service to maintain this relationship.[1]

An **industrial marketing transaction** takes place whenever a good or service is sold for any use other than personal consumption. In other words, any sale to an industrial user, wholesaler, retailer, or organization other than the ultimate consumer is an industrial sale. Exhibit 21-1 outlines the various industrial/organizational markets.

Manufacturers require raw materials, equipment, component parts, supplies, and services to produce both consumer *and* industrial products. Providing these inputs to manufacturers is one purpose of industrial marketing, but there is a vast range of other industrial marketing activities. Producers of other non-manufactured goods, such as farmers, also buy and use industrial products. Wholesalers and retailers purchase products for resale as well as equipment such as trucks, shelving, and typewriters. Hospitals, zoos, and other nonprofit organizations of all sorts use industrial goods and services to facilitate the performance of their functions. Federal, state, and local governments are industrial buyers. In fact, the federal government is the largest single buyer of industrial products. Because these sales are made to organizations of one kind or another, the term *organizational marketing* may be used in place of *industrial marketing.* The terms industrial sale and organizational sale are also interchangeable.

Marketing to organizations requires strategies specifically tailored to the needs of organizations. A wide array of marketing skills and activities is required for industrial marketing.

However, the sale of such disparate products as a pressurized-water reactor to a public utility constructing a nuclear power plant or coast-to-coast airline travel to a motion picture producer have common characteristics. This chapter investigates these characteristics with two goals in view. One goal is to provide a basic understanding of the characteristics of the industrial market. The other goal is understanding how the techniques and tools of effective marketing can be applied to the non-consumer marketplace.

THE NATURE OF INDUSTRIAL DEMAND

The nature of the demand for industrial goods and services differs greatly from the demand for most consumer goods. Some generalizations may be made about all industrial products and services because of the similar nature of industrial demand. Industrial demand is: (1) derived, (2) inelastic, and (3) fluctuating.

Derived Demand

Reductions in consumer demand for housing has a tremendous impact on the building supply products industry. The demand for aluminum depends on the demand for airplanes, trucks, and products packaged in aluminum. Downturns in the economy may cause people to cut back on their use of airlines which, in turn, reduces the need for airplane fuel and the parts used in airplane maintenance, as well as for the tools used for maintenance. Ultimately, even the demand for such mundane items as the brooms used to sweep out airline hangars will decline as airline usage declines. All of these examples demonstrate a basic truth—all demand for industrial products depends ultimately on consumer demand. It is *derived* from consumer demand. No business will buy raw materials or any other product used to run an organization unless its managers believe that consumers will buy the organization's products.

Exhibit 21-2 demonstrates the power of derived demand in the industrial marketplace. Notice that **derived demand** ultimately depends on consumer demand even when a particular purchasing situation is quite removed from consumers. No retailer would buy so much as a can of soup for resale unless it was thought that the soup could be sold to a customer. It may be less obvious that no manufacturer of cardboard box-making machines would buy even a pencil for use at the factory without believing that box makers will buy box-making machines, that packers will buy boxes, that wholesalers and retailers will buy boxed items, and that retailers will be able to sell those items to ultimate consumers.

Economists, noting that many organizations made up of farmers, wholesalers, retailers, and producers of all types of equipment depend on the successful sale of individual consumer products, have coined the phrase **acceleration principle** to describe the dramatic effects of derived demand. A small increase in demand at one level in the distribution system may accelerate the demand—that is, greatly increase the industrial demand at the next level in the chain. For example, if a wholesaler plans to maintain an inventory level equivalent to a two-months supply, consider what happens when consumer demand rises. A 10 percent increase in consumer de-

EXHIBIT 21-2

An Example of Derived Demand at Work in the Industrial Marketplace

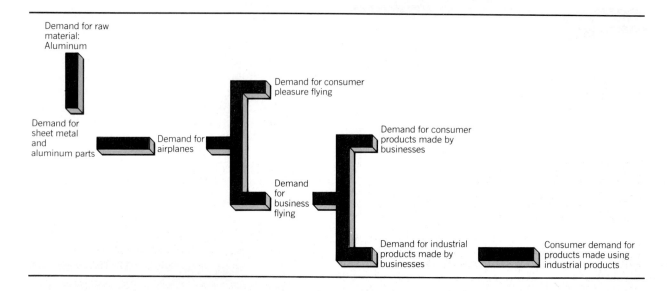

Demand for raw material: Aluminum

Demand for sheet metal and aluminum parts

Demand for airplanes

Demand for consumer pleasure flying

Demand for business flying

Demand for consumer products made by businesses

Demand for industrial products made by businesses

Consumer demand for products made using industrial products

mand will increase retailers' demands for inventory. Thus, at the wholesale level of the distribution chain, the demand based on the two-months supply standard will be dramatically increased. The acceleration principle holds for the purchase of industrial machinery for manufacturing, the inventory of component parts, and most other industrial products.

The Significance of Derived Demand. The effects of derived demand on their marketing efforts is important to industrial marketers, and not just because of its potentially devastating effects. Derived demand presents certain opportunities. Under some circumstances the industrial marketer can stimulate the demand for the *consumer* product on which demand for the industrial product depends. This draws demand from the consumer through the channel until it reaches the industrial seller. For example, advertisements suggesting that milk is better in unbreakable plastic jugs may be sponsored by the producers of plastic jugs or the manufacturers of machines that make plastic jugs. Recognizing a

trend of declining per capita beef consumption, the Beef Industry Council targeted advertisements to consumers in an attempt to reverse the trend. Pork producers and lamb producers have done much the same thing, even though these organizations represent farmers and ranchers who are several steps removed from the consumer in the channels of distribution.

The Beef Council experience suggests another advantage to dealing with derived demand. Alert industrial marketers, keeping an eye on the ultimate demand on which they depend, can foresee developments that may soon affect their businesses. In some cases, such marketers can take steps to influence these developments or to make adjustments that offset their efforts. Responding to trends in the marketplace is an important part of the job of *all* marketers, of course, but industrial marketers must pay special attention. Unfortunately, their distance from the consumers on whom they ultimately depend may make it more difficult for them to focus attention on developments that may affect their sales.

Lightweight aluminum saves energy in transportation.

If you've ever wondered how something so big got off the ground, part of the answer is aluminum.

Aluminum's high strength and light weight helped to make modern aviation possible.

Aluminum is important to *most* forms of transportation. Because taking the weight off planes, trucks...

and now cars, saves fuel.

Aluminum in transportation. It's a better way to get there—today.

ALCOA

We can't wait for tomorrow. For more information write Alcoa, 443-F Alcoa Building, Pittsburgh, PA 15219.

A case of derived demand.

E X P E R I E N C E   L A M B

An ordinary shish kabob made extraordinary with fresh American lamb. Tenderness with taste. The elegant addition to an international favorite. Experience Mideast Mystique lamb shish kabobs. Marinate 2 pounds of 1" lamb cubes overnight in 1/3 cup each lemon juice, olive oil, and onion, 1 garlic clove minced, 1 teaspoon savory and 1/2 teaspoon salt. Skewer lamb and vegetables. Broil, brushing with marinade.

lamb FRESH AMERICAN

Stimulating primary demand.

Price Inelasticity

If we isolate the influence of price on demand, when compared to the demand for consumer goods, the rises and falls in the demand for industrial goods are modest. Industry demand is relatively inelastic because demand is not likely to significantly change in the short run. There are two very good reasons for this inelasticity. First, industrial buyers are in a position to "pass along" price increases to their customers. If the price of the sheet metal used to make Jeep fenders goes up, American Motors, makers of Jeep, can raise the price of their pdocuts to cover the increased cost of the metal because the demand for Jeeps is strong. The second, less obvious, reason for price inelasticity is the tendency for the price of any one industrial product to be an almost insignificant part of the total price of the final product of which it is a part. When the price of sheet metal goes up, raising the cost of a fender by a few dollars, it has comparatively little effect on the total price of a finished Jeep.

Although industrial prices tend to be inelastic for the industry, buyers are not insensitive to them—especially if there are several competing sellers. Therefore, marketers must consider price in view of each customer's special situation.

DEPENDING ON DERIVED DEMAND MAY MEAN DEVELOPING PRIMARY DEMAND

Some suppliers of industrial products attempt to appeal directly to the consumers on whom the success of their industrial products ultimately depends. One firm to do this lately is G.D. Searle & Co., developers and marketers of NutraSweet™ brand sweetener, sold as a sweetening ingredient to such companies as General Foods for Kool-Aid. Once Searle received government approval to sell the low-calorie sweetener, makers of cereals, drinks, and desserts immediately expressed interest in the product. The company also sells its own consumer product containing NutraSweet for in-home use as a sugar substitute. In this case, the brand name Equal® is used.

With food makers expressing a desire to buy and use NutraSweet, some organizations would have concentrated all efforts on the industrial buyers. Not Searle. Following a pattern that has been used by other developers of new products, Searle ran a series of advertisements aimed at ordinary consumers. The purpose of these was to acquaint consumers with the fact that NutraSweet was a totally new kind of sweetener. The advertisements explained that NutraSweet is made of protein components, and that the human body treats these just as it would any other protein ingested. They advanced the claim that Nutra-Sweet tastes like sugar. Most importantly, the advertisements told consumers to look for products containing NutraSweet and showed packages of some of those products so consumers would know what to look for.

The campaign directed at consumers permits Searle to rightly claim some consumer familiarity with, and even loyalty to, NutraSweet. This encourages makers of drinks and other products to place the words "Made with NutraSweet" on their packages. This, in turn, reinforces the consumers' perception of the sweetener as something special. Searle sells NutraSweet to industrial buyers by selling it to consumers.

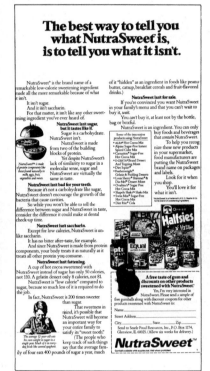

Source: From Jennifer Alter, "Searle Readies Aid for Sweetener Bids," *Advertising Age*, January 18, 1983, p. 47. Used with permission. Copyright 1983 by Crain Communications, Inc.

Fluctuating Demand

Most organizations prefer steady operating schedules. Thus, it might be expected that demand for industrial products would be more or less constant. Actually, when compared to the demand for consumer goods, the demand for industrial goods is characterized by *wide* fluctuations in demand. There are three logical reasons for this.

First, organizational purchases can usually be closely linked to the state of the economy. As the economy moves through its up and down cycles, demand for industrial products goes through cycles as well. During prosperous times, firms tend to maintain large inventories. When the economy slows or enters a turndown, retailers, wholesalers, manufacturers, and most other organizational customers tend to sell off or use up their existing inventories. They also tend to postpone purchases of new supplies, equipment, and other products. If the direction of the economy is uncertain, purchases are again postponed. This is especially true for machine tools, pumps, materials handling equipment, and other products that can be repaired and made to last until better economic times seem imminent.

Hence, industrial demand, influenced by environmental dynamics, can fluctuate widely.

Second, many industrial purchasers have a tendency to "stock up" on the products they buy. They then do not need to make further purchases until their stock is somewhat depleted. Third, many industrial products have long lives, as in the case of buildings and major equipment.

CHARACTERISTICS OF THE ORGANIZATIONAL MARKET

The agricultural, financial, and manufacturing industries are quite different from one another, yet they share some basic characteristics that are typical of industrial markets. Because these characteristics are far less frequently encountered in consumer markets, marketers should be aware of their special nature.

First, industrial markets tend to be more geographically concentrated than consumer markets. Second, they generally serve far fewer customers. For example, only a few companies make automobiles or tires. Even though some of these industries have moved production facilities to the Sun Belt, their headquarters remain mostly in their traditional centers, such as Detroit and Akron for automobiles and tires. Other industries have geographic centers, too. For example, several midwestern and far western cities remain the headquarters for airplane manufacture. Tulsa, Dallas, and Houston are major petroleum centers. New York and Chicago are important financial centers.

A third characteristic of industrial buyers is their preference for buying directly from the manufacturer or producer. This preference may derive from the desire to buy in large quantities or to avoid intermediaries in an effort to obtain a better price. It may also be a function of the technical complexity of many industrial products and the fact that many such products are made to order. For all of these reasons, the desire to deal directly with producers is understandable.

A fourth characteristic of industrial purchasers—their comparative expertise in buying—must be mentioned. They buy, almost always, in a scientific way, basing decisions on close analyses of the product being offered and careful comparisons with its competing products. Moreover, terms of sale, service, guarantees, and other such factors are likely to be carefully weighed. If a product is a highly technical one, the buyer will assign properly trained engineers or scientists to participate in the purchase decision. When a purchase decision is major, as it often is, a committee will often be formed to evaluate certain factors such as the industrial marketer's product, technical abilities, and position vis-à-vis competitors.

The characteristics of industrial customers mentioned here by no means constitute an exhaustive list of such factors, but there are enough for us to consider how industrial marketers deal with these special buyers. The fact that there are often relatively few buyers, coupled with the fact that they are likely to be geographically concentrated and prefer to deal directly with suppliers, suggests—indeed often mandates—the use of direct selling forces. The technical nature of many of the products and the expertise of the persons engaged in making purchase decisions demand a well-trained sales force with an extensive knowledge of the products they sell. Representing a maker of nuclear power plants is quite different from selling Legos or Loc Blocs to Christmas-shopping grandparents.

The various characteristics of industrial markets often combine to permit the marketer to identify almost all potential customers. Personal selling is usually expensive, but the opportunity to develop a list of nearly all potential customers can allow personal selling to be a cost-efficient marketing tool. A number of companies develop and sell lists of the names, addresses, and phone numbers of organizations by industry classification.

Changes in the Marketplace

The discussion of characteristics of the industrial market may give the impression that these attributes are somehow unchanging. This is not always the case. Industrial markets, like consumer markets, are dynamic. Effective industrial marketers must be alert to changes. For example, industrial production in the United States was once concentrated in a few North Central and Northeastern states. While these states are still important in this regard, more and more industry has moved to the Sun Belt where labor costs tend to be lower, where state and local governments are willing to give considerable incentives to firms willing to relocate, and where different life-styles may be available. Changes like these affect the work of industrial marketers as do such developments as fuel shortages, changes in the law, and challenges from overseas marketers.

ORGANIZATIONAL BUYING BEHAVIOR

Buying is a necessary activity for all formal organizations.[2] The purchasing of industrial goods and services, such as semiconductors or accounting services, may be a complex process. Purchasing agents and other organizational members determine the need to purchase products and services, engage in information-seeking activities, evaluate alternative purchasing actions, and negotiate the necessary arrangements with supplying organizations. Exhibit 21-3 shows that there are many activities in the buying process. Industrial buying takes place over time, involves communications among several organizational members, and demands financial relationships with suppliers. The organizational buying process is performed by knowledgeable individuals, attempting to be rational in their selection of alternative suppliers, brands, and quantities. Placing an order with a supplier is generally not a simple act. The steps to be followed in purchasing decisions and purchasing standards may be specifically spelled out in corporate manuals.

Multiple Decision-Making Responsibilities

Often, the responsibility for organizational buying is divided among several individuals. In general, as the complexity of the product under consideration increases, engineers and technicians will have a greater say in purchasing decisions. If the product is not complex, or if a regular pattern of purchase has been developed and agreed on, a purchasing agent is likely to have buying responsibility.

In any case, the buying decision affects many people in the organization and, therefore, many people will participate in it. These individuals may have some say in the purchase but they certainly will not always be in total agreement.

Consider the purchasing of air compressors for manufacturing plants. A study of the buying of these products discovered that the following individuals and groups were all involved in some part of the purchasing decision:[3]

- President
- Vice-President of Engineering

---

[2]This paragraph is based on F.E. Webster, Jr. and Y. Wind, *Organizational Buying Behavior* (Englewood Cliffs, N.J.: Prentice-Hall, 1972), p. 1.

[3]R.D. Buzzell, R.E.M. Nourse, J.B. Matthews, Jr., and T. Levitt, *Marketing: A Contemporary Analysis* (New York: McGraw-Hill, 1972), pp. 205–206.

■ Vice-President of Manufacturing

■ Plant Facilities Manager

■ Maintenance Supervisor

■ Chief Electrician

■ Purchasing Department Personnel

EXHIBIT 21-3

Buy Phases: Steps in an Organizational Buying Decision

---

1 Anticipation or recognition of a problem or need.

2 Recognition of likely solutions to the problem.

3 Determination of characteristics and quantity of needed items.

4 Development of specifications to guide the procurement.

5 Search for potential sources.

6 Acquisition and analysis of proposals.

7 Evaluation of proposals and selection of suppliers.

8 Selection of an order routine.

9 Performance of feedback and evaluation.

10 Evaluation of products and suppliers.

11 Use of evaluations as feedback to alter or adjust the buying process.

Source: Adapted from P.J. Robinson, C.W. Faris, and Y. Wind, *Industrial Buying and Creative Marketing* (Boston, Mass.: Allyn and Bacon, Inc., 1967), p. 14. Copyright Allyn and Bacon, Inc. Used with permission.

Three Kinds of Buying

As shown in Exhibit 21-3, organizational buying behavior may be viewed as a multi-stage, decision-making process. However, the amount of time and effort devoted to each of the stages or *buy phases* depends on a number of factors, such as the nature of the product, the costs involved, and the experience of the organization in buying the needed goods or services. Consider these three situations.

■ An organization buys goods and services on a regular basis from the same suppliers. Careful attention may have been given to selection of the suppliers at some earlier time, but the organization is well satisfied with both them and the products they offer. The organization buys from these suppliers virtually automatically. This is the **straight rebuy** situation. Everything from pencils to legal advice to equipment may be bought this way *if* the buyer is satisfied with the supplier's past performance.

■ An organization is discontented with current suppliers, or suspects that it may be in the organization's interest to "shop around." It is known what products are needed and who the likely suppliers might be. This is the **modified rebuy** situation. A firm might find itself in this mode regardless of the type of good or service under consideration.

■ An organization is facing a new problem or need, and is not certain as to what products will fill the need. Furthermore, the organization is not even aware of what suppliers might be able to fill the need. If the purchase is expected to be a very expensive one, the sense of concern and uncertainty is heightened. This is the **new task situation**.

In each situation, the length of the decision-making process as a whole will vary as will the time spent on each individual buying phase. These three separate kinds of purchases have been identified and associated with both specific types of industrial buyer behaviors and marketing activities.[4] Exhibit 21-4 summarizes the characteristics of these three categories of buying decisions. It is important to note that the key element that sets these categories apart from one another is buyer behavior patterns, not the complexity of the product involved or monetary concerns.

Understanding the types of buying situations and behaviors to be found in organizational buying is extremely important for indus-

---

[4] P.J. Robinson, C.W. Faris, Y. Wind, *Industrial Buying and Creative Marketing* (Boston, Mass.: Allyn and Bacon, 1967). Copyright Allyn and Bacon, Inc. Used with permission.

EXHIBIT 21-4

**Characteristics of the Straight Rebuy, Modified Rebuy,
and New Task Buying Situations**

Straight Rebuy

■ Continuing or recurring requirement, handled on a routine basis.

■ Usually the decision on each separate transaction is made in the purchasing department.

■ Formally or informally, a "list" of acceptable suppliers exists.

■ No supplier not on the "list" is considered.

■ Buyers have much relevant buying experience, and hence little new information is needed.

■ Appears to represent the bulk of the individual purchases within companies.

■ Item purchases, price paid, delivery time, etc., may vary from transaction to transaction, so long as these variations do not cause a new source of supply to be considered.

Modified Rebuy

■ May develop from either new task or straight rebuy situations.

■ The requirement is continuing or recurring or it may be expanded to a significantly larger level of operations.

■ The buying alternatives are known, but they are *changed*.

Modified Rebuy (continued)

■ Some additional information is needed before the decisions are made.

■ May arise because of outside events, such as an emergency or by the actions of a marketer.

■ May arise internally because of new buying influences, or for potential cost reductions, potential quality improvements, or potential service benefits.

■ Marketers who are not active suppliers try to convert the customer's straight rebuys into modified rebuys.

New Task

■ A requirement or problem that has not arisen before.

■ Little or no relevant past buying experience to draw upon.

■ A great deal of information is needed.

■ Must seek out alternative ways of solving the problem and alternative suppliers.

■ Occurs infrequently—but very important to marketers because it sets the pattern for the more routine purchases that will follow.

■ May be anticipated and developed by creative marketing.

Source: P.J. Robinson, C.W. Faris, and Y. Wind, *Industrial Buying and Creative Marketing* (Boston, Mass.: Allyn and Bacon, 1967), p. 28. Reproduced with permission.

---

trial marketers, just as consumer behavior patterns are important for consumer goods marketers. Each buying situation suggests a different marketing mix—an adjustment of the four major variables to fit particular circumstances. A marketing manager facing a *new buy* situation, for example, would understand that the target customer is uncertain of the steps to be taken to satisfy his or her organization's needs. Such a buyer probably would require a good deal of information about the supplier, its products, and its abilities to deliver and service the products. This suggests a marketing mix that stresses promotion, especially communication of information that will help the customer to evaluate alternatives and to understand why the particular supplier is the one to choose.

On the other hand, a buyer in a *modified rebuy* mode might require information of a particular type. This buyer knows something of what

HOW DIFFERENT MEMBERS OF AN ORGANIZATION EVALUATE A PRODUCT

It would be expected that different members of an organization would look for different things in any product to be purchased for organizational use. Many studies bear this out, though the factors important to each member of the organization vary considerably from product to product.

When a single product is under consideration, how widely might the focus on more important and less important factors vary? One study of a purchase decision involving an industrial cooling system grouped individuals into five categories and compared their areas of concern as shown

here. Of course, the marketing manager's task is to determine which variables are important to which influencers of the purchase and prepare the marketing mix accordingly.

Issues of Importance in the Formation of Individual Preferences

	Key Importance	Less Importance
Production engineers	Operating cost Energy savings Reliability Complexity	First cost Field proven
Corporate engineers	First cost Field proven Reliability Complexity	Energy savings Up-to-date
Plant managers	Operating cost Use of unproductive areas Up-to-date Power failure protection	First cost Complexity
Top managers	Up-to-date Energy savings Operating cost	Noise level in plant Reliability
Air conditioning consultants	Noise level in plant First cost Reliability	Up-to-date Energy savings Operating cost

Source: J. M. Choffray and G.L. Lilien, "Addressing Response to Industrial Marketing Strategy," *Journal of Marketing*, April 1978, p. 30. Used with permission.

is needed and who likely suppliers might be. In such a case, communications built around very specific problem areas might be appropriate. If the target buyer is shopping for new suppliers, the marketer must find out why. Have deliveries been spotty? Have there been product failures?

Are prices perceived as too high? The marketer must come up with responses to these problems that can show the target buyer why dealing with *this* marketing firm can answer those problems.

In the case of the *straight rebuy*, the marketer may be in the strong position of being the

EXHIBIT 21-5

Strategies Vendors Can Use in Three Types of Buying Decisions

Buying Situations	Supplier Status	
	In Supplier	**Out Supplier**
New task	Monitor changing or emerging purchasing needs in organization.	
	Isolate specific needs.	Isolate specific needs
	If possible, participate actively in early phases of buying process by supplying information and technical advice.	If possible, participate actively in early phases of buying process by supplying information and technical advice.
Straight rebuy	Reinforce buyer-seller relationship by meeting organization's expectations.	Convince organization that the potential benefits of reexamining requirements and suppliers exceed the costs.
	Be alert and responsive to changing needs of customer.	Attempt to gain a position on the organization's preferred list of suppliers even as a second or third choice.
Modified rebuy	Act immediately to remedy problems with customer.	Define and respond to the organization's problem with existing supplier.
	Reexamine and respond to customer needs.	Encourage organization to sample alternative offerings.

Source: P.J. Robinson, C.W. Faris, and Y. Wind, *Industrial Buying and Creative Marketing* (Boston, Mass.: Allyn and Bacon, 1967), p. 28. Copyright Allyn and Bacon, Inc. Used with permission.

supplier benefiting from the rebuy situation. In such circumstances, the marketer seeks to assure that the target customer does not become discontented but continues to make purchases on a regular basis from the same, good old supplier. A summary of how marketing efforts might vary from case to case is shown in Exhibit 21-5.

ORGANIZATIONAL BUYING MOTIVES

It is debatable whether rational buying criteria dominate organizational buying behavior to the exclusion of emotional motives. Reasonable observers must acknowledge that good salesmanship and effective advertisements often appeal to an industrial buyer's emotional need to buy "the best" or to take "pride" in the products purchased. There is one compelling argument that can lead students of industrial marketing to the belief that, while emotional buying motives may be identified, they are not the most important ones. The argument is that no industrial buyer would put his or her job and reputation on the line by purchasing a product *simply* because the salesperson provided the buyer with football tickets or some other gift. When the sale goes to the sales representative who offered a gift, that salesperson's product almost certainly met all the rational criteria by which the purchaser was expected to judge the product. That is, the emotional reasons to buy are almost always incidental to the purchase decision.

Typical Buying Criteria in the Industrial Marketplace

Although it might be possible to list nearly all possible rational reasons for buying, the importance of each factor varies from situation to situation, and some may never come into play in any given purchase decision. Our discussion here will focus on a few of the most influential purchasing criteria, but keep in mind each of these generally comes down to a *bottom line* criterion.

Product Characteristics. Industrial buyers are usually careful, yet organizations may make certain purchases without carefully analyzing the products they are buying simply because the costs and risks involved in making a bad choice are not very great. Paper clips and thumbtacks are pretty much all alike and, unless they turn out to be somehow defective, are often bought without close scrutiny. Most other goods and services bought by organizations are not like that, however. In fact, many products and services are made to the buyer's own specifications, indicating close consideration of exactly what is required to fulfill a given task.

Related Services. Service is an important variable in the purchasing of industrial products. Before the sale is consummated, the marketer may have to demonstrate the ability to provide rapid delivery, repair service, or technical support. After the sale, the supplier had better be able to deliver the promised services, since "downtime" costs money and may be a great source of customer frustration for industrial buyers of an office photocopier, a computer, or an assembly line conveyor system.

Prices. In spite of the relatively inelastic nature of industry demand, price can be the single most important determining factor in many organizational buying decisions to select a supplier. There is an old adage that says: "Farmers are price takers, not price makers." It suggests that farmers, themselves producers of industrial products, face keen competition in a marketplace where parity products (i.e., products which are more or less the same) are sold. Not all industrial marketers are quite so at the mercy of

DOCUTEL: ATM VERSUS EFTS

At one time, Docutel supplied virtually all automatic teller machines (ATMs) to banks. But Docutel found itself rapidly losing market share when large computer companies such as Burroughs, Honeywell, and IBM began to compete with it. What went wrong? Docutel continued to offer only one component part that solved banks' problems. The computer manufacturers began to look at the banks' total electronic funds transfer system (EFTS), and these competitors offered the banks a package of equipment representing a complete system of which the ATM was only one part. Docutel did not broadly interpret their customer's needs and the product required to satisfy those needs.

Source: Based on Derek F. Abell, "Strategic Windows," *Journal of Marketing*, July 1978, pp. 23–24.

Service is an important industrial buying motive.

TROUBLEMAKERS. MONEYMAKERS.

You can save money with French's durable plastic Freedom Shakers.
That's because with Freedom Shakers, no one needs to wash, dry,
refill or clean up any messes. When they're empty, just throw them away.
You'll also find customers are less likely to break them or take them.
So throw away your glass shaker troublemakers and get
French's disposable Freedom Shakers.
You'll be money ahead.
To calculate just how much you'll save, we'll send you a French's
Savings Estimate Form. You'll also receive a free pair of Freedom
Shakers. Get them both by calling 716/482-8000. Or write The R. T. French
Company, Foodservice Products Group, Dept. F0002. P.O. Box 22338.
Rochester, New York 14692.

Advertising addressed to industrial buyers, such as the restaurant industry, often addresses the buyer's concern with the profits. This R. T. French ad promises less trouble and more profit using durable plastic freedom shakers—an idea which is worth its salt.

market forces as are farmers, but many industrial goods and services face strong competition from products that are close substitutes. In such situations, price is likely to be the key to the completion of a sale. Organizational buyers often gather competitive bids from suppliers, further heightening the effects of competition on price.

Industrial buyers can be expected to analyze price carefully, examining not just the list price but also any discounts, terms of sale, and credit opportunities that accompany a purchase agreement. When this is coupled with a thorough knowledge of the product offered, detailed comparisons of value offered are possible, increasing potency of price as a buying criterion.

Other Reasons for Buying. In specific organizational situations, other rational criteria may come into play. When a fire extinguisher, smoke alarm, or sprinkling system is being purchased, a clear-cut motive is *safety*. When life insurance on key executives is bought, *security* might be the major motive. If safety equipment is bought, the motive might be *protection* against losing a safety-related law suit.

Yet even when these factors play a part in the decision, the questions of *what* sprinkler sys-

tem, *what* insurance policy, and *what* safety devices to buy remain. These questions are resolved in terms of the three major buying criteria discussed here: product, service, and price. Industrial marketers find this is to be true, time and again, even though the accent a particular buyer might place on one or the other of the three may vary. Some general patterns of emphasis are shown in Exhibit 21-6 and suggest factors to stress in marketing plans. For Copperweld Robotics, a producer of industrial robots, research showed that customers wanted answers to three questions in the following order: (1) Will it do the job? (2) What service is available? and (3) What is the price? Copperweld's director of marketing says that, for the industrial robot industry, "Service is absolutely the number one part of the marketing function because if one portion of the robot doesn't work, the whole line shuts down."[5]

The Bottom Line. In any organizational buying decision, each of the many motives that a buyer may have does not stand alone. They inter-

---

[5]Philip Maher, "Coming to Grips with the Robot Market," *Industrial Marketing*, January 1982, p. 98.

EXHIBIT 21-6

Shifts in Importance of the Three Major Organizational Buying Criteria

When competition or other factors make this criterion less important . . .	. . . these criteria are more important and are stressed by marketers
Product	Price and service
Price	Product and service
Service	Product and price

← Less important   More important →

play in the buyer's mind. Each contributes to the final decision and each affects the importance of the others (see Exhibit 21-6). Yet, as the following story about General Motors (GM) illustrates, they often boil down to one overriding factor: the need to operate an organization. General Motors' truck and coach division emphasizes issues like corrosion and fuel consumption in its advertising. The strategy is based on the belief that "GM customers don't buy these vehicles because they like them—they need them to make money."[6]

THE BUYING CENTER

How do industrial marketers manage to consider all the many persons involved in the organizational buying decision, their motives, and their special needs? It is a complicated and difficult task. However, the concept of the buying center helps to visualize the buying process and to organize the marketing manager's thinking as the marketing mix is developed.

The **buying center** in any organization is defined as "an informal, cross-departmental decision unit in which the primary objective is the acquisition, impartation, and processing of relevant purchasing-related information."[7] In somewhat simpler terms, the buying center includes all the people and groups that have a role in the decision-making processes of purchasing. Since they all have a part in the matter, they are seen as having common goals and as sharing in the risks associated with the ultimate decision. As the definition suggests, the membership in the buying center and the size of the center vary from organization to organization and from case to case. In smaller organizations, almost everyone may have some input into the buying process; in larger organizations, a more formal group may be identifiable. The buying center may range in size from a few people to perhaps 20.

When thinking in terms of a buying center, one must realize that the center is *not* identified on any organization chart. A committee seem-

[6]"GMC Truck Ads Focus on the Nuts and Bolts," *Advertising Age*, June 25, 1979, pp. 2–14.

[7]R.E. Spekman and L.W. Stern, "Environmental Uncertainty and Buying Group Structure: An Empirical Investigation," *Journal of Marketing*, Spring 1979, p. 56.

EXHIBIT 21-7

**Buying Center Membership and Shifts in Influence:
Hospital Purchase of an Intensive-Care Monitoring Unit**

Stages in Buying Process	Physicians	Nurses	Hospital Administrators	Engineers	Purchasing Department
1 Identification of a Need	High	Low	Moderate	Low	Low
2 Establishment of objectives	High	High	Moderate	Moderate	Low
3 Identification of alternatives/ evaluation of alternatives	High	High	Moderate	Moderate	Low
4 Choice of supplier	High	Low	High	Low	Moderate

Source: Gene R. Laczniak, "An Empirical Study of Hospital Buying," *Industrial Marketing Management*, January 1979, p. 61.

ingly created to decide on a purchase is likely to be but one part of the buying center. Its other members having informal, but nonetheless important, roles to play in the matter. Indeed, as the concept itself implies, the membership in the buying center may actually change as the decision-making process progresses. As the purchasing task moves from step to step, individuals with certain areas of expertise are likely to lose their membership in the buying center while others are added. It must be repeated that this membership is informal, so no announcements are likely to be made of who has been dropped and who has been added.

Structure and Roles in the Buying Center

The roles of members in the buying center have been closely studied. One such study involved the purchase of an expensive intensive-care monitoring device for a hospital. The buying situation for this hospital was of the new task buying variety. What sorts of individuals would influence this decision? From what parts of the hospital management and staff would they be drawn? How would their relative roles in the decision-making process change as the buying

task progressed from the first stages—identification of a need—to the last stage—actual selection of a supplier?

As you might guess, the individuals with influence in this decision-making process would not all be located in any one office or department. It was found that these five elements made up the buying center: physicians, nurses, hospital administrators, engineers, and the purchasing department. The questions facing a marketer of hospital equipment are not so easily answered. Do these individuals all have the same influence? Does the influence exerted change over time? The answers in this case are summarized in Exhibit 21-7.[8] Note how the patterns of influence change over time and how a marketer who chose to deal with any one buying center membership group, especially the purchasing department, would be wasting a good deal of effort and perhaps losing the sale in the process.

Buying centers include a wide variety of individuals. Each member has an official place within the organizational structure as well as an

---

[8]Gene R. Laczniak, "An Empirical Study of Hospital Buying," *Industrial Marketing Management*, January 1979, p. 61.

EXHIBIT 21-8

Five Roles Played Within a Buying Center

Role Title	Description of Role		
Users	These persons will actually use the products under consideration. If the question is a purchase of brooms and mops, the influence of the users may be nil. If the product considered plays a consequential role in the performance of a major function and is a key to organizational success, the user may be a major contributor to the decision. The user may be the one who initiates the purchase process and may even develop product specifications.	**Influencers**	Influencers affect the purchase decision by supplying information. It might be technical information, which aids in the evaluation process, but it could also be information on what course of action would be preferred by persons of position within the organization. Outsiders, such as consultants, may play the influencer role within the buying center.
Gatekeepers	These people control the flow of information to other buying center members. Many advertisements are directed to purchasing department members or to other target groups deemed important in the decision-making process. If these are passed on to some members of the organization but not to others, the gatekeeper has "opened the gate" to buying center membership to some individuals and effectively "closed the gate" to others. Any member of the organization, given the right circumstances, could play the gatekeeper role.	**Deciders**	Deciders make the actual purchase decision. The organization may not "officially" give them this power, but their role in the buying center does. The president of the company, aloof from all the evaluations and contacts with possible suppliers may make the final decision. The user or engineering expert who drew up the buying specifications may have performed the decider role by requesting a product that only one supplier could create.
		Buyers	The buyers have the formal authority to purchase the product. The purchasing agent may fill this role. However, by the time that role is performed by the PA, the decision has been made by the other members of the buying group, in effect reducing the actual purchase to a clerical task.

Source: From F.E. Webster and Y. Wind, *Organizational Buying Behavior* (Englewood Cliffs, N.J.: Prentice-Hall, 1972), pp. 77–80. Used with permission of Prentice-Hall, Inc. Copyright © 1972.

unofficial one in the buying center. The official organizational roles may influence those played within the buying center. In our hospital example, the formal organization of the hospital might require that all marketers of hospital equipment be screened by the purchasing department even though, as Exhibit 21-7 shows, the purchasing department actually has little influence over the decision-making process.

A scheme of buying center roles has been developed to show what kinds of activities are performed by buying center members. Five such roles are identified, but it should be kept in mind that one type of person within the organization may play more than a single role, and more than one role may be played by a single type of person. Consider the five buying center roles defined in Exhibit 21-8, and notice, for example, that doctors *and* nurses in our hospital case would have parts to play in several categories. Note that the importance of the role varies from decision to decision.

While the buying center is often loosely constructed and somewhat difficult for the industrial marketer to fully identify, its role in purchasing decisions is certainly potent. Therefore, it is in the marketing manager's best interest to devote time and effort to studying its ramifications in particular marketing situations.

CLASSIFYING INDUSTRIAL MARKETS

A wide variety of profit and not-for-profit institutions make up the markets for industrial products and services. Knowing how many of each kind of organization are in operation, where they are located, the size of the operations, and so on, can help to implement research activities and to plan marketing strategies. Fortunately, there is a great deal of data available on organizational markets. Although much of it is gathered by private companies, governmental agencies are also important sources of this information.

A major tool for use in researching the industrial marketplace is the **Standard Industrial Classification (SIC)** system. The SIC system is a numerical coding system developed by the federal government and is used to classify different segments of industry in terms of the type of economic activity in which they are engaged. The major divisions used in the system are shown in Exhibit 21-9. Since the SIC system involves code numbers, the codes can be lengthened to identify finer and finer gradations of differences within any particular field or industry.

Consider, for example, the industry that manufactures paper and allied products. This broad category is represented with the two-digit number 26. As shown in Exhibit 21-10, adding a third digit identifies specific manufacturing functions in the paper and allied products industry. A fourth digit more exactly locates the particular product category, and a fifth digit brings the process down to an even narrower product definition, in this case writing tablets. Additional digits define individual manufacturers and products. When people familiar with the SIC system use the word "industry," they are referring, in

effect, to a four-digit grouping in the SIC. For example, the code number 2648 is used to identify the "stationery products industry"; the fifth digit, or beyond, is used if the need for information is more narrowly defined.

EXHIBIT 21-9

Primary Divisions of Industrial Economic Activity and Their Criterion Data Measures

Division	Criterion to Measure Activity
Agriculture, forestry, and fishing, hunting, and trapping (except agricultural services)	Value of production
Mining	Value of production
Construction	Value of production
Manufacturing	Value of production
Transportation, communication, electric, gas, and sanitary services	Value of receipts or revenues
Wholesale trade	Value of sales
Retail trade	Value of sales
Finance, insurance, and real estate	Value of receipts
Services (including agricultural services)	Value of receipts or revenues
Public administration	Employment or payroll

EXHIBIT 21-10

**Selected SIC Codes for Major Group
Number 26—Paper and Allied Products**

Group Numbers	Product Code	Item Code
261 Pulp mills		
262 Paper mills, except building papermills		
263 Paperboard mills		
264 Converted paper and paperboard products, except containers and boxes	2648 Stationery products	26482 Tablets and related products
265 Paperboard containers and boxes		
266 Building paper and building board mills		

Source: Based on *Standard Industrial Classification Manual,* p. 100 and *1977 Census of Manufacturers,* Industry Series, Converted Paper and Paperboard Products.

The reason the SIC code system is important to marketers is that vast amounts of information are published by the federal government using the SIC code as a guide to that information. The Census of Retailing, the Census of Manufacturing, County Business Patterns, and many other useful government publications are based on the SIC system. Furthermore, because the system is so heavily employed in government statistics, it is also used by most private companies that generate marketing research data.

Government statistics reported by SIC codes are often utilized to calculate geographical market potential. For example, suppose a manufacturer of industrial lubricants wished to estimate the market potential in each sales territory.[9] In an effort to calculate an estimate of market potential, the company established the following procedure:

1 The company determined that industrial lubricant sales were concentrated in three industries: apparel products manufacturing (SIC 23), chemicals (SIC 28), and fabricated metals (SIC 34).

2 A survey of purchasing agents in each of these SIC industries was conducted. Purchasing

agents indicated their average annual rate o. purchase (in pounds) and the number of employees in their plants. On the basis of the survey the company estimated the current rate of purchase in pounds per employee for each type of industry.

3 Employment data for each industry were obtained on a county-by-county basis from *County Business Patterns.*

4 Market-potential estimates for each county were then derived as indicated in Exhibit 21-11 for Cook County, Illinois.

EXHIBIT 21-11

Market Potential for Cook County

SIC Code	Industry	Number of Employees	Pounds per Employee	Estimated Potential (pounds)
23	Apparel	18,066	30	41,890
28	Chemicals	32,661	50	1,633,050
34	Fabricated metals	87,101	65	5,661,565
				7,836,595

Source: Adapted from U.S. Department of Commerce, *Measuring Markets: A Guide to the Use of Federal and State Statistical Data* (Washington, D.C.: U.S. Government Printing Office, August 1974), p. 51.

[9] Adapted from U.S. Department of Commerce, *Measuring Markets: A Guide to the Use of Federal and State Statistical Data* (Washington, D.C.: U.S. Government Printing Office, August 1974), p. 51.

CLASSIFICATIONS OF INDUSTRIAL GOODS

Consumer products have been classified into the useful categories of convenience, shopping, and specialty goods. Industrial goods have also been classified. The categories used are these:

- Raw materials
- Installations
- Fabricating materials or component parts
- Process materials
- Accessory equipment
- Operating supplies
- Services

At first glance, these classifications seem product oriented rather than buyer oriented. However, buying habits and preferences vary between categories, and different marketing problems are associated with each of them. Each product type is discussed below and a *general* comparison of marketing mixes associated with each is presented.

Raw Materials

Raw materials are those products that are used to make other products. They are to become part of a finished good and the raw materials have been processed only slightly or not at all. Included in this class would be ingots of metals, logs, raw petroleum, truckloads of cement, and so on.[10]

The marketing activities associated with raw materials are focused largely on distribution. This is because raw materials tend to be bulky and yet relatively cheap considering their bulk. The emphasis is on handling these products as efficiently and cheaply as possible. To minimize the need to transport the materials, organiza-

---

[10]Certain kinds of raw materials are called *processed goods* in that they have been subject to some degree of processing. Boulders may have been processed to make road gravel, for example.

tions relying on bulky raw materials may choose to locate their processing plants near the source of supply. Thus, lumber mills are generally located relatively near forests. Oil refining plants are located close to oil-producing fields or near the ports through which foreign oil enters the country.

Another reason distribution is generally the major marketing concern in this product class is that raw materials are frequently already owned by the organizations that utilize them. Paper companies may own tracts of forests, metal-producing companies may operate their own mines, and petroleum companies may have their own oil fields. In cases such as these, the key marketing question is not one of promotion or price. Instead, concern will center around effective distribution. Even when raw materials are sold to other companies, the focus of attention is distribution because the buyers of these products want to hold material costs down and to be assured of steady supplies.

Installations

The industrial products known as **installations** are major investments. They tend to be expensive and have relatively long lives. A new building is an installation, as is a major computer system.

Because installations represent long-term and major investments, organizations usually consider them in a very carefully planned and executed buying process. The firm's most knowledgeable experts are likely to be assigned to the buying committee. The committee will exercise the utmost in caution and will scrutinize purchase possibilities, subjecting them to rigorous cost-benefit analyses.

Installations are often made-to-order. Thus, the ability to create the desired product and to deliver it by the deadlines promised is important to marketers of installations. Also important is the ability to keep costs in line because the supplier of the product may be expected to absorb any cost overruns. Price, however, is seldom the sole concern when installations are being evaluated. Quality and dependability are more important to most buyers. Organizational buyers are likely to feel, as might a consumer in a similar situation, that a relatively small addition to the price of an expensive product is well worth the extra cost if breakdowns and other annoying problems can be minimized.

It is unlikely that promotion, other than personal selling, would have much effect in generating sales for installations. These products are purchased infrequently and only after serious study has indicated that they are needed. However, advertising can be used to familiarize potential buyers with the supplying company's name or good reputation or to encourage inquiries. Advertising for installations usually appears in narrowly focused media. Giant rock crushers would be advertised in *Road and Gravel* magazine and automobile frame straighteners in *Bodyshop Business*. Direct mail is also a good possibility if likely buyers are easily identified through directories or mailing lists.

Personal selling is far more important than advertising. It frequently is necessary for a salesperson to spend months and even years in analyzing a target customer's business needs and in designing an installation or system appropriate to those needs. Team selling is often used. Although individuals selling installations are likely to be employed by the firm building those products, certain installations are sold through intermediaries. For example, a factory or office building might be sold by a real estate agent. Some other installations are relatively standardized. When a standard installation can be clearly and accurately described, a broker or other intermediary may participate in the selling process.

Fabricating Materials or Component Parts

Although the terms *fabricating materials* and *component parts* are often used interchangeably, there is a difference between them. **Fabricating materials** can be exemplified by sheet metal or cloth. **Component parts** include screws, bolts, batteries, and switches. Although there is

a distinction between the two, they are usually lumped together because they are purchased for the purpose of assembly and production. These products become part of the final product, but, unlike raw materials, they have already been subjected to considerable processing. For this reason, they are also called *manufactured materials and parts*.

A key concern to buyers of these parts and materials is whether they fit the buyer's specifications. If several suppliers are found to be able to satisfy specifications, the buyer is most likely to make the purchase selection based on factors such as price and certainty of delivery. For example, producers of lighting fixtures for homes or offices do not want to stop manufacturing or to fail to keep promised delivery dates because the suppliers of switches or bulbs did not meet delivery schedules. For these reasons, suppliers of component parts and materials usually deal directly with their customers. However, intermediaries may be used to reach smaller buyers, especially when the parts and materials are standardized.

Promoting these materials and parts involves many interesting possibilities. Some suppliers of parts and materials attempt to leap-frog their customers and go directly to consumers with suggestions to look for products that include parts made by those suppliers. Timken Roller Bearing Company has used this approach for decades, implying that lawn mowers and other machines made with Timken Bearings are higher in quality than those made by companies not wise enough to use the best possible bearings in their products. This may or may not affect many lawn mower sales, but it gives Timken salespeople an intriguing selling point when they approach potential customers.

Process Materials

Process materials, such as component parts and materials, are used in making other products, but they do not become part of those other products. For example, the acids used to clean machinery parts are process materials. Do not confuse process materials with process*ed* materials, another name for certain kinds of *raw materials*.

While some lawn mower and car buyers may care enough to look for a particular engine brand or battery, it seems unlikely that *anyone* would be impressed with the statement that a machine's wheel housings were dipped in Du-Pont hydrochloric acid rather than in Allied hydrochloric acid. Process materials are subject to almost no criteria other than meeting the buyer's specifications, price, and delivery schedule. Therefore, those are the key marketing variables. Contract buying, based almost exclusively on these two variables, is the rule. Direct sale is typical. For some of these materials, such as lubricating oil, there may be a widespread demand from small buyers. Intermediaries may be used to handle these customers.

Brand loyalty for process materials is negligible. Thus, advertising is seldom a component in the marketing mix. Some advertising may be used in carefully targeted media to help keep potential customers familiar with the marketing organization's name or to play up some differential advantage (e.g., delivery) the supplier has. For example, makers of chemicals used in the operation of sewerage treatment may run an occasional advertisement in *Sludge*, the magazine aimed at engineers concerned with environmental clean-up issues.

Accessory Equipment

Accessory equipment, sometimes called *minor equipment* to distinguish it more clearly from the major purchases known as installations, is the class of products that includes pick-up trucks, forklifts, desk-top calculators, and similar items. When compared to installations, this equipment has a relatively shorter life, cheaper unit prices, and is more standardized. Calculators and other office equipment can, for example, fill the needs of many different organizations and of different types of employees. These products, unlike more specialized products, have *horizontal demand.* That is, they can be used within many industries.

Because accessory equipment is frequently used and then replaced, the purchase of these items often becomes a straight rebuy. Purchasing agents may handle the buying with relatively little approval from equipment users, their supervisors, or buying committees. Some of these products, particularly the relatively standardized ones, can be sold through intermediaries. However, one characteristic of the market for many of these products is stiff competition, such as that found for office equipment, where both price and non-price competition can be significant. For example, photocopier manufacturers send direct sales representatives to call on target customers and draw attention to their cadres of trained service personnel.

Because the market is often broadly based, accessory advertising is commonly encountered in the general business press, including such periodicals as *The Wall Street Journal, Forbes,* and *Business Week.* It is also found in other media such as the general news magazines like *Newsweek,* and even on certain television programs likely to be seen by businesspeople.

Operating Supplies

Operating supplies have been called by some the convenience goods of industrial marketing. This is because these products, such as paper clips, stationery, thumbtacks, and cellophane tape, are characterized by low prices, standardized design, a rapid rate of consumption, and little or no buyer brand loyalty. Although some producers of these supplies may advertise their products as superior or as having some touch of class their competitors lack, most buyers are not greatly swayed by such claims.

After all, there is little reason for buyers to become excited about the contribution that operating supplies make to their operations. The products do not become part of the finished product. They are essentially unseen necessities that most purchasers would prefer to buy cheaply and with as little time commitment as possible. Barring some defect in the most recently received batch of staples or pencils, it is unlikely that these products will be given any thought at all. In a few special cases, some attention may be given to products in this class, as

MONSANTO EMPHASIZES BOTH ADVERTISING AND PERSONAL SELLING IN THE MARKETING OF THERMINOL HEAT TRANSFER FLUIDS

Therminol heat transfer fluids are used in many applications from chemical processing to offshore drilling, textile manufacturing to barge operations. The Monsanto product line consists of six fluids, each with a different operating temperature range. The company's commercial strategy focuses on the engineer early in the design phase of a new heat transfer system. The marketing strategy attempts to place Therminol engineering data in his hands.

Since there are tens of thousands of design engineers, in-depth or frequent contact by any sales force would be cost prohibitive. Magazine advertising with inquiry coupons is used to identify engineers and help Monsanto salesmen follow-up before

competition calls. When Therminol VP-1 was launched, it received modest magazine advertising support. Ads like this one ran frequently in chemical engineering journals.

The gross profit generated from a single coupon clipped from a Therminol VP-1 ad generated enough cash flow to pay for all the magazine advertising done for Therminol VP-1 . . . 12 times over. Returned coupons, followed up by the advertising department with literature, and later by the sales force with a personal call, led to very large first sales and subsequent reorders. The heat transfer fluids market is very competitive. If Monsanto hadn't gotten that order first, the competition would have.

Why the switch from Dowtherm A to Therminol VP-1?

Source: Adapted from Robert Isham, "Monsanto Traces Ads from Coupon to Bottom Line," *Industrial Marketing*, April 1982, p. 57. Used with permission.

---

when a lawyer selects a letterhead intended to give a good impression to clients. But even here, the lawyer has already established some standard of performance for the paper being bought and, beyond that, probably will stress price, convenience, and quantity discounts in making a selection.

The nature of competition in the operating supplies category is such that suppliers of these products may use a personal sales force to approach possible future customers or to service major accounts. Smaller accounts may be expected to visit the supplier's place of business or to call in their orders as new supplies are required. Operating supplies are used by almost every business or organization in the country.

Therefore, intermediaries are generally used in their sales and distribution.

Services

The organizational products category of **services** includes every type of service from maintenance of fleets of trucks to typewriter repair, and from janitorial services to medical services. The fact that the service is essentially inseparable from the individuals providing it is common to all service marketing. The performance expected from a cleaning service depends almost totally on the performance of janitors and their supervisors. The confidence so important in choosing a lawyer cannot be separated from the person

THE DIFFERENTIAL ADVANTAGE IN INDUSTRIAL MARKETING

For some industrial goods marketers, a differential advantage may be found in their products. IBM has a long history of being a leading producer of certain organizational products. Bell Telephone products have an excellent reputation for durability and dependability, a reputation that stands Bell sales representatives in good stead when they go up against competition. Promotion by itself is unlikely to provide an industrial marketer with a differential advantage, but can be used effectively to point out and ex-

plain other advantages.

The great significance of price and delivery is obvious to all organizations involved in industrial marketing. This may make it appear that no differential advantages are to be found among these marketing variables. Actually, these are the areas of opportunity for many industrial marketers. Efficient distribution can permit some marketers to lower their prices below those of competitors. Distribution may provide other differential advantages. An extensive warehousing system or

modern delivery techniques can allow the sales representative to promise immediate deliveries or to point out that his or her firm is the only one with a distribution point within hundreds of miles of the prospective customer.

While the constant mention of price and distribution may make it appear that the opportunities to offer a differential advantage to customers are limited, it in fact simply points out where those advantages should be sought.

---

selected to fill that role, nor from that person's performance when called upon for help. The distribution channels for such services are uniquely direct and the array of services purchased by organizations is great.

Service marketers must put themselves in the place of the buyer in an effort to determine what is important in the buying decision, as do marketers of other products. The businessperson contracting with a janitorial service may be interested in price, especially when competition

among such services is likely to be keen. However, the future buyer of a doctor's service or those of a management consultant will be more than a bit concerned with the service provider's record, reputation, education, and skills. A lawn treatment service may be chosen out of the telephone book by the plant manager, but many other services will not be chosen as a result of advertising efforts. The promotional efforts of professionals such as lawyers and doctors are often so subtle as to appear nonexistent.

SUMMARY

In this chapter the industrial or organizational marketplace has been explored along with buying practices and marketing efforts appropriate to this special market. The characteristics of the organizational market and the buying motives encountered in it differ significantly from those found in the consumer market. Nonetheless, application of effective marketing practices and concepts provides the key to an access into this market.

Demand for products in the industrial marketplace ultimately depends on consumer demand even when a particular purchasing decision is quite removed from consumers. Thus, consumer buying decisions can significantly affect a large number of industrial organizations. Also, the demand for industrial products is said to be price inelastic in that, as the prices for industrial products rise and fall, the amounts of those products demanded by industry buyers are not likely to change significantly. Finally, for a number of reasons, there are wide fluctuations, compared to consumer goods, in the demand for industrial goods.

Organizational buying behavior may be characterized as a multi-stage, decision-making process. The significance of each stage depends on the nature of the product, the costs involved, and the experience of the organization. Three separate buying situations—straight rebuy, modified rebuy, and new task—have been identified and are associated with specific types of industrial buyer behaviors. Each buying situation demands the implementation of a unique marketing mix.

Within an industrial or organizational buying decision, a wide range of purchasing motives and choice criteria may be at work. So-called "emotional" buying motives include such things as color preferences, status considerations, and product appearance. "Rational buying motives" or the major choice criteria might include product characteristics, related services, prices, safety, security, or the "bottom line."

Industrial or organizational buyers are both numerous and varied. A major tool used to understand the industrial marketplace is the Standard Industrial Classification System. The SIC is a numerical coding system designed to classify different segments of industry in terms of the type of economic activity in which they are engaged.

Industrial goods can be classified into the following useful categories: raw material, installations, fabricating materials, process materials, accessory equipment, operating supplies, and services.

The categories of industrial products, the three major buying situations in which organizations may find themselves, and the attitudes with which buyers approach their tasks have many parallels in the more familiar consumer market. As with consumer products marketing, effective industrial marketing managers aim to satisfy the wants and needs of their customers. Formulation of a marketing mix appropriate to the customer's situation rather than the preferences of the seller remains the basic goal of marketers whether the arena is that of the consumer or industrial market.

THE MOST IMPORTANT CONCEPT IN THIS CHAPTER

Industrial or organizational products range from bulky raw materials to intangible services; yet demand for these products is similar because industrial demand is derived, inelastic and fluctuating and because organizational buying behavior takes place over time, involves communications among several organizational members, and requires establishing financial relationships with suppliers.

KEY TERMS

Industrial marketing transaction

Derived demand

Acceleration principle

Straight rebuy

Modified rebuy

New task buy

Buying center

Users

Gatekeepers

Influencers

Deciders

Buyers

Standard Industrial Classification System (SIC)

Raw materials

Installations

Fabricating materials

Component parts

Process materials

Accessory equipment

Operating supplies

Services

QUESTIONS FOR DISCUSSION

1 Under what conditions would demand for an industrial product be inelastic with respect to price?

2 How does industrial marketing differ from consumer marketing?

3 Compare and contrast the consumer decision-making process and the industrial purchasing agent's decision-making process.

4 What variables might be useful to estimate demand for the following products?
(a) Paperclip sales
(b) Desk-top computers for industry
(c) Staplers
(d) Industrial lubricants for drill presses
(e) Forklift trucks

5 For the following products, indicate whether the buying task will be a straight rebuy, modified rebuy, or a new buying task?
(a) Lawn maintenance service for corporate headquarters
(b) Ball bearings as a component part
(c) Industrial robot for a production function
(d) Addition of personal computers for top-level executives

6 Identify the typical distribution and promotional strategies for each industrial product category given in the classification of industrial product scheme.

7 Try to identify how purchasing is carried out in your local university.

8 Are industrial marketers more likely to stress personal selling or advertising? Why?

CASE 21-1 Clark Industrial Lift Trucks*

As a major manufacturer of industrial lift trucks, Clark has built an image of marketing high-quality vehicles through a strong dealership operation. When top management began looking for new products and new markets to assure continued success, a search for an outside research firm began—a consulting firm that specialized in the application of consumer research techniques to industrial marketing problems.

Clark felt consumer research expertise would be a valuable asset in that numerous new product concepts needed market testing, a research problem common to the consumer area. However, the product concepts under consideration were quite technical in nature and would be marketed to sophisticated industrial buyers. Kennedy & Associates, the researcher, became involved with Clark's engineering staff. This involvement was critical in that technical features of the product concepts were not yet "locked in cement."

Some basic consumer research procedures were applied to evaluate and screen the new product concepts identified by Clark's marketing research department. Two critical questions had to be answered in reference to each product concept: (1) What are the preferences of the marketplace toward these new product concepts in comparison to existing products now being marketed? (2) What product attributes or features are considered by buyers in choosing one product over another?

Kennedy suggested product concept cards to ensure that various product concepts be clearly communicated to the individuals interviewed. Each concept card had an artist's rendition of what the product would look like and a

---

*Source: Excerpts from F. August and F.G. Cutler, "New Product Testing: Clark Uses Consumer Research Techniques," *Industrial Marketing*, August 1976, p. 68. Used with permission.

list of technical specifications considered important to buyers. Pricing information also was included. Products presently on the market were identified on similar product concept cards.

Personal interviews were conducted across the country with potential buyers of the new products. In each case, the individual was asked to look at a set of three concept cards—one representing a new product concept being considered by Clark, and a second and third representing actual existing products. Individuals were instructed to first rank the three products according to their preference and then identify their reasons for ranking the products as they did.

Clark was keenly interested in whether the suggested pricing of the new product concepts would be seen by the market as a positive or negative product feature. The concept cards elicited the answer to this critical question without asking directly "How important is price to you?" and then "What do you think about the price of Product X?" Direct questioning was not considered an appropriate and valid research approach to getting product feature importance ratings.

Focus group interviewing with customers also was used to get at underlying feelings toward existing products in the market and to identify customer needs that were being left unsatisfied. As in brainstorming type sessions, focus sessions allow participants to hear others talk about common problems and concerns, which often ignites ideas and comments not obtained otherwise.

Customers were brought in from various parts of the country for each of three sessions, which were videotaped for later analysis. The videotapes also were invaluable in communicating the needs of the customer to the engineering R&D department.

Questions

1 Identify the stage of new product development described in this case.

2 Evaluate Clark's techniques for developing new products.

CASE 21-2 Metheus*

Metheus Corporation is a rapidly expanding company engaged in the development and manufacture of computer-aided design tools for the electronics industry. The company is located in Hillsboro, Oregon, a suburb west of Portland.

The name Metheus is taken from the Greek Titans, Prometheus and Epimetheus, who were charged with providing tools for earth's inhabitants. Prometheus is traditionally associated with creativity and bold originality. The literal translation of *metheus* is "thinker."

The company's first product is a high-speed, high-resolution, color graphics display control-

---

*Source: Based on information supplied from the Metheus Corporation, Post Office Box 1049, Hillsborough, Oregon 97123.

ler. Development has been completed, and systems are currently being manufactured for sale to original equipment manufacturers (OEMs) and end users.

Metheus was founded in the spring of 1981 by Dr. Gene Chao, former director of Applied Research at Tektronix, Inc. Dr. Chao assembled key technical and managerial people, developed the company's business plan, initiated the search for investment capital, and incorporated the company in July 1981.

Key employees at Metheus have backgrounds primarily from Tektronix, Intel Corporation, and Floating Point Systems—three successful companies known for their technological leadership, strategic marketing, and ability to deliver quality products to the marketplace profitably and on time. The Metheus management team has excellent academic credentials and strong backgrounds in management, technical research, product development, marketing, manufacturing, and sales. Key people were selected for their proven abilities to get new products to market and successfully manage rapid growth.

In developing a compatible family of advanced computer graphics products, the company incorporated the latest developments in Large Scale Integration/Very Large Scale Integration technologies and innovative design techniques.

Question

What channel of distribution do you think the Metheus Corporation utilizes or should use? Explain why you have given this answer.

CHAPTER 22

Marketing in the Multinational Environment

CHAPTER SCAN

Throughout this textbook references have been made to marketing in the international as well as the domestic marketplace. However, the importance of this aspect of marketing requires that specific attention be given to it. This chapter focuses specifically on multinational marketing.

The approach taken in this chapter has two thrusts. One is to provide the reader with examples of marketing successes and failures on the international level. The other is to address international marketing from the point of view of an American organization seeking to develop non-domestic markets. This approach should serve to demonstrate the vast opportunities available to marketers on the international level, but also serve to show the many complexities that the effective marketer must unravel.

WHEN YOU HAVE STUDIED THIS CHAPTER, YOU WILL:

Be able to describe the impact of international marketing on our domestic economy and on the economies of our trading partners.

Be able to discuss the many cultural, linguistic, and political pitfalls that the successful international marketer must overcome.

Understand the powerful negative effects ethnocentrism can have on a multinational firm's marketing plans.

Be able to show the progression of steps a domestic marketer must complete in analyzing and developing overseas markets.

Have seen many examples of how otherwise clever American marketing organizations have failed to penetrate other nations' markets.

Have seen how the basic marketing mixes developed for domestic markets must be modified for use overseas, but that despite modification the principles of effective marketing still apply.

The world is passing through a transition period in the order of its economy that promises by far to be the most crucial in its entire history. As a result of the new conditions with which we are confronted and the ever broader front upon which the lines of economic struggle are deployed, we are rapidly becoming world-minded whether willingly or no. The lackadaisical and uninformed days and daze, under which trade was conducted in a world of static repose, no longer exists.

The world trader finds that the more clearly and completely he is able to analyze and interpret world conditions of economic, political, and social import—and they are all three inseparably correlated—the more successful he is in developing the world market along profitable and enduring lines. Today, more than ever before in the world's history, intelligent analysis of world trends as reflected by current events is indispensable to the successful conduct of all enterprise. "No one engaged in any form of commercial activity today, whether he is concerned with selling in markets outside of the domestic field or not, can afford to be other than thoroughly informed on the affairs of the world and their influence on its economy in general, and on our own domestic economy in particular."[1]

This sounds like a realistic assessment of the situation facing many marketers in the United States today. It is, however, interesting to note that this was written by V.D. Collins in 1935 in his book entitled *World Marketing.* Many marketers have not made too much progress in multinational marketing.

One of the reasons for this lack of progress is a failure on the part of many to adopt a global perspective. For many U.S. companies, the size and growth of the U.S. market have been such that a domestic orientation has been sufficient. Many consumers are unaware also of the kind of impact the world has on their daily lives. One out of every six jobs in the United States economy is dependent on world trade.

In this chapter we explore the nature of the world market and its importance to the continued success of many firms. We hope to provide you with an increased awareness of this importance and of how one might go about becoming involved in marketing products and services on a worldwide level.

A WORLD PERSPECTIVE

You may drive a Toyota, Renault, or Mercedes automobile. You may fill your tank at a Shell service station with gasoline refined from crude oil from Nigeria or Venezuela. You may sign the credit slip with a Bic pen. Each of these products comes from a non-U.S. company and is made available in the United States as a result of international marketing. Today, we live in a global village.[2] It is difficult to speak of matters that do not influence or are not themselves influenced by other areas of the world. Jet age transportation, television, computers, and other electronic technologies are reshaping and restructuring the patterns of business. The world is getting

smaller. Interaction between the people of various nations is increasing rapidly. Exchange between countries is commonplace. Multinational companies from Japan, the United States, or other developed nations feel completely at ease marketing their products in foreign markets. An organization that sells its products beyond its own nation's domestic market is a multinational marketer engaged in international marketing.

Multinational or **international marketing** involves the adoption of a marketing strategy that emphasizes a geographic market segmentation that distinguishes between domestic and foreign markets.

Not all U.S.-based firms choose to market their products outside the United States. A bagel

---

[1] V.D. Collins, *World Marketing* (Philadelphia, Pa.: J.B. Lippincott Company, 1935), p. 15.

[2] M. McLuhan and Q. Fiore, *War and Peace in the Global Village* (New York: Bantam Books, 1968).

bakery may limit its marketing to New York City. The organization's resources or market demand justifies this strategy. However, many firms find that it is advantageous to spend considerable time and effort marketing beyond their national boundaries. One can see that international markets may promise higher market potential than domestic markets by examining the following population estimates for the year 2000: India, 958 million; Mexico, 126 million; Brazil, 205 million; Indonesia, 198 million; Pakistan, 135 million; Nigeria, 154 million; and Bangladesh, 146 million.[3] For American producers of grain and livestock, these statistics reflect both a tremendous market potential, and a challenge for feeding the world. Population cannot be considered in and of itself. The population's ability and willingness to purchase are additional considerations. Procter & Gamble's Pampers disposable diaper, which has a 6 percent share of the disposable diaper market in Italy, could not be expected to do as well in Bangladesh, where per capita income is very low.[4]

The same fundamental, procedural marketing concepts that apply in domestic marketing apply in international marketing. The same basic marketing decisions have to be made in foreign markets: Target markets must be determined; marketing mix strategies must be planned and executed to appeal to these target markets; uncontrollable and environmental factors must be analyzed.

Although the basic marketing process is the same on a conceptual level, there are several strategic and tactical differences resulting from differences in cultural, economic, political, or legal environmental factors. Language barriers are the most obvious. Marketing in South America, for example, requires that strategies be executed in Spanish or Portuguese. In addition, different cultural values, political instability, and many other problems compound the complexity of uncontrollable factors.

Consider some of these environmental com-

Imports are the foreign products you purchase domestically. Exports are domestically produced products sold in foreign markets.

---

[3]Harm J. DeBlij, *Human Geography* (New York: John Wiley & Sons, 1982), p. 37.

[4]Elizabeth Guider, ''P&G Widens Market for Pampers in Italy,'' *Advertising Age,* December 14, 1981, p. 68.

plexities. If we compare the United States to Western Europe, we would generally conclude there are major differences. Europe consists of many different countries with many different languages and cultures. A number of different currencies exist; different sets of laws exist for each country; and each country generally appears to be quite different from the other. The United

EXHIBIT 22-1

A Comparison of European Nations and American States

European Nation	Square Miles	Comparable U.S. State	Square Miles
Belgium	11,779	Maryland	10,577
Denmark	16,633	Massachusetts	8,257
		New Hampshire	9,304
West Germany	96,011	Oregon	96,981
Italy	116,303	Arizona	113,909
Portugal	35,516	Indiana	36,291
Spain	194,885	Colorado	104,247
		Wyoming	97,914
United Kingdom (Great Britain and Northern Ireland)	94,222	Oregon	96,981

Source: From *World Almanac & Book of Facts, 1983* (New York: Newspaper Enterprise Association, 1983).

States, by comparison, appears to consist of a rather large, fairly homogeneous market. Although the states may vary slightly in terms of laws that affect business within each, these are only minor differences.

Let's look further at the size of these two markets. Exhibit 22-1 compares the countries in Europe to some of the states in the United States that are similar in geographic size. Imagine what it would be like if you had a company in Virginia and wanted to sell to a customer in Maryland. Imagine further that some people in Maryland spoke a different language, used a different currency, taxed you to export products into Maryland, and so on. Is this comparable to some of the situations faced in Western Europe? The answer is both yes and no. Although countries in Europe are quite similar in size to states in the United States, there are far more barriers between countries. Free trade exists among the states and they share a common set of laws, language, and cultural values. This certainly simplifies matters. Europe and parts of the rest of the world are moving increasingly in this direction.

THE IMPORTANCE OF WORLD MARKETING

Exhibit 22-2 shows the top 20 American companies that, on the basis of total export dollars, are most involved in multinational marketing or world trade. Certainly, the United States appears to be committed to multinational marketing. Although the United States is a large exporter in terms of absolute dollar volume, our degree of commitment is relatively low. American exports amount to slightly less than 7 percent of our gross national product (GNP). This compares to trading nations such as Japan (13 percent), West Germany (27 percent), the United Kingdom (20.5 percent), and Canada (29 percent).

The explanation for this small percentage is, in part, the result of the large and developed nature of the domestic market in the United States. No other country has such an extensive, well-developed domestic marketplace. Therefore,

EXHIBIT 22-2

The 20 Largest U.S. Multinationals

Rank	Company	Foreign Revenue (millions)	Total Revenue (millions)	Foreign as Percent of Total	Foreign Operating Profit* (millions)	Total Operating Profit* (millions)	Foreign as Percent of Total	Foreign Assets (millions)	Total Assets (millions)	Foreign as Percent of Total
1	Exxon	$69,386	$97,173	71.4%	$2,208	$4,343	50.8%	$29,914	$ 62,289	48.0%
2	Mobil	37,778[1]	60,969[1]	62.0	880[2]	1,380[2]	63.8	18,802	36,439	51.6
3	Texaco	31,118	46,986	66.2	833[2]	1,281[2]	65.0	12,956	27,114	47.8
4	Standard Oil Calif	16,957	34,362	49.3	404[2]	1,377[2]	29.3	8,861	23,465	37.8
5	Phibro-Salomon	16,600	26,703	62.2	218[2]	337[2]	64.7	4,600	39,669	11.6
6	Ford Motor	16,526	37,067	44.6	460[2]	−658[2]	P/D	14,327	21,956	65.3
7	IBM	15,336	34,364	44.6	1,646[2]	4,409[2]	37.3	14,122	32,541	43.4
8	General Motors	14,376	60,026	23.9	−107[2]	963[2]	D/P	12,288	41,363	29.7
9	Gulf Oil	11,513	28,427	40.5	300[2]	900[2]	33.3	7,625	20,436	37.3
10	E I du Pont de Nemours	11,057	33,223	33.3	488[6]	1,491[6]	32.7	5,911	24,343	24.3
11	Citicorp	10,865	17,814	61.0	448[2]	723[2]	62.0	73,316[4]	121,482[4]	60.4
12	Intl Tel & Tel[3]	9,824	21,922	44.8	851	1,194	71.3	9,914	29,172	34.0
13	BankAmerica	8,051	14,955	53.8	253[5]	389[5]	65.0	54,847[4]	119,869[4]	45.8
14	Chase Manhattan	6,207	10,171	61.0	215[2]	307[2]	70.0	41,387	80,863	51.2
15	Dow Chemical	5,544	10,618	52.2	143	356	40.2	5,260	11,807	44.5
16	General Electric	5,490[1]	27,192[1]	20.2	395[2]	1,817[2]	21.7	5,373	21,615	24.9
17	Sun Co.	4,901[1]	15,739[1]	31.1	54[6]	706[6]	7.7	2,399	12,019	20.0
18	Standard Oil Indiana	4,862[1]	28,389[1]	17.1	618[2]	1,826[2]	33.8	6,470	24,289	26.6
19	Occidental Petroleum	4,715[1]	18,527[1]	25.4	345[6]	548[6]	63.0	3,502	15,773	22.2
20	Safeway Stores	4,380	17,633	24.8	84[2]	160[2]	52.5	1,052	3,891	27.0

*Unless otherwise indicated. [1]Includes other income. [2]Net income. [3]Includes proportionate interest in unconsolidated subsidiaries or investments. [4]Average assets. [5]Income before security gains or losses. [6]Profit before interest and after taxes. P/D: Profit over deficit. D/P: Deficit over profit.

Source: From "Hard Times in Any Language," *Forbes*, July 4, 1983. Used with permission.

other nations have had to become involved in international marketing activities. For many, it is an absolute necessity.

There is also a major impact on the domestic economy of any nation as the volume of multinational marketing activity increases. Foreign products are imported into that country to fill needs not being satisfied by domestic manufacturers or producers. Because the United States cannot supply all of its oil-based needs, it must import oil from other nations. In this sense, imported products are necessary to a way of life. World trade does help some countries meet certain needs. With continued growth, world trade can be expected to raise the standard of living in many parts of the world.

In addition, world trade can stimulate and help improve domestic competition. Frequently

heard complaints about American automotive manufacturers are their lack of quality and their lack of attentiveness to market needs. Partly because of the tremendous inroads made by Japanese and European cars, American producers have recently begun to make major strides in remedying these deficiencies. Such improvements in domestic competition spur improvements in living standards as well as general economic well-being.

By encouraging domestic companies to increase their involvement in world trade, a nation can develop its own economy. Capital investments in domestic production and the inflow of revenues from the sale of products to other nations certainly can trigger domestic economic growth.

For some countries, however, the costs associated with involvement in world trade are high. As trade between developed and less-developed nations occurs, there is a tendency toward the emergence of cultural differences. A "culture shock"[5] may occur as the ideas, products, and life-styles of one culture begin to influence those of the other culture. Grumblings have been heard in more traditional societies about the decadent influences of Western products and life-styles that have begun to surface in these nations. Certainly, the possibility for unwanted cultural change exists when world trade increases.

Another cost is more directly measurable. Some nations experience trade deficits when the payments for imported goods and government payments made outside the country exceed revenues received for goods exported by that na-

tion. Consider the country's economy to be a large checkbook. When payments going out of the checkbook exceed the monies coming into the checkbook, there are difficulties. Such a deficit in the balance of payments of any country can clearly lead to domestic inflation as the domestic government manipulates its money supply, domestic spending, and taxes to help solve the deficit problem. The United States is one nation whose balance of payments annually shows a deficit, resulting in large part from overseas spending on the part of the U.S. government.

Clearly, multinational marketing is important to many nations for many reasons. Next we turn our attention to the decisions on the part of an individual firm investigating whether or not it should become involved in multinational marketing.

GETTING INVOLVED IN MULTINATIONAL MARKETING

Throughout most of this chapter, the perspective will be that of the U.S.-based company looking at the international marketplace. References made to a domestic company, then, will be made as if the United States were the location of the headquarters of the company planning international operations. This is done because most students using this textbook will operate from a U.S.-based perspective. On the other hand, the same concepts apply to any nation since companies from any country may be involved in virtually any international market.

Any domestic company may, at some point in its operations, have to consider whether or not it should get involved in international marketing. The decision sequence, is illustrated in Exhibit 22-3.

Decision 1: Do We Get Involved in International Marketing?

For many companies, especially in the United States, this decision is not easy. The market for products in the United States has been so large and has grown so much that many companies have found success by simply catering to the needs of this market. Indeed, many companies lack the financial or managerial ability to market products in even the entire United States, let alone to move into the international arena.

In addition, the U.S. government has not been a strong proponent of world trade. Some citizens have been quite critical of the government's lack of promotion of the United States in the world trade situation.[6] Whatever the reason,

---

[5]See, for instance, Philip Bock, *Culture Shock: A Reader in Modern Cultural Anthropology* (New York: Alfred A. Knopf, 1970).

[6]"Failure to Sell Abroad," *Business Week*, June 30, 1980.

EXHIBIT 22-3

The Decisions to Be Made When Getting Involved in International Marketing

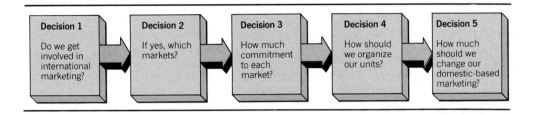

Decision 1	Decision 2	Decision 3	Decision 4	Decision 5
Do we get involved in international marketing?	If yes, which markets?	How much commitment to each market?	How should we organize our units?	How much should we change our domestic-based marketing?

EXHIBIT 22-4

Factors Influencing Whether or Not a Firm Becomes Involved in International Marketing

Encouraging Factors	Discouraging Factors
Saturated domestic market	Tariffs
Product is viewed by domestic market as obsolete	Import quotas
Domestic government or environment becomes anti-business	Other restrictive foreign government controls
Foreign market opportunities	
Foreign production opportunities	
Formation of economic communities	
GATT accords	

there is no question that the position of the United States in the world market is changing. Since the mid 1960s, the United States' share of the world market has fallen from 35 percent to 10 percent in consumer electronics, from 44 to 25 percent in automobiles, and from 26 to 17 percent in soybeans.[7] Recent events and patterns have begun to emerge to change this, but the effects of such changes are slow.

The economic theory of **comparative advantage** states that trade between two countries will benefit each country. Each country should specialize in the production of products in which it is most efficient. The production of other products is left to countries that are more efficient in such production. Thus, theoretically, an unre-stricted trade encourages international specialization and increased global efficiency.[8]

In the practice of international trade, the theory of comparative advantage tends to be applied only on a limited scale. The Japanese export steel, automobiles, and electronic technology. However, they must import natural resources and raw materials. Often, however, nationalism and other political motivations stand in the way of a full application of the theory of comparative advantage.

Factors Encouraging International Marketing. A number of factors exist that may encourage a company to get involved in multinational marketing. Exhibit 22-4 summarizes these

---

[7]"A Word from the Editors," *Best of Business*, Vol. 4, No. 2, Fall 1982, p. 4.

[8]Milton H. Spencer, *Contemporary Economics* (New York: Worth Publishers, 1980), p. 576.

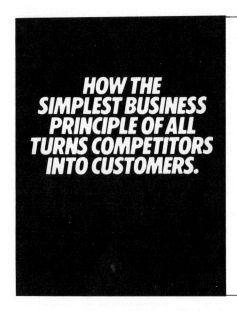

The theory of comparative advantage at work.

encouraging and discouraging factors. To begin with, certain considerations about the domestic market, such as market saturation, lack of new markets, or technological obsolescence, may encourage a domestic company to move into the international market. Whatever the reason, a saturated domestic market may lead a firm to consider the international market as an opportunity for extending the product life cycle. The obsolete product could be exported into overseas markets where it may be perceived as technologically acceptable.

In addition, there may be times when either the domestic government or the business climate become anti-business. In the United States, for example, there have been periods of strong pro-labor sentiment and periods of increased requirements on business that have hastened the entry of some businesses into international involvement in efforts to escape the effects of developments at home.

On the other hand, many factors encouraging world trade stem from foreign opportunities rather than domestic problems. Quite clearly, there are companies that view overseas opportunities the same way they view domestic opportunities—both are opportunities. Such companies are drawn into international trade because they see an opportunity and wish to take advantage of it. The opportunity may present itself in the form of market opportunities (new and untapped demand, growing market segments, etc.) or in the form of production opportunities (lower cost of labor, raw materials, and transportation costs, or more productive labor or facilities, and so on). Both opportunities can move an aggressive firm into the international arena.

Another major factor is the growing formation of economic communities. While many states in the United States are comparable in size to the nations in Europe, there is a common language, common currency, and fairly common trade laws. Worldwide, however, there are different languages, currencies, and trade laws between the nations. The formation of economic communities makes for greater commonality in trade among all the members of those communities and in the dealings that other nations experience with those community nations.

Perhaps the best known economic community is the **European Economic Community (EEC),** also known as the **Common Market.** Its members are Belgium, Denmark, France, West Germany, Ireland, Italy, Luxembourg, the Netherlands, and the United Kingdom. Rather than maintaining restrictions and tariffs or taxes on goods moved between nations (to be treated as exports or imports), the EEC has tried to reduce the number of tariffs and restrictions in hopes of achieving free trade in the same way trading between or among the states of the United States is experienced. This kind of activity certainly encourages trade between or among the countries who are members of the EEC. Another goal of the EEC is to promote trade from and with other nations. By trying to establish a common external tariff, EEC nations are promoting easier exporting to EEC nations in that a simplified tariff program and set of trade regulations result.

Not all economic communities have achieved the same degree of success. The **Latin American Free Trade Association (LAFTA)** was established with goals similar to those of the EEC. But political instabilities and economic difficulties in the area have dampened the enthusiasm of many and have weakened the abilities of LAFTA to further its cause.

The final encouraging factor is that economic communities are formed primarily by countries in the same area and with similar characteristics. The **General Agreements on Tariffs and Trade (GATT)** accords are a series of agreements reached by member nations who are not of the same general area of the world, but who simply want to encourage international trade. Several separate agreements have been signed by many industrialized and industrializing or developing nations in the Western world. The purpose of these accords has been to foster trade by reducing international trade restrictions and by achieving reductions in trade tariffs.

Factors Discouraging International Marketing. One of the dominant discouraging factors, mentioned several times thus far, is tariffs. **Tariffs** are taxes that are imposed by a nation on goods that are brought into that nation. In the domestic market, we see taxes levied selectively on products (such as gasoline, alcohol, and cigarettes) to raise revenues for some purpose. In the international market, however, taxes such as tariffs are usually levied by a government on selected products imported into that country for

the purpose of making that product more costly in the marketplace. Because the imported product is higher priced (as a result of the tariff), domestic production may be encouraged or consumption of the imported product may be discouraged. The existence of high, restrictive tariffs in some country may certainly discourage the companies of another nation from trading in that country.

Import quotas, or limits on a type of imported good, are another restrictive factor. Some countries, again trying to promote domestic production of some products or to discourage domestic consumption of some imported products, may impose quotas on selected products imported into those countries. Some quotas exist as absolute limits, and goods can only be imported until the set level is reached. After that, no further imports are allowed. Other quotas are established with tariffs in such a way that an extremely high tariff is levied on goods imported beyond the quota limit. The ultimate form of a quota is certainly an **embargo:** No goods from a particular country can be imported.

Recent activity in the automotive industry in the United States illustrates the use of quotas. Faced with increased competition from imported cars and increased pressure from automotive labor unions in the United States, Detroit and the U.S. government managed to get Japan to agree to a limit on the number of Japanese cars to be exported into the United States for a given period of time. Such a restriction is clearly a form of import quota. Recent moves by Honda and Volkswagen to establish production facilities in the United States are partly responses to such pressures.

Finally, foreign governments may impose a variety of other kinds of restrictive controls, discouraging companies from doing business in those markets. Sometimes countries will require that all trade with other nations be approved by some form of central ministry. This allows for the establishment of varying types of quotas and controls over goods brought into the country. Still other nations may establish boycotts or other barriers by the use of restrictive criteria set up to eliminate the importing of certain prod-

NONTARIFF BARRIERS: WHEN IS A SALAMI A BOLOGNA?

In France, it is illegal to advertise whiskey and gin—allegedly because they are bad for the health. Without the pressures of advertising, the French tend to drink domestic wines and brandies instead of importing scotch and gin.

Similar restrictions on trade exist in other countries. The United States, for example, prohibits the importation of French candies—presumably because their colorants are unsafe. Japan prohibits the exportation of calculators containing integrated circuits made in other countries. And The Netherlands prohibits exports of pharmaceuticals not manufactured by members of a Dutch trade association.

But perhaps most interesting is the question: When is a sausage not a sausage? The not-so-simple answer is: When it is exported and bumps into another country's definition of a sausage. The definition may be expressed in terms of size, shape, casing, color, the mix of ingredients, and, in some instances, the number of pieces per link. Anything that does not conform to a particular country's definition of a sausage is ruled a nonsausage and may not be imported.

Thus, the classic nontariff barrier is the provision of a German tariff law of 1902, now obsolete, affecting the import of cows. This granddaddy of nontariff barriers was designed to exclude Dutch and Russian cattle competitive with German types, but to allow entry of Swiss cattle. It did so with a definition that gave an extra low duty rate to "large dappled mountain cattle or brown cattle reared at a spot 300 meters above sea level and which have at least one month's grazing at a spot at least 800 meters above sea level."

The old German law, while not mentioning any country, achieved its aim with what amounted to a description of Swiss cattle-raising practices. Modern nontariff barriers, however, are not so diplomatic. The catalog of such barriers seems infinite, and as research develops, almost every country, including the United States, is seen to be a prime offender.

Source: From Milton H. Spencer, *Contemporary Economics* (New York: Worth Publishers, 1980), p. 578. Used with permission.

ucts. A local government may, for instance, establish buying criteria for food products such that food products shipped in from various countries may be prohibited.

All of these factors are of concern to a company in its initial decision regarding whether or not it wants to get involved in international marketing.

Decision 2: Which International Markets?

Having decided that it wishes to get involved in international marketing, the domestic company must identify which markets seem to be the likely targets. This involves much the same thinking as any segmentation decision. The company must decide if it wishes to concentrate its efforts in one or a few markets or if it wishes to pursue many targets. It must also decide whether sufficient potential exists in the possible targets, and what portion of that potential may be gained efficiently.

One author notes that the decision process should involve the following steps:[9]

1. Estimate the existing potential market.
2. Forecast the future potential market.
3. Forecast the sales to be expected.
4. Forecast the costs and profits involved.
5. Estimate the rate of return on investment.

Note that this process is really no different from that used in investigating any potential market. The factors being investigated may differ, but the process remains the same. However, to some extent, the criteria used in this evaluation may differ. Among the important criteria are such typical factors as market size, market growth, competitive activity, and costs of entry. Among the not-so-typical criteria are level of economic development, degree of political stability, existence of compatible marketing systems, political

---

[9]D.S.R. Leighton, "Deciding When to Enter International Markets," in *Handbook of Modern Marketing*, Victor Buell, ed. (New York: McGraw-Hill, 1970), Section 20, pp. 23–28.

regulations on businesses, and cultural compatibility.

The Cultural Environment. Culture basically consists of the values, beliefs, patterns of living, and social institutions shared by the members of a society. When we do business in the United States, we often take the cultural environment for granted. We assume that we know what these values and patterns are because we are so close to them. Yet a detailed analysis may show us to be wrong. There are variations, however minor, between various parts of even the United States. One author has proposed that the North American continent could be divided into nine more homogeneous "nations," each sharing its own peculiar culture.[10] Even between Americans and Canadians, where there is a good deal of cross-border flow of people, media, etc., there are differences in people. One study concludes that Canadians are more cautious, less optimistic, less self-confident, and less individualistic than Americans.[11] Therefore, we may be incorrect in ignoring the impact of variations in cultural elements even in North America. Clearly, we must pay attention to the influence of cultural factors in conducting business in other countries with which we are even less familiar.

Failure to fully understand a market and its cultural conditions can produce some unpredictable results. Consider, for instance, the following: One U.S. firm selling feminine sanitary napkins in several countries noticed a major increase in sales. Upon investigation, it was revealed that local farmers were buying them for use as dust masks.[12] Another U.S. company selling toothbrushes in South Vietnam during the Vietnam War years of the 1960s experienced a sales increase as the result of major purchases by the armies for use in cleaning weapons.[13]

More often than not, however, such failure to understand the market leads to unpleasant, rather than pleasant, results. One reason that many fail to fully understand overseas cultures and markets is that we tend to be ethnocentric. **Ethnocentrism** is the tendency to consider our own culture and way of life as the one which is the natural and normal way of doing things. We may mistakenly expect others to accept our feelings. To an extent, we are exporting our own biases into these foreign markets. This unconscious use of one's own cultural values as a reference point has been called the "self-reference criterion."[14]

This kind of myopia often results in mistakes. Large American-built cars are offered for sale in overcrowded European streets. English-based words are used to communicate with those in developing nations who are barely capable of reading their own languages. Foreign business people are expected to conduct business the same way we do in the United States. This cultural nearsightedness should be avoided by consciously recognizing its potentially biasing impact.

Business people may use this self-reference criterion or may be ethnocentric if they think their domestic strategy or reputation is better than any competitor in the host country.

Anheuser-Busch found that its premium-priced beer was not acceptable in the German market. Although its German joint venture partner, Berlinerkindle, was able to obtain excellent distribution (63 percent of food stores), monthly sales came to only 34 bottles per outlet. The price of Anheuser-Busch beer in Germany was 3.40 Deutschemarks ($1.55), twice that of ordinary beer and approximately 15 percent above the premium brands.[15] It was a mistake to think its positive appeal in America would warrant a premium price in Germany.

Foreign cultures should be analyzed so that differences between cultures may be understood. For example:

[10]"The Nine Nations of North America," *Marketing News,* January 21, 1983, pp. 1, 19, 20.

[11]S. Arnold and J. Barnes, "Canadians and Americans: Implications for Marketing," in D.N. Thompson, ed., *Problems in Canadian Marketing* (Chicago: American Marketing Association, 1977), pp. 3–27.

[12]David Ricks, *Big Business Blunders* (Homewood, Ill.: Dow-Jones-Irwin, 1983), p. 3.

[13]Ibid.

[14]James Lee, "Cultural Analysis in Overseas Operations," *Harvard Business Review,* March–April, 1966, pp. 106–114.

[15]Dagmar Mussey, "AB Test Goes Flat in Berlin," *Advertising Age,* November 23, 1981, p. 81.

■ Using green, the national color of Egypt, for packaging is considered in extremely poor taste in this African nation.[16]

■ Sending a woman sales representative to Libya, Iran, or other Middle East countries may show a lack of understanding of cultural values. The women's movement has not had much impact in many mid-Eastern countries.

■ Kentucky Fried Chicken had difficulty establishing franchises in Hong Kong. Chinese tastes preferred the cantonese drumsticks (kai pei and kai wick) braised with soy sauce and garlic sold on many Hong Kong sidestreets.[17]

■ The Simmons Mattress Company did not understand that Japanese retailers feel obligated to a supplier to whom a favor is owed. When retailers would not handle the product because of their feelings of obligation to traditional channel members, Simmons discovered the existence of these cultural values.[18]

Language, as we have mentioned earlier, is an important part of culture. The international marketer must be aware of the subtleties of the language. For example, the French word *tu* and the French word *vous* are both used for "you." However, the former is used to address a social equal or an inferior and the latter is used to signify formality and social respect. In Japan, "yes" may often be meant as "yes, I understand what you said," and not necessarily "yes, I agree." Numerous marketing mistakes have resulted from such misinterpretations. The Chevrolet brand name Nova translated into Spanish as "no go." The brand name of a British cosmetic product becomes "prostitute" when translated into Arabic. Herculon carpets becomes "the carpeting with the big derriere" when translated into Spanish.[19]

[16]*Business Week*, December 6, 1976, pp. 91–92.

[17]Nicky Careem, "Hong Kong Flocks to Kui Moo Ba under the Arches," *Advertising Age*, November 21, 1977, p. 87.

[18]"Simmons in Japan: No Bed of Roses," *Sales Management*, August 1, 1967, p. 28.

[19]Humberto Valencia, "Snafus Persist in Marketing to Hispanics," *Marketing News*, June 24, 1983, p. 3.

PAKU

The Japanese word for "to eat" is paku. This Japanese word and a tale about a ravenous Japanese folk character whose appetite could never be satisfied are the basis for creating a favorite of American video gamesmen, Pac-Man.

Source: "Pac-Man Fever," *Time*, April 5, 1982, p. 48.

The Political Environment. Another factor that is strongly related to the cultural environment in international operations relates to the political atmosphere of the various countries which the company is considering entering. One element of concern in the political environment is the *attitude of the government toward international trade.* Some nations are quite receptive to an infusion of foreign capital or products. Others are more protective of their own businesses and are not as receptive to foreign involvement in their nation. Zimbabwe, for example, recently changed its minerals policy and nationalized tantalum sales. At the same time, a new law set up a government minerals marketing corporation that receives a sales commission of 15 percent on each transaction.[20] Another example can be found in Japan. The Japanese government does not allow American automobile manufacturers to build plants in Japan. Furthermore, marketers must deal through trading companies and various middlemen that U.S. automobile manufacturers feel are counterproductive.[21]

Each country makes its own laws and policies regarding international trade. Laws about economic trade are often written to favor the host country's native companies. Such laws, in an attempt to stimulate the country's domestic economy, may restrict foreign operations. Laws may allow foreign firms to market only those

[20]"What's Chilling Business Interest in Zimbabwe?" *Business Week*, March 8, 1982, p. 52.

[21]Jack Givens, "Automobile Industry, Heal Thyselves," *Advertising Age*, September 29, 1980, p. 33.

AVOIDING FAUX PAS WHEN VISITING A FOREIGN COUNTRY

When you head for an unfamiliar country on short notice, some cramming on its customs could pay more dividends than a crash program in the language.

Unless you have been conjugating the local verbs for years, your business will probably be done in English. But while your foreign hosts won't expect you to spout the local patois, your innocent failures in nonverbal communication could offend them. Or you could misread their actions, with bad results.

Even a friendly grin can go wrong. Americans usually smile when shaking hands, but some German-speaking people find smiles too affectionate for new business acquaintances. So, while you're sizing up a German as a cold fish, he or she may be pegging you as the overly familiar type.

Try to break the ice in Germany with the "Wie geht's?" ("How goes it?") you got from watching war movies, and you'll be twice wrong. The expression is too informal and the question too personal for first encounters.

In Chinese-speaking areas, though, inquiring after a person's health is a proper first greeting, especially for the elderly.

But compliments are tricky in the Orient. You exchange them more readily there than in the U.S., but pay a Chinese-speaking person a compliment and he or she will surely decline it. Disagreeing is merely the way they accept praise. So if an Oriental compliments you, best be modest about it.

You can get into trouble by being too complimentary about objects in a Chinese or Japanese home; your host may feel obliged to give you the item.

The French are also evasive about compliments. They never say "merci" in response to praise, and if you respond to a compliment with "thanks," a French-speaking person could even interpret it as ridicule.

Formality is a must in France. Frenchmen who have worked side by side in an office for decades stick to formal pronouns when addressing each other, unless they also happen to have been school or military buddies.

And while using first names in business encounters is regarded as an American vice in many countries, nowhere is it found more offensive than in France.

Hand gestures are far from international. Italians wave goodbye with palm up and fingers moving back and forth—a beckoning signal to Americans. But when people wave the fingers with the palm down in China, Japan, and other Oriental areas, it's not goodbye—they mean "come here."

People who speak a romance language use more hand gestures than most Americans, but you can go wrong imitating them. For example, if you form a circle with thumb and forefinger, most Europeans will know you mean "it's the best," or "O.K." But in some Latin American countries the same gesture has a vulgar connotation.

The easiest place to have a gesture misunderstood abroad is in someone's home. Bearing gifts is expected in Japan, but can be considered a bribe in the Soviet Union. Portuguese and Brazilians like to bring foreigners home for dinner, but when it's time for you to go, politeness may compel them to insist that you stay. In some countries punctuality is expected; in others the custom is to arrive late. No matter where you go abroad, you can never assume that your best table manners will carry the day. You need a thorough rundown on local etiquette before your visit.

Someone at the country's nearest consulate or other agency will usually prove more than willing to point out ugly Americanisms for you. You can avoid embarrassment by speaking with nearly anyone native to the area.

Source: From *Business Week,* December 12, 1977, pp. 115–116. Reprinted with permission.

products that native companies are unable to produce without foreign capital, technology, or managerial expertise. Firms may be required to jointly own operations with host country citizens. Full foreign ownership may not be permitted. Venezuelan law provides a typical example of the latter point. Venezuela requires that companies, such as Sears, Roebuck and Company, be joint ventures with local investors (80 percent Venezuelan ownership). It is argued in such cases that national talent needs to be developed to manage retail operations.[22]

A government imposed **boycott** or embargo is an absolute banning of the purchase of certain products from another country.[23] *Boycotts* are usually the results of some political or social action, such as the Soviet invasion of Afghanistan. Governments may believe trading with the enemy is unwise. The Russians are not allowed to purchase U.S. military technology because its sale is prohibited.

Many political activities are oriented toward either encouraging domestic business and economic activity or discouraging and limiting trade with selected foreign nations.

Certainly another factor of interest in evaluating the likelihood of a country as a candidate for entry is the *degree of political stability.* Shortly after a new Italian government fixed prices on heating and diesel fuel, Standard Oil Company of Indiana pulled out of its Italian subsidiary Amoco Italia.[24] In the early 1980s, a McDonald's outlet and a Citibank branch were dynamited in El Salvador.[25] Global political developments that have an immediate connection to the company's native country may have a tremendous impact on the marketing within foreign countries. Estimating the political and economic stability of a country before risking investment is sound international management.[26]

The Economic Environment. Zimbabwe, Botswana, and Angola lack sophisticated distribution systems. A day at the market in Ethiopia hardly resembles an afternoon shopping trip in London or Rome. A country's state of economic development is a crucial environmental factor

to be accounted for in international marketing. Marketing in the developed countries of Western Europe is dramatically different from marketing in Third World nations such as Ethiopia or Nepal. Literacy, technology, distribution structure, and a number of other factors are all related to the level of economic development of the nation.

Stages of Economic Development. There are several ways of picturing the level of economic development of the nations of the world. One way is on the basis of development. Some nations, such as Sri Lanka or Nepal, may be portrayed as **undeveloped countries** because their standard of living is quite low and the economy is largely based on the land and agriculture. These countries do not possess sufficient purchasing power to allow them to be considered by many firms as viable markets.

Small-scale industry and limited market activity are characteristics of the **less-developed countries.** A limited number of small manufacturing, mining, or similar limited-technology companies may be developed, but marketing mechanisms, such as distribution networks and mass media vehicles, typically do not exist.

There is evidence of social change and increased market activity in the **developing countries.** Because of specialization of resources or domestic talent, selective industries begin to grow. A business-based middle class may start to emerge as entrepreneurs and develop successful businesses. Some of these businesses may be involved in exporting specialized products outside the nation. Others may import selected products as this type of economy developes limited target markets for goods from other nations. Many South American nations can be characterized as being in this stage.

In the **developed countries,** specialization is carried to its full level; full-scale marketing structures and activities are found; large markets exist for many products; and the nation is sufficiently developed that exporting and importing are reasonable possibilities. Canada, France, and West Germany are typical examples.

Exhibit 22-5 summarizes these stages and shows the appropriate marketing functions in these economies.

The view of nations as ranging from less de-

[22]*Business Week,* October 13, 1975, pp. 59–60.

[23]P.R. Cateora and J.M. Hess, *International Marketing* (Homewood, Ill.: Richard D. Irwin, 1975), pp. 59–60.

[24]"Indiana Standard May Trigger an Exodus," *Business Week,* January 25, 1982, p. 40.

[25]Steven Downer, "El Salvador Are Going, Going, Going, Gone?" *Advertising Age,* May 25, 1981, p. s-17.

[26]Lewis Kraar, "The Multinationals Get Smarter about Political Factors," *Fortune,* March 24, 1980, pp. 87–92.

EXHIBIT 22-5

Marketing Functions Performed at Different Levels of Development

Orientation	Functions	Stage of Economic Development
Traditional	Barter trade; exchange of goods; central markets prevalent; no specialization; no marketing activity; very rare trading in some form in most societies; for example, ancient Africa's salt trade	Undeveloped country
Self-sufficient	Degree of specialization; small-scale cottage industry; limited entrepreneurial activity; firms are labor intensive; producer is marketer	Less-developed country
Local markets	Specialization; industry is transitional but with some market orientation; separation of production and marketing; sellers' market conditions prevalent; limited marketing activities	Developing country
Regional, national, and international markets	Total specialization in production and marketing activities; complete market orientation; nations, regional, and export markets tapped; mass distribution practiced	Developed country

Source: From Kaynak Erdener, *Marketing in the Third World* (New York: Praeger, 1982), p. 29. Used with permission.

veloped to developed has been promoted by proponents of W.W. Rostow's "stages of growth" model.[27] According to this view, it is a logical transition for a nation to pursue economic development, and to follow a path roughly akin to those followed by the already developed nations.

However, it has also been argued that this may not be the case.[28] Instead, less-developed nations may prefer to avoid industrialization and some of its related consequences, both good and bad, in favor of such goals as isolationism and selective modernization. In this context, it may be that the role of international companies may *not* be one of promoting Western-oriented growth and development. In this sense, then, our view of economic stages may unfortunately imply that development is a natural and logical pattern.

---

[27]Walt W. Rostow, *The Stages of Economic Growth* (London: Cambridge University Press, 1960).

[28]Leslie M. Dawson, "Setting Multinational Industrial Marketing Strategies," *Industrial Marketing Management,* Vol. 9, 1980, pp. 179–186.

There are other economic factors to be considered as well. In evaluating a country in whatever stage of development, the marketer must consider the profitability of the various market targets and the income available in a country as key factors. Probably the best available indicator of total income is the gross national product (GNP) of each nation. This is the measure of the total value of the goods and services produced in that nation in a year. However, the GNP may be quite misleading. In the undeveloped, less-developed, and developing nations there are many activities done by the household unit itself—production of its own food, clothing, and perhaps shelter, among other things—that will not show in the national GNP since the value of such self-production cannot be computed. Especially in the developing nations, there may be pockets of wealth and production that account for major portions of that GNP. In such cases, even GNP per capita figures may be misleading. Exhibit 22-6 shows some GNP and GNP per capita figures for various nations. As you can see, the 1981 GNP per capita range in Europe is

EXHIBIT 22-6

**GNP and GNP per Capita for Selected Nations
in Organization for Economic Cooperation and Development (OECD)**

| Country | Gross National Product (GNP) | | | GNP per Capita | | | Inflation Rate,[2] 1980–1981 (percent) |
| | Total in Constant (1981) Dollars (billions)[1] | | | In Constant (1981) Dollars[1] | | | |
	1975	1980	1981	1975	1980	1981	
United States	2,411.5	2,882.9	2,937.7	11,166	12,663	12.783	9.4
OECD Europe	2,694.9	3,110.8	3,101.1	7,026	7,889	7,817	10.5
Belgium	83.2	95.8	95.2	8,489	9,713	9,655	5.0
Luxembourg[3]	3.4	3.9	3.8	9,444	10,694	10,472	6.2
Denmark	49.5	56.2	56.1	9,787	10,977	10,957	9.6
France	484.9	571.3	573.0	9,185	10,636	10,619	11.9
Germany, Fed. Rep.	578.2	688.6	686.5	9,352	11,185	11,132	4.3
Greece	31.5	39.0	38.8	3,482	4,046	3,996	19.9
Ireland	13.3	16.2	16.5	4,192	4,776	4,797	17.4
Italy	290.2	350.9	350.2	5,198	6,149	6,122	17.6
Netherlands	123.9	140.5	138.7	9,075	9,936	9,740	5.7
United Kingdom	470.6	510.2	499.2	8,418	9,118	8,941	11.4
Austria	55.1	65.4	65.5	7,327	8,712	8,722	5.5
Finland	40.4	47.0	47.4	8,567	9,833	9,875	11.2
Iceland	2.3	2.8	2.8	10,273	12,000	12,174	50.1
Norway	43.6	54.8	55.2	10,883	13,389	13,463	14.8
Portugal	17.5	22.5	22.9	1,853	2,276	2,306	17.6
Spain	166.5	183.9	184.5	4,676	4,914	4,900	13.3
Sweden	104.7	111.1	110.1	12,782	13,368	13,233	9.9
Switzerland	89.1	96.7	98.5	13,897	15,174	15,415	6.4
Turkey	47.0	54.0	56.2	1,174	1,202	1,212	36.4
Australia	133.4	151.3	158.9	9,688	10,351	10,693	8.8
Canada	229.0	266.0	274.0	10,073	11,108	11,318	10.0
Japan	853.9	1,095.0	1,126.8	7,654	9,377	9,578	2.8
New Zealand	22.9	23.8	24.7	7,422	7,643	7,891	15.8

[1]National currency values converted into dollars by the average 1981 Par Rate/Market Rate, as published by the International Monetary Fund, Washington, D.C.
[2]GNP or GDP (Gross Domestic Product) implicit price deflators; totals weighted by 1980 (base year) OECD weights.
[3]Gross domestic product.

Source: *Statistical Abstract of the United States 1982–83* (Washington, D.C.: U.S. Government Printing Office, 1983), p. 868.

quite broad, ranging from $1,212 in Turkey to $15,415 in Switzerland. As in all segmentation decisions, the marketer must investigate these and other economic factors influencing market profitability.

The Demographic Environment. It is expected that by 1988 the world's population will total 5 billion. This population is not evenly distributed over the continents but, instead, is concentrated in certain areas. Exhibit 22-7 shows

EXHIBIT 22-7

Population and Population Density for Selected Countries

Country	Population 1980 (millions)	Area (000 sq km)	Population Density (persons/square km)
Japan	118.7	372.3	319
Egypt	42.0	1001.4	42
Bangladesh	95.0	144.0	659
Netherlands	14.3	40.8	350
India	663.0	3287.6	202
Iran	37.0	1648.0	22
Nigeria	90.0	923.8	97
Colombia	27.2	1138.9	24
United States	225.2	9363.1	24
Ethiopia	31.0	1222.0	25
Argentina	27.1	2766.9	10

Source: H.J. DeBlij, *Human Geography* (New York: John Wiley & Sons, 1982), p. 31.

population and population density figures for various countries. The location of a nation's population, its demographic makeup, and its growth patterns all effect the potential profitability of marketing efforts.

The size of the family unit is also important. In India and Mexico, for instance, families are quite large, averaging five to six children per family. In these and similar countries, population growth often outruns the resource capabilities of the country, holding back economic growth and development.

Decision 3: How Much Commitment in Each Market?

Once a marketer has decided to become involved in international marketing, decisions must be made about the organization's degree of ownership and management involvement. Market potential, the organization's experience in international marketing, and host country policies often influence these decisions. These factors might cause a multinational marketer to use different strategies in different countries.

The types of involvement are: exporting, joint venturing, and direct investment. Each will be discussed separately.

Exporting. Moosehead Canadian Lager Beer is brewed and bottled in St. John, New Brunswick, Canada. Moosehead Brewery entered the international marketing business by utilizing All Brand Imports, Inc. of Rosalyn Heights, New York as a middleman for U.S. distribution. Moosehead is an exporter. By utilizing a foreign middleman, it passes on some of the risks of financial loss to the importer.

Exporting is probably the lowest level commitment that a company can make to international marketing. In this case, the company elects to sell some or all of its products overseas. Such sales may be accomplished either indirectly, through merchant or agent middlemen, or directly. There is no investment in either case in overseas plant or equipment.

With **indirect exporting,** a U.S. company may elect to periodically sell a portion of its inventory to some U.S.-based exporter. There is no systematic or well-planned effort to be in the international marketplace. Such companies view the international marketplace as a place to get rid of products. Others choose to export on a more continuous and planned basis.

Whatever the degree of indirect exporting, the U.S.-based company may use its domestic sales force to sell its products to a U.S.-based **buyer for export,** a type of merchant intermediary that exports a mix of products for sale in other markets. In addition, there are various types of export agents who may represent the manufacturer in overseas selling activities. These domestic-based manufacturers often treat such merchant middlemen as if they were domestic customers, serving them in essentially the same ways as other domestic customers.[29]

In the case of **direct exporting,** a firm may deal directly with overseas customers instead of using independent middlemen. Direct exporting may be used when a firm wants greater control over the foreign sale of its product. It is also possible that indirect exporters turn to this approach when the overseas market has grown to a sufficient size, or the risks have been reduced to a sufficiently low level, to warrant the use of direct exporting. The investment may be greater, but so is the potential for returns.

Such direct exporting may take several forms. Some companies use their own traveling salespeople who simply make occasional visits to overseas markets to try to sell the product there. These salespeople may meet with limited success unless they can cultivate the right prospects and unless they can be successful in understanding what is required to conduct business in another culture. Other companies may establish a domestic-based export department or division. The scope of this unit is determined in part by the degree of commitment the company feels toward international marketing.

Because of the often domestic-based perspective of these two types of direct export, they do not always meet with abundant success. Therefore, some other companies choose to establish overseas sales offices, branches, or distributors through which to sell their products. The key benefit of such organizations is their

Canon

キヤノン国際サービス網

CANON INTERNATIONAL SERVICE NETWORK
CANON'S WELTWEITES KUNDENDIENSTNETZ
RÉSEAU INTERNATIONAL DES SERVICES CANON
RED INTERNACIONAL DE SERVICIO DE CANON
SISTEMA INTERNAZIONALE SERVIZI CANON

Exporters may slightly modify products and instructional materials to suit each foreign market.

continued presence in the host country or overseas market. It can be expected that they may be in a better position to develop an understanding of the differences in foreign markets than would sales people making only occasional visits.

When the exporter does not make a major commitment to the overseas market, exported products are generally similar to the products marketed in the exporter's domestic market. For example, timber from the United States or diamonds from Western Australia are identical to the products sold in domestic markets. At the lowest level of change, packages and instruction manuals are often modified for the foreign market. The Canon list of international service networks for the Japanese-produced Canon camera is printed in six languages. Multinationals such as Canon may hire American advertising agencies to promote its exported products in the U.S.

Although exporting and importing may appear to be simple, the process can be quite complex. For example, a West German electrical utility sent uranium to be enriched in the Soviet Union. The Soviets, after being issued import licenses for enriched uranium, re-exported the materials to the United States to be fabricated into nuclear fuel for re-export to West Germany.[30]

---

[29]George Levy, *Multinational Product Strategy: A Typology for Worldwide Product Innovation and Diffusion* (New York: Praeger, 1976), pp. 74–77.

[30]"Soviet-U.S. Trade Busted by Transfer of Uranium," *Tulsa Tribune,* August 17, 1981, p. 11-b.

Joint Venturing. A level of involvement in international marketing that shows even greater commitment on the part of the domestic company is joint venturing. **Joint venturing** involves the joining of domestic and host companies to set up some production and marketing facilities in an overseas market. It differs from exporting in that with joint venturing some agreement exists for overseas production of the product.

There are several forms of joint venturing. One simple method involves **licensing.** With this form of business, a U.S.-based company (the licensor) wanting to do business in a particular overseas market may enter into a licensing agreement with an overseas company (the licensee) that permits the licensee to use the licensor's manufacturing processes, patents, trademarks, trade secrets, etc., in exchange for payment of a fee or royalty.

Licensing provides a means to conduct business in a country where the host country's laws discourage foreign ownership. One disadvantage of licensing is often the loss of managerial control. The foreign company makes key decisions for the licensor without the influence of that company. On the other hand, a licensee may provide a greater understanding of the local culture, experience with the distribution system, and the marketing skill required to be successful in the foreign market.

The Pac-Man arcade game was originally developed in Japan and was trademarked by Mamco, Ltd. of Japan. Mamco decided to license the rights to Pac-Man to Bally for development and use in the United States.[31] You know the rest of that story.

International franchising is a form of licensing in which the domestic-based company establishes overseas franchises in much the same way as it does in the domestic country. Because of the desire on the part of many franchisors for consistency, franchising agreements are most often found in markets where conditions are quite similar to those in the domestic market.

Some companies believe that the risks of licensing are too great and prefer to maintain greater marketing control. The companies may elect to use contract manufacturing overseas. Under **contract manufacturing,** a U.S.-based company would simply agree to permit an overseas manufacturer to produce the product. In a sense, this amounts to a type of private label manufacturing since the domestic company supplies the product specifications and the brand name, and the overseas company produces the product under that label for the domestic company. Overseas sales of the product are typically handled and controlled in some way by the domestic company. In Mexico and Spain, for instance, Sears may establish its own stores, but, rather than filling these stores with imported products, they often will use local manufacturers to produce Sears-label products to specifications.[32] In addition to increased marketing control, contract manufacturing offers the opportunity to utilize labor that may be less expensive in many overseas markets, thus yielding lower product prices or greater savings to the company.

A final form of joint venturing is the **joint ownership venture.** Under this arrangement, the domestic and foreign partners both invest capital and share ownership and control of the partnership in proportion to some agreed-on amount. Ownership is not always equally divided. More than two-thirds of Shell Oil is owned by Royal Dutch/Shell, a foreign (Netherlands-British) company.

A common reason for entering into joint ventures is that this may be required by countries that restrict foreign ownership of investments. In Mexico, there are restrictions barring 100 percent foreign ownership of Mexican advertising agencies. International agencies such as J. Walter Thompson Inc. must, therefore, be involved in joint ventures if they wish to operate in Mexico. In other countries, the government may require that the local company maintain a majority interest in the venture, keeping the foreign investor to less than 50 percent control in the company.

---

[31]"Pac-Man Fever," *Time*, April 5, 1982, p. 48.

[32]Philip Kotler, *Principles of Marketing* (Englewood Cliffs, N.J.: Prentice-Hall, 1980), p. 610.

Apollo Soyuz cigarettes commemorated a joint American-Soviet venture.

Another reason for joint ownership ventures is financial. A domestic company may wish to set up European operations, but may find it to be economically difficult. By joining with some European firm in a joint ownership venture the U.S. company may find its solution.

Clearly, a key to the success of a joint ownership venture, as with any type of partnership, is finding and keeping the right mix of companies. Overseas and American firms do not always have the same views. Europeans tend to be more engineering-oriented. Marketing often means sales to them. American companies often reverse this, putting marketing first. European companies may be more cautious in money matters. The list of differences continues. The point is that management becomes difficult when the partners disagree on fundamental components of the business. Finding the right partner reduces these differences.

Direct Foreign Investment. Exporting meets a foreign country's demand by utilizing excess capacity from domestic operations. If foreign market demand is great, a company may choose to directly invest in manufacturing and marketing operations in a host foreign country.

This form of business is called **direct foreign investment.**

Coca-Cola owns a bottling plant in Guangzhow (Canton), China. National Semiconductor Corporation has made a direct investment in manufacturing and marketing operations in Singapore and Hong Kong. Volkswagen built an automobile plant in Pennsylvania, hoping to minimize shipping expenses and political pressures associated with the selling of a foreign-made car to the U.S. market. Moreover, an organization that directly invests in plant operations in developing countries may take advantage of low-cost labor. Whatever the reason for direct investment in manufacturing facilities and marketing operations, this strategy reflects a long-term commitment to international marketing and is the greatest form of commitment to the world market discussed thus far.

There are a number of risks associated with a long-term direct investment strategy. The possible nationalization of a multinational's operations by a foreign power is one of these risks. For example, political unrest in Libya had a major impact on Exxon, Getty, and other oil companies.

Exhibit 22-8 summarizes the key points on the forms of international involvement we have discussed.

Decision 4: How Should We Organize for International Marketing?

Having decided to enter international marketing and having identified the markets which are the most likely candidates to enter, the marketer must decide on the nature of the organizational structure that will best match its commitment to those markets. The nature of the company's organization depends on the extent of its commitment.

Export Department or International Division? At the lowest level of involvement, companies may decide to establish an **export department** to deal either directly or indirectly (that is, through some form of merchant or agent intermediaries) with overseas customers.

EXHIBIT 22-8

Summary of Basic Multinational Strategies

Strategy	Location of Production Facility	Foreign Company's Primary Involvement	Ownership of Foreign Operation	Capital Outlay Required for Multinational
Exporting	Domestic	Middleman ensures foreign distribution and sales	Foreign channel ownership	Low
Licensing	Foreign country	Owns right to manufacture and use product name; local marketing	Joint according to contract	Low
Contractual agreements	Foreign company	Varies	Foreign ownership	Low
Joint ownership ventures	Foreign country	Partner	Partner	Moderate to high
Direct investment	Foreign country	Either foreign middlemen utilized or native sales force utilized	Complete domestic ownership	High

If the organization progresses beyond exporting to some form of investment or contract dealings with a foreign company, the export department may be insufficient. A larger **international department** or division may be required. Such units may conduct activities similar to those of the domestic division of the same company, but on a smaller scale. They may make production decisions but, more often than not, they will be conducting the international licensing or marketing of products. These divisions may be organized further into geographic territories (North American, Latin American, or European), product groupings, or customer groupings.

The Multinational Company Versus the International Company. Thus far we have been investigating the subject of international marketing and have been viewing this subject from the perspective of a U.S.-based company looking at foreign markets. To such a company,

these foreign markets are precisely that: foreign. They consider the U.S. market as "home" and consider the other countries as "different."

This is a major difference between the international marketer and the true multinational marketer. The multinational marketer does not have a home orientation. The geography of location in this sense is not a concern, unless it can be said that the *world* is "home" for the multinational. There is a fundamental difference in perspective here. The international marketer may view the world as "us" and "them," with "them" being the foreign markets. On the other hand, the multinational marketer views the world as "us." Opportunities exist anywhere, and the true multinational is not bound by geographical nearsightedness.

Multinational corporations tend to be large and to do business in many nations. In fact, total sales of some multinationals exceed the GNP of many smaller nations. Exhibit 22-9 shows some of the largest multinational companies in the

EXHIBIT 22-9

The 50 Largest Multinational Corporations in the World

Rank 1980	Rank 1979	Company	Headquarters	Sales ($000)
1	1	Exxon	New York	103,142,834
2	3	Royal Dutch/Shell Group	The Hague/London	77,114,243
3	4	Mobil	New York	59,510,000
4	2	General Motors	Detroit	57,728,500
5	7	Texaco	Harrison, N.Y.	51,195,830
6	6	British Petroleum	London	48,035,941
7	8	Standard Oil of California	San Francisco	40,479,000
8	5	Ford Motor	Dearborn, Mich.	37,085,000
9	13	ENI	Rome	27,186,939
10	9	Gulf Oil	Pittsburgh	26,483,000
11	10	International Business Machines	Armonk, N.Y.	26,213,000
12	14	Standard Oil (Ind.)	Chicago	26,133,080
13	15	Fiat	Turin (Italy)	25,155,000
14	11	General Electric	Fairfield, Conn.	24,959,000
15	16	Francaise des Pétroles	Paris	23,940,355
16	21	Atlantic Richfield	Los Angeles	23,744,302
17	12	Unilever	London/Rotterdam	23,607,516
18	26	Shell Oil	Houston	19,830,000
19	22	Renault	Paris	18,979,278
20	29	Petróleos de Venezuela	Caracas	18,818,931
21	18	International Telephone & Tel.	New York	18,529,655
22	32	Elf Aquitaine	Paris	18,430,074
23	20	Philips' Gloeilampenfabrieken	Eindhoven (Netherlands)	18,402,818
24	19	Volkswagenwerk	Wolfsburg (Germany)	18,339,046
25	36	Conoco	Stamford, Conn.	18,325,400

Source: "The 50 Largest Industrial Companies in the World," *Fortune Magazine,* August 10, 1981, p. 205; © 1981 Time Inc

world. Their organization and role in the world economy are quite complex.

Decision 5: How Much Should We Change Our Domestic-Based Marketing?

The international marketer must decide to what extent it should adjust its domestic marketing for each foreign market. The multinational also must determine to what extent market variations necessitate marketing adjustments.

The general approach many seem to take is the maintenance of a corporatewide strategy on a worldwide basis with tactical adjustments where local conditions warrant. If there were no strategic continuity of approach, the company would not gain a solid and cohesive worldwide identity. Instead, its identity would consist of the fragmented efforts and pieces put together in its various markets. There is value to coordinat-

Rank		Company	Headquarters	Sales ($000)
1980	**1979**			
26	23	Siemens	Munich	17,950,253
27	24	Daimler-Benz	Stuttgart	17,108,100
28	17	Peugeot	Paris	16,846,434
29	25	Hoechst	Frankfurt	16,480,551
30	27	Bayer	Leverkusen (Germany)	15,880,596
31	28	BASF	Ludwigshafen on Rhine	15,277,348
32	31	Thyssen	Duisburg (Germany)	15,235,998
33	47	Petrobrás (Petróleo Brasileiro)	Rio de Janeiro	14,836,326
34	●	PEMEX (Petróleos Mexicanos)	Mexico City	14,813,514
35	33	Nestlé	Vevey (Switzerland)	14,615,187
36	30	Toyota Motor	Toyota City (Japan)	14,233,779
37	38	Nissan Motor	Yokohama (Japan)	13,853,503
38	39	E.I. du Pont de Nemours	Wilmington, Del.	13,652,000
39	49	Phillips Petroleum	Bartlesville, Okla.	13,376,563
40	42	Imperial Chemical Industries	London	13,290,347
41	43	Tenneco	Houston	13,226,000
42	38	Nippon Steel	Tokyo	13,104,996
43	46	Sun	Radnor, Pa.	12,945,000
44	37	Hitachi	Tokyo	12,871,328
45	44	Matsushita Electric Industrial	Osaka (Japan)	12,684,404
46	34	U.S. Steel	Pittsburgh	12,492,100
47	48	Occidental Petroleum	Los Angeles	12,476,125
48	●	United Technologies	Hartford	12,323,994
49	45	Western Electric	New York	12,032,100
50	●	Standard Oil (Ohio)	Cleveland	11,023,196
		Totals		**1,203,998,984**

● = Companies were not in the top 50 in 1979.

ing and centralizing the strategic planning worldwide.

But this can be carried too far. Adjustments must be made for local conditions. U.S. automobile companies have been criticized because they have not adapted to Japanese desires. Japanese drive on the left side of the road and most Japanese prefer to have steering wheels on the right. No U.S. models available for shipment to Japan have made this adjustment. Therefore, it is desirable to adjust the strategic decisions in terms of the specific tactics used to implement strategic plans in each market. The costs of adjusting the strategy must be weighed against estimates of sales potentials.

International Marketing Research. Since one of the first steps in marketing is to conduct marketing research, a company will have to do research in identifying potential markets. Having decided to enter a market, it may need to do further research to clarify its specific courses of action.

But researchers encounter different circumstances in conducting research in many overseas nations. To begin with, there is rarely a wealth of available secondary data such as is found in the United States. American researchers are lucky. There are volumes of statistics and editorial literature about the people and the markets in the United States. In some countries, no census has ever been taken. In some of the developing nations, researchers are mistrusted. The view in these areas seems to be that anyone wanting to pry into another person's life must have less than honorable motives. Often, too, the lack of data and the different social patterns make it difficult for a researcher to use all the tools available. Carefully planned samples may be impossible to develop. Telephone directories certainly do not include all of the population and, in addition, may be woefully out of date. Street maps are unavailable in many cities in Latin America, Central America, and Asia. In fact, in some large metropolitan areas of the Near East and Asia, streets are unnamed or unidentified, and the houses on them are unnumbered.

Nevertheless, marketing research is clearly vital. Many research techniques that are needed to identify cultural differences have been borrowed from cultural anthropology.[33] Included among these studies is content analysis, especially the analysis of marketing communications used in particular nations. Standard research methods such as test marketing may be used. For example, Tang's promotion in Brazil emphasizes flavor and fun because test marketing showed that promoting the convenience aspect of the product as the drink of the American astronauts was a marketing disaster.

Research is becoming increasingly important even in the socialist or planned economies. In Czechoslovakia, for instance, there is a gov-ernment-controlled market and product research institute. Among its past activities was a study of the feasibility of introducing different brands of toilet soap geared toward different customer needs rather than having only one nonbranded product on the market.[34]

Product Planning. General Motors of Canada (GM) secured an order of slightly more than 25,000 Chevrolet Malibus to be shipped to Iraq. After receiving 13,500 cars, the customer in Iraq refused to accept delivery of the remainder of the order. The reason was that the cars were ill-suited for the hot, dusty, desert-like conditions in Iraq. Different clutches, supplemental air filters, and additional GM mechanics and engineers in Iraq were needed to help solve the problems.[35]

What GM failed to recognize in this case was how poorly the domestic-oriented product would suit local conditions. Apparently, GM was using the self-reference criterion. GM solved its problem by adjustment of the product.

There are basically three product-oriented adjustments that can be made in international marketing.[36] A company may elect to sell its *same product, unadjusted* in a market; it may sell its *same product, adapted* in a market; or it may sell a *new product invention* in a market.

The simplest strategy is probably to extend the same product into the international market. This may work well for some products but not for others. One reason for this has to do with the product itself. We have seen how risks increase in international marketing because of increased uncertainties and other factors. However, not all products have an equal amount of risk. Consider Exhibit 22-10. We can visualize products as vary-

[33]A brief summary of such methods can be found in J.F. Engel and R.D. Blackwell, *Consumer Behavior,* 4th ed. (Hinsdale, Ill.: Dryden, 1982), pp. 99–106.

[34]*Exporting to the Socialist Countries of Eastern Europe* (Geneva: International Trade Center UNCTAD/GATT, 1971), pp. 304–305.

[35]"GM Runs into a Middle East Crisis: It's Too Hot and Dusty in Baghdad," *The Wall Street Journal,* February 23, 1982, p. 37.

[36]Warren Keegan, "Multinational Product Planning: Strategic Alternatives," *Journal of Marketing,* Vol. 33, January 1969, pp. 58–62.

EXHIBIT 22-10

**Products Vary in Environmental
Sensitivity**

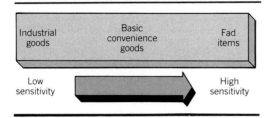

ing in terms of how sensitive they are to environmental conditions such as economic, cultural, and social factors.[37] On the one hand, industrial products are such that they may be used in very much the same way in all markets in the world. Therefore, their use (and thus the appropriate marketing of these) is not sensitive to the peculiarities of each separate culture or economy around the world. At the opposite extreme are fad items whose use and acceptance surely will change with different countries. For these products, the product use and marketing tactics are highly sensitive to local conditions. Highly sensitive products then would not be likely candidates for extension to foreign markets. Many industrial products, and many consumer products can be marketed directly into many nations.

Many products are best marketed with some sort of adaptation to local conditions. In 1973, Philip Morris Brazileira, the Brazil Division of Philip Morris, bought a small Brazilian cigarette manufacturer. Consumption of cigarettes in Brazil at that time was quite high, and Philip Morris was looking to gain a large share of this large market. Research showed, however, that existing Philip Morris' brands were too mild. The new company could help. The product was marketed as a low-tar and low-nicotine brand, since these were making major gains in the United States. Unfortunately, most Brazilians perceived these as diet cigarettes, and sales went nowhere.[38] The product and its marketing were not sufficiently adapted to the local market.

Campbell's Soup found that in order to penetrate the British market with its condensed soups, it had to add water, instead of selling the condensed version, to make the product look like and be priced like the soups already accepted in Britain.[39]

Product invention requires the development of a totally new product for the international market. This may take the form of backward invention (recreating or reintroducing a domestically obsolete product into another nation) or forward invention (the creation of a new product for the new market conditions). This is the costliest and riskiest product strategy, but the potential for rewards is also the greatest.

Promotion Planning. In much the same way as it faces decisions about extending or changing products, the firm must decide whether or not it needs to adapt its promotions, and if so, how. As noted above, many companies have decided to use a standardized overall approach or theme, yet adjust copy, colors, graphics, and so on, for local conditions. The Marlboro man is a rugged individualist all over the world. In Latin American magazines, he appears as a Latin cowboy type, much the same as the American version. But cowboys are not relevant in Hong Kong, so the Marlboro character is a more urban, rugged individual with a truck rather than a horse.[40]

Very few companies can effectively wage a single worldwide promotion. Some adjustments in language, graphic portrayal of people, and media are usually needed. At the simplest level, companies may have to change product names

[37]Warren Keegan, "A Conceptual Framework for Multinational Marketing," *Columbia Journal of World Business,* Vol. VII, No. 6, November–December 1977, p. 70.

[38]Edwin Gray, "Marketing Research Helped Philip Morris Penetrate the 'Impenetrable' Brazil Market," *Marketing News,* September 17, 1982, Sect. 2, pp. 7, 9.

[39]"The $30 Million Lesson," *Sales Management,* March 1, 1967, pp. 31–34.

[40]David A. Ricks, *Big Business Blunders* (Homewood, Ill.: Dow Jones-Irwin, 1983), p. 52.

or packages. A vitamin product was introduced into the South American market under the name "Fundavit," an English modification of terms suggesting that the product satisfied all the fundamental vitamin requirements. The name had to be changed when objections were raised that the product's name was too close to a Spanish term used to refer to an attractive female's derriere.[41]

Differences in media availability and literacy mean different media schedules. If the proportion of television households is low, mass marketing will need to find another medium. In countries where literacy is low, movie theater advertising may be an important medium. In many nations, the broadcast media (radio and television) are government controlled, and not always available to the marketer. Different media habits in each country also mean promotion strategy must be adjusted for these differences.

Price Planning. There is little likelihood that the marketer will have the option of extending the same price into many foreign nations. Variations in tariffs, currencies, and local competitive prices may mean that this marketing variable will often change from market to market, indicating that pricing decisions are not always easily made. In addition, high inflation exists in some areas of the world. Inflation in Brazil and Israel, for example, exceeded an annual rate of 100 percent during parts of 1981–1983. Often, too, manufacturers may not be able to control the margins and retail prices charged by the middlemen distributing or importing their products. International monetary exchange rates must be understood as well. Devaluation of the British pound is said to have contributed to the failure of Britain's Laker Airlines. **Devaluation** is a government act that decreases the value of the domestic currency relative to that of a foreign currency. In 1982, the Mexican peso was devaluated by almost 30 percent against the U.S. dollar.[42] This action made the Mexican peso worth less than before, thus raising the cost of goods im-

---

SCHWEPPING

Schwepps, the British tonic water and soft drinks company has decided to standardize advertising for its international brand. The basic advertising theme that will be used around the world contains the catchword "Schwepping" and a common product sequence filmed centrally. Schwepps had already standardized all labeling of its tonic water in its international markets for it had decided on creation of a new international word like "jogging" or "camping". Schwepps plans to overcome language barriers by promoting "Schwepping"—which is opening a bottle of Schwepps tonic (with the inevitable Schhh . . .) pouring it and drinking . . . enjoying the finest tonic water in the world . . . knowing how to make the most of one's pleasures.

Early testing of this campaign in the United States uncovered some confusion between the differences between "Schwepping" and "Schlepping," which had negative reactions, particularly in the Jewish community. This problem was resolved in American advertising by introducing a light jingle with the theme of "Schwepping it up."

In France the new word had to be registered by the company to avoid "franglais" problems. The Germans are still having trouble with the word "Schwepping" tacked on to the existing commercial.

Source: Adapted from Rod Chapman, "How Schwepping Was Born," *Advertising Age*, March 29, 1982, pp. m-2, m-3. Used with permission.

---

ported into Mexico and decreasing Mexicans' buying power—but making it more attractive for Americans to import Mexican goods because the American dollar could buy more Mexican products.

To cope with these factors, the marketer needs a full understanding of all of these influences. Cost-based pricing may be more commonly found overseas, since there are so many cost elements, including tariffs, intermediary margins, and value added taxes. However, such

---

[41]David Ricks, op. cit.

[42]"Devaluating the Peso Is Only the First Step," *Business Week*, March 8, 1982, p. 44.

is not always the case. In the past, some manufacturers have attempted to enter a market with a very low price to build market share or to simply get rid of excess inventory. **Dumping** is a colorful term describing the practice of pricing products sold in a foreign market for less than their comparable fair market value in the domestic market. This is often illegal. Nippon Electric Company was accused of dumping when it sold high-powered microwave amplifiers to Communications Satellite Corporation of the United States for nearly 40 percent less than fair market prices in Japan.[43]

Distribution Planning. It is difficult to generalize about the channels and means of distribution worldwide because so little standardization exists. Modern channels exist in some areas of the world, including selected urban pockets in some of the developing nations. An extension or adaptation of domestic practices may be effective in such cases. However, other nations maintain what seem to be rather archaic and economically inefficient systems.

Typically, the marketer must be concerned with adapting to the existing distribution structure of each nation. One American cosmetics company trying to sell its cosmetics in France did not use "perfumers"—small local retailers specializing in cosmetics who typically dictate French opinion on such matters. The American company thought it could sell to larger chain stores. The perfumers, however, were resentful of this snub by the Americans and managed to turn French opinion against the American brand.[44]

Variations such as this exist in the channel structures, the nature of retail outlets, and distribution systems. In Japan, Procter & Gamble must sell through a complex network of five types of wholesalers before their products even get to the retail level.[45]

In many markets overseas, small specialty retailers exist. Their prices may be quite high, and bargaining is expected. Food products are often purchased in small quantities for consumption that day, so large packages do not sell well. People simply do not have the storage or the refrigeration space to keep foods for any length of time. In fact, prepackaged foods may be looked on as suspect by those who prefer to carefully inspect their foods.

The total logistics systems must be considered as well. Domestically produced products often must be shipped several times. First, the domestic producer must ship the product to some dock or overseas shipping point. The goods must then be shipped from that point to another point of foreign entry. From there, they are shipped to either a regional warehouse or the foreign nation for which they are intended. Finally, the goods must be shipped to whatever type of unit may eventually sell the product. In addition, roads are not always well-constructed overseas; airlines are usually concentrated in urban centers; rail systems may or may not exist; and ports are not always capable of handling sizable amounts of cargo. Many differences in usage exist for these reasons. In Australia, for instance, nearly one-half of the ton-mile shipping is done via the coastal waterways because of the population concentration on the coasts of that nation.[46]

However, it should come as no surprise that more effective and efficient international marketing channels are evolving. The impact of free trade areas is increasing, as is international activity in many areas. Some of this activity is due to government intervention aimed at encouraging and stimulating economic growth. Great strides are being made. Consider how the following changes in Japanese channels will influence international marketing.

New types of establishments—which emphasize low pricing and innovative marketing policies—are steadily growing in importance. Supermarket-type outlets handle consumer sta-

---

[43]"Small Firm Fights Japanese Dumping," *INC,* May 1982, p. 28.

[44]David Ricks, op. cit., p. 120.

[45]William Hartley, "How Not to Do It: Cumbersome Japanese Distribution System Stumps U.S. Concerns," *The Wall Street Journal,* March 2, 1972, pp. 1, 8.

[46]Peter J. Rimmer, "Australia's Domestic Freight Transport Industry," in *Marketing* (Muncie, Ind.: Ball State University, Bureau of Business Research, 1979), p. 33.

EXHIBIT 22-11

The Spectrum of Markets and Marketing Functions in Eastern Europe

Market Types	A	B	C
Marketing functions	Decentralized self-management functioning within the constraints of a set of conditions	Planned economy functioning with central indirect levers	Direct planning system where a self-regulating market does not exist
Price	Except for certain state monopolies and certain prices established by the state at the maximum level prices are freely set in this market	A mixed price system whereupon fixed, limited, maximized, and free prices all play a role	Except for a part of agriculture and handicrafts, fixed prices uniformly set for the whole country
Location or distribution	Decentralized—centrally disapproved if does not fit the national economic plan	Decentralized, but centrally checked and approved	Totally centrally determined
Promotion	Decentralized at the enterprise level emphasizing promoting of the enterprise while informing consumers	Performed by industry and enterprise complexes independently	Mostly part of central plan
Product research	More emphasis on the prevailing consumption patterns as guidelines for national plans	Some market testing of products by major enterprises	Product research to prevent accumulation of unwanted goods in excess supply
Assortment	Decentralized and more consumer oriented	Partially decentralized, determined by enterprises with central approval	Determined by central authority and filtered down to the enterprise

Source: A. Coskun Samli, *Marketing and Distribution Systems in Eastern Europe* (New York: Praeger, 1978), p. 91.

ples at popular prices; networks of dealers for automobiles and electrical appliances sell mass-produced products; convenience stores are springing up to sell essentials in the early morning or late at night; and discount stores and mail-order businesses are using catalogues as well as mass communication media such as newspaper and TV advertising.

The growth of supermarkets is most impressive. The first Japanese supermarket opened in 1953; by 1979, the supermarket industry was competing for top place among retail businesses in sales volume. New supermarket branches have opened in provincial cities, so that national chains are emerging. While supermarkets follow low-pricing strategy, they are paying greater attention to attractive store design and merchandise displays. Their assortments are being broadened to nonfoods such as apparel, sundry household supplies, furniture, electrical appliances, and leisure goods. As mass sales outlets the Japanese supermarket chains have started direct buying at home and overseas.

U.S. producers and exporters who want to expand sales in the Japanese mass market should, therefore, consider developing products for distribution through supermarket channels. Similarly, there has been a recent proliferation of retail stores specializing in high-turnover, low-price products such as appliances, cameras, watches, golf equipment, eye glasses, and men's apparel. Such outlets might serve as important future sales outlets for U.S. manufacturers.

Confronted with such retail growth, department stores are emphasizing their capabilities as full-line retailers offering large assortments of diversified goods and services plus trained sales assistance. Although they tend to handle selected imported products, prestige as well as popular-grade imported products are expected to become more important as department stores search for merchandise capable of satisfying diverse consumer demands.[47]

Marketing Mix Planning. As we have seen, the marketing mix decisions essentially involve two steps: (1) investigation of local conditions, and (2) determination of the extent to which decisions made in one market may be transferred to another. Basically, this is the same as any segmentation decision: Segments may differ, and the marketing mix aimed at them may have to be altered somewhat. Even in segments such as the controlled economies of Eastern Europe, marketing plays a role and can be adapted to local conditions. Exhibit 22-11 illustrates marketing's role in those nations.

SUMMARY

In this chapter, we have discussed how marketing may be conducted on an international or multinational basis. The world is considerably smaller than many of us realize. Many nations of the world are comparable in size to states in the United States. Yet trade between or among such nations is complicated by differences in language, cultures, currencies, trade barriers, and governmental regulations. In spite of such difficulties, multinational marketing is increasing substantially. World trade helps a nation in that the nation's own economy may grow as domestic competition is increased and as imports improve the standard of living in those nations. However, world trade may also lead to undesirable cultural change, and trade deficits may result when the value of imported goods exceeds the value of a country's exports.

A five-step decision model was presented suggesting that a domestic company first makes a decision to get involved in international marketing, then decides which markets to enter, decides on its commitment to each market, determines how to organize its efforts, and, finally, determines how to adjust its marketing for each market.

The theory of comparative advantage suggests that nations become involved in international trade to take advantage of their specializations and to fill needs with the specialized outputs of other nations. Other encouraging factors were noted, as well as a set of factors discouraging multinational marketing.

In investigating the markets to enter, a firm must consider such factors as the cultural environment, the political environment, the economic environment, including the level of economic development, and the demographic environment. The specific concerns of each environment were noted.

A firm may choose to become involved in a foreign market on various levels. At the lowest level, it may choose to export, or it may elect joint venturing (such as licensing, franchising, contract manufacturing, or joint ownership venture). At the highest level, it may choose direct foreign investment.

To begin its involvement in overseas operations, the international company may establish an export department or an international department or division. Other companies, which are set up as truly multinational organizations having a global business perspective, choose to view the whole world as a potential market. Such companies do not have a domestic versus foreign perspective.

---

[47]Based on Frank Meissner, "Americans Must Practice the Marketing They Preach to Succeed in Japan's Mass Markets," *Marketing News*, October 17, 1982, p. 5.

Finally, we discussed the nature of marketing planning in international or multinational operations. We noted the difficulty of conducting marketing research in other nations because of the lack of data and poor status of research in general. Marketing mix decisions are often made with regard to a standard or global strategic approach and local adjustments in tactics. The question of whether an action should be extended intact into other nations, adapted somewhat, or created new or adjusted totally was investigated for each of the marketing mix elements. Specific concerns for each were noted.

THE MOST IMPORTANT CONCEPT IN THIS CHAPTER

The world is becoming a global village and multinational marketing is growing in importance as communications and transportation technologies improve. Differences (e.g., cultural) among countries must be recognized and marketing mixes should take these differences into account.

KEY TERMS

Multinational marketing

International marketing

Comparative advantage

European Economic Community (Common Market)

General Agreement on Tariffs and Trade (GATT)

Tariff

Import quotas

Embargo

Ethnocentrism

Boycott

Underdeveloped countries

Less-developed countries

Developing countries

Developed countries

Indirect exporting

Buyer for export

Direct exporting

Joint venturing

Licensing

International franchising

Contract manufacturing

Joint ownership venture

Direct foreign investment

Export department

International department

Devaluation

Dumping

QUESTIONS FOR DISCUSSION

1 What five decisions must be made before a firm decides to engage in international marketing?

2 What factors encourage and discourage international marketing?

3 What makes the multinational firms in Japan effective marketers?

4 What economic factors determine the marketing decision to export to certain countries?

5 What is a joint ownership venture? Find some examples.

6 Pick three countries, perhaps Greece, Brazil, and Hong Kong, and try to find out what the customs and courtesy for greetings are in these countries.

CASE 22-1 Toshiba International Corporation*

In 1982, the Instrumentation Division of Toshiba International Corporation was the first Japanese firm to establish a headquarters in Tulsa, Oklahoma. The operation included sales, service, assembly, and checkout for the company's computerized valve controls, mainly for petroleum processing and related industries. Now, the units are manufactured in Tokyo, but, according to Lewis Smith, Toshiba's Tulsa-based general manager, the company hopes to have some manufacturing in Tulsa within five years.

Toshiba's original decision to open up shop in Tulsa had a major effect on a small, relatively new advertising agency, Littlefield Marketing and Advertising.

When Smith decided on Tulsa, he knew he would need a local advertising firm to handle Toshiba's account. He looked in the yellow pages, but there were so many agencies he said he didn't know where to begin.

Instead of wading through the list, Smith called a friend who suggested David G. Littlefield's firm. The deal was made. Littlefield and James H. Davies, partner in a Tulsa design firm that handles Littlefield's artistic needs, soon visited their largest client's headquarters in Japan. Their Japanese hosts were so impressed by the Littlefield's agency that the company now will be responsible for producing Toshiba Instrumentation Division literature for all English-speaking countries.

Smith was hired by Toshiba International specifically to set up the Tulsa office. Both he and David W. Fahle, sales manager, were hired from Applied Automation, in San Francisco, a subsidiary of Phillips Petroleum Company.

Smith was given full control over choosing a location for the new headquarters. He narrowed it down to Houston and Tulsa before finally choosing the latter. A city with good access to engineers, the proper type of employees, a minimum of competition, good living conditions, and a central location were the factors influencing his decision.

"Our market stretches from western Canada down the West Coast of the U.S., through the Southwest and back up the East Coast. Tulsa was right in the middle of that U," Smith said.

Only two Japanese families have been transferred to Tulsa. Kosuke Miyoshi, director of Toshiba Corp., parent company of Toshiba International, felt that American personnel should be used when setting up operations in the United States.

The move into Tulsa represents the first time Toshiba International has marketed its instrumentation products in North America.

Questions

1 What type of market entry strategy is Toshiba employing?

2 What are its advantages? Disadvantages?

CASE 22-2 West Cigarettes

West cigarettes was introduced in the German market with a $22 million advertising campaign. This full-flavored cigarette was promoted with a "Going West, Feeling Free . . ." theme. The English language slogan "Let's Go West" was to appeal to German smokers in a manner similar to the Marlboro cowboy tradition. American trucking was utilized as a symbol of the modern-day cowboy. The advertising campaign was backed with a promotional tour of a real American truck visiting 100 German cities.

After one year on the market, West cigarettes has not met its sales goal of 1 percent share of the market.

Questions

1 Why do you think West cigarettes has not met its sales objectives?

2 What cultural factors may have played a part in the disappointing sales of West?

---

*Source: Adapted from "Japanese Firm Makes Home in Tulsa," *Tulsa World,* March 21, 1982, p. G-3. Used with permission.

CHAPTER 23

Marketing and Society

CHAPTER SCAN

This chapter addresses the matters known as marketing's social responsibilities. Many marketing decisions involve "trade-offs," such as deciding on the convenience of throw-away bottles versus possible littering or other environmental damage. This chapter discusses the difficulties involved in weighing the advantages and disadvantages of each such decision.

Marketing organizations must deal with many publics—competitors, consumers, and the public at large. In each case, the marketing concept provides guides, but not always answers, to problems that may develop. The marketing manager's own philosophies must influence his or her decisions.

Ultimately, the free market system will evaluate all marketing decisions.

**WHEN YOU HAVE STUDIED
THIS CHAPTER YOU WILL:**

Have an appreciation of the place of ethical behavior in marketing.

Understand the difficulties encountered in fulfilling marketing's responsibilities.

Be able to describe the several publics toward which marketers must act ethically.

Have a sense of the importance of the consumerism movement.

Be able to identify areas in which marketing's social responsibilities are particularly great.

Be able to explain how the free market system serves to guide and evaluate the decisions of marketing managers.

One Federal Express television commercial (Destination) was designed to communicate that Federal Express offers overnight delivery to "thousands more cities and communities . . . than the post office goes with Express Mail." The setting for the commercial is an old-fashioned post office. Two postal workers are discussing their retirement while standing behind a counter. A customer who is the first in a long line of customers asks about sending a package by Express Mail. The clerks laugh and reply, "We don't go there." The postal clerks who are portrayed as having no interest in waiting on the customer, finally pull the shade down in the customer's face. This commercial riled the U.S. Postal Service to such an extent that the Post Master General wrote to the President of Federal Express. The Post Master indicated that he thought it was unethical that the commercials "which depict postal employees as lazy, discourteous louts, totally disinterested in serving our customers," were being aired. The American Postal Workers Union also felt that the commercials insulted the integrity of the 670,000 postal workers. Federal Express's advertising agency claims the commercial was intended to be a light-hearted spoof, portraying humorous people in humorous situa-

tions in everyday life. The advertisement was to communicate and to emphasize the superior geographic coverage of Federal Express service compared with the Postal Service's Express Mail, simply a humorous comparison between the services of two competitive organizations.[1]

This story provides two insights. The first is that Federal Express, the Postal Service, and every profit and nonprofit organization operates within the context of a larger society and cannot be isolated from it. The second is that it is difficult to determine who is right and who is wrong in such situations. Perhaps you thought the commercial was clever. Perhaps you thought it wrongfully belittled innocent workers. In the absence of strict laws, the only answer to this debate is that Federal Express, operating within society, must weigh its actions carefully *and* be willing to accept the consequences of misjudging its own social responsibilities.

Social institutions, like individuals, must operate within society's rules of conduct. Some rules have been formalized into law, while others are so deeply ingrained in our culture that they are followed even though no law specifically mentions them. Others are simply general practices or rules-of-thumb.

SOCIAL RESPONSIBILITY

In recent years, much has been made of the social responsibility of business and other organizations, and of marketing in particular.

The term **social responsibility** designates the ethical consequences of how a particular individual's or organization's marketing activity might affect the interest of others.[2]

Social responsibility is broader than simple *legal* responsibility. Thus, social responsibility is more

difficult to deal with than law. For example, it is illegal to steal someone else's property, but what if you talk that person into giving you the property? What if you trick that person into signing the property over to you? What is the difference between telling a lie and avoiding the truth? At what point do good business practices become questionable?

Social Responsibility and Profit

Every aspect of marketing's social role is debatable. One of the more fundamental questions concerns the compatibility, or lack of it, between corporate social responsibility and the corporate

---

[1]"Mailmen Hit Federal Ad For Specious Delivery," *Ad Week*, May 24, 1982, p. 200.

[2]Keith Davis, "Understanding the Social Responsibility Puzzle," *Business Horizons*, Winter 1967, p. 45.

Photo: Frank Spinelli

POWERED BY THE DALLAS SYMPHONY

When American Airlines offered to help the Dallas Symphony Orchestra, they never dreamed it would result in sell-out performances on their 747's. Yet that's exactly what happened. Over a six-month period, American Airlines agreed to make cash contributions to the Dallas Symphony for each passenger who boarded the new daily 747 flight from Dallas to London. In no time they found that their sales were soaring as high as their planes.

The Business Committee for the Arts is helping companies of all sizes, from American Airlines to Pea Soup Andersen's Restaurants, discover that supporting the arts can give their business a lift. The Business Committee for the Arts will show you how collaboration with the arts can enhance your company's image, benefit your employees and offer tax advantages. To learn just how easily your business can form a successful partnership with the arts, contact the Business Committee for the Arts.

Don't be surprised if it helps your business take off.

BUSINESS COMMITTEE FOR THE ARTS • SUITE 510 • 1775 BROADWAY, NEW YORK, N.Y. 10019 • (212) 664-0600

THIS ADVERTISEMENT PREPARED AS A PUBLIC SERVICE BY OGILVY & MATHER

Social responsibility may be good for business.

profit motive. It has been argued that "welfare and society are not the corporation's business. Its business is making money, not sweet music."[3] A number of managers believe that profit-maximization is the only goal of business. It is believed that enhancing business' economic self-interest is best for the country. Social responsibility may place a company at a competitive disadvantage. For example, Ingersol-Rand developed a quiet air-compressor to silence noisy jack-hammers. Unfortunately, this product, which provided a clear social benefit in the form of noise abatement, had to be sold at a 25 percent premium because of its higher manufacturing cost.[4] In effect, the question becomes, "Would a buyer rather buy a jack-hammer for

---

[3]Theodore Levitt, "The Dangers of Social Responsibility, *Harvard Business Review*", September–October, 1958, p. 47.

[4]Laurence P. Feldman, "Societal Adaptation: A New Challenge for Marketing," *Journal of Marketing*, July 1971, pp. 54–60.

$5,000 or for $6,250?'' Similar problems face automobile manufacturers who believe that passenger-protecting air bags will save lives on the highway. Adding the bags might make the manufacturing costs of the auto $500 more expensive than the competitor's comparable model—and consumer's might not be willing to pay the difference. It is unlikely that one manufacturer will add an expensive safety feature to a product unless all competitors are forced to do the same. Like it or not, this kind of problem is usually settled by legislation requiring that socially desirable, but costly, features be added.

THE QUESTION OF ETHICS

Social responsibilities and problems of **ethics—** moral principles that guide our conduct—must be faced by any organization operating within a society. Ethical issues involve complex questions that cannot adequately be addressed here. In fact, addressing ethical problems frequently raises more questions than answers. But the heart of the issue is clearly this: There can be no absolute consensus on what should be done when ethical behavior is discussed. Different people, and even any *one* person, can evaluate a question using several different perspectives. However, there has been an undeniable trend toward broadening the social responsibility of marketing organizations beyond the limitations of their traditional roles as economic forces.

Some Fundamental Ethical Issues

Just as there are ethical aspects concerning all human interaction, there are a number of philosophical, ethical, and moral issues concerning marketing practices. There is no general agreement among philosophers about the answers to these ethical questions.

One assumption about ethics is that the rights and obligations of social institutions are dictated by the norms of society. **Norms** suggest what ought to be done under given circumstances. Ethical norms are guided by a **value system;** that is, by some system of preferences.[5]

---

[5]Kenneth E. Boulding, *Beyond Economics* (Ann Arbor, Mich.: University of Michigan Press, 1970), p. 227.

EXHIBIT 23-1

Marketing Decisions Are Influenced by Norms and Ethical Issues

Problems arise when two norms or values are in conflict. It may be that a corporation president—as well as society in general—values both high profits *and* a pollution-free environment. When one of these two goals or preferences in any way inhibits the achieving of the other goal, the businessman is faced with an ethical problem.

Exhibit 23-1 illustrates how norms and ethical issues influence our marketing decisions.

The Difficult Ethical Choice

The responsible marketing manager will be faced with an ethical problem when any goal or preference conflicts with another. Choosing between two values is rarely an simple, black-and-white decision. It is easy to imagine any number of such situations.

Although marketers and other business people often pride themselves on their rational, problem-solving abilities, one simple fact continues to plague the person seeking the ethical course of action in business. Simply put, there is no fixed measure or standard by which to judge actions. An engineer can calculate exactly how strong a steel girder is and a chemist can usually offer the right formulation of chemicals necessary to perform a task—but the business executive cannot be so precise. Even in instances where specific laws would seem to guide action, the laws and their application are almost always subject to debate.

Similarly unclear are the codes of ethics adopted by some professional business groups. Permanent, objective ethical standards are simply not available.[6] Beyond this, the available standards usually do not endure the test of time. What was ethical in the 1800s, the heyday of the "robber barons," is not seen as ethical today. Today's ethical decision may seem shockingly *un*ethical tomorrow.

ETHICAL DIMENSIONS OF THE MARKETING MIX

Throughout this book, we have seen that laws and regulations can affect and influence every aspect of the marketing mix. Similarly, ethical considerations can play a part in the development and implementation of that mix. Exhibit 23-2 presents some ethical questions that may be raised concerning all four major portions of the marketing mix. In considering them, remember that ethical issues are in fact philosophical in nature. There is no general agreement, even (or especially) among philosophers about answers to questions of ethics.[7]

---

[6]William Lazer, *Marketing Management: A Systems Perspective* (New York: John Wiley & Sons, 1971), p. 562.

[7]For an interesting discussion of ethical awareness among marketing executives see M.M. Pressley, D.J. Lincoln, and T. Little, "Ethical Beliefs and Personal Values of Top Level Executives," *Journal of Business Research*, December 1982.

EXHIBIT 23-2

Selected Ethical Questions Related to the Marketing Mix

Product

■ Who must accept responsibility for a faulty or hazardous product?

■ Is the package a source of information or a source of confusion for consumers?

Promotion

■ Can advertising persuade us to purchase products that we don't really want?

■ What effect does advertising have on children?

Price

■ Why do some pricing laws protect consumers while others protect business?

■ Do the poor really pay more?

Distribution

■ What are the ecological dimensions of channels of distribution?

■ What are the central issues in the debate that surrounds exclusive dealing and territorial restrictions?

Source: Adapted from R. Moyer and M.D. Hutt, *Macro Marketing: A Social Perspective*, 2nd ed. (New York: John Wiley & Sons, 1978), p. 9.

Some insist coal is good. Some insist coal is bad. We insist it's not that black or white.

Those who insist that coal is good point out that we have over 200 billion tons of economically recoverable coal in this country—enough to last us for at least three centuries at current consumption rates.

And, they further point out, although that represents 90% of our domestic energy resources, coal currently supplies less than 20% of our energy production.

It's true, that with greater usage, coal could give us as much as one half of the new energy we'll need between now and the year 2000—enough to help loosen the dangerous ties that bind us to expensive and insecure foreign oil.

But those who insist that coal is bad point to abandoned mines which scar the landscape and allow acid water to seep into streams.

And to the fact that coal contains ash and sulfur which, if not controlled, can pollute the air when burned.

Still, we at Atlantic Richfield's ARCO Coal Company believe that today the advantages of coal outweigh its disadvantages. And so do the many Americans who have invested with us.

That's because these days we have extremely tough environmental laws.

Laws that require the restoration of mined lands and the protection of air and water resources. Laws that ensure that coal mine areas are properly restored and that newly constructed or converted power plants reduce air pollution to protect health and welfare.

Of course, environmental controls are expensive. But they are a worthwhile investment when you consider that the cost of using coal is still less than half of the current cost of using oil.

And when you consider that coal can also be converted into transportation fuels such as gasoline and diesel fuel—reducing even more our dependence on foreign oil—it seems obvious that we ought to reassess our old prejudices against this most abundant of all fossil fuels.

At least Atlantic Richfield thinks so.

There are no easy answers.

ARCO ◆
Atlantic Richfield Company

Arco ran this ad in 1981, pointing out that ethical questions have no easy answers.

To Whom Is Marketing Responsible?

The question "To whom is marketing responsible?" can elicit several answers. One response is that marketing, as a function of a business or other organization, is responsible to the officers or owners of the business. This idea is not as narrow as it may seem, since if an organization breaks a law or "makes a mistake" its owners are often punished under the law or held as accountable in some other way. Thus, while it may be that organizations are responsible to the individuals who run them, it is also true that those people are responsible for the acts of their organizations.

One way of assigning marketing's locus of responsibility is to acknowledge that marketing has three publics to which it may be accountable: (1) competitors, (2) consumers, and (3) the general public. Because marketing interrelates with these three, there are three classes of issues dealing with social responsibility. As shown in Exhibit 23-3, these are fair *competitive* practices, *consumerism* issues, and issues dealing with what may be called *quality of life*. These issues are not exclusive of one another. There are many areas of overlap.

Where is government in all this? As Exhibit 23-3 illustrates, government is a social institution that oversees marketing and its three major publics. As such, it influences the interrelationships and may be called on by any public or any marketing organization to intervene when any other member of this scheme is thought to be behaving irresponsibly. Conflict and irresponsible behavior provide the impetus for most legislation.

EXHIBIT 23-3

The Three Publics and the Issues Constituting Marketing's Area of Responsibility

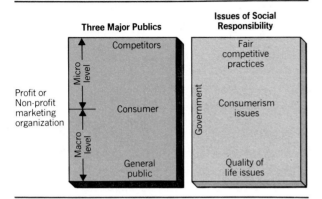

Macro-Responsibility

Our discussion of fair competitive practices and other areas of responsibility in marketing may have given the erroneous impression that marketing is obligated to act properly only toward its competitors or its clients. These matters, important though they are, are organizational responsibilities at the *micromarketing* level. That is, they concern one marketing organization interacting either with a customer or group of customers or a competitor or group of competitors. Marketing, as an aggregate social institution, has responsibilities at the broad societal or *macromarketing* level.

The study of marketing sometimes called *macromarketing* addresses the questions that concern the entire society and considers whether or not marketing performs adequately. In Exhibit 23-3, quality of life issues are of concern to the general public. In short, even if you are neither customer nor competitor of a given organization, organizations should respect your rights as a citizen. The general public is entitled to ask questions such as:

■ Is our marketing system adequate? Can it be improved at reasonable cost?

■ Is advertising wasteful? Does it cost consumers too much?

AMERICAN MARKETING ASSOCIATION CODE OF ETHICS

As a member of the American Marketing Association, I recognize the significance of my professional conduct and my responsibilities to society and to the other members of my profession.

1 By acknowledging my accountability to society as a whole as well as to the organization for which I work.

2 By pledging my efforts to assure that all presentations of goods, services, and concepts be made honestly and clearly.

3 By striving to improve marketing knowledge and practice in order to better serve society.

4 By supporting free consumer choice in circumstances that are legal and are consistent with generally accepted community standards.

5 By pledging to use the highest professional standards in my work and in competitive activity.

6 By acknowledging the right of the American Marketing Association, through established procedure, to withdraw my membership if I am found to be in violation of ethical standards of professional conduct.

Source: Reprinted by permission of the American Marketing Association.

■ Is our distribution system efficient?

■ Are products and packages polluting our environment unnecessarily?

■ Are there too many products? Do we *need* to offer automobiles in hundreds of colors?

Most individuals involved in marketing want to be socially productive. To achieve this goal, marketing managers must address social responsibility on the micro and macro levels. The concerns of each of the three major publics—competitors, customers, and general public—will be discussed below.

A responsible action toward consumers.

Responsible Action Toward Competitors

A capitalistic, free enterprise system values fair competition. This valuing of fair competition is reflected in our formal regulations. The Sherman Anti-Trust Act and many other laws were passed to encourage competition by assuring that monopolies, with a few exceptions, would not

develop by eliminating or controlling competitors. Laws of this type have been called *procompetitive* laws since they favor and foster competition.

Business practices, including marketing strategies and tactics, are considered to be socially unresponsible and undesirable if they seek to limit fair competition. For example, except in

WENDY'S AIN'T MAKING GRAMMATICAL PURISTS HAPPY

Wendy's advertising theme "Ain't No Reason To Go Any Place Else," has caused considerable controversy. Critics charge that using "ain't" and a double negative is bad grammar—and bad grammar is socially unresponsible. Wendy's says it is all good fun. They are injecting humor and humanity into their advertising by using the vernacular.

relatively rare situations, prices should reflect the forces of a freely competitive marketplace. Horizontal price fixing—competitors getting together to determine prices—violates this norm, and there are strict laws against the practice. Fines and even jail sentences are levied when executives are found guilty of the practice.

By current U.S. standards, most individuals feel that price collusion is *unethical*. Laws against the practice have settled the ethical issue here. But other, less clearly defined marketing practices, which are not against the law, are viewed by some as unfair or unethical. For example, some retailers selling well-known brands of athletic shoes offer consumers prices below the manufacturer's suggested retail prices. Certainly such a practice fits in the free competition tradition. But these retailers allege that the shoe manufacturers retaliate against price cutting with certain penalties, including shipping only irregular size shoes, delaying order shipment, and terminating dealership agreements.[8] Does the retailer owe responsible behavior to the consumer or to the manufacturer with whom some original understanding must have been made? Is the manufacturer responsible to company stockholders who want the firm to make as much money as possible? Or to the retailers who sell the product? Or to the consumers who value the manufacturer's name, believe its advertisements, and, after all, keep the company in business? Whatever your beliefs in the matter, you should realize there may be alternative positions taken by those with different values.

Even the propriety of 7-Up's caffeine-scare advertising strategy may be open to debate. When 7-Up began to stress caffeine . . . "Never Had It, Never Will," and "Crisp and Clean with No Caffeine," Pepsi claimed the ads were "a disservice to the public" since caffeine-related health concerns are "unsubstantiated."[9] Who is right?

A marketing practice may break a law that prohibits it exactly (as in the case of price fixing) *or* it may fall under a law that deals with a general issue, such as fraud, but does not mention the specific offending act. For example, coupon fraud thought to exceed $200 million annually, is a growing problem for the grocery industry.[10] Retailers, perhaps working with newspaper delivery people, may collect many coupons and request payment from manufacturers even though no purchases were made by consumers. Occasionally, manufacturers have circulated coupons for *non-existent* products in order to trap retailers who submit them claiming to have sold the product.

Marketing Criminals. Unfortunately, whether in dealings with competitors, consumers, or the environment, there are unscrupulous business people who do not follow the rules of the society in which they operate. Bluntly stated, there are marketing criminals. These individuals constitute a small minority among marketers, but it would be foolish to pretend that they do not exist. As is the usual case, those who willfully perform acts that are illegal or widely believed to be unfair receive the attention of the courts and the media, while stories about the honest competitor are not newsworthy.

[8] Robert Raissman, "Three Athletic Shoe Marketers Facing Stepped-Up FTC Inquiry," *Advertising Age*, April 5, 1982, p. 34.

[9] Janet Guyon, "7-Up Ads on Caffeine Rile Industry," *Wall Sreet Journal*, February 25, 1982, p. 25.

[10] Jennifer Alter, "Coupon Fraud: Big Business," *Advertising Age*, October 12, 1981, pp. 5–6.

THE PEPSI CHALLENGE

Industries often attempt to regulate the ethical behavior of companies within the industry. There are a number of trade associations with ethical codes, a number of review boards, and other vehicles for self-regulation. For instance, the National Advertising Division of the Council of Better Businesses reviews the appropriateness of advertising. Consider the following case concerning Pepsi Cola's and Coca-Cola's controversy concerning the Pepsi challenge.

The National Advertising Division of the Council of Better Business Bureaus has deemed that certain comparative claims made by Pepsi Cola Co. with respect to archrival Coca-Cola are misleading.

The Pepsi case involved three separate campaigns by BBDO, all of which were contested by Coke. The first was a TV commercial featuring actor Gabe Kaplan interviewing local volunteer firemen as they took the Pepsi Challenge. The second

campaign employed TV spots in a quick-cut montage format to show people choosing Pepsi over Coke. (Both the Kaplan and montage commercials carried the theme, "In tests like these nationwide, more people prefer Pepsi over Coke.") Lastly, local newspapers, radio, and outdoor (billboards) carried the results of informal "tastings" conducted in shopping mall booths. Results from seven locations were listed, with 60 percent preferring Pepsi, 38 percent Coke, and 2 percent undecided.

Coca-Cola complained that the firemen commercial was false and constituted an undisclosed dramatization; that this and the montage commercials misleadingly exaggerated consumer preferences for Pepsi; and that the taste booths were promotional gimmicks that produced false and misleading data. Pepsi denied these charges.

NAD concluded that neither Coke's nor Pepsi's voluminous research conclusively proved or dis-

proved the thesis that the montage commercials exaggerated the Pepsi margin of taste preference. However, the NAD decided that these commercials, including the firemen spots, were not conducted under the same controlled conditions as was the national taste test. Therefore, NAD ruled, it was misleading to state, "In tests like these," implying that the same procedures were followed.

As a result, Pepsi advised the NAD that future commercials supplied to local bottlers would not include numbers derived from shopping mall booths. The advertiser added that disputed montage commercials have since been replaced, for reasons unrelated to the complaint.

Finally, new ads that use the words "in tests like these" will superimpose a prominent message stating, "Nationwide, more people prefer the taste of Pepsi over Coke. Based on in-home nationwide taste tests."

Source: Excerpts from "Pepsi Modifies NAD-Challenged Claims," *Advertising Age*, December 21, 1981, p. 10. Copyright Crain Communications Inc © 1981

Responsible Action Toward Consumers

The consumerism movement is a reflection of business' lack of social responsibility to consumers, or rather the shirking of that responsibility by some marketers.[11] While there have been consumer movements from time to time in

American history, the current era has been by far the longest lasting and most significant one.

Consumerism is a broad social movement that grew out of the desire to protect individuals from practices which infringe on their rights as consumers.[12]

---

[11]This section follows arguments advanced by R. Moyer and M. Hutt, *Macro Marketing: A Social Perspective*, 2nd ed. (New York: John Wiley & Sons, 1978), pp. 170–171.

[12]George S. Day and David A. Aaker, "A Guide to Consumerism," *Journal of Marketing*, July 1970, p. 12.

Because the consumer movement is, at base, concerned with rights, it is frequently portrayed as starting with President John F. Kennedy's pronouncement of these four basic consumer rights:[13] (1) the *right to safety;* (2) the *right to be informed;* (3) the *right to choose;* and (4) the *right to be heard.*

Before dealing specifically with each of these four, it should be pointed out that if all organizations provided consumers with what they wanted (i.e., followed the marketing concept), the consumerism movement would have been unnecessary. However, no human system ever works perfectly, so to say that consumerism represents the failure of marketing goes a bit too far. The underlying truth of the marketing concept was ultimately vindicated when most organizations, after first trying to fight Ralph Nader and other consumerists, adopted a deeper concern for consumers as part of their marketing efforts.

The Right to Safety. Consumers have many expectations when they buy a product. They want it to work properly, to last as long as expected, and so on. But the most basic expectation is probably one of safety. Although most of us are willing to take certain reasonable risks, we assume we have a **right to safety**: We do not want our use of a product to place us unnecessarily in danger.

Procter & Gamble had to address questions of product safety when it appeared that use of its Rely tampon was related to deaths due to toxic shock syndrome.[14] Correlation does not prove causation, but P&G acted quickly to remove Rely from the market. The makers of Tylenol were confronted with a similar situation when some of that product was found to contain deadly cyanide. Tylenol was dealing with a more clear-cut situation: It was the victim of a murderer who did not conform to society's most fundamental norm. P&G's case was more difficult to deal with

---

[13]Consumer Advisory Council First Report, October 1963, pp. 6–28.

[14]Jennifer Alter, "Rely Verdict Leaves P&G, Others Unsure," *Advertising Age,* March 29, 1982, p. 10.

WHAT ARE THE MOST DANGEROUS PRODUCTS?

Much is made, especially in news stories, of the dangers of chemicals, pesticides, toys for infants, and nuclear energy plants. But do you know the five most dangerous products, according to the Consumer Products Safety Commission? They are: bicycles, stairs, doors, cleaning agents, and tables.

That bikes and cleaning products made the list is not too surprising. But tables, doors, and stairs? Should we ban stairs?

What this list shows is the importance of careful and proper usage of products. This is a difficult subject but few of us would blame Procter and Gamble if a child ate a spoonful of Tide or Cheer. The fault probably lies with the parent who left the detergent within the child's reach.

since the evidence was circumstantial. In both situations, however, the question is whether the companies were negligent in the production and sale of products. Should Tylenol have been packaged in tamper-proof bottles *before* somebody put poison in the capsules? Should P&G have marketed a product that could result in even one case of sickness or death in millions of uses? Should ketchup, mayonnaise, milk, mattresses, and Dr. Scholl's bunion pads all be tamper-proof to guard against all possible crazies?

Yes? It will be very expensive. No? You'll have to take risks.

Clearly some reasonable risks must be taken. Most would agree that consumers should be protected against products that are hazardous to life or health. In this, the right to safety is a move away from *caveat emptor* (let the buyer beware) to a philosophy that holds sellers responsible for their actions. Incidentally, in some instances, retailers have been held accountable for harmful products even though they "only sold" what manufacturers had produced.

Although we have many laws designed to protect consumers, faulty products are sometimes produced and consumers are sometimes injured. Even when products are properly constructed, manufacturers are now expected to further protect consumers by means of warnings, instructions on safe product use, and directions about what to do in certain problem situations. ("If swallowed, call physician immediately.") Although occasionally such requirements seem to go too far ("remove plastic wrapper from pizza before eating pizza"), it remains that unsafe products do not profit the marketer in the long run. Failure to protect customers is not consistent with the marketing concept.

The Right to Be Informed. A few years ago, a Chicagoan discovered that his Oldsmobile was equipped at the factory with an engine marked "Chevrolet." General Motors (GM) refused his demand for a "pure Oldsmobile," declaring that "switching engines" (which were all about the same anyway) had been a practice for years, necessitated by production schedules. The motorist sued. Ultimately, GM settled, out of court, with 66,000 owners of Buicks, Oldsmobiles, and Pontiacs who had been "deceived" in this manner. The buyers involved had insisted on their right to be informed of modifications made to the products they purchased. GM, by the way, soon began marking most of their engines generically as GM products.

Most would concur that the consumer has a right "to be protected against fraudulent, deceitful or grossly misleading information, advertising, labeling, or other practices, and to be given the facts one needs to make an informed choice."[15]

The right to be informed is reflected in laws and practices involving nutritional, product content and quality, and other information on labels, as well as requirements relating to truth-in-lending and package design.

Misleading Advertising. Because of its direct effects on buyers, one area of particular

concern is **misleading** or **deceptive advertising.** This emotional issue concerning the ethics of marketing is based on the fact that in almost all societies the truth is revered and lying is considered wrong. In the United States, the Federal Trade Commission Act of 1914 makes it illegal to have dishonest advertisements. Thus, laws and court cases aimed at ending the worst abuses have long been part of the American business scene.[16] Many recent incidents are traceable to consumerism and the right to be informed.

Identifying what is misleading or deceptive is not easy, however. Consider the following examples:

A Burger King commercial that portrays a little girl who says she has "A very big message for grownups." She indicates that a McDonald's Big Mac has 20 percent less meat than a Burger King Whopper. She closes the commercial saying "Unbelievable! Luckily I know a perfect way to show McDonald's how I feel. I go to Burger King!" McDonald's says it's unfair to compare a Big Mac with a Whopper, which costs 10 to 25 percent more than the McDonald's product.[17] McDonald's charges this is deceptive advertising and has taken its case to the courts.

Listerine advertisements suggested that the product was a cure for colds. The Federal Trade Commission determined that this was not true and forced Listerine's makers to run advertisements that cleared up any "misunderstanding."

Similarly, Profile, a "low-calorie" bread, was made to confess that its calorie-per-slice figure was low only because the bread was more thinly sliced than competitors' brands.

Bait and Switch. Although blatant deception is disapproved of by our society and legal system, hard and fast rules are difficult to develop and enforce. Advertising that attempts to employ the tactic known as **bait and switch** is a

---

[15]*Consumer Advisory Council First Report*, October 1963, pp. 6–28.

[16]For example, in the 1930s, the federal government refused to renew the broadcasting license of a radio station owner in Kansas City because of his insistence on advertising a return-to-youth operation consisting of installing goat glands in the bodies of human patients.

[17]"Burger King's Ads Cook Up a Storm," *Business Week*, October 11, 1982, p. 39.

case in point. Bait and switch involves advertising a product at an amazingly low price. Consumers, drawn to the store by the advertising, are "switched" to another, higher-priced item by salespeople who claim that the advertised item is, for some reason, no longer available.[18]

Although this tactic is clearly deceptive, proving intentional deception is difficult. Would anyone claim that the salesperson should not try to sell an item that was not mentioned in the store's advertisement? However, the sales tactic of trading up, whereby the salesperson tries to interest the customer in a higher-priced item than the customer first mentioned, is a regular practice. The marketing concept stresses honest attempts at customer satisfaction; the question of the ethics of switching revolves around intentions and the actual availability of the product. A salesperson may, though, point out a better, more expensive buying option. Again, questions of ethics are rarely straightforward and simple.

Puffery. Although the law prohibits advertisements that are blatantly deceptive, a gray area, known as *puffing,* exists. Movie producers often publicize their films and publishers sometimes advertise their books by using *puffs* or *trade puffing.* **Puffery** is the practice of making slight exaggerations, which society in general considers harmless. "Most exciting movie ever!" and "Funniest book you'll ever read" are examples. Some critics think they should be banned because they are not provable statements.

Where does puffing stop and lying begin? As in the case of Profile's low-calorie, thinly-sliced bread, the Federal Trade Commission or a judge may make the final decision.

The Right to Choose. The American marketing system, although often the subject of complaints, has generally respected the consumer's desire to have access to a wide variety of goods and services at competitive prices. **The right to choose** includes, however, the notion that the products offered for consideration will be fairly priced and of satisfactory quality.

One consumer right is the right to choose.

Perhaps the major issue in this area concerns **product obsolescence** or the consumer not having the choice to purchase the "old" model. For example, the word processor is making typewriters obsolete. Few people would criticize Raytheon for experimenting with high-frequency millimeter radio waves that eventually may transmit more information and more energy than today's microwaves.[19] Yet, some critics have said it is inappropriate for marketers to strive to make existing products obsolete or out-of-date. This criticism is most often given for **fashion obsolescence** rather than **technological obsolescence.**

The critics' underlying assumption is that consumers' functional needs are more important than social or emotional needs. However, individuals in our culture find "new" styles of apparel, or extra gadgets on appliances, or the latest automobile models more attractive. Although these style changes may not improve the performance of a product, they satisfy a number of psychological or social needs. New products yield the greatest profits. For this reason, marketers plan product obsolescence to help maintain an adequate level of profit and continue corporate survival.

---

[18]Since the advertised item is almost never actually sold, it is referred to as the "nailed down model."

[19]Frederick Rose, "Many Firms Increase Basic Research Outlays After Years of Neglect," *The Wall Street Journal,* December 3, 1981, p. 1.

"In the past 15 years, we've had 4 lawnmowers, 29 garden hoses and one refrigerator. A Frigidaire."

**FRIGIDAIRE
HERE TODAY, HERE TOMORROW.**

Frigidaire *One of the White Consolidated Industries*

Most products are subject to physical obsolescence. Frigidair has a product so durable they poke fun at other products with greater obsolescence.

Planned obsolescence is more controversial than **physical obsolescence.** When a lawn mower breaks down after six years, physical obsolescence occurs. Likewise, batteries do not last forever. Many products, however, are examples of planned obsolescence; they are designed not to last a long time. Although it may sound paradoxical, this is generally an attempt to satisfy consumer needs. For most consumers, purchasing a $100 lawn mower that lasts for six summers is preferable to spending $250 for one that lasts 30 years. Since not everyone has the same needs or values, this is an area of concern to consumers.

Occasionally, the American marketing system has not properly observed the consumer's right to choose. However, when a poor product is offered, or when a product is priced inappropriately high, a competitor will usually take advantage of the situation by offering a better product or lowering prices.

Our free enterprise system does, with rare exception, serve the consumer's right to choose, and serves it well. This right is interrelated to the need for competition. The Interstate Commerce Commission Act, the Sherman Act, the Clayton Act, the Federal Trade Commission Act, the Robinson-Patman Act, the Wheeler-Lea Act, and the Celler amendment to the Clayton Act all protect consumer choice. Each of these acts has been discussed elsewhere in this book.

The Right to Be Heard. Consumers should be assured that their interests and concerns will receive full and sympathetic consideration. **The right to be heard** should hold true even though the huge number of consumers (hundreds of millions) and transactions (hundreds of billions) would make perfect enforcement of that right by government impossible. Our system provides the setting for consumers, acting individually and as groups, to register their feelings. Such opportunities include complaints to sellers, letters to business executives, contact with legislators in government, and banding together into organizations to bring consumer issues to the attention of business and government. The success of individual consumers, professional advocates like Ralph Nader, and various consumer groups in bringing about changes in corporate policies and legislation shows the influence that organized, informed consumers can generate.[20]

Other Rights. Readers may wonder why President Kennedy's pronouncement did not include a "right to a clean environment." The answer, unfortunately and almost unbelievably, is that most people were not concerned with that issue until recently. Most people were ignorant of environmental and conservation issues. The few speakers and writers addressing such points as the danger of DDT or radiation were viewed, by the general population, as alarmists or fanatics.

Business people who think they are being driven crazy by consumerist legislation often

---

[20]R. Moyer and M.D. Hutt, *Macro Marketing: A Social Perspective*, 2nd ed. (New York: John Wiley & Sons, 1978), p. 171.

Who Cares?
We Do... That's Who

Every Skilcraft™ package is checked very carefully. Once in a while a less than perfect product goes out . . . or a part is missing. If there is a problem with your Skilcraft™ purchase, we'd like to correct it. Do not send back the product itself. Send the white card to tell us the problem and we'll take care of it right away.

Product Name _____

(Please do not mail product to us.)

Problem _____

_____

_____

Skilcraft™
Customer Service Department *(end panel of box)*
P.O. Box 705
Racine, Wisconsin 53401

Stock Number _____ Date of Purchase _____

Street Address _____

City _____ State _____

*Please print clearly;
this will be your mailing label.*
1001

Zip _____

A concerned marketer showed its respect for consumer rights.

point out that the four rights did not include the right of consumers to be protected from their own stupidity. Business people feel they should not have to label a toaster "Not for use in shower or tub or swimming pool."

Does Marketing Respect Consumer Rights?

Critics often charge that marketing organizations are not guided by true consumer orientation. A small minority of firms are not. Why a small minority? Because, as the marketing concept suggests, any organization that is not attempting to satisfy consumers is not likely to last long.

Thus, few firms, if any, purposely market products they believe are hazardous when properly used. Blatantly untruthful advertising exists, but it is a small percentage of all advertising. It would be less than true to say that every marketing organization has completely adopted a consumer-oriented marketing philosophy. Nevertheless, firms that tend to survive are not the

EXHIBIT 23-4

Measures Used to Ensure Consumer Protection

Prevention	Restitution	Punishment
Codes of conduct	Affirmative disclosure	Fines and incarceration
Disclosure of information requirements	Corrective advertising	Loss of profits
	Refunds of payments	Class action suits
Substantiation of advertising claims	Limitations on contracts—right to cancel	
	Arbitration	

Source: Based on Dorothy Cohen, "Remedies for Consumer Protection: Prevention, Restitution, or Punishment," *Journal of Marketing*, October 1975, p. 25.

shady, fly-by-night outfits. These organizations are ruined when dissatisfied customers "vote"—with their dollars and their feet—for some competing organization. Most of us have taken at least some satisfaction, and to some degree hurt an organization, by the statement, "I'll never go *there* again!" Our economic system works to en-courage consumer orientation. Organizations that survive over the long run are, virtually by definition, consumer oriented.

Society has means to ensure that organizations are consumer oriented. Exhibit 23-4 lists the preventive, restitutive and punishment measures that may be used.

QUALITY OF LIFE

As the United States, Canada, and other nations became more affluent, the values of their citizens changed. There has been increasing concern with **quality of life.** While that term is difficult to define precisely, it reflects a lessening of concern with being economically well-off and an increasing concern with a sense of well-being.[21]

When this sense is brought to bear on the business community, it translates into a feeling that organizations should be expected to be more than economically efficient. Business organizations are called on to serve customers by being economically efficient *and* preserve the environment *and* conserve natural resources—all at the same time.

Issues of quality of life spring from the idea that citizens have certain rights that no organization can be permitted to violate. Meeting quality of life expectations while fulfilling other missions has caused organizations many problems. Yet, if the demands of consumers, most of whom are interested in both quality of life issues and the demands of the law, are to be met, organizations must address these problems.

Ecology

Within the past 15 or 20 years, there has been a mounting realization that society must be concerned with ecology and protection of the environment. Do organizations, as important members of society, have a responsibility not to tamper with or damage the environment? Satisfaction of the general public, which wants a clean environment, is a major quality of life issue that marketers must understand. This is a complex issue since people want *more* than a clean environment. This fact loads environmental issues with trade-off considerations such as:

■ Marketers of electric power are told that nuclear plants are disruptive to the ecosystem and very dangerous. Yet people want low-priced electricity and do not want to burn "dirty coal," the use of which causes both pollution and disfigurement of the earth through mining.

■ Non-returnable cans and bottles may create litter problems and damage the environment in other ways. But people do not like the bother and expense associated with returnables and often throw them away for "convenience" sake.

■ People want and enjoy convenience in fast-food packaging but complain that too many wrappers cause litter problems.

The fact that marketing has a social responsibility to our environment is obvious. What is not obvious is how that responsibility will be met. It comes down to who will pay—in dollars and inconvenience—for a cleaner environment. Is society willing to pay a higher price for products that reduce pollution? Does society place a higher value on lower-priced automobiles or clean air?

---

[21]A. Campbell, P.E. Converse and W.L. Rogers, *The Quality of American Life* (New York: Russell Sage Foundation, 1976, p. 1.

We're doing something about your privacy

No job we do is more important than protecting your privacy. That's why we safeguard your telephone records and keep your telephone conversations private.

Here are some important points to remember about our commitment to your privacy.

• Southwestern Bell does not wiretap under any circumstances. We will assist authorized law enforcement officials in identifying lines when they place court-ordered wiretaps, but we do *not* place taps.

• Our employees are strictly prohibited from overhearing customer conversations, except when it is essential to the regular performance of their duties. Some repair workers, for instance, must check lines briefly to determine whether testing would interrupt a conversation in progress. Under no circumstances do employees listen for more than a few seconds.

• Billing records are released only upon receipt of proper legal process, subpoena, administrative summons or court order. We keep billing records for six months in accordance with regulatory requirements. Customers may review their own records if they wish.

Guarding your privacy is not just our policy. It's the way we do business every day.

A message from a telephone company.

Recycling

The issue of a cleaner environment can be partially solved by recycling waste products to make "new" products. Such a process can reduce trash and litter and conserve resources. The management of recycling from a marketing perspective has already been discussed in Chapter 12; it can be understood as a reverse in the flow of materials in the channel of distribution. Reusable materials are thus marketed through a backward channel. The consumer who drinks a can of beer can be the marketer of a raw material by recycling the empty can. The recycling process can reduce trash and litter and conserve natural resources. But the trade-off problem arises again. Consumers and organizations must bear the costs and effort of the recycling effort. And, in some cases, recycling has proved to be more expensive than continuing to operate in the old way. That is, the energy used in collecting, transporting, and reusing a can or bottle may make the recycled can more expensive than the new one.

Privacy

Americans are well aware of invasions of their privacy by means ranging from junk mail to telephone sales calls (especially when the caller is a tape-recorded message). The ringing phone or door bell always seems to coincide with dinner or a bath or the climbing of a ladder with a paint can in hand.

While most of these invasions of privacy may be harmless, they are annoying and **privacy issues** are an area that marketers must consider. Many consumers are no longer willing to pay the "cost" of such annoyances. This problem is particularly important to marketing researchers whose in-person, phone, or mail surveys cannot be done without public cooperation.

Public Standards

Matters of law and ethics are frequently decided on the basis of public standards or beliefs as to what is right and proper. More often, they are decided on the basis of what somebody *thinks* are the public standards. Certain advertisements, such as the Brooke Shields commercials for Calvin Klein blue jeans and the Jordache advertisements showing children in provocative poses, caused a stir because they were a challenge to public standards. Compari's advertising utilizes a headline with a double meaning: "Elizabeth Ashley talks about her 'first time'. When Compari says, "The first time is never the best," are they within the general public standards of society?

What do public standards dictate in deciding these marketing questions?

■ Is it socially responsible to name a perfume "Opium"?

■ Should liquor and cigarette advertising be allowed on television?

■ Should nudity be allowed in advertising, or in a brand name such as Nude Beer (sold in Maryland and Tennessee)?

■ Should cable TV companies be permitted to show "dirty movies?"

■ Should sellers of medicinal products be allowed to discuss bodily functions during TV and radio commercials?

■ Why don't the Poli-Grip commercials actually show users of the product putting in their false teeth?

■ Why, on TV, are toilet bowl cleaners only used on clean toilets?

The public's sense of decency is a tricky thing to deal with. Television networks are often accused of offering too much sex and violence. But the groups condemn shows ranging from *Dallas* to *Tom and Jerry*. Other groups condemn the self-proclaimed TV watchdogs saying no one should tell the American people what to do, and "if you don't like it, you don't have to look at it."

Issues of public standards and concerns are philosophical issues marketers must consider. They are not beyond answering. In many cases, one market segment may be offended in order to satisfy the needs of another market segment. One only needs to think of the controversy concerning the marketing of products such as Preparation-H. Clearly, many individuals find mass media advertising of this brand offensive while other segments of the population find the advertising perfectly acceptable. If some product offends you, would it be acceptable to adults in another market segment who find a need for the product?

The Quality of Children's Lives

Marketing to children has always been an area of controversy. It has been argued that advertising aimed at children fosters materialism, amplifies

status inequalities, encourages the consumption of high-sugar, low-nutritional value foods, and induces conflict within families.[22] It has been argued that children are susceptible, and, therefore, special protection should be provided for them. Others argue that children already understand the purpose of commercials and they must learn to be consumers. Marketing helps socialize them into the consumer role. Furthermore, parents—the ultimate arbitrators—have considerable influence on children.

[22]R.J. Adams, J.M. Browning, and M.R. Crask, "Some Attitudinal Correlates of Adult Opposition to Television Advertising Directed at Children," paper presented at the Southern Marketing Association Meeting, 1981.

Food products sold to children, because of their importance to growth and health, are special objects of concern. General Mills advertised Mr. Wonderful's Surprise as "the only cereal with a creamy filling" in a test market. Consumer groups complained that the product, like other sweetened cereals, was not nutritional. The cereal contained 30 percent sugar and 14 percent fat. General Mills argued, however, that their product should be considered as part of the child's total diet, and not as an item isolated "out of context."

Whichever side appeals to you in the cereal controversy, you probably can sympathize with the situation Jerry Della Femina, one of America's most successful and well-known advertising men, found himself in when he made a TV commercial for a toy rifle. It showed kids playing with the toy on a mound of dirt. Permission to run the advertisement was denied because it was decided that some kids might think the mound of dirt was included if you bought the gun. Della Femina's advertisement finally ran with the notation that the mound was *not* included with the toy gun.

Quality of Economic Life: The System's Efficiency

In Chapter 1, we saw that the task of marketing, from a macromarketing perspective, was the delivery of a standard of living. This is marketing's ultimate responsibility. Society expects marketing to be efficient and productive: to be without waste. Marketing's advocates say it is doing a wonderful job. Its critics say it is not. This debate has raged for years. On one side, it is argued that the marketing system in the United States, Canada, and other free markets has delivered a standard of living incomparable to any system in the world. A complex distribution system has developed to satisfy consumer needs. We have it made. On the other side, the marketing system has been criticized for saturating the public with the wrong bundle of goods—products that are frivolous and of little value to their users and to

TWO VIEWS

■ The "purpose of the product is not what the engineer explicitly says it is, but what the consumer implicitly demands that it shall be. Thus the consumer consumes not things, but expected benefits—not cosmetics, but the satisfactions of the allurements they promise; not quarter-inch drills, but quarter-inch holes; . . . not low-cal whipped cream, but self-rewarding indulgence combined with sophisticated convenience.

The significance of these distinctions is anything but trivial. Nobody knows this better, for example, than the creators of automobile ads. It is not the generic virtues that they tout, but more likely the car's capacity to enhance its user's status and his access to female prey.

Whether we are aware of it or not, we in effect expect and demand that advertising create these symbols for us to show us what life might be, to bring the possibilities that we cannot see before our eyes and screen out the stark reality in which we must live. We insist, as Gilbert puts it, that there be added a "touch of artistic verisimilitude to an otherwise bald and unconvincing narrative."

Source: Theodore Levitt, "The Morality (?) of Advertising," *Harvard Business Review,* Vol. 48, July–August, 1970, pp. 84–92. Reprinted with permission of the President and Fellows of Harvard University.

■ What does a man need—really need? A few pounds of food each day, heat and shelter, six feet to lie down in—and some form of working activity that will yield a sense of accomplishment. That's all—in a material sense. And we know it. But we are brainwashed by our economic system until we end up in a tomb beneath a pyramid of time payments, mortgages, preposterous gadgetry, playthings that divert our attention from the sheer idiocy of the charade.

Source: Sterling Hayden, *The Wanderer* (New York: Alfred Knopf, 1963).

society.[23] In other words, some believe that life would be improved without marketing's persuasive forces.

Marketing has been criticized for creating false needs. In particular, advertisers find that they are attacked for creating synthetic wants. One complaint that has been levied for years is that our relatively free marketing system saturates society with proliferations of products that are unnecessary or of little real value to buyers. The idea seems to be that life would be improved by controlling marketing. The point is often made by critics that Americans do not need hundreds of brands of cigarettes, 20 brands of gel toothpaste, 30 brands of detergent each packaged in eight sizes, and yet another "new" shampoo. Such excesses are portrayed as the creation of false needs.

Critics suggest that food, shelter, and clothing are all a human being needs. According to this view, marketing stimulates people to desire nonessential goods.

Yet, our discussions of market segmentation suggest that a wide variety of sizes, models, or brands is in the best interest of consumers. We do not all want red Toyotas just like our neighbors'. Furthermore, once the primary reason for buying a product is satisfied, secondary, possibly psychological, attributes become important.

Summarizing a complex issue, critics believe the emphasis on the marketing and consumption of products sacrifices other values, such as altruism. Marketers believe consumers' true values are being satisfied. Which view should be preferred? The answer lies within your value system, which is influenced by society's norms.

THE ETHICS OF PERSUASION

Another *macro* issue is the use of persuasion in marketing.[24] The most common target of critics is advertising. They argue that it is not right to use marketing skills, psychology, and expensive commercials to persuade consumers to buy a product, vote for a particular candidate, or give to a certain charity. However, most people would grant that *some* advertising is needed or we wouldn't know where to buy a product we want, whether a seller would accept a check, or what freeway exit leads to a motel. Thus the issue becomes one of *informative* versus *persuasive* advertising. Critics of advertising would say that informative advertisements are fine, and persuasive advertisements are wasteful and manipulative. There may be some merit in this argument,

but advertisements for an inferior product are almost certain to sell the product only *once*. Even the richest companies with the best sales records sometimes lose millions of dollars bringing products that fail into the marketplace. In fact, the quickest way to kill a poor product is to promote it aggressively. People will find out about its inferior nature just that much quicker.[25] This view conflicts sharply with H.G. Wells' claim that "Advertising is legalized lying."

The answer to questions about the proper use of persuasiveness will be influenced by your view of whether people are, or should be, able to exercise freedom of choice. Are consumers able to control their own destinies? Do you ever *not* buy products you see advertised? Why? Rethinking our discussions of the hierarchy of needs, selective perception, and other aspects of consumer behavior should help you make a decision on this issue.

[23]William Lazer, *Marketing, Marketing Management: A Systems Perspective* (New York: John Wiley & Sons, 1971), p. 563.

[24]Richard L. Johanneson, "Ethics of Persuasion: Some Perspectives," in Robert L. King, ed., *Marketing in the New Science of Planning* (Chicago, Ill.: American Marketing Association, 1968), pp. 541–546.

[25]David Ogilvy, *Confessions of an Advertising Man* (New York: Dell, 1963), p. 193.

MARKETING AND HIGHER PRICES

Marketing is an easy target for critics who claim its activities—such as advertising, designing packages, etc.—are a waste of time, money, and effort.

One of the charges against advertising is that it drains valuable resources into nonproductive activity. The increased costs of advertising are said to raise prices. This issue cannot be explored in depth here. We will, however, present the marketers' rebuttal of this issue: Advertising is a substitute for personal selling. The costs of advertising to a million individuals is substantially less than the cost of having personal sales representatives visit one million individuals. From this perspective, advertising is cost effective relative to personal selling. Efficiency must be related to alternative means for stimulating demand. In some instances, advertising lowers the cost of products. Here is what the president of Procter & Gamble believes:

Advertising used properly lowers costs to the consumer. This is a point that never seems to be understood adequately. By producing a large volume of sales for standardized items, advertising makes the mass production of such items possible. And mass production brings about savings in manufacturing costs; the high volume it creates also lowers distribution costs per unit.

For the retailer, advertising spurs a more rapid turnover of goods. This makes lower retail profit margins possible, thereby reducing prices for the consumer.[26]

Thus, although Procter & Gamble spends billions on advertising, imagine how much more it would cost to deal with each potential buyer of Tide, Cheer, Gleem, and Ivory soap individually.

It brings products that may be better than the ones now being sold to the consumer's attention. The new product may be less expensive or more efficient than the old one—advertising may have helped lower the consumer's costs. Beyond this, however, is a more powerful con-

cept. Advertising of a product like Tide or Cheer may stimulate demand for that product: It may result in a large volume of sales for a standardized product. This is the basis of mass production, and mass production results in great savings in manufacturing and distribution costs. In spurring a more rapid turnover of goods for wholesalers and retailers, advertising makes for still lower prices at the retail level. Of course, some advertising is wasteful but, believe it or not, advertising—used properly—lowers costs to consumers.

Does Distribution Cost Too Much?

A commonly heard cry is "eliminate the middleman!" Our previous discussions have explored the reasons for specialization in the distribution channel. A middleman may provide storage, selling, or other marketing functions more efficiently than either a manufacturer or a retailer. Eliminating the middleman does *not* eliminate the functions being performed by middlemen. Thus, a manufacturer who eliminates the use of wholesalers will have to perform the wholesaling function itself. This may cost *more* than using independent wholesalers because the wholesalers were better at their job than the manufacturer would or could be.

A critic might also note that some individual aspects of the distribution system are nonessential. Yet it has been shown over and over again that nonessentials such as convenience are important to consumers. The success of 7-Eleven, Quick-Trip, and other similar stores proves that consumers want, and will pay for, convenient location and quick service. The customers decide the trade-offs in this case, paying a little more money to avoid paying with their time. People can quickly and profoundly influence the distribution system simply by where they shop. It is arguable that distribution is the aspect of marketing that is *most* responsive to consumer demands. The high rate of business failure, especially among retailers, is a strong proof that middlemen *must* perform valuable functions if they are to survive.

---

[26]"Morgan's View of Advertising," *Advertising Age*, January 11, 1981, p. 52.

TAKE A STAND #3

With which side do you agree?

"Pointing out to the professional critics that their arguments are generally based on a misunderstanding of advertising seldom discourages further attacks. For fundamentally their quarrel is less with advertising than with the concept of free choice that underlies a free marketplace, the essential environment of advertising.

"The critics regard it as wasteful to have seven brands of bar soap competing for the consumer's favor with large advertising expenditures. I regard it as an opportunity, rare in the world today, for the consumer to learn about and choose exactly the features, color, fragrance, and shape he'd like.

"They see it as frivolous to introduce product features or conveniences that to them seem minor and add to the cost. I see it as offering a choice to those who consider the feature of convenience worth the price. They view as irresponsible the advertising of a product that under certain conditions of use or misuse or excessive use could possibly be dangerous to someone. As long as these conditions are sufficiently well known, I view it as part of the freedom to choose, to assume risk, to lead a free life.

"For these critics, the trouble with advertising is the trouble they perceive with the free marketplace and our whole economic system.

"In this much larger debate, I have heard their arguments and remain unconvinced, along with the vast majority of Americans."

Source: Excerpt used with permission from John O'Toole, "The Trouble with Advertising," as quoted in *Advertising Age*, March 1, 1982, p. m-33.

SUMMARY

This chapter dealt with a very challenging set of topics, including ethics, law, social responsibility, consumer rights, and efficiency in marketing. Providing a meaningful summary statement concerning such matters is as difficult as determining what is "right" and what is "wrong": as difficult, that is, as answering the questions this chapter has raised.

Ultimately, the answers to difficult societal questions must come from the society itself. How can the people decide issues and then voice their decision? They can and will do these things only if they are free to do so. Marketers know that "good" products drive out "bad" products if consumers are free to vote with their dollars. Similarly, in a free market, other problems marketers face are solved by a public free to make decisions. If John Kennedy's right to safety, right to be heard, right to choose, and right to be informed are respected, the free market will tell marketers what is right and what is wrong in their efforts to satisfy society's demands.

THE MOST IMPORTANT CONCEPT IN THIS CHAPTER

Issues of social responsibility in marketing arise because marketing is a social institution operating in a larger society. Failures by marketers to act responsibly can and will be corrected by a free society. Effective marketers must be guided by respect for society and a willingness to follow its suggestions. This is at the heart of the marketing concept—a concept that is, after all, good business.

KEY TERMS

Social responsibility

Ethics

Norms

Value system

Consumerism

The right to safety

The right to be informed

Misleading advertising

Deceptive advertising

Bait and switch

Puffery

The right to choose

Product obsolescence

Fashion obsolescence

Technological obsolescence

Planned obsolescence

Physical obsolescence

The right to be heard

Quality of life

Privacy issues

QUESTIONS FOR DISCUSSION

1 In what areas of marketing are there clear-cut ethical standards?

2 Discuss the relationship that exists among norms, ethical questions, and marketing actions.

3 In your own words, how would you define ethics?

4 Comment on the ethics of the following situations.
(a) A savings and loan utilizes its mortgage records to learn when homeowners' insurance policies expire. They then send a form letter recommending an insurance agency that represents the savings and loan as providing a competitive quotation for homeowner insurance policies.
(b) When 7-Up introduced its "no-caffeine" promotional campaign their advertising implied there was something undesirable about caffeine. Medical evidence concerning this issue is inconclusive. Is this ethical?
(c) A New Orleans brass shop doubles the price of its products. Then it announces a 65 percent off sale. Most of its customers are tourists who will visit the shop only once during a vacation visit. Is this ethical?
(d) In 1982 M&M's changed their regular-size package of M&M's weighing 1.69 ounces, or 4.81 grams, to a package that was marked brightly and indicated "Now even bigger pack," weighing 1.59 ounces, or 4.51 grams. Is this ethical?

5 What are the four basic rights of consumers?

6 Is marketing capable of manipulative persuasion? Discuss this issue by utilizing the example of efforts to persuade drivers to use seat belts.

7 Does distribution cost too much?

8 Is our marketing system efficient?

9 H.G. Wells said, "Advertising is legalized lying." Comment.

10 Identify some deceptive advertising on television. Why are they deceptive?

11 Make an argument for or against the passage of federal legislation requiring that air bags be placed in automobiles. What assumptions have you made about consumer behavior and human nature?

12 Is it ethical to advertise the following:
(a) A brand of cigarettes.
(b) A message to be careful while smoking that is delivered by a woman whose family perished and who was badly disfigured in a fire that started when her husband fell asleep while smoking a cigarette.

CASE 23-1 SCORE*

The Mountain View, California Chamber of Commerce has a special program to help people who are thinking of starting their own business or business persons who are looking for some guidance on how to overcome a knotty problem, such as marketing, inventory control, or pricing services.

SCORE, the Voluntary Service Corps of Retired Business Executives, is a program set up and sponsored by the federal Small Business Administration. Drawing on the talents of local business people who work as SCORE volunteers, the service is a free consulting service.

The basic service offered by SCORE is a free, one-hour confidential counseling session with a member of the SCORE team. After this general session, a person wanting more specific advice—for example, on restaurant management or store inventory—can also meet with one of SCORE's other volunteer specialists in that business.

A typical three-man team heading the Mountain View program might include chairman Jack Arnold, a retired electronics executive; Joe Frught, retired department store executive; and Edmund Backman, retired broker and attorney. These men are also members of REV—Retired Executive Volunteers—an organization of retired executives who have chosen to volunteer their time as unpaid consultants. The Chamber furnishes meeting space at its office.

Often, the would-be entrepreneur needs more direction, or needs to get both feet on the ground and think about the very practical issues of finance. According to SCORE chairman Arnold, "Very often a person may want to start a business and have financing that's nowhere near adequate, and have insufficient assets to secure a bank loan."

Existing businesses often come to SCORE looking for marketing help such as advice on how to determine their costs and set up a good pricing policy.

Questions

1 Why would REV members like Jack Arnold volunteer their time to SCORE?

2 Is SCORE a socially responsible organization? Why?

CASE 23-2 Saving the Harp Seal†

The fate of the harp seal, Canada's most publicized wildlife species, has become the subject of a complex and emotional debate between seal hunters and environmental groups. Since the early 1960s, North American conservationists have campaigned vigorously to abolish the early spring seal hunt in the northwest Atlantic, focusing on the clubbing to death of white-pelted harp seal pups in the Gulf of St. Lawrence but ignoring the hunts among smaller stocks in the White Sea and Greenland Sea.

The issue is not clear-cut, says Professor Lavigne, a zoologist at the University of Guelph, Ontario. But the general public has become confused by the deluge of superficial and often contradictory information furnished by experts and nonexperts to the news media. The amount of public attention focused on the controversy is excessive, considering that the harp seal is not an endangered species and the gross economic value of the sealing industry to Canada (estimated at between $1.5 and $5.5 million annually) is small.

"In reality," Lavigne contends, "multimillion dollar fish stocks off the east coast of Canada appear to be more depleted than the harp seal stock at the present time, but to date no organization has mounted a campaign to save herring or cod stocks from over-exploitation."

---

*Source: Based on materials supplied by J.B. Arnold.
†Source: From "The Perils of Symbolism," *The Wilson Quarterly,* Spring 1979, p. 43. Used with permission.

Why? Because the young, white harp seal pup has a photogenic appeal far superior to that of a cod or herring, the publicity helps generate contributions and support for environmental groups. The "self-perpetuating emotional debate" over the harp seal will serve no lasting purpose, says Lavigne, unless it helps create an informed concern for all over-exploited resources—something that has yet to happen.

Question

Are environmental groups that use the harp seal as a symbol of endangered species ethical marketers?

CASE 23-3 American Tourister

One American tourister advertisement showed a gorilla handling a suitcase made by American Tourister. WAGA-TV in Atlanta decided to test the truthfulness of the commercial.

The station gave Willie B., a 400-pound gorilla in the Atlanta zoo, a suitcase. The results? He proceeded to toss it around for a while, then ripped it to shreds.

An American Tourister spokesman who commented on the test indicated that the "friendly gorilla" advertisements were not intended to suggest that the luggage was "gorilla-proof." The aim was merely to show that 50 years of expertise produces luggage "tough and rugged enough to withstand rigorous use."

Questions

1 Was this commercial good advertising?

2 Is this advertisement deceptive?

CASE 23-4 Terry*

There is no story line running through the commercial. It shows a woman, clad only in a white shift, blonde hair astream behind her, cantering a dapple grey steed bareback along a silvery Andalusian beach. On the soundtrack, a male voice softly utters the words "noble," "invariable," and "with character," and finally, "the Carthusian horses . . . of Terry," as the spot ends with a cut to the gates of a Terry corral.

Before dismissing this advertisement as merely an insanely expensive way to market horseflesh, the puzzled foreigner should bear in mind two things: Terry, besides breeding and selling horses, also is a well-known distiller of brandy; and Radio-Television Espanola recently imposed a 100 percent surcharge on all liquor advertising.

Terry's girl on horseback was in fact introduced two years ago, when she rode for the marketer's brandy. In this latest campaign, though, the brandy is neither pictured nor mentioned. Apparently, the company feels that the pathways connecting the blonde, the horse, and the liquor have been so deeply carved into the Spanish consumer's brain as to make further reiteration unnecessary. What a resourceful way to market brandy, one thinks admiringly.

"But we're not selling brandy," says a spokesman for Terry. "You know, we do breed and sell horses, too. And our horse people say business has really picked up since we began advertising on TV." Though the spokesman insists the horse campaign was planned long before there was any talk of a TV liquor advertisement surcharge, it is a fact that horses figure prominently in Terry's current print advertisements for brandy.

---

*Source: Adapted with permission from Dwight Porter, "Terry Won't Be Saddled by Tas," *Advertising Age*, January 7, 1980, p. 72.

Question

What ethical questions should be resolved about this situation?

APPENDIX

Career Opportunities in Marketing

Marketing is a fascinating field. Students interested in a challenging career will find that marketing offers many opportunities that are hard to equal elsewhere. College students who have studied marketing provide a fresh source of talent for major U.S. corporations as well as smaller organizations. It is the purpose of this appendix to discuss briefly a variety of marketing careers and job opportunities available and to portray some of the excitement of marketing. We discuss these opportunities with two goals in mind. One is to show the variety of such opportunities. The other is to permit you to begin to think about other marketing courses that will help you decide which marketing career most appeals to you. Of course, a thorough portrait of these positions is not possible here. Think of these descriptions as summary statements that may start you on a deeper investigation of selected careers.

THE EXECUTIVE LEVEL

Our first look at a marketing position is one at the top. Consider the profile of a marketing vice-president, on page 683. Notice her career development and the path that she has taken to become successful.

PRODUCT AND BRAND MANAGEMENT

Jane Evans is a marketing executive responsible for several brands. Many corporations have individuals called brand managers or product managers who are responsible for all marketing activity associated with a *single brand,* or a small family of products. Typically, they would report to a vice-president like Ms. Evans.

The *brand manager,* sometimes called the *product manager,* is the marketing strategist who is typically viewed as a middle-level manager acting as the president of a "small company," which is operating within the larger organization. Phillip Morris has a brand manager for Miller Beer and another for Lite; Procter & Gamble has separate brand managers for Tide, Cheer, and Ivory Snow. The brand manager is a middle management coordinator who orchestrates the activities of marketing research, packaging design, production scheduling, distribution and sales activities, and advertising. Assisting the brand manager may be an *assistant brand manager* or a *brand assistant.* To work within a brand group, a manager would require a sound knowledge of marketing management and good human relations skills.

RETAIL MANAGEMENT

Jane Evans spent her first working years in retailing and the marketing skills she learned would have been very transferable to other areas of marketing management. A retailing career should be closely considered by the college-trained marketer for two very good reasons. One is that the number of opportunities in retailing are great. Millions upon millions of people work in the retailing industry. Rejecting a retailing career without careful thought about the supply and demand of jobs may be a mistake. The second reason that a career in retail marketing is attractive is that the opportunities for advancement into management are excellent. As a rule, a hard-working college graduate who is willing to put in the time and effort necessary is virtually guaranteed advancement into such management positions as *buyer, department manager, branch manager,* and *store manager.*

The old image of retailing as somehow staid and routine is no longer valid. Retailing has tripled in size since 1950. Competition has become increasingly vibrant. Failures of large conservative companies like W. T. Grant have shown retail marketers that simply offering merchandise for sale is not enough. Marketing, analyzing, and filling customer needs, is necessary for survival and success.

A career in this field typically involves some sales training and work at the start. Retailing has traditionally had a reputation for low wages but don't let that scare you away. Although salaries of those in management training positions may be less than those found in industrial sales or other fields, the salaries of managers can be quite high. One reason for this pattern seems to lie in the old maxim that "You either love retailing or you hate it." At the sales level, personnel

JANE EVANS—PROFILE OF A MARKETING VICE-PRESIDENT

Jane Evans was cut from a special cloth. It is ironic that the apparel business, a field devoted to adorning the feminine form, can boast of few women who wear the pants. Those who have made it to the top have done so by designing their own fashion lines. Jane Evans made it by design too, but her talent is as a marketer and manager. At 38, she is head of the General Mills Fashion Group, which includes Izod Lacoste, Lark luggage, Ship 'n Shore sportswear, Monet costume jewelry and Foot-Joy shoes. Evans earns more than $200,000 a year and has a hefty perk package including stock options tied to corporate performance.

Even before graduating from Vanderbilt University in 1965, she was recruited by Genesco, where she became assistant buyer for I. Miller, its retail shoe division. Maxey Jarman, Genesco's late eccentric chairman, liked Evans' ideas and moxie and, five years later, at 25, made her I. Miller's president. (During those years she met and married George Sheer, a shoe importer; they have a nine-year-old son, Jonathan.) At 29, she was recruited by the American Can Co. to become president of Butterick Fashion Marketing, the pattern company. After three years she left to rejuvenate Fingerhut, a mail-order retailer based in Minneapolis.

Evans credits her corporate climbs to her enormous energy, sunny disposition and inherent grasp of consumer marketing. She seems to know just what to do to turn an ailing business around. At I. Miller, she changed the dowdy company so it would appeal to younger customers. At Butterick, she redirected the sagging Vogue pattern line to attract working women who wanted elegant styles but simplified patterns.

Besides her other talents, Evans was tapped for the New York-based General Mills job because she is a team player. As she says: "I'm not a lone ranger." During the next year, Evans has her managerial work cut out for her. Responsible for five companies, she plans to strengthen her group's line of athletic wear, increase its accessories business through acquisitions and develop an entirely new clothing division for executive women.

Source: From "Marketing Master," *Money,* April 1983, p. 29. Used with permission.

turnover is admittedly quite high. Many who begin retailing careers find that some characteristics of work in this field (evening hours, weekend work) are not to their liking. Thus many retail employers tend to set low starting salaries but will provide major jumps in pay at regular intervals thereafter.

Increasingly, large retailers are developing "fast-track" programs for well-prepared college graduates, with salaries that are very attractive, even at the start. The men and women who land these spots are trained in many areas of sales and store management. They move from department to department, and from store to store, to quickly broaden their experience. Incidentally, while this pattern is by no means universal, many large retailers prefer to hire management trainees who were raised or went to school in the areas in which their stores are located. Thus, a department store in Omaha may try to recruit in Nebraska and Iowa, not in other areas, because of the likelihood that a person moving from another state may soon become "homesick" and, using the training gained in a well-run program, move to another job closer to home.

Evening hours, weekend work, the end-of-year rush leading up to Christmas, and the need to deal with every kind of consumer make retailing a special kind of marketing career. The ability to deal with the public and to bear with the difficulties associated with that are requisites in this career path. For the college-trained person, a desire to move into management is virtually a necessity since this is, as a rule, how attractive salaries will be earned.

There is the chance that you might want to

practice retail marketing as the owner of your own business. The rate of failure for new stores is quite high, however, and it should be noted that a person without experience and considerable capital backing will face major problems. Retailing's reputation for long hours does not begin to suggest the hours and effort that an independent store owner, or provider of a service to consumers, will have to put in to make a success of such a business. Still, the chance to build something of one's own, and to be one's own boss, is attractive to many. It can hold many financial and personal rewards.

ADVERTISING

President Franklin D. Roosevelt reputedly once said: "If I were starting life over again, I am inclined to think that I would go into the advertising business in preference to almost any other. . . . The general raising of the standards of modern civilization among all groups of people during the past half century would have been impossible without the spreading of the knowledge of higher standards by means of advertising."

Advertising and public relations work has been seen, in recent decades, as glamorous. Many students of marketing are attracted to these related fields in the communications business. But advertising work has many pressure-filled days and nights.

Advertising isn't for everyone. It's a tough, competitive field that demands dedication and hard work. To make it—to succeed—you need more than a degree.

You need a sense of creativity . . . a sense of humor . . . a sense of curiosity . . . a sense of adventure.

You should have an understanding of people and what motivates them . . . an understanding of the marketplace.

You'd better have a lot of enthusiasm and a lot of common sense.

You should be willing to work hard and learn constantly.

You've got to be intelligent. And most important, you've got to be flexible. Advertising isn't a 9 to 5 job, with day-to-day work neatly planned. It changes constantly, and you've got to be able to change with it, to adjust to changing deadlines, new directions.

Think you fit the description? Then welcome to an intriguing, exciting, rewarding career—to a business that's always challenging, never boring—and full of bright, lively, imaginative people, just like you![1]

In most companies, an individual or department is responsible for advertising. However, within a client company the *advertising manager* generally recommends how much to spend on advertising and what the advertising campaign strategy is expected to accomplish. Advertising managers work closely with the advertising agency. Companies generally hire advertising agencies to produce advertising campaigns. There are several jobs associated with work in advertising agencies such as *account executives, copywriters, art directors, media directors, media buyers,* and *marketing research workers.*

If you are interested in a career in an advertising agency don't pack your bags and drive to New York or Chicago just yet. Relatively few people with marketing careers, approximately 100,000 nationwide, are employed in advertising agencies.[2] Many people working in advertising are working in smaller cities and towns doing local or regional ads for a small advertising agency. Many are employed by local newspapers and TV or radio stations composing ads for paint stores and dry cleaners. Others sell advertising broadcast time or space in newspapers or on billboards. The jobs in advertising for large media users such as Procter and Gamble, the Ford Motor Company, and the U.S. Government are relatively few, but if you land one you are bound to have an exciting career.

Few trainees at advertising agencies receive attractive salaries. Like retailing, advertising re-

---

[1] Quoted from J. Walter Thompson, *Career Opportunities,* p. e.

[2] *Occupational Outlook Handbook,* 1982–83 edition, U.S. Department of Labor.

wards newcomers only after they have had a chance to prove themselves. Furthermore, since advertising is an exciting and challenging field, agencies usually have plenty of eager applicants competing for opening-level positions. Some agencies offer summer internships or training periods so that starry-eyed applicants can see the realities of the business before committing themselves to it. In short, advertising is an attractive career choice and can be very lucrative, but it is not what the movies make it out to be.

Jobs at an Advertising Agency[3]

The *account executive* is the agency's representative to the client—part business manager, part marketing consultant, part salesperson.

If you become an account executive, clients will look to you for counsel regarding their marketing problems. Creative people will look to you for product information, market analysis, and a timetable. Agency management will look to you to manage your account profitably.

A good account person is a capable organizer with an orderly business mind who thinks through a program in its entirety, who gets the basic facts, who diagnoses a business opportunity or problem accurately.

You determine relevant facts about the product or service and its competition, markets, distribution, and sales patterns. You study his-

tories of past performance to help plan more intelligently for the future. You then discuss this material with your colleagues—the writer, the art director, the market researcher. You should convey this information clearly so the agency team can analyze the material and agree on a general strategy.

Copywriters write the text of ads, called copy, and scripts for radio and TV ads. They have a way with words, but that is not enough. Copywriters must be able to write *persuasively* so "that the copy will trigger a consumer response." Good copywriting calls for creativity, imagination, and a sense of salesmanship.

Art directors are responsible for the visual appearance of ads, including the arrangement on the page, type style, photographs, and illustrations. Art directors often supervise those who lay out each ad, draw illustrations, and take photographs.

Media directors, media buyers, and their assistants buy space or time for ads in the appropriate media, which are any of the forms of communication used for advertising, including newspapers, magazines, radio, television, and billboards. The media director must not only recommend the most effective media for each client's advertising campaign but also the most effective publications, TV or radio stations, or billboard location. Beginners often start in the media department doing research on the relative effectiveness of various media for each client.

PUBLIC RELATIONS

Students landing positions in public relations are, as are workers in advertising, likely to have training in journalism and communications. However, business training and experience are also important since PR serves as the link between an organization and its various publics.

Some comprehension of such business functions as manufacturing, advertising, finance, and personnel is necessary since the PR specialist may one day have to explain these to various audiences.

Public relations people deal with news media, consumerists, politicians, and customers. They may also be responsible for publishing periodicals, books, and pamphlets for distribution within the organization as well as outside of it.

SALES AND SALES MANAGEMENT

The president of IBM, John R. Opel, began his career at IBM selling. He was so successful in sales that he was called to corporate headquarters to become assistant to Tom Watson, Jr., IBM's president and son of its founder. A job in personal selling is often utilized as a starting point for individuals expected to become corporate marketing managers. The salesperson must learn about the company's products and the company's customers to be effective. Selling is an effective training ground for sales management and other marketing management careers.

Many people associate "sales" with hucksterism or annoying door-to-door work. This is an unfortunate stereotype that does not portray the task of professional selling. There are more job opportunities in personal sales work than in any other area of marketing. Sales personnel may be called *sales representatives, territory managers, account managers,* or have some other title. Furthermore, many organizations, regardless of their long-range plans for entry-level people, expect incoming marketing trainees to at least get their feet wet in sales. This policy is hard to argue with since sales experience gives the newcomer a chance to learn the product line, to deal with customers and get an understanding of customer problems, and to become familiar with company methods and policies.

As the marketing concept has become adopted, the job of sales has become more and more professionalized. Salespeople are now front-line marketers and problem solvers. Most personal selling positions involve facilitating industrial transactions with manufacturers, wholesalers, retailers, governments, or other organizations. College-trained engineers, scientists, and business students are now the norm in sales, whereas years ago this was not the case. Forget the misconception about a fast-talking, used-car salesman and consider a career in sales.

People who enter careers in sales are likely to follow one of two basic career plans. For those who enjoy the day-to-day challenge of working "in the field" and the freedom from a "desk job," selling can be a lifelong career and can be a highly paid occupation that is satisfying to those who enjoy working with people. The second basic career plan is to move into sales management and become a district, regional, even national sales manager. Many individuals at executive levels in business organizations, including presidents and vice-presidents, started as salespeople and followed the sales route to the top. As we portrayed in Chapter 19, careers in sales vary tremendously.

In industrial products sales the industrial salesperson may require training or experience in discussing the technical aspects of the products sold. As a group, industrial salespeople are often expected to have a scientific or engineering background, to have experience in working with the products handled, or to have undergone some detailed training program. This, of course, reflects the type of buyer they are expected to deal with, the buyer who *really* knows what he or she wants in a product.

Since both major selling career paths begin in sales rather than in sales management, prospective salespeople, regardless of their ultimate goals, should be aware of the good points and the bad points associated with selling.

Personal salespeople gain many psychological and monetary rewards that are unavailable to most workers. They can take great pride in knowing their customers and in solving their problems. They are frequently presented with the challenge of meeting new people, of winning new customers, and of introducing new products or of opening up new territories. Many find it rewarding to represent a respected company and to know that that organization trusts them to represent it to the most important people—their customers. Personal salespeople can make excellent salaries, though this depends on their organization's compensation plans and, most importantly, their own efforts. Believe it or not, there are insurance sales representatives who earn more than a million dollars a year. But most important to many salespeople is the freedom they can enjoy and the chance to use their talents in new situations largely removed from the routine of "desk jockeys."

WILLIAM LENNARTZ, PRESIDENT OF COMPUTER POWER SYSTEMS CORPORATION

"Just about everything I've been able to accomplish I owe to my IBM training. I worked for IBM for 4 years after I graduated from the University of Colorado in 1963. I learned the computer business there. Then I saw an opportunity in the computer industry and started my own company. I sold it a few years ago to start my present business of selling power filtering and distribution units to computer users. I do a lot of top-level selling and I feel that it is directly responsible for much of my success."

Bill Lennartz does much more than just sell computer power units. He is on the 1984 Olympic committee responsible for licensing and merchandising relationships. He is also chairman of a group of citizens organized to raise a considerable sum of money to help support the Palos Verdes (California) public school system—a real selling task if there ever was one. In his "spare time," Bill is active in the Young Presidents Organization, which has resulted in his playing a most active and supportive role on the Advisory Council to the Entrepreneur Program at the University of Southern California.

Top-level selling, Bill says,

"Can be very effective or very detrimental to your organization. The fact that the president of the company is involved establishes the seriousness of the company in wanting to establish a relationship; and if the president of the selling company is talking to the president or high-level management of the buying company, then the middle or lower levels of management often react much more positively and quickly. If the president of the selling company is not successful in establishing a good relationship, then normally everything backfires."

Source: F.A. Russel, F.H. Beach, and R.H. Buskirk, *Selling: Principles and Practices* (New York: McGraw-Hill Book Company, 1982), p. 2. Used with permission.

There are, of course, some hardships. The "big money" may be slow coming to newcomers who have yet to learn the ropes, though many companies create remuneration plans that ameliorate this problem. Travel, with frequent nights away from home, is not uncommon and can be a special difficulty for people with family responsibilities. Selling can involve facing prospects who do not choose to buy the product offered and who, occasionally, may be downright hostile. There are many highs and lows associated with making and losing sales.

In all, selling is a career with great rewards, freedoms, and the chance to work for results that are clear for all to see. The sheer number of sales positions available requires any reader of *Marketing* to consider the sales field closely for career opportunities. The variety of sales jobs means the qualifications required to get one of these jobs also varies. They almost all require some human relations skills. For people willing to develop the skills necessary, building on their own aptitudes, selling is the right career choice.

Sales managers perform functions that are numerous and far reaching.[4] Sales management is one of the most responsible and challenging jobs in the whole company since the sales manager is held accountable for sales achievements in one territory, a region, or possibly the nation. The sales manager's task combines supervision and selling; the selling is concentrated on large, key accounts for the organization. The sales manager must be a teacher and motivator, an accountant, and a demand analyst.

Successful sales management usually leads to promotion, again to higher levels of responsibility. The sales manager of yesterday is becoming the marketing manager of today and tomorrow.

[4] Adapted from Oklahoma State University, *Marketing Department, Career Opportunities Guide.*

DISTRIBUTION/TRAFFIC MANAGER

Physical distribution is a major marketing activity. Each common carrier-airline and railroad offers numerous employment opportunities. So do public warehouses. Furthermore, most manufacturers and wholesalers have distribution traffic managers who are responsible for the management of inbound raw materials and component parts. People must manage the transportation of finished goods and the logistical considerations associated with warehousing, handling, and other transit issues concerning distribution. This is the job of the *traffic manager* or *distribution manager*.

Illustrative of careers in physical distribution are opportunities with a large railroad that hires college graduates as trainees for account service jobs. Trainees receive up to two years of training in the physical distribution problems of a particular industry, such as food processing. Once they have completed the training, the account service personnel begin calling on shippers who are current or prospective customers of the railroad. The *account service personnel* attempt to help the shippers solve their physical distribution problems. They seek ways of attaining benefits for shippers such as reduced distribution cost and faster delivery to customers. The aim of the account service personnel is to help shippers and, in the process, to develop goodwill and potential business for the railroad.

Account service personnel are highly paid. Their job duties are interesting and varied. Moreover, they have the opportunity to advance into managerial positions. Their positions are just part of one segment of the employment opportunities available in physical distribution.

MARKETING RESEARCH

Marketing researchers provide information to marketing managers. Marketing researchers provide forecasts and counseling based on information gathered by consumer surveys, analyses of sales trends, test markets, and other marketplace feedback. Marketing research is a growing field. Its importance has increased as the risks and expenses associated with marketing have grown. That's the good news.

Large firms specializing in marketing research are found in New York, Chicago, Los Angeles, and other major cities. But marketing research career opportunities exist outside of these firms. Manufacturers, industrial marketers, retailers, and even non-profit and governmental organizations employ researchers to both gather information and to interpret information gathered by external sources. Virtually each major city has field-interviewing services that conduct surveys. This is a great place to get some real-world experience during a summer or on a part-time basis.

Just as salespeople are stereotyped so are marketing researchers. Market researchers do not all wear glasses and sit in offices surrounded by charts and graphs. Many marketing research tasks do deal with statistical designs, but much of the job includes dealing with clients or internal users, describing alternative ways of gathering information, and explaining findings. The special focus of marketing research is on problem-solving. As such, this field is particularly rewarding for individuals who are inquisitive, analytical, and enjoy finding practical solutions to problems.

EXHIBIT A1

Career Field Course Guide[a]

Marketing Course at Your College or University	Advertising	Sales	Retailing	Distribution Management	Product Management	MBA Degree
Advertising/Promotion	x				x	x
Consumer Behavior	x	x	x		x	x
Channels-of-Distribution Strategy		x	x	x		
Logistics				x		
Marketing Research	x				x	x
Marketing Management and Strategy	x	x	x	x	x	x
Personal Selling	x	x	x			
Product Strategy					x	x
Sales Management		x		x		
Retailing			x			
Retail Management			x	x		

[a] Only five courses are checked for each field you may wish to take.

YOUR SECOND COURSE IN MARKETING

Once you have completed your first course in marketing, you may be interested in exploring individual marketing topics in greater detail. Most colleges and universities offer specialized courses in advertising, retailing, sales management, and other marketing topics. You may have already decided on a career in advertising and just can't wait until next semester to take an advertising class. For many students, this is a good idea. However, postponing a course in your specialty until you become better grounded in marketing's fundamentals may be a good idea.

Some courses, like consumer behavior, will be useful in understanding advertising, personal selling, and most other aspects of marketing. What is best to take will depend on how your university or college structures its marketing curriculum. The best advice might be to talk to your marketing advisor to determine which courses are best for you. Take his or her recommendation! However, the Career Field Course Guide in Exhibit A1 above may be helpful in selecting the electives to discuss with your academic advisor.

GLOSSARY

A

Acceleration Principle A phrase that describes the dramatic effects of derived demand. A small increase in demand at one level in the distribution system may greatly increase the industrial demand at another level of the channel system.

Accessory Equipment A type of industrial good, often more standardized and having a shorter life than installations. Examples: Fork-lifts, pick-up trucks, and calculators.

Accumulating Bulk Buying quantities of the same product from many small producers, then selling the assembled larger quantities to buyers interested in purchasing in sizable quantities. Example: A channel intermediary known as an assembler may buy quantities of apples from many small farms and subsequently sell the accumulated quantity to a food processor.

Acquisition Costs The expenses associated with obtaining inventory.

Administered Vertical Marketing System A type of channel arrangement in which coordination of the marketing activities is achieved through planning and management of a mutually beneficial program.

Advertising Any persuasive message carried by a paid medium for a sponsor of the message.

Advertising Appeal The central theme or idea of an advertisement. That portion of the advertising message that tells the potential buyer what the product offers and why that product should be of interest to the potential buyer.

Advertising Medium The vehicle, instrument, or means used to transmit a commercial message from a sender to a receiver. Examples: radio, television, and newspapers. Plural: Advertising Media.

Advertising Theme The portion of an advertising message that can be recognized as being the same in several different advertisements for the same product. The theme provides continuity among the advertisements.

Agent Intermediary Channel intermediary responsible for bringing buyers and sellers together or otherwise serving to help consummate a transaction. Agents never take title to the goods they deal in, but they sometimes take possession of those goods.

AIDA An acronym for Attention, Interest, Desire, and Action.

Air Freight A mode of transportation that involves the use of airplanes in the shipment of products.

Approach A step in the creative selling process that deals with making an initial contact and establishing rapport with the prospect.

Art From a marketing perspective, all aspects of an advertisement other than its verbal portions.

Aspirational Group A group to which an individual would like to belong.

Assembler A channel intermediary that specializes in accumulating bulk.

Association Advertising Format A type of advertising that concentrates on drawing an analogy or other relationship to convey its message. This creative strategy attempts to transfer the interest or excitement of some event, such as skydiving, to the product.

Assorting Function The creation of assortments of merchandise that would otherwise be unavailable. Example: Wholesalers and retailers buy goods from many suppliers and are thus able to offer wide assortments of goods to their own customers.

Attitude A learned predisposition to respond to a given object or idea in a consistently favorable or unfavorable manner.

Attribution Theory A theory of learning that stresses the importance of relating rewards or punishments received to actions performed.

Auction Company An agent intermediary who provides the service of bringing together buyers and sellers. These firms often assemble merchandise for sale in a central location and sell it by means of a bidding process.

Auxiliary Dimensions of a Product Packages, warranties, repair services, brand names, and sellers' reputations, as well as other features that augment the basic product itself.

B

Backward Channel A type of channel of distribution in which the product flows from the consumer to the producer as in the recycling process.

Bait Pricing A method of attracting customers by offering low-priced items for sale with the intent of selling more expensive goods rather than the advertised goods. This is called Bait and Switch if the low priced goods are not actually available.

Barter The exchange of goods and services without the use of money.

Basing Point Pricing Charging customers prices and shipping fees as if their orders had been shipped from a particular location. The actual place of shipment is not necessarily used to determine the prices and shipping charges.

Belief A cognitive understanding of the existence and characteristics of physical and social phenomena.

Benefit Segmentation A type of market segmentation in which customers are grouped according to the specific benefits they seek from a product.

Black Box A description of the unobservable psychological processes affecting consumer choice and behavior intended to suggest that researchers may observe the factors that influence behavior and the behaviors themselves, but not the internal workings of the consumer's mind.

Boycott The result of a decision not to buy certain domestic or imported products. Examples: The U.S. government might decree a boycott of the products of another country.

Brand A name, term, symbol, sign, design, or a unifying combination of these that identifies and distinguishes one product from a competing product.

Brand Extension A strategy of using well-known brand names or new products in other product lines.

Brand Image The complex interaction of symbols and meanings associated with a brand. Example: The Marlboro cigarette brand image is a masculine, rugged one.

Brand Manager A person within an organization responsible for planning and implementing the marketing programs associated with a single brand of product. Also called *Product Manager.*

Brand Mark Unique symbols that are part of the brand. Example: The five circles used by The International Olympics Committee.

Brand Name The verbal portion of a brand; the part that can be spoken.

Break-even Point The point at which an organization's revenues and costs are equal. Below this point no profit is made and loss occurs. Above this point profit is made.

Brokers Agent intermediaries whose major role is putting buyers and sellers in touch with one another and assisting with contractual arrangements. As agents, these intermediaries do not take title to the goods they deal in, though they may take possession.

Bulk-Breaking Function The sorting activity that consists of buying products in relatively large quantities then selling in smaller quantities. Example: Most wholesalers buy in relatively large quantities from producers then pass on smaller quantities to retailers. Also called *Breaking Bulk.*

Business Analysis Stage The stage in the development of a new product at which detailed analysis of the product occurs in an effort to determine its likely profitability.

Buyer Role played by the individual purchaser of a product. That person need not be the consumer of the product. Also, the title of a department store employee responsible for a department's buying and selling activities. A department manager.

Buyer Behavior The decision processes and purchasing activities associated with the acts of buying and using products. Also called *Consumer Behavior.*

Buyer for Export A company that purchases goods from domestic firms to sell in international markets.

Buying Center An informal, cross-departmental, decision-making unit in which the primary objective is the acquisition, impartation, and processing of relevant purchase-related information.

Buying Function One of the marketing functions performed by channel members. The buying function includes developing an assortment and consummating exchange with sellers.

C

Call Report A listing of the number of sales calls made, sales closed, and other activities of each salesperson over a certain period of time.

Cannibalization The introduction of a new product that appears to have detrimental effects on the sale of other products in the line. Example: A company's new brand of detergent may simply draw away buyers of the company's existing detergent brands.

Cash-and-Carry Wholesaler A limited-function wholesaler who does not provide delivery or credit services. Buyers would expect such a wholesaler to offer lower prices than a wholesaler who does offer delivery or credit.

Cash Discounts A price-discounting method that offers lower prices for timely payment of bills. The purpose of these discounts is to encourage prompt payment of invoices. Example: 2/10 net 30, an arrangement which offers a 2 percent discount if bills are paid within 10 days. The full or net amount is due in 30 days.

Catalog Showroom A self-service retail store that publishes a large catalog identifying products for sale. Customers select merchandise from the catalog and store employees retrieve selected items from storage. These stores are generally associated with discount prices.

Causal Research Research conducted with the specific intent to identify cause-and-effect relationships among variables.

Census A survey of all members of a population.

Chain Store One of a group of two or more stores of a similar type, centrally owned and operated.

Channel Conflict (Vertical Conflict) Refers to a situation in which the goals or behavior of channel members may be at odds with those of other members. Example: The behavior of a retailer may be to buy in small quantities, while the desire of a wholesaler may be to sell in large quantities.

Channel Cooperation The situation in which the marketing objectives and strategies of two or more channel members are harmonious.

Channel Interdependency The relationships between the various members of a channel of distribution.

Channel Leader (Channel Captain) The organization within a channel of distribution that is able to exert its power and influence over other channel members. Usually the activities of channel leaders serve to coordinate channel activities.

Channel of Distribution The complete sequence of marketing organizations involved in bringing a product from the producer to the ultimate consumer or business user. Also called the *Distribution Channel* or the *Trade Channel.*

Channel Power The influence of an intermediary within a channel of distribution.

Choice Criteria Attributes of a product, brand, or seller used by consumers to evaluate and select products or suppliers.

Closing The step in the transactional or sales process during which the salesperson attempts to obtain a commitment to buy from the prospect.

Closing Signals Signs revealed by potential buyers that indicate a readiness to buy.

Closure An element of the process of perception by means of which an individual completes an incomplete stimulus. Example: "Baseball, hot dogs, apple pie, and ? ."

Cluster Sampling An economically efficient sampling technique in which the primary sampling unit is not an individual element of the population but a large cluster of elements.

Coding The stage of the marketing research process at which information gathered is identified and classified by means of a symbol. Example: In a survey, "yes" or "no" responses are commonly coded as 1 and 2 for data-processing purposes.

Cognitive Dissonance A theory to explain the uncertainty and tension felt by individuals who fear, for example, that they have made incorrect decisions, and the behaviors that result from that concern. Example: After purchasing a new car, individuals may seek information confirming that the right choice was made and may avoid information suggesting that the wrong choice was made.

Cognitive Process The range of mental activities involving the interpretation of stimuli and the organization of thoughts and ideas.

Commercialization The stage in the product development process at which the decision is made to produce and market the product and thus to commit resources of all types to that effort.

Commercial Jingles Songs or other short verses having memory value that are used in advertisements.

Commission A payment, usually expressed as a percent of the selling price, made to a salesperson or channel intermediary.

Commission Merchant An agent intermediary given more marketing decision-making power by the sellers who use them than ordinary agents. Example: Commission merchants are often permitted to exercise

Commission with Draw A compensation plan for salespeople that is based on sales performance but provides for regular payments from a drawing account.

their own judgments in pricing the products sold.

Communication The process of exchanging information and of conveying meaning to others.

Communication Goals What the marketer wants the promotional message to accomplish. Some combination of: (1) generate attention, (2) be understood, (3) be believed, and (4) be remembered.

Comparative Advantage The economic concept that states that trade between two parties will benefit both because of the benefits associated with specialization of labor, economies of scale, or particular natural resources. Example: The United States might export agricultural products to Japan in return for Japanese-made electronic equipment, permitting both countries to do what they can do "best."

Comparative Advertising Advertising that directly contrasts one brand of a product with another competing brand.

Competitive Parity Basing marketing and other decisions on the activities of competitors. Example: One way to set a promotional budget is to match the budget of a competitor.

Complete Segmentation A situation in which each customer is treated as a distinct market segment.

Component Parts A type of industrial product that has undergone considerable processing before being incorporated into other goods. Examples: Spark plugs, screws, and wires that are used in the production of a generator.

Concentrated Marketing The development of a marketing mix and the direction of marketing efforts and resources with the intention of focusing fully on a selected market segment.

Conglomerchant A corporation operating a variety of retailing concerns, which may appear to be unrelated, by means of centralized management. The term is the retailing equivalent of the common term "conglomerate."

Consumer Behavior The decision processes and purchasing activities associated with the acts of buying and using products. Also called *Buyer Behavior*.

Consumer Market The market segment consisting of final consumers who will use a product or service to satisfy personal or household needs.

Consumer Product A good or service used by an individual or group to satisfy personal or household needs.

Consumerism A widespread social movement that grew out of the desire to protect individuals from practices that infringe on their rights as consumers.

Consummatory Messages Advertisements that suggest the benefits of some immediate action.

Consumption Patterns A segmentation variable that ranges from nonuse to heavy use of a product.

Continuous Innovation A process by which new products are developed that are characterized by minor alterations or improvements on existing products.

Contract Manufacturing In international marketing, an agreement in which a U.S.-based company agrees to permit an overseas manufacturer to produce and market a product in that country.

Contractual Vertical Marketing System A type of channel arrangement in which channel leadership is assigned through a legal agreement.

Control The management function consisting of (1) investigation, (2) determination that a plan is or is not being executed, and (3) evaluation of that execution in terms of planned performance levels.

Controllable Variables The marketing mix elements of product, price, place, and promotion.

Convenience Goods Relatively inexpensive, regularly purchased consumer products bought without a great deal of thought and with a minimum of shopping effort.

Convenience Sampling The sampling procedure by which the only criteria for selecting the people or items included in a study is ready availability. Example: Customers at a near-by shopping mall may be surveyed.

Conventional Channel A channel of distribution characterized by loosely aligned, relatively autonomous marketing organizations. Example: For many consumer products, the conventional channel of distribution is producer to wholesaler to retailer to consumer.

Cooperative Advertising An agreement by which the supplier and buyer of a product agree to share the cost of advertising that product.

Cooperative Organization A group of independent marketers (retailers) that have combined their financial and other resources in an effort to achieve such goals as lower cost of goods through a centralized wholesale buying center or more effective advertising.

Copy Any words contained within an advertisement.

Corporate Vertical Marketing Systems A type of channel in which one firm owns and operates the successive stages of distribution.

Creative Process The generation and development of ideas, especially of an advertising message or concept.

Creative Selling An adaptive process that tailors sales efforts and product offerings to specific customer needs. Example: A seller of computer systems would devote considerable effort to analyzing customers' needs and sell a computer system appropriate to those needs.

Credit Function A marketing activity performed by channel members. The credit function involves selling goods under any financial arrangement other than cash-and-carry.

Cross-Classification Matrix A marketing grid that helps isolate precise subdivisions within a market. Age groups, racial groups, income groups, and others can be identified using appropriate variables.

Cross Elasticity The relationship between the price elasticity of one product and that of substitutable or complementary products.

Cultural Environment That part of the environment that includes all factors other than elements of the physical environment. Example: Law, science, institutions, and customs are included in the cultural environment, while weather, mineral deposits, and other natural phenomena are not.

Culture Learned patterns of thought and behavior characteristic of a population or society.

Cumulative Quantity Discounts A price discount that grows larger as an increased volume of goods is purchased over a period of time. The intent is to encourage buyers to return to a particular supplier again and again.

Custom Marketing A marketing effort by which the organization seeks to satisfy each customer's unique set of needs. Each customer is, in effect, an individual market segment. Example: A builder of office complexes is likely to find that each developer wants a unique combination of buildings and features.

D

Data Recorded measures of phenomena.

Deceptive Advertising Promotional messages that mislead consumers.

Decider Role played in the buying process by the person who actually makes the final decision rather than simply contributes to the decision.

Decision-Making A cognitive process that combines memory, thinking, information processing, and the making of evaluative judgments.

Decoding The stage within the communication process at which the receiver of a message interprets the meaning of that message.

Delivered Pricing Setting a price that includes payment for delivering the product to the customer. Also called *Freight Allowed Pricing.*

Demand Curve A graphic representation of the relationship between various prices and the amount of product that will be desired at those prices. Also called the *Demand Schedule.*

Demarketing The marketing activity of discouraging demand for a product on either a temporary or permanent basis. This activity is associated with situations in which demand is high but supplies are inadequate to serve that demand.

Demographics The study and description of individuals and groups of people in terms of such variables as sex, race, marital status, and age. Demographic variables are frequently used as bases for market segmentation.

Demography The study of the size, composition, and distribution of human populations.

Demonstration Advertising Format A type of advertising that makes its sales pitch by showing a clear-cut example of how the product can be used to benefit the consumer by either dramatically illustrating product features or by proving some advertised claim.

Department Store A departmentalized retail outlet, often large, offering a wide variety of products and generally providing a full range of customer services.

Derived Demand Demand that occurs because of, or is based on, demand for another product. Example: The demand for industrial products depends on the demand for the consumer products which they are used to produce.

Descriptive Research Research designed to yield a description of the characteristics of a population or phenomenon. Example: Marketing researchers may wish to describe the type of consumer who buys a van rather than a car.

Desk Jobber A wholesaler, generally dealing in bulky products such as lumber, whose function is to handle customer orders and arrange for shipment of merchandise from the producer directly to the customer. These intermediaries take title to the goods they order but do not take possession. Also called a *Drop Shipper.*

Devaluation A government act that decreases the value of the domestic currency relative to that of a foreign currency.

Developed Countries Nations that are most economically advanced.

Developing Countries Nations that are characterized by social change, increasing market activity, specialization of resources, or domestic talent and the growth of selective industries.

Dialectic Theory A proposition formulated by the German philosopher Hegel, which states that the evolution of institutions follows a particular pattern, beginning with a thesis, which is then challenged by an antithesis; the interaction of the two finally yields a new institution—the synthesis.

Differentiated Marketing The marketing effort that involves an organization selecting more than one target market and then developing separate marketing mixes for each one.

Diffusion Process The spread of a new product through society.

Direct-Action Advertising Advertising designed to stimulate immediate buyer action. Example: "Final day of our going-out-of-business sale. This is your last chance."

Direct Exporting The direct sale of products to customers located outside of the domestic market.

Direct Foreign Investment Investing capital in production and marketing operations located in a host foreign country.

Direct-Response Retailers Mail-order specialty goods operations that feature goods not sold in stores. These firms emphasize advertising in the marketing mix to encourage customers to write or call a toll-free phone number to order the products.

Disaggregated Market A market with no groups or aggregates within it. The result is that products must be made to order for each buyer.

Discontinuous Innovation A product so new that no previous product performed an equivalent function. Such a product would require the development of new consumption or usage patterns.

Discount Store A retail outlet selling merchandise at low prices. Typically, low prices are achieved by cutting back on services and "extras" provided to customers.

Distribution Mix The sum total of the organization's methods of ensuring that its products are made available to its customers.

Distributor's Brand A brand name owned by a retailer, wholesaler, or other distributor rather than by a manufacturer. Also called a *Private Brand*. Example: Craftsman and Kenmore are brands that are owned by Sears and are distributor brands.

Diversion-in-Transit The privilege of directing a rail shipment to a specific destination that was not specified at the start of the trip.

Divisibility The quality of a product that provides an opportunity for consumers to try small amounts of a product.

Drive An internal stimulus arising from an unfulfilled motive.

Drop Shipper A wholesaler, generally dealing in bulky products such as lumber, whose function is to handle customer orders and arrange for shipment of merchandise from the producer directly to the customer. These intermediaries take title to the goods they order but do not take possession. Also called a *Desk Jobber.*

Dumping The practice of charging lower prices for products sold in foreign markets. May be illegal.

Dynamically Continuous Innovation A product that is different from previously available products but that does not strikingly change buying and usage patterns.

E

Early Adopter A group of consumers who purchase a particular product soon after it has been introduced. The early adopters enter the market after innovators have purchased the product.

Early Majority A group of consumers in the diffusion process. These shoppers are usually solid, middle-class consumers.

Economic Utility The ability of a good or service to satisfy a user's wants or needs. There are five subtypes of utility: form, place, time, information, and possession. Example: A pizza just coming out of the oven has more economic utility for a hungry person than does a collection of pizza ingredients.

Editing The stage in the marketing research process at which data are checked and readied for coding and analysis. Example: Editing would include discarding improperly filled in questionnaires.

Effective Marketing A consumer-oriented mix of business activities planned and implemented to facilitate the exchange or transfer of products, services, or ideas so that both parties profit in some way.

Eighty-Twenty Principle The term used to describe the phenomenon experienced by many organizations that a relatively small percentage of customers buy a disproportionately large share of the goods sold. Example: 80 percent of the sales may be accounted for by 20 percent of the customers.

Elasticity of Demand A measure of the degree to which a change in the price of a product affects the quantity demanded of that product. Such a measure does much to dictate prices and price competition strategies.

Embargo A governmental restriction that prohibits the importing of particular goods from particular countries.

Emotions A complex reaction of subjectively experienced feelings of attraction or repulsion. Examples: Love, anger, fear, hate.

Encoding The stage in the communication process at which the sender translates the idea to be communicated into words, pictures, gestures, numbers, or some other transmittable form.

Environmental Dynamics The changing

forces external to the organization that affect its behavior.

Ethics Moral principles that guide conduct.

Ethnocentrism The tendency to consider our own culture and way of life as the one most natural and the normal way of doing things.

European Economic Community (EEC) The group of European countries known as the Common Market which have cooperated to reduce the number of restrictions and tariffs on trading activities between the member countries. The EEC includes many of the countries of Western Europe. Membership does change from time to time.

Even Prices The converse of odd prices. While $1.99 would be considered an odd price, $2.00 would be an even price.

Evoked Set The set of products consumers think of when a particular stimulus is encountered.

Exclusive Dealing A situation which a distributor of a product carries only the products of one manufacturer and not those of competing manufacturers.

Exclusive Distribution A form of distribution which a supplier permits its products to be sold by a limited number of dealers. Example: There is seldom more than one or two Cadillac dealers in a community.

Exclusive Territory A geographical area assigned to a retailer, wholesaler, or other dealer, with the understanding that no other distributors will be assigned to operate within that territory.

Execution The coordination and control of the activities of people within an organization to assure that goals are achieved.

Execution Format The style or format by which an advertising message will be delivered. Example: The execution format might be "slice of life" or it may utilize a demonstration.

Experiment An artificial situation in which conditions are controlled to permit the manipulation of variables and the testing of a hypothesis.

Experimentation A research method that, by the manipulation of one variable while others are held constant, allows the determination of causal relationships among variables.

Exploratory Research Initial research steps taken to clarify and define the nature of a perceived problem

Exploration Stage The stage in the development of a new product, involving the search for product ideas consistent with the organization's objectives and mission.

Export Department An organizational unit that is developed to deal directly or indirectly with overseas customers.

Exporting Selling of domestically produced products in overseas markets.

F

Materials A partially processed industrial good that is used to produce and that becomes part of the final product. Example: Sheet metal that becomes part of an automobile's body.

Facilitating Agents Functional specialists who offer a service that aids the flow of goods and services through channels of distribution but who are not included within the channel itself. Examples: Banks and common carriers.

Family Brand A brand used to identify all members of a product line. Examples: Hunt's, Libby's, Minute Maid, Campbell's.

Family Life Cycle A series of stages through which most families pass. Examples: full nest, empty nest, and sole survivor.

Fantasy Advertising Format From a marketing perspective, a special type of the association advertising format that seeks to link the product with the target buyer's wildest dreams and hopes.

Fashion Obsolescence The pattern of products becoming "out of date" because of changes in the preferences for particular styles.

Federal Antitrust Legislation Federal laws that prohibit restraints of trade and monopoly, price fixing, price discrimination, deceptive practice, misrepresentations in the labeling of products, and other acts that tend to lessen competition.

Federal Trade Commission (FTC) An agency of the U.S. government established in 1914 and given broad powers to investigate "unfair methods of competition."

Feedback The communication of an individual's reaction back to the source of the message. The receiver becomes the source of the feedback information and the original sender becomes the receiver of the feedback.

Field Sales Managers District sales managers and regional sales managers directly concerned with salespeople in the field.

Flanker Brands Additions to a product line that are logical extensions within the same product category. Example: Ocean Spray adds Cranapple or Crangrape juice to its line of cranberry juice products.

Flexibility From a personal selling perspective, the ability of a salesperson to situationally adapt a sales presentation.

Focus Group Interview An unstructured and free-flowing discussion of a product or other concept with a small group of people. Example: A group of homemakers might be assembled for a discussion of vacuum cleaners and their comments recorded for later analysis.

Follow-up A step in the creative selling process after the sale is closed at which the salesperson contacts the buyer to make sure everything was handled properly and that the product was received in satisfactory condition. This activity may aid future sales efforts.

Form Utility A type of economic utility that involves the physical nature of particular products. Example: If most consumers add lemon flavoring and sweetener to instant ice tea, the inclusion of these three ingredients in a single product would provide form utility.

Four P's of Marketing Product, price, place, and promotion.

Franchise A contractual agreement between a franchisor, often a manufacturer or wholesaler, and a franchisee, typically an independent retailer.

Freight-Allowed Pricing Setting a price that includes payment for delivering the product to the customer. Also called *Delivered Pricing*.

Freight on Board (FOB) A term that identifies the point at which title passes from seller to buyer. At this point the buyer assumes shipping expenses and all further responsibility. Examples: FOB Pittsburgh, FOB Port of Entry, FOB Buyer's Plant.

Full-Line Pricing The approach to setting prices that recognizes that items in a product line should not be priced individually but should reflect some consideration of the prices of the other items in the line. Example: The price of G.M.'s Buick reflects the position of Buick in G.M.'s product line. Buicks are higher priced than Chevrolets or Pontiacs.

Full-Line Strategy The strategy of offering a large number of product variations to please a wide array of customer needs and wants. Example: Ford tractors are offered in sizes ranging from garden-size to sizes appropriate for major farming work.

Full-Service Merchant Wholesaler Wholesaler that maintains a sales force, offers goods delivery services, extends credit, provides information to customers, and offers other services.

Functional Discounts Reductions in price given to members of the trade for the activities they perform. Also called *Trade Discounts*.

G

Gatekeeper The individual, especially within the industrial buying center, who can control the flow of information to other individuals involved in making a purchase decision. Example: Salespeople may have to deal with a purchasing agent even though other officials make the actual purchase decision. The purchasing agent thus may influence the decision by passing on certain sales information and withholding other information.

General Agreement on Tariffs and Trade (GATT) A series of agreements and understandings intended to encourage international trade that have been reached by a number of trading nations around the world.

General Merchandise Retailer A retailer that carries a wide choice of merchandise, a selection that cuts across generic lines of goods. Example: The old-time general store carries food, hardware, clothing items, electrical supplies, drugstore items, and so on.

General Merchandise Wholesalers Wholesalers that sell a large number of different product types.

Generic Brand (See Generic Products)

Generic Brand Names Brand names that have become so commonly used that they now are part of the language and used to describe a product class rather than a particular manufacturer's product. Kerosene, cellophane, and aspirin all were once brand names but are now legally generic and open to use by any producer.

Generic Demand Demand for a product category without consideration for particular brands. Example: There is a demand for tomato sauce per se. This is generic demand.

Generic Products Products that carry neither a manufacturer's nor a distributor's brand. These goods are plainly packaged with stark black lettering that simply lists the contents.

H

Handling Objections A step in the creative selling process where the salesperson responds to questions or reservations expressed by potential buyers.

Hard Sell Aggressive persuasion that attempts to prove to a reluctant customer that he or she really needs the product offered even though the customer protests that such is not the case.

Holding Costs Costs incurred by an organization as a result of carrying inventory.

Horizontal Cooperative Promotion Promotional programs sponsored by channel members at the same level. Example: Downtown retailers sponsor ads designed to promote shopping downtown.

Hypermarket A huge retail outlet, typically a discount-oriented store, selling a wide variety of goods and performing some functions ordinarily performed by wholesalers.

Hypothesis A proposition that is empirically testable.

I

Image Building The promotional approach intended to generate consumer preference for one brand or product over another because of its symbolic value rather than because of its physical attributes.

Import Quotas Limits set on the amounts of certain types of goods that may be legally imported into a country. Example: Japan sets many import quotas on American agricultural products.

Independent Retailer A retail establishment that is not owned or controlled by any other organization. Example: The local grocery store may be independent, the local Sears certainly is not.

Indirect-Action Advertisement A type of advertising intended to stimulate sales over the longer run rather than to encourage immediate purchase.

Indirect Exporting Selling goods to an intermediary that specializes in selling products in international markets.

Individual Brand A brand assigned to a product within a product line that is not shared by other products in that line. Example: Procter and Gamble's detergent line includes individual brands like Tide, Cheer, Oxydol, and so on.

Industrial Market The market segment consisting of organizations who buy goods for use in the production of other products or for operating the organization.

Industrial Marketing Transaction Any sale to an organization rather than the ultimate consumer.

Industrial Products A broad array of goods and services that are used to produce other products and/or used to operate an organization. Example: Desks bought by the American Cancer Society for office use are industrial products.

Influencer A role played within a decision-making group, particularly the industrial buying center. The influencer supplies information and other inputs that affect the buying decision.

Informal Information System The information that a manager receives from interaction with the environment. This information comes to the manager on an unscheduled basis.

Information Utility A type of economic utility that involves the consumer's knowledge of a product's attributes.

Innovators That group of consumers who are the first to buy a product.

Installations A type of industrial good. A major piece of equipment that is typically expensive and expected to have a long life. Example: A new air conditioning system for a factory.

Institutional Advertising Advertising aimed not at communicating information about a product but intended to build a corporate image, to develop good will, or achieve some other nonproduct specific goal.

Instrumental Messages Advertisements that are intended to have some longer-term effect rather than inducing an immediate action.

Intensive Distribution The form of distribution whereby opportunities for customers to buy are maximized by the placing of the product in as many locations as possible. Example: Cigarettes are sold by most stores, by gas stations, by restaurants, and through vending machines.

International Department An organizational unit that manages the firm's international marketing operations.

International Franchising A form of licensing in which the domestic-based company establishes overseas franchises in much the same way as it does in the domestic country.

International Marketing The development and implementation of marketing strategies that emphasize geographic market segmentation and the distinction between foreign and domestic markets.

Interviewer Bias Intentional or unintentional actions of an interviewer that result in inaccurate responses by subjects. Example: An unpleasant interviewer may have the effect of biasing the responses of the people he talks to in that they respond quickly and inaccurately just to reduce the time required for the interview.

Inventory Control The activities involved in deciding questions of inventory size, placement, and delivery. The overall concern of inventory control is striking a balance between holding limited amounts of inventory so as to lower cost and having sufficient inventory to satisfy customer demand.

J

Jobber A wholesale intermediary in an industrial goods distribution channel.

Joint Decision-Making The discussion of buying choices and decisions among all individuals in a group. Example: Husband and wife may jointly decide on whether or not to build an addition onto their house.

Joint Ownership Venture An arrangement in which the domestic and foreign partners both invest capital and share ownership in a business operation.

Joint Venturing The arrangement between domestic and host companies to set up some production and marketing facilities in overseas markets.

Judgment Sample A nonprobability sampling technique whereby an experienced individual selects sample members based on some judgemental characteristic. Example: An experienced executive may decide that a sample of her five biggest customers will yield the data needed and that there is little payoff in interviewing all of her customers.

L

Label The paper or plastic sticker carrying product information that is affixed to a product.

Laboratory Experiment The manipulation of variables in a highly controlled environment with the goal of determining cause-and-effect relationships.

Laggards The last group of consumers in the adoption process. These consumers wait the longest period of time before trying the product.

Lanham Act A U.S. federal law declaring that brand names cannot be confusingly similar to registered trade marks. Example: A dog food named Pamina Puppy Chow, when Purina Puppy Chow is a registered name, would appear to violate the Lanham Act.

Late Majority A group of consumers in the adoption process. These shoppers are usually older, more conservative, and more traditional than the early majority.

Learning A change in behavior or cognitions brought about as a result of experience.

Less-developed Countries Nations that have progressed economically to the point where some small-scale industry and market activities exist.

Licensing Permission granted from the owner of a brand name or symbol to another organization seeking to use that name or symbol. Example: The owners of the Strawberry Shortcake name and figure license their use to makers of pajamas, lunch boxes, shampoo, and many other products.

Life-style Advertising A type of advertising that combines scenes or sequences of situations intended to reflect a particular target market's life-style.

Likert Scale A measure of attitudes. Given a statement to consider, respondents may then "agree strongly," "agree," "disagree," "disagree strongly," or express "no opinion."

Limited-Line Retailer A retail establishment that stocks only one or a few generic types of products. Often the limited-line retailer carries a good selection of products within the limited number of lines offered. Example: A store selling women's clothing is a limited-line retail store.

Limited-Line Strategy A type of product line strategy that involves offering a small number of product variations.

Limited-Service Wholesalers Wholesalers that offer less than full service. In return for lower prices, customers assume some of the marketing functions.

List Prices The basic price quotes prior to any adjustments. Often, the starting point for subsequent price negotiations.

Logistics The activities concerned with achieving a smoothly controlled flow of goods through an organization and its channels of distribution.

Logo A brand mark written in a distinctive way. Short for "logotype."

Loss Leader A product, typically a familiar and commonly purchased one, sold at a loss in an effort to attract buyers who may purchase other items that are profitable for the seller.

M

Macromarketing The societal view of marketing as the means by which a standard of living is delivered to society. Macromarketing focuses on the contributions and faults of the marketing system rather than on the marketing activities of individual organizations.

Mail-Order Wholesalers These wholesalers usually use a catalog to encourage orders by phone or through the mail. Goods are then delivered by mail.

Majority Fallacy The term used to describe the marketing effort that blindly pursues the largest, richest, or most easily accessible market segments without consideration of other, possibly more profitable segments that competitors might be ignoring.

Management The integration of human and material resources to achieve goals. The three general functions of the management process are planning, execution, and control.

Manufacturer An organization that recognizes a consumer need and produces a service or product that fills that need.

Manufacturer's Agent An independent agent intermediary who represents one manufacturer or a limited number of noncompeting suppliers within a limited geographic area. Agents may take possession of goods but do not take title.

Manufacturer's Brand A brand owned by the maker of the product. Also called a national brand. Example: Folger's, Tide, Charmin, and Coca-Cola are manufacturer's brands.

Manufacturer's Sales Branch A wholesaling establishment owned and maintained by the organization that produces the products sold. A distinguishing characteristic of the sales branch is that it carries an inventory.

Manufacturer's Sales Office A wholesaling establishment owned and maintained by the producer of the goods sold. Unlike the sales branch, the sales office does not carry inventory beyond, perhaps, some samples of merchandise.

Marginal Analysis The widely used attempt to determine the costs and revenues that are associated with the sale of each *additional* unit of a product. It also applies, for example, to attempting to determine the costs and benefits associated with each additional advertising dollar spent, or each new salesperson hired.

Marginal Cost The expense associated with producing one more unit of a good or service.

Marginal Revenue The revenue associated with selling one more unit of a good or service.

Market A market consists of a group of organizations and/or individuals who may want the product offered by the seller *and* who have the requisite purchasing power, the willingness to spend resources to buy the product, and the authority to make such an expenditure.

Market Development The broad marketing strategy of attempting to draw new customers to existing product offerings.

Market Factor A variable determined to be associated with sales that is analyzed in forecasting sales.

Market Factor Index A method utilized to forecast sales in which an association between sales and a number of other variables is analyzed.

Market Penetration The broad marketing strategy aimed at increasing the sales growth of an established product by increasing the product's usage rate in existing markets.

Market Potential The upper limit of industry demand. That is, the expected sales volume for *all* brands of a particular product.

Market Segmentation The identification within a larger market of any number of smaller, more homogeneous submarkets. Bases for segmentation might include geography, demographic or socioeconomic variables, psychographic variables, patterns of behavior, consumption patterns, consumer predispositions, and other relevant factors.

Market Segments Portions of a larger market identified and distinguished in termed of one or more characteristic variables.

Market Share The proportion of sales of a given product accounted for by a particular brand. That is, sales of one brand divided by total industry product sales. Also called share of market.

Marketing The activities involved in developing product, price, distribution, and promotional mixes that meet and satisfy the needs of customers. See "Effective Marketing."

Marketing Audit The careful analysis and evaluation of an organization's marketing resources, strengths, and weaknesses in light of opportunities and constraints presented by that organization's environment.

Marketing Concept The philosophy of management that stresses three basic elements: consumer orientation, emphasis on long-range profitability, and the integration of marketing and other organizational functions.

Marketing Dynamics The activities and changes that occur within an organization's marketing mix.

Marketing Information System (MIS) A continuing and interacting structure of people, equipment, and procedures designed to gather, sort, analyze, evaluate, and distribute pertinent, timely, and accurate information for use by marketing decision makers to improve their marketing planning, execution, and control.

Marketing Intelligence System The set of sources and procedures by which marketing executives obtain their everyday information about developments in the external environments of marketing. It is concerned with knowledge about competitors' activities, new market opportunities and developments, and related information. Example: A marketing manager may discover an important bit of marketing information while reading the morning paper. This is marketing intelligence, rather than marketing research, a more formal process.

Marketing Management A special application of general management techniques to the firm's marketing operations.

Marketing Mix The specific combination of interrelated and interdependent marketing activities engaged in by an organization. The basic elements of the marketing mix are the "4 P's" of product, price, place, and promotion. These elements are also referred to as marketing's controllable variables.

Marketing Myopia The failure of a firm to define its purpose on the basis of a consumer orientation.

Marketing Opportunity Analysis The diagnostic activity of interpreting the external environment of the organization. This includes the evaluation of organizational goals in terms of the environment.

Marketing Planning The design of marketing programs expected to be implemented in the future.

Marketing Research The systematic and objective process of gathering, recording, and analyzing data for marketing decision making.

Marketing Strategy Marketing strategy includes the identification and evaluation of opportunities, analysis of market segments, selection of a target market or of target markets, and planning an appropriate marketing mix.

Markup on Cost The amount of money a marketer has added to the cost of a good in order to arrive at a selling price, divided by the cost of the good.

Markup on Selling Price The amount of money a marketer has added to the cost of a good in order to arrive at the selling price, divided by the selling price of the good.

Materials Handling The use of muscle power, machinery, or other methods to identify, check, load, and unload goods.

Materials Management The distribution process that entails getting production materials to the factory or to other points of production and transporting semifinished goods within the manufacturing facility.

Meaningful Market Segments Market segments that can be distinguished from the overall market, are of significant size, are accessible, and are likely to respond favorably to the firm's marketing mix.

Media Selection Strategy Determining which media are most appropriate for a particular advertisement. Includes consideration of the message to be transmitted, the intended audience, the advertising objective, and budget.

Membership Group A group that an individual belongs to due to choice or chance.

Merchant Intermediary Any channel member other than the producer or final user of a product who performs marketing activities and who takes title to the product.

Merchant Wholesaler An independent middleman who sells merchandise and who may offer a variety of services to retailers or other nonconsumer buyers. The merchant wholesaler takes title to the goods that are offered for sale.

Missionary Sales Personnel Salespersons who perform the function of visiting prospective customers, distributing information to them, and handling questions and complaints. In this, the missionary performs more of a customer relations task than a selling task and rarely takes an order.

Modified Rebuy The buying situation that occurs when an industrial buyer is unhappy with current suppliers or their products and is "shopping around" rather than returning to regular suppliers.

Monopolistic Competition A type of competitive market structure where there are a large number of sellers and where some product differentiation exists.

Monopoly A type of competitive market structure where there is only one producer firm.

Montage Advertising Format A type of advertising that blends a number of situations, demonstrations, and other visual effects into one commercial.

Motivation An internal psychological drive state that causes the initiation of a behavior.

Motor Carrier A mode of transportation. Usually considered to be the trucking industry, but Greyhound's package service would also be classified as a motor carrier.

Multinational Marketing The marketing of products across national boundaries.

Multiple Channels The use of more than one channel of distribution by a manufacturer.

Multiple Channel Strategy A plan that determines how to distribute products through various channels.

Multiple Market Segmentation Choosing more than one target market segment and preparing a marketing mix for each.

N

National Brand A brand name that is actually owned by the manufacturer of a branded product and distributed by that manufacturer. Also called a manufacturer's brand. Examples: Texaco, Alpo, and Ultra Brite.

Need An innate desire that is basic to human beings. Example: The need for food and liquids.

New Product Any recently introduced product that offers some benefit that other product offerings do not offer.

New Task Buy An industrial buying situation in which the purchaser is seeking to fill a need never before addressed. Uncertainty and lack of information about products and suppliers characterize this situation.

Noise In communication theory, any interference or distraction that disrupts the communication process in any way.

Nonadopters The group of consumers who never buy the product under consideration.

Noncumulative Quantity Discount A price discount determined by the size of an individual purchase order. The larger the individual order the larger the discount on that order. The purpose of this discount is to encourage large order sizes.

Nonprice Competition Competition among firms where marketing variables other than price are emphasized.

Nonprobability Sample A type of sampling procedure where the units are selected on the basis of convenience or personal judgment.

Norm Rule of conduct to be followed in particular circumstances. Example: In some countries, bribes must be given to public officials in order that licenses can be obtained. In other countries, the giving and taking bribes is considered immoral.

O

Objection An honest reason for avoiding a purchase. Professional salespeople view the voicing of an objection as an opportunity to overcome that objection with additional information.

Observation The systematic noting and recording of verbal and nonverbal behaviors and communications by means of human or mechanical recorders of information.

Odd Prices A price that is a few cents less than the nearest round dollar price. The intent of the odd price is to psychologically "lower" the price of the item. Example: $1.98 rather than a flat $2.

Oligopoly A type of competitive market structure where the industry is controlled by a few large companies.

One-Price Policy The practice of charging a single price for a product regardless of the circumstances surrounding the sale, the quantity bought, or any other unique aspect of the exchange. The opposite of a variable price policy.

Operating Supplies A type of industrial good characterized by low price, standardized design, little brand loyalty, and frequent purchase. Examples: Paper clips, envelopes, sweeping compounds, and brooms.

Operational Planning A type of marketing planning that focuses on day-to-day functional activities.

Opinion Leaders Individuals in a group who, because of some quality or characteristic, are respected by other group members who are likely to follow their lead in particular matters.

Order Getters Salespeople who are primarily responsible for developing business for the firm. Order getters must seek out customers and creatively close sales.

Order Processing A systematic procedure followed to fill customer orders after these have been received by the sales office. The process begins when orders are received by the sales office and ends when merchandise has been shipped and bills sent to the customer.

Order Takers Salespeople who are primarily responsible for writing up orders, checking invoices, and assuring timely order process-

ing. Order takers usually do not spend much time prospecting for potential buyers.

Organizational Product A product used to satisfy the needs of a business or other organization. Also called an industrial product. Examples: Raw materials, office supplies, and fabricating materials bought by a profit or nonprofit organization.

Out-of-Stock Losses Losses of sales or customers that occur when a buyer demands a product that a supplier cannot provide in a timely manner due to lack of inventory.

Ownership Group An organization consisting of a number of stores, each with its own name and identity, which are in fact operated by a central owner. Example: The May Company and Allied Department Stores own and operate a wide range of department stores, each of which maintains its own local identity.

P

Package The outer wrapping surrounding a product, the main purposes of which are to protect the product, to identify the product, and, in the case of many goods, to promote the product and facilitate its use and handling.

Penetration Price A price that is set at a low level so that a product might quickly establish itself in the market. Most often employed when a new product faces an established competitive market.

Perceived Risk Consumers' perception that an action, particularly a purchase, might product consequences that are undesirable.

Percentage-of-Sales Method A procedure of determining a promotional budget. A simple percentage of company sales is used to compute the amount of the promotional budget. This method is said to be the most widely used promotional budgeting method because of its simplicity.

Perception The process of interpreting sensations and giving order and meaning to stimuli. In simpler terms, how we interpret the world around us.

Performance Monitoring Research Descriptive research that is continuously performed to provide feedback that enables the marketer to evaluate and monitor marketing programs.

Personal Selling Person-to-person dealings between a buyer and a seller where the purpose of the interaction is persuasion.

Personality The underlying disposition or dominant characteristics of individuals.

Physical Distribution That area of marketing concerned with physically moving products from the point of production to the place of consumption or other use.

Physical Distribution Concept An approach to handling problems of physical distribution that stresses that the PD system be designed and operated in such a way that *total* cost be minimized rather than the individual costs incurred in the process. Example: The *total* cost of distribution may be reduced even when a relatively expensive means of transportation is selected for use.

Physical Distribution Functions Includes bulk breaking, accumulating bulk, assorting, transporting, and storing.

Physical Distribution Management The broad range of activities concerned with the efficient movement of finished products from the point of production to the buyer. The design and administration of systems to control that process.

Physical Environment That part of the environment that consists of natural resources and the human population. Examples: Weather patterns, climate, mineral deposits, and so on.

Physical Obsolescence The breakdown of a product due to wear and tear.

Physiological Needs Aroused internal drives stemming from biological mechanisms.

Piggyback Service The use of flatcars to carry loaded truck trailers by rail.

Pioneering Advertising Advertising aimed at generating generic demand for a product, typically during the introduction stage of the product's life cycle. Also called primary demand advertising.

Pipelines A mode of transportation that involves the movement of products through pipes. Natural gas and crude petroleum are typically transported through pipelines.

Place (Distribution) One of the 4 P's of the marketing mix, this variable is concerned with the determination of how products may be delivered to the buyer, how quickly they should be moved, and any other aspects of distribution strategy.

Place Utility A type of economic utility that involves the geographic availability of goods.

Planned Obsolescence The practice of consciously attempting to make existing products out of date by frequently introducing new products at planned intervals of time.

Planning Horizon The length of time for which a particular plan applies.

Population In statistics, any complete group of entities sharing some common set of characteristics.

Possession Utility A type of economic utility that involves the completion of a desired exchange and the physical possession of the product by customers.

Positioning The technique, promotion by which a brand or product is portrayed to consumers as occupying a unique spot relative to its competition. Example: Nyquil is positioned as "*the* night-time medicine for colds."

Posttesting Research Research conducted after an advertisement has been used for a period of time to determine if its objectives are being met.

Prestige Assigned value judgments about a status or role. Example: Society has assigned more prestige to the occupation of the brain surgeon than to that of the manicurist.

Pretesting Research Research done in the earliest stages of the development of an advertisement that continues until the ad is ready for use.

Price A statement of value, usually in money terms, which can be used to relate the relative value of goods and services. Since price is an expression of a value exchanged, it can be expressed in time, votes, or other non-money terms. The purpose of price in the economy is to help allocate goods and services to various members of society.

Price Competition When competing products are not distinctive, the firms within the industry may emphasize lower prices in attempts to gain strategic advantage.

Price Inelasticity Price inelasticity of demand exists if the quantity of a product that is demanded does not change significantly when the price of that product changes. Example: A person needing a single dose of medicine per day to maintain health will buy only one dose per day even when the price goes up and will buy no more if the price declines.

Price Lining The setting of prices by a seller in accordance with certain "price points" believed to be attractive to buyers. Example: A retailer of men's suits may sell all suits at one of three or four "price points" such as $300, $250, $200, and $150.

Price Mix All elements of the price variable of an organization's marketing mix including the prices themselves, and any discounts, rebates, or other variations on prices.

Price Stabilization A pricing strategy of matching the competitor's price.

Pricing Objective The desired result associated with a particular pricing policy. The pricing objective must be consistent with the organization's other marketing objectives.

Primary Characteristics of a Product The basic features and aspects of a product. Example: Among the primary characteristics of the Rolls Royce are its prestige, its workmanship, its appearance, and its high price.

Primary Data Information gathered by researchers for a study in which they are involved. Original data rather than data generated by previous research.

Primary Demand Demand for a product class without consideration for brand. Example: Demand for gasoline rather than demand for Texaco. Also called generic demand.

Primary Demand Advertising A type of advertising that explains what a product is and how it works, and stimulates demand for the product category without concern for the different brands. Also called Pioneering Advertising.

Primary Group A relatively small group, such as one's family or close friends, where contact and influence endures over time. Also called an intimate group.

Privacy Issues The potential annoyances caused by marketers who make contacts with consumers.

Probability Sample A sample in which every member of the population has a known, nonzero probability of selection.

Problem Awareness The realization, as a result of stimuli, that a need is not completely satisfied. Example: The smell of food may make an individual aware of a feeling of hunger.

Problem Definition The first stage in the marketing research process.

Process Materials An industrial product used in the production of other products but that does not become part of that other product. Example: a chemical used to clean the fender of an automobile before it is painted.

Product A good or service, tangible or intangible, which an organization offers to its customers.

Product Advertising A promotional effort aimed at encouraging purchase of a particular product or service in the expectation that buyer action will follow. Example: "Sears is having a sale on home freezers this month only."

Product Categories Subsets of product types within product classes. Example: Light, heavy, and extra-light categories within the product class of beer.

Product Concept The marketing strategist's selection and blending of a product's primary characteristics and auxiliary dimensions into a basic idea emphasizing a particular set of consumer benefits.

Product Development The marketing functions associated with the generation of new products and their introduction to the marketplace.

Product Differentiation The marketing strategy of calling the attention of buyers to those aspects of a product that set it apart from its competitors.

Product Differentiation Campaign An approach to promotion which emphasizes some dimension of a product or the unique solution to a buyer problem that a product offers.

Product Diversification The strategy of marketing new products to new sets of customers. Example: A food producer may seek to grow by diversifying into paper products.

Product Life Cycle (PLC) A marketing management tool providing a graphic description of a product's sales history. The PLC is often depicted as having four stages: introduction, growth, maturity, and decline.

Product Line Within a firm's assortment, any group of products that are fairly closely related.

Product Manager A person within an organization responsible for planning and implementing the marketing programs associated with a single brand of product. Example: Procter & Gamble assigns a product manager to handle Cheer, another to handle Oxydol, and so on.

Product Mix The total product offering of a marketing firm. All products, regardless of type, are included in the product mix.

Product Obsolescence A condition that occurs when existing products become out of date due to the introduction of new products.

Product Portfolio Concept A marketing management tool that focuses on the interrelationships of different types of products within a product mix. As with a stocks and bonds portfolio, the emphasis is on the performance of the mix of products rather than on the performance of individual products. Typical product portfolio illustrations clas-

sify products into four quadrants based on high/low market share and high/low growth potential.

Product Strategy Planning and developing the mix of primary and auxiliary dimensions of a product's attributes.

Product Warranty A written guarantee of a product's integrity and the manufacturer's responsibility for repairing or replacing defective parts.

Production Era A period of time in business history when companies were oriented toward the production function.

Promotion The marketing communication process utilizing personal or nonpersonal means to remind, educate, inform, and persuade buyers or potential buyers of the organization's product. One of the 4 P's of the marketing mix.

Promotion Mix The totality of an organization's promotional effort, including advertising, personal selling, sales promotion, and publicity.

Promotion Strategy The overriding communication plan carried out by means of an organization's promotion mix.

Promotional Campaign A series of promotional activities aimed at achieving a specific objective.

Prospecting The activity of identifying likely customers from lists of previous buyers, referrals, government documents, and other sources.

Protection in Transit A function provided by packaging that reduces damage during delivery and storage prior to a product's use by final consumers.

Psychographics A basis for market segmentation stressing consumer ''life-style'' characteristics and buying patterns in pursuit of life goals.

Psychological Need A need resulting from the interaction of humans with their social environment.

Puffery The practice of making slight exaggerations in advertisements that society in general considers harmless.

Pull Strategy A marketing strategy that utilizes promotion to stimulate ultimate consumers or buyers to demand a product thereby "pulling" that product through the channel of distribution.

Purchase Satisfaction The feeling that the decision to buy was appropriate, which may occur after the product has been purchased.

Pure Competition A type of competitive market structure where there are no barriers to competition and price cannot be controlled by individual buyers or sellers.

Push Strategy A marketing strategy whereby a supplier promotes a product to other channel members rather than to the ultimate buyers of the product. Example: Some manufacturers of house paint promote heavily to retailers of paints, leaving the retailers to promote the product to consumers.

Q

Qualifying the Prospect A step in the creative selling process where the prospect's potential for buying is evaluated by the salesperson.

Quality Creep A phenomenon that can occur in the development of a product when planners succumb to the temptation to make the product better and better until ultimately the product may no longer fit the needs of the target market.

Quality of Life The sense of well-being perceived by citizens of a society.

Quota Bonus Plan A compensation plan for salespeople where a base salary is paid for sales activities. If sales exceed a certain amount (the quota), additional compensation (the bonus) is awarded.

Quota Sample A nonprobability sampling procedure that ensures representation of a portion of the population deemed to be important by the researchers.

R

Rack Jobber A type of limited-function merchant wholesaler who contracts with a retailer to place display racks in a store and to stock those racks with merchandise. The retailer typically receives an attractive commission for selling the merchandise.

Railroads A mode of transportation that involves the use of trains to ship products by rail.

Rating Scales A measurement device used in questionnaires to determine consumer attitudes. Examples: Likert Scale, Semantic Differential.

Raw Materials Those industrial products that are in an essentially unprocessed state and are used to produce other products. Example: Ingots of iron bought by producers of pipes and other metal products.

Reach The number of people exposed to an advertisement carried by a given medium.

Recall Tests Research done to determine the extent to which people can remember having seen particular ads.

Reference Groups Groups of people who influence the behavior of an individual because that individual aspires to be like the members of the groups. An individual may be a member of the groups or may be trying to become a member. In either case, the approval of the groups is being sought.

Reinforcement A reward or payoff that strengthens the stimulus-response process. Example: A consumer who is pleased with the way a product performed is likely to buy that product again.

Related Recall The ability of viewers of an advertisement to remember and repeat specific messages contained in the advertisement.

Relative Advantage Clear-cut benefits over other existing, competitive offerings.

Research Design The master plan specifying the methods and procedures for collecting and analyzing needed information.

Response An action induced by a stimulus. Example: The words "Watch out!" may cause a person to duck (Response).

Retail Sales Forces Salespeople working in a retail environment.

Retailer An individual or organization that sells products to ultimate consumers.

Retailing All activities concerned with the

sale of products to buyers who are the ultimate users of those products.

Return on Investment (ROI) The ratio of profits to assets (or net worth) for an organizational segment, company, or brand.

Return on Investment Price A price that has been set so that a desired return on investment is earned if the product is sold at that price.

Reverse Distribution The "backward channel of distribution." The flow of goods from consumer to producer. Recycling.

Right to Be Heard The interests and concerns of consumers should receive full consideration from marketers.

Right to Be Informed Consumers' right to obtain the information that is required to make an intelligent choice from among the products that are available.

Right to Choose There should be a variety of goods available so that consumers can select products that best meet particular needs.

Right to Safety Consumers have the right to expect the products they purchase to be free from unnecessary dangers.

Risk-taking Function A marketing function performed by channel members. Risk taking involves acting when the future is uncertain.

Robinson-Patman Act The U.S. federal law passed in 1936 that was intended to halt discriminatory pricing policies by specifying certain limited conditions under which a seller may sell to different buyers at different prices.

Role Appropriate cluster of behavior patterns associated with a position in a social setting. Examples: Sons, daughters, teachers, and doctors all have expected roles to perform.

S

Salary Plus Commission A compensation plan for salespeople that consists of a regular salary plus a payment for sales achieved.

Sales Correspondent A sales employee, at company headquarters or at a branch office, who answers queries concerning delivery schedules, service, installation, and so on.

Sales Era A period of time in business history when companies were oriented toward the sales function.

Sales Forecast Estimated sales volume for an organization or unit of an organization for a given future time period.

Sales Forecasting The process of predicting sales totals for specific future time periods. Accurate forecasting assists in the planning of all other marketing activities.

Sales Management The marketing management activity that deals with planning, direction, and control of the sales force or personal selling effort.

Sales Manager A marketing manager specifically responsible for recruiting, organizing, supervising, motivating, and evaluating a sales force.

Sales Objectives The sales volume or other sales tasks that are set as goals for the organization.

Sales Potential The maximum share of market a single organization can expect to receive during some future time period. Example: There will be millions of cars sold in the United States next year. The number that Ford can expect to sell is Ford's sales potential.

Sales Presentation The salesperson's attempt to communicate persuasively the product's benefits and to explain appropriate courses of action to the potential buyer.

Sales Promotion Those promotional activities, other than advertising, personal selling, and publicity, that stimulate consumer purchases and dealer effectiveness. Typically, a temporary offer of a reward to customers or dealers is made. Examples: Sales contests, sales meetings in desirable locations, and contests for consumers.

Sales Quota A level of sales volume to be achieved by a salesperson during a specific time period. Often a bonus of some sort is paid to salespeople who exceed that level.

Sales Team Members of the organization that assist the salesperson in the selling process.

Sales Territory The geographic area and/or specific accounts assigned to a sales person.

Sample A portion, subset, or part of a larger population.

Sampling Error The difference between the results of a study of a sample of a population and the results that would have been yielded by examining all members of the population (a census). That is, information gathered by examining a sample may not be "perfect" *because* a sample was used.

Science The accumulation of knowledge about humankind and its environment.

Scientific Observation The systematic recording of behavior, objects, or events as they are witnessed.

Scrambled Merchandising The offering for sale of products by a seller not traditionally associated with those products. Example: Drug stores selling electrical supplies, school supplies, and a selection of food products.

Screening Stage The stage in the development of new products involving analysis and evaluation of ideas to determine their reasonableness and appropriateness in light of organizational goals and objectives.

Seasonal Discount A reduction in price intended to encourage purchase of products during an inappropriate time of the year. Example: Resort hotels in Florida offer cheaper rates in summer than in winter.

Secondary Data Information that has been previously gathered for some reason other than the project at hand. Example: Government census data used by sales forecasters to estimate future demand for gasoline.

Secondary Group A group of people that influence the behavior of an individual but not as strongly as do that individual's primary or intimate groups. Example: One's family might be a primary group, one's classmates a secondary group.

Selective Demand Demand for a specific brand of product rather than for an entire product class.

Selective Distribution A strategy that restricts the sale of a product to a limited number of outlets.

Selective Perception The human tendency to screen out certain stimuli and to interpret other stimuli in light of personal backgrounds. Example: A voter who always votes Democratic is likely to ignore information about Republican candidates or interpret that information in a negative way.

Self-concept The individual's perception and appraisal of himself or herself.

Selling Agent An agent intermediary representing one or more producers of products on a commission basis and selling the producers' entire output of products. Much the same as a manufacturer's agent but not limited to a specific geographic area.

Selling Function One of the marketing functions performed by channel members. The selling function includes activities associated with providing a sales force or other promotional efforts.

Semantic Differential An attitude measurement scale consisting of a number of points arrayed between bipolar words or phrases permitting a respondent to indicate his or her perception of a product, store, or other concept being investigated. Example: A store might be described as
FRIENDLY — — — — — UNFRIENDLY.

Service Function Activities performed by channel members that increase the efficiency and effectiveness of the exchange process.

Service Mark Provides identification for services. While trademarks are used for products, service marks are employed to make particular services distinct. Examples: The NBC chimes, G.M.'s Mr. Goodwrench.

Services A category of industrial goods. Services represent activities performed on a contract basis by individuals not employed by the purchasing organization. Examples: Cleaning services, legal services, typewriter repair, etc.

Share of Market The amount of sales of a given product accounted for by a particular brand. That is, sales of one brand divided by total industry product sales. Also called Market Share.

Shopping Good A type of consumer good for which brand preference may be strong, for which consumers feel the need to make comparisons among products, and which are not bought on an everyday basis.

Simple Random Sample A sampling procedure that assures that each element in a population has an equal chance of being included in the sample chosen.

Single Product Strategy A type of product line strategy where only one product or only one product with very few model options is offered.

Skimming Price A relatively high price intended to "skim the cream" off the market. Typically such a price is charged at the start of a product's life cycle and assumes that demand for the product is strong enough to support such a price level.

Slice-of-Life Format A type of advertising that dramatizes a "typical" setting wherein people use the product.

Social Class A group of people who share similar levels of wealth, prestige, and power, and a set of related beliefs, attitudes, and values.

Social Needs Aroused internal drives stemming from interaction with the social environment.

Social Responsibility The ethical consequences of how an individual's or an organization's marketing activity might affect the interest of others.

Social Value A shared concept of what is seen as preferred behavior. Example: In ancient Sparta it was held that stealing was permissible as long as the thief was not caught.

Socialization Process The process by which society transmits its cultural values and norms to its members.

Socioeconomic Variables The broad range of factors that affect and prescribe an individual's or group's social position and economic standing within a larger community. These variables are frequently employed as a basis for marketing segmentation.

Sociology The field of learning that investigates human behavior through the study of social institutions and their interrelationships.

Soft Sell A promotional strategy that represents the converse of the hard sell. The soft sell is less blatant and less conspicuous than the hard sell.

Specialty Goods Consumer products that are not frequently bought, are likely to be expensive, and for which great care in purchase is likely.

Specialty Store A retail institution selling products limited to a narrow line of goods. Examples: Jewelry store, book store, fish store.

Specialty Wholesalers Wholesalers that offer a very narrow assortment of products. Example: A wholesaler that sells only jogging shoes.

Spokesperson A variation of the testimonial approach where an individual representing the company producing the product directly addresses the audience and urges the purchase of the product.

Standard Industrial Classification System (SIC) A numerical coding system developed by the U.S. government and widely employed by industrial marketers to classify organizations in terms of the economic activities in which they are engaged.

Status A socially defined position within a society held by an individual, organization, or object. Example: Garbage collectors and doctors both have jobs; the status associated with those jobs is assigned by the society in which they work.

Stimulus An aspect of the environment that triggers a behavioral response. Plural: stimuli.

Storage The physical distribution function of holding and housing goods in inventory.

Storyline Advertising Format A type of advertising that gives a history or tells a story about the product.

Straight Commission Plan A compensation plan that rewards only one thing—sales performance.

Straight Rebuy A type of industrial purchasing decision characterized by automatic and regular purchase of familiar products from regular suppliers.

Straight Salary Method A compensation plan that is not tied directly to sales performance.

Strategic Gap The difference between an organization's desired position in the market and its actual position.

Strategic Planning Determination of organizational objectives and of the means to be used to attain those objectives.

Strategy Basic organizational goals and objectives, the assignment of resources to be expended in pursuit of those objectives, and the courses of action to be followed in attaining those objectives.

Stratified Sampling A probability sampling procedure whereby subsamples are randomly drawn from samples identified as belonging to particular groups or strata. These groups or strata are believed to contain members who are more or less equal in terms of some characteristic. Example: The variable of age might be used to "stratify" a population into groups that might then be subjected to random sampling.

Subculture A group within a major culture that is distinct because of language variations, unique behavior, or other cultural differences.

Supermarket Any large, departmentalized retail establishment but especially one specializing primarily in food items.

Survey A research technique by which information is gathered from a sample of respondents. Surveys may be of the personal, telephone, or mail varieties.

Syncretic Decisions Those judgments made jointly by husband *and* wife.

Synthesis The third phase of the dialectic process involving the combination of differing concepts to form a new entity. In the development of retailing institutions, the evolution that occurs due to competition among institutions. Example: The department store challenged by the discount store leads to the development of the discount department store.

Systematic Error Incorrect information resulting from an imperfection in a research design or from a mistake in the execution of the research. That is, any mistake other than sampling error.

Systems Concept The idea that elements may be strongly interrelated and interact toward achieving a particular goal.

T

Tactic A specific action taken to execute a plan. The purpose of a tactic is to implement a strategy rather than to develop a plan of action.

Target Market A particular market or segment of a market toward which an organization directs its marketing plan. An organization may select and appeal to more than one target market.

Target Return Pricing The determination of a price level intended to yield a particular level of profit to the organization. Example: A price designed to yield a certain return on investment or a desired dollar profit.

Tariff A tax imposed by a state or nation on products brought into that state or nation. Such a tax is often intended to raise the price of imported goods thereby give a price advantage to domestic goods that they would not otherwise have.

Task Force A group of people within an organization assigned specific responsibility to complete a project. Example: A new product task force.

Task Method A method of setting a promotional analysis of the promotion's objectives. Also called the objective approach.

Technological Obsolescence The practice of making existing products out of date by introducing new products that are more technologically advanced.

Technology The application of scientific knowledge to practical purposes.

Testimonials A type of advertising in which an individual, usually a well-known person, makes a statement that he or she owns, uses, or supports the product.

Time Utility A type of economic utility that

involves the storage of goods so that they are available when needed. .

Total Cost From a physical distribution perspective, the entire range of associated costs that occur when a particular method of distribution is used.

Total Product The broad spectrum of tangible and intangible benefits a buyer might gain from a purchased product. Example: The purchase of a car brings with it a warranty, a "hot line" number for complaints, pride of ownership, and other benefits.

Trade Advertising Advertising aimed at buyers other than ultimate consumers. Trade advertising is aimed at wholesalers, distributors, retailers and others who are "in the trade."

Trade Discounts Price reductions given to dealers, installers, or others who are "in the trade" and *not* given to retail customers or others not "in the trade." Also called functional discounts as they are repayments for the performance of the wholesaling, retailing, and installation functions. Example: A discount on plumbing supplies given to a professional plumber.

Trademark A registered and legally protected brand name or brand mark.

Transportation The physical movement of products through a channel of distribution from producer to consumer and among channel intermediaries.

Trial Close A personal selling tactic intended to elicit from a client a signal indicating whether or not the client is ready to complete the transaction.

Trial Sampling Distribution of newly marketed products to enhance trialability and familiarity. "Free Samples."

Truck Wholesaler A limited-function merchant intermediary selling a limited line of merchandise and providing immediate delivery of that merchandise. Also called Truck Jobbers. Example: Distributors of snack foods to taverns.

Turnover The relative speed with which merchandise is sold, that is, stores selling expensive jewelry have a low turnover, food

stores generally have a high turnover. Also called stock turnover or stock turn.

Typing Contract An agreement between a buyer and a seller that requires the buyer to purchase certain additional items if that buyer wishes to buy other items offered for sale. Example: A seller of a popular photocopy machine may try to "tie" sales of paper, ink, and other supplies to the purchase of the copier.

U

Ultimate Consumer The individual, or family, or other group that actually uses a product or service. Example: An apple may travel from a farm through a series of intermediaries to a store and ultimately to the person who buys the apple for personal consumption. This last person is the ultimate consumer on whom the marketing system depends.

Underdeveloped Countries Nations that have economies based largely on primitive agriculture. Most of the residents have quite low standards of living.

Undifferentiated Marketing A marketing effort not targeted at a specific market segment but designed to appeal to a broad range of customers. This approach is appropriate if there should be a lack of diversity within a market.

Unfair Sales Practices Acts State laws that limit or prohibit the use of certain sales and marketing techniques. Most commonly, a law that specifies that certain types of merchandise must be sold at prescribed markups. This is sometimes called a minimum markup law. Example: A law that requires that all beer distributors mark up the products they sell at least 40 percent above cost.

Uniform Delivered Pricing A pricing practice whereby an organization charges the same price for a given product in all locations. Also called "Postage Stamp Pricing."

Universal Product Code (UPC) The array of black bars, readable by optical scanners, now found on many products. Intended to permit computerization of such tasks as checking out products in retail stores.

USP An acronym for "unique selling proposition." This concept involves identifying and promoting an aspect of the product that the competition does not or cannot easily offer.

Useless Quality Excessive quality built into a product. An electric saw built for professional carpenters has "useless quality" for most do-it-yourselfers.

V

Value (Economic) The power of one product to attract another product in exchange. Example: A new car purchased had sufficient value to attract the buyer's money, the money had the value sufficient to pay for the car.

Value (Social) A matter or goal that society views as important, reflecting the moral order of that society and its institutions. Example: Honesty.

Value System The system of preferences within a society that guides ethical norms.

Variable Price Policy A policy whereby different prices are charged to different customers. Example: Theaters often charge a lower admission price for matinees than for evening shows.

Venture Team A group of specialists from various functional areas of an organization who, in an entrepreneurial fashion, attempt to develop new products or business.

Vertical Cooperative Promotion An approach to promoting a product where channel members at different levels agree to jointly sponsor particular advertisements. Usually, the manufacturer agrees to pay for a portion of a retailer's advertising with the understanding that the ads will feature the manufacturer's product.

Vertical Marketing System (VMS) A vertical network of marketing establishments operating as a centrally coordinated distribution system. They may be linked by formal contracts such as franchises, by central ownership, or by the control of a channel leader. The three types of vertical marketing systems are corporate, contractual, and administered.

Voluntary Chain A group of independent retailers linked to a single wholesale supplier and operating much as a centrally owned chain store system might. Example: I.G.A. stores appear to be a chain but members of the chain are actually independently owned.

W

Warehouse Retailers Merchants that sell products from stores where the showroom facility doubles as a storage place for the retailer's stock. These stores are usually not very elaborately decorated and often feature a low price strategy.

Warehousing The marketing activity of holding and housing goods before shipment to buyers.

Warranty A guarantee of a product's integrity and of the manufacturer or supplier's responsibility for repairing and maintaining the product.

Water Transportation A mode of transportation that involves shipment by boat or barge.

Weakest Link Concept An idea that manufacturers should not make the various parts of a product of such high quality that they far outlast that part of the product that will be the first to wear out. Example: Home shop hobbyists will not pay to have the motor in an electric drill replaced, thus the housing of the rest of the tool should not be built to last "forever."

Wheel of Retailing A theory positing that new forms of retailing institutions enter the marketplace as low-status, low-margin, low-price operations, then gradually "trade up" to become higher-status, higher-margin, higher-price operations. This leaves a low-status spot for new low-price, low-margin retailers to occupy.

Wholesaler An organization or individual that

serves as an intermediary between manufacturer and retailer facilitating transfer of products and the title to them. Wholesalers neither consume nor produce the product, nor do they sell it to consumers.

Wholesaling All marketing activities associated with the sales of products to buyers who are not the ultimate users of those products.

Z

Zone Pricing The practice of varying prices according to the number of geographic areas through which a product passes in moving from seller to buyer. Example: The U.S. Postal Service charges for shipment of packages by the number of zone lines the package will cross on the way to its destination.

Photo Credits

Photo Credits—Color Plates

Photo Credits—Table of Contents

INDEX

Numbers in *italics* refer to cases that appear in the text.